MODERNISM IN LITERATURE

TODD K. BENDER University of Wisconsin, Madison

NANCY ARMSTRONG Instituo de Estudos Norte–Americanos
Universities of Coimbro and Oporto, Portugal

SUE M. BRIGGUM University of Wisconsin, Madison

FRANK A. KNOBLOCH University of Wisconsin, Madison

HOLT, RINEHART AND WINSTON
New York   Chicago   San Francisco   Atlanta
Dallas   Montreal   Toronto

Library of Congress Cataloging in Publication Data

Modernism in literature.

1. Literature, Modern—20th century.   2.   Modernism
(Literature)   I. Bender, Todd K.
PN6014.M325   808.8'01   76-43371
ISBN 0-03-015186-4

ACKNOWLEDGMENTS

The Associated Press for the story on page 13.

THOMAS HARDY: "Channel Firing" and "Convergence of the Twain" from *Collected Poems* by Thomas Hardy. Copyright 1925 by Macmillan Publishing Co., Inc. Reprinted by permission of Macmillan Publishing Co., Inc. and the Trustees of the Hardy Estate and Macmillan London and Basingstoke.

ROBERT FROST: "A Hillside Thaw," "Acquainted with the Night," "Two Tramps in Mud Time," "Desert Places," "Design," and "Directive" from *The Poetry of Robert Frost* edited by Edward Connery Lathem. Copyright 1923, 1928, 1930, 1939, 1947, © 1969 by Holt, Rinehart and Winston. Copyright 1936, 1951, © 1956, 1958 by Robert Frost. Copyright © 1964, 1967, 1975 by Lesley Frost Ballantine. Reprinted by permission of Holt, Rinehart and Winston, Publishers.

WILFRED OWEN: "Greater Love" and "Strange Meeting" from *Collected Poems* by Wilfred Owen. Copyright Chatto & Windus, Ltd. 1946, © 1963. Reprinted by permission of New Directions Publishing Corporation, The Owen Estate, and Chatto & Windus.

SHERWOOD ANDERSON: "The Book of the Grotesque," "Hands," and "Godliness" from *Winesburg, Ohio* by Sherwood Anderson. Copyright 1919 by B. W. Huebach, Inc. Copyright renewed 1947 by Eleanor Copenhaver Anderson. All rights reserved. Reprinted by permission of The Viking Press, Inc.

D. H. LAWRENCE: "The Odour of Chrysanthemums" from *The Complete Short Stories of D. H. Lawrence,* Volume II. All rights reserved. Reprinted by permission of The Viking Press, Inc. "The Woman Who Rode Away." Copyright 1928 by D. H. Lawrence and renewed 1956 by Frieda Lawrence Ravagli. Reprinted from *The Later D. H. Lawrence* by D. H. Lawrence, edited by William York Tindall, by permission of Alfred A. Knopf, Inc.

JEAN TOOMER: "Blood-Burning Moon" from *Cane* by Jean Toomer. Copyright 1923 by Boni & Liveright. Copyright renewed 1951 by Jean Toomer. Reprinted by permission of Liveright Publishing Corporation.

F. SCOTT FITZGERALD: "Winter Dreams" (copyright 1922 by Frances Scott Fitzgerald Lanahan) is reprinted by permission of Charles Scribner's Sons from *All the Sad Young Men.*

WILLIAM FAULKNER: "Barn Burning." Copyright 1939 and renewed 1967 by Estelle Faulkner and Jill Faulkner Summers. Reprinted from *Collected Stories of William Faulkner,* by William Faukner, by permission of Random House, Inc.

ERNEST HEMINGWAY: "The Snows of Kilimanjaro" (copyright 1936 by Ernest Hemingway) is reprinted by permission of Charles Scribner's Sons from *The Short Stories of Ernest Hemingway* by Ernest Hemingway.

JAMES T. FARRELL: "A Front-page Story" and "The Scoop." Reprinted from *The Short Stories of James T. Farrell* by permission of the publisher, Vanguard Press, Inc. Copyright 1935, 1937 by Vanguard Press, Inc. Copyright renewed 1963, 1965 by James T. Farrell.

RICHARD WRIGHT: "The Man Who Lived Underground" copyright © 1944 by L. B. Fischer Publishing Co. from *Eight Men* copyright © 1961, 1940 by Richard Wright, published originally by The World Publishing Company, with the permission of Thomas Y. Crowell Co., Inc.

FLANNERY O'CONNOR: "The Life You Save May Be Your Own." Copyright, 1953, by Flannery O'Connor. Reprinted from her volume, *A Good Man Is Hard to Find and Other Stories,* by permission of Harcourt Brace Jovanovich, Inc.

ALAN SILLITOE: "The Loneliness of the Long-Distance Runner." From *The Loneliness of the Long-Distance Runner* by Alan Sillitoe. Copyright © 1959 by Alan Sillitoe. Reprinted by permission of Alfred A. Knopf, Inc.

TERRY SOUTHERN: "Twirling at Ole Miss" from *Red Dirt Marijuana and Other Tastes.* Copyright © 1963 by Terry Southern. Reprinted by permission of The Sterling Lord Agency.

JOAN DIDION: "Some Dreamers of the Golden Dream" Reprinted by permission of Farrar, Straus & Giroux, Inc. from *Slouching towards Bethlehem* by Joan Didion. Copyright © 1966, 1968 by Joan Didion.

PREFACE

Modernism in Literature is designed for use in courses introducing the fundamentals of reading and writing about literature as well as in surveys of the modern age. We realize, of course, that no two instructors would put together the same anthology of modern literature, and we do not pretend to offer a "standard" reading list. We have tried to make a text flexible enough to accommodate both a variety of pedagogical approaches and a wide range of student abilities. Because there is more than enough material for two semesters' reading, each instructor can tailor the reading list to the needs of particular students, those new to college-level English or the experienced upper-class students who have chosen to focus on the twentieth century.

Our Contents includes selections from nearly all the major figures of the modern period and from the more interesting contemporary writers as well. Along with a broad selection of short stories, there are six works of novel or novella length, and in addition to poems of the length usually considered tolerable for undergraduates, we have included *The Waste Land,* complete with the author's notes, and an entire book from Williams' *Paterson.* Whenever possible we have chosen major works. Rather than one of Woolf's short stories, for example, you will find a chapter from the major document, *A Room of One's Own;* for the same reason, the first chapter of Joyce's *A Portrait of the Artist as a Young Man* accompanies one of the stories from *The Dubliners.* Our selection of classics is complemented by several experimental works rarely found in anthologies of this kind and by other pieces collected here for the first time. We consider some of the New Journalism, stories by South American fabulists, Rhys's long-overlooked novel, and Ondaatje's experimental narrative more interesting and teachable than the usual anthology selections. Although we have represented all the basic literary genres, the selection is obviously balanced in favor of fiction. The addition of one supplementary text, perhaps a collection of drama or contemporary poetry, will easily shift the balance in favor of the instructor's personal preference.

The three categories that organize these readings—Realism, Expressionism, and Impressionism—reflect our critical inclinations as well as the response of our students. We have found these conceptual categories superior to a straight historical arrangement in encouraging individual critical awareness. The categories are based on general literary principles that can be defined in terms of one author and applied to another, incrementally leading the student toward independent reading. Our organization remains flexible, however. In fact, some of our best class discussions developed when students disputed the placement of works in one category or another or when they challenged the distinctions between the categories themselves. We feel that this arrangement provokes fundamental considerations about the nature of art and leads students to original insights into the nature of modern culture, but if you find our orientation too technical, you can easily shift the focus from aesthetic movements to theme. The works under Realism explore possible relationships between man and a social or natural environment; in Expressionism, the artist represents the unique world of self; and Impressionism explores the act of perception as the individual mind and the objective world are conjoined.

Alternatively, if you wish to emphasize the nature of literature in general rather than the nature of modernism, the critical guide at the back of this book provides a ready-made program of study. A class can progress step-by-step through the nine aspects of literary language we have described and apply these concepts to an appropriate reading list. Modern literature is especially interesting for the very reason that it has not been irrevocably packaged and pigeonholed like the literary productions of earlier epochs, and while our organization seems logically coherent, pedagogically sound, and refreshingly new to us, it is primarily intended to encourage debate and critical activity on the part of students rather than to do the thinking for them.

We have designed our critical aids so as to incorporate within this single text the advantages of such supplements as the MLA style format, a glossary of literary terms, an introduction to critical approaches to literature, and a "how to write" handbook. More importantly, our critical aids are designed to bring students to a level of competence as quickly and easily as possible, first, by absolutely avoiding techniques and concepts we ourselves consider useless, and, secondly, by removing some of the mystery from the processes of literary study. Our "critical guide" is composed of nine conventions basic to the critical activity that can be mastered by the average student in a semester. This method enables the increasing number of students who have little prior training in English to progress rapidly toward proficient writing. Our Index of Useful Literary Terms is composed of terms that are less basic but still important in widening the scope of critical awareness with historical information or brief summaries of more specialized approaches to literature. These terms always include at least one application to a work in this text, and we've found that they provide convenient discussion or paper topics for the teacher to assign or for the ambitious student to discover on his own.

In presenting these aids, we have tried to remove the guesswork, the uncertain process of trial and error, which so often distresses the student of literature. To achieve this end, we have relied on examples to clarify our ideas. Exemplary work produced by real students in real introductory-level classrooms is worth more to other students than a thousand *dos* and *don'ts,* and accordingly we have devoted most of the space concerned with writing essays to essays written by our students. In the instructor's manual accompanying this text, we have also used the student as our guide and have repeated the questions and projects which have produced the best classroom results. Our critical aids are presented as useful suggestions, not iron-clad prescriptions. We feel that modern art raises more questions than it answers, and for us to pretend otherwise would be to falsify the nature of our material, denying the student the challenge and possibility for originality it affords.

We urge you to help us collect a more diverse selection of exemplary essays for use in future editions. Our editor at Holt, Rinehart and Winston is maintaining a file for those original undergraduate essays which you feel deserve recognition and provide sound models for other students to follow. Please send them to Harriett Prentiss, Senior Editor-English, Holt, Rinehart and Winston, 383 Madison Avenue, New York, N.Y. 10017.

Finally, we must take this opportunity to thank our students in English 208 at the University of Wisconsin-Madison for helping us select the readings and for giving us many good essays from which to choose examples, Professor Dennis Martin for his constructive criticism, and Harriett Prentiss, Susan Katz, and Ruth Chapman for their editorial assistance.

CONTENTS

Introduction to Modernism

The value of a traditional literary education is being rigorously questioned today. In "Real Students in Real Classrooms," Louis Kampf writes, "I can think of no decent justification for teaching composition or literature in terms of the profession's traditional objectives." Kampf argues that a literary education does not change the quality of an individual's life, nor does it promote social equality. "This is not to say," he adds, "that literacy is not a good thing. Obviously in an industrial society it's a necessity. However, literacy may be defined in various ways. Those who have power tend to do the defining." A working-class high school student views the study of literature as the totally arbitrary imposition of a middle-class liberal arts curriculum in this irreverent statement:

> School would be alright if you didn't have to take English. Social Studies I wouldn't mind being required, cause that's kinda interesting. But English, what real interest can you have about that? There might be some way you can make English interesting, but I can't see it. Cause I don't like reading a book and you're supposed to tell how good it is. And I don't think it's good. And I don't think it's right. Like, I

read *The Godfather* and I really like that book, but I can't do a book report on it cause it's not required for my Regents [test]. I don't care what anybody says, why should they tell me I should read a book and think it's good? I'll read what I want to read. It really pisses me off, this school. That's the only thing I can say. They're trying to teach me shit that I don't even want to know. The only reason I got to learn that shit is so I can take one exam and pass it. And one test doesn't mean shit.[1]

But to one college freshman, literature is not practical even in terms of middle-class goals:

I really don't think that lit. courses should be required. For someone who is pursuing a career in the field of science it is a waste of time and effort and distracts the student from his more important class. I think it is important to be able to write well and to be able to understand what is written, but there should be a course where you don't have to understand the deep thoughts of the works studied in this lit. class.

Until the 1960s, there was no serious challenge to teaching methods, selection of materials, or assumed motives for learning. Perhaps the teachers, the artists whose writings they taught, and the students who processed this information had similar social goals. Even more likely, few of them realized that any social goal at all was furthered by the study of literature. In recent years, however, the smooth transmission of knowledge, conventions, and values from one generation to the next has been disrupted by violent debate among teachers over teaching methods, grading procedures, and changes in the classic curriculum to incorporate black studies, women's studies, and maybe even *The Godfather*. These changes in the teachers' attitudes have been matched by the students' growing political awareness

and vocal irritation with old standards. These obvious shifts in the social framework within which the teaching of English takes place force us to question our old assumptions about the ultimate purpose of literary study.

Take, for example, this typical preface to a currently popular textbook which concludes with a sentimental appeal to the traditional humanitarian goal:

Most important of all, however, is that the book is aimed at the appreciation of good literature. Literature is the property of all; its appeal is to all. But literature, as an art, employs techniques and offers problems that can be understood only through analysis, and analysis means work. The immediate aim is to help the student in this work, but the primary object of the book is to promote the pleasurable study and, finally, the love of literature.

All the "buts" and "howevers" standing between the student and "the love of literature" invite a response to literary instruction resembling Huckleberry Finn's rejection of Miss Watson's impractical goals: "*She* was going to live so as to go to the good place. Well, I couldn't see no advantage in going where she was going, so I made up my mind I wouldn't try for it." Huck was asked to restrain his natural impulses in exchange for a lofty and mysterious goal, "the good place." The textbook author promises an equally mysterious, equally deferred gratification, "the love of literature." The path to the good place is difficult for all ("analysis means work"), and the author in fact assumes from the beginning that only a few will become competent readers and writers, as he confidentially admits in the privacy of his *Teacher's Manual*:

Indeed, if students were allowed to go through composition and literature classes without guidance, it is fair to

[1] Martha Hamilton, "Youth in Working-Class Suburbia," quoted in "Real Students in Real Classrooms" by Louis Kampf. *New Literary History*, Vol V, no 3 (Spring 1974).

say that perhaps ninety percent of all their writing would be synopsis or precis. . . . It is a fond hope that students will continue working on these problems after they leave our courses, but once they have received our grades they are on their own, out of reach of our voices.

Here he offers the more reasonable assumption that literature is *not* the property of all, nor is its appeal to all. In recent years, the fundamental dishonesty of these contradictory claims about the universal appeal of often difficult and specialized writing has inspired a cynicism in students and teachers alike, which can only obscure the genuine social advantages that do come with literacy and a literary education. Therefore, before we tell you what we think about literature, we want to explain the sometimes contradictory goals which we all, willingly or not, pursue as teachers and readers.

We ourselves belong to a group often called the literary establishment that includes critics, textbook writers, and teachers as well as the authors whose works we teach. Members of our group have certain ways of reading and talking about literature which we believe are better than those advocated by, say, popular book clubs. Even though there is disagreement within the literary establishment concerning the best way to read a particular work of literature, this group is differentiated from that of people who simply consume literature or respond to its art subjectively, reading for plot or for other "wrong" reasons. English professors communicate to students more or less forcibly, more or less intelligently, the ways in which highly literate people read and talk about literature. Even a teacher like Kampf who rejects the establishment, believing it fosters intellectual elitism and thus does not perform a valuable

service for the community, will have been educated in the values and terminology of that select group. To one degree or another, we all equate the educated voice with the voice of authority. The public wants its children to acquire it, and it pays teachers to perform this service.

You have recently decided to join a specific social group by coming to college or a university. Your group is divided between honors and "C" students, but society makes other, perhaps more telling distinctions on the basis of the kind of institution you are attending —the degree of its public prestige. *The Chronicle of Higher Education* (March 15, 1976) published results of a *Fortune* magazine poll: A tally of top corporate executives "showed that 35 percent graduated from Ivy League schools and another 45 percent from other private colleges and universities. Yet it is that kind of school, now costing upwards of $4,000 or $5,000 a year, that the average family can no longer afford." If you put this together with the fact that "the top 1 percent of our population own 28 percent of all personal wealth, and the top 10 percent just over 50 percent of it," you must conclude that the relationship between an individual's social class and type of education is frighteningly significant.

To see how the study of literature participates in this social stratification, we devised a rather unscientific survey to determine whether people are marked socially by the books they think are important. Of course we found it easy to distinguish the typical college student from the nonstudent and both from the literary specialist on the basis of their answers to the old question, "If you were stranded on a desert island, what five books would you wish you had with you?"

X	Y	Z
Bible	*Moby Dick*	*Remembrance of Things Past*
The Call of the Wild	*How to Survive on an Island*	*The Faerie Queene*
Love Story	*The Scarlet Letter*	*Ulysses*
Sears Catalogue	*Slaughterhouse Five*	*The Anatomy of Melancholy*
Run to Daylight: The Vince Lombardi Story	*The Story of 0* (in case it is lonely)	*The Decline and Fall of the Roman Empire*

Assuming that these people replied to our question with the titles of books they considered valuable, we drew several conclusions: First, some people value literature more highly than others, and second, groups within our society define good literature in radically different ways. Finally, the study of literature separates some from the vast majority (X), placing them in a much smaller group (Y), while a student whose wit, stamina, and money hold out may become one of the relatively few members of the literary establishment (Z).

Some obvious contradictions are emerging. The vast majority (X) sends its children to college in order that they appreciate *Moby Dick* and enter the economic progression that *The Chronicle of Higher Education* describes, yet the *Chronicle* article suggests that only a particular college education will be financially profitable. We, Parsons and Harvard teachers alike, serve that vast majority in its intention, but look at the amazing impracticality of our literary values as reflected in Z's reading list. Not one book on desert survival. The literary establishment somehow helps to create the social establishment but remains distinctly outside of it. One reason for this contradiction and its more than economic significance becomes clearer when we look at the history of the literature we choose to teach.

Each historical period has produced many more works of art than the few that were passed on to later generations.

Why certain writing survived and became designated as "good literature" is a complex subject, one whose major theme seems to be the shifting relationship between "good literature" and that which reflects the values of the social establishment. For example, statistics show an absolute correlation between the values of the dominant social class and the kinds of literature taught in United States public schools between 1836 and 1920: The American Book Company estimates that between those years 122,000,000 copies of the McGuffey *Reader* were sold in this country. According to *Historical Statistics of the United States*, approximately 7,500,000 people were enrolled in public school grades one through eight in any given year after 1870 (statistics for public school enrollment before that date were not compiled). The McGuffey *Reader* was comprised solely of literary and expository writings and excerpts such as Ben Franklin's *Poor Richard's Almanack*, Dickens' "The Death of Little Nell" from *The Old Curiosity Shop*, and fiction produced expressly for the *Reader* such as "Where There Is a Will There Is a Way" and "Lazy Ned." The statistics indicate that these literary selections were a primary part of the education of a substantial percentage of several generations of the population of the United States. The purpose served by the selection of subject matter and its commanding distribution is best expressed by Henry Vail, a partner in the firm which purchased publication rights to the *Reader* in the 1870s. In a letter, Vail explains the policies determining the book's major revisions in 1878:

> There was in the books [previous editions] much direct teaching of moral principle, with "thou shalt" and "thou shalt not." In the later revisions this gradually disappeared. The moral teaching was less direct but more effective. The pupil was left to make his own deductions. . . . The author and publishers were fully justified in their firm belief that the American people are a moral people and that they have a strong desire that their children be taught to become brave, patriotic, honest, self-reliant, temperate, and virtuous citizens.

The irony is, of course, that the *Reader* itself played a major role in determining those values shared by the great majority of the citizenry, which in turn determined the kind of literature that this public would desire to have its children read. The success of McGuffey's *Reader* in perpetuating the same values from generation to generation clearly demonstrates the political importance of its definition of good literature, and it shows why teachers may be considered useful tools for social mobility.

This kind of situation seems very distant to us today. Not only do we question the way conventional values are perpetuated in teaching, but we recognize that a standard reading list for twentieth century literature is impossible. Paradoxically, just as we have come to question the possibility of defining "good literature," we have also become aware of how absolutely necessary that definition can become. Periodically when governments have used control of literary production to establish totalitarian power, we have been forced into awareness of literature's influence over public values and thus over political circumstances. The Nazi book burnings and persecution of artists antagonistic to the Nazi state are common knowledge. Because uncontested, the

Führer's standard of beauty, the Aryan type, prevailed, playing no small part in creating the tolerance of the German public for mass annihilation of "inferior" types. Similarly, Stalin executed nearly a thousand artists and writers, nearly everybody of any reputation or talent, in order to solidify his political power in the U.S.S.R. Literature obviously has a broad political capacity to combat illegitimate power as well as to perpetuate power the public considers to be legitimate. Writers for McGuffey's *Reader* were valued to the degree they supported majority rule. In direct contrast, the twentieth century writers praised by the literary establishment uniformly attack the values of the majority.

James Joyce's *Ulysses* offers a classic example of minority attack in moral and legal rather than overtly political terms. The case reminds us that forms of literary censorship have existed in America and Britain as well. The fact that it took a major court decision to allow us to read Joyce's novel indicates that the difference in values between artist and community is no mere quibble over words but an extremely serious controversy. The decision of the United States district court delivered in 1933 by the Hon. John M. Woolsey which lifted the ban on *Ulysses* as a pornographic work concluded that events and words usually excluded from polite conversation may be essential to an honest depiction of human thoughts and emotions. The United States government had argued that *Ulysses* was obscene. Woolsey's decision in favor of the claimant determined that "unusual frankness" by itself does not constitute obscenity. Joyce's legal victory indicates that the minority can change majority values or at least its level of tolerance for moral questioning.

The variety of selections in this textbook indicates how far we have come since the Woolsey decision. But some of these stories would probably offend your parents, which reveals another contradiction. We have been hired by the public to teach its children how to survive in current society, yet we choose to accomplish this by offering writers who attack that society's standards. Why does the public want us to teach books it will never read and could never approve of? Our one tentative answer lies in the necessity of criticism for its own sake as social corrective and as intellectual exercise. This is the position of the innovative and "good" twentieth century artist, which we as teachers reflect.

This idea of the writer as minority critic has its roots in events of the previous century, and as nineteenth century specialists we find these historical roots particularly interesting. While the Mc-Guffey *Reader* reigned, minority reactions were forming that began in England with the Romantic movement and in the United States with the Transcendentalists. The end of the eighteenth century in England saw a transformation of the role of the artist in society. Poets such as Alexander Pope and Samuel Johnson had assumed, like the McGuffey editors, that art had a moral purpose. It was the poet's function to coax or scold readers into living up to the ideals of their culture by maintaining and perfecting social and religious institutions. William Wordsworth in his preface to the *Lyrical Ballads* in 1800 disputed this definition of the poet's role. Although he was a Cambridge-educated poet writing for the literate elite of his society, he reacted against his education when he praised a social ideal we call "cultural primitivism." Wordsworth's preface describes a fictional society, divorced from the traditional institutions of his readers, in which people live in a state of natural simplicity. He chooses a world of "humble and rustic life . . . because, in that condition, the essential passions of the heart find a better soil in which they can attain their maturity, are less under restraint, and speak a plainer and more emphatic language." Later in America, Henry David Thoreau made a personal as well as literary endorsement of cultural primitivism in his autobiography, *Walden*. Thoreau had abandoned the deadening materialism of the town to live in the woods, adopting the simple rustic life of a hermit. "I went to the woods," he says, "because I wished to live deliberately, to front only the essential facts of life, and see if I could not learn what it had to teach, and not, when I came to die, discover that I had not lived." Wordsworth and Thoreau, alienated from their materialistic middle-class society, yearned for one in which freedom, morality, and wisdom predominated. In this way, the English Romantics and American Transcendentalists established moral authority by opposing the established religious, political, and social values of their cultures. Literature as they defined it was truly a minority expression.

They felt, contrary to majority opinion, that human beings do not develop true identity through a process of education and socialization. The natural impulses and emotions which Wordsworth calls "the primary laws of our nature" are only obscured and repressed among the complexities of urban society. Rustics, savages, children, or hermits are more proper subjects for art, more worthy models of humanity, than educated gentlemen because the simple character yields a more realistic description of human nature. In his essay, "Civil Disobedience," Thoreau makes an even more direct assault on the values and institutions of his materialistic society by expressing a similar desire for realism. He says that people, in conforming to social institutions, have abandoned their real natures for a reduced, artificial one: "The mass of men serve the state thus, not as men mainly, but as machines, with their bodies." Moral art must recover a primary nature that society has repressed, and it must do so by repudiating approved forms of writing. Since old conventions, social and literary, obscure the primary truth, innovative art forms are necessary in order to convey the new realism.

The old urbane and polished verse forms were clearly inadequate to convey the values of the natural society. Wordsworth therefore argued for a kind of natural language in which the poet expressed primary truths "as far as was possible in a selection of language really used by men." Thoreau's fellow Transcendentalist, Ralph Waldo Emerson, saw a genuine moral necessity for honest language. In an essay in *Nature*, Emerson noted that language, like all social institutions, always expresses the values of the men who use it. Language in a materialistic society tends to be an instrument for repressing or corrupting natural virtue: "The corruption of man is followed by a corruption of language. When simplicity of character and the sovereignty of ideas is broken up by the prevalence of secondary desires—the desire of riches, of pleasure, of power, of praise—and duplicity and falsehood take place of simplicity and truth, the power over nature as an interpreter of the will is in a degree lost; new imagery ceases to be created, and old words are perverted to stand for things which are not." In order to prevent this falsification of truth, Emerson held, poets must overturn poetic conventions and repudiate the corrupt values of their audience.

The Romantics proposed a new concept of realism and a new literary language to convey it, but their realism was soon considered to be no more than an idealistic retreat into some "golden age" of the past. The assumptions of cultural primitivism that were central to the Romantic position were attacked on two fronts. Science radically altered the view that nature, especially human nature, was benign, and the facts of nineteenth century history seemed to verify science's conclusion. To begin with, Darwin's discoveries made it difficult for authors and readers to see nature as an innocent and harmonious garden. In *The Origin of Species* (1859), Darwin argued that all natural species, including *Homo sapiens*, originate "from a struggle for survival" where "new and improved varieties will inevitably supplant and exterminate the older, less improved, and intermediate varieties." The natural world is composed, then, not of morally superior creatures, but of those tough or cunning enough to compete successfully for food and to reproduce their kind. Darwin redefined nature as a ruthless system of domination: "As more individuals are produced than can possibly survive, there must in every case be a struggle for existence, either one individual with another of the same species, or with the individuals of distinct species, or with the physical conditions of life." This radical conflict between science and artistic and religious definitions of reality marks one of the major changes in cultural history that has produced contemporary attitudes and values. Most writers and readers today accept the authority of science over any other, just as science was enthusiastically accepted by the vast majority of the English and American public during the second half of the nineteenth century.

When Darwin redefined natural law as an amoral and materialistic process beyond human control, he not only discredited the idealism of the Romantics and Transcendentalists, but he also lent scientific validity to the optimistic materialism of the middle class. Herbert Spencer put Darwin's principles of evolution through natural selection together with the premises of the new sociology developed by Auguste Comte, transforming an unpleasantly deterministic idea of evolution into the ideal of progress. Darwin's theory showed that natural life developed toward more individuated, more specialized, so-called "higher" forms. As this happens, Spencer argued, larger and larger groups are formed, for the similarities within a group are always more significant than the differences between individuals. Spencer's translation of Darwin into social principles reconciled individualism with conformism by suggesting that the interests of each citizen as well as the interests of the state are served by free economic expansion. The individual would develop and improve through open competition. As each individual continued to benefit from free economic development, society would evolve into a complex but unified state based on voluntary cooperation rather than coercive authority. You can imagine how Spencer's principle of universal evolution pleased an aspiring middle class. He had concluded that government, the life of the individual, and even the arts were unified by a natural process that was "not an accident, not a thing within human control, but a beneficent necessity." When the idea of evolution was thus transformed into the idea of progress, science itself became a kind of faith. The majority now had an ethical justification for unbounded acquisition.

The acquisitive spirit found expression in rapid expansion of territory and a consequent increase in industrial capacity in both the British Empire and the American West. Writers responded to society's theme of progress as the novel, particularly the *Bildungsroman*, came into its own as an art form. The *Bildungsroman* traces the development of a hero from usually inauspicious beginnings through the course of his education to maturity. During this process of social experience, the hero sloughs off weakness and acquires virtue, finally evolving into a sensitive individual and responsible citizen. America's most famous examples, the Horatio Alger novels portray self-reliant heroes. Generally they show how a ragged city lad or poor farm boy possesses moral virtue, plenty of endurance, and the ability to make the most of an opportunity becomes a wealthy and powerful member of the middle class. In England, similar boys' books like *Tom Brown's School Days* let some unruly member of the middle class rise to become one of the leaders of the Empire through extravagant adherence to the virtues of justice, honesty, and obedience on the football field. While these popular heroic types consciously or unconsciously served the interests of the dominant social class, other writers of the same period, who will probably be more familiar to you, objected to these types on moral grounds. They felt that popular art as it reflected theories of optimistic, uncontrolled progress made the public complacent with dangerous falsehoods. The personal experience of these writers refuted the middle-class ideal. The British novelist Charles Dickens, for example, was forced into hard labor as a child when his father was thrown into debtors' prison. He began his writing career as a court reporter and saw at first hand poverty in London slums and corruption in England's prosperous bureaucracy. His experience totally contradicted assumptions about the benevolence of the Christian gentleman. In his best known *Bildungsroman, Great Expectations*, Dickens shows that it is impossible for his hero to develop morally and at the same time achieve social position. In order that Pip not be completely corrupted by wealth and position, Dickens has him save what is left of his soul by losing his fortune. When a fellow novelist convinced Dickens that the public would never accept an ending in which the hero is crushed both emotionally and economically as a result of his London education, Dickens offered a second, more polite ending that suggested that Pip's experience with greed and injustice was a valuable lesson that ultimately would lead to new maturity, respectability, and perhaps even a happy marriage. Mark Twain's *Huckleberry Finn* dramatizes a similar contradiction between public belief and realistic fact. Civilized adult society is revealed as increasingly mad and brutal with its feuds and legalized slavery, primitive in the Darwinian rather than the Romantic sense. As a consequence of his education into the facts of existence and the lies of society, Huck chooses an apparently lesser evil and "lights out for the territory," but the Twain who recorded the savagery of the frontier in *Roughing It* knew that human nature is essentially the same in the town and the wilderness.

As the century progressed, artists like Twain and Dickens, who associated good art with what were often pessimistic truths, found themselves in an increasingly antagonistic relationship with the ruling class. The facts of history were the weapons of their criticism. It became obvious that *laissez-faire* economic policy would not lead to an equitable distribution of wealth and justice. England emerged as an industrial giant, but for most people living standards did not improve with open competition. Stratification of the social classes only intensified as a result of warring economic interests. This conflict between masses of workers and an increasingly powerful capitalist elite produced what Prime Minister Benjamin Disraeli described as a society divided into "two nations, the rich and the poor." In America, unchecked industrialization created a new class of impoverished migrant and immigrant workers. The free competition that promised opportunity for wealth and power to all had placed many at the whim of laws of supply and demand, subjecting them to debilitating, monotonous labor in the factories.

Karl Marx in *Capital* (1867), applying the idea of evolution to economic history, came up with an interpretation of nineteenth century progress sharply at odds with middle-class optimism. Marx agreed with the Romantic writers in describing nineteenth century society as a wasteland where the dominant few prospered at the expense of the many and where humanitarian values were totally ignored. In contrast with the Romantics, however, Marx did not yearn for a less materialistic, more idealistic society. He rather welcomed the self-destructive tendencies he saw in capitalist England because he believed they would eventually produce a more advanced social order: "Along with the constantly diminishing number of magnates of Capital, who usurp and monopolize all advantages of this process of transformation, grows the mass of misery, oppression, slavery, degradation, exploitation; but with this, too, grows the revolt of the working class, a class always increasing in numbers, and disciplined, united, organized by the very mechanism of the process of capitalist production itself." When Marx went on to equate the collapse of capitalism with the end of everything the middle-class artist associated with culture, he said in effect that many of the artist's own values would be overturned along with middle-class dominance. Marx's purely materialistic interpretation of history was not seen as a positive alternative for artists until well into the twentieth century when writers from minority, ethnic, and politically oppressed groups were acknowledged and published.

The artist at the turn of the century saw social evils and documented them but found it difficult to propose alternatives as clearly positive as the Romantics' natural ideal. Not only was nature revealed as Darwinian battleground, but "nature" as the Romantics knew it was disappearing. The industrialized city was taking over the English landscape, and the economic system was steadily absorbing underdeveloped nations into the network of the Empire. In Joseph Conrad's novel, *Heart of Darkness*, the narrator finds himself hemmed in on one side by the "monstrous town" of London and by Africa as an example of ruthless European exploitation on the other. Technological advances of mixed blessing in America made civilization similarly inescapable. For example, four years after the Union Pacific Railroad was completed, four million buffalo had been killed, and the species was all but extinct within ten years. When natural resources disappear as quickly as the buffalo, Walden ponds become mere literary things of the past. Artists who want to represent human existence realistically have to consider the economic, social, and psychological stresses of industrial society. Stephen Crane's Maggie, typical of protagonists in turn-of-the-century American novels, "blossomed in a mud-puddle. She grew to be a most rare and wonderful production of a tenement district, a pretty girl." Nature is only a metaphor in a pervasively urban environment. Romantic natural idealism is impossible in an age experiencing the destruction of actual states of nature. The modern artist must therefore consider people in a city environment, without any humanitarian illusions. If the twentieth century writer retained any feeble hopes about a benevolent society, the universal carnage of the first World War and the equally universal devastation of economic depression destroyed them.

As writers shifted from natural optimism to critical realism, they retained one trait in common: They all opposed the assumptions of the majority and the conventions of its popular art. They were all participants in a kind of *avant garde*, criticizing what they felt to be false values in the hope of changing them. With Emerson, they felt a corrupt society fostered a corrupt language, which in turn perpetuated social lies. The artist had to create new conventions in language in order to reveal new truths about human nature. Expression of these primary truths took a number of forms. Some writers politically aligned themselves with exploited classes. Others viewed themselves as *poètes maudits*, "cursed" for their superior knowledge, alienated from the community at large, and appreciated only by future generations. This kind of writer recalls the nineteenth century French *avant garde* in its violent assault upon the public sensibility. Many French *nouveau riche* audiences, sitting in the theaters as politely as they would in church, were surprised when actors reversed the traditional audience prerogative and pelted the spectators themselves with cabbages. Later in England, Conrad compared his novels to barrels of gunpowder. The American Ezra Pound was at the center of a group who began their manifesto:

BLAST First (from politeness) ENGLAND

CURSE ITS CLIMATE FOR ITS SINS AND INFECTIONS

DISMAL SYMBOL, SET round our bodies,
of effeminate lout within.

VICTORIAN VAMPIRE, the LONDON cloud sucks
the TOWN'S heart.

While these attacks were generally levelled specifically at the middle class, virtually everybody was offended. It is no surprise that a genteel defender of culture, F. R. Leavis, was mystified: "Urban conditions, a sophisticated civilization, rapid change, and the mingling of cultures have destroyed the old rhythms and habits, and nothing ade-

quate has taken their place. The result is a sense, apparent in the serious literature of the day, that meaning and direction have vanished." Soviet author normally at odds with a critic like Leavis finds himself in agreement:

Modernism in any of its manifestations is bankrupt because it repudiates preceding experience, because it calls for the crushing of the conscious in conciouness, for an escape into a world which does not exist. From this stem the constant efforts of the modernists to shatter the mirror of life or at least to make it so dim that it reflects nothing, or almost nothing . . . 'I cannot imagine how one can get up in the morning and see the sun on the roofs of a city, or a wet, rainy day, or a child's fair head, or a sleeping woman in the dimness of a room, or the moisture of a sliced orange, or a bit of bread on a glazed plate . . . and start to make holes in a piece of old cardboard.' (from "The Art of Truth," in *Sputnik, A Digest of Soviet Press,* for national and international distribution, a kind of *Reader's Digest* in terms of its orthodox content.)

As the Soviet reaction suggests, modernist art may violate our ideas of what is real and therefore meaningful in human existence, or, as we see in Leavis' more troubled response, it may even force us to consider the possibility that meaning has vanished altogther. These critics are typical of readers of all classes and political inclinations who have found much of modern art obscure and irrelevant. When the artist feels continually the compulsion to create new and unexpected literary forms to convey new truths, the reader must work harder to follow these innovations. We live in an age in which artists have found innumerable ways to express their opposition to established values. Readers must therefore become increasingly critical of the validity of the art as well as its opposition. We cannot just accept the artist as spokesman for our society, nor can we accept society's definition of good literature.

As anthologists faced with this multiplicity of modernist technique and attitude, we had several options. We could have thrown up our hands and organized our material chronologically, but placing James Farrell's "Scoop" and Wallace Stevens' 'Idea of Order at Key West" together simply because they were written in the same year provides the student with as absurd a comparison as the conjunction of Joe Eszterhas and T. S. Eliot created by alphabetical order. To arrange the selections in thematic terms would stress content to the exclusion of any real consideration of technique. More importantly, it would tend to preempt the individual critical activity we have said is so important in the modern reader. So we decided to follow the lead of the writers themselves. Since they all seek to define the primary and make innovations in technique to this end, the spirit of modernism is best represented by categorizing the ways in which they themselves define "the real." Some writers, believing that the basis of reality is an objective material world, strive for a mimetric art that we generally call realism. Others, believing that the basis of reality resides in the individual perceiving mind, develop various modes of expressionism. Finally, those who think that reality resides primarily in the act of perception, the moment when mind encounters object, explore impressionism.

Artistic Model	Location of Reality	Relationship between Art and Reality
1. Realism	Objects in the external world	Art mirrors external objects
2. Expressionism	Subject: the perceiving mind	Art expresses author's state of mind
3. Impressionism	Act of perception: point of contact of subject and object	Art renders impressions, involving the audience in the artistic process of constructing a reality

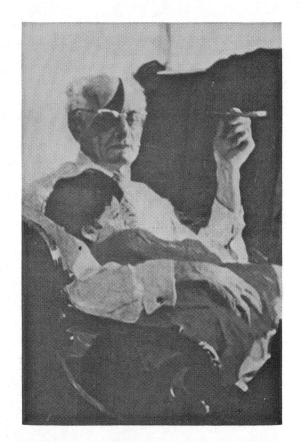

Grandfather and Granddaughter
(1957) by Vasili Yefanov. From
Sputnik: Digest of the Soviet Press,
August 1975.

Before the Storm *(1935) by*
Alexander Deineka. From Sputnik:
Digest of the Soviet Press,
August 1975.

1

Introduction to Realism

Consider the following article from The Associated Press, reprinted in part as it appeared in *The Capital Times* (Madison, Wisconsin) on June 25, 1975:

ARTIST PURCHASES HAND
BUT CAN'T SHOW IT
SYDNEY, Australia (AP)—The Sydney Opera House has refused to let a severed hand be shown at the house, but an art dealer says he has bought the hand and will display it for two weeks.

"In normal situations, the Opera House exercises no censorship over exhibits," a spokesman said. "But in this particular instance, the bounds of good taste have been exceeded."

An artist named Ivan Durrant said he paid a 24-year-old, left-handed medical student $133 last Sunday for the student's right hand. Art dealer Clive Evatt said he paid Durrant $600 to obtain the hand on behalf of an art collector.

Last month Durrant dumped the carcass of a slaughtered cow on the steps of the National Gallery in Melbourne to protest the eating of meat.

"The student came to me and said he wanted to amputate his hand as a protest in favor of his right to do as he wishes, even if it harms him," Durrant said. "He claimed it was hypocritical of me to kill the cow if I wouldn't condone his cutting off his hand. So I told him: 'If you are going to do it, I'd like to use the hand for my own things if you don't mind.' "

Durrant, an exponent of the New Realism movement in art, said exhibit of the hand—in a hand-size version of a glass-topped supermarket freezer—would be "shock therapy" for the public.

"Once people see an amputated hand, they'll know what a real amputated hand is," he explained. "Then when they see Vietnamese on television with their hands blown off, the real horror will come home to them."

What is it about this "artifact" that the Opera House spokesman found offensive? Many artists claim that they want their art to be "realistic." But if art is the *same* as reality, we do not recognize it as art. Art of course refers to reality, but it can never be the same. Take "photographic realism," for example. If we were to print our own photographs here, we would be surprised if you asked such questions as "are you people only two inches tall? Do you walk around inside a frame?" Photographic realism is clearly quite separate from the real object to which it refers, and similarly, literary realism is not to be confused with case histories of real people. Art by definition establishes distance from the real phenomena it describes, and the conventions which create that distance (such as the frame of a picture or the title of a book) make art possible.

Authors who choose literary realism do not want to destroy art by making it too real, yet they want to perform a more important function as artists than simply to express personal imaginings. The realist assumes with the scientist that the universe is comprised of natural objects, including people, that are governed by laws of cause and effect. To eliminate social irresponsibility produced by an ignorance of what is primary in human life, the artist at-tempts to select and arrange data that will reveal the laws which control our existence. Changes in social condi-tions and conventions always force the realist to modify existing literary con-ventions, and consequently many artists hailed in their day as extremely realistic seem ridiculously old-fashioned and artificial in a few years. If we can be-lieve Wordsworth's preface to his *Lyrical Ballads*, he intended to revolu-tionize the conventions of his day with his description of the cultural primitive, but his shepherds now seem wildly in-accurate images of real primitives. Whenever one set of ideas and tech-niques gives way to another, the newer claims to be "realistic."

Of course, all writers recognize the fundamental artificiality of their work, but realists feel that newer techniques are less deceptive and artificial than the old ones the public has grown to accept without question. While all forms of literary realism challenge accepted con-ventions to one degree or another, the *critical realists* see realistic representa-tion primarily in terms of direct expo-sure of the inaccuracy of accepted conventions. Wilfred Owen's "Greater Love," for example, systematically de-stroys the idealistic conventions of tradi-tional love poetry by showing their in-congruity with the hard facts of con-temporary existence. The reality of war is brought home to the British public through grotesque images of the battle-field. Similarly in "Winter Dreams," F. Scott Fitzgerald takes the glamor out of upper middle-class life. He has a young caddy aspire to what seems to be a paradise of country club membership and then achieve a disappointing suc-cess. The young princess he desires turns into a tired housewife, and the hero's successful empire is a chain of laundries. But in comparison with Fitzgerald's disillusionment, Richard Wright's representation of the dirty facts underlying "the good life" in "The Man Who Lived Underground" is shockingly realistic. The two authors share a desire to represent experience as it actually is for a typical individual, but they differ on what constitutes this experience. Because there are so many differing ideas of what is real and typical, we have decided to discuss realistic literature in terms of two basic theories of realism: Social realists take the behaviorist view that human existence is determined by the physical and social environment; psychological realists take the depth psychologist's view that subconscious instincts shape our social life.

Social realism is a consequence of the nineteenth century positivist reliance on the "scientific method." The *logical positivists* believed that there was a logic posited in all occurrences in the natural world. They maintained that since all knowledge is based on the careful and unbiased observation of natural phenomena, human behavior can be studied in much the same way as physical science, although the data behind human behavior are much more complex. If we study heredity and environment in detail, we can understand human behavior. Literary *naturalism* was an attempt to translate the scientific method into an artistic form. The movement's first spokesman, Emile Zola, described his objectives in this way: "We naturalists, we men of science, we must admit of nothing occult; men are but phenomena and the conditions of phenomena." Using character as a model of heredity and setting as if it were a direct copy of a human environment, the naturalist's fiction became a sort of experiment or demonstration of the interaction between man and nature. The high value placed upon scientific objectivity produced distinctive modifications in literary convention. The realist's narrative technique is modeled after that of historical or scientific discourse, systematically omitting direct allusion to the author or reader. The effect, according to critic Roland Barthes, is that "history seems to write itself" or not to be written at all, but to actually happen. The first sentence of James T. Farrell's "The Scoop" demonstrates the principle: "A large *Chicago Questioner* delivery truck parted the traffic as it roared northward toward the Clark Street Bridge." A causal sequence of this sort of narrative assertion then comprises the plot. The author does not say what *might* or *seemed* to have happened nor what did *not* happen; he asks no questions and cites no alternate possibilities. In keeping with this kind of plot, characters lack psychological complexity and potential for change or surprise. This rigid kind of determinism essentially distinguishes naturalism from other modes of realism. In the "A Front-Page Story," for example, Ruth Summer's character is established by her congenital homeliness, her defective heart, and her lower-class rural origin. In spite of the pathetic subject matter, this kind of fiction is true to the scientific mode, and we receive an entirely unsentimental account of her funeral: "Now she was a blue and bloated corpse, and her fatty arms gave one the impression of seminudity." This language resembles an autopsy report compared with Dickens' death of Little Nell: "She was dead. No sleep so beautiful and calm, so free from trace of pain, so fair to look upon. She seemed a creature fresh from the hand of God, and waiting for the breath of life; not one who had lived and suffered death. . . . She was dead. Dear, gentle, patient, noble Nell was dead." Farrell refrains from overt ethical judgment but his point is clear: Social position is a consequence of heredity and environment. Moral justice is only an abstraction.

To the degree that Farrell's art is a study in economic laws as defined by Marx, he is also a *Marxist realist,* one of the varieties of social realism. Notice the detailed analysis of social stratification and economic necessity in Alan Sillitoe's *The Loneliness of the Long-*

Distance Runner, another Marxist account. Social realist art does not always follow this kind of definite ideological prescription, but you will always be able to recognize social realism in general by the author's careful attention to detail. Detailed description is one of the best ways of convincing the reader that the thing described is genuine. The social realists usually describe the day-to-day life of ordinary lower or middle-class types, faithfully copying speech habits, vocabulary, and sentence structure, in order to capture language as it is really used. Just as a sociologist would record the style of dress of a certain group, so the author records its exact language. Joe Eszterhas' Charlie Simpson and Sillitoe's Smith speak unliterary language typical of their social classes, and this linguistic realism is common to much of modern literature.

Psychological realism, like social realism, is a consequence of nineteenth century science, but where the social realist sees behavior as a product of external forces, the psychological realist sees it as a consequence of inner psychological forces. Freud, the major authority for the psychological realist, concluded that the primary levels of consciousness were subject to the same determinism as nature and society. His Libido Theory identified two primary instincts, "the libido, sexual or life instincts . . . best comprised under the name of *eros*" that seek to prolong life and bring it to higher development, and the more "*destructive* or *aggressive* impulses." According to Freud, life "would consist in the manifestations of the conflict or interactions between the two classes of instincts"; the battle between these primary sexual and destructive instincts determines the nature of an individual's struggle for existence. Artists like William Faulkner and D. H. Lawrence, who assume the significance of primary levels of psychic activity, develop techniques to enable objective representation of unspoken life. The problem that confronts this kind of artist is how to objectify the flux of mental life while preserving the reader's sense of its absolute privacy. The writer striving for psychological realism must put into words thoughts, images, sensations, and emotions that are not necessarily verbal, and yet, in contrast to the traditional storyteller, not seem to intervene or interpret these phenomena. The reader must seem to gain direct experience of character rather than an artist's self-conscious observation of character. Lawrence solves this problem of direct observation of private thought by constructing a highly symbolic landscape to define the inner world of his characters. At the end of "The Woman Who Rode Away," the fantastic natural scene in its obviously sexual form reflects the inner drama of the thwarted sexuality which leads to the heroine's willing death. Other writers employ techniques of *stream of consciousness* for a more immediate and objective representation of the primary levels of psychic activity. The italicized portions of Faulkner's "Barn Burning," for example, demonstrate the use of interior monologue for purposes of psychological realism. Excerpts from Faulkner's *As I Lay Dying* and *The Sound and the Fury* (which unfortunately were not available for reprint) would offer other, more radically innovative examples of the stream-of-consciousness techniques developed to convey the private flux of mental life. The first chapter of *The Sound and the Fury* directly depicts the mental activities of a retarded adult, and in its obscurity it offers one of the greatest challenges for the reader in modern literature.

Realism in both social and psychological terms embodies a paradox: How can one achieve absolute objectivity? The social realist always selects and arranges material to support an idea or ideology. The psychological realist similarly selects, granting influence to particular schools of psychology. Both encounter a fundamental problem in attempting to create a scientific experiment with fictive data. The psychological realist can be no more successful in representing the mind than the social realist can be in representing the material world. No one can describe the private depths of the psyche without falsifying it, as Freud explains:

> How are we to arrive at a knowledge of the unconscious? It is of course only as something conscious that we know anything of it, after it has undergone transformation or translation into something conscious. . . . An instinct can never be an object of consciousness— only the idea that represents the instinct.*

If we regard the New Journalism as a form of realism, we see that its porpose is to be more honest than its objective forebears by exposing the paradox involved in any attempt to represent life in art. It is not surprising that a social realist thinks his art more real than impressionist or expressionist art, but it is important to note that even among journalists, all of whom purport to tell us what really happens out there in the world, the spirit of critical realism prevails, and a "new" group finds the methods of the old group conventional and unrealistic. The New Journalism derives its energy from a unique interplay of fiction and reportage, two modes of writing normally opposed in their aims. The subject matter is always an authentic contemporary event, and the story is replete with names, dates, and places that could be found in a newspaper. Consequently, this kind of story, in spokesman Tom Wolfe's words, "enjoys an advantage so obvious, so built-in, one almost forgets what a power it has: the simple fact that the reader knows *all this actually happened*." Besides satisfying our thirst for realism, this kind of story enjoys the advantages of fiction. An historical report would demand "objectivity," and any reference to the author would be avoided in order to convince us that the account is not merely his personal view of events. The New Journalist sees a fundamental deception in this convention. In his story, the author is represented as an engaged eye-witness, and the reader encounters personal attitudes and interpretations as they are formulated from the raw data of experience. Joan Didion's story involves the official newspaper accounts and subsequent legal judgment of a sensational California murder. The reporter's attempt to understand the event includes meticulous reconstruction of banal and sordid, seemingly irrelevant and unnewsworthy details of the actual experience. The result of this detail is an event sympathetically endowed with life and a reader moved to question supposedly objective newspaper accounts. Didion's narration has the authority of authenticity even though, like the novelist, she uses the subject matter as a vehicle for her own social views. Her "report" announces from the beginning its novelistic intention: "This is a story of love and death in the golden land. . . ."

The New Journalism is a popular art form; along with the cinema it has perhaps eclipsed the novel as the major conveyor of realism in our own era. In the attempt to compete with movies, magazines, and television for reader attention, a new kind of novel has emerged. A nonfiction novel like Truman Capote's *In Cold Blood*, a first cousin to the lively, irreverent, and often profane pieces of New Journalism, is a product of a new attitude toward literary as well as journalistic conventions.

---

* "The Unconscious" from *General Psychology Theory* by Sigmund Freud. New York: Collier-Macmillan, 1963, p. 116.

Thomas Hardy   (1840–1928)

CHANNEL FIRING

That night your great guns, unawares,
Shook all our coffins as we lay,
And broke the chancel window-squares,
We thought it was the Judgment-day

And sat upright. While drearisome   5
Arose the howl of wakened hounds:
The mouse let fall the altar-crumb,
The worms drew back into the mounds,

The glebe cow drooled. Till God called, "No;
It's gunnery practice out at sea   10
Just as before you went below;
The world is as it used to be:

"All nations striving strong to make
Red war yet redder. Mad as hatters
They do no more for Christés sake   15
Than you who are helpless in such matters.

"That this is not the judgment-hour
For some of them's a blessed thing,
For if it were they'd have to scour
Hell's floor for so much threatening. . . .   20

"Ha, ha. It will be warmer when
I blow the trumpet (if indeed
I ever do; for you are men,
And rest eternal sorely need)."

So down we lay again. "I wonder,   25
Will the world ever saner be,"
Said one, "than when He sent us under
In our indifferent century!"

And many a skeleton shook his head.
"Instead of preaching forty year,"   30
My neighbour Parson Thirdly said,
"I wish I had stuck to pipes and beer."

Again the guns disturbed the hour,
Roaring their readiness to avenge,
As far inland as Stourton Tower,   35
And Camelot, and starlit Stonehenge.

THE CONVERGENCE OF THE TWAIN

(Lines on the Loss of the "Titanic")

I

In a solitude of the sea
Deep from human vanity,
And the Pride of Life that planned her, stilly couches she.

II

Steel chambers, late the pyres
Of her salamandrine fires,
Cold currents thrid, and turn to rhythmic tidal lyres.

III

Over the mirrors meant
To glass the opulent
The sea-worm crawls—grotesque, slimed, dumb, indifferent.

IV

Jewels in joy designed
To ravish the sensuous mind
Lie lightless, all their sparkles bleared and black and blind.

V

Dim moon-eyed fishes near
Gaze at the gilded gear
And query: "What does this vaingloriousness down here?" ...

VI

Well: While was fashioning
This creature of cleaving wing,
The Immanent Will that stirs and urges everything

VII

Prepared a sinister mate
For her—so gaily great—
A Shape of Ice, for the time far and dissociate.

VIII

And as the smart ship grew
In stature, grace, and hue,
In shadowy silent distance grew the Iceberg too.

IX

Alien they seemed to be:
No mortal eye could see
The intimate welding of their later history,

X

Or sign that they were bent
By paths coincident
On being anon twin halves of one august event,

XI

Till the Spinner of the Years
Said "Now!" And each one hears,

And consummation comes, and jars two hemispheres.

Robert Frost (1874–1963)

A HILLSIDE THAW

To think to know the country and not know
The hillside on the day the sun lets go
Ten million silver lizards out of snow!
As often as I've seen it done before
I can't pretend to tell the way it's done.   5
It looks as if some magic of the sun
Lifted the rug that bred them on the floor
And the light breaking on them made them run.
But if I thought to stop the wet stampede,
And caught one silver lizard by the tail,   10
And put my foot on one without avail,
And threw myself wet-elbowed and wet-kneed
In front of twenty others' wriggling speed—
In the confusion of them all aglitter,
And birds that joined in the excited fun   15
By doubling and redoubling song and twitter—
I have no doubt I'd end by holding none.

It takes the moon for this. The sun's a wizard
By all I tell; but so's the moon a witch.
From the high west she makes a gentle cast   20
And suddenly, without a jerk or twitch,
She has her spell on every single lizard.
I fancied when I looked at six o'clock
The swarm still ran and scuttled just as fast.
The moon was waiting for her chill effect.   25
I looked at nine: the swarm was turned to rock
In every lifelike posture of the swarm,
Transfixed on mountain slopes almost erect.
Across each other and side by side they lay.
The spell that so could hold them as they were   30
Was wrought through trees without a breath of storm
To make a leaf, if there had been one, stir.
It was the moon's: she held them until day,
One lizard at the end of every ray.
The thought of my attempting such a stay!   35

ACQUAINTED WITH THE NIGHT

I have been one acquainted with the night.
I have walked out in rain—and back in rain.
I have outwalked the furthest city light.

I have looked down the saddest city lane.
I have passed by the watchman on his beat   5
And dropped my eyes, unwilling to explain.

I have stood still and stopped the sound of feet
When far away an interrupted cry
Came over houses from another street,

But not to call me back or say good-by;   10
And further still at an unearthly height
One luminary clock against the sky

Proclaimed the time was neither wrong nor right.
I have been one acquainted with the night.

TWO TRAMPS IN MUD TIME

Out of the mud two strangers came
And caught me splitting wood in the yard.
And one of them put me off my aim
By hailing cheerily "Hit them hard!"
I knew pretty well why he dropped behind   5
And let the other go on a way.
I knew pretty well what he had in mind:
He wanted to take my job for pay.

Good blocks of oak it was I split,
As large around as the chopping block;   10
And every piece I squarely hit
Fell splinterless as a cloven rock.
The blows that a life of self-control
Spares to strike for the common good,
That day, giving a loose to my soul,   15
I spent on the unimportant wood.

The sun was warm but the wind was chill.
You know how it is with an April day
When the sun is out and the wind is still,
You're one month on in the middle of May.   20
But if you so much as dare to speak,
A cloud comes over the sunlit arch,
A wind comes off a frozen peak,
And you're two months back in the middle of March.

A bluebird comes tenderly up to alight   25
And turns to the wind to unruffle a plume,
His song so pitched as not to excite
A single flower as yet to bloom.
It is snowing a flake: and he half knew
Winter was only playing possum.   30
Except in color he isn't blue,
But he wouldn't advise a thing to blossom.

The water for which we may have to look
In summertime with a witching wand,
In every wheelrut's now a brook,   35
In every print of a hoof a pond.
Be glad of water, but don't forget
The lurking frost in the earth beneath
That will steal forth after the sun is set
And show on the water its crystal teeth.   40

The time when most I loved my task
These two must make me love it more
By coming with what they came to ask.
You'd think I never had felt before
The weight of an ax-head poised aloft,   45
The grip on earth of outspread feet,
The life of muscles rocking soft
And smooth and moist in vernal heat.

Out of the woods two haulking tramps
(From sleeping God knows where last night,   50
But not long since in the lumber camps).
They thought all chopping was theirs of right.
Men of the woods and lumberjacks,
They judged me by their appropriate tool.
Except as a fellow handled an ax   55
They had no way of knowing a fool.

Nothing on either side was said.
They knew they had but to stay their stay
And all their logic would fill my head:
As that I had no right to play   60
With what was another man's work for gain.
My right might be love but theirs was need.
And where the two exist in twain
Theirs was the better right—agreed.

But yield who will to their separation,   65
My object in living is to unite
My avocation and my vocation
As my two eyes make one in sight.
Only where love and need are one,
And the work is play for mortal stakes,   70
Is the deed ever really done
For Heaven and the future's sakes.

DESERT PLACES

Snow falling and night falling fast, oh, fast
In a field I looked into going past,
And the ground almost covered smooth in snow,
But a few weeds and stubble showing last.

The woods around it have it—it is theirs.   5
All animals are smothered in their lairs.
I am too absent-spirited to count;
The loneliness includes me unawares.

And lonely as it is, that loneliness
Will be more lonely ere it will be less—   10
A blanker whiteness of benighted snow
With no expression, nothing to express.

They cannot scare me with their empty spaces
Between stars—on stars where no human race is.
I have it in me so much nearer home   15
To scare myself with my own desert places.

DESIGN

I found a dimpled spider, fat and white,
On a white heal-all, holding up a moth
Like a white piece of rigid satin cloth—
Assorted characters of death and blight
Mixed ready to begin the morning right,   5
Like the ingredients of a witches' broth—
A snow-drop spider, a flower like froth,
And dead wings carried like a paper kite.

What had that flower to do with being white,
The wayside blue and innocent heal-all?   10
What brought the kindred spider to that height,
Then steered the white moth thither in the night?
What but design of darkness to appall?—
If design govern in a thing so small.

DIRECTIVE

Back out of all this now too much for us,
Back in a time made simple by the loss
Of detail, burned, dissolved, and broken off
Like graveyard marble sculpture in the weather,
There is a house that is no more a house   5
Upon a farm that is no more a farm

And in a town that is no more a town.
The road there, if you'll let a guide direct you
Who only has at heart your getting lost,
May seem as if it should have been a quarry—   10
Great monolithic knees the former town
Long since gave up pretense of keeping covered.
And there's a story in a book about it:
Besides the wear of iron wagon wheels
The ledges show lines ruled southeast-northwest,   15
The chisel work of an enormous Glacier
That braced his feet against the Arctic Pole.
You must not mind a certain coolness from him
Still said to haunt this side of Panther Mountain.
Nor need you mind the serial ordeal   20
Of being watched from forty cellar holes
As if by eye pairs out of forty firkins.
As for the woods' excitement over you
That sends light rustle rushes to their leaves,
Charge that to upstart inexperience.   25
Where were they all not twenty years ago?
They think too much of having shaded out
A few old pecker-fretted apple trees.
Make yourself up a cheering song of how
Someone's road home from work this once was,   30
Who may be just ahead of you on foot
Or creaking with a buggy load of grain.
The height of the adventure is the height
Of country where two village cultures faded
Into each other. Both of them are lost.   35
And if you're lost enough to find yourself
By now, pull in your ladder road behind you
And put a sign up CLOSED to all but me.
Then make yourself at home. The only field
Now left's no bigger than a harness gall.   40
First there's the children's house of make-believe,
Some shattered dishes underneath a pine,
The playthings in the playhouse of the children.
Weep for what little things could make them glad.
Then for the house that is no more a house,   45
But only a belilaced cellar hole,
Now slowly closing like a dent in dough.
This was no playhouse but a house in earnest.
Your destination and your destiny's
A brook that was the water of the house,   50
Cold as a spring as yet so near its source,
Too lofty and original to rage.
(We know the valley streams that when aroused
Will leave their tatters hung on barb and thorn.)
I have kept hidden in the instep arch   55
Of an old cedar at the waterside
A broken drinking goblet like the Grail
Under a spell so the wrong ones can't find it,

So can't get saved, as Saint Mark says they mustn't.
(I stole the goblet from the children's playhouse.)   60
Here are your waters and your watering place.
Drink and be whole again beyond confusion.

Wilfred Owen (1893–1918)

GREATER LOVE

Red lips are not so red
  As the stained stones kissed by the English dead.
Kindness of wooed and wooer
Seems shame to their love pure.
O Love, your eyes lose lure   5
  When I behold eyes blinded in my stead!

Your slender attitude
  Trembles not exquisite like limbs knife-skewed,
Rolling and rolling there
Where God seems not to care;   10
Till the fierce love they bear
  Cramps them in death's extreme decrepitude.

Your voice sings not so soft,—
  Though even as wind murmuring through raftered loft,—
Your dear voice is not dear,   15
Gentle, and evening clear,
As theirs whom none now hear,
  Now earth has stopped their piteous mouths that coughed.

Heart, you were never hot
  Nor large, nor full like hearts made great with shot;   20
And though your hand be pale,
Paler are all which trail
Your cross through flame and hail:
  Weep, you may weep, for you may touch them not.

STRANGE MEETING

It seemed that out of battle I escaped
Down some profound dull tunnel, long since scooped
Through granites which titanic wars had groined.
Yet also there encumbered sleepers groaned,
Too fast in thought or death to be bestirred.   5
Then, as I probed them, one sprang up, and stared

With piteous recognition in fixed eyes,
Lifting distressful hands as if to bless.
And by his smile, I knew that sullen hall,
By his dead smile I knew we stood in Hell.   10
With a thousand pains that vision's face was grained;
Yet no blood reached there from the upper ground,
And no guns thumped, or down the flues made moan.
"Strange friend," I said, "here is no cause to mourn."
"None," said that other, "save the undone years,   15
The hopelessness. Whatever hope is yours,
Was my life also; I went hunting wild
After the wildest beauty in the world,
Which lies not calm in eyes, or braided hair,
But mocks the steady running of the hour,   20
And if it grieves, grieves richlier than here.
For of my glee might many men have laughed,
And of my weeping something had been left,
Which must die now. I mean the truth untold,
The pity of war, the pity war distilled.   25
Now men will go content with what we spoiled.
Or, discontent, boil bloody, and be spilled.
They will be swift with swiftness of the tigress,
None will break ranks, though nations trek from progress.
Courage was mine, and I had mystery: 30
Wisdom was mine, and I had mastery.
To miss the march of this retreating world
Into vain citadels that are not walled.
Then, when much blood had clogged their chariot-wheels
I would go up and wash them from sweet wells,   35
Even with truths that lie too deep for taint.
I would have poured my spirit without stint
But not through wounds; not on the cess of war.
Foreheads of men have bled where no wounds were.
I am the enemy you killed, my friend.   40
I knew you in this dark; for so you frowned
Yesterday through me as you jabbed and killed.
I parried; but my hands were loath and cold.
Let us sleep now . . . ."

Sherwood Anderson   (1876–1941)

From Winesburg, Ohio

THE BOOK OF THE GROTESQUE

The writer, an old man with a white mustache, had some difficulty in getting into bed. The windows of the house in which he lived were high and he wanted to look at the trees when he awoke in the morning. A carpenter came to fix the bed so that it would be on a level with the window.

Quite a fuss was made about the matter. The carpenter, who had been a soldier in the Civil War, came into the writer's room and sat down to talk of building a platform for the purpose of raising the bed. The writer had cigars lying about and the carpenter smoked.

For a time the two men talked of the raising of the bed and then they talked of other things. The soldier got on the subject of the war. The writer, in fact, led him to that subject. The carpenter had once been a prisoner in Andersonville prison and had lost a brother. The brother had died of starvation, and whenever the carpenter got upon that subject he cried. He, like the old writer, had a white mustache, and when he cried he puckered up his lips and the mustache bobbed up and down. The weeping old man with the cigar in his mouth was ludicrous. The plan the writer had for the raising of his bed was forgotten and later the carpenter did it in his own way and the writer, who was past sixty, had to help himself with a chair when he went to bed at night.

In his bed the writer rolled over on his side and lay quite still. For years he had been beset with notions concerning his heart. He was a hard smoker and his heart fluttered. The idea had got into his mind that he would some time die unexpectedly and always when he got into bed he thought of that. It did not alarm him. The effect in fact was quite a special thing and not easily explained. It made him more alive, there in bed, than at any other time. Perfectly still he lay and his body was old and not of much use any more, but something inside him was altogether young. He was like a pregnant woman, only that the thing inside him was not a baby but a youth. No, it wasn't a youth, it was a woman, young, and wearing a coat of mail like a knight. It is absurd, you see, to try to tell what was inside the old writer as he lay on his high bed and listened to the fluttering of his heart. The thing to get at is what the writer, or the young thing within the writer, was thinking about.

The old writer, like all of the people in the world, had got, during his long life, a great many notions in his head. He had once been quite handsome and a number of women had been in love with him. And then, of course, he had known people, many people, known them in a peculiarly intimate way that was different from the way in which you and I know people. At least that is what the writer thought and the thought pleased him. Why quarrel with an old man concerning his thoughts?

In the bed the writer had a dream that was not a dream. As he grew somewhat sleepy but was still conscious, figures began to appear before his eyes. He imagined the young indescribable thing within himself was driving a long procession of figures before his eyes.

You see the interest in all this lies in the figures that went before the eyes of the writer. They were all grotesques. All of the men and women the writer had ever known had become grotesques.

The grotesques were not all horrible. Some were amusing, some almost beautiful, and one, a woman all drawn out of shape, hurt the old man by her grotesqueness. When she passed he made a noise like a small dog whimpering. Had you come into the room you might have supposed the old man had unpleasant dreams or perhaps indigestion.

For an hour the procession of grotesques passed before the eyes of the old man, and then, although it was a painful thing to do, he crept out of bed and began to write. Some one of the grotesques had made a deep impression on his mind and he wanted to describe it.

At his desk the writer worked for an hour. In the end he wrote a book which he called "The Book of the Grotesque." It was never published, but I saw it once and it made an indelible impression on my mind. The book had one central thought that is very strange and has always remained with me. By remembering it I have been able to understand many people and things that I was never able to understand before. The thought was involved but a simple statement of it would be something like this:

That in the beginning when the world was young there were a great many thoughts but no such thing as a truth. Man made the truths himself and each truth was a composite of a great many vague thoughts. All about in the world were the truths and they were all beautiful.

The old man had listed hundreds of the truths in his book. I will not try to tell you all of them. There was the truth of virginity and the truth of passion, the truth of wealth and of poverty, of thrift and of profligacy, of carelessness and abandon. Hundreds and hundreds were the truths and they were all beautiful.

And then the people came along. Each as he appeared snatched up one of the truths and some who were quite strong snatched up a dozen of them.

It was the truths that made the people grotesques. The old man had quite an elaborate theory concerning the matter. It was his notion that the moment one of the people took one of the truths to himself, called it his truth, and tried to live his life by it, he became a grotesque and the truth he embraced became a falsehood.

You can see for yourself how the old man, who had spent all of his life writing and was filled with words, would write hundreds of pages concerning this matter. The subject would become so big in his mind that he himself would be in danger of becoming a grotesque. He didn't, I suppose, for the same reason that he never published the book. It was the young thing inside him that saved the old man.

Concerning the old carpenter who fixed the bed for the writer, I only mentioned him because he, like many of what are called very common people, became the nearest thing to what is understandable and lovable of all the grotesques in the writer's book.

HANDS

Upon the half decayed veranda of a small frame house that stood near the edge of a ravine near the town of Winesburg, Ohio, a fat little old man walked nervously up and down. Across a long field that had been seeded for clover but that had produced only a dense crop of yellow mustard weeds, he could see the public highway along which went a wagon filled with berry pickers returning from the fields. The berry pickers, youths and maidens, laughed and shouted boisterously. A boy clad in a blue shirt leaped from the wagon and attempted to drag after him one of the maidens, who screamed and protested shrilly. The feet of the boy in the road kicked up a cloud of dust that floated across the face of the departing sun. Over the long field came a thin girlish voice. "Oh, you Wing Biddlebaum, comb your hair, it's falling into your eyes," commanded the voice to the man, who was bald and whose nervous little hands fiddled about the bare white forehead as though arranging a mass of tangled locks.

Wing Biddlebaum, forever frightened and beset by a ghostly band of doubts, did not think of himself as in any way a part of the life of the town where he had lived for twenty years. Among all the people of Winesburg but one had come close to him. With

George Willard, son of Tom Willard, the proprietor of the New Willard House, he had formed something like a friendship. George Willard was the reporter on the *Winesburg Eagle* and sometimes in the evenings he walked out along the highway to Wing Biddlebaum's house. Now as the old man walked up and down on the veranda, his hands moving nervously about, he was hoping that George Willard would come and spend the evening with him. After the wagon containing the berry pickers had passed, he went across the field through the tall mustard weeds and climbing a rail fence peered anxiously along the road to the town. For a moment he stood thus, rubbing his hands together and looking up and down the road, and then, fear overcoming him, ran back to walk again upon the porch on his own house.

In the presence of George Willard, Wing Biddlebaum, who for twenty years had been the town mystery, lost something of his timidity, and his shadowy personality, submerged in a sea of doubts, came forth to look at the world. With the young reporter at his side, he ventured in the light of day into Main Street or strode up and down on the rickety front porch of his own house, talking excitedly. The voice that had been low and trembling became shrill and loud. The bent figure straightened. With a kind of wriggle, like a fish returned to the brook by the fisherman, Biddlebaum the silent began to talk, striving to put into words the ideas that had been accumulated by his mind during long years of silence.

Wing Biddlebaum talked much with his hands. The slender expressive fingers, forever active, forever striving to conceal themselves in his pockets or behind his back, came forth and became the piston rods of his machinery of expression.

The story of Wing Biddlebaum is a story of hands. Their restless activity, like unto the beating of the wings of an imprisoned bird, had given him his name. Some obscure poet of the town had thought of it. The hands alarmed their owner. He wanted to keep them hidden away and looked with amazement at the quiet inexpressive hands of other men who worked beside him in the fields, or passed, driving sleepy teams on country roads.

When he talked to George Willard, Wing Biddlebaum closed his fists and beat with them upon a table or on the walls of his house. The action made him more comfortable. If the desire to talk came to him when the two were walking in the fields, he sought out a stump or the top board of a fence and with his hands pounding busily talked with renewed ease.

The story of Wing Biddlebaum's hands is worth a book in itself. Sympathetically set forth it would tap many strange, beautiful qualities in obscure men. It is a job for a poet. In Winesburg the hands had attracted attention merely because of their activity. With them Wing Biddlebaum had picked as high as a hundred and forty quarts of strawberries in a day. They became his distinguishing feature, the source of his fame. Also they made more grotesque an already grotesque and elusive individuality. Winesburg was proud of the hands of Wing Biddlebaum in the same spirit in which it was proud of Banker White's new stone house and Wesley Moyer's bay stallion, Tony Tip, that had won the two-fifteen trot at the fall races in Cleveland.

As for George Willard, he had many times wanted to ask about the hands. At times an almost overwhelming curiosity had taken hold of him. He felt that there must be a reason for their strange activity and their inclination to keep hidden away and only a growing respect for Wing Biddlebaum kept him from blurting out the questions that were often in his mind.

Once he had been on the point of asking. The two were walking in the fields on a summer afternoon and had stopped to sit upon a grassy bank. All afternoon Wing Biddlebaum had talked as one inspired. By a fence he had stopped and beating like a giant wood-pecker upon the top board had shouted at George Willard, condemning his tendency to be too much influenced by the people about him. "You are destroying yourself," he cried. "You have the inclination to be alone and to dream and you are afraid of dreams. You want to be like others in town here. You hear them talk and you try to imitate them."

On the grassy bank Wing Biddle-baum had tried again to drive his point home. His voice became soft and remi-niscent, and with a sigh of contentment he launched into a long rambling talk, speaking as one lost in a dream.

Out of the dream Wing Biddlebaum made a picture for George Willard. In the picture men lived again in a kind of pastoral golden age. Across a green open country came clean-limbed young men, some afoot, some mounted upon horses. In crowds the young men came to gather about the feet of an old man who sat beneath a tree in a tiny garden and who talked to them.

Wing Biddlebaum became wholly in-spired. For once he forgot the hands. Slowly they stole forth and lay upon George Willard's shoulders. Something new and bold came into the voice that talked. "You must try to forget all you have learned," said the old man. "You must begin to dream. From this time on you must shut your ears to the roaring of the voices."

Pausing in his speech, Wing Biddle-baum looked long and earnestly at George Willard. His eyes glowed. Again he raised the hands to caress the boy and then a look of horror swept over his face.

With a convulsive movement of his body, Wing Biddlebaum sprang to his feet and thrust his hands deep into his trousers pockets. Tears came to his eyes. "I must be getting along home. I can talk no more with you," he said nervously.

Without looking back, the old man had hurried down the hillside and across a meadow, leaving George Willard per-plexed and frightened upon the grass slope. With a shiver of dread the boy arose and went along the road toward town. "I'll not ask him about his hands," he thought, touched by the memory of the terror he had seen in the man's eyes. "There's something wrong, but I don't want to know what it is. His hands have something to do with his fear of me and of everyone."

And George Willard was right. Let us look briefly into the story of the hands. Perhaps our talking of them will arouse the poet who will tell the hid-den wonder story of the influence for which the hands were but fluttering pennants of promise.

In his youth Wing Biddlebaum had been a school teacher in a town in Pennsylvania. He was not then known as Wing Biddlebaum, but went by the less euphonic name of Adolph Myers. As Adolph Myers he was much loved by the boys of his school.

Adolph Myers was meant by nature to be a teacher of youth. He was one of those rare, little-understood men who rule by a power so gentle that it passes as a lovable weakness. In their feeling for the boys under their charge such men are not unlike the finer sort of women in their love of men.

And yet that is but crudely stated. It needs the poet there. With the boys of his school, Adolph Myers had walked in the evening or had sat talking until dusk upon the schoolhouse steps lost in a kind of dream. Here and there went his hands, caressing the shoulders of the boys, playing about the tousled heads. As he talked his voice became soft and musical. There was a caress in that also. In a way the voice and the hands, the stroking of the shoulders and the touching of the hair were a part of the schoolmaster's effort to carry a dream into the young minds. By the caress that was in his fingers he expressed himself. He was one of those men in whom the force that creates life is diffused, not centralized. Under the caress of his hands doubt and disbelief went out of the minds of the boys and they began also to dream.

And then the tragedy. A half-witted boy of the school became enamored of the young master. In his bed at night he imagined unspeakable things and in the morning went forth to tell his dreams as facts. Strange, hideous accusations fell from his loose-hung lips. Through the Pennsylvania town went a shiver. Hidden, shadowy doubts that had been in men's minds concerning Adolph Myers were galvanized into beliefs.

The tragedy did not linger. Trembling lads were jerked out of bed and questioned. "He put his arms about me," said one. "His fingers were always playing in my hair," said another.

One afternoon a man of the town, Henry Bradford, who kept a saloon, came to the schoolhouse door. Calling Adolph Myers into the school yard he began to beat him with his fists. As his hard knuckles beat down into the frightened face of the schoolmaster, his wrath became more and more terrible. Screaming with dismay, the children ran here and there like disturbed insects. "I'll teach you to put your hands on my boy, you beast," roared the saloon keeper, who, tired of beating the master, had begun to kick him about the yard.

Adolph Myers was driven from the Pennsylvania town in the night. With lanterns in their hands a dozen men came to the door of the house where he lived alone and commanded that he dress and come forth. It was raining and one of the men had a rope in his hands. They had intended to hang the schoolmaster, but something in his figure, so small, white, and pitiful, touched their hearts and they let him escape. As he ran away into the darkness they repented of their weakness and ran after him, swearing and throwing sticks and great balls of soft mud at the figure that screamed and ran faster and faster into the darkness.

For twenty years Adolph Myers had lived alone in Winesburg. He was but forty but looked sixty-five. The name of Biddlebaum he got from a box of goods seen at a freight station as he hurried through an eastern Ohio town. He had an aunt in Winesburg, a black-toothed old woman who raised chickens, and with her he lived until she died. He had been ill for a year after the experience in Pennsylvania, and after his recovery worked as a day laborer in the fields, going timidly about and striving to conceal his hands. Although he did not understand what had happened he felt that the hands must be to blame. Again and again the fathers of the boys had talked of the hands. "Keep your hands to yourself," the saloon keeper had roared, dancing with fury in the schoolhouse yard.

Upon the veranda of his house by the ravine, Wing Biddlebaum continued to walk up and down until the sun had disappeared and the road beyond the field was lost in the grey shadows. Going into his house he cut slices of bread and spread honey upon them. When the rumble of the evening train that took away the express cars loaded with the day's harvest of berries had passed and restored the silence of the summer night, he went again to walk upon the veranda. In the darkness he could not see the hands and they became quiet. Although he still hungered for the presence of the boy, who was the medium through which he expressed his love of man, the hunger became again a part of his loneliness and his waiting. Lighting a lamp, Wing Biddle-baum washed the few dishes soiled by his simple meal and, setting up a fold-ing cot by the screen door that led to the porch, prepared to undress for the night. A few stray white bread crumbs lay on the cleanly washed floor by the table; putting the lamp upon a low stool he began to pick up the crumbs, carrying them to his mouth one by one with unbelievable rapidity. In the dense blotch of light beneath the table, the kneeling figure looked like a priest en-gaged in some service of his church. The nervous expressive fingers, flashing in and out of the light, might well have been mistaken for the fingers of the devotee going swiftly through decade after decade of his rosary.

GODLINESS
A Tale in Four Parts

PART ONE

There were always three or four old people sitting on the front porch of the house or puttering about the garden of the Bentley farm. Three of the old peo-ple were women and sisters to Jesse. They were a colorless, soft-voiced lot. Then there was a silent old man with thin white hair who was Jesse's uncle.

The farmhouse was built of wood, a board outer-covering over a framework of logs. It was in reality not one house but a cluster of houses joined together in a rather haphazard manner. Inside, the place was full of surprises. One went up steps from the living room into the dining room and there were always steps to be ascended or descended in passing from one room to another. At meal times the place was like a beehive. At one moment all was quiet, then doors began to open, feet clattered on stairs, a murmur of soft voices arose and people appeared from a dozen ob-scure corners.

Besides the old people, already men-tioned, many others lived in the Bent-ley house. There were four hired men, a woman named Aunt Callie Beebe, who was in charge of the housekeeping, a dull-witted girl named Eliza Stough-ton, who made beds and helped with the milking, a boy who worked in the stables, and Jesse Bentley himself, the owner and overlord of it all.

By the time the American Civil War had been over for twenty years, that part of Northern Ohio where the Bent-ley farms lay had begun to emerge from pioneer life. Jesse then owned machin-ery for harvesting grain. He had built modern barns and most of his land was drained with carefully laid tile drain, but in order to understand the man we will have to go back to an earlier day.

The Bentley family had been in Northern Ohio for several generations before Jesse's time. They came from New York State and took up land when the country was new and land could be had at a low price. For a long time they, in common with all the other Middle Western people, were very poor. The land they had settled upon was heavily wooded and covered with fallen logs and underbrush. After the long hard labor of clearing these away and cutting the timber, there were still the stumps to be reckoned with. Plows run through the fields caught on hidden roots, stones lay all about, on the low places water gathered, and the young corn turned yellow, sickened and died.

When Jesse Bentley's father and brothers had come into their ownership of the place, much of the harder part of the work of clearing had been done, but they clung to old traditions and worked like driven animals. They lived as practically all of the farming people of the time lived. In the spring and through most of the winter the highways leading into the town of Winesburg were a sea of mud. The four young men of the family worked hard all day in the fields, they ate heavily of coarse, greasy food, and at night slept like tired beasts on beds of straw. Into their lives came little that was not coarse and brutal and outwardly they were themselves coarse and brutal. On Saturday afternoons they hitched a team of horses to a three-seated wagon and went off to town. In town they stood about the stoves in the stores talking to other farmers or to the store keepers. They were dressed in overalls and in the winter wore heavy coats that were flecked with mud. Their hands as they stretched them out to the heat of the stoves were cracked and red. It was difficult for them to talk and so they for the most part kept silent. When they had bought meat, flour, sugar, and salt, they went into one of the Winesburg saloons and drank beer. Under the influence of drink the naturally strong lusts of their natures, kept suppressed by the heroic labor of breaking up new ground, were released. A kind of crude and animal-like poetic fervor took possession of them. On the road home they stood up on the wagon seats and shouted at the stars. Sometimes they fought long and bitterly and at other times they broke forth into songs. Once Enoch Bentley, the older one of the boys, struck his father, old Tom Bentley, with the butt of a teamster's whip, and the old man seemed likely to die. For days Enoch lay hid in the straw in the loft of the stable ready to flee if the result of his momentary passion turned out to be murder. He was kept alive with food brought by his mother, who also kept him informed of the injured man's condition. When all turned out well he emerged from his hiding place and went back to the work of clearing land as though nothing had happened.

.   .   .

The Civil War brought a sharp turn to the fortunes of the Bentleys and was responsible for the rise of the youngest son, Jesse. Enoch, Edward, Harry, and Will Bentley all enlisted and before the long war ended they were all killed. For a time after they went away to the South, old Tom tried to run the place, but he was not successful. When the last of the four had been killed he sent word to Jesse that he would have to come home.

Then the mother, who had not been well for a year, died suddenly, and the father became altogether discouraged. He talked of selling the farm and moving into town. All day he went about shaking his head and muttering. The work in the fields was neglected and weeds grew high in the corn. Old Tom hired men but he did not use them intelligently. When they had gone away to the fields in the morning he wandered into the woods and sat down on a log. Sometimes he forgot to come home at night and one of the daughters had to go in search of him.

When Jesse Bentley came home to the farm and began to take charge of things he was a slight, sensitive-looking man of twenty-two. At eighteen he had left home to go to school to become a scholar and eventually to become a minister of the Presbyterian Church. All through his boyhood he had been what in our country was called an "odd sheep" and had not got on with his brothers. Of all the family only his mother had understood him and she was now dead. When he came home to take charge of the farm, that had at that time grown to more than six hundred acres, everyone on the farms about and in the nearby town of Winesburg smiled at the idea of his trying to handle the work that had been done by his four strong brothers.

There was indeed good cause to smile. By the standards of his day Jesse did not look like a man at all. He was small and very slender and womanish of body and, true to the traditions of young ministers, wore a long black coat and a narrow black string tie. The neighbors were amused when they saw him, after the years away, and they were even more amused when they saw the woman he had married in the city.

As a matter of fact, Jesse's wife did soon go under. That was perhaps Jesse's fault. A farm in Northern Ohio in the hard years after the Civil War was no place for a delicate woman, and Katherine Bentley was delicate. Jesse was hard with her as he was with everybody about him in those days. She tried to do such work as all the neighbor women about her did and he let her go on without interference. She helped to do the milking and did part of the housework; she made the beds for the men and prepared their food. For a year she worked every day from sunrise until late at night and then after giving birth to a child she died.

As for Jesse Bentley—although he was a delicately built man there was something within him that could not easily be killed. He had brown curly hair and grey eyes that were at times hard and direct, at times wavering and uncertain. Not only was he slender but he was also short of stature. His mouth was like the mouth of a sensitive and very determined child. Jesse Bentley was a fanatic. He was a man born out of his time and place and for this he suffered and made others suffer. Never did he succeed in getting what he wanted out of life and he did not know what he wanted. Within a very short time after he came home to the Bentley farm he made everyone there a little afraid of him, and his wife, who should have been close to him as his mother had

been, was afraid also. At the end of two weeks after his coming, old Tom Bentley made over to him the entire ownership of the place and retired into the background. Everyone retired into the background. In spite of his youth and inexperience, Jesse had the trick of mastering the souls of his people. He was so in earnest in everything he did and said that no one understood him. He made everyone on the farm work as they had never worked before and yet there was no joy in the work. If things went well they went well for Jesse and never for the people who were his dependents. Like a thousand other strong men who have come into the world here in America in these later times, Jesse was but half strong. He could master others but he could not master himself. The running of the farm as it had never been run before was easy for him. When he came home from Cleveland where he had been in school, he shut himself off from all of his people and began to make plans. He thought about the farm night and day and that made him successful. Other men on the farms about him worked too hard and were too tired to think, but to think of the farm and to be everlastingly making plans for its success was a relief to Jesse. It partially satisfied something in his passionate nature. Immediately after he came home he had a wing built on to the old house and in a large room facing the west he had windows that looked into the barnyard and other windows that looked off across the fields. By the window he sat down to think. Hour after hour and day after day he sat and looked over the land and thought out his new place in life. The passionate burning thing in his nature flamed up and his eyes became hard. He wanted to make the farm produce as no farm in his state had ever produced before and then he wanted something else. It was the indefinable hunger within that made his eyes waver and that kept him always more and more silent before people. He would have given much to achieve peace and in him was a fear that peace was the thing he could not achieve.

All over his body Jesse Bentley was alive. In his small frame was gathered the force of a long line of strong men. He had always been extraordinarily alive when he was a small boy on the farm and later when he was a young man in school. In the school he had studied and thought of God and the Bible with his whole mind and heart. As time passed and he grew to know people better, he began to think of himself as an extraordinary man, one set apart from his fellows. He wanted terribly to make his life a thing of great importance, and as he looked about at his fellow men and saw how like clods they lived it seemed to him that he could not bear to become also such a clod. Although in his absorption in himself and in his own destiny he was blind to the fact that his young wife was doing a strong woman's work even after she had become large with child and that she was killing herself in his service, he did not intend to be unkind to her. When his father, who was old and twisted with toil, made over to him the ownership of the farm and seemed content to creep away to a corner and wait for death, he shrugged his shoulders and dismissed the old man from his mind.

In the room by the window overlooking the land that had come down to him sat Jesse thinking of his own affairs. In the stables he could hear the tramping of his horses and the restless movement of his cattle. Away in the fields he could see other cattle wandering over green hills. The voices of men, his men who worked for him, came in to him through the window. From the milkhouse there was the steady thump, thump of a churn being manipulated by the half-witted girl, Eliza Stoughton. Jesse's mind went back to the men of Old Testament days who had also owned lands and herds. He remembered how God had come down out of the skies and talked to these men and he wanted God to notice and to talk to him also. A kind of feverish boyish eagerness to in some way achieve in his own life the flavor of significance that had hung over these men took possession of him. Being a prayerful man he spoke of the matter aloud to God and the sound of his own words strengthened and fed his eagerness.

"I am a new kind of man come into possession of these fields," he declared. "Look upon me, O God, and look Thou also upon my neighbors and all the men who have gone before me here! O God, create in me another Jesse, like that one of old, to rule over men and to be the father of sons who shall be rulers!" Jesse grew excited as he talked aloud and jumping to his feet walked up and down in the room. In fancy he saw himself living in old times and among old peoples. The land that lay stretched out before him became of vast significance, a place peopled by his fancy with a new race of men sprung from himself. It seemed to him that in his day as in those other and older days, kingdoms might be created and new impulses given to the lives of men by the power of God speaking through a chosen servant. He longed to be such a servant. "It is God's work I have come to the land to do," he declared in a loud voice and his short figure straightened and he thought that something like a halo of Godly approval hung over him.

It will perhaps be somewhat difficult for the men and women of a later day to understand Jesse Bentley. In the last fifty years a vast change has taken place in the lives of our people. A revolution has in fact taken place. The coming of industrialism, attended by all the roar and rattle of affairs, the shrill cries of millions of new voices that have come among us from overseas, the going and coming of trains, the growth of cities, the building of the interurban car lines that weave in and out of towns and past farmhouses, and now in these later days the coming of the automobiles has worked a tremendous change in the lives and in the habits of thought of our people of Mid-America. Books, badly imagined and written though they may be in the hurry of our times, are in every household, magazines circulate by the millions of copies, newspapers are everywhere. In our day a farmer standing by the stove in the store in his village has his mind filled to overflowing with the words of other men. The newspapers and the magazines have pumped him full. Much of the old brutal ignorance that had in it also a kind of beautiful childlike innocence is gone forever. The farmer by the stove is brother to the men of the cities, and if you listen you will find him talking as glibly and as senselessly as the best city man of us all.

In Jesse Bentley's time and in the country districts of the whole Middle West in the years after the Civil War it was not so. Men labored too hard and were too tired to read. In them was no desire for words printed upon paper. As they worked in the fields, vague, half-formed thoughts took possession of them. They believed in God and in God's power to control their lives. In the little Protestant churches they gathered on Sunday to hear of God and his works. The churches were the center of the social and intellectual life of the times. The figure of God was big in the hearts of men.

And so, having been born an imaginative child and having within him a great intellectual eagerness, Jesse Bentley had turned wholeheartedly toward God. When the war took his brothers away, he saw the hand of God in that. When his father became ill and could no longer attend to the running of the farm, he took that also as a sign from God. In the city, when the word came to him, he walked about at night through the streets thinking of the matter and when he had come home and had got the work on the farm well under way, he went again at night to walk through the forests and over the low hills and to think of God.

As he walked the importance of his own figure in some divine plan grew in his mind. He grew avaricious and was impatient that the farm contained only six hundred acres. Kneeling in a fence corner at the edge of some meadow, he sent his voice abroad into the silence and looking up he saw the stars shining down at him.

One evening, some months after his father's death, and when his wife Katherine was expecting at any moment to be laid abed of childbirth, Jesse left his house and went for a long walk. The Bentley farm was situated in a tiny valley watered by Wine Creek, and Jesse walked along the banks of the stream to the end of his own land and on through the fields of his neighbors. As he walked the valley broadened and then narrowed again. Great open stretches of field and wood lay before him. The moon came out from behind clouds, and, climbing a low hill, he sat down to think.

Jesse thought that as the true servant of God the entire stretch of country through which he had walked should have come into his possession. He thought of his dead brothers and blamed them that they had not worked harder and achieved more. Before him in the moonlight the tiny stream ran down over stones, and he began to think of the men of old times who like himself had owned flocks and lands.

A fantastic impulse, half fear, half greediness, took possession of Jesse Bentley. He remembered how in the old Bible story the Lord had appeared to that other Jesse and told him to send his son David to where Saul and the men of Israel were fighting the Philistines in the Valley of Elah. Into Jesse's mind came the conviction that all of the Ohio farmers who owned land in the valley of Wine Creek were Philistines and enemies of God. "Suppose," he whispered to himself, "there should come from among them one who, like

Goliath the Philistine of Gath, could defeat me and take from me my possessions." In fancy he felt the sickening dread that he thought must have lain heavy on the heart of Saul before the coming of David. Jumping to his feet, he began to run through the night. As he ran he called to God. His voice carried far over the low hills. "Jehovah of Hosts," he cried, "send to me this night out of the womb of Katherine, a son. Let thy grace alight upon me. Send me a son to be called David who shall help me to pluck at last all of these lands out of the hands of the Philistines and turn them to Thy service and to the building of Thy kingdom on earth."

PART TWO

David Hardy of Winesburg, Ohio, was the grandson of Jesse Bentley, the owner of Bentley farms. When he was twelve years old he went to the old Bentley place to live. His mother, Louise Bentley, the girl who came into the world on that night when Jesse ran through the fields crying to God that he be given a son, had grown to womanhood on the farm and had married young John Hardy of Winesburg, who became a banker. Louise and her husband did not live happily together and everyone agreed that she was to blame. She was a small woman with sharp grey eyes and black hair. From childhood she had been inclined to fits of temper and when not angry she was often morose and silent. In Winesburg it was said that she drank. Her husband, the banker, who was a careful, shrewd man, tried hard to make her happy. When he began to make money he bought for her a large brick house on Elm Street in Winesburg and he was the first man in that town to keep a manservant to drive his wife's carriage.

But Louise could not be made happy. She flew into half insane fits of temper during which she was sometimes silent, sometimes noisy and quarrelsome. She swore and cried out in her anger. She got a knife from the kitchen and threatened her husband's life. Once she deliberately set fire to the house, and often she hid herself away for days in her own room and would see no one. Her life, lived as a half recluse, gave rise to all sorts of stories concerning her. It was said that she took drugs and that she hid herself away from people because she was often so under the influence of drink that her condition could not be concealed. Sometimes on summer afternoons she came out of the house and got into her carriage. Dismissing the driver she took the reins in her own hands and drove off at top speed through the streets. If a pedestrian got in her way she drove straight ahead and the frightened citizen had to escape as best he could. To the people of the town it seemed as though she wanted to run them down. When she had driven through several streets, tearing around corners and beating the horses with the whip, she drove off into the country. On the country roads after she had gotten out of sight of the houses she let the horses slow down to a walk and her wild, reckless mood passed. She became thoughtful and muttered words. Sometimes tears came into her eyes. And then when she came back into town she again drove furiously through the quiet streets. But for the influence of her husband and the respect he inspired in people's minds she would have been arrested more than once by the town marshal.

Young David Hardy grew up in the house with this woman and as can well be imagined there was not much joy in his childhood. He was too young then to have opinions of his own about people, but at times it was difficult for him not to have very definite opinions about the woman who was his mother. David was always a quiet, orderly boy and for a long time was thought by the people of Winesburg to be something of a dullard. His eyes were brown and as a child he had a habit of looking at things and people a long time without appearing to see what he was looking at. When he heard his mother spoken of harshly or when he overheard her berating his father, he was frightened and ran away to hide. Sometimes he could not find a hiding place and that confused him. Turning his face toward a tree or if he was indoors toward the wall, he closed his eyes and tried not to think of anything. He had a habit of talking aloud to himself, and early in life a spirit of quiet sadness often took possession of him.

On the occasions when David went to visit his grandfather on the Bentley farm, he was altogether contented and happy. Often he wished that he would never have to go back to town and once when he had come home from the farm after a long visit, something happened that had a lasting effect on his mind.

David had come back into town with one of the hired men. The man was in a hurry to go about his own affairs and left the boy at the head of the street in which the Hardy house stood. It was early dusk of a fall evening and the sky was overcast with clouds. Something happened to David. He could not bear to go into the house where his mother and father lived, and on an impulse he decided to run away from home. He intended to go back to the farm and to his grandfather, but lost his way and for hours he wandered weeping and frightened on country roads. It started to rain and lightning flashed in the sky. The boy's imagination was excited and he fancied that he could see and hear strange things in the darkness. Into his mind came the conviction that he was walking and running in some terrible void where no one had ever been before. The darkness about him seemed limitless. The sound of the wind blowing in trees was terrifying. When a team of horses approached along the road in which he walked he was frightened and climbed a fence. Through a field he ran until he

came into another road and getting upon his knees felt of the soft ground with his fingers. But for the figure of his grandfather, whom he was afraid he would never find in the darkness, he thought the world must be altogether empty. When his cries were heard by a farmer who was walking home from town and he was brought back to his father's house, he was so tired and excited that he did not know what was happening to him.

By chance David's father knew that he had disappeared. On the street he had met the farm hand from the Bentley place and knew of his son's return to town. When the boy did not come home an alarm was set up and John Hardy with several men of the town went to search the country. The report that David had been kidnapped ran about through the streets of Winesburg. When he came home there were no lights in the house, but his mother appeared and clutched him eagerly in her arms. David thought she had suddenly become another woman. He could not believe that so delightful a thing had happened. With her own hands Louise Hardy bathed his tired young body and cooked him food. She would not let him go to bed but, when he had put on his nightgown, blew out the lights and sat down in a chair to hold him in her arms. For an hour the woman sat in the darkness and held her boy. All the time she kept talking in a low voice. David could not understand what had so changed her. Her habitually dissatisfied face had become, he thought, the most peaceful and lovely thing he had ever seen. When he began to weep she held him more and more tightly. On and on went her voice. It was not harsh or shrill as when she talked to her husband, but was like rain falling on trees. Presently men began coming to the door to report that he had not been found, but she made him hide and be silent until she had sent them away. He thought it must be a game his mother and the men of the town were playing with him and laughed joyously. Into his mind came the thought that his having been lost and frightened in the darkness was an altogether unimportant matter. He thought that he would have been willing to go through the frightful experience a thousand times to be sure of finding at the end of the long black road a thing so lovely as his mother had suddenly become.

.   .   .

During the last years of young David's boyhood he saw his mother but seldom and she became for him just a woman with whom he had once lived. Still he could not get her figure out of his mind and as he grew older it became more definite. When he was twelve years old he went to the Bentley farm to live. Old Jesse came into town and fairly demanded that he be given charge of the boy. The old man was excited and determined on having his own way. He talked to John Hardy in the office of the Winesburg Savings Bank and then the two men went to the house on Elm Street to talk with Louise. They both expected her to make trouble but were mistaken. She was very quiet and when Jesse had explained his mission and had gone on at some length about the advantages to come through having the boy out of doors and in the quiet atmosphere of the old farmhouse, she nodded her head in approval. "It is an atmosphere not corrupted by my presence," she said sharply. Her shoulders shook and she semed about to fly into a fit of temper. "It is a place for a man child, although it was never a place for me," she went on. "You never wanted me there and of course the air of your house did me no good. It was like poison in my blood but it will be different with him."

Louise turned and went out of the room, leaving the two men to sit in embarrassed silence. As very often happened she later stayed in her room for

days. Even when the boy's clothes were packed and he was taken away she did not appear. The loss of her son made a sharp break in her life and she seemed less inclined to quarrel with her husband. John Hardy thought it had all turned out very well indeed.

And so young David went to live in the Bentley farmhouse with Jesse. Two of the old farmer's sisters were alive and still lived in the house. They were afraid of Jesse and rarely spoke when he was about. One of the women who had been noted for her flaming red hair when she was younger was a born mother and became the boy's caretaker. Every night when he had gone to bed she went into his room and sat on the floor until he fell asleep. When he became drowsy she became bold and whispered things that he later thought he must have dreamed.

Her soft low voice called him endearing names and he dreamed that his mother had come to him and that she had changed so that she was always as she had been that time after he ran away. He also grew bold and reaching out his hand stroked the face of the woman on the floor so that she was ecstatically happy. Everyone in the old house became happy after the boy went there. The hard insistent thing in Jesse Bentley that had kept the people in the house silent and timid and that had never been dispelled by the presence of the girl Louise was apparently swept away by the coming of the boy. It was as though God had relented and sent a son to the man.

The man who had proclaimed himself the only true servant of God in all the valley of Wine Creek, and who had wanted God to send him a sign of approval by way of a son out of the womb of Katherine, began to think that at last his prayers had been answered. Although he was at that time only fifty-five years old he looked seventy and was worn out with much thinking and scheming. The effort he had made to extend his land holdings had been successful and there were few farms in the valley that did not belong to him, but until David came he was a bitterly disappointed man.

There were two influences at work in Jesse Bentley and all his life his mind had been a battleground for these influences. First there was the old thing in him. He wanted to be a man of God and a leader among men of God. His walking in the fields and through the forests at night had brought him close to nature and there were forces in the passionately religious man that ran out to the forces in nature. The disappointment that had come to him when a daughter and not a son had been born to Katherine had fallen upon him like a blow struck by some unseen hand and the blow had somewhat softened his egotism. He still believed that God might at any moment make himself manifest out of the winds or the clouds, but he no longer demanded such recognition. Instead he prayed for it. Sometimes he was altogether doubtful and thought God had deserted the world. He regretted the fate that had not let him live in a simpler and sweeter time when at the beckoning of some strange cloud in the sky men left their lands and houses and went forth into the wilderness to create new races. While he worked night and day to make his farms more productive and to extend his holdings of land, he regretted that he could not use his own restless energy in the building of temples, the slaying of unbelievers and in general in the work of glorifying God's name on earth.

That is what Jesse hungered for and then also he hungered for something else. He had grown into maturity in America in the years after the Civil War and he, like all men of his time, had been touched by the deep influences that were at work in the country during those years when modern industrialism was being born. He began to buy machines that would permit him to do the work of the farms while employing fewer men and he sometimes thought that if he were a younger man he would give up farming altogether and start a factory in Winesburg for the making of machinery. Jesse formed the habit of reading newspapers and magazines. He invented a machine for the making of fence out of wire. Faintly he realized that the atmosphere of old times and places that he had always cultivated in his own mind was strange and foreign to the thing that was growing up in the minds of others. The beginning of the most materialistic age in the history of the world, when wars would be fought without patriotism, when men would forget God and only pay attention to moral standards, when the will to power would replace the will to serve and beauty would be well-nigh forgotten in the terrible headlong rush of mankind toward the acquiring of possessions, was telling its story to Jesse the man of God as it was to the men about him. The greedy thing in him wanted to make money faster than it could be made by tilling the land. More than once he went into Winesburg to talk with his son-in-law John Hardy about it. "You are a banker and you will have chances I never had," he said and his eyes shone. "I am thinking about it all the time. Big things are going to be done in the country and there will be more money to be made than I ever dreamed of. You get into it. I wish I were younger and had your chance." Jesse Bentley walked up and down in the bank office and grew more and more excited as he talked. At one time in his life he had been threatened with paralysis and his left side remained somewhat weakened. As he talked his left eyelid twitched. Later when he drove back home and when night came on and the stars came out it was harder to get back the old feeling of a close and personal God who lived in the sky overhead and who might at any moment reach out his hand, touch him on the shoulder, and appoint for him some heroic task to be done. Jesse's mind was fixed upon the things read in newspapers and magazines, on fortunes to be made almost without effort by shrewd men who bought and sold. For him the coming of the boy David did much to bring back with renewed force the old faith and it seemed to him that God had at last looked with favor upon him.

As for the boy on the farm, life began to reveal itself to him in a thousand new and delightful ways. The kindly attitude of all about him expanded his quiet nature and he lost the half timid, hesitating manner he had always had with his people. At night when he went to bed after a long day of adventures in the stables, in the fields, or driving about from farm to farm with his grandfather, he wanted to embrace everyone in the house. If Sherley Bentley, the woman who came each night to sit on the floor by his bedside, did not appear at once, he went to the head of the stairs and shouted, his young voice ringing through the narrow halls where for so long there had been a tradition of silence. In the morning when he awoke and lay still in bed, the sounds that came in to him through the windows filled him with delight. He thought with a shudder of the life in the house in Winesburg and of his mother's angry voice that had always made him tremble. There in the country all sounds were pleasant sounds. When he awoke at dawn the barnyard back of the house also awoke. In the house people stirred about. Eliza Stoughton the half-witted girl was poked in the ribs by a farm hand and giggled noisily, in some distant field a cow bawled and was answered by the cattle in the stables, and one of the farm hands spoke sharply to the horse he was grooming by the stable door. David leaped out of bed and ran to a window. All of the people stirring about excited his mind, and he won-

dered what his mother was doing in the house in town.

From the windows of his own room he could not see directly into the barnyard where the farm hands had now all assembled to do the morning chores, but he could hear the voices of the men and the neighing of the horses. When one of the men laughed, he laughed also. Leaning out at the open window, he looked into an orchard where a fat sow wandered about with a litter of tiny pigs at her heels. Every morning he counted the pigs. "Four, five, six, seven," he said slowly, wetting his finger and making straight up and down marks on the window ledge. David ran to put on his trousers and shirt. A feverish desire to get out of doors took possession of him. Every morning he made such a noise coming down stairs that Aunt Callie, the housekeeper, declared he was trying to tear the house down. When he had run through the long old house, shutting doors behind him with a bang, he came into the barnyard and looked about with an amazed air of expectancy. It seemed to him that in such a place tremendous things might have happened during the night. The farm hands looked at him and laughed. Henry Strader, an old man who had been on the farm since Jesse came into possession and who before David's time had never been known to make a joke, made the same joke every morning. It amused David so that he laughed and clapped his hands. "See, come here and look," cried the old man. "Grandfather Jesse's white mare has torn the black stocking she wears on her foot."

Day after day through the long summer, Jesse Bentley drove from farm to farm up and down the valley of Wine Creek, and his grandson went with him. They rode in a comfortable old phaeton drawn by the white horse. The old man scratched his thin white beard and talked to himself of his plans for increasing the productiveness of the fields they visited and of God's part in the plans all men made. Sometimes he looked at David and smiled happily and then for a long time he appeared to forget the boy's existence. More and more every day now his mind turned back again to the dreams that had filled his mind when he had first come out of the city to live on the land. One afternoon he startled David by letting his dreams take entire possession of him. With the boy as a witness, he went through a ceremony and brought about an accident that nearly destroyed the companionship that was growing up between them.

Jesse and his grandson were driving in a distant part of the valley some miles from home. A forest came down to the road and through the forest Wine Creek wriggled its way over stones toward a distant river. All the afternoon Jesse had been in a meditative mood and now he began to talk. His mind went back to the night when he had been frightened by thoughts of a giant that might come to rob and plunder him of his possessions, and again as on that night when he had run through the fields crying for a son, he became excited to the edge of insanity. Stopping the horse he got out of the buggy and asked David to get out also. The two climbed over a fence and walked along the bank of the stream. The boy paid no attention to the muttering of his grandfather, but ran along beside him and wondered what was going to happen. When a rabbit jumped up and ran away through the woods, he clapped his hands and danced with delight. He looked at the tall trees and was sorry that he was not a little animal to climb high in the air without being frightened. Stooping, he picked up a small stone and threw it over the head of his grandfather into a clump of bushes. "Wake up, little animal. Go and climb to the top of the trees," he shouted in a shrill voice.

Jesse Bentley went along under the trees with his head bowed and with his mind in a ferment. His earnestness affected the boy, who presently became silent and a little alarmed. Into the old man's mind had come the notion that now he could bring from God a word or a sign out of the sky, that the presence of the boy and man on their knees in some lonely spot in the forest would make the miracle he had been waiting for almost inevitable. "It was in just such a place as this that other David tended the sheep when his father came and told him to go down unto Saul," he muttered.

Taking the boy rather roughly by the shoulder, he climbed over a fallen log and when he had come to an open place among the trees he dropped upon his knees and began to pray in a loud voice.

A kind of terror he had never known before took possession of David. Crouching beneath a tree he watched the man on the ground before him and his own knees began to tremble. It seemed to him that he was in the presence not only of his grandfather but of someone else, someone who might hurt him, someone who was not kindly but dangerous and brutal. He began to cry and reaching down picked up a small stick, which he held tightly gripped in his fingers. When Jesse Bentley, absorbed in his own idea, suddenly arose and advanced toward him, his terror grew until his whole body shook. In the woods an intense silence seemed to lie over everything and suddenly out of the silence came the old man's harsh and insistent voice. Gripping the boy's shoulders, Jesse turned his face to the sky and shouted. The whole left side of his face twitched and his hand on the boy's shoulder twitched also. "Make a sign to me, God," he cried. "Here I stand with the boy David. Come down to me out of the sky and make Thy presence known to me."

With a cry of fear, David turned and, shaking himself loose from the hands that held him, ran away through the forest. He did not believe that the man who turned up his face and in a harsh voice shouted at the sky was his grandfather at all. The man did not look like his grandfather. The conviction that something strange and terrible had happened, that by some miracle a new and dangerous person had come into the body of the kindly old man, took possession of him. On and on he ran down the hillside, sobbing as he ran. When he fell over the roots of a tree and in falling struck his head, he arose and tried to run on again. His head hurt so that presently he fell down and lay still, but it was only after Jesse had carried him to the buggy and he awoke to find the old man's hand stroking his head tenderly that the terror left him. "Take me away. There is a terrible man back there in the woods," he declared firmly, while Jesse looked away over the tops of the trees and again his lips cried out to God. "What have I done that Thou dost not approve of me," he whispered softly, saying the words over and over as he drove rapidly along the road with the boy's cut and bleeding head held tenderly against his shoulder.

PART THREE

Surrender

The story of Louise Bentley, who became Mrs. John Hardy and lived with her husband in a brick house on Elm Street in Winesburg, is a story of misunderstanding.

Before such women as Louise can be understood and their lives made livable, much will have to be done. Thoughtful books will have to be written and thoughtful lives lived by people about them.

Born of a delicate and overworked mother, and an impulsive, hard, imaginative father, who did not look with favor upon her coming into the world, Louise was from childhood a neurotic, one of the race of over-sensitive women that in later days industrialism was to bring in such great numbers into the world.

During her early years she lived on the Bentley farm, a silent, moody child, wanting love more than anything else in the world and not getting it. When she was fifteen she went to live in Winesburg with the family of Albert Hardy, who had a store for the sale of buggies and wagons, and who was a member of the town board of education.

Louise went into town to be a student in the Winesburg High School and she went to live at the Hardys' because Albert Hardy and her father were friends.

Hardy, the vehicle merchant of Winesburg, like thousands of other men of his times, was an enthusiast on the subject of education. He had made his own way in the world without learning got from books, but he was convinced that had he but known books things would have gone better with him. To everyone who came into his shop he talked of the matter, and in his own household he drove his family distracted by his constant harping on the subject.

He had two daughters and one son, John Hardy, and more than once the daughters threatened to leave school altogether. As a matter of principle they did just enough work in their classes to avoid punishment. "I hate books and I hate anyone who likes books," Harriet, the younger of the two girls, declared passionately.

In Winesburg as on the farm Louise was not happy. For years she had dreamed of the time when she could go forth into the world, and she looked upon the move into the Hardy household as a great step in the direction of freedom. Always when she had thought of the matter, it had seemed to her that in town all must be gaiety and life, that there men and women must live happily and freely, giving and taking friendship and affection as one takes the feel of a wind on the cheek. After the silence and the cheerlessness of life in the Bentley house, she dreamed of stepping forth into an atmosphere that was warm and pulsating with life and reality. And in the Hardy household Louise might have got something of the thing for which she so hungered but for a mistake she made when she had just come to town.

Louise won the disfavor of the two Hardy girls, Mary and Harriet, by her application to her studies in school. She did not come to the house until the day when school was to begin and knew nothing of the feeling they had in the matter. She was timid and during the first month made no acquaintances. Every Friday afternoon one of the hired men from the farm drove into Winesburg and took her home for the weekend, so that she did not spend the Saturday holiday with the town people. Because she was embarrassed and lonely she worked constantly at her studies. To Mary and Harriet, it seemed as though she tried to make trouble for them by her proficiency. In her eagerness to appear well Louise wanted to answer every question put to the class by the teacher. She jumped up and down and her eyes flashed. Then when she had answered some question the others in the class had been unable to answer, she smiled happily. "See, I have done it for you," her eyes seemed to say. "You need not bother about the matter. I will answer all questions. For the whole class it will be easy while I am here."

In the evening after supper in the Hardy house, Albert Hardy began to praise Louise. One of the teachers had spoken highly of her and he was delighted. "Well, again I have heard of it," he began, looking hard at his daughters and then turning to smile at Louise. "Another of the teachers has told me of the good work Louise is doing. Everyone in Winesburg is telling me how smart she is. I am ashamed that they do not speak so of my own girls." Arising, the merchant marched about the room and lighted his evening cigar.

The two girls looked at each other and shook their heads wearily. Seeing their indifference the father became angry. "I tell you it is something for you two to be thinking about," he cried, glaring at them. "There is a big change coming here in America and in learning is the only hope of the coming generations. Louise is the daughter of a rich man but she is not ashamed to study. It should make you ashamed to see what she does."

The merchant took his hat from a rack by the door and prepared to depart for the evening. At the door he stopped and glared back. So fierce was his manner that Louise was frightened and ran upstairs to her own room. The daughters began to speak of their own affairs. "Pay attention to me," roared the merchant. "Your minds are lazy. Your indifference to education is affecting your characters. You will amount to nothing. Now mark what I say—Louise will be so far ahead of you that you will never catch up."

The distracted man went out of the house and into the street shaking with wrath. He went along muttering words and swearing, but when he got into Main Street his anger passed. He stopped to talk of the weather or the crops with some other merchant or with a farmer who had come into town and forgot his daughters altogether or, if he thought of them, only shrugged his shoulders. "Oh, well, girls will be girls," he muttered philosophically.

In the house when Louise came down into the room where the two girls sat, they would have nothing to do with her. One evening after she had been there for more than six weeks and was heartbroken because of the continued air of coldness with which she was always greeted, she burst into tears. "Shut up your crying and go back to your own room and to your books," Mary Hardy said sharply.

. . .

The room occupied by Louise was on the second floor of the Hardy house, and her window looked out upon an orchard. There was a stove in the room and every evening young John Hardy carried up an armful of wood and put it in a box that stood by the wall. During the second month after she came to the house, Louise gave up all hope of getting on a friendly footing with the Hardy girls and went to her own room as soon as the evening meal was at an end.

Her mind began to play with thoughts of making friends with John Hardy. When he came into the room with the wood in his arms, she pretended to be busy with her studies but watched him eagerly. When he had put the wood in the box and turned to go out, she put down her head and blushed. She tried to make talk but could say nothing, and after he had gone she was angry at herself for her stupidity.

The mind of the country girl became filled with the idea of drawing close to the young man. She thought that in him might be found the quality she had all her life been seeking in people. It seemed to her that between herself and all the other people in the world, a wall had been built up and that she was living just on the edge of some warm inner circle of life that must be quite open and understandable to others. She became obsessed with the thought that it wanted but a courageous act on her part to make all of her association with people something quite different, and that it was possible by such an act to pass into a new life as one opens a door and goes into a room. Day and night she thought of the matter, but although the thing she wanted so earnestly was something very warm and close it had as yet no conscious connection with sex. It had not become

that definite, and her mind had only alighted upon the person of John Hardy because he was at hand and unlike his sisters had not been unfriendly to her.

The Hardy sisters, Mary and Harriet, were both older than Louise. In a certain kind of knowledge of the world they were years older. They lived as all of the young women of Middle Western towns lived. In those days young women did not go out of our towns to Eastern colleges and ideas in regard to social classes had hardly begun to exist. A daughter of a laborer was in much the same social position as a daughter of a farmer or a merchant, and there were no leisure classes. A girl was "nice" or she was "not nice." If a nice girl, she had a young man who came to her house to see her on Sunday and on Wednesday evenings. Sometimes she went with her young man to a dance or a church social. At other times she received him at the house and was given the use of the parlor for that purpose. No one intruded upon her. For hours the two sat behind closed doors. Sometimes the lights were turned low and the young man and woman embraced. Cheeks became hot and hair disarranged. After a year or two, if the impulse within them became strong and insistent enough, they married.

One evening during her first winter in Winesburg, Louise had an adventure that gave her a new impulse to her desire to break down the wall that she thought stood between her and John Hardy. It was Wednesday and immediately after the evening meal Albert Hardy put on his hat and went away. Young John brought the wood and put it in the box in Louise's room. "You do work hard, don't you?" he said awkwardly, and then before she could answer he also went away.

Louise heard him go out of the house and had a mad desire to run after him. Opening her window she leaned out and called softly. "John, dear John, come back, don't go away." The night was cloudy and she could not see far into the darkness, but as she waited she fancied she could hear a soft little noise as of someone going on tiptoes through the trees in the orchard. She was frightened and closed the window quickly. For an hour she moved about the room trembling with excitement and when she could not longer bear the waiting, she crept into the hall and down the stairs into a closet-like room that opened off the parlor.

Louise had decided that she would perform the courageous act that had for weeks been in her mind. She was convinced that John Hardy had concealed himself in the orchard beneath her window and she was determined to find him and tell him that she wanted him to come close to her, to hold her in his arms, to tell her of his thoughts and dreams and to listen while she told him her thoughts and dreams. "In the darkness it will be easier to say things," she whispered to herself, as she stood in the little room groping for the door.

And then suddenly Louise realized that she was not alone in the house. In the parlor on the other side of the door a man's voice spoke softly and the door opened. Louise just had time to conceal herself in a little opening beneath the stairway when Mary Hardy, accompanied by her young man, came into the little dark room.

For an hour Louise sat on the floor in the darkness and listened. Without words Mary Hardy, with the aid of the man who had come to spend the evening with her, brought to the country girl a knowledge of men and women. Putting her head down until she was curled into a little ball she lay perfectly still. It seemed to her that by some strange impulse of the gods, a great gift had been brought to Mary Hardy and she could not understand the older woman's determined protest.

The young man took Mary Hardy into his arms and kissed her. When she struggled and laughed, he but held her the more tightly. For an hour the contest between them went on and then they went back into the parlor and Louise escaped up the stairs. "I hope you were quiet out there. You must not disturb the little mouse at her studies," she heard Harriet saying to her sister as she stood by her own door in the hallway above.

Louise wrote a note to John Hardy and late that night, when all in the house were asleep, she crept downstairs and slipped it under his door. She was afraid that if she did not do the thing at once her courage would fail. In the note she tried to be quite definite about what she wanted. "I want someone to love me and I want to love someone," she wrote. "If you are the one for me I want you to come into the orchard at night and make a noise under my window. It will be easy for me to crawl down over the shed and come to you. I am thinking about it all the time, so if you are to come at all you must come soon."

For a long time Louise did not know what would be the outcome of her bold attempt to secure for herself a lover. In a way she still did not know whether or not she wanted him to come. Sometimes it seemed to her that to be held tightly and kissed was the whole secret of life, and then a new impulse came and she was terribly afraid. The age-old woman's desire to be possessed had taken possession of her, but so vague was her notion of life that it seemed to her just the touch of John Hardy's hand upon her own hand would satisfy. She wondered if he would understand that. At the table next day while Albert Hardy talked and the two girls whispered and laughed, she did not look at John but at the table and as soon as possible escaped. In the evening she went out of the house until she was sure he had taken the wood to her room and gone away. When after several evenings of intense listening she heard no call from the darkness in the orchard, she was half beside herself with grief and decided that for her there was no way to break through the wall that had shut her off from the joy of life.

And then on a Monday evening two or three weeks after the writing of the note, John Hardy came for her. Louise had so entirely given up the thought of his coming that for a long time she did not hear the call that came up from the orchard. On the Friday evening before, as she was being driven back to the farm for the week-end by one of the hired men, she had on an impulse done a thing that had startled her, and as John Hardy stood in the darkness below and called her name softly and insistently, she walked about in her room and wondered what new impulse had led her to commit so ridiculous an act.

The farm hand, a young fellow with black curly hair, had come for her somewhat late on that Friday evening and they drove home in the darkness. Louise, whose mind was filled with thoughts of John Hardy, tried to make talk but the country boy was embarrassed and would say nothing. Her mind began to review the loneliness of her childhood and she remembered with a pang the sharp new loneliness that had just come to her. "I hate everyone," she cried suddenly, and then broke forth into a tirade that frightened her escort. "I hate father and old man Hardy, too," she declared vehemently. "I get my lessons there in the school in town but I hate that also."

Louise frightened the farm hand still more by turning and putting her cheek down upon his shoulder. Vaguely she hoped that he like that young man who had stood in the darkness with Mary would put his arms about her and kiss her, but the country boy was only alarmed. He struck the horse with the whip and began to whistle. "The road is rough, eh?" he said loudly. Louise was so angry that reaching up she snatched his hat from his head and threw it into the road. When he jumped out of the buggy and went to get it, she drove off and left him to walk the rest of the way back to the farm.

Louise Bentley took John Hardy to be her lover. That was not what she wanted but it was so the young man had interpreted her approach to him, and so anxious was she to achieve something else that she made no resistance. When after a few months they were both afraid that she was about to become a mother, they went one evening to the county seat and were married. For a few months they lived in the Hardy house and then took a house of their own. All during the first year Louise tried to make her husband understand the vague and intangible hunger that had led to the writing of the note and that was still unsatisfied. Again and again she crept into his arms and tried to talk of it, but always without success. Filled with his own notions of love between men and women, he did not listen but began to kiss her upon the lips. That confused her so that in the end she did not want to be kissed. She did not know what she wanted.

When the alarm that had tricked them into marriage proved to be groundless, she was angry and said bitter, hurtful things. Later when her son David was born, she could not nurse him and did not know whether she wanted him or not. Sometimes she stayed in the room with him all day, walking about and occasionally creeping close to touch him tenderly with her hands, and then other days came when she did not want to see or be near the tiny bit of humanity that had come into the house. When John Hardy reproached her for her cruelty, she laughed. "It is a man child and will get what it wants anyway," she said sharply. "Had it been a woman child there is nothing in the world I would not have done for it."

PART FOUR

Terror

When David Hardy was a tall boy of fifteen, he, like his mother, had an adventure that changed the whole current of his life and sent him out of his quiet corner into the world. The shell of the circumstances of his life was broken and he was compelled to start forth. He left Winesburg and no one there ever saw him again. After his disappearance, his mother and grandfather both died and his father became very rich. He spent much money in trying to locate his son, but that is no part of this story.

It was in the late fall of an unusual year on the Bentley farms. Everywhere the crops had been heavy. That spring, Jesse had bought part of a long strip of black swamp land that lay in the valley of Wine Creek. He got the land at a low price but had spent a large sum of money to improve it. Great ditches had to be dug and thousands of tile laid. Neighboring farmers shook their heads over the expense. Some of them laughed and hoped that Jesse would lose heavily by the venture, but the old man went silently on with the work and said nothing.

When the land was drained he planted it to cabbages and onions, and again the neighbors laughed. The crop was, however, enormous and brought high prices. In the one year Jesse made enough money to pay for all the cost of preparing the land and had a surplus that enabled him to buy two more farms. He was exultant and could not conceal his delight. For the first time in all the history of his ownership of the farms, he went among his men with a smiling face.

Jesse bought a great many new machines for cutting down the cost of labor and all of the remaining acres in the the strip of black fertile swamp land. One day he went into Winesburg and bought a bicycle and a new suit of clothes for David and he gave his two sisters money with which to go to a religious convention at Cleveland, Ohio.

In the fall of that year when the frost came and the trees in the forests along Wine Creek were golden brown, David spent every moment when he did not have to attend school, out in the open. Alone or with other boys he went every afternoon into the woods to gather nuts. The other boys of the countryside, most of them sons of laborers on the Bentley farms, had guns with which they went hunting rabbits and squirrels, but David did not go with them. He made himself a sling with rubber bands and a forked stick and went off by himself to gather nuts. As he went about thoughts came to him. He realized that he was almost a man and wondered what he would do in life, but before they came to anything, the thoughts passed and he was a boy again. One day he killed a squirrel that sat on one of the lower branches of a tree and chattered at him. Home he ran with the squirrel in hand. One of the Bentley sisters cooked the little animal and he ate it with great gusto. The skin he tacked on a board and suspended the board by a string from his bedroom window.

That gave his mind a new turn. After that he never went into the woods without carrying the sling in his pocket and he spent hours shooting at imaginary animals concealed among the brown leaves in the trees. Thoughts of his coming manhood passed and he was content to be a boy with a boy's impulses.

One Saturday morning when he was about to set off for the woods with the sling in his pocket and a bag for nuts on his shoulder, his grandfather stopped him. In the eyes of the old man was the strained serious look that always a little frightened David. At such times Jesse Bentley's eyes did not look straight ahead but wavered and seemed to be looking at nothing. Something like an invisible curtain appeared to have come between the man and all the rest of the world. "I want you to come with me," he said briefly, and his eyes looked over the boy's head into the sky. "We have something important to do today. You may bring the bag for nuts if you wish. It does not matter and anyway we will be going into the woods."

Jesse and David set out from the Bentley farmhouse in the old phaeton that was drawn by the white horse. When they had gone along in silence for a long way they stopped at the edge of a field where a flock of sheep were grazing. Among the sheep was a lamb that had been born out of season, and this David and his grandfather caught and tied so tightly that it looked like a little white ball. When they drove on again Jesse let David hold the lamb in his arms. "I saw it yestereday and it put me in mind of what I have long wanted to do," he said, and again he looked away over the head of the boy with the wavering, uncertain stare in his eyes.

After the feeling of exaltation that had come to the farmer as a result of his successful year, another mood had taken possession of him. For a long time he had been going about feeling very humble and prayerful. Again he walked alone at night thinking of God and as he walked he again connected his own figure with the figures of old days. Under the stars he knelt on the wet grass and raised up his voice in prayer. Now he had decided that like the men whose stories filled the pages of the Bible, he would make a sacrifice to God. "I have been given these abundant crops and God has also sent me a boy who is called David," he whispered to himself. "Perhaps I should have done

this thing long ago." He was sorry the idea had not come into his mind in the days before his daughter Louise had been born and thought that surely now when he had erected a pile of burning sticks in some lonely place in the woods and had offered the body of a lamb as a burnt offering, God would appear to him and give him a message.

More and more as he thought of the matter, he thought also of David and his passionate self-love was partially forgotten. "It is time for the boy to begin thinking of going out into the world and the message will be one concerning him," he decided. "God will make a pathway for him. He will tell me what place David is to take in life and when he shall set out on his journey. It is right that the boy should be there. If I am fortunate and an angel of God should appear, David will see the beauty and glory of God made manifest to man. It will make a true man of God of him also."

In silence Jesse and David drove along the road until they came to that place where Jesse had once before appealed to God and had frightened his grandson. The morning had been bright and cheerful, but a cold wind now began to blow and clouds hid the sun. When David saw the place to which they had come he began to tremble with fright, and when they stopped by the bridge where the creek came down from among the trees, he wanted to spring out of the phaeton and run away.

A dozen plans for escape ran through David's head, but when Jesse stopped the horse and climbed over the fence into the woods, he followed. "It is foolish to be afraid. Nothing will happen," he told himself as he went along with the lamb in his arms. There was something in the helplessness of the little animal held so tightly in his arms that gave him courage. He could feel the rapid beating of the beast's heart and that made his own heart beat less rapidly. As he walked swiftly along behind his grandfather, he untied the string with which the four legs of the lamb were fastened together. "If anything happens we will run away together," he thought.

In the woods, after they had gone a long way from the road, Jesse stopped in an opening among the trees where a clearing, overgrown with small bushes, ran up from the creek. He was still silent but began at once to erect a heap of dry sticks which he presently set afire. The boy sat on the ground with the lamb in his arms. His imagination began to invest every movement of the old man with significance and he became every moment more afraid. "I must put the blood of the lamb on the head of the boy," Jesse muttered when the sticks had begun to blaze greedily, and taking a long knife from his pocket he turned and walked rapidly across the clearing toward David.

Terror seized upon the soul of the boy. He was sick with it. For a moment he sat perfectly still and then his body stiffened and he sprang to his feet. His face became as white as the fleece of the lamb that, now finding itself suddenly released, ran down the hill. David ran also. Fear made his feet fly. Over the low bushes and logs he leaped frantically. As he ran he put his hand into his pocket and took out the branched stick from which the sling for shooting squirrels was suspended. When he came to the creek that was shallow and splashed down over the stones, he dashed into the water and turned to look back, and when he saw his grandfather still running toward him with the long knife held tightly in his hand he did not hesitate, but

reaching down, selected a stone and put it in the sling. With all his strength he drew back the heavy rubber bands and the stone whistled through the air. It hit Jesse, who had entirely forgotten the boy and was pursuing the lamb, squarely in the head. With a groan he pitched forward and fell almost at the boy's feet. When David saw that he lay still and that he was apparently dead, his fright increased immeasurably. It became an insane panic.

With a cry he turned and ran off through the woods weeping convulsively. "I don't care—I killed him, but I don't care," he sobbed. As he ran on and on he decided suddenly that he would never go back again to the Bentley farms or to the town of Winesburg. "I have killed the man of God and now I will myself be a man and go into the world," he said stoutly as he stopped running and walked rapidly down a road that followed the windings of Wine Creek as it ran through fields and forests into the west.

On the ground by the creek Jesse Bentley moved uneasily about. He groaned and opened his eyes. For a long time he lay perfectly still and looked at the sky. When at last he got to his feet, his mind was confused and he was not surprised by the boy's disappearance. By the roadside he sat down on a log and began to talk about God. That is all they ever got out of him. Whenever David's name was mentioned he looked vaguely at the sky and said that a messenger from God had taken the boy. "It happened because I was too greedy for glory," he declared, and would have no more to say in the matter.

D. H. Lawrence (1885–1930)

ODOUR OF CHRYSANTHEMUMS

I

The small locomotive engine, Number 4, came clanking, stumbling down from Selston with seven full wagons. It appeared round the corner with loud threats of speed, but the colt that it startled from among the gorse, which still flickered indistinctly in the raw afternoon, out-distanced it at a canter. A woman, walking up the railway line to Underwood, drew back into the hedge, held her basket aside, and watched the footplate of the engine advancing. The trucks thumped heavily past, one by one, with slow inevitable movement, as she stood insignificantly trapped between the jolting black wagons and the hedge; then they curved away towards the coppice where the withered oak leaves dropped noiselessly, while the birds, pulling at the scarlet hips beside the track, made off into the dusk that had already crept into the spinney. In the open, the smoke from the engine sank and cleaved to the rough grass. The fields were dreary and forsaken, and in the marshy strip that led to the whimsey, a reedy pit-pond, the fowls had already abandoned their run among the alders, to roost in the tarred fowl-house. The pit-bank loomed up beyond the pond, flames like red sores licking its ashy sides, in the afternoon's stagnant light. Just beyond rose the tapering chimneys and the clumsy black headstocks of Brinsley Colliery. The two wheels were spinning fast up against the sky, and the winding engine rapped out its little spasms. The miners were being turned up.

The engine whistled as it came into the wide bay of railway lines beside the colliery, where rows of trucks stood in harbour.

Miners, single, trailing and in groups, passed like shadows diverging home. At the edge of the ribbed level of sidings squat a low cottage, three steps down from the cinder track. A large bony vine clutched at the house, as if to claw down the tiled roof. Round the bricked yard grew a few wintry primroses. Beyond, the long garden sloped down to a bush-covered brook course. There were some twiggy apple trees, winter-crack trees, and ragged cabbages. Beside the path hung dishevelled pink chrysanthemums, like pink cloths hung on bushes. A woman came stooping out of the felt-covered fowl-house, half-way down the garden. She closed and padlocked the door, then drew herself erect, having brushed some bits from her white apron.

She was a tall woman of imperious mien, handsome, with definite black eyebrows. Her smooth black hair was parted exactly. For a few moments she stood steadily watching the miners as they passed along the railway: then she turned towards the brook course. Her face was calm and set, her mouth was closed with disillusionment. After a moment she called:

"John!" There was no answer. She

waited, and then said distinctly:

"Where are you?"

"Here!" replied a child's sulky voice from among the bushes. The woman looked piercingly through the dusk.

"Are you at that brook?" she asked sternly.

For answer the child showed himself before the raspberry-canes that rose like whips. He was a small, sturdy boy of five. He stood quite still, defiantly.

"Oh!" said the mother, conciliated. "I thought you were down at that wet brook—and you remember what I told you—"

The boy did not move or answer.

"Come, come on in," she said more gently, "it's getting dark. There's your grandfather's engine coming down the line!"

The lad advanced slowly, with resentful, taciturn movement. He was dressed in trousers and waistcoat of cloth that was too thick and hard for the size of the garments. They were evidently cut down from a man's clothes.

As they went slowly towards the house he tore at the ragged wisps of chrysanthemums and dropped the petals in handfuls among the path.

"Don't do that—it does look nasty," said his mother. He refrained, and she, suddenly pitiful, broke off a twig with three or four wan flowers and held them against her face. When mother and son reached the yard her hand hesitated, and instead of laying the flower aside, she pushed it in her apron-band. The mother and son stood at the foot of the three steps looking across the bay of lines at the passing home of the miners. The trundle of the small train was imminent. Suddenly the engine loomed past the house and came to a stop opposite the gate.

The engine-driver, a short man with round grey beard, leaned out of the cab high above the woman.

"Have you got a cup of tea?" he said in a cheery, hearty fashion.

It was her father. She went in, saying she would mash. Directly, she returned.

"I didn't come to see you on Sunday," began the little grey-bearded man.

"I didn't expect you," said his daughter.

The engine-driver winced; then, re-assuming his cheery, airy manner, he said:

"Oh, have you heard then? Well, and what do you think—?"

"I think it is soon enough," she replied.

At her brief censure the little man made an impatient gesture, and said coaxingly, yet with dangerous coldness:

"Well, what's a man to do? It's no sort of life for a man of my years, to sit at my own hearth like a stranger. And if I'm going to marry again it may as well be soon as late—what does it matter to anybody?"

The woman did not reply, but turned and went into the house. The man in the engine-cab stood assertive, till she returned with a cup of tea and a piece of bread and butter on a plate. She went up the steps and stood near the foot-plate of the hissing engine.

"You needn't 'a' brought me bread an' butter," said her father. "But a cup of tea"—he sipped appreciatively—"it's very nice." He sipped for a moment or two, then: "I hear as Walter's got another bout on," he said.

"When hasn't he?" said the woman bitterly.

"I heerd tell of him in the 'Lord Nelson' braggin' as he was going to spend that b—— afore he went: half a sovereign that was."

"When?" asked the woman.

"A' Sat'day night—I know that's true."

"Very likely," she laughed bitterly. "He gives me twenty-three shillings."

"Aye, it's a nice thing, when a man can do nothing with his money but make a beast of himself!" said the grey-whiskered man. The woman turned her head away. Her father swallowed the last of his tea and handed her the cup.

"Aye," he sighed, wiping his mouth. "It's a settler, it is—"

He put his hand on the lever. The little engine strained and groaned, and the train rumbled towards the crossing. The woman again looked across the metals. Darkness was settling over the spaces of the railway and trucks: the miners, in grey sombre groups, were still passing home. The winding engine pulsed hurriedly, with brief pauses. Elizabeth Bates looked at the dreary flow of men, then she went indoors. Her husband did not come.

The kitchen was small and full of firelight; red coals piled glowing up the chimney mouth. All the life of the room seemed in the white, warm hearth and the steel fender reflecting the red fire. The cloth was laid for tea; cups glinted in the shadows. At the back, where the lowest stairs protruded into the room, the boy sat struggling with a knife and a piece of white wood. He was almost hidden in the shadow. It was half-past four. They had but to await the father's coming to begin tea. As the mother watched her son's sullen little struggle with the wood, she saw herself in his silence and pertinacity; she saw the father in her child's indifference to all but himself. She seemed to be occupied by her husband. He had probably gone past his home, slunk past his own door, to drink before he came in, while his dinner spoiled and wasted in waiting. She glanced at the clock, then took the potatoes to strain them in the yard. The garden and fields beyond the brook were closed in uncertain darkness. When she rose with the saucepan, leaving the drain steaming into the night behind her, she saw the yellow lamps were lit along the high road that went up the hill away beyond the space of the railway lines and the field.

Then again she watched the men trooping home, fewer now and fewer.

Indoors the fire was sinking and the room was dark red. The woman put her saucepan on the hob, and set a batter-pudding near the mouth of the oven. Then she stood unmoving. Directly, gratefully, came quick young steps to the door. Someone hung on the latch a moment, then a little girl entered and began pulling off her outdoor things, dragging a mass of curls, just ripening from gold to brown, over her eyes with her hat.

Her mother chid her for coming late from school, and said she would have to keep her at home the dark winter days.

"Why, mother, it's hardly a bit dark yet. The lamp's not lighted, and my father's not home."

"No, he isn't. But it's a quarter to five! Did you see anything of him?"

The child became serious. She looked at her mother with large, wistful blue eyes.

"No, mother, I've never seen him. Why? Has he come up an' gone past, to Old Brinsley? He hasn't, mother, 'cos I never saw him."

"He'd watch that," said the mother bitterly, "he'd take care as you didn't see him. But you may depend upon it, he's seated in the 'Prince o' Wales.' He wouldn't be this late."

The girl looked at her mother piteously.

"Let's have our teas, mother, should we?" said she.

The mother called John to table. She opened the door once more and looked out across the darkness of the lines. All was deserted: She could not hear the winding-engines.

"Perhaps," she said to herself, "he's stopped to get some ripping done."

They sat down to tea. John, at the end of the table near the door, was almost lost in the darkness. Their faces were hidden from each other. The girl crouched against the fender slowly moving a thick piece of bread before the fire. The lad, his face a dusky mark on the shadow, sat watching her who was transfigured in the red glow.

"I do think it's beautiful to look in the fire," said the child.

"Do you?" said her mother. "Why?"

"It's so red, and full of little caves—and it feels so nice, and you can fair smell it."

"It'll want mending directly," replied her mother, "and then if your father comes he'll carry on and say there never is a fire when a man comes home sweating from the pit. A public-house is always warm enough."

There was silence till the boy said complainingly: "Make haste, our Annie."

"Well, I am doing! I can't make the fire do it no faster, can I?"

"She keeps wafflin' it about so's to make 'er slow," grumbled the boy.

"Don't have such an evil imagination, child," replied the mother.

Soon the room was busy in the darkness with the crisp sound of crunching. The mother ate very little. She drank her tea determinedly, and sat thinking. When she rose her anger was evident in the stern unbending of her head. She looked at the pudding in the fender, and broke out:

"It is a scandulous thing as a man can't even come home to his dinner! If it's crozzled up to a cinder I don't see why I should care. Past his very door he goes to get to a public-house, and here I sit with his dinner waiting for him—"

She went out. As she dropped piece after piece of coal on the red fire, the shadows fell on the walls, till the room was almost in total darkness.

"I canna see," grumbled the invisible John. In spite of herself, the mother laughed.

"You know the way to your mouth," she said. She set the dust-pan outside the door. When she came again like a shadow on the hearth, the lad repeated, complaining sulkily:

"I canna see."

"Good gracious!" cried the mother irritably, "you're as bad as your father if it's a bit dusk!"

Nevertheless, she took a paper spill from a sheaf on the mantelpiece and proceeded to light the lamp that hung from the ceiling in the middle of the room. As she reached up, her figure displayed itself just rounding with maternity.

"Oh, mother—!" exclaimed the girl.

"What?" said the woman, suspended in the act of putting the lamp-glass over the flame. The copper reflector shone handsomely on her, as she stood with uplifted arm, turning to face her daughter.

"You've got a flower in your apron!" said the child, in a little rapture at this unusual event.

"Goodness me!" exclaimed the woman, relieved. "One would think the house was afire." She replaced the glass and waited a moment before turning up the wick. A pale shadow was seen floating vaguely on the floor.

"Let me smell!" said the child, still rapturously, coming forward and putting her face to her mother's waist.

"Go along, silly!" said the mother, turning up the lamp. The light revealed their suspense so that the woman felt it almost unbearable. Annie was still bending at her waist. Irritably, the mother took the flowers out from her apron-band.

"Oh, mother—don't take them out!" Annie cried, catching her hand and trying to replace the sprig.

"Such nonsense!" said the mother, turning away. The child put the pale chrysanthemums to her lips, murmuring:

"Don't they smell beautiful!"

Her mother gave a short laugh.

"No," she said, "not to me. It was chrysanthemums when I married him, and chrysanthemums when you were born, and the first time they ever brought him home drunk, he'd got brown chrysanthemums in his button-hole."

She looked at the children. Their eyes and their parted lips were wondering. The mother sat rocking in silence for some time. Then she looked at the clock.

"Twenty minutes to six!" In a tone of fine bitter carelessness she continued: "Eh, he'll not come now till they bring him. There he'll stick! But he needn't come rolling in here in his pit-dirt, for *I* won't wash him. He can lie on the floor—Eh, what a fool I've been, what a fool! And this is what I came here for, to this dirty hole, rats and all, for him to slink past his very door. Twice last week—he's begun now—"

She silenced herself, and rose to clear the table.

While for an hour or more the children played, subduedly intent, fertile of imagination, united in fear of the mother's wrath, and in dread of their father's home-coming, Mrs. Bates sat in her rocking-chair making a 'singlet' of thick cream-coloured flannel, which gave a dull wounded sound as she tore off the grey edge. She worked at her sewing with energy, listening to the children, and her anger wearied itself, lay down to rest, opening its eyes from time to time and steadily watching, its ears raised to listen. Sometimes even her anger quailed and shrank, and the mother suspended her sewing, tracing the footsteps that thudded along the sleepers outside; she would lift her head sharply to bid the children 'hush', but she recovered herself in time, and the footsteps went past the gate, and the children were not flung out of their playworld.

But at last Annie sighed, and gave in. She glanced at her wagon of slip-pers, and loathed the game. She turned plaintively to her mother.

"Mother!"—but she was inarticulate.

John crept out like a frog from under the sofa. His mother glanced up.

"Yes," she said, "just look at those shirt-sleeves!"

The boy held them out to survey them, saying nothing. Then somebody called in a hoarse voice away down the line and suspense bristled in the room, till two people had gone by outside, talking.

"It is time for bed," said the mother.

"My father hasn't come," wailed Annie plaintively. But her mother was primed with courage.

"Never mind. They'll bring him when he does come—like a log." She meant there would be no scene. "And he may sleep on the floor till he wakes himself. I know he'll not go to work to-morrow after this!"

The children had their hands and faces wiped with a flannel. They were very quiet. When they had put on their nightdresses, they said their prayers, the boy mumbling. The mother looked down at them, at the brown silken bush of intertwining curls in the nape of the girl's neck, at the little black head of the lad, and her heart burst with anger at their father, who caused all three such distress. The children hid their faces in her skirts for comfort.

When Mrs. Bates came down, the room was strangely empty, with a ten-sion of expectancy. She took up her sewing and stitched for some time with-out raising her head. Meantime her anger was tinged with fear.

II

The clock struck eight and she rose suddenly, dropping her sewing on her chair. She went to the stair-foot door, opened it, listening. Then she went out, locking the door behind her.

Something scuffled in the yard, and she started, though she knew it was only the rats with which the place was over-run. The night was very dark. In the great bay of railway lines, bulked with trucks, there was no trace of light, only away back she could see a few yellow lamps at the pit-top, and the red smear of the burning pit-bank on the night. She hurried along the edge of the track, then, crossing the converging lines, came to the stile by the white gates, whence she emerged on the road. Then the fear which had led her shrank. People were walking up to New Brinsley; she saw the lights in the houses; twenty yards farther on were the broad windows of the "Prince of Wales," very warm and bright, and the loud voices of men could be heard distinctly. What a fool she had been to imagine that anything had happened to him! He was merely drinking over there at the "Prince of Wales." She faltered. She had never yet been to fetch him, and she never would go. So she continued her walk towards the long straggling line of houses, standing back on the highway. She entered a passage between the dwellings.

"Mr. Rigley?—Yes! Did you want him? No, he's not in at this minute."

The raw-boned woman leaned forward from her dark scullery and peered at the other, upon whom fell a dim light through the blind of the kitchen window.

"Is it Mrs. Bates?" she asked in a tone tinged with respect.

"Yes. I wondered if your Master was at home. Mine hasn't come yet."

"'Asn't 'e! Oh, Jack's been 'ome an' 'ad 'is dinner an' gone out. 'E's just gone for 'alf an hour afore bed-time. Did you call at the 'Prince of Wales'?"

"No—"

"No, you didn't like—! It's not very nice." The other woman was indulgent. There was an awkward pause. "Jack never said nothink about—about your Master," she said.

"No!—I expect he's stuck in there!"

Elizabeth Bates said this bitterly, and with recklessness. She knew that the woman across the yard was standing at her door listening, but she did not care. As she turned:

"Stop a minute! I'll just go an' ask Jack if 'e knows anythink," said Mrs. Rigley.

"Oh no—I wouldn't like to put—!"

"Yes, I will, if you'll just step inside an' see as th' childer doesn't come downstairs and set theirselves afire."

Elizabeth Bates, murmuring a remonstrance, stepped inside. The other woman apologized for the state of the room.

The kitchen needed apology. There were little frocks and trousers and childish undergarments on the squab and on the floor, and a litter of playthings everywhere. On the black American cloth of the table were pieces of bread and cake, crusts, slops, and a teapot with cold tea.

"Eh, ours is just as bad," said Elizabeth Bates, looking at the woman, not at the house. Mrs. Rigley put a shawl over her head and hurried out, saying:

"I shanna be a minute."

The other sat, noting with faint disapproval the general untidiness of the room. Then she fell to counting the shoes of various sizes scattered over the floor. There were twelve. She sighed and said to herself: "No wonder!"— glancing at the litter. There came the scratching of two pairs of feet on the yard, and the Rigleys entered. Elizabeth Bates rose. Rigley was a big man, with very large bones. His head looked particularly bony. Across his temple was a blue scar, caused by a wound got in the pit, a wound in which the coal-dust remained blue like tatooing.

"'Asna 'e come whoam yit?" asked the man, without any form of greeting, but with deference and sympathy. "I couldna say wheer he is—'e's non ower theer!"—he jerked his head to signify the "Prince of Wales."

"'E's 'appen gone up to th' 'Yew,'" said Mrs. Rigley.

There was another pause. Rigley had evidently something to get off his mind:

"Ah left 'im finishin' a stint," he began. "Loose-all 'ad bin gone about ten minutes when we com'n away, an' I shouted: 'Are ter comin,' Walt?' an' 'e said: 'Go on, Ah shanna be but a'ef a minnit,' so we com'n ter th' bottom, me an' Bowers, thinkin' as 'e wor just behint, an' 'ud come up i' th' next bantle—"

He stood perplexed, as if answering a charge of deserting his mate. Elizabeth Bates, now again certain of disaster, hastened to reassure him:

"I expect 'e's gone up to th' 'Yew Tree,' as you say. It's not the first time. I've fretted myself into a fever before now. He'll come home when they carry him."

"Ay, isn't it too bad!" deplored the other woman.

"I'll just step up to Dick's an' see if 'e *is* theer," offered the man, afraid of appearing alarmed, afraid of taking liberties.

"Oh, I wouldn't think of bothering you that far," said Elizabeth Bates, with emphasis, but he knew she was glad of his offer.

As they stumbled up the entry, Elizabeth Bates heard Rigley's wife run across the yard and open her neighbour's door. At this, suddenly all the blood in her body seemed to switch away from her heart.

"Mind!" warned Rigley. "Ah've said many a time as Ah'd fill up them ruts in this entry, sumb'dy 'll be breakin' their legs yit."

She recovered herself and walked quickly along with the miner.

"I don't like leaving the children in bed, and nobody in the house," she said.

"No, you dunna!" he replied courteously. They were soon at the gate of the cottage.

"Well, I shanna be many minnits. Dunna you be frettin' now, 'e'll be all right," said the butty.

"Thank you very much, Mr. Rigley," she replied.

"You're welcome!" he stammered, moving away. "I shanna be many minnits."

The house was quiet. Elizabeth Bates took off her hat and shawl, and rolled back the rug. When she had finished, she sat down. It was a few minutes past nine. She was startled by the rapid chuff of the winding-engine at the pit, and the sharp whirr of the brakes on the rope as it descended. Again she felt the painful sweep of her blood, and she put her hand to her side, saying aloud: "Good gracious!—it's only the nine o'clock deputy going down," rebuking herself.

She sat still, listening. Half an hour of this, and she was wearied out.

"What am I working myself up like this for?" she said pitiably to herself, "I s'll only be doing myself some damage."

She took out her sewing again.

At a quarter to ten there were footsteps. One person! She watched for the door to open. It was an elderly woman, in a black bonnet and a black woollen shawl—his mother. She was about sixty years old, pale, with blue eyes, and her face all wrinkled and lamentable. She shut the door and turned to her daughter-in-law peevishly.

"Eh, Lizzie, whatever shall we do, whatever shall we do!" she cried.

Elizabeth drew back a little, sharply.

"What is it, mother?" she said.

The elder woman seated herself in the sofa.

"I don't know, child, I can't tell you!" —she shook her head slowly. Elizabeth sat watching her, anxious and vexed.

"I don't know," replied the grandmother, sighing very deeply. "There's no end to my troubles, there isn't. The things I've gone through, I'm sure it's enough—!" She wept without wiping her eyes, the tears running.

"But, mother," interrupted Elizabeth, "what do you mean? What is it?"

The grandmother slowly wiped her eyes. The fountains of her tears were stopped by Elizabeth's directness. She wiped her eyes slowly.

"Poor child! Eh, you poor thing!"

she moaned. "I don't know what we're going to do, I don't—and you as you are—it's a thing, it is indeed!"

Elizabeth waited.

"Is he dead?" she asked, and at the words her heart swung violently, though she felt a slight flush of shame at the ultimate extravagance of the question. Her words sufficiently frightened the old lady, almost brought her to herself.

"Don't say so, Elizabeth! We'll hope it's not as bad as that; no, may the Lord spare us that, Elizabeth. Jack Rigley came just as I was sittin' down to a glass afore going to bed, an' 'e said: ''Appen you'll go down th' line, Mrs. Bates. Walt's had an accident. 'Appen you'll go an' sit wi' 'er till we can get him home.' I hadn't time to ask him a word afore he was gone. An' I put my bonnet on an' come straight down, Lizzie. I thought to myself: 'Eh, that poor blessed child, if anybody should come an' tell her of a sudden, there's no knowin' what'll 'appen to 'er.' You musn't let it upset you, Lizzie—or you know what to expect. How long is it, six months—or is it five, Lizzie? Ay!" —the old woman shook her head— "time slips on, it slips on! Ay!"

Elizabeth's thoughts were busy elsewhere. If he was killed—would she be able to manage on the little pension and what she could earn?—she counted up rapidly. If he was hurt—they wouldn't take him to the hospital—how tiresome he would be to nurse!—but perhaps she'd be able to get him away from the drink and his hateful ways. She would—while he was ill. The tears offered to come to her eyes at the picture. But what sentimental luxury was this she was beginning? She turned to consider the children. At any rate she was absolutely necessary for them. They were her business.

"Ay!" repeated the old woman, "it seems but a week or two since he brought me his first wages. Ay—he was a good lad, Elizabeth, he was, in his way.

I don't know why he got to be such a trouble, I don't. He was a happy lad at home, only full of spirits. But there's no mistake he's been a handful of trouble, he has! I hope the Lord'll spare him to mend his ways. I hope so, I hope so. You've had a sight o' trouble with him, Elizabeth, you have indeed. But he was a jolly enough lad wi' me, he was, I can assure you. I don't know how it is. . . ."

The old woman continued to muse aloud, a monotonous irritating sound, while Elizabeth thought concentratedly, startled once, when she heard the winding-engine chuff quickly, and the brakes skirr with a shriek. Then she heard the engine more slowly, and the brakes made no sound. The old woman did not notice. Elizabeth waited in suspense. The mother-in-law talked, with lapses into silence.

"But he wasn't your son, Lizzie, an' it makes a difference. Whatever he was, I remember him when he was little, an' I learned to understand him and to make allowances. You've got to make allowances for them—"

It was half-past ten, and the old woman was saying: "But it's trouble from beginning to end; you're never too old for trouble, never too old for that—" when the gate banged back, and there were heavy feet on the steps.

"I'll go, Lizzie, let me go," cried the old woman, rising. But Elizabeth was at the door. It was a man in pit-clothes.

"They're bringin' 'im, Missis," he said. Elizabeth's heart halted a moment. Then it surged on again, almost suffocating her.

"Is he—is it bad?" she asked.

The man turned away, looking at the darkness:

"The doctor says 'e'd been dead hours. 'E saw 'im i' th' lamp-cabin."

The old woman, who stood just behind Elizabeth, dropped into a chair, and folded her hands, crying: "Oh, my boy, my boy!"

"Hush!" said Elizabeth, with a sharp

twitch of a frown. "Be still, mother, don't waken th' children: I wouldn't have them down for anything!"

The old woman moaned softly, rocking herself. The man was drawing away. Elizabeth took a step forward.

"How was it?" she asked.

"Well, I couldn't say for sure," the man replied, very ill at ease. " 'E wor finishin' a stint an' th' butties 'ad gone, an' a lot o' stuff come down atop 'n 'im."

"And crushed him?" cried the widow, with a shudder.

"No," said the man, "it fell at th' back of 'im. 'E wor under th' face, an' it niver touched 'im. It shut 'im in. It seems 'e wor smothered."

Elizabeth shrank back. She heard the old woman behind her cry:

"What?—what did 'e say it was?"

The man replied, more loudly: " 'E wor smothered!"

Then the old woman wailed aloud, and this relieved Elizabeth.

"Oh, mother," she said, putting her hand on the old woman, "don't waken th' children, don't waken th' children."

She wept a little, unknowing, while the old mother rocked herself and moaned. Elizabeth remembered that they were bringing him home, and she must be ready. "They'll lay him in the parlour," she said to herself, standing a moment pale and perplexed.

Then she lighted a candle and went into the tiny room. The air was cold and damp, but she could not make a fire, there was no fireplace. She set down the candle and looked round. The candlelight glittered on the lustre-glasses, on the two vases that held some of the pink chrysanthemums, and on the dark mahogany. There was a cold, deathly smell of chrysanthemums in the room. Elizabeth stood looking at the flowers. She turned away, and calculated whether there would be room to lay him on the floor, between the couch and the chiffonier. She pushed the chairs aside. There would be room to lay him down and to step round him. Then she fetched the old red tablecloth, and another old cloth, spreading them down to save her bit of carpet. She shivered on leaving the parlour; so, from the dresser drawer she took a clean shirt and put it at the fire to air. All the time her mother-in-law was rocking herself in the chair and moaning.

"You'll have to move from there, mother," said Elizabeth. "They'll be bringing him in. Come in the rocker."

The old mother rose mechanically, and seated herself by the fire, continuing to lament. Elizabeth went into the pantry for another candle, and there, in the little pent-house under the naked tiles, she heard them coming. She stood still in the pantry doorway, listening. She heard them pass the end of the house, and come awkwardly down the three steps, a jumble of shuffling footsteps and muttering voices. The old woman was silent. The men were in the yard.

Then Elizabeth heard Matthews, the manager of the pit, say: "You go in first, Jim. Mind!"

The door came open, and the two women saw a collier backing into the room, holding one end of a stretcher, on which they could see the nailed pit-boots of the dead man. The two carriers halted, the man at the head stooping to the lintel of the door.

"Wheer will you have him?" asked the manager, a short, white-beared man.

Elizabeth roused herself and came from the pantry carrying the unlighted candle.

"In the parlour," she said.

"In there, Jim!" pointed the manager, and the carriers backed round into the tiny room. The coat with which they had covered the body fell off as they awkwardly turned through the two doorways, and the women saw their man, naked to the waist, lying stripped for work. The old woman began to moan in a low voice of horror.

"Lay th' stretcher at th' side," snapped the manager, "an' put 'im on th' cloths. Mind now, mind! Look you now—!"

One of the men had knocked off a vase of chrysanthemums. He stared awkwardly, then they set down the stretcher. Elizabeth did not look at her husband. As soon as she could get in the room, she went and picked up the broken vase and the flowers.

"Wait a minute!" she said.

The three men waited in silence while she mopped up the water with a duster.

"Eh, what a job, what a job, to be sure!" the manager was saying, rubbing his brow with trouble and perplexity. "Never knew such a thing in my life, never! He'd no busines to ha' been left. I never knew such a thing in my life! Fell over him clean as a whistle, an' shut him in. Not four foot of space, there wasn't—yet it scarce bruised him."

He looked down at the dead man, lying prone, half naked, all grimed with coal-dust.

" ' 'Sphyxiated', the doctor said. It *is* the most terrible job I've ever known. Seems as if it was done o' purpose. Clean over him, an' shut 'im in, like a mouse-trap"—he made a sharp, descending gesture with his hand.

The colliers standing by jerked aside their heads in hopeless comment.

The horror of the thing bristled upon them all.

Then they heard the girl's voice upstairs calling shrilly: "Mother, mother—who is it? Mother, who is it?"

Elizabeth hurried to the foot of the stairs and opened the door:

"Go to sleep!" she commanded sharply. "What are you shouting about? Go to sleep at once—there's nothing—"

Then she began to mount the stairs. They could hear her on the boards, and on the plaster floor of the little bedroom. They could hear her distinctly:

"What's the matter now?—what's the matter with you, silly thing?"—

her voice was much agitated, with an unreal gentleness.

"I thought it was some men come," said the plaintive voice of the child. "Has he come?"

"Yes, they've brought him. There's nothing to make a fuss about. Go to sleep now, like a good child."

They could hear her voice in the bedroom, they waited whilst she covered the children under the bedclothes.

"Is he drunk?" asked the girl, timidly, faintly.

"No! No—he's not! He—he's asleep."

"Is he asleep downstairs?"

"Yes—and don't make a noise."

There was silence for a moment, then the men heard the frightened child again:

"What's that noise?"

"It's nothing, I tell you, what are you bothering for?"

The noise was the grandmother moaning. She was oblivious of everything, sitting on her chair rocking and moaning. The manager put his hand on her arm and bade her "Sh—sh! !"

The old woman opened her eyes and looked at him. She was shocked by this interruption, and seemed to wonder.

"What time is it?" the plaintive thin voice of the child, sinking back unhappily into sleep, asked this last question.

"Ten o'clock," answered the mother more softly. Then she must have bent down and kissed the children.

Matthews beckoned to the men to come away. They put on their caps and took up the stretcher. Stepping over the body, they tiptoed out of the house. None of them spoke till they were far from the wakeful children.

When Elizabeth came down she found her mother alone on the parlour floor, leaning over the dead man, the tears dropping on him.

"We must lay him out," the wife said. She put on the kettle, then returning knelt at the feet, and began to unfasten the knotted leather laces. The room was clammy and dim with only one candle, so that she had to bend her face almost to the floor. At last she got off the heavy boots and put them away.

"You must help me now," she whispered to the old woman. Together they stripped the man.

When they arose, saw him lying in the naïve dignity of death, the women stood arrested in fear and respect. For a few moments they remained still, looking down, the old mother whimpering. Elizabeth felt countermanded. She saw him, now utterly inviolable he lay in himself. She had nothing to do with him. She could not accept it. Stooping, she laid her hand on him, in claim. He was still warm, for the mine was hot where he had died. His mother had his face between her hands, and was murmuring incoherently. The old tears fell in succession as drops from wet leaves; the mother was not weeping, merely her tears flowed. Elizabeth embraced the body of her husband, with cheek and lips. She seemed to be listening, inquiring, trying to get some connection. But she could not. She was driven away. He was impregnable.

She rose, went into the kitchen, where she poured warm water into a bowl, brought soap and flannel and a soft towel.

"I must wash him," she said.

Then the old mother rose stiffly, and watched Elizabeth as she carefully washed his face, carefully brushing the big blond moustache from his mouth with the flannel. She was afraid with a bottomless fear, so she ministered to him. The old woman, jealous, said:

"Let me wipe him!"—and she kneeled on the other side drying slowly as Elizabeth washed, her big black bonnet sometimes brushing the dark head of her daughter-in-law. They worked thus in silence for a long time. They never forgot it was death, and the touch of the man's dead body gave them strange emotions, different in each of the women; a great dread possessed them both, the mother felt the lie was given to her womb, she was denied; the wife felt the utter isolation of the human soul, the child within her was a weight apart from her.

At last it was finished. He was a man of handsome body, and his face showed no traces of drink. He was blond, full-fleshed, with fine limbs. But he was dead.

"Bless him," whispered his mother, looking always at his face, and speaking out of sheer terror. "Dear lad—bless him!" She spoke in a faint, sibilant ecstasy of fear and mother love.

Elizabeth sank down again to the floor, and put her face against his neck, and trembled and shuddered. But she had to draw away again. He was dead, and her living flesh had no place against his. A great dread and weariness held her: she was so unavailing. Her life was gone like this.

"White as milk he is, clear as a twelve-month baby, bless him, the darling!" the old mother murmured to herself. "Not a mark on him, clear and clean and white, beautiful as ever a child was made," she murmured with pride. Elizabeth kept her face hidden.

"He went peaceful, Lizzie—peaceful as sleep. Isn't he beautiful, the lamb? Ay—he must ha' made his peace, Lizzie. 'Appen he made it all right, Lizzie, shut in there. He'd have time. He wouldn't look like this if he hadn't made his peace. The lamb, the dear lamb. Eh, but he had a hearty laugh. I loved to hear it. He had the heartiest laugh, Lizzie, as a lad—"

Elizabeth looked up. The man's mouth was fallen back, slightly open under the cover of the moustache. The eyes, half shut, did not show glazed in the obscurity. Life with its smoky burning gone from him, had left him apart and utterly alien to her. And she knew what a stranger he was to her. In her womb was ice of fear, because of this separate stranger with whom she had been living as one flesh. Was this what it all meant—utter, intact separateness, obscured by heat of living? In dread she turned her face away. The fact was too deadly. There had been nothing between them, and yet they had come together, exchanging their nakedness repeatedly. Each time he had taken her, they had been two isolated beings, far apart as now. He was no more responsible than she. The child was like ice in her womb. For as she looked at the dead man, her mind, cold and detached, said clearly: "Who am I? What have I been doing? I have been fighting a husband who did not exist. *He* existed all the time. What wrong have I done? What was that I have been living with? There lies the reality, this man." And her soul died in her for fear: She knew she had never seen him, he had never seen her, they had met in the dark and had fought in the dark, not knowing whom they met nor whom they fought. And now she saw, and turned silent in seeing. For she had been wrong. She had said he was something he was not; she had felt familiar with him. Whereas he was apart all the while, living as she never lived, feeling as she never felt.

In fear and shame she looked at his naked body, that she had known falsely. And he was the father of her children. Her soul was torn from her body and stood apart. She looked at his naked body and was ashamed, as if she had denied it. After all, it was itself. It seemed awful to her. She looked at his face, and she turned her own face to the wall. For his look was other than hers, his way was not her way. She had denied him what he was—she saw it now. She had refused him as himself. And this had been her life, and his life. She was grateful to death, which restored the truth. And she knew she was not dead.

And all the while her heart was bursting with grief and pity for him. What had he suffered? What stretch of horror for this helpless man! She was rigid with agony. She had not been able to help him. He had been cruelly injured, this naked man, this other being, and she could make no reparation. There were the children—but the children belonged to life. This dead man had nothing to do with them. He and she were only channels through which life had flowed to issue in the children. She was a mother—but how awful she knew it now to have been a wife. And he, dead now, how awful he must have felt to be a husband. She felt that in the next world he would be a stranger to her. If they met there, in the beyond, they would only be ashamed of what had been before. The children had come, for some mysterious reason, out of both of them. But the children did not unite them. Now he was dead, she knew how eternally he was apart from her, how eternally he had nothing more to do with her. She saw this episode of her life closed. They had denied each other in life. Now he had withdrawn. An anguish came over her. It was finished then: it had become hopeless between them long before he died. Yet he had been her husband. But how little!

"Have you got his shirt, 'Lizabeth?"

Elizabeth turned without answering, though she strove to weep and behave as her mother-in-law expected. But she could not, she was silenced. She went into the kitchen and returned with the garment.

"It is aired," she said, grasping the cotton shirt here and there to try. She was almost ashamed to handle him; what right had she or anyone to lay hands on him; but her touch was humble on his body. It was hard work to clothe him. He was so heavy and inert. A terrible dread gripped her all the while: that he could be so heavy and utterly inert, unresponsive, apart. The horror of the distance between them was almost too much for her—it was so infinite a gap she must look across.

At last it was finished. They covered him with a sheet and left him lying, with his face bound. And she fastened the door of the little parlour, lest the children should see what was lying there. Then, with peace sunk heavy on her heart, she went about making tidy the kitchen. She knew she submitted to life, which was her immediate master. But from death, her ultimate master, she winced with fear and shame.

THE WOMAN WHO RODE AWAY

I

She had thought that this marriage, of all marriages, would be an adventure. Not that the man himself was exactly magical to her. A little, wiry, twisted fellow, twenty years older than herself, with brown eyes and greying hair, who had come to America a scrap of a wastrel, from Holland, years ago, as a tiny boy, and from the gold-mines of the west had been kicked south into Mexico, and now was more or less rich, owning silver-mines in the wilds of the Sierra Madre: It was obvious that the adventure lay in his circumstances, rather than his person. But he was still a little dynamo of energy, in spite of accidents survived, and what he had accomplished he had accomplished alone. One of those human oddments there is no accounting for.

When she actually *saw* what he had accomplished, her heart quailed. Great green-covered, unbroken mountain-hills, and in the midst of the lifeless isolation, the sharp pinkish mounds of the dried mud from the silver-works. Under the nakedness of the works, the walled-in, one-story adobe house, with its garden inside, and its deep inner veranda with tropical climbers on the sides. And when you looked up from this shut-in flowered patio, you saw the huge pink cone of the silver-mud refuse, and the machinery of the extracting plant against heaven above. No more.

To be sure, the great wooden doors were often open. And then she could stand outside, in the vast open world. And see great, void, tree-clad hills piling behind one another, from nowhere into nowhere. They were green in autumn-time. For the rest, pinkish, stark dry and abstract.

And in his battered Ford car her husband would take her into the dead, thrice-dead little Spanish town forgotten among the mountains. The great, sun-dried dead church, the dead portales, the hopeless covered market-place, where, the first time she went, she saw a dead dog lying between the meat-stalls and the vegetable array, stretched out as if for ever, nobody troubling to throw it away. Deadness within deadness.

Everybody feebly talking silver, and showing bits of ore. But silver was at a standstill. The great war came and went. Silver was a dead market. Her husband's mines were closed down. But she and he lived on in the adobe house under the works, among the flowers that were never very flowery to her.

She had two children, a boy and a girl. And her eldest, the boy, was nearly ten years old before she aroused from her stupor of subjected amazement. She was now thirty-three, a large, blue-eyed, dazed woman, beginning to grow stout. Her little, wiry, tough, twisted, brown-eyed husband was fifty-three, a man as tough as wire, tenacious as wire, still full of energy, but dimmed by the lapse of silver from the market, and by some curious inaccessibility on his wife's part.

He was a man of principles, and a

good husband. In a way, he doted on her. He never quite got over his dazzled admiration of her. But essentially, he was still a bachelor. He had been thrown out on the world, a little bachelor, at the age of ten. When he married he was over forty, and had enough money to marry on. But his capital was all a bachelor's. He was boss of his own works, and marriage was the last and most intimate bit of his own works.

He admired his wife to extinction, he admired her body, all her points. And she was to him always the rather dazzling Californian girl from Berkeley, whom he had first known. Like any sheikh, he kept her guarded among those mountains of Chihuahua. He was jealous of her as he was of his silver-mine: and that is saying a lot.

At thirty-three she really was still the girl from Berkeley, in all but physique. Her conscious development had stopped mysteriously with her marriage, completely arrested. Her husband had never become real to her, neither mentally nor physically. In spite of his late sort of passion for her, he never meant anything to her, physically. Only morally he swayed her, downed her, kept her in an invincible slavery.

So the years went by, in the adobe house strung round the sunny patio, with the silver-works overhead. Her husband was never still. When the silver went dead, he ran a ranch lower down, some twenty miles away, and raised pure-bred hogs, splendid creatures. At the same time, he hated pigs. He was a squeamish waif of an idealist, and really hated the physical side of life. He loved work, work, work, and making things. His marriage, his children, were something he was making, part of his business, but with a sentimental income this time.

Gradually her nerves began to go wrong: she must get out. She must get out. So he took her to El Paso for three months. And at least it was the United States.

But he kept his spell over her. The three months ended: back she was, just the same, in her adobe house among those eternal green or pinky-brown hills, void as only the undiscovered is void. She taught her children, she supervised the Mexican boys who were her servants. And sometimes her husband brought visitors, Spaniards or Mexicans or occasionally white men.

He really loved to have white men staying on the place. Yet he had not a moment's peace when they were there. It was as if his wife were some peculiar secret vein of ore in his mines, which no one must be aware of except himself. And she was fascinated by the young gentlemen, mining engineers, who were his guests at times. He, too, was fascinated by a real gentleman. But he was an old-timer miner with a wife, and if a gentleman looked at his wife, he felt as if his mine were being looted, the secrets of it pried out.

It was one of these young gentlemen who put the idea into her mind. They were all standing outside the great wooden doors of the patio, looking at the outer world. The eternal, motionless hills were all green, it was September, after the rains. There was no sign of anything, save the deserted mine, the deserted works, and a bunch of half-deserted miners' dwellings.

"I wonder," said the young man, "what there is behind those great blank hills."

"More hills," said Lederman. "If you go that way, Sonora and the coast. This way is the desert—you came from there —and the other way, hills and mountains."

"Yes, but what *lives* in the hills and the mountains? *Surely* there is something wonderful? It looks *so* like nowhere on earth: like being on the moon."

"There's plenty of game, if you want to shoot. And Indians, if you call *them* wonderful."

"Wild ones?"

"Wild enough."

"But friendly?"

"It depends. Some of them are quite wild, and they don't let anybody near. They kill a missionary at sight. And where a missionary can't get, nobody can."

"But what does the government say?"

"They're so far from everywhere, the government leaves 'em alone. And they're wily; if they think there'll be trouble, they send a delegation to Chihuahua and make a formal submission. The government is glad to leave it at that."

"And do they live quite wild, with their own savage customs and religion?"

"Oh yes. They use nothing but bows and arrows. I've seen them in town, in the Plaza, with funny sort of hats with flowers around them, and a bow in one hand, quite naked except for a sort of shirt, even in cold weather—striding round with their savage's bare legs."

"But don't you suppose it's wonderful, up there in their secret villages?"

"No. What would there be wonderful about it? Savages are savages, and all savages behave more or less alike: rather low-down and dirty, unsanitary, with a few cunning tricks, and struggling to get enough to eat."

"But surely they have old, old religions and mysteries—it *must* be wonderful, surely it must."

"I don't know about mysteries—howling and heathen practices, more or less indecent. No, I see nothing wonderful in that kind of stuff. And I wonder that you should, when you have lived in London or Paris or New York—"

"Ah, *everybody* lives in London or Paris or New York"—said the young man, as if this were an argument.

And this particular vague enthusiasm for unknown Indians found a full echo in the woman's heart. She was overcome by a foolish romanticism more unreal than a girl's. She felt it was her destiny to wander into the secret haunts of these timeless, mysterious, marvellous Indians of the mountains.

She kept her secret. The young man was departing, her husband was going with him down to Torreon, on business: would be away for some days. But before the departure, she made her husband talk about the Indians: about the wandering tribes, resembling the Navajo, who were still wandering free; and the Yaquis of Sonora; and the different groups in the different valleys of Chihuahua State.

There was supposed to be one tribe, the Chilchuis, living in a high valley to the south, who were the sacred tribe of all the Indians. The descendants of Montezuma and the old Aztec or Totonac kings still lived among them, and the old priests still kept up the ancient religion, and offered human sacrifices—so it was said. Some scientists had been to the Chilchui country, and had come back gaunt and exhausted with hunger and bitter privation, bringing various curious, barbaric objects of worship, but having seen nothing extraordinary in the hungry, stark village of savages.

Though Lederman talked in this offhand way, it was obvious he felt some of the vulgar excitement at the idea of ancient and mysterious savages.

"How far away are they?" she asked.

"Oh—three days on horseback—past Cuchitee and a little lake there is up there."

Her husband and the young man departed. The woman made her crazy plans. Of late, to break the monotony of her life, she had harassed her husband into letting her go riding with him, occasionally, on horseback. She was never allowed to go out alone. The country truly was not safe, lawless and crude.

But she had her own horse, and she dreamed of being free as she had been as a girl, among the hills of California.

Her daughter, nine years old, was now in a tiny convent in the little half-deserted Spanish mining-town five miles away.

"Manuel," said the woman to her house-servant, "I'm going to ride to the convent to see Margarita, and take her a few things. Perhaps I shall stay the night in the convent. You look after Freddy and see everything is all right till I come back."

"Shall I ride with you on the master's horse, or shall Juan?" asked the servant.

"Neither of you. I shall go alone."

The young man looked her in the eyes, in protest. Absolutely impossible that the woman should ride alone!

"I shall go alone," repeated the large, placid-seeming, fair-complexioned woman, with peculiar overbearing emphasis. And the man silently, unhappily yielded.

"Why are you going alone, mother?" asked her son, as she made up parcels of food.

"Am I *never* to be let alone? Not one moment of my life?" she cried, with sudden explosion of energy. And the child, like the servant, shrank into silence.

She set off without a qualm, riding astride on her strong roan horse, and wearing a riding-suit of coarse linen, a riding-skirt over her linen breeches, a scarlet neck-tie over her white blouse, and a black felt hat on her head. She had food in her saddle-bags, an army canteen with water, and a large, native blanket tied on behind the saddle. Peering into the distance, she set off from her home. Manuel and the little boy stood in the gateway to watch her go. She did not even turn to wave them farewell.

But when she had ridden about a mile, she left the wild road and took a small trail to the right, that led into another valley, over steep places and past great trees, and through another deserted mining settlement. It was September, the water was running freely in the little stream that had fed the now-abandoned mine. She got down to drink, and let the horse drink too.

She saw natives coming through the trees, away up the slope. They had seen her, and were watching her closely. She watched in turn. The three people, two women and a youth, were making a wide detour, so as not to come too close to her. She did not care. Mounting, she trotted ahead up the silent valley, beyond the silver-works, beyond any trace of mining. There was still a rough trail that led over rocks and loose stones into the valley beyond. This trail she had already ridden, with her husband. Beyond that she knew she must go south.

Curiously she was not afraid, although it was a frightening country, the silent, fatal-seeming mountain slopes, the occasional distant, suspicious, elusive natives among the trees, the great carrion birds occasionally hovering, like great flies, in the distance, over some carrion or some ranch-house or some group of huts.

As she climbed, the trees shrank and the trail ran through a thorny scrub, that was trailed over with blue convolvulus and an occasional pink creeper. Then these flowers lapsed. She was nearing the pine trees.

She was over the crest, and before her another silent, void, green-clad valley. It was past midday. Her horse turned to a little runlet of water, so she got down to eat her midday meal. She sat in silence looking at the motionless unliving valley, and at the sharp-peaked hills, rising higher to rock and pine trees, southwards. She rested two hours in the heat of the day, while the horse cropped around her.

Curious that she was neither afraid nor lonely. Indeed, the loneliness was like a drink of cold water to one who is very thirsty. And a strange elation sustained her from within.

She travelled on, and camped at night in a valley beside a stream, deep among the bushes. She had seen cattle and had crossed several trails. There must be a ranch not far off. She heard the strange wailing shriek of a mountain-lion, and the answer of dogs. But she sat by her small camp-fire in a secret hollow place and was not really afraid. She was buoyed up always by the curious, bubbling elation within her.

It was very cold before dawn. She lay wrapped in her blanket looking at the stars, listening to her horse shivering, and feeling like a woman who has died and passed beyond. She was not sure that she had not heard, during the night, a great crash at the centre of herself, which was the crash of her own death. Or else it was a crash at the centre of the earth, and meant something big and mysterious.

With the first peep of light she got up, numb with cold, and made a fire. She ate hastily, gave her horse some pieces of oil-seed cake, and set off again. She avoided any meeting—and since she met nobody, it was evident that she in turn was avoided. She came at last in sight of the village of Cuchitee, with its black houses with their reddish roofs, a sombre, dreary little cluster below another silent, long-abandoned mine. And beyond, a long, great mountain-side, rising up green and light to the darker, shaggier green of pine trees. And beyond the pine trees stretches of naked rock against the sky, rock slashed already and brindled with white stripes of snow. High up, the new snow had already begun to fall.

And now, as she neared, more or less, her destination, she began to go vague and disheartened. She had passed the little lake among yellowing aspen trees whose white trunks were round and suave like the white round arms of some woman. What a lovely place! In California she would have raved about it. But here she looked and saw that it was lovely, but she didn't care. She was weary and spent with her two nights in the open, afraid of the coming night. She didn't know where she was going, or what she was going for. Her horse plodded dejectedly on, towards that immense and forbidding mountain-slope, following a stony little

trail. And if she had had any will of her own left, she would have turned back, to the village, to be protected and sent home to her husband.

But she had no will of her own. Her horse splashed through a brook, and turned up a valley, under immense yellowing cottonwood trees. She must have been near nine thousand feet above sealevel, and her head was light with the altitude and with weariness. Beyond the cottonwood trees she could see, on each side, the steep sides of mountain-slopes hemming her in, sharp-plumaged with overlapping aspen, and, higher up, with sprouting, pointed spruce and pine tree. Her horse went on automatically. In this tight valley, on this slight trail, there was nowhere to go but ahead, climbing.

Suddenly her horse jumped, and three men in dark blankets were on the trail before her.

"Adios!" came the greeting, in the full, restrained Indian voice.

"Adios!" she replied, in her assured, American woman's voice.

"Where are you going?" came the quiet question, in Spanish.

The men in the dark sarapes had come closer, and were looking up at her.

"On ahead," she replied coolly, in her hard, Saxon Spanish.

These were just natives to her: dark-faced, strongly-built men in dark sarapes and straw hats. They would have been the same as the men who worked for her husband, except, strangely, for the long black hair that fell over their shoulders. She noted this long black hair with a certain distaste. These must be the wild Indians she had come to see.

"Where do you come from?" the same man asked. It was always the one man who spoke. He was young, with quick, large, bright black eyes that glanced sideways at her. He had a soft black moustache on his dark face, and a sparse tuft of beard, loose hairs on his chin. His long black hair, full of life, hung unrestrained on his shoulders. Dark as he was, he did not look as if he had washed lately.

His two companions were the same, but older men, powerful and silent. One had a thin black line of moustache, but was beardless. The other had the smooth cheeks and the sparse dark hairs marking the lines of his chin with the beard characteristic of the Indians.

"I come from far away," she replied, with half-jocular evasion.

This was received in silence.

"But where do you live?" asked the young man, with that same quiet insistence.

"In the north," she replied airily.

Again there was a moment's silence. The young man conversed quietly, in Indian, with his two companions.

"Where do you want to go, up this way?" he asked suddenly, with challenge and authority, pointing briefly up the trail.

"To the Chilchui Indians," answered the woman laconically.

The young man looked at her. His eyes were quick and black, and inhuman. He saw, in the full evening light, the faint sub-smile of assurance on her rather large, calm, fresh-complexioned face; the weary, bluish lines under her large blue eyes; and in her eyes, as she looked down at him, a half-childish, half-arrogant confidence in her own female power. But in her eyes also, a curious look of trance.

"*Usted es Señora?* You are a lady?" the Indian asked her.

"Yes, I am a lady," she replied complacently.

"With a family?"

"With a husband and two children, boy and girl," she said.

The Indian turned to his companion and translated, in the low, gurgling speech, like hidden water running. They were evidently at a loss.

"Where is your husband?" asked the young man.

"Who knows?" she replied airily.

"He has gone away on business for a week."

The black eyes watched her shrewdly. She, for all her weariness, smiled faintly in the pride of her own adventure and the assurance of her own womanhood, and the spell of the madness that was on her.

"And what do *you* want to do?" the Indian asked her.

"I want to visit the Chilchui Indians —to see their houses and to know their gods," she replied.

The young man turned and translated quickly, and there was a silence almost of consternation. The grave elder men were glancing at her sideways, with strange looks, from under their decorated hats. And they said something to the young man, in deep chest voices.

The latter still hesitated. Then he turned to the woman.

"Good!" he said. "Let us go. But we cannot arrive until to-morrow. We shall have to make a camp to-night."

"Good!" she said. "I can make a camp."

Without more ado, they set off at a good speed up the stony trail. The young Indian ran alongside her horse's head, the other two ran behind. One of them had taken a thick stick, and occasionally he struck her horse a resounding blow on the haunch, to urge him forward. This made the horse jump, and threw her back in the saddle, which, tired as she was, made her angry.

"Don't do that!" she cried, looking round angrily at the fellow. She met his black, large, bright eyes, and for the first time her spirit really quailed. The man's eyes were not human to her, and they did not see her as a beautiful white woman. He looked at her with a black, bright inhuman look, and saw no woman in her at all. As if she were some strange, unaccountable *thing*, incomprehensible to him, but inimical. She sat in her saddle in wonder, feeling once more as if she had died. And again he struck her horse, and jerked her badly in the saddle.

All the passionate anger of the spoilt white woman rose in her. She pulled her horse to a standstill, and turned with blazing eyes to the man at her bridle.

"Tell that fellow not to touch my horse again," she cried.

She met the eyes of the young man, and in their bright black inscrutability she saw a fine spark, as in a snake's eye, of derision. He spoke to his companion in the rear, in the low tones of the Indian. The man with the stick listened without looking. Then, giving a strange low cry to the horse, he struck it again on the rear, so that it leaped forward spasmodically up the stony trail, scattering the stones, pitching the weary woman in her seat.

The anger flew like a madness into her eyes, she went white at the gills. Fiercely she reined in her horse. But before she could turn, the young Indian had caught the reins under the horse's throat, jerked them forward, and was trotting ahead rapidly, leading the horse.

The woman was powerless. And along with her supreme anger there came a slight thrill of exultation. She knew she was dead.

The sun was setting, a great yellow light flooded the last of the aspens, flared on the trunks of the pine trees, the pine needles bristled and stood out with dark lustre, the rocks glowed with unearthly glamour. And through the effulgence the Indian at her horse's head trotted unweariedly on, his dark blanket swinging, his bare legs glowing with a strange transfigured ruddiness in the powerful light, and his straw hat with its half-absurd decorations of flowers and feathers shining showily above his river of long black hair. At times he would utter a low call to the horse, and then the other Indian, behind, would fetch the beast a whack with the stick.

The wonder-light faded off the mountains, the world began to grow dark, a cold air breathed down. In the sky, half a moon was srtuggling against the glow in the west. Huge shadows came down from steep rocky slopes. Water was rushing. The woman was conscious only of her fatigue, her unspeakable fatigue, and the cold wind from the heights. She was not aware how moonlight replaced daylight. It happened while she travelled unconscious with weariness.

For some hours they travelled by moonlight. Then suddenly they came to a standstill. The men conversed in low tones for a moment.

"We camp here," said the young man.

She waited for him to help her down. He merely stood holding the horse's bridle. She almost fell from the saddle, so fatigued.

They had chosen a place at the foot of rocks that still gave off a little warmth of the sun. One man cut pine boughs, another erected little screens of pine boughs against the rock for shelter, and put boughs of balsam pine for beds. The third made a small fire, to heat tortillas. They worked in silence.

The woman drank water. She did not want to eat—only to lie down.

"Where do I sleep?" she asked.

The young man pointed to one of the shelters. She crept in and lay inert. She did not care what happened to her, she was so weary, and so beyond everything. Through the twigs of spruce she could see the three men squatting round the fire on their hams, chewing the tortillas they picked from the ashes with their dark fingers, and drinking water from a gourd. They talked in low, muttering tones, with long intervals of silence. Her saddle and saddle-bags lay not far from the fire, unopened, untouched. The men were not interested in her nor her belongings. There they squatted with their hats on their heads, eating, eating mechanically, like animals, the dark sarape with its fringe falling to the ground before and be-hind, the powerful dark legs naked and squatting like an animal's showing the dirty white shirt and the sort of loin-cloth which was the only other gar-ment, underneath. And they showed no more sign of interest in her than if she had been a piece of venison they were bringing home from the hunt, and had hung inside a shelter.

After a while they carefully extin-guished the fire, and went inside their own shelter. Watching through the screen of boughs, she had a moment's thrill of fear and anxiety, seeing the dark forms cross and pass silently in the moonlight. Would they attack her now?

But no! They were as if oblivious to her. Her horse was hobbled; she could hear it hopping wearily. All was silent, mountain-silent, cold, deathly. She slept and woke and slept in a semi-conscious numbness of cold and fatigue. A long, long night, icy and eternal, and she aware that she had died.

II

Yet when there was a stirring, and a clink of flint and steel, and the form of a man crouching like a dog over a bone, at a red sputter of fire, and she knew it was morning coming, it seemed to her the night had passed too soon.

When the fire was going, she came out of her shelter with one real desire left: for coffee. The men were warming more tortillas.

"Can we make coffee?" she asked.

The young man looked at her, and she imagined the same faint spark of derision in his eyes. He shook his head.

"We don't take it," he said. "There is no time."

And the elder men, squatting on their haunches, looked up at her in the terrible paling dawn, and there was not even derision in their eyes. Only that intense, yet remote, inhuman glitter which was terrible to her. They were inaccessible.

They could not see her as a woman at all. As if she *were* not a woman. As if, perhaps, her whiteness took away all her womanhood, and left her as some giant, female white ant. That was all they could see in her.

Before the sun was up, she was in the saddle again, and they were climbing steeply, in the icy air. The sun came, and soon she was very hot, exposed to the glare in the bare places. It seemed to her they were climbing to the roof of the world. Beyond against heaven were slashes of snow.

During the course of the morning, they came to a place where the horse could go no farther. They rested for a time with a great slant of living rock in front of them, like the glossy breast of some earth-beast. Across this rock, along a wavering crack, they had to go. It seemed to her that for hours she went in torment, on her hands and knees, from crack to crevice, along the slanting face of this pure rock-moun-tain. An Indian in front and an Indian behind walked slowly erect, shod with sandals of braided leather. But she in her riding-boots dare not stand erect.

Yet what she wondered, all the time, was why she persisted in clinging and crawling along these mile-long sheets of rock. Why she did not hurl herself down, and have done! The world was below her.

When they emerged at last on a stony slope, she looked back and saw the third Indian coming carrying her saddle and saddle-bags on his back, the whole hung from a band across his fore-head. And he had his hat in his hand, as he stepped slowly, with the slow, soft, heavy tread of the Indian, unwav-ering in the chinks of rock, as if along a scratch in the mountain's iron shield.

The stony slope led downwards. The Indians seemed to grow excited. One ran ahead at a slow trot, disappearing round the curve of stones. And the track curved round and down till at last in the full blaze of the mid-morning sun, they could see a valley below them, between walls of rock, as in a great wide chasm let in the mountains. A green valley, with a river, and trees, and clusters of low flat sparkling houses. It was all tiny and perfect, three thousand feet below. Even the flat bridge over the stream, and the square with the houses around it, the bigger buildings piled up at opposite ends of the square, the tall cottonwood trees, the pastures and stretches of yellow-sere maize, the patches of brown sheep or goats in the distance, on the slopes, the railed enclosures by the stream-side. There it was, all small and perfect, looking magical, as any place will look magical, seen from the mountains above. The unusual thing was that the low houses glittered white, white-washed, looking like crystals of salt, or silver. This frightened her.

They began the long, winding descent at the head of the barranca, following the stream that rushed and fell. At first it was all rocks; then the pine trees began, and soon, the silver-limbed aspens. The flowers of autumn, big daisy-like flowers, and white ones, and many yellow flowers, were in profusion. But she had to sit down and rest, she was so weary. And she saw the bright flowers shadowily, as pale shadows hovering, as one who is dead must see them.

At length came grass and pasture-slopes between mingled aspen and pine trees. A shepherd, naked in the sun save for his hat and his cotton loin-cloth, was driving his brown sheep away. In a grove of trees they sat and waited, she and the young Indian. The one with the saddle had also gone forward.

They heard a sound of someone coming. It was three men, in fine sarapes of red and orange and yellow and black, and with brilliant feather head-dresses. The oldest had his grey hair braided with fur, and his red and orange-yellow sarape was covered with curious black markings, like a leopard-skin. The other two were not grey-haired, but they were elders too. Their blankets were in stripes, and their head-dresses not so elaborate.

The young Indian addressed the elders in a few quiet words. They listened without answering or looking at him or at the woman, keeping their faces averted and their eyes turned to the ground, only listening. And at length they turned and looked at the woman.

The old chief, or medicine-man, whatever he was, had a deeply wrinkled and lined face of dark bronze, with a few sparse grey hairs round the mouth. Two long braids of grey hair, braided with fur and coloured feather, hung on his shoulders. And yet, it was only his eyes that mattered. They were black and of extraordinary piercing strength, without a qualm of misgiving in their demonish, dauntless power. He looked into the eyes of the white woman with a long piercing look, seeking she knew not what. She summoned all her strength to meet his eyes and keep up her guard. But it was no good. He was not looking at her as one human being looks at another. He never even perceived her resistance or her challenge, but looked past them both, into she knew not what.

She could see it was hopeless to expect an human communication with this old being.

He turned and said a few words to the young Indian.

"He asks what do you seek here?" said the young man in Spanish.

"I? Nothing! I only came to see what it was like."

This was again translated, and the old man turned his eyes on her once more. Then he spoke again, in his low muttering tone, to the young Indian.

"He says, why does she leave her house with the white men? Does she want to bring the white man's God to the Chilchui?"

"No," she replied, foolhardy. "I came away from the white man's God myself. I came to look for the God of the Chilchui."

Profound silence followed, when this was translated. Then the old man spoke again, in a small voice almost of weariness.

"Does the white woman seek the gods of the Chilchui because she is weary of her own God?" came the question.

"Yes, she does. She is tired of the white man's God," she replied, thinking that was what they wanted her to say. She would like to serve the gods of the Chilchui.

She was aware of an extraordinary thrill of triumph and exultance passing through the Indians, in the tense silence that followed when this was translated. They they all looked at her with piercing black eyes, in which a steely covetous intent glittered incomprehensible. She was the more puzzled, as there was nothing sensual or sexual in the look. It had a terrible glittering purity that was beyond her. She was afraid, she would have been paralysed with fear, had not something died within her, leaving her with a cold, watchful wonder only.

The elders talked a little while, then the two went away, leaving her with the young man and the oldest chief. The old man now looked at her with a certain solicitude.

"He says are you tired?" asked the young man.

"Very tired," she said.

"The men will bring you a carriage," said the young Indian.

The carriage, when it came, proved to be a litter consisting of a sort of hammock of dark woollen frieze, slung on to a pole which was borne on the shoulders of two long-haired Indians. The woollen hammock was spread on the ground, she sat down on it, and the two men raised the pole to their shoulders. Swinging rather as if she were in a sack, she was carried out of the grove of trees, following the old chief, whose leopard-spotted blanket moved curiously in the sunlight.

They had emerged in the valley-head. Just in front were the maize-fields, with ripe ears of maize. The corn was not very tall, in this high altitude. The well-worn path went between it, and all she could see was the erect form of the old chief, in the flame and black sarape, stepping soft and heavy and swift, his head forward, looking neither to right nor left. Her bearers followed, stepping rhythmically, the long blue-black hair glistening like a river down the naked shoulders of the man in front.

They passed the maize, and came to a big wall or earth-work made of earth and adobe bricks. The wooden doors were open. Passing on, they were in a network of small gardens, full of flowers and herbs and fruit trees, each garden watered by a tiny ditch of running water. Among each cluster of trees and flowers was a small, glittering white house, windowless, and with closed door. The place was a network of little paths, small streams, and little bridges among square, flowering gardens.

Following the broadest path—a soft narrow track between leaves and grass, a path worn smooth by centuries of human feet, no hoof of horse nor any wheel to disfigure it—they came to the little river of swift bright water, and crossed on a log bridge. Everything was silent—there was not a human being anywhere. The road went on under magnificent cottonwood trees. It emerged suddenly outside the central plaza or square of the village.

This was a long oblong of low white houses with flat roofs, and two bigger buildings, having as it were little square huts piled on top of bigger long huts, stood at either end of the oblong, facing each other rather askew. Every little house was a dazzling white, save for the great round beam-ends which projected under the flat eaves, and for the flat roofs. Round each of the bigger buildings, on the outside of the square, was a stockyard fence, inside which was garden with trees and flowers, and various small houses.

Not a soul was in sight. They passed silently between the houses into the central square. This was quite bare and arid, the earth trodden smooth by endless generations of passing feet, passing across from door to door. All the doors of the windowless houses gave on to this blank square, but all doors were closed. The firewood lay near the threshhold, a clay oven was still smoking, but there was no sign of moving life.

The old man walked straight across the square to the big house at the end, where the two upper storeys, as in a house of toy bricks, stood each one smaller than the lower one. A stone staircase, outside, led up to the roof of the first storey.

At the foot of this staircase the litter-bearers stood still, and lowered the woman to the ground.

"You will come up," said the young Indian who spoke Spanish.

She mounted the stone stairs to the earthen roof of the first house, which formed a platform round the wall of the second storey. She followed around this platform to the back of the big house. There they descended again, into the garden at the rear.

So far they had seen no one. But now two men appeared, bare-headed, with long braided hair, and wearing a sort of white shirt gathered into a loin-cloth. These went along with the three new-comers, across the garden where red flowers and yellow flowers were blooming, to a long, low white house. There they entered without knocking.

It was dark inside. There was a low murmur of men's voices. Several men were present, their whiteshirts showing in the gloom, their dark faces invisible. They were sitting on a great log of smooth old wood, that lay along the far wall. And save for this log, the room seemed empty. But no, in the dark at one end was a couch, a sort of bed, and someone lying there, covered with furs.

The old Indian in the spotted sarape, who had accompanied the woman, now took off his hat and his blanket and his sandals. Laying them aside, he approached the couch, and spoke in a low voice. For some moments there was no answer. Then an old man with the snow-white hair hanging round his darkly-visible face, roused himself like a vision, and leaned on one elbow, looking vaguely at the company, in tense silence.

The grey-haired Indian spoke again, and then the young Indian, taking the woman's hand, led her forward. In her linen riding-habit, and black boots and hat, and her pathetic bit of a red tie, she stood there beside the fur-covered bed of the old, old man, who sat reared up, leaning on one elbow, remote as a ghost, his white hair streaming in disorder, his face almost black, yet with a far-off intentness, not of this world, leaning forward to look at her.

His face was so old, it was like dark glass, and the few curling hairs that sprang white from his lips and chin were quite incredible. The long white locks fell unbraided and disorderly on either side of the glassy dark face. And under a faint powder of white eye-brows, the black eyes of the old chief looked at her as if from the far, far dead, seeing something that was never to be seen.

At last he spoke a few deep, hollow words, as if to the dark air.

"He says, do you bring your heart to the god of the Chilchui?" translated the young Indian.

"Tell him yes," she said, automatically.

There was a pause. The old Indian spoke again, as if to the air. One of the men present went out. There was a silence as if of eternity in the dim room that was lighted only through the open door.

The woman looked round. Four old

men with grey hair sat on the log by the wall facing the door. Two other men, powerful and impassive, stood near the door. They all had long hair, and wore white shirts gathered into a loin-cloth. Their powerful legs were naked and dark. There was a silence like eternity.

At length the man returned, with white and dark clothing on his arm. The young Indian took them, and holding them in front of the woman, said:

"You must take off your clothes, and put these on."

"If all you men will go out," she said.

"No one will hurt you," he said quietly.

"Not while you men are here," she said.

He looked at the two men by the door. They came quickly forward, and suddenly gripped her arms as she stood, without hurting her, but with great power. Then two of the old men came, and with curious skill slit her boots down with keen knives, and drew them off, and slit her clothing so that it came away from her. In a few moments she stood there white and uncovered. The old man on the bed spoke, and they turned her round for him to see. He spoke again, and the young Indian deftly took the pins and comb from her fair hair, so that it fell over her shoulders in a bunchy tangle.

Then the old man spoke again. The Indian led her to the bedside. The white-haired, glassy-dark old man moistened his finger-tips at his mouth, and most delicately touched her on the breasts and on the body, then on the back. And she winced strangely each time, as the finger-tips drew along her skin, as if Death itself were touching her.

And she wondered, almost sadly, why she did not feel shamed in her nakedness. She only felt sad and lost. Because nobody felt ashamed. The elder men were all dark and tense with some other deep, gloomy, incomprehensible emo-

tion, which suspended all her agitation, while the young Indian had a strange look of ecstasy on his face. And she, she was only utterly strange and beyond herself, as if her body were not her own.

They gave her the new clothing: a long white cotton shift, that came to her knees: then a tunic of thick blue woollen stuff, embroidered with scarlet and green flowers. It was fastened over one shoulder only, and belted with a braid sash of scarlet and black wool.

When she was thus dressed, they took her away, barefoot, to a little house in the stockaded garden. The young Indian told her she might have what she wanted. She asked for water to wash herself. He brought it in a jar, together with a long wooden bowl. Then he fastened the gate-door of her house, and left her a prisoner. She could see through the bars of the gate-door of her house, the red flowers of the garden, and a humming-bird. Then from the roof of the big house she heard the long, heavy sound of a drum, unearthly to her in its summons, and an uplifted voice calling from the house top in a strange language, with a far-away emotionless intonation, delivering some speech or message. And she listened as if from the dead.

But she was very tired. She lay down on a couch of skins, pulling over her the blanket of dark wool, and she slept, giving up everything.

When she woke it was late afternoon, and the young Indian was entering with a basket-tray containing food, tortillas, and corn-mush with bits of meat, probably mutton, and a drink made of honey, and some fresh plums. He brought her also a long garland of red and yellow flowers with knots of blue buds at the end. He sprinkled the garland with water from a jar, then offered it to her, with a smile. He seemed very gentle and thoughtful, and on his face and in his dark eyes was a curious look of triumph and ecstasy, that frightened her a little. The glitter had gone from the black eyes, with their curving dark lashes, and he would look at her with this strange soft glow of ecstasy that was not quite human, and terribly impersonal, and which made her uneasy.

"Is there anything you want?" he said, in his low, slow, melodious voice, that always seemed withheld, as if he were speaking aside to somebody else, or as if he did not want to let the sound come out to her.

"Am I going to be kept a prisoner here?" she asked.

"No, you can walk in the garden to-morrow," he said softly. Always this curious solicitude.

"Do you like that drink?" he said, offering her a little earthenware cup. "It is very refreshing."

She sipped the liquor curiously. It was made with herbs and sweetened with honey, and had a strange, lingering flavour. The young man watched her with gratification.

"It has a peculiar taste," she said.

"It is very refreshing," he replied, his black eyes resting on her always with that look of gratified ecstasy. Then he went away. And presently she began to be sick, and to vomit violently, as if she had no control over herself.

Afterwards she felt a great soothing languor steal over her, her limbs felt strong and loose and full of languor, and she lay on her couch listening to the sounds of the village, watching the yellowing sky, smelling the scent of burning cedar wood, or pine wood. So distinctly she heard the yapping of tiny dogs, the shuffle of far-off feet, the murmur of voices, so keenly she detected the smell of smoke, and flowers, and evening falling, so vividly she saw the one bright star infinitely remote, stirring above the sunset, that she felt as if all her senses were diffused on the air, that she could distinguish the sound of evening flowers unfolding, and the actual crystal sound of the heavens, as the

vast belts of the world-atmosphere slid past one another, and as if the moisture ascending and the moisture descending in the air resounded like some harp in the cosmos.

She was a prisoner in her house, and in the stockaded garden, but she scarcely minded. And it was days before she realised that she never saw another woman. Only the men, the elderly men of the big house, that she imagined must be some sort of temple, and the men priests of some sort. For they always had the same colours, red, orange, yellow, and black, and the same grave, abstracted demeanour.

Sometimes an old man would come and sit in her room with her, in absolute silence. None spoke any language but Indian, save the one younger man. The older men would smile at her, and sit with her for an hour at a time, sometimes smiling at her when she spoke in Spanish, but never answering save with this slow, benevolent-seeming smile. And they gave off a feeling of almost fatherly solicitude. Yet their dark eyes, brooding over her, had something away in their depths that was awesomely ferocious and relentless. They would cover it with a smile, at once, if they felt her looking. But she had seen it.

Always they treated her with this curious impersonal solicitude, this utterly impersonal gentleness, as an old man treats a child. But underneath it she felt there was something else, something terrible. When her old visitor had gone away, in his silent, insidious, fatherly fashion, a shock of fear would come over her; though of what she knew not.

The young Indian would sit and talk with her freely, as if with great candour. But with him, too, she felt that everything real was unsaid. Perhaps it was unspeakable. His big dark eyes would rest on her almost cherishingly, touched with ecstasy, and his beautiful, slow, languorous voice would trail out its simple, ungrammatical Spanish. He told her he was the grandson of the old, old man, son of the man in the spotted sarape: and they were caciques, kings from the old, old days, before even the Spaniards came. But he himself had been in Mexico City, and also in the United States. He had worked as a labourer, building the roads in Los Angeles. He had travelled as far as Chicago.

"Don't you speak English, then?" she asked.

His eyes rested on her with a curious look of duplicity and conflict, and he mutely shook his head.

"What did you do with your long hair, when you were in the United States?" she asked. "Did you cut it off?"

Again, with the look of torment in his eyes, he shook his head.

"No," he said, in a low, subdued voice, "I wore a hat, and a handkerchief tied round my head."

And he relapsed into silence, as if of tormented memories.

"Are you the only man of your people who has been to the United States?" she asked him.

"Yes. I am the only one who has been away from here for a long time. The others come back soon, in one week. They don't stay away. The old men don't let them."

"And why did you go?"

"The old men want me to go—because I shall be the cacique—"

He talked always with the same naïveté, and almost childish candour. But she felt that this was perhaps just the effect of his Spanish. Or perhaps speech altogether was unreal to him. Anyhow, she felt that all the real things were kept back.

He came and sat with her a good deal—sometimes more than she wished —as if he wanted to be near her. She asked him if he was married. He said he was—with two children.

"I should like to see your children," she said.

But he answered only with that smile, a sweet, almost ecstatic smile, above which the dark eyes hardly change from their enigmatic abstraction.

It was curious, he would sit with her by the hour, without ever making her self-conscious, or sex-conscious. He seemed to have no sex, as he sat there so still and gentle and apparently submissive with his head bent a little forward, and the river of glistening black hair streaming maidenly over his shoulders.

Yet when she looked again, she saw his shoulders broad and powerful, his eyebrows black and level, the short, curved, obstinate black lashes over his lowered eyes, the small, fur-like line of moustache above his blackish, heavy lips, and the strong chin, and she knew that in some other mysterious way he was darkly and powerfully male. And he, feeling her watching him, would glance up at her swiftly with a dark lurking look in his eyes, which immediately he veiled with that half-sad smile.

The days and the weeks went by, in a vague kind of contentment. She was uneasy sometimes, feeling she had lost the power over herself. She was not in her own power, she was under the spell of some other control. And at times she had moments of terror and horror. But then these Indians would come and sit with her, casting their insidious spell over her by their very silent presence, their silent, sexless, powerful physical presence. As they sat they seemed to take her will away, leaving her will-less and victim to her own indifference. And the young man would bring her sweetened drink, often the same emetic drink, but sometimes other kinds. And after drinking, the languor filled her heavy limbs, her senses seemed to float in the air, listening, hearing. They had brought her a little female dog, which she called Flora. And once, in the trance of her senses, she felt she *heard* the little dog conceive, in her tiny womb, and begin to be complex, with young. And another day she could hear the vast sound of the earth going round, like some immense arrow-string booming.

But as the days grew shorter and colder, when she was cold, she would get a sudden revival of her will, and a desire to go out, to go away. And she insisted to the young man, she wanted to go out.

So one day, they let her climb to the topmost roof of the big house where she was, and look down the square. It was the day of the big dance, but not everybody was dancing. Women with babies in their arms stood in their door-ways, watching. Opposite, at the other end of the square, there was a throng before the other big house, and a small, brilliant group on the terrace roof of the first storey, in front of wide open doors of the upper storey. Through these wide open doors she could see fire glinting in darkness and priests in head-dresses of black and yellow and scarlet feathers, wearing robe-like blan-kets of black and red and yellow, with long green fringes, were moving about. A big drum was beating slowly and regularly, in the dense, Indian silence. The crowd below waited.

Then a drum started on a high beat, and there came the deep, powerful burst of men singing a heavy, savage music, like a wind roaring in some timeless forest, many mature men sing-ing in one breath, like the wind; and long lines of dancers walked out from under the big house. Men with naked, golden-bronze bodies and streaming black hair, tufts of red and yellow feathers on their arms, and kilts of white frieze with a bar of heavy red and black and green embroidery round their waists, bending slightly forward and stamping the earth in their ab-sorbed, monotonous stamp of the dance, a fox-fur, hung by the nose from their belt behind, swaying with the sumptu-ous swaying of a beautiful fox-fur, the tip of the tail writhing above the dancer's heels. And after each man, a woman with a strange elaborate head-dress of feathers and sea-shells, and wearing a short black tunic, moving erect, holding up tufts of feathers in each hand, swaying her wrists rhythm-ically and subtly beating the earth with her bare feet.

So, the long line of the dance unfurl-ing from the big house opposite. And from the big house beneath her, strange scent of incense, strange tense silence, then the answering burst of inhuman male singing, and the long line of the dance unfurling.

It went on all day, the insistence of the drum, the cavernous, roaring, storm-like sound of male singing, the inces-sant swinging of the fox-skins behind the powerful, gold-bronze, stamping legs of the men, the autumn sun from a perfect blue heaven pouring on the rivers of black hair, men's and women's, the valley all still, the walls of rock be-yond, the awful huge bulking of the mountain against the pure sky, its snow seething with sheer whiteness.

For hours and hours she watched, spellbound, and as if drugged. And in all the terrible persistence of the drum-ming and the primeval, rushing deep singing, and the endless stamping of the dance of fox-tailed men, the tread of heavy, bird-erect women in their black tunics, she seemed at last to feel her own death; her own obliteration. As if she were to be obliterated from the field of life again. In the strange towering symbols on the heads of the changeless, absorbed women she seemed to read once more the *Mene Mene Tekel Upharsin*. Her kind of womanhood, intensely personal and in-dividual, was to be obliterated again, and the great primeval symbols were to tower once more over the fallen in-dividual independence of woman. The sharpness and the quivering nervous consciousness of the highly-bred white woman was to be destroyed again, wom-anhood was to be cast once more into the great stream of impersonal sex and impersonal passion. Strangely, as if clairvoyant, she saw the immense sacrifice prepared. And she went back to her little house in a trance of agony.

After this, there was always a certain agony when she heard the drums at evening, and the strange uplifted savage sound of men singing round the drum, like wild creatures howling to the invisible gods of the moon and the vanished sun. Something of the chuckling, sobbing cry of the coyote, something of the exultant bark of the fox, the far-off wild melancholy exultance of the howling wolf, the torment of the puma's scream, and the insistence of the ancient fierce human male, with his lapses of tenderness and his abiding ferocity.

Sometimes she would climb the high roof after nightfall, and listen to the dim cluster of young men round the drum on the bridge just beyond the square, singing by the hour. Sometimes there would be a fire, and in the fire-glow, men in their white shirts or naked save for a loin-cloth, would be dancing and stamping like spectres, hour after hour in the dark cold air, within the fire-glow, forever dancing and stamping like turkeys, or dropping squatting by the fire to rest, throwing their blankets round them.

"Why do you all have the same colours?" she asked the young Indian."Why do you all have red and yellow and black, over your white shirts? And the women have black tunics?"

He looked into her eyes, curiously, and the faint, evasive smile came on to his face. Behind the smile lay a soft, strange malignancy.

"Because our men are the fire and the day-time, and our women are the spaces between the stars at night," he said.

"Aren't the women even stars?" she said.

"No. We say they are the spaces between the stars, that keep the stars apart."

He looked at her oddly, and again the touch of derision came into his eyes.

"White people," he said, "they know nothing. They are like children, always with toys. We know the sun, and we know the moon. And we say, when a white woman sacrifice herself to our gods, then our gods will begin to make the world again, and the white man's gods will fall to pieces."

"How sacrifice herself?" she asked quickly.

And he, as quickly covered, covered himself with a subtle smile.

"She sacrifice her own gods and come to our gods, I mean that," he said soothingly.

But she was not reassured. An icy pang of fear and certainty was at her heart.

"The sun he is alive at one end of the sky," he continued, "and the moon lives at the other end. And the man all the time have to keep the sun happy in his side of the sky, and the woman have to keep the moon quiet at her side of the sky. All the time she have to work at this. And the sun can't ever go into the house of the moon, and the moon can't ever go into the house of the sun, in the sky. So the woman, she asks the moon to come into her cave, inside her. And the man, he draws the sun down till he has the power of the sun. All the time he do this. Then when the man gets a woman, the sun goes into the cave of the moon, and that is how everything in the world starts."

She listened, watching him closely, as one enemy watches another who is speaking with double meaning.

"Then," she said, "why aren't you Indians masters of the white men?"

"Because," he said, "the Indian got weak, and lost his power with the sun, so the white man stole the sun. But they can't keep him—they don't know how. They got him, but they don't know what to do with him, like a boy who catch a big grizzly bear, and can't kill him, and can't run away from him. The grizzly bear eats the boy that catch him, when he want to run away from him. White men don't know what they are doing with the sun, and white women don't know what they do with the moon. The moon she got angry with white women, like a puma when someone kills her little ones. The moon, she bites white woman—here inside," and he pressed his side. "The moon, she is angry in a white woman's cave. The Indian can see it. And soon," he added, "the Indian women get the moon back and keep her quiet in their house. And the Indian men get the sun, and the power over all the world. White men don't know what the sun is. They never know."

He subsided into a curious exultant silence.

"But," she faltered, "why do you hate us so? Why do you hate me?"

He looked up suddenly with a light on his face, and a startling flame of a smile.

"No, we don't hate," he said softly, looking with a curious glitter into her face.

"You do," she said, forlorn and hopeless.

And after a moment's silence, he rose and went away.

III

Winter had now come, in the high valley, with snow that melted in the day's sun, and nights that were bitter cold. She lived on, in a kind of daze, feeling her power ebbing more and more away from her, as if her will were leaving her. She felt always in the same relaxed, confused, victimized state, unless the sweetened herb drink would numb her mind altogether, and release her senses into a sort of heightened, mystic acuteness and a feeling as if she were diffusing out deliciously into the harmony of things. This at length became the only state of consciousness she really recognized: this exquisite sense of bleeding out into the higher beauty and harmony of things. Then she could actually hear the great stars in heaven, which she saw through her door, speaking from their motion and brightness, saying things perfectly to the cosmos, as they trod in perfect ripples, like bells on the floor of heaven, passing one another and grouping in the timeless dance, with the spaces of dark between. And she could hear the snow on a cold, cloudy day twittering and faintly whistling in the sky, like birds that flock and fly away in autumn, suddenly calling farewell to the invisible moon, and slipping out of the plains of the air, releasing peaceful warmth. She herself would call to the arrested snow to fall from the upper air. She would call to the unseen moon to cease to be angry, to make peace again with the unseen sun like a woman who ceases to be angry in her house. And she would smell the sweetness of the moon relaxing to the sun in the wintry heaven, when the snow fell in a faint, cold-perfumed relaxation, as the peace of the sun mingled again in a sort of unison with the peace of the moon.

She was aware too of the sort of shadow that was on the Indians of the valley, a deep stoical disconsolation, almost religious in its depth.

"We have lost our power over the sun, and we are trying to get him back. But he is wild with us, and shy like a horse that has got away. We have to go through a lot." So the young Indian said to her, looking into her eyes with a strained meaning. And she, as if bewitched, replied:

"I hope you will get him back."

The smile of triumph flew over his face.

"Do you hope it?" he said.

"I do," she answered fatally.

"Then all right," he said. "We shall get him."

And he went away in exultance.

She felt she was drifting on some consummation, which she had no will to avoid, yet which seemed heavy and finally terrible to her.

It must have been almost December, for the days were short when she was taken again before the aged man, and stripped of her clothing, and touched with the old finger-tips.

The aged cacique looked her in the eyes, with his eyes of lonely, far-off, black intentness, and murmured something to her.

"He wants you to make the sign of peace," the young man translated, showing her the gesture. "Peace and farewell to him."

She was fascinated by the black, glass-like, intent eyes of the old cacique, that watched her without blinking, like a basilisk's, overpowering her. In their depths also she saw a certain fatherly compassion, and pleading. She put her hand before her face, in the required manner, making the sign of peace and farewell. He made the sign of peace back again to her, then sank among his furs. She thought he was going to die, and that he knew it.

There followed a day of ceremonial, when she was brought out before all the people, in a blue blanket with white fringe, and holding blue feathers in her hands. Before an altar of one house she was perfumed with incense and sprinkled with ash. Before the altar of the opposite house she was fumigated again with incense by the gorgeous, terrifying priests in yellow and scarlet and black, their faces painted with scarlet paint. And then they threw water on her. Meanwhile she was faintly aware of the fire on the altar, the heavy, heavy sound of a drum, the heavy sound of men beginning powerfully, deeply, savagely to sing, the swaying of the crowd of faces in the plaza below, and the formation for a sacred dance.

But at this time her commonplace consciousness was numb, she was aware of her immediate surroundings as shadows, almost immaterial. With refined and heightened senses she could hear the sound of the earth winging on its journey, like a shot arrow, the ripple-

rustling of the air, and the boom of the great arrow-string. And it seemed to her there were two great influences in the upper air, one golden towards the sun, and one invisible silver; the first travelling like rain ascending to the gold presence sunwards, the second like rain silverily descending the ladders of space towards the hovering, lurking clouds over the snowy mountain-top. Then between them, another presence, waiting to shake himself free of moisture, of heavy white snow that had mysteriously collected about him. And in summer, like a scorched eagle, he would wait to shake himself clear of the weight of heavy sunbeams. And he was coloured like fire. And he was always shaking himself clear, of snow or of heavy heat, like an eagle rustling.

Then there was a still stranger presence, standing watching from the blue distance, always watching. Sometimes running in upon the wind, or shimmering in the heat-waves. The blue wind itself, rushing, as it were, out of the holes into the sky, rushing out of the sky down upon the earth. The blue wind, the go-between, the invisible ghost that belonged to two worlds, that played upon the ascending and the descending chords of the rains.

More and more her ordinary personal consciousness had left her, she had gone into that other state of passional cosmic consciousness, like one who is drugged. The Indians, with their heavily religious natures, had made her succumb to their vision.

Only one personal question she asked the young Indian:

"Why am I the only one that wears blue?"

"It is the colour of the wind. It is the colour of what goes away and is never coming back, but which is always here, waiting like death among us. It is the colour of the dead. And it is the colour that stands away off, looking at us from the distance, that cannot come near to us. When we go near, it goes farther.

It can't be near. We are all brown and yellow and black hair, and white teeth and red blood. We are the ones that are here. You with blue eyes, you are the messengers from the far-away, you cannot stay, and now it is time for you to go back."

"Where to?" she asked.

"To the way-off things like the sun and the blue mother of rain, and tell them that we are the people on the world again, and we can bring the sun to the moon again, like a red horse to a blue mare; we are the people. The white women have driven back the moon in the sky, won't let her come to the sun. So the sun is angry. And the Indian must give the moon to the sun."

"How?" she said.

"The white woman got to die and go like a wind to the sun, tell him the Indians will open the gate to him. And the Indian women will open the gate to the moon. The white women don't let the moon come down out of the blue coral. The moon used to come down among the Indian women, like a white goat among the flowers. And the sun want to come down to the Indian men, like an eagle to the pine trees. The sun, he is shut out behind the white man, and the moon she is shut out behind the white woman, and they can't get away. They are angry, everything in the world gets angrier. The Indian says he will give the white woman to the sun, so the sun will leap over the white man and come to the Indian again. And the moon will be surprised, she will see the gate open, and she not know which way to go. But the Indian woman will call to the moon: *Come! Come! Come back into my grasslands. The wicked white woman can't harm you any more.* Then the sun will look over the heads of the white men, and see the moon in the pastures of our women, with the Red Men standing around like pine trees. Then he will leap over the heads of the white men, and come running past

to the Indians through the spruce trees. And we, who are red and black and yellow, we who stay, we shall have the sun on our right hand and the moon on our left. So we can bring the rain down out of the blue meadows, and up out of the black; and we can call the wind that tells the corn to grow, when we ask him, and we shall make the clouds to break, and the sheep to have twin lambs. And we shall be full of power, like a spring day. But the white people will be a hard winter, without snow—"

"But," said the white woman, "I don't shut out the moon—how can I?"

"Yes," he said, "you shut the gate, and then laugh, think you have it all your own way."

She could never quite understand the way he looked at her. He was always so curiously gentle, and his smile was so soft. Yet there was such a glitter in his eyes, and an unrelenting sort of hate came out of his words, a strange, profound, impersonal hate. Personally he liked her, she was sure. He was gentle with her, attracted by her in some strange, soft, passionless way. But impersonally he hated her with a mystic hatred. He would smile at her, winningly. Yet if, the next moment, she glanced round at him unawares, she would catch that gleam of pure after-hate in his eyes.

"Have I got to die and be given to the sun?" she asked.

"Some time," he said, laughing evasively. "Some time we all die."

They were gentle with her, and very considerate with her. Strange men, the old priests and the young cacique alike, they watched over her and cared for her like women. In their soft, insidious understanding, there was something womanly. Yet their eyes, with that strange glitter, and their dark, shut mouths that would open to the broad jaw, the small, strong, white teeth, had something very primitively male and cruel.

One wintry day, when snow was falling, they took her to a great dark chamber in the big house. The fire was burning in a corner on a high raised dais under a sort of hood or canopy of adobe-work. She saw in the fire-glow the glowing bodies of the almost naked priests, and strange symbols on the roof and walls of the chamber. There was no door or window in the chamber, they had descended by a ladder, from the roof. And the fire of pinewood danced continually, showing walls painted with strange devices, which she could not understand, and a ceiling of poles making a curious pattern of black and red and yellow, and alcoves or niches in which were curious objects she could not discern.

The older priests were going through some ceremony near the fire, in silence, intense Indian silence. She was seated on a low projection of the wall, opposite the fire, two men seated beside her. Presently they gave her a drink from a cup, which she took gladly, because of the semi-trance it would induce.

In the darkness and in the silence she was accurately aware of everything that happened to her: how they took off her clothes, and, standing her before a great, weird device on the wall, coloured blue and white and black, washed her all over with water and the amole infusion; washed even her hair, softly, carefully, and dried it on white cloths, till it was soft and glistening. Then they laid her on a couch under another great indecipherable image of red and black and yellow, and now rubbed all her body with sweet-scented oil, and massaged all her limbs, and her back, and her sides, with a long, strange, hypnotic massage. Their dark hands were incredibly powerful, yet soft with a watery softness she could not understand. And the dark faces, leaning near her white body, she saw were darkened with red pigment, with lines of yellow round the cheeks. And the dark eyes glittered absorbed, as the hands worked upon the soft white body of the woman.

They were so impersonal, absorbed in something that was beyond her. They never saw her as a personal woman: She could tell that. She was some mystic object to them, some vehicle of passions too remote for her to grasp. Herself in a state of trance, she watched their faces bending over her, dark, strangely glistening with the transparent red paint, and lined with bars of yellow. And in this weird, luminous-dark mask of living face, the eyes were fixed with an unchanging steadfast gleam, and the purplish-pigmented lips were closed in a full, sinister, sad grimness. The immense fundamental sadness, the grimness of ultimate decision, the fixity of revenge, and the nascent exultance of those that are going to triumph—these things she could read in their faces, as she lay and was rubbed into a misty glow by their uncanny dark hands. Her limbs, her flesh, her very bones at last seemed to be diffusing into a roseate sort of mist, in which her consciousness hovered like some sun-gleam in a flushed cloud.

She knew the gleam would fade, the cloud would go grey. But at present she did not believe it. She knew she was a victim; that all this elaborate work upon her was the work of victimizing her. But she did not mind. She wanted it.

Later, they put a short blue tunic on her and took her to the upper terrace, and presented her to the people. She saw the plaza below her full of dark faces and of glittering eyes. There was no pity: only the curious hard exultance. The people gave a subdued cry when they saw her, and she shuddered. But she hardly cared.

Next day was the last. She slept in a chamber of the big house. At dawn they put on her a big blue blanket with a fringe, and led her out into the plaza, among the throng of silent, dark-blanketed people. There was pure white snow on the ground, and the dark people in their dark-brown blankets looked like inhabitants of another world.

A large drum was slowly pounding,

and an old priest was declaiming from a house-top. But it was not till noon that a litter came forth, and the people gave that low, animal cry which was so moving. In the sack-like litter sat the old, old cacique, his white hair braided with a black braid and large turquoise stones. His face was like a piece of obsidian. He lifted his hand in token, and the litter stopped in front of her. Fixing her with his old eyes, he spoke to her for a few moments, in his hollow voice. No one translated.

Another litter came, and she was placed in it. Four priests moved ahead, in their scarlet and yellow and black, with plumed head-dresses. Then came the litter of the old cacique. Then the light drums began, and two groups of singers burst simultaneously into song, male and wild. And the golden-red, almost naked men, adorned with ceremonial feathers and kilts, the rivers of black hair down their backs, formed into two files and began to tread the dance. So they threaded out of the snowy plaza, in two long, sumptuous lines of dark red-gold and black and fur, swaying with a faint tinkle of bits of shell and flint, winding over the snow between the two bee-clusters of men who sang around the drums.

Slowly they moved out, and her litter, with its attendance of feathered, lurid dancing priests, moved after. Everybody danced the tread of the dance-step, even, subtly, the litter-bearers. And out of the plaza they went, past smoking ovens, on the trail to the great cottonwood trees, that stood like grey-silver lace against the blue sky, bare and exquisite above the snow. The river, diminished, rushed among fangs of ice. The chequer-squares of gardens within fences were all snowy, and the white houses now looked yellowish.

The whole valley glittered intolerably with pure snow, away to the walls of the standing rock. And across the flat cradle of snow-bed wound the long thread of the dance, shaking slowly and sumptuously in its orange and black motion. The high drums thudded quickly, and on the crystalline frozen air the swell and roar of the chant of savages was like an obsession.

She sat looking out of her litter with big, transfixed blue eyes, under which were the wan markings of her drugged weariness. She knew she was going to die, among the glisten of this snow, at the hands of this savage, sumptuous people. And as she stared at the blaze of the blue sky above the slashed and ponderous mountain, she thought: "I am dead already. What difference does it make, the transition from the dead I am to the dead I shall be, very soon?" Yet her soul sickened and felt wan.

The strange procession trailed on, in perpetual dance, slowly across the plain of snow, and then entered the slopes between the pine trees. She saw the copper-dark men dancing the dance-tread, onwards, between the copper-pale tree trunks. And at last, she, too, in her swaying litter, entered the pine trees.

They were travelling on and on, upwards, across the snow under the trees, past superb shafts of pale, flaked copper, the rustle and shake and tread of the threading dance, penetrating into the forest, into the mountain. They were following a stream-bed; but the stream was dry, like summer, dried up by the frozenness of the head-waters. There were dark, red-bronze willow bushes with wattles like wild hair, and pallid aspen trees looking cold flesh against the snow. Then jutting dark rocks.

At last she could tell that the dancers were moving forward no more. Nearer and nearer she came upon the drums, as to a lair of mysterious animals. Then through the bushes she emerged into a strange amphitheatre. Facing was a great wall of hollow rock, down the front of which hung a great dripping, fang-like spoke of ice. The ice came pouring over the rock from the precipice above, and then stood arrested, dripping out of high heaven, almost down to the hollow stones where the stream-pool should be below. But the pool was dry.

On either side the dry pool the lines of dancers had formed, and the dance was continuing without intermission, against a background of bushes.

But what she felt was that fanged inverted pinnacle of ice, hanging from the lip of the dark precipice above. And behind the great rope of ice she saw the leopard-like figures of priests climbing the hollow cliff face, to the cave that like a dark socket bored a cavity, an orifice, half-way up the crag.

Before she could realise, her litter-bearers were staggering in the footholds, climbing the rock. She, too, was behind the ice. There it hung, like a curtain that is not spread, but hangs like a great fang. And near above her was the orifice of the cave sinking dark into the rock. She watched it as she swayed upwards.

On the platform of the cave stood the priests, waiting in all their gorgeousness of feathers and fringed robes, watching her ascent. Two of them stooped to help her litter-bearer. And at length she was on the platform of the cave, far in behind the shaft of ice, above the hollow amphitheatre among the bushes below, where men were dancing, and the whole populace of the village was clustered in silence.

The sun was sloping down the afternoon sky, on the left. She knew that this was the shortest day of the year, and the last day of her life. They stood her facing the iridescent column of ice, which fell down marvellously arrested, away in front of her.

Some signal was given, and the dance below stopped. There was now absolute silence. She was given a little to drink, then two priests took off her mantle and her tunic, and in her strange pallor she stood there, between the lurid robes of the priests, beyond the pillar of ice, beyond and above the dark-faced people. The throng below gave the low, wild cry. Then the priest turned her round, so

she stood with her back to the open world, her long blonde hair to the people below. And they cried again.

She was facing the cave, inwards. A fire was burning and flickering in the depths. Four priests had taken off their robes, and were almost as naked as she was. They were powerful men in the prime of life, and they kept their dark, painted faces lowered.

From the fire came the old, old priest, with an incense-pan. He was naked and in a state of barbaric ecstasy. He fumigated his victim, reciting at the same time in a hollow voice. Behind him came another robeless priest, with two flint knives.

When she was fumigated, they laid her on a large flat stone, the four powerful men holding her by the outstretched arms and legs. Behind stood the aged man, like a skeleton covered with dark glass, holding a knife and transfixedly watching the sun; and behind him again was another naked priest, with a knife.

She felt little sensation, though she knew all that was happening. Turning to the sky, she looked at the yellow sun. It was sinking. The shaft of ice was like a shadow between her and it. And she realised that the yellow rays were filling half the cave, though they had not reached the altar where the fire was, at the far end of the funnel-shaped cavity.

Yes, the rays were creeping round slowly. As they grew ruddier, they penetrated farther. When the red sun was about to sink, he would shine full through the shaft of ice deep into the hollow of the cave, to the innermost.

She understood now that this was what the men were waiting for. Even those that held her down were bent and twisted round, their black eyes watching the sun with a glittering eagerness, and awe, and craving. The black eyes of the aged cacique were fixed like black mirrors on the sun, as if sightless, yet containing some terrible answer to the reddening winter planet. And all the eyes of the priests were fixed and glittering on the sinking orb, in the reddening, icy silence of the winter afternoon.

They were anxious, terribly anxious, and fierce. Their ferocity wanted something, and they were waiting the moment. And their ferocity was ready to leap out into a mystic exultance, of triumph. But they were anxious.

Only the eyes of the oldest man were not anxious. Black, and fixed, and as if sightless, they watched the sun, seeing beyond the sun. And in their black, empty concentration there was power, power intensely abstract and remote, but deep, deep to the heart of the earth, and the heart of the sun. In absolute motionlessness he watched till the red sun should send his ray through the column of ice. Then the old man would strike, and strike home, accomplish the sacrifice and achieve the power.

The mastery that man must hold, and that passes from race to race.

Jean Toomer (1894–1967)

BLOOD-BURNING MOON

I

Up from the skeleton stone walls, up from the rotting floor boards and the solid hand-hewn beams of oak of the pre-war cotton factory, dusk came. Up from the dusk the full moon came. Glowing like a fired pine-knot, it illumined the great door and soft showered the Negro shanties aligned along the single street of factory town. The full moon in the great door was an omen. Negro women improvised songs against its spell.

Louisa sang as she came over the crest of the hill from the white folks' kitchen. Her skin was the color of oak leaves on young trees in fall. Her breasts, firm and up-pointed like ripe acorns. And her singing had the low murmur of winds in fig trees. Bob Stone, younger son of the people she worked for, loved her. By the way the world reckons things, he had won her. By measure of that warm glow which came into her mind at thought of him, he had won her. Tom Burwell, whom the whole town called Big Boy, also loved her. But working in the fields all day, and far away from her, gave him no chance to show it. Though often enough of evenings he had tried to. Somehow, he never got along. Strong as he was with hands upon the ax or plow, he found it difficult to hold her. Or so he thought. But the fact was that he held her to factory town more firmly than he thought for. His black balanced, and pulled against, the white of Stone, when she thought of them. And her mind was vaguely upon them as she came over the crest of the hill, coming from the white folks' kitchen. As she sang softly at the evil of the full moon.

A strange stir was in her. Indolently, she tried to fix upon Bob or Tom as the cause of it. To meet Bob in the canebrake, as she was going to do an hour or so later, was nothing new. And Tom's proposal which she felt on its way to her could be indefinitely put off. Separately, there was no unusual significance to either one. But for some reason, they jumbled when her eyes gazed vacantly at the rising moon. And from the jumble came the stir that was strangely within her. Her lips trembled. The slow rhythm of her song grew agitant and restless. Rusty black and tan spotted hounds, lying in the dark corners of porches or prowling around back yards, put their noses in the air and caught its tremor. They began plaintively to yelp and howl. Chickens woke up and cackled. Intermittently, all over the countryside dogs barked and roosters crowed as if heralding a weird dawn or some ungodly awakening. The women sang lustily. Their songs were cotton-wads to stop their ears. Louisa came down into factory town and sank wearily upon the step before her home. The moon was rising towards a thick cloud-bank which soon would hide it.

Red nigger moon. Sinner!
Blood-burning moon. Sinner!
Come out that fact'ry door.

II

Up from the deep dusk of a cleared spot on the edge of the forest a mellow glow arose and spread fan-wise into the low-hanging heavens. And all around the air was heavy with the scent of boiling cane. A large pile of cane-stalks lay like ribboned shadows upon the ground. A mule, harnessed to a pole, trudged lazily round and round the pivot of the grinder. Beneath a swaying oil lamp, a Negro alternately whipped out at the mule, and fed cane-stalks to the grinder. A fat boy waddled pails of fresh ground juice between the grinder and the boiling stove. Steam came from the copper boiling pan. The scent of cane came from the copper pan and drenched the forest and the hill that sloped to factory town, beneath its fragrance. It drenched the men in circle seated around the stove. Some of them

chewed at the white pulp of stalks, but there was no need for them to, if all they wanted was to taste the cane. One tasted it in factory town. And from factory town one could see the soft haze thrown by the glowing stove upon the low-hanging heavens.

Old David Georgia stirred the thickening syrup with a long ladle, and ever so often drew it off. Old David Georgia tended his stove and told tales about the white folks, about moonshining and cotton picking, and about sweet nigger gals, to the men who sat there about his stove to listen to him. Tom Burwell chewed cane-stalk and laughed with the others till someone mentioned Louisa. Till someone said something about Louisa and Bob Stone, about the silk stockings she must have gotten from him. Blood ran up Tom's neck hotter than the glow that flooded from the stove. He sprang up. Glared at the men and said, "She's my gal." Will Manning laughed. Tom strode over to him. Yanked him up and knocked him to the ground. Several of Manning's friends got up to fight for him. Tom whipped out a long knife and would have cut them to shreds if they hadnt ducked into the woods. Tom had had enough. He nodded to Old David Georgia and swung down the path to factory town. Just then, the dogs started barking and the roosters began to crow. Tom felt funny. Away from the fight, away from the stove, chill got to him. He shivered. He shuddered when he saw the full moon rising towards the cloud-bank. He who didnt give a godam for the fears of old women. He forced his mind to fasten on Louisa. Bob Stone. Better not be. He turned into the street and saw Louisa sitting before her home. He went towards her, ambling, touched the brim of a marvelously shaped, spotted, felt hat, said he wanted to say something to her, and then found that he didnt know what he had to say, or if he did, that he couldnt say it. He shoved his big fists in his overalls, grinned, and started to move off.

"Youall want me, Tom?"

"Thats what us wants, sho, Louisa."

"Well, here I am—"

"An here I is, but that aint ahelpin none, all th same."

"You wanted to say something? . ."

"I did that, sho. But words is like th spots on dice: no matter how y fumbles em, there's times when they jes wont come. I dunno why. Seems like th love I feels fo yo done stole m tongue. I got it now. Whee! Louisa, honey, I oughtnt tell y, I feel I oughtnt cause yo is young an goes t church an I has had other gals, but Louisa I sho do love y. Lil gal, Ise watched y from them first days when youall sat right here befo yo door befo th well an sang sometimes in a way that like t broke m heart. Ise carried y with me into th fields, day after day, an after that, an I sho can plow when yo is there, an I can pick cotton. Yassur! Come near beatin Barlo yesterday. I sho did. Yassur! An next year if ole Stone'll trust me, I'll have a farm. My own. My bales will buy yo what y gets from white folks now. Silk stockings an purple dresses—course I dont believe what some folks been whisperin as t how y gets them things now. White folks always did do for niggers what they likes. An they jes cant help alikin yo, Louisa. Bob Stone likes y. Course he does. But not th way folks is awhisperin. Does he, hon?"

"I dont know what you mean, Tom."

"Course y dont. Ise already cut two niggers. Had t hon, t tell em so. Niggers always tryin t make somethin out a nothin. An then besides, white folks aint up t them tricks so much nowadays. Godam better not be. Leastawise not with yo. Cause I wouldnt stand f it. Nassur."

"What would you do, Tom?"

"Cut him jes like I cut a nigger."

"No, Tom—"

"I said I would an there aint no mo to it. But that aint th talk f now. Sing, honey Louisa, an while I'm listenin t y I'll be makin love."

Tom took her hand in his. Against the tough thickness of his own, hers felt soft and small. His huge body slipped down to the step beside her. The full moon sank upward into the deep purple of the cloud-bank. An old woman brought a lighted lamp and hung it on the common well whose bulky shadow squatted in the middle of the road, opposite Tom and Louisa. The old woman lifted the well-lid, took hold the chain, and began drawing up the heavy bucket. As she did so, she sang. Figures shifted, restless-like, between lamp and window in the front rooms of the shanties. Shadows of the figures fought each other on the gray dust of the road. Figures raised the windows and joined the old woman in song. Louisa and Tom, the whole street, singing:

Red nigger moon. Sinner!
Blood-burning moon. Sinner!
Come out that fact'ry door.

III

Bob Stone sauntered from his veranda out into the gloom of fir trees and magnolias. The clear white of his skin paled, and the flush of his cheeks turned purple. As if to balance this outer change, his mind became consciously a white man's. He passed the house with its huge open hearth which, in the days of slavery, was the plantation cookery. He saw Louisa bent over that hearth. He went in as a master should and took her. Direct, honest, bold. None of this sneaking that he had to go through now. The contrast was repulsive to' him. His family had lost ground. Hell no, his family still owned the niggers, practically. Damned if they did, or he wouldn't have to duck around so. What would they think if they knew? His mother? His sister? He shouldnt mention them, shouldnt think of them in this connection. There in the dusk he blushed at doing so. Fellows about town were all right, but how about his friends up North? He could see them incredible, repulsed. They didnt know. The thought first made him laugh. Then, with their eyes still upon him, he began to feel embarrassed. He felt the need of explaining things to them. Explain hell. They wouldnt understand, and moreover, who ever heard of a Southerner getting on his knees to any Yankee, or anyone. No sir. He was going to see Louisa tonight, and love her. She was lovely—in her way. Nigger way. What way was that? Damned if he knew. Must know. He'd known her long enough to know. Was there something about niggers that you couldnt know? Listening to them at church didnt tell you anything. Looking at them didnt tell you anything. Talking to them didnt tell you anything—unless it was gossip, unless they wanted to talk. Of course, about farming, and licker, and craps—but those werent nigger. Nigger was something more. How much more? Something to be afraid of, more? Hell no. Who ever heard of being afraid of a nigger? Tom Burwell. Cartwell had told him that Tom went with Louisa after she reached home. No sir. No nigger had ever been with his girl. He'd like to see one try. Some position for him to be in. Him, Bob Stone, of the old Stone family, in a scrap with a nigger over a nigger girl. In the good old days. . .Ha! Those were the days. His family had lost ground. Not so much, though. Enough for him to have to cut through old Lemon's canefield by way of the woods, that he might meet her. She was worth it. Beautiful nigger gal. Why nigger? Why not, just gal? No, it was because she was nigger that he went to her. Sweet. . . The scent of boiling cane came to him. Then he saw the rich glow of the stove. He heard the voices of the men circled around it. He was about to skirt the clearing when he heard his own name mentioned. He

stopped. Quivering. Leaning against a tree, he listened.

"Bad nigger. Yassur, he sho is one bad nigger when he gets started."

"Tom Burwell's been on th gang three times fo cuttin men."

"What y think he's agwine t do t Bob Stone?"

"Dunno yet. He aint found out. When he does—Baby!"

"Aint no tellin."

"Young Stone aint no quitter an I kin tell y that. Blood of th old uns in his veins."

"Thats right. He'll scrap, sho."

"Be gettin too hot f niggers round this away."

"Shut up, nigger. Y dont know what y talkin bout."

Bob Stone's ears burned as though he had been holding them over the stove. Sizzling heat welled up within him. His feet felt as if they rested on red-hot coals. They stung him to quick movement. He circled the fringe of the glowing. Not a twig cracked beneath his feet. He reached the path that led to factory town. Plunged furiously down it. Halfway along, a blindness within him veered him aside. He crashed into the bordering canebrake. Cane leaves cut his face and lips. He tasted blood. He threw himself down and dug his fingers in the ground. The earth was cool. Cane-roots took the fever from his hands. After a long while, or so it seemed to him, the thought came to him that it must be time to see Louisa. He got to his feet and walked calmly to their meeting place. No Louisa. Tom Burwell had her. Veins in his forehead bulged and distended. Saliva moistened the dried blood on his lips. He bit down on his lips. He tasted blood. Not his own blood; Tom Burwell's blood. Bob drove through the cane and out again upon the road. A hound swung down the path before him towards factory town. Bob couldnt see it. The dog loped aside to let him pass. Bob's blind rushing made him stumble over it. He fell with a thud that dazed him. The hound yelped. Answering yelps came from all over the countryside. Chickens cackled. Roosters crowed, heralding the bloodshot eyes of southern awakening. Singers in the town were silenced. They shut their windows down. Palpitant between the rooster crows, a chill hush settled upon the huddled forms of Tom and Louisa. A figure rushed from the shadow and stood before them. Tom popped to his feet.

"Whats y want?"

"I'm Bob Stone."

"Yassur—an I'm Tom Burwell. Whats y want?"

Bob lunged at him. Tom side-stepped, caught him by the shoulder, and flung him to the ground. Straddled him.

"Let me up."

"Yassur—but watch yo doins, Bob Stone."

A few dark figures, drawn by the sound of scuffle, stood about them. Bob sprang to his feet.

"Fight like a man, Tom Burwell, an I'll lick y."

Again he lunged. Tom side-stepped and flung him to the ground. Straddled him.

"Get off me, you godam nigger you."

"Yo sho has started somethin now. Get up."

Tom yanked him up and began hammering at him. Each blow sounded as if it smashed into a precious, irreplaceable soft something. Beneath them, Bob staggered back. He reached in his pocket and whipped out a knife.

"Thats my game, sho."

Blue flash, a steel blade slashed across Bob Stone's throat. He had a sweetish sick feeling. Blood began to flow. Then he felt a sharp twitch of pain. He let his knife drop. He slapped one hand against his neck. He pressed the other on top of his head as if to hold it down. He groaned. He turned, and staggered towards the crest of the hill in the direction of white town. Negroes who

had seen the fight slunk into their homes and blew the lamps out. Louisa, dazed, hysterical, refused to go indoors. She slipped, crumbled, her body loosely propped against the woodwork of the well. Tom Burwell leaned against it. He seemed rooted there.

Bob reached Broad Street. White men rushed up to him. He collapsed in their arms.

"Tom Burwell. . ."

White men like ants upon a forage rushed about. Except for the taut hum of their moving, all was silent. Shotguns, revolvers, rope, kerosene, torches. Two high-powered cars with glaring search-lights. They came together. The taut hum rose to a low roar. Then nothing could be heard but the flop of their feet in the thick dust of the road. The moving body of their silence preceded them over the crest of the hill into factory town. It flattened the Negroes beneath it. It rolled to the wall of the factory, where it stopped. Tom knew that they were coming. He couldnt move. And then he saw the search-lights of the two cars glaring down on him. A quick shock went through him, he stiffened. He started to run. A yell went up from the mob. Tom wheeled about and faced them. They poured down on him. They swarmed. A large man with dead-white face and flabby cheeks came to him and almost jabbed a gun-barrel through his guts.

"Hands behind y, nigger."

Tom's wrists were bound. The big man shoved him to the well. Burn him over it, and when the woodwork caved in, his body would drop to the bottom. Two deaths for a godam nigger. Louisa was driven back. The mob pushed in. Its pressure, its momentum was too great. Drag him to the factory. Wood and stakes already there. Tom moved in the direction indicated. But they had to drag him. They reached the great door. Too many to get in there. The mob divided and flowed around the walls to either side. The big man shoved him through the door. The mob pressed in from the sides. Taut humming. No words. A stake was sunk into the ground. Rotting floor boards piled around it. Kerosene poured on the rotting floor boards. Tom bound to the stake. His breast was bare. Nails scratches let little lines of blood trickle down and mat into the hair. His face, his eyes were set and stony. Except for irregular breathing, one would have thought him already dead. Torches were flung onto the pile. A great flare muffled in black smoke shot upward. The mob yelled. The mob was silent. Now Tom could be seen within the flames. Only his head, erect, lean, like a blackened stone. Stench of burning flesh soaked the air. Tom's eyes popped. His head settled downward. The mob yelled. Its yell echoed against the skeleton stone walls and sounded like a hun-

dred yells. Like a hundred mobs yelling. Its yell thudded against the thick front wall and fell back. Ghost of a yell slipped through the flames and out the great door of the factory. It fluttered like a dying thing down the single street of factory town. Louisa, upon the step before her home, did not hear it, but her eyes opened slowly. They saw the full moon glowing in the great door. The full moon, an evil thing, an omen, soft showering the homes of folks she knew. Where were they, these people? She'd sing, and perhaps they'd come out and join her. Perhaps Tom Burwell would come. At any rate, the full moon in the great door was an omen which she must sing to:

Red nigger moon. Sinner!
Blood-burning moon. Sinner!
Come out that fact'ry door.

F. Scott Fitzgerald (1896–1940)

WINTER DREAMS

Some of the caddies were poor as sin and lived in one-room houses with a neurasthenic cow in the front yard, but Dexter Green's father owned the second best grocery-store in Black Bear—the best one was "The Hub," patronized by the wealthy people from Sherry Island—and Dexter caddied only for pocket-money.

In the fall when the days became crisp and gray, and the long Minnesota winter shut down like the white lid of a box, Dexter's skis moved over the snow that hid the fairways of the golf course. At these times the country gave him a feeling of profound melancholy —it offended him that the links should lie in enforced fallowness, haunted by ragged sparrows for the long season. It

was dreary, too, that on the tees where the gay colors fluttered in summer there were now only the desolate sand-boxes knee-deep in crusted ice. When he crossed the hills the wind blew cold as misery, and if the sun was out he tramped with his eyes squinted up against the hard dimensionless glare.

In April the winter ceased abruptly. The snow ran down into Black Bear Lake scarcely tarrying for the early golfers to brave the season with red and black balls. Without elation, without an interval of moist glory, the cold was gone.

Dexter knew that there was something dismal about this northern spring, just as he knew there was something gorgeous about the fall. Fall made him clinch his hands and tremble and repeat idiotic sentences to himself, and make brisk abrupt gestures of command to imaginary audiences and armies. October filled him with hope which November raised to a sort of ecstatic triumph, and in this mood the fleeting brilliant impressions of the summer at Sherry Island were ready grist to his mill. He became a golf champion and defeated Mr. T. A. Hedrick in a marvellous match played a hundred times over the fairways of his imagination, a match each detail of which he changed about untiringly—sometimes he won with almost laughable ease, sometimes he came up magnificently from behind. Again, stepping from a Pierce-Arrow automobile, like Mr. Mortimer Jones, he strolled frigidly into the lounge of the Sherry Island Golf Club—or perhaps, surrounded by an admiring crowd, he gave an exhibition of fancy diving from the spring-board of the club raft. . . . Among those who watched him in open-mouthed wonder was Mr. Mortimer Jones.

And one day it came to pass that Mr. Jones—himself and not his ghost—came up to Dexter with tears in his eyes and said that Dexter was the —— best caddy in the club, and wouldn't he decide not to quit if Mr. Jones made it worth his while, because every other —— caddy in the club lost one ball a hole for him—regularly——

"No, sir," said Dexter decisively, "I don't want to caddy any more." Then, after a pause: "I'm too old."

"You're not more than fourteen. Why the devil did you decide just this morning that you wanted to quit? You promised that next week you'd go over to the State tournament with me."

"I decided I was too old."

Dexter handed in his "A Class" badge, collected what money was due him from the caddy master, and walked home to Black Bear Village.

"The best —— caddy I ever saw," shouted Mr. Mortimer Jones over a drink that afternoon. "Never lost a ball! Willing! Intelligent! Quiet! Honest! Grateful!"

The little girl who had done this was eleven—beautifully ugly as little girls are apt to be who are destined after a few years to be inexpressibly lovely and bring no end of misery to a great number of men. The spark, however, was perceptible. There was a general ungodliness in the way her lips twisted down at the corners when she smiled, and in the—Heaven help us!—in the almost passionate quality of her eyes. Vitality is born early in such women. It was utterly in evidence now, shining through her thin frame in a sort of glow.

She had come eagerly out on to the course at nine o'clock with a white linen nurse and five small new golf-clubs in a white canvas bag which the nurse was carrying. When Dexter first saw her she was standing by the caddy house, rather ill at ease and trying to conceal the fact by engaging her nurse in an obviously unnatural conversation graced by startling and irrelevant grimaces from herself.

"Well, it's certainly a nice day, Hilda," Dexter heard her say. She drew down the corners of her mouth, smiled, and glanced furtively around, her eyes in transit falling for an instant on Dexter.

Then to the nurse:

"Well, I guess there aren't very many people out here this morning, are there?"

The smile again—radiant, blatantly artificial—convincing.

"I don't know what we're supposed to do now," said the nurse looking nowhere in particular.

"Oh, that's all right. I'll fix it up."

Dexter stood perfectly still, his mouth slightly ajar. He knew that if he moved forward a step his stare would be in her line of vision—if he moved backward he would lose his full view of her face. For a moment he had not realized how young she was. Now he remembered having seen her several times the year before—in bloomers.

Suddenly, involuntarily, he laughed, a short abrupt laugh—then, startled by himself, he turned and began to walk quickly away.

"Boy!"

Dexter stopped.

"Boy——"

Beyond question he was addressed. Not only that, but he was treated to that absurd smile, that preposterous smile—the memory of which at least a dozen men were to carry into middle age.

"Boy, do you know where the golf teacher is?"

"He's giving a lesson."

"Well, do you know where the caddy-master is?"

"He isn't here yet this morning."

"Oh." For a moment this baffled her. She stood alternately on her right and left foot.

"We'd like to get a caddy," said the nurse. "Mrs. Mortimer Jones sent us out to play golf, and we don't know how without we get a caddy."

Here she was stopped by an ominous glance from Miss Jones, followed immediately by the smile.

"There aren't any caddies here except me," said Dexter to the nurse, "and I got to stay here in charge until the caddy-master gets here."

"Oh."

Miss Jones and her retinue now withdrew, and at a proper distance from Dexter became involved in a heated conversation, which was concluded by Miss Jones taking one of the clubs and hitting it on the ground with violence. For further emphasis she raised it again and was about to bring it down smartly upon the nurse's bosom, when the nurse seized the club and twisted it from her hands.

"You damn little mean old *thing*!" cried Miss Jones wildly.

Another argument ensued. Realizing that the elements of comedy were implied in the scene, Dexter several times began to laugh, but each time restrained the laugh before it reached audibility. He could not resist the monstrous conviction that the little girl was justified in beating the nurse.

The situation was resolved by the fortuitous apearance of the caddymaster, who was appealed to immediately by the nurse.

"Miss Jones is to have a little caddy, and this one says he can't go."

"Mr. McKenna said I was to wait here till you came," said Dexter quickly.

"Well, he's here now." Miss Jones smiled cheerfully at the caddy-master. Then she dropped her bag and set off at a haughty mince toward the first tee.

"Well?" The caddy-master turned to Dexter. "What you standing there like a dummy for? Go pick up the young lady's clubs."

"I don't think I'll go out to-day," said Dexter.

"You don't——"

"I think I'll quit."

The enormity of his decision frightened him. He was a favorite caddy, and the thirty dollars a month he earned through the summer were not to be made elsewhere around the lake. But he had received a strong emotional shock, and his perturbation required a violent and immediate outlet.

It is not so simple as that, either. As so frequently would be the case in the future, Dexter was unconsciously dictated to by his winter dreams.

II

Now, of course, the quality and the seasonability of these winter dreams varied, but the stuff of them remained. They persuaded Dexter several years later to pass up a business course at the State university—his father, prospering now, would have paid his way—for the precarious advantage of attending an older and more famous university in the East, where he was bothered by his scanty funds. But do not get the impression, because his winter dreams happened to be concerned at first with musings on the rich, that there was anything merely snobbish in the boy. He wanted not association with glittering things and glittering people—he wanted the glittering things themselves. Often he reached out for the best without knowing why he wanted it—and sometimes he ran up against the mysterious denials and prohibitions in which life indulges. It is with one of those denials and not with his career as a whole that this story deals.

He made money. It was rather amazing. After college he went to the city from which Black Bear Lake draws its wealthy patrons. When he was only twenty-three and had been there not quite two years, there were already people who liked to say: "Now *there's* a boy—" All about him rich men's sons were peddling bonds precariously, or investing patrimonies precariously, or plodding through the two dozen volumes of the "George Washington Commercial Course," but Dexter borrowed a thousand dollars on his college degree and his confident mouth, and bought a partnership in a laundry.

It was a small laundry when he went into it, but Dexter made a specialty of learning how the English washed fine woolen golf-stockings without shrinking them, and within a year he was catering to the trade that wore knickerbockers. Men were insisting that their Shetland hose and sweaters go to his laundry, just as they had insisted on a caddy who could find golf-balls. A little later he was doing their wives' lingerie as well—and running five branches in different parts of the city. Before he was twenty-seven he owned the largest string of laundries in his section of the country. It was then that he sold out and went to New York. But the part of his story that concerns us goes back to the days when he was making his first big success.

When he was twenty-three Mr. Hart —one of the gray-haired men who liked to say "Now there's a boy"—gave him a guest card to the Sherry Island Golf Club for a week-end. So he signed his name one day on the register, and that afternoon played golf in a foursome with Mr. Hart and Mr. Sandwood and Mr. T. A. Hedrick. He did not consider it necessary to remark that he had once carried Mr. Hart's bag over this same links, and that he knew every trap and gully with his eyes shut—but he found himself glancing at the four caddies who trailed them, trying to catch a gleam or gesture that would remind him of himself, that would lessen the gap which lay between his present and his past.

It was a curious day, slashed abruptly with fleeting, familiar impressions. One minute he had the sense of being a trespasser—in the next he was impressed by the tremendous superiority he felt toward Mr. T. A. Hedrick, who was a bore and not even a good golfer any more.

Then, because of a ball Mr. Hart lost near the fifteenth green, an enormous thing happened. While they were searching the stiff grasses of the rough there was a clear call of "Fore!" from behind a hill in their rear. And as they all turned abruptly from their search a bright new ball sliced abruptly over the hill and caught Mr. T. A. Hedrick in the abdomen.

"By Gad!" cried Mr. T. A. Hedrick, "they ought to put some of these crazy women off the course. It's getting to be outrageous."

A head and a voice came up together over the hill:

"Do you mind if we go through?"

"You hit me in the stomach!" declared Mr. Hedrick wildly.

"Did I?" The girl approached the group of men. "I'm sorry. I yelled 'Fore!' "

Her glance fell casually on each of the men—then scanned the fairway for her ball.

"Did I bounce into the rough?"

It was impossible to determine whether this question was ingenuous or malicious. In a moment, however, she left no doubt, for as her partner came up over the hill she called cheerfully:

"Here I am! I'd have gone on the green except that I hit something."

As she took her stance for a short mashie shot, Dexter looked at her closely. She wore a blue gingham dress, rimmed at throat and shoulders with a white edging that accentuated her tan. The quality of exaggeration, of thinness, which had made her passionate eyes and down-turning mouth absurd at eleven, was gone now. She was arrestingly beautiful. The color in her cheeks was centered like the color in a picture—it was not a "high" color, but a sort of fluctuating and feverish warmth, so shaded that it seemed at any moment it would recede and disappear. This color and the mobility of her mouth gave a continual impression of flux, of intense life, of passionate vitality—balanced only partially by the sad luxury of her eyes.

She swung her mashie impatiently and without interest, pitching the ball into a sand-pit on the other side of the green. With a quick, insincere smile and a careless "Thank you!" she went on after it.

"That Judy Jones!" remarked Mr. Hedrick on the next tee, as they waited —some moments—for her to play on ahead. "All she needs is to be turned up and spanked for six months and then to be married off to an old-fashioned cavalry captain."

"My God, she's good-looking!" said Mr. Sandwood, who was just over thirty.

"Good-looking!" cried Mr. Hedrick contemptuously, "she always looks as if she wanted to be kissed! Turning those big cow-eyes on every calf in town!"

It was doubtful if Mr. Hedrick intended a reference to the maternal instinct.

"She'd play pretty good golf if she'd try," said Mr. Sandwood.

"She has no form," said Mr. Hedrick solemnly.

"She has a nice figure," said Mr. Sandwood.

"Better thank the Lord she doesn't drive a swifter ball," said Mr. Hart, winking at Dexter.

Later in the afternoon the sun went down with a riotous swirl of gold and varying blues and scarlets, and left the the dry, rustling night of Western summer. Dexter watched from the veranda of the Golf Club, watched the even overlap of the waters in the little wind, silver molasses under the harvest-moon. Then the moon held a finger to her lips and the lake became a clear pool, pale and quiet. Dexter put on his bathing-suit and swam out to the farthest raft, where he stretched dripping on the wet canvas of the springboard.

There was a fish jumping and a star shining and the lights around the lake were gleaming. Over on a dark peninsula a piano was playing the songs of last summer and of summers before that—songs from "Chin-Chin" and "The Count of Luxemburg" and "The Chocolate Soldier"—and because the sound of a piano over a stretch of water had always seemed beautiful to Dexter he lay perfectly quiet and listened.

The tune the piano was playing at that moment had been gay and new five years before when Dexter was a sophomore at college. They had played it at a prom once when he could not afford the luxury of proms, and he had stood outside the gymnasium and listened. The sound of the tune precipitated in him a sort of ecstasy and it was with that ecstasy he viewed what happened to him now. It was a mood of intense appreciation, a sense that, for once, he was magnificently attuned to life and that everything about him was radiating a brightness and a glamour he might never know again.

A low, pale oblong detached itself suddenly from the darkness of the Island, spitting forth the reverberated sound of a racing motorboat. Two white streamers of cleft water rolled themselves out behind it and almost immediately the boat was beside him, drowning out the hot tinkle of the piano in the drone of its spray. Dexter raising himself on his arms was aware of a figure standing at the wheel, of two dark eyes regarding him over the lengthening space of water—then the boat had gone by and was sweeping in an immense and purposeless circle of spray round and round in the middle of the lake. With equal eccentricity one of the circles flattened out and headed back toward the raft.

"Who's that?" she called, shutting off her motor. She was so near now that Dexter could see her bathing-suit, which consisted apparently of pink rompers.

The nose of the boat bumped the raft, and as the latter tilted rakishly he was precipitated toward her. With different degrees of interest they recognized each other.

"Aren't you one of those men we played through this afternoon?" she demanded.

He was.

"Well, do you know how to drive a motor-boat? Because if you do I wish you'd drive this one so I can ride on the surf-board behind. My name is Judy Jones"—she favored him with an absurd smirk—rather, what tried to be a smirk, for, twist her mouth as she might, it was not grotesque, it was merely beautiful—"and I live in a house over there on the Island, and in that house there is a man waiting for me. When I drove up at the door he drove out of the dock because he says I'm his ideal."

There was a fish jumping and a star shining and the lights around the lake were gleaming. Dexter sat beside Judy Jones and she explained how her boat was driven. Then she was in the water, swimming to the floating surf-board with a sinuous crawl. Watching her was without effort to the eye, watching a branch waving or a sea-gull flying. Her arms, burned to butternut, moved sinuously among the dull platinum ripples, elbow appearing first, casting the forearm back with a cadence of falling water, then reaching out and down, stabbing a path ahead.

They moved out into the lake; turning, Dexter saw that she was kneeling on the low rear of the now uptilted surf-board.

"Go faster," she called, "fast as it'll go."

Obediently he jammed the lever forward and the white spray mounted at the bow. When he looked around again the girl was standing up on the rushing board, her arms spread wide, her eyes lifted toward the moon.

"It's awful cold," she shouted. "What's your name?"

He told her.

"Well, why don't you come to dinner to-morrow night?"

His heart turned over like the fly-wheel of the boat, and, for the second time, her casual whim gave a new direction to his life.

III

Next evening while he waited for her to come down-stairs, Dexter peopled the soft deep summer room and the sun-porch that opened from it with the men who had already loved Judy Jones. He knew the sort of men they were— the men who when he first went to college had entered from the great prep schools with graceful clothes and the deep tan of healthy summers. He had seen that, in one sense, he was better than these men. He was newer and stronger. Yet in acknowledging to himself that he wished his children to be like them he was admitting that he was but the rough, strong stuff from which they eternally sprang.

When the time had come for him to wear good clothes, he had known who were the best tailors in America, and the best tailors in America had made him the suit he wore this evening. He had acquired that particular reserve peculiar to his university, that set it off from other universities. He recognized the value to him of such a mannerism and he had adopted it; he knew that to be careless in dress and manner required more confidence than to be careful. But carelessness was for his children. His mother's name had been Krimelich. She was a Bohemian of the peasant class and she had talked broken English to the end of her days. Her son must keep to the set patterns.

At a little after seven Judy Jones came down-stairs. She wore a blue silk afternoon dress, and he was disappointed at first that she had not put on something more elaborate. This feeling was accentuated when, after a brief greeting, she went to the door of a butler's pantry and pushing it open called: "You can serve dinner, Martha." He had rather expected that a butler would announce dinner, that there would be a cocktail. Then he put these thoughts behind him as they sat down side by side on a lounge and looked at each other.

"Father and mother won't be here," she said thoughtfully.

He remembered the last time he had seen her father, and he was glad the parents were not to be here to-night—they might wonder who he was. He had been born in Keeble, a Minnesota village fifty miles farther north, and he always gave Keeble as his home instead of Black Bear Village. Country towns were well enough to come from if they weren't inconveniently in sight and used as footstools by fashionable lakes.

They talked of his university, which she had visited frequently during the past two years, and of the near-by city which supplied Sherry Island with its patrons, and whither Dexter would return next day to his prospering laundries.

During dinner she slipped into a moody depression which gave Dexter a feeling of uneasiness. Whatever petulance she uttered in her throaty voice worried him. Whatever she smiled at—at him, at a chicken liver, at nothing—it disturbed him that her smile could have no root in mirth, or even in amusement. When the scarlet corners of her lips curved down, it was less a smile than an invitation to a kiss.

Then, after dinner, she led him out on the dark sun-porch and deliberately changed the atmosphere.

"Do you mind if I weep a little?" she said.

"I'm afraid I'm boring you," he responded quickly.

"You're not. I like you. But I've just had a terrible afternoon. There was a man I cared about, and this afternoon he told me out of a clear sky that he was poor as a church-mouse. He'd never even hinted it before. Does this sound horribly mundane?"

"Perhaps he was afraid to tell you."

"Suppose he was," she answered. "He didn't start right. You see, if I'd thought of him as poor—well, I've been mad about loads of poor men, and fully intended to marry them all. But in this case, I hadn't thought of him that way, and my interest in him wasn't strong enough to survive the shock. As if a girl calmly informed her fiancé that she was a widow. He might not object to widows, but——"

"Let's start right," she interrupted herself suddenly. "Who are you, anyhow?"

For a moment Dexter hesitated. Then:

"I'm nobody," he announced. "My career is largely a matter of futures."

"Are you poor?"

"No," he said frankly, "I'm probably

making more money than any man my age in the Northwest. I know that's an obnoxious remark, but you advised me to start right."

There was a pause. Then she smiled and the corners of her mouth drooped and an almost imperceptible sway brought her closer to him, looking up into his eyes. A lump rose in Dexter's throat, and he waited breathless for the experiment, facing the unpredictable compound that would form mysteriously from the elements of their lips. Then he saw—she communicated her excitement to him, lavishly, deeply, with kisses that were not a promise but a fulfillment. They aroused in him not hunger demanding renewal but surfeit that would demand more surfeit . . . kisses that were like charity, creating want by holding back nothing at all.

It did not take him many hours to decide that he had wanted Judy Jones ever since he was a proud, desirous little boy.

IV

It began like that—and continued, with varying shades of intensity, on such a note right up to the dénouement. Dexter surrendered a part of himself to the most direct and unprincipled personality with which he had ever come in contact. Whatever Judy wanted, she went after with the full pressure of her charm. There was no divergence of method, no jockeying for position or premeditation of effects—there was a very little mental side to any of her affairs. She simply made men conscious to the highest degree of her physical loveliness. Dexter had no desire to change her. Her deficiencies were knit up with a passionate energy that transcended and justified them.

When, as Judy's head lay against his shoulder that first night, she whispered, "I don't know what's the matter with me. Last night I thought I was in love with a man and to-night I think I'm in love with you————"—it seemed to him a beautiful and romantic thing to say. It was the exquisite excitability that for the moment he controlled and owned. But a week later he was compelled to view this same quality in a different light. She took him in her roadster to a picnic supper, and after supper she disappeared, likewise in her roadster, with another man. Dexter became enormously upset and was scarcely able to be decently civil to the other people present. When she assured him that she had not kissed the other man, he knew she was lying—yet he was glad that she had taken the trouble to lie to him.

He was, as he found before the summer ended, one of a varying dozen who circulated about her. Each of them had at one time been favored above all others—about half of them still basked in the solace of occasional sentimental revivals. Whenever one showed signs of dropping out through long neglect, she granted him a brief honeyed hour, which encouraged him to tag along for a year or so longer. Judy made these forays upon the helpless and defeated without malice, indeed half unconscious that there was anything mischievous in what she did.

When a new man came to town every one dropped out—dates were automatically cancelled.

The helpless part of trying to do anything about it was that she did it all herself. She was not a girl who could be "won" in the kinetic sense—she was proof against cleverness, she was proof against charm; if any of these assailed her too strongly she would immediately resolve the affair to a physical basis, and under the magic of her physical splendor the strong as well as the brilliant played her game and not their own. She was entertained only by the gratification of her desires and by the direct exercise of her own charm. Perhaps from so much youthful love, so many youthful lovers, she had come, in self-defense, to nourish herself wholly from within.

Succeeding Dexter's first exhilaration came restlessness and dissatisfaction. The helpless ecstasy of losing himself in her was opiate rather than tonic. It was fortunate for his work during the winter that those moments of ecstasy came infrequently. Early in their acquaintance it had seemed for a while that there was a deep and spontaneous mutual atraction—that first August, for example—three days of long evenings on her dusky veranda, of strange wan kisses through the late afternoon, in shadowy alcoves or behind the protecting trellises of the garden arbors, of mornings when she was fresh as a dream and almost shy at meeting him in the clarity of the rising day. There was all the ecstasy of an engagement about it, sharpened by his realization that there was no engagement. It was during those three days that, for the first time, he had asked her to marry him. She said "maybe some day," she said "kiss me," she said "I'd like to marry you," she said "I love you"—she said—nothing.

The three days were interrupted by the arrival of a New York man who visited at her house for half September. To Dexter's agony, rumor engaged them. The man was the son of the president of a great trust company. But at the end of a month it was reported that Judy was yawning. At a dance one night she sat all evening in a motorboat with a local beau, while the New Yorker searched the club for her frantically. She told the local beau that she was bored with her visitor, and two days later he left. She was seen with him at the station, and it was reported that he looked very mournful indeed.

On this note the summer ended. Dexter was twenty-four, and he found himself increasingly in a position to do as he wished. He joined two clubs in the city and lived at one of them. Though he was by no means an integral part of the stag-lines at these clubs, he managed to be on hand at dances where Judy Jones was likely to appear. He could have gone out socially as much as he liked—he was an eligible young man, now, and popular with downtown fathers. His confessed devotion to Judy Jones had rather solidified his position. But he had no social aspirations and rather despised the dancing men who were always on tap for the Thursday or Saturday parties and who filled in at dinners with the younger married set. Already he was playing with the idea of going East to New York. He wanted to take Judy Jones with him. No disillusion as to the world in which she had grown up could cure his illusion as to her desirability.

Remember that—for only in the light of it can what he did for her be understood.

Eighteen months after he first met Judy Jones he became engaged to another girl. Her name was Irene Scheerer, and her father was one of the men who had always believed in Dexter. Irene was light-haired and sweet and honorable, and a little stout, and she had two suitors whom she pleasantly relinquished when Dexter formally asked her to marry him.

Summer, fall, winter, spring, another summer, another fall—so much he had given of his active life to the incorrigible lips of Judy Jones. She had treated him with interest, with encouragement, with malice, with indifference, with contempt. She had inflicted on him the innumerable little slights and indignities possible in such a case—as if in revenge for having ever cared for him at all. She had beckoned him and yawned at him and beckoned him again and he had responded often with bitterness and narrowed eyes. She had brought him ecstatic happiness and intolerable agony of spirit. She had caused him untold inconvenience and not a little trouble. She had insulted him, and she had ridden over him, and she had played his interest in her against his interest in his work—for fun. She had done everything to him except to criticise him—this she had not done—it seemed to him only because it might have sullied the utter indifference she manifested and sincerely felt toward him.

When autumn had come and gone again it occurred to him that he could not have Judy Jones. He had to beat this into his mind but he convinced himself at last. He lay awake at night for a while and argued it over. He told himself the trouble and the pain she had caused him, he enumerated her glaring deficiencies as a wife. Then he said to himself that he loved her, and after a while he fell asleep. For a week, lest he imagine her husky voice over the telephone or her eyes opposite him at lunch, he worked hard and late, and at night he went to his office and plotted out his years.

At the end of a week he went to a dance and cut in on her once. For almost the first time since they had met he did not ask her to sit out with him or tell her that she was lovely. It hurt him that she did not miss these things —that was all. He was not jealous when he saw that there was a new man to-night. He had been hardened against jealousy long before.

He stayed late at the dance. He sat for an hour with Irene Scheerer and talked about books and about music. He knew very little about either. But he was beginning to be master of his own time now, and he had a rather priggish notion that he—the young and already fabulously successful Dexter Green—should know more about such things.

That was in October, when he was twenty-five. In January, Dexter and Irene became engaged. It was to be announced in June, and they were to be married three months later.

The Minnesota winter prolonged itself interminably, and it was almost May when the winds came soft and the snow ran down into Black Bear Lake at last. For the first time in over a year Dexter was enjoying a certain tranquility of spirit. Judy Jones had been in Florida, and afterward in Hot Springs, and somewhere she had been engaged, and somewhere she had broken it off. At first, when Dexter had definitely given her up, it had made him sad that people still linked them together and asked for news of her, but when he began to be placed at dinner next to Irene Scheerer people didn't ask him about her any more—they told him about her. He ceased to be an authority on her.

May at last. Dexter walked the streets at night when the darkness was damp as rain, wondering that so soon, with so little done, so much of ecstasy had gone from him. May one year back had been marked by Judy's poignant, unforgivable, yet forgiven turbulence—it had been one of those rare times when he fancied she had grown to care for him. That old penny's worth of happiness he had spent for this bushel of content. He knew that Irene would be no more than a curtain spread behind him, a hand moving among gleaming teacups, a voice calling to children . . . fire and loveliness were gone, the magic of nights and the wonder of the varying hours and seasons . . . slender lips, down-turning, dropping to his lips and bearing him up into a heaven of eyes. . . . The thing was deep in him. He was too strong and alive for it to die lightly.

In the middle of May when the weather balanced for a few days on the thin bridge that led to deep summer he turned in one night at Irene's house. Their engagement was to be announced in a week now—no one would be surprised at it. And to-night they would sit together on the lounge at the University Club and look on for an hour at the dancers. It gave him a sense of solidity to go with her—she was so sturdily popular, so intensely "great."

He mounted the steps of the brownstone house and stepped inside.

"Irene," he called.

Mrs. Scheerer came out of the living-room to meet him.

"Dexter," she said, "Irene's gone up-stairs with a splitting headache. She wanted to go with you but I made her go to bed."

"Nothing serious, I——"

"Oh, no. She's going to play golf with you in the morning. You can spare her for just one night, can't you, Dexter?"

Her smile was kind. She and Dexter liked each other. In the living-room he talked for a moment before he said good-night.

Returning to the University Club, where he had rooms, he stood in the doorway for a moment and watched the dancers. He leaned against the door-post, nodded at a man or two—yawned.

"Hello, darling."

The familiar voice at his elbow startled him. Judy Jones had left a man and crossed the room to him—Judy Jones, a slender enamelled doll in cloth of gold: gold in a band at her head, gold in two slipper points at her dress's hem. The fragile glow of her face seemed to blossom as she smiled at him. A breeze of warmth and light blew through the room. His hands in the pockets of his dinner-jacket tightened spasmodically. He was filled with a sudden excitement.

"When did you get back?" he asked casually.

"Come here and I'll tell you about it."

She turned and he followed her. She had been away—he could have wept at the wonder of her return. She had passed through enchanted streets, doing things that were like provocative music. All mysterious happenings, all fresh and quickening hopes, had gone away with her, come back with her now.

She turned in the doorway.

"Have you a car here? If you haven't, I have."

"I have a coupé."

In then, with a rustle of golden cloth. He slammed the door. Into so many cars she had stepped—like this—like that—her back against the leather, so—her elbow resting on the door—waiting. She would have been soiled long since had there been anything to soil her—except herself—but this was her own self outpouring.

With an effort he forced himself to start the car and back into the street. This was nothing, he must remember. She had done this before, and he had put her behind him, as he would have crossed a bad account from his books.

He drove slowly down-town and, affecting abstraction, traversed the deserted streets of the business section, peopled here and there where a movie was giving out its crowd or where consumptive or pugilistic youth lounged in front of pool halls. The clink of glasses and the slap of hands on the bars issued from saloons, cloisters of glazed glass and dirty yellow light.

She was watching him closely and the silence was embarrassing, yet in this crisis he could find no casual word with which to profane the hour. At a convenient turning he began to zigzag back toward the University Club.

"Have you missed me?" she asked suddenly.

"Everybody missed you."

He wondered if she knew of Irene Scheerer. She had been back only a day—her absence had been almost contemporaneous with his engagement.

"What a remark!" Judy laughed sadly—without sadness. She looked at him searchingly. He became absorbed in the dashboard.

"You're handsomer than you used to be," she said thoughtfully. "Dexter, you have the most remembereable eyes."

He could have laughed at this, but he did not laugh. It was the sort of thing that was said to sophomores. Yet it stabbed at him.

"I'm awfully tired of everything, dar-ling." She called every one darling, en-downing the endearment with careless, individual comraderie. "I wish you'd marry me."

The directness of this confused him. He should have told her now that he was going to marry another girl, but he could not tell her. He could as easily have sworn that he had never loved her.

"I think we'd get along," she continued, on the same note, "unless probably you've forgotten me and fallen in love with another girl."

Her confidence was obviously enormous. She had said, in effect, that she found such a thing impossible to believe, that if it were true he had merely committed a childish indiscretion—and probably to show off. She would forgive him, because it was not a matter of any moment but rather something to be brushed aside lightly.

"Of course you could never love anybody but me," she continued, "I like the way you love me. Oh, Dexter, have you forgotten last year?"

"No, I haven't forgotten."

"Neither have I!"

Was she sincerely moved—or was she carried along by the wave of her own acting?

"I wish we could be like that again," she said, and he forced himself to answer:

"I don't think we can."

"I suppose not. . . . I hear you're giving Irene Scheerer a violent rush."

There was not the faintest emphasis on the name, yet Dexter was suddenly ashamed.

"Oh, take me home," cried Judy suddenly; "I don't want to go back to that idiotic dance—with those children."

Then, as he turned up the street that led to the residence district, Judy began to cry quietly to herself. He had never seen her cry before.

The dark street lightened, the dwellings of the rich loomed up around them, he stopped his coupé in front of the great white bulk of the Mortimer Joneses' house, somnolent, gorgeous, drenched with the splendor of the damp moonlight. Its solidity startled

him. The strong walls, the steel of the girders, the breadth and beam and pomp of it were there only to bring out the contrast with the young beauty beside him. It was sturdy to accentuate her slightness—as if to show what a breeze could be generated by a butterfly's wing.

He sat perfectly quiet, his nerves in wild clamor, afraid that if he moved he would find her irresistibly in his arms. Two tears had rolled down her wet face and trembled on her upper lip.

"I'm more beautiful than anybody else," she said brokenly, "why can't I be happy?" Her moist eyes tore at his stability—her mouth turned slowly downward with an exquisite sadness: "I'd like to marry you if you'll have me, Dexter. I suppose you think I'm not worth having, but I'll be so beautiful for you, Dexter."

A million phrases of anger, pride, passion, hatred, tenderness fought on his lips. Then a perfect wave of emotion washed over him, carrying off with it a sediment of wisdom, of convention, of doubt, of honor. This was his girl who was speaking, his own, his beautiful, his pride.

"Won't you come in?" He heard her draw in her breath sharply.

Waiting.

"All right," his voice was trembling, "I'll come in."

V

It was strange that neither when it was over nor a long time afterward did he regret that night. Looking at it from the perspective of ten years, the fact that Judy's flare for him endured just one month seemed of little importance. Nor did it matter that by his yielding he subjected himself to a deeper agony in the end and gave serious hurt to Irene Scheerer and to Irene's parents, who had befriended him. There was nothing sufficiently pictorial about

Irene's grief to stamp itself on his mind.

Dexter was at bottom hard-minded. The attitude of the city on his action was of no importance to him, not because he was going to leave the city, but because any outside attitude on the situation semed superficial. He was completely indifferent to popular opinion. Nor, when he had seen that it was no use, that he did not possess in himself the power to move fundamentally or to hold Judy Jones, did he bear any malice toward her. He loved her, and he would love her until the day he was too old for loving—but he could not have her. So he tasted the deep pain that is reserved only for the strong, just as he had tasted for a little while the deep happiness.

Even the ultimate falsity of the grounds upon which Judy terminated the engagement, that she did not want to "take him away" from Irene—Judy, who had wanted nothing else—did not revolt him. He was beyond any revulsion or any amusement.

He went East in February with the intention of selling out his laundries and settling in New York—but the war came to America in March and changed his plans. He returned to the West, handed over the management of the business to his partner, and went into the first officers' training-camp in late April. He was one of those young thousands who greeted the war with a certain amount of relief, welcoming the liberation from webs of tangled emotion.

VI

This story is not his biography, remember, although things creep into it which have nothing to do with those dreams he had when he was young. We are almost done with them and with him now. There is only one more incident to be related here, and it happens seven years farther on.

It took place in New York, where he had done well—so well that there were no barriers too high for him. He was thirty-two years old, and, except for one flying trip immediately after the war, he had not been West in seven years. A man named Devlin from Detroit came into his office to see him in a business way, and then and there this incident occurred, and closed out, so to speak, this particular side of his life.

"So you're from the Middle West," said the man Devlin with careless curiosity. "That's funny—I thought men like you were probably born and raised on Wall Street. You know—wife of one of my best friends in Detroit came from your city. I was an usher at the wedding."

Dexter waited with no apprehension of what was coming.

"Judy Simms," said Devlin with no particular interest; "Judy Jones she was once."

"Yes, I knew her." A dull impatience spread over him. He had heard, of course, that she was married—perhaps deliberately he had heard no more.

"Awfully nice girl," brooded Devlin meaninglessly, "I'm sort of sorry for her."

"Why?" Something in Dexter was alert, receptive at once.

"Oh, Lud Simms has gone to pieces in a way. I don't mean he ill-uses her, but he drinks and runs around——"

"Doesn't she run around?"

"No. Stays at home with her kids."

"Oh."

"She's a little too old for him," said Devlin.

"Too old!" cried Dexter. "Why, man, she's only twenty-seven."

He was possessed with a wild notion of rushing out into the streets and taking a train to Detroit. He rose to his feet spasmodically.

"I guess you're busy," Devlin apologized quickly. "I didn't realize——"

"No, I'm not busy," said Dexter, steadying his voice. "I'm not busy at all. Not busy at all. Did you say she was—twenty-seven? No, I said she was twenty-seven."

"Yes, you did," agreed Devlin dryly.

"Go on, then. Go on."

"What do you mean?"

"About Judy Jones."

Devlin looked at him helplessly.

"Well, that's—I told you all there is to it. He treats her like the devil. Oh, they're not going to get divorced or anything. When he's particularly outrageous she forgives him. In fact, I'm inclined to think she loves him. She was a pretty girl when she first came to Detroit."

A pretty girl! The phrase struck Dexter as ludicrous.

"Isn't she—a pretty girl, any more?"

"Oh, she's all right."

"Look here," said Dexter, sitting down suddenly. "I don't understand. You say she was a 'pretty girl' and now you say she's 'all right.' I don't understand what you mean—Judy Jones wasn't a pretty girl, at all. She was a great beauty. Why, I knew her, I knew her. She was——"

Devlin laughed pleasantly.

"I'm not trying to start a row," he said. "I think Judy's a nice girl and I like her. I can't understand how a man like Lud Simms could fall madly in love with her, but he did." Then he added: "Most of the women like her."

Dexter looked closely at Devlin, thinking wildly that there must be a reason for this, some insensitivity in the man or some private malice.

"Lots of women fade just like *that*," Devlin snapped his fingers. "You must have seen it happen. Perhaps I've forgotten how pretty she was at her wedding. I've seen her so much since then, you see. She has nice eyes."

A sort of dullness settled down upon Dexter. For the first time in his life he felt like getting very drunk. He knew that he was laughing loudly at something Devlin had said, but he did not know what it was or why it was funny. When, in a few minutes, Devlin went he lay down on his lounge and looked out the window at the New York skyline into which the sun was sinking in dull lovely shades of pink and gold.

He had thought that having nothing else to lose he was invulnerable at last—but he knew that he had just lost something more, as surely as if he had married Judy Jones and seen her fade away before his eyes.

The dream was gone. Something had been taken from him. In a sort of panic he pushed the palms of his hands into his eyes and tried to bring up a picture of the waters lapping on Sherry Island and the moonlit veranda, and gingham on the golf-links and the dry sun and the gold color of her neck's soft down. And her mouth damp to his kisses and her eyes plaintive with melancholy and her freshness like new fine linen in the morning. Why, these things were no longer in the world! They had existed and they existed no longer.

For the first time in years the tears were streaming down his face. But they were for himself now. He did not care about mouth and eyes and moving hands. He wanted to care, and he could not care. For he had gone away and he could never go back any more. The gates were closed, the sun was gone down, and there was no beauty but the gray beauty of steel that withstands all time. Even the grief he could have borne was left behind in the country of illusion, of youth, of the richness of life, where his winter dreams had flourished.

"Long ago," he said, "long ago, there was something in me, but now that thing is gone. Now that thing is gone, that thing is gone. I cannot cry. I cannot care. That thing will come back no more."

William Faulkner (1897–1962)

BARN BURNING

The store in which the Justice of the Peace's court was sitting smelled of cheese. The boy, crouched on his nail keg at the back of the crowded room, knew he smelled cheese, and more: From where he sat he could see the ranked shelves close-packed with the solid, squat, dynamic shapes of tin cans whose labels his stomach read, not from the lettering which meant nothing to his mind but from the scarlet devils and the silver curve of fish—this, the cheese which he knew he smelled and the hermetic meat which his intestines believed he smelled coming in intermittent gusts momentary and brief between the other constant one, the smell and sense just a little of fear because mostly of despair and grief, the old fierce pull of blood. He could not see the table where the Justice sat and before which his father and his father's enemy (*our enemy* he thought in that despair; *ourn! mine and hisn both! He's my father!*) stood, but he could hear them, the two of them that is, because his father had said no word yet:

"But what proof have you, Mr. Harris?"

"I told you. The hog got into my corn. I caught it up and sent it back to him. He had no fence that would hold it. I told him so, warned him. The next time I put the hog in my pen. When he came to get it I gave him enough wire to patch up his pen. The next time I put the hog up and kept it. I rode down to his house and saw the wire I gave him still rolled on to the spool in his yard. I told him he could have the hog when he paid me a dollar

pound fee. That evening a nigger came with the dollar and got the hog. He was a strange nigger. He said, "He say to tell you wood and hay kin burn.' I said, 'What?' 'That whut he say to tell you,' the nigger said. 'Wood and hay kin burn.' That night my barn burned. I got the stock out but I lost the barn."

"Where is the nigger? Have you got him?"

"He was a strange nigger, I tell you. I don't know what became of him."

"But that's not proof. Don't you see that's not proof?"

"Get that boy up here. He knows." For a moment the boy thought too that the man meant his older brother until Harris said, "Not him. The little one. The boy," and, crouching, small for his age, small and wiry like his father, in patched and faded jeans even too small for him, with straight, uncombed, brown hair and eyes gray and wild as storm scud, he saw the men between himself and the table part and become a lane of grim faces, at the end of which he saw the Justice, a shabby, collarless, graying man in spectacles, beckoning him. He felt no floor under his bare feet; he seemed to walk beneath the palpable weight of the grim turning faces. His father, stiff in his black Sunday coat donned not for the trial but for the moving, did not even look at him. *He aims for me to lie*, he thought, again with that frantic grief and despair. *And I will have to do hit.*

"What's your name, boy?" the Justice said.

"Colonel Sartoris Snopes," the boy whispered.

"Hey?" the Justice said. "Talk louder. Colonel Sartoris? I reckon anybody named for Colonel Sartoris in this country can't help but tell the truth, can they?" The boy said nothing. *Enemy! Enemy!* he thought; for a moment he could not even see, could not see that the Justice's face was kindly nor discern that his voice was troubled when he spoke to the man named Harris: "Do you want me to question this boy?" But he could hear, and during those subsequent long seconds while there was absolutely no sound in the crowded little room save that of quiet and intent breathing it was as if he had swung outward at the end of a grape vine, over a ravine, and at the top of the swing had been caught in a prolonged instant of mesmerized gravity, weightless in time.

"No!" Harris said violently, explosively. "Damnation! Send him out of here!" Now time, the fluid world, rushed beneath him again, the voices coming to him again through the smell of cheese and sealed meat, the fear and despair and the old grief of blood:

"This case is closed. I can't find against you, Snopes, but I can give you advice. Leave this country and don't come back to it."

His father spoke for the first time, his voice cold and harsh, level, without emphasis: "I aim to. I don't figure to stay in a country among people who . . ." he said something unprintable and vile, addressed to no one.

"That'll do," the Justice said. "Take your wagon and get out of this country before dark. Case dismissed."

His father turned, and he followed the stiff black coat, the wiry figure walking a little stiffly from where a Confederate provost's man's musket ball had taken him in the heel on a stolen horse thirty years ago, followed the two backs now, since his older brother had appeared from somewhere in the crowd, no taller than the father but thicker, chewing tobacco steadily, between the two lines of grim-faced men and out of the store and across the worn gallery and down the sagging steps and among the dogs and half-grown boys in the mild May dust, where as he passed a voice hissed:

"Barn burner!"

Again he could not see, whirling; there was a face in a red haze, moonlike, bigger than the full moon, the owner of it half again his size, he leaping in the red haze toward the face, feeling no blow, feeling no shock when his head struck the earth, scrabbling up and leaping again, feeling no blow this time either and tasting no blood, scrabbling up to see the other boy in full flight and himself already leaping into pursuit as his father's hand jerked him back, the harsh, cold voice speaking above him: "Go get in the wagon."

It stood in a grove of locusts and mulberries across the road. His two hulking sisters in their Sunday dresses and his mother and her sister in calico and sunbonnets were already in it, sitting on and among the sorry residue of the dozen and more movings which even the boy could remember—the battered stove, the broken beds and chairs, the clock inlaid with mother-of-pearl, which would not run, stopped at some fourteen minutes past two o'clock of a dead and forgotten day and time, which had been his mother's dowry. She was crying, though when she saw him she drew her sleeve across her face and began to descend from the wagon. "Get back," the father said.

"He's hurt. I got to get some water and wash his . . ."

"Get back in the wagon," his father said. He got in too, over the tail-gate. His father mounted to the seat where the older brother already sat and struck the gaunt mules two savage blows with the peeled willow, but without heat. It was not even sadistic; it was exactly that same quality which in later years would cause his descendants to over-run the engine before putting a motor car into motion, striking and reining back in the same movement. The wagon went on, the store with its quiet crowd of grimly watching men dropped behind; a curve in the road hid it. *Forever*, he thought. *Maybe he's done satisfied now, now that he has* . . . stopping himself, not to say it aloud even to himself. His mother's hand touched his shoulder.

"Does hit hurt?" she said.

"Naw," he said. "Hit don't hurt. Lemme be."

"Can't you wipe some of the blood off before hit dries?"

"I'll wash to-night," he said. "Lemme be, I tell you."

The wagon went on. He did not know where they were going. None of them ever did or ever asked, because it was always somewhere, always a house of sorts waiting for them a day or two days or even three days away. Likely his father had already arranged to make a crop on another farm before he . . . Again he had to stop himself. He (the father) always did. There was something about his wolflike independence and even courage when the advantage was at least neutral which impressed strangers, as if they got from his latent ravening ferocity not so much a sense of dependability as a feeling that his ferocious conviction in the rightness of his own actions would be of advantage to all whose interest lay with his.

That night they camped, in a grove of oaks and beeches where a spring ran. The nights were still cool and they had a fire against it, of a rail lifted from a nearby fence and cut into lengths—a small fire, neat, niggard almost, a shrewd fire; such fires were his father's habit and custom always, even in freezing weather. Older, the boy might have remarked this and wondered why not a big one; why should not a man who had not only seen the waste and extravagance of war, but who had in his blood an inherent voracious prodigality with material not his own, have burned everything in sight? Then he might

have gone a step farther and thought that that was the reason: that niggard blaze was the living fruit of nights passed during those four years in the woods hiding from all men, blue or gray, with his strings of horses (captured horses, he called them). And older still, he might have divined the true reason: that the element of fire spoke to some deep mainspring of his father's being, as the element of steel or of powder spoke to other men, as the one weapon for the preservation of integrity, else breath were not worth the breathing, and hence to be regarded with respect and used with discretion.

But he did not think this now and he had seen those same niggard blazes all his life. He merely ate his supper beside it and was already half asleep over his iron plate when his father called him, and once more he followed the stiff back, the stiff and ruthless limp, up the slope and on the starlit road where, turning, he could see his father against the stars but without face or depth—a shape black, flat, and bloodless as though cut from tin in the iron folds of the frockcoat which had not been made for him, the voice harsh like tin and without heat like tin:

"You were fixing to tell them. You would have told him." He didn't answer. His father struck him with the flat of his hand on the side of the head, hard but without heat, exactly as he had struck the two mules at the store, exactly as he would strike either of them with any stick in order to kill a horse fly, his voice still without heat or anger: "You're getting to be a man. You got to learn. You got to learn to stick to your own blood or you ain't going to have any blood to stick to you. Do you think either of them, any man there this morning, would? Don't you know all they wanted was a chance to get at me because they knew I had them beat? Eh?" Later, twenty years later, he was to tell himself, "If I had said they wanted only truth, justice, he would have hit me again." But now he said nothing. He was not crying. He just stood there. "Answer me," his father said.

"Yes," he whispered. His father turned.

"Get on to bed. We'll be there tomorrow."

Tomorrow they were there. In the early afternoon the wagon stopped before a paintless two-room house identical almost with the dozen others it had stopped before even in the boy's ten years, and again, as on the other dozen occasions, his mother and aunt got down and began to unload the wagon, although his two sisters and his father and brother had not moved.

"Likely hit ain't fitten for hawgs," one of the sisters said.

"Nevertheless, fit it will and you'll hog it and like it," his father said. "Get out of them chairs and help your Ma unload."

The two sisters got down, big, bovine, in a flutter of cheap ribbons; one of them drew from the jumbled wagon bed a battered lantern, the other a worn broom. His father handed the reins to the older son and began to climb stiffly over the wheel. "When they get unloaded, take the team to the barn and feed them." Then he said, and at first the boy thought he was still speaking to his brother: "Come with me."

"Me?" he said.

"Yes," his father said. "You."

"Abner," his mother said. His father paused and looked back—the harsh level stare beneath the shaggy, graying, irascible brows.

"I reckon I'll have a word with the man that aims to begin tomorrow owning me body and soul for the next eight months."

They went back up the road. A week ago—or before last night, that is —he would have asked where they were going, but not now. His father had struck him before last night but never before had he paused afterward

to explain why; it was as if the blow and the following calm, outrageous voice still rang, repercussed, divulging nothing to him save the terrible handicap of being young, the light weight of his few years, just heavy enough to prevent his soaring free of the world as it seemed to be ordered but not heavy enough to keep him footed solid in it, to resist it and try to change the course of its events.

Presently he could see the grove of oaks and cedars and the other flowering trees and shrubs where the house would be, though not the house yet. They walked beside a fence massed with honeysuckle and Cherokee roses and came to a gate swinging open between two brick pillars, and now, beyond a sweep of drive, he saw the house for the first time and at that instant he forgot his father and the terror and despair both, and even when he remembered his father again (who had not stopped) the terror and despair did not return. Because, for all the twelve movings, they had sojourned until now in a poor country, a land of small farms and fields and houses, and he had never seen a house like this before. *Hit's big as a courthouse* he thought quietly, with a surge of peace and joy whose reason he could not have thought into words, being too young for that: *They are safe from him. People whose lives are a part of this peace and dignity are beyond his touch, he no more to them than a buzzing wasp: capable of stinging for a little moment but that's all; the spell of this peace and dignity rendering even the barns and stable and cribs which belong to it impervious to the puny flames he might contrive . . .* this, the peace and joy, ebbing for an instant as he looked again at the stiff black back, the stiff and implacable limp of the figure which was not dwarfed by the house, for the reason that it had never looked big anywhere and which now, against the serene columned backdrop, had more than ever that impervious quality of something cut ruthlessly from tin, depthless, as though, sidewise to the sun, it would cast no shadow. Watching him, the boy remarked the absolutely undeviating course which his father held and saw the stiff foot come squarely down in a pile of fresh droppings where a horse had stood in the drive and which his father could have avoided by a simple change of stride. But it ebbed only for a moment, though he could not have thought this into words either, walking on in the spell of the house, which he could even want but without envy, without sorrow, certainly never with that ravening and jealous rage which unknown to him walked in the ironlike black coat before him: *Maybe he will feel it too. Maybe it will even change him now from what maybe he couldn't help but be.*

They crossed the portico. Now he could hear his father's stiff foot as it came down on the boards with clocklike finality, a sound out of all proportion to the displacement of the body it bore and which was not dwarfed either by the white door before it, as though it had attained to a sort of vicious and ravening minimum not to be dwarfed by anything—the flat, wide, black hat, the formal coat of broadcloth which had once been black but which had now that friction-glazed greenish cast of the bodies of old house flies, the lifted sleeve which was too large, the lifted hand like a curled claw. The door opened so promptly that the boy knew the Negro must have been watching them all the time, an old man with neat grizzled hair, in a linen jacket, who stood barring the door with his body, saying, "Wipe yo foots, white man, fo you come in here. Major ain't home nohow."

"Get out of my way, nigger," his father said, without heat too, flinging the door back and the Negro also and entering, his hat still on his head. And now the boy saw the prints of the stiff foot on the doorjamb and saw them appear on the pale rug behind the machinelike deliberation of the foot which seemed to bear (or transmit) twice the weight which the body compassed. The Negro was shouting "Miss Lula! Miss Lula!" somewhere behind them, then the boy, deluged as though by a warm wave by a suave turn of carpeted stair and a pendant glitter of chandeliers and a mute gleam of gold frames, heard the swift feet and saw her too, a lady—perhaps he had never seen her like before either—in a gray, smooth gown with lace at the throat and an apron tied at the waist and the sleeves turned back, wiping cake or biscuit dough from her hands with a towel as she came up the hall, looking not at his father at all but at the tracks on the blond rug with an expression of incredulous amazement.

"I tried," the Negro cried. "I tole him to . . ."

"Will you please go away?" she said in a shaking voice. "Major de Spain is not at home. Will you please go away?"

His father had not spoken again. He did not speak again. He did not even look at her. He just stood stiff in the center of the rug, in his hat, the shaggy iron-gray brows twitching slightly above the pebble-colored eyes as he appeared to examine the house with brief deliberation. Then with the same deliberation he turned; the boy watched him pivot on the good leg and saw the stiff foot drag round the arc of the turning, leaving a final long and fading smear. His father never looked at it, he never once looked down at the rug. The negro held the door. It closed behind them, upon the hysteric and indistinguishable woman-wail. His father stopped at the top of the steps and scraped his boot clean on the edge of it. At the gate he stopped again. He stood for a moment, planted stiffly on the stiff foot, looking back at the house. "Pretty and white, ain't it?" he said.

"That's sweat. Nigger sweat. Maybe it ain't white enough yet to suit him. Maybe he wants to mix some white sweat with it."

Two hours later the boy was chopping wood behind the house within which his mother and aunt and the two sisters (the mother and aunt, not the two girls, he knew that; even at this distance and muffled by walls the flat loud voices of the two girls emanated an incorrigible idle inertia) were setting up the stove to prepare a meal, when he heard the hooves and saw the linen-clad man on a fine sorrel mare, whom he recognized even before he saw the rolled rug in front of the Negro youth following on a fat bay carriage horse—a suffused, angry face vanishing, still at full gallop, beyond the corner of the house where his father and brother were sitting in the two tilted chairs; and a moment later, almost before he could have put the axe down, he heard the hooves again and watched the sorrel mare go back out of the yard, already galloping again. Then his father began to shout one of the sisters' names, who presently emerged backward from the kitchen door dragging the rolled rug along the ground by one end while the other sister walked behind it.

"If you ain't going to tote, go on and set up the wash pot," the first said.

"You, Sarty!" the second shouted. "Set up the wash pot!" His father appeared at the door, framed against that shabbiness, as he had been against that other bland perfection, impervious to either, the mother's anxious face at his shoulder.

"Go on," the father said. "Pick it up." The two sisters stooped, broad, lethargic; stooping, they presented an incredible expanse of pale cloth and a flutter of tawdry ribbons.

"If I thought enough of a rug to have to git hit all the way from France I wouldn't keep hit where folks coming in would have to tromp on hit," the first said. They raised the rug.

"Abner," the mother said. "Let me do it."

"You go back and git dinner," his father said. "I'll tend to this."

From the woodpile through the rest of the afternoon the boy watched them, the rug spread flat in the dust beside the bubbling wash-pot, the two sisters stooping over it with that profound and lethargic reluctance, while the father stood over them in turn, implacable and grim, driving them though never raising his voice again. He could smell the harsh homemade lye they were using; he saw his mother come to the door once and look toward them with an expresion not anxious now but very like despair; he saw his father turn, and he fell to with the axe and saw from the corner of his eye his father raise from the ground a flattish fragment of field stone and examine it and return to the pot, and this time his mother actually spoke: "Abner. Abner. Please don't. Please, Abner."

Then he was done too. It was dusk; the whippoorwills had already begun. He could smell coffee from the room where they would presently eat the cold food remaining from the mid-afternoon meal, though when he entered the house he realized they were having coffee again probably because there was a fire on the hearth, before which the rug now lay spread over the backs of the two chairs. The tracks of his father's foot were gone. Where they had been were now long, water-cloudy scoriations resembling the sporadic course of a lilliputian mowing machine.

It still hung there while they ate the cold food and then went to bed, scattered without order or claim up and down the two rooms, his mother in one bed, where his father would later lie, the older brother in the other, himself, the aunt, and the two sisters on pallets on the floor. But his father was not in bed yet. The last thing the boy remembered was the depthless, harsh silhouette of the hat and coat bending over the rug and it seemed to him that he had not even closed his eyes when the silhouette was standing over him, the fire almost dead behind it, the stiff foot prodding him awake. "Catch up the mule," his father said.

When he returned with the mule his father was standing in the black door, the rolled rug over his shoulder. "Ain't you going to ride?" he said.

"No. Give me your foot."

He bent his knee into his father's hand, the wiry, surprising power flowed smoothly, rising, he rising with it, on to the mule's bare back (they had owned a saddle once; the boy could remember it though not when or where) and with the same effortlessness his father swung the rug up in front of him. Now in the starlight they retraced the afternoon's path, up the dusty road rife with honeysuckle, through the gate and up the black tunnel of the drive to the lightless house, where he sat on the mule and felt the rough warp of the rug drag across his thighs and vanish.

"Don't you want me to help?" he whispered. His father did not answer and now he heard again that stiff foot striking the hollow portico with that wooden and clocklike deliberation, that outrageous overstatement of the weight it carried. The rug, hunched, not flung (the boy could tell that even in the darkness) from his father's shoulder struck the angle of wall and floor with a sound unbelievably loud, thunderous, then the foot again, unhurried and enormous; a light came on in the house and the boy sat, tense, breathing steadily and quietly and just a little fast, though the foot itself did not increase its beat at all, descending the steps now; now the boy could see him.

"Don't you want to ride now?" he whispered. "We kin both ride now," the light within the house altering now, flaring up and sinking. *He's coming down the stairs now*, he thought. He had already ridden the mule up be-

side the horse block; presently his father was up behind him and he doubled the reins over and slashed the mule across the neck, but before the animal could begin to trot the hard, thin arm came round him, the hard, knotted hand jerking the mule back to a walk.

In the first red rays of the sun they were in the lot, putting plow gear on the mules. This time the sorrel mare was in the lot before he heard it at all, the rider collarless and even bareheaded, trembling, speaking in a shaking voice as the woman in the house had done, his father merely looking up once before stooping again to the hame he was buckling, so that the man on the mare spoke to his stooping back:

"You must realize you have ruined that rug. Wasn't there anybody here, any of your women . . ." he ceased, shaking, the boy watching him, the older brother leaning now in the stable door, chewing, blinking slowly and steadily at nothing apparently. "It cost a hundred dollars. But you never had a hundred dollars. You never will. So I'm going to charge you twenty bushels of corn against your crop. I'll add it in your contract and when you come to the commissary you can sign it. That won't keep Mrs. de Spain quiet but maybe it will teach you to wipe your feet off before you enter her house again."

Then he was gone. The boy looked at his father, who still had not spoken or even looked up again, who was now adjusting the logger-head in the hame.

"Pap," he said. His father looked at him—the inscrutable face, the shaggy brows beneath which the gray eyes glinted coldly. Suddenly the boy went toward him, fast, stopping as suddenly. "You done the best you could!" he cried. "If he wanted hit done different why didn't he wait and tell you how? He won't git no twenty bushels! He won't git none! We'll gether hit and hide hit! I kin watch . . ."

"Did you put the cutter back in that straight stock like I told you?"

"No, sir," he said.

"Then go do it."

That was Wednesday. During the rest of that week he worked steadily, at what was within his scope and some which was beyond it, with an industry that did not need to be driven nor even commanded twice; he had this from his mother, with the difference that some at least of what he did he liked to do, such as splitting wood with the half-size axe which his mother and aunt had earned, or saved money somehow, to present him with at Christmas. In company with the two older women (and on one afternoon, even one of the sisters), he built pens for the shoat and the cow which were a part of his father's contract with the landlord, and one afternoon, his father being absent, gone somewhere on one of the mules, he went to a field.

They were running a middle buster now, his brother holding the plow straight while he handled the reins, and walking beside the straining mule, the rich black soil shearing cool and damp against his bare ankles, he thought *Maybe this is the end of it. Maybe even that twenty bushels that seems hard to have to pay for just a rug will be a cheap price for him to stop forever and always from being what he used to be*; thinking, dreaming now, so that his brother had to speak sharply to him to mind the mule: *Maybe he even won't collect the twenty bushels. Maybe it will all add up and balance and vanish—corn, rug, fire; the terror and grief, the being pulled two ways like between two teams of horses—gone, done with for ever and ever.*

Then it was Saturday; he looked up from beneath the mule he was harnessing and saw his father in the black coat and hat. "Not that," his father said. "The wagon gear." And then, two hours later, sitting in the wagon bed behind his father and brother on the seat, the wagon accomplished a final curve, and he saw the weathered paintless store with its tattered tobacco- and patent-medicine posters and the tethered wagons and saddle animals below the gallery. He mounted the gnawed steps behind his father and brother, and there again was the lane of quiet, watching faces for the three of them to walk through. He saw the man in spectacles sitting at the plank table and he did not need to be told this was a Justice of the Peace; he sent one glare of fierce, exultant, partisan defiance at the man in collar and cravat now, whom he had seen but twice before in his life, and that on a galloping horse, who now wore on his face an expression not of rage but of amazed unbelief which the boy could not have known was at the incredible circumstance of being sued by one of his own tenants, and came and stood against his father and cried at the Justice: "He ain't done it! He ain't burnt . . ."

"Go back to the wagon," his father said.

"Burnt?" the Justice said. "Do I understand this rug was burned too?"

"Does anybody here claim it was?" his father said. "Go back to the wagon." But he did not, he merely retreated to the rear of the room, crowded as that other had been, but not to sit down this time, instead, to stand pressing among the motionless bodies, listening to the voices:

"And you claim twenty bushels of corn is too high for the damage you did to the rug?"

"He brought the rug to me and said he wanted the tracks washed out of it. I washed the tracks out and took the rug back to him."

"But you didn't carry the rug back to him in the same condition it was in before you made the tracks on it."

His father did not answer, and now for perhaps half a minute there was no sound at all save that of breathing, the faint, steady suspiration of complete and intent listening.

"You decline to answer that, Mr. Snopes?" Again his father did not answer. "I'm going to find against you,

Mr. Snopes. I'm going to find that you were responsible for the injury to Major de Spain's rug and hold you liable for it. But twenty bushels of corn seems a little high for a man in your circumstances to have to pay. Major de Spain claims it cost a hundred dollars. October corn will be worth about fifty cents. I figure that if Major de Spain can stand a ninety-five dollar loss on something he paid cash for, you can stand a five-dollar loss you haven't earned yet. I hold you in damages to Major de Spain to the amount of ten bushels of corn over and above your contract with him, to be paid to him out of your crop at gathering time. Court adjourned."

It had taken no time hardly, the morning was but half begun. He thought they would return home and perhaps back to the field, since they were late, far behind all other farmers. But instead his father passed on behind the wagon, merely indicating with his hand for the older brother to follow with it, and crossed the road toward the blacksmith shop opposite, pressing on after his father, overtaking him, speaking, whispering up at the harsh, calm face beneath the weathered hat: "He won't git no ten bushels neither. He won't git one. We'll . . ." until his father glanced for an instant down at him, the face absolutely calm, the grizzled eyebrows tangled above the cold eyes, the voice almost pleasant, almost gentle:

"You think so? Well, we'll wait till October anyway."

The matter of the wagon—the setting of a spoke or two and the tightening of the tires—did not take long either, the business of the tires accomplished by driving the wagon into the spring branch behind the shop and letting it stand there, the mules nuzzling into the water from time to time, and the boy on the seat with the idle reins, looking up the slope and through the sooty tunnel of the shed where the slow hammer rang and where his father sat on an upended cypress bolt, easily, either talking or listening, still sitting there when the boy brought the dripping wagon up out of the branch and halted it before the door.

"Take them on to the shade and hitch," his father said. He did so and returned. His father and the smith and a third man squatting on his heels inside the door were talking, about crops and animals; the boy, squatting too in the ammoniac dust and hoof-parings and scales of rust, heard his father tell a long and unhurried story out of the time before the birth of the older brother even when he had been a professional horsetrader. And then his father came up beside him where he stood before a tattered last year's circus poster on the other side of the store, gazing rapt and quiet at the scarlet horses, the incredible poisings and convolutions of tulle and tights and the painted leers of comedians, and said, "It's time to eat."

But not at home. Squatting beside his brother against the front wall, he watched his father emerge from the store and produce from a paper sack a segment of cheese and divide it carefully and deliberately into three with his pocket knife and produce crackers from the same sack. They all three squatted on the gallery and ate, slowly, without talking; then in the store again, they drank from a tin dipper tepid water smelling of the cedar bucket and of living beech trees. And still they did not go home. It was a horse lot this time, a tall rail fence upon and along which men stood and sat and out of which one by one horses were led, to be walked and trotted and then cantered back and forth along the road while the slow swapping and buying went on and the sun began to slant westward, they—the three of them—watching and listening, the older brother with his muddy eyes and his steady, inevitable tobacco, the father commenting now and then on certain of the animals, to no one in particular.

It was after sundown when they

reached home. They ate supper by lamplight, then, sitting on the doorstep, the boy watched the night fully accomplish, listening to the whippoorwills and the frogs, when he heard his mother's voice: "Abner! No! No! Oh, God. Oh, God. Abner!" and he rose, whirled, and saw the altered light through the door where a candle stub now burned in a bottle neck on the table and his father, still in the hat and coat, at once formal and burlesque as though dressed carefully for some shabby and ceremonial violence, emptying the reservoir of the lamp back into the five-gallon kerosene can from which it had been filled, while the mother tugged at his arm until he shifted the lamp to the other hand and flung her back, not savagely or viciously, just hard, into the wall, her hands flung out against the wall for balance, her mouth open and in her face the same quality of hopeless despair as had been in her voice. Then his father saw him standing in the door.

"Go to the barn and get that can of oil we were oiling the wagon with," he said. The boy did not move. Then he could speak.

"What . . ." he cried. "What are you . . ."

"Go get that oil," his father said. "Go."

Then he was moving, running, outside the house, toward the stable; this the old habit, the old blood which he had not been permitted to choose for himself, which had been bequeathed him willy nilly and which had run for so long (and who knew where, battening on what of outrage and savagery and lust) before it came to him. *I could keep on*, he thought. *I could run on and on and never look back, never need to see his face again. Only I can't. I can't*, the rusted can in his hand now, the liquid splashing in it as he ran back to the house and into it, into the sound of his mother's weeping in the next room, and handed the can to his father.

"Ain't you going to even send a nigger?" he cried. "At least you sent a nigger before!"

This time his father didn't strike him. The hand came even faster than the blow had, the same hand which had set the can on the table with almost excruciating care flashing from the can toward him too quick for him to follow it, gripping him by the back of his shirt and on to tiptoe before he had seen it quit the can, the face stooping at him in breathless and frozen ferocity, the cold, dead voice speaking over him to the older brother who leaned against the table, chewing with that steady, curious, sidewise motion of cows:

"Empty the can into the big one and go on. I'll catch up with you."

"Better tie him up to the bedpost," the brother said.

"Do like I told you," the father said. Then the boy was moving, his bunched shirt and the hard, bony hand between his shoulder-blades, his toes just touching the floor, across the room and into the other one, past the sisters sitting with spread heavy thighs in the two chairs over the cold hearth, and to where his mother and aunt sat side by side on the bed, the aunt's arms about his mother's shoulders.

"Hold him," the father said. The aunt made a startled movement. "Not you," the father said. "Lennie. Take hold of him. I want to see you do it." His mother took him by the wrist. "You'll hold him better than that. If he gets loose don't you know what he is going to do? He will go up yonder." He jerked his head toward the road. "Maybe I'd better tie him."

"I'll hold him," his mother whispered.

"See you do then." Then his father was gone, the stiff foot heavy and measured upon the boards, ceasing at last.

Then he began to struggle. His mother caught him in both arms, he jerking and wrenching at them. He would be stronger in the end, he knew that. But he had no time to wait for it.

"Lemme go!" he cried. "I don't want to have to hit you!"

"Let him go!" the aunt cried. "If he don't go, before God, I am going up there myself!"

"Don't you see I can't?" his mother cried. "Sarty! Sarty! No! No! Help me, Lizzie!"

Then he was free. His aunt grasped at him but it was too late. He whirled, running, his mother stumbled forward on to her knees behind him, crying to the nearer sister: "Catch him, Net! Catch him!" But that was too late too, the sister (the sisters were twins, born at the same time, yet either of them now gave the impression of being, encompassing as much living meat and volume and weight as any other two of the family) not yet having begun to rise from the chair, her head, face, alone merely turned, presenting to him in the flying instant an astonishing expanse of young female features untroubled by any surprise even, wearing only an expression of bovine interest. Then he was out of the room, out of the house, in the mild dust of the starlit road and the heavy rifeness of honeysuckle, the pale ribbon unspooling with terrific slowness under his running feet, reaching the gate at last and turning in, running, his heart and lungs drumming, on up the drive toward the lighted house, the lighted door. He did not knock, he burst in, sobbing for breath, incapable for the moment of speech; he saw the astonished face of the Negro in the linen jacket without knowing when the Negro had appeared.

"De Spain!" he cried, panted. "Where's . . ." then he saw the white man too emerging from a white door down the hall. "Barn!" he cried. "Barn!"

"What?" the white man said. "Barn?"

"Yes!" the boy cried. "Barn!"

"Catch him!" the white man shouted.

But it was too late this time too. The Negro grasped his shirt, but the entire sleeve, rotten with washing, carried away, and he was out that door too and in the drive again, and had actually never ceased to run even while he was screaming into the white man's face.

Behind him the white man was shouting, "My horse! Fetch my horse!" and he thought for an instant of cutting across the park and climbing the fence into the road, but he did not know the park nor how high the vine-massed fence might be and he dared not risk it. So he ran on down the drive, blood and breath roaring; presently he was in the road again though he could not see it. He could not hear either; the galloping mare was almost upon him before he heard her, and even then he held his course, as if the very urgency of his wild grief and need must in a moment more find him wings, waiting until the ultimate instant to hurl himself aside and into the weed-choked roadside ditch as the horse thundered past and on, for an instant in furious silhouette against the stars, the tranquil early summer night sky which, even before the shape of the horse and rider vanished, stained abruptly and violently upward: a long, swirling roar incredible and soundless, blotting the stars, and he springing up and into the road again, running again, knowing it was too late yet still running even after he heard the shot and, an instant later, two shots, pausing now without knowing he had ceased to run, crying "Pap! Pap!" running again before he knew he had begun to run, stumbling, tripping over something and scrabbling up again without ceasing to run, looking backward over his shoulder at the glare as he got up, running on among the invisible trees, panting, sobbing, "Father! Father!"

At midnight he was sitting on the crest of a hill. He did not know it was midnight and he did not know how far he had come. But there was no glare behind him now and he sat now, his back toward what he had called home for four days anyhow, his face toward the dark woods which he would enter when breath was strong again, small, shaking steadily in the chill darkness, hugging himself into the remainder of his thin, rotten shirt, the grief and despair now no longer terror and fear but just grief and despair. *Father. My Father*, he thought. "He was brave!" he cried suddenly, aloud but not loud, no more than a whisper: "He was! He was in the war! He was in Colonel Sartoris' cav'ry!" not knowing that his father had gone to that war a private in the fine old European sense, wearing no uniform, admitting the authority of and giving fidelity to no man or army or flag, going to war as Malbrouck himself did: for booty—it meant nothing and less than nothing to him if it were enemy booty or his own.

The slow constellations wheeled on. It would be dawn and then sun-up after a while and he would be hungry. But that would be tomorrow and now he was only cold, and walking would cure that. His breathing was easier now and he decided to get up and go on, and then he found that he had been asleep because he knew it was almost dawn, the night almost over. He could tell that from the whippoorwills. They were everywhere now among the dark trees below him, constant and inflectioned and ceaseless, so that, as the instant for giving over to the day birds drew nearer and nearer, there was no interval at all between them. He got up. He was a little stiff, but walking would cure that too as it would the cold, and soon there would be the sun. He went on down the hill, toward the dark woods within which the liquid silver voices of the birds called unceasing—the rapid and urgent beating of the urgent and quiring heart of the late spring night. He did not look back.

Ernest Hemingway (1899–1961)

THE SNOWS OF KILIMANJARO

Kilimanjaro is a snow covered mountain 19,710 feet high, and is said to be the highest mountain in Africa. Its western summit is called the Masai "Ngàje Ngài," the House of God. Close to the western summit there is the dried and frozen carcass of a leopard. No one has explained what the leopard was seeking at that altitude.

"The marvellous thing is that it's painless," he said. "That's how you know when it starts."

"Is it really?"

"Absolutely. I'm awfully sorry about the odor though. That must bother you."

"Don't! Please don't."

"Look at them," he said. "Now is it sight or is it scent that brings them like that?"

The cot the man lay on was in the wide shade of a mimosa tree and as he looked out past the shade onto the glare of the plain there were three of the big birds squatted obscenely, while in the sky a dozen more sailed, making quick-moving shadows as they passed.

"They've been there since the day the truck broke down," he said. "Today's the first time any have lit on the ground. I watched the way they sailed very carefully at first in case I ever wanted to use them in a story. That's funny now."

"I wish you wouldn't," she said.

"I'm only talking," he said. "It's much easier if I talk. But I don't want to bother you."

"You know it doesn't bother me," she said. "It's that I've gotten so very nervous not being able to do anything. I think we might make it as easy as we can until the plane comes."

"Or until the plane doesn't come."

"Please tell me what I can do. There must be something I can do."

"You can take the leg off and that might stop it, though I doubt it. Or you can shoot me. You're a good shot now. I taught you to shoot, didn't I?"

"Please don't talk that way. Couldn't I read to you?"

"Read what?"

"Anything in the book bag that we haven't read."

"I can't listen to it," he said. "Talking is the easiest. We quarrel and that makes the time pass."

"I don't quarrel. I never want to quarrel. Let's not quarrel any more. No matter how nervous we get. Maybe they will be back with another truck today. Maybe the plane will come."

"I don't want to move," the man said. "There is no sense in moving now except to make it easier for you."

"That's cowardly."

"Can't you let a man die as comfortably as he can without calling him names? What's the use of slanging me?"

"You're not going to die."

"Don't be silly. I'm dying now. Ask those bastards." He looked over to where the huge, filthy birds sat, their naked heads sunk in the hunched feathers. A fourth planed down, to run quick-legged and then waddle slowly toward the others.

"They are around every camp. You never notice them. You can't die if you don't give up."

"Where did you read that? You're such a bloody fool."

"You might think about some one else."

"For Christ's sake," he said, "That's been my trade."

He lay then and was quiet for a while and looked across the heat shimmer of the plain to the edge of the bush. There were a few Tommies that showed minute and white against the yellow and, far off, he saw a herd of zebra, white against the green of the bush. This was a pleasant camp under big trees against a hill, with good water, and close by, a nearly dry water hole where sand grouse flighted in the mornings.

"Wouldn't you like me to read?" she asked. She was sitting on a canvas chair beside his cot. "There's a breeze coming up."

"No thanks."

"Maybe the truck will come."

"I don't give a damn about the truck."

"I do."

"You give a damn about so many things that I don't."

"Not so many, Harry."

"What about a drink?"

"It's supposed to be bad for you. It said in Black's to avoid all alcohol. You shouldn't drink."

"Molo!" he shouted.

"Yes Bwana."

"Bring whiskey-soda."

"Yes Bwana."

"You shouldn't," she said. "That's what I mean by giving up. It says it's bad for you. I know it's bad for you."

"No," he said. "It's good for me."

So now it was all over, he thought. So now he would never have a chance to finish it. So this was the way it ended in a bickering over a drink. Since the gangrene started in his right leg he had no pain and with the pain the horror had gone and all he felt now was a great tiredness and anger that this was the end of it. For this, that now was coming, he had very little curiosity. For years it had obsessed him; but now it meant nothing in itself. It was strange how easy being tired enough made it.

Now he would never write the things that he had saved to write until he knew enough to write them well. Well, he would not have to fail at trying to write them either. Maybe you could never write them, and that was why you put them off and delayed the starting. Well he would never know, now.

"I wish we'd never come," the woman said. She was looking at him holding the glass and biting her lip. "You never would have gotten anything like this in Paris. You always said you loved Paris. We could have stayed in Paris or gone anywhere. I'd have gone anywhere. I said I'd go anywhere you wanted. If you wanted to shoot we could have gone shooting in Hungary and been comfortable."

"Your bloody money," he said.

"That's not fair," she said. "It was always yours as much as mine. I left everything and I went wherever you wanted to go and I've done what you wanted to do. But I wish we'd never come here."

"You said you loved it."

"I did when you were all right. But now I hate it. I don't see why that had to happen to your leg. What have we done to have that happen to us?"

"I suppose what I did was to forget to put iodine on it when I first scratched it. Then I didn't pay any attention to it because I never infect. Then, later, when it got bad, it was probably using that weak carbolic solution when the other antiseptics ran out that paralyzed the minute blood vessels and started the gangrene." He looked at her, "What else?"

"I don't mean that."

"If we would have hired a good mechanic instead of a half baked kikuyu driver, he would have checked the oil and never burned out that bearing in the truck."

"I don't mean that."

"If you hadn't left your own people,

your goddamned Old Westbury, Saratoga, Palm Beach people to take me on——"

"Why, I loved you. That's not fair. I love you now. I'll always love you. Don't you love me?"

"No," said the man. "I don't think so. I never have."

"Harry, what are you saying? You're out of your head."

"No. I haven't any head to go out of."

"Don't drink that," she said. "Darling, please don't drink that. We have to do everything we can."

"You do it," he said. "I'm tired."

Now in his mind he saw a railway station at Karagatch and he was standing with his pack and that was the headlight of the Simplon-Orient cutting the dark now and he was leaving Thrace then after the retreat. That was one of the things he had saved to write, with, in the morning at breakfast, looking out the window and seeing snow on the mountains in Bulgaria and Nansen's Secretary asking the old man if it were snow and the old man looking at it and saying, No, that's not snow. It's too early for snow. And the Secretary repeating to the other girls, No, you see. It's not snow and them all saying, It's not snow we were mistaken. But it was the snow all right and he sent them on into it when he evolved exchange of populations. And it was snow they tramped along in until they died that winter.

It was snow too that fell all Christmas week that year up in the Gauertal, that year they lived in the woodcutter's house with the big square porcelain stove that filled half the room, and they slept on mattresses filled with beech leaves, the time the deserter came with his feet bloody in the snow. He said the police were right behind him and they gave him woolen socks and held the gendarmes talking until the tracks had drifted over.

In Schrunz, on Christmas day, the

snow was so bright it hurt your eyes when you looked out from the weinstube and saw every one coming home from church. That was where they walked up the sleigh-smoothed urine-yellowed road along the river with the steep pine hills, skis heavy on the shoulder, and where they ran that great run down the glacier above the Madlener-haus, the snow as smooth to see as cake frosting and as light as powder and he remembered the noiseless rush the speed made as you dropped down like a bird.

They were snow-bound a week in the Madlener-haus that time in the blizzard playing cards in the smoke by the lantern light and the stakes were higher all the time as Herr Lent lost more. Finally he lost it all. Everything, the skischule money and all the season's profit and then his capital. He could see him with his long nose, picking up the cards and then opening, "Sans Voir." There was always gambling then. When there was no snow you gambled and when there was too much you gambled. He thought of all the time in his life he had spent gambling.

But he had never written a line of that, nor of that cold, bright Christmas day with the mountains showing across the plain that Barker had flown across the lines to bomb the Austrian officers' leave train, machine-gunning them as they scattered and ran. He remembered Barker afterwards coming into the mess and starting to tell about it. And how quiet it got and then somebody saying, "You bloody murderous bastard."

Those were the same Austrians they killed then that he skied with later. No not the same. Hans, that he skied with all that year, had been in the Kaiser-Jägers and when they went hunting hares together up the little valley above the saw-mill they had talked of the fighting on Pasubio and of the attack on Pertica and Asalone and he had never written a word of that. Nor of Monte Corno, nor the Siete Commum, nor of Arsiedo.

How many winters had he lived in the Vorarlberg and the Arlberg? It was four and then he remembered the man who had the fox to sell when they had walked into Bludenz, that time to buy presents, and the cherry-pit taste of good kirsch, the fast-slipping rush of running powder-snow on crust, singing "Hi! Ho! said Rolly!" as you ran down the last stretch to the steep drop, taking it straight, then running the orchard in three turns and out across the ditch and onto the icy road behind the inn. Knocking your bindings loose, kicking the skis free and leaning them up against the wooden wall of the inn, the lamplight coming from the window, where inside, in the smoky, new-wine smelling warmth, they were playing the accordion.

"Where did we stay in Paris?" he asked the woman who was sitting by him in a canvas chair, now, in Africa.

"At the Crillon. You know that."

"Why do I know that?"

"That's where we always stayed."

"No. Not always."

"There and at the Pavillion Henri-Quatre in St. Germain. You said you loved it there."

"Love is a dunghill," said Harry. "And I'm the cock that gets on it to crow."

"If you have to go away," she said, "is it absolutely necessary to kill off everything you leave behind? I mean do you have to take away everything? Do you have to kill your horse, and your wife and burn your saddle and your armour?"

"Yes," he said. "Your damned money was my armour. My Swift and my Armour."

"Don't."

"All right. I'll stop that. I don't want to hurt you."

"It's a little bit late now."

"All right then. I'll go on hurting you. It's more amusing. The only thing

I ever really liked to do with you I can't do now."

"No, that's not true. You liked to do many things and everything you wanted to do I did."

"Oh, for Christ sake stop bragging, will you?"

He looked at her and saw her crying.

"Listen," he said. "Do you think that it is fun to do this? I don't know why I'm doing it. It's trying to kill to keep yourself alive, I imagine. I was all right when we started talking. I didn't mean to start this, and now I'm crazy as a coot and being as cruel to you as I can be. Don't pay any attention, darling, to what I say. I love you, really. You know I love you. I've never loved any one else the way I love you."

He slipped into the familiar lie he made his bread and butter by.

"You're sweet to me."

"You bitch," he said. "You rich bitch. That's poetry. I'm full of poetry now. Rot and poetry. Rotten poetry."

"Stop it. Harry, why do you have to turn into a devil now?"

"I don't like to leave anything," the man said. "I don't like to leave things behind."

.   .   .

It was evening now and he had been asleep. The sun was gone behind the hill and there was a shadow all across the plain and the small animals were feeding close to camp; quick dropping heads and switching tails, he watched them keeping well out away from the bush now. The birds no longer waited on the ground. They were all perched heavily in a tree. There were many more of them. His personal boy was sitting by the bed.

"Memsahib's gone to shoot," the boy said. "Does Bwana want?"

"Nothing."

She had gone to kill a piece of meat and, knowing how he liked to watch the game, she had gone well away so she would not disturb this little pocket of the plain that he could see. She was always thoughtful, he thought. On anything she knew about, or had read, or that she had ever heard.

It was not her fault that when he went to her he was already over. How could a woman know that you meant nothing that you said; that you spoke only from habit and to be comfortable? After he no longer meant what he said, his lies were more successful with women than when he had told them the truth.

It was not so much that he lied as that there was no truth to tell. He had had his life and it was over and then he went on living it again with different people and more money, with the best of the same places, and some new ones.

You kept from thinking and it was all marvellous. You were equipped with good insides so that you did not go to pieces that way, the way most of them had, and you made an attitude that you cared nothing for the work you used to do, now that you could no longer do it. But, in yourself, you said that you would write about these people; about the very rich; that you were really not of them but a spy in their country; that you would leave it and write of it and for once it would be written by some one who knew what he was writing of. But he would never do it, because each day of not writing, of comfort, of being that which he despised, dulled his ability and softened his will to work so that, finally, he did no work at all. The people he knew now were all much more comfortable when he did not work. Africa was where he had been happiest in the good time of his life, so he had come out here to start again. They had made this safari with the minimum of comfort. There was no hardship; but there was no luxury and he had thought that he could get back into training that way. That in some way he could work the fat off his soul the way a fighter went into the mountains to work and train in order to burn it out of his body.

She had liked it. She said she loved it. She loved anything that was exciting, that involved a change of scene, where there were new people and where things were pleasant. And he had felt the illusion of returning strength of will to work. Now if this was how it ended, and he knew it was, he must not turn like some snake biting itself because its back was broken. It wasn't this woman's fault. If it had not been she it would have been another. If he lived by a lie he should try to die by it. He heard a shot beyond the hill.

She shot very well this good, this rich bitch, this kindly caretaker and destroyer of his talent. Nonsense. He had destroyed his talent himself. Why should he blame this woman because she kept him well? He had destroyed his talent by not using it, by betrayals of himself and what he believed in, by drinking so much that he blunted the edge of his perceptions, by laziness, by sloth, and by snobbery, by pride and by prejudice, by hook and by crook. What was this? A catalogue of old books? What was his talent anyway? It was a talent all right but instead of using it, he had traded on it. It was never what he had done, but always what he could do. And he had chosen to make his living with something else instead of a pen or a pencil. It was strange, too, wasn't it, that when he fell in love with another woman, that woman should always have more money than the last one? But when he no longer was in love, when he was only lying, as to this woman, now, who had the most money of all, who had all the money there was, who had had a husband and children, who had taken lovers and been dissatisfied with them, and who loved him dearly as a writer, as a man, as a companion and as a proud possession; it was strange that when he did not love her at all and was lying, that he should be able to give her more for her money than when he had really loved.

We must all be cut out for what we do, he thought. However you make your living is where your talent lies. He had sold vitality, in one form or another, all his life and when your affections are not too involved you give much better value for the money. He had found that out but he would never write that, now, either. No, he would not write that, although it was well worth writing.

Now she came in sight, walking across the open toward the camp. She was wearing jodphurs and carrying her rifle. The two boys had a Tommie slung and they were coming along behind her. She was still a good-looking woman, he thought, and she had a pleasant body. She had a great talent and appreciation for the bed, she was not pretty, but he liked her face, she read enormously, liked to ride and shoot and, certainly, she drank too much. Her husband had died when she was still a comparatively young woman and for a while she had devoted herself to her two just-grown children, who did not need her and were embarrassed at having her about, to her stable of horses, to books, and to bottles. She liked to read in the evening before dinner and she drank Scotch and soda while she read. By dinner she was fairly drunk and after a bottle of wine at dinner she was usually drunk enough to sleep.

That was before the lovers. After she had the lovers she did not drink so much because she did not have to be drunk to sleep. But the lovers bored her. She had been married to a man who had never bored her and these people bored her very much.

Then one of her two children was killed in a plane crash and after that was over she did not want the lovers, and drink being no anæsthetic she had to make another life. Suddenly, she had been acutely frightened of being alone. But she wanted some one that she respected with her.

It had begun very simply. She liked what he wrote and she had always envied the life he led. She thought he did exactly what he wanted to. The steps by which she had acquired him and the way in which she had finally fallen in love with him were all part of a regular progression in which she had built herself a new life and he had traded away what remained of his old life.

He had traded it for security, for comfort too, there was no denying that, and for what else? He did not know. She would have bought him anything he wanted. He knew that. She was a damned nice woman too. He would as soon be in bed with her as any one; rather with her, because she was richer, because she was very pleasant and appreciative and because she never made scenes. And now this life that she had built again was coming to a term because he has not used iodine two weeks ago when a thorn had scratched his knee as they moved forward trying to photograph a herd of waterbuck standing, their heads up, peering while their nostrils searched the air, their ears spread wide to hear the first noise that would send them rushing into the bush. They had bolted, too, before he got the picture.

Here she came now.

He turned his head on the cot to look toward her. "Hello," he said.

"I shot a Tommy ram," she told him. "He'll make you good broth and I'll have them mash some potatoes with the Klim. How do you feel?"

"Much better."

"Isn't that lovely? You know I thought perhaps you would. You were sleeping when I left."

"I had a good sleep. Did you walk far?"

"No. Just around behind the hill. I made quite a good shot on the Tommy."

"You shoot marvellously, you know."

"I love it. I've loved Africa. Really. If you're all right it's the most fun that I've ever had. You don't know the fun it's been to shoot with you. I've loved the country."

"I love it too."

"Darling, you don't know how mar-

vellous it is to see you feeling better. I couldn't stand it when you felt that way. You won't talk to me like that again, will you? Promise me?"

"No," he said. "I don't remember what I said."

"You don't have to destroy me. Do you? I'm only a middle-aged woman who loves you and wants to do what you want to do. I've been destroyed two or three times already. You wouldn't want to destroy me again, would you?"

"I'd like to destroy you a few times in bed," he said.

"Yes. That's the good destruction. That's the way we're made to be destroyed. The plane will be here to-morrow."

"How do you know?"

"I'm sure. It's bound to come. The boys have the wood all ready and the grass to make the smudge. I went down and looked at it again today. There's plenty of room to land and we have the smudges ready at both ends."

"What makes you think it will come tomorrow?"

"I'm sure it will. It's overdue now. Then, in town, they will fix up your leg and then we will have some good destruction. Not that dreadful talking kind."

"Should we have a drink? The sun is down."

"Do you think you should?"

"I'm having one."

"We'll have one together. *Molo, letti dui whiskey-soda!*" she called.

"You'd better put on your mosquito boots," he told her.

"I'll wait till I bathe . . ."

While it grew dark they drank and just before it was dark and there was no longer enough light to shoot, a hyena crossed the open on his way around the hill.

"That bastard crosses there every night," the man said. "Every night for two weeks."

"He's the one makes the noise at night. I don't mind it. They're a filthy animal though."

Drinking together, with no pain now except the discomfort of lying in the one position, the boys lighting a fire, its shadow jumping on the tents, he could feel the return of acquiescence in this life of pleasant surrender. She *was* very good to him. He had been cruel and unjust in the afternoon. She was a fine woman, marvellous really. And just then it occurred to him that he was going to die.

It came with a rush; not as a rush of water nor of wind; but of a sudden evil-smelling emptiness and the odd thing was that the hyena slipped lightly along the edge of it.

"What is it, Harry?" she asked him.

"Nothing," he said. "You had better move over to the other side. To windward."

"Did Molo change the dressing?"

"Yes. I'm just using the boric now."

"How do you feel?"

"A little wobbly."

"I'm going in to bathe," she said. "I'll be right out. I'll eat with you and then we'll put the cot in."

So, he said to himself, we did well to stop the quarrelling. He had never quarrelled much with this woman, while with the woman that he loved he had quarrelled so much they had finally, always, with the corrosion of the quarrelling, killed what they had together. He had loved too much, demanded too much, and he wore it all out.

He thought about alone in Constantinople that time, having quarrelled in Paris before he had gone out. He had whored the whole time and then, when that was over, and he had failed to kill his loneliness, but only made it worse, he had written her, the first one, the one who left him, a letter telling her how he had never been able to kill it. . . . How when he thought he saw her outside the Regence one time it made him go all faint and sick inside, and that he would follow a woman who looked like her in some way, along the Boulevard, afraid to see it was not she, afraid to lose the feeling it gave him. How every one he had slept with had only made him miss her more. How what she had done could never matter since he knew he could not cure himself of loving her. He wrote this letter at the Club, cold sober, and mailed it to New York asking her to write him at the office in Paris. That seemed safe. And that night missing her so much it made him feel hollow sick inside, he wandered up past Taxim's, picked a girl up and took her out to supper. He had gone to a place to dance with her afterward, she danced badly, and left her for a hot Armenian slut, that swung her belly against him so it almost scalded. He took her away from a British gunner subaltern after a row. The gunner asked him outside and they fought in the street on the cobbles in the dark. He'd hit him twice, hard, on the side of the jaw and when he didn't go down he knew he was in for a fight. The gunner hit him in the body, then beside his eye. He swung with his left again and landed and the gunner fell on him and grabbed his coat and tore the sleeve off and he clubbed him twice behind the ear and then smashed him with his right as he pushed him away. When the gunner went down his head hit first and he ran with the girl because they heard the M.P.'s coming. They got into a taxi and drove out to Rimmily Hissa along the Bosphorus, and around, and back in the cool night and went to bed and she felt as over-ripe as she looked but smooth, rose-petal, syrupy, smooth-bellied, big-breasted and needed no pillow under her buttocks, and he left her before she was awake looking blousy enough in the first daylight and turned up at the Pera Palace with a black eye, carrying his coat because one sleeve was missing.

That same night he left for Anatolia and he remembered, later on that trip, riding all day through fields of the poppies that they raised for opium and how strange it made you feel, finally, and all the distances seemed wrong, to where they had made the attack with the newly arrived Constantine officers, that did not know a god-damned thing, and the artillery had fired into the troops and the British observer had cried like a child.

That was the day he'd first seen dead men wearing white ballet skirts and up-turned shoes with pompons on them. The Turks had come steadily and lump-ily and he had seen the skirted men running and the officers shooting into them and running then themselves and he and the British observer had run too until his lungs ached and his mouth was full of the taste of pennies and they stopped behind some rocks and there were the Turks coming as lumpily as ever. Later he had seen the things that he could never think of and later still he had seen much worse. So when he got back to Paris that time he could not talk about it or stand to have it mentioned. And there in the café as he passed was that American poet with a pile of saucers in front of him and a stupid look on his potato face talking about the Dada movement with a Roumanian who said his name was Tristan Tzara, who always wore a mon-ocle and had a headache, and, back at the apartment with his wife that now he loved again, the quarrel all over, the madness all over, glad to be home, the office sent his mail up to the flat. So then the letter in answer to the one he'd written came in on a platter one morning and when he saw the hand-writing he went cold all over and tried to slip the letter underneath another. But his wife said, "Who is that letter from, dear?" and that was the end of the beginning of that.

He remembered the good times with them all, and the quarrels. They always picked the finest places to have the quarrels. And why had they always quarrelled when he was feeling best? He had never written any of that be-cause, at first, he never wanted to hurt

any one and then it seemed as though there was enough to write without it. But he had always thought that he would write it finally. There was so much to write. He had seen the world change; not just the events; although he had seen many of them and had watched the people, but he had seen the subtler change and he could re-member how the people were at dif-ferent times. He had been in it and he had watched it and it was his duty to write of it; but now he never would.

"How do you feel?" she said. She had come out from the tent now after her bath.

"All right."

"Could you eat now?" He saw Molo behind her with the folding table and the other boy with the dishes.

"I want to write," he said.

"You ought to take some broth to keep your strength up."

"I'm going to die tonight," he said. "I don't need my strength up."

"Don't be melodramatic, Harry, please," she said.

"Why don't you use your nose? I'm rotted half way up my thigh now. What the hell should I fool with broth for? Molo, bring whiskey-soda."

"Please take the broth," she said gently.

"All right."

The broth was too hot. He had to hold it in the cup until it cooled enough to take it and then he just got it down without gagging.

"You're a fine woman," he said. "Don't pay any attention to me."

She looked at him with her well-known, well-loved face from *Spur* and *Town and Country,* only a little the worse for drink, only a little the worse for bed, but *Town and Country* never showed those good breasts and those useful thighs and those lightly small-of-back-caressing hands, and as he looked and saw her well known pleasant smile, he felt death come again. This time there was no rush. It was a puff, as of a wind that makes a candle flicker and the flame go tall.

"They can bring my net out later and hang it from the tree and build the fire up. I'm not going in the tent tonight. It's not worth moving. It's a clear night. There won't be any rain."

So this was how you died, in whispers that you did not hear. Well, there would be no more quarrelling. He could promise that. The one experience that he had never had he was not going to spoil now. He probably would. You spoiled everything. But perhaps he wouldn't.

"You can't take dictation, can you?"

"I never learned," she told him.

"That's all right."

There wasn't time, of course, although it seemed as though it telescoped so that you might put it all into one paragraph if you could get it right.

There was a log house, chinked white with mortar, on a hill above the lake. There was a bell on a pole by the door to call the people in to meals. Behind the house were fields and behind the fields was the timber. A line of lombardy poplars ran from the house to the dock. Other poplars ran along the point. A road went up to the hills along the edge of the timber and along that road he picked blackberries. Then that log house was burned down and all the guns that had been on deer foot racks above the open fire place were burned and afterwards their barrels, with the lead melted in the magazines, and the stocks burned away, lay out on the heap of ashes that were used to make lye for the big iron soap kettles, and you asked Grandfather if you could have them to play with, and he said, no. You see they were his guns still and he never bought any others. Nor did he hunt any more. The house was rebuilt in the same place out of lumber now and painted white and from its porch you saw the poplars and the lake beyond; but there
were never any more guns. The barrels of the guns that had hung on the deer feet on the wall of the log house lay out there on the heap of ashes and no one ever touched them.

In the Black Forest, after the war, we rented a trout stream and there were two ways to walk to it. One was down the valley from Triberg and around the valley road in the shade of the trees that bordered the white road, and then up a side road that went up through the hills past many small farms, with the big Schwarzwald houses, until that road crossed the stream. That was where our fishing began.

The other way was to climb steeply up to the edge of the woods and then go across the top of the hills through the pine woods, and then out to the edge of a meadow and down across this meadow to the bridge. There were birches along the stream and it was not big, but narrow, clear and fast, with pools where it had cut under the roots of the birches. At the Hotel in Triberg the proprietor had a fine season. It was very pleasant and we were all great friends. The next year came the inflation and the money he had made the year before was not enough to buy supplies to open the hotel and he hanged himself.

You could dictate that, but you could not dictate the Place Contrescarpe where the flower sellers dyed their flowers in the street and the dye ran over the paving where the autobus started and the old men and the women, always drunk on wine and bad marc; and the children with their noses running in the cold; the smell of dirty sweat and poverty and drunkenness at the Café des Amateurs and the whores at the Bal Musette they lived above. The Concierge who entertained the trooper of the Garde Republicaine in her loge, his horse-hair-plumed helmet on a chair. The locataire across the hall whose husband was a bicycle racer and her joy that morning at the Cremerie when she had opened

L'Auto and seen where he placed third in Paris-Tours, his first big race. She had blushed and laughed and then gone upstairs crying with the yellow sporting paper in her hand. The husband of the woman who ran the Bal Musette drove a taxi and when he, Harry, had to take an early plane the husband knocked upon the door to wake him and they each drank a glass of white wine at the zinc of the bar before they started. He knew his neighbors in that quarter then because they all were poor.

Around that Place *there were two kinds; the drunkards and the sportifs. The drunkards killed their poverty that way; the sportifs took it out in exercise. They were the descendants of the Communards and it was no struggle for them to know their politics. They knew who had shot their fathers, their relatives, their brothers, and their friends when the Versailles troops came in and took the town after the Commune and executed any one they could catch with calloused hands, or who wore a cap, or carried any other sign he was a working man. And in that poverty, and in that quarter across the street from a Boucherie Chevaline and a wine co-operative he had written the start of all he was to do. There never was another part of Paris that he loved like that, the sprawling trees, the old white plastered houses painted brown below, the long green of the autobus in that round square, the purple flower dye upon the paving, the sudden drop down the hill of the rue Cardinal Lemoine to the River, and the other way the narrow crowded world of the rue Mouffetard. The street that ran up toward the Pantheon and the other that he always took with the bicycle, the only asphalted street in all that quarter, smooth under the tires, with the high narrow houses and the cheap tall hotel where Paul Verlaine had died. There were only two rooms in the apartments where they lived and he had a room on the top floor of that hotel that cost him sixty francs a month where he did his writing,*
and from it he could see the roofs and chimney pots and all the hills of Paris.

From the apartment you could only see the wood and coal man's place. He sold wine too, bad wine. The golden horse's head outside the Boucherie Chevaline where the carcasses hung yellow gold and red in the open window, and the green painted co-operative where they bought their wine; good wine and cheap. The rest was plaster walls and the windows of the neighbors. The neighbors who, at night, when some one lay drunk in the street, moaning and groaning in that typical French ivresse *that you were propaganded to believe did not exist, would open their windows and then the murmur of talk.*

"Where is the policeman? When you don't want him the bugger is always there. He's sleeping with some concierge. Get the Agent." *Till some one threw a bucket of water from a window and the moaning stopped. "What's that? Water. Ah, that's intelligent." And the windows shutting. Marie, his femme de ménage, protesting against the eight-hour day saying, "If a husband works until six he gets only a little drunk on the way home and does not waste too much. If he works only until five he is drunk every night and one has no money. It is the wife of the working man who suffers from this shortening of hours."*

"Wouldn't you like some more broth?" the woman asked him now.

"No, thank you very much. It is awfully good."

"Try just a little."

"I would like a whiskey-soda."

"It's not good for you."

"No. It's bad for me. Cole Porter wrote the words and the music. This knowledge that you're going mad for me."

"You know I like you to drink."

"Oh yes. Only it's bad for me."

When she goes, he thought. I'll have

all I want. Not all I want but all there is. Ayee he was tired. Too tired. He was going to sleep a little while. He lay still and death was not there. It must have gone around another street. It went in pairs, on bicycles, and moved absolutely silently on the pavements.

No, he had never written about Paris. Not the Paris that he cared about. But what about the rest that he had never written?

What about the ranch and the silvered gray of the sage brush, the quick, clear water in the irrigation ditches, and the heavy green of the alfalfa. The trail went up into the hills and the cattle in the summer were shy as deer. The bawling and the steady noise and slow moving mass raising a dust as you brought them down in the fall. And behind the mountains, the clear sharpness of the peak in the evening light and, riding down along the trail in the moonlight, bright across the valley. Now he remembered coming down through the timber in the dark holding the horse's tail when you could not see and all the stories that he meant to write.

About the half-wit chore boy who was left at the ranch that time and told not to let any one get any hay, and that old bastard from the Forks who had beaten the boy when he had worked for him stopping to get some feed. The boy refusing and the old man saying he would beat him again. The boy got the rifle from the kitchen and shot him when he tried to come into the barn and when they came back to the ranch he'd been dead a week, frozen in the corral, and the dogs had eaten part of him. But what was left you packed on a sled wrapped in a blanket and roped on and you got the boy to help you haul it, and the two of you took it out over the road on skis, and sixty miles down to town to turn the boy over. He having no idea that he would be arrested. Thinking he had done his duty and that you were his friend and he

would be rewarded. He'd helped to haul the old man in so everybody could know how bad the old man had been and how he'd tried to steal some feed that didn't belong to him, and when the sheriff put the handcuffs on the boy he couldn't believe it. Then he'd started to cry. That was one story he had saved to write. He knew at least twenty good stories from out there and he had never written one. Why?

"You tell them why," he said.

"Why what, dear?"

"Why nothing."

She didn't drink so much, now, since she had him. But if he lived he would never write about her, he knew that now. Nor about any of them. The rich were dull and they drank too much, or they played too much backgammon. They were dull and they were repetitious. He remembered poor Julian and his romantic awe of them and how he had started a story once that began, "The very rich are different from you and me." And how some one had said to Julian, Yes, they have more money. But that was not humorous to Julian. He thought they were a special glamourous race and when he found they weren't it wrecked him just as much as any other thing that wrecked him.

He had been contemptuous of those who wrecked. You did not have to like it because you understood it. He could beat anything, he thought, because no thing could hurt him if he did not care.

All right. Now he would not care for death. One thing he had always dreaded was the pain. He could stand pain as well as any man, until it went on too long, and wore him out, but here he had something that had hurt frightfully and just when he had felt it breaking him, the pain had stopped.

He remembered long ago when Williamson, the bombing officer, had been hit by a stick bomb some one in a German patrol had thrown as he was com-

ing in through the wire that night and, screaming, had begged every one to kill him. He was a fat man, very brave, and a good officer, although addicted to fantastic shows. But that night he was caught in the wire, with a flare lighting him up and his bowels spilled out into the wire, so when they brought him in, alive, they had to cut him loose. Shoot me, Harry. For Christ sake shoot me. They had had an argument one time about our Lord never sending you anything you could not bear and some one's theory had been that meant that at a certain time the pain passed you out automatically. But he had always remembered Williamson, that night. Nothing passed out Williamson until he gave him all his morphine tablets that he had always saved to use himself and then they did not work right away.

Still this now, that he had, was very easy; and if it was no worse as it went on there was nothing to worry about. Except that he would rather be in better company.

He thought a little about the company that he would like to have.

No, he thought, when everything you do, you do too long, and do too late, you can't expect to find the people still there. The people all are gone. The party's over and you are with your hostess now.

I'm getting as bored with dying as with everything else, he thought.

"It's a bore," he said out loud.

"What is, my dear?"

"Anything you do too bloody long."

He looked at her face between him and the fire. She was leaning back in the chair and the firelight shone on her pleasantly lined face and he could see that she was sleepy. He heard the hyena make a noise just outside the range of the fire.

"I've been writing," he said. "But I got tired."

"Do you think you will be able to sleep?"

"Pretty sure. Why don't you turn in?"

"I like to sit here with you."

"Do you feel anything strange?" he asked her.

"No. Just a little sleepy."

"I do," he said.

He had just felt death come by again.

"You know the only thing I've never lost is curiosity," he said to her.

"You've never lost anything. You're the most complete man I've ever known."

"Christ," he said. "How little a woman knows. What is that? Your intuition?"

Because, just then, death had come and rested its head on the foot of the cot and he could smell its breath.

"Never believe any of that about a scythe and a skull," he told her. "It can be two bicycle policemen as easily, or be a bird. Or it can have a wide snout like a hyena."

It had moved up on him now, but it had no shape any more. It simply occupied space.

"Tell it to go away."

It did not go away but moved a little closer.

"You've got a hell of a breath," he told it. "You stinking bastard."

It moved up closer to him still and now he could not speak to it, and when it saw he could not speak it came a little closer, and now he tried to send it away without speaking, but it moved in on him so its weight was all upon his chest, and while it crouched there and he could not move, or speak, he heard the woman say, "Bwana is asleep now. Take the cot up very gently and carry it into the tent."

He could not speak to tell her to make it go away and it crouched now, heavier, so he could not breathe. And then, while they lifted the cot, suddenly it was all right and the weight went from his chest.

It was morning and had been morning for some time and he heard the plane. It showed very tiny and then made a wide circle and the boys ran out and lit the fires, using kerosene, and piled on grass so there were two big smudges at each end of the level place and the morning breeze blew them toward the camp and the plane circled twice more, low this time, and then glided down and levelled off and landed smoothly and, coming walking toward him, was old Compton in slacks, a tweed jacket and a brown felt hat.

"What's the matter, old cock?" Compton said.

"Bad leg," he told him. "Will you have some breakfast?"

"Thanks. I'll just have some tea. It's the Puss Moth you know. I won't be able to take the Memsahib. There's only room for one. Your lorry is on the way."

Helen had taken Compton aside and was speaking to him. Compton came back more cheery than ever.

"We'll get you right in," he said. "I'll be back for the Mem. Now I'm afraid I'll have to stop at Arusha to refuel. We'd better get going."

"What about the tea?"

"I don't really care about it you know."

The boys had picked up the cot and carried it around the green tents and down along the rock and out onto the plain and along past the smudges that were burning brightly now, the grass all consumed, and the wind fanning the fire, to the little plane. It was difficult getting him in, but once in he lay back in the leather seat, and the leg was stuck straight out to one side of the seat where Compton sat. Compton started the motor and got in. He waved to Helen and to the boys and, as the clatter moved into the old familiar roar, they swung around with Compie watching for wart-hog holes and roared, bumping, along the stretch between the fires and with the last bump rose and he saw them all standing below, waving, and the camp beside the hill, flattening now, and the plain spreading, clumps of trees, and the bush flattening, while

the game trails ran now smoothly to the dry waterholes, and there was a new water that he had never known of. The zebra, small rounded backs now, and the wildebeeste, big-headed dots seeming to climb as they moved in long fingers across the plain, now scattering as the shadow came toward them, they were tiny now, and the movement had no gallop, and the plain as far as you could see, gray-yellow now and ahead old Compie's tweed back and the brown felt hat. Then they were over the first hills and the wildebeeste were trailing up them, and then they were over mountains with sudden depths of green-rising forest and the solid bamboo slopes, and then the heavy forest again, sculptured into peaks and hollows until they crossed, and hills sloped down and then another plain, hot now, and purple brown, bumpy with heat and Compie looking back to see how he was riding. Then there were other mountains dark ahead.

And then instead of going on to Arusha they turned left, he evidently figured that they had the gas, and looking down he saw a pink sifting cloud, moving over the ground, and in the air, like the first snow in a blizzard, that comes from nowhere, and he knew the locusts were coming up from the South. Then they began to climb and they were going to the East it seemed, and then it darkened and they were in a storm, the rain so thick it seemed like flying through a waterfall, and then they were out and Compie turned his head and grinned and pointed and there, ahead, all he could see, as wide as all the world, great, high, and unbelievably white in the sun, was the square top of Kilimanjaro. And then he knew that there was where he was going.

Just then the hyena stopped whimpering in the night and started to make a strange, human, almost crying sound. The woman heard it and stirred uneasily. She did not wake. In her dream she was at the house on Long Island and it was the night before her daughter's début. Somehow her father was there and he had been very rude. Then the noise the hyena made was so loud she woke and for a moment she did not know where she was and she was very afraid. Then she took the flashlight and shone it on the other cot that they had carried in after Harry had gone to sleep. She could see his bulk under the mosquito bar but somehow he had got-ten his leg out and it hung down alongside the cot. The dressings had all come down and she could not look at it.

"Molo," she called, "Molo! Molo!"

Then she said, "Harry, Harry!" Then her voice rising, "Harry! Please, Oh Harry!"

There was no answer and she could not hear him breathing.

Outside the tent the hyena made the same strange noise that had awakened her. But she did not hear him for the beating of her heart.

James T. Farrell   (1904–   )

A FRONT-PAGE STORY

The undertaking parlor seemed oppressively formal and impersonal, with its subdued lights, its dull green carpet, waxed flooring, scrupulously polished but stiff-backed chairs, weighty sofas, and potted green plants set upon marble-topped tables. And shadowed toward the rear of this room of artificial sublimity Ruth Summer was laid out in a sleeveless pink taffeta dress with a shoulder corsage. She had been a short dumpy girl with thin, stringy, blonde hair, and a commonplace oval face. Now, she was a blue and bloated corpse, and her fatty bloodless arms gave one the impression of semi-nudity. The dress had evidently been her best party frock, purchased after stinting sacrifices, and lovingly doted over. It had been saved and preserved for those parties and affairs which she had been only infrequently able to attend, and when she had worn it in life, it must have hung like a sack on her squat figure, the inappropriate type of dress that just such a monotonous and uninspired girl would wear. In death, it draped her like a last treachery.

The young campus reporter for *The Chicago Questioner* studied this twenty-one-year-old corpse, feeling like an imposter. Near him stood a small and repressed group which spoke in semi-articulate whispers. In its center was Ruth Summer's father, a tall, homespun man with unpressed clothes, lop-sided shoulders, and a genial but rutted visage. He had just arrived by train to send his daughter's body back home to Iowa for burial, and he was speaking with Ruth's tall, homely cousin, the woman at whose house Ruth had boarded. The cousin was explaining that if Ruth had only taken her into confidence, such foolhardiness might have been prevented. Three of Ruth's student friends, bucolic carbon copies of the dead girl's own personality, completed the group. As they listened to the conversation between the father and the cousin, their faces were intent and bewildered. The young campus reporter continued staring at the corpse, surreptitiously straining to hear and remember every word of the conversation. He recalled the statement which the tall, homely cousin had inadvertently made, prior to the father's arrival:

"It was literal suicide."

He approached the group, his presence causing an additional awkwardness among them. Replying to the question of one of the student friends, he re-explained that he had been in several classes with Ruth. The confused father drew a frayed newspaper clipping from his worn wallet and, without comment, handed it around. The young reporter read it last, and as he read slowly, he forced himself in the effort of remembering as much of it, verbatim, as he could. It recorded that Ruth Summer, honor student and valedictory orator at the town high school, was leaving to attend the University, and that all her many friends, admirers, and classmates predicted for her a brilliant academic career at this famous Temple of Truth. After having read the clipping twice, he returned it to the father, and shook his head with sad expressiveness. No one spoke. No one looked at anyone else. The young reporter, after shuffling his feet nervously and turning his face aside to blow his nose, stated that he would be going. The father thanked him for having remembered his daughter, and the tall cousin reiterated this expression of gratitude. The three student friends stared after him with puzzled suspicion. After a final glance at the dead girl, in her sleeveless frock, he departed.

Outside on the Midway he paused to jot down as much as he could remember from the clipping the father had shown him. He perceived that he was using, for his notes, the blank sides of an official release from the Department of Public Relations. He knew what the release contained: a eulogistic description of the commencement exercises, six and a half mimeographed pages of sugared words reflecting praise upon the University. That he should be using this release for his notes was, like the dress, another accidental irony. Even after her death this simple, betrayed girl must be humiliated. He stuffed the papers back in his pocket, lit a cigarette, and, walking toward the line of Gothic University Towers, attempted to think of other subjects. The Midway, and the buildings in the distance of several blocks, glowed and were mellow under a spreading June twilight, and the sky was calm. All about him were the heedless echoes of living people, children playing on the shaven grass in the center of the Midway, strolling pedestrians, a succession of whizzing automobiles, a jazz song audible from a radio within an opened window, an Illinois Central Suburban electric train, drawing into and out of the Midway station, an airplane rumbling overhead, causing people to pause and gape skyward with dreamy oblivious eyes and opened mouths.

He crossed over to the north side of the Midway and passed the white-stoned million-dollar Gothic chapel in which, on the previous day, the graduation exercises had been conducted, and he briefly glanced upward at the high and serene white-stoned tower. He entered a long, low and ornate hall dedicated to the recreation and social life of the female students. It was here that Ruth Summer had worked for two years as a checkroom girl. And it was from a garrulous elderly woman in this building that he had indirectly received the tip on the story. He nodded and smiled at the blue-uniformed guard who stood inside the door at the edge of the broad lobby, a rubicund jolly-faced man decrepit with age. Casually, he sauntered to the bulletin board, and paused as if he were interested in the few tacked-on announcements and notices. Copies of the University annual lay on a table which stood near the checkroom on his left, half-concealed by a post. Since he had to procure one immediately and he did not have the ten dollars to purchase it, a copy would have to be stolen. Once before he had had to steal one in the same manner. He glanced about the lobby, as if he were seeking some girl. He walked to the table, quickly snatched a copy, and proceeded around behind the checkroom where there were telephone booths and a cloister. In one of the telephone booths he concealed the annual under his jacket, holding it in place with a stiffened left arm. Coming out of the telephone booth, he sat at the edge of the lobby for several moments, arose, and drifted toward the door, while the guard was answering questions.

A few paces down from the building he removed the annual and placed it under his left arm. He knew that it contained a photograph of Ruth Summer, but he had no curiosity to look at the picture.

He walked with a slackened pace. This one was a front-page scoop, and he experienced none of that quickening sense of keenness, that thrilling feeling of a dog on the hunt, which he should have. He harbored no illusions that he was more than a part-time campus reporter, whose principal duty was that of supplying *The Chicago Questioner* with a steady succession of leg pictures of prominent and attractive campus girls. And he had no ambitions of becoming a newspaper man, particularly one employed by *The Chicago Questioner* and working under Kelly Malloy, the triple-chinned editor. Withal, his work had permitted him to return to classes this last quarter. He desired to retain it, and to do so, he could not permit such stories to pass. If he did, they would be picked up by someone else, and then he would have to explain to Kelly Malloy why he was missing them.

As it was, Kelly was continuing his job largely on sufferance. Bobby Wallace, the ex-baseball writer who was now the University's Director of Public Relations, was tight on news, and barely deigned to recognize the existence of the campus reporter. Rather, he sent news in official releases, and whenever he needed a reporter or photographer, he telephoned the City Desk. He had

countered Bobby's tactics by turning in as many ridiculous stories about the University as he could, and most of them had been printed. But it still seemed to puzzle Kelly Malloy that Bobby should always be telephoning for reporters and photographers. This story would settle all grudges with The Department of Public Relations. It was a sole measure of compensation for not having ignored the story, in the hope that no one else would have dug it up.

He sat on the steps of the main library building, smoking, shrinking from the moment when he would go inside to the phone booth and call up the City Desk. In quick, epitomizing mental pictures, he had a sense of Ruth Summer's whole university career. He could visualize this unostentatious, unsung, practically unknown small town girl against various familiar campus backgrounds. He could see her during that now forgotten freshman week of four years ago, when she had matriculated. He could sense that lost and lonely feeling that must have been hers as she stood in slow-moving lines, waiting to interview her dean, waiting to register for courses, waiting to apply for work at The Bureau of Vocational Guidance, waiting to pay her fees. He could see her sitting in chapel during that important first week, when deans and administrators officially welcomed the class of 1929, with lip-service to TRUTH, with clichés describing benefits and privileges which the University so altruistically placed at the disposal of its students, with stale stereotypes expressing the formal ideals of the institution. And he could see her attentively listening and literal-mindedly accepting their words, determining that she would make the most of her opportunity. Likewise could he see her in classrooms, with a loose-leaf notebook before her, diligently copying notes from lectures. And again in the library studying. She had majored in Education, and had planned to become a teacher, and he could see her poring over her assignments in one of her text-books, perhaps a text-book with some such title as *The Theory and Method of The Theory and Practice of Teaching High-School English.* He wondered how many hours she had stolen from sleep, from fun, from dreams, from her life, to devote to her courses in Education. How much of her short life had she given to such problems as the scientific method of grading high-school English papers, to drawing up reading lists for English courses in junior high schools, to the laborious listing of the titles of innocuous books which she herself had no time to read, to considerations of the quantity of fresh air to be permitted twenty-five students, to theoretical discussions of the value and efficacy of using the True and False method in conducting examinations. And again, he could see her on some rare evening of relaxation, when she would have been able to attend an International Club Dance—affairs generally considered freak shows by the prominent campus men and women—when she would have stood like a wall-flower, perhaps in her sleeveless pink taffeta dress, waiting for someone to ask her to dance, watching dance after dance without any invitation, or, if she were dancing, moving so woodenly and awkwardly that she became a trial to her partner. He could see her again, emerging from the office of her doctor at the beginning of her junior year, pondering and brooding on the words she just heard, knowing that she had such a very weak heart that she could not hope for a long life, and that any undue excitement or violent exercise would induce her death. He was forced, from his reflection, to admire her persistence and courage in continuing with full-time schedules and going on with her work as checkroom girl and waitress, despite the doctor's warning. He could see her, constantly tired, moving from classroom to library, to hasty meals, to work, and then home to her room for study until she dropped off into a sleep of physical exhaustion. He

could see her, a plainly dressed girl, proceeding along a campus walk, moving by the lilac trees on a sunny spring day, just another grind driving herself toward her goal of an education and a degree, smothering impulse after impulse to dally and deviate from her purposes. He attempted to imagine how she must have felt on such occasions, when she would have passed some athlete or club girl who had sat near her in a class, and who passed her by outside without even a formal nod of recognition. He thought of this dead girl, and of her career, that had been so completely fruitless. All her work and study, the more than a thousand dollars which she had paid for tuition, the strain of her effort to obtain an education—all fruitless.

And yesterday, a cold and rainy day, she had gone out to the sand dunes with a newly found friend who had been ignorant of the condition of her heart. While the successful members of her class were in the million-dollar chapel, listening to oratory on the subject of TRUTH, EDUCATION, and CITIZENSHIP, and receiving their degrees, she was out on the sand dunes, her unattractive body clothed in a swimming suit. She had known what the consequences of her gesture would be.

"It was literal suicide."

She had known that if she ran about the dunes, and that if she risked plunging into the icy waters of Lake Michigan, she would not return alive. It had been with a final desperation, nursing a final disappointment, that she had gone on this expedition. Her friend had been first in the water. Ruth had run among the dunes, shouting. She had stopped for a moment to wave to her friend while the latter swam outward. Shouting and laughing, she had pitched down to the shore line. She had collapsed in shallow water, and a wave had washed over her and dragged her to the shore where she had lain, buffeted by the steady charge of waves until her friend, coming in unaware, had discovered her. She had been dead for over an hour when a doctor had examined the body, diagnosing heart failure as the cause of death.

The young campus reporter tossed aside a half-smoked cigarette butt, and stood up. Twilight had settled and it was almost completely dark. The Midway was wrapped in an atmosphere of loneliness, with its passing automobiles, its blinking traffic signals, and its sauntering pedestrians. He turned toward the door of the building. He had forgotten that it was closed, so he walked over to an open hall at the other end of the campus, to telephone.

The City Desk gave him a rewrite man. He stated the facts simply, one by one. She had come to the University with the reputation of being a brilliant student at her small town high school. She had worked her way through school as a waitress and checkroom girl. This June, she had expected to graduate. She had been too busy to have many friends, or much fun during her four years. A few days before graduation she had received a formal notice informing her that she would not be permitted to graduate because she lacked one grade point, and that her average, therefore, did not qualify her for a degree. She had told none of her friends of this development, and had proceeded with her graduation plans. She had paid for her cap and gown, and had sat with the graduating class for the official picture. She had attended the annual senior class breakfast, held one day before commencement exercises. Then on the day of graduation, she had gone out to the sand dunes in the rain, and had attempted to run and swim. For two years, she had been the victim of severe heart attacks, and was under the care of a doctor. She knew that her action would result in death. Now her father was in town, and in the morning she was being returned home in a coffin without the degree for which she had struggled.

The rewrite man asked how the facts had been gotten.

"By lying," the campus reporter answered.

"Come on, I'm busy. How did you get them?"

"I posed as a friend, and spoke with her cousin, her father, and some of her friends. And I saw her laid out in the undertaking parlor."

"Anything else?"

"Yes, she lived with her cousin, and the cousin stated that 'It was literal suicide.' "

"Sounds like it was. How about her picture?"

"It's in the latest annual. I got a copy, and I'm sending it down in a cab."

"Swell stuff, kid! That's good work. I'll have to remind Kelly about it tomorrow."

"And listen! Give her a break. It'll be the first one she ever had. Try and keep out too much of the sob stuff. If you make it too gooey, the story will be spoiled."

"Yeh, it's pretty sad. All right, and are you sure you got it all in now? Nothing else?"

"You got it."

"Well, listen while I repeat it for you."

After hanging up, the campus reporter telephoned for a taxi cab. Waiting for the cab he looked across the street at the gymnasium, which stood darkened and clothed in shadows. He gave the driver the annual, instructed him to get it down to the city desk of *The Chicago Questioner* as quickly as possible, and that he would be paid down there. He watched the cab shoot off. In the morning, his story and Ruth's picture would be on the front page, and the girl's body would be on the train, moving toward home. And the father, with the unpressed suit, the lop-sided shoulders, and the genial but rutted face, would be sitting by the train window, looking out, a bewildered man.

He walked eastward, reflecting on

the final meanings of this girl's life. Bobby Wallace would read the story, and become furious. He would receive a telephone call from the office of the vice-president, and he would be called on the carpet to explain why such unfavorable news had gotten into the papers, and particularly at this time, following the commencement exercises, and all the favorable national publicity which the University had received following its recent surprising appointment of the new "boy president" from Yale. Bobby would have to say that he knew nothing about it. He would have to confess defeat. Then the dean of women would get him and demand an explanation. And even the chairman of the board of trustees, Morton G. Quick, the stockyards capitalist and power behind the University throne, would telephone Bobby and ask about the story. Bobby would telephone Kelly and brand the story as a lie, and the campus reporter as a liar. Kelly would chuckle to himself, his three chins moving, and answer ambiguously. Ruth Summer, who in life had merely been one undistinguished student out of about five thousand, a name on reports, a source of one hundred dollars tuition fees every quarter, a student employee with a name on payrolls, a student who must have a desk in various classrooms, and, finally, a member of the class of 1929 who had had to be formally notified that she lacked the prerequisites for graduation—in death, she would be an embarrassment to all the institution's officialdom. To the campus reporter, she was a scoop, a means of preserving his job, and the instrument of settling his grievances with The Department of Public Relations. To *The Chicago Questioner*, she was a front-page story, exciting the staff for the space of a few moments while the story was written and turned in. To the editors of the other papers, she would be a source of annoyance, something they had missed, and her story in *The Questioner* would be turned over to their rewrite men to be hashed up for their own editions. To a nameless taxi-driver, she was a long and easy haul from The University all the way downtown, with no passenger to watch whether or not he took a long route to jack up his fare.

And while she had become or was becoming all these various meanings, she lay in that oppressive undertaking parlor, blue and bloated in a sleeveless pink taffeta party frock, and all the fruitless dignity and courage of her life was betrayed, even after her death.

THE SCOOP

A large *Chicago Questioner* delivery truck parted the traffic as it roared northward toward the Clark Street bridge. It shook the street, emitted carbon monoxide gas from its exhaust pipe, punctuated the atmosphere with the shrillness of an open cutout. And thundered onward.

It was the first truck to be used for deliveries. Dennis McDermott, a circulation slugger, stood on the tail gate and hung onto a stout rope. Husky and handsome, he expressed his pride in a characteristic leering frown. He enjoyed the honor of having been assigned to this new truck while the other sluggers remained at work on horse-drawn vehicles.

Bumping, the truck rattled over the Clark Street bridge. Dennis was tearing through the scenes of his boyhood. He had grown up on the Near North Side, been educated on its streets, and he had served as an altar boy at the Holy Name Cathedral. Nuns had even looked at him with masked wonderment, incapable of understanding why such an intelligent-looking boy, who seemed so holy and so devout in his acolyte's cassock, should always be fighting the way he was. That had been before he had been ejected from school for the third and final time in his seventh grade. His father had been an Irish immigrant and an unskilled worker. A precinct captain in Bart Gallivan's organization had gotten him a job as a street cleaner, and that had elevated Dennis' father to one of the most minor positions in the neighborhood political aristocracy. Dennis had always had before him the example of the local hoodlums, and in his small-boy manner he had emulated them, leading his gang in expeditions to roll drunks, and in fights against neighborhood gangs of Jews and wops. Reckless and possessed of volatile courage, he had grown up to be a tough guy, hired as a slugger and strikebreaker, employed in the taxicab wars, and then by *The Questioner* in the newspaper circulation war. Twice, he had been arrested in hold-ups. Duke O'Connell, from Dennis' own neighborhood, had become State's Attorney, and he had sprung Dennis both times. He stood on the tail gate of the truck, delivering papers to the old corners, even to corners where he had sold newspapers himself. And just as earlier sluggers had gypped him by subtracting papers from his order and charging him for them, so he was now gypping newsboys who were acquiring an education similar to his own in the same kind of system.

He clutched his supporting ropes more tightly as the truck curved about a corner. It drew up to a newsstand and Dennis flung down a bundle containing forty-five copies of the paper.

"How many?" asked the newsboy, a tired-looking kid of twelve or thirteen with a hole in the knee of his left stocking.

"What you ordered. Fifty!" Dennis said in his habitually bullying voice.

"Last night there were only forty-five. I counted 'em," the kid said with a nervous and uncertain air of defiance.

"I said there was fifty!"

"Well, I counted 'em!" the kid said, a whine creeping into his voice.

Dennis squeezed the boy's left ear between two strong fingers, and asked him how many there had been.

"I counted 'em!" the kid said, his voice cracking.

Dennis gave him a back-handed slap in the mouth and said that there had been fifty copies. He collected for the papers and jumped on the truck as the sniffling newsboy opened the bundle.

"How's it going, Wop?" Dennis asked Rocko Martini at the next stop.

"All right, Irish," Rocko replied, winking.

While Rocko opened his bundle of papers, Dennis quickly said that he and a pal were pulling an easy house job on Saturday night and they needed somebody for a lookout. He'd been watching Rocko, and he knew he was all right. If Rocko wanted, they'd let him in with a fourth of the take. Rocko agreed, and Dennis made a date to meet him after work to give him the lowdown.

After two uneventful stops, the truck drew up to a stand where two newsboys were jawing each other. Dennis leaped down and stood over them, sneering, his hands on his hips. He noticed that a freckle-faced kid had a bundle of *The Chicago Clarion*.

"What's the idea, huh?"

"This guy's trying to bust into my business," *The Questioner* kid said.

Dennis looked at the freckle-faced boy, and the latter drew back a few paces.

"This is my corner, ain't it, Denny?"

"Well, I can sell my papers where I wanna. It's a free country, ain't it?"

"So that's the story!" Dennis said, grabbing the freckled kid's papers, and shoving him. The kid reached for his papers. Dennis twisted his arm, booted his tail, and warned him not to be seen selling papers on this corner again. He tore the papers up and told *The Questioner* kid to let him know if the punk came back.

Dennis delivered papers to Shorty Ellis, the punk he didn't like. Ellis was always giving *The Questioner* inside place on his stand. He told his driver to go around the block, and jumped off the tail gate. He sauntered back to Ellis. He pointed to the copies of *The Questioner* which were placed on the inside.

"Didn't I tell you where to place our papers?"

"Well, Muggs was around and told me to place his in the same spot."

"He did?"

"Yes."

"What did I tell you?"

"I don't see why you guys can't leave a kid alone to sell his papers."

"You don't, huh!" Dennis said, catching a look in Ellis' eyes that he didn't like.

"Change 'em!"

"And then Muggs'll be around and crack my puss."

"Change 'em!"

Ellis did not obey the command. Dennis slapped his face. Touching the red flush on his cheek, Ellis drew back, pulled out a pocket knife and, waving it before him defensively, told Dennis to let him alone. Dennis advanced on the boy. Ellis, still brandishing his knife, scratched Dennis' wrists. Dennis lost his temper and flashed a razor.

When the boy again struck out defensively, Dennis slashed his throat, almost from ear to ear. The boy fell, his head nearly dismembered, his blood gushing over the sidewalk. Dennis looked around. No one had seen the fracas. He knew the kid would die quickly. He hastened away and leaped onto his truck. It raced back to *The Questioner* office. He saw the night editor, Kelly Malloy, who had worked himself up from a copy boy and was now only in his thirties. Malloy always talked hard, but he had a soft, womanish face. He had been given the job in a change that was calculated to jack up circulation, and Dennis was the best circulation man on the force. When Dennis assured him for the fourth time that no one had seen him slash the boy, he breathed a sigh of relief. Then he slapped his hands together and said that the story was worth an extra. He became a dynamo of energy.

Very soon Dennis was back on the truck with an extra which bore the headline:

NEWSBOY MURDERED; SLAYER
UNAPPREHENDED
*North-Side Boy Slashed With Razor In
Suspected Neighborhood Gang Fight*

At that time *The Questioner* was conducting, as a circulation stunt, one of its wars on crime. On the editorial page of the extra there was a flamboyant editorial demanding that the police enforce the laws and reduce crime.

Richard Wright (1908–1960)

THE MAN WHO LIVED UNDERGROUND

I've got to hide, he told himself. His chest heaved as he waited, crouching in a dark corner of the vestibule. He was tired of running and dodging. Either he had to find a place to hide, or he had to surrender. A police car swished by through the rain, its siren rising sharply. They're looking for me all over . . .

He crept to the door and squinted through the fogged plate glass. He stiffened as the siren rose and died in the distance. Yes, he had to hide, but where? He gritted his teeth. Then a sudden movement in the street caught his attention. A throng of tiny columns of water snaked into the air from the perforations of a manhole cover. The columns stopped abruptly, as though the perforations had become clogged; a gray spout of sewer water jutted up from underground and lifted the circular metal cover, juggled it for a moment, then let it fall with a clang.

He hatched a tentative plan: he would wait until the siren sounded far off, then he would go out. He smoked and waited, tense. At last the siren gave him his signal; it wailed, dying, going away from him. He stepped to the sidewalk, then paused and looked curiously at the open manhole, half expecting the cover to leap up again. He went to the center of the street and stooped and peered into the hole, but could see nothing. Water rustled in the black depths.

He started with terror; the siren sounded so near that he had the idea that he had been dreaming and had awakened to find the car upon him. He dropped instinctively to his knees and his hands grasped the rim of the manhole. The siren seemed to hoot directly above him and with a wild gasp of exertion he snatched the cover far enough off to admit his body. He swung his legs over the opening and lowered himself into watery darkness. He hung for an eternal moment to the rim by his finger tips, then he felt rough metal prongs and at once he knew that sewer workmen used these ridges to lower themselves into manholes. Fist over fist, he let his body sink until he could feel no more prongs. He swayed in dank space; the siren seemed to howl at the very rim of the manhole. He dropped and was washed violently into an ocean of warm, leaping water. His head was battered against a wall and he wondered if this were death. Frenziedly his fingers clawed and sank into a crevice. He steadied himself and measured the strength of the current with his own muscular tension. He stood slowly in water that dashed past his knees with fearful velocity.

He heard a prolonged scream of brakes and the siren broke off. Oh, God! They had found him! Looming above his head in the rain a white face hovered over the hole. "How did this damn thing get off?" he heard a policeman ask. He saw the steel cover move slowly until the hole looked like a quarter moon turned black. "Give me a hand here," someone called. The cover clanged into place, muffling the sights and sounds of the upper world. Knee-deep in the pulsing current, he breathed with aching chest, filling his lungs with the hot stench of yeasty rot.

From the perforations of the manhole cover, delicate lances of hazy violet sifted down and wove a mottled pattern upon the surface of the streaking current. His lips parted as a car swept past along the wet pavement overhead, its heavy rumble soon dying out, like the hum of a plane speeding through a dense cloud. He had never thought that cars could sound like that; everything seemed strange and unreal under here. He stood in darkness for a long time, knee-deep in rustling water, musing.

The odor of rot had become so general that he no longer smelled it. He got his cigarettes, but discovered that his matches were wet. He searched and found a dry folder in the pocket of his shirt and managed to strike one; it flared weirdly in the wet gloom, glowing greenishly, turning red, orange, then yellow. He lit a crumpled cigarette; then, by the flickering light of the match, he looked for support so that he would not have to keep his muscles flexed against the pouring water. His pupils narrowed and he saw to either side of him two steaming walls that rose and curved inward some six feet above his head to form a dripping, mouse-colored dome. The bottom of the sewer was a sloping V-trough. To the left, the sewer vanished in ashen fog. To the right was a steep down-curve into which water plunged.

He saw now that had he not regained his feet in time, he would have been swept to death, or had he entered any other manhole he would have probably drowned. Above the rush of the current he heard sharper juttings of water; tiny streams were spewing into the sewer from smaller conduits. The match died; he struck another and saw a mass of debris sweep past him and clog the throat of the down-curve. At once the water began rising rapidly. Could he climb out before he drowned? A long hiss sounded and the debris was sucked from sight; the current lowered. He understood now what had made the water toss the manhole cover; the down-curve had become temporarily obstructed and the perforations had become clogged.

He was in danger; he might slide into a down-curve; he might wander with a lighted match into a pocket of gas and blow himself up; or he might contract some horrible disease ... Though he wanted to leave, an irrational impulse held him rooted. To the left, the convex ceiling swooped to a height of less than five feet. With cigarette slanting from pursed lips, he waded with taut muscles, his feet sloshing over the slimy bottom, his shoes sinking into spongy slop, the slate-colored water cracking in creamy foam against his knees. Pressing his flat left palm against the lowered ceiling, he struck another match and saw a metal pole nestling in a niche of the wall. Yes, some sewer workman had left it. He reached for it, then jerked his head away as a whisper of scurrying life whisked past and was still. He held the match close and saw a huge rat, wet with slime, blinking beady eyes and baring tiny fangs. The light blinded the rat and the frizzled head moved aimlessly. He grabbed the pole and let it fly against the rat's soft body; there was shrill piping and the grizzly body splashed into the dun-colored water and was snatched out of sight, spinning in the scuttling stream.

He swallowed and pushed on, following the curve of the misty cavern, sounding the water with the pole. By the faint light of another manhole cover he saw, amid loose wet brick, a hole with walls of damp earth leading into blackness. Gingerly he poked the pole into it; it was hollow and went beyond the length of the pole. He shoved the pole before him, hoisted himself upward, got to his hands and knees, and crawled. After a few yards he paused, struck to wonderment by the silence; it seemed that he had traveled a million miles away from the world. As he inched forward again he could sense the bottom of the dirt tunnel becoming dry and lowering slightly. Slowly he rose and to his astonishment he stood erect. He could not hear the rustling of the water now and he felt confoundingly alone, yet lured by the darkness and silence.

He crept a long way, then stopped, curious, afraid. He put his right foot forward and it dangled in space; he drew back in fear. He thrust the pole outward and it swung in emptiness. He trembled, imagining the earth crumbling and burying him alive. He scratched a match and saw that the dirt floor sheered away steeply and widened into a sort of cave some five feet below him. An old sewer, he muttered. He cocked his head, hearing a feathery cadence which he could not identify. The match ceased to burn.

Using the pole as a kind of ladder, he slid down and stood in darkness. The air was a little fresher and he could still hear vague noises. Where was he? He felt suddenly that someone was standing near him and he turned sharply, but there was only darkness. He poked cautiously and felt a brick wall; he followed it and the strange sounds grew louder. He ought to get out of here. This was crazy. He could not remain here for any length of time; there was no food and no place to sleep. But the faint sounds tantalized him; they were strange but familiar. Was it a motor? A baby crying? Music? A siren? He groped on, and the sounds came so clearly that he could feel the pitch and timbre of human voices. Yes, singing! That was it! He listened with open mouth. It was a church service. Enchanted, he groped toward the waves of melody.

Jesus, take me to your home above
And fold me in the bosom of Thy
love . . .

The singing was on the other side of a brick wall. Excited, he wanted to watch the service without being seen. Whose church was it? He knew most of the churches in this area above ground, but the singing sounded too strange and detached for him to guess. He looked to the left, to the right, down to the black dirt, then upward and was startled to see a bright sliver of light slicing the darkness like the blade of a razor. He struck one of his two remaining matches and saw rusty pipes running along an old concrete ceiling. Photographically he located the exact position of the pipes in his mind. The match flame sank and he sprang upward; his hands clutched a pipe. He swung his legs and tossed his body onto the bed of pipes and they creaked, swaying up and down; he thought that the tier was about to crash, but nothing happened. He edged to the crevice and saw a segment of black men and women, dressed in white robes, singing, holding tattered songbooks in their black palms. His first impulse was to laugh, but he checked himself.

What was he doing? He was crushed with a sense of guilt. Would God strike him dead for that? The singing swept on and he shook his head, disagreeing in spite of himself. They oughn't to

do that, he thought. But he could think of no reason *why* they should not do it. Just singing with the air of the sewer blowing in on them . . . He felt that he was gazing upon something abysmally obscene, yet he could not bring himself to leave.

After a long time he grew numb and dropped to the dirt. Pain throbbed in his legs and a deeper pain, induced by the sight of those black people groveling and begging for something they could never get, churned in him. A vague conviction made him feel that those people should stand unrepentant and yield no quarter in singing and praying, yet *he* had run away from the police, had pleaded with them to believe in *his* innocence. He shook his head, bewildered.

How long had he been down here? He did not know. This was a new kind of living for him; the intensity of feelings he had experienced when looking at the church people sing made him certain that he had been down here a long time, but his mind told him that the time must have been short. In this darkness the only notion he had of time was when a match flared and measured time by its fleeting light. He groped back through the hole toward the sewer and the waves of song subsided and finally he could not hear them at all. He came to where the earth hole ended and he heard the noise of the current and time lived again for him, measuring the moments by the wash of water.

The rain must have slackened, for the flow of water had lessened and came only to his ankles. Ought he to go up into the streets and take his chances on hiding somewhere else? But they would surely catch him. The mere thought of dodging and running again from the police made him tense. No, he would stay and plot how to elude them. But what could he do down here? He walked forward into the sewer and came to another manhole cover; he stood beneath it, debating. Fine pencils of gold spilled suddenly from the little circles in the manhole cover and trembled on the surface of the current. Yes, street lamps . . . It must be night . . .

He went forward for about a quarter of an hour, wading aimlessly, poking the pole carefully before him. Then he stopped, his eyes fixed and intent. What's that? A strangely familiar image attracted and repelled him. Lit by the yellow stems from another manhole cover was a tiny nude body of a baby snagged by debris and half-submerged in water. Thinking that the baby was alive, he moved impulsively to save it, but his roused feelings told him that it was dead, cold, nothing, the same nothingness he had felt while watching the men and women singing in the church. Water blossomed about the tiny legs, the tiny arms, the tiny head, and rushed onward. The eyes were closed, as though in sleep; the fists were clenched, as though in protest; and the mouth gaped black in a soundless cry.

He straightened and drew in his breath, feeling that he had been staring for all eternity at the ripples of veined water skimming impersonally over the shriveled limbs. He felt as condemned as when the policeman had accused him. Involuntarily he lifted his hand to brush the vision away, but his arm fell listlessly to his side. Then he acted; he closed his eyes and reached forward slowly with the soggy shoe of his right foot and shoved the dead baby from where it had been lodged. He kept his eyes closed, seeing the little body twisting in the current as it floated from sight. He opened his eyes, shivered, placed his knuckles in the sockets, hearing the water speed in the somber shadows.

He tramped on, sensing at times a sudden quickening in the current as he passed some conduit whose waters were swelling the stream that slid by his feet. A few minutes later he was standing under another manhole cover, listening to the faint rumble of noises above ground. Streetcars and trucks, he mused. He looked down and saw a stagnant pool of gray-green sludge; at intervals a balloon pocket rose from the scum, glistening a bluish-purple, and burst. Then another. He turned, shook his head, and tramped back to the dirt cave by the church, his lips quivering.

Back in the cave, he sat and leaned his back against a dirt wall. His body was trembling slightly. Finally his senses quieted and he slept. When he awakened he felt stiff and cold. He had to leave this foul place, but leaving meant facing those policemen who had wrongly accused him. No, he could not go back above ground. He remembered the beating they had given him and how he had signed his name to a confession, a confession which he had not even read. He had been too tired when they had shouted at him, demanding that he sign his name; he had signed it to end his pain.

He stood and groped about in the darkness. The church singing had stopped. How long had he slept? He did not know. But he felt refreshed and hungry. He doubled his fist nervously, realizing that he could not make a decision. As he walked about he stumbled over an old rusty iron pipe. He picked it up and felt a jagged edge. Yes, there was a brick wall and he could dig into it. What would he find? Smiling, he groped to the brick wall, sat, and began digging idly into damp cement. I can't make any noise, he cautioned himself. As time passed he grew thirsty, but there was no water. He had to kill time or go aboveground. The cement came out of the wall easily; he extracted four bricks and felt a soft draft blowing into his face. He stopped, afraid. What was beyond? He waited a long time and nothing happened; then he began digging again, soundlessly, slowly; he enlarged the hole and crawled through into a dark room and collided with another wall. He felt his way to the right; the wall ended and his fingers toyed in space, like the antennae of an insect.

He fumbled on and his feet struck something hollow, like wood. What's this? He felt with his fingers. Steps . . . He stooped and pulled off his shoes and mounted the stairs and saw a yellow chink of light shining and heard a low voice speaking. He placed his eye to a keyhole and saw the nude waxen figure of a man stretched out upon a white table. The voice, low-pitched and vibrant, mumbled indistinguishable words, neither rising nor falling. He craned his neck and squinted to see the man who was talking, but he could not locate him. Above the naked figure was suspended a huge glass container filled with a blood-red liquid from which a white rubber tube dangled. He crouched closer to the door and saw the tip end of a black object lined with pink satin. A coffin, he breathed. This is an undertaker's establishment . . . A fine-spun lace of ice covered his body and he shuddered. A throaty chuckle sounded in the depths of the yellow room.

He turned to leave. Three steps down it occurred to him that a light switch should be nearby; he felt along the wall, found an electric button, pressed it, and a blinding glare smote his pupils so hard that he was sightless, defenseless. His pupils contracted and he wrinkled his nostrils at a peculiar odor. At once he knew that he had been dimly aware of this odor in the darkness, but the light had brought it sharply to his attention. Some kind of stuff they use to embalm, he thought. He went down the steps and saw piles of lumber, coffins, and a long workbench. In one corner was a tool chest. Yes, he could use tools, could tunnel through walls with them. He lifted the lid of the chest and saw nails, a hammer, a crowbar, a screwdriver, a light bulb, and a long length of electric wire. Good! He would lug these back to his cave.

He was about to hoist the chest to his shoulders when he discovered a door behind the furnace. Where did it lead? He tried to open it and found it securely bolted. Using the crowbar so as to make no sound, he pried the door open; it swung on creaking hinges, outward. Fresh air came to his face and he caught the faint roar of faraway sound. Easy now, he told himself. He widened the door and a lump of coal rattled toward him. A coalbin . . . Evidently the door led into another basement. The roaring noise was louder now, but he could not identify it. Where was he? He groped slowly over the coal pile, then ranged in darkness over a gritty floor. The roaring noise seemed to come from above him, then below. His fingers followed a wall until he touched a wooden ridge. A door, he breathed.

The noise died to a low pitch; he felt his skin prickle. It seemed that he was playing a game with an unseen person whose intelligence outstripped his. He put his ear to the flat surface of the door. Yes, voices . . . Was this a prize fight stadium? The sound of the voices came near and sharp, but he could not tell if they were joyous or despairing. He twisted the knob until he heard a soft click and felt the springy weight of the door swinging toward him. He was afraid to open it, yet captured by curiosity and wonder. He jerked the door wide and saw on the far side of the basement a furnace glowing red. Ten feet away was still another door, half ajar. He crossed and peered through the door into an empty, high-ceilinged corridor that terminated in a dark complex of shadow. The belling voices rolled about him and his eagerness mounted. He stepped into the corridor and the voices swelled louder. He crept on and came to a narrow stairway leading circularly upward; there was no question but that he was going to ascend those stairs.

Mounting the spiraled staircase, he heard the voices roll in a steady wave, then leap to crescendo, only to die away, but always remaining audible. Ahead of him glowed red letters: E—X—I—T. At the top of the steps he paused in front of a black curtain that fluttered uncertainly. He parted the folds and looked into a convex depth that gleamed with clusters of shimmering lights. Sprawling below him was a stretch of human faces, tilted upward, chanting, whistling, screaming, laughing. Dangling before the faces, high upon a screen of silver, were jerking shadows. A movie, he said with slow laughter breaking from his lips.

He stood in a box in the reserved section of a movie house and the impulse he had had to tell the people in the church to stop their singing seized him. These people were laughing at their lives, he thought with amazement. They were shouting and yelling at the animated shadows of themselves. His compassion fired his imagination and he stepped out of the box, walked out upon thin air, walked on down to the audience; and, hovering in the air just above them, he stretched out his hand to touch them . . . His tension snapped and he found himself back in the box, looking down into the sea of faces. No; it could not be done; he could not awaken them. He sighed. Yes, these people were children, sleeping in their living, awake in their dying.

He turned away, parted the black curtain, and looked out. He saw no one. He started down the white stone steps and when he reached the bottom he saw a man in trim blue uniform coming toward him. So used had he become to being underground that he thought that he could walk past the man, as though he were a ghost. But the man stopped. And he stopped.

"Looking for the men's room, sir?" the man asked, and, without waiting for an answer, he turned and pointed. "This way, sir. The first door to your right."

He watched the man turn and walk up the steps and go out of sight. Then he laughed. What a funny fellow! He went back to the basement and stood in the red darkness, watching the glowing embers in the furnace. He went to the sink and turned the faucet and the water flowed in a smooth silent stream that looked like a spout of blood. He brushed the mad image from his mind and began to wash his hands leisurely, looking about for the usual bar of soap. He found one and rubbed it in his palms until a rich lather bloomed in his cupped fingers, like a scarlet sponge. He scrubbed and rinsed his hands meticulously, then hunted for a towel; there was none. He shut off the water, pulled off his shirt, dried his hands on it; when he put it on again he was grateful for the cool dampness that came to his skin.

Yes, he was thirsty; he turned on the faucet again, bowled his fingers and when the water bubbled over the brim of his cupped palms, he drank in long, slow swallows. His bladder grew tight; he shut off the water, faced the wall, bent his head, and watched a red stream strike the floor. His nostrils wrinkled against acrid wisps of vapor; though he had tramped in the waters of the sewer, he stepped back from the wall so that his shoes, wet with sewer slime, would not touch his urine.

He heard footsteps and crawled quickly into the coalbin. Lumps rattled noisily. The footsteps came into the basement and stopped. Who was it? Had someone heard him and come down to investigate? He waited, crouching, sweating. For a long time there was silence, then he heard the clang of metal and a brighter glow lit the room. Somebody's tending the furnace, he thought. Footsteps came closer and he stiffened. Looming before him was a white face lined with coal dust, the face of an old man with watery blue eyes. Highlights spotted his gaunt cheekbones, and he held a huge shovel. There was a screechy scrape of metal against stone, and the old man lifted a shovelful of coal and went from sight.

The room dimmed momentarily, then a yellow glare came as coal flared at the furnace door. Six times the old man came to the bin and went to the furnace with shovels of coal, but not once did he lift his eyes. Finally he dropped the shovel, mopped his face with a dirty handkerchief, and sighed: "Wheeew!" He turned slowly and trudged out of the basement, his footsteps dying away.

He stood, and lumps of coal clattered down the pile. He stepped from the bin and was startled to see the shadowy outline of an electric bulb hanging above his head. Why had not the old man turned it on? Oh, yes . . . He understood. The old man had worked here for so long that he had no need for light; he had learned a way of seeing in his dark world, like those sightless worms that inch along underground by a sense of touch.

His eyes fell upon a lunch pail and he was afraid to hope that it was full. He picked it up; it was heavy. He opened it. *Sandwiches!* He looked guiltily around; he was alone. He searched farther and found a folder of matches and a half-empty tin of tobacco; he put them eagerly into his pocket and clicked off the light. With the lunch pail under his arm, he went through the door, groped over the pile of coal, and stood again in the lighted basement of the undertaking establishment. I've got to get those tools, he told himself. And turn off that light. He tiptoed back up the steps and switched off the light; the invisible voice still droned on behind the door. He crept down and, seeing with his fingers, opened the lunch pail and tore off a piece of paper bag and brought out the tin and spilled grains of tobacco into the makeshift concave. He rolled it and wet it with spittle, then inserted one end into his mouth and lit it: he sucked smoke that bit his lungs. The nicotine reached his brain, went out along his

arms to his finger tips, down to his stomach, and over all the tired nerves of his body.

He carted the tools to the hole he had made in the wall. Would the noise of the falling chest betray him? But he would have to take a chance; he had to have those tools. He lifted the chest and shoved it; it hit the dirt on the other side of the wall with a loud clatter. He waited, listening; nothing happened. Head first, he slithered through and stood in the cave. He grinned, filled with a cunning idea. Yes, he would now go back into the basement of the undertaking establishment and crouch behind the coal pile and dig another hole. Sure! Fumbling, he opened the tool chest and extracted a crowbar, a screwdriver, and a hammer; he fastened them securely about his person.

With another lumpish cigarette in his flexed lips, he crawled back through the hole and over the coal pile and sat, facing the brick wall. He jabbed with the crowbar and the cement sheered away; quicker than he thought, a brick came loose. He worked an hour; the other bricks did not come easily. He sighed, weak from effort. I ought to rest a little, he thought. I'm hungry. He felt his way back to the cave and stumbled along the wall till he came to the tool chest. He sat upon it, opened the lunch pail, and took out two thick sandwiches. He smelled them. Pork chops . . . His mouth watered. He closed his eyes and devoured a sandwich, savoring the smooth rye bread and juicy meat. He ate rapidly, gulping down lumpy mouthfuls that made him long for water. He ate the other sandwich and found an apple and gobbled that up too, sucking the core till the last trace of flavor was drained from it. Then, like a dog, he ground the meat bones with his teeth, enjoying the salty, tangy marrow. He finished and stretched out full length on the ground and went to sleep. . . .

. . . His body was washed by cold

water that gradually turned warm and he was buoyed upon a stream and swept out to sea where waves rolled gently and suddenly he found himself walking upon the water how strange and delightful to walk upon the water and he came upon a nude woman holding a nude baby in her arms and the woman was sinking into the water holding the baby above her head and screaming *help* and he ran over the water to the woman and he reached her just before she went down and he took the baby from her hands and stood watching the breaking bubbles where the woman sank and he called *lady* and still no answer yes dive down there and rescue that woman but he could not take this baby with him and he stooped and laid the baby tenderly upon the surface of the water expecting it to sink but it floated and he leaped into the water and held his breath and strained his eyes to see through the gloomy volume of water but there was no woman and he opened his mouth and called *lady* and the water bubbled and his chest ached and his arms were tired but he could not see the woman and he called again *lady lady* and his feet touched sand at the bottom of the sea and his chest felt as though it would burst and he bent his knees and propelled himself upward and water rushed past him and his head bobbed out and he breathed deeply and looked around where was the baby the baby was gone and he rushed over the water looking for the baby calling *where is it* and the empty sky and sea threw back his voice *where is it* and he began to doubt that he could stand upon the water and then he was sinking and as he struggled the water rushed him downward spinning dizzily and he opened his mouth to call for help and water surged into his lungs and he choked. . . .

He groaned and leaped erect in the dark, his eyes wide. The images of terror that thronged his brain would not let him sleep. He rose, made sure that the tools were hitched to his belt, and groped his way to the coal pile and found the rectangular gap from which he had taken the bricks. He took out the crowbar and hacked. Then dread paralyzed him. How long had he slept? Was it day or night now? He had to be careful. Someone might hear him if it were day. He hewed softly for hours at the cement, working silently. Faintly quivering in the air above him was the dim sound of yelling voices. Crazy people, he muttered. They're still there in that movie . . .

Having rested, he found the digging much easier. He soon had a dozen bricks out. His spirits rose. He took out another brick and his fingers fluttered in space. Good! What lay ahead of him? Another basement? He made the hole larger, climbed through, walked over an uneven floor and felt a metal surface. He lighted a match and saw that he was standing behind a furnace in a basement; before him, on the far side of the room, was a door. He crossed and opened it; it was full of odds and ends. Daylight spilled from a window above his head.

Then he was aware of a soft, continuous tapping. What was it? A clock? No, it was louder than a clock and more irregular. He placed an old empty box beneath the window, stood upon it, and looked into an areaway. He eased the window up and crawled through; the sound of the tapping came clearly now. He glanced about; he was alone. Then he looked upward at a series of window ledges. The tapping identified itself. That's a typewriter, he said to himself. It seemed to be coming from just above. He grasped the ridges of a rain pipe and lifted himself upward; through a half-inch opening of window he saw a doorknob about three feet away. No, it was not a doorknob; it was a small circular disk made of stainless steel with many fine markings upon it. He held his breath, an eerie white hand, seemingly detached from its arm, touched the metal knob and whirled it, first to the left, then to the right. It's a safe! . . . Suddenly he could see the dial no more; a huge metal door swung slowly toward him and he was looking into a safe filled with green wads of paper money, rows of coins wrapped in brown paper, and glass jars and boxes of various sizes. His heart quickened. Good Lord! The white hand went in and out of the safe, taking wads of bills and cylinders of coins. The hand vanished and he heard the muffled click of the big door as it closed. Only the steel dial was visible now. The typewriter still tapped in his ears, but he could not see it. He blinked, wondering if what he had seen was real. There was more money in that safe than he had seen in all his life.

As he clung to the rain pipe, a daring idea came to him and he pulled the screwdriver from his belt. If the white hand twirled that dial again, he would be able to see how far to left and right it spun and he would have the combination! His blood tingled. I can scratch the numbers right here, he thought. Holding the pipe with one hand, he made the sharp edge of the screwdriver bite into the brick wall. Yes, he could do it. Now, he was set. Now, he had a reason for staying here in the underground. He waited for a long time, but the white hand did not return. Goddamn! Had he been more alert, he could have counted the twirls and he would have had the combination. He got down and stood in the areaway, sunk in reflection.

How could he get into that room? He climbed back into the basement and saw wooden steps leading upward. Was that the room where the safe stood? Fearing that the dial was now being twirled, he clambered through the window, hoisted himself up the rain pipe, and peered; he saw only the naked gleam of the steel dial. He got down and doubled his fists. Well, he would explore the basement. He re-turned to the basement room and mounted the steps to the door and squinted through the keyhole; all was dark, but the tapping was still some-where near, still faint and directionless. He pushed the door in; along one wall of a room was a table piled with radios and electrical equipment. A radio shop, he muttered.

Well, he could rig up a radio in his cave. He found a sack, slid the radio into it, and slung it across his back. Closing the door, he went down the steps and stood again in the basement, disappointed. He had not solved the problem of the steel dial and he was irked. He set the radio on the floor and again hoisted himself through the win-dow and up the rain pipe and squinted; the metal door was swinging shut. God-damn! He's worked the combination again. If I had been patient, I'd have had it! How could he get into that room? He *had* to get into it. He could jimmy the window, but it would be much better if he could get in without any traces. To the right of him, he cal-culated, should be the basement of the building that held the safe; therefore, if he dug a hole right *here,* he ought to reach his goal.

He began a quiet scraping; it was hard work, for the bricks were not damp. He eventually got one out and lowered it softly to the floor. He had to be careful; perhaps people were be-yond this wall. He extracted a second layer of brick and found still another. He gritted his teeth, ready to quit. I'll dig one more, he resolved. When the next brick came out he felt air blowing into his face. He waited to be chal-lenged, but nothing happened.

He enlarged the hole and pulled himself through and stood in quiet darkness. He scratched a match to flame and saw steps; he mounted and peered through a keyhole: Darkness . . . He strained to hear the typewriter, but there was only silence. Maybe the office had closed? He twisted the knob and swung the door in; a frigid blast made him shiver. In the shadows before him were halves and quarters of hogs and lambs and steers hanging from metal hooks on the low ceiling, red meat encased in folds of cold white fat. Fronting him was frost-coated glass from behind which came indistinguishable sounds. The odor of fresh raw meat sickened him and he backed away. A meat market, he whispered.

He ducked his head, suddenly blinded by light. He narrowed his eyes; the red-white rows of meat were drenched in yellow glare. A man wearing a crimson-spotted jacket came in and took down a bloody meat cleaver. He eased the door to, holding it ajar just enough to watch the man, hoping that the darkness in which he stood would keep him from being seen. The man took down a hunk of steer and placed it upon a bloody wooden block and bent forward and whacked it with the cleaver. The man's face was hard, square, grim; a jet of mustache smudged his upper lip and a glistening cowlick of hair fell over his left eye. Each time he lifted the cleaver and brought it down upon the meat, he let out a short, deep-chested grunt. After he had cut the meat, he wiped blood off the wooden block with a sticky wad of gunny sack and hung the cleaver upon a hook. His face was proud as he placed the chunk of meat in the crook of his elbow and left.

The door slammed and the light went off; once more he stood in shadow. His tension ebbed. From behind the frosted glass he heard the man's voice: "Forty-eight cents a pound, ma'am." He shuddered, feeling that there was something he had to do. But what? He stared fixedly at the cleaver, then he sneezed and was terrified for fear that the man had heard him. But the door did not open. He took down the cleaver and examined the sharp edge smeared with cold blood. Behind the ice-coated glass a cash register rang with a vibrating, musical tinkle.

Absent-mindedly holding the meat cleaver, he rubbed the glass with his thumb and cleared a spot that enabled him to see into the front of the store. The shop was empty, save for the man who was now putting on his hat and coat. Beyond the front window a wan sun shone in the streets; people passed and now and then a fragment of laughter or the whir of a speeding auto came to him. He peered closer and saw on the right counter of the shop a mosquito netting covering pears, grapes, lemons, oranges, bananas, peaches, and plums. His stomach contracted.

The man clicked out the light and he gritted his teeth, muttering, Don't lock the ice box door . . . The man went through the door of the shop and locked it from the outside. Thank God! Now, he would eat some more! He waited, trembling. The sun died and its rays lingered on in the sky, turning the streets to dusk. He opened the door and stepped inside the shop. In reverse letters across the front window was: NICK'S FRUITS AND MEATS. He laughed, picked up a soft ripe yellow pear and bit into it; juice squirted; his mouth ached as his saliva glands reacted to the acid of the fruit. He ate three pears, gobbled six bananas, and made away with several oranges, taking a bite out of their tops and holding them to his lips and squeezing them as he hungrily sucked the juice.

He found a faucet, turned it on, laid the cleaver aside, pursed his lips under the stream until his stomach felt about to burst. He straightened and belched, feeling satisfied for the first time since he had been underground. He sat upon the floor, rolled and lit a cigarette, his bloodshot eyes squinting against the film of drifting smoke. He watched a patch of sky turn red, then purple; night fell and he lit another cigarette, brooding. Some part of him was trying to remember the world he had left, and another part of him did not want to remember it. Sprawling before him in his mind was his wife, Mrs. Wooten for whom he worked, the three policemen who had picked him up. . . . He possessed them now more completely than he had ever possessed them when he had lived above ground. How this had come about he could not say, but he had no desire to go back to them. He laughed, crushed the cigarette, and stood up.

He went to the front door and gazed out. Emotionally he hovered between the world aboveground and the world underground. He longed to go out, but sober judgment urged him to remain here. Then impulsively he pried the lock loose with one swift twist of the crowbar; the door swung outward. Through the twilight he saw a white man and a white woman coming toward him. He held himself tense, waiting for them to pass; but they came directly to the door and confronted him.

"I want to buy a pound of grapes," the woman said.

Terrified, he stepped back into the store. The white man stood to one side and the woman entered.

"Give me a pound of the dark ones," the woman said.

The white man came slowly forward, blinking his eyes.

"Where's Nick?" the man asked.

"Were you just closing?" the woman asked.

"Yes, ma'am," he mumbled. For a second he did not breathe, then he mumbled again: "Yes, ma'am."

"I'm sorry," the woman said.

The street lamps came on, lighting the store somewhat. Ought he run? But that would raise an alarm. He moved slowly, dreamily, to a counter and lifted up a bunch of grapes and showed them to the woman.

"Fine," the woman said. "But isn't that more than a pound?"

He did not answer. The man was staring at him intently.

"Put them in a bag for me," the woman said, fumbling with her purse.

"Yes, ma'am."

He saw a pile of paper bags under a narrow ledge; he opened one and put the grapes in.

"Thanks," the woman said, taking the bag and placing a dime in his dark palm.

"Where's Nick?" the man asked again. "At supper?"

"Sir? Yes, sir," he breathed.

They left the store and he stood trembling in the doorway. When they were out of sight, he burst out laughing and crying. A trolley car rolled noisily past and he controlled himself quickly. He flung the dime to the pavement with a gesture of contempt and stepped into the warm night air. A few shy stars trembled above him. The look of things was beautiful, yet he felt a lurking threat. He went to an unattended newsstand and looked at a stack of papers. He saw a headline: HUNT NEGRO FOR MURDER.

He felt that someone had slipped up on him from behind and was stripping off his clothes; he looked about wildly, went quickly back into the store, picked up the meat cleaver where he had left it near the sink, then made his way through the icebox to the basement. He stood for a long time, breathing heavily. They know I didn't do anything, he muttered. But how could he prove it? He had signed a confession. Though innocent, he felt guilty, condemned. He struck a match and held it near the steel blade, fascinated and repelled by the dried blotches of blood. Then his fingers gripped the handle of the cleaver with all the strength of his body, he wanted to fling the cleaver from him, but he could not. The match flame wavered and fled; he struggled through the hole and put the cleaver in the sack with the radio. He was determined to keep it, for what purpose he did not know.

He was about to leave when he remembered the safe. Where was it? He wanted to give up, but felt that he ought to make one more try. Opposite the last hole he had dug, he tunneled again, plying the crowbar. Once he was so exhausted that he lay on the concrete floor and panted. Finally he made another hole. He wriggled through and his nostrils filled with the fresh smell of coal. He struck a match; yes, the usual steps led upward. He tiptoed to a door and eased it open. A fair-haired white girl stood in front of a steel cabinet, her blue eyes wide upon him. She turned chalky and gave a high-pitched scream. He bounded down the steps and raced to his hole and clambered through, replacing the bricks with nervous haste. He paused hearing loud voices.

"What's the matter, Alice?"

"A man . . ."

"What man? Where?"

"A man was at that door . . ."

"Oh, nonsense!"

"He was looking at me through the door!"

"Aw, you're dreaming."

"I *did* see a man!"

The girl was crying now.

"There's nobody here."

Another man's voice sounded.

"What is it, Bob?"

"Alice says she saw a man in here, in that door!"

"Let's take a look."

He waited, poised for flight. Footsteps descended the stairs.

"There's nobody down here."

"The window's locked."

"And there's no door."

"You ought to fire that dame."

"Oh, I don't know. Women are that way."

"She's too hysterical."

The men laughed. Footsteps sounded again on the stairs. A door slammed. He sighed, relieved that he had escaped. But he had not done what he had set out to do; his glimpse of the room had been too brief to determine if the safe was there. He had to know. Boldly he groped through the hole once more; he reached the steps and pulled off his shoes and tip-toed up and peered through the keyhole. His head accidentally touched the door and it swung silently in a fraction of an inch; he saw the girl bent over the cabinet, her back to him. Beyond her was the safe. He crept back down the steps, thinking exultingly: I found it!

Now he had to get the combination. Even if the window in the areaway was locked and bolted, he could gain entrance when the office closed. He scoured through the holes he had dug and stood again in the basement where he had left the radio and the cleaver. Again he crawled out of the window and lifted himself up the rain pipe and peered. The steel dial showed lonely and bright, reflecting the yellow glow of an unseen light. Resigned to a long wait, he sat and leaned against the wall. From far off came the faint sounds of life aboveground; once he looked with a baffled expression at the dark sky. Frequently he rose and climbed the pipe to see the white hand spin the dial, but nothing happened. He bit his lip with impatience. It was not the money that was luring him, but the mere fact that he could get it with impunity. Was the hand now twirling the dial? He rose and looked, but the white hand was not in sight.

Perhaps it would be better to watch continuously? Yes; he slung to the pipe and watched the dial until his eyes thickened with tears. Exhausted, he stood again in the areaway. He heard a door being shut and he clawed up the pipe and looked. He jerked tense as a vague figure passed in front of him. He stared unblinkingly, hugging the pipe with one hand and holding the screwdriver with the other, ready to etch the combination upon the wall. His ears caught: *Dong . . . Dong . . . Dong . . . Dong . . . Dong . . . Dong . . . Dong . . .* Seven o'clock, he whispered. Maybe they were closing now? What kind of store would be open as late as this? he wondered. Did anyone live in the rear? Was there a night watchman? Perhaps the safe was *already* locked for the night! Goddamn! While he had been eating in that shop, they had locked up everything. . . Then, just as he was about to give up, the white hand touched the dial and turned it once to the right and stopped at six. With quivering fingers, he etched 1–R–6 upon the brick wall with the tip of the screwdriver. The hand twirled the dial twice to the left and stopped at two, and he engraved 2–L–2 upon the wall. The dial was spun four times to the right and stopped at six again; he wrote 4–R–6. The dial rotated three times to the left and was centered straight up and down; he wrote 3–L–0. The door swung open and again he saw the piles of green money and the rows of wrapped coins. I got it, he said grimly.

Then he was stone still, astonished. There were two hands now. A right hand lifted a wad of green bills and deftly slipped it up the sleeve of the left arm. The hands trembled; again the right hand slipped a packet of bills up the left sleeve. He's stealing, he said to himself. He grew indignant, as if the money belonged to him. Though *he* had planned to steal the money, he despised and pitied the man. He felt that his stealing the money and the man's stealing were two entirely different things. He wanted to steal the money merely for the sensation involved in getting it, and he had no intention whatever of spending a penny of it; but he knew that the man who was now stealing it was going to spend it, perhaps for pleasure. The huge steel door closed with a soft click.

Though angry, he was somewhat satisfied. The office would close soon. I'll clean the place out, he mused. He imagined the entire office staff cringing with fear; the police would question everyone for a crime they had not committed, just as they had questioned him. And they would have no idea of how the money had been stolen until they discovered the holes he had tunneled in the walls of the basements. He

lowered himself and laughed mischievously, with the abandoned glee of an adolescent.

He flattened himself against the wall as the window above him closed with rasping sound. He looked; somebody was bolting the window securely with a metal screen. That won't help you, he snickered to himself. He clung to the rain pipe until the yellow light in the office went out. He went back into the basement, picked up the sack containing the radio and cleaver, and crawled through the two holes he had dug and groped his way into the basement of the building that held the safe. He moved in slow motion, breathing softly. Be careful now, he told himself. There might be a night watchman. . . . In his memory was the combination written in bold white characters as upon a blackboard. Eel-like he squeezed through the last hole and crept up the steps and put his hand on the knob and pushed the door in about three inches. Then his courage ebbed; his imagination wove dangers for him.

Perhaps the night watchman was waiting in there, ready to shoot. He dangled his cap on a forefinger and poked it past the jamb of the door. If anyone fired, they would hit his cap; but nothing happened. He widened the door, holding the crowbar high above his head, ready to beat off an assailant. He stood like that for five minutes; the rumble of a streetcar brought him to himself. He entered the room. Moonlight floated in from a side window. He confronted the safe, then checked himself. Better take a look around first . . . He stepped about and found a closed door. Was the night watchman in there? He opened it and saw a washbowl, a faucet, and a commode. To the left was still another door that opened into a huge dark room that seemed empty; on the far side of that room he made out the shadow of still another door. Nobody's here, he told himself. He turned back to the safe and fingered the dial; it spun with ease. He laughed and twirled it just for fun. Get to work, he told himself. He turned the dial to the figures he saw on the blackboard of his memory; it was so easy that he felt that the safe had not been locked at all. The heavy door eased loose and he caught hold of the handle and pulled hard, but the door swung open with a slow momentum of its own. Breathless, he gaped at wads of green bills, rows of wrapped coins, curious glass jars full of white pellets, and many oblong green metal boxes. He glanced guiltily over his shoulder; it seemed impossible that someone should not call to him to stop.

They'll be surprised in the morning, he thought. He opened the top of the sack and lifted a wad of compactly tied bills; the money was crisp and new. He admired the smooth, cleancut edges. The fellows in Washington sure know how to make this stuff, he mused. He rubbed the money with his fingers, as though expecting it to reveal hidden qualities. He lifted the wad to his nose and smelled the fresh odor of ink. Just like any other paper, he mumbled. He dropped the wad into the sack and picked up another. Holding the bag, he thought and laughed.

There was in him no sense of possessiveness; he was intrigued with the form and color of the money, with the manifold reactions which he knew that men aboveground held toward it. The sack was one-third full when it occurred to him to examine the denominations of the bills; without realizing it, he had put many wads of one-dollar bills into the sack. Aw, nuts, he said in disgust. Take the big ones . . . He dumped the one-dollar bills onto the floor and swept all the hundred-dollar bills he could find into the sack, then he raked in rolls of coins with crooked fingers.

He walked to a desk upon which sat a typewriter, the same machine which the blond girl had used. He was fascinated by it; never in his life had he

used one of them. It was a queer instrument of business, something beyond the rim of his life. Whenever he had been in an office where a girl was typing, he had almost always spoken in whispers. Remembering vaguely what he had seen others do, he inserted a sheet of paper into the machine; it went in lopsided and he did not know how to straighten it. Spelling in a soft diffident voice, he pecked out his name on the keys: *freddaniels*. He looked at it and laughed. He would learn to type correctly one of these days.

Yes, he would take the typewriter too. He lifted the machine and placed it atop the bulk of money in the sack. He did not feel that he was stealing, for the cleaver, the radio, the money, and the typewriter were all on the same level of value, all meant the same thing to him. They were the serious toys of the men who lived in the dead world of sunshine and rain he had left, the world that had condemned him, branded him guilty.

But what kind of a place is this? He wondered. What was in that dark room to his rear? He felt for his matches and found that he had only one left. He leaned the sack against the safe and groped forward into the room, encountering smooth, metallic objects that felt like machines. Baffled, he touched a wall and tried vainly to locate an electric switch. Well, he *had* to strike his last match. He knelt and struck it, cupping the flame near the floor with his palms. The place seemed to be a factory, with benches and tables. There were bulbs with green shades spaced about the tables; he turned on a light and twisted it low so that the glare was limited. He saw a half-filled packet of cigarettes and appropriated it. There were stools at the benches and he concluded that men worked here at some trade. He wandered and found a few half-used folders of matches. If only he could find more cigarettes! But there were none.

But what kind of a place was this?

On a bench he saw a pad of paper captioned: PEER'S — MANUFACTURING JEWELERS. His lips formed an "O," then he snapped off the light and ran back to the safe and lifted one of the glass jars and stared at the tiny white pellets. Gingerly he picked up one and found that it was wrapped in tissue paper. He peeled the paper and saw a glittering stone that looked like glass, glinting white and blue sparks. Diamonds, he breathed.

Roughly he tore the paper from the pellets and soon his palm quivered with precious fire. Trembling, he took all four glass jars from the safe and put them into the sack. He grabbed one of the metal boxes, shook it, and heard a tinny rattle. He pried off the lid with the screwdriver. Rings! Hundreds of them . . . Were they worth anything? He scooped up a handful and jets of fire shot fitfully from the stones. These are diamonds too, he said. He pried open another box. Watches! A chorus of soft, metallic ticking filled his ears. For a moment he could not move, then he dumped all the boxes into the sack.

He shut the safe door, then stood looking around, anxious not to overlook anything. Oh! He had seen a door in the room where the machines were. What was in there? More valuables? He re-entered the room, crossed the floor, and stood undecided before the door. He finally caught hold of the knob and pushed the door in; the room beyond was dark. He advanced cautiously inside and ran his fingers along the wall for the usual switch, then he was stark still. *Something had moved in the room!* What was it? Ought he to creep out, taking the rings and diamonds and money? Why risk what he already had? He waited and the ensuing silence gave him confidence to explore further. Dare he strike a match? Would not a match flame make him a good target? He tensed again as he heard a faint sigh; he was now convinced that there was something alive near him, something that lived and breathed. On tiptoe he felt slowly along the wall, hoping that he would not collide with anything. Luck was with him; he found the light switch.

No; don't turn the light on . . . Then suddenly he realized that he did not know in what direction the door was. Goddamn! He had to turn the light on or strike a match. He fingered the switch for a long time, then thought of an idea. He knelt upon the floor, reached his arm up to the switch and flicked the button, hoping that if anyone shot, the bullet would go above his head. The moment the light came on he narrowed his eyes to see quickly. He sucked in his breath and his body gave a violent twitch and was still. In front of him, so close that it made him want to bound up and scream, was a human face.

He was afraid to move lest he touch the man. If the man had opened his eyes at that moment, there was no telling what he might have done. The man —long and rawboned—was stretched out on his back upon a little cot, sleeping in his clothes; his head cushioned by a dirty pillow, his face, clouded by a dark stubble of beard, looked straight up to the ceiling. The man sighed, and he grew tense to defend himself; the man mumbled and turned his face away from the light. I've got to turn off that light, he thought. Just as he was about to rise, he saw a gun and cartridge belt on the floor at the man's side. Yes, he would take the gun and cartridge belt, not to use them, but just to keep them, as one takes a memento from a country fair. He picked them up and was about to click off the light when his eyes fell upon a photograph perched upon a chair near the man's head; it was the picture of a woman, smiling, shown against a background of open fields; at the woman's side were two young children, a boy and a girl. He smiled indulgently; he could send a bullet into that man's brain and time would be over for him. . . .

He clicked off the light and crept

silently back into the room where the safe stood; he fastened the cartridge belt about him and adjusted the holster at his right hip. He strutted about the room on tiptoe, lolling his head nonchalantly, then paused abruptly, pulled the gun, and pointed it with grim face toward an imaginary foe. "Boom!" he whispered fiercely. Then he bent forward with silent laughter. That's just like they do it in the movies, he said.

He contemplated his loot for a long time, then got a towel from the washroom and tied the sack securely. When he looked up he was momentarily frightened by his shadow looming on the wall before him. He lifted the sack, dragged it down the basement steps, lugged it across the basement, gasping for breath. After he had struggled through the hole, he clumsily replaced the bricks, then tussled with the sack until he got it to the cave. He stood in the dark, wet with sweat, brooding about the diamonds, the rings, the watches, the money; he remembered the singing in the church, the people yelling in the movie, the dead baby, the nude man stretched out upon the white table. . . . He saw these items hovering before his eyes and felt that some dim meaning linked them together, that some magical relationship made them kin. He stared with vacant eyes, convinced that all of these images, with their tongueless reality, were striving to tell him something. . . .

Later, seeing with his fingers, he untied the sack and set each item neatly upon the dirt floor. Exploring, he took the bulb, the socket, and the wire out of the tool chest; he was elated to find a double socket at one end of the wire. He crammed the stuff into his pockets and hoisted himself upon the rusty pipes and squinted into the church; it was dim and empty. Somewhere in this wall were live electric wires; but where? He lowered himself, groped and tapped the wall with the butt of the screwdriver, listening vainly for hollow sounds. I'll just take a chance and dig, he said.

For an hour he tried to dislodge a brick, and when he struck a match, he found that he had dug a depth of only an inch! No use in digging here, he sighed. By the flickering light of a match, he looked upward, then lowered his eyes, only to glance up again, startled. Directly above his head, beyond the pipes, was a wealth of electric wiring. I'll be damned, he snickered.

He got an old dull knife from the chest and, seeing again with his fingers, separated the two strands of wire and cut away the insulation. Twice he received a slight shock. He scraped the wiring clean and managed to join the two twin ends, then screwed in the bulb. The sudden illumination blinded him and he shut his lids to kill the pain in his eyeballs. I've got that much done, he thought jubilantly.

He placed the bulb on the dirt floor and the light cast a blatant glare on the bleak clay walls. Next he plugged one end of the wire that dangled from the radio into the light socket and bent down and switched on the button; almost at once there was the harsh sound of static, but no words or music. Why won't it work? he wondered. Had he damaged the mechanism in any way? Maybe it needed grounding? Yes . . . He rummaged in the tool chest and found another length of wire, fastened it to the ground of the radio, and then tied the opposite end to a pipe. Rising and growing distinct, a slow strain of music entranced him with its measured sound. He sat upon the chest, deliriously happy.

Later he searched again in the chest and found a half-gallon can of glue; he opened it and smelled a sharp odor. Then he recalled that he had not even looked at the money. He took a wad of green bills and weighed it in his palm, then broke the seal and held one of the bills up to the light and studied it closely. *The United States of America will pay to the bearer on demand one hundred dollars,* he head in slow speech; then: *This note is legal tender for all debts, public and private. . . .* He broke into a musing laugh, feeling that he was reading of the doings of people who lived on some far-off planet. He turned the bill over and saw on the other side of it a delicately beautiful building gleaming with paint and set amidst green grass. He had no desire whatever to count the money; it was what it stood for—the various currents of life swirling aboveground—that captivated him. Next he opened the rolls of coins and let them slide from their paper wrappings to the ground; the bright, new gleaming pennies and nickles and dimes piled high at his feet, a glowing mound of shimmering copper and silver. He sifted them through his fingers, listening to their tinkle as they struck the conical heap.

Oh, yes! He had forgotten. He would now write his name on the typewriter. He inserted a piece of paper and poised his fingers to write. But what was his name? He stared, trying to remember. He stood and glared about the dirt cave, his name on the tip of his lips. But it would not come to him. Why was he here? Yes, he had been running away from the police. But why? His mind was blank. He bit his lips and sat again, feeling a vague terror. But why worry? He laughed, then pecked slowly: *itwasalonghotday.* He was determined to type the sentence without making any mistakes. How did one make capital letters? He experimented and luckily discovered how to lock the machine for capital letters and then shift it back to lower case. Next he discovered how to make spaces, then he wrote neatly and correctly: *It was a long hot day.* Just why he selected that sentence he did not know; it was merely the ritual of performing the thing that appealed to him. He took the sheet out of the machine and looked around with stiff

neck and hard eyes and spoke to an imaginary person:

"Yes, I'll have the contracts ready tomorrow."

He laughed. That's just the way they talk, he said. He grew weary of the game and pushed the machine aside. His eyes fell upon the can of glue, and a mischievous idea bloomed in him, filling him with nervous eagerness. He leaped up and opened the can of glue, then broke the seals on all the wads of money. I'm going to have some wallpaper, he said with a luxurious, physical laugh that made him bend at the knees. He took the towel with which he had tied the sack and balled it into a swab and dipped it into the can of glue and dabbed glue onto the wall; then he pasted one green bill by the side of another. He stepped back and cocked his head. Jesus! That's funny. . . . He slapped his thighs and guffawed. He had triumphed over the world aboveground! He was free! If only people could see this! He wanted to run from this cave and yell his discovery to the world.

He swabbed all the dirt walls of the cave and pasted them with green bills; when he had finished the walls blazed with a yellow-green fire. Yes, this room would be his hide-out; between him and the world that had branded him guilty would stand this mocking symbol. He had not stolen the money; he had simply picked it up, just as a man would pick up firewood in a forest. And that was how the world aboveground now seemed to him, a wild forest filled with death.

The walls of money finally palled on him and he looked about for new interests to feed his emotions. The cleaver! He drove a nail into the wall and hung the bloody cleaver upon it. Still another idea welled up. He pried open the metal boxes and lined them side by side on the dirt floor. He grinned at the gold and fire. From one box he lifted up a fistful of ticking gold watches and dangled them by their gleaming chains. He stared with an idle smile, then began to wind them up; he did not attempt to set them at any given hour, for there was no time for him now. He took a fistful of nails and drove them into the papered walls and hung the watches upon them, letting them swing down by their glittering chains, trembling and ticking busily against the backdrop of green with the lemon sheen of the electric light shining upon the metal watch casings, converting the golden disks into blobs of liquid yellow. Hardly had he hung up the last watch than the idea extended itself; he took more nails from the chest and drove them into the green paper and took the boxes of rings and went from nail to nail and hung up the golden bands. The blue and white sparks from the stones filled the cave with brittle laughter, as though enjoying his hilarious secret. People certainly can do some funny things, he said to himself.

He sat upon the tool chest, alternately laughing and shaking his head soberly. Hours later he became conscious of the gun sagging at his hip and he pulled it from the holster. He had seen men fire guns in movies, but somehow his life had never led him into contact with firearms. A desire to feel the sensation others felt in firing came over him. But someone might hear . . . Well, what if they did? They would not know where the shot had come from. Not in their wildest notions would they think that it had come from under the streets! He tightened his fingers on the trigger; there was a deafening report and it seemed that the entire underground had caved in upon his eardrums; and in the same instant there flashed an orange-blue spurt of flame that died quickly but lingered on as a vivid after-image. He smelled the acrid stench of burnt powder filling his lungs and he dropped the gun abruptly.

The intensity of his feelings died and he hung the gun and cartridge belt upon the wall. Next he lifted the jars of diamonds and turned them bottom upward, dumping the white pellets upon the ground. One by one he picked them up and peeled the tissue paper from them and piled them in a neat heap. He wiped his sweaty hands on his trousers, lit a cigarette, and commenced playing another game. He imagined that he was a rich man who lived aboveground in the obscene sunshine and he was strolling through a park of a summer morning, smiling, nodding to his neighbors, sucking an after-breakfast cigar. Many times he crossed the floor of the cave, avoiding the diamonds with his feet, yet subtly gauging his footsteps so that his shoes, wet with sewer slime, would strike the diamonds at some undetermined moment. After twenty minutes of sauntering, his right foot smashed into the heap and diamonds lay scattered in all directions, glinting with a million tiny chuckles of icy laughter. Oh, shucks, he mumbled in mock regret, intrigued by the damage he had wrought. He continued walking, ignoring the brittle fire. He felt that he had a glorious victory locked in his heart.

He stooped and flung the diamonds more evenly over the floor and they showered rich sparks, collaborating with him. He went over the floor and trampled the stones just deeply enough for them to be faintly visible, as though they were set deliberately in the prongs of a thousand rings. A ghostly light bathed the cave. He sat on the chest and frowned. Maybe *any*thing's right, he mumbled. Yes, if the world as men had made it was right, then anything else was right, any act a man took to satisfy himself, murder, theft, torture.

He straightened with a start. What was happening to him? He was drawn to these crazy thoughts, yet they made him feel vaguely guilty. He would stretch out upon the ground, then get up; he would want to crawl again through the holes he had dug, but would restrain himself; he would think of going again up into the streets, but fear would hold him still. He stood in the middle of the cave, surrounded by green walls and a laughing floor, trembling. He was going to do something, but what? Yes, he was afraid of himself, afraid of doing some nameless thing.

To control himself, he turned on the radio. A melancholy piece of music rose. Brooding over the diamonds on the floor was like looking up into a sky full of restless stars; then the illusion turned into its opposite: he was high up in the air looking down at the twinkling lights of a sprawling city. The music ended and a man recited news events. In the same attitude in which he had contemplated the city, so now, as he heard the cultivated tone, he looked down upon land and sea as men fought, as cities were razed, as planes scattered death upon open towns, as long lines of trenches wavered and broke. He heard the names of generals and the names of mountains and the names of countries and the names and numbers of divisions that were in action on different battle fronts. He saw black smoke billowing from the stacks of warships as they neared each other over wastes of water and he heard their huge guns thunder as red-hot shells screamed across the surface of night seas. He saw hundreds of planes wheeling and droning in the sky and heard the clatter of machine guns as they fought each other and he saw planes falling in plumes of smoke and blaze of fire. He saw steel tanks rumbling across fields of ripe wheat to meet other tanks and there was a loud clang of steel as numberless tanks collided. He saw troops with fixed bayonets charging in waves against other troops who held fixed bayonets and men groaned as steel ripped into their bodies and they went down to die. . . . The voice on the radio faded and he was staring at the diamonds on the floor at his feet.

He shut off the radio, fighting an irrational compulsion to act. He walked aimlessly about the cave, touching the walls with his fingertips. Suddenly he stood still. *What was the matter with him?* Yes, he knew. . . . It was these walls; these crazy walls were filling him with a wild urge to climb out into the dark sunshine aboveground. Quickly he doused the light to banish the shouting walls, then sat again upon the tool chest. Yes, he was trapped. His muscles were flexed taut and sweat ran down his face. He knew now that he could not stay here and he could not go out. He lit a cigarette with shaking fingers; the match flame revealed the green-papered walls with militant distinctness; the purple on the gun barrel glinted like a threat; the meat cleaver brooded with its eloquent splotches of blood; the mound of silver and copper smoldered angrily; the diamonds winked at him from the floor; and the gold watches ticked and trembled, crowning time the king of consciousness, defining the limits of living. . . . The match blaze died and he bolted from where he stood and collided brutally with the nails upon the walls. The spell was broken. He shuddered, feeling that, in spite of his fear, sooner or later he would go up into that dead sunshine and somehow say something to somebody about all this.

He sat again upon the tool chest. Fatigue weighed upon his forehead and eyes. Minutes passed and he relaxed. He dozed, but his imagination was alert. He saw himself rising, wading again in the sweeping water of the sewer; he came to a manhole and climbed out and was amazed to discover that he had hoisted himself into a room filled with armed policemen who were watching him intently. He jumped awake in the dark; he had not moved. He sighed, closed his eyes, and slept again; this time his imagination designed a scheme of protection for him. His dreaming made him feel that he was standing in a room watching over his own nude body lying stiff and cold upon a white table. At the far end of the room he saw a crowd of people huddled in a corner, afraid of his body. Though lying dead upon the table, he was standing in some mysterious way at his side, warding off the people, guarding his body, and laughing to himself as he observed the situation. They're scared of me, he thought.

He awakened with a start, leaped to his feet, and stood in the center of the black cave. It was a full minute before he moved again. He hovered between sleeping and waking, unprotected, a prey of wild fears. He could neither see nor hear. One part of him was asleep; his blood coursed slowly and his flesh was numb. On the other hand he was roused to a strange, high pitch of tension. He lifted his fingers to his face, as though about to weep. Gradually his hands lowered and he struck a match, looking about, expecting to see a door through which he could walk to safety; but there was no door, only the green walls and the moving floor. The match flame died and it was dark again.

Five minutes later he was still standing when the thought came to him that he had been asleep. Yes . . . But he was not yet fully awake; he was still queerly blind and deaf. How long had he slept? Where was he? Then suddenly he recalled the green-papered walls of the cave and in the same instant he heard loud singing coming from the church beyond the wall. Yes, they woke me up, he muttered. He hoisted himself and lay atop the bed of pipes and brought his face to the narrow slit. Men and women stood here and there between pews. A song ended and a young black girl tossed back her head and closed her eyes and broke plaintively into another hymn:

Glad, glad, glad, oh, so glad
I got Jesus in my soul . . .

Those few words were all she sang, but what her words did not say, her emotions said as she repeated the lines, varying the mood and tempo, making her tone express meanings which her conscious mind did not know. Another woman melted her voice with the girl's, and then an old man's voice merged with that of the two women. Soon the entire congregation was singing:

Glad, glad, glad, oh, so glad
I got Jesus in my soul . . .

They're wrong, he whispered in the lyric darkness. He felt that their search for a happiness they could never find made them feel that they had committed some dreadful offense which they could not remember or understand. He was now in possession of the feeling that had gripped him when he had first come into the underground. It came to him in a series of questions: Why was this sense of guilt so seemingly innate, so easy to come by, to think, to feel, so verily physical? It seemed that when one felt this guilt one was retracing in one's feelings a faint pattern designed long before; it seemed that one was always trying to remember a gigantic shock that had left a haunting impression upon one's body which one could not forget or shake off, but which had been forgotten by the conscious mind, creating in one's life a state of eternal anxiety.

He had to tear himself away from this; he got down from the pipes. His nerves were so taut that he seemed to feel his brain pushing through his skull. He felt that he had to do something, but he could not figure out what it was. Yet he knew that if he stood here until he made up his mind, he would never move. He crawled through the hole he had made in the brick wall and the exertion afforded him respite from tension. When he entered the basement of the radio store, he stopped in fear, hearing loud voices.

"Come on, boy! Tell us what you did with the radio!"

"Mister, I didn't steal the radio! I swear!"

He heard a dull thumping sound and he imagined a boy being struck violently.

"Please, mister!"

"Did you take it to a pawn shop?"

"No, sir! I didn't steal the radio! I got a radio at home," the boy's voice pleaded hysterically. "Go to my home and look!"

There came to his ears the sound of another blow. It was so funny that he had to clap his hand over his mouth to keep from laughing out loud. They're beating some poor boy, he whispered to himself, shaking his head. He felt a sort of distant pity for the boy and wondered if he ought to bring back the radio and leave it in the basement. No. Perhaps it was a good thing that they were beating the boy; perhaps the beating would bring to the boy's attention, for the first time in his life, the secret of his existence, the guilt that he could never get rid of.

Smiling, he scampered over a coal pile and stood again in the basement of the building where he had stolen the money and jewelry. He lifted himself into the areaway, climbed the rain pipe, and squinted through a two-inch opening of window. The guilty familiarity of what he saw made his muscles tighten. Framed before him in a bright tableau of daylight was the night watchman sitting upon the edge of a chair, stripped to the waist, his head sagging forward, his eyes red and puffy. The watchman's face and shoulders were stippled with red and black welts. Back of the watchman stood the safe, the steel door wide open showing the empty vault. Yes, they think he did it, he mused.

Footsteps sounded in the room and a man in a blue suit passed in front of him, then another, then still another. Policemen, he breathed. Yes, they were trying to make the watchman confess, just as they had once made him confess to a crime he had not done. He stared

into the room, trying to recall something. Oh . . . Those were the same policemen who had beaten him, had made him sign that paper when he had been too tired and sick to care. Now, they were doing the same thing to the watchman. His heart pounded as he saw one of the policemen shake a finger into the watchman's face.

"Why don't you admit it's an inside job, Thompson?" the policeman said.

"I've told you all I know," the watchman mumbled through swollen lips.

"But nobody was here but you!" the policeman shouted.

"I was sleeping," the watchman said. "It was wrong, but I was sleeping all that night!"

"Stop telling us that lie!"

"It's the truth!"

"When did you get the combination?"

"I don't know how to open the safe," the watchman said.

He clung to the rain pipe, tense; he wanted to laugh, but he controlled himself. He felt a great sense of power; yes, he could go back to the cave, rip the money off the walls, pick up the diamonds and rings, and bring them here and write a note, telling them where to look for their foolish toys. No . . . What good would that do? It was not worth the effort. The watchman was guilty; although he was not guilty of the crime of which he had been accused, he was guilty, had always been guilty. The only thing that worried him was that the man who had been really stealing was not being accused. But he consoled himself: they'll catch him sometime during his life.

He saw one of the policemen slap the watchman across the mouth.

"Come clean, you bastard!"

"I've told you all I know," the watchman mumbled like a child.

One of the policemen went to the rear of the watchman's chair and jerked it from under him; the watchman pitched forward upon his face.

"Get up!" a policeman said.

Trembling, the watchman pulled himself up and sat limply again in the chair.

"Now, are you going to talk?"

"I've told you all I know," the watchman gasped.

"Where did you hide the stuff?"

"I didn't take it!"

"Thompson, your brains are in your feet," one of the policemen said. "We're going to string you up and get them back into your skull."

He watched the policemen clamp handcuffs on the watchman's wrists and ankles; then they lifted the watchman and swung him upside-down and hoisted his feet to the edge of a door. The watchman hung, head down, his eyes bulging. They're crazy, he whispered to himself as he clung to the ridges of the pipe.

"You going to talk?" a policeman shouted into the watchman's ear.

He heard the watchman groan.

"We'll let you hang there till you talk, see?"

He saw the watchman close his eyes.

"Let's take 'im down. He passed out," a policeman said.

He grinned as he watched them take the body down and dump it carelessly upon the floor. The policeman took off the handcuffs.

"Let 'im come to. Let's get a smoke," a policeman said.

The three policemen left the scope of his vision. A door slammed. He had an impulse to yell to the watchman that he could escape through the hole in the basement and live with him in the cave. But he wouldn't understand, he told himself. After a moment he saw the watchman rise and stand, swaying from weakness. He stumbled across the room to a desk, opened a drawer, and took out a gun. He's going to kill himself, he thought, intent, eager, detached, yearning to see the end of the man's actions. As the watchman stared vaguely about he lifted the gun to his temple; he stood like that for some

minutes, biting his lips until a line of blood etched its way down a corner of his chin. No, he oughtn't do that, he said to himself in a mood of pity.

"Don't!" he half whispered and half yelled.

The watchman looked wildly about; he had heard him. But it did not help; there was a loud report and the watchman's head jerked violently and he fell like a log and lay prone, the gun clattering over the floor.

The three policemen came running into the room with drawn guns. One of the policemen knelt and rolled the watchman's body over and stared at a ragged, scarlet hole in the temple.

"Our hunch was right," the kneeling policeman said. "He was guilty, all right."

"Well, this ends the case," another policeman said.

"He knew he was licked," the third one said with grim satisfaction.

He eased down the rain pipe, crawled back through the holes he had made, and went back into his cave. A fever burned in his bones. He had to act, yet he was afraid. His eyes stared in the darkness as though propped open by invisible hands, as though they had become lidless. His muscles were rigid and he stood for what seemed to him a thousand years.

When he moved again his actions were informed with precision, his muscular system reinforced from a reservoir of energy. He crawled through the hole of earth, dropped into the gray sewer current, and sloshed ahead. When his right foot went forward at a street intersection, he fell backward and shot down into water. In a spasm of terror his right hand grabbed the concrete ledge of a down-curve and he felt the streaking water tugging violently at his body. The current reached his neck and for a moment he was still. He knew that if he moved clumsily he would be sucked under. He held onto the edge with both hands and slowly pulled himself up. He sighed, standing once more in the sweeping water, thankful that he had missed death.

He waded on through sludge, moving with care, until he came to a web of light sifting down from a manhole cover. He saw steel hooks running up the side of the sewer wall; he caught hold and lifted himself and put his shoulder to the cover and moved it an inch. A crash of sound came to him as he looked into a hot glare of sunshine through which blurred shapes moved. Fear scalded him and he dropped back into the pallid current and stood paralyzed in the shadows. A heavy car rumbled past overhead, jarring the pavement, warning him to stay in his world of dark light, knocking the cover back into place with an imperious clang.

He did not know how much fear he felt, for fear claimed him completely; yet it was not a fear of the police or of people, but a cold dread at the thought of the actions he knew he would perform if he went out into that cruel sunshine. His mind said no; his body said yes; and his mind could not understand his feelings. A low whine broke from him and he was in the act of uncoiling. He climbed upward and heard the faint honking of auto horns. Like a frantic cat clutching a rag, he clung to the steel prongs and heaved his shoulder against the cover and pushed it off halfway. For a split second his eyes were drowned in the terror of yellow light and he was in a deeper darkness than he had ever known in the underground.

Partly out of the hole, he blinked, regaining enough sight to make out meaningful forms. An odd thing was happening: No one was rushing forward to challenge him. He had imagined the moment of his emergence as a desperate tussle with men who wanted to cart him off to be killed; instead, life froze about him as the traffic stopped. He pushed the cover aside, stood, swaying in a world so fragile that he expected it to collapse and drop him into some deep void. But nobody seemed to pay him heed. The cars were now swerving to shun him and the gaping hole.

"Why in hell don't you put up a red light, dummy?" a raucous voice yelled.

He understood; they thought that he was a sewer workman. He walked toward the sidewalk, weaving unsteadily through the moving traffic.

"Look where you're going, nigger!"

"That's right! Stay there and get killed!"

"You blind, you bastard?"

"Go home and sleep your drunk off!"

A policeman stood at the curb, looking in the opposite direction. When he passed the policeman, he feared that he would be grabbed, but nothing happened. Where was he? Was this real? He wanted to look about to get his bearings, but felt that something awful would happen to him if he did. He wandered into a spacious doorway of a store that sold men's clothing and saw his reflection in a long mirror: his cheekbones protruded from a hairy black face; his greasy cap was perched askew upon his head and his eyes were red and glassy. His shirt and trousers were caked with mud and hung loosely. His hands were gummed with a black stickiness. He threw back his head and laughed so loudly that passers-by stopped and stared.

He ambled on down the sidewalk, not having the merest notion of where he was going. Yet, sleeping within him, was the drive to go somewhere and say something to somebody. Half an hour later his ears caught the sound of spirited singing.

> The Lamb, the Lamb, the Lamb
> I hear thy voice a-calling
> The Lamb, the Lamb, the Lamb
> I feel thy grace a-falling

A church! He exclaimed. He broke into a run and came to brick steps leading downward to a subbasement. This is it! The church into which he had peered. Yes, he was going in and tell them. What? He did not know; but, once face to face with them, he would think of what to say. Must be Sunday, he mused. He ran down the steps and jerked the door open; the church was crowded and a deluge of song swept over him.

The Lamb, the Lamb, the Lamb
Tell me again your story
The Lamb, the Lamb, the Lamb
Flood my soul with your glory

He stared at the singing faces with a trembling smile.

"Say!" he shouted.

Many turned to look at him, but the song rolled on. His arm was jerked violently.

"I'm sorry, Brother, but you can't do that in here," a man said.

"But, mister!"

"You can't act rowdy in God's house," the man said.

"He's filthy," another man said.

"But I want to tell 'em," he said loudly.

"He stinks," someone muttered.

The song had stopped, but at once another one began.

Oh, wondrous sight upon the cross
Vision sweet and divine
Oh, wondrous sight upon the cross
Full of such love sublime

He attempted to twist away, but other hands grabbed him and rushed him into the doorway.

"Let me alone!" he screamed, struggling.

"Get out!"

"He's drunk," somebody said. "He ought to be ashamed!"

"He acts crazy!"

He felt that he was failing and he grew frantic.

"But, mister, let me tell—"

"Get away from this door, or I'll call the police!"

He stared, his trembling smile fading in a sense of wonderment.

"The police," he repeated vacantly. "Now, get!"

He was pushed toward the brick steps and the door banged shut. The waves of song came.

Oh, wondrous sight, wondrous sight
Lift my heavy heart above
Oh, wondrous sight, wondrous sight
Fill my weary soul with love

He was smiling again now. Yes, the police . . . That was it! Why had he not thought of it before? The idea had been deep down in him, and only now did it assume supreme importance. He looked up and saw a street sign: COURT STREET — HARTSDALE AVENUE. He turned and walked northward, his mind filled with the image of the police station. Yes, that was where they had beaten him, accused him, and had made him sign a confession of his guilt. He would go there and clear up everything, make a statement. What statement? He did not know. He was the statement, and since it was all so clear to him, surely he would be able to make it clear to others.

He came to the corner of Hartsdale Avenue and turned westward. Yeah, there's the station. . . A policeman came down the steps and walked past him without a glance. He mounted the stone steps and went through the door, paused; he was in a hallway where several policemen were standing, talking, smoking. One turned to him.

"What do you want, boy?"

He looked at the policeman and laughed.

"What in hell are you laughing about?" the policeman asked.

He stopped laughing and stared. His whole being was full of what he wanted to say to them, but he could not say it.

"Are you looking for the Desk Sergeant?"

"Yes, sir," he said quickly; then: "Oh, no, sir."

"Well, make up your mind, now."

Four policemen grouped themselves around him.

"I'm looking for the men," he said.

"What men?"

Peculiarly, at that moment he could not remember the names of the policemen; he recalled their beating him, the confession he had signed, and how he had run away from them. He saw the cave next to the church, the money on the walls, the guns, the rings, the cleaver, the watches, and the diamonds on the floor.

"They brought me here," he began.

"When?"

His mind flew back over the blur of the time lived in the underground blackness. He had no idea of how much time had elapsed, but the intensity of what had happened to him told him that it could not have transpired in a short space of time, yet his mind told him that time must have been brief.

"It was a long time ago." He spoke like a child relating a dimly remembered dream. "It was a long time," he repeated, following the promptings of his emotions. "They beat me . . . I was scared . . . I ran away."

A policeman raised a finger to his temple and made a derisive circle.

"Nuts," the policeman said.

"Do you know what place this is, boy?"

"Yes, sir. The police station," he answered sturdily, almost proudly.

"Well, who do you want to see?"

"The men," he said again, feeling that surely they knew the men. "You know the men," he said in a hurt tone.

"What's your name?"

He opened his lips to answer and no words came. He had forgotten. But what did it matter if he had? It was not important.

"Where do you live?"

"Where did he live? It had been so long ago since he had lived up here in this strange world that he felt it was foolish even to try to remember. Then for a moment the old mood that had dominated him in the underground surged back. He leaned forward and spoke eagerly.

"They said I killed the woman."

"What woman?" a policeman asked.

"And I signed a paper that said I was guilty," he went on, ignoring their questions. "Then I ran off . . ."

"Did you run off from an institution?"

"No, sir," he said, blinking and shaking his head. "I came from under the ground. I pushed off the manhole cover and climbed out . . ."

"All right, now," a policeman said, placing an arm about his shoulder. "We'll send you to the psycho and you'll be taken care of."

"Maybe he's a Fifth Columnist!" a policeman shouted.

There was laughter and, despite his anxiety, he joined in. But the laughter lasted so long that it irked him.

"I got to find those men," he protested mildly.

"Say, boy, what have you been drinking?"

"Water," he said. "I got some water in a basement."

"Were the men you ran away from dressed in white, boy?"

"No, sir," he said brightly. "They were men like you."

An elderly policeman caught hold of his arm.

"Try and think hard. Where did they pick you up?"

He knitted his brows in an effort to remember, but he was blank inside. The policeman stood before him demanding logical answers and he could no longer think with his mind; he thought with his feelings and no words came.

"I was guilty," he said. "Oh, no, sir. I wasn't then, I mean, mister!"

"Aw, talk sense. Now, where did they pick you up?"

He felt challenged and his mind began reconstructing events in reverse; his feelings ranged back over the long hours and he saw the cave, the sewer, the bloody room where it was said that a woman had been killed.

"Oh, yes, sir," he said, smiling. "I was coming from Mrs. Wooten's."

"Who is she?"

"I work for her."

"Where does she live?"

"Next door to Mrs. Peabody, the woman who was killed."

The policemen were very quiet now, looking at him intently.

"What do you know about Mrs. Peabody's death, boy?"

"Nothing, sir. But they said I killed her. But it doesn't make any difference. I'm guilty!"

"What are you talking about, boy?"

His smile faded and he was possessed with memories of the underground; he saw the cave next to the church and his lips moved to speak. But how could he say it? The distance between what he felt and what these men meant was vast. Something told him, as he stood there looking into their faces, that he would never be able to tell them, that they would never believe him even if he told them.

"All the people I saw was guilty," he began slowly.

"Aw, nuts," a policeman muttered.

"Say," another policeman said, "that Peabody woman was killed over on Winewood. That's Number Ten's beat."

"Where's Number Ten?" a policeman asked.

"Upstairs in the swing room," someone answered.

"Take this boy up, Sam," a policeman ordered.

"O.K. Come along, boy."

An elderly policeman caught hold of his arm and led him up a flight of wooden stairs, down a long hall, and to a door.

"Squad Ten!" the policeman called through the door.

"What?" a gruff voice answered.

"Someone to see you!"

"About what?"

The old policeman pushed the door in and then shoved him into the room.

He stared, his lips open, his heart barely beating. Before him were the three policemen who had picked him up and had beaten him to extract the confession. They were seated about a small table, playing cards. The air was blue with smoke and sunshine poured through a high window, lighting up fantastic smoke shapes. He saw one of the policemen look up; the policeman's face was tired and a cigarette dropped limply from one corner of his mouth and both of his fat, puffy eyes were squinting and his hands gripped his cards.

"Lawson!" the man exclaimed.

The moment the man's name sounded he remembered the names of all of them: Lawson, Murphy, and Johnson. How simple it was. He waited, smiling, wondering how they would react when they knew that he had come back.

"Looking for me?" the man who had been called Lawson mumbled, sorting his cards. "For what?"

So far only Murphy, the red-headed one, had recognized him.

"Don't you-all remember me?" he blurted, running to the table.

All three of the policemen were looking at him now. Lawson, who seemed the leader, jumped to his feet.

"Where in hell have you been?"

"Do you know 'im, Lawson?" the old policeman asked.

"Huh?" Lawson frowned. "Oh, yes. I'll handle 'im." The old policeman left the room and Lawson crossed to the door and turned the key in the lock. "Come here boy," he ordered in a cold tone.

He did not move; he looked from face to face. Yes, he would tell them about his cave.

"He looks batty to me," Johnson said, the one who had not spoken before.

"Why in hell did you come back here?" Lawson said.

"I—I just didn't want to run away no more," he said. "I'm all right, now." He paused; the men's attitude puzzled him.

"You've been hiding, huh?" Lawson asked in a tone that denoted that he had not heard his previous words. "You told us you were sick, and when we left you in the room, you jumped out of the window and ran away."

Panic filled him. Yes, they were indifferent to what he would say! They were waiting for him to speak and they would laugh at him. He had to rescue himself from this bog; he had to force the reality of himself upon them.

"Mister, I took a sackful of money and pasted it on the walls . . ." he began.

"I'll be damned," Lawson said.

"Listen," said Murphy, "let me tell you something for your own good. We don't want you, see? You're free, free as air. Now go home and forget it. It was all a mistake. We caught the guy who did the Peabody job. He wasn't colored at all. He was an Eyetalian."

"Shut up!" Lawson yelled. "Have you no sense!"

"But I want to tell 'im," Murphy said.

"We can't let this crazy fool go," Lawson exploded. "He acts nuts, but this may be a stunt . . ."

"I was down in the basement," he began in a childlike tone, as though repeating a lesson learned by heart; "and I went into a movie . . ." His voice failed. He was getting ahead of his story. First, he ought to tell them about the singing in the church, but what words could he use? He looked at them appealingly. "I went into a shop and took a sackful of money and diamonds and watches and rings . . . I didn't steal 'em, I'll give 'em all back. I just took 'em to play with . . ." He paused, stunned by their disbelieving eyes.

Lawson lit a cigarette and looked at him coldly.

"What did you do with the money?" he asked in a quiet, waiting voice.

"I pasted the hundred-dollar bills on the walls."

"What walls?" Lawson asked.

"The walls of the dirt room," he said, smiling, "the room next to the church. I hung up the rings and the watches and I stamped the diamonds into the dirt . . ." He saw that they were not understanding what he was saying. He grew frantic to make them believe, his voice tumbled on eagerly. "I saw a dead baby and a dead man . . ."

"Aw, you're nuts," Lawson snarled, shoving him into a chair.

"But mister . . ."

"Johnson, where's the paper he signed?" Lawson asked.

"What paper?"

"The confession, fool!"

Johnson pulled out his billfold and extracted a crumpled piece of paper.

"Yes, sir, mister," he said, stretching forth his hand. "That's the paper I signed . . ."

Lawson slapped him and he would have toppled had his chair not struck a wall behind him. Lawson scratched a match and held the paper over the flame; the confession burned down to Lawson's fingertips.

He stared, thunderstruck; the sun of the underground was fleeting and the terrible darkness of the day stood before him. They did not believe him, but he *had* to make them believe him!

"But, mister . . ."

"It's going to be all right, boy," Lawson said with a quiet, soothing laugh. "I've burned your confession, see? You didn't sign anything." Lawson came close to him with the black ashes cupped in his palm. "You don't remember a thing about this, do you?"

"Don't you-all be scared of me," he pleaded, sensing their uneasiness. "I'll sign another paper, if you want me to. I'll show you the cave."

"What's your game, boy?" Lawson asked suddenly.

"What are you trying to find out?" Johnson asked.

"Who sent you here?" Murphy demanded.

"Nobody sent me, mister," he said. "I just want to show you the room . . ."

"Aw, he's plumb bats," Murphy said. "Let's ship 'im to the psycho."

"No," Lawson said. "He's playing a game and I wish to God I knew what it was."

There flashed through his mind a definite way to make them believe him; he rose from the chair with nervous excitement.

"Mister, I saw the night watchman blow his brains out because you accused him of stealing," he told them. "But he didn't steal the money and diamonds. I took 'em."

Tigerishly Lawson grabbed his collar and lifted him bodily.

"Who told you about that?"

"Don't get excited, Lawson," Johnson said. "He read about it in the papers."

Lawson flung him away.

"He couldn't have," Lawson said, pulling papers from his pocket. "I haven't turned in the reports yet."

"Then how *did* he find out?" Murphy asked.

"Let's get out of here," Lawson said with quick resolution. "Listen, boy, we're going to take you to a nice, quiet place, see?"

"Yes, sir," he said. "And I'll show you the underground."

"Goddamn," Lawson muttered, fastening the gun at his hip. He narrowed his eyes at Johnson and Murphy. "Listen," he spoke just above a whisper, "say nothing about this, you hear?"

"O.K.," Johnson said.

"Sure," Murphy said.

Lawson unlocked the door and Johnson and Murphy led him down the stairs. The hallway was crowded with policemen.

"What have you got there, Lawson?"

"What did he do, Lawson?"

"He's psycho, ain't he, Lawson?"

Lawson did not answer; Johnson and Murphy led him to the car parked at the curb, pushed him into the back seat. Lawson got behind the steering wheel and the car rolled forward.

"What's up, Lawson?" Murphy asked.

"Listen," Lawson began slowly, "we tell the papers that he spilled about the Peabody job, then he escapes. The Wop is caught and we tell the papers that we steered them wrong to trap the real guy, see? Now this dope shows up and acts nuts. If we let him go, he'll squeal that we framed him, see?"

"I'm all right, mister," he said, feeling Murphy's and Johnson's arm locked rigidly into his. "I'm guilty . . . I'll show you everything in the underground. I laughed and laughed . . ."

"Shut that fool up!" Lawson ordered.

Johnson tapped him across the head with a blackjack and he fell back against the seat cushion, dazed.

"Yes, sir," he mumbled. "I'm all right."

The car sped along Hartsdale Avenue, then swung onto Pine Street and rolled to State Street, then turned south. It slowed to a stop, turned in the middle of a block, and headed north again.

"You're going around in circles, Lawson," Murphy said.

Lawson did not answer; he was hunched over the steering wheel. Finally he pulled the car to a stop at a curb.

"Say, boy, tell us the truth," Lawson asked quietly. "Where did you hide?"

"I didn't hide, mister."

The three policemen were staring at him now; he felt that for the first time they were willing to understand him.

"Then what happened?"

"Mister, when I looked through all of those holes and saw how people were living, I loved 'em . . ."

"Cut out that crazy talk!" Lawson snapped. "Who sent you back here?"

"Nobody, mister."

"Maybe he's talking straight," Johnson ventured.

"All right," Lawson said. "Nobody hid you. Now, tell us *where* you hid."

"I went underground . . ."

"What goddam underground do you keep talking about?"

"I just went . . ." He paused and looked into the street, then pointed to a manhole cover. "I went down in there and stayed."

"In the *sewer*?"

"Yes, sir."

The policemen burst into a sudden laugh and ended quickly. Lawson swung the car around and drove to Woodside Avenue; he brought the car to a stop in front of a tall apartment building.

"What're we going to do, Lawson?" Murphy asked.

"I'm taking him up to my place," Lawson said. "We've got to wait until night. There's nothing we can do now."

They took him out of the car and led him into a vestibule.

"Take the steps," Lawson muttered.

They led him up four flights of stairs and into the living room of a small apartment. Johnson and Murphy let go of his arms and he stood uncertainly in the middle of the room.

"Now, listen, boy," Lawson began, "forget those wild lies you've been telling us. Where did you hide?"

"I just went underground, like I told you."

The room rocked with laughter. Lawson went to a cabinet and got a bottle of whiskey; he placed glasses for Johnson and Murphy. The three of them drank.

He felt that he could not explain himself to them. He tried to muster all the sprawling images that floated in him; the images stood out sharply in his mind, but he could not make them have the meaning for others that they had for him. He felt so helpless that he began to cry.

"He's nuts, all right," Johnson said. "All nuts cry like that."

Murphy crossed the room and slapped him.

"Stop that raving!"

A sense of excitement flooded him; he ran to Murphy and grabbed his arm.

"Let me show you the cave," he said. "Come on, and you'll see!"

Before he knew it a sharp blow had clipped him on the chin; darkness covered his eyes. He dimly felt himself being lifted and laid out on the sofa. He heard low voices and struggled to rise, but hard hands held him down. His brain was clearing now. He pulled to a sitting posture and stared with glazed eyes. It had grown dark. How long had he been out?

"Say, boy," Lawson said soothingly, "will you show us the underground?"

His eyes shone and his heart swelled with gratitude. Lawson believed him! He rose, glad; he grabbed Lawson's arm, making the policeman spill whisky from the glass to his shirt.

"Take it easy, goddammit," Lawson said.

"Yes, sir."

"O.K. We'll take you down. But you'd better be telling us the truth, you hear?"

He clapped his hands in wild joy.

"I'll show you everything!"

He had triumphed at last! He would now do what he had felt was compelling him all along. At last he would be free of his burden.

"Take 'im down," Lawson ordered.

They led him down to the vestibule; when he reached the sidewalk he saw that it was night and a fine rain was falling.

"It's just like when I went down," he told them.

"What?" Lawson asked.

"The rain," he said, sweeping his arm in a wide arc. "It was raining when I went down. The rain made the water rise and lift the cover off."

"Cut it out," Lawson snapped.

They did not believe him now, but they would. A mood of high selflessness throbbed in him. He could barely contain his rising spirits. They would see what he had seen; they would feel what he had felt. He would lead them through all the holes he had dug and .... He wanted to make a hymn, prance about in physical ecstasy, throw his arm about the policeman in fellowship.

"Get into the car," Lawson ordered.

He climbed in and Johnson and Murphy sat at either side of him; Lawson slid behind the steering wheel and started the motor.

"Now, tell us where to go," Lawson said.

"It's right around the corner from where the lady was killed," he said.

The car rolled slowly and he closed his eyes, remembering the song he had heard in the church, the song that had wrought him to such a high pitch of terror and pity. He sang softly, lolling his head:

Glad, glad, glad, oh, so glad
I got Jesus in my soul . . .

"Mister," he said, stopping his song, "you ought to see how funny the rings look on the wall." He giggled. "I fired a pistol, too. Just once, to see how it felt."

"What do you suppose he's suffering from?" Johnson asked.

"Delusions of grandeur, maybe," Murphy said.

"Maybe it's because he lives in a white man's world," Lawson said.

"Say, boy, what did you eat down there?" Murphy asked, prodding Johnson anticipatorily with his elbow.

"Pears, oranges, bananas, and pork chops," he said.

The car filled with laughter.

"You didn't eat any watermelon?" Lawson asked, smiling.

"No, sir," he answered calmly. "I didn't see any."

The three policemen roared harder and louder.

"Boy, you're sure some case," Murphy said, shaking his head in wonder.

The car pulled to a curb.

"All right, boy," Lawson said. "Tell us where to go."

He peered through the rain and saw where he had gone down. The streets, save for a few dim lamps glowing softly through the rain, were dark and empty.

"Right there, mister," he said, pointing.

"Come on; let's take a look," Lawson said.

"Well, suppose he did hide down there," Johnson said, "what is that supposed to prove?"

"I don't believe he hid down there," Murphy said.

"It won't hurt to look," Lawson said. "Leave things to me."

Lawson got out of the car and looked up and down the street.

He was eager to show them the cave now. If he could show them what he had seen, then they would feel what he had felt and they in turn would show it to others and those others would feel as they had felt, and soon everybody would be governed by the same impulse of pity.

"Take 'im out," Lawson ordered.

Johnson and Murphy opened the door and pushed him out; he stood trembling in the rain, smiling. Again Lawson looked up and down the street; no one was in sight. The rain came down hard, slanting like black wires across the wind-swept air.

"All right," Lawson said. "Show us."

He walked to the center of the street, stopped and inserted a finger in one of the tiny holes of the cover and tugged but he was too weak to budge it.

"Did you really go down in there, boy?" Lawson asked; there was a doubt in his voice.

"Yes, sir. Just a minute. I'll show you."

"Help 'im get that damn thing off," Lawson said.

Johnson stepped forward and lifted the cover; it clanged against the wet pavement. The hole gaped round and black.

"I went down in there," he announced with pride.

Lawson gazed at him for a long time without speaking, then he reached his right hand to his holster and drew his gun.

"Mister, I got a gun just like that down there," he said, laughing and looking into Lawson's face. "I fired it once then hung it on the wall. I'll show you."

"Show us how you went down," Lawson said quietly.

"I'll go down first, mister, and then you-all can come after me, hear?" he spoke like a little boy playing a game.

"Sure, sure," Lawson said soothingly. "Go ahead. We'll come."

He looked brightly at the policemen; he was bursting with happiness. He bent down and placed his hands on the rim of the hole and sat on the edge, his feet dangling into watery darkness. He heard the familiar drone of the gray current. He lowered his body and hung for a moment by his fingers, then he went downward on the steel prongs, hand over hand, until he reached the last rung. He dropped and his feet hit the water and he felt the stiff current trying to suck him away. He balanced himself quickly and looked back upward at the policemen.

"Come on, you-all!" he yelled, casting his voice above the rustling at his feet.

The vague forms that towered above him in the rain did not move. He laughed, feeling that they doubted him. But, once they saw the things he had done, they would never doubt again.

"Come on! The cave isn't far!" he yelled. "But be careful when your feet hit the water, because the current's pretty rough down here!"

Lawson still held the gun. Murphy and Johnson looked at Lawson quizzically.

"What are we going to do, Lawson?" Murphy asked.

"We are not going to follow that crazy nigger down into that sewer, are we?" Johnson asked.

"Come on, you-all!" he begged in a shout.

He saw Lawson raise the gun and point it directly at him. Lawson's face twitched, as though he were hesitating.

Then there was a thunderous report and a streak of fire ripped through his chest. He was hurled into the water, flat on his back. He looked in amazement at the blurred white faces looming above him. They shot me, he said to himself. The water flowed past him, blossoming in foam about his arms, his legs, and his head. His jaw sagged and his mouth gaped soundless. A vast pain gripped his head and gradually squeezed out consciousness. As from a great distance he heard hollow voices.

"What did you shoot him for, Lawson?"

"I had to."

"Why?"

"You've got to shoot his kind. They'd wreck things."

As though in a deep dream, he heard a metallic clank; they had replaced the manhole cover, shutting out forever the sound of wind and rain. From overhead came the muffled roar of a powerful motor and the swish of a speeding car. He felt the strong tide pushing him slowly into the middle of the sewer, turning him about. For a split second there hovered before his eyes the glittering cave, the shouting walls, and the laughing floor. . . . Then his mouth was full of thick, bitter water. The current spun him around. He sighed and closed his eyes, a whirling object rushing alone in the darkness, veering, tossing, lost in the heart of the earth.

Flannery O'Connor (1925–1964)

THE LIFE YOU SAVE MAY BE YOUR OWN

The old woman and her daughter were sitting on their porch when Mr. Shiftlet came up their road for the first time. The old woman slid to the edge of her chair and leaned forward, shading her eyes from the piercing sunset with her hand. The daughter could not see far in front of her and continued to play with her fingers. Although the old woman lived in this desolate spot with only her daughter and she had never seen Mr. Shiftlet before, she could tell, even from a distance, that he was a tramp and no one to be afraid of. His left coat sleeve was folded up to show there was only half an arm in it and his gaunt figure listed slightly to the side as if the breeze were pushing him. He had on a black town suit and a brown felt hat that was turned up in the front and down in the back and he carried a tin tool box by a handle. He came on, at an amble, up her road, his face turned toward the sun which appeared to be balancing itself on the peak of a small mountain.

The old woman didn't change her position until he was almost into her yard; then she rose with one hand fisted on her hip. The daughter, a large girl in a short blue organdy dress, saw him all at once and jumped up and began to stamp and point and make excited speechless sounds.

Mr. Shiftlet stopped just inside the yard and set his box on the ground and tipped his hat at her as if she were not in the least afflicted; then he turned toward the old woman and swung the hat all the way off. He had long black slick hair that hung flat from a part in the middle to beyond the tips of his ears on either side. His face descended in forehead for more than half its length and ended suddenly with his features just balanced over a jutting steel-trap jaw. He seemed to be a young man but he had a look of composed dissatisfaction as if he understood life thoroughly.

"Good evening," the old woman said. She was about the size of a cedar fence post and she had a man's gray hat pulled down low over her head.

The tramp stood looking at her and didn't answer. He turned his back and faced the sunset. He swung both his whole and his short arm up slowly so that they indicated an expanse of sky and his figure formed a crooked cross. The old woman watched him with her arms folded across her chest as if she were the owner of the sun, and the daughter watched, her head thrust forward and her fat helpless hands hanging at the wrists. She had long pink-gold hair and eyes as blue as a peacock's neck.

He held the pose for almost fifty seconds and then he picked up his box and came on to the porch and dropped down on the bottom step. "Lady," he said in a firm nasal voice, "I'd give a fortune to live where I could see me a sun do that every evening."

"Does it every evening," the old woman said and sat back down. The daughter sat down too and watched him with a cautious sly look as if he were a bird that had come up very close. He leaned to one side, rooting in his pants pocket, and in a second he brought out a package of chewing gum and offered her a piece. She took it and unpeeled it and began to chew without taking her eyes off him. He offered the old woman a piece but she only raised her upper lip to indicate she had no teeth.

Mr. Shiftlet's pale sharp glance had already passed over everything in the yard—the pump near the corner of the house and the big fig tree that three or four chickens were preparing to roost in—and had moved to a shed where he saw the square rusted back of an automobile. "You ladies drive?" he asked.

"That car ain't run in fifteen year," the old woman said. "The day my husband died, it quit running."

"Nothing is like it used to be, lady," he said. "The world is almost rotten."

"That's right," the old woman said. "You from around here?"

"Name Tom T. Shiftlet," he murmured, looking at the tires.

"I'm pleased to meet you," the old woman said. "Name Lucynell Crater and daughter Lucynell Crater. What you doing around here, Mr. Shiftlet?"

He judged the car to be about a 1928 or '29 Ford. "Lady," he said, and turned and gave her his full attention, "lemme tell you something. There's one of these doctors in Atlanta that's taken a knife and cut the human heart—the human heart," he repeated, leaning forward, "out of a man's chest and held it in his hand," and he held his hand out, palm up, as if it were slightly weighted with the human heart, "and studied it like it was a day-old chicken, and, lady," he said, allowing a long significant pause in which his head slid forward and his clay-colored eyes brightened, "he don't know no more about it than you or me."

"That's right," the old woman said.

"Why, if he was to take that knife and cut into every corner of it, he still wouldn't know no more than you or me. What you want to bet?"

"Nothing," the old woman said wisely. "Where you come from, Mr. Shiftlet?"

He didn't answer. He reached into his pocket and brought out a sack of tobacco and a package of cigarette papers and rolled himself a cigarette, expertly with one hand, and attached it in a hanging position to his upper lip. Then he took a box of wooden matches from his pocket and struck one on his shoe. He held the burning match as if he were studying the mystery of flame while it traveled dangerously toward his skin. The daughter began to make loud noises and to point to his hand and shake her finger at him, but when the flame was just before touching him, he leaned down with his hand cupped over it as if he were going to set fire to his nose and lit the cigarette.

He flipped away the dead match and blew a stream of gray into the evening. A sly look came over his face. "Lady," he said, "nowadays, people'll do anything anyways. I can tell you my name is Tom T. Shiftlet and I come from Tarwater, Tennessee, but you never have seen me before: how you know I ain't lying? How you know my name ain't Aaron Sparks, lady, and I come from Singleberry, Georgia, or how you know it's not George Speeds and I come from Lucy, Alabama, or how you know I ain't Thompson Bright from Toolafalls, Mississippi?"

"I don't know nothing about you," the old woman muttered, irked.

"Lady," he said, "people don't care how they lie. Maybe the best I can tell you is, I'm a man; but listen, lady," he said and paused and made his tone more ominous still, "what is a man?"

The old woman began to gum a seed. "What you carry in that tin box, Mr. Shiftlet?" she asked.

"Tools," he said, put back. "I'm a carpenter."

"Well, if you come out here to work, I'll be able to feed you and give you a place to sleep but I can't pay. I'll tell you that before you begin," she said.

There was no answer at once and no particular expression on his face. He leaned back against the two-by-four that helped support the porch roof. "Lady," he said slowly, "there's some men that some things mean more to them than money." The old woman rocked without comment and the daughter watched the trigger that moved up and down in his neck. He told the old woman then that all most people were interested in was money, but he asked what a man was made for. He asked her if a man was made for money, or what. He asked her what she thought she was made for but she didn't answer, she only sat rocking and wondered if a one-armed man could put a new roof on her garden house. He asked a lot of questions that she didn't answer. He told her that he was twenty-eight years old and had lived a varied life. He had been a gospel singer, a foreman on the railroad, an assistant in an undertaking parlor, and he had come over the radio for three months with Uncle Roy and his Red Creek Wranglers. He said he had fought and bled in the Arm Service of his country and visited every foreign land and that everywhere he had seen people that didn't care if they did a thing one way or another. He said he hadn't been raised thataway.

A fat yellow moon appeared in the branches of the fig tree as if it were going to roost there with the chickens. He said that a man had to escape to the country to see the world whole and that he wished he lived in a desolate place like this where he could see the sun go down every evening like God make it to do.

"Are you married or are you single?" the old woman asked.

There was a long silence. "Lady," he asked finally, "where would you find an innocent woman today? I wouldn't have any of this trash I could just pick up."

The daughter was leaning very far down, hanging her head almost between her knees, watching him through a triangular door she had made in her overturned hair; and she suddenly fell in a heap on the floor and began to whimper. Mr. Shiftlet straightened her out and helped her get back in the chair.

"Is she your baby girl?" he asked.

"My only," the old woman said, "and she's the sweetest girl in the world. I wouldn't give her up for nothing on earth. She's smart too. She can sweep the floor, cook, wash, feed the chickens, and hoe. I wouldn't give her up for a casket of jewels."

"No," he said kindly, "don't ever let any man take her away from you."

"Any man come after her," the old woman said, "'ll have to stay around the place."

Mr. Shiftlet's eye in the darkness was focused on a part of the automobile bumper that glittered in the distance. "Lady," he said, jerking his short arm up as if he could point with it to her house and yard and pump, "there ain't a broken thing on this plantation that I couldn't fix for you, one-arm jackleg or not. I'm a man," he said with a sullen dignity, "even if I ain't a whole one. I got," he said, tapping his knuckles on the floor to emphasize the immensity of what he was going to say, "a moral intelligence!" and his face pierced out of the darkness into a shaft of doorlight and he stared at her as if he were astonished himself at this impossible truth.

The old woman was not impressed with the phrase. "I told you you could hang around and work for food," she said, "if you don't mind sleeping in that car yonder."

"Why listen, Lady," he said with a grin of delight, "the monks of old slept in their coffins!"

"They wasn't as advanced as we are," the old woman said.

The next morning he began on the roof of the garden house while Lucynell, the daughter, sat on a rock and watched him work. He had not been around a week before the change he had made in the place was apparent. He had patched the front and back steps, built a new hog pen, restored a fence, and taught Lucynell, who was completely deaf and had never said a word in her life, to say the word "bird." The big rosy-faced girl followed him everywhere, saying "Burrttddt ddbirrrttdt," and clapping her hands. The old woman watched from a distance, secretly pleased. She was ravenous for a son-in-law.

Mr. Shiftlet slept on the hard narrow back seat of the car with his feet out the side window. He had his razor and a can of water on a crate that served him as a bedside table and he put up a piece of mirror against the back glass and kept his coat neatly on a hanger that he hung over one of the windows.

In the evenings he sat on the steps and talked while the old woman and Lucynell rocked violently in their chairs on either side of him. The old woman's three mountains were black against the dark blue sky and were visited off and on by various planets and by the moon after it had left the chickens. Mr. Shiftlet pointed out that the reason he had improved this plantation was because he had taken a personal interest in it. He said he was even going to make the automobile run.

He had raised the hood and studied the mechanism and he said he could tell that the car had been built in the days when cars were really built. You take now, he said, one man puts in one bolt and another man puts in another bolt and another man puts in another bolt so that it's a man for a bolt. That's why you have to pay so much for a car: You're paying all those men. Now if you didn't have to pay but one man, you could get you a cheaper car and one that had had a personal interest taken in it, and it would be a better car. The old woman agreed with him that this was so.

Mr. Shiftlet said that the trouble with the world was that nobody cared, or stopped and took any trouble. He said he never would have been able to teach Lucynell to say a word if he hadn't cared and stopped long enough.

"Teach her to say something else," the old woman said.

"What you want her to say next?" Mr. Shiftlet asked.

The old woman's smile was broad and toothless and suggestive. "Teach her to say, 'sugarpie,'" she said.

Mr. Shiftlet already knew what was on her mind.

The next day he began to tinker with the automobile and that evening he told her that if she would buy a fan belt, he would be able to make the car run.

The old woman said she would give him the money. "You see that girl yonder?" she asked, pointing to Lucynell who was sitting on the floor a foot away, watching him, her eyes blue even in the dark. "If it was ever a man wanted to take her away, I would say, 'No man on earth is going to take that sweet girl of mine away from me!' but if he was to say, 'Lady, I don't want to take her away, I want her right here,' I would say, 'Mister, I don't blame you none. I wouldn't pass up a chance to live in a permanent place and get the sweetest girl in the world myself. You ain't no fool,' I would say."

"How old is she?" Mr. Shiftlet asked casually.

"Fifteen, sixteen," the old woman said. The girl was nearly thirty but because of her innocence it was impossible to guess.

"It would be a good idea to paint it too," Mr. Shiftlet remarked. "You don't want it to rust out."

"We'll see about that later," the old woman said.

The next day he walked into town and returned with the parts he needed, and a can of gasoline. Late in the afternoon, terrible noises issued from the shed and the old woman rushed out of the house, thinking Lucynell was somewhere having a fit. Lucynell was sitting on a chicken crate, stamping her feet and screaming, "Burrddtttt! bddurrddtttt!" but her fuss was drowned out by the car. With a volley of blasts it emerged from the shed, moving in a fierce and stately way. Mr. Shiftlet was in the driver's seat, sitting very erect. He had an expression of serious modesty on his face as if he had just raised the dead.

That night, rocking on the porch, the old woman began her business at once. "You want you an innocent woman, don't you?" she asked sympathetically. "You don't want none of this trash."

"No'm, I don't," Mr. Shiftlet said.

"One that can't talk," she continued, "can't sass you back or use foul language. That's the kind for you to have. Right there," and she pointed to Lucynell sitting cross-legged in her chair, holding both feet in her hands.

"That's right," he admitted. "She wouldn't give me any trouble."

"Saturday," the old woman said, "you and her and me can drive into town and get married."

Mr. Shiftlet eased his position on the steps.

"I can't get married right now," he said. "Everything you want to do takes money and I ain't got any."

"What you need with money?" she asked.

"It takes money," he said. "Some people'll do anything anyhow these days, but the way I think, I wouldn't marry no woman that I couldn't take on a trip like she was somebody. I mean take her to a hotel and treat her. I wouldn't marry the Duchesser Windsor," he said firmly, "unless I could take her to a hotel and give her something good to eat. I was raised thataway and there ain't a thing I can do about it. My old mother taught me how to do."

"Lucynell don't even know what a hotel is," the old woman muttered. "Listen here, Mr. Shiftlet," she said, sliding forward in her chair, "you'd be getting a permanent house and a deep well and the most innocent girl in the world. You don't need no money. Lemme tell you something: There ain't

any place in the world for a poor disabled friendless drifting man."

The ugly words settled in Mr. Shiftlet's head like a group of buzzards in the top of a tree. He didn't answer at once. He rolled himself a cigarette and lit it and then he said in an even voice, "Lady, a man is divided into parts, body and spirit."

The old woman clamped her gums together.

"A body and a spirit," he repeated. "The body, lady, is like a house: It don't go anywhere; but the spirit, lady, is like a automobile: always on the move, always . . ."

"Listen, Mr. Shiftlet," she said, "my well never goes dry and my house is always warm in the winter and there's no mortgage on a thing about this place. You can go to the courthouse and see for yourself. And yonder under that shed is a fine automobile." She laid the bait carefully. "You can have it painted by Saturday. I'll pay for the paint."

In the darkness, Mr. Shiftlet's smile stretched like a weary snake waking up by a fire. "Yes'm," he said softly.

After a second he recalled himself and said, "I'm only saying a man's spirit means more to him than anything else. I would have to take my wife off for the weekend without no regards at all for cost. I got to follow where my spirit says to go."

"I'll give you fifteen dollars for a weekend trip," the old woman said in a crabbed voice. "That's the best I can do."

"That wouldn't hardly pay for more than the gas and the hotel," he said. "It wouldn't feed her."

"Seventeen-fifty," the old woman said. "That's all I got so it isn't any use you trying to milk me. You can take a lunch."

Mr. Shiftlet was deeply hurt by the word "milk." He didn't doubt that she had more money sewed up in her mattress but he had already told her he was not interested in her money. "I'll make that do," he said, and rose and walked off without treating with her further.

On Saturday the three of them drove into town in the car that the paint had barely dried on and Mr. Shiftlet and Lucynell were married in the Ordinary's office while the old woman witnessed. As they came out of the courthouse, Mr. Shiftlet began twisting his neck in his collar. He looked morose and bitter as if he had been insulted while someone held him. "That didn't satisfy me none," he said. "That was just something a woman in an office did, nothing but paper work and blood tests. What do they know about my blood? If they was to take my heart and cut it out," he said, "they wouldn't know a thing about me. It didn't satisfy me at all."

"It satisfied the law," the old woman said sharply.

"The law," Mr. Shiftlet said, and spit. "It's the law that don't satisfy me."

He had painted the car dark green with a yellow band around it just under the windows. The three of them climbed in the front seat and the old woman said, "Don't Lucynell look pretty? Looks like a baby doll." Lucynell was dressed up in a white dress that her mother had uprooted from a trunk and there was a Panama hat on her head with a bunch of red wooden cherries on the brim. Every now and then her placid expression was changed by a sly isolated little thought like a shoot of green in the desert. "You got a prize!" the old woman said.

Mr. Shiftlet didn't even look at her.

They drove back to the house to let the old woman off and pick up the lunch. When they were ready to leave, she stood staring in the window of the car, with her fingers clenched around the glass. Tears began to seep sideways out of her eyes and run along the dirty creases in her face. "I ain't ever been parted with her for two days before," she said.

Mr. Shiftlet started the motor.

"And I wouldn't let no man have her but you because I seen you would do right. Goodbye, Sugarbaby," she said, clutching at the sleeve of the white dress. Lucynell looked straight at her and didn't seem to see her there at all. Mr. Shiftlet eased the car forward so that she had to move her hands.

The early afternoon was clear and open and surrounded by pale blue sky. The hills flattened under the car one after another and the climb and dip and swerve went entirely to Mr. Shiftlet's head so that he forgot his morning bitterness. He had always wanted an automobile but he had never been able to afford one before. He drove very fast because he wanted to make Mobile by nightfall.

Occasionally he stopped his thoughts long enough to look at Lucynell in the seat beside him. She had eaten the lunch as soon as they were out of the yard and now she was pulling the cherries off the hat one by one and throwing them out the window. He became depressed in spite of the car. He had driven about a hundred miles when he decided that she must be hungry again and at the next small town they came to, he stopped in front of an aluminum-painted eating place called The Hot Spot and took her in and ordered her a plate of ham and grits. The ride had made her sleepy and as soon as she got up on the stool, she rested her head on the counter and shut her eyes. There was no one in The Hot Spot but Mr. Shiftlet and the boy behind the counter, a pale youth with a greasy rag hung over his shoulder. Before he could dish up the food, she was snoring gently.

"Give it to her when she wakes up," Mr. Shiftlet said. "I'll pay for it now."

The boy bent over her and stared at the long pink-gold hair and the half-shut sleeping eyes. Then he looked up and stared at Mr. Shiftlet. "She looks like an angel of Gawd," he murmured.

"Hitch-hiker," Mr. Shiftlet explained. "I can't wait. I got to make Tuscaloosa."

The boy bent over again and very carefully touched his fingers to a strand of the golden hair and Mr. Shiftlet left.

He was more depressed than ever as he drove on by himself. The late afternoon had grown hot and sultry and the country had flattened out. Deep in the sky a storm was preparing very slowly and without thunder as if it meant to drain every drop of air from the earth before it broke. There were times when Mr. Shiftlet preferred not to be alone. He felt too that a man with a car had a responsibility to others and he kept his eye out for a hitch-hiker. Occasionally he saw a sign that warned: "Drive carefully. The life you save may be your own."

The narrow road dropped off on either side into dry fields and here and there a shack or a filling station stood in a clearing. The sun began to set directly in front of the automobile. It was a reddening ball that through his windshield was slightly flat on the bottom and top. He saw a boy in overalls and a gray hat standing on the edge of the road and he slowed the car down and stopped in front of him. The boy didn't have his hand raised to thumb the ride, he was only standing there, but he had a small cardboard suitcase and his hat was set on his head in a way to indicate that he had left somewhere for good. "Son," Mr. Shiftlet said, "I see you want a ride."

The boy didn't say he did or he didn't but he opened the door of the car and got in, and Mr. Shiftlet started driving again. The child held the suitcase on his lap and folded his arms on top of it. He turned his head and looked out the window away from Mr. Shiftlet. Mr. Shiftlet felt oppressed. "Son," he said after a minute, "I got the best old mother in the world so I reckon you only got the second best."

The boy gave him a quick dark glance and then turned his face back out the window.

"It's nothing so sweet," Mr. Shiftlet continued, "as a boy's mother. She taught him his first prayers at her knee, she give him love when no other would, she told him what was right and what wasn't, and she seen that he done the right thing. Son," he said, "I never rued a day in my life like the one I rued when I left that old mother of mine."

The boy shifted in his seat but he didn't look at Mr. Shiftlet. He unfolded his arms and put one hand on the door handle.

"My mother was a angel of Gawd," Mr. Shiftlet said in a very strained voice. "He took her from heaven and giver to me and I left her." His eyes were instantly clouded over with a mist of tears. The car was barely moving.

The boy turned angrily in the seat. "You go to the devil!" he cried. "My old woman is a flea bag and yours is a stinking pole cat!" and with that he flung the door open and jumped out with his suitcase into the ditch.

Mr. Shiftlet was so shocked that for about a hundred feet he drove along slowly with the door still open. A cloud, the exact color of the boy's hat and shaped like a turnip, had descended over the sun, and another, worse looking, crouched behind the car. Mr. Shiftlet felt that the rottenness of the world was about to engulf him. He raised his arm and let it fall again to his breast. "Oh, Lord!" he prayed. "Break forth and wash the slime from this earth!"

Alan Sillitoe (1928–)

THE LONELINESS OF THE LONG-DISTANCE RUNNER

I

As soon as I got to Borstal they made me a long-distance cross-country runner. I suppose they thought I was just the build for it because I was long and skinny for my age (and still am) and in any case I didn't mind it much, to tell you the truth, because running had always been made much of in our family, especially running away from the police. I've always been a good runner, quick and with a big stride as well, the only trouble being that no matter how fast I run, and I did a very fair lick even though I do say so myself, it didn't stop me getting caught by the cops after that bakery job.

You might think it a bit rare, having long-distance cross-country runners in Borstal, thinking that the first thing a long-distance runner would do when they set him loose at them fields and woods would be to run as far away from the place as he could get on a bellyful of Borstal slumgullion—but you're wrong, and I'll tell you why. The first thing is that them bastards over us aren't as daft as they most of the time look, and for another thing I am not so daft as I would look if I tried to make a break for it on my long-distance running, because to abscond and then get caught is nothing but a mug's game, and I'm not falling for it. Cunning is what counts in this life, and even that you've got to use in the slyest way you can; I'm telling you straight: they're cunning, and I'm cunning. If only "them" and "us" had the same ideas

we'd get on like a house on fire, but they don't see eye to eye with us and we don't see eye to eye with them, so that's how it stands and how it will always stand. The one fact is that all of us are cunning, and because of this there's no love lost between us. So the thing is that they know I won't try to get away from them: They sit there like spiders in that crumbly manor house, perched like jumped-up jackdaws on the roof, watching out over the drives and fields like German generals from the tops of tanks. And even when I jog-trot on behind a wood and they can't see me anymore they know my sweeping-brush head will bob along that hedge-top in an hour's time and that I'll report to the bloke on the gate. Because when on a raw and frosty morning I get up at five o'clock and stand shivering my belly off on the stone floor and all the rest still have another hour to snooze before the bells go, I slink downstairs through all the corridors to the big outside door with a permit running-card in my fist, I feel like the first and last man on the world, both at once, if you can believe what I'm trying to say. I feel like the first man because I've hardly got a stitch on and am sent against the frozen fields in a shimmy and shorts—even the first poor bastard dropped on to the earth in midwinter knew how to make a suit of leaves, or how to skin a pterodactyl for a topcoat. But there I am, frozen stiff, with nothing to get me warm except a couple of hours' long-distance running before breakfast, not even a slice of bread-and-sheepdip. They're training me up fine for the big sports day when all the pig-faced snotty-nosed dukes and ladies—who can't add two and two together and would mess themselves like loonies if they didn't have slavies to beck-and-call—come and make speeches to us about sports being just the thing to get us leading an honest life and keep our itching finger-ends off them shop locks and safe handles and hairgrips to open gas meters. They give us a bit of blue ribbon and a cup for a prize after we've shagged ourselves out running or jumping, like race horses, only we don't get so well looked-after as race horses, that's the only thing.

So there I am, standing in the doorway in shimmy and shorts, not even a dry crust in my guts, looking out at frosty flowers on the ground. I suppose you think this is enough to make me cry? Not likely. Just because I feel like the first bloke in the world wouldn't make me bawl. It makes me feel fifty times better than when I'm cooped up in that dormitory with three hundred others. No, it's sometimes when I stand there feeling like the *last* man in the world that I don't feel so good. I feel like the last man in the world because I think that all those three hundred sleepers behind me are dead. They sleep so well I think that every scruffy head's kicked the bucket in the night and I'm the only one left, and when I look out into the bushes and frozen ponds I have the feeling that it's going to get colder and colder until everything I can see, meaning my red arms as well, is going to be covered with a thousand miles of ice, all the earth, right up to the sky and over every bit of land and sea. So I try to kick this feeling out and act like I'm the first man on earth. And that makes me feel good, so as soon as I'm steamed up enough to get this feeling in me, I take a flying leap out of the doorway, and off I trot.

I'm in Essex. It's supposed to be a good Borstal, at least that's what the governor said to me when I got here from Nottingham. "We want to trust you while you are in this establishment," he said, smoothing out his newspaper with lily-white workless hands, while I read the big words upside down: *Daily Telegraph.* "If you play ball with us, we'll play ball with you." (Honest to God, you'd have thought it was going to be one long tennis match.) "We want hard honest work and we want good athletics," he said as well. "And if you give us both these things you can be sure we'll do right by you and send you back into the world an honest man." Well, I could have died laughing, especially when straight after this I hear the barking sergeant-major's voice calling me and two others to attention and marching us off like we was Grenadier Guards. And when the governor kept saying how "we" wanted you to do this, and "we" wanted you to do that, I kept looking round for the other blokes, wondering how many of them there was. Of course, I knew there were thousands of them, but as far as I knew only one was in the room. And there *are* thousands of them, all over the poxeaten country, in shops, offices, railway stations, cars, houses, pubs—In-law blokes like you and them, all on the watch for Out-law blokes like me and us—and waiting to 'phone for the coppers as soon as we make a false move. And it'll always be there, I'll tell you that now, because I haven't finished making all my false moves yet, and I dare say I won't until I kick the bucket. If the In-laws are hoping to stop me making false moves they're wasting their time. They might as well stand me up against a wall and let fly with a dozen rifles. That's the only way they'll stop me, and a few million others. Because I've been doing a lot of thinking since coming here. They can spy on us all day to see if we're pulling our puddings and if we're working good or doing our "athletics" but they can't make an X-ray of our guts to find out what we're telling ourselves. I've been asking myself all sorts of questions, and thinking about my life up to now. And I like doing all this. It's a treat. It passes the time away and don't make Borstal seem half so bad as the boys in our street used to say it was. And this long-distance running lark is the best of all, because it makes me think so good that I learn things even better than when I'm on my bed at night. And apart from that, what with thinking so much while I'm running I'm getting to be one of the best runners in the Borstal. I can go my five miles round better than anybody else I know.

So as soon as I tell myself I'm the first man ever to be dropped into the world, and as soon as I take that first flying leap out into the frosty grass of an early morning when even birds haven't the heart to whistle, I get to thinking, and that's what I like. I go my rounds in a dream, turning at lane or footpath corners without knowing I'm turning, leaping brooks without knowing they're there, and shouting good morning to the early cow-milker without seeing him. It's a treat, being a long-distance runner, out in the world by yourself with not a soul to make you bad-tempered or tell you what to do or that there's a shop to break and enter a bit back from the next street. Sometimes I think that I've never been so free as during that couple of hours when I'm trotting up the path out of the gates and turning by that bare-faced, big-bellied oak tree at the lane end. Everything's dead, but good, because it's dead before coming alive, not dead after being alive. That's how I look at it. Mind you, I often feel frozen stiff at first. I can't feel my hands or feet or flesh at all, like I'm a ghost who wouldn't know the earth was under him if he didn't see it now and again through the mist. But even though some people would call this frost-pain

suffering if they wrote about it to their mams in a letter, I don't, because I know that in half an hour I'm going to be warm, that by the time I get to the main road and am turning on to the wheatfield footpath by the bus stop I'm going to feel as hot as a potbellied stove and as happy as a dog with a tin tail.

It's a good life, I'm saying to myself, if you don't give in to coppers and Borstal-bosses and the rest of them bastard-faced In-laws. Trot-trot-trot. Puff-puff-puff. Slap-slap-slap go my feet on the hard soil. Swish-swish-swish as my arms and side catch the bare branches of a bush. For I'm seventeen now, and when they let me out of this—if I don't make a break and see that things turn out otherwise—they'll try to get me in the army, and what's the difference between the army and this place I'm in now? They can't kid me, the bastards. I've seen the barracks near where I live, and if there weren't swaddies on guard outside with rifles you wouldn't know the difference between their high walls and the place I'm in now. Even though the swaddies come out at odd times a week for a pint of ale, so what? Don't I come out three mornings a week on my long-distance running, which is fifty times better than boozing. When they first said that I was to do my long-distance running without a guard pedalling beside me on a bike I couldn't believe it; but they called it a progressive and modern place, though they can't kid me because I know it's just like any other Borstal, going by the stories I've heard, except that they let me trot about like this. Borstal's Borstal no matter what they do; but anyway I moaned about it being a bit thick sending me out so early to run five miles on an empty stomach, until they talked me round to thinking it wasn't so bad—which I knew all the time—until they called me a good sport and patted me on the back when I said I'd do it and that I'd try to win them the Borstal Blue Ribbon Prize Cup For Long-Distance Cross-

Country Running (All England). And now the governor talks to me when he comes on his rounds, almost as he'd talk to his prize race horse, if he had one.

"All right, Smith?" he asks.

"Yes, sir," I answer.

He flicks his grey moustache: "How's the running coming along?"

"I've set myself to trot round the grounds after dinner just to keep my hand in, sir," I tell him.

The pot-bellied pop-eyed bastard gets pleased at this: "Good show. I know you'll get us that cup," he says.

And I swear under my breath: "Like boggery, I will." No, I won't get them that cup, even though the stupid tash-twitching bastard has all his hopes in me. Because what does his barmy hope mean? I ask myself. Trot-trot-trot, slap-slap-slap, over the stream and into the wood where it's almost dark and frosty-dew twigs sting my legs. It don't mean a bloody thing to me, only to him, and it means as much to him as it would mean to me if I picked up the racing paper and put my bet on a hoss I didn't know, had never seen, and didn't care a sod if I ever did see. That's what it means to him. And I'll lose that race, because I'm not a race horse at all, and I'll let him know it when I'm about to get out—if I don't sling my hook even before the race. By Christ I will. I'm a human being and I've got thoughts and secrets and bloody life inside me that he doesn't know is there, and he'll never know what's there because he's stupid. I suppose you'll laugh at this, me saying the governor's a stupid bastard when I know hardly how to write and he can read and write and add-up like a professor. But what I say is true right enough. He's stupid, and I'm not, because I can see further into the likes of him than he can see into the likes of me. Admitted, we're both cunning, but I'm more cunning and I'll win in the end even if I die in gaol at eighty-two, because I'll have more fun and fire out

of my life than he'll ever get out of his. He's read a thousand books I suppose, and for all I know he might even have written a few, but I know for a dead cert, as sure as I'm sitting here, that what I'm scribbling down is worth a million to what he could ever scribble down. I don't care what anybody says, but that's the truth and can't be denied. I know when he talks to me and I look into his army mug that I'm alive and he's dead. He's as dead as a doornail. If he ran ten yards he'd drop dead. If he got ten yards into what goes on in my guts he'd drop dead as well—with surprise. At the moment it's dead blokes like him as have the whip-hand over blokes like me, and I'm almost dead sure it'll always be like that, but even so, by Christ, I'd rather be like I am—always on the run and breaking into shops for a packet of fags and a jar of jam—than have the whip-hand over somebody else and be dead from the toenails up. Maybe as soon as you get the whip-hand over somebody you do go dead. By God, to say that last sentence has needed a few hundred miles of long-distance running. I could no more have said that at first than I could have took a million-pound note from my back pocket. But it's true, you know, now I think of it again, and has always been true, and always will be true, and I'm surer of it every time I see the governor open that door and say Goodmorning lads.

As I run and see my smoky breath going out into the air as if I had ten cigars stuck in different parts of my body I think more on the little speech the governor made when I first came. Honesty. Be honest. I laughed so much one morning I went ten minutes down in my timing because I had to stop and get rid of the stitch in my side. The governor was so worried when I got back late that he sent me to the doctor's for an X-ray and heart check. Be honest. It's like saying: Be dead, like me, and then you'll have no more pain of leaving your nice slummy house for Borstal or prison. Be honest and settle down in a cosy six pounds a week job. Well, even with all this long-distance running I haven't yet been able to decide what he means by this, although I'm just about beginning to—and I don't like what it means. Because after all my thinking I found that it adds up to something that can't be true about me, being born and brought up as I was. Because another thing people like the governor will never understand is that I *am* honest, that I've never been anything else but honest, and that I'll always be honest. Sounds funny. But it's true because I know what honest means according to me and he only knows what it means according to him. I think my honesty is the only sort in the world, and he thinks his is the only sort in the world as well. That's why this dirty great walled-up and fenced-up manor house in the middle of nowhere has been used to coop-up blokes like me. And if I had the whip-hand I wouldn't even bother to build a place like this to put all the cops, governors, posh whores, penpushers, army officers, Members of Parliament in; no, I'd stick them up against a wall and let them have it, like they'd have done with blokes like us years ago, that is, if they'd ever known what it means to be honest, which they don't and never will so help me God Almighty.

I was nearly eighteen months in Borstal before I thought about getting out. I can't tell you much about what it was like there because I haven't got the hang of describing buildings or saying how many crumby chairs and slatted windows make a room. Neither can I do much complaining, because to tell you the truth I didn't suffer in Borstal at all. I gave the same answer a pal of mine gave when someone asked him how much he hated it in the army. "I didn't hate it," he said. "They fed me, gave me a suit, and pocket-money, which was a bloody sight more than I

ever got before, unless I worked myself to death for it, and most of the time they wouldn't let me work but sent me to the dole office twice a week." Well, that's more or less what I say. Borstal didn't hurt me in that respect, so since I've got no complaints I don't have to describe what they gave us to eat, what the dorms were like, or how they treated us. But in another way Borstal does something to me. No, it doesn't get my back up, because it's always been up, right from when I was born. What it does do is show me what they've been trying to frighten me with. They've got other things as well, like prison and, in the end, the rope. It's like me rushing up to thump a man and snatch the coat off his back when, suddenly, I pull up because he whips out a knife and lifts it to stick me like a pig if I come too close. That knife is Borstal, clink, the rope. But once you've seen the knife you learn a bit of unarmed combat. You have to, because you'll never get that sort of knife in your own hands, and this unarmed combat doesn't amount to much. Still, there it is, and you keep on rushing up to this man, knife or not, hoping to get one of your hands on his wrist and the other on his elbow both at the same time, and press back until he drops the knife.

You see, by sending me to Borstal they've shown me the knife, and from now on I know something I didn't know before: that it's war between me and them. I always knew this, naturally, because I was in Remand Homes as well and the boys there told me a lot about their brothers in Borstal, but it was only touch and go then, like kittens, like boxing-gloves, like dobbie. But now that they've shown me the knife, whether I ever pinch another thing in my life again or not, I know who my enemies are and what war is. They can drop all the atom bombs they like for all I care: I'll never call it war and wear a soldier's uniform, because I'm in a different sort of war, that they think is child's play. The war they think is war is suicide, and those that go and get killed in war should be put in clink for attempted suicide because that's the feeling in blokes' minds when they rush to join up or let themselves be called up. I know, because I've thought how good it would be sometimes to do myself in and the easiest way to do it, it occurred to me, was to hope for a big war so's I could join up and get killed. But I got past that when I knew I already was in a war of my own, that I was born into one, that I grew up hearing the sound of "old soldiers" who'd been over the top at Dartmoor, half-killed at Lincoln, trapped in no-man's-land at Borstal, that sounded louder than any Jerry bombs. Government wars aren't my wars; they've got nowt to do with me, because my own war's all that I'll ever be bothered about. I remember when I was fourteen and I went out into the country with three of my cousins, all about the same age, who later went to different Borstals, and then to different regiments, from which they soon deserted, and then to different gaols where they still are as far as I know. But anyway, we were all kids then, and wanted to go out to the woods for a change, to get away from the roads of stinking hot tar one summer. We climbed over fences and went through fields, scrumping a few sour apples on our way, until we saw the wood about a mile off. Up Colliers' Pad we heard another lot of kids talking in high-school voices behind a hedge. We crept up on them and peeped through the brambles, and saw they were eating a picnic, a real posh spread out of baskets and flasks and towels. There must have been about seven of them, lads and girls sent out by their mams and dads for the afternoon. So we went on our bellies through the hedge like crocodiles and surrounded them, and then dashed into the middle, scattering the fire and batting their tabs and snatching up all there was to eat,

then running off over Cherry Orchard fields into the wood with a man chasing us who'd come up while we were ransacking their picnic. We got away all right, and had a good feed into the bargain, because we'd been clambed to death and couldn't wait long enough to get our chops ripping into them thin lettuce and ham sandwiches and creamy cakes.

Well, I'll always feel during every bit of my life like those daft kids should have felt before we broke them up. But they never dreamed that what happened was going to happen, just like the governor of this Borstal who spouts to us about honesty and all that wappy stuff don't know a bloody thing, while I know every minute of my life that a big boot is always likely to smash any nice picnic I might be barmy and dishonest enough to make for myself. I admit that there've been times when I've thought of telling the governor all this so as to put him on his guard, but when I've got as close as seeing him I've changed my mind, thinking to let him either find out for himself or go through the same mill as I've gone through. I'm not hard-hearted (in fact I've helped a few blokes in my time with the odd quid, lie, fag, or shelter from the rain when they've been on the run) but I'm boggered if I'm going to risk being but in the cells just for trying to give the governor a bit of advice he don't deserve. If my heart's soft I know the sort of people I'm going to save it for. And any advice I'd give the governor wouldn't do him the least bit of good; it'd only trip him up sooner than if he wasn't told at all, which I suppose is what I want to happen. But for the time being I'll let things go on as they are, which is something else I've learned in the last year or two. (It's a good job I can only think of these things as fast as I can write with this stub of pencil that's clutched in my paw, otherwise I'd have dropped the whole thing weeks ago.)

By the time I'm half-way through my morning course, when after a frost-bitten dawn I can see a phlegmy bit of sunlight hanging from the bare twigs of beech and sycamore, and when I've measured my half-way mark by the short-cut scrimmage down the steep bush-covered bank and into the sunken lane, when still there's not a soul in sight and not a sound except the neighing of a piebald foal in a cottage stable that I can't see, I get to thinking the deepest and daftest of all. The governor would have a fit if he could see me sliding down the bank because I could break my neck or ankle, but I can't not do it because it's the only risk I take and the only excitement I ever get, flying flat-out like one of them pterodactyls from the 'Lost World' I once heard on the wireless, crazy like a cut-balled cockerel, scratching myself to bits and almost letting myself go but not quite. It's the most wonderful minute because there's not one thought or word or picture of anything in my head while I'm going down. I'm empty, as empty as I was before I was born, and I don't let myself go, I suppose, because whatever it is that's farthest down inside me don't want me to die or hurt myself bad. And it's daft to think deep, you know, because it gets you nowhere, though deep is what I am when I've passed this half-way mark because the long-distance run of an early morning makes me think that every run like this is a life—a little life, I know—but a life as full of misery and happiness and things happening as you can ever get really around yourself—and I remember that after a lot of these runs I thought that it didn't need much know-how to tell how a life was going to end once it had got well started. But as usual I was wrong, caught first by the cops and then by my own bad brain, I could never trust myself to fly scot-free over these traps, was always tripped up sooner or later no matter how many I got over to the good without even

knowing it. Looking back I suppose them big trees put their branches to their snouts and gave each other the wink, and there I was whizzing down the bank and not seeing a bloody thing.

II

I don't say to myself: "You shouldn't have done the job and then you'd have stayed away from Borstal"; no, what I ram into my runner-brain is that my luck had no right to scram just when I was on my way to making the coppers think I hadn't done the job after all. The time was autumn and the night foggy enough to set me and my mate Mike roaming the streets when we should have been rooted in front of the telly or stuck into a plush posh seat at the pictures, but I was restless after six weeks away from any sort of work, and well you might ask me why I'd been bone-idle for so long because normally I sweated my thin guts out on a milling-machine with the rest of them, but you see, my dad died from cancer of the throat, and mam collected a cool five hundred in insurance and benefits from the factory where he'd worked, "for your bereavement," they said, or words like that.

Now I believe, and my mam must have thought the same, that a wad of crisp blue-back fivers ain't a sight of good to a living soul unless they're flying out of your hand into some shopkeeper's till, and the shopkeeper is passing you tip-top things in exchange over the counter, so as soon as she got the money, mam took me and my five brothers and sisters out to town and got us dolled-up in new clothes. Then she ordered a twenty-one-inch telly, a new carpet because the old one was covered with blood from dad's dying and wouldn't wash out, and took a taxi home with bags of grub and a new fur coat. And do you know—you wain't believe me when I tell you—she'd still near three hundred left in her bulging handbag the next day, so how could any of us go to work after that? Poor old dad, he didn't get a look in, and he was the one who'd done the suffering and dying for such a lot of lolly.

Night after night we sat in front of the telly with a ham sandwich in one hand, a bar of chocolate in the other, and a bottle of lemonade between our boots, while mam was with some fancy-man upstairs on the new bed she'd ordered, and I'd never known a family as happy as ours was in that couple of months when we'd got all the money we needed. And when the dough ran out I didn't think about anything much, but just roamed the streets—looking for another job, I told mam—hoping I suppose to get my hands on another five hundred nicker so's the nice life we'd got used to could go on and on for ever. Because it's surprising how quick you can get used to a different life. To begin with, the adverts on the telly had shown us how much more there was in the world to buy than we'd ever dreamed of when we'd looked into shop windows but hadn't seen all there was to see because we didn't have the money to buy it with anyway. And the telly made all these things seem twenty times better than we'd ever thought they were. Even adverts at the cinema were cool and tame, because now we were seeing them in private at home. We used to cock our noses up at things in shops that didn't move, but suddenly we saw their real value because they jumped and glittered around the screen and had some pasty-faced tart going head over heels to get her nail-polished grabbers on to them or her lipstick lips over them, not like the crumby adverts you saw on posters or in newspapers as dead as doornails; these were flickering around loose, half-open packets and tins, making you think that all you had to do was finish opening them before they were yours, like seeing an unlocked safe through a shop window with the man gone away for a cup of tea without thinking to guard his lolly. The films they showed were good as well, in that way, because we couldn't get our eyes unglued from the cops chasing the robbers who had satchel-bags crammed with cash and looked like getting away to spend it—until the last moment. I always hoped they would end up free to blow the lot, and could never stop wanting to put my hand out, smash into the screen (it only looked a bit of rag-screen like at the pictures) and get the copper in a half-nelson so's he'd stop following the bloke with the money-bags. Even when he'd knocked off a couple of bank clerks I hoped he wouldn't get nabbed. In fact then I wished more than ever he wouldn't be-cause it meant the hot-chair if he did, and I wouldn't wish that on anybody no matter what they'd done, because I'd read in a book where the hot-chair worn't a quick death at all, but that you just sat there scorching to death until you were dead. And it was when these cops were chasing the crooks that we played some good tricks with the telly, because when one of them opened his big gob to spout about getting their man I'd turn the sound down and see his mouth move like a goldfish or mackerel or a minnow mim-icking what they were supposed to be acting—it was so funny the whole fam-ily nearly went into fits on the brand-new carpet that hadn't yet found its way to the bedroom. It was the best of all though when we did it to some Tory telling us about how good his government was going to be if we kept on voting for them—their slack chops rolling, opening and bumbling, hands lifting to twitch moustaches and touching their buttonholes to make sure the flower hadn't wilted, so that you could see they didn't mean a word they said, especially with not a murmur coming out because we'd cut off the sound. When the governor of the Borstal first talked to me I was reminded of those times so much that I nearly killed myself trying not to laugh. Yes, we played so many good stunts on the box of tricks that mam used to call us the Telly Boys, we got so clever at it.

My pal Mike got let off with probation because it was his first job—anyway the first they ever knew about—and because they said he would never have done it if it hadn't been for me talking him into it. They said I was a menace to honest lads like Mike—hands in his pockets so that they looked stone-empty, head bent forward as if looking for half-crowns to fill 'em with, a ripped jersey on and his hair falling into his eyes so that he could go up to women and ask them for a shilling because he was hungry—and that I was the brains behind the job, the guiding light when it came to making up anybody's mind, but I swear to God I worn't owt like that because really I ain't got no more brains than a gnat after hiding the money in the place I did. And I—being cranky like I am—got sent to Borstal because to tell you the honest truth I'd been to Remand Homes before—though that's another story and I suppose if ever I tell it it'll be just as boring as this one is. I was glad though that Mike got away with it, and I only hope he always will, not like silly bastard me.

So on this foggy night we tore ourselves away from the telly and slammed the front door behind us, setting off up our wide street like slow tugs on a river that'd broken their hooters, for we didn't know where the housefronts began what with the perishing cold mist all around. I was snatched to death without an overcoat: Mam had forgotten to buy me one in the scrummage of shopping, and by the time I thought to remind her of it the dough was all gone. So we whistled "The Teddy Boys Picnic" to keep us warm, and I told myself that I'd get a coat soon if it was the last thing I did. Mike said he

thought the same about himself, adding that he'd also get some brand-new glasses with gold rims, to wear instead of the wire frames they'd given him at the school clinic years ago. He didn't twig it was foggy at first and cleaned his glasses every time I pulled him back from a lamp-post or car, but when he saw the lights on Alfreton Road looking like octopus eyes he put them in his pocket and didn't wear them again until we did the job. We hadn't got two ha-pennies between us, and though we weren't hungry we wished we'd got a bob or two when we passed the fish and chip shops because the delicious sniffs of salt and vinegar and frying fat made our mouths water. I don't mind telling you we walked the town from one end to the other and if our eyes worn't glued to the ground looking for lost wallets and watches they was swivelling around house windows and shop doors in case we saw something easy and worth nipping into.

Neither of us said as much as this to each other, but I know for a fact that that was what we was thinking. What I don't know—and as sure as I sit here I know I'll never know—is which of us was the first bastard to latch his peepers on to that baker's backyard. Oh yes, it's all right me telling myself it was me, but the truth is that I've never known whether it was Mike or not, because I do know that I didn't see the open window until he stabbed me in the ribs and pointed it out. "See it?" he said.

"Yes," I told him, "so let's get cracking."

"But what about the wall though?" he whispered, looking a bit closer.

"On your shoulders," I chipped in.

His eyes were already up there: "Will you be able to reach?" It was the only time he ever showed any life.

"Leave it to me," I said, ever-ready. "I can reach anywhere from your ham-hock shoulders."

Mike was a nipper compared to me,

but underneath the scruffy draught-board jersey he wore were muscles as hard as iron, and you wouldn't think to see him walking down the street with glasses on and hands in pockets that he'd harm a fly, but I never liked to get on the wrong side of him in a fight because he's the sort that don't say a word for weeks on end—sits plugged in front of the telly, or reads a cowboy book, or just sleeps—when suddenly BIFF—half kills somebody for almost nothing at all, such as beating him in a race for the last Football Post on a Saturday night, pushing in before him at a bus stop, or bumping into him when he was day-dreaming about Dolly-on-the-Tub next door. I saw him set on a bloke once for no more than fixing him in a funny way with his eyes, and it turned out that the bloke was cock-eyed but nobody knew it because he'd just that day come to live in our street. At other times none of these things would matter a bit, and I suppose the only reason why I was pals with him was because I didn't say much from one month's end to another either.

He puts his hands up in the air like he was being covered with a Gatling-Gun, and moved to the wall like he was going to be mowed down, and I climbed up him like he was a stile or step-ladder, and there he stood, the palms of his upshot maulers flat and turned out so's I could step on 'em like they was the adjustable jackspanner under a car, not a sound of a breath nor the shiver of a flinch coming from him. I lost no time in any case, took my coat from between my teeth, chucked it up to the glass-topped wall (where the glass worn't too sharp because the jags had been worn down by years of ac-cidental stones) and was sitting astrad-dle before I knew where I was. Then down the other side, with my legs rammed up into my throat when I hit the ground, the crack coming about as hard as when you fall after a high parachute drop, that one of my mates

told me was like jumping off a twelve-foot wall, which this must have been. Then I picked up my bits and pieces and opened the gate for Mike, who was still grinning and full of life because the hardest part of the job was already done. "I came, I broke, I entered," like that clever-dick Borstal song.

I didn't think about anything at all, as usual, because I never do when I'm busy, when I'm draining pipes, looting sacks, yaling locks, lifting latches, forc-ing my bony hands and lanky legs into making something move, hardly feeling my lungs going in-whiff and out-whaff, not realizing whether my mouth is clamped tight or gaping, whether I'm hungry, itching from scabies, or whether my flies are open and flashing dirty words like muck and spit into the late-night final fog. And when I don't know anything about all this then how can I honest-to-God say I think of any-thing at such times? When I'm wonder-ing what's the best way to get a window open or how to force a door, how can I be thinking or have anything on my mind? That's what the four-eyed white-smocked bloke with the note-book couldn't understand when he asked me questions for days and days after I got to Borstal; and I couldn't explain it to him then like I'm writing it down now; and even if I'd been able to maybe he still wouldn't have caught on because I don't know whether I can understand it myself even at this moment, though I'm doing my best you can bet.

So before I knew where I was I was inside the baker's office watching Mike picking up that cash box after he'd struck a match to see where it was, wearing a tailor-made fifty-shilling grin on his square crew-cut nut as his paws closed over the box like he'd squash it to nothing. "Out," he suddenly said, shaking it so's it rattled. "Let's scram."

"Maybe there's some more," I said, pulling half a dozen drawers out of a rollertop desk.

"No," he said, like he'd already been

twenty years in the game, "this is the lot," patting his tin box, "this is it."

I pulled out another few drawers, full of bills, books and letters. "How do you know, you loony sod?"

He barged past me like a bull at a gate. "Because I do."

Right or wrong, we'd both got to stick together and do the same thing. I looked at an ever-loving babe of a brand-new typewriter, but knew it was too traceable, so blew it a kiss, and went out after him. "Hang on," I said, pulling the door to, "we're in no hurry."

"Not much we aren't," he says over his shoulder.

"We've got months to splash the lolly," I whispered as we crossed the yard, "only don't let that gate creak too much or you'll have the narks tuning-in."

"You think I'm barmy?" he said, creaking the gate so that the whole street heard.

I don't know about Mike, but now I started to think of how we'd get back safe through the streets with that money-box up my jumper. Because he'd clapped it into my hand as soon as we'd got to the main road, which might have meant that he'd started thinking as well, which only goes to show how you don't know what's in anybody else's mind unless you think about things yourself. But as far as my thinking went at that moment it wasn't up to much, only a bit of fright that wouldn't budge not even with a hot blow-lamp, about what we'd say if a copper asked us where we were off to with that hump in my guts.

"What is it?" he'd ask, and I'd say: "A growth." "What do you mean, a growth, my lad?" he'd say back, narky like. I'd cough and clutch myself like I was in the most tripe-twisting pain in the world, and screw my eyes up like I was on my way to the hospital, and Mike would take my arm like he was the best pal I'd got. "Cancer," I'd manage to say to Narker, which would make his slow punch-drunk brain suspect a thing or two. "A lad of your age?" So I'd groan

again, and hope to make him feel a real bully of a bastard, which would be impossible, but anyway: "It's in the family. Dad died of it last month, and I'll die of it next month by the feel of it." "What, did he have it in the guts?" "No, in the throat. But it's got me in the stomach." Groan and cough. "Well, you shouldn't be out like this if you've got cancer, you should be in the hospital." I'd get ratty now: "That's where I'm trying to go if only you'd let me and stop asking so many questions. Aren't I, Mike?" Grunt from Mike as he unslung his cosh. Then just in time the copper would tell us to get on our way, kind and considerate all of a sudden, saying that the outpatient department of the hospital closes at twelve, so hadn't he better call us a taxi? He would if we liked, he says, and he'd pay for it as well. But we tell him not to bother, that he's a good bloke even if he is a copper, that we know a short cut anyway. Then just as we're turning a corner he gets it into his big batchy head that we're going the opposite way to the hospital, and calls us back. So we'd start to run . . . if you can call all that thinking.

Up in my room Mike rips open that money-box with a hammer and chisel, and before we know where we are we've got seventy-eight pounds fifteen and fourpence ha'penny *each* lying all over my bed like tea spread out on Christmas Day: cake and trifle, salad and sandwiches, jam tarts and bars of chocolate: all shared and shared alike between Mike and me because we believed in equal work and equal pay, just like the comrades my dad was in until he couldn't do a stroke anymore and had no breath left to argue with. I thought how good it was that blokes like that poor baker didn't stash all his cash in one of the big marble-fronted banks that take up every corner of the town, how lucky for us that he didn't trust them no matter how many millions of tons of concrete or how many iron bars and boxes they were made of, or how many coppers kept their blue pop-eyed peepers glued on to them, how smashing it was that he believed in money-boxes when so many shop-keepers thought it old-fashioned and tried to be modern by using a bank, which wouldn't give a couple of sin-cere, honest, hardworking, conscientious blokes like Mike and me a chance.

Now you'd think, and I'd think, and anybody with a bit of imagination would think, that we'd done as clean a job as could ever be done, that, with the baker's shop being at least a mile from where we lived, and with not a soul having seen us, and what with the fog and the fact that we weren't more than five minutes in the place, that the coppers should never have been able to trace us. But then, you'd be wrong, I'd be wrong, and everybody else would be wrong, no matter how much imagina-tion was diced out between us.

Even so, Mike and I didn't splash the money about, because that would have made people think straightaway that we'd latched on to something that didn't belong to us. Which wouldn't do at all, because even in a street like ours there are people who love to do a good turn for the coppers, though I never know why they do. Some people are so mean-gutted that even if they've only got tuppence more than you and they think you're the sort that would take it if you have half the chance, they'd get you put inside if they saw you ripping lead out of a lavatory, even if it weren't their lavatory—just to keep their tup-pence out of your reach. And so we didn't do anything to let on about how rich we were, nothing like going down town and coming back dressed in brand-new Teddy boy suits and carrying a set of skiffle-drums like another pal of ours who'd done a factory office about six months before. No, we took the odd bobs and pennies out and folded the notes into bundles and stuffed them up the drainpipe outside the door in the backyard. "Nobody'll ever think of

looking for it there," I said to Mike. "We'll keep it doggo for a week or two, then take a few quid a week out till it's all gone. We might be thieving bastards, but we're not green."

Some days later a plain-clothes dick knocked at the door. And asked for me. I was still in bed, at eleven o'clock, and had to unroll myself from the com-fortable black sheets when I heard mam calling me. "A man to see you," she said. "Hurry up, or he'll be gone."

I could hear her keeping him at the back door, nattering about how fine it had been but how it looked like rain since early this morning—and he didn't answer her except to snap out a snotty yes or no. I scrambled into my trousers and wondered why he'd come—know-ing it was a copper because "a man to see you" always meant just that in our house—and if I'd had any idea that one had gone to Mike's house as well at the same time I'd have twigged it to be be-cause of that hundred and fifty quid's worth of paper stuffed up the drain-pipe outside the back door about ten inches away from that plain-clothed cop-per's boot, where mam still talked to him thinking she was doing me a favor, and I wishing to God she'd ask him in, though on second thoughts realizing that that would seem more suspicious than keeping him outside, because they know we hate their guts and smell a rat if they think we're trying to be nice to them. Mam wasn't born yester-day, I thought, thumping my way down the creaking stairs.

I'd seen him before: Borstal Bernard in nicky-hat, Remand Home Ronald in rowing-boat boots, Probation Pete in a pit-prop machintosh, three-months clink in collar and tie (all this out of a Bor-stal skiffle-ballad that my new mate made up, and I'd tell you it in full but it doesn't belong in this story), a 'tec, who'd never had as much in his pockets as that drainpipe had up its jackses. He was like Hitler in the face, right down to the paint-brush tash, except that being six-foot tall made him seem worse. But

I straightened my shoulders to look into his illiterate blue eyes—like I always do with any copper.

Then he started asking me questions, and my mother from behind said: "He's never left that television set for the last three months, so you've got nowt on him, mate. You might as well look for somebody else, because you're wasting the rates you get out of my rent and the income-tax that comes out of my pay-packet standing there like that"—which was a laugh because she'd never paid either to my knowledge, and never would, I hoped.

"Well, you know where Papplewick Street is, don't· you?" the copper asked me, taking no notice of mam.

"Ain't it off Alfreton Road?" I asked him back, helpful and bright.

"You know there's a baker's half-way down on the left-hand side, don't you?"

"Ain't it next door to a pub, then?" I wanted to know.

He answered me sharp: "No, it bloody well ain't." Coppers always lose their tempers as quick as this, and more often than not they gain nothing by it. "Then I don't know it," I told him, saved by the bell.

He slid his big boot round and round on the doorstep. "Where were you last Friday night?" Back in the ring, but this was worse than a boxing match.

I didn't like him trying to accuse me of something he wasn't sure I'd done. "Was I at that baker's you mentioned? Or in the pub next door?"

"You'll get five years in Borstal if you don't give me a straight answer," he said, unbuttoning his mac even though it was cold where he was standing.

"I was glued to the telly, like mam says," I swore blind. But he went on and on with his loony questions: "Have you got a television?"

The things he asked wouldn't have taken in a kid of two, and what else could I say to the last one except: "Has the aerial fell down? Or would you like to come in and see it?"

He was liking me even less for saying that. "We know you weren't listening to the television set last Friday, and so do you, don't you?"

"P'raps not, but I was *looking* at it, because some times we turn the sound down for a bit of fun." I could hear mam laughing from the kitchen, and I hoped Mike's mam was doing the same if the cops had gone to him as well.

"We know you weren't in the house," he said, starting up again, cranking himself with the handle. They always say "We" "We," never "I" "I"—as if they feel braver and righter knowing there's a lot of them against only one.

"I've got witnesses," I said to him. "Mam for one. Her fancy-man, for two. Ain't that enough? I can get you a dozen more, or thirteen altogether, if it was a baker's that got robbed."

"I don't want no lies," he said, not catching on about the baker's dozen. Where do they scrape cops up from any way? "All I want is to get from you where you put that money."

Don't get mad, I kept saying to myself, don't get mad—hearing mam setting out cups and saucers and putting the pan on the stove for bacon. I stood back and waved him inside like I was a butler. "Come and search the house. If you've got a warrant."

"Listen, my lad," he said like the dirty bullying jumped-up bastard he was, "I don't want too much of your lip, because if we get you down to the Guildhall you'll get a few bruises and black-eyes for your trouble." And I knew he wasn't kidding either, because I'd heard about all them sort of tricks. I hoped one day though that him and all his pals would be the ones to get the black-eyes and kicks; you never knew. It might come sooner than anybody thinks, like in Hungary. "Tell me where the money is, and I'll get you off with probation."

"What money?" I asked him, because I'd heard that one before as well.

"You know what money."

"Do I look as though I'd know owt about money?" I said, pushing my fist through a hole in my shirt.

"The money that was pinched, that you know all about," he said. "You can't trick me, so it's no use trying."

"Was it three-and-eightpence ha'-penny?" I asked.

"You thieving young bastard. We'll teach you to steal money that doesn't belong to you."

I turned my head around: "Mam," I called out, "get my lawyer on the blower, will you?"

"Clever, aren't you?" he said in a very unfriendly way, "but we won't rest until we clear all this up."

"Look," I pleaded, as if about to sob my socks off because he'd got me wrong, "it's all very well us talking like this, it's like a game almost, but I wish you'd tell me what it's all about, because honest-to-God I've just got out of bed and here you are at the door talking about me having pinched a lot of money, money that I don't know anything about."

He swung around now as if he'd trapped me, though I couldn't see why he might think so. "Who said anything about money? I didn't. What made you bring money into this little talk we're having?"

"It's you," I answered, thinking he was going barmy and about to start foaming at the chops, "you've got money on the brain, like all policemen. Baker's shops as well."

He screwed his face up. "I want an answer from you: Where's that money?"

But I was getting fed-up with all this. "I'll do a deal."

Judging by his flash-bulb face he thought he was suddenly on to a good thing. "What sort of a deal?"

So I told him: "I'll give you all the money I've got, one and fourpence ha' penny, if you stop this third-degree and let me go in and get my breakfast. Honest, I'm clambed to death. I ain't had a bite since yesterday. Can't you hear my guts rollin'?"

His jaw dropped, but on he went, pumping me for another half hour. A routine check-up, as they say on the pictures. But I knew I was winning on points.

Then he left, but came back in the afternoon to search the house. He didn't find a thing, not a French farthing. He asked me questions again and I didn't tell him anything except lies, lies, lies, because I can go on doing that forever without batting an eyelid. He'd got nothing on me and we both of us knew it, otherwise I'd have been down at the Guildhall in no time, but he kept on keeping on because I'd been in a Remand Home for a high-wall job before; and Mike was put through the same mill because all the local cops knew he was my best pal.

When it got dark me and Mike were in our parlor with a low light on and the telly off, Mike taking it easy in the rocking chair and me slouched out on the settee, both of us puffing a packet of Woods. With the door bolted and curtains drawn we talked about the dough we'd crammed up the drainpipe. Mike thought we should take it out and both of us do a bunk to Skegness or Cleethorpes for a good time in the arcades, living like lords in a boarding house near the pier, then at least we'd both have had a big beano before getting sent down.

"Listen, you daft bleeder," I said, "we aren't going to get caught at all, *and* we'll have a good time, later." We were so clever we didn't even go out to the pictures, though we wanted to.

In the morning old Hitler-face questioned me again, with one of his pals this time, and the next day they came, trying as hard as they could to get something out of me, but I didn't budge an inch. I know I'm showing off when I say this, but in me he'd met his match, and I'd never give in to questions no matter how long it was kept up. They searched the house a couple of times as well, which made me think they thought they really had something to go by, but I know now that they hadn't, and that it was all buckshee speculation. They turned the house upside down and inside out like an old sock, went from top to bottom and front to back but naturally didn't find a thing. The copper even poked his face up the front-room chimney (that hadn't been used or swept for years) and came down looking like Al Jolson so that he had to swill himself clean at the scullery sink. They kept tapping and pottering around the big aspidistra plant that grandma had left to mam, lifting it up from the table to look under the cloth, putting it aside so's they could move the table and get at the boards under the rug—but the big headed stupid ignorant bastards never once thought of emptying the soil out of the plant pot, where they'd have found the crumpled-up money-box that we'd buried the night we did the job. I suppose it's still there, now I think about it, and I suppose mam wonders now and again why the plant don't prosper like it used to—as if it could with a fistfull of thick black tin lapped around its guts.

The last time he knocked at our door was one wet morning at five minutes to nine and I was sleep-logged in my crumby bed as usual. Mam had gone to work that day so I shouted for him to hold on a bit, and then went down to see who it was. There he stood, six-feet tall and sopping wet, and for the first time in my life I did a spiteful thing I'll never forgive myself for: I didn't ask him to come in out of the rain, because I wanted him to get double pneumonia and die. I suppose he could have pushed by me and come in if he'd wanted, but maybe he'd got used to asking questions on the doorstep and didn't want to be put off by changing his ground even though it was raining. Not that I don't like being spiteful because of any barmy principle I've got, but this bit of spite, as it turned out, did me no good at all. I should have treated him as a brother I hadn't seen for twenty years and dragged him in

for a cup of tea and a fag, told him about the picture I hadn't seen the night before, asked him how his wife was after her operation and whether they'd shaved her moustache off to make it, and then sent him happy and satisfied out by the front door. But no, I thought, let's see what he's got to say for himself now.

He stood a little to one side of the door, either because it was less wet there, or because he wanted to see me from a different angle, perhaps having found it monotonous to watch a bloke's face always telling lies from the same side. "You've been identified," he said, twitching raindrops from his tash. "A woman saw you and your mate yesterday and she swears blind you are the same chaps she saw going into that bakery."

I was dead sure he was still bluffing, because Mike and I hadn't even seen each other the day before, but I looked worried. "She's a menace then to innocent people, whoever she is, because the only bakery I've been in lately is the one up our street to get some cutbread on tick for mam."

He didn't bite on this. "So now I want to know where the money is"— as if I hadn't answered him at all.

"I think mam took it to work this morning to get herself some tea in the canteen." Rain was splashing down so hard I thought he'd get washed away if he didn't come inside. But I wasn't much bothered, and went on: "I remember I put it in the telly-vase last night—it was my only one-and-three and I was saving it for a packet of tips this morning—and I nearly had a jibbering black fit just now when I saw it had gone. I was reckoning on it for getting me through today because I don't think life's worth living without a fag, do you?"

I was getting into my stride and began to feel good, twigging that this would be my last pack of lies, and that if I kept it up for long enough this time I'd have the bastards beat: Mike and me would be off to the coast in a few weeks time having the fun of our lives, playing at penny football and latching on to a couple of tarts that would give us all they were good for. "And this weather's no good for picking-up fag-ends in the street," I said, "because they'd be sopping wet. Course, I know you could dry 'em out near the fire, but it don't taste the same you know, all said and done. Rainwater does summat to 'em that don't bear thinkin' about: it turns 'em back into hoss-tods without the taste though."

I began to wonder, at the back of my brainless eyes, why old copper-lugs didn't pull me up sharp and say he hadn't got time to listen to all this, but he wasn't looking at me anymore, and all my thoughts about Skegness went bursting to smithereens in my sludgy loaf. I could have dropped into the earth when I saw what he'd fixed his eyes on.

He was looking at *it,* an ever-loving fiver, and I could only jabber: "The one thing is to have some real fags because new hoss-tods is always better than stuff that's been rained on and dried, and I know how you feel about not being able to find money because one-and-three's one-and-three in anybody's pocket, and naturally if I see it knocking around I'll get you on the blower tomorrow straightaway and tell you where you can find it."

I thought I'd go down in a fit: three green-backs as well had been washed down by the water, and more were following, lying flat at first after their fall, then getting tilted at the corners by wind and rainspots as if they were alive and wanted to get back into the dry snug drainpipe out of the terrible weather, and you can't imagine how I wished they'd be able to. Old Hitler-face didn't know what to make of it but just kept staring down and down, and I thought I'd better keep on talking, though I knew it wasn't much good now.

"It's a fact, I know, that money's hard to come by and half-crowns don't get

found on bus seats or in dustbins, and I didn't see any in bed last night because I'd 'ave known about it, wouldn't I? You can't sleep with things like that in the bed because they're too hard, and anyway at first they're. . ." It took Hitler-boy a long time to catch on; they were beginning to spread over the yard a bit, reinforced by the third color of a ten-bob note, before his hand clamped itself on to my shoulder.

III

The pop-eyed potbellied governor said to a pop-eyed potbellied Member of Parliament who sat next to his pop-eyed potbellied whore of a wife that I was his only hope for getting the Borstal Blue Ribbon Prize Cup For Long-Distance Cross-Country Running (all England), which I was, and it set me laughing to myself inside, and I didn't say a word to any potbellied pop-eyed bastard that might give them real hope, though I knew the governor anyway took my quietness to mean he'd got that cup already stuck on the bookshelf in his office among the few other mildewed trophies.

"He might take up running in a sort of professional way when he gets out," and it wasn't until he'd said this and I'd heard it with my own flap-tabs that I realized it might be possible to do such a thing, run for money, trot for wages on piece work at a bob a puff rising bit by bit to a guinea a gasp and retiring through old age at thirty-two because of lace-curtain lungs, a football heart, and legs like varicose beanstalks. But I'd have a wife and car and get my grinning long-distance clock in the papers and have a smashing secretary to answer piles of letters sent by tarts who'd mob me when they saw who I was as I pushed my way into Woolworth's for a packet of razor blades and a cup of tea. It was something to think about all right, and sure enough the governor knew he'd got me when he said, turning to me as if I would at any rate have to be consulted about it all: "How does this matter strike you, then, Smith, my lad?"

A line of potbellied pop-eyes gleamed at me and a row of goldfish mouths opened and wiggled gold teeth at me, so I gave them the answer they wanted because I'd hold my trump card until later. "It'd suit me fine, sir," I said.

"Good lad. Good show. Right spirit. Splendid."

"Well," the governor said, "get that cup for us today and I'll do all I can for you. I'll get you trained so that you whack every man in the Free World." And I had a picture in my brain of me running and beating everybody in the world, leaving them all behind until only I was trot-trotting across a big wide moor alone, doing a marvellous speed as I ripped between boulders and reed-clumps, when suddenly: CRACK! CRACK!—bullets that can go faster than any man running, coming from a copper's rifle planted in a tree, winged me and split my gizzard in spite of my perfect running, and down I fell.

The potbellies expected me to say something else. "Thank you, sir," I said.

Told to go, I trotted down the pavilion steps, out on to the field because the big cross-country was about to begin and the two entries from Gunthorpe had fixed themselves early at the starting line and were ready to move off like white kangaroos. The sports ground looked a treat: with big tea-tents all round and flags flying and seats for families—empty because no mam or dad had known what opening day meant—and boys still running heats for the hundred yards, and lords and ladies walking from stall to stall, and the Borstal Boys Brass Band in blue uniforms; and up on the stands the brown jackets of Hucknall as well as our own grey blazers, and then the Gunthrope lot with shirt sleeves rolled. The blue sky was full of sunshine and it couldn't

have been a better day, and all of the big show was like something out of Ivanhoe that we'd seen on the pictures a few days before.

"Come on, Smith," Roach the sports master called to me, "we don't want you to be late for the big race, eh? Although I dare say you'd catch them up if you were." The others cat-called and grunted at this, but I took no notice and placed myself between Gunthorpe and one of the Aylesham trusties, dropped on my knees and plucked a few grass blades to suck on the way round. So the big race it was, for them, watching from the grandstand under a fluttering Union Jack, a race for the governor, that he had been waiting for, and I hoped he and all the rest of his pop-eyed gang were busy placing big bets on me, hundred to one to win, all the money they had in their pockets, all the wages they were going to get for the next five years, and the more they placed the happier I'd be. Because here was a dead cert going to die on the big name they'd built for him, going to go down dying with laughter whether it choked him or not. My knees felt the cool soil pressing into them, and out of my eye's corner I saw Roach lift his hand. The Gunthorpe boy twitched before the signal was given; somebody cheered too soon; Medway bent forward; then the gun went, and I was away.

We went once around the field and then along a half-mile drive of elms, being cheered all the way, and I seemed to feel I was in the lead as we went out by the gate and into the lane, though I wasn't interested enough to find out. The five-mile course was marked by splashes of whitewash gleaming on gateposts and trunks and stiles and stones, and a boy with a waterbottle and bandage-box stood every half-mile waiting for those that dropped out or fainted. Over the first stile, without trying, I was still nearly in the lead but one; and if any of you want tips about running, never be in a hurry, and never let any of the other runners know you are in a hurry even if you are. You can always overtake on long-distance running without letting the others smell the hurry in you; and when you've used your craft like this to reach the two or three up front then you can do a big dash later that puts everybody else's hurry in the shade because you've not had to make haste up till then. I ran to a steady jog-trot rhythm, and soon it was so smooth that I forgot I was running, and I was hardly able to know that my legs were lifting and falling and my arms going in and out, and my lungs didn't seem to be working at all, and my heart stopped that wicked thumping I always get at the beginning of a run. Because you see I never race at all; I just run, and somehow I know that if I forget I'm racing and only jog-trot along until I don't know I'm running I always win the race. For when my eyes recognize that I'm getting near the end of the course—by seeing a stile or cottage corner—I put on a spurt, and such a fast big spurt it is because I feel that up till then I haven't been running and that I've used up no energy at all. And I've been able to do this because I've been thinking; and I wonder if I'm the only one in the running business with this system of forgetting that I'm running because I'm too busy thinking; and I wonder if any of the other lads are on to the same lark, though I know for a fact that they aren't. Off like the wind along the cobbled footpath and rutted lane, smoother than the flat grass track on the field and better for thinking because it's not too smooth, and I was in my element that afternoon knowing that nobody could beat me at running but intending to beat myself before the day was over. For when the governor talked to me of being honest when I first came in he didn't know what the word meant or he wouldn't have had me here in this race, trotting along in shimmy and shorts and sunshine. He'd

have had me where I'd have had him if I'd been in his place: in a quarry breaking rocks until he broke his back. At least old Hitler-face the plain-clothes dick was honester than the governor, because he at any rate had had it in for me and I for him, and when my case was coming up in court a copper knocked at our front door at four o'clock in the morning and got my mother out of bed when she was paralytic tired, reminding her she had to be in court at dead on half past nine. It was the finest bit of spite I've ever heard of, but I would call it honest, the same as my mam's words were honest when she really told that copper what she thought of him and called him all the dirty names she'd ever heard of, which took her half an hour and woke the terrace up.

I trotted on along the edge of a field bordered by the sunken lane, smelling green grass and honeysuckle, and I felt as though I came from a long line of whippets trained to run on two legs, only I couldn't see a toy rabbit in front and there wasn't a collier's cosh behind to make me keep up the pace. I passed the Gunthorpe runner whose shimmy was already black with sweat and I could just see the corner of the fenced-up copse in front where the only man I had to pass to win the race was going all out to gain the half-way mark. Then he turned into a tongue of trees and bushes where I couldn't see him anymore, and I couldn't see anybody, and I knew what the loneliness of the long-distance runner running across country felt like, realizing that as far as I was concerned this feeling was the only honesty and realness there was in the world and I knowing it would be no different ever, no matter what I felt at odd times, and no matter what anybody else tried to tell me. The runner behind me must have been a long way off because it was so quiet, and there was even less noise and movement than there had been at five o'clock of a frosty winter morning. It was hard to understand, and all I knew was that you had to run, run, run, without knowing why you were running, but on you went through fields you didn't understand and into woods that made you afraid, over hills without knowing you'd been up and down, and shooting across streams that would have cut the heart out of you had you fallen into them. And the winning post was no end to it, even though crowds might be cheering you in, because on you had to go before you got your breath back, and the only time you stopped really was when you tripped over a tree trunk and broke your neck or fell into a disused well and stayed dead in the darkness forever. So I thought: they aren't going to get me on this racing lark, this running and trying to win, this jog-trotting for a bit of blue ribbon, because it's not the way to go on at all, though they swear blind that it is. You should think about nobody and go your own way, not on a course marked out for you by people holding mugs of water and bottles of iodine in case you fall and cut yourself so that they can pick you up—even if you want to stay where you are—and get you moving again.

On I went, out of the wood, passing the man leading without knowing I was going to do so. Flip-flap, flip-flap, jog-trot, jog-trot, crunchslap-crunchslap, across the middle of a broad field again, rhythmically running in my greyhound effortless fashion, knowing I had won the race though it wasn't half over, won it if I wanted it, could go on for ten or fifteen or twenty miles if I had to and drop dead at the finish of it, which would be the same, in the end, as living an honest life like the governor wanted me to. It amounted to: win the race and be honest, and on trot-trotting I went, having the time of my life, loving my progress because it did me good and set me thinking which by now I liked to do, but not caring at all when I remembered that I had to win this race as well as run it. One of the two, I had

to win the race or run it, and I knew I could do both because my legs had carried me well in front—now coming to the short cut down the bramble bank and over the sunken road—and would carry me further because they seemed made of electric cable and easily alive to keep on slapping at those ruts and roots, but I'm not going to win because the only way I'd see I came in first would be if winning meant that I was going to escape the coppers after doing the biggest bank job of my life, but winning means the exact opposite, no matter how they try to kill or kid me, means running right into their white-gloved wall-barred hands and grinning mugs and staying there for the rest of my natural long life of stone-breaking anyway, but stone-breaking in the way I want to do it and not in the way they tell me.

Another honest thought that comes is that I could swing left at the next hedge of the field, and under its cover beat my slow retreat away from the sports ground winning post. I could do three or six or a dozen miles across the turf like this and cut a few main roads behind me so's they'd never know which one I'd taken; and maybe on the last one when it got dark I could thumb a lorry-lift and get a free ride north with somebody who might not give me away. But no, I said I wasn't daft didn't I? I won't pull out with only six months left, and besides there's nothing I want to dodge and run away from; I only want a bit of my own back on the In-laws and Potbellies by letting them sit up there on their big posh seats and watch me lose this race, though as sure as God made me I know that when I do lose I'll get the dirtiest crap and kitchen jobs in the months to go before my time is up. I won't be worth a threpp'ny-bit to anybody here, which will be all the thanks I get for being honest in the only way I know. For when the governor told me to be honest it was meant to be in his way not mine, and if I kept on being honest in the way he wanted and won my race for him he'd see I got the cushiest six months still left to run; but in my own way, well, it's not allowed, and if I find a way of doing it such as I've got now then I'll get what-for in every mean trick he can set his mind to. And if you look at it in my way, who can blame him? For this is war—and ain't I said so?—and when I hit him in the only place he knows he'll be sure to get his own back on me for not collaring that cup when his heart's been set for ages on seeing himself standing up at the end of the afternoon to clap me on the back as I take the cup from Lord Earwig or some such chinless wonder with a name like that. And so I'll hit him where it hurts a lot, and he'll do all he can to get his own back, tit for tat, though I'll enjoy it most because I'm hitting first, and be-cause I planned it longer. I don't know why I think these thoughts are better than any I've ever had, but I do, and I don't care why. I suppose it took me a long time to get going on all this be-cause I've had no time and peace in all my bandit life, and now my thoughts are coming pat and the only trouble is I often can't stop, even when my brain feels as if it's got cramp, frostbite and creeping paralysis all rolled into one and I have to give it a rest by slap-dashing down through the brambles of the sunken lane. And all this is another uppercut I'm getting in first at people like the governor, to show how—if I can—his races are never won even though some bloke always comes un-knowingly in first, how in the end the governor is going to be doomed while blokes like me will take the pickings of his roasted bones and dance like maniacs around his Borstal's ruins. And so this story's like the race and once again I won't bring off a winner to suit the governor; no, I'm being honest like he told me to, without him knowing what he means, though I don't suppose he'll ever come in with a story of his own, even if he reads this one of mine and knows who I'm talking about.

I've just come up out of the sunken lane, kneed and elbowed, thumped and bramble-scratched, and the race is two-thirds over, and a voice is going like a wireless in my mind saying that when you've had enough of feeling good like the first man on earth of a frosty morn-ing, and you've known how it is to be taken bad like the last man on earth on a summer's afternoon, then you get at last to being like the only man on earth and don't give a bogger about either good or bad, but just trot on with your slippers slapping the good dry soil that at least would never do you a bad turn. Now the words are like coming from a crystal-set that's broken down, and something's happening inside the shell-case of my guts that bothers me and I don't know why or what to blame it on, a grinding near my ticker as though a bag of rusty screws is loose inside me and I shake them up every time I trot forward. Now and again I break my rhythm to feel my left shoulder-blade by swinging a right hand across my chest as if to rub the knife away that has somehow got stuck there. But I know it's nothing to bother about, that more likely it's caused by too much thinking that now and again I take for worry. For sometimes I'm the greatest worrier in the world I think (as you twigged I'll bet from me having got this story out) which is funny anyway because my mam don't know the mean-ing of the word so I don't take after her; though dad had a hard time of worry all his life up to when he filled his bedroom with hot blood and kicked the bucket that morning when nobody was in the house. I'll never forget it, straight I won't, because I was the one that found him and I often wished I hadn't. Back from a session on the fruit-machines at the fish-and-chip shop, jingling my three-lemon loot to a nail-dead house, as soon as I got in I knew something was wrong, stood leaning my head against the cold mirror above the mantelpiece trying not to open my eyes and see my stone-cold clock—because I knew I'd gone as white as a piece of chalk since coming in as if I'd been got at by a Dracula-vampire and even my penny-pocket winnings kept quiet on purpose.

Gunthorpe nearly caught me up. Birds were singing from the briar hedge, and a couple of thrushies flew like lightning into some thorny bushes. Corn had grown high in the next field and would be cut down soon with scythes and mowers; but I never wanted to notice much while running in case it put me off my stroke, so by the haystack I decided to leave it all behind and put on such a spurt, in spite of nails in my guts, that before long I'd left both Gunthorpe and the birds a good way off; I wasn't far now from going into that last mile and a half like a knife through margarine, but the quietness I suddenly trotted into between two pickets was like opening my eyes underwater and looking at the pebbles on a stream bottom, reminding me again of going back that morning to the house in which my old man had croaked, which is funny because I hadn't thought about it at all since it happened and even then I didn't brood much on it. I wonder why? I suppose that since I started to think on these long-distance runs I'm liable to have anything crop up and pester at my tripes and innards, and now that I see my bloody dad behind each grass-blade in my barmy runner-brain I'm not so sure I like to think and that it's such a good thing after all. I choke my phlegm and keep on running anyway and curse the Borstal-builders and their athletics—flappity-flap, slop-slop, crunchslap-crunchslap-crunchslap—who've maybe got their own back on me from the bright beginning by sliding magic-lantern slides into my head that never stood a chance before. Only if I take whatever comes like this in my runner's stride can I keep on keeping on like my old self and beat them back; and now I've thought on this far I know I'll win, in the crunchslap end. So anyway after a bit I went upstairs one step at a time not thinking anything about how I should find dad and what I'd do when I did. But now I'm making up for it by going over the rotten life mam led him ever since I can remember, knocking-on with different men even when he was alive and fit and she not caring whether he knew it or not, and most of the time he wasn't so blind as she thought and cursed and roared and threatened to punch her tab, and I had to stand up to stop him even though I knew she deserved it. What a life for all of us. Well, I'm not grumbling, because if I did I might just as well win this bleeding race, which I'm not going to do, though if I don't lose speed I'll win it before I know where I am, and then where would I be?

Now I can hear the sportsground noise and music as I head back for the flags and the lead-in drive, the fresh new feel of underfoot gravel going against the iron muscles of my legs. I'm nowhere near puffed despite that bag of nails that rattles as much as ever, and I can still give a big last leap like gale-force wind if I want to, but everything is under control and I know now that there ain't another long-distance cross-country running runner in England to touch my speed and style. Our doddering bastard of a governor, our half-dead gangrened gaffer is hollow like an empty petrol drum, and he wants me and my running life to give him glory, to put in him blood and throbbing veins he never had, wants his potbellied pals to be his witnesses as I gasp and stagger up to his winning post so's he can say: "My Borstal gets that cup, you see. I win my bet, because it pays to be honest and try to gain the prizes I offer to my lads, and they know it, have known it all along. They'll always be honest now, because I made them so." And his pals will think: "He trains his lads to live right, after all; he deserves a medal but we'll get him made a Sir"—and at this very moment as the birds come back to whistling I can tell myself I'll never care a sod what any of the chinless spineless In-laws think or say. They've seen me and they're cheering now and loudspeakers set around the field like elephant's ears are spreading out the big news that I'm well in the lead, and can't do anything else but stay there. But I'm still thinking of the Out-law death my dad died, telling the doctors to scat from the house when they wanted him to finish up in hospital (like a bleeding guinea-pig, he raved at them). He got up in bed to throw them out and even followed them down the stairs in his shirt though he was no more than skin and stick. They tried to tell him he'd want some drugs but he didn't fall for it, and only took the pain-killer that mam and I got from a herb-seller in the next street. It's not till now that I know what guts he had, and when I went into the room that morning he was lying on his stomach with the clothes thrown back, looking like a skinned rabbit, his grey head resting just on the edge of the bed, and on the floor must have been all the blood he'd had in his body, right from his toe-nails up, for nearly all of the lino and carpet was covered in it, thin and pink.

And down the drive I went, carrying a heart blocked up like Boulder Dam across my arteries, the nail-bag clamped down tighter and tighter as though in a wood-work vice, yet with my feet like birdwings and arms like talons ready to fly across the field except that I didn't want to give anybody that much of a show, or win the race by accident. I smell the hot dry day now as I run towards the end, passing a mountain-heap of grass emptied from cans hooked on to the fronts of lawnmowers pushed by my pals; I rip a piece of tree-bark with my fingers and stuff it in my mouth, chewing wood and dust and maybe maggots as I run until I'm nearly

sick, yet swallowing what I can of it just the same because a little birdie whistled to me that I've got to go on living for at least a bloody sight longer yet but that for six months I'm not going to smell that grass or taste that dusty bark or trot this lovely path. I hate to have to say this but something bloody-well made me cry, and crying is a thing I haven't bloody-well done since I was a kid of two or three. Because I'm slowing down now for Gunthorpe to catch me up, and I'm doing it in a place just where the drive turns in to the sportsfield—where they can see what I'm doing, especially the governor and his gang from the grandstand, and I'm going so slow I'm almost marking time. Those on the nearest seats haven't caught on yet to what's happening and are still cheering like mad ready for when I make that mark, and I keep on wondering when the bleeding hell Gunthorpe behind me is going to nip by on to the field because I can't hold this up all day, and I think Oh Christ it's just my rotten luck that Gunthorpe's dropped out and that I'll be here for half an hour before the next bloke comes up, but even so, I say, I won't budge, I won't go for that last hundred yards if I have to sit down cross-legged on the grass and have the governor and his chinless wonders pick me up and carry me there, which is against their rules so you can bet they'd never do it be-cause they're not clever enough to break the rules—like I would be in their place—even though they are their own. No, I'll show him what honesty means if it's the last thing I do, though I'm sure he'll never understand because if he and all them like him did it'd mean they'd be on my side which is impossi-ble. By God I'll stick this out like my dad stuck out his pain and kicked them doctors down the stairs: if he had guts for that then I've got guts for this and here I stay waiting for Gunthorpe or Aylesham to bash that turf and go right slap-up against that bit of clothes-line stretched across the winning post.

As for me, the only time I'll hit that clothes-line will be when I'm dead and a comfortable coffin's been got ready on the other side. Until then I'm a long-distance runner, crossing country all on my own no matter how bad it feels.

The Essex boys were shouting themselves blue in the face telling me to get a move on, waving their arms, standing up and making as if to run at that rope themselves because they were only a few yards to the side of it. You cranky lot, I thought, stuck at that winning post, and yet I knew they didn't mean what they were shouting, were really on my side and always would be, not able to keep their maulers to themselves, in and out of cop-shops and clink. And there they were now having the time of their lives letting themselves go in cheering me which made the governor think they were heart and soul on his side when he wouldn't have thought any such thing if he'd had a grain of sense. And I could hear the lords and ladies now from the grandstand, and could see them standing up to wave me in: "Run!" they were shouting in their posh voices. "Run!" But I was deaf, daft and blind, and stood where I was, still tasting the bark in my mouth and still blubbing like a baby, blubbing now out of gladness that I'd got them beat at last.

Because I heard a roar and saw the Gunthorpe gang throwing their coats up in the air and I felt the pat-pat of feet on the drive behind me getting closer and closer and suddenly a smell of sweat and a pair of lungs on their last gasp passed me by and went swinging on towards that rope, all shagged out and rocking from side to side, grunting like a Zulu that didn't know any better, like the ghost of me at ninety when I'm heading for that fat upholstered coffin. I could have cheered him myself: "Go on, go on, get cracking. Knot yourself up on that piece of tape." But he was already there, and so I went on, trot-trotting after him until I got to

the rope, and collapsed, with a murderous sounding roar going up through my ears while I was still on the wrong side of it.

It's about time to stop; though don't think I'm not still running, because I am, one way or another. The governor at Borstal proved me right; he didn't respect my honesty at all; not that I expected him to, or tried to explain it to him, but if he's supposed to be educated then he should have more or less twigged it. He got his own back right enough, or thought he did, because he had me carting dustbins about every morning from the big full-working kitchen to the garden-bottoms where I had to empty them; and in the afternoon I spread out slops over spuds and carrots growing in the allotments. In the evenings I scrubbed floors, miles and miles of them. But it wasn't a bad life for six months, which was another thing he could never understand and would have made it grimmer if he could, and it was worth it when I look back on it, considering all the thinking I did, and the fact that the boys caught on to me losing the race on purpose and never had enough good words to say about me, or curses to throw out (to themselves) at the governor.

The work didn't break me; if anythink it made me stronger in many ways, and the governor knew, when I left, that his spite had got him nowhere. For since leaving Borstal they tried to get me in the army, but I didn't pass the medical and I'll tell you why. No sooner was I out, after that final run and six-months hard, than I went down with pleurisy, which means as far as I'm concerned that I lost the governor's race all right, and won my own twice over, because I know for certain that if I hadn't raced my race I wouldn't have got this pleurisy, which keeps me out of khaki but doesn't stop me doing the sort of work my itchy fingers want to do.

I'm out now and the heat's switched on again, but the rats haven't got me for the last big thing I pulled. I counted six hundred and twenty-eight pounds and am still living off it because I did the job all on my own, and after it I had the peace to write all this, and it'll be money enough to keep me going until I finish my plans for doing an even bigger snatch, something up my sleeve I wouldn't tell to a living soul. I worked out my systems and hiding-places while pushing scrubbing-brushes around them Borstal floors, planned my outward life of innocence and honest work, yet at the same time grew perfect in the razor-edges of my craft for what I knew I had to do once free; and what I'll do again if netted by the poaching coppers.

In the meantime (as they say in one or two books I've read since, useless though because all of them ended on a winning post and didn't teach me a thing) I'm going to give this story to a pal of mine and tell him that if I do get captured again by the coppers he can try and get it put into a book or something, because I'd like to see the governor's face when he reads it, if he does, which I don't suppose he will; even if he did read it though I don't think he'd know what it was all about. And if I don't get caught the bloke I give this story to will never give me away; he's lived in our terrace for as long as I can remember, and he's my pal. That I do know.

Terry Southern (1926–)

from Red Dirt Marijuana and Other Tastes

TWIRLING AT OLE MISS

In an age gone stale through the complex of bureaucratic interdependencies, with its tedious labyrinth of technical specialization, each contingent upon the next, and all aimed to converge into a single totality of meaning, it is a refreshing moment indeed when one comes across an area of human endeavor absolutely sufficient unto itself, pure and free, no strings attached—the cherished and almost forgotten *l'art pour l'art*. Such is the work being carried forward now at the Dixie National Baton Twirling Institute, down at the campus of Ole Miss—a visit to which is well worthwhile these days, if one can keep one's wits about.

In my case, it was the first trip South in many years, and I was duly apprehensive. For one thing, the Institute is located just outside Oxford, Mississippi —and, by grotesque coincidence, Faulkner's funeral had been held only the day before my arrival, lending a grimly surreal aura to the nature of my assignment . . . namely, to get the story of the Baton Twirling Institute. Would reverting to the Texas twang and callousness of my youth suffice to see me through?

Arriving in Oxford then, on a hot midday in July, after the three-hour bus ride from Memphis, I stepped off in front of the Old Colonial Hotel and meandered across the sleepy square toward the only sign of life at hand—the proverbial row of shirt-sleeved men sitting on benches in front of the county courthouse, a sort of permanent jury.

"Howdy," I say, striking an easy stance, smiling friendly-like. "Whar the school?"

The nearest regard me in narrow surmise: They are quick to spot the stranger here, but a bit slow to cotton. One turns to another.

"What's that he say, Ed?"

Big Ed shifts his wad, sluices a long spurt of juice into the dust, gazes at it reflectively before fixing me again with gun-blue-cold eyes.

"Reckon you mean, 'Whar the school *at?*', don't you, stranger?"

Next to the benches, and about three feet apart, are two public drinking fountains, and I notice that the one boldly marked "For Colored" is sitting squarely in the shadow cast by the justice symbol on the courthouse façade—to be entered later, of course, in my writer's notebook, under "Imagery, sociochiaroscurian, hack."

After getting directions (rather circuitous, I thought—being farther put off by what I understood, though perhaps in error, as a fleeting reference to "the Till case") I decided to take a cab, having just seen one park on the opposite side of the square.

"Which is nearer," I asked the driver, "Faulkner's house or his grave?"

"Wal," he said without looking around, "now that would take a little studyin', if you were gonna hold a man to it, but offhand I'd say they were pretty damn near the same—about ten minutes from where we're sittin' and fifty cents each. They're in opposite directions."

I sensed the somehow questionable irony of going from either to the Baton Twirling Institute, and so decided to get over to the Institute first and get on with the coverage.

"By the way," I asked after we'd started, "where can a man get a drink of whiskey around here?" It had just occurred to me that Mississippi is a dry state.

"Place over on the county line," said the driver, "about eighteen miles; cost you four dollars for the trip, eight for the bottle."

"I see."

He half turned, giving me a curious look.

"Unless, of course, you'd like to try some 'nigger-pot.'"

"Nigger-Pot? Great God yes, man," I said in wild misunderstanding, "let's go!"

It soon developed, of course, that what he was thinking about was the unaged and uncolored corn whiskey privately made in the region, and also known as "white lightning." I started to demur, but as we were already in the middle of the colored section, thought best to go through with it. Why not begin the sojourn with a genuine Dixieland experience—the traditional jug of corn?

As it happened the distiller and his wife were in the fields when we reached the house, or hut as it were, where we were tended by a Negro boy of about nine.

"This here's a mighty fine batch," he said, digging around in a box of kindling wood and fetching out unlabeled pints of it.

The taxi driver, who had come inside with me, cocked his head to one side and gave a short laugh, as to show we were not so easily put upon.

"Why, boy," he said, "I wouldn't have thought you was a drinkin' man."

"Nosuh, I ain't no drinkin' man, but I sure know how it suppose to taste—that's 'cause times nobody here I have to *watch* it and I have to *taste* it too, see it workin' right. We liable lose the whole batch I don't know how it suppose to taste. You all taste it," he added, holding out one of the bottles and shaking it in my happy face. "You see if that ain't a fine batch!"

Well, it had a pretty good taste all right—a bit edgy perhaps, but plenty of warmth and body. And I did have to admire the pride the young fellow took in his craft. You don't see much of that these days—especially among nine-year-olds. So I bought a couple of bottles, and the driver bought one, and we were off at last for the Institute.

The Dixie National Baton Twirling Institute holds its classes in a huge, sloping, fairyland grove on the campus of Ole Miss, and it resembles something from another age. The classes had already begun when I stepped out of the cab, and the sylvan scene which stretched before me, of some seven hundred girls, nymphs and nypmhets all, cavorting with their staffs in scanty attire beneath the broadleaf elms, was a sight to spin the senses and quicken the blood. Could I but have donned satyr's garb and rushed savagely among them! But no, there was this job o' work to get on with—dry, factual reportage—mere donkey work, in fact. I decided the correct procedure was to first get some background material, and to this end I sought out Don Sartell, "Mister Baton" himself, Director of the Institute. Mr. Sartell is a handsome and personable young man from north of the Mason-Dixon line, highly intelligent, acutely atuned to the needs of the young, and, needless to say, extremely dexterous *avec les doigts.* (By way of demonstrating the latter he once mastered a year's typing course in a quick six hours—or it may have been six days, though I do recall that it was an impressive and well-documented achievement.)

"Baton twirling," he tells me straight off, "is the second largest girl's youth movement in America—the first, of course, being the Girl Scouts." (Veteran legman, I check this out later. Correct.) "The popularity of baton twirling," he expains, "has a threefold justification: (1) it is a sport which can be practiced alone; (2) it does not, unlike other solo sports (sailing, skiing, shooting, etc.), require expensive equipment; and (3) it does not, again like the aforementioned, require travel, but, on the contrary, may be practiced in one's own living room or backyard."

"Right," I say. "So far, so good, Mister Baton—but what about the intrinsics? I mean, just what is the point of it all?"

"The point, aside from the simple satisfaction of mastering a complex and highly evolved skill, is the development of self-confidence, poise, ambidexterity, disciplined coordination, et cetera."

I asked if he would like a drink of nigger-pot. He declined graciously: he does not drink or smoke. My place, I decided, is in the grove, with the groovy girls—so, limbering up my 600-page, eight-dollar copy of *Who's Who in Baton Twirling*, I take my leave of the excellent fellow and steal toward the sylvan scene below, ready for anything.

The development of American baton twirling closely parallels the history of emancipation of our women. A larger version of this same baton (metal with a knob on the end) was first used, of course, to direct military marching bands, or, prior to that, drum corps—the baton being manipulated in a fairly straight-forward, dum-de-dum, up-and-down manner. The idea of *twirling* it—and finally even *flinging* it—is, obviously, a delightfully girlish notion.

Among those most keenly interested in mastering the skill today are drum majorettes from the high schools and colleges of the South and Midwest, all of which have these big swinging bands and corps of majorettes competing during the half at football games. In the South, on the higher-educational level, almost as much expense and training goes into these groups as into the football team itself, and, to persons of promise and accomplishment in the field, similar scholarships are available. Girls who aspire to become majorettes —and it is generally considered the smartest status a girl can achieve on the Southern campus—come to the Institute for preschool training. Or, if she is already a majorette, she comes to sharpen her technique. Many schools send a girl, or a small contingent of them, to the Institute to pick up the latest routines so that they can come back and teach the rest of the corps what they have learned. Still others are training to be professionals and teachers of baton twirling. Most of these girls come every year—I talked to one from Honey Pass, Arkansas, a real cutie pie, who had been there for eight consecutive years, from the time she was nine. When I asked if she would like a drink of pot, she replied pertly: "N . . . o . . . spells 'No'!" Such girls are usually championship material, shooting for the Nationals.

Competitions to determine one's degree of excellence are held regularly under the auspices of the National Baton Twirling Association, and are of the following myriad categories: *Advanced Solo; Intermediate Solo; Beginners Solo; Strutting Routine; Beginners Strutting Routine; Military Marching; Flag; Two-Baton; Fire Baton; Duet; Trio; Team; Corps; Boys; Out-of-State;* and others. Each division is further divided into age groups: 0–6, 7–8, 9–10, 11–12, 13–14, 15–16, 17 and over. The winner in each category receives a trophy, and the first five runners-up receive medals. This makes for quite a bit of hardware riding on one session, so that a person in the baton-twirling game does not go too long without at least token recognition—and the general run of *Who's Who* entries ("eight trophies, seventy-three medals") would make someone like Audie Murphy appear rudely neglected.

The rules of competition, however, are fairly exacting. Each contestant appears singly before a Judge and Scorekeeper, and while the Judge observes and relays the grading to the Scorekeeper, the girl goes through her routine for a closely specified time. In Advanced Solo, for example, the routine must have a duration of not less than two minutes and twenty seconds, and not more than two and thirty. She is scored on general qualities relating to her degree of accomplishment—including *showmanship, speed,* and *drops,* the latter, of course, counting against her, though not so much as one might suppose. Entrance fees average about two dollars for each contestant. Some girls use their allowance to pay it.

In the Institute's grove—not unlike the fabled Arcadia—the groups are ranged among the trees in various states of learning. The largest, most central and liveliest of these groups is the one devoted to the mastery of Strutting. Practice and instruction in Strutting are executed to records played over a public-address system at an unusually loud volume—a sort of upbeat rock and roll with boogie-woogie overtones. *Dixie, The Stripper,* and *Potato Peel* were the three records in greatest use for this class—played first at half speed, to learn the motions, then blasted at full tempo. Strutting is, of course, one of the most fantastic body-movement phenomena one is likely to see anywhere. The deliberate narcissistic intensity it requires must exceed even that of the Spanish flamenco dancer. High-style (or "all-out") Strutting is to be seen mainly in the South, and what it resembles more than anything else is a very contemporary burlesque-house number—with the grinds in and the bumps out. It is the sort of dance one associates with jaded and sequin-covered washed-out blondes in their very late thirties—but Ole Miss, as is perhaps well known, is in "the heartland of beautiful girls," having produced two Miss Americas and any number of runners-up, and to watch a hundred of their nymphets practice the Strut, in bathing suits, short shorts, and other such skimp, is a visual treat which cuts anything the Twist may offer the viewer. It is said, incidentally, that the best Strutting is done at the colored schools of the South, and that of these the greatest of all is to be seen at Alabama State Teachers College. That jazz trends have decisively influenced the style of Strutting in recent years in readily acknowledged, and is highly apparent indeed.

At the Institute, the instructor of the Strut stands on a slightly raised platform facing her class, flanked by her two assistants. She wears dark glasses, tight rolled shorts, and looks to be about 34-22-34. She's a swinger from Pensacola, Florida, a former National Senior Champion and Miss Majorette of America, now turned pro. When not at the Dixie Institute at the University of Mississippi, or a similar establishment, she gives private lessons at her own studio, for four to six dollars an hour, and drives a Cadillac convertible.

As for other, more academic, aspects of baton twirling, an exhibition was given the first evening by members of the cadre—all champions, and highly skilled indeed. It is really quite amazing what can be done with a baton, and no one could have been more surprised than your correspondent. The members of the cadre can literally walk those sticks over every inch of the body, almost it seems without touching them. This is especially effective at night when they use a thing called the "fire baton," with a torch flaming at each end.

Instruction in speed and manipulation of this sort is a long and nerve-racking process. There is something almost insane about the amount of sheer effort and perseverance which seems to go into achieving even a nominal degree of real excellence—and practice of four hours a day is not uncommon. And yet the genuine and really impressive skill which is occasionally displayed makes it difficult to consider the art as so totally ridiculous as one would have previously believed—though, of course, another might argue that such achieved excellence only makes it more ridiculous—or perhaps not so much ridiculous as absurd. In fact, in the existentialist sense, it might well be considered as the final epitome of the absurd—I mean, people starving in India and that sort of thing, and then others spending four hours a day skillfully flinging a metal stick about. *Ça alors!* In any case it has evolved now into a highly developed art and a

tightly organized movement—though by no means one which has reached full flower. For one thing, a nomenclature—that hallmark of an art's maturity —has not yet been wholly formalized. Theoretically, at least, there should be a limit to the number of possible manipulations, each of which could legitimately be held as distinct from all others—that is to say, a repertory which woud remain standard and unchanged for a period of time. The art of baton twirling has not yet reached that stage, however, and innovations arise with such frequency that there does not exist at present any single manual, or similiarly doctrinaire work, on the subject. Doubtless this is due in large part to the comparative newness of the art as a large and intensely active pastime—the Dixie National Baton Twirling Institute, for example, having been founded as recently as 1951. The continuing evolution of the art as a whole is reflected in the names of the various manipulations. Alongside the commonplace (or classic) designations, such as *arabesque, tour-jeté, cradles,* etc., are those of more exotic or contemporary flavor: *bat, walk-over, pretzel,* and the like . . . and all, old or new, requiring countless hours of practice.

During the twirling exhibition I fell into conversation with a couple of graduate law students, and afterward went along with them to the campus coffee shop, "Rebel Devil" or whatever it is called—nearly all shops there have the word "Rebel" in them—and we had an interesting talk. Ole Miss prides itself, among other things, on having the only law school in the state which is accredited by the American Bar Association—so that these two graduate law students were not without some claim to representing a certain level of relative advancement in the community of scholars. They were clean-cut young men in their mid-twenties, dressed in summer suits of tasteful cut. In answer to a question of mine, we talked about

Constitutional Law for ten minutes before I realized they were talking about *State* Constitutional Law. When it became apparent what I was driving at, however, they were quick to face the issue squarely.

"*We* nevuh had no Negra problem heah," said one of them, shaking his head sadly. He was a serious man wearing glasses and the mein of a Harvard divinity student. "Theah just *weren't* no problem—wasn't till these *agi-ta-tors* came down heah started all this problem business."

They were particularly disturbed about the possible "trouble, an' I mean *real* trouble" which would be occasioned by the attempted registration of a Negro student [James Meredith] which was threatening to take place quite soon, during that very summer session, in fact. As it happened, the authorities managed to delay it; I did, however, get a preview of things to come.

"Why they'll find *dope* in his room the first night he's heah," the other student said, "dope, a gun, something—*anything*, just plant it in theah an' *find* it! And out he'll go!"

They assured me that they themselves were well above this sort of thing, and were, in fact, speaking as mature and nonviolent persons.

"But now these heah young *unduh* graduates, they're hot-headed. Why, do you know how *they* feel? What *they* say?"

Then to the tune of *John Brown's Body*, the two graduate law students begin to sing, almost simultaneously: "*Oh we'll bury all the niggers in the Mississippi mud . . . ,*" singing it rather loudly it seemed to me—I mean if they were just documenting a point in a private conversation—or perhaps they were momentarily carried away, so to speak. In any event, and despite a terrific effort at steely Zen detachment, the incident left me somewhat depressed, so I retired early, to my comfortable room in the Alumni House, where I

sipped the white corn and watched television. But I was not destined to escape so easily, for suddenly who should appear on the screen but old Governor Faubus himself—in a gubernatorial campaign rant—with about six cross-purpose facial tics going strong, and in general looking as mad as a hatter. At first I actually mistook it for a rather tasteless and heavy-handed parody of the governor. It could not, I thought, really be Faubus, because why would the network carry an Arkansas primary campaign speech in Mississippi? Surely not just for laughs. Later I learned that while there is such a thing in television as a *nation*wide hookup for covering events of national importance, there is also such a thing as a *South*wide hookup.

The Institute's mimeographed schedule, of which I had received a copy, read for the next day as follows:

7:30	Up and at 'em
8–9	Breakfast—University Cafeteria
9–9:30	Assembly, Limber up, Review—Grove
9:30–10:45	Class No. 4
10:45–11:30	Relax—Make Notes
11:30–12:45	Class No. 5
1–2:30	Lunch—University Cafeteria
2:30–4	Class No. 6
4–5:30	Swim Hour
6:30–7:30	Supper—University Cafeteria
7:30	Dance—Tennis Court
11	Room Check
11:30	Lights Out (NO EXCEPTIONS)

The "*Up and at 'em*" seemed spirited enough; as did the "NO EXCEPTIONS" being in heavy capitals; but the rest somehow offered little promise, so, after a morning cup of coffee, I walked over to the library, just to see if they really had any books there—other than books on Constitutional Law, that is. Indeed they did, and quite a modern and comfortable structure it was, too, air-conditioned (as was, incidentally, my room at the Alumni House) and well-lighted throughout. After looking around for a bit, I carefully opened a mint first-edition copy of *Light in August*, and found "nigger-lover" scrawled across the title page. I decided I must be having a run of bad luck as, a few minutes later, I suffered still another minor trauma on the steps of the library. It was one of those incredible bits of irony which sometimes do occur in life, but are never suitable for fiction— for I had completely put the title-page incident out of my mind and was sitting on the steps of the library, having a smoke, when this very amiable gentleman of middle age paused in passing to remark on the weather (102°) and to inquire in an oblique and courteous way as to the nature of my visit. An immaculate, pink-faced man, with pince-nez spectacles attached by a silver loop to his lapel, nails buffed to a gleam, he carried a smart leather briefcase and a couple of English-literature textbooks which he rested momentarily on the balustrade as he continued to smile down on me with what seemed to be extraordinary happiness.

"My, but it's a mighty warm day, an' that's no lie," he said, withdrawing a dazzling white-linen handkerchief and touching it carefully to his brow, ". . . an' I expect you all from up Nawth," he added with a twinkle, "find it especially so!" Then he quite abruptly began to talk of the "natural tolerance" of the people of Mississippi, speaking in joyfully objective tones, as though it were, even to him, an unfailing source of mystery and delight.

"Don't mind nobody's business but yoah own!" he said, beaming and nodding his head—and it occurred to me this might be some kind of really weirdly obscured threat, the way he was smiling; but no, evidently he was just remarkably good-natured. " 'Live an' let live!' That's how the people of Mississippi feel—always have! Why, look at William Faulkner, with all his notions,

an' him livin' right ovah heah in Oxford all the time an' nobody botherin' him—just let him go his own way— why we even let him teach heah at the University one yeah! That's right! I know it! Live an' let live—you can't beat it! I'll see you now, you heah?" And his face still a glittering mask of joviality, he half raised his hand in good-by and hurried on. Who was this strange, happy educator? Was it he who had defaced the title page? His idea of tolerance and his general hilarity gave one pause. I headed back to the grove, hoping to recover some equilibrium. There, things seemed to be proceeding pretty much as ever.

"Do you find that your costume is an advantage in your work?" I asked the first seventeen-year-old Georgia Peach I came across, she wearing something like a handkerchief-size Confederate flag.

"Yessuh, I *do*," she agreed, with friendly emphasis, tucking her little blouse in a bit more snugly all around, and continuing to speak in that oddly rising inflection peculiar to girls of the South, making parts of a reply sound like a question: "Why, back home near Macon . . . Macon, Georgia? At Robert E. Lee High? . . . we've got these outfits with *tassels!* And a little red-and-gold skirt? . . . that, you know, sort of *flares out?* Well, now they're awful pretty, and of course they're *short* and everything, but I declare those tassels and that little skirt get in my way!"

The rest of the day passed without untoward incident, with my observing the Strut platform for a while, then withdrawing to rest up for the Dance, and perhaps catch the Faub on video again.

The Dance was held on a boarded-over outdoor tennis court, and was a swinging affair. The popular style of dancing in the white South is always in advance of that in the rest of white America; and, at any given moment, it most nearly resembles that which is occurring at the same time in Harlem, which is invariably the forerunner of whatever is to become the national style. I mused on this, standing there near the court foul line, and (in view of the day's events) pursued it to an interesting generalization: perhaps *all* the remaining virtues, or let us say, positive traits, of the white Southerner —folk song, poetic speech, and the occasional warmth and simplicity of human relationships—would seem rather obviously to derive from the colored culture there. Due to my magazine assignment, I could not reveal my findings over the public-address system at the dance—and, in fact, thought best to put them from my mind entirely, and get on with the coverage—and, to that end, had a few dances and further questioned the girls. Their view of the world was quite extraordinary. For most, New York was like another country—queer, remote, and of small import in the scheme of things. Several girls spoke spiritedly of wanting to "get into television," but it always developed that they were talking about programs produced in Memphis. Memphis, in fact, was definitely the mecca, yardstick and *summum bonum.* As the evening wore on, I found it increasingly difficult, despite the abundance of cutie pieness at hand, to string along with these values, and so finally decided to wrap it

up. It should be noted too, that girls at the Dixie National are under extremely close surveillance both in the grove and out.

The following day I made one last tour, this time noting in particular the instruction methods for advanced twirling techniques: *1-, 2-, 3-finger rolls, wrist rolls, waist roll, neck roll, etc.* A pretty girl of about twelve was tossing a baton sixty feet straight up, a silver whir in the Mississippi sunlight, and she beneath it spinning like an ice skater, and catching it behind her back, not having moved an inch. She said she had practiced it an hour a day for six years. Her hope was to become "the best there is at the high toss and spin" —and she was now up to seven complete turns before making the catch. Was there a limit to the height and number of spins one could attain? No, she guessed not.

After lunch I packed, bid adieu to the Dixie National and boarded the bus for Memphis. As we crossed the Oxford square and passed the courthouse, I saw the fountain was still shaded, although it was now a couple of hours later than the time before. Perhaps it is always shaded—cool and inviting, it could make a person thirsty just to see it.

Joan Didion (1935–)

SOME DREAMERS OF THE GOLDEN DREAM

This is a story about love and death in the golden land, and begins with the country. The San Bernardino Valley lies only an hour east of Los Angeles by the

San Bernardino Freeway but is in certain ways an alien place: not the coastal California of the subtropical twilights and the soft westerlies off the Pacific but a harsher California, haunted by the Mojave just beyond the mountains, devastated by the hot dry Santa Ana wind that comes down through the passes at 100 miles an hour and whines through the eucalyptus windbreaks and works on the nerves. October is the bad month for the wind, the month when breathing is difficult and the hills blaze up spontaneously. There has been no rain since April. Every voice seems a scream. It is the season of suicide and divorce and prickly dread, wherever the wind blows.

The Mormons settled this ominous country, and then they abandoned it, but by the time they left the first orange tree had been planted and for the next hundred years the San Bernardino Valley would draw a kind of people who imagined they might live among the talismanic fruit and prosper in the dry air, people who brought with them Midwestern ways of building and cooking and praying and who tried to graft those ways upon the land. The graft took in curious ways. This is the California where it is possible to live and die without ever eating an artichoke, without ever meeting a Catholic or a Jew. This is the California where it is easy to Dial-A-Devotion, but hard to buy a book. This is the country in which a belief in the literal interpretation of Genesis has slipped imperceptibly into a belief in the literal interpretation of *Double Indemnity,* the country of the teased hair and the Capris and the girls for whom all life's promise comes down to a waltz-length white wedding dress and the birth of a Kimberly or a Sherry or a Debbi and a Tijuana divorce and a return to hairdressers' school. "We were just crazy kids," they say without regret, and look to the future. The future always looks good in the golden land, because no one remembers the past. Here is where the hot wind blows and the old ways do not seem relevant, where the divorce rate is double the national average and where one person in every thirty-eight lives in a trailer.

Here is the last stop for all those who come from somewhere else, for all those who drifted away from the cold and the past and the old ways. Here is where they are trying to find a new life style, trying to find it in the only places they know to look: the movies and the newspapers. The case of Lucille Marie Maxwell Miller is a tabloid monument to that new life style.

Imagine Banyan Street first, because Banyan is where it happened. The way to Banyan is to drive west from San Bernardino out Foothill Boulevard, Route 66: past the Santa Fe switching yards, the Forty Winks Motel. Past the motel that is nineteen stucco tepees: "SLEEP IN A WIGWAM—GET MORE FOR YOUR WAMPUM." Past Fontana Drag City and the Fontana Church of the Nazarene and the Pit Stop A Go-Go; past Kaiser Steel, through Cucamonga, out to the Kapu Kai Restaurant-Bar and Coffee Shop, at the corner of Route 66 and Carnelian Avenue. Up Carnelian Avenue from the Kapu Kai, which means "Forbidden Seas," the subdivision flags whip in the harsh wind. "HALF-ACRE RANCHES! SNACK BARS! TRAVERTINE ENTRIES! $95 DOWN." It is the trail of an intention gone haywire, the flotsam of the New California. But after a while the signs thin out on Carnelian Avenue, and the houses are no longer the bright pastels of the Springtime Home owners but the faded bungalows of the people who grow a few grapes and keep a few chickens out here, and then the hill gets steeper and the road climbs and even the bungalows are few, and here— desolate, roughly surfaced, lined with eucalyptus and lemon groves—is Banyan Street.

Like so much of this country, Banyan suggests something curious and unnatural. The lemon groves are sunken, down a three- or four-foot retaining wall, so that one looks directly into their dense foliage, too lush, unsettlingly glossy, the greenery of nightmare; the fallen eucalyptus bark is too dusty, a place for snakes to breed. The stones look not like natural stones but like the rubble of some unmentioned upheaval. There are smudge pots, and a closed cistern. To one side of Banyan there is the flat valley, and to the other the San Bernardino Mountains, a dark mass looming too high, too fast, nine, ten, eleven thousand feet, right there above the lemon groves. At midnight on Banyan Street there is no light at all, and no sound except the wind in the eucalyptus and a muffled barking of dogs. There may be a kennel somewhere, or the dogs may be coyotes.

Banyan Street was the route Lucille Miller took home from the twenty-four-hour Mayfair Market on the night of October 7, 1964, a night when the moon was dark and the wind was blowing and she was out of milk, and Banyan Street was where, at about 12:30 A.M., her 1964 Volkswagen came to a sudden stop, caught fire, and began to burn. For an hour and fifteen minutes Lucille Miller ran up and down Banyan calling for help, but no cars passed and no help came. At three o'clock that morning, when the fire had been put out and the California Highway Patrol officers were completing their report, Lucille Miller was still sobbing and incoherent, for her husband had been asleep in the Volkswagen. "What will I tell the children, when there's nothing left, nothing left in the casket," she cried to the friend called to comfort her. "How can I tell them there's nothing left?"

In fact there was something left, and a week later it lay in the Draper Mortuary Chapel in a closed bronze coffin blanketed with pink carnations. Some 200 mourners heard Elder Robert E. Denton of the Seventh-Day Adventist Church of Ontario speak of "the temper of fury that has broken out among us." For Gordon Miller, he said, there would be "no more death, no more heartaches, no more misunderstandings." Elder Ansel Bristol mentioned the "pe-culiar" grief of the hour. Elder Fred Jensen asked "what shall it profit a man, if he shall gain the whole world, and lose his own soul?" A light rain fell, a blessing in a dry season, and a female vocalist sang "Safe in the Arms of Jesus." A tape recording of the service was made for the widow, who was being held without bail in the San Bernardino County Jail on a charge of first-degree murder.

Of course she came from somewhere else, came off the prairie in search of something she had seen in a movie or heard on the radio, for this is a Southern California story. She was born on January 17, 1930, in Winnipeg, Manitoba, the only child of Gordon and Lily Maxwell, both school-teachers and both dedicated to the Seventh-Day Adventist Church, whose members observe the Sabbath on Saturday, believe in an apocalyptic Second Coming, have a strong missionary tendency, and, if they are strict, do not smoke, drink, eat meat, use makeup, or wear jewelry, including wedding rings. By the time Lucille Maxwell enrolled at Walla Walla College in College Place, Washington, the Adventist school where her parents then taught, she was an eighteen-year-old possessed of unremarkable good looks and remarkable high spirits. "Lucille wanted to see the world," her father would say in retrospect, "and I guess she found out."

The high spirits did not seem to lend themselves to an extended course of study at Walla Walla College, and in the spring of 1949 Lucille Maxwell met and married Gordon ("Cork") Miller, a twenty-four-year-old graduate of Walla Walla and of the University of Oregon dental school, then stationed at Fort Lewis as a medical officer. "Maybe you could say it was love at first sight," Mr. Maxwell recalls. "Before they were ever formally introduced, he sent Lucille a dozen and a half roses with a card that said even if she didn't come out on a date with him, he hoped she'd find the roses pretty anyway." The Maxwells remember their daughter as a "radiant" bride.

Unhappy marriages so resemble one another that we do not need to know too much about the course of this one. There may or may not have been trouble on Guam, where Cork and Lucille Miller lived while he finished his Army duty. There may or may not have been problems in the small Oregon town where he first set up private practice. There appears to have been some disappointment about their move to California: Cork Miller had told friends that he wanted to become a doctor, that he was unhappy as a dentist and planned to enter the Seventh-Day Adventist College of Medical Evangelists at Loma Linda, a few miles south of San Bernardino. Instead he bought a dental practice in the west end of San Bernardino County, and the family settled there, in a modest house on the kind of street where there are always tricycles and revolving credit and dreams about bigger houses, better streets. That was 1957. By the summer of 1964 they had achieved the bigger house on the better street and the familiar accouterments of a family on its way up: the $30,000 a year, the three children for the Christmas card, the picture window, the family room, the newspaper photographs that showed "Mrs. Gordon Miller, Ontario Heart Fund Chairman. . . ." They were paying the familiar price for it. And they had reached the familiar season of divorce.

It might have been anyone's bad summer, anyone's siege of heat and nerves and migraine and money worries, but this one began particularly early and particularly badly. On April 24 an old friend, Elaine Hayton, died suddenly; Lucille Miller had seen her only the night before. During the month of May, Cork Miller was hospitalized briefly with a bleeding ulcer, and his usual reserve deepened into depression. He

told his accountant that he was "sick of looking at open mouths," and threatened suicide. By July 8, the conventional tensions of love and money had reached the conventional impasse in the new house on the acre lot at 8488 Bella Vista, and Lucille Miller filed for divorce. Within a month, however, the Millers seemed reconciled. They saw a marriage counselor. They talked about a fourth child. It seemed that the marriage had reached the traditional truce, the point at which so many resign themselves to cutting both their losses and their hopes.

But the Millers' season of trouble was not to end that easily. October 7 began as a commonplace enough day, one of those days that sets the teeth on edge with its tedium, its small frustrations. The temperature reached 102° in San Bernardino that afternoon, and the Miller children were home from school because of Teachers' Institute. There was ironing to be dropped off. There was a trip to pick up a prescription for Nembutal, a trip to a self-service dry cleaner. In the early evening, an unpleasant accident with the Volkswagen: Cork Miller hit and killed a German shepherd, and afterward said that his head felt "like it had a Mack truck on it." It was something he often said. As of that evening Cork Miller was $63,479 in debt, including the $29,637 mortgage on the new house, a debt load which seemed oppressive to him. He was a man who wore his responsibilities uneasily, and complained of migraine headaches almost constantly.

He ate alone that night, from a TV tray in the living room. Later the Millers watched John Forsythe and Senta Berger in *See How They Run,* and when the movie ended, about eleven, Cork Miller suggested that they go out for milk. He wanted some hot chocolate. He took a blanket and pillow from the couch and climbed into the passenger seat of the Volkswagen. Lucille Miller remembers reaching over to lock his door as she backed down the driveway.

By the time she left the Mayfair Market, and long before they reached Banyan Street, Cork Miller appeared to be asleep.

There is some confusion in Lucille Miller's mind about what happened between 12:30 A.M., when the fire broke out, and 1:50 A.M., when it was reported. She says that she was driving east on Banyan Street at about 35 m.p.h. when she felt the Volkswagen pull sharply to the right. The next thing she knew the car was on the embankment, quite near the edge of the retaining wall, and flames were shooting up behind her. She does not remember jumping out. She does remember prying up a stone with which she broke the window next to her husband, and then scrambling down the retaining wall to try to find a stick. "I don't know how I was going to push him out," she says. "I just thought if I had a stick, I'd push him out." She could not, and after a while she ran to the intersection of Banyan and Carnelian Avenue. There are no houses at that corner, and almost no traffic. After one car had passed without stopping, Lucille Miller ran back down Banyan toward the burning Volkswagen. She did not stop, but she slowed down, and in the flames she could see her husband. He was, she said, "just black."

At the first house up Sapphire Avenue, half a mile from the Volkswagen, Lucille Miller finally found help. There Mrs. Robert Swenson called the sheriff, and then, at Lucille Miller's request, she called Harold Lance, the Millers' lawyer and their close friend. When Harold Lance arrived he took Lucille Miller home to his wife, Joan. Twice Harold Lance and Lucille Miller returned to Banyan Street and talked to the Highway Patrol officers. A third time Harold Lance returned alone, and when he came back he said to Lucille Miller, "O.K. . . . you don't talk any more."

When Lucille Miller was arrested the next afternoon, Sandy Slagle was with her. Sandy Slagle was the intense, relentlessly loyal medical student who used to baby-sit for the Millers, and had been living as a member of the family since she graduated from high school in 1959. The Millers took her away from a difficult home situation, and she thinks of Lucille Miller not only as "more or less a mother or a sister" but as "the most wonderful character" she has ever known. On the night of the accident, Sandy Slagle was in her dormitory at Loma Linda University, but Lucille Miller called her early in the morning and asked her to come home. The doctor was there when Sandy Slagle arrived, giving Lucille Miller an injection of Nembutal. "She was crying as she was going under," Sandy Slagle recalls. "Over and over she'd say, 'Sandy, all the hours I spent trying to save him and now what are they trying to *do* to me?' "

At 1:30 that afternoon, Sergeant William Paterson and Detectives Charles Callahan and Joseph Karr of the Central Homicide Division arrived at 8488 Bella Vista. "One of them appeared at the bedroom door," Sandy Slagle remembers, "and said to Lucille, 'You've got ten minutes to get dressed or we'll take you as you are.' She was in her nightgown, you know, so I tried to get her dressed."

Sandy Slagle tells the story now as if by rote, and her eyes do no waver. "So I had her panties and bra on her and they opened the door again, so I got some Capris on her, you know, and a scarf." Her voice drops. "And then they just took her."

The arrest took place just twelve hours after the first report that there had been an accident on Banyan Street, a rapidity which would later prompt Lucille Miller's attorney to say that the entire case was an instance of trying to justify a reckless arrest. Actually what first caused the detectives who arrived on Banyan Street toward dawn that morning to give the accident more than routine attention were certain apparent physical inconsistencies. While Lucille Miller had said that she was driving about 35 m.p.h. when the car swerved to a stop, an examination of the cooling Volkswagen showed that it was in low gear, and that the parking rather than the driving lights were on. The front wheels, moreover, did not seem to be in exactly the position that Lucille Miller's description of the accident would suggest, and the right rear wheel was dug in deep, as if it had been spun in place. It seemed curious to the detectives, too, that a sudden stop from 35 m.p.h.—the same jolt which was presumed to have knocked over a gasoline can in the back seat and somehow started the fire—should have left two milk cartons up right on the back floorboard, and the remains of a Polaroid camera box lying apparently undisturbed on the back seat.

No one, however, could be expected to give a precise account of what did and did not happen in a moment of terror, and none of these inconsistencies seemed in themselves incontrovertible evidence of criminal intent. But they did interest the Sheriff's Office, as did Gordon Miller's apparent unconsciousness at the time of the accident, and the length of time it had taken Lucille Miller to get help. Something, moreover, struck the investigators as wrong about Harold Lance's attitude when he came back to Banyan Street the third time and found the investigation by no means over. "The way Lance was acting," the prosecuting attorney said later, "they thought maybe they'd hit a nerve."

And so it was that on the morning of October 8, even before the doctor had come to give Lucille Miller an injection to calm her, the San Bernardino County Sheriff's Office was trying to construct another version of what might have happened between 12:30 and 1:50 A.M. The hypothesis they would eventually present was based on the somewhat tortuous premise that Lucille Miller had undertaken a plan which failed: a plan to stop the car on the lonely road, spread gasoline over her presumably drugged husband, and, with a stick on the accelerator, gently "walk" the Volkswagen over the embankment, where it would tumble four feet down the retaining wall into the lemon grove and almost certainly explode. If this happened, Lucille Miller might then have somehow negotiated the two miles up Carnelian to Bella Vista in time to be home when the accident was discovered. This plan went awry, according to the Sheriff's Office hypothesis, when the car would not go over the rise of the embankment. Lucille Miller might have panicked then—after she had killed the engine the third or fourth time, say, out there on the dark road with the gasoline already spread and the dogs baying and the wind blowing and the unspeakable apprehension that a pair of headlights would suddenly light up Banyan Street and expose her there—and set the fire herself.

Although this version accounted for some of the physical evidence—the car in low because it had been started from a dead stop, the parking lights on because she could not do what needed doing without some light, a rear wheel spun in repeated attempts to get the car over the embankment, the milk cartons upright because there had been no sudden stop—it did not seem on its own any more or less credible than Lucille Miller's own story. Moreover, some of the physical evidence did seem to support her story: a nail in a front tire, a nine-pound rock found in the car, presumably the one with which she had broken the window in an attempt to save her husband. Within a few days an autopsy had established that Gordon Miller was alive when he burned, which did not particularly help the State's case, and that he had enough Nembutal and Sandoptal in his blood to put the average person to sleep, which did: on the other hand Gordon Miller habitually took both Nembutal and Fiorinal (a common headache prescription which contains Sandoptal), and had been ill besides.

It was a spotty case, and to make it work at all the State was going to have to find a motive. There was talk of unhappiness, talk of another man. That kind of motive, during the next few weeks, was what they set out to establish. They set out to find it in accountants' ledgers and double-indemnity clauses and motel registers, set out to determine what might move a woman who believed in all the promises of the middle class—a woman who had been chairman of the Heart Fund and who always knew a reasonable little dressmaker and who had come out of the bleak wild of prairie fundamentalism to find what she imagined to be the good life—what should drive such a woman to sit on a street called Bella Vista and look out her new picture window into the empty California sun and calculate how to burn her husband alive in a Volkswagen. They found the wedge they wanted closer at hand than they might have at first expected, for, as testimony would reveal later at the trial, it seemed that in December of 1963 Lucille Miller had begun an affair with the husband of one of her friends, a man whose daughter called her "Auntie Lucille," a man who might have seemed to have the gift for people and money and the good life that Cork Miller so noticeably lacked. The man was Arthwell Hayton, a well-known San Bernardino attorney and at one time a member of the district attorney's staff.

In some ways it was the conventional clandestine affair in a place like San Bernardino, a place where little is bright or graceful, where it is routine to misplace the future and easy to start looking for it in bed. Over the seven weeks that it would take to try Lucille Miller for murder, Assistant District Attorney Don A. Turner and defense attorney Edward P. Foley would between them

unfold a curiously predictable story. There were the falsified motel registrations. There were the lunch dates, the afternoon drives in Arthwell Hayton's red Cadillac convertible. There were the interminable discussions of the wronged partners. There were the confidantes ("I knew everything," Sandy Slagle would insist fiercely later. "I knew every time, places, everything") and there were the words remembered from bad magazine stories ("Don't kiss me, it will trigger things," Lucille Miller remembered telling Arthwell Hayton in the parking lot of Harold's Club in Fontana after lunch one day) and there were the notes, the sweet exchanges: "Hi Sweetie Pie! You are my cup of tea!! Happy Birthday—you don't look a day over 29!! Your baby, Arthwell."

And, toward the end, there was the acrimony. It was April 24, 1964, when Arthwell Hayton's wife, Elaine, died suddenly, and nothing good happened after that. Arthwell Hayton had taken his cruiser, *Captain's Lady,* over to Catalina that weekend; he called home at nine o'clock Friday night, but did not talk to his wife because Lucille Miller answered the telephone and said that Elaine was showering. The next morning the Haytons' daughter found her mother in bed, dead. The newspapers reported the death as accidental, perhaps the result of an allergy to hair spray. When Arthwell Hayton flew home from Catalina that weekend, Lucille Miller met him at the airport, but the finish had already been written.

It was in the breakup that the affair ceased to be in the conventional mode and began to resemble instead the novels of James M. Cain, the movies of the late 1930s, all the dreams in which violence and threats and blackmail are made to seem commonplaces of middle-class life. What was most startling about the case that the State of California was preparing against Lucille Miller was something that had nothing to do with law at all, something that never appeared in the eight-column afternoon headlines but was always there between them: the revelation that the dream was teaching the dreamers how to live. Here is Lucille Miller talking to her lover sometime in the early summer of 1964, after he had indicated that, on the advice of his minister, he did not intend to see her any more: "First, I'm going to go to that dear pastor of yours and tell him a few things. . . . When I do tell him that, you won't be in the Redlands Church any more. . . . Look, Sonny Boy, if you think your reputation is going to be ruined, your life won't be worth two cents." Here is Arthwell Hayton, to Lucille Miller: "I'll go to Sheriff Frank Bland and tell him some things that I know about you until you'll wish you'd never heard of Arthwell Hayton." For an affair between a Seventh-Day Adventist dentist's wife and a Seventh-Day Adventist personal-injury lawyer, it seems a curious kind of dialogue.

"Boy, I could get that little boy coming and going," Lucille Miller later confided to Erwin Sprengle, a Riverside contractor who was a business partner of Arthwell Hayton's and a friend to both the lovers. (Friend or no, on this occasion he happened to have an induction coil attached to his telephone in order to tape Lucille Miller's call.) "And he hasn't got one thing on me that he can prove. I mean, I've got concrete— he has nothing concrete." In the same taped conversation with Erwin Sprengle, Lucille Miller mentioned a tape that she herself had surreptitiously made, months before, in Arthwell Hayton's car.

"I said to him, I said 'Arthwell, I just feel like I'm being used.' . . . He started sucking his thumb and he said 'I love you. . . . This isn't something that happened yesterday. I'd marry you tomorrow if I could. I don't love Elaine.' He'd love to hear that played back, wouldn't he?"

"Yeah," drawled Sprengle's voice on the tape. "That would be just a little incriminating, wouldn't it?"

"Just a *little* incriminating," Lucille Miller agreed. "It really *is*."

Later on the tape, Sprengle asked where Cork Miller was.

"He took the children down to the church."

"You didn't go?"

"No."

"You're naughty."

It was all, moreover, in the name of "love"; everyone involved placed a magical faith in the efficacy of the very word. There was the significance that Lucille Miller saw in Arthwell's saying that he "loved" her, that he did not "love" Elaine. There was Arthwell insisting, later, at the trial, that he had never said it, that he may have "whispered sweet nothings in her ear" (as her defense hinted that he had whispered in many ears), but he did not remember bestowing upon her the special seal, saying the word, declaring "love." There was the summer evening when Lucille Miller and Sandy Slagle followed Arthwell Hayton down to his new boat in its mooring at Newport Beach and untied the lines with Arthwell aboard, Arthwell and a girl with whom he later testified he was drinking hot chocolate and watching television. "I did that on purpose," Lucille Miller told Erwin Sprengle later, "to save myself from letting my heart do something crazy."

January 11, 1965, was a bright warm day in Southern California, the kind of day when Catalina floats on the Pacific horizon and the air smells of orange blossoms and it is a long way from the bleak and difficult East, a long way from the cold, a long way from the past. A woman in Hollywood staged an all-night sit-in on the hood of her car to prevent repossession by a finance company. A seventy-year-old pensioner drove his station wagon at five miles an hour past three Gardena poker parlors and emptied three pistols and a twelve-gauge shotgun through their windows, wounding twenty-nine people. "Many young women become prostitutes just to have enough money to play cards," he explained in a note. Mrs. Nick Adams said that she was "not surprised" to hear her husband announce his divorce plans on the Les Crane Show, and, farther north, a sixteen-year-old jumped off the Golden Gate Bridge and lived.

And, in the San Bernardino County Courthouse, the Miller trial opened. The crowds were so bad that the glass courtroom doors were shattered in the crush, and from then on identification disks were issued to the first forty-three spectators in line. The line began forming at 6 A.M., and college girls camped at the courthouse all night, with stores of graham crackers and No-Cal.

All they were doing was picking a jury, those first few days, but the sensational nature of the case had already suggested itself. Early in December there had been an abortive first trial, a trial at which no evidence was ever presented because on the day the jury was seated the San Bernardino *Sun-Telegram* ran an "inside" story quoting Assistant District Attorney Don Turner, the prosecutor, as saying, "We are looking into the circumstances of Mrs. Hayton's death. In view of the current trial concerning the death of Dr. Miller, I do not feel I should comment on Mrs. Hayton's death." It seemed that there had been barbituates in Elaine Hayton's blood, and there had seemed some irregularity about the way she was dressed on that morning when she was found under the covers, dead. Any doubts about the death at the time, however, had never gotten as far as the Sheriff's Office. "I guess somebody didn't want to rock the boat," Turner said later. "These were prominent people."

Although all of that had not been in the *Sun-Telegram's* story, an immediate mistrial had been declared. Almost as immediately, there had been another development: Arthwell Hayton had asked newspapermen to an 11 A.M. Sunday morning press conference in his office. There had been television cameras, and flash bulbs popping. "As you gentlemen may know," Hayton had said, striking a note of stiff bonhomie, "there are very often women who become amorous toward their doctor or lawyer. This does not mean on the physician's or lawyer's part that there is any romance toward the patient or client."

"Would you deny that you were having an affair with Mrs. Miller?" a reporter had asked.

"I would deny that there was any romance on my part whatsoever."

It was a distinction he would maintain through all the wearing weeks to come.

So they had come to see Arthwell, these crowds who now milled beneath the dusty palms outside the courthouse, and they had also come to see Lucille, who appeared as a slight, intermittently pretty woman, already pale from lack of sun, a woman who would turn thirty-five before the trial was over and whose tendency toward haggardness was beginning to show, a meticulous woman who insisted, against her lawyer's advice, on coming to court with her hair piled high and lacquered. "I would've been happy if she'd come in with it hanging loose, but Lucille wouldn't do that," her lawyer said. He was Edward P. Foley, a small, emotional Irish Catholic who several times wept in the courtroom. "She has a great honesty, this woman," he added, "but this honesty about her appearance always worked against her."

By the time the trial opened, Lucille Miller's appearance included maternity clothes, for an official examination on December 18 had revealed that she was then three and a half months pregnant, a fact which made picking a jury even more difficult than usual, for Turner was asking the death penalty. "It's unfortunate but there it is," he would say of the pregnancy to each juror in turn, and finally twelve were seated, seven of them women, the youngest forty-one, an assembly of the very peers—housewives, a machinist, a truck driver, a grocery-store manager, a filing clerk—above whom Lucille Miller had wanted so badly to rise.

That was the sin, more than the adultery, which tended to reinforce the one for which she was being tried. It was implicit in both the defense and the prosecution that Lucille Miller was an erring woman, a woman who perhaps wanted too much. But to the prosecution she was not merely a woman who would want a new house and want to go to parties and run up high telephone bills ($1152 in ten months), but a woman who would go so far as to murder her husband for his $80,000 in insurance, making it appear an accident in order to collect another $40,000 in double indemnity and straight accident policies. To Turner she was a woman who did not want simply her freedom and a reasonable alimony (she could have had that, the defense contended, by going through with her divorce suit), but wanted everything, a woman motivated by "love and greed." She was a "manipulator." She was a "user of people."

To Edward Foley, on the other hand, she was an impulsive woman who "couldn't control her foolish little heart." Where Turner skirted the pregnancy, Foley dwelt upon it, even calling the dead man's mother down from Washington to testify that her son had told her they were going to have another baby because Lucille felt that it would "do much to weld our home again in the pleasant relations that we used to have." Where the prosecution saw a "calculator," the defense saw a "blabbermouth," and in fact Lucille Miller did emerge as an ingenuous conversationalist. Just as, before her husband's death, she had confided in her

friends about her love affair, so she chatted about it after his death, with the arresting sergeant. "Of course Cork lived with it for years, you know," her voice was heard to tell Sergeant Paterson on a tape made the morning after her arrest. "After Elaine died, he pushed the panic button one night and just asked me right out, and that, I think, was when he really—the first time he really faced it." When the sergeant asked why she had agreed to talk to him, against the specific instructions of her lawyers, Lucille Miller said airily, "Oh, I've always been basically quite an honest person. . . . I mean I can put a hat in the cupboard and say it cost ten dollars less, but basically I've always kind of just lived my life the way I wanted to, and if you don't like it you can take off."

The prosecution hinted at men other than Arthwell, and even, over Foley's objections, managed to name one. The defense called Miller suicidal. The prosecution produced experts who said that the Volkswagen fire could not have been accidental. Foley produced witnesses who said that it could have been. Lucille's father, now a junior-high-school teacher in Oregon, quoted Isaiah to reporters: *"Every tongue that shall rise against thee in judgment thou shalt condemn."* "Lucille did wrong, her affair," her mother said judiciously. "With her it was love. But with some I guess it's just passion." There was Debbie, the Millers' fourteen-year-old, testifying in a steady voice about how she and her mother had gone to a supermarket to buy the gasoline can the week before the accident. There was Sandy Slagle, in the courtroom every day, declaring that on at least one occasion Lucille Miller had prevented her husband not only from committing suicide but from committing suicide in such a way that it would appear an accident and ensure the double-indemnity payment. There was Wenche Berg, the pretty twenty-seven-year-old Norwegian governess to Arthwell Hayton's children, testifying that Arthwell had instructed her not to allow Lucille Miller to see or talk to the children.

Two months dragged by, and the headlines never stopped. Southern California's crime reporters were headquartered in San Bernardino for the duration: Howard Hertel from the *Times*, Jim Bennett and Eddy Jo Bernal from the *Herald-Examiner*. Two months in which the Miller trial was pushed off the *Examiner's* front page only by the Academy Award nominations and Stan Laurel's death. And finally, on March 2, after Turner had reiterated that it was a case of "love and greed," and Foley had protested that his client was being tried for adultery, the case went to the jury.

They brought in the verdict, guilty of murder in the first degree, at 4:50 P.M. on March 5. "She didn't do it," Debbie Miller cried, jumping up from the spectators' section. "She didn't *do* it." Sandy Slagle collapsed in her seat and began to scream. "Sandy, for God's sake please *don't*," Lucille Miller said in a voice that carried across the courtroom, and Sandy Slagle was momentarily subdued. But as the jurors left the courtroom she screamed again: "You're murderers. . . . Every last one of you is a *murderer*." Sheriff's deputies moved in then, each wearing a string tie that read "1965 SHERIFF'S RODEO," and Lucille Miller's father, that sad-faced junior-high-school teacher who believed in the word of Christ and the dangers of wanting to see the world, blew her a kiss off his fingertips.

The California Institution for Women at Frontera, where Lucille Miller is now, lies down where Euclid Avenue turns into country road, not too many miles from where she once lived and shopped and organized the Heart Fund Ball. Cattle graze across the road, and Rainbirds sprinkle the alfalfa. Frontera has a softball field and tennis courts, and looks as if it might be a California junior college, except that the trees are not yet high enough to conceal the concertina wire around the top of the Cyclone fence. On visitors' day there are big cars in the parking area, big Buicks and Pontiacs that belong to grandparents and sisters and fathers (not many of them belong to husbands), and some of them have bumper stickers that say "SUPPORT YOUR LOCAL POLICE."

A lot of California murderesses live here, a lot of girls who somehow misunderstood the promise. Don Turner put Sandra Garner here (and her husband in the gas chamber at San Quentin) after the 1959 desert killings known to crime reporters as "the soda-pop murders." Carole Tregoff is here, and has been ever since she was convicted of conspiring to murder Dr. Finch's wife in West Covina, which is not too far from San Bernardino. Carole Tregoff is in fact a nurse's aide in the prison hospital, and might have attended Lucille Miller had her baby been born at Frontera; Lucille Miller chose instead to have it outside, and paid for the guard who stood outside the delivery room in St. Bernardine's Hospital. Debbie Miller came to take the baby home from the hospital, in a white dress with pink ribbons, and Debbie was allowed to choose a name. She named the baby Kimi Kai. The children live with Harold and Joan Lance now, because Lucille Miller will probably spend ten years at Frontera. Don Turner waived his original request for the death penalty (it was generally agreed that he had demanded it only, in Edward Foley's words, "to get anybody with the slightest trace of human kindness in their veins off the jury"), and settled for life imprisonment with the possibility of parole. Lucille Miller does not like it at Frontera, and has had trouble adjusting. "She's going to have to learn humility," Turner says. "She's going to have to use her ability to charm, to manipulate."

The new house is empty now, the house on the street with the sign that says

PRIVATE ROAD
BELLA VISTA
DEAD END

The Millers never did get it landscaped, and weeds grow up around the fieldstone siding. The television aerial has toppled on the roof, and a trash can is stuffed with the debris of family life: a cheap suitcase, a child's game called "Lie Detector." There is a sign on what would have been the lawn, and the sign reads "ESTATE SALE." Edward Foley is trying to get Lucille Miller's case appealed, but there have been delays. "A trial always comes down to a matter of sympathy," Foley says wearily now. "I couldn't create sympathy for her." Everyone is a little weary now, weary and resigned, everyone except Sandy Slagle, whose bitterness is still raw. She lives in an apartment near the medical school in Loma Linda, and studies reports of the case in *True Police Cases* and *Official Detective Stories*. "I'd much rather we not talk about the Hayton business too much," she tells visitors, and she keeps a tape recorder running. "I'd rather talk about Lucille and what a wonderful person she is and how her rights were violated." Harold Lance does not talk to visitors at all. "We don't want to give away what we can sell," he explains pleasantly; an attempt was made to sell Lucille Miller's personal story to *Life*, but *Life* did not want to buy it. In the district attorney's offices they are prosecuting other murders now, and do not see why the Miller trial attracted so much attention. "It wasn't a very interesting murder as murders go," Don Turner says laconically. Elaine Hayton's death is no longer under investigation. "We know everything we want to know," Turner says.

Arthwell Hayton's office is directly below Edward Foley's. Some people around San Bernardino say that Arthwell Hayton suffered; others say that he did not suffer at all. Perhaps he did not, for time past is not believed to have any bearing upon time present or future, out in the golden land where every day the world is born anew. In any case, on October 17, 1965, Arthwell Hayton married again, married his children's pretty governess, Wenche Berg, at a service in the Chapel of the Roses at a retirement village near Riverside. Later the newlyweds were feted at a reception for seventy-five in the dining room of Rose Garden Village. The bridegroom was in black tie, with a white carnation in his buttonhole. The bride wore a long white *peau de soie* dress and carried a shower bouquet of sweetheart roses with stephanotis streamers. A coronet of seed pearls held her illusion veil.

Joe Eszterhas (1944–)

CHARLIE SIMPSON'S APOCALYPSE

Right after the sun comes up, first thing folks do around Harrisonville, Missouri, is go up to the barn and see if the mare is still there. Horse-thieves drive around the gravel roads and brushy hills in tractor-trailers looking to rustle lazyboned nags. Then they grind them up into bags of meat jelly for the dogfood people. It's getting so that a man can't live in peace anywhere, not even on his own plot of land.

Harrisonville is 40 miles southeast

of Kansas City along Interstate 71, just down the blacktop from the red-brick farmhouse where Harry S Truman, haberdasher and President, was born. The little town is filled with weeping willows, alfalfa, Longhorn steer, and Black Whiteface cows. Life should be staid and bucolic, a slumbering leftover of what everyone who buys the $3.00 Wednesday-night Catfish Dinner at Scotts' Bar B-Q calls Them Good Old Days. But it isn't like that anymore. There's always some botheration to afflict a man these days and if it isn't the horse-thieves or the velvetleaf that plagued the soybeans last year, then it's them vagrant tornadoes.

They call this lush area Twister Alley. Of all the woebegone acreage in America, Harrisonville and the fast-blink single-gas-station towns clustered about it—Peculiar, Lone Jack, Gunn City—attract more funnel clouds and 90 mph whirlwinds each hardluck year than anyplace else. The whirlwinds sweep down across greenbacked rows of wheat and corn, tottering power lines and flame onto dried haystacks—raising hell two or three times a season with the insurance rates and the little money a farming man has left after Uncle Sam takes his share. For some reason the land provokes these killer-storms and, out around a bonfire on a warm spring night, a man can sit around with his Mail Pouch and wait for jagged strips of angry lightning to neon the wisteria and the hollyhock.

Except for the twisters, the horse-thieves and the velvetleaf, it is like any other tacky, jaundiced Southern town. It carries a weighty but atrophied Dixie tradition, having once been a proud link of the Confederacy, although it is not very far from the Kansas border-town where John Brown, saintly revolutionary murderer, launched his blood-bath a century ago. Its most famous citizen is a machinist named Jerry Binder, who won a ballyhooed $5000 suggestion award from Trans World Airlines for improving the turbine of the JT3D

jet engine. Billy Quantrill's Civil War raiders once raped and ravaged here to historical acclaim and Harry "Harri-cula" Truman, or just plain "Harry S." (as they say at Scott's Bar B-Q) visited here one Appreciation Day not long after he dropped the Aye-tomic Bomb. Harry S chewed saucy chicken wings on the courthouse steps and told the folks the White House was nothin' but a big white jail.

Harrisonville serves as Cass County's seat—population 4700—and by 1980 will be only a few miles south of the exact demographic center of America. It will be at the very heart of the calcified Heartland, a patriotic footnote which pleases the town's flaccid watery-eyed mayor and dentist, Dr. M. O. Raine, to no end.

This spring the last snowfall was shoveled away on April Fool's Day and folks started getting ready for the summer: The Harrisonville Fire Department tested its six Civil Defense Air Raid-Tornado Warning sirens and even the 89-year-old Harrisonville Hotel, the oldest building in town, its roof damaged by generations of funnelclouds, got a homey face-lift. Its eroded brick was scraped and washed down. The Missouri Turkey Shoot Season was opening; the American Legion Building at 303 Pearl Street, a mausoleum of cigar butts, housed a nightly clap-happy gospel meeting—"Do You Want To Be Saved?"—and the Peculiar Panthers knocked off the favored Harrisonville Wildcat basketball team 66–55. The Chamber of Commerce announced "real-big, real-good" news—the long-delayed acquisition of a shiny new cherry-topped 1972 ambulance.

Less than a month later on a muggy thunderheaded warm day, Friday, April 21st, at 5:55 PM, the Civil Defense sirens let out a high-pitched scream that cut across the wheatfields for miles around. Folks hurried to their citizens' band radios to await emergency instructions.

They thought it was another god-damn tornado.

They couldn't understand the breathless disjointed words which G. M. Allen, town banker and fire chief, garbled at his white-helmeted Civil Defense volunteers in the hamlets and hollows around town.

What in tarnation was G. M. talking about? "Hippies . . . Killed two policemen . . . Dead . . . M-1 carbine . . . Blood all over the place . . . the Simpson boy . . . Come on into town . . . Bring your guns . . . There's more of 'em . . . Yo, a revolution."

I. CHARLIE SIMPSON'S MAD-DOG DANCE

On Friday, April 21st:

Astronaut John W. Young leaped off the moondust and exuberantly saluted the American flag. At North Carolina State University, a thousand kids danced around a hand-painted sign that said: NIXON'S MACHINE IS FALLING. In Lawrence, Kansas, 600 persons met in front of Strong Hall to plan an antiwar march.

At 5:55 PM on the town square in Harrisonville, Missouri, Charles Simpson, 24 years old, 6'3", 180 pounds, flowing shoulder length gunmetal black hair, known to his friends as "Ootney," leaped out of a red Volkswagen. He was an asthmatic who liked Henry David Thoreau and had eyes like razor slits. The car was driven by a friend, John Risner, 26, a pallid Navy veteran, the son of a former deputy sheriff, beer-bellied, wire-bearded, blue jeaned, wearing a picaresque black felt English derby hat. The car had a peace symbol on its windshield.

Charles Simpson jumped out of the car on Independence Avenue, less than a thousand feet across the street from the Allen Bank and Trust Company, a modernized plate-glass structure facing the courthouse. It was minutes away from closing. Simpson was a farmboy who grew up in the apple-knocker village of Holden 24 miles away, the son of a totally disabled World War II combat veteran. He started walking south on Independence Avenue. He was wearing knee-popped bellbottoms, a waist-length Army fatigue jacket, and yellowed dry-goods boots caked with mud and cowflop. He had high jutting cheekbones, a hooked and fist-kissed nose, a swarthy complexion, and uneven calcimine-white teeth. His eyes were coal-black and slanted. There was whipcord in his muscles but he looked a little funny when he suddenly crossed the street and started running.

As he loped across Independence onto Pearl Street, he reached under his patched Army jacket and took out an M-1 semi-automatic carbine with clip and over 140 rounds of ammunition. It was the same weapon which National Guardsmen used at Kent State University in 1970, killing four students and wounding nine. He had used the combat-regulation weapon in the fields around town with his friends Rise Risner, target-shooting overfed squirrels, moonlighting packrats, and non-returnable bottles of Budweiser beer.

On this Friday afternoon, as Charles Simpson reached for the M-1 under his fatigue jacket, he saw two brown-uniformed members of the Harrisonville Police Department—Donald Marler, 26, and Francis Wirt, 24, a Vietnam veteran, back from the war only four months and a policeman less than a month. They were part of the department's foot-patrol, recently pressured by the town's businessmen to keep an ever-alert eye on the square. Both men were armed with holstered police-regulation .38s. Both men knew Simpson.

As Friday afternoon traffic backed up around the square—the shops were closing and each of the town square's four corners is red-lighted—Charles Simpson leaned into a crouch and aimed his semi-automatic carbine waist-high at the two policemen. They were less than 100 feet away. He fired a quick burst of bullets. The two policemen went down poleaxed. A lady 20 feet from the gunfire fainted and her car rammed into the Happiness-Is-Tastee-Freeze delivery truck in front of her.

Simpson ran toward the two policemen sprawled on the concrete. Both were moaning, bleeding badly, unable to return fire. He stood rigidly over both men, pointing the muzzle down over first one and then the other, and fired two more staccato bursts into their bodies at point-blank range. The bullets, made for war zones, ripped into and through the bodies. Patrolman Marler was hit twice in the chest, twice in the abdomen, and once in each hand. Wirt was shot twice in the abdomen and three times in the right arm. His elbow looked as if it had been fragged.

Simpson spinned, turning to the Allen Bank and Trust Company, and ran inside. He didn't say anything. He didn't aim the carbine at anyone. He pointed it willy-nilly toward a rear wall covered with advertising slogans—INVEST IN AMERICA, BUY U.S. SAVINGS BONDS—and fired again. Bullets ricocheted around the floor and walls, wounding two cashiers. Simpson turned again, ran outside, waving the rifle in front of him, and ran west on Pearl, heading toward the town's water tower —HI THERE! CLASS OF '69—and the Cass County Sheriff's Office. He was a death-dealing whirligig. He had a shit-fire grin on his face.

The sheriff's office is about a thousand feet west on Pearl Street from the Allen Bank. Across the street from it is the Capitol Cleaners, which holds a monopoly on the town's laundry trade, offers STARCH BARGAINS.

As Charles Simpson dashed from the bank to the sheriff's office down the narrow street, a 58-year-old man with boils on his neck named Orville T. Allen was getting out of his battered pick-up truck in front of the cleaners. He had operated a dry-cleaning store in

nearby Garden City for 27 years and was there to pick up some part-time weekend laundry.

Charles Simpson saw Orville Allen across the street, a man in faded khaki pants he had never seen before, and aimed his carbine. The burst caught Allen in the chest. He dropped to the pavement, twisted on the ground, turned his bleeding chest to the sky, and clasped his hands in prayer. "God," he moaned. A trail of blood trickled across the street toward the sheriff's office.

Sheriff Bill Gough, 46, a hulking and slow-footed man, had just taken off his holstered .38 revolver and was sitting down reading that week's issue of the Democrat-Missourian. The paper had come out that noon and carried a front-page story about an 18-year-old Kansas kid the sheriff's deputies had arrested for possession of marijuana. Gough heard something rat-tat-tat outside his office as he scanned the paper, but he didn't think it was gunfire. He thought it was some fool beating a piece of tin with a stick. He went outside, unarmed, to see what all the commotion was about.

As he got outside, he saw Simpson coming toward him, the M-1 aimed head-high. He tried to duck but wasn't quite fast enough (although the savage reflex twist of his big body probably saved his life). He was hit in the right shoulder and the left leg but staggered inside his office. His wife, sitting at a desk, screamed. He knocked her to the floor, grabbed his revolver, and flung himself behind a desk with such force that his elbows were purple for weeks. Covered with his own blood, Sheriff Gough aimed the revolver at the door and waited for Simpson to open it. His hands shook. He was afraid he'd lose control and wildly pull the trigger before Simpson stuck his head inside.

But when he hit Gough in the street, Simpson spinned around and, waving the gun wildy in the air, started trotting back toward the square. Allen's body lay a few feet away from him. Suddenly, in front of the Harrisonville Retirement Home, a dim gray-slab matchbox of a building across the street from Allen's bleeding body, he stopped. He bent down, put the carbine inside his mouth, sucking the barrel. He fired his last burst. He blew the top of his head off. His mad-dog dance was over.

He had fired more than 40 rounds. Four people were dead, three wounded. The town's shiny new Chamber of Commerce ambulance drove around the square and collected bodies. As the Civil Defense sirens screamed and G. M. Allen's volunteer firemen hosed down the bloodstains, gun-wielding deputies and policemen grabbed all the longhairs around the square and took them to Bill Gough's jail.

II. THE HIPPIES, AND G. M. ALLEN

All roads lead to the square, an editorial in J. W. Brown's shopping-news weekly, the Cass County Democrat-Missourian, once said with prophetic innocence. "At least that's what it seems like to outsiders. The Square seems to us to be a big chunk out of the past, sitting in the middle of the present. The cobblestone streets, the old hotel and courthouse, are probably taken for granted by the townspeople." Charles Ootney Simpson's fierce assault on the town square was the final escalation of a guerrilla war of raw nerves and icy glares. It was fought for control of a seemingly insignificant logistical area: courthouse steps, shrubbery encircling it, and sidewalks facing its entrances on Wall and Pearl Streets. To understand the fated intensity of this cornpone guerrilla war, one must understand the uniquely claustrophobic architecture of the square itself and its place in Harrisonville's rustic-schizoid tradition.

The courthouse anchors the square, surrounded on four sides by contrasting clapboard and imitation brick shops. It is the epicenter of a tight and walled-in rectangle decorated by butterflies and honey-bees. The cobblestoned pavement on the four streets surrounding it—Wall to the south, Lexington to the east, Pearl to the north, Independence to the west—is chokingly narrow. It is less than 30 feet from the courthouse curb to any of the businesses on its sides. The streets were designed for horses and buggies, not delivery trucks. All the streets are one-way in a looping arc; you have to drive through Lexington and Pearl to get to Independence. Since the streets are so narrow, the shops on all sides—like South Side Prescriptions, Felix Hacker's Paint Supplies, Ballon's Dry Goods and Wright's Shoe Palace—are literally but steps away from whatever is happening around the courthouse. If someone sitting on the courthouse steps shouts an epithet—"Off the pigs," for example—the shout will echo dramatically, reverberating through the little stores where, in years past, only the cash registers made noise.

The courthouse was built in the first decade of the 20th century. It is red-brick, three stories tall, topped by a cupolaed belltower and a flagpole. The bells ring once a year—on the Fourth of July. The flagpole is bare; a new one splits the grass in front of the War Veterans statue and flies the flag 24 hours a day. The building sits atop a mound-like elevation exactly 16 steps above the neatly-swept sidewalk. A black iron railing leads to the south side doors, which are flanked by four columnar graystone pillars. The elevation transforms the courthouse steps into a stage. If Old Lloyd Foster, for example, who ebulliently runs South Side Prescriptions, glances out his store window at the courthouse, he is looking up. The building is at the tip of his nose.

On the Wall Street side of the courthouse there is a fixed metal sign that says: LEARN TO LEAD! ARMY NCO CANDIDATE SCHOOL. The same kind of sign on the Independence Street side in blue and red says: THE MARINE CORPS BUILDS MEN—2735 B TROOP. Six feet of manicured grass and shrubbery surround the building on all sides. The clock atop the belltower is dead. It's been stuck for more than a decade. For some bizarre reason, the clock's hands paralyzed at different times—it is 2:20 to the south, 6:25 to the east, 1:20 to the west. The northern clock face has been removed—pigeons flutter there. A deeply-carved inscription above the southern doors says: A PUBLIC OFFICE IS A PUBLIC TRUST.

The courthouse steps and the town square have served for generations as a place of public lolling. Saturday-night hoedowns were celebrated there; its four streets were barricaded and strung with multi-colored lightbulbs. Three times a year there was a carnival. And gradually the town fathers—meaning the bankers, aldermen, and Chamber of Commerce officials (the mayor was always a yoyo)—accepted too that the courthouse steps and shrubbery served as a haven for grizzled lushes to gulp their pints of Missouri corn whiskey. Every small town has its drunks, but they always become harmless and somewhat valuable characters, walking examples to contrast with God-fearing lives. The old bullshit artists are happy enough just to be left alone. They exude alcohol and sour courtesy, never fuss anyone, and the judges and deputies avert their eyes and walk smugly past them to wood-paneled chambers where decanters of aged bourbon are kept out of sight.

In the late summer of 1971, the town drunks abandoned the courthouse steps and claimed they were being spooked out. The figures now lazing in the shade and dangling their legs were a bewildering new phenomenon and no one knew quite what to make of them. They were townie kids who had grown up around Cass County and played for the Harrisonville Wildcats, getting their first fifths of sourmash from tight-mouthed Old Lloyd Foster. But when Old Lloyd looked across at these home-grown kids now, they gave him a fright. They were different. They had changed. They were their own kids but . . . somehow they weren't their own kids anymore. They wore their hair long and untrimmed and grew chinbound moustaches and billowing beards. They wore all manners of beegum strawhats and cropduster clothes—always bluejeans and a lot of Army jackets, engineer's boots, and $2 teeny-shoes which Old Lloyd's son, Don, sold them at the Sears Country Catalog Store. They played riotous Frisbee in the middle of the street and collected wilted flowers in back of Vann's Florist Shop and decked themselves out with dead roses and carnations. They wore "love crosses" around their necks from which Jesus' body had been blasphemously ripped away.

Some of the women who came in once a week to Connie's Beauty Salon said they called them filthy names and scratched their privates. Some of the policemen said they called them "Pigs" face to face and were always talking about their godalmighty "Civil Liberties." Some of the businessmen claimed the one word they heard echoing around the square from morning 'til closing was a four-letter word they couldn't even repeat out loud what with women and children in town. "There was no doubt about it," said 60-year-old J. W. Brown, editor and publisher of the Democrat-Missourian, a flatulent pipe-smoking country gentleman. "What we had here were our own hippies, settin' up there, raisin' hell, callin' our women names, drinkin' wine and smokin' some of that marijuana. I even heard tell they was right up there in the bushes havin' sexual intercourse. Yes sir, Sex-You-All intercourse. Now those old drunks who used to set up there, those old boys never did any of that."

Sex-You-All debauchery 16 steps above ground level right at the nosetips of righteous town merchants is not what the new courthouse squatters had in mind. Not at all. They were there in the beginning because there was no other place to go. Where could you go in Harrisonville?—this small time place haunted by homilies, platitudes, and bushwah. Into Guido's Pizza Parlor? Well, maybe but couldn't stay there too long. As time went by Win Allen, the kingpin, Rise Risner, Ootney Simpson, George Russell, Harry Miller, and the Thompson Brothers hung around the square because it got to be an entertaining mock-serious game. They were liberating Harrisonville, Missouri, showing the Sho-Me State some puffed-up balls. They were fighting their revolution against people they had cowedly called "Sir" all their teenage lives.

Beer-bellied Rise Risner and Gary Hale, a reedy and subdued James Taylor look-alike, went off to the Navy as cowlicked country boys and came back dazedly turned-on, rejecting everything around them. They were home but home sure as hell didn't feel like home.

Liberating Harrisonville meant a lot of mind-blowing. They soon found themselves romantic figures, idolized by some of the high school kids. They conducted hoohawing teach-ins in front of the War-Vets statue as Legionnaires stood around on the sidewalk in their peaked caps and called it "jackrollin' the blind." They'd read selections from Abbie Hoffman, Timothy Leary, and Bobby Seale in stentorian tones, lifting their voices to phrases like "Off the pigs!" and "Up against the wall, motherfucker!"

They had Dylan and Jimi Hendrix tapes in their cars and boomed "Stone Free" and "Lay Lady Lay" in the night. They smoked as much dope as was available and there was always more than enough. The Army had planted crops of hemp during World War II and five-foot high marijuana plants shadowed the wheatfields.

Snake-charmed, the high school kids started imitating them, of course, using words like "motherfucker" and acting heavylidded in civics class just for the aggravation of it. The principal, an ex-Marine, freaked, naturally, and zeroed-in on the new villains at council meetings when the school budget was discussed and the vandalism dollar-damage was counted. Only the year before, the principal fired a matronly English-teacher who made *Stranger in a Strange Land* required reading. The townspeople picked up the taboo; the lady was once seen going into a liquor store and the town's elders were soon saying she was fucking and sucking all the seniors in her classes.

So these plowboy hippies—who were convinced, perhaps from experience, that their elders still cornholed cows when they got horny—came to dominate the town's consciousness and its square. And of all the revolutionaries and sugartits cavorting around the square, two seemed the most frightening—the Simpson boy, who'd always rub his pecker when a woman went by, and The Nigger, one of the town's six blacks. Win Allen, 24, frail and birdlike, with bloodshot eyes and a habit of slurring his words, made no secret of the fact he was shanghaied into Uncle Sam's Army, went AWOL, and managed to con himself a dishonorable discharge. He was a Bad Nigger as opposed to his younger brother, Butch, 17, a walking bowling ball who played forward for the Harrisonville Wildcats scoring an average 15 points a game. Butch was a Good Nigger. But Win (short for Edwin) had an Afro popout hairdo and was always up there on the steps, holding hands with a white girl, talking about Love, and waving books like *The Fire Next Time* and *Do It!*

Every time one of Bill Davis' policemen or Bill Gough's deputies passed the square, Win Allen would cheerfully yell: "Hey, here comes The Pigs." He even spoke his special blackevil language, and pretty soon half the kids in the high school were using this garbled childrenese, not just ordinary hippie words the townspeople heard in television commercials but words they'd never heard before. Words like "bro" and "gritting down" (eating) and "Crib" and "P-ing down" (sexual intercourse) and "bogosity" (anything he disagreed with). But the single phrase which all the kids were using was just gibberish for anything that Win liked. When Win liked something as much as he liked P-ing down, he said: "Most ricky-tick." "Most ricky-tick" was being heard all over town. A high school senior even used it in an essay on "The Prospect of Marriage." The townspeople would go home at night, after having to endure the raucous courthouse shenanigans all day, and their own kids would say bogosity and gritting down and most ricky-tick.

Some action clearly had to be taken. G. M. Allen, fire-chief, got up at a special Chamber of Commerce meeting and said with hawkshaw eloquence: "I'm an American, damn it, and I'm proud to be an American and I don't go for all this hangin' the flag upside-down stuff."

G. M. Allen had another reason for urging civic action, a pocketbook reason. Rise Risner and Charles Simpson and Win Allen and the rest of that pestiferous crew had become an economic menace. Business was off all over town, from the Capot Department Store to alderman Luke Scavuzzo's grocery. Some of the people who shuffled in to make their monthly mortgage payments to G. M. Allen's bank told him they were afraid to come into town. The hippies. The hippies were scaring business away. Harrisonville just couldn't sit around and let itself get overrun, G. M. Allen said.

The aldermen agreed that action had become a matter of local survival, although one of them, sucking his teeth, pointed out alternatives—"Don't stretch the blanket, now, G. M."—explaining the financial setback. There was a nationwide economic crisis and wage-price freeze and 11 miles down Interstate 71 one of those deluxe glass and chromium shopping centers, calling itself Truman Corners, had just opened up. Maybe folks were shopping there.

"Maybe so," G. M. Allen told the tooth-sucker, "but they'd be leavin' their money here if it weren't for them hippies," and the Chamber of Commerce spring offensive, to recapture the town square for the old drunks, was under way.

III. THE BATTLE OF THE TOWN SQUARE

Actually, the aldermen had two offensives to mount at the same time, and they were both G. M. Allen's hardnosed command: Operation Hippie and Operation Tornado.

To facilitate the war against tornadoes, G. M. Allen thought it would be a civic coup if the Fire-Fighters Association of Missouri—tornado-watchers of the entire state—held their annual convention in Harrisonville. The aldermen, perhaps contemplating the weekend revenue from 500 firefighters and their wives gratefully applauded G. M.'s boosterism. G. M. lined the convention up for Friday, April 21st. There would be a tornado committee meeting Saturday morning and a brass-band parade Saturday afternoon. Doris' House of Charm announced it would offer a "Fireladies' Shampoo Special" for its beehive-headed lady tourists. As a further step, G. M. ran off hundreds of emergency doomsday leaflets and distributed them in the stores around the square. His directive began: "When a tornado is spotted in the Harrisonvile area, six sirens around the *city* will sound a long *blast* for three minutes. Our air-raid emergency *bombing warning* differs from a storm warning by sounding an up-and-down warbling *blast* rather than a long continuing *blast*. BE ALERT, G. M. ALLEN, FIRE CHIEF."

To facilitate the offensive against hippies, G. M. figured it was necessary that everyone in town understand the critical nature of the crisis. He arranged with the Kiwanis Club to import a "drug addict expert." The "drug addict expert" was Robert Williams, the police chief from Grandview. Chief Williams, a man of profound second-hand insight, heard about drugs and hippies all the time from his police friends in Kansas City.

"It's approaching a crisis stage," he told the Kiwanians. "Police can't even eliminate the problem. We've got to wake up and take a hard stand. What we've got to do is stand up and inject some old-fashioned moral values before all our young fall victim to those older marauders who prey on them." The Harrisonville Community Betterment Council appointed a Drug-Abuse Committee.

Late at night on March 23rd, G. M. Allen, a delegation of town businessmen, and members of the city council met with police officials at G. M.'s Citizens National Bank on Wall Street. A list of crimes the hippies were suspected of was compiled. Someone broke into the courthouse one night by forcing open a window and crept up three flights to the belltower. Nothing was damaged, or stolen, but three marijuana cigarette butts were found on the floor. The caller always used the word "motherfucker" and threatened "torching." In nearby Archie, a carload of the hippies —Risner, Simpson, Win Allen—were seen driving through and that same day bomb threats were reported at the Archie State Bank and the Archie Elementary School. And they all knew, G. M. Allen scowlingly said, about the obstruction of traffic in the square.

The mobilization meeting agreed on some immediate measures: The shrubbery around the courthouse would be trimmed so there couldn't be anymore

sexual intercourse going on up there. Superwatted bright lights, the kind used in urban high-crime areas, would be erected around the square. Chief Davis promised a new foot patrol, two of his nine men acting as roving beatmen, walking in circles around the square 12 hours a day. A list of city ordinances —"Ordinances, man," Win Allen would say, "dig?"—was drawn up for city council approval.

"Vulgar, profane, or indecent" language in public was punishable by a $500 fine or 60 days in the county jail or both. Picketing and parades were illegal unless authorized by the city attorney or Chief Davis. And the topper, a declaration of virtual martial law: Any assembly of three or more persons in the town square was declared an illegal assembly punishable by a $1000 fine.

G. M. Allen, the little man with bifocals and the Alfred E. Newman haircut that stopped a full inch above his red-veined ears, was happy as a clam. He had a responsibility as fire chief and Civil Defense coordinator and he intended to live up to it. "You listen to TV, it used to be cowboys and indians, now it's 'Kill the Cops,'" he'd say. He was a World War II combat veteran who'd raised four decent lawabiding kids and, even though his youngest daughter had gone to school with Risner and Win Allen and had liked them, even though she was "a little bit oversold on Civil Rights," G. M. Allen was convinced that what they'd decided in his bank that night was for the betterment not only of Harrisonville but of America too. "If they don't believe in America," he told the meeting, "they should get the hell out."

Hours after the anti-hippie-frisbee-promiscuity meeting ended, a 30-pound-slab of concrete was tossed through the $495 plate-glass window fronting G. M. Allen's bank. He sputtered down half a block to see J. W. Brown at the

Democrat-Missourian and ordered a boldset black-bordered ad. He was petrified with emotion. The Citizens National Bank was offering a $500 reward for "information leading to the arrest and conviction of the person or persons who maliciously broke our window."

For Rise Risner, Gary Hale, Win Allen, and Ootney Simpson, the "shit coming down from the black sky" was a routine part of "life in the Hick City."

During the second week of April, as the foot patrols made ten minute reconnaisance sorties around the square, Win Allen came up with what he told Charles Simpson was "Dee-Vine Inspiration." Saturday, the 22nd, would be a national day of protest against the War in Vietnam. Win Allen decided he was going to organize Harrisonville's own anti-war march, a ragamuffin parade of cow-dunged kids screaming anti-imperialist slogans right under the Harrisonville brownshirts' noses. On Wednesday, April 19th, Win Allen and Ootney Simpson, friendly, grinning, and wary, marched to the office of the city attorney and asked for a parade permit. They were told they didn't need one. "We want somethin' in writin', not jive," Win said. "Go ahead and march," the ferret-faced attorney smiled. But he'd give them no paper.

Charles Simpson, who trusted his instincts, was sure it was a boobytrap. "The fuckers'll just bust us," he said.

But Win's dreams escalated: The march would protest not only the war but the new town ordinances. Win could carry a sign that said DOWN WITH NIXON'S WAR and Ootney would carry a sign that said DOWN WITH G. M. ALLEN'S WAR.

"It's gonna be most ricky-tick," Allen said.

"Crazy fuckin' niggers," Simpson laughed.

G. M. Allen heard about the anti-war march The Nigger and the hippies were planning and went to see Chief Davis about it. He wasn't going to have his big weekend spoiled. The Fire-Fighters Association of Missouri would be in town and each of the forty departments was going to bring its fire engine. At two o'clock Saturday afternoon, after they finished caucusing over the tornadoes, all those beautiful firetrucks, their sirens blasting, would be driven around the square.

All the firefighters would be in their starched parade outfits and the sidewalks would be filled with farmers who'd come into town to see the firetrucks and would spend a few dollars while they were there. It would be the biggest thing on the square since the horseshoe-pitching contests they used to hold. G. M. Allen was damned if he was going to let those spitshined firetrucks be set upon by an army of crablice—hometown purvoids spewing filth, contumely, and treason.

The day after the haggling session with the city attorney was spent coordinating Saturday's anti-war march. Win Allen and Ootney Simpson discussed logistics with Rise, Gary Hale and the others—and just about everyone agreed that it was a trap, the march certain to end inside Sheriff Gough's roach-crawling jail. But no one cared. They were high on their own daydreams. They'd march anyway. Fuck it: The theatrical aspects were simply too tempting, too ricky-tick to worry about the whip and thud of the brownshirts' new Japanese billyclubs. They would march up Wall Street, gathering at Guido's Pizza Place minutes before the firefighters' cortege was to assemble near the Missouri Farm Association silo. The square would be decked with bunting and the farmers would be tip-toeing around the sidewalks waiting for the sirens when, led by Win Allen, led by a nigger, the outlaws would shamble into that red-white-blue arena, blowing minds, ruining everything, filling the square with clenched fists and that eyeteeth-rattling cry: "ONE TWO THREE FOUR WE DON'T WANT YOUR FUCKIN' WAR."

Word went out Thursday to the timid and sheepish "Teeny Bros" at the high school that all those interested in coming to jail for the war should come down to the square after school and Win or Rise or Ootney would give them the lowdown. A lot of kids showed up because the Teeny Bros themselves were in the process of launching a guerrilla action of their own, a pep-rally protest against Bar B-Q Ham on Cheese Bun, Chicken Fried Steak-w-cream-gravy, and Cheeseburger Noodle Loaf. The Teeny Bros were actually threatening to take to the streets carrying big signs that said, NO MORE BAR B-Q HAM and waving the signs in front of the struck-dumb principal's office.

The Teeny Bros drifted into town that afternoon, keeping a paranoid eye out for the foot patrols, and organized themselves into action groups. The freshmen and sophomores—"The Snots"—would all paint signs. The Snots were more than anxious to paint words like NO MORE WAR and demonstrate their militance. As the day wore on and the foot patrols told Chief Davis there seemed to be a pow-wow of outlaws in town, some of the outlaws got bored and went home while other part-time badmen slouched by, having heard about Win's Dee-Vine Inspiration from some squiggly-excited Teeny Bro. Charles Simpson went home around 4 o'clock to his Holden farmhouse, reluctantly, going along with Win's fantasy, noting the ironies offered by the prospect of the two parades. The firefighters would be cheered because they drove shiny engines; the outlaws would go to jail because they dreamed of a warless world. "Fuck it, they'll just bust us," Ootney told Win Allen again, "the whole shit just turns my teeth sour." Ootney was tired. He was going home and he was going to mow down some squirrels with his itty-bitty machine gun.

Harry Miller was one of the hangers-on who slouched by—about an hour after Ootney left to do battle with his doomed squirrels. Harry Miller drove into the square, nodding respectfully at the brownshirts, and then catfooted over to Rise and Win and some of the others. Everything looked cool: Win was chasing dragonflies.

Harry Miller is 24 years old and his jeans are too tight because there is a gut bulging at his belt. His face is puffy and there is a Brando-like sluggishness, a hovering petulance, about him. He doesn't rattle very easily and he looks like he can take care of himself—a veteran of bicep-building Army infantry training. He looks like a young Bill Haley. His hair is parted in the middle and shoved to the sides but his hair isn't long enough and sometimes a few hairs dangle into the forehead forming perfect curleycues.

It was near 5:30. The air was stuffed with heat and they were thirsty. Win and Rise and Gary Hale and Harry Miller and George Russell and John Thompson, their smart-cracking court-jester, walked across the street to Lloyd Foster's drug store. One of the Teeny Bros whose mother had given him allowance money that day was sent inside to spend it on a carton of Pepsi-Cola.

"Here we are," Harry Miller says, "standin' not only exactly under the drug store's roof but out in front, near the Sears store, which Old Lloyd's boy, Don, runs. So we're waitin' for this kid to bring us some bellywash. We are standin' right beside a mailbox which is public property. OK, out of nowhere, Don Foster drives up. Man, I seen that car comin', you could tell he was gonna do somethin', it was in his eyes, like he already knew he was gonna do this. OK, when he comes over there, there were already police parked on the other side of the square so we couldn't see 'em. Don Foster pulls up and he immediately jumps out and storms up. He's a big guy, wears nice cowboy boots, got sideburns, carries a pencil behind his ear, walks around wantin' everybody to cut down trees.

"So he storms up and he starts sayin', 'Get away from my store.' He says to Win, 'Get your black ass out of here.' So he starts violently throwin' shit and John Thompson says, 'Listen, man, we pay taxes, I'm not gettin' out of here.' So the Foster dude says, 'Oh, you wanna fight, I'll fight you.' So he pushes John with both hands, just pushes John and knocks him back. John weighs about 40 pounds less than the dude and most of his weight is stuck up on top of his head in his hair. Well, right then I caught a sense, I knew exactly what was gonna happen. OK, so then the old man, Old Lloyd, comes runnin' out and starts throwin' some bogus shit. I don't know what he was sayin', just yellin' and screamin'. Somehow Don Foster got a hold of John again and pushed him again.

"So I got in between them. I says to Foster, 'Man, leave us alone, you're tryin' to fight us, you wanna get us throwed in jail, just leave our asses alone, we're not goin' to jail for you.' And he says: 'You get out of the way or I'll smack your ass, buddy.' So I got out of the way and they got off by theirselves again and started pilin' at it. So his father, Old Lloyd, says: 'By Gawd, I'm gonna call the police.' So he walks back to his store, takes about four steps, doesn't even get to his phone, turns back out again watchin' them hassle, and here comes the police already turnin' the corner of the courthouse, boogeyin' from the courthouse. OK, after they turn the courthouse, it is like 50 feet before the first one gets to the fight—here's John and this Don Foster on the ground.

"The Foster dude is on top smackin' John beside the head. John's on the bottom gettin' ahold of him by the neck and the ear. So here's Sgt. Jim Harris, the police officer, the other two pigs are behind him OK, so Harris is 500 feet away, his club in the air, runnin' right at him. Here's John on the bot-

tom with Foster on top of him. So Harris twists around and leans down so he can hit John even with Foster on top of him. He hits John in the shoulder and across the side of the face. Foster jumped off and the other two policemen picked up Foster's jacket for him. Foster got his jacket and walked up beside his old man and Old Lloyd starts pointin' at us, sayin' 'Him and him and him' and points to Win and says: 'The Nigger, The Nigger, The Nigger,' over and over again. So the pigs put us all under arrest for disturbin' the peace and start walkin' us over to the jail in the sheriff's office. Eight of us: Rise and Win and Gary Hale and John Thompson and George Russell and some of the others.

"On the way over there, one of the pigs decides he's gonna have a little fun with Win, so he sticks Win in the spine with his nightstick as hard as he can. When Win turns around the pig yells. 'The Nigger's resistin' arrest.' When we get to the jail we says, 'We wanna file a complaint against the Foster dude for pushin' John,' 'cause I mean, if they're gonna play that game on you, you might as well play it back on them. Chief Davis is there and the sheriff is there and Sgt. Jim Harris is there and they all said they didn't have the authority for us to file a complaint.

"So we had to just scream, say, 'Goddamnit, I want a damn report! I wanna file a complaint!' I mean we had to scream for 15, 20 minutes. Finally they brought the city attorney down and he gives us two sheets of paper with nothin' on it except the top says 'Municipal Court' and some bogus printed stuff. But all they had us do was sign our names on it and that couldn't— man, when you file a complaint there's somethin' wrote down there and you read it, so that couldn't have been any real complaint form. OK, so that was just to get us to shut up. They throw us in jail and we knew it was bogus, we just took it as it was, $110 apiece. Then our Nigger, he was about the last one to come in. We hollered across the monkeybars over to his cell and we say —'Hey, Win, how we gonna get out?' And he says: 'You know, I don't know, my bail's $1100.'

"That jail is like the inside of a toilet bowl in a place where everybody's got the backdoor trots, know what I mean? We had to take a shit, well, we had to get a Look Magazine and tear the pages and put it on the seat it was so grubby. The shitter didn't really have a seat on it. They had some drunks over in the bullpen but they didn't say nothin' to us, nobody said nothin'.

"There were cops crawlin' out of the ratholes, we must have scared the pricks off of 'em. Here's eight guys in jail, right? They had six Highway Patrolmen there, they had five guys from the city police department, they had five guys from the sheriff's department, about seven policemen from the surrounding towns in the county."

"The chief of the fire department," Harry Miller says, "yes siree, G. M. Allen comes in all aflutter. Had this little red firehat on, Number 4. He says, 'Did you get 'em all? Anybody hurt?' G. M. walks up and down real slow, lookin' at us, lookin' us over, lookin' us in the hair, and then he says: 'Where's The Nigger? I got somethin' to say to The Nigger.'"

Win Allen says: "Dig, here I am, under arrest, in the clink. And this dude comes up to me in his little cute firehat and I expect him to say somethin' to me about what happened. So he comes up to me, gets real friendly allasudden and whispers, 'Win, I want you to come see me tomorrow about that bill you owe me.' He has the fuckin' audacity to come to me in the clink and talk to me about a loan my family owes him."

A 16-year-old dimple-cheeked high school dropout named Robin Armstrong, a strangely vague and muted farmgirl whose father blew his brains out two years ago—'I'm fed up with everything; people are just so fuckin'

ignorant anymore"—was standing in front of the firetruck. All of her friends were in jail and she was screaming, "You fuckin' pigs!" and the firemen were clutching their gleaming hatchets.

Her mother drove up then and Robin Armstrong, trembling with fear and fury, started running like a panicked jackrabbit down an alley.

"I saw it from the window," Harry Miller says. "Robin starts boogeyin' in between the jail and the rest home, she's gonna run down this old road because she don't want her mother to capture her ass. So the firetruck has a tank with 200 pounds of pressure in it and you know that big hose they have —well, they open that big hose up and hit Robin in the back with it and knock her on the ground. They skidded her face across the gravel."

Mrs. Armstrong, 40ish and sagging but dressed as if she still knew how to please, went up to her sobbing daughter whose mouth was bleeding, and slapped her hard. She called her daughter a "little hoor" and then she sashayed back to the fireman who was still holding the hose. And then she thanked him.

The outlaws spent their night in the crabseat wiping their asses with Look Magazine and organizing their Saturday parade, wondering all the time how they'd make bail. One of their bros was up all night, making phone calls and asking the parents to bail their kids out and getting nowhere. They didn't want to spend their money.

As the sun came up, red-eyed Ootney Simpson had figured out only one way to get his friends out of jail. At 11 o'clock Friday morning, Ootney Simpson, smiling like a dimwit fool, worn down to the edge, showed up at the sheriff's office. The outlaw looked the sheriff in the eye and put $1500 in cash on the counter. It was his life's savings, the bankroll for the plot of land he dreamed about. His dream was dead. A sweat of fatigue caked his face.

"Simpson's the name," the dreamer said, "revolution's my game. Free the People!"

IV. OOTNEY SIMPSON'S DREAM

They called him "Ootney" because of a shriveled old geezer named Jimbob Jones who runs a carry-out grocery on Number Seven Highway about four miles from town. Jimbob Jones took a weird shine to Charles Simpson and whenever he and his friends would wander in for their quarters of strawberry wine and sixpacks of beer, Jimbob Jones would cackle: "Well, looky here, Rootin' Tootin' Mr. Simpson." So Rise and Win called him "Rootin' Tootin'" at first, and then "Tootney" and gradually bastardized it into Ootney.

When Ootney showed up at the jail that Friday morning with his packet of liberating $100 bills, Rise and Win weren't surprised. It was just like Ootney—whenever something had to be done, Ootney was there to do it. As his father says, "All his life he'd go out there in the hayfield and keep up with the best of 'em."

He was of the hayfield and the barn, grew to manhood there and loved it. He lived in Holden, a town smaller and even more backwoods then Harrisonville, a place where the cemetery is still called "the boneyard," a police station is a "booby hutch," and the mentally retarded are "cabbageheads."

Ootney's father, Charles B. Simpson, is 53 years old and looks 75. He looks like a man who is going to die and has looked that way for years. He stands 5'9", weighs 102 pounds, sports a Hitler moustache, a red baseball cap, and a cardigan sweater which the moths have savored for years. He walks with face-twisted pain and a briar walking stick with a vulcanized rubber tip, his leg having been broken into pieces by shrapnel on the African front in WWII.

He raised three kids and supported a wife, did as much work as he could, pinched pennies, lived on hot dogs and beans, and waited for the disability checks. Four years ago his wife left him and, except for Charles, the kids got married and left him too.

The corpse-faced veteran and his boy were never too close and it was only in the past year or so that they did much talking. It was hard for the old man to move and he spent long hours sitting in his rocking chair in the room with the calico rug and the big calendar filled with bone-chilling winter scenes. He sat in the rocking chair with his baseball cap pulled over his grey eyes, the cane draped over a thigh, staring at the walls and the dates on the calendar. The boy would come into the room, his long hippie hair in his face, squat down on the rug, and they would talk. They talked about the land and the crops and the war, about policemen and guns and steer, about Henry David Thoreau and Abbie Hoffman and General of the Army Douglas MacArthur. "The boy expressed his feelings too plain," the old man says, "you can't do that."

He was always telling the old man about Thoreau and although the old man didn't know too much about him, he listened. Thoreau lived by a pond and his friends were plants and animals. He didn't pay his taxes because he wouldn't support a government which practiced slavery.

The old man didn't have too much to say about Henry David Thoreau but a man talking to his son has to have something to say, so he told the boy stories about General Douglas MacArthur. The old man admired General Douglas MacArthur as much as the boy admired Henry David Thoreau. So he told his stories. How General MacArthur won the Philippines from the Japs. How he could have beat the Chinese across the Yalu River if Harry S. Truman hadn't had stopped him. How Harry S Truman once wanted to be a piano player in a whorehouse and that's where he belonged. How General Douglas MacArthur should have been President and the country wouldn't be in the fix that it's in.

The old man didn't know exactly what the boy did all the time in Harrisonville. One time Al Wakeman, the Holden police chief, came over and told the old man to keep his damn boy the hell out of trouble. Charles was always roaring up and down the streets on his motorcycle. "Disturbing the peace," the chief said.

Ever since he was a kid, Ootney had a bad case of asthma. He'd have an attack and his nose and throat would swell up, shutting most of his breathing off. That kept him out of the Army. "One shot-to-hell veteran's enough in the family," the old man says. "He went to high school but he didn't graduate —he had mumps real bad his senior year." Rise Risner adds: "He just farted school off. He said, 'Man, you fuckers are just teachin' me a bunch of lies, you're not teachin' me anything I wanna learn.' He finally got into a big hassle with a teacher one day, just never did go back. He was real intelligent, he could see through shit. He'd always tell you the truth, even if it hurt. He'd say, 'Look you motherfucker, you've been layin' down some phony shit.' "

When he dropped out of high school, Ootney Simpson went to work at a foundry in Kingsville. He was bored with the job but worked at it for more than a year. He said he wanted to save enough money to build himself the world's most souped-up drag racer. "He saved up a bunch of money," Rise says, "and he got fired 'cause he took off one weekend. He told his supervisor, 'Well, I'm not gonna be at work a few days.' So he came back and they said, 'Well, you know, since you didn't notify anybody that you were gonna be haulin' ass for these few days, you're fired.' So he started thinkin'. He went back raisin'

hell. He went right into the personnel department and said, 'Look you motherfuckers, I did notify you. I want this changed. I still wanna be fired but I want this to read that I notified you and you let me go,' and so after that he started collectin' unemployment."

Ootney was spending a lot of time in those days with his younger brother, Elwyn, 23. "Bubber" looks like a chunkier Ootney—the same coal-black eyes, hair as long and parted the same way down the middle. Bubber also worked at the foundry and, together, they were building their dream drag racer, blowing most of their money on new manifolds and sparkling chrome treasures.

Win Allen says, "Like the cat and Bubber, they used to race their drags in Kansas City, makin' cars and doin' some racin' and then one day Bubber, says, 'We're just gettin' screwed, people are just takin' our money,' and so they stopped racin'." Rise adds: "They put $10,000 into their dream car, Ootney was just floatin' along, searchin', he broke his back on that car. And they put ten grand into it and that's when Bubber got married and Bubber's wife said, 'All right, you gotta get rid of that race car.' Well, Ootney and Bubber were in a partnership, you know, he says to his wife, 'OK, honey, I'll get rid of that racin' machine for you.' And they sold the major part of it for $1000. So they took a $9000 beatin' right there.

"Bubber and Ootney broke bad after that, like Bubber's wife was always hasslin' Charles even. Bubber picked up all this pseudo-shit—shit like trailers and pickup trucks. Like he was working 16 hours a day in two different foundries. He worked at one in Harrisonville and he got off work there at 3:30 and he had to haul ass to punch in on time to get to the other foundry by 4. Just to feed his wife. Well, that's about when Ootney's head started to spin. He didn't give a fuck about the money, but he just knew that whatever he was searchin' for he couldn't find at a drag strip. That's when he started showin' up around the square with us and gettin' into readin'.

"After a while he started talkin' to us about Thoreau," Rise says, "and he said the only thing he and Thoreau differed on was women. Like Ootney man, he dug on women. I mean he didn't fall in love with 'em or get stuck on 'em he just dug to fuck, just P-down, man. He just loved it. He could fuck all night and he still couldn't have enough. He was crazy about it. But he said he had to have women around him all the time and that's the only thing he and Thoreau differed on because Thoreau says in one of his books, he goes, 'A woman would be a foe to my career,' and Ootney goes, 'Old Henry David, he must not have liked to fuck.'

"If Ootney felt like takin' off his clothes, he didn't give a fuck who was there, no, he'd take his clothes off and jump in a river and take a bath or somethin'. Nothin' embarrassed him, nothin' natural. And he was crazy-good with women. Any woman you ever seen in your life, Ootney Simpson could scheme her into the fuckin' bedroom. It was like he was above women, they owed it to him to fuck him. He was a peach, true beautifulness. He had this long black hair and he had this big beard for a while that was like right under his eyes, hair all over him, skinny. His eyes had a sparkle, the whites were real big, this hooked nose, a real freak, a freak all the way. When he let his beard grow, the only thing you could see was the eyes—just the whites of 'em, 'cause the rest of him was dark. Sometimes he wore great big baggy Army pants. He was a real killer, man.

"He was real weird in a lot of healthy ways. Like he hated telephones. He'd fuckin' drive 40 miles to tell a dude some little-ass thing rather than call him on the phone. He hated phones. He said, 'If you can't look a man in the eyes when you're talkin' to him to tell

him somethin', it ain't worth nothin'.' He said, 'Anything that you lay on somebody that you feel is a part of you, you gotta look them in the eyes, feel their soul right there.' "

Harry Miller says, "He was full of feelings, just look at him and you could tell. Just look at his face and you'd say, 'Man, that guy there, he'll give me a dollar to get somethin' to eat.' It seems like anytime somebody was depressed, he was around to help them out. His feelings were so sensitive, like you couldn't gross him out, but he had such feeling for his friends. He could stand 50 feet away and somebody would jump up on you and the vibes from Ootney would knock him down. If we were havin' a hassle in town, fuckin' Ootney would pick up the vibes 30 miles away.

"Some of his fuckin' acts you could never forget," says Harry. "One time an ex-Marine from out of Vietnam, been home three months, comes up to Pat and Ernie's Bar and drinks 15 beers and an old guy that we used to know in high school brings him over to Rise's house, we called it the Hippie House, and Ootney is there. So they come in and the Marine starts throwin' down shit about—'Gawddamn, you don't faaght for your country, ya oughtta be shawt.' I was in bed but Ootney heard it. This guy was gonna fire on Rise's ass. Ootney gets up stark nekid, walks in there, and comes down into shit like Rubin jumpin' a Chicago pig's ass or somethin'. And jumps all over the Marine. He looks the dude back about three steps and he grabs his prick and shakes it at the Marine and turns around and just shoots him the moon and then he gives him the finger. Man, that Marine, he ran away."

Rise says, "But he was always gettin' into some shit. Like there was a cloud over him and it rained pigs everytime Ootney made a move. Like even when he wanted to do nothin' but listen to a rock and roll concert. He dug Black Sabbath. Black Sabbath cost him $150. He went up to Kansas City to see 'em and, first, he lost his ticket so he had to buy another ticket when he got up there and there was another dude there, a friend of ours who didn't have any money and didn't have a ticket either. So Ootney bought him a ticket. Plus all the other shit, miscellaneous money bullshit from that day. Then after the concert he was takin' a piss outside, you know, in the street, and he got busted for his piss and it cost him $100.

"Another time he was with a dude and the dude was drivin' through Kingsville, the town where the foundry is, and the pigs busted this guy for a faulty exhaust or somethin'. And so they were sittin' in the pig's cruiser and they had to wait for the county pigs to get there and give them the ticket because those pigs were just flunkies or somethin'. So Ootney says to the pig, 'Am I under arrest?' And the pigs goes, 'No, you're not under arrest.' So Ootney gets the keys from the dude who drove the car and he just jumps in and speeds away at like 100 mph, makin' a U-turn and givin' the pigs the finger and everythin'. He keeps racin' on at 100 mph and the pigs put out a roadblock for him 'cause he's tearin' up the countryside. He stops off at his place in Holden and puts his brother Bubber's motorcycle helmet on and some gloves and comes roarin' back to Kingsville 'cause he knows the pigs must be after him. Well, he roars right around that roadblock at 100 mph and drives right back up to where his friend is sittin' in the pig's car. One of the pigs pulls out his gun and he was pointin' the gun and shakin' and sayin', 'Get your ass over here, Simpson.' And Ootney has on this helmet and gloves and he just freaked them out. 'Course he spent that night in jail too."

Win Allen says, "Like the time we were over in Holden and I was found guilty of contempt of court, that was an outtasight scene right there. Like Rise and Ootney and I and his brother Bubber were there and Bubber had a traffic violation that he was found guilty of and he didn't do nothin' wrong. So when the judge tells him that he's guilty, seeing that I dig on freedom of speech, I say, 'Bullshit' and the judge fined me. After a while the judge calls me up there and he says, 'Do you know the prior defendant?' And I say, 'Yeah, I know him, he's a citizen of America.' So after a while one of the pigs says, 'Boy, come along with me.' 'Boy,' dig? And I was gonna slide with him you know. So Ootney says, 'Stop the music, I'll pay the nigger's fine.' They freaked out. They didn't know how to react. They smiled. Ootney says, 'We'll teach the nigger a lesson once we got him into his cage.' Sheeit, we laughed all the way out of town. The judge musta thought Ootney was gonna cut my dick off and put it down my throat or somethin'."

Over and over again, in the past few months, Charles Simpson told his friends about the plot of land that he was going to buy. "I'm gonna live just like Thoreau," he told them, "just like old Henry David." He'd laugh. "Fuck all you longhaired hippie dudes."

"He was gonna buy these 12 acres," Rise says, "aw, fuck, that's all he did for a couple months—just dream about and plan his land. That's all he wanted and the fuckin' redneck farmer told him, 'Yeah, I'll sell it to you.' It is a shitty piece of land but Ootney liked it, just rocks and all barren, real freak's land. The redneck tells him, 'All we gotta do now is send off to the capital and get a few papers, make out the forms and everything' and so Charles, he had the money, he made all the arrangements, all he had to do is give the redneck the money and take over. It would be his land. He used to take us out there and we'd sit around on the rocks and smoke a few joints and Ootney would say, 'Welcome to my land, this is my land.' Well, somethin' happens and the redneck goes, 'Aw, hell, I don't wanna sell it, there's too much red tape and I don't wanna sell it to no hippie anyway.' That broke Ootney's back."

On Wednesday, April 19th, Charles Simpson found out he couldn't have his barren rock-filled dreamworld. On Friday, the 21st, he withdrew his dream money to bail out his outlaw friends.

He went home and told his father he'd gotten the money from the bank and the shot-apart, ashen-faced old man sitting in the rocking chair said:

"What about the land?"

"It don't matter now."

He reached into a closet and took out the M-1 semi-automatic carbine he had bought from a friend and said he was leaving for Harrisonville to get his friends out of jail.

"What you takin' the gun for?" the old man asked.

"Gonna shoot me some targets," his boy said.

V. THE SHIT COMES DOWN FROM THE SKY

"Simpson's my name, revolution's my game" didn't go over very well with Sheriff Bill Gough, but he didn't say anything about it. Those longhairs were making noise all morning and driving him batty. It would be a real pleasure to get them out of his jail. He'd take those friendly old juiceheads any day. It looked like a long weekend was cropping, what with the fire fighters coming in that night and those crazy longhairs still talking—right in jail—about holding their protest march tomorrow.

So he didn't give the Simpson boy any trouble when he asked, "Free the People!" in a shade louder voice than the sheriff liked to hear in his office. He counted the stacks of bills and looked up just how much the bond was and told his deputy to start getting the long-

hairs out of their cells. Simpson had a big grin on his face, but he looked like he hadn't slept for weeks. The whites of his eyes were more red than white and his hands were skittery. When the Anderson boy came in, Simpson looked at him as if he were going to kill him and before the sheriff could do anything, Simpson had the Anderson boy by the lapels. "Now listen here," the sheriff said, "you fight in here, both of you are gonna go to jail. I don't care how much money you got."

Rise Risner had just been brought out of his cell and was standing next to the counter when John Anderson walked through the door. "Anderson works at TWA with some computers, but he always made out that he was a friend of ours, rappin' to us and stuff. Anderson was there the night before, Thursday, when we were being taken to jail. Well, he had enough money on him to get some of us and he didn't do it. He didn't want to spend his damn money. Ootney found out about it and when he saw Anderson he said, 'Look you fucker, you're supposed to be a friend of ours. I don't want you to ever fuck me over like that.' "

Ootney looked strungout to everyone. "He was tired, yeah," Win Allen says, "but it was more. He was pissed off bad. I think the money had a lot to do with it—like, this was the money he was gonna buy his land with, dig, and it had turned into jail money. And he was pissed off about me, too. Like Charles really dug me. So when he found out my bond was so high, a thousand dollars more than the others, that really pissed him off bad. He told me after he got us out, he said, 'Nigger, if your face was as white as my ass, you wouldn't be havin' all this shit.' He goes, 'These fuckin' crackers, they gonna lynch you up against a tree one night." Then he laughed. Ootney was like that. He was jolly and jivin' but the vibes were like off center, it was like there was a bomb inside his head."

Standing around the water tower outside the jail, they decided it was more important than ever to stage their anti-war march. They went to George Russell's house, where Ootney "leaned up against a wall and looked like he was gonna fall asleep."

"You fuckin' jailbirds kept me up all night," he said.

"Ootney lost his beauty sleep," they hooted.

Rise says, "We were real determined we had to be in that square the next day marchin' with those signs and screamin'. The bust was the best example of the kind of shit we had all felt. Old Lloyd just had to point his finger and say 'Him and Him' and it was enough to send us all to the crabseat."

Win Allen decided they'd hand pamphlets out Saturday as they marched around the square "so the Truth can be put up on the walls." Hasty essays had to be written about war, repression, racism, and the new town ordinances.

"Come on, Ootney," Win said. "Help us write some of this shit."

"OK," Simpson said. "I'll write how much I like fuckin'."

They raspberried him and threw him lip-smacking mock farts, figuring, as Rise says, "We better leave Old Ootney alone 'cause he looked pretty tired." But Simpson brightened after a while and, before the meeting ended, offered to help after all. A friend of his in Holden had a mimeo-machine and he would take the essays over there and have them run off.

"Ootney's the production manager," Rise yelled, and, as the others laughed, Simpson came alive, dancing around, his fists flying, shadowboxing Rise's belly.

"Come on, come on," he yelled, "Charles Simpson's gonna take on all you creepo fuckers."

Rise says, "After a while we split up and Ootney took the stuff we wrote up and he was gonna take it over to Holden to the friend of his that had the machine. He asked me if I wanted to go over there with him and I said sure. We piled on into his 1952 Chevy. That was Ootney's batmobile. It was an old, fallin' apart car that made a lot of noise. He loved the car, said it was a real Hippie car. So we drove on out and we got outside a place called Strasburg and the goddamn car blows up. So we sat there not believin' it, you know, here we are and I just got out of jail and Ootney didn't get any sleep and now the goddamn car blows. Well, we couldn't believe it. We were so pissed off we couldn't do nothin' but stand there and mumble and say fuck it and laugh.

"So we decided we were gonna hitchhike into Holden and then hitchhike back to Harrisonville. Ootney had his sleeping bag in the back and the M-1 but I didn't think nothin' of it 'cause he and I were always goin' target shootin' with the thing. So he puts the rifle into his sleepin' bag and we're standin' there hitchhikin' and the car's still smokin'. Then this dude from Harrisonvile that we know comes along and picks us up. He's goin' back to Harrisonville so he drives us back there and we get my car. We drive into Holden and drop the shit off with the mimeo guy and then we had nothin' to do. So Ootney says, 'Let's just take the gun and shoot some target practice.' We were gonna spend the night out in the woods.

As Charles Simpson and Rise Risner drove from Holden to Harrisonville late Friday afternoon, they talked. The radio was thumping and Rise only half-listened. The conversation was like a hundred others they had had. "Nothing much," Rise says, "Just a lot of shit, rap talk. Maybe he was trying to tell me somethin', but if he did, maybe I wasn't listenin' that close."

They talked about astrology. Ootney was a Pisces and as they speeded past the wheatfields and around the greening countryside, he talked to Rise about being a Pisces, about how he'd read a book that said he'd be nothing but a dreamer all his life and he'd never make any money. He said that this book said a Pisces was "self-destructive."

"So what does that mean?" Rise asked.

"I don't know," Ootney laughed. "Maybe it means I'm fucked up."

"Yeah, it means you'll fuck yourself to death," Rise said.

They talked, too, about dope. Ootney said he hadn't done any dope for sometime and didn't want to do any dope, "because everytime I smoke a joint I think about how everybody's fuckin' us over and I get all depressed and down."

As Rise drove into town, he heard Charles Simpson say a few quiet sentences that would forever stick in his mind.

"Everytime I turn around, I'm gettin' fucked up somehow. My old man's dyin' and my old lady leaves and the pigs are always hasslin' me. Shit, I can't buy a piece of land even when I got the money. I can't drive around without my car blowin' up on me. It's always the same shit. Ain't it ever gonna stop?"

"When we got into town," Rise says, "We were stopped at the red light and the radio was playin' the new Stones song. I was beatin' on the dash and sayin' 'Tumblin'-tumblin',' and all of a sudden Charles jumps out of the car and runs up the street. He was out of the car and halfway up the street before I even knew what happened. And I freaked right there. What the fuck was he doin'? He had the fuckin' gun. What the fuck was he runnin' up the street for with that fuckin' gun in his jacket?"

Rise panicked. He made a U-turn, stepped on the gas, and "started boogeyin' out of Harrisonville, goin' the other direction."

When Simpson jumped out of the car, Charles Hale, Gary's younger brother, saw him and ran up to him. He asked Simpson if he had seen Gary.

"He just shook his head," Charles Hale says, "the only thing I noticed

was, he had this great big beautiful smile on his face."

Gary Hale was on the other side of the square with Win Allen and some of the others. "So all of a sudden," Win says, "We heard this *rat-tat-tat-tat-tat* like. And I said, 'Hey Gary, that sound like some caps, man, like somebody bustin' some caps,' and he said, 'That's what it sounds like to me.' We looked at one another and we got vibes instantly, we said, 'Wait a minute, man, who's all here?' So then we see people startin' to run and we started boogeyin' and we heard these two pigs were shot. And then we heard, 'There's a dirty hippie down there, dead,' and we all— like we saw Charles' body—and like we couldn't identify with that blood."

Rise drove around for a while, scared, and then, finally, drove back to the square. "By the time I got there the two dead pigs had been taken off the street but Charles was still lyin' in the street where he had shot himself, all covered up. All I could see was his boots stickin' out from under the plastic bag. My knees just kind of buckled and I was leaned up against this building and I just kind of went down. I just passed out on the sidewalk and I lay there a few seconds. There's this woman who runs the cleaners and I've known her all my life and she goes:

" 'Well, he tried to shoot me, Johnny' and I didn't say anything.

" 'Why did he try to shoot me, Johnny? I didn't do anythin' to him,' and I just screamed, 'Shut up, goddamn you, just shut up.' "

G. M. Allen was about to leave the bank for the day when he saw people running and heard the police sirens. He ran over to the other side of the square, saw the people in front of the Allen Bank and Trust Company, and heard about the two policemen killed and the Simpson boy in the alley with his head blown off. He wasn't surprised. He expected something like this all along. He felt it in his bones. He turned and headed back to his office as fast as he could. He had to activate the Civil Defense sirens and get on the CB band and tell his volunteers to get into town. Gary Hale saw him rushing across the square and went up to him.

"You satisfied now?" Gary Hale said, "You see what you've done?"

"Get out of my way, little bastard," G. M. Allen said.

He got to his office and as he pushed the button and the sirens started screaming, G. M. Allen had a comforting thought.

It was 6 o'clock and the firefighters coming for their convention would be checking into their motels. They'd have more than enough manpower in Harrisonville that night to handle whatever would happen. 500 firefighters from all across the State of Missouri would be there.

And right then G.M. Allen said a prayer. He thanked the Lord for giving him the wisdom to plan the convention for the right time—"when the hippies started doing their killing."

VI. LIFE AMONG THE RAZORBACKS

Firefighters watchdogged the street corners that night with hatchets and shotguns in their hands. The square was barricaded and police cruisers shadowed all the streets leading into town. A rifleman armed with a carbine very much like Charles Simpson's perched in the courthouse belltower, which commands an overview and a clear shot to every cranny of the square. Around 11 o'clock a thunderstorm rolled in with its gnarled bolts of field-lightning and the rain sent the gunmen scurrying to their cars.

About an hour after the shooting, Win Allen was walking across the square and a policeman went up to him and said, "You got two of ours, now it's time we get some of you." When a curfew was announced that night, Win

and Rise and the others got out of town fast and decided to stay out.

"There was blood in those people's eyes," Rise says, "It was like we'd all pulled that trigger, not just Ootney. They couldn't do anything to Ootney because he was smart and blew his brains out, but we are still there. I was really scared. Those people were crazy. The pigs were lookin' at us like they could hardly wait to tickle their triggers. We knew that if any of us like made the smallest wrong move, one of us would be dead and they'd just make up some bogosity and get away with callin' it justifiable murder."

G. M. Allen says, "I was just happy we had all those men in town. Besides that, we had policemen come from as far as 50 miles away. We didn't know what to expect, but we were ready. We thought some of the hippies might wanna shoot some more policemen or some innocent people. It didn't make sense, not any of it, unless you figure the whole thing was planned and Simpson was just talked into killin' those policemen for the sake of their revolution."

On Saturday, the 22nd, the national day of protest to end the Vietnam War, the curfew was lifted—but only during the day, until six o'clock that night. Some of the firefighters and policemen got some rest, but gunmen still patrolled all sides of the square and a rifleman still stood guard in the belltower, using binoculars to scan the alleys and the rooftops. Harrisonville's first antiwar protest was, naturally, canceled, and after only brief debate, the firefighters decided to cancel their parade.

"You mean we drove those trucks all the way out here for nothin'?" a firefighter asked G. M. Allen.

"It ain't fair, sure," G. M. Allen said, "but I figure a lot of people are gonna be too scared to come into town."

He was wrong. Except for the longhairs, everyone within a hundred miles seemed to drive to Harrisonville that day. Traffic was backed up for half a mile, all the way to the FINA gas station, and people stood in clusters around the spots which had been pools of blood the day before.

In the course of florid descriptions, rumor fed upon rumor. The Simpson boy had eaten LSD just before he did his killing. The gun was traced to the Black Panther Party in Chicago. Simpson had belonged to a Communist hippie group in Kansas City. FBI men were coming into town. The longhairs had decided to kill the whole town, just like Charlie Manson had killed those people in California. They found some dynamite hidden in the MFA silo. The courthouse would be burned that night. The hippies had a list with the names of townspeople who were going to be killed on it. The National Guard was coming in.

And the pickup trucks carrying whole families of people who hardly ever came to town kept coming in on this day. Excited little kids stood by the Retirement Home's grey walls and asked, "Is this where he killed himself, mommy?"

Saturday night, the gunman in the belltower saw something move on the roof of the Harrisonville Hotel. He yelled to the firefighters across the street and, within minutes, the hotel was surrounded by dozens of men carrying all sorts of weapons—from Colt .45s to mail-order Lee Harvey Oswald specials. "Give yourself up," a deputy's bullhorn echoed. "You're surrounded.

There was a crash on the sidewalk and an old wino who'd found a comfortable place for the night yelled, "Don't shoot, don't shoot, I'm comin' " and miraculously no shots were fired. The doddering old drunk had dropped his pint of whiskey from the rooftop in pants-pissed fear and a deputy was assigned to sweep the glass off the street.

The burials were held Monday. Patrolman Donald Lee Marler's was the first. More than 50 policemen came to the funeral, some of them from Kansas City. Marler's open casket was in the church foyer but was closed minutes before his wife and family got there. The minister said, "The fact that everyone dies is proof that all have sinned. But God says it does not end there. Our friend took the short cut home." The city council held a meeting before Marlers' funeral and voted to pay for both Marler's and Wirt's funerals. A reporter asked if the curfew would be extended and Mayor M. O. Raine, the dentist who'd once pulled one of Charles Simpson's teeth, said, "This is a black day and I don't like to have too many decisions made when people are so emotional, so I'm not gonna make that decision now."

Charles Simpson was buried last—in Chilhowee, a tiny town not far from Holden, where his grandparents are buried. Rise Risner, who was one of the pallbearers, says, "There was a whole lot of people there, I think about half of 'em were pigs because a lot of 'em had cameras. This dude, this minister, like you could tell he wasn't too happy about havin' to bury Ootney. He was just goin' through the motions, like he was the one who got stuck with buryin' a sack of shit. That's what the vibe was, that's what his face said. The minister was talkin' about how Jesus died and all this shit and he didn't say one fuckin' thing about Charles. They didn't have anything about him even, they didn't say one fuckin' thing about his life. Nothin'. He was rappin' shit about fuckin' burying Jesus and 'He rose' and all this shit. I thought he was talkin' about Charles for a long time until I found out what he was talkin' about. John Thompson was singin' 'Blowin' in the Wind' and we all chimed in."

After the ceremony, as they were bringing the casket out of the church, in the glare of television cameras and wire service photographers, the pallbearers clenched their fists and held them to the sky, their other hand on the wooden box that had Charles Simpson's body in it. "We gave the power fist 'cause we figured that would be a way of showin' everybody that Ootney was a brother," Rise says, "No matter what kind of shit they were sayin' about him. He was one of us. We did it 'cause we loved him."

Some of the townspeople saw and others heard about the pallbearers' clenched fists and, at first, no one knew what to make of it. But then G. M. Allen told Mayor Raine he heard it meant someone else was going to die and Mayor Raine told some of the councilmen and by nightfall the word was out all over town. The hippies were going to kill another policeman. So the curfew was extended still another night and the rifleman still crouched in the belltower.

The curfew was lifted, finally, the next day, but Win Allen and Rise Risner and Gary Hale and the others still didn't feel safe going into town. They drove out to the City Park about a mile from town and were surrounded by guns within minutes.

"You gonna get your asses outta here," a policeman told Rise Risner, "or we gonna get even."

Win and Rise collected all of their friends and left town, camping out in an open and nearly inaccessible field about six miles away. "I was afraid they'd come to one of our houses like one of those lynching parties on TV and just take us," Rise says. "It was cold out there and it rained and we were wet as hell, but we were alive."

By Friday, feelings ran so ugly that the Rev. W. T. Niermeier, who had sermonized at Patrolman Marler's funeral, wrote a column for the Democrat-Missourian that said:

"A word of God for our community at this time. Recompense to no man evil for evil. Live peaceably with all men. Dearly beloved, avenge not yourselves. Thou shalt not follow a multitude to do evil."

That day's Democrat-Missourian carried a news story about the shooting but nothing about the circumstances. "Well, I didn't want to write too much about Simpson," said J. W. Brown, the editor, "not after all the trouble he caused us. I figured folks just wouldn't want to read about him and if folks don't want to read about somethin', I don't print it." That same day, the newspaper was awarded its 16th Blue Ribbon Weekly Newspaper citation by the Missouri Press Association—for "outstanding performance in the field of journalism."

The next issue of the paper carried a new two-column ad. The ad was the result of the funerals J. W. Brown had to attend that week. He talked to some of the directors and they determined that the funeral homes didn't do much advertising in the Democrat-Missourian and the next week, the bold black-bordered ad, which in a perverse way Charles Simpson had solicited, said

A HOUSE WITHOUT A WOMAN is like a body without soul or spirit. Benjamin Franklin's words of wisdom recognize that a house becomes a home through the loving touch of a woman and the warm glow of a friendly hearth. Likewise, we believe, a funeral director becomes more than a business man since his prime object is to be of service to those in need. It is with humble pride that we serve the citizens of this community.

Friday afternoon, a week after the shooting, G. M. Allen was talking to one of his friends about the list the hippies were supposed to have with the names of the people they were going to kill on it. G. M. Allen said he heard that he was Number One on that list. "I don't hold too much by it," G. M. Allen said, "maybe there isn't even any list—but, by God, they try somethin'—well, I was in the Infantry during the War, they better think about that."

A few days after that, Luke Scavuzzo, who runs Scavuzzo's Grocery and is an alderman, was doing a radio talk show in Kansas City and he said: "Maybe some people in town pushed those kids too much." Now, Luke Scavuzzo said, "Some people have learned they better *ease up.*" By nightfall, town scuttlebutt held that Luke Scavuzzo was saying they were going to "*give up.*" The next day about 20 people came in to tell Luke Scavuzzo they weren't going to buy his groceries anymore because of what he said.

"Luke had to go around for a whole week tellin' everybody he never said that," G. M. Allen says, "He should have known better. Nobody's gonna give up or ease up. Are we supposed to wait around till someone else gets killed?"

A few weeks after Ootney Simpson fired his M-1 on the town square, the Civil Defense sirens screamed again and people ran to their citizens' band radios expecting to hear the worst of their fears confirmed. More trouble. Another killing. The voice of G. M. Allen was as breathless and garbled as the last time. But this time there was little to worry about. It came out of the east and overturned a mobile home and knocked down some outhouses and then it was gone.

Just another goddamn tornado.

I got into Harrisonville about two weeks after the shooting. The first person I saw was Win Allen. He was lying on the courthouse steps, pressed flat with his face to the cement. He didn't move and he stayed that way, as still as the pennies on a dead man's eyes. Win and Rise and the others had decided it was safe enough to go back into town. The old mock-heroic game for the town square would go on. Four dead men weren't going to get in the way.

I got out of the car and walked into the drug store for a pack of Luckies and an old man behind the counter was staring out the window at Win Allen. He watched me get out of the car and his eyes must have picked out the Missouri plates on it because when I walked in his tone was conspiratorial

and trusting. "See that nigger boy up there," Lloyd Foster said, "he's been climbin' those steps every day for four days now and just layin' down up there. He goes up there and he looks around and he puts his fist up in the air and then he lays down on top of his face. He pretends he's dead. They say it's a way of rememberin' the crazy hippie that killed our policemen."

I was wearing a tie and a blue blazer and the next few days I wore the same get-up, exaggerating the effect, walking around with a fat Special Corona 77 cigar sticking out of my mouth. I sought out townspeople in the most razorbacked bars in town, buying them beer and malt liquor and getting them to talk. I slicked my hair back above my ears and bought a bottle of gooey hair-oil and—with cigar and coat and tie—I must have looked respectable enough to them because pretty soon they were buying me beers. I told them I was from a magazine in San Francisco and forgot to say which one. I think the cigar and the slick hair got through. When I got back to the motel at night and looked in the mirror I saw some guy I remembered from somewhere but I couldn't place him.

When I was finished talking to the townspeople I drove back to my motel and washed my hair and changed. I put my jeans on and let my hair fall down over my ears and put on my leather jacket and drove back into town. I was getting pretty tired of cigars anyway. I found Win Allen and told him I was from *Rolling Stone* and wanted to talk about Charles Simpson, and Win Allen almost cried he was so happy. "Man," Win said, "we been watchin' you watchin' us and we figured you was FBI. With that cee-gar." We laughed.

That night we gathered near the square—one of the cops I'd talked to spotted me and gave me a fixed hard glare—and drove about ten miles out of town into the middle of a wheatfield. We found a clearing that suited us and built a bonfire. It was a cloudy spring

night, about 70 degrees, and the lightning was already playing patterns off
to the east. There were about a dozen
of us and we had eight or nine bottles
of red wine and a dozen six-packs of
beer. We also had a bagful of tongue-
burning Missouri weed.

The fire was roaring and Rise Risner's red Volkswagen, which had been
pulled as close as possible, played Dylan, Hendrix, and, what the hell, Jose
Feliciano. The people here were Charles
Simpson's best friends. We were talking about a man who had killed three
innocent people in cold blood. They
were calling him a brother and telling
me how much he loved people and how
he believed in The Cause.

"Sometimes Ootney said he thought
violence was the only kind of revolution there was," Rise said. "But dig,"
Win said, "as far as violent revolution
—anytime someone infringes on me
and fucks me, it makes me mad, that's
the way Charles was thinkin' too."

"A lot of freaks you meet in places,"
Rise said, "somebody will rip them off
or something and they'll haul ass. But
we're not that way. We're country boys.
We're willin' to fight the motherfuckers if they wanna fight us."

"Ootney was smart," Rise said, "he
killed himself to keep the pigs from
havin' the satisfaction of killin' him or
lockin' him up in some honky jail. He
was into so much cosmic shit, man. He
was so heavy with that, it was a religion to him. Like some religions say
self-destruction is the best thing you
can do for your God, that's why they
burn themselves. I know Ootney had
to feel the same thing."

"One time Ootney was in a black
neighborhood," Win said, "and somebody said somethin' about Jesus to him
and Ootney said, 'The only way that
Jesus and I differ is that he was willin'
to die for the people around him and
I'm not ready for that yet.'"

"I think he was Jesus," Rise said, "as
far as I'm concerned he was Jesus."

"Because that cat just laid down
truth, man," Win said. "Everything that
came out of his mouth was truth and
supposedly like Jesus laid down the
same thing. And when he got up the
stuff to die for The Cause, Charles became of the same instance. He was
groovy, outtasight, he had so much
compassion for people, sentimental
about a lot of things, sensitive."

It had been a long few days and I
had scrutinized too many vivid details
of four vicious killings and something
in my mind flailed out now—Jesus
Simpson, murderer, cold-blooded killer,
compassionate, sensitive, sentimental.
It could have been the fatigue or the
Missouri weed or the beer mixed with
wine, but I saw too many grotesqueries
leaping about in that blazing bonfire.

"As far as I'm concerned," Rise said,
"Charles isn't dead. It is just somethin'
Charles wanted to do and if Charles
wanted to do it, I can't say anything
about it."

"Yeah," I said, "but what about the
people killed and their wives and kids?
Don't you care about that?"

"Well, you know," Rise said, "how
can I criticize it. It's Charles' thing. Like
it was a far-out thing to do."

We were gathered around this bonfire on a spring night in Missouri and
the date was the fourth of May, 1972.
I'd never had much luck with the
fourth of May. On this day in 1971, I
was standing around a green field at
Kent State University listening to
requiems and eulogies. And on this day
in 1970 I was running dazedly around
those same lush fields looking at pools
of blood and asking National Guardsmen why they had killed four innocent
kids.

And now I was talking to some kids
asking them why one of their best
friends killed three innocent people
with the same kind of gun the Guardsmen used and all they could say to me
was:

"Like it was a far-out thing to do."

I told them the story of my May 4ths and Win Allen said:

"Well, dig, man, now it's four to three."

"Right on," Rise said.

"Old Ootney," Win said, "Old Ootney. That gun was outtasight, man. Like the first time I went to his crib I saw it and I said, 'Ootney, is that yours?' and he said, 'Yeah, a friend of mine gave it to me,' and I said: 'Wow, man, sometime when you and I go fishin' and out in the woods, maybe I can dig on it.' Like Charles had this Buck knife with a holster on it and this most beautiful fishin' pole and he said—he said whenever he went home, he just fondled the stuff all the time, felt it up and dug it."

"Yeah," Rise said, "Ootney loved nature."

Billboard for the First New York Film Festival,
1963, Oil on canvas, 9' 6" x 15'. Hirshhorn
Museum and Sculpture Garden, Smithsonian
Institution.

Two Women in the Country by Willem de
Kooning (1954). Oil, enamel, and charcoal
on canvas, 46 x 46". Hirshhorn Museum and
Sculpture Garden, Smithsonian Institution.

2

Introduction to Expressionism

Although "expressionism" historically denotes a movement that originated in Germany in the early twentieth century, the term might be used generally to apply to artists who seek to express the nature of the perceiver rather than the object perceived. In this sense, there are nearly as many modes of expressionism as there are expressionist artists. Whether they call themselves symbolists, imagists, surrealists, or absurdists, they all seek to represent a unique human mind rather than the material world it observes. This search may result in a depiction of the artist's own creative processes or delve into a pre-conscious form of mental activity. In the process, the artist is exalted either as creator of language conventions or as the one person capable of going beyond verbal conventions in order to represent psychic truth. Delineation of the different schools is difficult since each writer tended to experiment with various techniques, but the basic position of the expressionist artist might be summarized in terms of the "art for art's sake" movement that formed at the turn of the century in opposition to the principles of literary realism.

These writers maintained that although reality seems to be composed of things outside of our consciousness, we cannot perceive or understand that world objectively. While writers of literary realism assumed that direct observation would yield some knowledge of the universal laws governing human experience, members of the "art for art's sake" movement argued that even direct observations and sensations do not bring knowledge of the world. Walter Pater, one of the originators of this movement in England, claimed that if we analyze the way we perceive physical things, we will see how subjective our experience of the world really is. In *The Renaissance*, he argues that all our ideas are derived from primary impressions of the world outside and that "experience, already reduced to a group of impressions, is ringed round for each one of us by that thick wall of personality through which no real voice has ever pierced on its way to us, or from us to that which we can only conjecture to be without. Every one of those impressions is the impression of the individual in his isolation, each mind keeping as a solitary prisoner its own dream of a world." Pater suggests that we understand the world only as we reconstruct it in our minds. Since we each live in a world of our own making, it follows that artists can imitate only their own personalities in works of art. And why should they want to do otherwise? According to Pater, not only is self-expression more true to reality than pseudo-objective description, it *is* reality and therefore valuable for its own sake.

An artist who assumes that only the subjective experience is real will naturally conclude that representation of an artist's highly developed imaginative processes is the most worthy subject. An appropriate novel would therefore trace the development of the artistic mind. Joyce called his *Künstlerroman*, or novel of artistic development, *A Portrait of the Artist*. You have seen a similar kind of novel in the realist's *Bildungsroman*. Faukner's short *Bildungsroman*, "Barn Burning," for example, traces the tensions and conflicts repressed in the development of a social personality. Joyce is not interested in the development of this sort of representative social type, however; he modifies the *Bildungsroman* to show how the unique consciousness of the artist develops, particularly how the artist acquires language. His hero acquires conventional words, images, symbols, and myths, but his unique artistic powers become evident when he distorts the conventions of his culture to construct his own experience of the world. At the end of his development, the artist leaves the babble and chaos of Ireland in order to reshape his personal experience into an ordered and meaningful art form.

Stephen's promise at the end of the novel "to forge in the smithy of my soul the uncreated consciousness of my race" indicates one way for the modern artist to cope with an intolerable universe. If the material world is chaotic, art can provide meaning and order. Poets in the *symbolist* tradition assume that the artist can create symbols of lasting value, symbols that can lend order to a disintegrating culture the way religion once did. Symbolism began as an international movement with Edgar Allen Poe in America. He was followed by the French poets Baudelaire, Verlaine, Rimbaud, and Mallarmé, and their concept was adopted in turn by English poets in the "art for art's sake" movement. These poets all wished to create an art that reflected the abstract perfection of music rather than the story line of narrative poetry.

Yeats's gyre is a useful example of the way an abstract symbol is developed by an artist influenced by the symbolists. Throughout his career, Yeats constructed an elaborate universe of poetic symbols. In many of his poems we find language that does not refer to things in the common world we inhabit but expressing the imaginary world of the poet. We all understand symbols like a cross and a dollar sign—they have public associations with the ideas of Christianity and money. A symbol like Yeats's gyre in "The Second Coming" and "Sailing to Byzantium," however, lacks these public associations. The image of the gyre, commonly indicating only a spiral motion or form, takes on special significance as it is repeated in new forms in different poems. Yeats's gyre comes to stand for his theory of history as a progression from periods of intense order to periods of anarchy that, in turn, give birth to new and vital cultures. The initiated reader of Yeats will attribute this symbolic significance to any image of a cone-shaped or whirling object in Yeats's poetry, whether or not its special significance can be derived from the particular poem in which it is found. This symbol when related to others often borrowed from Christian and other mythologies forms a symbolic system or private mythology. Such a system attempts to reconstruct the entire universe according to the desires and needs of the individual poet's imagination, heedless of its intelligibility to the reading public. The obscurity involved in this kind of symbol system suggests a hazard of technique that intensifies in subsequent expressionist movements. If only subjective experience can be expressed in art because we each can understand only our own experience, how can ideas be communicated from one person to another? Won't every symbol be only one person's private association?

Although the *imagists* encountered similar charges of obscurity, their movement began in an attempt to avoid the confusion and vagueness of abstract language. The subjective perceiver was to be represented in concrete terms, without reference to any personal mythology. Wallace Stevens' "Thirteen Ways of Looking at a Black-bird," for example, shows how the nature of a tangible object, a blackbird, changes as it is contemplated from different perspectives by the artist. The emphasis is on the perspective rather than the object, and Stevens' poetic blackbird actually has very little to do with any real bird. It is simply a medium for the poet to express his ideas, and Stevens indicates the importance of these ideas when he states that "Poetry is the supreme fiction." There are many detailed fictions that attempt to give an ordered and precise view of reality. In Stevens' view, religion is one of the more notable attempts, but poetry is supreme because all order is created by the human imagination. Only poetry acknowledges this truth. T. S. Eliot's speaker in *The Waste Land* is basically in agreement about the personal source of poetry and its cultural role: It is only after renovating the private psychological and spiritual landscape that the poet can create images of order and unity for the public. This renovation never occurs in *The Waste Land*, however, for the speaker remains in a state of emotional paralysis, unable to perceive anything vital or unified in his environment. Unlike the symbolists, the imagists acknowledged that the facts of history and science had taken the mystery out of the universe. They would posit no semidivine theory of gyres to revitalize the wasteland.

In order to express this emotional paralysis in concrete rather than vague or sentimental terms, Eliot devised what he termed the "objective correlative." As he describes the concept, the poet chooses "a set of objects, a situation, a chain of events which shall be the formula of the *particular* emotion; such that when the external facts, which must terminate in sensory experience, are given, the emotion is immediately evoked." This set of objects is then a concrete way of dramatizing the shifting states of consciousness in an individual. Look at the beginning of

"The Love Song of J. Alfred Prufrock." The poem opens with the strange comparison of an evening sky and "a patient etherized upon a table." The next extravagant metaphor, comparing the fog to a prowling cat, makes it obvious that Eliot's images have ceased to describe weather conditions in London and actually express the emotions of the perceiver making the comparison. The imagist poet recognizes that the mind in an emotional state expresses itself in terms of a complex of images that are not arranged according to natural relationships or chronology. A model imagist poem like "In a Station of the Metro" will simply present the reader with two normally unrelated images from which the reader is to reconstruct the mental process of the observer. One of the central contributions of imagism to modern art is the concept of the concrete image as "that which presents an intellectual and emotional complex in an instant of time," as Ezra Pound explains it. Even a brief look at Pound's "Canto I" will reveal a problem many imagist poems present for the reader, however. The poems fragment the continuity of space and time and violate ordinary syntax in order to represent this emotional complex precisely, but as a result the reader finds it difficult to follow the subjective associations of the poet. In *The Waste Land*, the poet's literary associations are so diverse that the author provides notes for the reader.

You will have difficulty negotiating the literary allusions and innovative language of Pound and Eliot. Theoretically you should be on more common ground with the *surrealist* poets because they seek a spontaneous, unsophisticated, unliterary expression, but paradoxically, their experiments in this direction produced poetic language that was no less obscure than imagism and symbolism. Like the psychological realists, the surrealists were fascinated with Freud's theories concerning the irrational and creative forces that inhabit every human mind, but unlike the realists, they were interested in the unique and even aberrant individual rather than the common type. The poetic consciousness was as important to the surrealists as to other expressionists because only the artist could break conventions and explore inner forces generally unacknowledged. Only the artist could overthrow the tyranny of rational thinking and conventional writing and express the primitive, irrational, and eccentric aspects of the personality. Because of their fascination with the subconscious, the surrealists were particularly interested in Freud's theories concerning presocial erotic instincts, and the content of their work reflects this concern for the primary libidinal levels of psychic activity. They also admired the British Romantic artists for advocating political revolt, valuing imagination over reason, and expressing normally suppressed impulses in their Gothic fiction.

The surrealists acknowledged direct roots in the Dada movement which flourished around the first World War. The dadaists had sought to destroy all preexisting artistic, social, ethical, and logical conventions in order to express the absurdity of contemporary existence. As one adherent, George Grosz, concluded, "Nothing was holy to us . . . We spat upon everything, including ourselves. Our symbol was nothingness, a vacuum, a void. . . ." The surrealists, feeling that some positive value could be found in the liberated subconscious, broke with the nihilistic dadaists in 1922. Their position was expressed by André Breton in his 1924 manifesto: "I believe in the future resolution of these two states—outwardly so contradictory—which are dream and reality, into a sort of absolute reality, a *surreality*."

Surrealists art attempts to express this absolute reality by freeing the mind from its traditional rational structures.

Their artistic inspiration derives from recollection of dreams, trancelike states, hallucinations, and from attempts at automatic or unconscious writing. Their goal was a chance or unwilled juxtaposition of visual images. For example, at the beginning of Thomas' "The Mouse and the Woman," the "world outside" is separate from the world within the madhouse, but soon "under the sun the iron bars melted." The two worlds become indistinguishable. Because this story of a madman-artist is a mixture of dream and reality, we can't tell which elements describe his hallucinations and which actually occur. Because he destroys the distinction between these two basic categories by which normal people organize reality, Thomas' fiction seems to be controlled by some mysterious demonic force, and we have the uncomfortable sense of being excluded from its meaning. Delving into the depths of personality, the artist may find knowledge even more personal and obscure than Yeats's vision or Eliot's juxtaposition of images. Thomas characteristically makes the most ordinary words seem part of a foreign language in order to show us the poet's imagination freed from conventional reality. Primary psychic expression may even involve the uniquely prelogical perspective of a foetus, as in Thomas' "Before I knocked and flesh made enter." And if Thomas' verse seems relatively incomprehensible to you, look at E. E. Cummings' "Anyone Lived in a Pretty How Town." For years linguists have been concocting theories to explain the unique grammar of this poem. Perhaps the purest form of subjective expression is the automatic writing of French surrealists, but this uncontrolled verbal outpouring toward which surrealism aspired eliminates any kind of meaning. Like the severed hand, this kind of expression violates our sense of what art is, and we reject it as meaningless. But if uncontrolled language does not communicate and if, as the surrealists theorize, artfully controlled language invariably suppresses or falsifies the primary psychic experience, then how does the artist express subjective reality?

Using science-fiction fantasy, artists like Harlan Ellison rudely distort conventional representations of their society in order to show a violent psychic response. The subjective response is not meaningless; it is definably subversive. The future in these stories is a version of the present perversely manipulated by the artist's unique attitudes and emotions. In "A Boy and His Dog," Ellison gives us a post-World War III society that has been reconstructed so that social and psychological elements normally repressed in our own world have gained dominance. These repressed elements wreak their vengeance on sterile middle-class culture in the form of an extravagant rape. The story's technique is in keeping with its content, for Ellison uses strongly colloquial language and "pornographic" descriptions to attack the polite literary conventions which currently obstruct the free expression of the artist.

The confessional poets following in the footsteps of Robert Lowell use psychological rather than political fantasy. Anne Sexton and Sylvia Plath, for example, use language to discover and exorcise the traumatic experiences of childhood buried in the subconscious. This use of poetic language offers therapeutic escape from the dark and destructive impulses Ellison celebrates, and it provides the confessional poets with an artistic control and a social form for what would otherwise be madness.

Yet other artists dramatize the absurdity of the very attempt to communicate personal expression in language. Since dramatic form enables the artist to present actions as well as speech, playwrights like Beckett and Pinter can show how inadequate language is to express what is private and primary. In these works, language is deliberately emptied of meaning. "Act without Words" demonstrates Beckett's hostility toward language, for true to its title the play allows objects and actions to speak for themselves without the interference of a verbal message. Pinter similarly uses silence to expose the deceptions of language. His main character, a matchseller, never speaks during the play. The gentleman character's speech disintegrates in the presence of this demonic figure, while the lady of the house dresses the matchseller up as her husband and gives him a false name. In the deliberately antiliterary tradition of the Theater of the Absurd, drama represents reality as a strange game with incomprehensible rules. In Absurdism, the desire for expressive language leads to a preference for silence.

William Butler Yeats (1865–1939)

SEPTEMBER 1913

What need you, being come to sense,
But fumble in a greasy till
And add the halfpence to the pence
And prayer to shivering prayer, until
You have dried the marrow from the bone?   5
For men were born to pray and save:
Romantic Ireland's dead and gone,
It's with O'Leary in the grave.

Yet they were of a different kind,
The names that stilled your childish play,   10
They have gone about the world like wind,
But little time had they to pray
For whom the hangman's rope was spun,
And what, God help us, could they save?
Romantic Ireland's dead and gone,   15
It's with O'Leary in the grave.

Was it for this the wild geese spread
The grey wing upon every tide;
For this that all that blood was shed,
For this Edward Fitzgerald died,   20
And Robert Emmet and Wolfe Tone,
All that delirium of the brave?
Romantic Ireland's dead and gone,
It's with O'Leary in the grave.

Yet could we turn the years again,   25
And call those exiles as they were
In all their loneliness and pain,
You'd cry, "Some woman's yellow hair

Has maddened every mother's son":
They weighed so lightly what they gave.   30
But let them be, they're dead and gone,
They're with O'Leary in the grave.

THE WILD SWANS AT COOLE

The trees are in their autumn beauty,
The woodland paths are dry,
Under the October twilight the water
Mirrors a still sky;
Upon the brimming water among the stones   5
Are nine-and-fifty swans.

The nineteenth autumn has come upon me
Since I first made my count;
I saw, before I had well finished,
All suddenly mount   10
And scatter wheeling in great broken rings
Upon their clamorous wings.

I have looked upon those brilliant creatures,
And now my heart is sore.
All's changed since I, hearing at twilight,   15
The first time on this shore,
The bell-beat of their wings above my head,
Trod with a lighter tread.

Unwearied still, lover by lover,
They paddle in the cold   20
Companionable streams or climb the air;
Their hearts have not grown old;
Passion or conquest, wander where they will,
Attend upon them still.

But now they drift on the still water,   25
Mysterious, beautiful;
Among what rushes will they build,
By what lake's edge or pool
Delight men's eyes when I awake some day
To find they have flown away?   30

EASTER 1916

I have met them at close of day
Coming with vivid faces
From counter or desk among grey
Eighteenth-century houses.
I have passed with a nod of the head   5

Or polite meaningless words,
Or have lingered awhile and said
Polite meaningless words,
And thought before I had done
Of a mocking tale or a gibe   10
To please a companion
Around the fire at the club,
Being certain that they and I
But lived where motley is worn:
All changed, changed utterly: 15
A terrible beauty is born.

That woman's days were spent
In ignorant good-will,
Her nights in argument
Until her voice grew shrill.   20
What voice more sweet than hers
When, young and beautiful,
She rode to harriers?
This man had kept a school
And rode our wingèd horse;   25
This other his helper and friend
Was coming into his force;
He might have won fame in the end,
So sensitive his nature seemed,
So daring and sweet his thought.   30
This other man I had dreamed
A drunken, vainglorious lout.
He had done most bitter wrong
To some who are near my heart,
Yet I number him in the song;   35
He, too, has resigned his part
In the casual comedy;
He, too, has been changed in his turn,
Transformed utterly:
A terrible beauty is born.   40

Hearts with one purpose alone
Through summer and winter seem
Enchanted to a stone
To trouble the living stream.
The horse that comes from the road,   45
The rider, the birds that range
From cloud to tumbling cloud,
Minute by minute they change;
A shadow of cloud on the stream
Changes minute by minute;   50
A horse-hoof slides on the brim,
And a horse plashes within it;
The long-legged moor-hens dive,
And hens to moor-cocks call;
Minute by minute they live: 55
The stone's in the midst of all.

Too long a sacrifice
Can make a stone of the heart.
O when may it suffice?
That is Heaven's part, our part   60
To murmur name upon name,
As a mother names her child
When sleep at last has come
On limbs that had run wild.
What is it but nightfall?   65
No, no, not night but death;
Was it needless death after all?
For England may keep faith
For all that is done and said.
We know their dream; enough   70
To know they dreamed and are dead;
And what if excess of love
Bewildered them till they died?
I write it out in a verse—
MacDonagh and MacBride   75
And Connolly and Pearse
Now and in time to be,
Wherever green is worn,
Are changed, changed utterly:
A terrible beauty is born.   80

THE SECOND COMING

Turning and turning in the widening gyre
The falcon cannot hear the falconer;
Things fall apart; the centre cannot hold;
Mere anarchy is loosed upon the world,
The blood-dimmed tide is loosed, and everywhere   5
The ceremony of innocence is drowned;
The best lack all conviction, while the worst
Are full of passionate intensity.

Surely some revelation is at hand;
Surely the Second Coming is at hand.   10
The Second Coming! Hardly are those words out
When a vast image out of *Spiritus Mundi*
Troubles my sight: somewhere in sands of the desert
A shape with lion body and the head of a man,
A gaze blank and pitiless as the sun,   15
Is moving its slow thighs, while all about it
Reel shadows of the indignant desert birds.
The darkness drops again; but now I know
That twenty centuries of stony sleep
Were vexed to nightmare by a rocking cradle,   20
And what rough beast, its hour come round at last,
Slouches towards Bethlehem to be born?

SAILING TO BYZANTIUM

That is no country for old men. The young
In one another's arms, birds in the trees
—Those dying generations—at their song,
The salmon-falls, the mackerel-crowded seas,
Fish, flesh, or fowl, commend all summer long   5
Whatever is begotten, born, and dies.
Caught in that sensual music all neglect
Monuments of unaging intellect.

An aged man is but a paltry thing,
A tattered coat upon a stick, unless   10
Soul clap its hands and sing, and louder sing
For every tatter in its mortal dress,
Nor is there singing school but studying
Monuments of its own magnificence;
And therefore I have sailed the seas and come   15
To the holy city of Byzantium.

O sages standing in God's holy fire
As in the gold mosaic of a wall,
Come from the holy fire, perne in a gyre,
And be the singing-masters of my soul.   20
Consume my heart away; sick with desire
And fastened to a dying animal
It knows not what it is; and gather me
Into the artifice of eternity.

Once out of nature I shall never take   25
My bodily form from any natural thing,
But such a form as Grecian goldsmiths make
Of hammered gold and gold enamelling
To keep a drowsy emperor awake;
Or set upon a golden bough to sing   30
To lords and ladies of Byzantium
Of what is past, or passing, or to come.

LEDA AND THE SWAN

A sudden blow: the great wings beating still
Above the staggering girl, her thighs caressed
By the dark webs, her nape caught in his bill,
He holds her helpless breast upon his breast.

How can those terrified vague fingers push   5
The feathered glory from her loosening thighs?
And how can body, laid in that white rush,
But feel the strange heart beating where it lies?

A shudder in the loins engenders there
The broken wall, the burning roof and tower   10
And Agamemnon dead.
                    Being so caught up,
So mastered by the brute blood of the air,
Did she put on his knowledge with his power
Before the indifferent beak could let her drop?   15

AMONG SCHOOL CHILDREN

I walk through the long schoolroom questioning;
A kind old nun in a white hood replies;
The children learn to cipher and to sing,
To study reading-books and history,
To cut and sew, be neat in everything   5
In the best modern way—the children's eyes
In momentary wonder stare upon
A sixty-year-old smiling public man.

I dream of a Ledæan body, bent
Above a sinking fire, a tale that she   10
Told of a harsh reproof, or trivial event
That changed some childish day to tragedy—
Told, and it seemed that our two natures blent
Into a sphere from youthful sympathy,
Or else, to alter Plato's parable,   15
Into the yolk and white of the one shell.

And thinking of that fit of grief or rage
I look upon one child or t'other there
And wonder if she stood so at that age—
For even daughters of the swan can share   20
Something of every paddler's heritage—
And had that colour upon cheek or hair,
And thereupon my heart is driven wild:
She stands before me as a living child.

Her present image floats into the mind—   25
Did Quattrocento finger fashion it
Hollow of cheek as though it drank the wind
And took a mess of shadows for its meat?
And I though never of Ledæan kind
Had pretty plumage once—enough of that,   30
Better to smile on all that smile, and show
There is a comfortable kind of old scarecrow.

What youthful mother, a shape upon her lap
Honey of generation had betrayed,
And that must sleep, shriek, struggle to escape   35

As recollection or the drug decide,
Would think her son, did she but see that shape
With sixty or more winters on its head,
A compensation for the pang of his birth,
Or the uncertainty of his setting forth? 40

Plato thought nature but a spume that plays
Upon a ghostly paradigm of things;
Solider Aristotle played the taws
Upon the bottom of a king of kings;
World-famous golden-thighed Pythagoras 45
Fingered upon a fiddle stick or strings
What a star sang and careless Muses heard:
Old clothes upon old sticks to scare a bird.

Both nuns and mothers worship images,
But those the candles light are not as those 50
That animate a mother's reveries,
But keep a marble or a bronze repose.
And yet they too break hearts—O Presences
That passion, piety or affection knows,
And that all heavenly glory symbolise— 55
O self-born mockers of man's enterprise;

Labour is blossoming or dancing where
The body is not bruised to pleasure soul,
Nor beauty born out of its own despair,
Nor blear-eyed wisdom out of midnight oil. 60
O chestnut-tree, great-rooted blossomer,
Are you the leaf, the blossom or the bole?
O body swayed to music, O brightening glance,
How can we know the dancer from the dance?

BYZANTIUM

The unpurged images of day recede;
The Emperor's drunken soldiery are abed;
Night resonance recedes, night-walker's song
After great cathedral gong;
A starlit or a moonlit dome disdains
All that man is,
All mere complexities,
The fury and the mire of human veins.

Before me floats an image, man or shade,
Shade more than man, more image than a shade; 10
For Hades' bobbin bound in mummy-cloth
May unwind the winding path;
A mouth that has no moisture and no breath

Breathless mouths may summon;
I hail the superhuman;   15
I call it death-in-life and life-in-death.

Miracle, bird or golden handiwork,
More miracle than bird or handiwork,
Planted on the star-lit golden bough,
Can like the cocks of Hades crow,   20
Or, by the moon embittered, scorn aloud
In glory of changeless metal
Common bird or petal
And all complexities of mire or blood.

At midnight on the Emperor's pavement flit   25
Flames that no faggot feeds, nor steel has lit,
Nor storm disturbs, flames begotten of flame,
Where blood-begotten spirits come
And all complexities of fury leave,
Dying into a dance,   30
An agony of trance,
An agony of flame that cannot singe a sleeve.

Astraddle on the dolphin's mire and blood,
Spirit after spirit! The smithies break the flood,
The golden smithies of the Emperor!   35
Marbles of the dancing floor
Break bitter furies of complexity,
Those images that yet
Fresh images beget,
That dolphin-torn, that gong-tormented sea.   40

CRAZY JANE TALKS WITH THE BISHOP

I met the Bishop on the road
And much said he and I.
"Those breasts are flat and fallen now,
Those veins must soon be dry;
Live in a heavenly mansion,   5
Not in some foul sty."

"Fair and foul are near of kin,
And fair needs foul," I cried.
"My friends are gone, but that's a truth
Nor grave nor bed denied,   10
Learned in bodily lowliness
And in the heart's pride.

"A woman can be proud and stiff
When on love intent;
But Love has pitched his mansion in   15

The place of excrement;
For nothing can be sole or whole
That has not been rent."

THE CIRCUS ANIMALS' DESERTION

1

I sought a theme and sought for it in vain,
I sought it daily for six weeks or so.
Maybe at last, being but a broken man,
I must be satisfied with my heart, although
Winter and summer till old age began   5
My circus animals were all on show,
Those stilted boys, that burnished chariot,
Lion and woman and the Lord knows what.

2

What can I but enumerate old themes?
First that sea-rider Oisin led by the nose   10
Through three enchanted islands, allegorical dreams,
Vain gaiety, vain battle, vain repose,
Themes of the embittered heart, or so it seems,
That might adorn old songs or courtly shows;
But what cared I that set him on to ride,   15
I, starved for the bosom of his faery bride?

And then a counter-truth filled out its play,
The Countess Cathleen was the name I gave it;
She, pity-crazed, had given her soul away,
But masterful Heaven had intervened to save it.   20
I thought my dear must her own soul destroy,
So did fanaticism and hate enslave it,
And this brought forth a dream and soon enough
This dream itself had all my thought and love.

And when the Fool and Blind Man stole the bread   25
Cuchulain fought the ungovernable sea;
Heart-mysteries there, and yet when all is said
It was the dream itself enchanted me:
Character isolated by a deed
To engross the present and dominate memory.   30
Players and painted stage took all my love,
And not those things that they were emblems of.

3

Those masterful images because complete
Grew in pure mind, but out of what began?
A mound of refuse or the sweeping of a street,   35
Old kettles, old bottles, and a broken can,

Old iron, old bones, old rags, that raving slut
Who keeps the till. Now that my ladder's gone,
I must lie down where all the ladders start,
In the foul rag-and-bone shop of the heart.   40

Wallace Stevens (1879–1955)

SUNDAY MORNING

1

Complacencies of the peignoir, and late
Coffee and oranges in a sunny chair,
And the green freedom of a cockatoo
Upon a rug mingle to dissipate
The holy rush of ancient sacrifice.   5
She dreams a little, and she feels the dark
Encroachment of that old catastrophe,
As a calm darkens among water-lights.
The pungent oranges and bright, green wings
Seem things in some procession of the dead,   10
Winding across wide water, without sound.
The day is like wide water, without sound,
Stilled for the passing of her dreaming feet
Over the seas, to silent Palestine,
Dominion of the blood and sepulchre.   15

2

Why should she give her bounty to the dead?
What is divinity if it can come
Only in silent shadows and in dreams?
Shall she not find in comforts of the sun,
In pungent fruit and bright, green wings, or else   20
In any balm or beauty of the earth,
Things to be cherished like the thought of heaven?
Divinity must live within herself:
Passions of rain, or moods in falling snow;
Grievings in loneliness, or unsubdued   25
Elations when the forest blooms; gusty
Emotions on wet roads on autumn nights;
All pleasures and all pains, remembering
The bough of summer and the winter branch.
These are the measures destined for her soul.   30

3

Jove in the clouds had his inhuman birth.
No mother suckled him, no sweet land gave

Large-mannered motions to his mythy mind.
He moved among us, as a muttering king,
Magnificent, would move among his hinds,   35
Until our blood, commingling, virginal,
With heaven, brought such requital to desire
The very hinds discerned it, in a star.
Shall our blood fail? Or shall it come to be
The blood of paradise? And shall the earth   40
Seem all of paradise that we shall know?
The sky will be much friendlier then than now,
A part of labor and a part of pain,
And next in glory to enduring love,
Not this dividing and indifferent blue.   45

4

She says, "I am content when wakened birds,
Before they fly, test the reality
Of misty fields, by their sweet questionings;
But when the birds are gone, and their warm fields
Return no more, where, then, is paradise?"   50
There is not any haunt of prophecy,
Nor any old chimera of the grave,
Neither the golden underground, nor isle
Melodious, where spirits gat them home,
Nor visionary south, nor cloudy palm   55
Remote on heaven's hill, that has endured
As April's green endures; or will endure
Like her remembrances of awakened birds,
Or her desire for June and evening, tipped
By the consummation of the swallow's wings.   60

5

She says, "But in contentment I still feel
The need of some imperishable bliss."
Death is the mother of beauty; hence from her,
Alone, shall come fulfilment to our dreams
And our desires. Although she strews the leaves   65
Of sure obliteration on our paths,
The path sick sorrow took, the many paths
Where triumph rang its brassy phrase, or love
Whispered a little out of tenderness,
She makes the willow shiver in the sun   70
For maidens who were wont to sit and gaze
Upon the grass, relinquished to their feet.
She causes boys to pile new plums and pears
On disregarded plate. The maidens taste
And stray impassioned in the littering leaves.   75

6

Is there no change of death in paradise?
Does ripe fruit never fall? Or do the boughs

Hang always heavy in that perfect sky,
Unchanging, yet so like our perishing earth,
With rivers like our own that seek for seas   80
They never find, the same receding shores
That never touch with inarticulate pang?
Why set the pear upon those river-banks
Or spice the shores with odors of the plum?
Alas, that they should wear our colors there,   85
The silken weavings of our afternoons,
And pick the strings of our insipid lutes!
Death is the mother of beauty, mystical,
Within whose burning bosom we devise
Our earthly mothers waiting, sleeplessly.   90

7

Supple and turbulent, a ring of men
Shall chant in orgy on a summer morn
Their boisterous devotion to the sun,
Not as a god, but as a god might be,
Naked among them, like a savage source.   95
Their chant shall be a chant of paradise,
Out of their blood, returning to the sky;
And in their chant shall enter, voice by voice,
The windy lake wherein their lord delights,
The trees, like serafin, and echoing hills,   100
That choir among themselves long afterward.
They shall know well the heavenly fellowship
Of men that perish and of summer morn.
And whence they came and whither they shall go
The dew upon their feet shall manifest.   105

8

She hears, upon that water without sound,
A voice that cries, "The tomb in Palestine
Is not the porch of spirits lingering.
It is the grave of Jesus, where he lay."
We live in an old chaos of the sun,   110
Or old dependency of day and night,
Or island solitude, unsponsored, free,
Of that wide water, inescapable.
Deer walk upon our mountains, and the quail
Whistle about us their spontaneous cries;   115
Sweet berries ripen in the wilderness;
And, in the isolation of the sky,
At evening, casual flocks of pigeons make
Ambiguous undulations as they sink,
Downward to darkness, on extended wings.   120

DOMINATION OF BLACK

At night, by the fire,
The colors of the bushes
And of the fallen leaves,
Repeating themselves,
Turned in the room,   5
Like the leaves themselves
Turning in the wind.
Yes: but the color of the heavy hemlocks
Came striding.
And I remembered the cry of the peacocks.   10

The colors of their tails
Were like the leaves themselves
Turning in the wind,
In the twilight wind.
They swept over the room,   15
Just as they flew from the boughs of the hemlocks
Down to the ground.
I heard them cry—the peacocks.
Was it a cry against the twilight
Or against the leaves themselves   20
Turning in the wind,
Turning as the flames
Turned in the fire,
Turning as the tails of the peacocks
Turned in the loud fire,   25
Loud as the hemlocks
Full of the cry of the peacocks?
Or was it a cry against the hemlocks?

Out of the window,
I saw how the planets gathered   30
Like the leaves themselves
Turning in the wind.
I saw how the night came,
Came striding like the color of the heavy hemlocks.
I felt afraid.   35
And I remembered the cry of the peacocks.

THIRTEEN WAYS OF LOOKING
AT A BLACKBIRD

I
Among twenty snowy mountains,
The only moving thing
Was the eye of the blackbird.

II

I was of three minds,
Like a tree
In which there are three blackbirds.

III

The blackbird whirled in the autumn winds.
It was a small part of the pantomime.

IV

A man and a woman
Are one.
A man and a woman and a blackbird
Are one.

V

I do not know which to prefer,
The beauty of inflections
Or the beauty of innuendoes,
The blackbird whistling
Or just after.

VI

Icicles filled the long window
With barbaric glass.
The shadow of the blackbird
Crossed it, to and fro.
The mood
Traced in the shadow
An indecipherable cause.

VII

O thin men of Haddam,
Why do you imagine golden birds?
Do you not see how the blackbird
Walks around the feet
Of the women about you?

VIII

I know noble accents
And lucid, inescapable rhythms;
But I know, too,
That the blackbird is involved
In what I know.

IX

When the blackbird flew out of sight,
It marked the edge
Of one of many circles.

X

At the sight of blackbirds
Flying in a green light,

Even the bawds of euphony
Would cry out sharply.

XI

He rode over Connecticut
In a glass coach.
Once, a fear pierced him,
In that he mistook
The shadow of his equipage
For blackbirds.

XII

The river is moving.
The blackbird must be flying.

XIII

It was evening all afternoon.
It was snowing
And it was going to snow.
The blackbird sat
In the cedar-limbs.

A HIGH-TONED
OLD CHRISTIAN WOMAN

Poetry is the supreme fiction, madame.
Take the moral law and make a nave of it
And from the nave build haunted heaven. Thus,
The conscience is converted into palms,
Like windy citherns hankering for hymns.
We agree in principle. That's clear. But take
The opposing law and make a peristyle,
And from the peristyle project a masque
Beyond the planets. Thus, our bawdiness,
Unpurged by epitaph, indulged at last,
Is equally converted into palms,
Squiggling like saxophones. And palm for palm,
Madame, we are where we began. Allow,
Therefore, that in the planetary scene
Your disaffected flagellants, well-stuffed,
Smacking their muzzy bellies in parade,
Proud of such novelties of the sublime,
Such tink and tank and tunk-a-tunk-tunk,
May, merely may, madame, whip from themselves
A jovial hullabaloo among the spheres.
This will make widows wince. But fictive things
Wink as they will. Wink most when widows wince.

THE EMPEROR OF ICE-CREAM

Call the roller of big cigars,
The muscular one, and bid him whip
In kitchen cups concupiscent curds.
Let the wenches dawdle in such dress
As they are used to wear, and let the boys
Bring flowers in last month's newspapers.
Let be be finale of seem.
The only emperor is the emperor of ice-cream.

Take from the dresser of deal,
Lacking the three glass knobs, that sheet
On which she embroidered fantails once
And spread it so as to cover her face.
If her horny feet protrude, they come
To show how cold she is, and dumb.
Let the lamp affix its beam.
The only emperor is the emperor of ice-cream.

THE IDEA OF ORDER AT KEY WEST

She sang beyond the genius of the sea.
The water never formed to mind or voice,
Like a body wholly body, fluttering
Its empty sleeves; and yet its mimic motion
Made constant cry, caused constantly a cry,
That was not ours although we understood,
Inhuman, of the veritable ocean.

The sea was not a mask. No more was she.
The song and water were not medleyed sound
Even if what she sang was what she heard,
Since what she sang was uttered word by word.
It may be that in all her phrases stirred
The grinding water and the gasping wind;
But it was she and not the sea we heard.

For she was the maker of the song she sang.
The ever-hooded, tragic-gestured sea
Was merely a place by which she walked to sing.
Whose spirit is this? we said, because we knew
It was the spirit that we sought and knew
That we should ask this often as she sang.

If it was only the dark voice of the sea
That rose, or even colored by many waves;
If it was only the outer voice of sky

And cloud, of the sunken coral water-walled,
However clear, it would have been deep air,
The heaving speech of air, a summer sound
Repeated in a summer without end
And sound alone. But it was more than that,
More even than her voice, and ours, among
The meaningless plungings of water and the wind,
Theatrical distances, bronze shadows heaped
On high horizons, mountainous atmospheres
Of sky and sea.

          It was her voice that made
The sky acutest at its vanishing.
She measured to the hour its solitude.
She was the single artificer of the world
In which she sang. And when she sang, the sea,
Whatever self it had, became the self
That was her song, for she was the maker. Then we,
As we beheld her striding there alone,
Knew that there never was a world for her
Except the one she sang and, singing, made.

Ramon Fernandez, tell me, if you know,
Why, when the singing ended and we turned
Toward the town, tell why the glassy lights,
The lights in the fishing boats at anchor there,
As the night descended, tilting in the air,
Mastered the night and portioned out the sea,
Fixing emblazoned zones and fiery poles,
Arranging, deepening, enchanting night.

Oh! Blessed rage for order, pale Ramon,
The maker's rage to order words of the sea,
Words of the fragrant portals, dimly-starred,
And of ourselves and of our origins,
In ghostlier demarcations, keener sounds.

FAREWELL TO FLORIDA

I

Go on, high ship, since now, upon the shore,
The snake has left its skin upon the floor.
Key West sank downward under massive clouds
And silvers and greens spread over the sea. The moon
Is at the mast-head and the past is dead.
Her mind will never speak to me again.
I am free. High above the mast the moon
Rides clear of her mind and the waves make a refrain
Of this: that the snake has shed its skin upon
The floor. Go on through the darkness. The waves fly back.

II

Her mind had bound me round. The palms were hot
As if I lived in ashen ground, as if
The leaves in which the wind kept up its sound
From my North of cold whistled in a sepulchral South
Her South of pine and coral and coraline sea,
Her home, not mine, in the ever-freshened Keys,
Her days, her oceanic nights, calling
For music, for whisperings from the reefs.
How content I shall be in the North to which I sail
And to feel sure and to forget the bleaching sand . . .

III

I hated the weathery yawl from which the pools
Disclosed the sea floor and the wilderness
Of waving weeds. I hated the vivid blooms
Curled over the shadowless hut, the rust and bones,
The trees like bones and the leaves half sand, half sun.
To stand here on the deck in the dark and say
Farewell and to know that that land is forever gone
And that she will not follow in any word
Or look, nor ever again in thought, except
That I loved her once . . . Farewell. Go on, high ship.

IV

My North is leafless and lies in a wintry slime
Both of men and clouds, a slime of men in crowds.
The men are moving as the water moves,
This darkened water cloven by sullen swells
Against your sides, then shoving and slithering,
The darkness shattered, turbulent with foam.
To be free again, to return to the violent mind
That is their mind, these men, and that will bind
Me round, carry me, misty deck, carry me
To the cold, go on, high ship, go on, plunge on.

POETRY IS A DESTRUCTIVE FORCE

That's what misery is,
Nothing to have at heart.
It is to have or nothing.

It is a thing to have,
A lion, an ox in his breast.
To feel it breathing there.

Corazon, stout dog,
Young ox, bow-legged bear,
He tastes its blood, not spit.

He is like a man
In the body of a violent beast.
Its muscles are his own . . .

The lion sleeps in the sun.
Its nose is on its paws.
It can kill a man.

William Carlos Williams (1883–1963)

PATERSON, BOOK II

SUNDAY IN THE PARK

I
    Outside

                  outside myself

                              there is a world,
    he rumbled, subject to my incursions
    —a world   5

                  (to me) at rest,

                         which I approach
concretely—

                  The scene's the Park
                  upon the rock,   10
                  female to the city

    —upon whose body Paterson instructs his thoughts
    (concretely)

                        —late spring,
             a Sunday afternoon!   15

    —and goes by the footpath to the cliff (counting:
    the proof)

                  himself among the others,
    —treads there the same stones
    on which their feet slip as they climb,   20
    paced by their dogs!

    laughing, calling to each other—

                Wait for me!

.   .   the ugly legs of the young girls,
pistons too powerful for delicacy!   .   25
the men's arms, red, used to heat and cold,
to toss quartered beeves and   .

Yah! Yah! Yah! Yah!

—over-riding
the risks: 30
pouring down!
For the flower of a day!

Arrived breathless, after a hard climb he,
looks back (beautiful but expensive!) to
the pearl-grey towers! Re-turns   35
and starts, possessive, through the trees,

— that love,
that is not, is not in those terms
to which I'm still the positive
in spite of all;   40
the ground dry, — passive-possessive

Walking —

Thickets gather about groups of squat sand-pine,
all but from bare rock   .   .

—a scattering of man-high cedars (sharp cones),   45
antlered sumac   .

—roots, for the most part, writhing
upon the surface
(so close are we to ruin every
day!)   50
searching the punk-dry rot

Walking —

The body is tilted slightly forward from the basic standing
position and the weight thrown on the ball of the foot,
while the other thigh is lifted and the leg and opposite   55
arm are swung forward (fig. 6B). Various muscles, aided   .

Despite my having said that I'd never write to you again, I do so now because I
find, with the passing of time, that the outcome of my failure with you has been
the complete damming up of all my creative capacities in a particularly disastrous
manner such as I have never before experienced.   60
For a great many weeks now (whenever I've tried to write poetry) every thought
I've had, even every feeling, has been struck off some surface crust of myself which
began gathering when I first sensed that you were ignoring the real contents of
my last letters to you, and which finally congealed into some impenetrable sub-

stance when you asked me to quit corresponding with you altogether without   65
even an explanation.

That kind of blockage, exiling one's self from one's self—have you ever experienced it? I dare say you have, at moments; and if so, you can well understand
what a serious psychological injury it amounts to when turned into a permanent
day-to-day condition.   70

How do I love you? These!

(He hears! Voices . indeterminate! Sees them
moving, in groups, by twos and fours — filtering
off by way of the many bypaths.)

I asked him, What do you do?   75

He smiled patiently, The typical American question.
In Europe they would ask, What are you doing? Or,
What are you doing now?

What do I do? I listen, to the water falling. (No
sound of it here but with the wind!) This is my entire   80
occupation.

No fairer day ever dawned anywhere than May 2, 1880, when the German
Singing Societies of Paterson met on Garret Mountain, as they did many years
before on the first Sunday in May.

However the meeting of 1880 proved a fatal day, when William Dalzell, who   85
owned a piece of property near the scene of the festivities, shot John Joseph Van
Houten. Dalzell claimed that the visitors had in previous years walked over his
garden and was determined that this year he would stop them from crossing any
part of his grounds.

Immediately after the shot the quiet group of singers was turned into an in-   90
furiated mob who would take Dalzell into their own hands. The mob then proceeded to burn the barn into which Dalzell had retreated from the angry group.

Dalzell fired at the approaching mob from a window in the barn and one of the
bullets struck a little girl in the cheek. . . . Some of the Paterson Police rushed
Dalzell out of the barn [to] the house of John Ferguson some half furlong away.   95

The crowd now numbered some ten thousand,
"a great beast!"
for many had come from the city to join the conflict.
The case looked serious, for the Police were greatly out-numbered. The crowd then
tried to burn the Ferguson house and Dalzell went to the house of John Mc-   100
Guckin. While in this house it was that Sergeant John McBride suggested that it
might be well to send for William McNulty, Dean of Saint Joseph's Catholic
Church.

In a moment the Dean set on a plan. He proceeded to the scene in a hack.
Taking Dalzell by the arm, in full view of the infuriated mob, he led the man to   105
the hack and seating himself by his side, ordered the driver to proceed. The
crowd hesitated, bewildered between the bravery of the Dean and   .

Signs everywhere of birds nesting, while
in the air, slow, a crow zigzags
with heavy wings before the wasp-thrusts   110
of smaller birds circling about him
that dive from above stabbing for his eyes

Walking—

      he leaves the path, finds hard going
      across-field, stubble and matted brambles   115
      seeming a pasture—but no pasture
      —old furrows, to say labor sweated or
      had sweated here   .
                              a flame,
      spent.   120
          The file-sharp grass   .

      When! from before his feet, half tripping,
      picking a way, there starts   .
                  a flight of empurpled wings!
      —invisibly created (their   125
      jackets dust-grey) from the dust kindled
      to sudden ardor!

              They fly away, churring! until
      their strength spent they plunge
      to the coarse cover again and disappear   130
      —but leave, livening the mind, a flashing
      of wings and a churring song   .

      AND a grasshopper of red basalt, boot-long,
      tumbles from the core of his mind,
      a rubble-bank disintegrating beneath a   135
      tropic downpour

      Chapultepec! grasshopper hill!

      —a matt stone solicitously instructed
      to bear away some rumor
      of the living presence that has preceded   140
      it, out-precedented its breath   .

      These wings do not unfold for flight—
      no need!
      the weight (to the hand) finding
      a counter-weight or counter buoyancy   145
      by the mind's wings   .

      He is afraid! What then?

      Before his feet, at each step, the flight
      is renewed. A burst of wings, a quick
      churring sound   :   150
          couriers to the ceremonial of love!

      —aflame in flight!
          —aflame only in flight!

No flesh but the caress!

He is led forward by their announcing wings.   155

If that situation with you (your ignoring those particular letters and then your final note) had belonged to the inevitable lacrimae rerum (as did, for instance, my experience with Z.) its result could not have been (as it *has* been) to destroy the validity for me myself *of* myself, because in that case nothing to do with my sense of personal identity would have been maimed—the cause of one's frustra-   160 tions in such instances being not *in* one's self nor in the other person but merely in the sorry scheme of things. But since your ignoring those letters was not "natural" in that sense (or rather since to regard it as unnatural I am forced, psy- chologically, to feel that what I wrote you about, was sufficiently trivial and un- important and absurd to merit your evasion) it could not but follow that that   165 whole side of life connected with those letters should in consequence take on for my own self that same kind of unreality and inaccessibility which the inner lives of other people often have for us.

    —his mind a red stone carved to be
    endless flight   .   170
    Love that is a stone endlessly in flight,
    so long as stone shall last bearing
    the chisel's stroke   .

    .   .   and is lost and covered
    with ash, falls from an undermined bank   175
    and — begins churring!
    AND DOES, the stone after the life!

    The stone lives, the flesh dies
    —we know nothing of death.

    —boot long   180
    window-eyes that front the whole head,
              Red stone! as if
    a light still clung in them   .

    Love

                combating sleep   185
                _____

                the sleep
    piecemeal

Shortly after midnight, August 20, 1878, special officer Goodridge, when, in front of the Franklin House, heard a strange squealing noise down towards Ellison Street. Running to see what was the matter, he found a cat at bay under the water   190 table at Clark's hardware store on the corner, confronting a strange black animal too small to be a cat and entirely too large for a rat. The officer ran up to the spot and the animal got in under the grating of the cellar window, from which it frequently poked its head with a lightning rapidity. Mr. Goodridge made several strikes at it with his club but was unable to hit it. Then officer Keyes came along   195 and as soon as he saw it, he said it was a mink, which confirmed the theory that

Mr. Goodridge had already formed. Both tried for a while to hit it with their
clubs but were unable to do so, when finally officer Goodridge drew his pistol and
fired a shot at the animal. The shot evidently missed its mark, but the noise and
powder so frightened the little joker that it jumped out into the street, and made   200
down into Ellison Street at a wonderful gait, closely followed by the two officers.
The mink finally disappeared down a cellar window under the grocery store below
Spangermacher's lager beer saloon, and that was the last seen of it. The cellar was
examined again in the morning, but nothing further could be discovered of the
little critter that had caused so much fun.   205

Without invention nothing is well spaced,
unless the mind change, unless
the stars are new measured, according
to their relative positions, the
line will not change, the necessity   210
will not matriculate: unless there is
a new mind there cannot be a new
line, the old will go on
repeating itself with recurring
deadliness: without invention   215
nothing lies under the witch-hazel
bush, the alder does not grow from among
the hummocks margining the all
but spent channel of the old swale,
the small foot-prints   220
of the mice under the overhanging
tufts of the bunch-grass will not
appear: without invention the line
will never again take on its ancient
divisions when the word, a supple word,   225
lived in it, crumbled now to chalk.

Under the bush they lie protected
from the offending sun—
11 o'clock
        They seem to talk   230
—a park, devoted to pleasure : devoted to   .   grasshoppers!

3 colored girls, of age! stroll by
—their color flagrant,
        their voices vagrant
their laughter wild, flagellant, dissociated   235
from the fixed scene   .

But the white girl, her head
upon an arm, a butt between her fingers
lies under the bush   .   .

Semi-naked, facing her, a sunshade   240
over his eyes,
he talks with her

—the jalopy half hid
behind them in the trees—
I bought a new bathing suit, just   245

pants and a brassier   :
the breasts and
the pudenda covered—beneath

the sun in frank vulgarity.
Minds beaten thin   250
by waste—among

the working classes SOME sort
of breakdown
has occurred. Semi-roused

they lie upon their blanket   255
face to face,
mottled by the shadows of the leaves

upon them, unannoyed,
at least here unchallenged.
Not undignified.   .   .   260

talking, flagrant beyond all talk
in perfect domesticity—
And having bathed

and having eaten (a few
sandwiches)   265
their pitiful thoughts do meet

in the flesh—surrounded
by churring loves! Gay wings
to bear them (in sleep)

—their thoughts alight,   270
away
    .   .   among the grass

Walking   —

across the old swale—a dry wave in the ground
tho' marked still by the line of Indian alders   275

    .   .   they (the Indians) would weave
in and out, unseen, among them along the stream

    .   come out whooping between the log
house and men working the field, cut them
off! they having left their arms in the block-   280

house, and—without defense—carry them away
into captivity. One old man   .

>   Forget it! for God's sake, Cut
>   out that stuff   .

Walking   —   285

>   he rejoins the path and sees, on a treeless
>   knoll—the red path choking it—
>   a stone wall, a sort of circular
>   redoubt against the sky, barren and
>   unoccupied. Mount. Why not?   290

>   A chipmunk,
>   with tail erect, scampers among the stones.

>   (Thus the mind grows, up flinty pinnacles)

>   but as he leans, in his stride,
>   at sight of a flint arrow-head   295
>   (it is not)
>   —there
>   in the distance, to the north, appear
>   to him the chronic hills

>   Well, so they are.   300

>   He stops short:
>   Who's here?

>   To a stone bench, to which she's leashed, within the wall
a man in tweeds—a pipe hooked in his jaw—is combing out a new-washed
Collie bitch. The deliberate comb-strokes part the long hair—even her face   305
he combs though her legs tremble slightly—until it lies, as he designs, like
ripples in white sand giving off its clean-dog odor. The floor, stone slabs, she
stands patiently before his caresses in that bare "sea chamber"

>   to the right
>   from this vantage, the observation tower   310
>   in the middle distance stands up prominently
>   from its pubic grove

DEAR B. Please excuse me for not having told you this when I was over to your
house. I had no courage to answer your questions so I'll write it. Your dog *is*
going to have puppies although I prayed she would be okay. It wasn't that she   315
was left alone as she never was but I used to let her out at dinner time while I
hung up my clothes. At the time, it was on a Thursday, my mother-in-law had
some sheets and table cloths out on the end of the line. I figured the dogs
wouldn't come as long as I was there and none came thru my yard or near the
apartment. He must have come between your hedge and the house. *Every few*   320
seconds I would run to the end of the line or peek under the sheets to see if
Musty was alright. She was until I looked a minute too late. I took sticks and
stones after the dog but he wouldn't beat it. George gave me plenty of hell and

I started praying that I had frightened the other dog so much that nothing had
happened. I know you'll be cursing like a son-of-a-gun and probably won't ever   325
speak to me again for not having told you. Don't think I haven't been worrying
about Musty. She's occupied my mind every day since that awful event. You
won't think so highly of me now and feel like protecting me. Instead I'll bet you
could kill . . .

And still the picnickers come on, now   330
early afternoon, and scatter through the
trees over the fenced-in acres   .

Voices!   .
multiple and inarticulate   .   voices
clattering loudly to the sun, to   335
the clouds. Voices!
assaulting the air gaily from all sides.

—among which the ear strains to catch
the movement of one voice among the rest
—a reed-like voice   340
                    of peculiar accent

Thus she finds what peace there is, reclines,
before his approach, stroked
by their clambering feet—for pleasure

It is all for   345
pleasure   .   their feet   .   aimlessly
          wandering

The "great beast" come to sun himself
                              as he may
.   .   their dreams mingling,   350
aloof

Let us be reasonable!

Sunday in the park,
limited by the escarpment, eastward; to
the west abutting on the old road: recreation   355
with a view! the binoculars chained
to anchored stanchions along the east wall—
          beyond which, a hawk
                    soars!

—a trumpet sounds fitfully.   360

Stand at the rampart (use a metronome
if your ear is deficient, one made in Hungary
if you prefer)
and look away north by east where the church
spires still spend their wits against   365

the sky   to the ball-park
in the hollow with its minute figures running
—beyond the gap where the river
plunges into the narrow gorge, unseen

—and the imagination soars, as a voice   370
beckons, a thundrous voice, endless
—as sleep: the voice
that has ineluctably called them—
               that unmoving roar!
churches and factories   375
          (at a price)
together, summoned them from the pit .

—his voice, one among many (unheard)
moving under all.

           The mountain quivers.   380
Time! Count! Sever and mark time!

So during the early afternoon, from place
to place he moves,
his voice mingling with other voices
—the voice in his voice   385
opening his old throat, blowing out his lips,
kindling his mind (more
than his mind will kindle)

         —following the hikers.

At last he comes to the idlers' favorite   390
haunts, the picturesque summit, where
the blue-stone (rust-red where exposed)
has been faulted at various levels
         (ferns rife among the stones)
into rough terraces and partly closed in   395
dens of sweet grass, the ground gently sloping.

Loiterers in groups straggle
over the bare rock-table—scratched by their
boot-nails more than the glacier scratched
them—walking indifferent through   400
each other's privacy   .

         —in any case,
the center of movement, the core of gaiety.

Here a young man, perhaps sixteen,
is sitting with his back to the rock among   405
some ferns playing a guitar, dead pan   .

The rest are eating and drinking.

The big guy

in the black hat is too full to move   .

but Mary

is up!

       Come on! Wassa ma'? You got
broken leg?

It is this air!

             the air of the Midi
and the old cultures intoxicates them:
present!

     —lifts one arm holding the cymbals
of her thoughts, cocks her old head
and dances! raising her skirts:

La la la la!

What a bunch of bums! Afraid somebody see
you?   .
    Blah!
           Excrementi!
               —she spits.
Look a' me, Grandma! Everybody too damn
lazy.

This is the old, the very old, old upon old,
the undying: even to the minute gestures,
the hand holding the cup, the wine
spilling, the arm stained by it:

Remember

    the peon in the lost
    Eisenstein film drinking

    from a wine-skin with the abandon
    of a horse drinking

    so that it slopped down his chin?
    down his neck, dribbling

    over his shirt-front and down
    onto his pants—laughing, toothless?

Heavenly man!

—the leg raised, verisimilitude   .
even to the coarse contours of the leg, the
bovine touch! The leer, the cave of it,

the female of it facing the male, the satyr—
    (Priapus!)
with that lonely implication, goatherd
and goat, fertility, the attack, drunk,
cleansen   .   450

               Rejected. Even the film
suppressed   :   but   .   persistent

The picnickers laugh on the rocks celebrating
the varied Sunday of their loves with
its declining light—   455

Walking —

    look down (from a ledge) into this grassy
den
        (somewhat removed from the traffic)
                  above whose brows   460
a moon! where she lies sweating at his side:

             She stirs, distraught,
against him—wounded (drunk), moves
against him (a lump) desiring,
against him, bored   .   465

flagrantly bored and sleeping, a
beer bottle still grasped spear-like
in his hand   .

while the small, sleepless boys, who
have climbed the columnar rocks   470
overhanging the pair (where they lie
overt upon the grass, besieged—

careless in their narrow cell under
the crowd's feet) stare down,
                  from history!   475
at them, puzzled and in the sexless
light (of childhood) bored equally,
go charging off   .

          There where
the movement throbs openly   480
and you can hear the Evangelist shouting!

           —moving nearer
    she—lean as a goat—leans
    her lean belly to the man's backside
    toying with the clips of his   485
    suspenders   .

—to which he adds his useless voice:
until there moves in his sleep
a music that is whole, unequivocal (in
his sleep, sweating in his sleep—laboring   490
against sleep, agasp!)
                    —and does not waken.

Sees, alive (asleep)
              —the fall's roar entering
his sleep (to be fulfilled)   495
                          reborn
in his sleep—scattered over the mountain
severally   .
          —by which he woos her, severally.
And the amnesic crowd (the scattered),   500
called about — strains
to catch the movement of one voice   .

                              hears,
              Pleasure! Pleasure!

                              —feels,   505
half dismayed, the afternoon of complex
voices its own—
                    and is relieved
                          (relived)

          A cop is directing traffic   510
          across the main road up
          a little wooded slope toward
          the conveniences:

                          oaks, choke-cherry,
dogwoods, white and green, iron-wood   :   515
humped roots matted into the shallow soil
—mostly gone: rock out-croppings
polished by the feet of the picnickers:
sweetbarked sassafras   .

leaning from the rancid grease: 520
                          deformity—

—to be deciphered (a horn, a trumpet!)
an elucidation by multiplicity,
a corrosion, a parasitic curd, a clarion
for belief, to be good dogs   :   525

NO DOGS ALLOWED AT LARGE IN THIS PARK

II
    Blocked.
              (Make a song out of that: concretely)
    By whom?

In its midst rose a massive church.   .   .   And it all came to me then—that
those poor souls had nothing else in the world, save that church, between them   5
and the eternal stony, ungrateful and unpromising dirt they lived by .   .   .   .   ,

      Cash is mulct of them that others may live
      secure
      .   .   and knowledge restricted.

      An orchestral dullness overlays their world   10

I see they—the Senate, is trying to block Lilienthal and deliver "the bomb" over
to a few industrialists. I don't think they will succeed but . . that is what I mean
when I refuse to get excited over the cry, Communist! they use to blind us. It's
terrifying to think how easily we can be destroyed, a few votes. Even though
Communism is a threat, are Communists any *worse* than the guilty bastards trying   15
in that way to undermine us?

        We leap awake and what we see
        fells us   .

        Let terror twist the world!

Faitoute, sick of his diversions but proud of women,   20
his requites, standing with his back
to the lions' pit,
                 (where the drunken
lovers slept, now, both of them)
                           indifferent,   25
started again wandering—foot pacing foot outward
into emptiness   .   .

      Up there.
           The cop points.
                 A sign nailed   30
to a tree: Women.

              You can see figures
moving beyond the screen of the trees and, close
at hand, music blurts out suddenly.

Walking —   35
                         a
      cramped arena has been left clear at the base
of the observation tower near the urinals. This
is the Lord's line: Several broken benches
drawn up in a curving row against the shrubbery   40
face the flat ground, benches on which
a few children have been propped by the others
against their running off   .

      Three middle aged men with iron smiles
      stand behind the benches—backing (watching)   45

the kids, the kids and several women—and
holding,
            a cornet, clarinet and trombone,
severally, in their hands, at rest.
                    There is also,   50
played by a woman, a portable organ   .   .

            Before them an old man,
wearing a fringe of long white hair, bareheaded,
his glabrous skull reflecting the sun's
light and in shirtsleeves, is beginning to   55
speak—
        calling to the birds and trees!

Jumping up and down in his ecstasy he beams
into the empty blue, eastward, over the parapet
toward the city   .   .   60

    .   .   .   .

There are people—especially among women—who can speak only to one person.
And I am one of those women. I do not come easily to confidences (though it
cannot but seem otherwise to you). I could not possibly convey to any one of
those people who have crossed my path in these few months, those particular
phases of my life which I made the subject of my letters to you. I must let my-   65
self be entirely misunderstood and misjudged in all my economic and social
maladjustments, rather than ever attempt to communicate to anyone else what I
wrote to you about. And so my having heaped these confidences upon you
(however tiresome you may have found them and however far I may yet need
to go in the attainment of *complete* self-honesty which is difficult for anyone)   70
was enough in itself to have caused my failure with you to have so disastrous
an effect upon me.

    Look, there lies the city!

                —calling with his back
to the paltry congregation, calling the winds;   75
a voice calling, calling   .

Behind him the drawn children whom his suit
of holy proclamation so very badly fits,
winkless, under duress, must feel
their buttocks ache on the slats of the sodden   80
benches.
        But as he rests, they sing—when
prodded—as he wipes his prismed brow.
                    The light
fondles it as if inclined to form a halo—   85

Then he laughs:

            One sees him first. Few listen.
Or, in fact, pay the least
attention, walking about, unless some Polock

with his mouth open tries to make it out,   90
as if it were some Devil (looks into the faces
of a young couple passing, laughing
together, for some hint) What kind of priest
is this? Alarmed, goes off scowling, looking
back.   95
        This is a Protestant! protesting—as
though the world were his own   .

                     —another,
twenty feet off, walks his dog absorbedly
along the wall top—thoughtful of the dog—   100
at the cliff's edge above a fifty foot drop   .

.   .   alternately the harangue, followed
by horn blasts surmounting
what other sounds   .   they quit now
as the entranced figure of a man resumes—   105

But his decoys bring in no ducks—other than
the children with their dusty little minds
and happiest *non sequiturs.*

             No figure
from the clouds seems brought hovering near   110

   The detectives found a note on the kitchen table addressed to a soldier from
Fort Bragg, N. C. The contents of the letter showed that she was in love with
the soldier, the detective said.

This is what the preacher said: Don't think
about me. Call me a stupid old man, that's   115
right. Yes, call me an old bore who talks until
he is hoarse when nobody wants to listen. That's
the truth. I'm an old fool and I know it.

               BUT   .   !
You can't ignore the words of Our Lord Jesus   120
Christ who died on the Cross for us that we
may have Eternal Life! Amen.

          Amen! Amen!

shouted the disciples standing behind the
benches. Amen!   125

     —the spirit of our Lord that gives
the words of even such a plain, ignorant fellow
as I a touch of His Own blessed dignity and
and strength among you   .   .

I tell you—lifting up his arms—I bring   130
the riches of all the ages to you here today.

  It was windless and hot in the sun
  where he was standing bareheaded.

     Great riches shall be yours!
I wasn't born here. I was born in what we call   135
over here the Old Country. But it's the same
people, the same kind of people there as here
and they're up to the same kind of tricks as over
here—only, there isn't as much money
over there—and that makes the difference.   140

My family were poor people. So I started to work
when I was pretty young.
   —Oh, it took me a long time! but
one day I said to myself, Klaus, that's my name,
Klaus, I said to myself, you're a success.   145
   You have worked hard but you have been
lucky.
       You're
rich—and now we're going to enjoy ourselves.

Hamilton saw more clearly than anyone else with what urgency the new   150
government must assume authority over the States if it was to survive. He never
trusted the people, "a great beast," as he saw them and held Jefferson to be little
better if not worse than any.

  So I came to America!

Especially in the matter of finances a critical stage presented itself. The States   155
were inclined to shrug off the debt incurred during the recent war—each state
preferring to undertake its own private obligations separately. Hamilton saw that
if this were allowed to ensue the effect would be fatal to future credit. He came
out with vigor and cunning for "Assumption," assumption by the Federal Government of the national debt, and the granting to it of powers of taxation without   160
which it could not raise the funds necessary for this purpose. A storm followed in
which he found himself opposed by Madison and Jefferson.

  But when I got here I soon found out that I
  was a pretty small frog in a mighty big pool. So
  I went to work all over again. I suppose   165
  I was born with a gift for that sort of thing.
  I throve and I gloried in it. And I thought then
  that I was happy. And I was — as happy
  as money could make me.

    But did it make me GOOD?   170

   He stopped to laugh, healthily, and
   his wan assistants followed him,
   forcing it out—grinning against
   the rocks with wry smiles   .

           NO! he shouted, bending   175
at the knees and straightening himself up
violently with the force of his emphasis—like
Beethoven getting a crescendo out of an
orchestra—NO!

It did *not* make me good. (His clenched fists   180
were raised above his brows.) I kept on making
money, more and more of it, but it didn't make
me good.

           America the golden!
             with trick and money   185
                 damned
           like Altgeld sick
               and molden
           we love thee bitter
                 land   190

           Like Altgeld on the
                 corner
           seeing the mourners
                 pass
           we bow our heads   195
               before thee
           and take our hats
               in hand

                         And so
one day I heard a voice . . . a voice—just   200
as I am talking to you here today   .   .

  .   .   .   .

  .   .   .   .   .   And the voice said,
Klaus, what's the matter with you? You're not
happy. I am happy! I shouted back,
I've got everything I want. No, it said.   205
Klaus, that's a lie. You're not happy.
And I had to admit it was the truth. I wasn't
happy. That bothered me a lot. But I was pig-
headed and when I thought it over I said
to myself, Klaus, you must be getting old   210
to let things like that worry you.

  .   .   .   .   .   .   then one day
our blessed Lord came to me and put His hand
on my shoulder and said, Klaus, you old fool,
you've been working too hard. You look   215
tired and worried. Let me help you.

I am worried, I replied, but I don't know what to
do about it. I got everything that money can
buy but I'm not happy, that's the truth.

And the Lord said to me, Klaus, get rid of your   220
money. You'll never be happy until you do that.

As a corollary to the famous struggle for assumption lay the realization among
many leading minds in the young republic that unless industry were set upon its
feet, unless manufactured goods could be produced income for taxation would
be a myth.   225
   The new world had been looked on as a producer of precious metals, pelts and
raw materials to be turned over to the mother country for manufactured articles
which the colonists had no choice but to buy at advanced prices. They were prevented from making woolen, cotton or linen cloth for sale. Nor were they allowed
to build furnaces to convert the native iron into steel.   230
   Even during the Revolution Hamilton had been impressed by the site of the
Great Falls of the Passaic. His fertile imagination envisioned a great manufacturing center, a great Federal City, to supply the needs of the country. Here
was water-power to turn the mill wheels and the navigable river to carry manufactured goods to the market centers: a national manufactury.   235

   Give up my money!

                —with monotonous insistence
   the falls of his harangue hung featureless
   upon the ear, yet with a certain strangeness
   as if arrested in space   240

                That would be a hard thing
   for me to do. What would my rich friends say?
   They'd say, That old fool Klaus Ehrens must
   be getting pretty crazy, getting rid of his
   cash. What! give up the thing I'd struggled all   245
   my life to pile up—so I could say I was rich?
   No! that I couldn't do. But I was troubled
   in mind.

                He paused to wipe his brow while
   the singers struck up a lively hymn tune.   250

                I couldn't eat, I couldn't
   sleep for thinking of my trouble so that
   when the Lord came to me the third time I was
   ready and I kneeled down before Him
   and said, Lord, do what you will with me!   255

   Give away your money, He said, and I
   will make you the richest man in the world!
   And I bowed my head and said to Him, Yea, Lord.
   And His blessed truth descended upon me and filled
   me with joy, such joy and such riches as I   260
   had never in my life known to that day and I said
   to Him, Master!
                In the Name of the Father
   and the Son and the Holy Ghost.
                        Amen.   265

Amen! Amen! echoed the devout assistants.
        Is this the only beauty here?
        And is this beauty—
        torn to shreds by the
        lurking schismatists?   270

        Where is beauty among
        these trees?
        Is it the dogs the owners
        bring here to dry their coats?

        These women are not   275
        beautiful and reflect
        no beauty but gross   .   .
        Unless it is beauty   ;

        to be, anywhere,
        so flagrant in desire   .   280
        The beauty of holiness,
        if this it be,

        is the only beauty
        visible in this place
        other than the view   285
        and a fresh budding tree.

So I started to get rid of my money. It didn't take
me long I can tell you! I threw it away with both
hands. And I began to feel better   .   .   .   .

      —and leaned on the parapet, thinking   290

      From here, one could see him—that
      tied man, that cold blooded
      murderer   .   April! in the distance
      being hanged. Groups at various
      vantages along the cliff   .   having   295
      gathered since before daybreak
      to witness it.

                One kills
for money but doesn't always get it.

      Leans on the parapet thinking, while   300
      the preacher, outnumbered, addresses
      the leaves in the patient trees   :

          The gentle Christ
          child of Pericles
          and femina practa   305

Split between
Athens and
the amphyoxus

The gentle Christ—
weed and worth   310
wistfully forthright

Weeps and is
remembered as of
the open tomb

—threw it away with both hands.   .   until   315
it was gone

         —he made a wide motion with both
hands as of scattering money to the winds—

—but the riches that had been given me are
beyond all counting. You can throw them   320
carelessly about you on all sides—and still
you will have more. For God Almighty has
boundless resources and never fails. There is no
end to the treasures of our Blessed Lord who
died on the Cross for us that we may be saved.   325
Amen.

The Federal Reserve System is a private enterprise . . . a private monopoly . . .
(with power) . . . given to it by a spineless Congress . . . to issue and regulate
all our money.
   They create money from nothing and lend it to private business (the same   330
money over and over again at a high rate of interest), and also to the Government
whenever it needs money in war and peace; for which we, the people, representing
the Government (in this instance at any rate) must pay interest to the banks
in the form of high taxes.

The bird, the eagle, made himself   335
small—to creep into the hinged egg
until therein he disappeared, all
but one leg upon which a claw opened
and closed wretchedly gripping
the air, and would not—for all   340
the effort of the struggle, remain
inside   .

   Witnessing the Falls Hamilton was impressed by this show of what in those
times was overwhelming power . . . planned a stone aqueduct following a proposed boulevard, as the crow flies, to Newark with outlets every mile or two   345
along the river for groups of factories: The Society for Useful Manufactures:
SUM, they called it.
   The newspapers of the day spoke in enthusiastic terms of the fine prospects of
the "National Manufactory" where they fondly believed would be produced all

cotton, cassimeres, wall papers, books, felt and straw hats, shoes, carriages, pottery,   350
bricks, pots, pans and buttons needed in the United States. But L'Enfant's plans
were more magnificent than practical and Peter Colt, Treasurer of the State of
Connecticut, was chosen in his place.
.   .   .   .   .   The prominent purpose of the Society
was the manufacture of cotton goods.   355

     Washington at his first inaugural
      .   .   .   .   .   wore
     a coat of Crow-black homespun woven
     in Paterson   .   .   .   .   .

In other words, the Federal Reserve Banks constitute a Legalized National   360
Usury System, whose Customer No. 1 is our Government, the richest country in
the world. Every one of us is paying tribute to the money racketeers on every
dollar we earn through hard work.
.   .   .   .   In all our great bond issues the interest is always greater
than the principle. All of the great public works cost more than twice the actual   365
cost, on that account. Under the present system of doing business we SIMPLY ADD
120 to 150 per cent to the stated cost.
The people must pay anyway; why should they be compelled to pay twice?
THE WHOLE NATIONAL DEBT IS MADE UP ON INTEREST CHARGES. If the people
ever get to thinking of bonds and bills at the same time, the game is up.   370

          If there is subtlety,
    you are subtle. I beg your indulgence:
    no prayer should cause you anything
    but tears. I had a friend   .   .
    let it pass. I remember when as a child   375
    I stopped praying and shook with fear
    until sleep—your sleep calmed me —

    You also, I am sure, have read
    Frazer's Golden Bough. It does you
    justice—a prayer such as might be made   380
    by a lover who
    appraises every feature of his bride's
    comeliness, and terror—
    terror to him such as one, a man
    married, feels toward his bride—   385

    You are the eternal bride and
    father—quid pro quo,
    a simple miracle that knows
    the branching sea, to which the oak
    is coral, the coral oak.   390
    The Himalayas and prairies
    of your features amaze and delight—

    Why should I move from this place
    where I was born? knowing
    how futile would be the search   395

for you in the multiplicity
of your debacle. The world spreads
for me like a flower opening—and
will close for me as might a rose—

wither and fall to the ground   400
and rot and be drawn up
into a flower again. But you
never wither—but blossom
all about me. In that I forget
myself perpetually—in your   405
composition and decomposition
I find my   .   .

                        despair!

.   .   .   .

Whatever your reasons were for that note of yours and for your indifferent evasion
of my letters just previous to that note—the one thing that I still wish more   410
than any other is that I could see you. It's tied up with even more than I've said
here. And more importantly, it is the *one* impulse I have that breaks through
that film, that crust, which has gathered there so fatally between my true self
and that which can make only mechanical gestures of living. But even if you
should grant it, I wouldn't want to see you unless with some little warmth of   415
friendliness and friendship on your part. . . . Nor should I want to see you at
your office under any circumstances. That is not what I mean (because I have
no specific matter to see you about now as I had when I first called upon you as
a complete stranger, not as I could have had, just before your last note when I
wanted so badly to have you go over some of my most faulty poems with me),   420
I have been feeling (with that feeling increasingly stronger) that I shall never
again be able to recapture any sense of my own personal identity (without
which I cannot write, of course—but in itself far more important than the
writing) until I can recapture some faith in the reality of my own thoughts and
ideas and problems which were turned into dry sand by your attitude toward   425
those letters and by that note of yours later. That is why I cannot throw off my
desire to see you—not impersonally, but in the most personal ways, since I could
never have written you at all in a completely impersonal fashion.

III

                 Look for the nul
                 defeats it all

                 the N of all
                 equations   .

                 that rock, the blank   5
                 that holds them up

                 which pulled away—
                 the rock's

                 their fall. Look
                 for that nul   10

that's past all
seeing

the death of all
that's past

all being   .   15

But Spring shall come and flowers will bloom
and man must chatter of his doom   .   .

The descent beckons
           as the ascent beckoned
                      Memory is a kind   20
of accomplishment
           a sort of renewal
                      even
an initiation, since the spaces it opens are new
places   25
           inhabited by hordes
                      heretofore unrealized,
of new kinds—
           since their movements
                      are towards new objectives   30
(even though formerly they were abandoned)

No defeat is made up entirely of defeat—since
the world it opens is always a place
           formerly
                      unsuspected. A   35
world lost,
           a world unsuspected
                      beckons to new places
and no whiteness (lost) is so white as the memory
of whiteness   .   40

With evening, love wakens
           though its shadows
                      which are alive by reason
of the sun shining—
           grow sleepy now and drop away   45
                      from desire

Love without shadows stirs now
           beginning to waken
                      as night
advances.   50

The descent
           made up of despairs
                      and without accomplishment

realizes a new awakening :
which is a reversal   55
of despair.
For what we cannot accomplish, what
is denied to love,
what we have lost in the anticipation—
a descent follows,   60
endless and indestructible   .

Listen! —

the pouring water!
The dogs and trees
conspire to invent   65
a world—gone!

Bow, wow! A
departing car scatters gravel as it
picks up speed!

Outworn! *le pauvre petit ministre*   70
did his best, they cry,
but though he sweat for all his worth
no poet has come   .

Bow, wow! Bow, wow!

Variously the dogs barked, the trees   75
stuck their fingers to their noses. No
poet has come, no poet has come.
—soon no one in the park but
guilty lovers and stray dogs   .

Unleashed!   80

Alone, watching the May moon above the
trees   .

At nine o'clock the park closes. You
must be out of the lake, dressed, in
your cars and going: they change into   85
their street clothes in the back seats
and move out among the trees   .

The "great beast" all removed
before the plunging night, the crickets'
black wings and hylas wake   .   90

Missing was the thing Jim had found in Marx and Veblen and Adam Smith and Darwin—the dignified sound of a great, calm bell tolling the morning of a new age   .   ,   instead, the slow complaining of a door loose on its hinges.

Faitoute, conscious by moments,   95
rouses by moments, rejects him finally
and strolls off   .

That the poem,
the most perfect rock and temple, the highest
falls, in clouds of gauzy spray, should be   100
so rivaled   .   that the poet,
in disgrace, should borrow from erudition (to
unslave the mind): railing at the vocabulary
(borrowing from those he hates, to his own
disfranchisement)   .   105
—discounting his failures   .
seeks to induce his bones to rise into a scene,
his dry bones, above the scene, (they will not)
illuminating it within itself, out of itself
to form the colors, in the terms of some   110
back street, so that the history may escape
the panders

.   .   accomplish the inevitable
poor, the invisible, thrashing, breeding
.   debased city   115

Love is no comforter, rather a nail in the
skull

.   reversed in the mirror of its
own squalor, debased by the divorce from learning,
its garbage on the curbs, its legislators   120
under the garbage, uninstructed, incapable of
self instruction   .

a thwarting, an avulsion   :

—flowers uprooted, columbine, yellow and red,
strewn upon the path; dogwoods in full flower,   125
the trees dismembered; it women
shallow, its men steadfastly refusing—at
the best   .

The language   .   words
without style! whose scholars (there are none)   130
.   or dangling, about whom
the water weaves its strands encasing them
in a sort of thick lacquer, lodged
under its flow   .

Caught (in mind)   135
beside the water he looks down, listens!
But discovers, still, no syllable in the confused

uproar: missing the sense (thought he tries)
untaught but listening, shakes with the intensity
of his listening   .   140

Only the thought of the stream comforts him,
its terrifying plunge, inviting marriage—and
a wreath of fur   .

And She   —

   Stones invent nothing, only a man invents.   145
   What answer the waterfall? filling
   the basin by the snag-toothed stones?

And He   —

   Clearly, it is the new, uninterpreted, that
   remoulds the old, pouring down   .   150

And she   —

   It has not been enacted in our day!

             Le
pauvre petit ministre, swinging his arms, drowns
under the indifferent fragrance of the bass-wood   155
trees   .

My feelings about you now are those of anger and indignation; and they enable
me to tell you a lot of things straight from the shoulder, without my usual tongue
tied round-aboutness.
 You might as well take all your own literature and everyone else's and toss it   160
into one of those big garbage trucks of the Sanitation Department, so long as
the people with the top-cream minds and the "finer" sensibilities use those minds
and sensibilities not to make themselves more humane human beings than the
average person, but merely as means of ducking responsibility toward a better
understanding of their fellow men, except theoretically—which doesn't mean a   165
God damned thing.

   .   and there go the Evangels! (their organ
   loaded into the rear of a light truck) scooting
   down-hill   .   the children
   are at least getting a kick out of *this!*   170

   His anger mounts. He is chilled to the bone.
   As there appears a dwarf, hideously deformed—
   he sees squirming roots trampled
   under the foliage of his mind by the holiday
   crowds as by the feet of the straining   175
   minister. From his eyes sparrows start and
   sing. His ears are toadstools, his fingers have
   begun to sprout leaves (his voice is drowned
   under the falls)   .

Poet, poet! sing your song, quickly! or   180
not insects but pulpy weeds will blot out
your kind.
               He all but falls   .   .

And She   —

     Marry us! Marry us!   185
            Or! be dragged down, dragged
    under and lost

     She was married with empty words:
                  better to
                stumble at   190
               the edge
                 to fall
                   fall
              and be

             —divorced   195

    from the insistence of place—
                from knowledge,
    from learning—the terms
    foreign, conveying no immediacy, pouring down.

              —divorced   200
    from time (no invention more), bald as an
    egg   .

       and leaped (or fell) without a
    language, tongue-tied
             the language worn out   ,   205

    The dwarf lived there, close to the waterfall—
    saved by his protective coloring.

    Go home. Write. Compose   .

    Ha!

    Be reconciled, poet, with your world, it is   210
    the only truth!

    Ha!

    —the language is worn out.

And She   —
     You have abandoned me!   215

                    —at the magic sound of the stream
                    she threw herself upon the bed—
                    a pitiful gesture! lost among the words:
                    Invent (if you can) discover or
                    nothing is clear—will surmount   220
                    the drumming in your head. There will be
                    nothing clear, nothing clear   .

            He fled pursued by the roar.

    Seventy-five of the world's leading scholars, poets and philosophers gathered at
Princeton last week   .   .   .   225

                        Faitoute ground his heel
            hard down on the stone:

    Sunny today, with the highest temperature near 80 degrees; moderate southerly
winds. Partly cloudy and continued warm tomorrow, with moderate southerly
winds.   230

                    Her belly   .   her belly is like
                    a cloud   .   a cloud
                                    at evening   .

            His mind would reawaken:

He   Me with my pants, coat and vest still on!   235

She   And me still in my galoshes!

                    —the descent follows the ascent—to wisdom
                    as to despair.   240
                    A man is under the crassest necessity
                    to break down the pinnacles of his moods
                    fearlessly —
                    to the bases; base! to the screaming dregs,
                    to have known the clean air   245
                    From that base, unabashed, to regain
                    the sun kissed summits of love!

                                        —obscurely
                    in to scribble   .   and a war won!

                    —saying over to himself a song written   250
                    previously   .   inclines to believe
                    he sees, in the structure, something
                                            of interest!

            On this most voluptuous night of the year
            the term of the moon is yellow with no light   255

the air's soft, the night bird has
only one note, the cherry tree in bloom

makes a blur on the woods, its perfume
no more than half guessed moves in the mind.
No insect is yet awake, leaves are few.   260
In the arching trees there is no sleep.

The blood is still and indifferent, the face
does not ache nor sweat soil nor the
mouth thirst. Now love might enjoy its play
and nothing disturb the full octave of its run.   265

Her belly   .   her belly is like a white cloud   .   a
white cloud at evening   .   before the shuddering night!

My attitude toward woman's wretched position in society and my ideas about
all the changes necessary there, were interesting to you, weren't they, in so far as
they made for *literature?* That my particular emotional orientation, in wrenching   270
myself free from patterned standardized feminine feelings, enabled me to do
some passably good work with *poetry*—all that was fine, wasn't it—something for
you to sit up and take notice of! And you saw in one of my first letters to you
(the one you had wanted to make use of, then, in the Introduction to your
Paterson) an indication that my thoughts were to be taken seriously, because   275
that too could be turned by you into literature, as something disconnected from
life.

But when my actual personal life crept in, stamped all over with the *very same*
attitudes and sensibilities and preoccupations that you found quite admirable as
literature—that was an entirely different matter, wasn't it? No longer admirable,   280
but, on the contrary, deplorable, annoying, stupid, or in some other way unpardonable; because those very ideas and feelings which make one a writer
with some kind of new vision, are often the *very same ones* which, in living
itself, make one clumsy, awkward, absurd, ungrateful, confidential where most
people are reticent, and reticent where one should be confidential, and which   285
cause one, all too often, to step on the toes of other people's sensitive egos as a
result of one's stumbling earnestness or honesty carried too far. And that they
are the very same ones—that's important, something to be remembered at all
times, especially by writers like yourself who are so sheltered from life in the raw
by the glass-walled conditions of their own safe lives.   290

Only my writing (when I write) is myself: only that is the real me in any
essential way. Not because I bring to literature and to life two different incon-
sistent sets of values, as you do. No, *I* don't do that; and I feel that when anyone
does do it, literature is turned into just so much intellectual excrement fit for
the same stinking hole as any other kind.   295

But in writing (as in all forms of creative art) one derives one's unity of
being and one's freedom to be one's self, from one's relationship to those particular externals (language, clay, paints, et cetera) over which one has complete
control and the shaping of which lies entirely in one's own power; whereas in
living, one's shaping of the externals involved there (of one's friendships, the   300
structure of society, et cetera) is no longer entirely within one's own power but
requires the cooperation and the understanding and the humanity of others in
order to bring out what is best and most real in one's self.

That's why all that fine talk of yours about woman's need to "sail free in her
own element" as a *poet,* becomes nothing but empty rhetoric in the light of   305

your behavior towards me. No woman will ever be able to do that, completely, until she is able *first* to "sail free in her own element" in living itself—which means in her relationships with men even before she can do so in her relation- ships with other women. The members of any underprivileged class distrust and hate the "outsider" who is *one of them,* and women therefore—women in general—will never be content with their lot until the light seeps down to them, not from one of their own, but from the eyes of changed male attitudes toward them—so that in the meantime, the problems and the awareness of a woman like myself are looked upon even more unsympathetically by other women than by men.

And that, my dear doctor, is another reason why I needed of you a very different kind of friendship from the one you offered me.

I still don't know of course the specific thing that caused the cooling of your friendliness toward me. But I do know that if you were going to bother with me *at all,* there were only two things for you to have considered: (1) that I was, as I still am, a woman dying of loneliness—yes, really dying of it almost in the same way that people die slowly of cancer or consumption or any other such disease (and with all my efficiency in the practical world continually undermined by that loneliness); and (2) that I needed desperately, and still do, some ways and means of leading a *writer's* life, either by securing some sort of writer's job (or any other job having to do with my cultural interests) or else through some kind of literary journalism such as the book reviews—because only in work and jobs of that kind, can I turn into assets what are liabilities for me in jobs of a different kind.

Those were the two problems of mine that you continually and almost de- liberately placed in the background of your attempts to help me. And yet they were, and remain, much greater than whether or not I get my poetry published. I didn't need the *publication* of my poetry with your name lent to it, in order to go on writing poetry, half as much as I needed your friendship in other ways (the very ways you ignored) in order to write it. I couldn't, for that reason, have brought the kind of responsiveness and appreciation that you expected of me (not with any real honesty) to the kind of help from you which I needed so much less than the kind you withheld.

Your whole relationship with me amounted to pretty much the same thing as your trying to come to the aid of a patient suffering from pneumonia by handing her a box of aspirin or Grove's cold pills and a glass of hot lemonade. I couldn't tell you that outright. And how were you, a man of letters, to have realized it when the imagination, so quick to assert itself most powerfully in the creation of a piece of literature, seems to have no power at all in enabling writers in your circumstances to fully understand the maladjustment and impotencies of a woman in my position?

When you wrote to me up in W. about that possible censor job, it seemed a very simple matter to you, didn't it, for me to make all the necessary inquiries about the job, arrange for the necessary interviews, start work (if I was hired) with all the necessary living conditions for holding down such a job, and thus find my life all straightened out in its practical aspects, at least—as if by magic?

But it's never so simple as that to get on one's feet even in the most ordinary practical ways, for anyone on *my* side of the railway tracks—which isn't your side, nor the side of your great admirer, Miss Fleming, nor even the side of those well cared for people like S. T. and S. S. who've spent most of their lives with some Clara or some Jeanne to look after them even when they themselves have been flat broke.

A completely down and out person with months of stripped, bare hardship behind him needs all kinds of things to even get himself in shape for looking for a respectable, important white-collar job. And then he needs ample funds for eating and sleeping and keeping up appearances (especially the latter) while going around for various interviews involved. And even if and when a job of that kind is obtained, he still needs the eating and the sleeping and the carfares and the keeping up of appearances and what not, waiting for his first pay check and even perhaps for the second pay check since the first one might have to go almost entirely for back rent or something else of that sort.

And all that takes a hell of a lot of money (especially for a woman)—a lot more than ten dollars or twenty five dollars. Or else it takes the kind of very close friends at whose apartment one is quite welcome to stay for a month or two, and whose typewriter one can use in getting off some of the required letters asking for interviews, and whose electric iron one can use in keeping one's clothes pressed, et cetera—the kind of close friends that I don't have and never have had, for reasons which you know.

Naturally, I couldn't turn to *you*, a stranger, for any such practical help on so large a scale; and it was stupid of me to have minimized the extent of help I needed when I asked you for that first money-order that got stolen and later for the second twenty-five dollars—stupid because it was misleading. But the different kind of help I asked for, *finally* (and which you placed in the background) would have been an adequate substitute, because I could have carried out *those* plans which I mentioned to you in the late fall (the book reviews, supplemented by almost any kind of part-time job, and later some articles, and maybe a month at Yaddo this summer) *without* what it takes to get on one's feet in other very different ways. And the, eventually, the very fact that my name had appeared here and there in the book review sections of a few publications (I'd prefer not to *use* poetry that way) would have enabled me to obtain certain kinds of jobs (such as an O.W.I. job for instance) without all that red tape which affects only obscure, unknown people.

The anger and the indignation which I feel towards you now has served to pierce through the rough ice of that congealment which my creative faculties began to suffer from as a result of that last note from you. I find myself thinking and feeling in terms of poetry again. But over and against that is the fact that I'm even more lacking in anchorage of any kind than when I first got to know you. My loneliness is a million fathoms deeper, and my physical energies even more seriously sapped by it; and my economic situation is naturally worse, with living costs so terribly high now, and with my contact with your friend Miss X having come off so badly.

However, she may have had another reason for paying no attention to that note of mine—perhaps the reason of having found out that your friendliness toward me had cooled—which would have made a difference to her, I suppose, since she is such a great "admirer" of yours. But I don't know. That I'm in the dark about, too; and when I went up to the "Times" last week, to try, on my own, to get some of their fiction reviews (the "Times" publishes so many of those), nothing came of that either. And it's *writing* that I want to do—not operating a machine or a lathe, because with literature more and more tied up with the social problems and social progress (for me, in my way of thinking) any contribution I might be able to make to the welfare of humanity (in war-time or peace-time) would have to be as a writer, and not as a factory worker.

When I was very young, ridiculously young (of school-girl age) for a critical role, with my mind not at all developed and all my ideas in a state of first-week embryonic formlessness, I was able to obtain book-reviews from any number of magazines without any difficulty—and *all* of them books by writers of accepted importance (such as Cummings, Babette Deutsch, H. D.) whereas now when my ideas have matured, and when I really have something to say, I can get no work of that kind at all. And why is that? It's because in all those intervening years, I have been forced, as a woman not content with woman's position in the world, to do a lot of pioneer *living* which writers of your sex and with your particular social background do not have thrust upon them, and which the members of my own sex frown upon (for reasons I've already referred to)—so that at the very moment when I wanted to return to writing from living (with my ideas clarified and enriched by living) there I was (and still am)—because of that living— completely in exile socially.   420

I glossed over and treated very lightly (in my first conversation with you) those literary activities of my early girlhood, because the work in itself was not much better than that which any talented college freshman or precocious prep-school senior contributes to her school paper. But, after all, that work, instead of   425 appearing in a school paper where it belonged, was taken so seriously by editors of the acceptably important literary publications of that time, that I was able to average as much as $15 a week, very easily, from it. And I go into that now and stress it here; because you can better imagine, in the light of that, just how I feel in realizing that on the basis of just a few superficials (such as possessing   430 a lot of appealingly youthful sex-appeal and getting in with the right set) I was able to maintain my personal identity as a writer in my relationship to the world, whereas now I am cut off from doing so because it was necessary for me in my living, to strip myself of those superficials.

You've never had to live, Dr. P—not in any of the by-ways and dark under-   435 ground passages where life so often has to be tested. The very circumstances of your birth and social background provided you with an escape from life in the raw; and you confuse that protection from life with an *inability* to live—and are thus able to regard literature as nothing more than a desperate last extremity resulting from that illusionary inability to live. (I've been looking at some of your   440 autobiographical works, as this indicates.)

But living (unsafe living, I mean) isn't something one just sits back and decides about. It happens to one, in a small way, like measles; or in a big way, like a leaking boat or an earthquake. Or else it doesn't happen. And when it does, then one must bring, as I must, one's life to literature; and when it doesn't then   445 one brings to life (as you do) purely literary sympathies and understandings, the insights and humanity of words on paper *only*—and also, alas, the ego of the literary man which most likely played an important part in the change of your attitude toward me. That literary man's ego wanted to help me in such a way, I think, that my own achievements might serve as a flower in his buttonhole, if   450 that kind of help had been enough to make me bloom.

But I have no blossoms to bring to any man in the way of either love *or* friendship. That's one of the reasons why I didn't want that introduction to my poems. And I'm not wanting to be nasty or sarcastic in the last lines of this letter. On the contrary a feeling of profound sadness has replaced now the anger and   455 the indignation with which I started to write all this. I wanted your friendship more than I ever wanted anything else (yes, *more,* and I've wanted other things badly) I wanted it desperately, not because I have a single thing with which to adorn any man's pride—but just because I haven't.

Yes, the anger which I imagined myself to feel on all the previous pages, was   460 false. I am too unhappy and too lonely to be angry; and if some of the things to which I have called your attention here should cause any change of heart in you regarding me, that would be just about the only thing I can conceive of as occurring in my life right now.

La votre   465

C.

P. S. That I'm back here at 21 Pine Street causes me to add that that mystery as to who forged the "Cress" on that money order and also took one of Brown's checks (though his was *not* cashed, and therefore replaced later) never did get cleared up. And the janitor who was here at the time, is dead now. I don't think   470 it was he took any of the money. But still I was rather glad that the post-office didn't follow it through because just in case Bob did have anything to do with it, he would have gotten into serious trouble—which I shouldn't have welcomed, because he was one of those miserably underpaid negroes and an awfully decent human being in lots of ways. But now I wish it *had* been followed through *after* he died (which was over two months ago) because the crooks may have been those low vile upstate farm people whose year-round exploitation of down and out farm help ought to be brought to light in some fashion, and because if they *did* steal the money order and were arrested for it, that in itself would have brought to the attention of the proper authorities all their other illegal activities as well: And yet that kind of justice doesn't interest me greatly. What's at the root of this or that crime or antisocial act, both psychologically and environmentally, always interests me more. But as I make that last statement, I'm reminded of how much I'd like to do a lot of things with *people* in some prose—some stories, maybe a novel. I can't tell you how much I want the living which I need in order to write. And I simply can't achieve them entirely alone. I don't even possess a typewriter now, nor have even a rented one—and I can't think properly except on a typewriter. I can do poetry (though only the first draft) in long-hand, and letters. But for any prose writing, other than letters, I can't do any work without a typewriter. But that of course is the least of my problems—the typewriter; at least the easiest to do something about.

475
480
485
490

C.

Dr. P.:

This is the simplest, most outright letter I've ever written to you; and you ought to read it all the way through, and carefully, because it's about you, as a writer, and about the ideas regarding women that you expressed in your article on A.N., and because in regard to myself, it contains certain information which I did not think it necessary to give you before, and which I do think now you ought to have. And if my anger in the beginning makes you too angry to go on from there— well, that anger of mine isn't there in the last part, now as I attach this post-script.

495
500

C.

And if you don't feel like reading it even for those reasons, will you then do so, *please,* merely out of fairness to me—much time and much thought and much unhappiness having gone into those pages.

D. H. Lawrence (1885–1930)

SNAKE

A snake came to my water-trough
On a hot, hot day, and I in pyjamas for the heat,
To drink there.

In the deep, strange-scented shade of the great dark carob-tree
I came down the steps with my pitcher
And must wait, must stand and wait, for there he was at the trough before me.

He reached down from a fissure in the earth-wall in the gloom
And trailed his yellow-brown slackness soft-bellied down, over the edge of
    the stone trough

5

And rested his throat upon the stone bottom,   10
And where the water had dripped from the tap, in a small clearness,
He sipped with his straight mouth,
Softly drank through his straight gums, into his slack long body,
Silently.

Someone was before me at my water-trough,   15
And I, like a second comer, waiting.

He lifted his head from his drinking, as cattle do,
And looked at me vaguely, as drinking cattle do,
And flickered his two-forked tongue from his lips, and mused a moment,
And stooped and drank a little more,   20
Being earth-brown, earth-golden from the burning bowels of the earth
On the day of Sicilian July, with Etna smoking.

The voice of my education said to me
He must be killed,
For in Sicily the black, black snakes are innocent, the gold are venomous.   25

And voices in me said, If you were a man
You would take a stick and break him now, and finish him off.

But must I confess how I liked him,
How glad I was he had come like a guest in quiet, to drink at my water-trough
And depart peaceful, pacified, and thankless,   30
Into the burning bowels of this earth?

Was it cowardice, that I dared not kill him?
Was it perversity, that I longed to talk to him?
Was it humility, to feel so honoured?
I felt so honoured.   35

And yet those voices:
If you were not afraid, you would kill him!

And truly I was afraid, I was most afraid,
But even so, honoured still more
That he should seek my hospitality   40
From out the dark door of the secret earth.

He drank enough
And lifted his head, dreamily, as one who has drunken,
And flickered his tongue like a forked night on the air, so black,
Seeming to lick his lips,   45
And looked around like a god, unseeing, into the air,
And slowly turned his head,
And slowly, very slowly, as if thrice adream,
Proceeded to draw his slow length curving round
And climb again the broken bank of my wall-face.   50

And as he put his head into that dreadful hole,
And as he slowly drew up, snake-easing his shoulders, and entered farther,
A sort of horror, a sort of protest against his withdrawing into that
    horrid black hole,
Deliberately going into the blackness, and slowly drawing himself after,   55
Overcame me now his back was turned.

I looked round, I put down my pitcher,
I picked up a clumsy log
And threw it at the water-trough with a clatter.

I think it did not hit him,   60
But suddenly that part of him that was left behind convulsed in
    undignified haste,
Writhed like lightning, and was gone
Into the black hole, the earth-lipped fissure in the wall-front,
At which, in the intense still noon, I stared with fascination.   65

And immediately I regretted it.
I thought how paltry, how vulgar, what a mean act!
I despised myself and the voices of my accursed human education.

And I thought of the albatross,
And I wished he would come back, my snake.   70

For he seemed to me again like a king,
Like a king in exile, uncrowned in the underworld,
Now due to be crowned again.

And so, I missed my chance with one of the lords
Of life.   75
And I have something to expiate;
A pettiness.

BAVARIAN GENTIANS

Not every man has gentians in his house
in soft September, at slow, sad Michaelmas.

Bavarian gentians, big and dark, only dark
darkening the day-time, torch-like with the smoking blueness of Pluto's gloom,
ribbed and torch-like, with their blaze of darkness spread blue   5
down flattening into points, flattened under the sweep of white day
torch-flower of the blue-smoking darkness, Pluto's dark-blue daze,
black lamps from the halls of Dis, burning dark blue,
giving off darkness, blue darkness, as Demeter's pale lamps give off light,
lead me then, lead the way.   10

Reach me a gentian, give me a torch!
let me guide myself with the blue, forked torch of this flower

down the darker and darker stairs, where blue is darkened on blueness
even where Persephone goes, just now, from the frosted September
to the sightless realm where darkness is awake upon the dark   15
and Persephone herself is but a voice
or a darkness invisible enfolded in the deeper dark
of the arms Plutonic, and pierced with the passion of dense gloom,
among the splendour of torches of darkness, shedding darkness on the lost
      bride and her groom.   20

Ezra Pound (1885–1972)

THE GARDEN

> *En robe de parade.*
>   —Samain

Like a skein of loose silk blown against a wall
She walks by the railing of a path in Kensington Gardens,
And she is dying piece-meal
    of a sort of emotional anæmia.

And round about there is a rabble   5
Of the filthy, sturdy, unkillable infants of the very poor.
They shall inherit the earth.

In her is the end of breeding.
Her boredom is exquisite and excessive.
She would like some one to speak to her,   10
And is almost afraid that I
    will commit that indiscretion.

IN A STATION OF THE METRO

The apparition of these faces in the crowd;
Petals on a wet, black bough.

CANTO I

And then went down to the ship,
Set keel to breakers, forth on the godly sea, and
We set up mast and sail on that swart ship,

Bore sheep aboard her, and our bodies also
Heavy with weeping, and winds from sternward   5
Bore us out onward with bellying canvas,
Circe's this craft, the trim-coifed goddess.
Then sat we amidships, wind jamming the tiller,
Thus with stretched sail, we went over sea till day's end.
Sun to his slumber, shadows o'er all the ocean,   10
Came we then to the bounds of deepest water,
To the Kimmerian lands, and peopled cities
Covered with close-webbed mist, unpierced ever
With glitter of sun-rays
Nor with stars stretched, nor looking back from heaven   15
Swartest night stretched over wretched men there.
The ocean flowing backward, came we then to the place
Aforesaid by Circe.
Here did they rites, Perimedes and Eurylochus,
And drawing sword from my hip   20
I dug the ell-square pitkin;
Poured we libations unto each the dead,
First mead and then sweet wine, water mixed with white flour
Then prayed I many a prayer to the sickly death's-heads;
As set in Ithaca, sterile bulls of the best   25
For sacrifice, heaping the pyre with goods,
A sheep to Tiresias only, black and a bell-sheep.
Dark blood flowed in the fosse,
Souls out of Erebus, cadaverous dead, of brides
Of youths and of the old who had borne much;   30
Souls stained with recent tears, girls tender,
Men many, mauled with bronze lance heads,
Battle spoil, bearing yet dreary arms,
These many crowded about me; with shouting,
Pallor upon me, cried to my men for more beasts;   35
Slaughtered the herds, sheep slain of bronze;
Poured ointment, cried to the gods,
To Pluto the strong, and praised Proserpine;
Unsheathed the narrow sword,
I sat to keep off the impetuous impotent dead,   40
Till I should hear Tiresias.
But first Elpenor came, our friend Elpenor,
Unburied, cast on the wide earth,
Limbs that we left in the house of Circe,
Unwept, unwrapped in sepulchre, since toils urged other.   45
Pitiful spirit. And I cried in hurried speech:
"Elpenor, how art thou come to this dark coast?
"Cam'st thou afoot, outstripping seamen?"
                And he in heavy speech:
"Ill fate and abundant wine. I slept in Circe's ingle.   50
"Going down the long ladder unguarded,
"I fell against the buttress,
"Shattered the nape-nerve, the soul sought Avernus.
"But thou, O King, I bid remember me, unwept, unburied,

"Heap up mine arms, be tomb by sea-bord, and inscribed: 55
" '*A man of no fortune, and with a name to come.*'
"And set my oar up, that I swung mid fellows."

And Anticlea came, whom I beat off, and then Tiresias Theban,
Holding his golden wand, knew me, and spoke first:
"A second time? why? man of ill star,   60
"Facing the sunless dead and this joyless region?
"Stand from the fosse, leave me my bloody bever
"For soothsay."
        And I stepped back,
And he strong with the blood, said then: "Odysseus   65
"Shalt return through spiteful Neptune, over dark seas,
"Lose all companions." Then Anticlea came.
Lie quiet Divus. I mean, that is Andreas Divus,
In officina Wecheli, 1538, out of Homer.
And he sailed, by Sirens and thence outward and away   70
And unto Circe.
        Venerandam,
In the Cretan's phrase, with the golden crown, Aphrodite,
Cypri munimenta sortita est, mirthful, oricalchi, with golden
Girdle and breast bands, thou with dark eyelids   75
Bearing the golden bough of Argicida. So that:

T. S. Eliot (1888–1965)

THE LOVE SONG
OF J. ALFRED PRUFROCK

S'io credesse che mia risposta fosse
A persona che mai tornasse al mondo,
Questa fiamma staria senza piu scosse.
Ma perciocche giammai di questo fondo
Non torno vivo alcun, s'i'odo il vero,
Senza tema d'infamia ti rispondo.

Let us go then, you and I,
When the evening is spread out against the sky
Like a patient etherised upon a table;
Let us go, through certain half-deserted streets,
The muttering retreats   5
Of restless nights in one-night cheap hotels
And sawdust restaurants with oyster-shells:
Streets that follow like a tedious argument
Of insidious intent

To lead you to an overwhelming question. . .   10
Oh, do not ask, "What is it?"
Let us go and make our visit.

    In the room the women come and go
Talking of Michelangelo.

    The yellow fog that rubs its back upon the window-panes,   15
The yellow smoke that rubs its muzzle on the window-panes
Licked its tongue into the corners of the evening,
Lingered upon the pools that stand in drains,
Let fall upon its back the soot that falls from chimneys,
Slipped by the terrace, made a sudden leap,   20
And seeing that it was a soft October night,
Curled once about the house, and fell asleep.

    And indeed there will be time
For the yellow smoke that slides along the street,
Rubbing its back upon the window-panes;   25
There will be time, there will be time
To prepare a face to meet the faces that you meet;
There will be time to murder and create,
And time for all the works and days of hands
That lift and drop a question on your plate;   30
Time for you and time for me,
And time yet for a hundred indecisions,
And for a hundred visions and revisions,
Before the taking of a toast and tea.

    In the room the women come and go   35
Talking of Michelangelo.

    And indeed there will be time
To wonder, "Do I dare?" and, "Do I dare?"
Time to turn back and descend the stair,
With a bald spot in the middle of my hair—   40
[They will say: "How his hair is growing thin!"]
My morning coat, my collar mounting firmly to the chin,
My necktie rich and modest, but asserted by a simple pin—
[They will say: "But how his arms and legs are thin!"]
Do I dare   45
Disturb the universe?
In a minute there is time
For decisions and revisions which a minute will reverse.

    For I have known them all already, known them all:—
Have known the evenings, mornings, afternoons,   50
I have measured out my life with coffee spoons;
I know the voices dying with a dying fall
Beneath the music from a farther room.
    So how should I presume?

And I have known the eyes already, known them all— 55
The eyes that fix you in a formulated phrase,
And when I am formulated, sprawling on a pin,
When I am pinned and wriggling on the wall,
Then how should I begin
To spit out all the butt-ends of my days and ways? 60
  And how should I presume?

And I have known the arms already, known them all—
Arms that are braceleted and white and bare
[But in the lamplight, downed with light brown hair!]
Is it perfume from a dress 65
That makes me so digress?
Arms that lie along a table, or wrap about a shawl.
  And should I then presume?
  And how should I begin?

                    .   .   .

Shall I say, I have gone at dusk through narrow streets 70
And watched the smoke that rises from the pipes
Of lonely men in shirt-sleeves, leaning out of windows? . . .

  I should have been a pair of ragged claws
Scuttling across the floors of silent seas.

                    .   .   .

And the afternoon, the evening, sleeps so peacefully! 75
Smoothed by long fingers,
Asleep . . . tired . . . or it malingers,
Stretched on the floor, here beside you and me.
Should I, after tea and cakes and ices,
Have the strength to force the moment to its crisis? 80
But though I have wept and fasted, wept and prayed,
Though I have seen my head [grown slightly bald] brought in upon a platter,
I am no prophet—and here's no great matter;
I have seen the moment of my greatness flicker,
And I have seen the eternal Footman hold my coat, and snicker, 85
And in short, I was afraid.

  And would it have been worth it, after all,
After the cups, the marmalade, the tea,
Among the porcelain, among some talk of you and me,
Would it have been worth while,
To have bitten off the matter with a smile, 90
To have squeezed the universe into a ball
To roll it toward some overwhelming question,
To say: "I am Lazarus, come from the dead,
Come back to tell you all, I shall tell you all"—
If one, settling a pillow by her head, 95
  Should say: "That is not what I meant at all.
  That is not it, at all."

  And would it have been worth it, after all,
Would it have been worth while,
After the sunsets and the dooryards and the sprinkled streets, 100

After the novels, after the teacups, after the skirts that trail along the floor—
And this, and so much more?—
It is impossible to say just what I mean!
But as if a magic lantern threw the nerves in patterns on a screen:
Would it have been worth while   105
If one, settling a pillow or throwing off a shawl,
And turning toward the window, should say:
    "That is not it at all,
    That is not what I meant, at all."

No! I am not Prince Hamlet, nor was meant to be;   110
Am an attendant lord, one that will do
To swell a progress, start a scene or two,
Advise the prince; no doubt, an easy tool,
Deferential, glad to be of use,
Politic, cautious, and meticulous;   115
Full of high sentence, but a bit obtuse;
At times, indeed, almost ridiculous—
Almost, at times, the Fool.

    I grow old . . . I grow old . . .
I shall wear the bottoms of my trousers rolled.   120

    Shall I part my hair behind? Do I dare to eat a peach?
I shall wear white flannel trousers, and walk upon the beach.
I have heard the mermaids singing, each to each.

    I do not think that they will sing to me.

    I have seen them riding seaward on the waves   125
Combing the white hair of the waves blown back
When the wind blows the water white and black.

    We have lingered in the chambers of the sea
By sea-girls wreathed with seaweed red and brown
Till human voices wake us, and we drown.   130

THE WASTE LAND

> "Nam Sibyllam quidem Cumis ego ipse oculis meis vidi in ampulla pendere, et cum
> illi pueri dicerent: Σίβυλλα τί θέλεις; respondebat illa: ἀποθανεῖν θέλω."

For Ezra Pound
il miglior fabbro.

I. The Burial of the Dead

April is the cruellest month, breeding
Lilacs out of the dead land, mixing
Memory and desire, stirring

Dull roots with spring rain.
Winter kept us warm, covering   5
Earth in forgetful snow, feeding
A little life with dried tubers.
Summer surprised us, coming over the Starnbergersee
With a shower of rain; we stopped in the colonnade,
And went on in sunlight, into the Hofgarten,   10
And drank coffee, and talked for an hour.
Bin gar keine Russin, stamm' aus Litauen, echt deutsch.
And when we were children, staying at the archduke's,
My cousin's, he took me out on a sled,
And I was frightened. He said, Marie,   15
Marie, hold on tight. And down we went.
In the mountains, there you feel free.
I read, much of the night, and go south in the winter.

    What are the roots that clutch, what branches grow
Out of this stony rubbish? Son of man,   20
You cannot say, or guess, for you know only
A heap of broken images, where the sun beats,
And the dead tree gives no shelter, the cricket no relief,
And the dry stone no sound of water. Only
There is shadow under this red rock,   25
(Come in under the shadow of this red rock),
And I will show you something different from either
Your shadow at morning striding behind you
Or your shadow at evening rising to meet you;
I will show you fear in a handful of dust.   30
            Frisch weht der Wind
            Der Heimat zu
            Mein Irisch Kind,
            Wo weilest du?
"You gave me hyacinths first a year ago;   35
"They called me the hyacinth girl."
—Yet when we came back, late, from the Hyacinth garden,
Your arms full, and your hair wet, I could not
Speak, and my eyes failed, I was neither
Living nor dead, and I knew nothing,   40
Looking into the heart of light, the silence.
Oed' und leer das Meer.

    Madame Sosostris, famous clairvoyante,
Had a bad cold, nevertheless
Is known to be the wisest woman in Europe,   45
With a wicked pack of cards. Here, said she,
Is your card, the drowned Phoenician Sailor,
(Those are pearls that were his eyes. Look!)
Here is Belladonna, the Lady of the Rocks,
The lady of situations.
Here is the man with three staves, and here the Wheel,   50
And here is the one-eyed merchant, and this card,

Which is blank, is something he carries on his back,
Which I am forbidden to see. I do not find
The Hanged Man. Fear death by water.
I see crowds of people, walking round in a ring.   55
Thank you. If you see dear Mrs. Equitone,
Tell her I bring the horoscope myself:
One must be so careful these days.

    Unreal City,
Under the brown fog of a winter dawn,   60
A crowd flowed over London Bridge, so many,
I had not thought death had undone so many.
Sighs, short and infrequent, were exhaled,
And each man fixed his eyes before his feet.
Flowed up the hill and down King William Street,   65
To where Saint Mary Woolnoth kept the hours
With a dead sound on the final stroke of nine.
There I saw one I knew, and stopped him, crying: "Stetson!
"You who were with me in the ships at Mylae!
"That corpse you planted last year in your garden,   70
"Has it begun to sprout? Will it bloom this year?
"Or has the sudden frost disturbed its bed?
"Oh keep the Dog far hence, that's friend to men,
"Or with his nails he'll dig it up again!
"You! hyprocrite lecteur!—mon semblable,—mon frère!"   75

II. A Game of Chess

The Chair she sat in, like a burnished throne,
Glowed on the marble, where the glass
Held up by standards wrought with fruited vines
From which a golden Cupidon peeped out
(Another hid his eyes behind his wing)   80
Doubled the flames of sevenbranched candelabra
Reflecting light upon the table as
The glitter of her jewels rose to meet it,
From satin cases poured in rich profusion;
In vials of ivory and coloured glass   85
Unstoppered, lurked her strange synthetic perfumes,
Unguent, powdered, or liquid—trouble, confused
And drowned the sense in odours; stirred by the air
That freshened from the window, these ascended
In fattening the prolonged candle-flames,   90
Flung their smoke into the laquearia,
Stirring the pattern on the coffered ceiling.
Huge sea-wood fed with copper
Burned green and orange, framed by the coloured stone,
In which sad light a carvèd dolphin swam.   95
Above the antique mantel was displayed
As though a window gave upon the sylvan scene
The change of Philomel, by the barbarous king
So rudely forced; yet there the nightingale

Filled all the desert with inviolable voice   100
And still she cried, and still the world pursues,
"Jug Jug" to dirty ears.
And other withered stumps of time
Were told upon the walls; staring forms
Leaned out, leaning, hushing the room enclosed.   105
Footsteps shuffled on the stair.
Under the firelight, under the brush, her hair
Spread out in fiery points
Glowed into words, then would be savagely still.

   "My nerves are bad to-night. Yes, bad. Stay with me.   110
"Speak to me. Why do you never speak. Speak.
   "What are you thinking of? What thinking? What?
"I never know what you are thinking. Think."

   I think we are in rats' alley
Where the dead men lost their bones.   115

   "What is that noise?"
                  The wind under the door.
"What is that noise now? What is the wind doing?"
                 Nothing again nothing.
                            "Do   120
"You know nothing? Do you see nothing? Do you remember
"Nothing?"
     I remember
Those are pearls that were his eyes.
"Are you alive, or not? Is there nothing in your head?"   125
                             But
O O O O that Shakespeherian Rag—
It's so elegant
So intelligent
"What shall I do now? What shall I do?"   130
"I shall rush out as I am, and walk the street
"With my hair down, so. What shall we do to-morrow?
"What shall we ever do?"
                   The hot water at ten.
And if it rains, a closed car at four.   135
And we shall play a game of chess,
Pressing lidless eyes and waiting for a knock upon the door.

   When Lil's husband got demobbed, I said—
I didn't mince my words, I said to her myself,
HURRY UP PLEASE ITS TIME   140
Now Albert's coming back, make yourself a bit smart.
He'll want to know what you done with that money he gave you
To get yourself some teeth. He did, I was there.
You have them all out, Lil, and get a nice set,
He said, I swear, I can't bear to look at you.   145
And no more can't I, I said, and think of poor Albert,

He's been in the army four years, he wants a good time,
And if you don't give it him, there's others will, I said.
Oh is there, she said. Something o' that, I said.
Then I'll know who to thank, she said, and give me a straight look.   150
HURRY UP PLEASE ITS TIME
If you don't like it you can get on with it, I said.
Others can pick and choose if you can't.
But if Albert makes off, it won't be for lack of telling.
You ought to be ashamed, I said, to look so antique.   155
(And her only thirty-one.)
I can't help it, she said, pulling a long face,
It's them pills I took, to bring it off, she said.
(She's had five already, and nearly died of young George.)
The chemist said it would be all right, but I've never been the same.   160
You are a proper fool, I said.
Well, if Albert won't leave you alone, there it is, I said,
What you get married for if you don't want children?
HURRY UP PLEASE ITS TIME
Well, that Sunday Albert was home, they had a hot gammon,   165
And they asked me in to dinner, to get the beauty of it hot—
HURRY UP PLEASE ITS TIME
HURRY UP PLEASE ITS TIME
Goonight Bill. Goonight Lou. Goonight May. Goonight.
Ta ta. Goonight. Goonight.   170
Good night, ladies, good night, sweet ladies, good night, good night.

III. The Fire Sermon

The river's tent is broken: the last fingers of leaf
Clutch and sink into the wet bank. The wind
Crosses the brown land, unheard. The nymphs are departed.
Sweet Thames, run softly, till I end my song.   175
The river bears no empty bottles, sandwich papers,
Silk handkerchiefs, cardboard boxes, cigarette ends
Or other testimony of summer nights. The nymphs are departed.
And their friends, the loitering heirs of city directors;
Departed, have left no addresses.   180
By the waters of Leman I sat down and wept . . .
Sweet Thames, run softly till I end my song,
Sweet Thames, run softly, for I speak not loud or long.
But at my back in a cold blast I hear
The rattle of the bones, and chuckle spread from ear to ear.   185
A rat crept softly through the vegetation
Dragging its slimy belly on the bank
While I was fishing in the dull canal
On a winter evening round behind the gashouse
Musing upon the king my brother's wreck   190
And on the king my father's death before him.
White bodies naked on the low damp ground
And bones cast in a little low dry garret,
Rattled by the rat's foot only, year to year.
But at my back from time to time I hear   195

The sound of horns and motors, which shall bring
Sweeney to Mrs. Porter in the spring.
O the moon shone bright on Mrs. Porter
And on her daughter
They wash their feet in soda water   200
Et O ces voix d'enfants, chantant dans la coupole!

    Twit twit twit
Jug jug jug jug jug jug
So rudely forc'd.
Tereu   205

    Unreal City
Under the brown fog of a winter noon
Mr. Eugenides, the Smyrna merchant
Unshaven, with a pocket full of currants
C.i.f. London: documents at sight,   210
Asked me in demotic French
To luncheon at the Cannon Street Hotel
Followed by a weekend at the Metropole.

    At the violet hour, when the eyes and back
Turn upward from the desk, when the human engine waits   215
Like a taxi throbbing waiting,
I Tiresias, though blind, throbbing between two lives,
Old man with wrinkled female breasts, can see
At the violet hour, the evening hour that strives
Homeward, and brings the sailor home from sea,   220
The typist home at teatime, clears her breakfast, lights
Her stove, and lays out food in tins.
Out of the window perilously spread
Her drying combinations touched by the sun's last rays,
On the divan are piled (at night her bed)   225
Stockings, slippers, camisoles, and stays.
I Tiresias, old man with wrinkled dugs
Perceived the scene, and foretold the rest—
I too awaited the expected guest.
He, the young man carbuncular, arrives,   230
A small house agent's clerk, with one bold stare,
One of the low on whom assurance sits
As a silk hat on a Bradford millionaire.
The time is now propitious, as he guesses,
The meal is ended, she is bored and tired,   235
Endeavours to engage her in caresses
Which still are unreproved, if undesired.
Flushed and decided, he assaults at once;
Exploring hands encounter no defence;
His vanity requires no response,   240
And makes a welcome of indifference.
(And I Tiresias have foresuffered all
Enacted on this same divan or bed;

I who have sat by Thebes below the wall
And walked among the lowest of the dead.)   245
Bestows one final patronising kiss,
And gropes his way, finding the stairs unlit ...

   She turns and looks a moment in the glass,
Hardly aware of her departed lover;
Her brain allows one half-formed thought to pass: 250
"Well now that's done: and I'm glad it's over."
When lovely woman stoops to folly and
Paces about her room again, alone,
She smoothes her hair with automatic hand,
And puts a record on the gramophone.   255

   "This music crept by me upon the waters"
And along the Strand, up Queen Victoria Street.
O City city, I can sometimes hear
Beside a public bar in Lower Thames Street,
The pleasant whining of a mandoline   260
And a clatter and a chatter from within
Where fishermen lounge at noon: where the walls
Of Magnus Martyr hold
Inexplicable splendour of Ionian white and gold.

          The river sweats   265
          Oil and tar
          The barges drift
          With the turning tide
          Red sails
          Wide   270
          To leeward, swing on the heavy spar.
          The barges wash
          Drifting logs
          Down Greenwich reach
          Past the Isle of Dogs.   275
                    Weialala leia
                    Wallala leialala

          Elizabeth and Leicester
          Beating oars
          The stern was formed   280
          A gilded shell
          Red and gold
          The brisk swell
          Rippled both shores
          Southwest wind   285
          Carried down stream
          The peal of bells
          White towers
                    Weialala leia
                    Wallala leialala   290

"Trams and dusty trees.
Highbury bore me. Richmond and Kew
Undid me. By Richmond I raised my knees
Supine on the floor of a narrow canoe."

"My feet are at Moorgate, and my heart   295
Under my feet. After the event
He wept. He promised 'a new start.'
I made no comment. What should I resent?"

"On Margate Sands.
I can connect   300
Nothing with nothing.
The broken fingernails of dirty hands.
My people humble people who expect
Nothing."
          la la   305

To Carthage then I came

Burning burning burning burning
O Lord Thou pluckest me out
O Lord Thou pluckest

burning   310

IV. Death by Water

Phlebas the Phoenician, a fortnight dead,
Forgot the cry of gulls, and the deep sea swell
And the profit and loss.
                    A current under sea
Picked his bones in whispers. As he rose and fell   315
He passed the stages of his age and youth
Entering the whirlpool.
                    Gentile or Jew
O you who turn the wheel and look to windward,
Consider Phlebas, who was once handsome and tall as you.   320

V. What the Thunder Said

After the torchlight red on sweaty faces
After the frosty silence in the gardens
After the agony in stony places
The shouting and the crying
Prison and palace and reverberation   325
Of thunder of spring over distant mountains
He who was living is now dead
We who were living are now dying
With a little patience

Here is no water but only rock   330
Rock and no water and the sandy road

The road winding above among the mountains
Which are mountains of rock without water
If there were water we should stop and drink
Amongst the rock one cannot stop or think   335
Sweat is dry and feet are in the sand
If there were only water amongst the rock
Dead mountain mouth of carious teeth that cannot spit
Here one can neither stand nor lie nor sit
There is not even silence in the mountains   340
But dry sterile thunder without rain
There is not even solitude in the mountains
But red sullen faces sneer and snarl
From doors of mudcracked houses
                              If there were water   345
   And no rock
   If there were rock
   And also water
   And water
   A spring   350
   A pool among the rock
   If there were the sound of water only
   Not the cicada
   And dry grass singing
   But sound of water over a rock   355
    Where the hermit-thrush sings in the pine trees
    Drip drop drip drop drop drop drop
    But there is no water

   Who is the third who walks always beside you?
When I count, there are only you and I together   360
But when I look ahead up the white road
There is always another one walking beside you
Gliding wrapt in a brown mantle, hooded
I do not know whether a man or a woman
—But who is that on the other side of you?   365

   What is that sound high in the air
Murmur of maternal lamentation
Who are those hooded hordes swarming
Over endless plains, stumbling in cracked earth
Ringed by the flat horizon only   370
What is the city over the mountains
Cracks and reforms and bursts in the violet air
Falling towers
Jerusalem Athens Alexandria
Vienna London   375
Unreal

   A woman drew her long black hair out tight
And fiddled whisper music on those strings
And bats with baby faces in the violet light

Whistled, and beat their wings 380
And crawled head downward down a blackened wall
And upside down in air were towers
Tolling reminiscent bells, that kept the hours
And voices singing out of empty cisterns and exhausted wells.

   In this decayed hole among the mountains 385
In the faint moonlight, the grass is singing
Over the tumbled graves, about the chapel
There is the empty chapel, only the wind's home.
It has no windows, and the door swings,
Dry bones can harm no one. 390
Only a cock stood on the rooftree
Co co rico co co rico
In a flash of lightning. Then a damp gust
Bringing rain

   Ganga was sunken, and the limp leaves 395
Waited for rain, while the black clouds
Gathered far distant, over Himavant.
The jungle crouched, humped in silence.
Then spoke the thunder
Da 400
Datta: what have we given?
My friend, blood shaking my heart
The awful daring of a moment's surrender
Which an age of prudence can never retract
By this, and this only, we have existed 405
Which is not to be found in our obituaries
Or in memories draped by the beneficient spider
Or under seals broken by the lean solicitor
In our empty rooms
Da 410
Dayadhvam: I have heard the key
Turn in the door once and turn once only
We think of the key, each in his prison
Thinking of the key, each confirms a prison
Only at nightfall, aethereal rumours 415
Revive for a moment a broken Coriolanus
Da
Damyata: The boat responded
Gaily, to the hand expert with sail and oar
The sea was calm, your heart would have responded 420
Gaily, when invited, beating obedient
To controlling hands

          I sat upon the shore
Fishing, with the arid plain behind me
Shall I at least set my hands in order? 425
London Bridge is falling down falling down falling down
Poi s'ascose nel foco che gli affina

Quando fiam uti chelidon—O swallow swallow
Le Prince d'Aquitaine à la tour abolie
These fragments I have shored against my ruins   430
Why then Ile fit you. Hieronymo's mad againe.
Datta. Dayadhvam. Damyata.
       Shantih   shantih   shantih

NOTES ON "THE WASTE LAND"

Not only the title, but the plan and a good deal of the incidental symbolism of the poem were suggested by Miss Jessie L. Weston's book on the Grail legend: *From Ritual to Romance* (Cambridge). Indeed, so deeply am I indebted, Miss Weston's book will elucidate the difficulties of the poem much better than my notes can do; and I recommend it (apart from the great interest of the book itself) to any who think such elucidation of the poem worth the trouble. To another work of anthropology I am indebted in general, one which has influenced our generation profoundly; I mean *The Golden Bough;* I have used especially the two volumes *Adonis, Attis, Osiris.* Anyone who is acquainted with these works will immediately recognise in the poem certain references to vegetation ceremonies.

I. The Burial of the Dead
Line 20. Cf. Ezekiel II, i.
23. Cf. Ecclesiastes XII, v.
31. V. Tristan und Isolde, I, verses 5–8.
42. Id. III, verse 24.
46. I am not familiar with the exact constitution of the Tarot pack of cards, from which I have obviously departed to suit my own convenience. The Hanged Man, a member of the traditional pack, fits my purpose in two ways: because he is associated in my mind with the Hanged God of Frazer, and because I associate him with the hooded figure in the passage of the disciples to Emmaus in Part V. The Phoenician Sailor and the Merchant appear later; also the "crowds of people," and Death by Water is executed in Part IV. The Man with Three Staves (an authentic member of the Tarot pack) I associate, quite arbitrarily, with the Fisher King himself.
60. Cf. Baudelaire:
    "Fourmillante cité, cité pleine de rêves,
    "Où le spectre en plein jour raccroche le passant."
63. Cf. Inferno III, 55–57:
             "si lunga tratta
    di gente, ch'io non avrei mai creduto
    che morte tanta n'avesse disfatta."
64. Cf. Inferno IV, 25–27:
    "Quivi, secondo che per ascoltare,
    "non avea pianto, ma' che di sospiri,
    "che l'aura eterna facevan tremare."
68. A phenomenon which I have often noticed.
74. Cf. the Dirge in Webster's *White Devil.*
76. V. Baudelaire, Preface to *Fleurs du Mal.*

II. A Game of Chess
77. Cf. *Antony and Cleopatra,* II, ii, l. 190.
92. Laquearia. V. *Aeneid,* I, 726:
    dependent lychni laquearibus aureis incensi, et noctem flammis funalia vincunt.
98. Sylvan scene. V. Milton, *Paradise Lost,* IV, 140.
99. V. Ovid, *Metamorphoses,* VI, Philomela.
100. Cf. Part III, l. 204.

115. Cf. Part III, l. 195.
118. Cf. Webster: "Is the wind in that door still?"
126. Cf. Part I, l. 37, 48.
138. Cf. the game of chess in Middleton's *Women beware Women.*

III. The Fire Sermon

176. V. Spenser, *Prothalamion.*
192. Cf. *The Tempest,* I, ii.
196. Cf. Marvell, *To His Coy Mistress.*
197. Cf. Day, *Parliament of Bees:*
> "When of the sudden, listening, you shall hear,
> "A noise of horns and hunting, which shall bring
> "Actaeon to Diana in the spring,
> "Where all shall see her naked skin . . ."

199. I do not know the origin of the ballad from which these lines are taken: it was reported to me from Sydney, Australia.

202. V. Verlaine, *Parsifal.*

210. The currants were quoted at a price "carriage and insurance free to London"; and the Bill of Lading etc. were to be handed to the buyer upon payment of the sight draft.

218. Tiresias, although a mere spectator and not indeed a "character," is yet the most important personage in the poem, uniting all the rest. Just as the one-eyed merchant, seller of currants, melts into the Phoenician Sailor, and the latter is not wholly distinct from Ferdinand Prince of Naples, so all the women are one woman, and the two sexes meet in Tiresias. What Tiresias *sees,* in fact, is the substance of the poem. The whole passage from Ovid is of great anthropological interest:

> ". . . Cum Iunone iocos et maior vestra profecto est
> Quam, quae contingit maribus," dixisse, "voluptas."
> Illa negat; placuit quae sit sententia docti
> Quaerere Tiresiae: venus huic erat utraque nota.
> Nam duo magnorum viridi coeuntia silva
> Corpora serpentum baculi violaverat ictu
> Deque viro factus, mirabile, femina septem
> Egerat autumnos; octavo rursus eosdem
> Vidit et "est vestrae si tanta potentia plagae,"
> Dixit "ut auctoris sortem in contraria mutet,
> Nunc quoque vos feriam!" percussis anguibus isdem
> Forma prior rediit genetivaque venit imago.
> Arbiter hic igitur sumptus de lite iocosa
> Dicta Iovis firmat; gravius Saturnia iusto
> Nec pro materia fertur doluisse suique
> Iudicis aeterna damnavit lumina nocte,
> At pater omnipotens (neque enim licet inrita cuiquam
> Facta dei fecisse deo) pro lumine adempto
> Scire futura dedit poenamque levavit honore.

221. This may not appear as exact as Sappho's lines, but I had in mind the "longshore" or "dory" fisherman, who returns at nightfall.

253. V. Goldsmith, the song in *The Vicar of Wakefield.*

257. V. *The Tempest,* as above.

264. The interior of St. Magnus Martyr is to my mind one of the finest among Wren's interiors. See *The Proposed Demolition of Nineteen City Churches:* (P. S. King & Son, Ltd.).

266. The Song of the (three) Thames-daughters begins here. From line 292 to 306 inclusive they speak in turn. V. *Götterdämmerung,* III, i: the Rhine-daughters.

279. V. Froude, *Elizabeth,* Vol. I, ch. iv, letter of De Quadra to Philip of Spain:
"In the afternoon we were in a barge, watching the games on the river. (The queen) was alone with Lord Robert and myself on the poop, when they began to talk nonsense, and

went so far that Lord Robert at last said, as I was on the spot there was no reason why they should not be married if the queen pleased."

293. Cf. *Purgatorio*, V, 133:
"Ricorditi di me, che son la Pia;
"Siena mi fe', disfecemi Maremma."

307. V. St. Augustine's *Confessions:* "to Carthage then I came, where a cauldron of unholy loves sang all about mine ears."

308. The complete text of the Buddha's Fire Sermon (which corresponds in importance to the Sermon on the Mount) from which these words are taken, will be found translated in the late Henry Clarke Warren's *Buddhism in Translation* (Harvard Oriental Series). Mr. Warren was one of the great pioneers of Buddhist studies in the Occident.

309. From St. Augustine's *Confessions* again. The collocation of these two representatives of eastern and western asceticism, as the culmination of this part of the poem, is not an accident.

V. What the Thunder Said

In the first part of Part V three themes are employed: the journey to Emmaus, the approach to the Chapel Perilous (see Miss Weston's book) and the present decay of eastern Europe.

357. This is *Turdus aonalaschkae pallasii*, the hermit-thrush which I have heard in Quebec Province. Chapman says (*Handbook of Birds of Eastern North America*) "it is most at home in secluded woodland and thickety retreats. . . . Its notes are not remarkable for variety or volume, but in purity and sweetness of tone and exquisite modulation they are unequalled." Its "water-dripping song" is justly celebrated.

360. The following lines were stimulated by the account of one of the Antarctic expeditions (I forget which, but I think one of Shackleton's): it was related that the party of explorers, at the extremity of their strength, had the constant delusion that there was *one more member* than could actually be counted.

367–77. Cf. Hermann Hesse, *Blick ins Chaos:* "Schon ist halb Europa, schon ist zumindest der halbe Osten Europas auf dem Wege zum Chaos, fährt betrunken im heiligem Wahn am Abgrund entlang und singt dazu, singt betrunken und hymnisch wie Dmitri Karamasoff sang. Ueber diese Lieder lacht der Bürger beleidigt, der Heilige und Seher hört sie mit Tränen."

402. "Datta, dayadhvam, damyata" (Give, sympathise, control). The fable of the meaning of the Thunder is found in the *Brihadaranyaka—Upanishad*, 5, 1. A translation is found in Deussen's *Sechzig Upanishads des Veda*, p. 489.

408. Cf. Webster, *The White Devil*, V, vi:
". . . they'll remarry
Ere the worm pierce your winding-sheet, ere the spider
Make a thin curtain for your epitaphs."

412. Cf. *Inferno*, XXXIII, 46:
"ed io sentii chiavar l'uscio di sotto
all'orribile torre."
Also F. H. Bradley, *Appearance and Reality*, p. 346.

"My external sensations are no less private to myself than are my thoughts or my feelings. In either case my experience falls within my own circle, a circle closed on the outside; and, with all its elements alike, every sphere is opaque to the others which surround it. . . . In brief, regarded as an existence which appears in a soul, the whole world for each is peculiar and private to that soul."

425. V. Weston: *From Ritual to Romance;* chapter on the Fisher King.

428. V. *Purgatorio*, XXVI, 148.
" 'Ara vos prec per aquella valor
'que vos guida al som de l'escalina,
'sovegna vos a temps de ma dolor.'
Poi s'ascose nel foco che gli affina."

429. V. *Pervigilium Veneris*. Cf. Philomela in Parts II and III.

430. V. Gerard de Nerval, Sonnet *El Desdichado.*
432. V. Kyd's *Spanish Tragedy.*
434. Shantih. Repeated as here, a formal ending to an Upanishad. "The Peace which passeth understanding" is our equivalent to this word.

E. E. Cummings   (1894–1962)

A MAN WHO HAD FALLEN AMONG THIEVES

a man who had fallen among thieves
lay by the roadside on his back
dressed in fifteenthrate ideas
wearing a round jeer for a hat

fate per a somewhat more than less   5
emancipated evening
had in return for consciousness
endowed him with a changeless grin

whereon a dozen staunch and leal
citizens did graze at pause   10
then fired by hypercivic zeal
sought newer pastures or because

swaddled with a frozen brook
of pinkest vomit out of eyes
which noticed nobody he looked   15
as if he did not care to rise

one hand did nothing on the vest
its wideflung friend clenched weakly dirt
while the mute trouserfly confessed
a button solemnly inert.   20

Brushing from whom the stiffened puke
i put him all into my arms
and staggered banged with terror through
a million billion trillion stars

BUFFALO BILL'S

Buffalo Bill's
defunct
        who used to
        ride a watersmooth-silver
                          stallion   5

and break onetwothreefourfive pigeonsjustlikethat
                                        Jesus

he was a handsome man
                    and what i want to know is
how do you like your blueeyed boy   10
Mister Death

ANYONE LIVED IN A PRETTY HOW TOWN

anyone lived in a pretty how town
(with up so floating many bells down)
spring summer autumn winter
he sang his didn't he danced his did.

Women and men (both little and small)   5
cared for anyone not at all
they sowed their isn't they reaped their same
sun moon stars rain

children guessed (but only a few
and down they forgot as up they grew   10
autumn winter spring summer)
that noone loved him more by more

when by now and tree by leaf
she laughed his joy she cried his grief
bird by snow and stir by still   15
anyone's any was all to her

someones married their everyones
laughed their cryings and did their dance
(sleep wake hope and then) they
said their nevers they slept their dream   20

stars rain sun moon
(and only the snow can begin to explain
how children are apt to forget to remember
with up so floating many bells down)

one day anyone died i guess   25
(and noone stooped to kiss his face)
busy folk buried them side by side
little by little and was by was

all by all and deep by deep
and more by more they dream their sleep   30
noone and anyone earth by april
wish by spirit and if by yes.

Women and men (both dong and ding)
summer autumn winter spring
reaped their sowing and went their came   35
sun moon stars rain

Hart Crane   (1899–1932)

from *The Bridge*

TO BROOKLYN BRIDGE

How many dawns, chill from his rippling rest
The seagull's wings shall dip and pivot him,
Shedding white rings of tumult, building high
Over the chained bay waters Liberty—

Then, with inviolate curve, forsake our eyes   5
As apparitional as sails that cross
Some page of figures to be filed away;
—Till elevators drop us from our day . . .

I think of cinemas, panoramic sleights
With multitudes bent toward some flashing scene   10
Never disclosed, but hastened to again,
Foretold to other eyes on the same screen;

And Thee, across the harbor, silver-paced
As though the sun took step of thee, yet left
Some motion ever unspent in thy stride,—   15
Implicitly thy freedom staying thee!

Out of some subway scuttle, cell or loft
A bedlamite speeds to thy parapets,
Tilting there momently, shrill shirt ballooning,
A jest falls from the speechless caravan.   20

Down Wall, from girder into street noon leaks,
A rip-tooth of the sky's acetylene;
All afternoon the cloud-flown derricks turn . . .
Thy cables breathe the North Atlantic still.

And obscure as that heaven of the Jews,   25
Thy guerdon . . . Accolade thou dost bestow
Of anonymity time cannot raise:
Vibrant reprieve and pardon thou dost show.

O harp and altar, of the fury fused,
(How could mere toil align thy choiring strings!)   30
Terrific threshold of the prophet's pledge,
Prayer of pariah, and the lover's cry,—

Again the traffic lights that skim thy swift
Unfractioned idiom, immaculate sigh of stars,
Beading thy path—condense eternity: 35
And we have seen night lifted in thine arms.

Under thy shadow by the piers I waited;
Only in darkness is thy shadow clear.
The City's fiery parcels all undone,
Already snow submerges an iron year . . .   40

O Sleepless as the river under thee,
Vaulting the sea, the prairies' dreaming sod,
Unto us lowliest sometime sweep, descend
And of the curveship lend a myth to God.

VAN WINKLE

Macadam, gun-grey as the tunny's belt,
Leaps from Far Rockaway to Golden Gate:
Listen! the miles a hurdy-gurdy grinds—
Down gold arpeggios mile on mile unwinds.

*Streets spread
past store and
factory—sped
by sunlight
and her   5
smile . . .*

Times earlier, when you hurried off to school,
—It is the same hour though a later day—
You walked with Pizarro in a copybook,
And Cortes rode up, reining tautly in—
Firmly as coffee grips the taste,—and away!

There was Priscilla's cheek close in the wind,   10
And Captain Smith, all beard and certainty,
And Rip Van Winkle bowing by the way,—
"Is this Sleepy Hollow, friend—?" And he—

*Like Memory,
she is time's
truant, shall
take you by   15
the hand . . .*

*And Rip forgot the office hours,
            and he forgot the pay;
Van Winkle sweeps a tenement
            way down on Avenue A,—*

The grind-organ says . . . Remember, remember
The cinder pile at the end of the backyard
Where we stoned the family of young   20
Garter snakes under . . . And the monoplanes
We launched—with paper wings and twisted
Rubber bands . . . Recall—recall

                        the rapid tongues
That flittered from under the ash heap day   25
After day whenever your stick discovered
Some sunning inch of unsuspecting fibre—
It flashed back at your thrust, as clean as fire.

And Rip was slowly made aware
that he, Van Winkle, was not here   30
nor there. He woke and swore he'd seen Broadway
a Catskill daisy chain in May—

So memory, that strikes a rhyme out of a box,
Or splits a random smell of flowers through glass—
Is it the whip stripped from the lilac tree   35
One day in spring my father took to me,
Or is it the Sabbatical, unconscious smile
My mother almost brought me once from church
And once only, as I recall—?

It flickered through the snow screen, blindly   40
It forsook her at the doorway, it was gone
Before I had left the window. It
Did not return with the kiss in the hall.

Macadam, gun-grey as the tunny's belt,
Leaps from Far Rockaway to Golden Gate. . . .   45
Keep hold of that nickel for car-change, Rip,—
Have you got your *"Times"*—?
And hurry along, Van Winkle—it's getting late!

THE RIVER

Stick your patent name on a signboard
brother—all over—going west—young man
Tintex—Japalac—Certain-teed Overalls ads   *. . . and past*
and lands sakes! under the new playbill ripped   *the din and*
in the guaranteed corner—see Bert Williams what?   *slogans of*   5
Minstrels when you steal a chicken just   *the year—*
save me the wing for if it isn't
Erie it ain't for miles around a
Mazda—and the telegraphic night coming on Thomas

a Ediford—and whistling down the tracks   10
a headlight rushing with the sound—can you
imagine—while an EXpress makes time like
SCIENCE—COMMERCE and the HOLYGHOST
RADIO ROARS IN EVERY HOME WE HAVE THE NORTHPOLE
WALLSTREET AND VIRGINBIRTH WITHOUT STONES OR   15
WIRES OR EVEN RUNning brooks connecting ears
and no more sermons windows flashing roar
breathtaking—as you like it . . . eh?
                    So the 20th Century—so
whizzed the Limited—roared by and left   20
three men, still hungry on the tracks, ploddingly

watching the tail lights wizen and converge, slipping gimleted and neatly out of sight.

•   •   •

The last bear, shot drinking in the Dakotas
Loped under wires that span the mountain stream.   25
Keen instruments, strung to a vast precision   *to those*
Bind town to town and dream to tacking dream.   *whose addresses*
But some men take their liquor slow—and count   *are never near*
—Though they'll confess no rosary nor clue—
The river's minute by the far brook's year.   30
Under a world of whistles, wires and steam
Caboose-like they go ruminating through
Ohio, Indiana—blind baggage—
To Cheyenne tagging . . . Maybe Kalamazoo.

Time's rendings, time's blendings they construe   35
As final reckonings of fire and snow;
Strange bird-wit, like the elemental gist
Of unwalled winds they offer, singing low
My Old Kentucky Home and *Casey Jones,*
Some Sunny Day. I heard a road-gang chanting so.   40
And afterwards, who had a colt's eyes—one said,
"Jesus! Oh I remember watermelon days!" And sped
High in a cloud of merriment, recalled
"—And when my Aunt Sally Simpson smiled," he drawled—
"It was almost Louisiana, long ago."   45
"There's no place like Booneville though, Buddy,"
One said, excising a last burr from his vest,
"—For early trouting." Then peering in the can,
"—But I kept on the tracks." Possessed, resigned,
He trod the fire down pensively and grinned,   50
Spreading dry shingles of a beard. . . .

Behind

My father's cannery works I used to see
Rail-squatters ranged in nomad raillery,
The ancient men—wifeless or runaway   55
Hobo-trekkers that forever search
An empire wilderness of freight and rails.
Each seemed a child, like me, on a loose perch,
Holding to childhood like some termless play.
John, Jake or Charley, hopping the slow freight   60
—Memphis to Tallahassee—riding the rods,
Blind fists of nothing, humpty-dumpty clods.

Yet they touch something like a key perhaps.
From pole to pole across the hills, the states
—They know a body under the wide rain;   *but who have*   65
Youngsters with eyes like fjords, old reprobates   *touched her,*
With racetrack jargon, dotting immensity   *knowing her*
They lurk across her, knowing her yonder breast   *without name*

Snow-silvered, sumac-stained or smoky blue—
Is past the valley-sleepers, south or west.   70
—As I have trod the rumorous midnights, too,

And past the circuit of the lamp's thin flame
(O Nights that brought me to her body bare!)
Have dreamed beyond the print that bound her name.
Trains sounding the long blizzards out—I heard   75
Wail into distances I knew were hers.
Papooses crying on the wind's long mane
Screamed redskin dynasties that fled the brain,
—Dead echoes! But I knew her body there,
Time like a serpent down her shoulder, dark,   80
And space, an eaglet's wing, laid on her hair.

Under the Ozarks, domed by Iron Mountain,
The old gods of the rain lie wrapped in pools
Where eyeless fish curvet a sunken fountain   *nor the*
And re-descend with corn from querulous crows.   *myths of her*   85
Such pilferings make up their timeless eatage,   *fathers . . .*
Propitiate them for their timber torn
By iron, iron—always the iron dealt cleavage!
They doze now, below axe and powder horn.

And Pullman breakfasters glide glistening steel   90
From tunnel into field—iron strides the dew—
Straddles the hill, a dance of wheel on wheel.
You have a half-hour's wait at Siskiyou,
Or stay the night and take the next train through.
Southward, near Cairo passing, you can see   95
The Ohio merging,—borne down Tennessee;
And if it's summer and the sun's in dusk
Maybe the breeze will lift the River's musk
—As though the waters breathed that you might know
Memphis Johnny, Steamboat Bill, Missouri Joe.   100
Oh, lean from the window, if the train slows down,
As though you touched hands with some ancient clown,
—A little while gaze absently below
And hum *Deep River* with them while they go.

Yes, turn again and sniff once more—look see,   105
O Sheriff, Brakeman and Authority—
Hitch up your pants and crunch another quid,
For you, too, feed the River timelessly.
And few evade full measure of their fate;
Always they smile out eerily what they seem.   110
I could believe he joked at heaven's gate—
Dan Midland—jolted from the cold brake-beam.

Down, down—born pioneers in time's despite,
Grimed tributaries to an ancient flow—
They win no frontier by their wayward plight,   115
But drift in stillness, as from Jordan's brow.

You will not hear it as the sea; even stone
Is not more hushed by gravity . . . But slow,
As loth to take more tribute—sliding prone
Like one whose eyes were buried long ago   120

The River, spreading, flows—and spends your dream.
What are you, lost within this tideless spell?
You are your father's father, and the stream—
A liquid theme that floating niggers swell.

Damp tonnage and alluvial march of days—   125
Nights turbid, vascular with silted shale
And roots surrendered down of moraine clays:
The Mississippi drinks the farthest dale.

O quarrying passion, undertowed sunlight!
The basalt surface drags a jungle grace   130
Ochreous and lynx-barred in lengthening might;
Patience! and you shall reach the biding place!

Over De Soto's bones the freighted floors
Throb past the City storied of three thrones.
Down two more turns the Mississippi pours   135
(Anon tall ironsides up from salt lagoons)

And flows within itself, heaps itself free.
All fades but one thin skyline 'round . . . Ahead
No embrace opens but the stinging sea;
The River lifts itself from its long bed,   140

Poised wholly on its dream, a mustard glow
Tortured with history, its one will—flow!
—The Passion spreads in wide tongues, choked and slow,
Meeting the Gulf, hosannas silently below.

THE DANCE

The swift red flesh, a winter king—
Who squired the glacier woman down the sky?
She ran the neighing canyons all the spring;
She spouted arms; she rose with maize—to die.

And in the autumn drouth, whose burnished hands
With mineral wariness found out the stone
Where prayers, forgotten, streamed the mesa sands?
He holds the twilight's dim, perpetual throne.

Mythical brows we saw retiring—loth,
Disturbed and destined, into denser green.
Greeting they sped us, on the arrow's oath:
Now lie incorrigibly what years between . . .

*Then you shall
see her truly
—your blood
remembering
its first
invasion of her   5
secrecy, its
first encounters
with her kin,
her chieftain
lover . . . his
shade that
haunts the   10
lakes and hills*

There was a bed of leaves, and broken play;
There was a veil upon you, Pocahontas, bride—
O Princess whose brown lap was virgin May;   15
And bridal flanks and eyes hid tawny pride.

I left the village for dogwood. By the canoe
Tugging below the mill-race, I could see
Your hair's keen crescent running, and the blue
First moth of evening take wing stealthily.   20

What laughing chains the water wove and threw!
I learned to catch the trout's moon whisper; I
Drifted how many hours I never knew,
But, watching, saw that fleet young crescent die,—

And one star, swinging, take its place, alone,   25
Cupped in the larches of the mountain pass—
Until, immortally, it bled into the dawn.
I left my sleek boat nibbling margin grass . . .

I took the portage climb, then chose
A further valley-shed; I could not stop.   30
Feet nozzled wat'ry webs of upper flows;
One white veil gusted from the very top.

O Appalachian Spring! I gained the ledge;
Steep, inaccessible smile that eastward bends
And northward reaches in that violet wedge   35
Of Adirondacks!—wisped of azure wands,

Over how many bluffs, tarns, streams I sped!
—And knew myself within some boding shade:—
Grey tepees tufting the blue knolls ahead,
Smoke swirling through the yellow chestnut glade . . .   40

A distant cloud, a thunder-bud—it grew,
That blanket of the skies: the padded foot
Within,—I heard it; 'til its rhythm drew,
—Siphoned the black pool from the heart's hot root!

A cyclone threshes in the turbine crest,   45
Swooping in eagle feathers down your back;
Know, Maquokeeta, greeting; know death's best;
—Fall, Sachem, strictly as the tamarack!

A birch kneels. All her whistling fingers fly.
The oak grove circles in a crash of leaves;   50
The long moan of a dance is in the sky.
Dance, Maquokeeta: Pocahontas grieves . . .

And every tendon scurries toward the twangs
Of lightning deltaed down your saber hair.
Now snaps the flint in every tooth; red fangs
And splay tongues thinly busy the blue air . .   55

Dance, Maquokeeta! snake that lives before,
That casts his pelt, and lives beyond! Sprout, horn!
Spark, tooth! Medicine-man, relent, restore—
Lie to us,—dance us back the tribal morn!

Spears and assemblies: black drums thrusting on—   60
O yelling battlements,—I, too, was liege
To rainbows currying each pulsant bone:
Surpassed the circumstance, danced out the siege!

And buzzard-circleted, screamed from the stake;
I could not pick the arrows from my side.   65
Wrapped in that fire, I saw more escorts wake—
Flickering, sprint up the hill groins like a tide.

I heard the hush of lava wrestling your arms,
And stag teeth foam about the raven throat;
Flame cataracts of heaven in seething swarms   70
Fed down your anklets to the sunset's moat.

O, like the lizard in the furious noon,
That drops his legs and colors in the sun,
—And laughs, pure serpent, Time itself, and moon
Of his own fate, I saw thy change begun!   75

And saw thee dive to kiss that destiny
Like one white meteor, sacrosanct and blent
At last with all that's consummate and free
There, where the first and last gods keep thy tent.

       •   •   •

Thewed of the levin, thunder-shod and lean,   80
Lo, through what infinite seasons dost thou gaze—
Across what bivouacs of thine angered slain,
And see'st thy bride immortal in the maize!

Totem and fire-gall, slumbering pyramid—
Though other calendars now stack the sky,   85
Thy freedom is her largesse, Prince, and hid
On paths thou knewest best to claim her by.

High unto Labrador the sun strikes free
Her speechless dream of snow, and stirred again,
She is the torrent and the singing tree;   90
And she is virgin to the last of men . . .

West, west and south! winds over Cumberland
And winds across the llano grass resume
Her hair's warm sibilance. Her breasts are fanned
O stream by slope and vineyard—into bloom!   95

And when the caribou slant down for salt
Do arrows thirst and leap? Do antlers shine
Alert, star-triggered in the listening vault
Of dusk?—And are her perfect brows to thine?

We danced, O Brave, we danced beyond their farms,   100
In cobalt desert closures made our vows . . .
Now is the strong prayer folded in thine arms,
The serpent with the eagle in the boughs.

W. H. Auden (1907–1973)

Musée des Beaux Arts

About suffering they were never wrong,
The Old Masters: how well they understood
Its human position; how it takes place
While someone else is eating or opening a window or just walking dully along;
How, when the aged are reverently, passionately waiting   5
For the miraculous birth, there always must be
Children who did not specially want it to happen, skating
On a pond at the edge of the wood:

They never forgot
That even the dreadful martyrdom must run its course   10
Anyhow in a corner, some untidy spot
Where the dogs go on with their doggy life and the torturer's horse
Scratches its innocent behind on a tree.

In Brueghel's *Icarus,* for instance: how everything turns away
Quite leisurely from the disaster; the ploughman may   15
Have heard the splash, the forsaken cry,
But for him it was not an important failure; the sun shone
As it had to on the white legs disappearing into the green
Water; and the expensive delicate ship that must have seen
Something amazing, a boy falling out of the sky,   20
Had somewhere to get to and sailed calmly on.

IN MEMORY OF W. B. YEATS

(d. Jan. 1939)

I

He disappeared in the dead of winter:
The brooks were frozen, the airports almost deserted,
And snow disfigured the public statues;
The mercury sank in the mouth of the dying day.
What instruments we have agree   5
The day of his death was a dark cold day.

Far from his illness
The wolves ran on through the evergreen forests,
The peasant river was untempted by the fashionable quays;
By mourning tongues   10
The death of the poet was kept from his poems.

But for him it was his last afternoon as himself,
An afternoon of nurses and rumours;
The provinces of his body revolted,
The squares of his mind were empty,   15
Silence invaded the suburbs,
The current of his feeling failed; he became his admirers.

Now he is scattered among a hundred cities
And wholly given over to unfamiliar affections,
To find his happiness in another kind of wood   20
And be punished under a foreign code of conscience.
The words of a dead man
Are modified in the guts of the living.

But in the importance and noise of to-morrow
When the brokers are roaring like beasts on the floor of the Bourse,   25
And the poor have the sufferings to which they are fairly accustomed,
And each in the cell of himself is almost convinced of his freedom,
A few thousand will think of this day
As one thinks of a day when one did something slightly unusual.
What instruments we have agree   30
The day of his death was a dark cold day.

II

You were silly like us; your gift survived it all:
The parish of rich women, physical decay,
Yourself. Mad Ireland hurt you into poetry.
Now Ireland has her madness and her weather still,   35
For poetry makes nothing happen: it survives
In the valley of its making where executives
Would never want to tamper, flows on south
From ranches of isolation and the busy griefs,
Raw towns that we believe and die in; it survives,   40
A way of happening, a mouth.

III

Earth, receive an honoured guest:
William Yeats is laid to rest.
Let the Irish vessel lie
Emptied of its poetry.   45

In the nightmare of the dark
All the dogs of Europe bark,
And the living nations wait,
Each sequestered in its hate;

Intellectual disgrace   50
Stares from every human face,
And the seas of pity lie
Locked and frozen in each eye.

Follow, poet, follow right
To the bottom of the night,   55
With your unconstraining voice
Still persuade us to rejoice;

With the farming of a verse
Make a vineyard of the curse,
Sing of human unsuccess   60
In a rapture of distress;

In the deserts of the heart
Let the healing fountain start,
In the prison of his days
Teach the free man how to praise.   65

IN MEMORY OF SIGMUND FREUD
(d. Sept. 1939)

When there are so many we shall have to mourn,
when grief has been made so public, and exposed
        to the critique of a whole epoch
        the frailty of our conscience and anguish,

of whom shall we speak? For every day they die   5
among us, those who were doing us some good,
        who knew it was never enough but
        hoped to improve a little by living.

Such was this doctor: still at eighty he wished
to think of our life from whose unruliness   10
        so many plausible young futures
        with threats or flattery ask obedience,

but his wish was denied him: he closed his eyes
upon that last picture, common to us all,
        of problems like relatives gathered   15
        puzzled and jealous about our dying.

For about him till the very end were still
those he had studied, the fauna of the night,
        and shades that still waited to enter
        the bright circle of his recognition   20

turned elsewhere with their disappointment as he
was taken away from his life interest
    to go back to the earth in London,
an important Jew who died in exile.

Only Hate was happy, hoping to augment   25
his practice now, and his dingy clientele
    who think they can be cured by killing
and covering the gardens with ashes.

They are still alive, but in a world he changed
simply by looking back with no false regrets;   30
    all he did was to remember
like the old and be honest like children.

He wasn't clever at all: he merely told
the unhappy Present to recite the Past
    like a poetry lesson till sooner   35
or later it faltered at the line where

long ago the accusations had begun,
and suddenly knew by whom it had been judged,
    how rich life had been and how silly,
and was life-forgiven and more humble,   40

able to approach the Future as a friend
without a wardrobe of excuses, without
    a set mask of rectitude or an
embarrassing over-familiar gesture.

No wonder the ancient cultures of conceit   45
in his technique of unsettlement foresaw
    the fall of princes, the collapse of
their lucrative patterns of frustration:

if he succeeded, why, the Generalised Life
would become impossible, the monolith   50
    of State be broken and prevented
the co-operation of avengers.

Of course they called on God, but he went his way
down among the lost people like Dante, down
    to the stinking fosse where the injured   55
lead the ugly life of the rejected,

and showed us what evil is, not, as we thought,
deeds that must be punished, but our lack of faith,
    our dishonest mood of denial,
the concupiscence of the oppressor.   60

If some traces of the autocratic pose,
the paternal strictness he distrusted, still
    clung to his utterance and features,
  it was a protective coloration

for one who'd lived among enemies so long: 65
if often he was wrong and, at times, absurd,
    to us he is no more a person
  now but a whole climate of opinion

under whom we conduct our different lives:
Like weather he can only hinder or help,   70
    the proud can still be proud but find it
  a little harder, the tyrant tries to

make do with him but doesn't care for him much:
he quietly surrounds all our habits of growth
    and extends, till the tired in even   75
  the remotest miserable duchy

have felt the change in their bones and are cheered,
till the child, unlucky in his little State,
    some hearth where freedom is excluded,
  a hive whose honey is fear and worry,   80

feels calmer now and somehow assured of escape,
while, as they lie in the grass of our neglect,
    so many long-forgotten objects
  revealed by his undiscouraged shining

are returned to us and made precious again;   85
games we had thought we must drop as we grew up,
    little noises we dared not laugh at,
  faces we made when no one was looking.

But he wishes us more than this. To be free
is often to be lonely. He would unite   90
    the unequal moieties fractured
  by our own well-meaning sense of justice,

would restore to the larger the wit and will
the smaller possesses but can only use
    for arid disputes, would give back to   95
  the son the mother's richness of feeling:

but he would have us remembered most of all
to be enthusiastic over the night,
    not only for the sense of wonder
  it alone has to offer, but also   100

because it needs our love. With large sad eyes
its delectable creatures look up and beg
  us dumbly to ask them to follow:
  they are exiles who long for the future

that lies in our power, they too would rejoice   105
if allowed to serve enlightenment like him,
  even to bear our cry of "Judas,"
  as he did and all must bear who serve it.

THE SHIELD OF ACHILLES

  She looked over his shoulder
   For vines and olive trees,
  Marble well-governed cities
   And ships upon untamed seas,
  But there on the shining metal   5
   His hands had put instead
  An artificial wilderness
   And a sky like lead.

A plain without a feature, bare and brown,
 No blade of grass, no sign of neighbourhood,   10
Nothing to eat and nowhere to sit down,
 Yet, congregated on its blankness, stood
 An unintelligible multitude,
A million eyes, a million boots in line,
Without expression, waiting for a sign.   15

Out of the air a voice without a face
 Proved by statistics that some cause was just
In tones as dry and level as the place:
 No one was cheered and nothing was discussed;
 Column by column in a cloud of dust   20
They marched away enduring a belief
Whose logic brought them, somewhere else, to grief.

  She looked over his shoulder
   For ritual pieties,
  White flower-garlanded heifers,   25
   Libation and sacrifice,
  But there on the shining metal
   Where the altar should have been,
  She saw by his flickering forge-light
   Quite another scene.   30

Barbed wire enclosed an arbitrary spot
 Where bored officials lounged (one cracked a joke)
And sentries sweated for the day was hot:
 A crowd of ordinary decent folk

Watched from without and neither moved nor spoke 35
As three pale figures were led forth and bound
To three posts driven upright in the ground.

The mass and majesty of this world, all
   That carries weight and always weighs the same
Lay in the hands of others; they were small 40
   And could not hope for help and no help came:
   What their foes liked to do was done, their shame
Was all the worst could wish; they lost their pride
And died as men before their bodies died.

     She looked over his shoulder 45
       For athletes at their games,
     Men and women in a dance
       Moving their sweet limbs
     Quick, quick, to music,
       But there on the shining shield 50
     His hands had set no dancing-floor
       But a weed-choked field.

A ragged urchin, aimless and alone,
   Loitered about that vacancy, a bird
Flew up to safety from his well-aimed stone: 55
   That girls are raped, that two boys knife a third,
   Were axioms to him, who'd never heard
Of any world where promises were kept,
Or one could weep because another wept.

     The thin-lipped armourer, 60
       Hephaestos hobbled away,
     Thetis of the shining breasts
       Cried out in dismay
     At what the god had wrought
     To please her son, the strong 65
     Iron-hearted man-slaying Achilles
       Who would not live long.

One rational voice is dumb. Over his grave
the household of Impulse mourns one dearly loved:
    sad is Eros, builder of cities,
    and weeping anarchic Aphrodite. 70

Theodore Roethke   (1908–1963)

ORCHIDS

They lean over the path,
Adder-mouthed,
Swaying close to the face,
Coming out, soft and deceptive,
Limp and damp, delicate as a young bird's tongue;   5
Their fluttery fledgling lips
Move slowly,
Drawing in the warm air.

And at night,
The faint moon falling through whitewashed glass,   10
The heat going down
So their musky smell comes even stronger,
Drifting down from their mossy cradles:
So many devouring infants!
Soft luminescent fingers,   15
Lips neither dead nor alive,
Loose ghostly mouths,
Breathing.

UNFOLD! UNFOLD!

1

By snails, by leaps of frog, I came here, spirit.
Tell me, body without skin, does a fish sweat?
I can't crawl back through those veins,
I ache for another choice.
The cliffs! The cliffs! They fling me back.   5
Eternity howls in the last crags,
The field is no longer simple:
It's a soul's crossing time.
The dead speak noise.

2

It's time you stood up and asked   10
                    —Or sat down and did.
A tongue without song
                    —Can still whistle in a jug.

You're blistered all over
          —Who cares? The old owl?   15
When you find the wind
          —Look for the white fire.

   3
What a whelm of proverbs, Mr. Pinch!
Are the entrails clear, immaculate cabbage?
The last time I nearly whispered myself away.   20
I was far back, farther than anybody else.
On the jackpine plains I hunted the bird nobody knows;
Fishing, I caught myself behind the ears.
Alone, in a sleep-daze, I stared at billboards;

I was privy to oily fungus and the algae of standing waters;   25
Honored, on my return, by the ancient fellowship of rotten stems.
I was pure as a worm on a leaf; I cherished the mold's children.
Beetles sweetened my breath.
I slept like an insect.

I met a collector of string, a shepherd of slow forms.   30
My mission became the salvation of minnows.
I stretched like a board, almost a tree.
Even thread had a speech.

Later, I did and I danced in the simple wood.
A mouse taught me how, I was a happy asker.   35
Quite-by-chance brought me many cookies.
I jumped in butter.
Hair had kisses.

   4
Easy the life of the mouth. What a lust for ripeness!
All openings praise us, even oily holes.   40
The bulb unravels. Who's floating? Not me.
The eye perishes in the small vision.
What else has the vine loosened?
I hear a dead tongue halloo.

   5
Sing, sing, you symbols! All simple creatures,   45
All small shapes, willow-shy,
In the obscure haze, sing!

A light song comes from the leaves.
A slow sigh says yes. And light sighs;
A low voice, summer-sad.   50
Is it you, cold father? Father,
For whom the minnows sang?

     A house for wisdom; a field for revelation.
     Speak to the stones, and the stars answer.
     At first the visible obscures: 55
     Go where light is.

This fat can't laugh.
Only my salt has a chance.
I'll seek my own meekness.
What grace I have is enough.   60
The lost have their own pace.
The stalks ask something else.
What the grave says,
The nest denies.

In their harsh thickets   65
The dead thrash.
They help.

Dylan Thomas (1914–1953)

BEFORE I KNOCKED

Before I knocked and flesh let enter,
With liquid hands tapped on the womb,
I who was shapeless as the water
That shaped the Jordan near my home
Was brother to Mnetha's daughter   5
And sister to the fathering worm.

I who was deaf to spring and summer,
Who knew not sun nor moon by name,
Felt thud beneath my flesh's armour,
As yet was in a molten form,   10
The leaden stars, the rainy hammer
Swung by my father from his dome.

I knew the message of the winter,
The darted hail, the childish snow,
And the wind was my sister suitor;   15
Wind in me leaped, the hellborn dew;
My veins flowed with the Eastern weather;
Ungotten I knew night and day.

As yet ungotten, I did suffer;
The rack of dreams my lily bones   20
Did twist into a living cipher.
And flesh was snipped to cross the lines
Of gallow crosses on the liver
And brambles in the wringing brains.

My throat knew thirst before the structure   25
Of skin and vein around the well
Where words and water make a mixture

Unfailing till the blood runs foul;
My heart knew love, my belly hunger;
I smelt the maggot in my stool.   30

And time cast forth my mortal creature
To drift or drown upon the seas
Acquainted with the salt adventure
Of tides that never touch the shores.
I who was rich was made the richer   35
By sipping at the vine of days.

I, born of flesh and ghost, was neither
A ghost nor man, but mortal ghost.
And I was struck down by death's feather.
I was mortal to the last   40
Long breath that carried to my father
The message of his dying Christ

You who bow down at cross and altar,
Remember me and pity Him
Who took my flesh and bone for armour   45
And doublecrossed my mother's womb.

THE FORCE THAT THROUGH THE GREEN FUSE DRIVES THE FLOWER

The force that through the green fuse drives the flower
Drives my green age; that blasts the roots of trees
Is my destroyer.
And I am dumb to tell the crooked rose
My youth is bent by the same wintry fever.   5

The force that drives the water through the rocks
Drives my red blood; that dries the mouthing streams
Turns mine to wax.
And I am dumb to mouth unto my veins
How at the mountain spring the same mouth sucks.   10

The hand that whirls the water in the pool
Stirs the quicksand; that ropes the blowing wind
Hauls my shroud sail.
And I am dumb to tell the hanging man
How of my clay is made the hangman's lime.   15

The lips of time leech to the fountain head;
Love drips and gathers, but the fallen blood
Shall calm her sores.
And I am dumb to tell a weather's wind
How time has ticked a heaven round the stars.   20

And I am dumb to tell the lover's tomb
How at my sheet goes the same crooked worm.

A REFUSAL TO MOURN THE DEATH,
BY FIRE, OF A CHILD IN LONDON

Never until the mankind making
Bird beast and flower
Fathering and all humbling darkness
Tells with silence the last light breaking
And the still hour   5
Is come of the sea tumbling in harness

And I must enter again the round
Zion of the water bead
And the synagogue of the ear of corn
Shall I let pray the shadow of a sound   10
Or sow my salt seed
In the least valley of sackcloth to mourn

The majesty and burning of the child's death.
I shall not murder
The mankind of her going with a grave truth   15
Nor blaspheme down the stations of the breath
With any further
Elegy of innocence and youth.

Deep with the first dead lies London's daughter,
Robed in the long friends,   20
The grains beyond age, the dark veins of her mother,
Secret by the unmourning water
Of the riding Thames.
After the first death, there is no other.

FERN HILL

Now as I was young and easy under the apple boughs
About the lilting house and happy as the grass was green,
        The night above the dingle starry,
            Time let me hail and climb
        Golden in the heydays of his eyes,   5
And honoured among wagons I was prince of the apple towns
And once below a time I lordly had the trees and leaves
            Trail with daisies and barley
        Down the rivers of the windfall light.

And as I was green and carefree, famous among the barns   10
About the happy yard and singing as the farm was home,
    In the sun that is young once only,
        Time let me play and be
     Golden in the mercy of his means,
And green and golden I was huntsman and herdsman, the calves   15
Sang to my horn, the foxes on the hills barked clear and cold,
        And the sabbath rang slowly
    In the pebbles of the holy streams.

All the sun long it was running, it was lovely, the hay
Fields high as the house, the tunes from the chimneys, it was air   20
    And playing, lovely and watery
        And fire green as grass.
    And nightly under the simple stars
As I rode to sleep the owls were bearing the farm away,
All the moon long I heard, blessed among stables, the nightjars   25
    Flying with the ricks, and the horses
      Flashing into the dark.

And then to awake, and the farm, like a wanderer white
With the dew, come back, the cock on his shoulder: it was all
    Shining, it was Adam and maiden,   30
      The sky gathered again
    And the sun grew round that very day.
So it must have been after the birth of the simple light
In the first, spinning place, the spellbound horses walking warm
    Out of the whinnying green stable   35
      On to the fields of praise.

And honoured among foxes and pheasants by the gay house
Under the new made clouds and happy as the heart was long,
    In the sun born over and over,
      I ran my heedless ways,   40
    My wishes raced through the house high hay
And nothing I cared, at my sky blue trades, that time allows
In all his tuneful turning so few and such morning songs
    Before the children green and golden
    Follow him out of grace,   45

Nothing I cared, in the lamb white days, that time would take me
Up to the swallow thronged loft by the shadow of my hand,
    In the moon that is always rising,
      Nor that riding to sleep
    I should hear him fly with the high fields   50
And wake to the farm forever fled from the childless land.
Oh as I was young and easy in the mercy of his means,
      Time held me green and dying
    Though I sang in my chains like the sea.

Robert Lowell (1917-)

SKUNK HOUR

for Elizabeth Bishop

Nautilus Island's hermit
heiress still lives through winter in her Spartan cottage;
her sheep still graze above the sea.
Her son's a bishop. Her farmer
is first selectman in our village;   5
she's in her dotage.

Thirsting for
the hierarchic privacy
of Queen Victoria's century,
she buys up all   10
the eyesores facing her shore,
and lets them fall.

The season's ill—
we've lost our summer millionaire,
who seem to leap from an L. L. Bean   15
catalogue. His nine-knot yawl
was auctioned off to lobstermen.
A red fox stain covers Blue Hill.

And now our fairy
decorator brightens his shop for fall;   20
his fishnet's filled with orange cork,
orange, his cobbler's bench and awl;
there is no money in his work,
he'd rather marry.

One dark night,   25
my Tudor Ford climbed the hill's skull;
I watched for love-cars. Lights turned down,
they lay together, hull to hull,
where the graveyard shelves on the town. . . .
My mind's not right.   30

A car radio bleats,
"Love, O careless Love. . . ." I hear
my ill-spirit sob in each blood cell,

as if my hand were at its throat. . . .
I myself am hell;   35
nobody's here—

only skunks, that search
in the moonlight for a bite to eat.
They march on their soles up Main Street:
white stripes, moonstruck eyes' red fire   40
under the chalk-dry and spar spire
of the Trinitarian Church.

I stand on top
of our back steps and breathe the rich air—
a mother skunk with her column of kittens swills the garbage pail.   45
She jabs her wedge-head in a cup
of sour cream, drops her ostrich tail,
and will not scare.

FOR THE UNION DEAD

"Relinquunt Omnia Servare Rem Publicam."

The old South Boston Aquarium stands
in a Sahara of snow now. Its broken windows are boarded.
The bronze weathervane cod has lost half its scales.
The airy tanks are dry.

Once my nose crawled like a snail on the glass;   5
my hand tingled
to burst the bubbles
drifting from the noses of the cowed, compliant fish.

My hand draws back. I often sigh still
for the dark downward and vegetating kingdom   10
of the fish and reptile. One morning last March,
I pressed against the new barbed and galvanized

fence on the Boston Common. Behind their cage,
yellow dinosaur steamshovels were grunting
as they cropped up tons of mush and grass   15
to gouge their underworld garage.

Parking spaces luxuriate like civic
sandpiles in the heart of Boston.
A girdle of orange, Puritan-pumpkin colored girders
braces the tingling Statehouse,   20

shaking over the excavations, as it faces Colonel Shaw
and his bell-cheeked Negro infantry

on St. Gaudens' shaking Civil War relief,
propped by a plank splint against the garage's earthquake.

Two months after marching through Boston,   25
half the regiment was dead;
at the dedication,
William James could almost hear the bronze Negroes breathe.

Their monument sticks like a fishbone
in the city's throat.   30
Its Colonel is as lean
as a compass-needle.

He has an angry wrenlike vigilance,
a greyhound's gentle tautness;
he seems to wince at pleasure,   35
and suffocate for privacy.

He is out of bounds now. He rejoices in man's lovely,
peculiar power to choose life and die—
when he leads his black soldiers to death,
he cannot bend his back.   40

On a thousand small town New England greens,
the old white churches hold their air
of sparse, sincere rebellion; frayed flags
quilt the graveyards of the Grand Army of the Republic.

The stone statues of the abstract Union Soldier   45
grow slimmer and younger each year—
wasp-waisted, they doze over muskets
and muse through their sideburns ...

Shaw's father wanted no monument
except the ditch,   50
where his son's body was thrown
and lost with his "niggers."

The ditch is nearer.
There are no statues for the last war here;
on Boylston Street, a commercial photograph   55
shows Hiroshima boiling

over a Mosler Safe, the "Rock of Ages"
that survived the blast. Space is nearer.
When I crouch to my television set,
the drained faces of Negro school-children rise like balloons.   60

Colonel Shaw
is riding on his bubble,
he waits
for the blessèd break.

The Aquarium is gone. Everywhere,   65
giant finned cars nose forward like fish;
a savage servility
slides by on grease.

Lawrence Ferlinghetti (1919–)

from *A Coney Island of the Mind*

THE POET'S EYE OBSCENELY SEEING

The poet's eye obscenely seeing
sees the surface of the round world
        with its drunk rooftoops
        and wooden oiseaux on clotheslines
        and its clay males and females   5
        with hot legs and rosebud breasts
        in rollaway beds
and its trees full of mysteries
and its Sunday parks and speechless statues
and its America   10
        with its ghost towns and empty Ellis Islands
and its surrealist landscape of
              mindless prairies
              supermarket suburbs
              steamheated cemeteries   15
              cinerama holy days
              and protesting cathedrals
a kissproof world of plastic toiletseats tampax and taxis
        drugged store cowboys and las vegas virgins
        disowned indians and cinemad matrons   20
        unroman senators and conscientious non-objectors
and all the other fatal shorn-up fragments
of the immigrant's dream come too true
        and mislaid
           among the sunbathers   25

THEY WERE PUTTING UP THE STATUE

      They were putting up the statue
        of Saint Francis
     in front of the church
       of Saint Francis
         in the city of San Francisco   5

in a little side street
                    just off the Avenue
                                        where no birds sang
        and the sun was coming up on time
                                        in its usual fashion   10
                and just beginning to shine
                                on the statue of Saint Francis
                where no birds sang

And a lot of old Italians
                            were standing all around   15
            in the little side street
                            just off the Avenue
        watching the wily workers
                        who were hoisting up the statue
with a chain and a crane   20
                    and other implements
And a lot of young reporters
                        in button-down clothes
    were taking down the words
                        of one young priest   25
    who was propping up the statue
                            with all his arguments

        And all the while
                    while no birds sang
                                any Saint Francis Passion   30
and while the lookers kept looking
                        up at Saint Francis
        with his arms outstretched
                            to the birds which weren't there
    a very tall and very purely naked   35
                            young virgin
        with very long and very straight
                        straw hair
        and wearing only a very small
                            bird's nest   40
            in a very existential place
                        kept passing thru the crowd
                                        all the while
                and up and down the steps
                            in front of Saint Francis   45
        her eyes downcast all the while
                            and singing to herself

DON'T LET THAT HORSE
EAT THAT VIOLIN

Don't let that horse
    eat that violin

 cried Chagall's mother

      But he
   kept right on   5
     painting

And became famous

And kept on painting
    The Horse With Violin In Mouth

And when he finally finished it   10
he jumped up upon the horse
      and rode away
    waving the violin

And then with a low bow gave it
to the first naked nude he ran across   15

And there were no strings
     attached

READING YEATS I DO NOT
THINK OF IRELAND

    Reading Yeats I do not think
         of Ireland
  but of midsummer New York
       and of myself back then
   reading that copy I found   5
      on the Thirdavenue El

   the El
     with its flyhung fans
  and its signs reading
     SPITTING IS FORBIDDEN   10

   the El
     careening thru its thirdstory world
  with its thirdstory people
      in their thirdstory doors
  looking as if they had never heard   15
      of the ground

                an old dame
                        watering her plant
        or a joker in a straw
                        putting a stickpin in his peppermint tie   20
and looking just like he had nowhere to go
                                but coneyisland

        or an undershirted guy
                        rocking in his rocker
watching the El pass by   25
                as if he expected it to be different
        each time

        Reading Yeats I do not think
                                of Arcady
    and of its woods which Yeats thought dead   30
                                I think instead
        of all the gone faces
                getting off at midtown places
        with their hats and their jobs
                and of that lost book I had   35
                        with its blue cover and its white inside
        where a pencilhand had written
                        HORSEMAN, PASS BY!

Allen Ginsberg (1926-)

SUNFLOWER SUTRA

I walked on the banks of the tincan banana dock and sat down under the huge
    shade of a Southern Pacific locomotive to look at the sunset over the box
    house hills and cry.
Jack Kerouac sat beside me on a busted rusty iron pole, companion, we
    thought the same thoughts of the soul, bleak and blue and sad-eyed, sur-   5
    rounded by the gnarled steel roots of trees of machinery.
The oily water on the river mirrored by the red sky, sun sank on top of final
    Frisco peaks, no fish in that stream, no hermit in those mounts, just our-
    selves rheumy-eyed and hungover like old bums on the riverbank, tired
    and wily.   10
Look at the Sunflower, he said, there was a dead gray shadow against the sky,
    big as a man, sitting dry on top of a pile of ancient sawdust —
— I rushed up enchanted — it was my first sunflower, memories of Blake —
    my visions — Harlem
and Hells of the Eastern rivers, bridges clanking, Joes Greasy Sandwiches, dead   15
    baby carriages, black treadless tires forgotten and unretreaded, the poem
    of the riverbank, condoms & pots, steel knives, nothing stainless, only the
    dank muck and the razor sharp artifacts passing into the past —

and the gray Sunflower poised against the sunset, crackly bleak and dusty with
    the smut and smog and smoke of olden locomotives in its eye —   20
corolla of bleary spikes pushed down and broken like a battered crown, seeds
    fallen out of its face, soon-to-be-toothless mouth of sunny air, sunrays
    obliterated on its hairy head like a dried wire spiderweb,
leaves stuck out like arms out of the stem, gestures from the sawdust root,
    broke pieces of plaster fallen out of the black twigs, a dead fly in its ear,   25
Unholy battered old thing you were, my sunflower O my soul, I loved you then!
The grime was no man's grime but death and human locomotives,
all that dress of dust, that veil of darkened railroad skin, that smog of cheek,
    that eyelid of black mis'ry, that sooty hand or phallus or protuberance of
    artificial worse-than-dirt — industrial — modern — all that civilization   30
    spotting your crazy golden crown —
and those blear thoughts of death and dusty loveless eyes and ends and
    withered roots below, in the home-pile of sand and sawdust, rubber dollar
    bills, skin of machinery, the guts and innards of the weeping coughing car,
    the empty lonely tincans with their rusty tongues alack, what more could   35
    I name, the smoked ashes of some cock cigar, the cunts of wheelbarrows
    and the milky breasts of cars, wornout asses out of chairs & sphincters of
    dynamos — all these
entangled in your mummied roots — and you there standing before me in
    the sunset, all your glory in your form!   40
A perfect beauty of a sunflower! a perfect excellent lovely sunflower
    existence! a sweet natural eye to the new hip moon, woke up alive and
    excited grasping in the sunset shadow sunrise golden monthly breeze!
How many flies buzzed round you innocent of your grime, while you cursed
    the heavens of the railroad and your flower soul?   45
Poor dead flower? when did you forget you were a flower? when did you look
    at your skin and decide you were an impotent dirty old locomotive? the
    ghost of a locomotive? the specter and shade of a once powerful mad
    American locomotive?
You were never no locomotive, Sunflower, you were a sunflower!   50
And you Locomotive, you are a locomotive, forget me not!
So I grabbed up the skeleton thick sunflower and stuck it at my side like a
    scepter,
and deliver my sermon to my soul, and Jack's soul too, and anyone who'll
    listen,   55
— We're not our skin of grime, we're not our dread bleak dusty imageless
    locomotive, we're all beautiful golden sunflowers inside, we're blessed by
    our own seed & golden hairy naked accomplishment-bodies growing into
    mad black formal sunflowers in the sunset, spied on by our eyes under the
    shadow of the mad locomotive riverbank sunset Frisco hilly tincan evening   60
    sitdown vision.

Gregory Corso (1930–)

MARRIAGE

for Mr. and Mrs. Mike Goldberg

Should I get married? Should I be good?
Astound the girl next door
with my velvet suit and faustus hood?
Don't take her to movies but to cemeteries
tell all about werewolf bathtubs and forked clarinets   5
then desire her and kiss her and all the preliminaries
and she going just so far and I understanding why
not getting angry saying You must feel! It's beautiful to feel!
Instead take her in my arms
lean against an old crooked tombstone   10
and woo her the entire night the constellations in the sky —

When she introduces me to her parents
back straightened, hair finally combed, strangled by a tie,
should I sit knees together on their 3rd-degree sofa
and not ask Where's the bathroom?   15
How else to feel other than I am,
a young man who often thinks Flash Gordon soap —
O how terrible it must be for a young man
seated before a family and the family thinking
We never saw him before! He wants our Mary Lou!   20
After tea and homemade cookies they ask What do you do?
Should I tell them? Would they like me then?
Say All right get married, we're losing a daughter
but we're gaining a son —
And should I then ask Where's the bathroom?   25

O God, and the wedding! All her family and her friends
and only a handful of mine all scroungy and bearded
just waiting to get at the drinks and food —
And the priest! he looking at me as if I masturbated
asking me Do you take this woman   30
for your lawful wedded wife?
And I, trembling what to say, say Pie Glue!
I kiss the bride all those corny men slapping me on the back:
She's all yours, boy! Ha-ha-ha!
And in their eyes you could see   35
some obscene honeymoon going on —

Then all that absurd rice and clanky cans and shoes
Niagara Falls! Hordes of us! Husbands! Wives! Flowers!
All streaming into cozy hotels
All going to do the same thing tonight   40
The indifferent clerk he knowing what was going to happen
The lobby zombies they knowing what
The whistling elevator man he knowing
The winking bellboy knowing
Everybody knows! I'd be almost inclined not to do anything!   45
Stay up all night! Stare that hotel clerk in the eye!
Screaming: I deny honeymoon! I deny honeymoon!
running rampant into those almost climactic suites
yelling Radio belly! Cat shovel!
O I'd live in Niagara forever! in a dark cave beneath the Falls   50
I'd sit there the Mad Honeymooner
devising ways to break marriages, a scourge of bigamy
a saint of divorce —

But I should get married I should be good
How nice it'd be to come home to her   55
and sit by the fireplace and she in the kitchen
aproned young and lovely wanting my baby
and so happy about me she burns the roast beef
and comes crying to me and I get up from my big papa chair
saying Christmas teeth! Radiant brains! Apple deaf!   60
God what a husband I'd make! Yes, I should get married!
So much to do! like sneaking into Mr. Jones' house late at night
and cover his golf clubs with 1920 Norwegian books
Like hanging a picture of Rimbaud on the lawnmower
Like pasting Tannu Tuva postage stamps   65
all over the picket fence
Like when Mrs. Kindhead comes to collect
for the Community Chest
grab her and tell her There are unfavorable omens in the sky!
And when the mayor comes to get my vote tell him   70
When are you going to stop people killing whales!
And when the milkman comes leave him a note in the bottle
Penguin dust, bring me penguin dust, I want penguin dust —

Yet if I should get married and it's Connecticut and snow
and she gives birth to a child and I am sleepless, worn,   75
up for nights, head bowed against a quiet window,
the past behind me,
finding myself in the most common of situations
a trembling man
knowledged with responsibility not twig-smear   80
nor Roman coin soup —
O what would that be like!
Surely I'd give it for a nipple a rubber Tacitus
For a rattle a bag of broken Bach records
Tack Della Francesca all over its crib   85

Sew the Greek alphabet on its bib
And build for its playpen a roofless Parthenon —

No, I doubt I'd be that kind of father
not rural not snow no quiet window
but hot smelly tight New York City   90
seven flights up, roaches and rats in the walls
a fat Reichian wife screeching over potatoes Get a job!
And five nose-running brats in love with Batman
And the neighbors all toothless and dry haired
like those hag masses of the 18th century   95
all wanting to come in and watch TV
The landlord wants his rent
Grocery store Blue Cross Gas & Electric Knights of Columbus
Impossible to lie back and dream Telephone snow,
ghost parking —   100
No! I should not get married I should never get married!

But — imagine if I were married to a beautiful
sophisticated woman
tall and pale wearing an elegant black dress
and long black gloves   105
holding a cigarette holder in one hand
and a highball in the other
and we lived high up in a penthouse with a huge window
from which we could see all of New York
and even farther on clearer days   110
No, can't imagine myself married to that pleasant prison dream —

O but what about love? I forget love
not that I am incapable of love
it's just that I see love as odd as wearing shoes —
I never wanted to marry a girl who was like my mother   115
And Ingrid Bergman was always impossible
And there's maybe a girl now but she's already married
And I don't like men and —
but there's got to be somebody!
Because what if I'm 60 years old and not married,   120
all alone in a furnished room with pee stains on my underwear
and everybody else is married! All the universe married but me!

Ah, yet well I know that were a woman possible
as I am possible
then marriage would be possible —   125
Like SHE in her lonely alien gaud waiting her Egyptian lover
so I wait — bereft of 2,000 years and the bath of life.

Anne Sexton (1928–1974)

from *Transformations*

CINDERELLA

You always read about it:
the plumber with twelve children
who wins the Irish Sweepstakes.
From toilets to riches.
That story.   5

Or the nursemaid,
some luscious sweet from Denmark
who captures the oldest son's heart.
From diapers to Dior.
That story.   10

Or a milkman who serves the wealthy,
eggs, cream, butter, yogurt, milk,
the white truck like an ambulance
who goes into real estate
and makes a pile.   15
From homogenized to martinis at lunch.

Or the charwoman
who is on the bus when it cracks up
and collects enough from the insurance.
From mops to Bonwit Teller.   20
That story.

Once
the wife of a rich man was on her deathbed
and she said to her daughter Cinderella:
Be devout. Be good. Then I will smile   25
down from heaven in the seam of a cloud.
The man took another wife who had
two daughters, pretty enough
but with hearts like blackjacks.
Cinderella was their maid.   30
She slept on the sooty hearth each night
and walked around looking like Al Jolson.
Her father brought presents home from town,
jewels and gowns for the other women
but the twig of a tree for Cinderella.   35

She planted that twig on her mother's grave
and it grew to a tree where a white dove sat.
Whenever she wished for anything the dove
would drop it like an egg upon the ground.
The bird is important, my dears, so heed him.   40

Next came the ball, as you all know.
It was a marriage market.
The prince was looking for a wife.
All but Cinderella were preparing
and gussying up for the big event.   45
Cinderella begged to go too.
Her stepmother threw a dish of lentils
into the cinders and said: Pick them
up in an hour and you shall go.
The white dove brought all his friends;   50
all the warm wings of the fatherland came,
and picked up the lentils in a jiffy.
No, Cinderella, said the stepmother,
you have no clothes and cannot dance.
That's the way with stepmothers.   55

Cinderella went to the tree at the grave
and cried forth like a gospel singer:
Mama! Mama! My turtledove,
send me to the prince's ball!
The bird dropped down a golden dress   60
and delicate little gold slippers.
Rather a large package for a simple bird.
So she went. Which is no surprise.
Her stepmother and sisters didn't
recognize her without her cinder face   65
and the prince took her hand on the spot
and danced with no other the whole day.

As nightfall came she thought she'd better
get home. The prince walked her home
and she disappeared into the pigeon house   70
and although the prince took an axe and broke
it open she was gone. Back to her cinders.
These events repeated themselves for three days.
However on the third day the prince
covered the palace steps with cobbler's wax   75
and Cinderella's gold shoe stuck upon it.

Now he would find whom the shoe fit
and find his strange dancing girl for keeps.
He went to their house and the two sisters
were delighted because they had lovely feet.   80
The eldest went into a room to try the slipper on
but her big toe got in the way so she simply

sliced it off and put on the slipper.
The prince rode away with her until the white dove
told him to look at the blood pouring forth.   85
That is the way with amputations.
They don't just heal up like a wish.
The other sister cut off her heel
but the blood told as blood will.
The prince was getting tired.   90
He began to feel like a shoe salesman.
But he gave it one last try.
This time Cinderella fit into the shoe
like a love letter into its envelope.

At the wedding ceremony   95
the two sisters came to curry favor
and the white dove pecked their eyes out.
Two hollow spots were left
like soup spoons.

Cinderella and the prince   100
lived, they say, happily ever after,
like two dolls in a museum case
never bothered by diapers or dust,
never arguing over the timing of an egg,
never telling the same story twice,   105
never getting a middle-aged spread,
their darling smiles pasted on for eternity.
Regular Bobbsey Twins.
That story.

BRIAR ROSE (SLEEPING BEAUTY)

Consider
a girl who keeps slipping off,
arms limp as old carrots,
into the hypnotist's trance,
into a spirit world   5
speaking with the gift of tongues.
She is stuck in the time machine,
suddenly two years old sucking her thumb,
as inward as a snail,
learning to talk again.   10
She's on a voyage.
She is swimming further and further back,
up like a salmon,
struggling into her mother's pocketbook.
Little doll child,   15
come here to Papa.
Sit on my knee.
I have kisses for the back of your neck.

A penny for your thoughts, Princess.
I will hunt them like an emerald.   20
Come be my snooky
and I will give you a root.
That kind of voyage,
rank as honeysuckle.

Once   25
a king had a christening
for his daughter Briar Rose
and because he had only twelve gold plates
he asked only twelve fairies
to the grand event.   30
The thirteenth fairy,
her fingers as long and thin as straws,
her eyes burnt by cigarettes,
her uterus an empty teacup,
arrived with an evil gift.   35
She made this prophecy:
The princess shall prick herself
on a spinning wheel in her fifteenth year
and then fall down dead.
Kaputt!   40
The court fell silent.
The king looked like Munch's *Scream*.
Fairies' prophecies,
in times like those,
held water.   45
However the twelfth fairy
had a certain kind of eraser
and thus she mitigated the curse
changing that death
into a hundred-year sleep.   50

The king ordered every spinning wheel
exterminated and exorcized.
Briar Rose grew to be a goddess
and each night the king
bit the hem of her gown   55
to keep her safe.
He fastened the moon up
with a safety pin
to give her perpetual light
He forced every male in the court   60
to scour his tongue with Bab-o
lest they poison the air she dwelt in.
Thus she dwelt in his odor.
Rank as honeysuckle.

On her fifteenth birthday   65
she pricked her finger
on a charred spinning wheel

and the clocks stopped.
Yes indeed. She went to sleep.
The king and queen went to sleep,   70
the courtiers, the flies on the wall.
The fire in the hearth grew still
and the roast meat stopped crackling.
The trees turned into metal
and the dog became china.   75
They all lay in a trance,
each a catatonic
stuck in the time machine.
Even the frogs were zombies.
Only a bunch of briar roses grew   80
forming a great wall of tacks
around the castle.
Many princes
tried to get through the brambles
for they had heard much of Briar Rose   85
but they had not scoured their tongues
so they were held by the thorns
and thus were crucified.
In due time
a hundred years passed   90
and a prince got through.
The briars parted as if for Moses
and the prince found the tableau intact.
He kissed Briar Rose
and she woke up crying: 95
Daddy! Daddy!
Presto! She's out of prison!
She married the prince
and all went well
except for the fear —   100
the fear of sleep.

Briar Rose
was an insomniac . . .
She could not nap
or lie in sleep   105
without the court chemist
mixing her some knock-out drops
and never in the prince's presence.
If it is to come, she said,
sleep must take me unawares   110
while I am laughing or dancing
so that I do not know that brutal place
where I lie down with cattle prods,
the hole in my cheek open.
Further, I must not dream   115
for when I do I see the table set
and a faltering crone at my place,

her eyes burnt by cigarettes
as she eats betrayal like a slice of meat.

I must not sleep   120
for while asleep I'm ninety
and think I'm dying.
Death rattles in my throat
like a marble.
I wear tubes like earrings.   125
I lie as still as a bar of iron.
You can stick a needle
through my kneecap and I won't flinch.
I'm all shot up with Novocain.
This trance girl   130
is yours to do with.
You could lay her in a grave,
an awful package,
and shovel dirt on her face
and she'd never call back: Hello there!   135
But if you kissed her on the mouth
her eyes would spring open
and she'd call out: Daddy! Daddy!
Presto!
She's out of prison.   140

There was a theft.
That much I am told.
I was abandoned.
That much I know.
I was forced backward.   145
I was forced forward.
I was passed hand to hand
like a bowl of fruit.
Each night I am nailed into place
and I forget who I am.   150
Daddy?
That's another kind of prison.
It's not the prince at all,
but my father
drunkenly bent over my bed,   155
circling the abyss like a shark,
my father thick upon me
like some sleeping jellyfish.

What voyage this, little girl?
This coming out of prison?   160
God help —
this life after death?

Ted Hughes (1930–)

from *Crow*

IN LAUGHTER

Cars collide and erupt luggage and babies
In laughter
The steamer upends and goes under saluting like a stuntman
In laughter
The nosediving aircraft concludes with a boo   5
In laughter
People's arms and legs fly off and fly on again
In laughter
The haggard mask on the bed rediscovers its pang
In laughter, in laughter   10
The meteorite crashes
With extraordinarily ill luck on the pram

The ears and eyes are bundled up
Are folded up in the hair,
Wrapped in the carpet, the wallpaper, tied with the lampflex   15
Only the teeth work on
And the heart, dancing on in its open cave
Helpless on the strings of laughter
While the tears are nickle-plated and come through doors with a bang

And the wails stun with fear   20
And the bones
Jump from the torment flesh has to stay for

Stagger some distance and fall in full view

Still laughter scampers around on centipede boots
Still it runs all over on caterpillar tread   25
And rolls back onto the mattress, legs in the air

But it's only human

And finally it's had enough—enough!
And slowly sits up, exhausted,
And slowly starts to fasten buttons,   30
With long pauses,

Like somebody the police have come for.

APPLE TRAGEDY

So on the seventh day
The serpent rested,
God came up to him.
"I've invented a new game," he said.

The serpent stared in surprise   5
At this interloper.
But God said: "You see this apple?
I squeeze it and look—cider."

The serpent had a good drink
And curled up into a questionmark.   10
Adam drank and said: "Be my god."
Eve drank and opened her legs

And called to the cockeyed serpent
And gave him a wild time.
God ran and told Adam   15
Who in drunken rage tried to hang himself in the orchard.

The serpent tried to explain, crying "Stop"
But drink was splitting his syllable.
And Eve started screeching: "Rape! Rape!"
And stamping on his head.   20

Now whenever the snake appears she screeches
"Here it comes again; Help! O Help!"
Then Adam smashes a chair on its head,
And God says: "I am well pleased"

And everything goes to hell.   25

Peter Redgrove (1932-)

THIRTEEN WAYS OF LOOKING AT A BLACKBOARD

I
The blackboard is clean.
The master must be coming.

II
The vigilant mosquito bites on a rising pitch.
The chalk whistles over the blackboard.

III

Among twenty silent children
The only moving thing
Is the chalk's white finger.

IV

O young white cricketers,
Aching for the greensward,
Do you not see how my moving hand
Whitens the black board?

V

A man and a child
Are one.
A man and a child and a blackboard
Are three.

VI

Some wield their sticks of chalk
Like torches in dark rooms.
I make up my blackboard
Like the face of an actor.

VII

I was of three minds
Like a room
In which there are three blackboards.

VIII

I dream.
I am an albino.

IX

I wake.
I forget a word.
The chalk snaps on the blackboard.

X

Twenty silent children
Staring at the blackboard.
On one wall of each of twenty nurseries
The light has gone out.

XI

He ambles among the white rocks of Dover,
Crushing pebbles with black boots.
He is a small blackboard
Writing on chalk.

XII

It is the Christmas holidays.
The white snow lies in the long black branches.
The black board

In the silent schoolroom
Perches on two stubby branches.

XIII
The flesh that is white
Wastes over the bones that are chalk,
Both in the day
And through the black night.

Sylvia Plath (1932–1963)

SOW

God knows how our neighbor managed to breed
His great sow:
Whatever his shrewd secret, he kept it hid

In the same way
He kept the sow—impounded from public stare,   5
Prize ribbon and pig show.

But one dusk our questions commended us to a tour
Through his lantern-lit
Maze of barns to the lintel of the sunk sty door

To gape at it: 10
This was no rose-and-larkspurred china suckling
With a penny slot
For thrifty children, nor dolt pig ripe for heckling,
About to be
Glorified for prime flesh and golden crackling   15

In a parsley halo;
Nor even one of the common barnyard sows,
Mire-smirched, blowzy,

Maunching thistle and knotweed on her snout-cruise—
Bloat tun of milk   20
On the move, hedged by a litter of feat-foot ninnies

Shrilling her hulk
To halt for a swig at the pink teats. No. This vast
Brobdingnag bulk

Of a sow lounged belly-bedded on that black compost,   25
Fat-rutted eyes
Dream-filmed. What a vision of ancient hoghood must

Thus wholly engross
The great grandam!—our marvel blazoned a knight,
Helmed, in cuirass,   30

Unhorsed and shredded in the grove of combat
By a grisly-bristled
Boar, fabulous enough to straddle that sow's heat.

But our farmer whistled,
Then, with a jocular fist thwacked the barrel nape,   35
and the green-copse-castled

Pig hove, letting legend like dried mud drop,
Slowly, grunt
On grunt, up in the flickering light to shape

A monument   40
Prodigious in gluttonies as that hog whose want
Made lean Lent

Of kitchen slops and, stomaching no constraint,
Proceeded to swill
The seven troughed seas and every earthquaking continent.   45

DADDY

You do not do, you do not do
Any more, black shoe
In which I have lived like a foot
For thirty years, poor and white,
Barely daring to breathe or Achoo!   5

Daddy, I have had to kill you.
You died before I had time—
Marble-heavy, a bag full of God,
Ghastly statue with one grey toe
Big as a Frisco seal   10

And a head in the freakish Atlantic
Where it pours bean green over blue
In the waters off beautiful Nauset.
I used to pray to recover you.
Ach, du!   15

In the German tongue, in the Polish town
Scraped flat by the roller
Of wars, wars, wars.
But the name of the town is common.
My Polack friend   20

Says there are a dozen or two.
So I never could tell where you
Put your foot, your root,
I never could talk to you.
The tongue stuck in my jaw.   25

It stuck in a barb wire snare.
Ich, ich, ich, ich!
I could hardly speak.
I thought every German was you.
And the language obscene   30

An engine, an engine
Chuffing me off like a Jew.
A Jew to Dachau, Auschwitz, Belsen.
I began to talk like a Jew.
I think I may well be a Jew.   35

The snows of the Tyrol, the clear beer of Vienna
Are not very pure or true.
With my gypsy ancestress and my weird luck
And my Tarot pack and my Tarot pack
I may be a bit of a Jew.   40

I have always been scared of *you,*
With your Luftwaffe, your gobbledygoo.
And your neat moustache
And your Aryan eye, bright blue.
Panzer-man, panzer-man, o You!   45

Not God but a swastika
So black no sky could squeak through.
Every woman adores a Fascist,
The boot in the face, the brute
Brute heart of a brute like you.   50

You stand at the blackboard, daddy,
In the picture I have of you,
A cleft in your chin instead of your foot
But no less a devil for that, no not
Any less the black man who   55

Bit my pretty red heart in two.
I was ten when they buried you.
At twenty I tried to die
And get back, back, back to you.
I thought even the bones would do.   60

But they pulled me out of the sack,
And they stuck me together with glue.
And then I knew what to do.
I made a model of you,
A man in black with a Meinkampf look   65

And a love of the rack and the screw.
And I said I do, I do.
So daddy, I'm finally through.
The black telephone's off at the root,
The voices just can't worm through.　70

If I've killed one man, I've killed two—
The vampire who said he was you
And drank my blood for a year—
Seven years, if you want to know.
Daddy, you can lie back now.　75

There's a stake in your fat black heart
And the villagers never liked you.
They are dancing and stamping on you.
They always *knew* it was you.
Daddy, daddy, you bastard, I'm through.　80

H. G. Wells (1866–1946)

THE TIME MACHINE

An Invention

> Fool! All that is at all
> Lasts ever past recall.
> —Robert Browning

I. THE INVENTOR

The man who made the Time Machine—the man I shall call the Time Traveler—was well known in scientific circles a few years since, and the fact of his disappearance is also well known. He was a mathematician of peculiar subtlety, and one of our most conspicuous investigators in molecular physics. He did not confine himself to abstract science. Several ingenious, and one or two profitable, patents were his: very profitable they were, these last, as his handsome house at Richmond testified. To those who were his intimates, however, his scientific investigations were as nothing to his gift of speech. In the after-dinner hours he was ever a vivid and variegated talker, and at times his fantastic, often paradoxical, conceptions came so thick and close as to form one continuous discourse. At these times he was as unlike the popular conception of a scientific investigator as a man could be. His cheeks would flush, his eyes grow bright; and the stranger the ideas that sprang and crowded in his brain, the happier and the more animated would be his exposition.

Up to the last there was held at his house a kind of informal gathering, which it was my privilege to attend, and where, at one time or another, I have met most of our distinguished literary and scientific men. There was a plain dinner at seven. After that we would adjourn to a room of easy-chairs and little tables, and there, with libations of alcohol and reeking pipes, we would invoke the god. At first the conversation was mere fragmentary chatter, with some local *lacunae* of digestive silence; but toward nine or half-past nine, if the god was favorable, some particular topic would triumph by a kind of natural selection, and would become the common interest. So it was, I remember, on the last Thursday but one of all—the Thursday when I first heard of the Time Machine.

I had been jammed in a corner with a gentleman who shall be disguised as Filby. He had been running down Milton—the public neglects poor Filby's little verses shockingly; and as I could think of nothing but the relative status of Filby and the man he criticized, and was much too timid to discuss that, the arrival of that moment of fusion, when our several conversations were suddenly merged into a general discussion, was a great relief to me.

"What's that is nonsense?" said a well-known Medical Man, speaking across Filby to the Psychologist.

"He thinks," said the Psychologist, "that Time's only a kind of Space."

"It's not thinking," said the Time Traveler; "it's knowledge."

"Foppish affectation," said Filby, still harping upon his wrongs; but I feigned a great interest in this question of Space and Time.

"Kant——" began the Psychologist.

"Confound Kant!" said the Time Traveler. "I tell you I'm right. I've got experimental proof of it. I'm not a metaphysician." He addressed the Medical Man across the room, and so brought the whole company into his own circle. "It's the most promising departure in experimental work that has ever been

made. It will simply revolutionize life. Heaven knows what life will be when I've carried the thing through."

"As long as it's not the water of immortality I don't mind," said the distinguished Medical Man. "What is it?"

"Only a paradox," said the Psychologist.

The Time Traveler said nothing in reply, but smiled and began tapping his pipe upon the fender curb. This was the invariable presage of a dissertation.

"You have to admit that time is a spatial dimension," said the Psychologist, emboldened by immunity and addressing the Medical Man, "and then all sorts of remarkable consequences are found inevitable. Among others, that it becomes possible to travel about in time."

The Time Traveler chuckled. "You forget that I'm going to prove it experimentally."

"Let's have your experiment," said the Psychologist.

"I think we'd like the argument first," said Filby.

"It's this," said the Time Traveler. "You must follow me carefully. I shall have to controvert one or two ideas that are almost universally accepted. The geometry, for instance, they taught you at school is founded on a misconception."

"Is not that rather a large thing to expect us to begin upon?" said Filby.

"I do not mean to ask you to accept anything without reasonable ground for it. You will soon admit as much as I want from you. You know, of course, that a mathematical line, a line of thickness *nil*, has no real existence. They taught you that? Neither has a mathematical plane. These things are mere abstractions."

"That is all right," said the Psychologist.

"Nor, having only length, breadth, and thickness, can a cube have a real existence."

"There I object," said Filby.

"Of course a solid body may exist. All real things——"

"So most people think. But wait a moment. Can an instantaneous cube exist?"

"Don't follow you," said Filby.

"Can a cube that does not last for any time at all, have a real existence?"

Filby became pensive.

"Clearly," the Philosophical Inventor proceeded, "any real body must have extension in *four* directions: it must have Length, Breadth, Thickness, and — Duration. But through a natural infirmity of the flesh, which I will explain to you in a moment, we incline to overlook the fact. There are really four dimensions, three which we call the three planes of Space, and a fourth, Time. There is, however, a tendency to draw an unreal distinction between the former three dimensions and the latter, because it happens that our consciousness moves intermittently in one direction along the latter from the beginning to the end of our lives."

"That," said a Very Young Man, making spasmodic efforts to relight his cigar over the lamp: "that—very clear indeed."

"Now, it is very remarkable that this is so extensively overlooked," continued the Philosophical Inventor, with a slight accession of cheerfulness. "Really this is what is meant by the Fourth Dimension, though some people who talk about the Fourth Dimension do not know they mean it. It is only another way of looking at Time. *There is no difference between Time and any of the three dimensions of Space except that our consciousness moves along it.* But some foolish people have got hold of the wrong side of that idea. You have all heard what they have to say about this Fourth Dimension?"

"I have not," said the Provincial Mayor.

"It is simply this, That space, as our mathematicians have it, is spoken of as having three dimensions, which one may call Length, Breadth, and Thickness, and is always definable by reference to these planes, each at right angle to the others. But some philosophical people have been asking why *three* dimensions particularly—why not another direction at right angles to the other three?—and have even tried to construct a Four-Dimensional geometry. Professor Simon Newcomb was expounding this to the New York Mathematical Society only a month or so ago. You know how on a flat surface, which has only two dimensions, we can represent a figure of a Three-Dimensional solid, and similarly they think that by models of three dimensions they could represent one of four—if they could master the perspective of the thing. See?"

"I think so," murmured the Provincial Mayor; and, knitting his brows, he lapsed into an introspective state, his lips moving as one who repeats mystic words. "Yes, I think I see it now," he said after some time, brightening in a quite transitory manner.

"Well, I do not mind telling you I have been at work upon this geometry of Four Dimensions for some time. Some of my results are curious: for instance, here is a portrait of a man at eight years old, another at fifteen, another at seventeen, another at twenty-three, and so on. All these are evidently sections, as it were, Three-Dimensional representations of his Four-Dimensional being, which is a fixed and unalterable thing.

"Scientific people," proceeded the Philosopher, after the pause required for the proper assimilation of this, "know very well that Time is only a kind of Space. Here is a popular scientific diagram, a weather record. This line I trace with my finger shows the movement of the barometer. Yesterday it was so high, yesterday night it fell, then this morning it rose again, and so gently upward to here. Surely the mercury did not trace this line in any of the dimensions of space generally recognized? But certainly it traced such a line, and that line, therefore, we must conclude, was along the Time Dimension."

"But," said the Medical Man, staring hard at a coal in the fire, "if Time is really only a fourth dimension of Space, why is it, and why has it always been, regarded as something different? And why cannot we move about in Time as we move about in the other dimensions of Space?"

The Philosophical Person smiled. "Are you so sure we can move freely in Space? Right and left we can go, backward and forward freely enough, and men always have done so. I admit we move freely in two dimensions. But how about up and down? Gravitation limits us there."

"Not exactly," said the Medical Man. "There are balloons."

"But before the balloons, save for spasmodic jumping and the inequalities of the surface, man had no freedom of vertical movement."

"Still they could move a little up and down," said the Medical Man.

"Easier, far easier, down than up."

"And you cannot move at all in Time. You cannot get away from the present moment."

"My dear sir, that is just where you are wrong. That is just where the whole world has gone wrong. We are always getting away from the present moment. Our mental existences, which are immaterial and have no dimensions, are passing along the Time Dimension with a uniform velocity from the cradle to the grave. Just as we should travel *down* if we began our existence fifty miles above the earth's surface."

"But the great difficulty is this," interrupted the Psychologist: "You *can* move about in all directions of Space, but you cannot move about in Time."

"That is the germ of my great discovery. But you are wrong to say that we cannot move about in Time. For instance, if I am recalling an incident very vividly I go back to the instant of its occurrence; I become absent-minded, as you say. I jump back for a moment. Of course we have no means of staying back for any length of time any more than a savage or an animal has of staying six feet above the ground. But a civilized man is better off than the savage in this respect. He can go up against gravitation in a balloon, and why should we not hope that ultimately he may be able to stop or accelerate his drift along the Time Dimension; or even to turn about and travel the other way?"

"Oh, *this*," began Filby, "is all——"

"Why not?" said the Philosophical Inventor.

"It's against reason," said Filby.

"What reason?" said the Philosophical Inventor.

"You can show black is white by argument," said Filby, "but you will never convince me."

"Possibly not," said the Philosophical Inventor. "But now you begin to see the object of my investigations into the geometry of Four Dimensions. Long ago I had a vague inkling of a machine——"

"To travel through Time!" said the Very Young Man.

"That shall travel indifferently in any direction of Space and Time, as the driver determines."

Filby contented himself with laughter.

"It would be remarkably convenient," the Psychologist suggested. "One might travel back and witness the battle of Hastings."

"Don't you think you would attract attention?" said the Medical Man. "Our ancestors had no great tolerance for anachronisms."

"One might get one's Greek from the very lips of Homer and Plato," the Very Young Man thought.

"In which case they would certainly

plow you for the little-go. The German scholars have improved Greek so much."

"Then, there is the future," said the Very Young Man. "Just think! One might invest all one's money, leave it to accumulate at interest, and hurry on ahead."

"To discover a society," said I, "erected on a strictly communistic basis."

"Of all the wild extravagant theories ——" began the Psychologist.

"Yes, so it seemed to me, and so I never talked of it until——"

"Experimental verification!" cried I. "You are going to verify *that!*"

"The experiment!" cried Filby, who was getting brain-weary.

"Let's see your experiment, anyhow," said the Psychologist, "though it's all humbug, you know."

The Time Traveler smiled round at us. Then, still smiling faintly, and with his hands deep in his trousers pockets, he walked slowly out of the room, and we heard his slippers shuffling down the long passage to his laboratory.

The Psychologist looked at us. "I wonder what he's got?"

"Some sleight-of-hand trick or other," said the Medical Man, and Filby tried to tell us about a conjuror he had seen at Burslem, but before he had finished his preface the Time Traveler came back, and Filby's anecdote collapsed.

The thing the Time Traveller held in his hand was a glittering metallic framework, scarcely larger than a small clock, and very delicately made. There was ivory in it, and some transparent crystalline substance. And now I must be explicit, for this that follows —unless his explanation is to be accepted—is an absolutely unaccountable thing. He took one of the small octagonal tables that were scattered about the room, and set it in front of the fire, with two legs on the hearthrug. On this table he placed the mechanism. Then

he drew up a chair and sat down. The only other object on the table was a small shaded lamp, the bright light of which fell upon the model. There were also perhaps a dozen candles about, two in brass candlesticks upon the mantel and several in sconces, so that the room was brilliantly illuminated. I sat in a low armchair nearest the fire, and I drew this forward so as to be almost between the Time Traveler and the fireplace. Filby sat behind him, looking over his shoulder. The Medical Man and the Rector watched him in profile from the right, the Psychologist from the left. We were all on the alert. It appears incredible to me that any kind of trick, however subtly conceived and however adroitly done, could have been played upon us under these conditions.

The Time Traveler looked at us and then at the mechanism.

"Well?" said the Psychologist.

"This little affair," said the Time Traveler, resting his elbows upon the table and pressing his hands together above the apparatus, "is only a model. It is my plan for a machine to travel through Time. You will notice that it looks singularly askew, and that there is an odd twinkling appearance about this bar, as though it was in some way unreal." He pointed to the part with his finger. "Also, here is one little white lever, and here is another."

The Medical Man got up out of his chair and peered into the thing. "It's beautifully made," he said.

"It took two years to make," retorted the Time Traveler. Then, when we had all done as the Medical Man, he said: "Now I want you clearly to understand that this lever, being pressed over, sends the machine gliding into the future, and this other reverses the motion. This saddle represents the seat of a time traveler. Presently I am going to press the lever, and off the machine will go. It will vanish, pass into future time, and disappear. Have a good look at the thing. Look at the table too, and satisfy yourselves there is no trickery. I don't want to waste this model, and then be told I'm a quack."

There was a minute's pause perhaps. The Psychologist seemed about to speak to me, but changed his mind. Then the Time Traveler put forth his finger toward the lever. "No," he said suddenly; "lend me your hand." And turning to the Psychologist, he took that individual's hand in his own and told him to put out his forefinger. So that it was the Psychologist himself who sent forth the model Time Machine on its interminable voyage. We all saw the lever turn. I am absolutely certain there was no trickery. There was a breath of wind, and the lamp flame jumped. One of the candles on the mantel was blown out, and the little machine suddenly swung round, became indistinct, was seen as a ghost for a second perhaps, as an eddy of faintly glittering brass and ivory; and it was gone—vanished! Save for the lamp the table was bare.

Everyone was silent for a minute. Then Filby said he was d———d.

The psychologist recovered from his stupor, and suddenly looked under the table. At that the Time Traveler laughed cheerfully. "Well?" he said, with a reminiscence of the Psychologist. Then, getting up, he went to the tobacco jar on the mantel, and with his back to us began to fill his pipe.

We stared at each other.

"Look here," said the Medical Man, "are you in earnest about this? Do you seriously believe that that machine has traveled into Time?"

"Certainly," said the Time Traveler, stooping to light a spill at the fire. Then he turned, lighting his pipe, to look at the Psychologist's face. (The Psychologist, to show that he was not unhinged, helped himself to a cigar and tried to light it uncut.) "What is more, I have a big machine nearly finished in there,"—he indicated the laboratory,— "and when that is put together I mean to have a journey on my own account."

"You mean to say that that machine has traveled into the future?" said Filby.

"Into the future or the past—I don't, for certain, know which."

After an interval the Psychologist had an inspiration.

"It must have gone into the past if it has gone anywhere," he said.

"Why?" said the Time Traveler.

"Because I presume that it has not moved in space, and if it traveled into the future it would still be here all this time, since it must have traveled through this time."

"But," said I, "if it traveled into the past it would have been visible when we came first into this room; and last Thursday when we were here; and the Thursday before that; and so forth!"

"Serious objections," remarked the Rector with an air of impartiality, turning toward the Time Traveler.

"Not a bit," said the Time Traveler, and, to the Psychologist: "You think. You can explain that. It's presentation below the threshold, you know, diluted presentation."

"Of course," said the Psychologist, and reassured us. "That's a simple point in psychology. I should have thought of it. It's plain enough, and helps the paradox delightfully. We cannot see it, nor can we appreciate this machine, any more than we can the spoke of a wheel spinning, or a bullet flying through the air. If it is traveling through time fifty times or a hundred times faster than we are, if it gets through a minute while we get through a second, the impression it creates will of course be only one-fiftieth or one-hundredth of what it would make if it were not traveling in time. That's plain enough." He passed his hand through the space in which the machine had been. "You see?" he said laughing.

We sat and stared at the vacant table for a minute or so. Then the Time Traveler asked us what we thought of it all.

"It sounds plausible enough tonight," said the Medical Man; "but wait until tomorrow. Wait for the common sense of the morning."

"Would you like to see the Time Machine itself?" asked the Time Traveler. And therewith, taking the lamp in his hand, he led the way down the long, draughty corridor to his laboratory. I remember vividly the flickering light, his queer, broad head in silhouette, the dance of the shadows, how we all followed him, puzzled but incredulous, and how there in the laboratory we beheld a larger edition of the little mechanism which we had seen vanish from before our eyes. Parts were of nickel, parts of ivory, parts had certainly been filed or sawn out of rock crystal. The thing was generally complete, but the twisted crystalline bars lay unfinished upon the bench beside some sheets of drawings, and I took one up for a better look at it. Quartz it seemed to be.

"Look here," said the Medical Man, "are you perfectly serious? Or is this a trick—like that ghost you showed us last Christmas?"

"Upon that machine," said the Time Traveler, holding the lamp aloft, "I intend to explore Time. Is that plain? I was never more serious in my life."

II. THE TIME TRAVELER RETURNS

I think that at that time none of us quite believed in the Time Machine. The fact is, the Time Traveler was one of those men who are too clever to be believed; you never felt that you saw all round him; you always suspected some subtle reserve, some ingenuity in ambush, behind his lucid frankness. Had Filby shown the model and explained the matter in the Time Traveler's words, we should have shown *him* far less skepticism. The point is, we should have seen his motives—a pork-butcher could understand Filby. But the Time Traveler had more than a touch of whim among his elements, and we distrusted him. Things that would have made the fame of a clever man seemed tricks in his hands. It is a mistake to do things too easily. The serious people who took him seriously never felt quite sure of his deportment; they were somehow aware that trusting their reputations for judgment with him was like furnishing a nursery with eggshell china. So I don't think any of us said very much about time traveling in the interval between that Thursday and the next, though its odd potentialities ran, no doubt, in most of our minds: its plausibility, that is, its practical incredibleness, the curious possibilities of anachronism and of utter confusion it suggested. For my own part, I was particularly preoccupied with the trick of the model. That I remember discussing with the Medical Man, whom I met on Friday at the Linnæan. He said he had seen a similar thing at Tübingen, and laid considerable stress on the blowing-out of the candle. But how the trick was done he could not explain.

The next Thursday I went again to Richmond—I suppose I was one of the Time Traveler's most constant guests—and, arriving late, found four or five men already assembled in his drawing room. The Medical Man was standing before the fire with a sheet of paper in one hand and his watch in the other. I looked round for the Time Traveler, and—

"It's half-past seven now," said the Medical Man. "I suppose we'd better have dinner?"

"Where's———?" said I, naming our host.

"You've just come? It's rather odd. He's unavoidably detained. He asks me in his note to lead off with dinner at seven if he's not back. Says he'll explain when he comes."

"It's seems a pity to let the dinner spoil," said the Editor of a well-known daily paper; and thereupon the Doctor rang the bell.

The Psychologist was the only person besides the Doctor and myself who had attended the previous dinner. The other men were Blank, the Editor aforementioned, a certain journalist, and another—a quiet, shy man with a beard—whom I didn't know, and who, as far as my observation went, never opened his mouth all the evening. There was some speculation at the dinner-table about the Time Traveler's absence, and I suggested time traveling, in a half-jocular spirit. The Editor wanted that explained to him, and the Psychologist volunteered a wooden account of the "ingenious paradox and trick" we had witnessed that day week. He was in the midst of his exposition when the door from the corridor opened slowly and without noise. I was facing the door, and saw it first.

"Hallo!" I said. "At last!"

And the door opened wider, and the Time Traveler stood before us. I gave a cry of surprise.

"Good Heavens, man! what's the matter?" cried the Medical Man, who saw him next. And the whole tableful turned toward the door.

He was in an amazing plight. His coat was dusty and dirty, and smeared with green down the sleeves; his hair disordered, and as it seemed to me grayer—either with dust and dirt or because its color had actually faded. His face was ghastly pale; his chin had a brown cut on it—a cut half-healed; his expression was haggard and drawn, as by intense suffering. For a moment he hesitated in the doorway, as if he had been dazzled by the light. Then he came into the room. He walked with just such a limp as I have seen in foot-sore tramps. We stared at him in silence, expecting him to speak.

He said not a word, but came painfully to the table, and made a motion toward the wine. The Editor filled a glass of champagne and pushed it to-

ward him. He drained it, and it seemed to do him good; for he looked round the table, and the ghost of his old smile flickered across his face.

"What on earth have you been up to, man?" said the Doctor.

The Time Traveler did not seem to hear. "Don't let me disturb you," he said, with a certain faltering articulation. "I'm all right." He stopped, held out his glass for more, and took it off at a draught. "That's good," he said. His eyes grew brighter, and a faint color came into his cheeks. His glance flickered over our faces with a certain dull approval, and then went round the warm and comfortable room. Then he spoke again, still as it were feeling his way among his words. "I'm going to wash and dress, and then I'll come down and explain things. Save me some of that mutton. I'm starving for a bit of meat."

He looked across at the Editor, who was a rare visitor, and hoped he was all right. The Editor began a question.

"Tell you presently," said the Time Traveler. "I'm—funny! Be all right in a minute."

He put down his glass, and walked toward the staircase door. Again I remarked his lameness and the soft padding sound of his footfall, and standing up in my place I saw his feet as he went out. He had nothing on them but a pair of tattered, blood-stained socks. Then the door closed upon him. I had half a mind to follow, till I remembered how he detested any fuss about himself. For a minute, perhaps, my mind was wool gathering. Then, "Remarkable Behavior of an Eminent Scientist," I heard the Editor say, thinking (after his wont) in headlines. And this brought my attention back to the bright dinner table.

"What's the game?" said the Journalist. "Has he been doing the Amateur Cadger? I don't follow."

I met the eye of the Psychologist, and read my own interpretation in his face. I thought of the Time Traveler limping painfully upstairs. I don't think anyone else had noticed his lameness.

The first to recover completely from this surprise was the Medical Man, who rang the bell—the Time Traveler hated to have servants waiting at dinner—for a hot plate. At that the Editor turned to his knife and fork with a grunt, and the Silent Man followed suit. The dinner was resumed. Conversation was exclamatory for a little while, with gaps of wonderment; and then the Editor got fervent in his curiosity.

"Does our friend eke out his modest income with a crossing, or has he his Nebuchadnezzar phases?" he inquired.

"I feel assured it's this business of the Time Machine," I said, and took up the Psychologist's account of our previous meeting.

The new guests were frankly incredulous. The Editor raised objections.

"What *was* this time traveling? A man couldn't cover himself with dust by rolling in a paradox, could he?"

And then, as the idea came home to him, he resorted to caricature. Hadn't they any clothes-brushes in the Future? The Journalist, too, would not believe at any price, and joined the Editor in the easy work of heaping ridicule on the whole thing. They were both the new kind of Journalist—very joyous, irreverent young men. "Our Special Correspondent in the Day After To-Morrow reports," the Journalist was saying—or rather shouting—when the Time Traveler came back. He was dressed in ordinary evening clothes, and nothing save his haggard look remained of the change that had startled me.

"I say," said the Editor hilariously, "these chaps here say you have been traveling into the middle of next week! Tell us all about little Rosebery, will you? What will you take for the lot?"

The Time Traveler came to the place reserved for him without a word. He smiled quietly, in his old way.

"Where's my mutton?" he said. "What a treat it is to stick a fork into meat again!"

"Story!" cried the Editor.

"Story be d———d!" said the Time Traveler. "I want something to eat. I won't say a word until I get some peptone into my arteries. Thanks! And the salt."

"One word," said I. "Have you been time traveling?"

"Yes," said the Time Traveler, with his mouth full, nodding his head.

"I'd give a shilling a line for a verbatim note," said the Editor. The Time Traveler pushed his glass toward the Silent Man and rang it with his finger nail; at which the Silent Man, who had been staring at his face, started convulsively, and poured him wine. The rest of the dinner was uncomfortable. For my own part, sudden questions kept on rising to my lips, and I dare say it was the same with the others. The Journalist tried to relieve the tension by telling anecdotes of Hettie Potter. The Time Traveler devoted his attention to his dinner, and displayed the appetite of a tramp. The Medical Man smoked a cigarette, and watched the Time Traveler through his eyelashes. The Silent Man seemed even more clumsy than usual, and drank champagne with regularity and determination out of sheer nervousness. At last the Time Traveler pushed his plate away, and looked round us.

"I suppose I must apologize," he said. "I was simply starving. I've had a most amazing time." He reached out his hand for a cigar, and cut the end. "But come into the smoking room. It's too long a story to tell over greasy plates." And ringing the bell in passing, he led the way into the adjoining room.

"You have told Blank and Dash and Chose about the machine?" he said to me, leaning back in his easychair and naming the three new guests.

"But the thing's a mere paradox," said the Editor.

"I can't argue to-night. I don't mind

telling you the story, but I can't argue. I will," he went on, "tell you the story of what has happened to me, if you like, but you must refrain from interruptions. I want to tell it. Badly. Most of it will sound like lying. So be it! It's true—every word of it, all the same. I was in my laboratory at four o'clock, and since then—— I've lived eight days—such days as no human being ever lived before! I'm nearly worn out, but I shan't sleep till I've told this thing over to you. Then I shall go to bed. But no interruptions! Is it agreed?"

"Agreed!" said the Editor, and the rest of us echoed "Agreed!" And with that the Time Traveler began his story as I have set it forth. He sat back in his chair at first, and spoke like a weary man. Afterward he got more animated. In writing it down I feel with only too much keenness the inadequacy of pen and ink—and, above all, my own inadequacy—to express its quality. You read, I will suppose, attentively enough; but you cannot see the speaker's white, sincere face in the bright circle of the little lamp, nor hear the intonation of his voice. You cannot know how his expression followed the turns of his story! Most of us hearers were in shadow, for the candles in the smoking room had not been lighted, and only the face of the Journalist and the legs of the Silent Man from the knees downward were illuminated. At first we glanced now and again at each other. After a time we ceased to do that, and looked only at the Time Traveler's face.

III. THE STORY BEGINS

"I told some of you last Thursday of the principles of the Time Machine, and showed you the actual thing itself, incomplete, in the workshop. There it is now, a little travel-worn, truly; and one of the ivory bars is cracked, and a brass rail bent; but the rest of it is sound enough. I expected to finish it on Friday; but on Friday, when the putting together was nearly done, I found that one of the nickel bars was exactly one inch too short, and this I had to get remade; so that the thing was not complete until this morning. It was at ten o'clock today that the first of all Time Machines began its career. I gave it a last tap, tried all the screws again, put one more drop of oil on the quartz rod, and sat myself in the saddle. I suppose a suicide who holds a pistol to his skull feels much the same wonder at what will come next as I felt then. I took the starting lever in one hand and the stopping one in the other, pressed the first, and almost immediately the second. I seemed to reel; I felt a nightmare sensation of falling; and, looking round, I saw the laboratory exactly as before. Had anything happened? For a moment I suspected that my intellect had tricked me. Then I noted the clock. A moment before, as it seemed, it had stood at a minute or so past ten; now it was nearly half-past three!

"I drew a breath, set my teeth, gripped the starting lever with both my hands, and went off with a thud. The laboratory got hazy and went dark. Mrs. Watchett came in, and walked, apparently without seeing me, toward the garden door. I suppose it took her a minute or so to traverse the place, but to me she seemed to shoot across the room like a rocket. I pressed the lever over to its extreme position. The night came like the turning out of a lamp, and in another moment came tomorrow. The laboratory grew faint and hazy, then fainter and ever fainter. To-morrow night came black, then day again, night again, day again, faster and faster still. An eddying murmur filled my ears and a strange, dumb confusedness descended on my mind.

"I am afraid I cannot convey the peculiar sensations of time-traveling. They are excessively unpleasant. There is a feeling exactly like that one has upon a switchback—of a helpless headlong motion! I felt the same horrible anticipation, too, of an imminent smash. As I put on pace, day followed night, like the flap, flap, flap of some rotating body. The dim suggestion of the laboratory seemed presently to fall away from me, and I saw the sun hopping swiftly across the sky, leaping it every minute, and every minute marking a day. I supposed the laboratory had been destroyed, and I had come into the open air. I had a dim impression of scaffolding, but I was already going too fast to be conscious of any moving things. The slowest snail that ever crawled dashed by too fast for me. The twinkling succession of darkness and light was excessively painful to the eye. Then in the intermittent darkness, I saw the moon spinning swiftly through her quarters from new to full, and had a faint glimpse of the circling stars. Presently, as I went on, still gaining velocity, the palpitation of night and day merged into one continuous grayness; the sky took on a wonderful deepness of blue, a splendid luminous color like that of early twilight; the jerking sun became a streak of fire, a brilliant arch in space, the moon a fainter fluctuating band; and I could see nothing of the stars, save now and then a brighter circle flickering in the blue.

"The landscape was misty and vague. I was still on the hillside upon which this house now stands, and the shoulder rose above me gray and dim. I saw trees growing and changing like puffs of vapor, now brown, now green; they grew, spread, fluctuated, and passed away. I saw huge buildings rise up faint and fair, and pass like dreams. The whole surface of the earth seemed changing—melting and flowing under my eyes. The little hands upon the dials that registered my speed raced round faster and faster. Presently I noted that the sun belt swayed up and down, from solstice to solstice, in a minute or less, and that, consequently, my pace was over a year a minute; and minute by minute the white snow flashed across the world and vanished, and was followed by the bright, brief green of spring.

"The unpleasant sensations of the start were less poignant now. They merged at last into a kind of hysterical exhilaration. I remarked, indeed, a clumsy swaying of the machine, for which I was unable to account. But my mind was too confused to attend to it, so with a kind of madness growing upon me I flung myself into futurity. At first I scarce thought of stopping, scarce thought of anything but these new sensations. But presently a fresh series of impressions grew up in my mind,—a certain curiosity, and therewith a certain dread,—until they at last took complete possession of me. What strange developments of humanity, what wonderful advances upon our rudimentary civilization, I thought, might not appear when I came to look nearly into the dim, elusive world that raced and fluctuated before my eyes! I saw great and splendid architectures rising about me, more massive than any buildings of our own time, and yet, as it seemed, built of glimmer and mist. I saw a richer green flow up the hillside, and remain there without any wintry intermission. Even through the veil of my confusion the earth seemed very fair. And so my mind came round to the business of stopping.

"The peculiar risk lay in the possibility of my finding some substance in the space which I, or the machine, occupied. So long as I traveled at a high velocity through time, this scarcely mattered: I was, so to speak, attenuated—was slipping like a vapor through the interstices of intervening substances! But to come to a stop involved the jamming of myself, molecule by molecule, into whatever lay in my way, meant bringing my atoms into such intimate contact with those of the obstacle that a profound chemical reaction—possibly a far-reaching explosion—would result, and blow myself and my apparatus out of the Rigid Universe—out of all possible dimensions—into the Unknown.

This possibility had occurred to me again and again while I was making the machine; but then I had cheerfully accepted it as an unavoidable risk—one of the risks a man has got to take! Now the risk was inevitable, I no longer saw it in the same cheerful light. The fact is that, insensibly, the absolute strangeness of everything, the sickly jarring and swaying of the machine, above all the feeling of prolonged falling, had absolutely upset my nerve. I told myself that I could never stop, and with a gust of petulance I resolved to stop forthwith. Like an impatient fool, I lugged over the lever, and incontinently the thing went reeling over, and I was flung headlong through the air.

"There was the sound of a clap of thunder in my ears. I may have been stunned for a moment. A pitiless hail was hissing round me, and I was sitting on soft turf in front of the overset machine. Everything still seemed gray, but presently I remarked that the confusion in my ears was gone. I looked round me. I was on what seemed to be a little lawn in a garden, surrounded by rhododendron bushes, and I noticed that their mauve and purple blossoms were dropping in a shower under the beating of the hailstones. The rebounding, dancing hail hung in a little cloud over the machine, and drove along the ground like smoke. In a moment I was wet to the skin. 'Fine hospitality,' said I, 'to a man who has traveled innumerable years to see you!'

"Presently I thought what a fool I was to get wet. I stood up and looked round me. A colossal figure, carved apparently in some white stone, loomed indistinctly beyond the rhododendrons through the hazy downpour. But all else of the world was invisible.

"My sensations would be hard to describe. As the columns of hail grew thinner, I saw the white figure more distinctly. It was very large, for a silver birch tree touched its shoulder. It was of white marble, in shape something like a winged sphinx, but the wings, instead of being carried vertically at the sides, were spread so that it seemed to hover. The pedestal, it appeared to me, was of bronze, and was thick with verdigris. It chanced that the face was toward me; the sightless eyes seemed to watch me; there was the faint shadow of a smile on the lips. It was greatly weatherworn, and that imparted an unpleasant suggestion of disease. I stood looking at it for a little space—half a minute, perhaps, or half an hour. It seemed to advance and to recede as the hail drove before it denser or thinner. At last I tore my eyes from it for a moment, and saw that the hail curtain had worn threadbare, and that the sky was lightening with the promise of the sun.

"I looked up again at the crouching white shape, and the full temerity of my voyage came suddenly upon me. What might appear when that hazy curtain was altogether withdrawn? What might not have happened to men? What if cruelty had grown into a common passion? What if in this interval the race had lost its manliness, and had developed into something inhuman, unsympathetic, and overwhelmingly powerful? I might seem some old-world savage animal, only the more dreadful and disgusting for our common likeness—a foul creature to be incontinently slain.

"Already I saw other vast shapes—huge buildings with intricate parapets and tall columns, with a wooded hillside dimly creeping in upon me through the lessening storm. I was seized with a panic fear. I turned frantically to the Time Machine, and strove hard to readjust it. As I did so the shafts of the sun smote through the thunderstorm. The gray downpour was swept aside and vanished like the trailing garments of a ghost. Above me, in the intense blue of the summer sky, some faint brown shreds of clouds whirled into nothingness. The great buildings about me stood out clear and distinct, shining with the wet of the thunderstorm, and picked out in white by the unmelted hailstones piled along their courses. I felt naked in a strange world. I felt as perhaps a bird may feel in the clear air, knowing the hawk wings above and will swoop. My fear grew to frenzy. I took a breathing space, set my teeth, and again grappled fiercely, wrist and knee, with the machine. It gave under my desperate onset and turned over. It struck my chin violently. One hand on the saddle, the other on the lever, I stood panting heavily in attitude to mount again.

"But with this recovery of a prompt retreat my courage recovered. I looked more curiously and less fearfully at this world of the remote future. In a circular opening, high up in the wall of the nearer house, I saw a group of figures clad in rich soft robes. They had seen me, and their faces were directed toward me.

"Then I heard voices approaching me. Coming through the bushes by the white sphinx were the heads and shoulders of men running. One of these emerged in a pathway leading straight to the little lawn upon which I stood with my machine. He was a slight creature—perhaps four feet high—clad in a purple tunic, girdled at the waist with a leather belt. Sandals or buskins—I could not clearly distinguish which—were on his feet; his legs were bare to the knees, and his head was bare. Noticing that, I noticed for the first time how warm the air was.

"He struck me as being a very beautiful and graceful creature, but indescribably frail. His flushed face reminded me of the more beautiful kind of consumptive—that hectic beauty of which we used to hear so much. At the sight of him I suddenly regained confidence. I took my hands from the machine.

IV. THE GOLDEN AGE

"In another moment we were standing face to face, I and this fragile thing out of futurity. He came straight up to me and laughed into my eyes. The absence of any sign of fear from his bearing struck me at once. Then he turned to the two others who were following him and spoke to them in a strange and very sweet and liquid tongue.

"There were others coming, and presently a little group of perhaps eight or ten of these exquisite creatures were about me. One of them addressed me. It came into my head, oddly enough, that my voice was too harsh and deep for them. So I shook my head, and pointing to my ears, shook it again. He came a step forward, hesitated, and then touched my hand. Then I felt other soft little tentacles upon my back and shoulders. They wanted to make sure I was real. There was nothing in this at all alarming. Indeed, there was something in these pretty little people that inspired confidence—a graceful gentleness, a certain childlike ease. And besides, they looked so frail that I could fancy myself flinging the whole dozen of them about like ninepins. But I made a sudden motion to warn them when I saw their little pink hands feeling at the Time Machine. Happily then, when it was not too late, I thought of a danger I had hitherto forgotten, and reaching over the bars of the machine I unscrewed the little levers that would set it in motion, and put these in my pocket. Then I turned again to see what I could do in the way of communication.

"And then, looking more nearly into their features, I saw some further peculiarities in their Dresden china type of prettiness. Their hair, which was uniformly curly, came to a sharp end at the neck and cheek; there was not the faintest suggestion of it on the face, and their ears were singularly minute. The mouths were small, with bright red, rather thin lips, and the little chins ran to a point. The eyes were large and mild; and—this may seem egotism on my part—I fancied even then that there was a certain lack of the interest I might have expected in them.

"As they made no effort to communicate with me, but simply stood round me smiling and speaking in soft cooing notes to each other, I began the conversation. I pointed to the Time Machine and to myself. Then, hesitating for a moment how to express Time, I pointed to the sun. At once a quaintly pretty little figure in checkered purple and white, followed my gesture, and then astonished me by imitating the sound of thunder.

"For the moment I was staggered, though the import of his gesture was plain enough. The question had come into my mind abruptly: Were these creatures fools? You may hardly understand how it took me. You see I had always anticipated that the people of the year Eight Hundred Thousand odd would be incredibly in front of us in knowledge, art, everything. Then one of them suddenly asked me a question that showed him to be on the intellectual level of one of our five-year-old children—asked me, in fact, if I had come from the sun in a thunderstorm! It let loose the judgment I had suspended upon their clothes, their frail, light limbs, and fragile features. A flow of disappointment rushed across my mind. For a moment I felt that I had built the Time Machine in vain.

"I nodded, pointed to the sun, and gave them such a vivid rendering of a thunderclap as startled them. They all withdrew a pace or so and bowed. Then came one laughing toward me, carrying a chain of beautiful flowers, altogether new to me, and put it about my neck. The idea was received with melodious applause; and presently they were all running to and fro for flowers, and laughingly flinging them upon me until I was almost smothered with blossom. You who have never seen the like can scarcely imagine what delicate and wonderful flowers countless years of culture had created. Then someone suggested that their plaything should be exhibited in the nearest building, and so I was led past the sphinx of white marble, which had seemed to watch me all the while with a smile at my astonishment, toward a vast gray edifice of fretted stone. As I went with them the memory of my confident anticipations of a profoundly grave and intellectual posterity came, with irresistible merriment, to my mind.

"The building had a large entry and was altogether of colossal dimensions. I was naturally most occupied with the growing crowd of little people, and with the big open portals that yawned before me shadowy and mysterious. My general impression of the world I saw over their heads was of a tangled waste of beautiful bushes and flowers, a long neglected and yet weedless garden. I saw a number of tall spikes of strange white flowers, measuring a foot perhaps across the spread of the waxen petals. They grew scattered, as if wild, among the variegated shrubs, but, as I say, I did not examine them closely at this time. The Time Machine was left deserted on the turf among the rhododendrons.

"The arch of the doorway was richly carved, but naturally I did not observe the carving very narrowly, though I fancied I saw suggestions of old Phœnician decorations as I passed through, and it struck me that they were very badly broken and weather-worn. Several more brightly clad people met me in the doorway, and so we entered, I, dressed in dingy nineteenth century garments, looking grotesque enough, garlanded with flowers, and surrounded by an eddying mass of bright, soft-colored robes and shining white limbs, in a melodious whirl of laughter and laughing speech.

"The big doorway opened into a proportionately great hall hung with brown. The roof was in shadow, and the windows, partially glazed with colored glass, and partially unglazed, admitted a tempered light. The floor was made up of huge blocks of some very hard white metal, not plates nor slabs—blocks, and it was so much worn, as I judged by the going to and fro of past generations, as to be deeply channeled along the more frequented ways. Transverse to the length were innumerable tables made of slabs of polished stone, raised, perhaps, a foot from the floor, and upon these were heaps of fruits. Some I recognized as a kind of hypertrophied raspberry and orange, but for the most part they were strange.

"Between the tables were scattered a great number of cushions. Upon these my conductors seated themselves, signing for me to do likewise. With a pretty absence of ceremony they began to eat the fruit with their hands, flinging peel, and stalks, and so forth, into the round openings in the sides of the tables. I was not loth to follow their example, for I felt thirsty and hungry. As I did so I surveyed the hall at my leisure.

"And perhaps the thing that struck me most was its dilapidated look. The stained-glass windows, which displayed only a geometrical pattern, were broken in many places, and the curtains that hung across the lower end were thick with dust. And it caught my eye that the corner of the marble table near me was fractured. Nevertheless, the general effect was extremely rich and picturesque. There were, perhaps, a couple of hundred people dining in the hall, and most of them, seated as near to me as they could come, were watching me with interest, their little eyes shining over the fruit they were eating. All were clad in the same soft, and yet strong, silky material.

"Fruit, by the bye, was all their diet. These people of the remote future were strict vegetarians, and while I was with them, in spite of some carnal cravings, I had to be frugivorous also. Indeed, I found afterward that horses, cattle, sheep, dogs, had followed the ichthyosaurus into extinction. But the fruits were very delightful; one, in particular, that seemed to be in season all the time I was there,—a floury thing in a three-sided husk,—was especially good, and I made it my staple. At first I was puzzled by all these strange fruits, and by the strange flowers I saw, but later I began to perceive their import.

"However, I am telling you of my fruit dinner in the distant future now. So soon as my appetite was a little checked, I determined to make a resolute attempt to learn the speech of these new men of mine. Clearly that was the next thing to do. The fruits seemed a convenient thing to begin upon, and holding one of these up I began a series of interrogative sounds and gestures. I had some considerable difficulty in conveying my meaning. At first my efforts met with a stare of surprise or inextinguishable laughter, but presently a fair-haired little creature seemed to grasp my intention and repeated a name. They had to chatter and explain their business at great length to each other, and my first attempts to make their exquisite little sounds of the language caused an immense amount of genuine, if uncivil amusement. However, I felt like a schoolmaster amid children, and persisted, and presently I had a score of noun substantives at least, at my command; and then I got to demonstrative pronouns, and even the verb 'to eat.' But it was slow work, and the little people soon tired and wanted to get away from my interrogations, so I determined, rather of necessity, to let them give their lessons in little doses when they felt inclined. And very little doses I found they were before long, for I never met people more indolent or more easily fatigued.

V. SUNSET

"A queer thing I soon discovered about my little hosts, and that was their lack of interest. They would come to me with eager cries of astonishment, like children, but, like children, they would soon stop examining me, and wander away after some other toy. The dinner and my conversational beginnings ended, I noted for the first time that almost all those who had surrounded me at first were gone. It is odd, too, how speedily I came to disregard these little people. I went out through the portal into the sunlit world again as soon as my hunger was satisfied. I was continually meeting more of these men of the future, who would follow me a little distance, chatter and laugh about me, and, having smiled and gesticulated in a friendly way, leave me again to my own devises.

"The calm of evening was upon the world as I emerged from the great hall, and the scene was lit by the warm glow of the setting sun. At first things were very confusing. Everything was so entirely different from the world I had known—even the flowers. The big building I had left was situated on the slope of a broad river valley, but the Thames had shifted, perhaps a mile from its present position. I resolved to mount to the summit of a crest, possibly a mile and a half away, from which I could get a wider view of this our planet in the year 802,701, A.D For that, I should explain, was the date the little dials of my machine recorded.

"As I walked I was watchful of every impression that could possibly help to explain the condition of ruinous splendor in which I found the world—for ruinous it was. A little way up the hill, for instance, was a great heap of granite, bound together by masses of aluminum, a vast labyrinth of precipitous walls and crumbled heaps, amid which were thick heaps of very beautiful pagoda-like plants—nettles possibly, but wonderfully tinted with brown about the leaves, and incapable of stinging. It was evidently the derelict remains of some vast structure, built to what end I could not determine. It was here that I was destined, at a later date, to have a very strange experience—the first intimation of a still stranger discovery—but of that I will speak in its proper place.

"Looking round, with a sudden thought, from a terrace on which I had rested for a while, I realized that there were no small houses to be seen. Apparently the single house, and possibly even the household, had vanished. Here and there among the greenery were palace-like buildings, but the house and the cottage, which form such characteristic features of our own English landscape, had disappeared.

" 'Communism,' said I to myself.

"And on the heels of that came another thought. I looked at the half dozen little figures that were following me. Then, in a flash, I perceived that all had the same form of costume, the same soft hairless visage, and the same girlish rotundity of limb. It may seem strange, perhaps, that I had not noticed this before. But everything was so strange. Now, I saw the fact plainly enough. In costume, and in all the differences of texture and bearing that now mark off the sexes from each other, these people of the future were alike. And the children seemed to my eyes to be but the miniatures of their parents. I judged then that children of that time were extremely precocious, physically at least, and I found afterward abundant verification of my opinion.

"Seeing the ease and security in which these people were living, I felt that this close resemblance of the sexes was, after all, what one would expect; for the strength of a man and the softness of a woman, the institution of the family, and the differentiation of occupations are mere militant necessities of an age of physical force. Where population is balanced and abundant, much child-bearing becomes an evil rather than a blessing to the State; where violence comes but rarely and offspring are secure, there is less necessity—indeed there is no necessity—of an efficient family, and the specialization of the sexes with reference to their children's needs disappears. We see some beginnings of this even in our own time, and in this future age it was complete. This, I must remind you, was my speculation at the time. Later, I was to appreciate how far it fell short of the reality.

"While I was musing upon these things, my attention was attracted by a pretty little structure, like a well under a cupola. I thought in a transitory way of the oddness of wells still existing, and then resumed the thread of my speculations. There were no large buildings toward the top of the hill, and as my walking powers were evidently miraculous, I was presently left alone for the first time. With a strange sense of freedom and adventure I pushed up to the crest.

"There I found a seat of some yellow metal that I did not recognize, corroded in places with a kind of pinkish rust and half smothered in soft moss, the arm rests cast and filed into the resemblance of griffins' heads. I sat down on it, and I surveyed the broad view of our old world under the sunset of that long day. It was as sweet and fair a view as I have ever seen. The sun had already gone below the horizon and the west was flaming gold, touched with some horizontal bars of purple and crimson. Below was the valley of the Thames, in which the river lay like a band of burnished steel. I have ready spoken of the great palaces dotted about among the variegated greenery, some in ruins and some still occupied. Here and there rose a white or silvery figure in the waste garden of the earth, here and there came the sharp vertical line of some cupola or obelisk. There were no hedges, no signs of proprietary rights, no evidences of agriculture; the whole earth had become a garden.

"So watching, I began to put my interpretation upon the things I had seen, and as it shaped itself to me that evening, my interpretation was something in this way (afterward I found I had got only a half truth, or only a glimpse of one facet of the truth):

"It seemed to me that I had happened upon humanity upon the wane. The ruddy sunset set me thinking of the sunset of mankind. For the first time I began to realize an odd consequence of the social effort in which we are at present engaged. And yet, come to think, it is a logical consequence enough. Strength is the outcome of need; security sets a premium on feebleness. The work of ameliorating the conditions of life—the true civilizing process that makes life more and more secure—had gone steadily on to a climax. One triumph of a united humanity over Nature had followed another. Things that are now mere dreams had become projects deliberately put in hand and carried forward. And the harvest was what I saw!

"After all, the sanitation and the agriculture of to-day are still in the rudimentary stage. The science of our time has attacked but a little department of the field of human disease, but, even so, it spreads its operations very steadily and persistently. Our agriculture and horticulture destroy just here and there a weed and cultivate perhaps a score or so of wholesome plants, leaving the greater number to fight out a balance as they can. We improve our favorite plants and animals—and how few they are—gradually by selective breeding; now a new and better peach, now a seedless grape, now a sweeter and larger flower, now a more convenient breed of cattle. We improve them gradually, because our ideals are vague and tentative, and our knowledge is very limited; because Nature, too, is shy and slow in our clumsy hands. Some day all this will be better organized, and still better. That is the drift of the current in spite of the eddies. The whole world will be intelligent, educated, and cooperating; things will move faster and faster toward the subjugation of Nature. In the end, wisely and carefully we shall readjust the balance of animal and vegetable life to suit our human needs.

"This adjustment, I say, must have been done, and done well: done indeed for all time, in the space of Time across which my machine had leaped. The air was free from gnats, the earth from weeds or fungi; everywhere were fruits and sweet and delightful flowers; brilliant butterflies flew hither and thither. The ideal of preventive medicine was attained. Diseases had been stamped out. I saw no evidence of any contagious diseases during all my stay. And I shall have to tell you later that even the processes of putrefaction and decay had been profoundly affected by these changes.

"Social triumphs, too, had been effected. I saw mankind housed in splendid shelters, gloriously clothed, and as yet I had found them engaged in no toil. There were no signs of struggle, neither social nor economical struggle. The shop, the advertisement, traffic, all that commerce which constitutes the body of our world, was gone. It was natural on that golden evening that I should jump at the idea of a social paradise.

"The difficulty of increasing population had been met, I guessed, and population had ceased to increase.

"But with this change in condition comes inevitably adaptations to the change. What, unless biological science is a mass of errors, is the cause of human intelligence and vigor? Hardship and freedom: conditions under which the active, strong, and subtle survive and the weaker go to the wall; conditions that put a premium upon the loyal alliance of capable men, upon self-restraint, patience, and decision. And the institution of the family, and the emotions that arise therein, the fierce jealousy, the tenderness for offspring, parental self-devotion, all found their justification and support in the imminent dangers of the young. *Now* where are those imminent dangers? There is a sentiment arising, and it will grow, against connubial jealousy, against fierce maternity, against passion of all sorts; unnecessary things now, and things that

make us uncomfortable, savage survivals, discords in a refined and pleasant life.

"I thought of the physical slightness of the people, their lack of intelligence, and those big abundant ruins, and it strengthened my belief in a perfect conquest of Nature. For after the battle comes Quiet. Humanity had been strong, energetic, and intelligent, and had used all its abundant vitality to alter the conditions under which it lived. And now came the reaction of the altered conditions.

"Under the new conditions of perfect comfort and security, that restless energy, that with us is strength, would become weakness. Even in our own time certain tendencies and desires, once necessary to survival, are a constant source of failure. Physical courage and the love of battle, for instance, are no great help—may even be hindrances—to a civilized man. And in a state of physical balance and security, power, intellectual as well as physical, would be out of place. For countless years I judged there had been no danger of war or solitary violence, no danger from wild beasts, no wasting disease to require strength of constitution, no need of toil. For such a life, what we should call the weak are as well equipped as the strong, are, indeed, no longer weak. Better equipped indeed they are, for the strong would be fretted by an energy for which there was no outlet. No doubt the exquisite beauty of the buildings I saw was the outcome of the last surgings of the now purposeless energy of mankind before it settled down into perfect harmony with the conditions under which it lived—the flourish of that triumph which began the last great peace. This has ever been the fate of energy in security; it takes to art and to eroticism, and then come languor and decay.

"Even this artistic impetus would at last die away—had almost died in the Time I saw. To adorn themselves with flowers, to dance, to sing in the sunlight;

so much was left of the artistic spirit, and no more. Even that would fade in the end into a contented inactivity. We are kept keen on the grindstone of pain and necessity, and it seemed to me that here was that hateful grindstone broken at last!

"As I stood there in the gathering dark I thought that in this simple explanation I had mastered the problem of the world—mastered the whole secret of these delicious people. Possibly the checks they had devised for the increase of population had succeeded too well, and their numbers had rather diminished than kept stationary. That would account for the abandoned ruins. Very simple was my explanation, and plausible enough—as most wrong theories are.

"As I stood there musing over this too perfect triumph of man, the full moon, yellow and gibbous, came up out of an overflow of silver light in the northeast. The bright little figures ceased to move about below, a noiseless owl flitted by, and I shivered with the chill of the night. I determined to descend and find where I could sleep.

"I looked for the building I knew. Then my eye traveled along to the figure of the white sphinx upon the pedestal of bronze, growing distinct as the light of the rising moon grew brighter. I could see the silver birch against it. There was the tangle of rhododendron bushes, black in the pale light, and there was the little lawn. I looked at the lawn again. A queer doubt chilled my complacency. 'No,' said I stoutly to myself, 'that was not the lawn.'

"But it *was* the lawn. For the white leprous face of the sphinx was toward it. Can you imagine what I felt as this conviction came home to me? But you cannot. The Time Machine was gone!

"At once, like a lash across the face, came the possibility of losing my own age, of being left helpless in this strange new world. The bare thought of it was an actual physical sensation. I could feel it grip me at the throat and stop my breathing.

VI. THE MACHINE IS LOST

"In another moment I was in a passion of fear, and running with great, leaping strides down the slope. Once I fell headlong and cut my face. I lost no time in stanching the blood, but jumped up and ran on, with a warm trickle down my cheek and chin. All the time I ran I was saying to myself: 'They have moved it a little—pushed it under the bushes out of the way.' Nevertheless, I ran with all my might. All the time, with the certainty that sometimes comes with excessive dread, I knew that such assurance was folly, knew instinctively that the machine was removed out of my reach.

"My breath came with pain. I suppose I covered the whole distance, from the hill crest to the little lawn, two miles perhaps, in ten minutes. And I am not a young man. I cursed aloud as I ran at my confident folly in leaving the machine, wasting good breath thereby. I cried aloud, and none answered. Not a creature seemed to be stirring in that moonlit world.

"When I reached the lawn my worst fears were realized. Not a trace of the thing was to be seen. I felt faint and cold when I faced the empty space among the black tangle of bushes. I ran round it furiously, as if the thing might be hidden in a corner, and then stopped abruptly with my hands clutching my hair. Above me towered the sphinx upon the bronze pedestal, white, shining, leprous in the light of the rising moon. It seemed to smile in mockery of my dismay.

"I might have consoled myself by imagining the little people had put the mechanism in some shelter for me, had not I felt assured of their physical and intellectual inadequacy. That is what dismayed me: the sense of some hitherto unsuspected power through whose intervention my invention had vanished. Yet of one thing I felt assured: unless some other age had produced its exact duplicate, the machine could not have moved in Time. The attachment of the levers—I will show you the method later—prevented anyone from tampering with it in that way when they were removed. It had been moved, and was hid, only in Space. But, then, where could it be?

"I think I must have had a kind of frenzy. I remember running violently in and out among the moonlit bushes all round the sphinx, and startling some white animal that in the dim light I took for a small deer. I remember, too, late that night, beating the bushes with my clenched fists until my knuckles were gashed and bleeding from the broken twigs.

"Then, sobbing and raving in my anguish of mind, I went down to the great building of stone. The big hall was dark, silent, and deserted. I slipped on the uneven floor and fell over one of the malachite tables, almost breaking my shin. I lit a match and went on past the dusty curtains of which I have told you.

"There I found a second great hall covered with cushions, upon which perhaps a score or so of the little people were sleeping. I have no doubt they found my second appearance strange enough, coming suddenly out of the quiet darkness with inarticulate noises and the splutter and flare of a match. For they had forgotten about matches. 'Where is my Time Machine?' I began, bawling like an angry child, laying hands upon them and shaking them up together. It must have been very queer to them. Some laughed, most of them looked sorely frightened. When I saw them standing round me, it came into my head that I was doing as foolish a thing as it was possible for me to do under the circumstances, in trying to revive the sensation of fear. For reasoning from the daylight behavior I thought that fear must be forgotten.

"Abruptly I dashed down the match, and knocking one of the people over in my course, went blundering across the big dining hall again out under the moonlight. I heard cries of terror and their little feet running and stumbling this way and that. I do not remember all I did as the moon crept up the sky. I suppose it was the unexpected nature of my loss that maddened me. I felt hopelessly cut off from my own kind, a strange animal in an unknown world. I must have raved to and fro, screaming and crying upon God and Fate. I have a memory of horrible fatigue, as the long night of despair wore away, of looking in this impossible place and that, of groping among moonlit ruins and touching strange creatures in the black shadows; at last, of lying on the ground near the sphinx and weeping with absolute wretchedness, even anger at the folly of leaving the machine having leaked away with my strength. I had nothing left but misery.

"Then I slept, and when I woke again it was full day, and a couple of sparrows were hopping around me upon the turf within reach of my arm.

"I sat up in the freshness of the morning trying to remember how I had got there, and why I had such a profound sense of desertion and despair. Then things came clear in my mind. With the plain, reasonable daylight I could look my circumstances fairly in the face. I saw the wild folly of my frenzy overnight, and I could reason with myself.

" 'Suppose the worst,' said I, 'suppose the machine altogether lost—perhaps destroyed. It behooves me to be calm and patient, to learn the way of the people, to get a clear idea of the method of my loss and the means of getting materials and tools; so that in the end, perhaps, I may make another. That would be my only hope, a poor hope, perhaps, but better than despair. And, after all, it was a beautiful and curious world.

" 'But probably the machine has only been taken away. Still, I must be calm and patient, find its hiding place, and recover it by force or cunning.' And with that I scrambled to my feet and looked about me, wondering where I could bathe. I felt weary, stiff, and travel-soiled. The freshness of the morning made me desire an equal freshness. I had exhausted my emotion. Indeed, as I went about my business, I found myself wondering at my intense excitement overnight.

"That morning I made a careful ex-amination of the ground about the little lawn. I wasted some time in futile questionings conveyed as well as I was able to such of the little people as came by. They all failed to understand my gestures—some were simply stolid; some thought it was a jest, and laughed at me. I had the hardest task in the world to keep my hands off their pretty, laughing faces. It was a foolish impulse, but the devil begotten of fear and blind anger was ill curbed, and still eager to take advantage of my per-plexity. The turf gave better counsel. I found a groove ripped in it, about midway between the pedestal of the sphinx and the marks of my feet where, on arrival, I had struggled with the overturned machine. There were other signs of the removal of a heavy body about, of queer, narrow footprints like those I could imagine made by a sloth. This directed my closer attention to the pedestal. It was, as I think I have said, of bronze. It was not a mere block, but highly decorated with deep-framed pan-els on either side. I went and rapped at these. The pedestal was hollow. Ex-amining the panels with care, I found them discontinuous with the frames. There were no handles nor keyholes, but possibly the panels, if they were doors, as I supposed, opened from within. One thing was clear enough to my mind. It took no very great mental

effort to infer that my Time Machine was inside that pedestal. But how it got there was a different problem.

"I saw the heads of two orange-clad people coming through the bushes and under some blossom-covered apple trees toward me. I turned, smiling, to them, and beckoned them to me. They came, and then, pointing to the bronze ped-estal, I tried to intimate my wish to open it. But at my first gesture toward this, they behaved very oddly. I don't know how to convey their expression to you. Suppose you were to use a grossly improper gesture to a delicate-minded woman—it is how she would look. They went off as if they had received the last possible insult.

"However, I wanted access to the Time Machine; so I tried a sweet-looking little chap in white next, with exactly the same result. Somehow, his manner made me ashamed of myself. But, as I say, I wanted the Time Machine. I tried one more. As he turned off like the others, my temper got the better of me. In three strides I was after him, had him by the loose part of his robe round the neck, and began dragging him to-ward the sphinx. Then I saw the horror and repugnance of his face, and all of a sudden I let him go.

"But I was not beaten yet. I banged with my fist at the bronze panels. I thought I heard something stir inside— to be explicit, I thought I heard a sound like a chuckle—but I must have been mistaken. Then I got a big pebble from the river, and came and hammered till I had flattened a coil in the decorations, and the verdegris came off in powdery flakes. The delicate little people must have heard me hammering in gusty outbreaks a mile away on either hand, but nothing came of it. I saw a crowd of them upon the slopes, looking fur-tively at me. At last, hot and tired, I sat down to watch the place. But I was too restless to watch long, and, besides, I am too Occidental for a long vigil. I could work at a problem for years, but to wait inactive for twenty-four hours—that is another matter.

"I got up after a time, and began walking aimlessly through the bushes toward the hill again.

" 'Patience,' said I to myself. 'If you want your machine again, you must leave that sphinx alone. If they mean to take your machine away, it's little good your wrecking their bronze panels, and if they don't, you will get it back so soon as you can ask for it. To sit among all those unknown things before a puzzle like that is hopeless. That way lies monomania. Face this world. Learn its ways; watch it; be careful of too hasty guesses at its meaning. In the end you will find clues to it all.'

"Then suddenly the humor of the situation came into my mind: the thought of the years I had spent in study and toil to get into the future age, and now my passion of anxiety to get out of it. I had made myself the most complicated and the most hopeless trap that ever a man devised. Although it was at my own expense, I could not help myself. I laughed aloud.

"Going through the big palace it seemed to me that the little people avoided me. It may have been my fancy, or it may have had something to do with my hammering at the gates of bronze. Yet I felt tolerably sure of the avoidance. I was careful, however, to show no concern, and to abstain from any pursuit of them, and in the course of a day or two things got back to the old footing.

VII. THE STRANGE ANIMAL

"I made what progress I could in the language, and in addition I pushed my explorations here and there. Either I missed some subtle point or their language was excessively simple, almost exclusively composed of concrete substantives and verbs. There seemed to be few, if any, abstract terms, or little use of figurative language. Their sentences were usually simple and of two words, and I failed to convey or understand any but the simplest propositions. I determined to put the thought of my Time Machine, and the mystery of the bronze doors under the sphinx, as much as possible in a corner of my memory until my growing knowledge would lead me back to them in a natural way. Yet a certain feeling you may understand tethered me in a circle of a few miles round the point of my arrival.

"So far as I could see, all the world displayed the same exuberant richness as the Thames valley. From every hill I climbed I saw the same abundance of splendid buildings, endlessly varied in material and style, the same clustering thickets of evergreens, the same blossom-laden trees and tree ferns. Here and there water shone like silver, and beyond, the land rose into blue undulating hills and so faded into the serenity of the sky.

"A peculiar feature that presently attracted my attention was certain circular wells that appeared to sink to a profound depth. One lay by the path up the hill which I had followed during my first walk. These wells were rimmed with bronze, curiously wrought, and often protected by small cupolas from the rain. Sitting by the side of these, and peering down, I failed to see any gleam of water, and could catch no reflection from a lighted match. I heard a peculiar dull sound; thud, thud, thud, like the beating of some big engine, and I discovered from the flaring of the match that a steady current of air set down the shaft.

"Moreover, I carelessly threw a scrap of paper into the throat of the well, and instead of fluttering slowly down, it was at once sucked swiftly out of sight. After a time, too, I came to connect with these wells certain tall towers that stood here and there upon the hill slopes. Above these there was often apparent a peculiar flicker of the air, much as one sees it on a hot day above a sun-scorched beach.

"Putting these things together there certainly seemed to me a strong suggestion of an extensive system of subterraneous ventilation, though its true import was difficult to imagine. I was at first inclined to associate it with the sanitary apparatus of these people. It was the obvious suggestion of these things, but it was absolutely wrong.

"And here I must admit that I learned very little of drains, and bells, and modes of conveyance and the like conveniences during my time in this real future. In some of the fictitious visions of Utopias and coming times I have read, there is a vast amount of detail about building construction and social arrangements and so forth. But while such details are easy enough to obtain when the whole world lies in one's imagination, they are altogether inaccessible to a real traveler amid such realities as surrounded me. Conceive what tale of London a negro from Central Africa would take back to his tribe. What would he know of railway companies, of social movements, of telephone and telegraph wires, of the parcels delivery company, and postal orders? And yet we at least would be willing enough to explain these things. And even of what he knew, how much could he make his untraveled friend believe? Then think how little is the gap between a negro and a man of our times, and how wide the interval between myself and the Golden Age people. I was sensible of much that was unseen, and which contributed to my comfort, but save for a general impression of automatic organization, I fear I can convey very little of the difference to your minds.

"In the matter of sepulcher, for instance, I could see no traces of crematoria or anything suggestive of tombs. But it occurred to me that possibly cemeteries or crematoria existed at some spot beyond the range of my explorations. This again was a question I deliberately put to myself, and upon which my curiosity was at first entirely defeated. Neither were there any old or infirm among them.

"I must confess that my satisfaction with my first theories at an automatic civilization and a decadent humanity did not endure. Yet I could think of none other. Let me put my difficulties. The several big palaces I had explored were mere living places, great dining halls and sleeping apartments. I could find no machinery, no appliances of any kind. Yet these people were clothed in pleasant fabrics that must at times need renewal, their sandals though without ornament were fairly complex specimens of metal work. Somehow such things must be made. And the little people displayed no vestige of the creative tendencies of our time. There were no shops, no workshops, no indications of importations from any other part of the earth. They spent all their time in playing gently, in bathing in the river, in making love in a half playful fashion, in eating fruit, and sleeping. I could not see how things were kept going.

"Then again about the Time Machine. Something, I knew not what, had taken it into the hollow pedestal of the sphinx. Why? For the life of me I could not imagine.

"Then there were those wells without water, those flickering pillars. I felt I missed a clue somewhere. I felt—how shall I say it? Suppose you found an inscription with sentences here and there in excellent plain English, and interpolated therewith others made up of words, even of letters, absolutely unknown to you. That was how the world of 802,701 presented itself to me on the third day of my stay.

"On that day, too, I made a friend—of a sort. It happened that as I was watching some of the little people bathing in a shallow of the river, one of them was seized with cramp and began drifting down the stream. The main current of the stream ran rather swiftly there, but not too swiftly for even a moderate swimmer. It will give you an idea, therefore, of the strange want of ideas of these people, when I tell you that none made the slightest attempt to rescue the weakly, crying little creature who was drowning before their eyes.

"When I realized this I hurriedly slipped off my garments, and wading in from a point lower down, caught the poor little soul and brought her to land.

"A little rubbing of the limbs soon brought her round, and I had the satisfaction of seeing that she was all right before I left her. I had got to such a low estimate of these little folks that I did not expect gratitude. In that, however, I was wrong.

"The incident happened in the morning. In the afternoon I met my little woman, as I believe it was, when I was returning toward my center from one of my explorations, and she received me with cries of delight and presented me with a big garland of flowers—evidently prepared for me.

"The action took my imagination. Very possibly I had been feeling desolate. At any rate I did my best to display my appreciation of the gift.

"We were soon seated together in a little stone arbor, engaged in a conversation that was chiefly smiles.

"The little creature's friendliness affected me exactly as a child's might. We passed each other flowers and she kissed my hands. I did the same to hers. Then I tried conversation and found out her name was Weena, which, though I don't know what it meant, somehow seemed appropriate enough. That was the beginning of a queer friendship that lasted altogether a week and ended—as I will tell you.

"She was exactly like a child. She wanted to be with me always. She tried to follow me everywhere, and it went to my heart to tire her out upon my next exploration and leave her behind at last exhausted, and calling after me rather plaintively. But the problems of the world had to be mastered. I had not, I said to myself, come into the future to carry on a miniature flirtation. Yet her distress when I left her was very great, her expostulations at the parting sometimes frantic, and I think altogether I had as much trouble as comfort from her affection. And yet she was, somehow, a very great comfort.

"I thought it was mere childish affection that made her cling to me. Until it was too late, I did not clearly know what I had inflicted upon her when I left her. Nor, until it was too late, did I clearly understand what she was to me. For the little doll of a creature, by merely seeming fond of me and showing in her weak futile way that she cared for me, presently gave my return to the neighborhood of the white sphinx, almost the feeling of coming home. I would watch for her little figure of white and gold so soon as I came over the hill.

"It was from her, too, that I learned that fear had not altogether left the world. She was fearless enough in the daylight, and she had the oddest confidence in me—for once in a foolish moment I made threatening grimaces at her, and she simply laughed at them. But she dreaded the dark, dreaded shadows, dreaded black things. Darkness to her was the one fearful thing. It was a singularly passionate dread, and it set me thinking and observing. I discovered then, among other things, that these little people gathered into the great houses after dark, and slept a number together. To enter upon them without a light was to put them into a tumult of apprehension. I never found one out of doors or one sleeping alone within doors after dark.

"Yet I was still such a blockhead that I missed the lesson of that fear, and in spite of Weena's evident distress insisted upon sleeping away from these slumbering heaps of humanity. It troubled her greatly, but usually her odd affection for me triumphed, and for five of the nights of our acquaintance, including the last night of all, she slept with her head pillowed beside mine. But my story slips away from me as I speak of her.

"It must have been on the night before I rescued Weena that I woke up about dawn. I had been restless, dreaming most disagreeably that I was drowned and that sea anemones were feeling over my face with their soft palps. I awoke with a start, and with an odd fancy that some grayish animal had just rushed out of the chamber in which I slept.

"I tried to get to sleep again, but I felt restless and uncomfortable. It was that dim gray hour when things are just creeping out of the darkness, when everything is colorless and clear-cut and yet unreal. I got up and went down into the great hall and out upon the flagstones in front of the palace. I thought I would make a virtue of necessity and see the sunrise.

"The moon was setting, and the dying moonlight and first pallor of dawn mingled together in a ghastly half-light. The bushes were inky black, the ground a somber gray, the sky colorless and cheerless. And up the hill slope I thought I saw ghosts. Three several times as I scanned the slope I saw white figures. Twice I fancied I saw a solitary white ape-like creature running rather quickly up the hill, and once near the ruins I saw a group of two carrying some dark body. They moved hastily. I did not see what became of them. It seemed that they vanished among the bushes.

"The dawn was still indistinct, you must understand. I was feeling that chill, uncertain, early morning feeling you may have experienced. I doubted my eyes. As the eastern sky grew brighter, and the light of the day increased, and vivid coloring came back to the world once more, I scanned the view keenly,

but I saw no confirmation of my white figures. They were mere creatures of the half light.

" 'They must have been ghosts,' said I; 'I wonder whence they dated.'

"For a queer notion of Grant Allen's came into my head and amused me. If each generation dies and leaves ghosts, he argues, the world at last will get overcrowded with them. On that theory they would have become very thick in eight hundred thousand years from now, and it was no great wonder to see four all at once. But the jest was unsatisfactory, and I was thinking of these figures all the morning until the rescue of Weena drove the subject out of my head. I associated them in some indefinite way with the white animal I had startled in my first passionate search for the Time Machine. But Weena was a pleasant substitute for such a topic.

"These ghostly shapes were soon destined to take possession of my mind in a far more vivid fashion. I think I have said how much hotter than our own was the weather of this future age. I cannot account for it. It may be the sun was hotter, or else the earth was nearer the sun. It is usual to assume that the sun will go on cooling steadily in the future, but people unfamiliar with such speculations as those of the younger Darwin, forget that the planets must ultimately, one by one, fall back into the parent body. As these catastrophes occur the sun will blaze out again with renewed energy. It may be that some inner planet had suffered this fate. Whatever the reason, the fact remains that the sun was very much hotter than it is now.

"It was one very hot morning, my fourth morning, I think, as I was seeking a refuge from the heat and glare in a colossal ruin near the great house where I sheltered, that this remarkable incident occurred. Clambering among these heaps of masonry, I found a long narrow gallery, the end and side windows of which were blocked by fallen masses of masonry and which by contrast with the brilliance outside seemed at first impenetrably dark to me.

"I entered it groping, for the change from light to blackness made spots of color swim before me. Suddenly I halted spell-bound. A pair of eyes, luminous by reflection against the daylight without, was watching me out of the obscurity!

"The old instinctive dread of wild animals came upon me. I clenched my hands and steadfastly looked into the glaring eyeballs. I feared to turn. Then the thought of the absolute security in which humanity appeared to be living came to my mind. Then I remembered that strange dread of the dark.

"Overcoming my fear to some extent, I advanced a step, and spoke. I will admit that my voice was hoarse and ill controlled. I put out my hand, and touched something soft.

"At once the eyes darted sideways, and something white ran past me. I turned, with my heart in my mouth, and saw a queer little ape-like figure, with the head held down in a peculiar manner, running across the sunlit space behind me. It blundered against a block of granite, staggered aside, and in a moment was hidden in a black shadow beneath another pile of ruined masonry.

"My impression of it was of course very imperfect. It was of a dull white color, and had strange, large, grayish-red eyes. There was some flaxen hair on its head and down its back. But, as I say, it went too fast for me to see distinctly. I cannot even say whether it ran on all fours, or only with its forearms held very low.

"After a momentary hesitation I followed the creature into the second heap of ruins. I could not find it there at first, but after a time, in the profound obscurity I came upon one of those round, well-like openings, of which I have told you, half closed by a fallen pillar. A sudden thought came to me. Could the thing have vanished down the shaft? I lit a match, and, looking down, saw a small white moving figure, with large bright eyes, that regarded me steadfastly as it retreated.

"The thing made me shudder. It was so like a human spider. It was clambering down the wall of the shaft, and now I noticed for the first time a number of metal projections for foot and hand, forming a kind of ladder down.

"Suddenly the light burned my fingers and fell out of my hand, going out as it dropped; and when I had lit another, the little monster had disappeared.

"I do not know how long I sat peering down the portentous well. Very slowly could I persuade myself that the thing I had seen was a man. But gradually the real truth dawned upon me; that man had not remained one species, but had differentiated into two distinct animals; that my graceful children of the upperworld were not the only descendants of the men of my generation, but that this bleached, nocturnal thing that had flashed before me, was also heir to our age.

"I thought of the flickering pillars, and of my theory of an underground ventilation. I began to suspect their true import.

"But what was this creature doing in my scheme of a perfectly balanced organization? How was it related to the indolent serenity of the beautiful overworld people? And what was hidden down below there? I sat upon the edge of the well, telling myself I had nothing to fear in descending, and that there I must go for the solution of my difficulties, and withal I was absolutely afraid to go down.

"As I hesitated, two of the beautiful upperworld people came running in their amorous sport, across the daylight into the shadow. One pursued the other, flinging flowers at her as he ran. They seemed disappointed when they found me with my arm against the overturned pillar, peering down the well. Apparently, it was considered bad form to notice these apertures, for when I pointed to it, and tried to frame a question about it in their tongue, they seemed distressed, and turned away. They were, however, interested by my matches, and I struck several to amuse them.

"However, all my attempts to woo them toward the subject I wanted failed; and presently I left them. I resolved to go back to Weena, and see what I could get from her.

"But my mind was already in revolution, my guesses and impressions slipping and sliding to a new adjustment. I had now the clue to these wells, to the ventilating towers, to the problem of the ghosts, and a hint, indeed, of the meaning of the bronze gates and the fate of the Time Machine. Vaguely indeed, there came a suggestion toward the economic problem that had puzzled me.

"Here was the new view: Evidently this second species of man was subterranean. There were three circumstances in particular that made me think its rare emergence upon the surface was the outcome of long subterraneous habit. In the first place, the bleached appearance, common in most animals that lived largely in the dark—the white fish of the Kentucky caves, for instance. Then the large eyes and their capacity for reflecting the light—a common feature of nocturnal eyes, witness the owl and the cat. And finally the evident confusion in the sunlight, the hasty flight toward dark shadow, and the carriage of the head while in the light, reinforced the idea of an extremely sensitive retina.

"Beneath my feet, then, the earth must be tunneled out to an enormous extent, and in these caverns the new race lived. The presence of ventilating shafts and wells all along the hill slopes—everywhere, in fact, except along the river valley—showed how universally the ramifications of the underworld extended.

"And it was natural to assume that it was in the underworld that the necessary work of the overworld was performed. This was so plausible that I accepted it unhesitatingly. From that I went on to assume how the splitting of the human species came about. I dare say you will anticipate what shape my theory took, though I soon felt it was still short of the truth of the case.

"But at first, starting from the problems of our own age, it seemed as clear as daylight to me that the gradual widening of the present merely temporary and social difference of the capitalist from the laborer was the key to the explanation. No doubt it will seem grotesque enough to you and wildly incredible, and yet even now there are circumstances that point in the way things have gone. There is a tendency plainly enough to utilize underground space for the less ornamental purposes of civilization; there is the Metropolitan Railway in London, for instance, and all these new electric railways; there are subways, and underground workrooms, restaurants, and so forth. Evidently, I thought, this tendency had increased until industry had gradually lost sight of the day, going into larger and larger underground factories, in which the workers would spend an increasing amount of their time. Even now, an East End worker lives in such artificial conditions as practically to be cut off from the natural surface of the earth and the clear sky altogether.

"Then again, the exclusive tendency of richer people, due, no doubt, to the increasing refinement of their education and the widening gulf between them and the rude violence of the poor, is already leading to the closing of considerable portions of the surface of the country against these latter. About London, for instance, perhaps half the prettier country is shut up from such intrusion. And the same widening gulf, due to the length and expense of the higher educational process and the increased facilities for, and temptation to-ward, forming refined habits among the rich, will make that frequent exchange between class and class, that promotion and intermarriage which at present re-tards the splitting of our species along the lines of social stratification, less and less frequent.

"So, in the end, you would have above ground the Haves, pursuing health, com-fort, and beauty, and below ground the Have-nots; the workers, getting contin-ually adapted to their labor. No doubt, once they were below ground, consid-erable rents would be charged for the ventilation of their caverns. Workers who struck work would starve or be suffocated for arrears of ventilator rent; workers who were so constituted as to be miserable and rebellious would die. In the end, if the balance was held permanent, the survivors would become as well adapted to the conditions of their subterranean life as the overworld people were to theirs, and as happy in their way. It seemed to me that the refined beauty of the overworld, and the etiolated pallor of the lower, fol-lowed naturally enough.

"The great triumph of humanity I had dreamed of now took a different shape in my mind. It had been no triumph of universal education and gen-eral co-operation, such as I had imagined at the first. Instead, I saw a real aristoc-racy, armed with a perfected science and working out to a logical conclusion the industrial system of today. The tri-umph of the overworld humanity had not been simply a triumph over nature, but a triumph over nature and their fellowmen.

"I must warn you this was my theory at the time. I had no convenient Cicerone on the pattern of the Utopian books. My explanation may be absolutely wrong. I still think it the most plausible one. But even on this supposition the balanced civilization that was at last at-tained must have long since passed its zenith, and was now far gone in decay.

The too perfect security of the over-world had led these to a slow movement of degeneration at last—to a general dwindling of size, strength, and in-telligence. That I already saw clearly enough, but what had happened to the lower world I did not yet suspect. Yet from what I had seen of the Morlocks,—that, by the bye, was the name by which these creatures were called,—I could imagine the modification of the human type was far more profound in the un-derworld than among the Eloi, the beautiful races that I already knew.

"Then came some troublesome doubts. Why had the Morlocks taken my Time Machine? For I felt sure these under-people had taken it. Why, too, if the Eloi were masters, could they not restore the thing to me? And why were the Eloi so afraid of the dark?

"I determined, as I have said ,to question Weena about this underworld, but here again I was disappointed. At first she would not understand my ques-tions, and then she refused to answer. She shivered as though the topic was unendurable. And when I pressed her, perhaps a little harshly, she burst into tears.

"They were the only tears I ever saw in that future age, except my own. When I saw them I ceased abruptly to trouble about the Morlocks, and was only concerned in driving these signs of her human inheritance out of her eyes again. And presently she was smil-ing and clapping her hands while I solemnly burnt a match.

VIII. THE MORLOCKS

"It may seem odd to you, but it was two days before I could follow up the clue of these Morlocks in what was mani-festly the proper way, and descend into the well. I felt a peculiar shrinking from their pallid bodies. They were just the half-bleached color of the worms and things one sees preserved in spirit in a zoological museum. And they were cold to the touch. Probably my shrinking was largely due to the sympathetic influence of the Eloi, whose disgust of the Morlocks I now began to appreciate.

"The next night I did not sleep very well. Possibly my health was a little disordered. I was oppressed with doubt and perplexity. Once or twice I had a feeling of intense fear for which I could perceive no definite reason. I remember creeping noiselessly into the great hall where the little people were sleeping in the moonlight—that night it was that Weena was among them—and feeling reassured by their presence. It occurred to me even then that when in the course of a few days the moon passed through its last quarter and the nights became dark, the appearance of these unpleasant creatures from below, these whitened Lemurs, these new vermin that had replaced the old, might be more abundant.

"On both these days I had the restless feeling of one who shirks an inevitable duty. I felt assured that the Time Machine was only to be recovered by boldly penetrating these subterranean mysteries. Yet I could not face it. If I had only had a companion it would have been different. But I was so horribly alone, and even to clamber down into the darkness of the well appalled me.

"I don't know if you will understand my feeling, but I never felt quite safe at my back.

"It was this restless feeling, perhaps, that drove me further than I had hitherto gone in my exploring expeditions. Going to the southwestward toward the rising country that is now called Combe Wood, I observed far off, in the direction of nineteenth century Banstead, a vast green pile, of a different character from any I had hitherto seen. It was larger than even the largest of the palaces or ruins I knew, and the façade appeared to me Oriental in its character. The face of it had the luster as well

as the pale green tint, a kind of bluish green, of a certain type of Chinese porcelain. The difference in appearance in the building suggested a difference in its use. I was minded to push on and explore it. But the day was growing late and I had come upon the sight of the place after a long and tiring circuit. I resolved to postpone this examination for the following day, and returned to the welcome and caresses of little Weena.

"But the next morning I was in a mood of remorse for my hesitation in descending the well and facing the Morlocks in their caverns. I perceived my curiosity regarding this great pile of Green Porcelain was a mere self-deception to shirk the experience I dreaded by another day. I resolved I would make the descent without further waste of time, and started out in the early morning toward a well near the ruins of granite and aluminum.

"Little Weena ran by my side. She followed me to the well dancing, but when she saw me lean over the mouth and look downward, she seemed strangely disconcerted.

" 'Good-by, little Weena,' said I, kissing her, and then putting her down I began to feel over the parapet for the climbing hooks—rather hastily, for I feared my courage might leak away.

"At first Weena watched me in amazement, and then she gave a most piteous cry, and running to me began to pull at me with her little hands. I think her opposition nerved me rather to proceed. I shook her off, perhaps a little roughly, and in another moment I was in the throat of the well.

"I saw her agonized face over the parapet, and smiled to reassure her. Then I had to look down at the unstable hooks by which I hung.

"I had to clamber down a shaft of perhaps two hundred yards. The descent was effected by means of metallic bars projecting from the sides of the well, and since they were adapted to the needs of a creature much smaller and lighter than myself, I was speedily cramped and fatigued by the descent. And not simply fatigued. My weight suddenly bent one of the hooks and almost swung me off it down into the blackness beneath.

"For a moment I hung by one hand, and after that experience I did not dare to rest again, and though my arms and back were presently acutely painful, I continued to clamber with as quick a motion as possible down the sheer descent. Glancing upward I saw the aperture, a mere small blue disk above me, in which a star was visible, and little Weena's head appeared as a round black projection. The thudding sound of some machine below me grew louder and more oppressive. Everything save that minute circle above was profoundly dark. When I looked up again Weena had disappeared.

"I was in an agony of discomfort. I had some thought of trying to go up the shaft again, and leave the underworld alone. But while I turned this over in my mind I continued to descend.

"It was with intense relief that I saw dimly coming up a foot to the right of me, a slender loophole in the wall of the shaft, and swinging myself in, found it was the aperture of a narrow horizontal tunnel in which I could lie down and rest.

"It was not too soon. My arms ached, my back was cramped, and I was trembling with the prolonged fear of falling. Besides this, the unbroken darkness had had a distressing effect upon my eyes. The air was full of the throbbing and hum of the machinery that pumped the air down the shaft.

"I do not know how long I lay in that tunnel. I was roused by a soft hand touching my face. Starting up in the darkness, I snatched at my matches and hastily striking one saw three grotesque, white creatures, similar to the one I had seen above ground in the ruin, hastily retreating before the light. Living as they did in what appeared to me impenetrable darkness, their eyes were abnormally large and sensitive, just as are the eyes of the abyssal fishes or of any purely nocturnal creatures, and they reflected the light in the same way. I have no doubt they could see me in that rayless obscurity, and they did not seem to have any fear of me apart from the light. But so soon as I struck a match in order to see them, they fled incontinently, vanishing up dark gutters and tunnels from which their eyes glared at me in the strangest fashion.

"I tried to call to them, but what language they had was apparently a different one from that of the overworld people. So that I was needs left to my own unaided exploration. The thought of flight rather than exploration was even at that time in my mind.

" 'You are in for it now,' said I to myself, and went on.

"Feeling my way along this tunnel of mine, the confused noise of machinery grew louder, and presently the walls fell away from me and I came to a large open space, and striking another match saw I had entered a vast arched cavern extending into darkness, at last, beyond the range of my light.

"The view I had of this cavern was as much as one could see in the burning of a match. Necessarily my memory of it is very vague. Great shapes like big machines rose out of the dim and threw grotesque black shadows, in which the spectral Morlocks sheltered from the glare. The place, by the bye, was very stuffy and oppressive, and the faint *halitus* of freshly shed blood was in the air. Some way down the central vista was a little table of white metal upon which a meal seemed to be spread. The Morlocks at any rate were carnivorous. Even at the time I remember thinking what large animal could have survived to furnish the red joint I saw. It was all very indistinct, the heavy smell, the big unmeaning shapes, the white figures lurking in the shadows, and only waiting for the darkness to come at me again. Then the match burned down and stung my fingers and fell, a wriggling red spot in the black.

"I have thought since how particularly ill equipped I was. When I had started with the Time Machine. I had started with the absurd assumption that the men of the future would certainly be infinitely in front of us in all their appliances. I had come without arms, without medicine, without anything to smoke,—at times I missed tobacco frightfully,—even without enough matches. If I had only thought of a kodak! I could have flashed that glimpse of the underworld in a second and examined it at leisure. But as it was, I stood there with only the weapons and powers that Nature had endowed me with—hands, feet, and teeth—except four safety matches that still remained to me.

"I was afraid to push my way in among all this machinery in the dark, and it was only with my last glimpse of light I discovered that my store of matches had run low. It had never occurred to me until that moment that there was any need to economize them, and I had wasted almost half of the box in astonishing the above-ground people, to whom fire was a novelty. As I say, I had four left.

"Then while I stood in the dark a hand touched mine; then some lank fingers came feeling over my face. I was sensible of a dull, unpleasant odor. I fancy I detected the breathing of a number of those little beings about me. I felt the box of matches in my hand being gently disengaged, and other hands behind me plucking at my clothing.

"The sense of these unseen creatures examining me was indescribably unpleasant. The sudden realization of my ignorance of their ways of thinking and possible actions came home to me very vividly in the darkness. I shouted at them as loudly as I could. They started away from me, and then I could feel them approaching me again. They clutched at me more boldly, whispering odd sounds to each other. I shivered violently and shouted again, rather discordantly. This time they were not so seriously alarmed and made a queer laughing noise as they came toward me again.

"I will confess I was horribly frightened. I determined to strike another match and escape under its glare. Eking it out with a scrap of paper from my pocket, I made good my retreat to the narrow tunnel. But hardly had I entered this when my light was blown out, and I could hear them in the blackness rustling like wind among leaves and pattering like the rain, as they hurried after me.

"In a moment I was clutched by several hands again, and there was no mistake now that they were trying to draw me back. I struck another light and waved it in their dazzled faces. You can scarcely imagine how nauseatingly inhuman those pale, chinless faces and great lidless, pinkish-gray eyes seemed, as they stared stupidly, evidently blinded by the light.

"So I gained time and retreated again, and when my second match had ended struck my third. That had almost burned through as I reached the opening of the tunnel upon the well. I lay down on the edge, for the throbbing whirl of the air-pumping machine below made me giddy, and felt sideways for the projecting hooks. As I did so my feet were grasped from behind and I was violently tugged backward. I lit my last match—and it incontinently went out. But I had my hand on the climbing bars now, and kicking violently disengaged myself from the clutches of the Morlocks, and was speedily clambering up the shaft again.

"They remained peering and blinking up the shaft, except one little wretch who followed me for some way, and indeed well-nigh captured my boot as a trophy.

"That upward climb seemed unending. While I still had the last twenty or thirty feet of it above me, a deadly nausea came upon me. I had the greatest difficulty in keeping my hold. The last few yards was a frightful struggle against this faintness. Several times my head swam and I felt all the sensations of falling.

"At last I got over the well mouth somehow and staggered out of the ruin into the blinding sunlight. I fell upon my face. Even the soil seemed sweet and clean.

"Then I remember Weena kissing my hands and ears, and the voices of others of the Eloi. Then probably I was insensible for a time.

IX. WHEN THE NIGHT CAME

"Now, indeed, I seemed to be in a worse case than before. Hitherto, except during my night's anguish at the loss of the Time Machine, I had felt a sustaining hope of ultimate escape, but my hope was staggered by these new discoveries. Hitherto, I had merely thought myself impeded by the childish simplicity of the little people and by some unknown forces which I had only to understand in order to overcome. But there was an altogether new element in the sickening quality of the Morlocks, something inhuman and malign. Instinctively I loathed them. Before, I had felt as a man might feel who had fallen into a pit; my concern was with the pit and how to get out again. But now I felt like a beast in a trap, whose enemy would presently come.

"The enemy I dreaded may surprise you. It was the darkness of the new moon. Weena had put this into my head by some, at first, incomprehensible remarks about the Dark Nights. It was not now such a very difficult problem to guess what the coming Dark Nights

might mean. The moon was on the wane; each night there was a longer interval of darkness. And I now understood, to some slight degree, at least, the reason of the fear of the little upperworld people for the dark. I wondered vaguely what foul villainy it might be that the Morlocks did under the darkness of the new moon.

"Whatever the origin of the existing conditions, I felt pretty sure now that my second hypothesis was all wrong. The upperworld people might once have been the favored aristocracy of the world, and the Morlocks their mechanical servants, but that state of affairs had passed away long since. The two species that had resulted from the evolution of man were sliding down toward, or had already arrived at, an altogether new relationship. The Eloi, like the Carlovingian kings, had decayed to a mere beautiful futility. They still possessed the earth on sufferance, since the Morlocks, subterranean for innumerable generations, had come at last to find the daylit surface unendurable. And the Morlocks made their garments, I inferred, and maintained them in their habitual need, perhaps through the survival of an old habit of service. They did it, as a standing horse paws with his foot, or as a man enjoys killing animals in sport—because ancient and departed necessities had impressed it on the organism. But clearly the old order was already in part reversed. The Nemesis of the delicate ones was creeping on apace. Ages ago, thousands of generations ago, man had thrust his brother man out of the ease and sunlight of life. And now that brother was coming back—changed. Already the Eloi had begun to learn one old lesson anew. They were becoming acquainted again with Fear.

"Then suddenly came into my head the memory of the meat I had seen in the underworld. It seemed odd how this memory floated into my mind, not stirred up, as it were, by the current of my meditations, but coming in almost like a question from outside. I tried to recall the form of it. I had a vague sense of something familiar, but at that time I could not tell what it was.

"Still, however helpless the little people might be in the presence of their mysterious Fear, I was differently constituted. I came out of this age of ours, this ripe prime of the human race, when fear does not paralyze and mystery has lost its terrors. I at least would defend myself. Without further delay I determined to make myself arms and a fastness where I might sleep with some security. From that refuge as a base I could face the strange world with some confidence again, a confidence I had lost now that I realized to what uncanny creatures I nightly lay exposed. I felt I could never sleep again until my bed was secure from them. I shuddered with horror to think how they must already have examined me during my sleep.

"I wandered during the afternoon along the valley of the Thames, but found nothing that commended itself to my mind as a sufficiently inaccessible retiring place. All the buildings and trees seemed easily practicable to such dexterous climbers as the Morlocks—to judge by their wells—must be. Then the tall pinnacles of the Palace of Green Porcelain, and the polished gleam of its walls, came back to my memory, and in the evening, taking Weena like a child upon my shoulder, I went up the hills toward the southwest.

"Now the distance I had reckoned was seven or eight miles, but it must have been nearer eighteen. I had first seen the Palace on a moist afternoon when distances are deceptively diminished. In addition, the heel of one of my shoes was loose, and a nail was working through the sole,—they were comfortable old shoes I wear about indoors,—so that I was lame. It was already long past sunset before I came in sight of the Palace, standing out in black silhouette against the pale yellow of the sky.

"Weena had been hugely delighted when first I carried her, but after a time she desired me to let her down and ran along by the side of me, occasionally darting off on either hand to pick flowers to stick in my pockets. My pockets had always puzzled Weena, but at the last she had concluded they were an eccentric kind of vases for floral decoration. At least she utilized them for that purpose.

"And that reminds me! As I changed my jacket I found——"

(The Time Traveler paused, put his hand into his pocket, and silently placed two withered flowers, not unlike very large white mallows, upon the little table. Then he resumed his narrative.)

"As the hush of evening crept over the world and we proceeded over the hill-crest toward Wimbledon, Weena became tired and wanted to return to the house of gray stone. But I pointed out the distant pinnacles of the Palace of Green Porcelain to her, and contrived to make her understand that we were seeking a refuge there from her Fear.

"You know that great pause that comes upon things before the dusk. Even the breeze stops in the trees. There is to me always an air of expectation about that evening stillness. The sky was clear, remote, and empty. save for a few horizontal bars far down in the sunset.

"That night the expectation took the color of my fears. In the darkling calm my senses seemed preternaturally sharpened. I fancied I could even feel the hollowness of the ground beneath my feet, could indeed almost see through it, the Morlocks in their ant-hill going hither and thither and waiting for the dark. In this excited state I fancied that they would take my invasion of their burrows as a declaration of war. And why had they taken my Time Machine?

"So we went on in the quiet, and the twilight deepened into night. The clear blue of the distance faded and one star after another came out. The ground grew dim and the trees black. Weena's fears and her fatigue grew upon her. I took her in my arms and talked to her and caressed her. Then as the darkness grew profounder she put her arms round my neck, and closing her eyes tightly pressed her face against my shoulder.

"We went down a long slope into a valley, and there in the dimness I almost walked into a little river. This I waded, and went up the opposite side of the valley, past a number of sleeping houses, and by a statue that appeared to me in the indistinct light to represent a faun, or some such figure, minus the head. Here, too, were acacias. So far, I had seen nothing of the Morlocks, but it was yet early in the night, and the darker hours before the old moon rose were still to come.

"From the brow of the next hill I saw a thick wood spreading wide and black before me. At this I hesitated. I could see no end to it either to the right or to the left. Feeling tired,—my feet, in particular, were very sore,—I carefully lowered Weena from my shoulder as I halted, and sat down upon the turf. I could no longer see the Palace of Green Porcelain, and I was in doubt of my direction.

"I looked into the thickness of the wood, and thought of what it might hide. Under that dense tangle of branches one would be out of sight of the stars. Even were there no other lurking danger there,—a danger I did not care to let my imagination loose upon,—there would still be all the roots to stumble over, and the tree boles to strike myself against. I was very tired, too, after the excitements of the day, and I decided that I would not face it, but would pass the night upon the open hill.

"Weena, I was glad to discover, was fast asleep. I carefully wrapped her in my jacket, and sat down beside her to wait for the moonrise. The hillside upon which I sat was quiet and deserted, but from the black of the wood there came now and then a stir of living things.

"Above me shone the stars, for the night was clear. I felt a certain sense of friendly comfort in their twinkling. All the old constellations had gone from the sky, however, for that slow movement that is imperceptible in a dozen human lifetimes, had long ago rearranged them in unfamiliar groupings. But the Milky Way, it seemed to me, was still the same tattered streamer of star dust as of yore. Southward—as I judged it—was a very bright red star that was new to me. It was even more splendid than our own green Sirius. Amid all these scintillating points of light, one planet shone kindly and steadily like the face of an old friend.

"Looking at these stars suddenly dwarfed my own troubles and all the gravities of terrestrial life. I thought of their unfathomable distance, and the slow, inevitable drift of their movements out of the unknown past into the unknown future. I thought of the great precessional cycle that the pole of the earth describes in the heavens. Only forty times had that silent revolution occurred during all the years I had traversed. And during those few revolutions, all the activity, all the traditions, the carefully planned organizations, the nations, languages, literature, aspirations, even the mere memory of man as I knew man, had been swept out of existence. Instead were these frail creatures who had forgotten their high ancestry, and the white animals of which I went in fear. Then I thought of the great fear there was between these two species, and for the first time, with a sudden shiver, came the clear knowledge of what the meat I had seen might be. Yet it was too horrible! I looked at little Weena sleeping beside me, her face white and starlike under the stars, and forthwith dismissed the thought from my mind.

"Through that long night I kept my

mind off the Morlocks as well as I could, and whiled away the time by trying to fancy I could find traces of the old constellations among the new confusion. The sky kept very clear, except a hazy cloud or so. No doubt I dozed at times. Then, as my vigil wore on, came a faintness in the eastward sky like the reflection of some colorless fire, and the old moon rose thin and peaked and white. And close behind and overtaking it and overflowing it the dawn came, pale at first and then growing pink and warm.

"No Morlocks had approached us. Indeed, I had seen none upon the hill that night. And in the confidence of renewed day it almost seemed to me that my fear had been unreasonable. I stood up, and found my foot with the loose heel swollen at the ankle and painful under the heel. I sat down again, took off my shoes, and flung them away.

"I awakened Weena, and forthwith we went down into the wood, now green and pleasant, instead of black and forbidding. And there we found some fruit wherewith to break our fast. We soon met others of the dainty ones, laughing and dancing in the sunlight, as though there was no such thing in nature as the night.

"Then I thought once more of the meat that I had seen. I felt assured now of what it was, and, from the bottom of my heart, I pitied this last feeble rill from the great flood of humanity. Clearly, somewhere in the long ages of human decay, the food of the Morlocks had run short. Possibly they had lived on rats and suchlike vermin. Even now, man is far less discriminating and exclusive in his food than he was, far less than any monkey. His prejudice against human flesh is no deep-seated instinct. And so these inhuman sons of men——

"I tried to look at the thing in a scientific spirit. After all, these were scarcely to be counted human beings; less human

they were and more remote than our cannibal ancestors of three or four thousand years ago. And the minds that would have made this state torment were gone. Why should I trouble? The Eloi were mere fatted cattle, which the antlike Morlocks preserved and preyed upon, probably saw to the breeding of. And there was Weena dancing by my side!

"Then I tried to preserve myself from the horror that was coming upon me by regarding it as a rigorous punishment of human selfishness; man had been content to live in ease and delight upon the labors of his fellow-men; had taken Necessity as his watchword and excuse, and in fullness of time Necessity had come home to him. I tried even a Carlyle-like scorn of these wretched aristocrats in decline.

"But this attitude of mind was impossible. However great their intellectual degradation, the Eloi had kept too much of the human form not to claim my sympathy, and to make me perforce a participant in their degradation and their Fear.

"I had at this time very vague ideas of what course I should pursue. My first idea was to secure some safe place of refuge for Weena and myself, and to make myself such arms of metal or stone as I could contrive. That necessity was immediate. In the next place, I hoped to procure some means of fire, so that I should have the weapon of a torch at hand, for nothing, I knew, would be more efficient against these Morlocks. Then I wanted to arrange some contrivance to break open the doors of bronze under the white sphinx. I had in mind a battering ram. I had a persuasion that if I could enter these doors and carry a blaze of light before me, I should discover the Time Machine and escape. I could not imagine the Morlocks were powerful enough to remove it far. Weena I had resolved to bring with me to our own Time.

"Turning such schemes over in my

mind, I pursued our way toward the building which my fancy had chosen as our dwelling-place.

X. THE PALACE OF GREEN PORCELAIN

"This Palace of Green Porcelain, when we approached it about noon, was, I found, deserted and falling into ruin. Only ragged vestiges of glass remained in its windows, and great sheets of the green facing had fallen away in places from the corroded metallic framework. It lay very high upon a turfy down, and, looking northeastward before I entered it, I was surprised to see a large estuary, or an arm of the sea, where I judged Wandsworth and Battersea must once have been. I thought then—though I never followed the thought up—of what might have happened, or might be happening, to the living things in the sea.

"The material of the Palace proved, on examination, to be indeed porcelain, and above the face of it I saw an inscription in some unknown characters. I thought, rather foolishly, that Weena might help me to interpret this, but I only learned that the bare idea of writing had never entered her head. She always seemed to me, I fancy, more human than she was, perhaps because her affection was so human.

"Within the big valves of the door—which were open and broken—we found, instead of the customary hall, a long gallery lit by many side windows. Even at the first glance I was reminded of a museum. The tiled floor was thick with dust, and a remarkable array of miscellaneous objects were shrouded in the same gray covering. Clearly, the place had been derelict for a very considerable time.

"Then I perceived, standing strange and gaunt in the center of the hall, what was clearly the lower part of the skeleton of some huge animal. As I approached this I recognized by the oblique feet that it was some extinct creature after the fashion of the *megatherium*. The skull and the upper bones lay beside it in the thick dust, and in one place where rain water had dripped through some leak in the roof, the skeleton had decayed away. Further along the gallery was the huge skeleton barrel of a *brontosaurus*. My museum hypothesis was confirmed. Going toward the side of the gallery I found what appeared to be sloping shelves, and clearing away the thick dust, I found the old familiar glass cases of our own time. But these must have been air-tight to judge from the fair preservation of some of their contents.

"Clearly we stood among the ruins of some latter day South Kensington. Here apparently was the Paleontological Section, and a very splendid array of fossils it must have been; though the inevitable process of decay that had been warded off for a time, and had, through the extinction of bacteria and fungi, lost ninety-nine-hundredths of its force, was nevertheless, with extreme sureness, if with extreme slowness, at work again upon all its treasures. Here and there I found traces of the little people in the shape of rare fossils broken to pieces or threaded in strings upon reeds. And the cases had in some instances been bodily removed—by the Morlocks, as I judged.

"The place was very silent. The thick dust deadened our footsteps. Weena, who had been rolling a sea urchin down the sloping glass of a case, presently came, as I stared about me, and very quietly took my hand and stood beside me.

"At first I was so much surprised by this ancient monument of an intellectual age that I gave no thought to the possibilities it presented me. Even my preoccupation about the Time Machine and the Morlocks receded a little from my mind. The curiosity concerning human destiny that had led to my time traveling was removed. Now, judging from the size of the place, this Palace of Green Porcelain had a great deal more in it than a gallery of paleontology; possibly historical galleries, it might be even a library. To me, at least in my present circumstances, these would be vastly more interesting than this spectacle of old-time geology in decay.

"Exploring, I found another short gallery running transversely to the first. This appeared to be devoted to minerals, and the sight of a block of sulphur set my mind running on gunpowder. But I could find no saltpeter; indeed no nitrates of any kind. Doubtless they had deliquesced ages ago. Yet the sulphur hung in my mind and set up a train of thinking. As for the rest of the contents of that place, though on the whole they were the best preserved of all I saw—I had little interest. I am no specialist in mineralogy, and I soon went on down a very ruinous aisle running parallel to the first hall I had entered.

"Apparently this section had been devoted to Natural History, but here everything had long since passed out of recognition. A few shriveled vestiges of what had once been stuffed animals, dried-up mummies in jars that had once held spirit, a brown dust of departed plants, that was all. I was sorry for this, because I should have been glad to trace the patient readjustments by which the conquest of animated nature had been attained.

"From this we come to a gallery of simply colossal proportions, but singularly ill lit, and with its floor running downward at a slight angle from the end at which I entered it. At intervals there hung white globes from the ceiling,—many of them cracked and smashed,—which suggested that originally the place had been artificially lit.

Here I was more in my element, for I found rising on either side of me the huge bulks of big machines, all greatly corroded, and many broken down, but some still fairly complete in all their parts. You know I have a certain weakness for mechanism, and I was inclined to linger among these, the more so since for the most part they had the interest of puzzles, and I could make only the vaguest guesses of what they were for. I fancied if I could solve these puzzles I should find myself in the possession of powers that might be of use against the Morlocks.

"Suddenly Weena came very close to my side, so suddenly that she startled me.

"Had it not been for her I do not think I should have noticed that the floor of the gallery sloped at all* The end I had entered was quite above ground, and was lit by rare slit-like windows. As one went down the length of the place, the ground came up against these windows, until there was at last a pit like the 'area' of a London house, before each, and only a narrow line of daylight at the top. I went slowly along, puzzling about the machines, and had been too intent upon them to notice the gradual diminution of the light, until Weena's increasing apprehension attracted my attention.

"Then I saw that the gallery ran down at last into a thick darkness. I hesitated about proceeding, and then as I looked around me, I saw that the dust was here less abundant and its surface less even. Further away toward the dim, it appeared to be broken by a number of small narrow footprints. At that my sense of the immediate presence of the Morlocks revived. I felt that I was wasting my time in my academic examination of this machinery. I called to mind that it was already far advanced in the afternoon, and that I had still no

---

* It may be, of course, that the floor did not slope, but that the museum was built upon the side of the hill.—*Editor.*

weapon, no refuge, and no means of making a fire. And then, down in the remote black of the gallery, I heard a peculiar pattering and those same odd noises I had heard down the well.

"I took Weena's hand. Then struck with a sudden idea, I left her, and turned to a machine from which projected a lever not unlike those in a signal box. Clambering upon the stand of the machine and grasping this lever in my hands, I put all my weight upon it sideways. Weena, deserted in the central aisle, began suddenly to whimper. I had judged the strength of the lever pretty correctly, for it snapped after a minute's strain, and I rejoined Weena with a mace in my hand more than sufficient, I judged, for any Morlock skull I might encounter.

"And I longed very much to kill a Morlock or so. Very inhuman, you may think, to want to go killing one's own descendants, but it was impossible somehow to feel any humanity in the things. Only my disinclination to leave Weena, and a persuasion that if I began to slake my thirst for murder my Time Machine might suffer, restrained me from going straight down the gallery and killing the brutes I heard there.

"Mace in one hand and Weena in the other we went out of that gallery and into another still larger, which at the first glance reminded me of a military chapel hung with tattered flags. The brown and charred rags that hung from the sides of it, I presently recognized as the decaying vestiges of books. They had long since dropped to pieces and every semblance of print had left them. But here and there were warped and cracked boards and metallic clasps that told the tale well enough.

"Had I been a literary man I might perhaps have moralized upon the futility of all ambition, but as it was, the thought that struck me with keenest force, was the enormous waste of labor rather than of hope, to which this somber gallery of rotting paper testi-

fied. At the time I will confess, though it seems a petty trait now, that I thought chiefly of the Philosophical Transactions, and my own seventeen papers upon physical optics.

"Then going up a broad staircase we came to what may once have been a gallery of technical chemistry. And here I had not a little hope of discovering something to help me. Except at one end where the roof had collapsed, this gallery was well preserved. I went eagerly to every unbroken case. And at last, in one of the really air-tight cases, I found a box of matches. Very eagerly I tried them. They were perfectly good. They were not even damp.

"At that discovery I suddenly turned 'Dance!' I cried to her in her own tongue. For now I had a weapon indeed against the horrible creatures we feared. And so in that derelict museum, upon the thick soft coating of dust, to Weena's huge delight, I solemnly performed a sort of composite dance, whistling 'The Land of the Leal' as cheerfully as I could. In part it was a modest cancan, in part a step dance, in part a skirt dance,—so far as my tail coat permitted,—and in part original. For naturally I am inventive, as you know.

"Now, I still think that for this box of matches to have escaped the wear of time for immemorial years was a strange, and for me, a most fortunate thing. Yet oddly enough I found here a far more unlikely substance, and that was camphor. I found it in a sealed jar, that, by chance, I supposed had been really hermetically sealed. I fancied at first the stuff was paraffin wax, and smashed the jar accordingly. But the odor of camphor was unmistakable. It struck me as singularly odd, that among the universal decay, this volatile substance had chanced to survive, perhaps through many thousand years. It reminded me of a sepia painting I had once seen done from the ink of a fossil Belemnite that must have perished and become fossilized millions of years ago. I was about to throw this camphor on one side, and then remembering that it was inflammable and burnt with a good bright flame, I put it into my pocket.

"I found no explosives, however, or any means of breaking down the bronze doors. As yet my iron crowbar was the most hopeful thing I had chanced upon. Nevertheless I left that gallery greatly elated by my discoveries.

"I cannot tell you the whole story of my exploration through that long afternoon. It would require a great effort of memory to recall it at all in the proper order. I remember a long gallery containing the rusting stands of arms of all ages, and that I hesitated between my crowbar and a hatchet or a sword. I could not carry both, however, and my bar of iron, after all, promised best against the bronze gates. There were rusty guns, pistols, and rifles here; most of them were masses of rust, but many of aluminum, and still fairly sound. But any cartridges or powder there may have been had rotted into dust. One corner I saw was charred and shattered; perhaps, I thought, by an explosion among the specimens there. In another place was a vast array of idols—Polynesian, Mexican, Grecian, Phœnician, every country on earth, I should think. And here, yielding to an irresistible impulse, I wrote my name upon the nose of a steatite monster from South America that particularly took my fancy.

"As the evening drew on my interest waned. I went through gallery after gallery, dusty, silent, often ruinous, the exhibits sometimes were mere heaps of rust and lignite, sometimes fresher. In one place I suddenly found myself near a model of a tin mine, and then by the merest accident I discovered in an airtight case two dynamite cartridges; I shouted 'Eureka!' and smashed the case joyfully. Then came a doubt. I hesitated, and then selecting a little side gallery I made my essay. I never felt such a bitter disappointment as I did then, waiting five, ten, fifteen minutes for the explosion that never came. Of course the things were dummies, as I might have guessed from their presence there. I really believe had they not been so, I should have rushed off incontinently there and then, and blown sphinx, bronze doors, and, as it proved, my chances of finding the Time Machine all together into nonexistence.

"It was after that, I think, that we came to a little open court within the palace, turfed and with three fruit trees. There it was we rested and refreshed ourselves.

"Toward sunset I began to consider our position. Night was now creeping upon us and my inaccessible hiding-place was still to be found. But that troubed me very little now. I had in my possession a thing that was perhaps the best of all defenses against the Morlocks. I had matches again. I also had the camphor in my pocket if a blaze were required. It seemed to me that the best thing we could do would be to pass the night in the open again, protected by a fire.

"In the morning there was the Time Machine to obtain. Toward that as yet I had only my iron mace. But now with my growing knowledge I felt very differently toward the bronze doors than I had done hitherto. Up to this I had refrained from forcing them, largely because of the mystery on the other side. They had never impressed me as being very strong, and I hoped to find my bar of iron not altogether inadequate for the work.

XI. IN THE DARKNESS OF THE FOREST

"We emerged from the Palace of Green Porcelain while the sun was still in part above the horizon. I was determined to reach the white sphinx early the next morning, and I proposed before the dusk came to push through the woods that had stopped me on the previous journey. My plan was to go as far as possible that night, and then, building a fire about us, to sleep under the protection of its glare. Accordingly as we went along I gathered any sticks or dried grass I saw, and presently had my arms full of such litter. So loaded, our progress was slower than I had anticipated, and besides, Weena was tired. I, too, began to suffer from sleepiness, and it was fully night before we reached the wood.

"Now, upon the shrubby hill upon the edge of this, Weena would have stopped, fearing the darkness before us. But a singular sense of impending calamity, that should indeed have served me as a warning, drove me onward. I had been without sleep for the length of a night and two days, and I was feverish and irritable. I felt sleep coming upon me, and with it the Morlocks.

"While we hesitated I saw among the bushes up the slope behind us, and dim against the sky, three crouching figures. There was scrub and long grass all about us, and I did not feel safe from their insidious approach. The forest, I calculated, was rather less than a mile in breadth. If we could get through it, the hillside beyond was bare, and to me it seemed an altogether safer resting-place. I thought that with my matches and the camphor I could contrive to keep my path illuminated through the woods. Yet it was evident that if I was to flourish matches with my hands I should have to abandon my firewood. So rather reluctantly I put this down.

"Then it came into my head that I would amaze our friends behind by lighting it. Ultimately I was to discover the atrocious folly of this proceeding, but just then it came to my mind as an ingenious move for covering our retreat.

"I don't know if you have ever thought what a rare thing in the absence of man and in a temperate climate, flames must be. The sun's heat is rarely strong enough to burn even when focussed by dewdrops, as is sometimes the case in more tropical districts. Lightning may blast and blacken, but it rarely gives rise to widespread fire. Decaying vegetation may occasionally smoulder with the heat of its fermentation, but this again rarely results in flames. Now, in this decadent age the art of fire-making had been altogether forgotten on the earth. The red tongues that went licking up my heap of wood were an altogether new and strange thing to Weena.

"She wanted to run to it and play with it. I believe she would have cast herself into it had I not restrained her. But I caught her up and in spite of her struggles plunged boldly before me into the wood. For a little way the glare of my fire lit the path. Looking back presently I could see, through the crowded tree stems, that from my heap of sticks the blaze had spread to some bushes adjacent, and a curved line of fire was creeping up the grass of the hill. I laughed at that.

"Then I turned toward the dark trees before me again. It was very black and Weena clung to me convulsively, but there was still, as my eyes grew accustomed to the darkness, sufficient light for me to avoid blundering against the stems. Overhead it was simply black, except when here and there a gap of remote blue sky shone down upon me. I lit none of my matches because I had no hand free. Upon my left arm I carried my little one, in my right hand I had the iron bar I had wrenched from the machine.

"For some way I heard nothing but the crackling twigs under my feet, the faint rustle of the breeze above, and my breathing and the throb of the blood vessels in my ears. Then I seemed to hear a pattering about me.

"I pushed on grimly. The pattering became more distinct, and then I heard the same queer sounds and voices I had heard before in the underworld. There were evidently several of the Morlocks, and they were closing in upon me.

"In another minute I felt a tug at my coat, then something at my arm. Weena shivered violently and became quite still.

"It was time for a match. But to get at that I must put her down. I did so, and immediately as I fumbled with my pocket a struggle began in the darkness about my knees, perfectly silent on her part and with the same peculiar cooing sounds on the part of the Morlocks. Soft little hands, too, were creeping over my coat and back, touching even my neck.

"The match scratched and fizzed. I held it flaring, and immediately the white backs of the Morlocks became visible as they fled amid the trees. I hastily took a lump of camphor from my pocket and prepared to light it as soon as the match waned.

"Then I looked at Weena. She was lying clutching my feet and quite motionless, with her face to the ground. With a sudden fright I stooped to her. She seemed scarcely to breathe. I lit the block of camphor and flung it to the ground, and as it spit and flared up and drove back the Morlocks and the shadows, I knelt down and lifted up Weena. The wood behind seemed full of the stir and murmur of a great company of creatures.

"Apparently she had fainted. I put her carefully upon my shoulder and rose to push on, and then came a horrible realization.

"While maneuvering with my matches and Weena, I had turned myself about several times, and now I had not the faintest idea in what direction my path lay. For all I knew I might be facing back toward the Palace of Green Porcelain.

"I found myself in a cold perspiration. I had to think rapidly what to do. I determined to build a fire and encamp where we were. I put the motionless Weena down upon a turfy bole. Very hastily, as my first lump of camphor waned, I began collecting sticks and leaves.

"Here and there out of the darkness round me the eyes of the Morlocks shone like carbuncles.

"Presently the camphor flickered and went out. I lit a match, and as I did so saw two white forms that had been approaching Weena dash hastily back. One was so blinded by the light that he came straight for me, and I felt his bones grind under the blow of my fist. He gave a whoop of dismay, staggered a little way, and fell down.

"I lit another piece of camphor and went on gathering my bonfire. Presently I noticed how dry was some of the foliage above me, for since I had arrived on the Time Machine, a matter of a week, no rain had fallen. So instead of casting about among the trees for fallen twigs I began leaping up and dragging down branches. Very soon I had a choking smoky fire of green wood and dry sticks, and could save my other lumps of camphor.

"Then I turned to where Weena lay beside my iron mace. I tried what I could to revive her, but she lay like one dead. I could not even satisfy myself whether or not she breathed.

"Now the smoke of the fire beat over toward me, and it must have made me suddenly heavy. Moreover the vapor of camphor was in the air. My fire would not want replenishing for an hour or so. I felt very weary after my exertion and sat down. The wood, too, was full of a slumberous murmur that I did not understand.

"I seemed merely to nod and open my eyes. Then it was all dark around me, and the Morlocks had their hands upon me. Flinging off their clinging fingers I hastily felt in my pocket for the match-box, and—it had gone! Then they gripped and closed with me again.

"In a moment I knew what had happened. I had slept, and my fire had gone out, and the bitterness of death came over my soul. The forest seemed full of the smell of burning wood. I was caught by the neck, by the hair, by the arms, and pulled down. It was indescribably horrible in the darkness to feel all these soft creatures heaped upon me. I felt as if I was in a monstrous spider's web. I was overpowered. Down I went.

"I felt some little teeth nipping at my neck. Abruptly I rolled over, and as I did so, my hand came against my iron lever. Somehow this gave me strength for another effort. I struggled up, shaking off these human rats from me, and then holding the bar short, I thrust where I judged their faces might be. I could feel the succulent giving of flesh and bone under my blows, and for a moment I was free.

"The strange exultation that so often seems to accompany fighting came upon me. I knew that both I and Weena were lost, but I determined to make the Morlocks pay for their meat. I stood with my back to a tree swinging the iron bar before me. The whole wood was full of the stir and cries of them.

"A minute passed. Their voices seemed to rise to a higher pitch of excitement and their movements became faster. Yet none came within reach of me. I stood glaring at the blackness. Then suddenly came hope.

"What if the Morlocks had no courage?

"And close on the heels of that came a strange thing. The darkness seemed to grow luminous. Very dimly I began to see the Morlocks about me,—three, battered at my feet,—and then I perceived with incredulous surprise that the others were running, in an incessant stream, as it seemed to me, from behind me, and away through the wood in front of me. And their backs seemed no longer white, but reddish.

"Then as I stood agape I saw, across a gap of starlight between the branches, a little red spark go drifting and vanish. And at that I understood the smell of burning wood, the slumberous murmur that was growing now into a gusty roaring, the red glow, and the flight of the Morlocks.

"Stepping out from behind my tree and looking back, I saw through the back pillars of the nearer trees the flames of the burning forest. No doubt it was my first fire coming after me. With that I hastily looked round for Weena, but she was gone. The hissing and crackling behind me, the explosive thud as each fresh tree burst into flame, left little time for reflection. With my iron bar still in hand I followed in the path of the Morlocks.

"It was a close race. Once the flames crept forward so swiftly on my right as I ran, that I was outflanked and had to strike off to the left. But at last I emerged upon a small open place, and as I did so, a Morlock came blundering toward me and passed me, and went on straight into the fire.

"And now I was to see the most weird and horrible scene, I think, of all that I beheld in that future age.

"This whole space was as bright as day with the reflection of the fire. In the center was a small hillock or tumulus surmounted by a scorched hawthorn. Beyond this hill was another arm of the burning forest from which yellow tongues were already writhing, and completely encircling the space with a fence of fire. Upon the hillside were perhaps thirty or forty Morlocks, dazzled by the light and heat of the fire, which was now very bright and hot, blundering hither and thither against each other in their bewilderment. At first I did not realize their blindness, and struck furiously at them with my bar in a frenzy of fear as they approached me, killing one and crippling several others. But when I had watched the gestures of one of them groping under the hawthorn against the red sky, and heard the moans to which they all gave vent, I was assured of their absolute helplessness and refrained from striking any of them again. Yet every now and then one would come straight toward me, setting loose a quivering horror, that made me quick to elude him. At one time the flames died down somewhat, and I feared these foul creatures would presently be able to see me, and I was even thinking of beginning the fight by killing some of them before this should happen, but the fire burst out again brightly and I stayed my hand. I walked about the hill among them and avoiding them, looking for some trace of Weena, but I found nothing.

"At last I sat down upon the summit of the hillock and watched this strange incredible company of the blind, groping to and fro and making uncanny noises to one another, as the glare of the fire beat upon them. The coiling uprush of smoke streamed across the sky, and through the rare tatters of that red canopy, remote as though they belonged to another universe, shone the little stars. Two or three Morlocks came blundering into me and I drove them off, trembling myself as I did so, with blows of my fists. For the most of that night I was persuaded it was a nightmare. I bit myself and screamed aloud in a passionate desire to awake. I beat on the ground with my hands, and got up, and sat down again, and wandered here and there, and again sat down on the crest of the hill. Then I would fall to rubbing my eyes and calling upon God to let me awake. Thrice I saw Morlocks put their heads down in a kind of agony and rush into the flames. But at last, above the subsiding red of the fire, above the streaming masses of black smoke and the whitening and blackening tree stumps, and the diminishing number of these dim creatures, came the white light of the day.

"I searched again over the open space for some traces of Weena, but could find none. I had half feared to discover her mangled remains, but clearly they had left her poor little body in the forest. I cannot describe how it relieved me to think that it had escaped the awful fate to which it seemed destined. As I thought of that I was almost moved to begin a massacre of the defenseless abominations about me, but I contained myself. This hillock, as I have said, was a kind of island in the forest. From its summit I could now make out, through a haze of smoke, the Palace of Green Porcelain, and from that I could get my bearings for the white sphinx. And so leaving the remnant of these damned souls going hither and thither and moaning, as the day grew clearer, I tied some grass about my feet and limped on across smoking ashes and among black stems that still pulsated internally with fire, toward the hiding place of the Time Machine.

"I walked slowly, for I was almost exhausted as well as lame, and I felt the most intense wretchedness on account of the horrible death of little Weena, which then seemed an overwhelming calamity. Yet even now, as I tell you of it in this old familiar room, it seems more like the sorrow of a dream than an actual loss. But it left me absolutely lonely again that morning—terribly alone. I began to think of this house of mine, of this fireside, of some of you, and with such thoughts came a longing that was pain.

"As I walked over the smoking ashes under the bright morning sky I made a discovery. In my trouser pocket were still some loose matches. The box must have leaked before it was lost!

XII. THE TRAP OF THE WHITE SPHINX

"So about eight or nine in the morning I came to the same seat of yellow metal from which I had viewed the world upon the evening of my arrival. I thought of my hasty conclusions upon that evening and could not refrain from laughing bitterly at my confidence. Here was the same beautiful scene, the same abundant foliage, the same splendid palaces and magnificent ruins, the same silver river running between its fertile banks. The gay robes of the beautiful people moved hither and thither among the trees. Some were bathing in exactly the place where I had saved Weena, and that suddenly gave me a keen stab of pain. And like blots upon the landscape rose the cupolas above the ways to the underworld. I understood now what all the beauty of the overworld people covered. Very pleasant was their day, as pleasant as the day of the cattle in the field. Like the cattle they knew of no enemies, and provided against no needs. And their end was the same.

"I grieved to think how brief the dream of the human intellect had been. It had committed suicide. It had set itself steadfastly toward comfort and ease, a balanced society with security and permanence as its watchwords, it had attained its hopes—to come to this at last. Once, life and property must have reached almost absolute safety. The rich had been assured of his wealth and comfort, the toiler assured of his life and work. No doubt in that perfect world there had been no unemployed problem, no social question left unsolved. And a great quiet had followed.

"It is a law of nature we overlook that intellectual versatility is the compensation for change, danger, and trouble. An animal perfectly in harmony with its environment is a perfect mechanism. Nature never appeals to intelligence until habit and instinct are useless. There is no intelligence where there is no change and no need of change. Only those animals partake of intelligence that have to meet a huge variety of needs and dangers.

"So, as I see it, the upperworld man had drifted toward his feeble prettiness, and the underworld to mere mechanical industry. But that perfect state had lacked one thing even of mechanical perfection—absolute permanency. Apparently as time went on the feeding of the underworld, however it was effected, had become disjointed. Mother Necessity, who had been staved off for a few thousand years, came back again, and she began below. The underworld, being in contact with machinery which, however perfect, still needs some little thought outside of habit, had probably retained, perforce, rather more initiative, if less of every other human character, than the upper. And when other meat failed them, they turned to what old habit had hitherto forbidden. So I say I saw it in my last view of the world of 810,701. It may be as wrong an explanation as mortal wit could invent. It is how the thing shaped itself to me, and as that I give it to you.

"After the fatigues, excitements, and terrors of the past days, and in spite of my grief, this seat and the tranquil view and the warm sunlight were very pleasant. I was very tired and sleepy, and soon my theorizing passed into dozing. Catching myself at that I took my own hint, and spreading myself out upon the turf, I had a long and refreshing sleep.

"I awoke a little before sunsetting. I now felt safe against being caught napping by the Morlocks, and stretching myself I came on down the hill toward the white sphinx. I had my crowbar in one hand, and the other played with the matches in my pocket.

"And now came a most unexpected thing. As I approached the pedestal of the sphinx I found the bronze panels were open. They had slid down into grooves.

"At that I stopped short before them, hesitating to enter.

"Within was a small apartment, and on a raised place in the corner of this was the Time Machine. I had the small levers in my pocket. So here, after all my elaborate preparations for the siege of the white sphinx, was a meek surrender. I threw my iron bar away, almost sorry not to use it.

"A sudden thought came into my head as I stooped toward the portal. For once at least I grasped the mental operations of the Morlocks. Suppressing a strong inclination to laugh, I stepped through the bronze frame and up to the Time Machine. I was surprised to find it had been carefully oiled and cleaned. I have suspected since that the Morlocks had even partially taken it to pieces while trying in their dim way to grasp its purpose.

"Now, as I stood and examined it, finding a pleasure in the mere touch of the contrivance, the thing I had expected happened. The bronze panels suddenly slid up and struck the frame with a clang. I was in the dark—trapped. So the Morlocks thought. At that I chuckled gleefully.

"I could already hear their murmuring laughter as they came toward me. Very calmly I tried to strike the match. I had only to fix on the levers and depart then like a ghost. But I had overlooked one little thing. The matches were of that abominable kind that light only on the box.

"You may imagine how all my calm vanished. The little brutes were close upon me. One touched me. I made a sweeping blow in the dark at them with the lever, and began to scramble into the saddle of the Machine. Then came one hand upon me and then another.

"Then I had simply to fight against their persistent fingers for my levers, and at the same time feel for the studs over which these fitted. One, indeed, they almost got away from me. As it slipped from my hand I had to butt in the dark with my head—I could hear the Morlock's skull ring—to recover it. It was a nearer thing than the fight in the forest, I think, this last scramble.

"But at last the lever was fixed and pulled over. The clinging hands slipped from me. The darkness presently fell from my eyes. I found myself in the same gray light and tumult I have already described.

XIII. THE FURTHER VISION

"I have already told you of the sickness and confusion that comes with time traveling. And this time I was not seated properly in the saddle, but sideways and in an unstable fashion. For an indefinite time I clung to the machine as it swayed and vibrated, quite unheeding how I went, and when I brought myself to look at the dials again I was amazed to find where I had arrived. One dial records days, another thousands of days, another millions of days, and another thousands of millions. Now instead of reversing the levers I had pulled them over so as to go forward with them, and when I came to look at these indicators I found that the thousands hand was sweeping round as fast as the seconds hand of a watch, into futurity.

"Very cautiously, for I remembered my former headlong fall, I began to reverse my motion. Slower and slower went the circling hands, until the thousands one seemed motionless and the daily one was no longer a mere mist upon its scale. Still slower, until the gray haze around me became distincter, and dim outlines of a low hill and a sea became visible.

"But as my motion became slower there was, I found, no blinking change of day and night. A steady twilight brooded over the earth. And the band of light that had indicated the sun had, I now noticed, become fainter, had faded indeed to invisibility in the east, and in the west was increasingly broader and redder. The circling of the stars growing slower and slower had given place to creeping points of light. At last, some time before I stopped, the sun, red and very large, halted motionless upon the horizon, a vast dome glowing with a dull heat. The work of the tidal drag was accomplished. The earth had come to rest with one face to the sun even as in our own time the moon faces the earth.

"I stopped very gently and sat upon the Time Machine looking round me.

"The sky was no longer blue. Northeastward it was inky black, and out of the blackness shone brightly and steadily the pale white stars. Overhead it was a deep Indian red, and starless, and southeastward it grew brighter to where, cut by the horizon, lay the motionless hull of the huge red sun.

"The rocks about me were of a harsh reddish color, and all the trace of life that I could see at first was the intensely green vegetation that covered every projecting point on its southeastern side. It was the same rich green that one sees on forest moss or on the lichen in caves, plants which, like these, grow in a perpetual twilight.

"The Machine was standing on a sloping beach. The sea stretched away to the southwest to rise into a sharp bright horizon against the wan sky. There were no breakers and no waves, for not a breath of wind was stirring. Only a slight oily swell rose and fell like a gentle breathing, and showed that the eternal sea was still moving and living. And along the margin where the water sometimes broke was a thick incrustation of salt—pink under the lurid sky.

"There was a sense of oppression in my head and I noticed that I was breathing very fast. The sensations remind me of my only experience of mountaineering, and from that I judged the air was more rarified than it is now.

"Far away up the desolate slope I heard a harsh scream, and saw a thing like a huge white butterfly go slanting and fluttering up into the sky and, circling, disappear over some low hillocks beyond.

"The sound of its voice was so dismal that I shivered, and seated myself more firmly upon the Machine.

"Looking round me I saw that, quite near to me, what I had taken to be a reddish mass of rock was moving slowly toward me. Then I saw the thing was really a monstrous crab-like creature. Can you imagine a crab as large as yonder table, with its numerous legs moving slowly and uncertainly, its big claws swaying, its long antennæ like carters' whips, waving and feeling, and its stalked eyes gleaming at you on either side of its metallic front? Its back was corrugated and ornamented with ungainly bosses, and a greenish incrustation blotched it here and there. I could see the numerous palps of its complicated mouth flickering and feeling as it approached.

"As I stared at this sinister apparition crawling toward me, I felt a tickling on my cheeks as though a fly had alighted there.

"I tried to brush it away with my hand, but in a moment it returned, and almost immediately after another came near my ear. I struck at this and caught something threadlike. It was drawn swiftly out of my hand. With a frightful qualm I turned and saw I had grasped the antennæ of another monster crab that stood immediately behind me. Its evil eyes were wriggling on their stalks, its mouth was all alive with appetite, and its vast ungainly claws, smeared with green slime, were descending upon me.

"In a moment my hand was on the lever of the Time Machine, and I had placed a month between myself and these monsters. But I found I was still on the same beach and I saw them distinctly now as soon as I stopped. Dozens of them seemed to be crawling here and there in the somber light among the foliated sheets of intense green.

"I cannot convey the sense of abominable desolation that hung over the world. The red eastern sky, the northward blackness, the salt Dead Sea, the stony beach crawling with these foul, slow-stirring monsters, the uniform, poisonous-looking green of the lichenous plants, the thin air that hurt one's lungs; all contributed to an appalling effect.

"I moved on a hundred years, and there was the same red sun, the same dying sea, the same chill air, and the same crowd of earthly crustacea creeping in and out among the green weed and the red rocks.

"So I traveled, stopping ever and again, in great strides of a thousand years or more, drawn on by the mystery of the earth's fate, tracing with a strange fascination how the sun was growing larger and duller in the westward sky, and the life of the old earth ebbing out. At last, more than thirty million years hence, the huge red-hot dome of the sun had come to obscure nearly a sixth part of the darkling heavens. Then it was I stopped, for the crawling multitude of crabs had disappeared, and the red beach, save for its livid green liverworts and lichens, seemed lifeless again.

"As soon as I stopped a bitter cold assailed me. The air felt keenly cold, and rare white flakes ever and again came eddying down. To the northeastward the glare of snow lay under the starlight of the sable sky, and I could see an undulating crest of pinkish white hillocks. There were fringes of ice along the sea margin, drifting masses further out, but the main expanse of that salt ocean, all bloody under the eternal sunset, was still unfrozen.

"I looked about me to see if any traces of animals remained. A certain indefinable apprehension still kept me in the saddle of the Machine. I saw nothing moving, on earth or sky or sea. The green slime on the rocks alone testified that life was not extinct. A shallow sandbank had appeared in the sea and the water had receded from the beach. I fancied I saw some black object flopping about upon this bank, but it became motionless as I looked at it, and I judged my eye had been deceived

and that the object was merely a rock. The stars in the sky were intensely bright and seemed to me to twinkle very little.

"Suddenly I noticed that the circular outline, westward, of the sun had changed, that a concavity, a bay, had appeared in the curve. I saw this grow larger. For a minute, perhaps, I stared aghast at this blackness that was creeping over the day, and then I realized that an eclipse was beginning. No doubt, now that the moon was creeping ever nearer to the earth, and the earth to the sun, eclipses were of frequent occurrence.

"The darkness grew apace, a cold wind began to blow in freshening gusts from the east, and then the white flakes that were falling out of the air increased. The tide was creeping in with a ripple and a whisper. Beyond these lifeless sounds the world was silent—silent! It would be hard to convey to you the stillness of it. All the sounds of man, the bleating of sheep, the cries of birds, the hum of insects, the stir that makes the background of our lives, were over. As the darkness thickened the eddying flakes became more abundant, dancing before my eyes; and the cold of the air more intense. At last, swiftly, one after the other, the white peaks of the distant hills vanished into blackness. The breeze grew to a moaning wind. I saw the black central shadow of the eclipse sweeping toward me. In another moment the pale stars alone were visible. All else was rayless obscurity. The sky was absolutely black.

"A horror of this great darkness came upon me. The cold that smote to my marrow, and the pain I felt in breathing, overcame me. I shivered and a deadly nausea seized me. Then like a red-hot bow in the sky appeared the edge of the sun.

"I got off the Machine to recover myself. I felt giddy and incapable of facing the return journey. As I stood sick and confused I saw again the moving thing upon the shoal—there was no mistake now that it was a moving thing—against the red water of the sea. It was a round thing, of the size of a football perhaps, or bigger; it seemed black against the weltering blood-red water, and it was hopping fitfully about. Then I felt I was fainting. A terrible dread of lying helpless in that remote twilight sustained me while I clambered upon the saddle.

"So I came home. For a long time I must have been insensible upon the Machine. The blinking succession of the days and nights was resumed, the sun grew golden again, the sky blue. I breathed with greater freedom. The fluctuating contours of the land ebbed and flowed. The hands spun backward upon the dials. At last I saw again the dim shadows of homes, the evidences of decadent humanity. These, too, changed and passed, and others came. Presently when the millions dial was at zero I slackened speed, and began to recognize our own pretty and familiar architecture. The thousands hand ran back to the starting point, the night and day flapped slower and slower. Then the old walls of the laboratory came round me. Very gently now I diminished the pace of the mechanism.

"I saw one little thing that seemed odd to me. I think I have told you that when I set out, before my velocity became very high, Mrs. Watchett had walked across the room, traveling, as it seemed to me, like a rocket. As I returned I passed again across that minute when she traversed the laboratory. But now every motion appeared to be the exact inversion of her previous one. The door at the lower end opened and she glided quietly up the laboratory, back foremost, and disappeared behind the door by which she had previously entered.

"Then I stopped the Machine, and saw about me again the old familiar laboratory, my tools, my appliances, just as I had left them. I got off the thing very shakily and sat down upon my bench. For several minutes I trembled violently. Then I became calmer. Around me was my old workshop again, exactly as it had been. I might have slept there and the whole thing have been a dream.

"And yet not exactly. The thing had started from the southeast corner of the laboratory. It had come to rest again in the northwest, against the wall, where you will find it. That gives you the exact distance from my little lawn to the pedestal of the white sphinx.

"For a time my brain became stagnant. Presently I got up and came through the passage here, limping, because my heel was still painful, and feeling sorely begrimed. I saw the *Pall Mall Gazette* on the table by the door. I found the date was indeed today, and looking at the timepiece, saw the hour was almost eight o'clock. I heard your voices and the clatter of plates. I hesitated—I felt so sick and weak. Then I sniffed good wholesome meat, and opened the door. You know the rest. I washed and dined, and now I am telling you the story."

"I know," he said after a while, "that all this will be absolutely incredible to you, but to me the one incredible thing is that I am here tonight in this old familiar room, looking into your wholesome faces, and telling you all these strange adventures."

He looked at the Medical Man.

"No; I cannot expect you to believe it. Take it as a lie, or a prophecy. Say I dreamed it in the workshop. Consider I have been speculating upon the destinies of our race, until I have hatched this fiction. Treat my assertion of its truth as a mere stroke of art to enhance its interest. And taking it as a story, what do you think of it?"

He took up his pipe and began in his old accustomed manner to tap upon the bars of the grate.

XIV. AFTER THE TIME TRAVELER'S STORY

"There was a momentary stillness. Then chairs began to creak and shoes to scrape upon the carpet. I took my eyes off the Time Traveler's face and looked round at his audience. They were in the dark and little spots of color swam before them. The Medical Man seemed absorbed in the contemplation of our host. The Editor was looking hard at the end of his cigar—the sixth. The Journalist fumbled for his watch. The others as far as I remember were motionless.

The Editor stood up with a sigh. "What a pity it is you're not a writer of stories!" he said, putting his hand on the Time Traveler's shoulder.

"You don't believe it?"

"Well——"

"I thought not." The Time Traveler turned round to us. "Where are the matches?" he said. He lit one and spoke over his pipe, puffing, "To tell you all the truth—I hardly believe it myself—and yet——"

His eyes fell with a mute inquiry upon the withered white flowers upon the little table. Then he turned over the hand holding his pipe, and I saw he was looking at some half healed scars on his knuckles.

The Medical Man rose, came to the lamp, and examined the flowers. "The gynecium's odd," he said.

The Psychologist leaned forward to see, holding out his hand for a specimen.

"I'm hanged if it isn't a quarter to one," said the Journalist. "How shall we get home?"

"Plenty of cabs at the station," said the Psychologist.

"It's a curious thing," said the Medical Man; "but I certainly don't know the natural order of these flowers. May I have them?"

The Time Traveler hesitated. Then suddenly, "Certainly not."

"Where did you really get them?" said the Medical Man.

The Time Traveler put his hand to his head. He spoke like one who was trying to keep hold of an idea that eluded him. "They were put into my pocket by Weena—when I traveled into Time." He stared round the room. "I'm d——d if it isn't all going. This room and you and the atmosphere of everyday is too much for my memory. Did I ever make a Time Machine, or a model of a Time Machine, or is it all only a dream? They say life is a dream, a precious poor dream at times—but I can't stand another that won't fit. It's madness. And where did the dream come from? I must look at that Machine. If there *is* one."

He caught up the lamp swiftly and carried it flaring redly through the door into the corridor.

We followed him.

There in the flickering light of the lamp was the Machine, sure enough, squat, ugly, and askew, a thing of brass, ebony, ivory, and translucent, glimmering quartz. Solid to the touch—for I put out my hand and felt the rail of it—and with brown spots and smears upon the ivory, and bits of grass and moss upon the lower parts, and one rail bent awry.

The Time Traveler put the lamp down on the bench, and ran his hand along the broken rail.

"It's all right now," he said. "The story I told you was true. I'm sorry to have brought you out here—in the cold."

He took up the lamp, and in an absolute silence we returned to the smoking room.

The Time Traveler came into the hall with us and helped the Editor on with his coat. The Medical Man looked into our host's face and, with a certain hesitation, told him he was suffering from overwork, at which he laughed hugely. I remember him standing in the open doorway bawling good-night.

I shared a cab with the Editor. He thought the tale a "gaudy lie." For my own part I was unable to come to any conclusion about the matter. The story was so fantastic and incredible, the telling so credible and sober. I lay awake most of the night thinking about it. I determined to go next day and see the Time Traveler again.

I was told he was in the laboratory, and being on easy terms in the house I went up to him. The laboratory, however, was empty. I stared for a minute at the Time Machine and put out my hand and touched a lever. At that the squat, substantial looking mass swayed like a bough shaken by the wind. Its instability startled me extremely, and I had a queer reminiscence of childish days when I used to be forbidden to meddle. I came back through the corridor. The Time Traveler met me in the smoking room. He was coming from the house. He had a small camera under one arm and a knapsack under the other. He laughed when he saw me and gave me an elbow to shake.

"I'm frightfully busy," he said; "with that thing in there."

"But is it not some hoax?" said I. "Do you really travel through Time?"

"Really and truly I do." And he looked frankly into my eyes.

He hesitated. His eye wandered round the room. "I only want half an hour," he said. "I know why you came, and it's awfully good of you. There's some magazines here. If you'll stop to lunch I'll prove this time traveling to you up to the hilt. Specimens and all. If you'll forgive my leaving you now?"

I consented, hardly comprehending then the full import of his words, and he nodded and went on down the corridor. I heard the door of the laboratory slam, seated myself in a chair, and took up the *New Review*. What was he going to do before lunch time? Then suddenly I was reminded by an advertisement that I had promised to meet Richardson the publisher at two. I looked at my watch, and saw I could barely save that engagement. I got up and went down the passage to tell the Time Traveler.

As I took hold of the handle of the door I heard an exclamation oddly truncated at the end, and a click and a thud. A gust of air whirled round me as I opened the door, and from within came the sound of broken glass falling on the floor. The Time Traveler was not there. I seemed to see a ghostly indistinct figure sitting in a whirling mass of black and brass for a moment, a figure so transparent that the bench behind with its sheets of drawings was absolutely distinct; but this phantasm I immediately perceived was illusory. The Time Machine had gone. Save for a subsiding stir of dust the central space of the laboratory was empty. A pane of the skylight had apparently just been blown in.

I felt an unreasonable amazement. I knew that something strange had happened, and for a moment could not distinguish what the strange thing might be. As I stood staring, the door into the garden opened, and the man-servant appeared.

We looked at each other. Then ideas began to come.

"Has Mr. —— gone out that way?" said I.

"No, sir. No one has come out this way. I was expecting to find him here."

At that I understood. At the risk of disappointing Richardson I remained waiting for the Time Traveler, waiting for the second, perhaps still stranger, story, and the specimens and photographs he would bring with him.

But I am beginning to fear now that I must wait a lifetime for that. The Time Traveler vanished three years ago. Up to the present he has not returned, and when he does return he will find his home in the hands of strangers and his little gathering of auditors broken up forever. Filby has exchanged poetry for playwriting, and is a rich man—as literary men go—and extremely unpopular. The Medical Man is dead, the Journalist is in India, and the Psychologist has succumbed to paralysis. Some of the other men I used to meet there have dropped as completely out of existence as if they, too, had traveled off upon some similar anachronisms. And so, ending in a kind of dead wall, the story of the Time Machine must remain for the present at least.

James Joyce (1882–1941)

AN ENCOUNTER

It was Joe Dillon who introduced the Wild West to us. He had a little library made up of old numbers of *The Union Jack, Pluck* and *The Halfpenny Marvel.* Every evening after school we met in his back garden and arranged Indian battles. He and his fat young brother Leo the idler held the loft of the stable while we tried to carry it by storm; or we fought a pitched battle on the grass. But, however well we fought, we never won siege or battle and all our bouts ended with Joe Dillon's war dance of victory. His parents went to eight-o'clock mass every morning in Gardiner Street and the peaceful odor of Mrs. Dillon was prevalent in the hall of the house. But he played too fiercely for us who were younger and more timid. He looked like some kind of an Indian when he capered round the garden, an old tea-cosy on his head, beating a tin with his fist and yelling:

—Ya! yaka, yaka, yaka!

Everyone was incredulous when it was reported that he had a vocation for the priesthood. Nevertheless it was true.

A spirit of unruliness diffused itself among us and, under its influence, differences of culture and constitution were waived. We banded ourselves together, some boldly, some in jest and some almost in fear: and of the number of these latter, the reluctant Indians who were afraid to seem studious or lacking in robustness, I was one. The adventures related in the literature of the Wild West were remote from my nature but, at least, they opened doors of escape. I like better some American detective stories which were traversed from time to time by unkempt fierce and beautiful girls. Though there was nothing wrong in these stories and though their intention was sometimes literary they were circulated secretly at school. One day when Father Butler was hearing the four pages of Roman History clumsy Leo Dillon was discovered with a copy of *The Halfpenny Marvel.*

—This page or this page? This page? Now, Dillon, up! *Hardly had the day . . .* Go on! What day? *Hardly had the day dawned . . .* Have you studied it? What have you there in your pocket?

Everyone's heart palpitated as Leo Dillon handed up the paper and everyone assumed an innocent face. Father Butler turned over the pages, frowning.

—What is this rubbish? he said. *The Apache Chief!* Is this what you read instead of studying your Roman History? Let me not find any more of this wretched stuff in this college. The man who wrote it, I suppose, was some wretched scribbler that writes these things for a drink. I'm surprised at boys like you, educated, reading such stuff. I could understand it if you were . . . National School boys. Now, Dillon,

I advise you strongly, get at your work or . . .

This rebuke during the sober hours of school paled much of the glory of the Wild West for me and the confused puffy face of Leo Dillon awakened one of my consciences. But when the restraining influence of the school was at a distance I began to hunger again for wild sensations, for the escape which those chronicles of disorder alone seemed to offer me. The mimic warfare of the evening became at last as wearisome to me as the routine of school in the morning because I wanted real adventures to happen to myself. But real adventures, I reflected, do not happen to people who remain at home: they must be sought abroad.

The summer holidays were near at hand when I made up my mind to break out of the weariness of school-life for one day at least. With Leo Dillon and a boy named Mahony I planned a day's miching. Each of us saved up sixpence. We were to meet at ten in the morning on the Canal Bridge. Mahony's big sister was to write an excuse for him and Leo Dillon was to tell his brother to say he was sick. We arranged to go along the Wharf Road until we came to the ships, then to cross in the ferryboat and walk out to see the Pigeon House. Leo Dillon was afraid we might meet Father Butler or someone out of the college; but Mahony asked, very sensibly, what would Father Butler be doing out at the Pigeon House. We were reassured: and I brought the first stage of the plot to an end by collecting sixpence from the other two, at the same time showing them my own sixpence. When we were making the last arrangements on the eve we were all vaguely excited. We shook hands, laughing, and Mahony said:

—Till to-morrow, mates.

That night I slept badly. In the morning I was firstcomer to the bridge as I lived nearest. I hid my books in the long grass near the ashpit at the end of the garden where nobody ever came and hurried along the canal bank. It was a mild sunny morning in the first week of June. I sat up on the coping of the bridge admiring my frail canvas shoes which I had diligently pipeclayed overnight and watching the docile horses pulling a tramload of business people up the hill. All the branches of the tall trees which lined the mall were gay with little light green leaves and the sunlight slanted through them on to the water. The granite stone of the bridge was beginning to be warm and I began to pat it with my hands in time to an air in my head. I was very happy.

When I had been sitting there for five or ten minutes I saw Mahony's grey suit approaching. He came up the hill, smiling, and clambered up beside me on the bridge. While we were waiting he brought out the catapult which bulged from his inner pocket and explained some improvements which he had made in it. I asked him why he had brought it and he told me he had brought it to have some gas with the birds. Mahony used slang freely, and spoke of Father Butler as Bunsen Burner. We waited on for a quarter of an hour more but still there was no sign of Leo Dillon. Mahony, at last, jumped down and said:

—Come along. I knew Fatty'd funk it.

—And his sixpence . . . ? I said.

—That's forfeit, said Mahony. And so much the better for us—a bob and a tanner instead of a bob.

We walked along the North Strand Road till we came to the Vitriol Works and then turned to the right along the Wharf Road. Mahony began to play the Indian as soon as we were out of public sight. He chased a crowd of ragged girls, brandishing his unloaded catapult and, when two ragged boys began, out of chivalry, to fling stones at us, he proposed that we should charge them. I objected that the boys were too small, and so we walked on, the ragged troop screaming after us: *Swaddlers! Swaddlers!* thinking that we were Protestants because Mahony, who was dark-complexioned, wore the silver badge of a cricket club in his cap. When we came to the Smoothing Iron we arranged a siege; but it was a failure because you must have at least three. We revenged ourselves on Leo Dillon by saying what a funk he was and guessing how many he would get at three o'clock from Mr. Ryan.

We came then near the river. We spent a long time walking about the noisy streets flanked by high stone walls, watching the working of cranes and engines and often being shouted at for our immobility by the drivers of groaning carts. It was noon when we reached the quays and, as all the laborers seemed to be eating their lunches, we bought two big currant buns and sat down to eat them on some metal piping beside the river. We pleased ourselves with the spectacle of Dublin's commerce—the barges signalled from far away by their curls of woolly smoke, the brown fishing fleet beyond Ringsend, the big white sailing-vessel which was being discharged on the opposite quay. Mahony said it would be right skit to run away to sea on one of those big ships and even I, looking at the high masts, saw, or imagined, the geography which had been scantily dosed to me at school gradually taking substance under my eyes. School and home seemed to recede from us and their influences upon us seemed to wane.

We crossed the Liffey in the ferry-boat, paying our toll to be transported in the company of two laborers and a little Jew with a bag. We were serious to the point of solemnity, but once during the short voyage our eyes met and we laughed. When we landed we watched the discharging of the graceful three-master which we had observed from the other quay. Some bystander said that she was a Norwegian vessel. I went to the stern and tried to decipher the legend upon it but, failing to do so, I came back and examined the foreign sailors to see had any of them green eyes for I had some confused notion. . . . The sailors' eyes were blue and grey and even black. The only sailor whose eyes could have been called green was a tall man who amused the crowd on the quay by calling out cheerfully every time the planks fell:

—All right! All right!

When we were tired of this sight we wandered slowly into Ringsend. The day had grown sultry, and in the windows of the grocers' shops musty biscuits lay bleaching. We bought some biscuits and chocolate which we ate sedulously as we wandered through the squalid streets where the families of the fishermen live. We could find no dairy and so we went into a huckster's shop and bought a bottle of raspberry lemonade each. Refreshed by this, Mahony chased a cat down a lane, but the cat escaped into a wide field. We both felt rather tired and when we reached the field we made at once for a sloping bank over the ridge of which we could see the Dodder.

It was too late and we were too tired to carry out our project of visiting the Pigeon House. We had to be home before four o'clock lest our adventure should be discovered. Mahony looked regretfully at his catapult and I had to suggest going home by train before he regained any cheerfulness. The sun went in behind some clouds and left us to our jaded thoughts and the crumbs of our provisions.

There was nobody but ourselves in the field. When we had lain on the bank for some time without speaking I saw a man approaching from the far end of the field. I watched him lazily as I chewed one of those green stems on which girls tell fortunes. He came along by the bank slowly. He walked with one hand upon his hip and in the other hand he held a stick with which he tapped the turf lightly. He was shabbily dressed in a suit of greenish-black and wore what we used to call a jerry hat with a high crown. He seemed to be fairly old for his moustache was ashen-grey. When he passed at our feet he glanced up at us quickly and then continued his way. We followed him with our eyes and saw that when he had gone on for perhaps fifty paces he turned about and began to retrace his steps. He walked towards us very slowly, always tapping the ground with his stick, so slowly that I thought he was looking for something in the grass.

He stopped when he came level with us and bade us good-day. We answered him and he sat down beside us on the slope slowly and with great care. He began to talk of the weather, saying that it would be a very hot summer and adding that the seasons had changed greatly since he was a boy—a long time ago. He said that the happiest time of one's life was undoubtedly one's schoolboy days and that he would give anything to be young again. While he expressed these sentiments which bored us a little we kept silent. Then he began to talk of school and of books. He asked us whether we had read the poetry of Thomas Moore or the works of Sir Walter Scott and Lord Lytton. I pretended that I had read every book he mentioned so that in the end he said:

—Ah, I can see you are a bookworm like myself. Now, he added, pointing to Mahony who was regarding us with open eyes, he is different; he goes in for games.

He said he had all Sir Walter Scott's works and all Lord Lytton's works at home and never tired of reading them. Of course, he said, there were some of Lord Lytton's works which boys couldn't read. Mahony asked why couldn't boys read them—a question which agitated and pained me because I was afraid the man would think I was as stupid as Mahony. The man, however, only smiled. I saw that he had great gaps in his mouth between his yellow teeth.

Then he asked us which of us had the most sweethearts. Mahony mentioned lightly that he had three totties. The man asked me how many had I. I answered that I had none. He did not believe me and said he was sure I must have one. I was silent.

—Tell us, said Mahony pertly to the man, how many have you yourself?

The man smiled as before and said that when he was our age he had lots of sweethearts.

—Every boy, he said, has a little sweetheart.

His attitude on this point struck me as strangely liberal in a man of his age. In my heart I thought that what he said about boys and sweethearts was reasonable. But I disliked the words in his mouth and I wondered why he shivered once or twice as if he feared something or felt a sudden chill. As he proceeded I noticed that his accent was good. He began to speak to us about girls, saying what nice soft hair they had and how soft their hands were and how all girls were not so good as they seemed to be if one only knew. There was nothing he liked, he said, so much as looking at a nice young girl, at her nice white hands and her beautiful soft hair. He gave me the impression that he was repeating something which he had learned by heart or that, magnetized by some words of his own speech, his mind was slowly circling round and round in the same orbit. At times he spoke as if he were simply alluding to some fact that everybody knew, and at times he lowered his voice and spoke mysteriously as if he were telling us something secret which he did not wish others to overhear. He repeated his phrases over and over again, varying them and surrounding them with his monotonous voice. I continued to gaze towards the foot of the slope, listening to him.

After a long while his monologue paused. He stood up slowly, saying that he had to leave us for a minute or so, a few minutes, and, without changing the direction of my gaze, I saw him walking slowly away from us towards the near end of the field. We remained silent when he had gone. After a silence of a few minutes I heard Mahony exclaim:

—I say! Look what he's doing!

As I neither answered nor raised my eyes Mahony exclaimed again:

—I say . . . He's a queer old josser!

—In case he asks us for our names, I said, let you be Murphy and I'll be Smith.

We said nothing further to each other. I was still considering whether I would go away or not when the man came back and sat down beside us again. Hardly had he sat down when Mahony, catching sight of the cat which had escaped him, sprang up and pursued her across the field. The man and I watched the chase. The cat escaped once more and Mahony began to throw stones at the wall she had escaladed. Desisting from this, he began to wander about the far end of the field, aimlessly.

After an interval the man spoke to me. He said that my friend was a very rough boy and asked did he get whipped often at school. I was going to reply indignantly that we were not National School boys to be *whipped,* as he called it; but I remained silent. He began to speak on the subject of chastizing boys. His mind, as if magnetized again by his speech, seemed to circle slowly round and round its new center. He said that when boys were that kind they ought to be whipped and well whipped. When a boy was rough and unruly there was nothing would do him any good but a good sound whipping. A slap on the hand or a box on the ear was no good: what he wanted was to get a nice warm whipping. I was surprised at this sentiment and involuntarily glanced up at

his face. As I did so I met the gaze of a pair of bottle-green eyes peering at me from under a twitching forehead. I turned my eyes away again.

The man continued his monologue. He seemed to have forgotten his recent liberalism. He said that if ever he found a boy talking to girls or having a girl for a sweetheart he would whip him and whip him; and that would teach him not to be talking to girls. And if a boy had a girl for a sweetheart and told lies about it then he would give him such a whipping as no boy ever got in this world. He said that there was nothing in this world he would like so well as that. He described to me how he would whip such a boy as if he were unfolding some elaborate mystery. He would love that, he said, better than anything in this world; and his voice, as he led me monotonously through the mystery, grew almost affectionate and seemed to plead with me that I should understand him.

I waited till his monologue paused again. Then I stood up abruptly. Lest I should betray my agitation I delayed a few moments pretending to fix my shoe properly and then, saying that I was obliged to go, I bade him good-day. I went up the slope calmly but my heart was beating quickly with fear that he would seize me by the ankles. When I reached the top of the slope I turned round and, without looking at him, called loudly across the field:

Murphy!

My voice had an accent of forced bravery in it and I was ashamed of my paltry stratagem. I had to call the name again before Mahony saw me and hallooed in answer. How my heart beat as he came running across the field to me! He ran as if to bring me aid. And I was penitent; for in my heart I had always despised him a little.

from A PORTRAIT OF THE ARTIST AS A YOUNG MAN

CHAPTER I

Once upon a time and a very good time it was there was a moocow coming down along the road and this moocow that was coming down along the road met a nicens little boy named baby tuckoo. . . .

His father told him that story: his father looked at him through a glass: he had a hairy face.

He was baby tuckoo. The moocow came down the road where Betty Byrne lived: she sold lemon platt.

O, the wild rose blossoms
On the little green place.

He sang that song. That was his song.

O, the green wothe botheth

When you wet the bed first it is warm then it gets cold. His mother put on the oilsheet. That had the queer smell.

His mother had a nicer smell than his father. She played on the piano the sailor's hornpipe for him to dance. He danced:

Tralala lala
Tralala tralaladdy
Tralala lala
Tralala lala.

Uncle Charles and Dante clapped. They were older than his father and mother but uncle Charles was older than Dante.

Dante had two brushes in her press. The brush with the maroon velvet back was for Michael Davitt and the brush with the green velvet back was for Parnell. Dante gave him a cachou every time he brought her a piece of tissue paper.

The Vances lived in number seven. They had a different father and mother. They were Eileen's father and mother. When they were grown up he was going to marry Eileen. He hid under the table. His mother said:

—O, Stephen will apologize.

Dante said:

—O, if not, the eagles will come and pull out his eyes.

Pull out his eyes,
Apologize,
Apologize,
Pull out his eyes.

Apologize,
Pull out his eyes,
Pull out his eyes,
Apologize.

* * *

The wide playgrounds were swarming with boys. All were shouting and the prefects urged them on with strong cries. The evening air was pale and chilly and after every charge and thud of the footballers the greasy leather orb flew like a heavy bird through the grey light. He kept on the fringe of his line, out of sight of his prefect, out of the reach of the rude feet, feigning to run now and then. He felt his body small and weak amid the throng of players and his eyes were weak and watery. Rody Kickham was not like that: he would be captain of the third line all the fellows said.

Rody Kickham was a decent fellow but Nasty Roche was a stink. Rody Kickham had greaves in his number and a hamper in the refectory. Nasty Roche had big hands. He called the Friday pudding dog-in-the-blanket. And one day he had asked:

—What is your name?

Stephen had answered:

—Stephen Dedalus.

Then Nasty Roche had said:

—What kind of a name is that?

And when Stephen had not been able to answer Nasty Roche had asked:

—What is your father?

Stephen had answered:

—A gentleman.

Then Nasty Roche had asked:

—Is he a magistrate?

He crept about from point to point on the fringe of his line, making little runs now and then. But his hands were bluish with cold. He kept his hands in the sidepockets of his belted grey suit. That was a belt round his pocket. And belt was also to give a fellow a belt. One day a fellow had said to Cantwell:

—I'd give you such a belt in a second.

Cantwell had answered:

—Go and fight your match. Give Cecil Thunder a belt. I'd like to see you. He'd give you a toe in the rump for yourself.

That was not a nice expression. His mother had told him not to speak with the rough boys in the college. Nice mother! The first day in the hall of the castle when she had said goodbye she had put up her veil double to her nose to kiss him: and her nose and eyes were red. But he had pretended not to see that she was going to cry. She was a nice mother but she was not so nice when she cried. And his father had given him two fiveshilling pieces for pocket money. And his father had told him if he wanted anything to write home to him and, whatever he did, never to peach on a fellow. Then at the door of the castle the rector had shaken hands with his father and mother, his soutane fluttering in the breeze, and the car had driven off with his father and mother on it. They had cried to him from the car, waving their hands:

—Goodbye, Stephen, goodbye!

—Goodbye, Stephen, goodbye!

He was caught in the whirl of a scrimmage and, fearful of the flashing eyes and muddy boots, bent down to look through the legs. The fellows were struggling and groaning and their legs were rubbing and kicking and stamping. Then Jack Lawton's yellow boots dodged out the ball and all the other boots and legs ran after. He ran after them a little way and then stopped. It was useless to run on. Soon they would be going home for the holidays. After supper in the studyhall he would change the number pasted up inside his desk from seventyseven to seventysix.

It would be better to be in the studyhall than out there in the cold. The sky was pale and cold but there were lights in the castle. He wondered from which window Hamilton Rowan had thrown his hat on the haha and had there been flowerbeds at that time under the windows. One day when he had been called to the castle the butler had shown him the marks of the soldiers' slugs in the wood of the door and had given him a piece of shortbread that the community ate. It was nice and warm to see the lights in the castle. It was like something in a book. Perhaps Leicester Abbey was like that. And there were nice sentences in Doctor Cornwell's Spelling Book. They were like poetry but they were only sentences to learn the spelling from.

Wolsey died in Leicester Abbey
Where the abbots buried him.
Canker is a disease of plants,
Cancer one of animals.

It would be nice to lie on the hearthrug before the fire, leaning his head upon his hands, and think on those sentences. He shivered as if he had cold slimy water next his skin. That was mean of Wells to shoulder him into the square ditch because he would not swop his little snuffbox for Wells's seasoned hacking chestnut, the conqueror of forty. How cold and slimy the water had been! A fellow had once seen a big rat jump into the scum. Mother was sitting at the fire with Dante waiting for Brigid to bring in the tea. She had her feet on the fender and her jewelly slippers were so hot and they had such a lovely warm smell! Dante knew a lot of things. She had taught him where the Mozambique Channel was and what was the longest river in America and what was the name of the highest mountain in the moon. Father Arnall knew more than Dante because he was a priest but both his father and uncle Charles said that Dante was a clever woman and a wellread woman. And when Dante made that noise after dinner and then put up her hand to her mouth: that was heartburn.

A voice cried far out on the playground:

—All in!

Then other voices cried from the lower and third lines:

—All in! All in!

The players closed around, flushed and muddy, and he went among them, glad to go in. Rody Kickham held the ball by its greasy lace. A fellow asked him to give it one last: but he walked on without even answering the fellow. Simon Moonan told him not to because the prefect was looking. The fellow turned to Simon Moonan and said:

—We all know why you speak. You are McGlade's suck.

Suck was a queer word. The fellow called Simon Moonan that name because Simon Moonan used to tie the prefect's false sleeves behind his back and the prefect used to let on to be angry. But the sound was ugly. Once he had washed his hands in the lavatory of the Wicklow Hotel and his father pulled the stopper up by the chain after and the dirty water went down through the hole in the basin. And when it had all gone down slowly the hole in the basin had made a sound like that: suck. Only louder.

To remember that and the white look of the lavatory made him feel cold and then hot. There were two cocks that you turned and water came out: cold and hot. He felt cold and then a little hot: and he could see the names printed on the cocks. That was a very queer thing.

And the air in the corridor chilled him too. It was queer and wettish. But soon the gas would be lit and in burning it made a light noise like a little song. Always the same: and when the fellows stopped talking in the playroom you could hear it.

It was the hour for sums. Father Arnall wrote a hard sum on the board and then said:

—Now then, who will win? Go ahead, York! Go ahead, Lancaster!

Stephen tried his best but the sum was too hard and he felt confused. The little silk badge with the white rose on it that was pinned on the breast of his jacket began to flutter. He was no good at sums but he tried his best so that York might not lose. Father Arnall's face looked very black but he was not in a wax: he was laughing. Then Jack Lawton cracked his fingers and Father Arnall looked at his copybook and said:

—Right. Bravo Lancaster! The red rose wins. Come on now, York! Forge ahead!

Jack Lawton looked over from his side. The little silk badge with the red rose on it looked very rich because he had a blue sailor top on. Stephen felt his own face red too, thinking of all the bets about who would get first place in elements, Jack Lawton or he. Some weeks Jack Lawton got the card for first and some weeks he got the card for first. His white silk badge fluttered and fluttered as he worked at the next sum and heard Father Arnall's voice. Then all his eagerness passed away and he felt his face quite cool. He thought his face must be white because it felt so cool. He could not get out the answer for the sum but it did not matter. White roses and red roses: those were beautiful colors to think of. And the cards for first place and second place and third place were beautiful colors too: pink and cream and lavender. Lavender and cream and pink roses were beautiful to think of. Perhaps a wild rose might be like those colors and he remembered the song about the wild rose blossoms on the little green place. But you could not have a green rose. But perhaps somewhere in the world you could.

The bell rang and then the classes began to file out of the rooms and along the corridors towards the refectory. He sat looking at the two prints of butter on his plate but could not eat the damp bread. The tablecloth was damp and limp. But he drank off the hot weak tea which the clumsy scullion, girt with a white apron, poured into his cup. He wondered whether the scullion's apron was damp too or whether all white things were cold and damp. Nasty Roche and Saurin drank cocoa that their people sent them in tins. They said they could not drink the tea; that it was hogwash. Their fathers were magistrates, the fellows said.

All the boys seemed to him very strange. They had all fathers and mothers and different clothes and voices. He longed to be at home and lay his head on his mother's lap. But he could not: and so he longed for the play and study and prayers to be over and to be in bed.

He drank another cup of hot tea and Fleming said:

—What's up? Have you a pain or what's up with you?

—I don't know, Stephen said.

—Sick in your breadbasket, Fleming said, because your face looks white. It will go away.

—O yes, Stephen said.

But he was not sick there. He thought that he was sick in his heart if you could be sick in that place. Fleming was very decent to ask him. He wanted to cry. He leaned his elbows on the table and shut and opened the flaps of his ears. Then he heard the noise of the refectory every time he opened the flaps of his ears. It made a roar like a train at night. And when he closed the flaps the roar was shut off like a train going into a tunnel. That night at Dalkey the train had roared like that and then, when it went into the tunnel, the roar stopped. He closed his eyes and the train went on, roaring and then stopping; roaring again, stopping. It was nice to hear it roar and stop and then roar out of the tunnel again and then stop.

Then the higher line fellows began to come down along the matting in the middle of the refectory, Paddy Rath and Jimmy Magee and the Spaniard who was allowed to smoke cigars and the little Portuguese who wore the woolly cap. And then the lower line tables and the tables of the third line. And every single fellow had a different way of walking.

He sat in a corner of the playroom pretending to watch a game of dominos and once or twice he was able to hear for an instant the little song of the gas. The prefect was at the door with some boys and Simon Moonan was knotting his false sleeves. He was telling them something about Tullabeg.

Then he went away from the door and Wells came over to Stephen and said:

—Tell us, Dedalus, do you kiss your mother before you go to bed?

Stephen answered:

—I do.

Wells turned to the other fellows and said:

—O, I say, here's a fellow says he kisses his mother every night before he goes to bed.

The other fellows stopped their game and turned round, laughing. Stephen blushed under their eyes and said:

—I do not.

Wells said:

—O, I say, here's a fellow says he doesn't kiss his mother before he goes to bed.

They all laughed again. Stephen tried to laugh with them. He felt his whole body hot and confused in a moment. What was the right answer to the question? He had given two and still Wells laughed. But Wells must know the right answer for he was in third of grammar. He tried to think of Wells's mother but he did not dare to raise his eyes to Wells's face. He did not like Wells's face. It was Wells who had shouldered him into the square ditch the day before because he would not swop his little snuffbox for Wells's seasoned hacking chestnut, the conqueror of forty. It was a mean thing to do; all the fellows said it was. And how cold and slimy the water had been! And a fellow had once seen a big rat jump plop into the scum.

The cold slime of the ditch covered his whole body; and, when the bell rang for study and the lines filed out of the playrooms, he felt the cold air of the corridor and staircase inside his clothes. He still tried to think what was the right answer. Was it right to kiss his mother or wrong to kiss his mother? What did that mean, to kiss? You put your face up like that to say goodnight and then his mother put her face down. That was to kiss. His mother put her lips on his cheek; her lips were soft and they wetted his cheek; and they made a tiny little noise: kiss. Why did people do that with their two faces?

Sitting in the studyhall he opened the lid of his desk and changed the number pasted up inside from seventyseven to seventysix. But the Christmas vacation was very far away: but one time it would come because the earth moved round always.

There was a picture of the earth on the first page of his geography: a big ball in the middle of clouds. Fleming had a box of crayons and one night during free study he had colored the earth green and the clouds maroon. That was like the two brushes in Dante's press, the brush with the green velvet back for Parnell and the brush with the maroon velvet back for Michael Davitt. But he had not told Fleming to color them those colors. Fleming had done it himself.

He opened the geography to study the lesson; but he could not learn the names of places in America. Still they were all different places that had those different names. They were all in different countries and the countries were in continents and the continents were in the world and the world was in the universe.

He turned to the flyleaf of the geography and read what he had written there: himself, his name and where he was.

> Stephen Dedalus
> Class of Elements
> Clongowes Wood College
> Sallins
> County Kildare
> Ireland
> Europe
> The World
> The Universe

That was in his writing: and Fleming one night for a cod had written on the opposite page:

> Stephen Dedalus is my name,
> Ireland is my nation.
> Clongowes is my dwellingplace
> And heaven my expectation.

He read the verses backwards but then they were not poetry. Then he read the flyleaf from the bottom to the top till he came to his own name. That was he: and he read down the page again. What was after the universe? Nothing. But was there anything round the universe to show where it stopped before the nothing place began? It could not be a wall but there could be a thin thin line there all round everything. It was very big to think about everything and everywhere. Only God could do that. He tried to think what a big thought that must be but he could think only of God. God was God's name just as his name was Stephen. Dieu was the French for God and that was God's name too; and when anyone prayed to God and said Dieu then God knew at once that it was a French person that was praying. But though there were different names for God in all the different languages in the world and God understood what all the people who prayed said in their different languages still God remained always the same God and God's real name was God.

It made him very tired to think that way. It made him feel his head very big. He turned over the flyleaf and looked wearily at the green round earth in the middle of the maroon clouds. He wondered which was right, to be for the green or for the maroon, because Dante had ripped the green velvet back off the brush that was for Parnell one day with her scissors and had told him that Parnell was a bad man. He wondered if they were arguing at home about that. That was called politics. There were two sides in it: Dante was on one side and his father and Mr. Casey were on the other side but his mother and uncle Charles were on no side. Every day there was something in the paper about it.

It pained him that he did not know well what politics meant and that he did not know where the universe ended. He felt small and weak. When would he be like the fellows in poetry and rhetoric? They had big voices and big boots and they studied trigonometry. That was very far away. First came the vacation and then the next term and then vacation again and then again another term and then again the vacation. It was like a train going in and out of tunnels and that was like the noise of the boys eating in the refectory when you opened and closed the flaps of the ears. Term, vacation; tunnel, out; noise, stop. How far away it was! It was better to go to bed to sleep. Only prayers in the chapel and then bed. He shivered and yawned. It would be lovely in bed after the sheets got a bit hot. First they were so cold to get into. He shivered to think how cold they were first. But then they got hot and then he could sleep. It was lovely to be tired. He yawned again. Night prayers and then bed: he shivered and wanted to yawn. It would be lovely in a few minutes. He felt a warm glow creeping up from the cold shivering sheets, warmer and warmer till he felt warm all over, ever so warm; ever so warm and yet he shivered a little and still wanted to yawn.

The bell rang for night prayers and he filed out of the studyhall after the others and down the staircase and along the corridors to the chapel. The corridors were darkly lit and the chapel was darkly lit. Soon all would be dark and sleeping. There was cold night air in the chapel and the marbles were the color the sea was at night. The sea was cold day and night: but it was colder at night. It was cold and dark under the seawall beside his father's house. But the kettle would be on the hob to make punch.

The prefect of the chapel prayed above his head and his memory knew the responses:

O Lord, open our lips
And our mouth shall announce Thy
    praise.
Incline unto our aid, O God!
O Lord, make haste to help us!

There was a cold night smell in the chapel. But it was a holy smell. It was not like the smell of the old peasants who knelt at the back of the chapel at Sunday mass. That was a smell of air and rain and turf and corduroy. But they were very holy peasants. They breathed behind him on his neck and sighed as they prayed. They lived in Clane, a fellow said: there were little cottages there and he had seen a woman standing at the halfdoor of a cottage with a child in her arms, as the cars had come past from Sallins. It would be lovely to sleep for one night in that cottage before the fire of smoking turf, in the dark lit by the fire, in the warm dark, breathing the smell of the peasants, air and rain and turf and corduroy. But, O, the road there between the trees was dark! You would be lost in the dark.

It made him afraid to think of how it was.

He heard the voice of the prefect of the chapel saying the last prayer. He prayed it too against the dark outside under the trees.

Visit, we beseech Thee, O Lord, this habitation and drive away from it all the snares of the enemy. May Thy holy angels dwell herein to preserve us in peace and may Thy blessing be always upon us through Christ, Our Lord.
Amen.

His fingers trembled as he undressed himself in the dormitory. He told his fingers to hurry up. He had to undress and then kneel and say his own prayers and be in bed before the gas was lowered so that he might not to go hell when he died. He rolled his stockings off and put on his nightshirt quickly and knelt trembling at his bedside and repeated his prayers quickly quickly, fearing that the gas would go down. He felt his shoulders shaking as he murmured:

God bless my father and my mother
*   and spare them to me!*
God bless my little brothers and sisters
*   and spare them to me!*
God bless Dante and uncle Charles and
*   spare them to me!*

He blessed himself and climbed quickly into bed and, tucking the end of the nightshirt under his feet, curled himself together under the cold white sheets, shaking and trembling. But he would not go to hell when he died; and the shaking would stop. A voice bade the boys in the dormitory good night. He peered out for an instant over the coverlet and saw the yellow curtains round and before his bed that shut him off on all sides. The light was lowered quietly.

The prefect's shoes went away. Where? Down the staircase and along the corridors or to his room at the end? He saw the dark. Was it true about the black dog that walked there at night with eyes as big as carriagelamps? They said it was the ghost of a murderer. A long shiver of fear flowed over his body. He saw the dark entrance hall of the castle. Old servants in old dress were in the ironingroom above the staircase. It was long ago. The old servants were quiet. There was a fire there but the hall was still dark. A figure came up the staircase from the hall. He wore the white cloak of a marshal; his face was pale and strange; he held his hand pressed to his side. He looked out of strange eyes at the old servants. They looked at him and saw their master's face and cloak and knew that he had received his deathwound. But only the dark was where they looked: only dark silent air. Their master had received his deathwound on the battlefield of Prague far away over the sea. He was standing on the field; his hand was pressed to his side; his face was pale and strange and he wore the white cloak of a marshal.

O how cold and strange it was to think of that! All the dark was cold and strange. There were pale strange faces there, great eyes like carriagelamps. They were the ghosts of murderers, the figures of marshals who had received their deathwound on battlefields far away over the sea. What did they wish to say that their faces were so strange?

Visit, we beseech Thee, O Lord, this habitation and drive away from it all . . .

Going home for the holidays! That would be lovely: the fellows had told him. Getting up on the cars in the early wintry morning outside the door of the castle. The cars were rolling on the gravel. Cheers for the rector!

Hurray! Hurray! Hurray!

The cars drove past the chapel and all caps were raised. They drove merrily along the country roads. The drivers pointed with their whips to Bodenstown. The fellows cheered. They passed the farmhouse of the Jolly Farmer. Cheer after cheer after cheer. Through Clane they drove, cheering and cheered.

The peasant women stood at the half-doors, the men stood here and there. The lovely smell there was in the wintry air: the smell of Clane: rain and wintry air and turf smoldering and corduroy.

The train was full of fellows: a long long chocolate train with cream facings. The guards went to and fro opening, closing, locking, unlocking the doors. They were men in dark blue and silver; they had silvery whistles and their keys made a quick music: click, click: click, click.

And the train raced on over the flat lands and past the Hill of Allen. The telegraphpoles were passing, passing. The train went on and on. It knew. There were colored lanterns in the hall of his father's house and ropes of green branches. There were holly and ivy round the pierglass and holly and ivy, green and red, twined round the chandeliers. There were red holly and green ivy round the old portraits on the walls. Holly and ivy for him and for Christmas.

Lovely . . .

All the people. Welcome home, Stephen! Noises of welcome. His mother kissed him. Was that right? His father was a marshal now: higher than a magistrate. Welcome home, Stephen!

Noises . . .

There was a noise of curtainrings running back along the rods, of water being splashed in the basins. There was a noise of rising and dressing and washing in the dormitory: a noise of clapping of hands as the prefect went up and down telling the fellows to look sharp. A pale sunlight showed the yellow curtains drawn back, the tossed beds. His bed was very hot and his face and body were very hot.

He got up and sat on the side of his bed. He was weak. He tried to pull on his stocking. It had a horrid rough feel. The sunlight was queer and cold.

Fleming said:

—Are you not well?

He did not know; and Fleming said:

—Get back into bed. I'll tell McGlade you're not well.

—He's sick.

—Who is?

—Tell McGlade.

—Get back into bed.

—Is he sick?

A fellow held his arms while he loosened the stocking clinging to his foot and climbed back into the hot bed.

He crouched down between the sheets, glad of their tepid glow. He heard the fellows talk among themselves about him as they dressed for mass. It was a mean thing to do, to shoulder him into the square ditch, they were saying.

Then their voices ceased; they had gone. A voice at his bed said:

—Dedalus, don't spy on us, sure you won't?

Wells's face was there. He looked at it and saw that Wells was afraid.

—I didn't mean to. Sure you won't?

His father had told him, whatever he did, never to peach on a fellow. He shook his head and answered no and felt glad. Wells said:

—I didn't mean to, honor bright. It was only for cod. I'm sorry.

The face and the voice went away. Sorry because he was afraid. Afraid that it was some disease. Canker was a disease of plants and cancer one of animals: or another different. That was a long time ago then out on the playgrounds in the evening light, creeping from point to point on the fringe of his line, a heavy bird flying low through the grey light. Leicester Abbey lit up. Wolsey died there. The abbots buried him themselves.

It was not Wells's face, it was the prefect's. He was not foxing. No, no: he was sick really. He was not foxing. And he felt the prefect's hand on his forehead; and he felt his forehead warm and damp against the prefect's cold damp hand. That was the way a rat felt, slimy and damp and cold. Every rat had two eyes to look out of. Sleek slimy coats, little little feet tucked up to jump, black shiny eyes to look out of. They could understand how to jump. But the minds of rats could not understand trigonometry. When they were dead they lay on their sides. Their coats dried then. They were only dead things.

The prefect was there again and it was his voice that was saying that he was to get up, that Father Minister had said he was to get up and dress and go to the infirmary. And while he was dressing himself as quickly as he could the prefect said:

—We must pack off to Brother Michael because we have the colly-wobbles! Terrible thing to have the collywobbles! How we wobble when we have the collywobbles!

He was very decent to say that. That was all to make him laugh. But he could not laugh because his cheeks and lips were all shivery: and then the prefect had to laugh by himself.

The prefect cried:

—Quick march! Hayfoot! Strawfoot!

They went together down the stair-case and along the corridor and past the bath. As he passed the door he remembered with a vague fear the warm turf-colored bogwater, the warm moist air, the noise of plunges, the smell of the towels, like medicine.

Brother Michael was standing at the door of the infirmary and from the door of the dark cabinet on his right came a smell like medicine. That came from the bottles on the shelves. The prefect spoke to Brother Michael and Brother Michael answered and called the prefect sir. He had reddish hair mixed with grey and a queer look. It was queer that he would always be a brother. It was queer too that you could not call him sir because he was a brother and had a different kind of look. Was he not holy enough or why could he not catch up on the others?

There were two beds in the room and in one bed there was a fellow: and when they went in he called out:

—Hello! It's young Dedalus! What's up?

—The sky is up, Brother Michael said.

He was a fellow out of the third of grammar and, while Stephen was un-dressing, he asked Brother Michael to bring him a round of buttered toast.

—Ah, do! he said.

—Butter you up! said Brother Mi-chael. You'll get your walking papers in the morning when the doctor comes.

—Will I? the fellow said. I'm not well yet.

Brother Michael repeated:

—You'll get your walking papers, I tell you.

He bent down to rake the fire. He had a long back like the long back of a tramhorse. He shook the poker gravely and nodded his head at the fel-low out of third of grammar.

Then Brother Michael went away and after a while the fellow out of third of grammar turned in towards the wall and fell asleep.

That was the infirmary. He was sick then. Had they written home to tell his mother and father? But it would be quicker for one of the priests to go himself to tell them. Or he would write a letter for the priest to bring.

Dear Mother
    I am sick. I want to go home. Please come and take me home. I am in the infirmary.
                        Your fond son,
                                Stephen

How far away they were! There was cold sunlight outside the window. He wondered if he would die. You could die just the same on a sunny day. He might die before his mother came. Then he would have a dead mass in the chapel like the way the fellows had told him it was when Little had died. All the fellows would be at the mass, dressed in black, all with sad faces. Wells too would be there but no fellow would look at him. The rector would be there in a cope of black and gold and there would be tall yellow candles on the altar and round the catafalque. And they would carry the coffin out of the chapel slowly and he would be buried in the little graveyard of the community off the main avenue of limes. And Wells would be sorry then for what he had done. And the bell would toll slowly.

He could hear the tolling. He said over to himself the song that Brigid had taught him.

> Dingdong! The castle bell!
> Farewell, my mother!
> Bury me in the old churchyard
> Beside my eldest brother.
> My coffin shall be black,
> Six angels at my back,
> Two to sing and two to pray
> And two to carry my soul away.

How beautiful and sad that was! How beautiful the words were where they said *Bury me in the old churchyard!* A tremor passed over his body. How sad and how beautiful! He wanted to cry quietly but not for himself: for the words, so beautiful and sad, like music. The bell! The bell! Farewell! O farewell!

The cold sunlight was weaker and Brother Michael was standing at his bedside with a bowl of beeftea. He was glad for his mouth was hot and dry. He could hear them playing on the playgrounds. And the day was going on in the college just as if he were there.

Then Brother Michael was going away and the fellow out of third of grammar told him to be sure and come back and tell him all the news in the paper. He told Stephen that his name was Athy and that his father kept a lot of racehorses that were spiffing jumpers and that his father would give a good tip to Brother Michael any time he wanted it because Brother Michael was very decent and always told him the news out of the paper they got every day up in the castle. There was every kind of news in the paper: accidents, shipwrecks, sports and politics.

—Now it is all about politics in the paper, he said. Do your people talk about that too?

—Yes, Stephen said.

—Mine too, he said.

Then he thought for a moment and said:

—You have a queer name, Dedalus, and I have a queer name too, Athy. My name is the name of a town. Your name is like Latin.

Then he asked:

—Are you good at riddles?

Stephen answered:

—Not very good.

Then he said:

—Can you answer me this one? Why is the county Kildare like the leg of a fellow's breeches?

Stephen thought what could be the answer and then said:

—I give it up.

—Because there is a thigh in it, he said. Do you see the joke? Athy is the town in the county Kildare and a thigh is the other thigh.

—O, I see, Stephen said.

—That's an old riddle, he said.

After a moment he said:

—I say!

—What? asked Stephen.

—You know, he said, you can ask that riddle another way?

—Can you? said Stephen.

—The same riddle, he said. Do you know the other way to ask it?

—No, said Stephen.

—Can you not think of the other way? he said.

He looked at Stephen over the bedclothes as he spoke. Then he lay back on the pillow and said:

—There is another way but I won't tell you what it is.

Why did he not tell it? His father, who kept the racehorses, must be a magistrate too like Saurin's father and Nasty Roche's father. He thought of his own father, of how he sang songs while his mother played and of how he always gave him a shilling when he asked for sixpence and he felt sorry for him that he was not a magistrate like the other boys' fathers. Then why was he sent to that place with them? But his father had told him that he would be no stranger there because his granduncle had presented an address to the liberator there fifty years before. You could know the people of that time by their old dress. It seemed to him a solemn time: and he wondered if that was the time when the fellows in Clongowes wore blue coats with brass buttons and yellow waistcoats and caps of rabbitskin and drank beer like grownup people and kept greyhounds of their own to course the hares with.

He looked at the window and saw that the daylight had grown weaker. There would be cloudy grey light over the playgrounds. There was no noise on the playgrounds. The class must be doing the themes or perhaps Father Arnall was reading a legend out of the book.

It was queer that they had not given him any medicine. Perhaps Brother Michael would bring it back when he came. They said you got stinking stuff to drink when you were in the infirmary. But he felt better now than before. It would be nice getting better slowly. You could get a book then. There was a book in the library about Holland. There were lovely foreign names in it and pictures of strangelooking cities and ships. It made you feel so happy.

How pale the light was at the window! But that was nice. The fire rose and fell on the wall. It was like waves. Someone had put coal on and he heard voices. They were talking. It was the noise of the waves. Or the waves were talking among themselves as they rose and fell.

He saw the sea of waves, long dark waves rising and falling, dark under the moonless night. A tiny light twinkled at the pierhead where the ship was entering: and he saw a multitude of people gathered by the waters' edge to see the ship that was entering their harbor. A tall man stood on the deck, looking out towards the flat dark land: and by the light at the pierhead he saw his face, the sorrowful face of Brother Michael.

He saw him lift his hand towards the people and heard him say in a loud voice of sorrow over the waters:

—He is dead. We saw him lying upon the catafalque.

A wail of sorrow went up from the people.

—Parnell! Parnell! He is dead!

They fell upon their knees, moaning in sorrow.

And he saw Dante in a maroon velvet dress and with a green velvet mantle hanging from her shoulders walking proudly and silently past the people who knelt by the waters' edge.

A great fire, banked high and red, flamed in the grate and under the ivy-twined branches of the chandelier the Christmas table was spread. They had come home a little late and still dinner was not ready: but it would be ready in a jiffy, his mother had said. They were waiting for the door to open and for the servants to come in, holding the big dishes covered with their heavy metal covers.

All were waiting: uncle Charles, who sat far away in the shadow of the window, Dante and Mr. Casey, who sat in the cosychairs at either side of the hearth, Stephen, seated on a chair between them, his feet resting on the toasted boss. Mr. Dedalus looked at himself in the pierglass above the mantelpiece, waxed out his mustache-ends and then, parting his coattails, stood with his back to the glowing fire: and still, from time to time, he withdrew a hand from his coattail to wax out one of his mustache-ends. Mr. Casey leaned his head to one side and, smiling, tapped the gland of his neck with his fingers. And Stephen smiled too for he knew now that it was not true that Mr. Casey had a purse of silver in his throat. He smiled to think how the silvery noise which Mr. Casey used to make had deceived him. And when he had tried to open Mr. Casey's hand to see if the purse of silver was hidden there he had seen that the fingers could not be straightened out: and Mr. Casey had told him that he had got those three cramped fingers making a birthday present for Queen Victoria.

Mr. Casey tapped the gland of his neck and smiled at Stephen with sleepy eyes: and Mr. Dedalus said to him:

—Yes. Well now, that's all right. O, we had a good walk, hadn't we, John? Yes . . . I wonder if there's any likelihood of dinner this evening. Yes. . . . O, well now, we got a good breath of ozone round the Head today. Ay, bedad.

He turned to Dante and said:

—You didn't stir out at all, Mrs. Riordan?

Dante frowned and said shortly:

—No.

Mr. Dedalus dropped his coattails and went over to the sideboard. He brought forth a great stone jar of whisky from the locker and filled the decanter slowly, bending now and then to see how much he had poured in. Then replacing the jar in the locker he poured a little of the whisky into two glasses, added a little water and came back with them to the fireplace.

—A thimbleful, John, he said, just to whet your appetite.

Mr. Casey took the glass, drank, and placed it near him on the mantelpiece. Then he said:

—Well, I can't help thinking of our friend Christopher manufacturing . . .

He broke into a fit of laughter and coughing and added:

—. . . manufacturing that champagne for those fellows.

Mr. Dedalus laughed loudly.

—Is it Christy? he said. There's more cunning in one of those warts on his bald head than in a pack of jack foxes.

He inclined his head, closed his eyes, and, licking his lips profusely, began to speak with the voice of the hotel-keeper.

—And he has such a soft mouth when he's speaking to you, don't you know. He's very moist and watery about the dewlaps, God bless him.

Mr. Casey was still struggling through his fit of coughing and laughter. Stephen, seeing and hearing the hotel-keeper through his father's face and voice, laughed.

Mr. Dedalus put up his eyeglass and, staring down at him, said quietly and kindly:

—What are you laughing at, you little puppy, you?

The servants entered and placed the dishes on the table. Mrs. Dedalus followed and the places were arranged.

—Sit over, she said.

Mr. Dedalus went to the end of the table and said:

—Now, Mrs. Riordan, sit over. John, sit you down, my hearty.

He looked round to where uncle Charles sat and said:

—Now then, sir, there's a bird here waiting for you.

When all had taken their seats he laid his hand on the cover and then said quickly, withdrawing it:

—Now, Stephen.

Stephen stood up in his place to say the grace before meals:

Bless us, O Lord, and these Thy gifts which through Thy bounty we are about to receive through Christ Our Lord.
Amen.

All blessed themselves and Mr. Dedalus with a sigh of pleasure lifted from the dish the heavy cover pearled around the edge with glistening drops.

Stephen looked at the plump turkey which had lain, trussed and skewered, on the kitchen table. He knew that his father had paid a guinea for it in Dunn's of D'Olier Street and that the man had prodded it often at the breastbone to show how good it was: and he remembered the man's voice when he had said:

—Take that one, sir. That's the real Ally Daly.

Why did Mr. Barrett in Clongowes call his pandybat a turkey? But Clongowes was far away: and the warm heavy smell of turkey and ham and celery rose from the plates and dishes and the great fire was banked high and red in the grate and the green ivy and red holly made you feel so happy and when dinner was ended the big plumpudding would be carried in, studded with peeled almonds and sprigs of holly, with bluish fire running around it and a little green flag flying from the top.

It was his first Christmas dinner and he thought of his little brothers and sisters who were waiting in the nursery, as he had often waited, till the pudding came. The deep low collar and the Eton jacket made him feel queer and oldish: and that morning when his mother had brought him down to the parlor, dressed for mass, his father had cried. That was because he was thinking of his own father. And uncle Charles had said so too.

Mr. Dedalus covered the dish and began to eat hungrily. Then he said:

—Poor old Christy, he's nearly lopsided now with roguery.

—Simon, said Mrs. Dedalus, you haven't given Mrs. Riordan any sauce.

Mr. Dedalus seized the sauceboat.

—Haven't I? he cried. Mrs. Riordan, pity the poor blind.

Dante covered her plate with her hands and said:

—No, thanks.

Mr. Dedalus turned to uncle Charles.

—How are you off, sir?

—Right as the mail, Simon.

—You, John?

—I'm all right. Go on yourself.

—Mary? Here, Stephen, here's something to make your hair curl.

He poured sauce freely over Stephen's plate and set the boat again on the table. Then he asked uncle Charles was it tender. Uncle Charles could not speak because his mouth was full but he nodded that it was.

—That was a good answer our friend made to the canon. What? said Mr. Dedalus.

—I didn't think he had that much in him, said Mr. Casey.

—*I'll pay you your dues, father, when you cease turning the house of God into a pollingbooth.*

—A nice answer, said Dante, for any man calling himself a catholic to give to his priest.

—They have only themselves to blame, said Mr. Dedalus suavely. If they took a fool's advice they would confine their attention to religion.

—It is religion, Dante said. They are doing their duty in warning the people.

—We go to the house of God, Mr. Casey said, in all humility to pray to our Maker and not to hear election addresses.

—It is religion, Dante said again. They are right. They must direct their flocks.

—And preach politics from the altar, is it? asked Mr. Dedalus.

—Certainly, said Dante. It is a question of public morality. A priest would not be a priest if he did not tell his flock what is right and what is wrong.

Mrs. Dedalus laid down her knife and fork, saying:

—For pity's sake and for pity sake let us have no political discussion on this day of all days in the year.

—Quite right, ma'am, said uncle Charles. Now, Simon, that's quite enough now. Not another word now.

—Yes, yes, said Mr. Dedalus quickly.

He uncovered the dish boldly and said:

—Now then, who's for more turkey?

Nobody answered. Dante said:

—Nice language for any catholic to use!

—Mrs. Riordan, I appeal to you, said Mrs. Dedalus, to let the matter drop now.

Dante turned on her and said:

—And am I to sit here and listen to the pastors of my church being flouted?

—Nobody is saying a word against them, said Mr. Dedalus, so long as they don't meddle in politics.

—The bishops and priests of Ireland have spoken, said Dante, and they must be obeyed.

—Let them leave politics alone, said Mr. Casey, or the people may leave their church alone.

—You hear? said Dante turning to Mrs. Dedalus.

—Mr. Casey! Simon! said Mrs. Dedalus. Let it end now.

—Too bad! Too bad! said uncle Charles.

—What? cried Mr. Dedalus. Were we to desert him at the bidding of the English people?

—He was no longer worthy to lead, said Dante. He was a public sinner.

—We are all sinners and black sinners, said Mr. Casey coldly.

—*Woe be to the man by whom the scandal cometh!* said Mrs. Riordan. *It would be better for him that a millstone were tied about his neck and that he were cast into the depth of the sea rather than that he should scandalize one of these, my least little ones.* That is the language of the Holy Ghost.

—And very bad language if you ask me, said Mr. Dedalus coolly.

—Simon! Simon! said uncle Charles. The boy.

—Yes, yes, said Mr. Dedalus. I meant about the . . . I was thinking about the bad language of that railway porter. Well now, that's all right. Here, Stephen, show me your plate, old chap. Eat away now. Here.

He heaped up the food on Stephen's plate and served uncle Charles and Mr. Casey to large pieces of turkey and splashes of sauce. Mrs. Dedalus was eating little and Dante sat with her hands in her lap. She was red in the face. Mr. Dedalus rooted with the carvers at the end of the dish and said:

—There's a tasty bit here we call the pope's nose. If any lady or gentleman . . .

He held a piece of fowl up on the prong of the carvingfork. Nobody spoke. He put it on his own plate, saying:

—Well, you can't say but you were asked. I think I had better eat it myself because I'm not well in my health lately.

He winked at Stephen and, replacing the dishcover, began to eat again.

There was a silence while he ate. Then he said:

—Well, now, the day kept up fine after all. There were plenty of strangers down too.

Nobody spoke. He said again:

—I think there were more strangers down than last Christmas.

He looked round at the others whose faces were bent towards their plates and, receiving no reply, waited for a moment and said bitterly:

—Well, my Christmas dinner has been spoiled anyhow.

—There could be neither luck nor grace, Dante said, in a house where there is no respect for the pastors of the church.

Mr. Dedalus threw his knife and fork noisily on his plate.

—Respect! he said. Is it for Billy with the lip or for the tub of guts up in Armagh? Respect!

—Princes of the church, said Mr. Casey with slow scorn.

—Lord Leitrim's coachman, yes, said Mr. Dedalus.

—They are the Lord's anointed, Dante said. They are an honor to their country.

—Tub of guts, said Mr. Dedalus coarsely. He has a handsome face, mind you, in repose. You should see that fellow lapping up his bacon and cabbage of a cold winter's day. O Johnny!

He twisted his features into a grimace of heavy bestiality and made a lapping noise with his lips.

—Really, Simon, said Mrs. Dedalus,

you should not speak that way before Stephen. It's not right.

—O, he'll remember all this when he grows up, said Dante hotly—the language he heard against God and religion and priests in his own home.

—Let him remember too, cried Mr. Casey to her from across the table, the language with which the priests and the priests' pawns broke Parnell's heart and hounded him into his grave. Let him remember that too when he grows up.

—Sons of bitches! cried Mr. Dedalus. When he was down they turned on him to betray him and rend him like rats in a sewer. Low-lived dogs! And they look it! By Christ, they look it!

—They behaved rightly, cried Dante. They obeyed their bishops and their priests. Honor to them!

—Well, it is perfectly dreadful to say that not even for one day in the year, said Mrs. Dedalus, can we be free from these dreadful disputes!

Uncle Charles raised his hands mildly and said:

—Come now, come now, come now! Can we not have our opinions whatever they are without this bad temper and this bad language? It is too bad surely.

Mrs. Dedalus spoke to Dante in a low voice but Dante said loudly:

—I will not say nothing. I will defend my church and my religion when it is insulted and spit on by renegade catholics.

Mr. Casey pushed his plate rudely into the middle of the table and, resting his elbows before him, said in a hoarse voice to his host:

—Tell me, did I tell you that story about a very famous spit?

—You did not, John, said Mr. Dedalus.

—Why then, said Mr. Casey, it is a most instructive story. It happened not long ago in the county Wicklow where we are now.

He broke off and, turning towards Dante, said with quiet indignation:

—And I may tell you, ma'am, that I,

if you mean me, am no renegade catholic. I am a catholic as my father was and his father before him and his father before him again when we gave up our lives rather than sell our faith.

—The more shame to you now, Dante said, to speak as you do.

—The story, John, said Mr. Dedalus smiling. Let us have the story anyhow.

—Catholic indeed! repeated Dante ironically. The blackest protestant in the land would not speak the language I have heard this evening.

Mr. Dedalus began to sway his head to and fro, crooning like a country singer.

—I am no protestant, I tell you again, said Mr. Casey flushing.

Mr. Dedalus, still crooning and swaying his head, began to sing in a grunting nasal tone:

O, come all you Roman catholics
That never went to mass.

He took up his knife and fork again in good humor and set to eating, saying to Mr. Casey:

—Let us have the story, John. It will help us to digest.

Stephen looked with affection at Mr. Casey's face which stared across the table over his joined hands. He liked to sit near him at the fire, looking up at his dark fierce face. But his dark eyes were never fierce and his slow voice was good to listen to. But why was he then against the priests? Because Dante must be right then. But he had heard his father say that she was a spoiled nun and that she had come out of the convent in the Alleghanies when her brother had got the money from the savages for the trinkets and the chainies. Perhaps that made her severe against Parnell. And she did not like him to play with Eileen because Eileen was a protestant and when she was young she knew children that used to play with protestants and the protestants used to make fun of the litany of the Blessed Virgin. *Tower of Ivory*, they used to say, *House of Gold!* How could a woman be a tower of ivory or a house of gold? Who was right then? And he remembered the evening in the infirmary in Clongowes, the dark waters, the light at the pierhead and the moan of sorrow from the people when they had heard.

Eileen had long white hands. One evening when playing tig she had put her hands over his eyes: long and white and thin and cold and soft. That was ivory: a cold white thing. That was the meaning of *Tower of Ivory.*

—The story is very short and sweet. Mr. Casey said. It was one day down in Arklow, a cold bitter day, not long before the chief died. May God have mercy on him!

He closed his eyes wearily and paused. Mr. Dedalus took a bone from his plate and tore some meat from it with his teeth, saying:

—Before he was killed, you mean.

Mr. Casey opened his eyes, sighed and went on:

—It was down in Arklow one day. We were down there at a meeting and after the meeting was over we had to make our way to the railway station through the crowd. Such booing and baaing, man, you never heard. They called us all the names in the world. Well there was one old lady, and a drunken old harridan she was surely, that paid all her attention to me. She kept dancing along beside me in the mud bawling and screaming into my face: *Priest-hunter! The Paris Funds! Mr. Fox! Kitty O'Shea!*

—And what did you do, John? asked Mr. Dedalus.

—I let her bawl away, said Mr. Casey. It was a cold day and to keep up my heart I had (saving your presence, ma'am) a quid of Tullamore in my mouth and sure I couldn't say a word in any case because my mouth was full of tobacco juice.

—Well, John?

—Well. I let her bawl away, to her heart's content, *Kitty O'Shea* and the rest of it till at last she called that lady a name that I won't sully this Christmas board nor your ears, ma'am, nor my own lips by repeating.

He paused. Mr. Dedalus, lifting his head from the bone, asked:

—And what did you do, John?

—Do! said Mr. Casey. She stuck her ugly old face up at me when she said it and I had my mouth full of tobacco juice. I bent down to her and *Phth!* says I to her like that.

He turned aside and made the act of spitting.

—*Phth!* says I to her like that, right into her eye.

He clapped a hand to his eye and gave a hoarse scream of pain.

—*O Jesus, Mary and Joseph!* says she. *I'm blinded! I'm blinded and drownded!*

He stopped in a fit of coughing and laughter, repeating:

—*I'm blinded entirely.*

Mr. Dedalus laughed loudly and lay back in his chair while uncle Charles swayed his head to and fro.

Dante looked terribly angry and repeated while they laughed:

—Very nice! Ha! Very nice!

It was not nice about the spit in the woman's eye. But what was the name the woman had called Kitty O'Shea that Mr. Casey would not repeat? He thought of Mr. Casey walking through the crowds of people and making speeches from a wagonette. That was what he had been in prison for and he remembered that one night Sergeant O'Neill had come to the house and had stood in the hall, talking in a low voice with his father and chewing nervously at the chinstrap of his cap. And that night Mr. Casey had not gone to Dublin by train but a car had come to the door and he had heard his father say something about the Cabinteely road.

He was for Ireland and Parnell and so was his father: and so was Dante too for one night at the band on the esplanade she had hit a gentleman on the head with her umbrella because he had taken off his hat when the band played *God save the Queen* at the end.

Mr. Dedalus gave a snort of contempt.

—Ah, John, he said. It is true for them. We are an unfortunate priestridden race and always were and always will be till the end of the chapter.

Uncle Charles shook his head, saying:

—A bad business! A bad business!

Mr. Dedalus repeated:

—A priestridden Godforsaken race!

He pointed to the portrait of his grandfather on the wall to his right.

—Did you see that old chap up there, John? he said. He was a good Irishman when there was no money in the job. He was condemned to death as a whiteboy. But he had a saying about our clerical friends, that he would never let one of them put his two feet under his mahogany.

Dante broke in angrily:

—If we are a priestridden race we ought to be proud of it! They are the apple of God's eye. *Touch them not,* says Christ, *for they are the apple of My eye.*

—And can we not love our country then? asked Mr. Casey. Are we not to follow the man that was born to lead us?

—A traitor to his country! replied Dante. A traitor, an adulterer! The priests were right to abandon him. The priests were always the true friends of Ireland.

—Were they, faith? said Mr. Casey.

He threw his fists on the table and, frowning angrily, protruded one finger after another.

—Didn't the bishops of Ireland betray us in the time of the union when bishop Lanigan presented an address of loyalty to the Marquess Cornwallis? Didn't the bishops and priests sell the aspirations of their country in 1829 in return for cathoic emancipation? Didn't they denounce the fenian movement from the pulpit and in the confession-box? And didn't they dishonor the ashes of Terence Bellew MacManus?

His face was glowing with anger and Stephen felt the glow rise to his own cheek as the spoken words thrilled him. Mr. Dedalus uttered a guffaw of coarse scorn.

—O, by God, he cried, I forgot little old Paul Cullen! Another apple of God's eye!

Dante bent across the table and cried to Mr. Casey:

—Right! Right! They were always right! God and morality and religion come first.

Mrs. Dedalus, seeing her excitement, said to her:

—Mrs. Riordan, don't excite yourself answering them.

—God and religion before everything! Dante cried. God and religion before the world!

Mr. Casey raised his clenched fist and brought it down on the table with a crash.

—Very well, then, he shouted hoarsely, if it comes to that, no God for Ireland!

—John! John! cried Mr. Dedalus, seizing his guest by the coatsleeve.

Dante stared across the table, her cheeks shaking. Mr. Casey struggled up from his chair and bent across the table towards her, scraping the air from before his eyes with one hand as though he were tearing aside a cobweb.

—No God for Ireland! he cried. We have had too much God in Ireland. Away with God!

—Blasphemer! Devil! screamed Dante, starting to her feet and almost spitting in his face.

Uncle Charles and Mr. Dedalus pulled Mr. Casey back into his chair again, talking to him from both sides reasonably. He stared before him out of his dark flaming eyes, repeating:

—Away with God, I say!

Dante shoved her chair violently aside and left the table, upsetting her napkinring which rolled slowly along the carpet and came to rest against the foot of an easychair. Mrs. Dedalus rose quickly and followed her towards the door. At the door Dante turned round violently and shouted down the room, her cheeks flushed and quivering with rage:

—Devil out of hell! We won! We crushed him to death! Fiend!

The door slammed behind her.

Mr. Casey, freeing his arms from his holders, suddenly bowed his head on his hands with a sob of pain.

—Poor Parnell! he cried loudly. My dead king!

He sobbed loudly and bitterly.

Stephen, raising his terrorstricken face, saw that his father's eyes were full of tears.

The fellows talked together in little groups.

One fellow said:

—They were caught near the Hill of Lyons.

—Who caught them?

—Mr. Gleeson and the minister. They were on a car.

The same fellow added:

—A fellow in the higher line told me.

Fleming asked:

—But why did they run away, tell us?

—I know why, Cecil Thunder said. Because they had fecked cash out of the rector's room.

—Who fecked it?

—Kickham's brother. And they all went shares in it.

But that was stealing. How could they have done that?

—A fat lot you know about it, Thunder! Wells said. I know why they scut.

—Tell us why.

—I was told not to, Wells said.

—O, go on, Wells, all said. You might tell us. We won't let it out.

Stephen bent forward his head to hear. Wells looked round to see if anyone was coming. Then he said secretly:

—You know the altar wine they keep in the press in the sacristy?

—Yes.

—Well, they drank that and it was found out who did it by the smell. And that's why they ran away, if you want to know.

And the fellow who had spoken first said:

—Yes, that's what I heard too from the fellow in the higher line.

The fellows were all silent. Stephen stood among them, afraid to speak, listening. A faint sickness of awe made him feel weak. How could they have done that? He thought of the dark silent sacristy. There were dark wooden presses there where the crimped surplices lay quietly folded. It was not the chapel but still you had to speak under your breath. It was a holy place. He remembered the summer evening he had been there to be dressed as boatbearer, the evening of the procession to the little altar in the wood. A strange and holy place. The boy that held the censer had swung it gently to and fro near the door with the silvery cap lifted by the middle chain to keep the coals lighting. That was called charcoal: and it had burned quietly as the fellow had swung it gently and had given off a weak sour smell. And then when all were vested he had stood holding out the boat to the rector and the rector had put a spoonful of incense in it and it had hissed on the red coals.

The fellows were talking together in little groups here and there on the playground. The fellows seemed to him to have grown smaller: that was because a sprinter had knocked him down the day before, a fellow out of second of grammar. He had been thrown by the fellow's machine lightly on the cinderpath and his spectacles had been broken in three pieces and some of the grit of the cinders had gone into his mouth.

That was why the fellows seemed to him smaller and farther away and the goalposts so thin and far and the soft grey sky so high up. But there was no play on the football grounds for cricket was coming: and some said that Barnes would be the prof and some said it would be Flowers. And all over the playgrounds they were playing rounders and bowling twisters and lobs. And from here and from there came the sounds of the cricketbats through the soft grey air. They said: pick, pack, pock, puck: like drops of water in a fountain slowly falling in the brimming bowl.

Athy, who had been silent, said quietly:

—You are all wrong.

All turned towards him eagerly.

—Why?

—Do you know?

—Who told you?

Tell us, Athy.

Athy pointed across the playground to where Simon Moonan was walking by himself kicking a stone before him.

—Ask him, he said.

The fellows looked there and then said:

—Why him?

—Is he in it?

—Tell us, Athy. Go on. You might if you know.

Athy lowered his voice and said:

—Do you know why those fellows scut? I will tell you but you must not let on you know.

He paused for a moment and then said mysteriously:

—They were caught with Simon Moonan and Tusker Boyle in the square one night.

The fellows looked at him and asked:

—Caught?

—What doing?

Athy said:

—Smuggling.

All the fellows were silent: and Athy said:

—And that's why.

Stephen looked at the faces of the fellows but they were all looking across the playground. He wanted to ask some-body about it. What did that mean about the smuggling in the square? Why did the five fellows out of the higher line run away for that? It was a joke, he thought. Simon Moonan had nice clothes and one night he had shown him a ball of creamy sweets that the fellows of the football fifteen had rolled down to him along the carpet in the middle of the refectoy when he was at the door. It was the night of the match against the Bective Rangers and the ball was made just like a red and green apple only it opened and it was full of the creamy sweets. And one day Boyle had said that an elephant had two tuskers instead of two tusks and that was why he was called Tusker Boyle but some fellows called him Lady Boyle because he was always at his nails, paring them.

Eileen had long thin cool white hands too because she was a girl. They were like ivory; only soft. That was the meaning of *Tower of Ivory* but protestants could not understand it and made fun of it. One day he had stood beside her looking into the hotel grounds. A waiter was running up a trail of bunting on the flagstaff and a fox terrier was scampering to and fro on the sunny lawn. She had put her hand into his pocket where his hand was and he had felt how cool and thin and soft her hand was. She had said that pockets were funny things to have: and then all of a sudden she had broken away and had run laughing down the sloping curve of the path. Her fair hair had streamed out behind her like gold in the sun. *Tower of Ivory. House of Gold.* By thinking of things you could understand them.

But why in the square? You went there when you wanted to do something. It was all thick slabs of slate and water trickled all day out of tiny pinholes and there was a queer smell of stale water there. And behind the door of one of the closets there was a drawing in red pencil of a bearded man in a Roman dress with a brick in each hand

and underneath was the name of the drawing:

Balbus was building a wall.

Some fellows had drawn it there for a cod. It had a funny face but it was very like a man with a beard. And on the wall of another closet there was written in backhand in beautiful writing:

Julius Cæsar wrote The Calico Belly.

Perhaps that was why they were there because it was a place where some fellows wrote things for cod. But all the same it was queer what Athy said and the way he said it. It was not a cod because they had run away. He looked with the others in silence across the playground and began to feel afraid.

At last Fleming said:

—And we are all to be punished for what other fellows did?

—I won't come back, see if I do, Cecil Thunder said. Three days' silence in the refectory and sending us up for six and eight every minute.

—Yes, said Wells. And old Barrett has a new way of twisting the note so that you can't open it and fold it again to see how many ferulae you are to get. I won't come back too.

—Yes, said Cecil Thunder, and the prefect of studies was in second of grammar this morning.

—Let us get up a rebellion, Fleming said. Will we?

All the fellows were silent. The air was very silent and you could hear the cricketbats but more slowly than before: pick, pock.

Wells asked:

—What is going to be done to them?

—Simon Moonan and Tusker are going to be flogged, Athy said, and the fellows in the higher line got their choice of flogging or being expelled.

—And which are they taking? asked the fellow who had spoken first.

—All are taking expulsion except Corrigan, Athy answered. He's going to be flogged by Mr. Gleeson.

—Is it Corrigan that big fellow? said Fleming. Why, he'd be able for two of Gleeson!

—I know why, Cecil Thunder said. He is right and the other fellows are wrong because a flogging wears off after a bit but a fellow that has been expelled from college is known all his life on account of it. Besides Gleeson won't flog him hard.

—It's best of his play not to, Fleming said.

—I wouldn't like to be Simon Moonan and Tusker, Cecil Thunder said. But I don't believe they will be flogged. Perhaps they will be sent up for twice nine.

—No, no, said Athy. They'll both get it on the vital spot.

Wells rubbed himself and said in a crying voice:

—Please, sir, let me off!

Athy grinned and turned up the sleeves of his jacket, saying:

It can't be helped;
It must be done.
So down with your breeches
And out with your bum.

The fellows laughed; but he felt that they were a little afraid. In the silence of the soft grey air he heard the cricket-bats from here and from there: pock. That was a sound to hear but if you were hit then you would feel a pain. The pandybat made a sound too but not like that. The fellows said it was made of whalebone and leather with lead inside: and he wondered what was the pain like. There were different kinds of pains for all the different kinds of sounds. A long thin cane would have a high whistling sound and he wondered what was that pain like. It made him shivery to think of it and cold: and what Athy said too. But what was there to laugh at in it? It made him shivery: but that was because you always felt like a shiver when you let down your trousers. It was the same in the bath when you undressed yourself. He wondered who had to let them down, the master or the boy himself. O how could they laugh about it that way?

He looked at Athy's rolledup sleeves and knuckly inky hands. He had rolled up his sleeves to show how Mr. Gleeson would roll up his sleeves. But Mr. Gleeson had round shiny cuffs and clean white wrists and fattish white hands and the nails of them were long and pointed. Perhaps he pared them too like Lady Boyle. But they were terribly long and pointed nails. So long and cruel they were though the white fattish hands were not cruel but gentle. And though he trembled with cold and fright to think of the cruel long nails and of the high whistling sound of the cane and of the chill you felt at the end of your shirt when you undressed yourself yet he felt a feeling of queer quiet pleasure inside him to think of the white fattish hands, clean and strong and gentle. And he thought of what Cecil Thunder had said; that Mr. Gleeson would not flog Corrigan hard. And Fleming had said he would not because it was best of his play not to. But that was not why.

A voice from far out on the playground cried:

—All in!

And other voices cried:

—All in! All in!

During the writing lesson he sat with his arms folded, listening to the slow scraping of the pens. Mr. Harford went to and fro making little signs in red pencil and sometimes sitting beside the boy to show him how to hold the pen. He had tried to spell out the headline for himself though he knew already what it was for it was the last of the book. *Zeal without prudence is like a ship adrift.* But the lines of the letters were like fine invisible threads and it was only by closing his right eye tight and staring out of the left eye that he could make out the full curves of the capital.

But Mr. Harford was very decent and never got into a wax. All the other masters got into dreadful waxes. But why

were they to suffer for what fellows in the higher line did? Wells had said that they had drunk some of the altar wine out of the press in the sacristy and that it had been found out who had done it by the smell. Perhaps they had stolen a monstrance to run away with it and sell it somewhere. That must have been a terrible sin, to go in there quietly at night, to open the dark press and steal the flashing gold thing into which God was put on the altar in the middle of flowers and candles at benediction while the incense went up in clouds at both sides as the fellow swung the censer and Dominic Kelly sang the first part by himself in the choir. But God was not in it of course when they stole it. But still it was a strange and a great sin even to touch it. He thought of it with deep awe; a terrible and strange sin: it thrilled him to think of it in the silence when the pens scraped lightly. But to drink the altar wine out of the press and be found out by the smell was a sin too: but it was not terrible and strange. It only made you feel a little sickish on account of the smell of the wine. Because on the day when he had made his first holy communion in the chapel he had shut his eyes and opened his mouth and put out his tongue a little: and when the rector had stooped down to give him the holy communion he had smelt a faint winy smell off the rector's breath after the wine of the mass. The word was beautiful: wine. It made you think of dark purple because the grapes were dark purple that grew in Greece outside houses like white temples. But the faint smell off the rector's breath had made him feel a sick feeling on the morning of his first communion. The day of your first communion was the happiest day of your life. And once a lot of generals had asked Napoleon what was the happiest day of his life. They thought he would say the day he won some great battle or the day he was made an emperor. But he said:

—Gentlemen, the happiest day of my life was the day on which I made my first holy communion.

Father Arnall came in and the Latin lesson began and he remained still, leaning on the desk with his arms folded. Father Arnall gave out the themebooks and he said that they were scandalous and that they were all to be written out again with the corrections at once. But the worst of all was Fleming's theme because the pages were stuck together by a blot: and Father Arnall held it up by a corner and said it was an insult to any master to send him up such a theme. Then he asked Jack Lawton to decline the noun *mare* and Jack Lawton stopped at the ablative singular and could not go on with the plural.

—You should be ashamed of yourself, said Father Arnall sternly. You, the leader of the class!

Then he asked the next boy and the next and the next. Nobody knew. Father Arnall became very quiet, more and more quiet as each boy tried to answer and could not. But his face was black-looking and his eyes were staring though his voice was so quiet. Then he asked Fleming and Fleming said that that word had no plural. Father Arnall suddenly shut the book and shouted at him:

—Kneel out there in the middle of the class. You are one of the idlest boys I ever met. Copy out your themes again the rest of you.

Fleming moved heavily out of his place and knelt between the two last benches. The other boys bent over their themebooks and began to write. A silence filled the classroom and Stephen, glancing timidly at Father Arnall's dark face, saw that it was a little red from the wax he was in.

Was that a sin for Father Arnall to be in a wax or was he allowed to get into a wax when the boys were idle because that made them study better or was he only letting on to be in a wax? It was because he was allowed because a priest would know what a sin was and would not do it. But if he did it one time by mistake what would he do to go to confession? Perhaps he would go to confession to the minister. And if the minister did it he would go to the rector: and the rector to the provincial: and the provincial to the general of the jesuits. That was called the order: and he had heard his father say that they were all clever men. They could all have become highup people in the world if they had not become jesuits. And he wondered what Father Arnall and Paddy Barrett would have become and what Mr. McGlade and Mr. Gleeson would have become if they had not become jesuits. It was hard to think what because you would have to think of them in a different way with different colored coats and trousers and with beards and moustaches and different kinds of hats.

The door opened quietly and closed. A quick whisper ran through the class: the prefect of studies. There was an instant of dead silence and then the loud crack of a pandybat on the last desk. Stephen's heart leapt up in fear.

—Any boys want flogging here, Father Arnall? cried the prefect of studies. Any lazy idle loafers that want flogging in this class?

He came to the middle of the class and saw Fleming on his knees.

—Hoho! he cried. Who is this boy? Why is he on his knees? What is your name, boy?

—Fleming, sir.

—Hoho, Fleming! An idler of course. I can see it in your eye. Why is he on his knees, Father Arnall?

—He wrote a bad Latin theme, Father Arnall said, and he missed all the questions in grammar.

—Of course he did! cried the prefect of studies. Of course he did! A born idler! I can see it in the corner of his eye.

He banged his pandybat down on the desk and cried:

—Up, Fleming! Up, my boy!

Fleming stood up slowly.

—Hold out! cried the prefect of studies.

Fleming held out his hand. The pandybat came down on it with a loud smacking sound: one, two, three, four, five, six.

—Other hand!

The pandybat came down again in six loud quick smacks.

—Kneel down! cried the prefect of studies.

Fleming knelt down squeezing his hands under his armpits, his face contorted with pain, but Stephen knew how hard his hands were because Fleming was always rubbing rosin into them. But perhaps he was in great pain for the noise of the pandies was terrible. Stephen's heart was beating and fluttering.

—At your work, all of you! shouted the prefect of studies. We want no lazy idle loafers here, lazy idle little schemers. At your work, I tell you. Father Dolan will be in to see you every day. Father Dolan will be in tomorrow.

He poked one of the boys in the side with the pandybat, saying:

—You, boy! When will Father Dolan be in again?

—Tomorrow, sir, said Tom Furlong's voice.

—Tomorrow and tomorrow and tomorrow, said the prefect of studies. Make up your minds for that. Every day Father Dolan. Write away. You, boy, who are you?

Stephen's heart jumped suddenly.

—Dedalus, sir.

—Why are you not writing like the others?

—I . . . my , . .

He could not speak with fright.

—Why is he not writing, Father Arnall?

—He broke his glasses, said Father Arnall, and I exempted him from work.

—Broke? What is this I hear? What is this your name is? said the prefect of studies.

Dedalus, sir.

—Out here, Dedalus. Lazy little schemer. I see schemer in your face. Where did you break your glasses?

Stephen stumbled into the middle of the class, blinded by fear and haste.

—Where did you break your glasses? repeated the prefect of studies.

—The cinderpath, sir.

—Hoho! The cinderpath! cried the prefect of studies. I know that trick.

Stephen lifted his eyes in wonder and saw for a moment Father Dolan's whitegrey not young face, his baldy whitegrey head with fluff at the sides of it, the steel rims of his spectacles and his no-colored eyes looking through the glasses. Why did he say he knew that trick?

—Lazy idle little loafer! cried the prefect of studies. Broke my glasses! An old schoolboy trick! Out with your hand this moment!

Stephen closed his eyes and held out in the air his trembling hand with the palm upwards. He felt the prefect of studies touch it for a moment at the fingers to straighten it and then the swish of the sleeve of the soutane as the pandybat was lifted to strike. A hot burning stinging tingling blow like the loud crack of a broken stick made his trembling hand crumple together like a leaf in the fire: and at the sound and the pain scalding tears were driven into his eyes. His whole body was shaking with fright, his arm was shaking and his crumpled burning livid hand shook like a loose leaf in the air. A cry sprang to his lips, a prayer to be let off. But though the tears scalded his eyes and his limbs quivered with pain and fright he held back the hot tears and the cry that scalded his throat.

—Other hand! shouted the prefect of studies.

Stephen drew back his maimed and quivering arm and held out his left hand. The soutane sleeve swished again as the pandybat was lifted and a loud clashing sound and a fierce maddening tingling burning pain made his hand shrink together with the palms and fingers in a livid quivering mass. The scalding water burst forth from his eyes and, burning with shame and agony and fear, he drew back his shaking arm in terror and burst out into a whine of pain. His body shook with a palsy of fright and in shame and rage he felt the scalding cry come from his throat and the scalding tears falling out of his eyes and down his flaming cheeks.

—Kneel down! cried the prefect of studies.

Stephen knelt down quickly pressing his beaten hands to his sides. To think of them beaten and swollen with pain all in a moment made him feel so sorry for them as if they were not his own but someone else's that he felt sorry for. And as he knelt, calming the last sobs in his throat and feeling the burning tingling pain pressed in to his sides, he thought of the hands which he had held out in the air with the palms up and of the firm touch of the prefect of studies when he had steadied the shaking fingers and of the beaten swollen reddened mass of palm and fingers that shook helplessly in the air.

—Get at your work, all of you, cried the prefect of studies from the door. Father Dolan will be in every day to see if any boy, any lazy idle little loafer wants flogging. Every day. Every day.

The door closed behind him.

The hushed class continued to copy out the themes. Father Arnall rose from his seat and went among them, helping the boys with gentle words and telling them the mistakes they had made. His voice was very gentle and soft. Then he returned to his seat and said to Fleming and Stephen:

—You may return to your places, you two.

Fleming and Stephen rose and, walking to their seats, sat down. Stephen, scarlet with shame, opened a book quickly with one weak hand and bent down upon it, his face close to the page.

It was unfair and cruel because the doctor had told him not to read without glasses and he had written home to his father that morning to send him a new pair. And Father Arnall had said that he need not study till the new glasses came. Then to be called a schemer before the class and to be pandied when he always got the card for first or second and was the leader of the Yorkists! How could the prefect of studies know that it was a trick? He felt the touch of the prefect's fingers as they had steadied his hand and at first he had thought he was going to shake hands with him because the fingers were soft and firm: but then in an instant he had heard the swish of the soutane sleeve and the crash. It was cruel and unfair to make him kneel in the middle of the class then: and Father Arnall had told them both that they might return to their places without making any difference between them. He listened to Father Arnall's low and gentle voice as he corrected the themes. Perhaps he was sorry now and wanted to be decent. But it was unfair and cruel. The prefect of studies was a priest but that was cruel and unfair. And his whitegrey face and the nocolored eyes behind the steel-rimmed spectacles were cruel looking because he had steadied the hand first with his firm soft fingers and that was to hit it better and louder.

—It's a stinking mean thing, that's what it is, said Fleming in the corridor as the classes were passing out in file to the refectory, to pandy a fellow for what is not his fault.

—You really broke your glasses by accident, didn't you? Nasty Roche asked.

Stephen felt his heart filled by Fleming's words and did not answer.

—Of course he did! said Fleming. I wouldn't stand it. I'd go up and tell the rector on him.

—Yes, said Cecil Thunder eagerly, and I saw him lift the pandybat over his shoulder and he's not allowed to do that.

—Did they hurt much? Nasty Roche asked.

—Very much, Stephen said.

—I wouldn't stand it, Fleming repeated, from Baldyhead or any other Baldyhead. It's a stinking mean low trick, that's what it is. I'd go straight up to the rector and tell him about it after dinner.

—Yes, do. Yes, do, said Cecil Thunder.

—Yes, do. Yes, go up and tell the rector on him, Dedalus, said Nasty Roche, because he said that he'd come in tomorrow again to pandy you.

—Yes, yes. Tell the rector, all said.

And there were some fellows out of second of grammar listening and one of them said:

—The senate and the Roman people declared that Dedalus had been wrongly punished.

It was wrong; it was unfair and cruel: and, as he sat in the refectory, he suffered time after time in memory the same humiliation until he began to wonder whether it might not really be that there was something in his face which made him look like a schemer and he wished he had a little mirror to see. But there could not be; and it was unjust and cruel and unfair.

He could not eat the blackish fish fritters they got on Wednesdays in Lent and one of his potatoes had the mark of the spade in it. Yes, he would do what the fellows had told him. He would go up and tell the rector that he had been wrongly punished. A thing like that had been done before by somebody in history, by some great person whose head was in the books of history. And the rector would declare that he had been wrongly punished because the senate and the Roman people always declared that the men who did that had been wrongly punished. Those were the great men whose names were in Richmal Magnall's Questions. History was all about those men and what they did and that was what Peter Parley's Tales

about Greece and Rome were all about. Peter Parley himself was on the first page in a picture. There was a road over a heath with grass at the side and little bushes: and Peter Parley had a broad hat like a protestant minister and a big stick and he was walking fast along the road to Greece and Rome.

It was easy what he had to do. All he had to do was when the dinner was over and he came out in his turn to go on walking but not out to the corridor but up the staircase on the right that led to the castle. He had nothing to do but that: to turn to the right and walk fast up the staircase and in half a minute he would be in the low dark narrow corridor that led through the castle to the rector's room. And every fellow had said that it was unfair, even the fellow out of second of grammar who had said that about the senate and the Roman people.

What would happen? He heard the fellows of the higher line stand up at the top of the refectory and heard their steps as they came down the matting: Paddy Rath and Jimmy Magee and the Spaniard and the Portuguese and the fifth was big Corrigan who was going to be flogged by Mr. Gleeson. That was why the prefect of studies had called him a schemer and pandied him for nothing: and, straining his weak eyes, tired with the tears, he watched big Corrigan's broad shoulders and big hanging black head passing in the file. But he had done something and besides Mr. Gleeson would not flog him hard: and he remembered how big Corrigan looked in the bath. He had skin the same color as the turfcolored bogwater in the shallow end of the bath and when he walked along the side his feet slapped loudly on the wet tiles and at every step his thighs shook a little because he was fat.

The refectory was half empty and the fellows were still passing out in file. He could go up the staircase because there was never a priest or a prefect outside the refectory door. But he could not go. The rector would side with the prefect of studies and think it was a schoolboy trick and then the prefect of studies would come in every day the same only it would be worse because he would be dreadfully waxy at any fellow going up to the rector about him. The fellows had told him to go but they would not go themselves. They had forgotten all about it. No, it was best to forget all about it and perhaps the prefect of studies had only said he would come in. No, it was best to hide out of the way because when you were small and young you could often escape that way.

The fellows at his table stood up. He stood up and passed out among them in the file. He had to decide. He was coming near the door. If he went on with the fellows he could never go up to the rector because he could not leave the playground for that. And if he went and was pandied all the same all the fellows would make fun and talk about young Dedalus going up to the rector to tell on the prefect of studies.

He was walking down along the matting and he saw the door before him. It was impossible: he could not. He thought of the baldy head of the prefect of studies with the cruel nocolored eyes looking at him and he heard the voice of the prefect of studies asking him twice what his name was. Why could he not remember the name when he was told the first time? Was he not listening the first time or was it to make fun out of the name? The great men in the history had names like that and nobody made fun of them. It was his own name that he should have made fun of if he wanted to make fun. Dolan: it was like the name of a woman that washed clothes.

He had reached the door and, turning quickly up to the right, walked up the stairs and, before he could make up his mind to come back, he had entered the low dark narrow corridor that led to the castle. And as he crossed the threshold of the door of the corridor he saw, without turning his head to look, that all the fellows were looking after him as they went filing by.

He passed along the narrow dark corridor, passing little doors that were the doors of the rooms of the community. He peered in front of him and right and left through the gloom and thought that those must be portraits. It was dark and silent and his eyes were weak and tired with tears so that he could not see. But he thought they were the portraits of the saints and great men of the order who were looking down on him silently as he passed: saint Ignatius Loyola holding an open book and pointing to the words *Ad Majorem Dei Gloriam* in it, saint Francis Xavier pointing to his chest, Lorenzo Ricci with his berretta on his head like one of the prefects of the lines, the three patrons of holy youth, saint Stanislaus Kostka, saint Aloysius Gonzaga and blessed John Berchmans, all with young faces because they died when they were young, and Father Peter Kenny sitting in a chair wrapped in a big cloak.

He came out on the landing above the entrance hall and looked about him. That was where Hamilton Rowan had passed and the marks of the soldiers' slugs were there. And it was there that the old servants had seen the ghost in the white cloak of a marshal.

An old servant was sweeping at the end of the landing. He asked him where was the rector's room and the old servant pointed to the door at the far end and looked after him as he went on to it and knocked.

There was no answer. He knocked again more loudly and his heart jumped when he heard a muffled voice say:

—Come in!

He turned the handle and opened the door and fumbled for the handle of the green baize door inside. He found it and pushed it open and went in.

He saw the rector sitting at a desk

writing. There was a skull on the desk and a strange solemn smell in the room like the old leather of chairs.

His heart was beating fast on account of the solemn place he was in and the silence of the room: and he looked at the skull and at the rector's kind-looking face.

—Well, my little man, said the rector, what is it?

Stephen swallowed down the thing in his throat and said:

—I broke my glasses, sir.

The rector opened his mouth and said:

—O!

Then he smiled and said:

—Well, if we broke our glasses we must write home for a new pair.

—I wrote home, sir, said Stephen, and Father Arnall said I am not to study till they come.

—Quite right! said the rector.

Stephen swallowed down the thing again and tried to keep his legs and his voice from shaking.

—But, sir . . .

—Yes?

—Father Dolan came in today and pandied me because I was not writing my theme.

The rector looked at him in silence and he could feel the blood rising to his face and the tears about to rise to his eyes.

The rector said:

—Your name is Dedalus, isn't it?

—Yes, sir.

—And where did you break your glasses?

—On the cinderpath, sir. A fellow was coming out of the bicycle house and I fell and they got broken. I don't know the fellow's name.

The rector looked at him again in silence. Then he smiled and said:

—O, well, it was a mistake; I am sure Father Dolan did not know.

—But I told him I broke them, sir, and he pandied me.

—Did you tell him that you had written home for a new pair? the rector asked.

—No, sir.

—O well then, said the rector, Father Dolan did not understand. You can say that I excuse you from your lessons for a few days.

Stephen said quickly for fear his trembling would prevent him:

—Yes, sir, but Father Dolan said he will come in tomorrow to pandy me again for it.

—Very well, the rector said, it is a mistake and I shall speak to Father Dolan myself. Will that do now?

Stephen felt the tears wetting his eyes and murmured:

—O yes sir, thanks.

The rector held his hand across the side of the desk where the skull was and Stephen, placing his hand in it for a moment, felt a cool moist palm.

—Good day now, said the rector, withdrawing his hand and bowing.

—Good day, sir, said Stephen.

He bowed and walked quietly out of the room, closing the doors carefully and slowly.

But when he had passed the old servant on the landing and was again in the low narrow dark corridor he began to walk faster and faster. Faster and faster he hurried on through the gloom excitedly. He bumped his elbow against the door at the end and, hurrying down the staircase, walked quickly through the two corridors and out into the air.

He could hear the cries of the fellows on the playgrounds. He broke into a run and, running quicker and quicker, ran across the cinderpath and reached the third line playground, panting.

The fellows had seen him running. They closed round him in a ring, pushing one against another to hear.

—Tell us! Tell us!

—What did he say?

—Did you go in?

—What did he say?

—Tell us! Tell us!

He told them what he had said and

what the rector had said and, when he had told them, all the fellows flung their caps spinning up into the air and cried:

—Hurroo!

They caught their caps and sent them up again spinning skyhigh and cried again:

—Hurroo! Hurroo!

They made a cradle of their locked hands and hoisted him up among them and carried him along till he struggled to get free. And when he had escaped from them they broke away in all directions, flinging their caps again into the air and whistling as they went spinning up and crying:

—Hurroo!

And they gave three groans for Baldyhead Dolan and three cheers for Conmee and they said he was the decentest rector that was ever in Clongowes.

The cheers died away in the soft grey air. He was alone. He was happy and free: but he would not be anyway proud with Father Dolan. He would be very quiet and obedient: and he wished that he could do something kind for for him to show him that he was not proud.

The air was soft and grey and mild and evening was coming. There was the smell of evening in the air, the smell of the fields in the country where they digged up turnips to peel them and eat them when they went out for a walk to Major Barton's, the smell there was in the little wood beyond the pavilion where the gallnuts were.

The fellows were practising long shies and bowing lobs and slow twisters. In the soft grey silence he could hear the bump of the balls: and from here and from there through the quiet air the sound of the cricket bats: pick, pack, pock, puck: like drops of water in a fountain falling softly in the briming bowl.

Samuel Beckett (1906–)

ACT WITHOUT WORDS I

A Mime for One Player

Translated from the French by the author.

Desert. Dazzling light.

The man is flung backwards on stage from right wing. He falls, gets up immediately, dusts himself, turns aside, reflects.

Whistle from right wing.

He reflects, goes out right.

Immediately flung back on stage he falls, gets up immediately, dusts himself, turns aside, reflects.

Whistle from left wing.

He reflects, goes out left.

5

10

Immediately flung back on stage he falls,
gets up immediately, dusts himself, turns
aside, reflects.

Whistle from left wing.   15

He reflects, goes toward left wing,
hesitates, thinks better of it, halts, turns
aside, reflects.

A little tree descends from flies, lands. It
has a single bough some three yards from   20
ground and at its summit a meager tuft of
palms casting at its foot a circle of shadow.

He continues to reflect.

Whistle from above.

He turns, sees tree, reflects, goes to it, sits   25
down in its shadow, looks at his hands.

A pair of tailor's scissors descends from
flies, comes to rest before tree, a yard from
ground.

He continues to look at his hands.   30

Whistle from above.

He looks up, sees scissors, takes them and
starts to trim his nails.

The palms close like a parasol, the shadow
disappears.   35

He drops scissors, reflects.

A tiny carafe, to which is attached a huge
label inscribed WATER, descends from
flies, comes to rest some three yards from
ground.   40

He continues to reflect.

Whistle from above.

He looks up, sees carafe, reflects, gets up,
goes and stands under it, tries in vain to
reach it, renounces, turns aside, reflects.   45

A big cube descends from flies, lands.

He continues to reflect.

Whistle from above.

He turns, sees cube, looks at it, at carafe,
reflects, goes to cube, takes it up, carries   50
it over and sets it down under carafe, tests
its stability, gets up on it, tries in vain to
reach carafe, renounces, gets down,
carries cube back to its place, turns aside,
reflects.   55

A second smaller cube descends from flies,
lands.

He continues to reflect.

Whistle from above.

He turns, sees second cube, looks at it, at   60

carafe, goes to second cube, takes it up,
carries it over and sets it down under
carafe, tests its stability, gets up on it, tries
in vain to reach carafe, renounces, gets
down, takes up second cube to carry it   65
back to its place, hesitates, thinks better of
it, sets it down, goes to big cube, takes it
up, carries it over and puts it on small one,
tests their stability, gets up on them, the
cubes collapse, he falls, gets up   70
immediately, brushes himself, reflects.

He takes up small cube, puts it on big one,
tests their stability, gets up on them and is
about to reach carafe when it is pulled
up a little way and comes to rest beyond   75
his reach.

He gets down, reflects, carries cubes back
to their place, one by one, turns aside,
reflects.

A third still smaller cube descends from   80
flies, lands.

He continues to reflect.

Whistle from above.

He turns, sees third cube, looks at it,
reflects, turns aside, reflects.   85

The third cube is pulled up and disappears
in flies.

Beside carafe a rope descends from flies,
with knots to facilitate ascent.

He continues to reflect.   90

Whistle from above.

He turns, sees rope, reflects, goes to it,
climbs up it and is about to reach carafe
when rope is let out and deposits him
back on ground.   95

He reflects, looks around for scissors, sees
them, goes and picks them up, returns to
rope and starts to cut it with scissors.

The rope is pulled up, lifts him off ground,
he hangs on, succeeds in cutting rope,   100
falls back on ground, drops scissors, falls,
gets up again immediately, brushes
himself, reflects.

The rope is pulled up quickly and
disappears in flies.   105

With length of rope in his possession he
makes a lasso with which he tries to
lasso carafe.

The carafe is pulled up quickly and
disappears in flies.   110

He turns aside, reflects.

He goes with lasso in his hand to tree,
looks at bough, turns and looks at cubes,
looks again at bough, drops lasso, goes to
cubes, takes up small one, carries it over   115
and sets it down under bough, goes back
for big one, takes it up and carries it over
under bough, makes to put it on small one,
hesitates, thinks better of it, sets it down,
takes up small one and puts it on big one,   120
tests their stability, turns aside and stoops
to pick up lasso.
    The bough folds down against trunk.
    He straightens up with lasso in his hand,
turns and sees what has happened.   125
    He drops lasso, turns aside, reflects.
    He carries back cubes to their place, one
by one, goes back for lasso, carries it over
to cubes and lays it in a neat coil on
small one.   130
    He turns aside, reflects.
    Whistle from right wing.
    He reflects, goes out right.
    Immediately flung back on stage he falls,
gets up immediately, brushes himself,   135
turns aside, reflects.
    Whistle from left wing.
    He does not move.
    He looks at his hands, looks around for
scissors, sees them, goes and picks them   140
up, starts to trim his nails, stops, reflects,
runs his finger along blade of scissors,
goes and lays them on small cube, turns
aside, opens his collar, frees his neck
and fingers it.   145
    The small cube is pulled up and
disappears in flies, carrying away rope
and scissors.
    He turns to take scissors, sees what has
happened.   150
    He turns aside, reflects.
    He goes and sits down on big cube.
    The big cube is pulled from under him.
He falls. The big cube is pulled up and
disappears in flies.   155
    He remains lying on his side, his face
towards auditorium, staring before him.
    The carafe descends from flies and comes
to rest a few feet from his body.
    He does not move.   160
    Whistle from above.
    He does not move.

The carafe descends further, dangles and
plays about his face.
　　He does not move.   165
　　The carafe is pulled up and disappears
in flies.
　　The bough returns to horizontal,
the palms open, the shadow returns.
　　Whistle from above.   170
　　He does not move.
　　The tree is pulled up and disappears in
flies.
　　He looks at his hands.

CURTAIN

Dylan Thomas (1914–1953)

THE MOUSE AND THE WOMAN

1

In the eaves of the lunatic asylum were birds who whistled the coming in of spring. A madman, howling like a dog from the top room, could not disturb them, and their tunes did not stop when he thrust his hands through the bars of the window near their nests and clawed the sky. A fresh smell blew with the winds around the white building and its grounds. The asylum trees waved green hands over the wall to the world outside.

In the gardens the patients sat and looked up at the sun or upon the flowers or upon nothing, or walked sedately along the paths, hearing the gravel crunch beneath their feet with a hard, sensible sound. Children in print dresses might be expected to play, not noisily, upon the lawn. The building, too, had a sweet expression, as though it knew only the kind things of life and the polite emotions. In a middle room sat a child who had cut off his double thumb with a scissors.

A little way off the main path leading from house to gate, a girl, lifting her arms, beckoned to the birds. She enticed the sparrows with little movements of her fingers, but to no avail. It must be spring, she said. The sparrows sang exultantly, and then stopped.

The howling in the top room began again. The madman's face was pressed close to the bars of the window. Opening his mouth wide, he bayed up at the sun, listening to the inflections of his voice with a remorseless concentration. With his unseeing eyes fixed on the green garden, he heard the revolution of the years as they moved softly back. Now there was no garden. Under the sun the iron bars melted. Like a flower, a new room pulsed and opened.

2

Waking up when it was still dark, he turned the dream over and over on the tip of his brain until each little symbol became heavy with a separate meaning. But there were symbols he could not remember, they came and went so quickly among the rattle of leaves, the gestures of women's hands spelling on the sky, the falling of rain and the humming wind. He remembered the oval of her face and the color of her eyes. He remembered the pitch of her voice, though not what she said. She moved again wearily up and down the same ruler of turf. What she said fell with the leaves, and spoke in the wind whose brother rattled the panes like an old man.

There had been seven women, in a mad play by a Greek, each with the same face, crowned by the same hoop of mad, black hair. One by one they trod the ruler of turf, then vanished. They turned the same face to him, intolerably weary with the same suffering.

The dream had changed. Where the women were was an avenue of trees. And the trees leant forward and interlaced their hands, turning into a black forest. He had seen himself, absurd in his nakedness, walk into the depths. Stepping on a dead twig, he was bitten.

Then there was her face again. There was nothing in his dream but her tired face. And the changes of the details of the dream and the celestial changes, the levers of the trees and the toothed twigs, these were the mechanisms of her delirium. It was not the sickness of sin that was upon her face. Rather it was the sickness of never having sinned and of never having done well.

He lit the candle on the little deal table by his bedside. Candle light threw the shadows of the room into confusion, and raised up the warped men of shadow out of the corners. For the first time he heard the clock. He had been deaf until then to everything except the wind outside the window and the clean winter sounds of the night-world. But now the steady tick tock tick sounded like the heart of someone hidden in his room. He could not hear the night birds now. The loud clock drowned their crying, or the wind was too cold for them and made commotion among their feathers. He remembered the dark hair of the woman in the trees and of the seven women treading the ruler of turf.

He could no longer listen to the speaking of reason. The pulse of a new heart beat at his side. Contentedly he let the dream dictate its rhythm. Often he would rise when the sun had dropped down, and, in the lunatic blackness under the stars, walk on the hill, feeling the wind finger his hair and at his nostrils. The rats and the rabbits on his towering hill came out in the dark, and the shadows consoled them for the night of the harsh sun. The dark woman, too, had risen out of darkness, pulling down the stars in their hundreds and showing him a mystery that hung and shone higher in the night of the sky than all the planets crowding beyond the curtains.

He fell to sleep again and woke in the sun. As he dressed, the dog scratched at the door. He let it in and felt its wet muzzle in his hand. The weather was hot for a midwinter day. The little wind there was could not relieve the sharpness of the heat. With the opening of the bedroom window, the uneven beams of the sun twisted his images into the hard lines of light.

He tried not to think of the woman as he ate. She had risen out of the depths of darkness. Now she was lost again. She is drowned, dead, dead. In the clean glittering of the kitchen, among the white boards, the oleographs of old women, the brass candlesticks, the plates on the shelves, and the sounds of kettle and clock, he was caught between believing in her and denying her. Now he insisted on the lines of her neck. The wilderness of her hair rose over the dark surface. He saw her flesh in the cut bread; her blood, still flowing through the channels of her mysterious body, in the spring water.

But another voice told him that she was dead. She was a woman in a mad story. He forced himself to hear the voice telling that she was dead. Dead, alive, drowned, raised up. The two voices shouted across his brain. He could not bear to think that the last spark in her had been put out. She is alive, alive, cried the two voices together.

As he tidied the sheets on his bed, he saw a block of paper, and sat down at the table with a pencil poised in his hand. A hawk flew over the hill. Seagulls, on spread, unmoving wings, cried past the window. A mother rat, in a hole in the hillside near the holes of rabbits, suckled its young as the sun climbed higher in the clouds.

He put the pencil down.

3

One winter morning, after the last crowing of the cock, in the walks of his garden, had died to nothing, she who for so long had dwelt with him appeared in all the wonder of her youth. She had cried to be set free, and to walk in his dreams no longer. Had she not been in the beginning, there would have been no beginning. She had moved in his belly when he was a boy, and stirred in his boy's loins. He at last gave birth to her who had been with him from the beginning. And with him dwelt a dog, a mouse, and a dark woman.

4

It is not a little thing, he thought, this writing that lies before me. It is the telling of a creation. It is the story of birth. Out of him had come another. A being had been born, not out of the womb, but out of the soul and the spinning head. He had come to the cottage

on the hill that the being within him might ripen and be born away from the eyes of men. He understood what the wind that took up the woman's cry had cried in his last dream. Let me be born, it had cried. He had given a woman being. His flesh would be upon her, and the life that he had given her would make her walk, talk, and sing. And he knew, too, that it was upon the block of paper she was made absolute. There was an oracle in the lead of the pencil.

In the kitchen he cleaned up after his meal. When the last plate had been washed, he looked around the room. In the corner near the door was a hole no bigger than a half-crown. He found a tiny square of tin and nailed it over the hole, making sure that nothing could go in or come out. Then he donned his coat and walked out on to the hill and down towards the sea.

Broken water leapt up from the inrushing tide and fell into the crevices of the rocks, making innumerable pools. He climbed down to the half-circle of beach, and the clusters of shells did not break when his foot fell on them. Feeling his heart knock at his side, he turned to where the greater rocks climbed perilously up to the grass. There, at the foot, the oval of her face towards him, she stood and smiled. The spray brushed her naked body, and the creams of the sea ran unheeded over her feet. She lifted her hand. He crossed to her.

5

In the cool of the evening they walked in the garden behind the cottage. She had lost none of her beauty with the covering up of her nakedness. With slippers on her feet she stepped as gracefully as when her feet were bare. There was a dignity in the poise of her head, and her voice was clear as a bell. Walking by her side along the narrow path, he heard no discord in the crying together of the gulls. She pointed out bird and bush with her finger, illuminating a new loveliness in the wings and leaves, in the sour churning of water over pebbles, and a new life along the dead branches of the trees.

It is quiet here, she said as they stood looking out to sea and the dark coming over the land. Is it always as quiet?

Not when the storms come in with the tide, he said. Boys play behind the hill, lovers go down to the shore.

Late evening turned to night so suddenly that, where she stood, stood a shadow under the moon. He took its hand, and they ran together to the cottage.

It was lonely for you before I came, she said.

As a cinder hissed into the grate, he moved back in his chair, making a startled gesture with his hand.

How quickly you become frightened, she said, I am frightened of nothing.

But she thought over her words and spoke again, this time in a low voice.

One day I may have no limbs to walk with, no hands to touch with. No heart under my breast.

Look at the million stars, he said. They make some pattern on the sky. It is a pattern of letters spelling a word. One night I shall look up and read the word.

But she kissed him and calmed his fear.

6

The madman remembered the inflections of her voice, heard, again, her frock rustling, and saw the terrible curve of her breast. His own breathing thundered in his ears. The girl on the bench beckoned to the sparrows. Somewhere a child purred, stroking the black columns of a wooden horse that neighed and then lay down.

7

They slept together on the first night, side by side in the dark, their arms around one another. The shadows in the corner were trimmed and shapely in her presence, losing their old deformity. And the stars looked in upon them and shone in their eyes.

Tomorrow you must tell me what you dream, he said.

It will be what I have always dreamed, she said. Walking on a little length of grass, up and down, up and down, till my feet bleed. Seven images of me walking up and down.

It is what I dream. Seven is a number in magic.

Magic? she said.

A woman makes a wax man, puts a pin in its chest; and the man dies. Someone has a little devil, tells it what to do. A girl dies, you see her walk. A woman turns into a hill.

She let her head rest on his shoulder, and fell to sleep.

He kissed her mouth, and passed his hand through her hair.

She was asleep, but he did not sleep. Wide awake, he stared into darkness. Now he was drowned in terror, and the sucking waters closed over his skull.

I, I have a devil, he said.

She stirred at the noise of his voice, and then again her head was motionless and her body straight along the curves of the cool bed.

I have a devil, but I do not tell it what to do. It lifts my hand. I write. The words spring into life. She, then, is a woman of the devil.

She made a contented sound, nestled ever nearer to him. Her breath was warm on his neck, and her foot lay on his like a mouse. He saw that she was beautiful in her sleep. Her beauty could not have sprouted out of evil. God, whom he had searched for in his loneliness, had formed her for his mate as Eve for Adam out of Adam's rib.

He kissed her again, and saw her smile as she slept.

God at my side, he said.

He had not slept with Rachel and woken with Leah. There was the pallor of dawn on her cheeks. He touched them lightly with a finger-nail. She did not stir.

But there had been no woman in his dreams. Not even a thread of woman's hair had dangled from the sky. God had come down in a cloud and the cloud had changed to a snakes' nest. Foul hissing of snakes had suggested the sound of water, and he had been drowned. Down and down he had fallen, under green shiftings and the bubbles that fishes blew from their mouths, down and down on to the bony floors of the sea.

Then against a white curtain of people had moved and moved to no purpose but to speak mad things.

What did you find under the tree?

I found an airman.

No, no, under the other tree?

I found a bottle of foetus.

No, no, under the other tree?

I found a mouse-trap.

He had been invisible. There had been nothing but his voice. He had flown across back gardens, and his voice, caught in a tangle of wireless aerials, had bled as though it were a thing of substance. Men in deck-chairs were listening to the loud-speakers speaking:

What did you find under the tree?

I found a wax man.

No, no, under the other tree?

He could remember little else except the odds and ends of sentences, the movement of a turning shoulder, the sudden flight or drop of syllables. But slowly the whole meaning edged into his brain. He could translate every symbol of his dreams, and he lifted the pencil so that they might stand hard and clear upon the paper. But the words would not come. He thought he heard the scratching of velvet paws behind a panel. But when he sat still and listened close, there was no sound.

She opened her eyes.

What are you doing? she said.

He put down the paper, and kissed her before they rose to dress.

What did you dream last night? he asked her, when they had eaten.

Nothing. I slept, that is all. What did you dream?

Nothing, he said.

8

There was creation screaming in the steam of the kettle, in the light making mouths on the china and the floor she swept as a child sweeps the floor of a doll's house. There was nothing to see in her but the ebb and flood of creation, only the transcendent sweep of being and living in the careless fold of flesh from shoulder-bone to elbow. He could not tell, after the horror he had found in the translating symbols, why the sea should point to the fruitful and unfailing stars with the edge of each wave, and an image of fruition disturb the moon in its dead course.

She moulded his images that evening. She lent light, and the lamp was dim beside her who had the oil of life glistening in every pore of her hand.

And now in the garden they remembered how they had walked in the garden for the first time.

You were lonely before I came.

How quickly you become frightened.

She had lost none of her beauty with the covering up of her nakedness. Though he had slept at her side, he had been content to know the surface of her. Now he stripped her of her clothes and laid her on a bed of grass.

9

The mouse had waited for this consummation. Wrinkling its eyes, it crept stealthily along the tunnel, littered with scraps of half-eaten paper, behind the kitchen wall. Stealthily, on tiny, padded paws, it felt its way through darkness, its nails scraping on the wood. Stealthily, it worked its way between the walls, screamed at the blind light through the chinks, and filed through the square of tin. Moonlight dropped slowly into the space where the mouse, working its destruction, inched into light. The last barrier fell away. And on the clean stones of the kitchen floor the mouse stood still.

10

That night he told of the love in the garden of Eden.

A garden was planted eastward, and Adam lived in it. Eve was made for him, out of him, bone of his bones, flesh of his flesh. They were as naked as you upon the seashore, but Eve could not have been as beautiful. They ate with the devil, and saw that they were naked, and covered up their nakedness. In their good bodies they saw evil for the first time.

Then you saw evil in me, she said, when I was naked. I would as soon be naked as be clothed. Why did you cover up my nakedness?

It was not good to look upon, he said.

But it was beautiful. You yourself said that it was beautiful, she said.

It was not good to look upon.

You said the body of Eve was good. And yet you say I was not good to look upon. Why did you cover up my nakedness?

It was not good to look upon.

11

Welcome, said the devil to the madman. Cast your eyes upon me. I grow and grow. See how I multiply. See my sad, Grecian stare. And the longing to be born in my dark eyes. Oh, that was the best joke of all.

I am an asylum boy tearing the wings of birds. Remember the lions that were crucified. Who knows that it was not I who opened the door to the tomb for Christ to struggle out?

But the madman had heard that welcome time after time. Ever since the evening of the second day after their love in the garden, when he had told her that her nakedness was not good to look upon, he had heard the welcome ring out in the sliding rain, and seen the welcome words burnt into the sea. He had known at the ringing of the first syllable in his ears that nothing on the earth could save him, and that the mouse would come out.

But the mouse had come out already.

The madman cried down at the beckoning girl to whom, now, a host of birds edged closer on a bough.

12

Why did you cover up my nakedness?

It was not good to look upon.

Why, then, No, no, under the other tree?

It was not good, I found a wax cross.

As she had questioned him, not harshly, but with bewilderment, that he whom she loved should find her nakedness unclean, he heard the broken pieces of the old dirge break into her questioning.

Why, then, she said, No, no, under the other tree?

He heard himself reply, It was not good, I found a talking thorn.

Real things kept changing place with unreal, and, as a bird burst into song, he heard the springs rattle far back in its throat.

She left him with a smile that still poised over a question, and, crossing the strip of hill, vanished into the half-dark where the cottage stood like another woman. But she returned ten times, in ten different shapes. She breathed at his ear, passed the back of her hand over his dry mouth, and lit the lamp in the cottage room more than a mile away.

It grew darker as he stared at the stars. Wind cut through the new night. Very suddenly a bird screamed over the trees, and an owl, hungry for mice, hooted in the mile-away wood.

There was contradiction in heartbeat and green Sirius, an eye in the east. He put his hand to his eyes, hiding the star, and walked slowly towards the lamp burning far away in the cottage. And all the elements come together, of wind and sea and fire, of love and the passing of love, closed in a circle around him.

She was not sitting by the fire, as he had expected her to be, smiling upon the folds of her dress. He called her name at the foot of the stairs. He looked into the empty bedroom, and called her name in the garden. But she had gone, and all the mystery of her presence had left the cottage. And the shadows that he thought had departed when she had come crowded the corners, muttering in women's voices among themselves. He turned down the wick in the lamp. As he climbed upstairs, he heard the corner voices become louder and louder until the whole cottage reverberated with them, and the wind could not be heard.

13

With tears in his cheeks and with a hard pain in his heart, he fell to sleep, coming at last to where his father sat in an alcove carved in a cloud.

Father, he said, I have been walking over the world, looking for a thing worthy of love, but I drove it away and go now from place to place, moaning my hideousness, hearing my own voice in the voices of the corncrakes and the frogs, seeing my own face in the riddled faces of the beasts.

He held out his arms, waiting for words to fall from that old mouth hidden under a white beard frozen with tears. He implored the old man to speak.

Speak to me, your son. Remember how we read the classic books together on the terraces. Or on an Irish harp you would pluck tunes until the geese, like the seven geese of the Wandering Jew, rose squawking into the air. Father, speak to me, your only son, a prodigal out of the herbaceous spaces of small towns, out of the smells and sounds of the city, out of the thorny desert and the deep sea. You are a wise old man.

He implored the old man to speak, but, coming closer to him and staring into his face, he saw the stains of death upon mouth and eyes and a nest of mice in the tangle of the frozen beard.

It was weak to fly, but he flew. And it was a weakness of the blood to be invisible, but he was invisible. He reasoned and dreamed unreasonably at the same time, knowing his weakness and the lunacy of flying but having no strength to conquer it. He flew like a bird over the fields, but soon the bird's body vanished, and he was a flying voice. An open window beckoned him by the waving of its blinds, as a scarecrow beckons a wise bird by its ragged waving, and into the open window he flew, alighting on a bed near a sleeping girl.

Awake, girl, he said. I am your lover come in the night.

She awoke at his voice.

Who called me?

I called you.

Where are you?

I am upon the pillow by your head, speaking into your ear.

Who are you?

I am a voice.

Stop calling into my ear, then, and hop into my hand so that I may touch you and tickle you. Hop into my hand, voice.

He lay still and warm in her palm.

Where are you?

I am in your hand.

Which hand?

The hand on your breast, left hand. Do not make a fist or you will crush me. Can you not feel me warm in your hand? I am close to the roots of your fingers.

Talk to me.

I had a body, but was always a voice. As I truly am, I come to you in the night, a voice on your pillow.

I know what you are. You are the still, small voice I must not listen to. I have been told not to listen to that still, small voice that speaks in the night. It is wicked to listen. You must not come here again. You must go away.

But I am your lover.

I must not listen, said the girl and suddenly clenched her hand.

14

He could go into the garden, regardless of rain, and bury his face in the wet earth. With his ears pressed close to the earth, he would hear the great heart, under soil and grass, strain before breaking. In dreams he would say to some figure, Lift me up. I am only ten pounds now. I am lighter. Six pounds. Two pounds. My spine shows through my breast. The secret of that alchemy that had turned a little revolution of the unsteady senses into a golden moment was lost as a key is lost in undergrowth. A secret was confused among the night, and the confusion of the last madness before the grave would come down like an animal on the brain.

He wrote upon the block of paper, not knowing what he wrote, and dreading the words that looked up at him at last and could not be forgotten.

15

And this is all there was to it: a woman had been born, not out of the womb, but out of the soul and the spinning head. And he who had borne her out of darkness loved his creation, and she loved him. But this is all there was to it: a miracle befell a man. He fell in love with it, but could not keep it, and the miracle passed. And with him dwelt a dog, a mouse, and a dark woman. The woman went away, and the dog died.

16

He buried the dog at the end of the garden. Rest in peace, he told the dead dog. But the grave was not deep enough and there were rats in the underhanging of the bank who bit through the sack shroud.

17

Upon town pavements he saw the woman step loose, her breasts firm under a coat on which the single hairs from old men's heads lay white on black. Her life, he knew, was only a life of days. Her spring had passed with him. After the summer and the autumn, unhallowed time between full life and death, there would be winter corrugating charm. He who knew the subtleties of every reason, and sensed the four together in every symbol of the earth, would disturb the chronology of the seasons. Winter must not appear.

18

Consider now the old effigy of time, his long beard whitened by an Egyptian sun, his bare feet watered by the Sargasso sea. Watch me belabor the old fellow. I have stopped his heart. It split like a chamber pot. No, this is no rain falling. This is the wet out of the cracked heart.

Parhelion and sun shine in the same sky with the broken moon. Dizzy with the chasing of moon by sun, and by the twinkling of so many stars, I run upstairs to read again of the love of some man for a woman. I tumble down to see the half-crown hole in the kitchen wall stabbed open, and the prints of a mouse's pads on the floor.

Consider now the old effigies of the seasons. Break up the rhythm of the old figures' moving, the spring trot, summer canter, sad stride of autumn, and winter shuffle. Break, piece by piece, the continuous changing of motion into a spindle-shanked walking.

Consider the sun for whom I know no image but the old image of a shot eye, and the broken moon.

19

Gradually the chaos became less, and the things of the surrounding world were no longer wrought out of their own substance into the shapes of his thoughts. Some peace fell about him, and again the music of creation was to be heard trembling out of crystal water, out of the holy sweep of the sky down to the wet edge of the earth where a sea flowed over. Night came slowly, and the hill rose to the unrisen stars. He turned over the block of paper and upon the last page wrote in a clear hand:

20

The woman died.

21

There was dignity in such a murder. And the hero in him rose up in all his holiness and strength. It was just that he who had brought her forth from darkness should pack her away again. And it was just that she would die not knowing what hand out of the sky struck upon her and laid her low.

He walked down the hill, his steps slow as in procession, and his lips smiling at the dark sea. He climbed on to the shore, and, feeling his heart knock at his side, turned to where the greater rocks climbed perilously to the grass. There at the foot, her face towards him, she lay and smiled. Sea-water ran unheeded over her nakedness. He crossed to her, and touched her cold cheek with his nails.

22

Acquainted with the last grief, he stood at the open window of his room. And the night was an island in a sea of mystery and meaning. And the voice out of the night was a voice of acceptance. And the face of the moon was the face of humility.

He knew the last wonder before the grave and the mystery that bewilders and incorporates the heavens and the earth. He knew that he had failed before the eye of God and the eye of Sirius to hold his miracle. The woman had shown him that it was wonderful to live. And now, when at last he knew how wonderful, and how pleasant the blood in the trees, and how deep the well of the clouds, he must close his eyes and die. He opened his eyes, and looked up at the stars. There were a million stars spelling the same word. And the word of the stars was written clearly upon the sky.

23

Alone in the kitchen, among the broken chairs and china, stood the mouse that had come out of the hole. Its paws rested lightly upon the floor painted all over with the grotesque figures of birds and girls. Stealthily, it crept back into the hole. Stealthily, it worked its way between the walls. There was no sound in the kitchen but the sound of the mouse's nails scraping upon wood.

24

In the eaves of the lunatic asylum the birds still whistled, and the madman, pressed closed to the bars of the window near their nest, bayed up at the sun.

Upon the bench some distance from the main path, the girl was beckoning to the birds, while on a square of lawn danced three old women, hand in hand, simpering in the wind, to the music of an Italian organ from the world outside.

Spring is come, said the warders.

Harold Pinter (1930–)

A SLIGHT ACHE

A country house, with two chairs and a table laid for breakfast at the center of the stage. These will later be removed and the action will be focused on the scullery on the right and the study on the left, both indicated with a minimum of scenery and props. A large well kept garden is suggested at the back of the stage with flower beds, trimmed hedges, etc. The garden gate, which cannot be seen by the audience, is off right.

FLORA *and* EDWARD *are discovered sitting at the breakfast table.*
EDWARD *is reading the paper.*

FLORA Have you noticed the honeysuckle this morning?

EDWARD The what?

FLORA The honeysuckle.

EDWARD Honeysuckle? Where?

FLORA By the back gate, Edward.

EDWARD Is that honeysuckle? I thought it was . . . convolvulus, or something.

FLORA But you know it's honeysuckle.

EDWARD I tell you I thought it was convolvulus.

[*Pause.*]

FLORA It's in wonderful flower.

EDWARD I must look.

FLORA The whole garden's in flower this morning. The clematis. The convolvulus. Everything. I was out at seven. I stood by the pool.

EDWARD Did you say—that the convolvulus was in flower?

FLORA Yes.

EDWARD But good God, you just denied there was any.

FLORA I was talking about the honeysuckle.

EDWARD About the what?

FLORA [*calmly*]: Edward—you know that shrub outside the toolshed . . .

EDWARD Yes, yes.

FLORA That's convolvulus.

EDWARD That?

FLORA Yes.

EDWARD Oh.

[*Pause.*]

I thought it was japonica.

FLORA Oh, good Lord no.

EDWARD Pass the teapot, please.

[*Pause. She pours tea for him.*]

I don't see why I should be expected to distinguish between these plants. It's not my job.

FLORA You know perfectly well what grows in your garden.

EDWARD Quite the contrary. It is clear that I don't.

[*Pause.*]

FLORA [*rising*] I was up at seven. I

stood by the pool. The peace. And everything in flower. The sun was up. You should work in the garden this morning. We could put up the canopy.

EDWARD The canopy? What for?

FLORA To shade you from the sun.

EDWARD Is there a breeze?

FLORA A light one.

EDWARD It's very treacherous weather, you know.

[*Pause.*]

FLORA Do you know what today is?

EDWARD Saturday.

FLORA It's the longest day of the year.

EDWARD Really?

FLORA It's the height of summer to-day.

EDWARD Cover the marmalade.

FLORA What?

EDWARD Cover the pot. There's a wasp. [*He puts the paper down on the table.*] Don't move. Keep still. What are you doing?

FLORA Covering the pot.

EDWARD Don't move. Leave it. Keep still.

[*Pause.*]

Give me the 'Telegraph'.

FLORA Don't hit it. It'll bite.

EDWARD Bite? What do you mean, bite? Keep still.

[*Pause.*]

It's landing.

FLORA It's going in the pot.

EDWARD Give me the lid.

FLORA It's in.

EDWARD Give me the lid.

FLORA I'll do it.

EDWARD Give it to me! Now . . . Slowly . . .

FLORA What are you doing?

EDWARD Be quiet. Slowly . . . carefully . . . on . . . the . . . pot! Ha-ha-ha. Very good.

[*He sits on a chair to the right of the table.*]

FLORA Now he's in the marmalade.

EDWARD Precisely.

[*Pause. She sits on a chair to the left of the table and reads the 'Telegraph'.*]

FLORA Can you hear him?

EDWARD Hear him?

FLORA Buzzing?

EDWARD Nonsense. How can you hear him? It's an earthenware lid.

FLORA He's becoming frantic.

EDWARD Rubbish. Take it away from the table.

FLORA What shall I do with it?

EDWARD Put it in the sink and drown it.

FLORA It'll fly out and bite me.

EDWARD It will not bite you! Wasps don't bite. Anyway, it won't fly out. It's stuck. It'll drown where it is, in the marmalade.

FLORA What a horrible death.

EDWARD On the contrary.

[*Pause.*]

FLORA Have you got something in your eyes?

EDWARD No. Why do you ask?

FLORA You keep clenching them, blinking them.

EDWARD I have a slight ache in them.

FLORA Oh, dear.

EDWARD Yes, a slight ache. As if I hadn't slept.

FLORA Did you sleep, Edward?

EDWARD Of course I slept. Uninterrupted. As always.

FLORA And yet you feel tired.

EDWARD I didn't say I felt tired. I merely said I had a slight ache in my eyes.

FLORA Why is that, then?

EDWARD I really don't know.

[*Pause.*]

FLORA Oh goodness!

EDWARD What is it?

FLORA I can see it. It's trying to come out.

EDWARD How can it?

FLORA Through the hole. It's trying to crawl out, through the spoon-hole.

EDWARD Mmmnn, yes. Can't do it, of course. [*Silent pause.*] Well, let's kill it, for goodness' sake.

FLORA Yes, let's. But how?

EDWARD Bring it out on the spoon and squash it on a plate.

FLORA   It'll fly away. It'll bite.

EDWARD   If you don't stop saying that word I shall leave this table.

FLORA   But wasps do bite.

EDWARD   They don't bite. They sting. It's snakes . . . that bite.

FLORA   What about horseflies?
[Pause.]

EDWARD   [to himself]   Horseflies suck.
[Pause.]

FLORA   [tentatively]   If we . . . if we wait long enough, I suppose it'll choke to death. It'll suffocate in the marmalade.

EDWARD   [briskly]   You do know I've got work to do this morning, don't you? I can't spend the whole day worrying about a wasp.

FLORA   Well, kill it.

EDWARD   You want to kill it?

FLORA   Yes.

EDWARD   Very well. Pass me the hot water jug.

FLORA   What are you going to do?

EDWARD   Scald it. Give it to me.
[She hands him the jug. Pause.]
Now . . .

FLORA   [whispering]   Do you want me to lift the lid?

EDWARD   No, no, no. I'll pour down the spoon hole. Right . . . down the spoonhole.

FLORA   Listen!

EDWARD   What?

FLORA   It's buzzing.

EDWARD   Vicious creatures.
[Pause.]
Curious, but I don't remember seeing any wasps at all, all summer, until now. I'm sure I don't know why. I mean, there must have been wasps.

FLORA   Please.

EDWARD   This couldn't be the first wasp, could it?

FLORA   Please.

EDWARD   The first wasp of summer? No. It's not possible.

FLORA   Edward.

EDWARD   Mmmmmnnn?

FLORA   Kill it.

EDWARD   Ah, yes. Tilt the pot. Tilt.

Aah . . . down here . . . right down . . . blinding him . . . that's . . . it.

FLORA   Is it?

EDWARD   Lift the lid. All right, I will. There he is! Dead. What a monster.
[He squashes it on a plate.]

FLORA   What an awful experience.

EDWARD   What a beautiful day it is. Beautiful. I think I shall work in the garden this morning. Where's that canopy?

FLORA   It's in the shed.

EDWARD   Yes, we must get it out. My goodness, just look at that sky. Not a cloud. Did you say it was the longest day of the year today?

FLORA   Yes.

EDWARD   Ah, it's a good day. I feel it in my bones. In my muscles. I think I'll stretch my legs in a minute. Down to the pool. My God, look at that flowering shrub over there. Clematis. What a wonderful . . . [He stops suddenly.]

FLORA   What?
[Pause.]
Edward, what is it?
[Pause.]
Edward . . .

EDWARD   [thickly]   He's there.

FLORA   Who?

EDWARD   [low, murmuring]   Blast and damn it, he's there, he's there at the back gate.

FLORA   Let me see.
[She moves over to him to look. Pause.]
[Lightly.]   Oh, it's the matchseller.

EDWARD   He's back again.

FLORA   But he's always there.

EDWARD   Why? What is he doing there?

FLORA   But he's never disturbed you, has he? The man's been standing there for weeks. You've never mentioned it.

EDWARD   What is he doing there?

FLORA   He's selling matches, of course.

EDWARD   It's ridiculous. What's the time?

FLORA   Half past nine.

EDWARD . . What in God's name is he doing with a tray full of matches at half past nine in the morning?

FLORA   He arrives at seven o'clock.

EDWARD   Seven o'clock?

FLORA   He's always there at seven.

EDWARD   Yes, but you've never . . . actually seen him arrive?

FLORA   No, I . . .

EDWARD   Well, how do you know he's . . . not been standing there all night? [*Pause.*]

FLORA   Do you find him interesting, Edward?

EDWARD   [*casually*] Interesting? No. No, I . . . don't find him interesting.

FLORA   He's a very nice old man, really.

EDWARD   You've spoken to him?

FLORA   No. No, I haven't spoken to him. I've nodded.

EDWARD   [*pacing up and down*] For two months he's been standing on that spot, do you realize that? Two months. I haven't been able to step outside the back gate.

FLORA   Why on earth not?

EDWARD   [*to himself*] It used to give me great pleasure, such pleasure, to stroll along through the long grass, out through the back gate, pass into the lane. That pleasure is now denied me. It's my own house, isn't it? It's my own gate.

FLORA   I really can't understand this, Edward.

EDWARD   Damn. And do you know I've never seen him sell one box? Not a box. It's hardly surprising. He's on the wrong road. It's not a road at all. What is it? It's a lane, leading to the monastery. Off everybody's route. Even the monks take a short cut to the village, when they want to go . . . to the village. No one goes up it. Why doesn't he stand on the main road if he wants to sell matches, by the *front* gate? The whole thing's preposterous.

FLORA   [*going over to him*] I don't know why you're getting so excited about it. He's a quiet, harmless old man, going about his business. He's quite harmless.

EDWARD   I didn't say he wasn't harmless. Of course he's harmless. How could he be other than harmless? [*Fade out and silence.*]

[FLORA'S *voice, far in the house, drawing nearer.*]

FLORA   [*off*]   Edward, where are you? Edward? Where are you, Edward? [*She appears.*] Edward? Edward, what are you doing in the scullery?

EDWARD   [*looking through the scullery window*]   Doing?

FLORA   I've been looking everywhere for you. I put up the canopy ages ago. I came back and you were nowhere to be seen. Have you been out?

EDWARD   No.

FLORA   Where have you been?

EDWARD   Here.

FLORA   I looked in your study. I even went into the attic.

EDWARD   [*tonelessly*]   What would I be doing in the attic?

FLORA   I couldn't imagine what had happened to you. Do you know it's twelve o'clock?

EDWARD   Is it?

FLORA   I even went to the bottom of the garden, to see if you were in the toolshed.

EDWARD   [*tonelessly*]   What would I be doing in the toolshed?

FLORA   You must have seen me in the garden. You can see through this window.

EDWARD   Only part of the garden.

FLORA   Yes.

EDWARD   Only a corner of the garden. A very small corner.

FLORA   What are you doing in here?

EDWARD   Nothing. I was digging out some notes, that's all.

FLORA   Notes?

EDWARD   For my essay.

FLORA   Which essay?

EDWARD My essay on space and time.

FLORA But . . . I've never . . . I don't know that one.

EDWARD You don't know it?

FLORA I thought you were writing one about the Belgian Congo.

EDWARD I've been engaged on the dimensionality and continuity of space . . . and time . . . for years.

FLORA And the Belgian Congo?

EDWARD [shortly] Never mind about the Belgian Congo.

[Pause.]

FLORA But you don't keep notes in the scullery.

EDWARD You'd be surprised. You'd be highly surprised.

FLORA Good Lord, what's that? Is that a bullock let loose? No. It's the matchseller! My goodness, you can see him . . . through the hedge. He looks bigger. Have you been watching him? He looks . . . like a bullock.

[Pause.]

Edward?

[Pause.]

[Moving over to him.] Are you coming outside? I've put up the canopy. You'll miss the best of the day. You can have an hour before lunch.

EDWARD I've no work to do this morning.

FLORA What about your essay? You don't intend to stay in the scullery all day, do you?

EDWARD Get out. Leave me alone.

[A slight pause.]

FLORA Really Edward. You've never spoken to me like that in all your life.

EDWARD Yes, I have.

FLORA Oh, Weddie. Beddie-Weddie . . .

EDWARD Do not call me that!

FLORA Your eyes are bloodshot.

EDWARD Damn it.

FLORA It's too dark in here to peer . . .

EDWARD Damn.

FLORA It's so bright outside.

EDWARD Damn.

FLORA And it's dark in here.

[Pause.]

EDWARD Christ blast it!

FLORA You're frightened of him.

EDWARD I'm not.

FLORA You're frightened of a poor old man. Why?

EDWARD I am not!

FLORA He's a poor, harmless old man.

EDWARD Aaah my eyes.

FLORA Let me bathe them.

EDWARD Keep away.

[Pause.]

[Slowly.] I want to speak to that man. I want to have a word with him.

[Pause.]

It's quite absurd, of course. I really can't tolerate something so . . . absurd, right on my doorstep. I shall not tolerate it. He's sold nothing all morning. No one passed. Yes. A monk passed. A non-smoker. In a loose garment. It's quite obvious he was a non-smoker but still, the man made no effort. He made no effort to clinch a sale, to rid himself of one of his cursed boxes. His one chance, all morning, and he made no effort.

[Pause.]

I haven't wasted my time. I've hit, in fact, upon the truth. He's not a matchseller at all. The bastard isn't a matchseller at all. Curious I never realized that before. He's an impostor. I watched him very closely. He made no move towards the monk. As for the monk, the monk made no move towards him. The monk was moving along the lane. He didn't pause, or halt, or in any way alter his step. As for the matchseller—how ridiculous to go on calling him by that title. What a farce. No, there is something very false about that man. I intend to get to the bottom of it. I'll soon get rid of him. He can go and ply his trade somewhere else. Instead of standing like a bullock . . . a bullock, outside my back gate.

FLORA But if he isn't a matchseller, what is his trade?

EDWARD We'll soon find out.

FLORA You're going out to speak to him?

EDWARD Certainly not! Go out to *him*? Certainly . . . not. I'll invite him in here. Into my study. Then we'll . . . get to the bottom of it.

FLORA Why don't you call the police and have him removed?

[*He laughs. Pause.*]

Why don't you call the police, Edward? You could say he was a public nuisance. Athough I . . . I can't say I find him a nuisance.

EDWARD Call him in.

FLORA Me?

EDWARD Go out and call him in.

FLORA Are you serious?

[*Pause.*]

Edward, I could call the police. Or even the vicar.

EDWARD Go and get him.

[*She goes out. Silence.* EDWARD *waits.*]

FLORA [*in the garden*] Good morning.

We haven't met. I live in this house here. My husband and I.

[*Pause.*]

I wonder if you could . . . would you care for a cup of tea?

[*Pause.*]

Or a glass of lemon? It must be so dry, standing here.

[*Pause.*]

Would you like to come inside for a little while? It's much cooler. There's something we'd very much like to . . . tell you, that will benefit you. Could you spare a few moments? We won't keep you long.

[*Pause.*]

Might I buy your tray of matches, do you think? We've run out, completely, and we always keep a very large stock. It happens that way, doesn't it? Well, we can discuss it inside. Do come. This way. Ah, now, do come. Our house is full of curios, you know. My husband's been rather a collector. We have goose for lunch. Do you care for goose?

[*She moves to the gate.*]

Come and have lunch with us. This way. That's . . . right. May I take your arm? There's a good deal of *nettle* inside the gate. [*The* MATCH-SELLER *appears.*] Here. This way. Mind now. Isn't it beautiful weather? It's the longest day of the year today.

[*Pause.*]

That's honeysuckle. And that's convolvulus. There's clematis. And do you see that plant by the conservatory? That's japonica.

[*Silence. She enters the study.*]

FLORA He's here.

EDWARD I know.

FLORA He's in the hall.

EDWARD I know he's here. I can smell him.

FLORA Smell him?

EDWARD I smelt him when he came under my window. Can't you smell the house now?

FLORA What are you going to do with him. Edward? You won't be rough with him in any way? He's very old. I'm not sure if he can hear, or even see. And he's wearing the oldest—

EDWARD I don't want to know what he's wearing.

FLORA But you'll see for yourself in a minute, if you speak to him.

EDWARD I shall.

[*Slight pause.*]

FLORA He's an old man. You won't . . . be rough with him?

EDWARD If he's so old, why doesn't he seek shelter . . . from the storm?

FLORA But there's no storm. It's summer, the longest day . . .

EDWARD There was a storm, last week. A summer storm. He stood without moving, while it raged about him.

FLORA When was this?

EDWARD He remained quite still while it thundered all about him.

[*Pause.*]

FLORA Edward . . . are you sure it's wise to bother about all this?

EDWARD Tell him to come in.

FLORA I . . .

EDWARD Now.

[*She goes and collects the* MATCH-SELLER.]

FLORA Hullo. Would you like to go in? I won't be long. Up these stairs here.

[*Pause.*]

You can have some sherry before lunch.

[*Pause.*]

Shall I take your tray? No. Very well, take it with you. Just . . . up those stairs. The door at the . . .

[*She watches him move.*]

the door . . .

[*Pause.*]

the door at the top. I'll join you . . . later. [*She goes out.*]

[*The* MATCHSELLER *stands on the threshold of the study.*]

EDWARD [*cheerfully*] Here I am Where are you?

[*Pause.*]

Don't stand out there, old chap. Come into my study. [*He rises.*] Come in.

[*The* MATCHSELLER *enters.*]

That's right. Mind how you go. That's . . . it. Now, make yourself comfortable. Thought you might like some refreshment, on a day like this. Sit down, old man. What will you have? Sherry? Or what about a double scotch? Eh?

[*Pause.*]

I entertain the villagers annually, as a matter of fact. I'm not the squire, but they look upon me with some regard. Don't believe we've got a squire here any more, actually. Don't know what became of him. Nice old man he was. Great chess-player, as I remember. Three daughters. The pride of the county. Flaming red hair. Alice was the eldest. Sit yourself down, old chap. Eunice I think was number two. The youngest one was the best of the bunch. Sally. No, no, wait a minute, no, it wasn't Sally, it was . . . Fanny. Fanny. A flower. You must be a stranger here. Unless you lived here once, went on a long voyage and have lately returned. Do you know the district?

[*Pause.*]

Now, now, you musn't . . . stand about like that. Take a seat. Which one would you prefer? We have a great variety, as you see. Can't stand uniformity. Like different seats, different backs. Often when I'm working, you know, I draw up one chair, scribble a few lines, put it by, draw up another, sit back, ponder, put it by . . . [*absently*] . . . sit back . . . put it by . . .

[*Pause.*]

I write theological and philosophical essays . . .

[*Pause.*]

Now and again I jot down a few observations on certain tropical phenomena—not from the same standpoint, of course. [*Silent pause.*] Yes. Africa, now. Africa's always been my happy hunting ground. Fascinating country. Do you know it? I get the impression that you've . . . been around a bit. Do you by any chance know the Membunza Mountains? Great range south of Katambaloo. French Equatorial Africa, if my memory serves me right. Most extraordinary diversity of flora and fauna. Especially fauna. I understand in the Gobi Desert you can come across some very strange sights. Never been there myself. Studied the maps though. Fascinating things, maps.

[*Pause.*]

Do you live in the village? I don't often go down, of course. Or are you passing through? On your way to another part of the country? Well, I can tell you, in my opinion you won't find many prettier parts than here. We win the first prize regularly, you know, the best kept village in the area. Sit down.

[*Pause.*]

I say, can you hear me?

[*Pause.*]

I said, I say, can you hear me?

[*Pause.*]

You possess most extraordinary repose, for a man of your age, don't you? Well, perhaps that's not quite the right word . . . repose. Do you find it chilly in here? I'm sure it's chillier in here than out. I haven't been out yet, today, though I shall probably spend the whole afternoon working, in the garden, under my canopy, at my table, by the pool.

[*Pause.*]

Oh, I understand you met my *wife*? Charming woman, don't you think? Plenty of grit there, too. Stood by me through thick and thin, that woman. In season and out of season. Fine figure of a woman she was, too, in her youth. Wonderful carriage, flaming red hair. [*He stops abruptly.*]

[*Pause.*]

Yes, I . . . I was in much the same position myself then as you are now, you understand. Struggling to make my way in the world. I was in commerce too. [*With a chuckle.*] Oh, yes, I know what it's like—the weather, the rain, beaten from pillar to post, up hill and down dale . . . the rewards were few . . . winters in hovels . . . up till all hours working at your thesis . . . yes, I've done it all. Let me advise you. Get a good woman to stick by you. Never mind what the world says. Keep at it. Keep your shoulder to the wheel. It'll pay dividends.

[*Pause.*]

[*With a laugh.*] You must excuse my chatting away like this. We have few visitors this time of the year. All our friends summer abroad. I'm a home bird myself. Wouldn't mind taking a trip to Asia Minor, mind you, or to certain lower regions of the Congo, but Europe? Out of the question. Much too noisy. I'm sure you agree. Now look, what will you have to drink? A glass of ale? Curaçao Fockink Orange? Ginger beer? Tia Maria? A Wachenheimer Fuchsmantel Reisling Beeren Auslese? Gin and it? Chateauneuf-du-Pape? A little Asti Spumante? Or what do you say to a straightforward Piesporter Goldtropfschen Feine A u s l e s e (Reichsgraf von Kesselstaff)? Any preference?

[*Pause.*]

You look a trifle warm. Why don't you take off your balaclava? I'd find that a little itchy myself. But then I've aways been one for freedom of movement. Even in the depth of winter I wear next to nothing.

[*Pause.*]

I say, can I ask you a personal question? I don't want to seem inquisitive but aren't you rather on the wrong road for matchselling? Not terribly busy, is it? Of course you may not care for petrol fumes or the noise of traffic. I can quite understand that.

[*Pause.*]

Do forgive me peering but is that a glass eye you're wearing?

[*Pause.*]

Do take off your balaclava, there's a good chap, put your tray down and take your ease, as they say in this part of the world. [*He moves towards him.*] I must say you keep quite a good stock, don't you? Tell me, between ourselves, are those boxes full, or are there just a few half-empty ones among them? Oh yes, I used to be in commerce. Well now, before the good lady sounds the gong for petit déjeuner will you join me in an apéritif? I recommend a glass of cider. Now . . . just a minute . . . I know I've got some—Look out! Mind your tray!

[*The tray falls, and the matchboxes.*]

Good God, what . . . ?

[*Pause.*]

You've dropped your tray.

[*Pause. He picks the matchboxes up.*]

[*Grunts.*] Eh, these boxes are all wet. You've no right to sell wet matches, you know. Uuuuugggh. This feels suspiciously like fungus. You won't get very far in this trade if you don't take care of your goods. [*Grunts, rising.*] Well, here you are.

[*Pause.*]

Here's your tray.

[*He puts the tray into the* MATCH-SELLER'S *hands, and sits. Pause.*]

Now listen, let me be quite frank with you, shall I? I really cannot understand why you don't sit down. There are four chairs at your disposal. Not to mention the hassock. I can't possibly talk to you unless you're settled. Then and only then can I speak to you. Do you follow me? You're not being terribly helpful. [*Slight pause.*] You're sweating. The sweat's pouring out of you. Take off that balaclava.

[*Pause.*]

Go into the corner then. Into the corner. Go on. Get into the shade of the corner. Back. Backward.

[*Pause.*]

Get back!

[*Pause.*]

Ah, you understand me. Forgive me for saying so, but I had decided that you had the comprehension of a bullock. I was mistaken. You understand me perfectly well. That's right. A little more. A little to the right. Aaah. Now you're there. In shade, in shadow. Good-o. Now I can get down to brass tacks. Can't I?

[*Pause.*]

No doubt you're wondering why I invited you into this house? You may think I was alarmed by the look of you. You would be quite mistaken. I was not alarmed by the look of you. I did not find you at all alarming.

No, no. Nothing outside this room has ever alarmed me. You disgusted me, quite forcibly, if you want to know the truth.

[*Pause.*]

Why did you disgust me to that extent? That seems to be a pertinent question. You're no more disgusting than Fanny, the squire's daughter, after all. In appearance you differ but not in essence. There's the same . . .

[*Pause.*]

The same . . .

[*Pause.*]

[*In a low voice.*] I want to ask you a question. Why do you stand outside my back gate, from dawn till dusk, why do you pretend to sell matches, why . . . ? What is it, damn you. You're shivering. You're sagging. Come here, come here . . . mind your tray! [EDWARD *rises and moves behind a chair.*] Come, quick, quick. There. Sit here. Sit . . . sit in this.

[*The* MATCHSELLER *stumbles and sits. Pause.*]

Aaaah! You're sat. At last. What a relief. You must be tired. [*Slight pause.*] Chair comfortable? I bought it in a sale. I bought all the furniture in this house in a sale. The same sale. When I was a young man. You too, perhaps. You too, perhaps.

[*Pause.*]

At the same time, perhaps!

[*Pause.*]

[*Muttering.*] I must get some air. I must get a breath of air.

[*He goes to the door.*]

Flora!

FLORA Yes?

EDWARD [*with great weariness*] Take me into the garden.

[*Silence. They move from the study door to a chair under a canopy.*]

FLORA Come under the canopy.

EDWARD Ah. [*He sits.*]

[*Pause.*]

The peace. The peace out here.

FLORA Look at our trees.

EDWARD Yes.

FLORA Our own trees. Can you hear the birds?

EDWARD No, I can't hear them.

FLORA But they're singing, high up, and flapping.

EDWARD Good. Let them flap.

FLORA Shall I bring your lunch out here? You can have it in peace, and a quiet drink, under your canopy. [*Pause.*]

How are you getting on with your old man?

EDWARD What do you mean?

FLORA What's happening? How are you getting on with him?

EDWARD Very well. We get on remarkably well. He's a little . . . reticent. Somewhat withdrawn. It's understandable. I should be the same, perhaps, in his place. Though, of course, I could not possibly find myself in his place.

FLORA Have you found out anything about him?

EDWARD A little. A little. He's had various trades, that's certain. His place of residence is unsure. He's . . . he's not a drinking man. As yet, I haven't discovered the reason for his arrival here. I shall in due course . . . by nightfall.

FLORA Is it necessary?

EDWARD Necessary?

FLORA [*quickly sitting on the right arm of the chair.*] I could show him out now, it wouldn't matter. You've seen him, he's harmless, unfortunate . . . old, that's all. Edward—listen—he's not here through any . . . design, or anything, I know it. I mean, he might just as well stand outside our back gate as anywhere else. He'll move on. I can . . . make him. I promise you. There's no point in upsetting yourself like this. He's an old man, weak in the head . . . that's all. [*Pause.*]

EDWARD You're deluded.

FLORA Edward—

EDWARD [*rising*] You're deluded. And stop calling me Edward.

FLORA You're not still frightened of him?

EDWARD Frightened of him? Of *him*? Have you *seen* him? [*Pause.*]

He's like jelly. A great bullockfat of jelly. He can't see straight. I think as a matter of fact he wears a glass eye. He's almost stone deaf . . . almost . . . not quite. He's very nearly dead on his feet. Why should he frighten me? No, you're a woman, you know nothing. [*Slight pause.*] But he possesses other faculties. Cunning. The man's an impostor and he knows I know it.

FLORA I'll tell you what. Look. Let me speak to him. I'll speak to him.

EDWARD [*quietly*] And I know he knows I know it.

FLORA I'll find out all about him, Edward. I promise you I will.

EDWARD And he knows I know.

FLORA Edward! Listen to me! I can find out all about him, I promise you. I shall go and have a word with him now. I shall . . . get to the bottom of it.

EDWARD You? It's laughable.

FLORA You'll see—he won't bargain for me. I'll surprise him. He'll . . . he'll admit everything.

EDWARD [*softly*] He'll admit everything, will he?

FLORA You wait and see, you just—

EDWARD [*hissing*] What are you plotting?

FLORA I know exactly what I shall—

EDWARD What are you plotting? [*He seizes her arms.*]

FLORA Edward, you're hurting me! [*Pause.*]

[*With dignity.*] I shall wave from the window when I'm ready. Then you can come up. I shall get to the truth of it, I assure you. You're much too heavy-handed, in every way. You should trust your wife more, Edward. You should trust her judgment, and

have a greater insight into her capabilities. A woman . . . a woman will often succeed, you know, where a man must invariably fail.
[*Silence. She goes into the study.*]
Do you mind if I come in?
[*The door closes.*]
Are you comfortable?
[*Pause.*]
Oh, the sun's shining directly on you. Wouldn't you rather sit in the shade?
[*She sits down.*]
It's the longest day of the year today, did you know that? Actually the year has flown. I can remember Christmas and that dreadful frost. And the floods! I hope you weren't here in the floods. We were out of danger up here, of course, but in the valleys whole families I remember drifted away on the current. The country was a lake. Everything stopped. We lived on our own preserves, drank elderberry wine, studied other cultures.
[*Pause.*]
Do you know, I've got a feeling I've seen you before, somewhere. Long before the flood. You were much younger. Yes, I'm really sure of it. Between ourselves, were you ever a poacher? I had an encounter with a poacher once. It was a ghastly rape, the brute. High up on a hillside cattle track. Early spring. I was out riding on my pony. And there on the verge a man lay—ostensibly injured, lying on his front, I remember, possibly the victim of a murderous assault, how was I to know? I dismounted, I went to him, he rose, I fell, my pony took off, down to the valley. I saw the sky through the trees, blue. Up to my ears in mud. It was a desperate battle.
[*Pause.*]
I lost.
[*Pause.*]
Of course, life was perilous in those days. It was my first canter unchaperoned.
[*Pause.*]

Years later, when I was a Justice of the Peace for the county, I had him in front of the bench. He was there for poaching. That's how I know he was a poacher. The evidence though was sparse, inadmissible, I acquitted him, letting him off with a caution. He'd grown a red beard, I remember. Yes. A bit of a stinker.
[*Pause.*]
I say, you are perspiring, aren't you? Shall I mop your brow? With my chiffon? Is it the heat? Or the closeness? Or confined space? Or . . . ?
[*She goes over to him.*] Actually, the day is cooling. It'll soon be dusk. Perhaps it is dusk. May I? You don't mind?
[*Pause. She mops his brow.*]
Ah, there, that's better. And your cheeks. It is a woman's job, isn't it? And I'm the only woman on hand. There.
[*Pause. She leans on the arm of chair.*]
[*Intimately.*] Tell me, have you a woman? Do you like women? Do you ever . . . think about women?
[*Pause.*]
Have you ever . . . stopped a woman?
[*Pause.*]
I'm sure you must have been quite attractive once. [*She sits.*] Not any more, of course. You've got a vile smell. Vile. Quite repellent, in fact.
[*Pause.*]
Sex, I suppose, means nothing to you. Does it ever occur to you that sex is a very vital experience for other people? Really, I think you'd amuse me if you weren't so hideous. You're probably quite amusing in your own way. [*seductively*] Tell me all about love. Speak to me of love.
[*Pause.*]
God knows what you're saying at this very moment. It's quite disgusting. Do you know when I was a girl I loved . . . I loved . . . I simply adored . . . what *have* you got on, for goodness sake? A jersey? It's clogged. Have

you been rolling in mud? [*Slight pause.*] You haven't been rolling in mud, have you? [*She rises and goes over to him.*] And what have you got under your jersey? Let's see. [*Slight pause.*] I'm not tickling you, am I? No. Good . . . Lord, is this a vest? That's quite original. Quite original. [*She sits on the arm of his chair.*] Hmmnn, you're a solid old boy, I must say. Not at all like a jelly. All you need is a bath. A lovely lathery bath. And a good scrub. A lovely lathery scrub. [*Pause.*] Don't you? It will be a pleasure. [*She throws her arms round him.*] I'm going to keep you. I'm going to keep you, you dreadful chap, and call you Barnabas. Isn't it dark, Barnabas? Your eyes, your eyes, your great big eyes.

[*Pause.*]

My husband would never have guessed your name. Never. [*She kneels at his feet. Whispering.*] It's me you were waiting for, wasn't it? You've been standing waiting for me. You've seen me in the woods, picking daisies, in my apron, my pretty daisy apron, and you came and stood, poor creature, at my gate, till death us do part. Poor Barnabas. I'm going to put you to bed. I'm going to put you to bed and watch over you. But first you must have a good whacking great bath. And I'll buy you pretty little things that will suit you. And little toys to play with. On your deathbed. Why shouldn't you die happy?

[*A shout from the hall.*]

EDWARD Well?

[*Footsteps upstage.*]

Well?

FLORA Don't come in.

EDWARD Well?

FLORA He's dying.

EDWARD Dying? He's not dying.

FLORA I tell you, he's very ill.

EDWARD He's not dying! Nowhere near. He'll see you cremated.

FLORA The man is desperately ill!

EDWARD Ill? You lying slut. Get back to your trough!

FLORA Edward . . .

EDWARD [*violently*] To your trough! [*She goes out. Pause.*]

[*Coolly.*] Good evening to you. Why are you sitting in the gloom? Oh, you've begun to disrobe. Too warm? Let's open these windows, then, what?

[*He opens the windows.*]

Pull the blinds.

[*He pulls the blinds.*]

And close . . . the curtains . . . again.

[*He closes the curtains.*]

Ah. Air will enter through the side chinks. Of the blinds. And filter through the curtains. I hope. Don't want to suffocate, do we?

[*Pause.*]

More comfortable? Yes. You look different in darkness. Take off all your togs, if you like. Make yourself at home. Strip to your buff. Do as you would in your own house.

[*Pause.*]

Did you say something?

[*Pause.*]

Did you say something?

[*Pause.*]

Anything? Well then, tell me about your boyhood. Mmnn?

[*Pause.*]

What did you do with it? Run? Swim? Kick the ball? You kicked the ball? What position? Left back? Goalie? First reserve?

[*Pause.*]

I used to play myself. Country house matches, mostly. Kept wicket and batted number seven.

[*Pause.*]

Kept wicket and batted number seven. Man called—Cavendish, I think had something of your style. Bowled left arm over the wicket, always kept his cap on, quite a dab hand at solo whist, preferred a good round of prop and cop to anything else.

[*Pause.*]
On wet days when the field was swamped.
[*Pause.*]
Perhaps you don't play cricket.
[*Pause.*]
Perhaps you never met Cavendish and never played cricket. You look less and less like a cricketeer the more I see of you. Where did you live in those days? God damn it, I'm entitled to know something about you! You're in my blasted house, on my territory, drinking my wine, eating my duck! Now you've had your fill you sit like a hump, a mouldering heap. In my room. My den. I can rem ... [*He stops abruptly.*]
[*Pause.*]
You find that funny? Are you grinning?
[*Pause.*]
[*In disgust.*]   Good Christ, is that a grin on your face? [*Further disgust.*] It's lopsided. It's all—down on one side. You're grinning. It amuses you, does it? When I tell you how well I remember this room, how well I remember this den. [*Muttering.*] Ha. Yesterday now, it was clear, clearly defined, so clearly.
[*Pause.*]
The garden, too, was sharp, lucid, in the rain, in the sun.
[*Pause.*]
My den, too, was sharp, arranged for my purpose ... quite satisfactory.
[*Pause.*]
The house too, was polished, all the banisters were polished, and the stair rods, and the curtain rods.
[*Pause.*]
My desk was polished, and my cabinet.
[*Pause.*]
I was polished. [*Nostalgic.*] I could stand on the hill and look through my telescope at the sea. And follow the path of the three-masted schooner, feeling fit, well aware of my sinews, their suppleness, my arms lifted holding the telescope, steady, easily, no trembling, my aim was perfect, I could pour hot water down the spoon-hole, yes, easily, no difficulty, my grasp firm, my command established, my life was accounted for, I was ready for my excursions to the cliff, down the path to the back gate, through the long grass, no need to watch for the nettles, my progress was fluent, after my long struggling against all kinds of usurpers, disreputables, lists, literally list of people anxious to do me down, and my reputation down, my command was established, all summer I would breakfast, survey my landscape, take my telescope, examine the overhanging of my hedges, pursue the narrow lane past the monastery, climb the hill, adjust the lens [*he mimes a telescope*], watch the progress of the three-masted schooner, my progress was as sure, as fluent ...
[*Pause. He drops his arms.*]
Yes, yes, you're quite right, it is funny.
[*Pause.*]
Laugh your bloody head off! Go on. Don't mind me. No need to be polite.
[*Pause.*]
That's right.
[*Pause.*]
You're quite right, it is funny. I'll laugh with you!
[*He laughs.*]
Ha-ha-ha! Yes! You're laughing with me, I'm laughing with you, we're laughing together!
[*He laughs and stops.*]
[*Brightly.*]   Why did I invite you into this room? That's your next question, isn't it? Bound to be.
[*Pause.*]
Well, why not, you might say? My oldest acquaintance. My nearest and dearest. My kith and kin. But surely correspondence would have been as satisfactory . . . more satisfactory? We could have exchanged postcards,

couldn't we? What? Views, couldn't we? Of sea and land, city and village, town and country, autumn and winter . . . clocktowers . . . museums . . . citadels . . . bridges . . . rivers . . .
[*Pause.*]
Seeing you stand, at the back gate, such close proximity, was not at all the same thing.
[*Pause.*]
What are you doing? You're taking off your balaclava . . . you've decided not to. No, very well then, all things considered, did I then invite you into this room with express intention of asking you to take off your balaclava, in order to determine your resemblance to—some other person? The answer is no, certainly not, I did not, for when I first saw you you wore no balaclava. No head covering of any kind, in fact. You looked quite different without a head—I mean without a hat—I mean without a headcovering, of any kind. In fact every time I have seen you you have looked quite different to the time before.
[*Pause.*]
Even now you look different. Very different.
[*Pause.*]
Admitted that sometimes I viewed you through dark glasses, yes, and sometimes through light glasses, and on other occasions bare eyed, and on other occasions through the bars of the scullery window, or from the roof, the roof, yes in driving snow, or from the bottom of the drive in thick fog, or from the roof again in blinding sun, so blinding, so hot, that I had to skip and jump and bounce in order to remain in one place. Ah, that's good for a guffaw, is it? That's good for a belly laugh? Go on, then. Let it out. Let yourself go, for God's . . . [*He catches his breath.*] You're crying . . .
[*Pause.*]

[*Moved.*] You haven't been laughing. You're crying.
[*Pause.*]
You're weeping. You're shaking with grief. For me. I can't believe it. For my plight. I've been wrong.
[*Pause.*]
[*Briskly.*] Come, come, stop it. Be a man. Blow your nose for goodness sake. Pull yourself together.
[*He sneezes.*]
Ah.
[*He rises. Sneeze.*]
Ah. Fever. Excuse me.
[*He blows his nose.*]
I've caught a cold. A germ. In my eyes. It was this morning. In my eyes. My eyes.
[*Pause. He falls to the floor.*]
Not that I had any difficulty in seeing you, no, no, it was not so much my sight, my sight is excellent—in winter I run about with nothing on but a pair of polo shorts—no, it was not so much any deficiency in my sight as the airs between me and my object —don't weep—the change of air, the currents obtaining in the space between me and my object, the shades they make, the shapes they take, the quivering, the eternal quivering— please stop crying—nothing to do with heat-haze. Sometimes, of course, I would take shelter, shelter to compose myself. Yes, I would seek a tree, a cranny of bushes, erect my canopy and so make shelter. And rest. [*Low murmur.*] And then I no longer heard the wind or saw the sun. Nothing entered, nothing left my nook. I lay on my side in my polo shorts, my fingers lightly in contact with the blades of grass, the earthflowers, the petals of the earthflowers flaking, lying on my palm, the underside of all the great foliage dark, above me, but it is only afterwards I say the foliage was dark, the petals flaking, then I said nothing, I remarked nothing, things happened upon me, then in

my times of shelter, the shades, the petals, carried themselves, carried their bodies upon me, and nothing entered my nook, nothing left it.
[*Pause.*]
But then, the time came. I saw the wind. I saw the wind, swirling, and the dust at my back gate, lifting, and the long grass, scything together . . .
[*Slowly, in horror.*] You *are* laughing. You're laughing. Your face. Your body. [*Overwhelming nausea and horror.*] Rocking . . . gasping . . . rocking . . . shaking . . . rocking . . . heaving . . . rocking . . . You're laughing at me! Aaaaahhhh!
[*The* MATCHSELLER *rises. Silence.*]
You look younger. You look extraordinarily . . . youthful.
[*Pause.*]
You want to examine the garden? It must be very bright, in the moonlight. [*Becoming weaker.*] I would like to join you . . . explain . . . show you . . . the garden . . . explain . . . The plants . . . where I run . . . my track . . . in training . . . I was number one sprinter at Howells . . . when a stripling . . . no more than a stripling . . . licked . . . men twice my strength . . . when a stripling . . . like yourself.
[*Pause.*]

[*Flatly.*]   The pool must be glistening. In the moonlight. And the lawn. I remember it well. The cliff. The sea. The three-masted schooner.
[*Pause.*]
[*With great, final effort—a whisper.*]
Who are you?
FLORA [*off*]   Barnabas?
[*Pause. She enters.*]
Ah, Barnabas. Everything is ready.
[*Pause.*]
I want to show you my garden, your garden. You must see my japonica, my convolvulus . . . my honeysuckle, my clematis.
[*Pause.*]
The summer is coming. I've put up your canopy for you. You can lunch in the garden, by the pool. I've polished the whole house for you.
[*Pause.*]
Take my hand.
[*Pause. The* MATCHSELLER *goes over to her.*]
Yes. Oh, wait a moment.
[*Pause.*]
Edward. Here is your tray.

She crosses to EDWARD *with the tray of matches, and puts it in his hands. Then she and the* MATCHSELLER *start to go out as the curtain falls slowly.*

Harlan Ellison (1934-)

A BOY AND HIS DOG

I

I was out with Blood, my dog. It was his week for annoying me; he kept calling me Albert. He thought that was pretty damned funny. Payson Terhune: ha ha. I'd caught a couple of water rats for him, the big green and ochre ones, and someone's manicured poodle, lost off a leash in one of the downunders; he'd eaten pretty good, but he was cranky. "Come on, son of a bitch," I demanded, "find me a piece of ass."

Blood just chuckled, deep in his dog-throat. "You're funny when you get horny," he said.

Maybe funny enough to kick him up-side his sphincter asshole, that refugee from a dingo-heap.

"Find! I ain't kidding!"

"For shame, Albert. After all I've taught you. Not 'I *ain't* kidding'. I'm *not* kidding."

He knew I'd reached the edge of my patience. Sullenly, he started casting. He sat down on the crumbled remains of the curb, and his eyelids flickered and closed, and his hairy body tensed. After a while he settled down on his front paws, and scraped them forward till he was lying flat, his shaggy head on the outstretched paws. The tense-ness left him and he began trembling, almost the way he trembled just pre-paratory to scratching a flea. It went on that way for almost a quarter of an hour, and finally he rolled over and lay on his back, his naked belly toward the night sky, his front paws folded mantis-like, his hind legs extended and open. "I'm sorry," he said. "There's nothing."

I could have gotten mad and booted him, but I knew he had tried. I wasn't happy about it, I really wanted to get laid, but what could I do? "Okay," I said, with resignation, "forget it."

He kicked himself onto his side and quickly got up.

"What do you want to do?" he asked.

"Not much we *can* do, is there?" I was more than a little sarcastic. He sat down again, at my feet, insolently hum-ble.

I leaned against the melted stub of a lamppost, and thought about girls. It was painful. "We can always go to a show," I said. Blood looked around the street, at the pools of shadow lying in the weed-overgrown craters, and didn't say anything. The whelp was waiting for me to say okay, let's go. He liked movies as much as I did.

"Okay, let's go."

He got up and followed me, his tongue hanging, panting with happi-ness. Go ahead and laugh, you egg-sucker. No popcorn for *you*!

Our Gang was a roverpak that had never been able to cut it simply forag-ing, so they'd opted for comfort and gone a smart way to getting it. They were movie-oriented kids, and they'd taken over the turf where the Metro-pole Theater was located. No one tried to bust their turf, because we all needed the movies, and as long as Our Gang had access to films, and did a better job of keeping the films going, they pro-vided a service, even for solos like me and Blood. *Especially* for solos like us.

They made me check my .45 and the Browning .22 long at the door. There was a little alcove right beside the ticket booth. I bought my tickets first; it cost me a can of Oscar Meyer Philadelphia Scrapple for me, and a tin of sardines for Blood. Then the Our Gang guards with the bren guns motioned me over to the alcove and I checked my heat. I saw water leaking from a broken pipe in the ceiling and I told the checker, a kid with big leathery warts all over his face and lips, to move my weapons where it was dry. He ignored me. "Hey you! Motherfuckin' toad, move my stuff over the other side . . . it goes to rust fast . . . an' it picks up any spots, man, I'll break your bones!"

He started to give me jaw about it, looked at the guards with the brens, knew if they tossed me out I'd lose my price of admission whether I went in or not, but they weren't looking for any action, probably understrength, and gave him the nod to let it pass, to do what I said. So the toad moved my Browning to the other end of the gun rack, and pegged my .45 under it.

Blood and me went into the theater.

"I want popcorn."

"Forget it."

"Come on, Albert. Buy me popcorn."

"I'm tapped out. You can live without popcorn."

"You're just being a shit."

I shrugged: sue me.

We went in. The place was jammed. I was glad the guards hadn't tried to take anything but guns. My spike and knife felt reassuring, lying-up in their oiled sheaths at the back of my neck. Blood found two together, and we moved into the row, stepping on feet. Someone cursed and I ignored him. A Doberman growled. Blood's fur stirred, but he let it pass. There was always *some* hardcase on the muscle, even in neutral ground like the Metropole.

(I heard once about a get-it-on they'd had at the old Loew's Granada, on the South Side. Wound up with ten or twelve rovers and their mutts dead, the theater burned down and a couple of good Cagney films lost in the fire. After that was when the roverpaks had got up the agreement that movie houses were sanctuaries. It was better now, but there was always somebody too messed in the mind to come soft.)

It was a triple feature. "Raw Deal" with Dennis O'Keefe, Claire Trevor, Raymond Burr and Marsha Hunt was the oldest of the three. It'd been made in 1948, seventy-six years ago, god only knows how the damn thing'd hung together all that time; it slipped sprockets and they had to stop the movie all the time to re-thread it. But it was a good movie. About this solo who'd been japped by his roverpak and was out to get revenge. Gangsters, mobs, a lot of punching and fighting. Real good.

The middle flick was a thing made during the Third War, in '07, two years before I was even born, thing called "Smell of a Chink". It was mostly gut-spilling and some nice hand-to-hand. Beautiful scene of skirmisher greyhounds equipped with napalm throwers, jellyburning a Chink town. Blood dug it, even though we'd seen this flick before. He had some kind of phony shuck going that these were ancestors of his,

and *he* knew and *I* knew he was making it up.

"Wanna burn a baby, hero?" I whispered to him. He got the barb and just shifted in his seat, didn't say a thing, kept looking pleased as the dogs worked their way through the town. I was bored stiff.

I was waiting for the main feature.

Finally it came on. It was a beauty, a beaver flick made in the late 1970's. It was called "Big Black Leather Splits". Started right out very good. These two blondes in black leather corsets and boots laced all the way up to their crotches, with whips and masks, got this skinny guy down and one of the chicks sat on his face while the other one went down on him. It got really hairy after that.

All around me there were solos playing with themselves. I was about to jog it a little myself when Blood leaned across and said, real soft, the way he does when he's onto something unusually smelly, "There's a chick in here."

"You're nuts," I said.

"I tell you I smell her. She's in here, man."

Without being conspicuous, I looked around. Almost every seat in the theater was taken with solos or their dogs. If a chick had slipped in there'd have been a riot. She'd have been ripped to pieces before any single guy could have gotten into her. "Where?" I asked, softly. All around me, the solos were beating-off, moaning as the blondes took off their masks and one of them worked the skinny guy with a big wooden ram strapped around her hips.

"Give me a minute," Blood said. He was really concentrating. His body was tense as a wire. His eyes were closed, his muzzle quivering. I let him work.

It was possible. Just maybe possible. I knew that they made really dumb flicks in the downunders, the kind of crap they'd made back in the 1930's and '40's, real clean stuff with even married people sleeping in twin beds. Myrna Loy and George Brent kind of flicks. And I knew that once in a while a chick from one of the really strict middle-class downunders would cumup, to see what a hairy flick was like. I'd heard about it, but it'd never happened in any theater *I'd* ever been in.

And the chances of it happening in the Metropole, particularly, were slim. There was a lot of twisty trade came to the Metropole. Now, understand, I'm not specially prejudiced against guys corning one another . . . hell, I can understand it. There just aren't enough chicks anywhere. But I can't cut the jockey-and-boxer scene because it gets some weak little boxer hanging on you, getting jealous, you have to hunt for him and all he thinks he has to do is bare his ass to get all the work done for him. It's as bad as having a chick dragging along behind. Made for a lot of bad blood and fights in the bigger roverpaks, too. So I just never swung that way. Well, not *never*, but not for a long time.

So with all the twisties in the Metropole, I didn't think a chick would chance it. Be a toss-up who'd tear her apart first: the boxers or the straights.

And if she *was* here, why couldn't any of the other dogs smell her . . . ?"

"Third row in front of us," Blood said. "Aisle seat. Dressed like a solo."

"How's come *you* can whiff her and no other dog's caught her?"

"You forget who I am, Albert."

"I didn't forget, I just don't believe it."

Actually, bottom-line, I guess I *did* believe it. When you'd been as dumb as I'd been and a dog like Blood'd taught me so much, a guy came to believe *everything* he said. You don't argue with your teacher.

Not when he'd taught you how to read and write and add and subtract and everything else they used to know that meant you were smart (but doesn't mean much of anything now, except

it's good to know it, I guess).

(The reading's a pretty good thing. It comes in handy when you can find some canned goods someplace, like in a bombed-out supermarket; makes it easier to pick out stuff you like when the pictures are gone off the labels. Couple of times the reading stopped me from taking canned beets. Shit, I *hate* beets!)

So I guess I *did* believe why he could whiff a maybe chick in there, and no other mutt could. He'd told me all about *that* a million times. It was his favorite story. History he called it. Christ, I'm not *that* dumb! I knew what history was. That was all the stuff that happened before now.

But I liked hearing history straight from Blood, instead of him making me read one of those crummy books he was always dragging in. And *that* particular history was all about him, so he laid it on me over and over, till I knew it by heart . . . no, the word was *rote*. Not *wrote*, like writing, that was something else. I knew it by rote, like it means you got it word-for-word.

And when a mutt teaches you everything you know, and he tells you something rote, I guess finally you *do* believe it. Except I'd never let that leg-lifter know it.

II

What he'd told me rote was:

Over fifty years ago, in Los Angeles, before the Third War even got going completely, there was a man named Buesing who lived in Cerritos. He raised dogs as watchmen and sentries and attackers. Dobermans, Danes, Schnauzers and Japanese akitas. He had one 4-year-old German shepherd bitch named Ginger. She worked for the Los Angeles Police Department's narcotics division. She could smell out marijuana. No matter how well it was hidden. They ran a test on her: there were 25,000 boxes in an auto parts warehouse. Five of them had been planted with marijuana that had been sealed in cellophane, wrapped in tin foil and heavy brown paper, and finally hidden in three separate sealed cartons. Within seven minutes Ginger found all five packages. At the same time that Ginger was working, ninety-two miles further north, in Santa Barbara, cetologists had drawn and amplified dolphin spinal fluid and injected it into Chacma baboons and dogs. Altering surgery and grafting had been done. The first successful product of this cetacean experimentation had been a 2-year-old male Puli named Ahbhu, who had communicated sense-impressions telepathically. Cross-breeding and continued experimentation had produced the first skirmisher dogs, just in time for the Third War. Telepathic over short distances, easily trained, able to track gasoline or troops or poison gas or radiation when linked with their human controllers, they had become the shock commandos of a new kind of war. The selective traits had bred true. Dobermans, greyhounds, akitas, pulis and schnauzers had steadily become more telepathic.

Ginger and Ahbhu had been Blood's ancestors.

He had told me so, a thousand times. Had told me the story just that way, in just those words, a thousand times, as it had been told to him. I'd never believed him till now.

Maybe the little bastard *was* special.

I checked out the solo scrunched down in the aisle seat three rows ahead of me. I couldn't tell a damned thing. The solo had his (her?) cap pulled way down, fleece jacket pulled way up.

"Are you sure?"

"As sure as I can be. It's a girl."

"If it is, she's playing with herself just like a guy."

Blood snickered. "Surprise," he said sarcastically.

The mystery solo sat through "Raw Deal" again. It made sense, if that was a girl. Most of the solos and all of the members of roverpaks left after the beaver flick. The theater didn't fill up much more, it gave the streets time to empty, he/she could make his/her way back to wherever he/she had come from. I sat through "Raw Deal" again myself. Blood went to sleep.

When the mystery solo got up, I gave him/her time to get weapons if any'd been checked, and start away. Then I pulled Blood's big shaggy ear and said, "Let's do it." He slouched after me, up the aisle.

I got my guns and checked the street. Empty.

"Okay, nose," I said, "where'd he go?"

"Her. To the right."

I started off, loading the Browning from my bandolier. I still didn't see anyone moving among the bombed-out shells of the buildings. This section of the city was crummy, really bad shape. But then, with Our Gang running the Metropole, they didn't have to repair anything else to get their livelihood. It was ironic; the Dragons had to keep an entire power plant going to get tribute from the other roverpaks; Ted's Bunch had to mind the reservoir; the Bastinados worked like fieldhands in the marijuana gardens; the Barbados Blacks lost a couple of dozen members every year cleaning out the radiation pits all over the city; and Our Gang only had to run that movie house.

Whoever their leader had been, however many years ago it had been that the roverpaks had started forming out of foraging solos, I had to give it to him: he'd been a flinty sharp mother. He knew what services to deal in.

"She turned off here," Blood said.

I followed him as he began loping, toward the edge of the city and the bluish-green radiation that still flickered from the hills. I knew he was right, then. The only thing out here was the access dropshaft to the downunder. It was a girl, all right.

The cheeks of my ass tightened as I thought about it. I was going to get laid. It had been almost a month, since Blood had whiffed that solo chick in the basement of the Market Basket. She'd been filthy, and I'd gotten the crabs from her, but she'd been a woman, all right, and once I'd tied her down and clubbed her a couple of times she'd been pretty good. She'd liked it, too, even if she did spit on me and tell me she'd kill me if she ever got loose. I left her tied up, just to be sure. She wasn't there when I went back to look, week before last.

"Watch out," Blood said, dodging around a crater almost invisible against the surrounding shadows. Something stirred in the crater.

Trekking across the nomansland I realized why it was that all but a handful of solos or members of roverpaks were guys. The War had killed off most of the girls, and that was the way it always was in wars . . . at least that's what Blood told me. The things getting born were seldom male *or* female, and had to be smashed against a wall as soon as they were pulled out of the mother.

The few chicks who hadn't gone downunder with the middle-classers were hard, solitary bitches like the one in the Market Basket; tough and stringy and just as likely to cut off your meat with a razor blade once they let you get in. Scuffling for a piece of ass had gotten harder and harder, the older I'd gotten.

But every once in a while a chick got tired of being roverpak property, or a raid was got-up by five or six roverpaks and some unsuspecting downunder was taken, or—like this time, yeah—some middle-class chick from a downunder got hot pants to find out what a beaver flick looked like, and cumup.

I was going to get laid. Oh boy, I couldn't wait!

III

Out here it was nothing but empty corpses of blasted buildings. One entire block had been stomped flat, like a steel press had come down from Heaven and given one solid wham! and everything was powder under it. The chick was scared and skittish, I could see that. She moved erratically, looking back over her shoulder and to either side. She knew she was in dangerous country. Man, if she'd only known *how* dangerous.

There was one building standing all alone at the end of the smash-flat block, like it had been missed and chance let it stay. She ducked inside, and a minute later I saw a bobbing light. Flashlight? Maybe.

Blood and I crossed the street and came up into the blackness surrounding the building. It was what was left of a YMCA.

That meant "Young Men's Christian Association." Blood taught me to read.

So what the hell was a young men's christian association? Some times being able to read makes more questions than if you were stupid.

I didn't want her getting out; inside there was as good a place to screw her as any, so I put Blood on guard right beside the steps leading up into the shell, and I went around the back. All the doors and windows had been blown out, of course. It wasn't no big trick getting in. I pulled myself up to the ledge of a window, and dropped down inside. Dark inside. No noise, except the sound of her, moving around on the other side of the old YMCA. I didn't know if she was heeled or not, and I wasn't about to take any chances. I bowslung the Browning and took out the .45 automatic. I didn't have to snap back the action—there was always a slug in the chamber.

I started moving carefully through the room. It was a locker room of some kind. There was glass and debris all over the floor, and one entire row of metal lockers had the paint blistered off their surfaces; the flash blast had caught them through the windows, a lot of years ago. My sneakers didn't make a sound coming through the room.

The door was hanging on one hinge, and I stepped over—through the inverted triangle. I was in the swimming pool area. The big pool was empty, with tiles buckled down at the shallow end. It stunk bad in there; no wonder, there were dead guys, or what was left of them, along one wall. Some lousy cleaner-up had stacked them, but hadn't buried them. I pulled my bandana up around my nose and mouth, and kept moving.

Out the other side of the pool place, and through a little passage with popped light bulbs in the ceiling. I didn't have any trouble seeing. There was moonlight coming through busted windows and a chunk was out of the ceiling. I could hear her real plain now, just on the other side of the door at the end of the passage. I hung close to the wall, and stepped down to the door. It was open a crack, but blocked by a fall of lath and plaster from the wall. It would make noise when I went to pull it open, that was for certain. I had to wait for the right moment.

Flattened against the wall, I checked out what she was doing in there. It was a gymnasium, big one, with climbing ropes hanging down from the ceiling. She had a big square eight-cell flashlight sitting up on the croup of a vaulting horse. There were parallel bars and a horizontal bar about eight feet high, the high-tempered steel all rusty now. There were swinging rings and a trampoline and a big wooden balancing beam. Over to one side there were wall-bars and balancing benches, horizontal and oblique ladders, and a couple of stacks of vaulting boxes. I made a note to remember this joint. It was better for working-out than the jerry-rigged gym I'd set up in an old auto wrecking yard. A guy has to keep in shape, if he's going to be a solo.

She was out of her disguise. Standing there in the skin, shivering. Yeah, it was chilly, and I could see a pattern of chicken-skin all over her. She was maybe five six or seven, with nice tits and kind of skinny legs. She was brushing out her hair. It hung way down the back. The flashlight didn't make it clear enough to tell if she had red hair or chestnut, but it wasn't blonde, which was good, and that was because I dug redheads. She had nice tits, though. I couldn't see her face, the hair was hanging down all smooth and wavy and cut off her profile.

The crap she'd been wearing was thrown around on the floor, and what she was going to put on was up on the vaulting horse. She was standing in little shoes with a kind of a funny heel on them.

I couldn't move. I suddenly realized I couldn't move. She was nice, really nice. I was getting a real big kick out of just standing there and seeing the way her waist fell inward and her hips fell outward, the way the muscles at the side of her tits pulled up when she reached to the top of her head to brush all that hair down. It was really weird, the kick I was getting out of standing and just staring at a chick do that. Kind of very, well, woman stuff. I liked it a lot.

I'd never ever stopped and just looked at a chick like that. All the ones I'd ever seen had been scumbags that Blood had smelled out for me, and I'd snatchn'grabbed them. Or the big chicks in the beaver flicks. Not like this one, kind of soft and very smooth, even with the goose bumps. I could of watched her all night.

She put down the brush, and reached over and took a pair of panties off the pile of clothes, and wriggled into them. Then she got her bra and put it on. I never knew the way chicks did it. She put it on backwards, around her waist, and it had a hook on it. Then she slid it around till the cups were in front, and kind of pulled it up under and scooped herself into it, first one, then the other; then she pulled the straps over her shoulder. She reached for her dress, and I nudged some of the lath and plaster aside, and grabbed the door to give it a yank.

She had the dress up over her head, and her arms up inside the material, and when she stuck her head in, and was all tangled there for a second, I yanked the door and there was a crash as chunks of wood and plaster fell out of the way, and a heavy scraping, and I jumped inside and was on her before she could get out of the dress.

She started to scream, and I pulled the dress off her with a ripping sound, and it all happened for her before she knew what that crash and scrape was all about.

Her face was wild. Just wild. Big eyes: I couldn't tell what color they were because they were in shadow. Real fine features, a wide mouth, little nose, cheekbones just like mine, real high and prominent and a dimple in her right cheek. She stared at me really scared.

And then . . . and this is really weird . . . I felt like I should *say* something to her. I don't know what. Just something. It made me uncomfortable, to see her scared, but what the hell could I do about *that*, I mean, I was going to rape her, after all, and I couldn't very well tell her not to be shrinky about it. She was the one cumup, after all. But even so, I wanted to say hey, don't be scared, I just want to lay you. (That never happened before. I never wanted to *say* anything to a chick, just get in, and that was that.)

But it passed, and I put my leg behind hers and tripped her back, and she went down in a pile. I leveled the .45 at her, and her mouth kind of opened in a little o shape. "Now I'm gonna go

over there and get one of them wrestling mats, so it'll be better, comfortable, uh-huh? You make a move off that floor and I shoot a leg out from under you, and you'll get screwed just the same, except you'll be without a leg." I waited for her to let me know she was onto what I was saying, and she finally nodded real slow, so I kept the automatic on her, and went over to the big dusty stack of mats, and pulled one off.

I dragged it over to her, and flipped it so the cleaner side was up, and used the muzzle of the .45 to maneuver her onto it. She just sat there on the mat, with her hands behind her, and her knees bent, and stared at me.

I unzipped my pants and started pulling them down off one side, when I caught her looking at me real funny. I stopped with the jeans. "What're *you* lookin' at?"

I was mad. I didn't know why I was mad, but I was.

"What's your name?" she asked. Her voice was very soft, and kind of furry, like it came up through her throat that was all lined with fur or something.

She kept looking at me, waiting for me to answer.

"Vic," I said. She looked like she was waiting for more.

"Vic what?"

I didn't know what she meant for a minute, then I did. "Vic. Just Vic. That's all."

"Well, what're your mother and father's names?"

Then I started laughing, and working my jeans down again. "Boy, are you a dumb bitch," I said, and laughed some more. She looked hurt. It made me mad again. "Stop lookin' like that, or I'll bust out your teeth!"

She folded her hands in her lap.

I got the pants down around my ankles. They wouldn't come off over the sneakers. I had to balance on one foot and scuff the sneaker off the other foot. It was tricky, keeping the .45 on her and getting the sneaker off at the same time. But I did it.

I was standing there buck-naked from the waist down and she had sat forward a little, her legs crossed, hands still in her lap. "Get that stuff off," I said.

She didn't move for a second, and I thought she was going to give me trouble. But then she reached around behind and undid the bra. Then she tipped back and slid the panties off her ass.

Suddenly, she didn't look scared any more. She was watching me very close and I could see her eyes were blue now. Now this is the really weird thing . . .

I couldn't do it. I mean, not exactly. I mean, I *wanted* to fuck her, see, but she was all soft and pretty and she kept *looking* at me, and no solo I ever met would believe me, but I heard myself *talking* to her, still standing there like some kind of wetbrain, one sneaker off and jeans down around my ankle. "What's *your* name?"

"Quilla June Holmes."

"That's a weird name."

"My mother says it's not that uncommon, back in Oklahoma."

"That where your folks come from?" She nodded. "Before the Third War."

"They must be pretty old by now."

"They are, but they're okay. I guess."

We were just frozen there, talking to each other. I could tell she was cold, because she was shivering. "Well," I said, sort of getting ready to drop down beside her, "I guess we better—"

Damn it! That damned Blood! Right at that moment he came crashing in from outside. Came skidding through the lath, and plaster, raising dust, slid along on his ass till he got to us. "*Now* what?" I demanded.

"Who're you talking to?" the girl asked.

"Him. Blood."

"*The dog!?!*"

Blood stared at her and then ignored her. He started to say something, but the girl interrupted him, "Then it's true what they say . . . you can all talk to animals . . ."

"You going to listen to her all night, or do you want to hear why I came in?"

"Okay, why're you here?"

"You're in trouble, Albert."

"Come *on*, forget the mickeymouse. What's up?"

Blood twisted his head toward the front door of the YMCA. "Roverpak. Got the building surrounded. I make it fifteen or twenty, maybe more."

"How the hell'd they know we was here?"

Blood looked chagrined. He drooped his head.

"Well?"

"Some other mutt must've smelled her in the theater."

"Great."

"Now what?"

"Now we stand 'em off, that's what. You got any better suggestions?"

"Just one."

I waited. He grinned.

"Pull your pants up."

IV

The girl, this Quilla June, was pretty safe. I made her a kind of a shelter out of wrestling mats, maybe a dozen of them. She wouldn't get hit by a stray bullet, and if they didn't go right for her, they wouldn't find her. I climbed one of the ropes hanging down from the girders and laid out up there with the Browning and a couple of handfuls of reloads. I wished to God I'd had an automatic, a bren or a Thompson. I checked the .45, made sure it was full, with one in the chamber, and set the extra clips down on the girder. I had a clear line-of-fire all around the gym.

Blood was lying in shadow right near the front door. He'd suggested I try and pick off any dogs with the roverpak first, if I could. That would allow him to operate freely.

That was the least of my worries.

I'd wanted to hole up in another room, one with only a single entrance, but I had no way of knowing if the rovers were already in the building, so I did the best I could with what I had. Everything was quiet. Even that Quilla June. It'd taken me valuable minutes to convince her she'd damned well better hole up and not make any noise; she was better off with me than with twenty of *them*. "If you ever wanna see your mommy and daddy again," I warned her. After that she didn't give me no trouble, packing her in with mats.

Quiet.

Then I heard two things, both at the same time. From back in the swimming pool I heard boots crunching plaster. Very soft. And from one side of the front door I heard a tinkle of metal striking wood. So they were going to try a yoke. Well, I was ready.

Quiet again.

I sighted the Browning on the door to the pool room. It was still open from when I'd come through. Figure him at maybe five-ten, and drop the sights a foot and a half, and I'd catch him in the chest. I'd learned long ago you don't try for the head. Go for the widest part of the body: the chest and stomach. The trunk.

Suddenly, outside, I heard a dog bark, and part of the darkness near the front door detached itself and moved inside the gym. Directly opposite Blood. I didn't move the Browning.

The rover at the front door moved a step along the wall, away from Blood. Then he cocked back his arm and threw something—a rock, a piece of metal, something—across the room, to draw fire. I didn't move the Browning.

When the thing he'd thrown hit the floor, two rovers jumped out of the swimming pool door, one on either side of it, rifles down, ready to spray. Before they could open up, I'd squeezed off the first shot, tracked across and put a second shot into the other one. They both went down. Dead hits, right in the heart. Bang, they were down, neither one moved.

The mother by the door turned to split, and Blood was on him. Just like that, out of the darkness, riiiip!

Blood leaped, right over the crossbar of the guy's rifle held at ready, and sank his fangs into the rover's throat. The guy screamed, and Blood dropped, carrying a piece of the guy with him. The guy was making awful bubbling sounds and went down on one knee. I put a slug into his head, and he fell forward.

It went quiet again.

Not bad. Not bad atall atall. Three takeouts and they still didn't know our positions. Blood had fallen back into the murk by the entrance. He didn't say a thing, but I knew what he was thinking; maybe that was three out of seventeen, or three out of twenty, or twenty-two. No way of knowing; we could be faced-off in here for a week and never know if we'd gotten them all, or some, or none. They could go and get poured full again, and I'd find myself run out of slugs and no food and that girl, that Quilla June, crying and making me divide my attention, and daylight—and they'd be still laying out there, waiting till we got hungry enough to do something dumb, or till we ran out of slugs, and then they'd cloud up and rain all over us.

A rover came dashing straight through the front door at top speed, took a leap, hit on his shoulders, rolled, came up going in a different direction and snapped off three rounds into different corners of the room before I could track him with the Browning. By that time he was close enough under me where I didn't have to waste a .22 slug. I picked up the .45 without a sound and blew the back off his head. Slug went in neat, came out and took most of his hair with it. He fell right down.

"Blood! The rifle!"

Came out of the shadows, grabbed it up in his mouth and dragged it over to the pile of wrestling mats in the far corner. I saw an arm poke out from the mass of mats, and a hand grabbed the rifle, dragged it inside. Well, it was at least safe there, till I needed it. Brave little bastard: he scuttled over to the dead rover and started worrying the ammo bandolier off his body. It took him a while; he could have been picked off from the doorway or outside one of the windows, but he did it. Brave little bastard. I had to remember to get him something good to eat, when we got out of this. I smiled, up there in the darkness: *if* we get out of this, I wouldn't have to worry about getting him something tender. It was lying all over the floor of that gymnasium.

Just as Blood was dragging the bandolier back into the shadows, two of them tried it with their dogs. They came through a ground floor window, one after another, hitting and rolling and going in opposite directions, as the dogs—a mother-ugly akita, big as a house, and a Doberman bitch the color of a turd—shot through the front door and split in the unoccupied two directions. I caught one of the dogs, the akita, with the .45 and it went down thrashing. The Doberman was all over Blood.

But firing, I'd given away my position. One of the rovers fired from the hip and .30–06 soft-nosed slugs spanged off the girders around me. I dropped the automatic, and it started to slip off the girder as I reached for the Browning. I made a grab for the .45 and that was the only thing saved me. I fell forward to clutch at it, it slipped away and hit the gym floor with a crash, and the rover fired at where I'd been. But I

was flat on the girder, arm dangling, and the crash startled him. He fired at the sound, and right at that instant I heard another shot, from a Winchester, and the other rover, who'd made it safe into the shadows, fell forward holding a big pumping hole in his chest. That Quilla June had shot him, from behind the mats.

I didn't even have time to figure out what the fuck was happening . . . Blood was rolling around with the Doberman and the sounds they were making were awful . . . the rover with the .30–06 chipped off another shot and hit the muzzle of the Browning, protruding over the side of the girder, and wham it was gone, falling down. I was naked up there without clout, and the son-ofabitch was hanging back in shadow waiting for me.

Another shot from the Winchester, and the rover fired right into the mats. She ducked back behind, and I knew I couldn't count on her for anything more. But I didn't need it; in that second, while he was focused on her, I grabbed the climbing rope, flipped myself over the girder, and howling like a burnpit-screamer, went sliding down, feeling the rope cutting my palms. I got down far enough to swing, and kicked off. I swung back and forth, whipping my body three different ways each time, swinging out and over, way over, each time. The sonofabitch kept firing, trying to track a trajectory, but I kept spinning out of his line of fire. Then he was empty, and I kicked back as hard as I could, and came zooming in toward his corner of shadows, and let loose all at once and went ass-over-end into the corner, and there he was, and I went right into him and he spanged off the wall, and I was on top of him, digging my thumbs into his eye-sockets. He was screaming and the dogs were screaming and that girl was screaming, and I pounded the motherfucker's head against the floor till he stopped moving, then I grabbed up the empty .30–06 and whipped his head till I knew he wasn't gonna give me no more aggravation.

Then I found the .45 and shot the Doberman.

Blood got up and shook himself off. He was cut up bad. "Thanks," he mumbled, and went over and lay down in the shadows to lick himself off.

I went and found that Quilla June, and she was crying. About all the guys we'd killed. Mostly about the one *she'd* killed. I couldn't get her to stop bawling, so I cracked her across the face, and told her she'd saved my life, and that helped some.

Blood came dragassing over. "How're we going to get out of this, Albert?"

"Let me think."

I thought and knew it was hopeless. No matter how many we got, there'd be more. And it was a matter of *macho* now. Their honor.

"How about a fire?" Blood suggested.

"Get away while it's burning?" I shook my head. "They'll have the place staked-out all around. No good."

"What if we don't leave? What if we burn up with it?"

I looked at him. Brave . . . and smart as hell.

V

We gathered all the lumber and mats and scaling ladders and vaulting boxes and benches and anything else that would burn, and piled the garbage against a wooden divider at one end of the gym. Quilla June found a can of kerosene in a storeroom, and we set fire to the whole damn pile. Then we followed Blood to the place he'd found for us. The boiler room way down under the YMCA. We all climbed into the empty boiler, and dogged down the door, leaving a release vent open for air. We had one mat in there with us, and all the ammo we could carry, and the extra rifles and sidearms the rovers'd had on them.

"Can you catch anything?" I asked Blood.

"A little. Not much. I'm reading one guy. The building's burning good."

"You be able to tell when they split?"

"Maybe. *If* they split."

I settled back. Quilla June was shaking from all that had happened. "Just take it easy," I told her. "By morning the place'll be down around our ears and they'll go through the rubble and find a lot of dead meat and maybe they won't look too hard for a chick's body. And everything'll be all right . . . if we don't get choked off in here."

She smiled, very thin, and tried to look brave. She was okay, that one. She closed her eyes and settled back on the mat and tried to sleep. I was beat. I closed my eyes, too.

"Can you handle it?" I asked Blood.

"I suppose. You better sleep."

I nodded, eyes still closed, and fell on my side. I was out before I could think about it.

When I came back, I found the girl, that Quilla June, snuggled up under my armpit, her arm around my waist, dead asleep. I could hardly breathe. It was like a furnace; hell, it *was* a furnace. I reached out a hand and the wall of the boiler was so damned hot I couldn't touch it. Blood was up on the mattress with us. That mat had been the only thing'd kept us from being singed good. He was asleep, head buried in his paws. She was aleep, still naked.

I put a hand on her tit. It was warm. She stirred and cuddled into me closer. I got a hard on.

Managed to get my pants off, and rolled on top of her. She woke up fast when she felt me pry her legs apart, but it was too late by then. "Don't . . . *stop* . . . what are you doing . . . no, don't . . ."

But she was half-asleep, and weak, and I don't think she really wanted to fight me anyhow.

She cried when I broke her, of

course, but after that it was okay. There was blood all over the wrestling mat. And Blood just kept sleeping.

It was really different. Usually, when I'd get Blood to track something down for me, it'd be grab it and punch it and get away fast before something bad could happen. But when she came, she rose up off the mat, and hugged me around the back so hard I thought she'd crack my ribs, and then she settled back down slow slow slow, like I do when I'm doing leg-lifts in the makeshift gym I rigged in the auto wrecking yard. And her eyes were closed, and she was relaxed looking. And happy. I could tell.

We did it a lot of times, and after a while it was her idea, but I didn't say no. And then we lay out side-by-side and talked.

She asked me about how it was with Blood, and I told her how the skirmisher dogs had gotten telepathic, and how they'd lost the ability to hunt food for themselves, so the solos and rover-paks had to do it for them, and how dogs like Blood were good at finding chicks for solos like me. She didn't say anything to that.

I asked her about what it was like where she lived, in one of the down-unders.

"It's nice. But it's always very quiet. Everyone is very polite to everyone else. It's just a small town."

"Which one you live in?"

"Topeka. It's real close to here."

"Yeah, I know. The access dropshaft is only about half a mile from here. I went out there once, to take a look around."

"Have you ever been in a down-under?"

"No. But I don't guess I want to be, either."

"Why? It's very nice. You'd like it."

"Shit."

"That's very crude."

"*I'm* very crude."

"Not all the time."

I was getting mad. "Listen, you ass, what's the matter with you? I grabbed you and pushed you around, I raped you half a dozen times, so what's so good about me, huh? What's the matter with you, don't you even have enough smarts to know when somebody's—"

She was smiling at me. "I didn't mind. I liked doing it. Want to do it again?"

I was really shocked. I moved away from her. "What the hell is wrong with you? Don't you know that a chick from a downunder like you can be really mauled by solos? Don't you know chicks get warnings from their parents in the downunders, 'Don't cumup, you'll get snagged by them dirty, hairy, slobbering solos!' Don't you know that?"

She put her hand on my leg and started moving it up, the fingertips just brushing my thigh. I got another hard on. "My parents never said that about solos," she said. Then she pulled me over her again, and kissed me and I couldn't stop from getting in her again.

God, it just went on like that for hours. After a while Blood turned around and said, "I'm not going to keep pretending I'm asleep. I'm hungry. And I'm hurt."

I tossed her off me—she was on top by this time—and examined him. The Doberman had taken a good chunk out of his right ear, and there was a rip right down his muzzle, and blood-matted fur on one side. He was a mess. "Jesus, man, you're a mess," I said.

"You're no savory rose garden yourself, Albert!" he snapped. I pulled my hand back.

"Can we get out of here?" I asked him.

He cast around, and then shook his head. "I can't get any readings. Must be a pile of rubble on top of this boiler. I'll have to go out and scout."

We kicked that around for a while, and finally decided if the building was razed, and had cooled a little, the rover-pak would have gone through the ashes by now. The fact that they hadn't tried the boiler indicated that we were prob-ably buried pretty good. Either that, or the building was still smoldering over-head. In which case, they'd still be out there, waiting to sift the remains.

"Think you can handle it, the condi-tion you're in?"

"I guess I'll *have* to, won't I?" Blood said. He was really surly. "I mean, what with you busy coitusing your brains out, there won't be much left for staying alive, will there?"

I sensed real trouble with him. He didn't like Quilla June. I moved around him and undogged the boiler hatch. It wouldn't open. So I braced my back against the side, and jacked my legs up, and gave it a slow, steady shove.

Whatever had fallen against it from outside, resisted for a minute, then started to give, then tumbled away with a crash. I pushed the door open all the way, and looked out. The upper floors had fallen in on the basement, but by the time they'd given, they'd been mostly cinder and lightweight rubble. Everything was smoking out there. I could see daylight through the smoke.

I slipped out, burning my hands on the outside lip of the hatch. Blood fol-lowed. He started to pick his way through the debris. I could see that the boiler had been almost completely cov-ered by the gunk that had dropped from above. Chances were good the roverpak had taken a fast look, figured we'd been fried, and moved on. But I wanted Blood to run a recon, anyway. He started off, but I called him back. He came.

"What is it?"

I looked down at him. "I'll tell you what it is, man. You're acting very shitty."

"Sue me."

"Goddamit, dog, what's got your ass up?"

"Her. That nit chick you've got in there."

"So what? Big deal . . . I've had chicks before."

"Yeah, but never any that hung on like this one. I warn you, Albert, she's going to make trouble."

"Don't be dumb!" He didn't reply. Just looked at me with anger, and then scampered off to check out the scene. I crawled back inside and dogged the hatch. She wanted to make it again. I said I didn't want to; Blood had brought me down. I was bugged. And I didn't know which one to be pissed off at.

But God she was pretty.

She kind of pouted, and settled back with her arms wrapped around her. "Tell me some more about the down-under," I said.

At first she was cranky, wouldn't say much, but after a while she opened up and started talking freely. I was learn-ing a lot. I figured I could use it some time, maybe.

There were only a couple of hundred downunders in what was left of the United States and Canada. They'd been sunk on the sites of wells or mines or other kinds of deep holes. Some of them, out in the west, were in natural cave formations. They went way down, maybe two to five miles. They were like big caissons, stood on end. And the peo-ple who'd settled them were squares of the worst kind. Southern Baptists, Fundamentalists, lawanorder goofs, real middle-class squares with no taste for the wild life. And they'd gone back to a kind of life that hadn't existed for a hundred and fifty years. They'd gotten the last of the scientists to do the work, invent the how and why, and then they'd run them out. They didn't want any progress, they didn't want any dis-sent, they didn't want anything that would make waves. They'd had enough of that. The best time in the world had been just before the First War, and they figured if they could keep it like that, they could live quiet lives and sur-vive. Shit! I'd go nuts in one of the downunders.

Quilla June smiled, and snuggled up again, and this time I didn't turn her off. She started touching me again, down there and all over, and then she said, "Vic?"

"Uh-huh."

"Have you ever been in love?"

"What?"

"In love. Have you ever been in love with a girl?"

"Well, I damn well guess I haven't!"

"Do you know what love is?"

"Sure. I guess I do."

"But if you've never been in love . . . ?"

"Don't be dumb. I mean, I've never had a bullet in the head, and I know I wouldn't like it."

"You don't know what love is, I'll bet."

"Well, if it means living in a down-under, I guess I just don't wanna find out." We didn't go on with the conversation much after that. She pulled me down and we did it again. And when it was over, I heard Blood scratching at the boiler. I opened the hatch and he was standing out there. "All clear," he said.

"You sure?"

"Yeah, yeah, I'm sure. Put your pants on," he said it with a sneer in the tone, "and come on out here. We have to talk some stuff."

I looked at him, and he wasn't kidding. I got my jeans and sneakers on, and climbed down out of the boiler.

He trotted ahead of me, away from the boiler, over some blacksoot beams, and outside the gym. It was down. Looked like a rotted stump tooth.

"Now what's lumbering you?" I asked him.

He scampered up on a chunk of concrete till he was almost nose-level with me.

"You're going dumb on me. Vic."

I knew he was serious. No Albert shit, straight Vic. "How so?"

"Last night, man. We could have cut out of there and left her for them. *That* would have been smart."

"I wanted her."

"Yeah, I know. That's what I'm talking about. It's today now, not last night. You've had her about a half a hundred times. Why're we hanging around?"

"I want some more."

Then he got angry. "Yeah, well, listen, chum . . . *I* want a few things myself. I want something to eat, and I want to get rid of this pain in my side, and I want away from this turf. Maybe they *don't* give up this easily."

"Take it easy. We can handle all that. Don't mean she can't go with us."

"*Doesn't* mean," he corrected me. "And so *that's* the new story. Now we travel three, is that right?"

I was getting *tres* uptight myself. "You're starting to sound like a damn poodle!"

"And you're starting to sound like a boxer."

I hauled back to crack him one. He didn't move. I dropped the hand. I'd never hit Blood. I didn't want to start now.

"Sorry," he said, softly.

"That's okay."

But we weren't looking at each other.

"Vic, man, you've got a responsibility to me, you know."

"You don't have to tell me that."

"Well, I guess maybe I do. Maybe I have to remind you of some stuff. Like the time that burnpit-screamer came up out of the street and made a grab for you."

I shuddered. The motherfucker'd been green. Righteous stone green, glowing like fungus. My gut heaved, just thinking.

"And I went for him, right?"

I nodded. Right, mutt, right.

"And I could have been burned bad, and died, and that would've been all of it for me, right or wrong, isn't that true?" I nodded again. I was getting pissed off proper. I didn't like being made to feel guilty. It was a fifty-fifty with Blood and me. He knew that. "But I did it, right?" I remembered the way the green thing had screamed. Christ, it was like ooze and eyelashes.

"Okay, okay, don't hanger me."

"*Harangue*, not hanger."

"Well WHATEVER!" I shouted. "Just knock off the crap, or we can forget the whole fucking arrangement!"

Then Blood blew. "Well, maybe we *should*, you simple *dumb putz!*"

"What's a *putz*, you little turd . . . is that something bad . . . yeah, it must be . . . you watch your fucking mouth, son of a bitch, I'll kick your ass!"

We sat there and didn't talk for fifteen minutes. Neither one of us knew which way to go.

Finally, I backed off a little. I talked soft and I talked slow. I was about up to here with him, but told him I was going to do right by him, like I always had, and he threatened me, saying I'd damned well better because there were a couple of very hip solos making it around the city, and they'd be delighted to have a sharp tail-scent like him. I told him I didn't like being threatened, and he'd better watch his fucking step or I'd break his leg. He got furious and stalked off. I said screw you and went back to the boiler to take it out on that Quilla June again.

But when I stuck my head inside the boiler, she was waiting, with a pistol one of the dead rovers had supplied. She hit me good and solid over the right eye with it, and I fell straight forward across the hatch, and was out cold.

VI

"I told you she was no good." He watched me as I swabbed out the cut with disinfectant from my kit, and painted the gash with iodine. He smirked when I flinched.

I put away the stuff, and rummaged around in the boiler, gathering up all the spare ammo I could carry, and ditching the Browning in favor of the heavier .30–06. Then I found something that must've slipped out of her clothes.

It was a little metal plate, about 3 inches long and an inch-and-a-half high. It had a whole string of numbers on it, and there were holes in it, in random patterns. "What's this?" I asked Blood.

He looked at it, sniffed it.

"Must be an identity card of some kind. Maybe it's what she used to get out of the downunder."

That made my mind up.

I jammed it in a pocket and started out. Toward the access dropshaft.

"Where the hell are you going?" Blood yelled after me.

"Come on back, you'll get killed out there!

"I'm hungry, dammit! I'm wooded.

"Albert, you simpleton! Come back here!"

I kept right on walking. I was gonna find that bitch and brain her. Even if I had to go downunder to find her.

It took me an hour to walk to the access downshaft leading down to Topeka. I thought I saw Blood following, but hanging back a ways. I didn't give a damn. I was mad.

Then, there it was. A tall, straight, featureless pillar of shining black metal. It was maybe twenty feet in diameter, perfectly flat on top, disappearing straight into the ground. It was a cap, that was all. I walked straight up to it, and fished around in the pocket for that metal card. Then something was tugging at my right pants leg.

"Listen, you moron, you can't go down there!"

I kicked him off, but he came right back.

"Listen to me!"

I turned around and stared at him.

Blood sat down; the powder puffed up around him. "Albert . . ."

"My name is Vic, you little eggsucker."

"Okay, okay, no fooling around. Vic." His tone softened. "Vic. Come on, man." He was trying to get through to me. I was really boiling, but he was trying to make sense. I shrugged, and crouched down beside him.

"Listen, man," Blood said, "this chick has bent you way out of shape. You *know* you can't go down there. It's all square and settled and they know everyone; they hate solos. Enough rover-paks have raided downunder and raped their women, and stolen their food, they'll have defenses set up. They'll *kill* you, man!"

"What the hell do you care? You're always saying you'd be better off without me." He sagged at that.

"Vic, we've been together almost three years. Good and bad. But this can be the worst. I'm scared, man. Scared you won't come back. And I'm hungry, and I'll have to go find some dude who'll take me on . . . and you know most solos are in paks now, I'll be low mutt. I'm not that young any more. And I'm hurt pretty bad."

I could dig it. He was talking sense. But all I could think of was how that bitch, that Quilla June, had rapped me. And then there were images of her soft tits, and the way she made little sounds when I was in her, and I shook my head, and knew I had to go get even.

"I got to do it, Blood. I got to."

He breathed deep, and sagged a little more. He knew it was useless. "You don't even see what she's done to you, Vic. That metal card, it's too easy, as if she *wanted* you to follow."

I got up. "I'll try to get back quick. Will you wait . . . ?"

He was silent a long while, and I waited. Finally, he said, "For a while. Maybe I'll be here, maybe not."

I understood. I turned around and started walking around the pillar of black metal. Finally, I found a slot in the pillar, and slipped the metal card into it. There was a soft humming sound, then a section of the pillar di-lated. I hadn't even seen the lines of

the sections. A circle opened and I took a step through. I turned and there was Blood, watching me. We looked at each other, all the while that pillar was humming.

"So long, Vic."

"Take care of yourself, Blood."

"Hurry back."

"Do my best.'

"Yeah. Right."

Then I turned around and stepped inside. The access portal irised closed behind me.

VII

I should have known. I should have suspected. Sure, every once in a while a chick came up to see what it was like on the surface, what had happened to the cities; sure, it happened. Why, I'd believed her when she'd told me, cud-dled up beside me in that steaming boiler, that she'd wanted to see what it was like when a girl did it with a guy, that all the flicks she'd seen in Topeka were sweet and solid and dull, and the girls in her school'd talked about beaver flicks, and one of them had a little eight-page comic book and she'd read it with wide eyes . . . sure, I'd believed her. It was logical. I should have suspected something when she left that metal i.d. plate behind. It was too easy. Blood'd tried to tell me. Dumb? Yeah!

The second that access iris swirled closed behind me, the humming got louder, and some cool light grew in the walls. Wall. It was a circular compart-ment with only two sides to the wall: *in*side and *out*side. The wall pulsed up light and the humming got louder, and the floor I was standing on dilated just the way the outside port had done. But I was standing there, like a mouse in a cartoon, and as long as I didn't look down I was cool, I wouldn't fall.

Then I started settling. Dropped through the floor, the iris closed over-head, I was dropping down the tube, picking up speed but not too much, just dropping steadily. Now I knew what a dropshaft was.

Down and down I went and every once in a while I'd see something like 10 LEV or ANTIPOLL 55 or BREEDER-CON or PUMP SE 6 on the wall, faintly I could make out the sectioning of an iris . . . but I never stopped dropping.

Finally, I dropped all the way to the bottom and there was TOPEKA CITY LIMITS POP. 22,860 on the wall, and I settled down without any strain, bending a little from the knees to cushion the impact, but even that wasn't much.

I used the metal plate again, and the iris—a much bigger one this time—swirled open, and I got my first look at a downunder.

It stretched away in front of me, twenty miles to the dim shining horizon of tin can metal where the wall behind me curved and curved and curved till it made one smooth, encircling circuit and came back around around around to where I stood, staring at it. I was down at the bottom of a big metal tube that stretched up to a ceiling an eighth of a mile overhead, twenty miles across. And in the bottom of that tin can, someone had built a town that looked for all the world like a photo out of one of the water-logged books in the library on the surface. I'd seen a town like this in the books. Just like this. Neat little houses, and curvy little streets, and trimmed lawns, and a business section and everything else that a Topeka would have.

Except a sun, except birds, except clouds, except rain, except snow, except cold, except wind, except ants, except dirt, except mountains, except oceans, except big fields of grain, except stars, except the moon, except forests, except animals running wild, except . . .

Except freedom.

They were canned down here, like dead fish. Canned.

I felt my throat tighten up. I wanted to get out. Out! I started to tremble, my hands were cold and there was sweat on my forehead. This had been insane, coming down here. I had to get out. *Out!*

I turned around, to get back in the dropshaft, and then it grabbed me.

That bitch Quilla June! I shoulda suspected!

The thing was low, and green, and boxlike, and had cables with mittens on the ends instead of arms, and it rolled on tracks, and it grabbed me.

It hoisted me up on its square flat top, holding me with them mittens on the cables, and I couldn't move, except to try kicking at the big glass eye in the front, but it didn't do any good. It didn't bust. The thing was only about four feet high, and my sneakers almost reached the ground, but not quite, and it started moving off into Topeka, hauling me along with it.

People were all over the place. Sitting in rockers on their front porches, raking their lawns, hanging around the gas station, sticking pennies in gumball machines, painting a white stripe down the middle of the road, selling newspapers on a corner, listening to an oompah band on a shell in a park, playing hopscotch and pussy-in-the-corner, polishing a fire engine, sitting on benches, reading, washing windows, pruning bushes, tipping hats to ladies, collecting milk bottles in wire carrying racks, grooming horses, throwing a stick for a dog to retrieve, diving into a communal swimming pool, chalking vegetable prices on a slate outside a grocery, walking hand-in-hand with a girl, all of them watching me go past on that metal motherfucker.

I could hear Blood speaking, saying just what he'd said before I'd entered the dropshaft: *It's all square and settled and they know everyone; they hate solos. Enough roverpaks have raided*

*downunders and raped their women, and
stolen their food, they'll have defenses
set up. They'll kill you, man!*

Thanks, mutt.

Goodbye.

VIII

The green box tracked through the
business section and turned in at a
shopfront with the words BETTER
BUSINESS BUREAU on the window.
It rolled right inside the open door, and
there were half a dozen men and old
men and very old men in there, waiting for me. Also a couple of women.
The green box stopped.

One of them came over and took the
metal plate out of my hand. He looked
at it, then turned around and gave it
to the oldest of the old men, a withered
toad wearing baggy pants and a green
eyeshade and garters that held up the
sleeves of his striped shirt. "Quilla June,
Lew," the guy said to the old man. Lew
took the metal plate and put it in the
top left drawer of a rolltop desk. "Better take his guns, Aaron," the old coot
said. And the guy who'd taken the plate
cleaned me.

"Let him loose, Aaron," Lew said.

Aaron stepped around the back of
the green box and something clicked,
and the cable-mittens sucked back inside the box, and I got down off the
thing. My arms were numb where the
box had held me. I rubbed one, then
the other, and I glared at them.

"Now, boy . . ." Lew started.

"Suck wind, asshole!"

The women blanched. The men
tightened their faces.

"I told you it wouldn't work," another
of the old men said to Lew.

"Bad business, this," said one of the
younger ones.

Lew leaned forward in his straight-
back chair and pointed a crumbled finger at me. "Boy, you better be nice."

"I hope all your fuckin' children are
hare-lipped!"

"This is no good, Lew!" another man
said.

"Guttersnipe," a woman with a beak
snapped.

Lew stared at me. His mouth was a
nasty little black line. I knew the son-
ofabitch didn't have a tooth in his
crummy head that wasn't rotten and
smelly. He stared at me with vicious
little eyes. God he was ugly, like a toad
ready to snaffle a fly off the wall with
his tongue. He was getting set to say
something I wouldn't like. "Aaron,
maybe you'd better put the sentry back
on him." Aaron moved to the green box.

"Okay, hold it," I said, holding up
my hand.

Aaron stopped, looked at Lew, who
nodded. Then Lew leaned real far
forward again, and aimed that bird-claw
at me. "You ready to behave yourself,
son?"

"Yeah, I guess."

"You'd better be dang sure."

"Okay. I'm *dang* sure. Also *fuckin'*
sure!"

"And you'll watch your mouth."

I didn't reply. Old coot.

"You're a bit of an experiment for
us, boy. We tried to get one of you
down here other ways. Sent up some
good folks to capture one of you little
scuts, but they never came back. Fig-
gered it was best to lure you down to
us."

I sneered. That Quilla June. I'd take
care of her!

One of the women, a little younger
than Bird-Beak, came forward and
looked into my face. "Lew, you'll never
get this one to cow-tow. He's a filthy
little killer. Look at those eyes."

"How'd you like the barrel of a rifle
jammed up your ass, bitch?" She
jumped back. Lew was angry again.
"Sorry," I said, real quickly, "I don't
like bein' called names. *Macho*, y'know?"

He settled back and snapped at the

woman. "Mez, leave him alone. I'm tryin' to talk a bit of sense here. You're only making it worse."

Mez went back and sat with the others. Some Better Business Bureau these creeps were!

"As I was saying, boy: you're an experiment for us. We've been down here in Topeka close to twenty years. It's nice down here. Quiet, orderly, nice people, who respect each other, no crime, respect for the elders, and just all around a good place to live. We're growin' and we're prosperin'."

I waited.

"But, well, we find now that some of our folks can't have no more babies, and the women that do, they have mostly girls. We need some men. Certain special kind of men."

I started laughing. This was too good to be true. They wanted me for stud service. I couldn't stop laughing.

"Crude!" one of the women said, scowling.

"This's awkward enough for us, boy, don't make it no harder." Lew was embarrassed.

Here I'd spent most of Blood's and my time aboveground hunting up tail, and down here they wanted me to service the local ladyfolk. I sat down on the floor and laughed till tears ran down my cheeks.

Finally, I got up and said, "Sure. Okay. But if I do, there's a couple of things *I* want."

Lew looked at me close.

"The first thing I want is that Quilla June. I'm gonna fuck her blind, and then I'm gonna bang her on the head the way she did me!"

They huddled for a while, then came out and Lew said, "We can't tolerate any violence down here, but I s'pose Quilla June's as good a place to start as any. She's capable, isn't she, Ira?"

A skinny, yellow-skinned man nodded. He didn't look happy about it. Quilla June's old man, I bet.

"Well, let's get started," I said. "Line 'em up." I started to unzip my jeans.

The women screamed, the men grabbed me, and they hustled me off to a boarding house where they gave me a room, and they said I should get to know Topeka a little bit before I went to work, because it was, uh, er, well, awkward, and they had to get the folks in town to accept what was going to have to be done . . . on the assumption, I suppose, that if I worked out okay, they'd import a few more young bulls from aboveground, and turn us loose.

So I spent some time in Topeka, getting to know the folks, seeing what they did, how they lived. It was nice, real nice. They rocked in rockers on the front porches, they raked their lawns, they hung around the gas station, they stuck pennies in gumball machines, they painted white stripes down the middle of the road, they sold newspapers on the corners, they listened to oompah bands on a shell in the park, they played hopscotch and pussy-in-the-corner, they polished fire engines, they sat on benches reading, they washed windows and pruned bushes, they tipped their hats to ladies, they collected milk bottles in wire carrying racks, they groomed horses and threw sticks for their dogs to retrieve, they dove into the communal swimming pool, they chalked vegetable prices on a slate outside the grocery, they walked hand-in-hand with some of the ugliest chicks I've ever seen, *and they bored the ass off me.*

Inside a week I was ready to scream.

I could feel that tin can closing in on me.

I could feel the weight of the earth over me.

They ate artificial shit: artificial peas and fake meat and make-believe chicken and ersatz corn and bogus bread and it all tasted like chalk and dust to me.

Polite? Christ, you could puke from the lying, hypocritical crap they called civility. Hello Mr. This and Hello Mrs. That. And how are you? And how is little Janie? And how is business? And are you going to the sodality meeting Thursday? And I started gibbering in my room at the boarding house.

The clean, sweet, neat, lovely way they lived was enough to kill a guy. No wonder the men couldn't get it up and make babies that had balls instead of slots.

The first few days, everyone watched me like I was about to explode and cover their nice whitewashed fences with shit. But after a while, they got used to seeing me. Lew took me over to the Mercantile, and got me fitted out with a pair of bib overalls and a shirt that any solo could've spotted a mile away. That Mez, that dippy bitch who'd called me a killer, she started hanging around, finally said she wanted to cut my hair, make me look civilized. But I was hip to where she was at. Wasn't a bit of the mother in her.

"What'sa'matter, cunt," I pinned her. "Your old man isn't taking care of you?"

She tried to stick her fist in her mouth, and I laughed like a loon. "Go cut off *his* balls, baby. My hair stays the way it is." She cut and run. Went like she had a diesel tail-pipe.

It went on like that for a while. Me just walking around, them coming and feeding me, keeping all their young meat out of my way till they got the town stacked-away for what was coming with me.

Jugged like that, my mind wasn't right for a while. I got all claustrophobed, clutched, went and sat under the porch in the dark, at the rooming house. Then that passed, and I got piss-mean, snapped at them, then surly, then quiet, then just mud dull. Quiet.

Finally, I started getting hip to the possibilities of getting out of there. It began with me remembering the poodle I'd fed Blood one time. It had to come

from a downunder. And it couldn't of got up through the dropshaft. So that meant there were other ways out.

They gave me pretty much the run of the town, as long as I kept my manners around me and didn't try anything sudden. That green sentry box was always somewhere nearby.

So I found the way out. Nothing so spectacular; it just had to be there, and I found it.

Then I found out where they kept my weapons, and I was ready. Almost.

IX

It was a week to the day when Aaron and Lew and Ira came to get me. I was pretty goofy by that time. I was sitting out on the back porch of the boarding house, smoking a corncob pipe with my shirt off, catching some sun. Except there wasn't no sun. Goofy.

They came around the house. "Morning, Vic," Lew greeted me. He was hobbling along with a cane, the old fart. Aaron gave me a big smile. The kind you'd give a big black bull about to stuff his meat into a good breed cow. Ira had a look that you could chip off and use in your furnace.

"Well, howdy, Lew. Mornin' Aaron, Ira."

Lew seemed right pleased by that.

Oh, you lousy bastards, just you wait!

"You 'bout ready to go meet your first lady?"

"Ready as I'll ever be, Lew," I said, and got up.

"Cool smoke, ain't it?" Aaron said.

I took the corncob out of my mouth. "Pure dee-light." I smiled. I hadn't even lit the fucking thing.

They walked me over to Marigold Street and as we came up on a little house with yellow shutters and a white picket fence, Lew said, "This's Ira's house. Quilla June is his daughter."

"Well, land sakes," I said, wide-eyed.

Ira's lean jaw muscles jumped.

We went inside.

Quilla June was sitting on the settee with her mother, an older version of her, pulled thin as a withered muscle. "Miz Holmes," I said, and made a little curtsy. She smiled. Strained, but smiled.

Quilla June sat with her feet right together, and her hands folded in her lap. There was a ribbon in her hair. It was blue.

Matched her eyes.

Something went thump in my gut.

"Quilla June," I said.

She looked up. "Mornin', Vic."

Then everyone sort of stood around looking awkward, and finally Ira began yapping and yipping about get in the bedroom and get this unnatural filth over with so they could go to Church and pray the Good Lord wouldn't Strike All Of Them Dead with a bolt of lightning in the ass, or some crap like that.

So I put out my hand, and Quilla June reached for it without looking up, and we went in the back, into a small bedroom, and she stood there with her head down.

"You didn't tell 'em, did you?" I asked.

She shook her head.

And suddenly, I didn't want to kill her at all. I wanted to hold her. Very tight. So I did. And she was crying into my chest, and making little fists beating on my back, and then she was looking up at me and running her words all together: "Oh, Vic, I'm sorry, so sorry, I didn't mean to, I had to, I was sent out to, I was so scared, and I love you and now they've got you down here, and it isn't dirty, is it, it isn't the way my Poppa says it is, is it?"

I held her and kissed her and told her it was okay, and then I asked her if she wanted to come away with me, and she said yes yes yes she really did. So I told her I might have to hurt her Poppa to get away, and she got a look in her eyes that I knew real well.

For all her propriety, Quilla June Holmes didn't much like her prayer-shouting Poppa.

I asked her if she had anything heavy, like a candlestick or a club, and she said no. So I went rummaging around in that back bedroom, and found a pair of her Poppa's socks, in a bureau drawer. I pulled the big brass balls off the headboard of the bed, and dropped them into the sock. I hefted it. Oh. Yeah.

She stared at me with big eyes. "What're you going to do?"

"You want to get out of here?"

She nodded.

"Then just stand back behind the door. No, wait a minute, I got a better idea. Get on the bed."

She lay down on the bed. "Okay," I said, "now pull up your skirt, pull off your pants, and spread out." She gave me a look of pure horror. "Do it," I said. "If you want out."

So she did it, and I rearranged her so her knees were bent and her legs open at the thighs, and I stood to one side of the door, and whispered to her, "Call your Poppa. Just him."

She hesitated a long moment, then she called out, in a voice she didn't have to fake, "Poppa! Poppa, come here, please!" Then she clammed her eyes shut tight.

Ira Holmes came through the door, took one look at his secret desire, his mouth dropped open, I kicked the door closed behind him and walloped him as hard as I could. He squished a little, and spattered the bedspread, and went very down.

She opened her eyes when she heard the thunk! and when the stuff spattered her legs she leaned over and puked on the floor. I knew she wouldn't be much good to me in getting Aaron into the room, so I opened the door, stuck my head around, looked worried, and said, "Aaron, would you come here a minute, please?" He looked at Lew, who was rapping with Mrs. Holmes about what was going on in the back bedroom, and when Lew nodded him on, he came into the room. He took a look at Quilla June's naked bush, at the blood on the wall and bedspread, at Ira on the floor, and opened his mouth to yell, just as I whacked him. It took two more to get him down, and then I had to kick him in the chest to put him away. Quilla June was still puking.

I grabbed her by the arm and swung her up off the bed. At least she was being quiet about it, but man did she stink.

"Come on!"

She tried to pull back, but I held on, and opened the bedroom door. As I pulled her out, Lew stood up, leaning on his cane. I kicked the cane out from under the old fart and down he went in a heap. Mrs. Holmes was staring at us, wondering where her old man was: "He's back in there," I said, heading for the front door. "The Good Lord got him in the head."

Then we were out in the street, Quilla June stinking along behind me, dry-heaving and bawling and probably wondering what had happened to her underpants.

They kept my weapons in a locked case at the Better Business Bureau, and we detoured around by my boarding house where I pulled the crowbar I'd swiped from the gas station out from under the back porch. Then we cut across behind the Grange and into the business section, and straight into the BBB. There was a clerk who tried to stop me, and I split his gourd with the crowbar. Then I pried the latch off the cabinet in Lew's office, and got the .30–06 and my .45 and all the ammo, and my spike, and my knife, and my kit, and loaded up. By that time Quilla June was able to make some sense.

"Where we gonna go, where we gonna go, oh Poppa Poppa Poppa . . . !"

"Hey, listen, Quilla June, Poppa me

no Poppas. You said you wanted to be with me . . . well, I'm goin'! *Up*, baby, and if you wanna go with me, you better stick close."

She was too scared to object.

I stepped out the front of the shop-front, and there was that green box sentry, coming on like a whippet. It had its cables out, and the mittens were gone. It had hooks.

I dropped to one knee, wrapped the sling of the .30–06 around my forearm, sighted clean, and fired dead at the big eye in the front. One shot, spang!

Hit that eye, the thing exploded in a shower of sparks, and the green box swerved and went through the front window of The Mill End Shoppe, screeching and crying and showering the place with flames and sparks. Nice.

I turned around to grab Quilla June, but she was gone. I looked off down the street, and here came all the vigilantes, Lew hobbling along with his cane like some kind of weird grasshopper.

And right then the shots started. Big, booming sounds. The .45 I'd given Quilla June. I looked up, and on the porch around the second floor, there she was, the automatic down on the railing like a pro, sighting into that mob and snapping off shots like maybe Wild Bill Elliott in a 40's Republic flick.

But dumb! Mother, dumb! Wasting time on that, when we had to get away.

I found the outside staircase going up there, and took it three steps at a time. She was smiling and laughing, and every time she'd pick one of those boobs out of the pack her little tongue-tip would peek out of the corner of her mouth, and her eyes would get all slick and wet and wham! down the boob would go.

She was really into it.

Just as I reached her, she sighted down on her scrawny mother. I slammed the back of her head and she missed the shot, and the old lady did a little dance-step and kept coming. Quilla

June whipped her head around at me, and there was kill in her eyes. "You made me miss." The voice gave me a chill.

I took the .45 away from her. Dumb. Wasting ammunition like that.

Dragging her behind me, I circled the building, found a shed out back, dropped down onto it and had her follow. She was scared at first, but I said, "Chick can shoot her old lady as easy as you do shouldn't be worried about a drop this small." She got out on the ledge, other side of the railing and held on. "Don't worry," I said, "you won't wet your pants. You haven't got any."

She laughed, like a bird, and dropped. I caught her, we slid down the shed door, and took a second to see if that mob was hard on us. Nowhere in sight.

I grabbed Quilla June by the arm and started off toward the south end of Topeka. It was the closest exit I'd found in my wandering, and we made it in about fifteen minutes, panting and weak as kittens.

And there it was.

A big air-intake duct.

I pried off the clamps with the crowbar, and we climbed up inside. There were ladders going up. There had to be. It figured, Repairs. Keep it clean. Had to be. We started climbing.

It took a long, long time.

Quilla June kept asking me, from down behind me, whenever she got too tired to climb, "Vic, do you love me?" I kept saying yes. Not only because I meant it. It helped her keep climbing.

X

We came up a mile from the access dropshaft. I shot off the filter covers and the hatch bolts, and we climbed out. They should have known better down there. You don't fuck around with Jimmy Cagney.

They never had a chance.

Quilla June was exhausted. I didn't blame her. But I didn't want to spend the night out in the open; there were things out there I didn't like to think about meeting even in daylight. It was getting on toward dusk.

We walked toward the access dropshaft.

Blood was waiting.

He looked weak. But he'd waited.

I stooped down and lifted his head. He opened his eyes, and very softly he said, "Hey."

I smiled at him. Jesus, it was good to see him. "We made it back, man."

He tried to get up, but he couldn't. The wounds on him were in ugly shape. "Have you eaten?" I asked.

"No. Grabbed a lizard yesterday . . . or maybe it was day before. I'm hungry, Vic."

Quilla June came up then, and Blood saw her. He closed his eyes. "We'd better hurry, Vic," she said. "Please. They might come up from the dropshaft."

I tried to lift Blood. He was dead weight. "Listen, Blood, I'll leg it into the city and get some food. I'll come back quick. You just wait here."

"Don't go in there, Vic," he said. "I did a recon the day after you went down. They found out we weren't fried in that gym. I don't know how. Maybe mutts smelled our track. I've been keeping watch, and they haven't tried to come out after us. I don't blame them. You don't know what it's like out here at night, man . . . you don't know . . ."

He shivered.

"Take it easy, Blood."

"But they've got us marked lousy in the city, Vic. We can't go back there. We'll have to make it someplace else."

That put it on a different stick. We couldn't go back, and with Blood in that condition we couldn't go forward. And I knew, good as I was solo, I couldn't make it without him. And there wasn't anything out here to eat. He had to have food, at once, and some medical care. I had to do something. Something good, something fast.

"Vic," Quilla June's voice was high and whining, "come *on!* Leave him. He'll be all right. We have to hurry."

I looked up at her. The sun was going down. Blood trembled in my arms.

She got a pouty look on her face. "If you love me, you'll come *on!*"

I couldn't make it alone out there without him. I knew it. If I loved her. She asked me, in the boiler, do you know what love is?

It was a small fire, not nearly big enough for any roverpak to spot from the outskirts of the city. No smoke. And after Blood had eaten his fill, I carried him to the air-duct a mile away, and we spent the night inside, on a little ledge. I held him all night. He slept good. In the morning, I fixed him up pretty good. He'd make it; he was strong.

He ate again. There was plenty left from the night before. I didn't eat. I wasn't hungry.

We started off across the blast wasteland that morning. We'd find another city, and make it.

We had to move slow, because Blood was still limping. It took a long time before I stopped hearing her calling in my head. Asking me, asking me: *do you know what love is?*

Sure I know.

A boy loves his dog.

Sunday Afternoon on the
Island of la Grande Gatte
(1884-1886) *by Georges
Seurat. Oil on canvas, 81
x 120⅜". Helen Birch
Bartlett Memorial Collec-
tion, 1926.224, The Art
Institute of Chicago. Detail
below.*

3
Introduction to Impressionism

Literary impressionism, like realism and expressionism, developed from the tradition of empiricism. David Hume, one of the ancestors of the nineteenth-century empiricists, established the philosophical base for this literary form in *A Treatise on Human Nature* (1793). He asserted that "all perceptions of the human mind resolve themselves into two distinct kinds, which I shall call *impressions* and *ideas*." The sensory impressions of experience are direct and primary, whereas ideas are either vague memories or complex combinations of impressions. A centaur, for example, is a construction combining the idea of a horse with the idea of a man, and these ideas in turn derive from primary impressions. Sensory impressions are obviously more direct and accurate, and since they are closer to the object, they are more valuable as a source of truth. Nineteenth-century scientific method and scientific explanations of human behavior are based on Hume's priorities.

In nineteenth-century France, two innovative schools of art were founded upon this philosophical tradition: the naturalistic writers and the impressionist painters. Both the novels of Zola and the paintings of Monet, Manet, Degas and Seurat were expressly "scientific," anti-romantic, and anti-academic. Literary naturalism proposed to communicate a scientifically valid truth or a natural law as revealed in the observation of actual things. Actual things sometimes violate polite conventions, however, and Zola was never admitted into the French Academy. In England, translations of his novels were attacked for obscenity. French impressionist paintings, like Zola's writings, also offended official aesthetic standards. Both the naturalist and the impressionist essentially chose ordinary moments from ordinary experience, rejecting the formal postures of aristocratic life encouraged at the academies. The impressionists so violated conventional notions of realism in art that in 1863 they were excluded from the "establishment" show at the Salon des Beaux Arts. In vigorous protest they displayed their work in the "Salon des Refusés" ("Gallery of the Rejected"). This counter-exhibition is said to have begun the impressionist period.

The impressionist painters were influenced by the new experiments in photography and the physics of light. Seurat, for example, developed a theory of *pointillism* and optical mixture of color based on scientific studies such as Von Helmholtz' on the nature of color and the propagation of light. Seurat contended that an optical mixture was brighter than any physical mixture of pigment; for example, the green produced by mixing blue and yellow paints together is much less bright than the illusion of green created when unmixed dots of blue and yellow paint fuse on the observer's retina. These scientifically based theories of form and color led Seurat to fill canvases with miniscule dots of color that, when observed at a distance of about six feet, merge in the eye to form glistening images. Such a pointillist painting is just a cluster of dots; its recognizable form is constructed only on the retina of the viewer's eye.

The impressionists' experiments with perception are in keeping with the new science and Hume's notion of the primacy of the impression in creating ideas, and they dramatize the role of the viewer in determining the meaning of a painting. Literary impressionists place a similar emphasis upon the perceiver in their attempt to resolve the problems we have seen confronting the realists and expressionists. Realistic authors seek to represent what is "out there," but they will always be bound by principles of selection that make objectivity impossible. Expressionists, in seeking to represent the mind, can represent nothing but their own mental processes, distorted by translation into language which is by nature a public rather than private convention. Total subjectivity is impossible. The impressionists, like the expressionists, recognize the subjectivity of perception, but like the realists, they have a social purpose and devise means of conveying what is real.

Impressionists Ford Madox Ford, Joseph Conrad, and Henry James create the illusion of reality by combining description of an objective, material world with its effect on the individual perceiver. Ford in his biography of Joseph Conrad recalled their theory of the real in life and in art[1]:

We [Conrad and Ford] agreed that the general effect of a novel must be the general effect that life makes on mankind. A novel must therefore not be a narration, a report. Life does not say to you: In 1914 my next door neighbor, Mr. Slack, erected a greenhouse and painted it with Cox's green aluminium paint. . . . If you think about the matter you will remember, in various unordered pictures, how one day Mr. Slack appeared in his garden and contemplated the wall of his house. You will then try to remember the year of that occurrence and you will fix it as August 1914 because having had the foresight

[1] Ford Madox Ford, *Joseph Conrad*. New York: Octagon Books, 1924. Used with permission.

to bear the municipal stock of the city of Liege you were able to afford a first-class season ticket for the first time in your life. You will remember Mr. Slack—then much thinner because it was before he found out where to buy that cheap Burgundy of which he has since drunk an inordinate quantity though whiskey you think would be much better for him! Mr. Slack again came into his garden, this time with a pale, weaselly-faced fellow, who touched his cap from time to time. Mr. Slack will point to his house wall several times at different points, the weaselly fellow touching his cap at each pointing. Some days after, coming back from business you will have observed against Mr. Slack's wall. . . . At this point you will remember that you were then the manager of the fresh-fish branch of Messrs. Catlin and Clovis in Fenchurch Street. . . . What a change since then! Millicent had not yet put her hair up. . . . You will remember how Millicent's hair looked, rather pale and burnished in plaits. You will remember how it now looks, henna'd: and you will see in one corner of your mind's eye a little picture of Mr. Mills the vicar talking—oh, very kindly—to Millicent after she has come back from Brighton. . . . But perhaps you had better not risk that. You remember some of the things said by means of which Millicent has made you cringe—and her expression! . . . Cox's Aluminium Paint! . . . You remember the half empty tin that Mr. Slack showed you— he had a most undignified cold—with the name in a horse-shoe over a blue circle that contained a red lion asleep in front of a real-gold sun . . . .

The sentence beginning "In 1914 . . ." resembles the assertions of James T. Farrell's story, "The Scoop." These "reports" by an all-knowing narrator are not limited to the impressions of a particular perceiver at the time of the event. Notice how the impressionist transforms the historical assertions that "In 1914 my next door neighbor, Mr. Slack, erected a greenhouse and painted it with Cox's green aluminium paint."

In the impressionist version, it is almost impossible to decide what event is being described because the key verbs, "erected" and "painted," have been omitted. However, the impressionist has obviously added more than has been taken away. Note the dashes, exclamations and ellipses as well as the apparently extraneous disgressions about municipal stocks and cheap burgundy. All these additions serve to tell us more about the personality of the narrator than about Mr. Slack. The pauses, the sense of excitement, the mental lapses, and the apparently arbitrary order of impressions are in stark contrast with the original sentence and the Farrell story. Notice also that the speaker alludes to what is *not* there with remarks like "but perhaps you had better not risk that" and a reference to the whiskey Mr. Slack does not drink. All these features would be excluded by the social realist as irrelevant.

Life does not narrate but renders impressions, and therefore, Ford says, an author "must write . . . as if . . . rendering the impressions of a person present at the scene." As we can see in the above passage, those impressions include not just recollections of the green paint but also apparent digressions, like the reference to first-class season tickets or Millicent's remarks. The impressionists defend deviation from conventional narrative on psychological grounds: "a person present at a scene does not see everything and is above all not able to remember immensely long passages of dialogue." A long speech by a character will lose readers' good faith: they will not believe anyone can remember that much. The effect of life, the illusion of reality, then, is not produced by the report or the corrected chronicle, but by the impression in all of its detail and seeming irrelevance.

The structure of the traditional novel consequently undergoes radical changes. Plot disappears, or it is no longer a tidy causal sequence of reported events. In Conrad's *Heart of Darkness*, the narrator's description of Marlow's tale as an "inconclusive" experience is a description of typical impressionist art:

> The yarns of seamen have a direct simplicity, the whole meaning of which lies within the shell of a cracked nut. But Marlow was not typical (if his propensity to spin yarns be excepted), and to him the meaning of an episode was not inside like a kernel but outside, enveloping the tale which brought it out only as a glow brings out a haze, in the likeness of one of these misty halos that sometimes are made visible by the spectral illumination of moonshine.

A character is no longer defined only by description of outward appearance but by psychological reaction to events as reflected in a record of personal impressions. Thus the narrator's description of Marlow as seated like a Buddha tells us more about his own attitudes toward Marlow than about Marlow himself. Similarly, Marlow's tale tells us about himself and his own attempt to make sense out of his experience. For example, Marlow's attitude toward Kurtz is contradictory: Should he admire Kurtz for his boldness in discovering the most primary truths of his own nature, or should he condemn him for abandoning the restraint which preserves civilization? This kind of narration is often called "unreliable narration," but although this is a useful term, a too literal interpretation of "unreliable" can be misleading.

In a courtroom, for example, witnesses are called unreliable when their testimony does not match proven facts, perhaps because of dishonesty or ignorance. But impressionist fiction is different: There is no "real" event reported by its characters, and no recourse to evidence outside of their testimony. In reality the jury's judgment that a report is unreliable means that it does not correspond to the real event. In fiction the reader's judgment that a narrator's report is "unreliable" means that it has internal contradictions or seems incomplete. Since the author has withheld judgment, readers are put into constructive roles. They have to judge for themselves as in life, but without life's real event.

Conventional narrations can be "solved." Detective stories, for example, generally have single, clear-cut solutions. But impressionist fiction usually defies solution; platoons of literary scholars construct conflicting versions of the basic meaning of the works. Since one person is necessarily limited and cannot see or remember everything, the narrator in an impressionist work is limited and subject to criticism by outside observers. The impressionist writer will often widen the scope of the immediate impressions of a character by supplying us with a character's reveries or recollections, increasing the potential for ambiguity. The author may set traps and puzzles for which there are no solutions. Actions in the work as well as their significance may be unresolved, forcing readers to make over and over again the possible critical structures which *are* the impressionist work of art. Each reader must create the meaning of the work by synthesizing the verbal data given, often with few guides for separating the irrelevant from the essential. The open-ended activity impressionism requires of the reader has even led to charges that it is trivial, frustrating, and dishonest.

Just as the impressionist painter makes the viewer conscious that he is looking at pigment and not a real scene, the literary impressionst makes us conscious of words and how they are arranged. The impressionist's written representations of the way reality affects the minds of their characters, and the multiple ways readers reconstruct that reality, inevitably lead to awareness that language is always separate from experience. The relationship between any word and the world is basically arbitrary, whether the object to be represented is a fact of material or subjective experience. Jean Rhys's *Wide Sargasso Sea* constructs a new version of what is already a literary version of experience, Charlotte Brontë's *Jane Eyre*, and a reader familiar with Brontë's novel will also be aware that Rhys's language refers not to life but to a representation of life. It is fiction twice removed. Michael Ondaatje does the same thing with an historical figure. Try as we may to find the real Billy the Kid, we find just a composite of literary sources; the original human reality has been irretrievably lost.

We might regard the impressionist novel as the last vestige of literary empiricism and the beginning of relativistic fiction. Writers may not be able to convey the reality of the material world nor of subjective experience, but they can create works which frankly admit that endless versions of any given event are possible and that language can refer to nothing but itself. The novels that follow in this tradition are informed with relativistic doubt: Can we know the experience of another? Can we generalize about human experience at all?

Ford Madox Ford (1873–1939)

WHAT THE ORDERLY DOG SAW

A Winter Landscape

I

The seven white peacocks against the castle wall
In the high trees and the dusk are like tapestry,
The sky being orange, the high wall a purple barrier
The canal, dead silver in the dusk
   And you are far away.   5
Yet I can see infinite miles of mountains.
Little lights shining in rows in the dark of them;
Infinite miles of marshes.
Thin wisps of mist, shimmering like blue webs
Over the dusk of them, great curves and horns of sea   10
And dusk and dusk and the little village
   And you, sitting in the firelight.

II

Around me are the two hundred and forty men of B Company
Mud-coloured.
Going about their avocations,   15
Resting between their practice of the art
Of killing men,
As I too rest between my practice

Of the Art of killing men.
Their pipes glow above the mud and their mud colour, moving   20
    like fireflies beneath the trees,
I too being mud-coloured
Beneath the trees and the peacocks.
When they come up to me in the dusk
They start, stiffen and salute, almost invisibly.   25
And the forty-two prisoners from the Battalion guardroom
Crouch over the tea cans in the shadow of the wall.
And the bread hunks glimmer, beneath the peacocks,
    And you are far away.

III
Presently I shall go in,   30
I shall write down the names of the forty-two
Prisoners in the Battalion guardroom
On fair white foolscap.
Their names, rank, and regimental numbers,
Corps, Companies, Punishments and Offences,   35
Remarks, and By whom Confined.
Yet in spite of all I shall see only
The infinite miles of dark mountain,
The infinite miles of dark marshland,
Great curves and horns of sea   40
The little village.
And you,
Sitting in the firelight.

Joseph Conrad   (1857–1924)

HEART OF DARKNESS

I

The *Nellie,* a cruising yawl, swung to her anchor without a flutter of the sails, and was at rest. The flood had made, the wind was nearly calm, and being bound down the river, the only thing for it was to come to and wait for the turn of the tide.

The sea-reach of the Thames stretched before us like the beginning of an interminable waterway. In the offing the sea and the sky were welded together without a joint, and in the luminous space the tanned sails of the barges drifting up with the tide seemed to stand still in red clusters of canvas sharply peaked, with gleams of varnished sprits. A haze rested on the low shores that ran out to sea in vanishing flatness. The air was dark above Gravesend, and farther back still seemed condensed into a mournful gloom, brooding motionless over the biggest, and the greatest, town on earth.

The Director of Companies was our

captain and our host. We four affectionately watched his back as he stood in the bows looking to seaward. On the whole river there was nothing that looked half so nautical. He resembled a pilot, which to a seaman is trustworthiness personified. It was difficult to realize his work was not out there in the luminous estuary, but behind him, within the brooding gloom.

Between us there was, as I have already said somewhere, the bond of the sea. Besides holding our hearts together through long periods of separation, it had the effect of making us tolerant of each other's yarns—and even convictions. The Lawyer—the best of old fellows—had, because of his many years and many virtues, the only cushion on deck, and was lying on the only rug. The Accountant had brought out already a box of dominoes, and was toying architecturally with the bones. Marlow sat cross-legged right aft, leaning against the mizzen-mast. He had sunken cheeks, a yellow complexion, a straight back, an ascetic aspect, and, with his arms dropped, the palms of hands outwards, resembled an idol. The Director, satisfied the anchor had good hold, made his way aft and sat down amongst us. We exchanged a few words lazily. Afterwards there was silence on board the yacht. For some reason or other we did not begin that game of dominoes. We felt meditative, and fit for nothing but placid staring. The day was ending in a serenity of still and exquisite brilliance. The water shone pacifically; the sky, without a speck, was a benign immensity of unstained light; the very mist on the Essex marshes was like a gauzy and radiant fabric, hung from the wooded rises inland, and draping the low shores in diaphanous folds. Only the gloom to the west, brooding over the upper reaches, became more somber every minute, as if angered by the approach of the sun.

And at last, in its curved and imperceptible fall, the sun sank low, and from glowing white changed to a dull red without rays and without heat, as if about to go out suddenly, stricken to death by the touch of that gloom brooding over a crowd of men.

Forthwith a change came over the waters, and the serenity became less brilliant but more profound. The old river in its broad reach rested unruffled at the decline of day, after ages of good service done to the race that peopled its banks, spread out in the tranquil dignity of a waterway leading to the uttermost ends of the earth. We looked at the venerable stream not in the vivid flush of a short day that comes and departs for ever, but in the august light of abiding memories. And indeed nothing is easier for a man who has, as the phrase goes, "followed the sea" with reverence and affection, than to evoke the great spirit of the past upon the lower reaches of the Thames. The tidal current runs to and fro in its unceasing service, crowded with memories of men and ships it has borne to the rest of home or to the battles of the sea. It had known and served all the men of whom the nation is proud, from Sir Francis Drake to Sir John Franklin, knights all, titled and untitled—the great knights-errant of the sea. It had borne all the ships whose names are like jewels flashing in the night of time, from the *Golden Hind* returning with her round flanks full of treasure, to be visited by the Queen's Highness and thus pass out of the gigantic tale, to the *Erebus* and *Terror,* bound on other conquests—and that never returned. It had known the ships and the men. They had sailed from Deptford, from Greenwich, from Erith—the adventurers and the settlers; kings' ships and the ships of men on 'Change; captains, admirals, the dark "interlopers" of the Eastern trade, and the commissioned "generals" of East India fleets. Hunters for gold or pursuers of fame, they all had gone out on that stream, bearing the sword, and often the torch, messengers of the might within the land, bearers of a spark from the sacred fire. What greatness had not floated on the ebb of that river into the mystery of an unknown earth! . . . The dreams of men, the seed of commonwealths, the germs of empires.

The sun set; the dusk fell on the stream, and lights began to appear along the shore. The Chapman lighthouse, a three-legged thing erect on a mud-flat, shone strongly. Lights of ships moved in the fairway—a great stir of lights going up and going down. And farther west on the upper reaches the place of the monstrous town was still marked ominously on the sky, a brooding gloom in sunshine, a lurid glare under the stars.

"And this also," said Marlow suddenly, "has been one of the dark places of the earth."

He was the only man of us who still "followed the sea." The worst that could be said of him was that he did not represent his class. He was a seaman, but he was a wanderer too, while most seamen lead, if one may so express it, a sedentary life. Their minds are of the stay-at-home order, and their home is always with them—the ship; and so is their country—the sea. One ship is very much like another, and the sea is always the same. In the immutability of their surroundings the foreign shores, the foreign faces, the changing immensity of life, glide past, veiled not by a sense of mystery but by a slightly disdainful ignorance; for there is nothing mysterious to a seaman unless it be the sea itself, which is the mistress of his existence and as inscrutable as Destiny. For the rest, after his hours of work, a casual stroll or a casual spree on shore suffice to unfold for him the secret of a whole continent, and generally he finds the secret not worth knowing. The yarns of seamen have a direct simplicity, the whole meaning of which lies within the shell of a cracked nut. But Marlow was not typical (if his propensity to spin yarns be excepted), and to him the meaning of an episode was not inside like a kernel but outside, enveloping the tale which brought it out only as a glow brings out a haze, in the likeness of one of these misty halos that sometimes are made visible by the spectral illumination of moonshine.

His remark did not seem at all surprising. It was just like Marlow. It was accepted in silence. No one took the trouble to grunt even; and presently he said, very slow:

"I was thinking of very old times, when the Romans first came here, nineteen hundred years ago—the other day. . . . Light came out of this river since—you say Knights? Yes; but it is like a running blaze on a plain, like a flash of lightning in the clouds. We live in the flicker—may it last as long as the old earth keeps rolling! But darkness was here yesterday. Imagine the feelings of a commander of a fine—what d'ye call 'em?—trireme in the Mediterranean, ordered suddenly to the north; run overland across the Gauls in a hurry; put in charge of one of these craft the legionaries—a wonderful lot of handy men they must have been too—used to build, apparently by the hundred, in a month or two, if we may believe what we read. Imagine him here—the very end of the world, a sea the color of lead, a sky the color of smoke, a kind of ship about as rigid as a concertina—and going up this river with stores, or orders, or what you like. Sandbanks, marshes, forests, savages —precious little to eat fit for a civilized man, nothing but Thames water to drink. No Falernian wine here, no going ashore. Here and there a military camp lost in a wilderness, like a needle in a bundle of hay—cold, fog, tempests, disease, exile, and death— death skulking in the air, in the water, in the bush. They must have been dying like flies here. Oh yes—he did it. Did it very well, too, no doubt, and without thinking much about it either, except afterwards to brag of what he had gone through in his time, perhaps. They were men enough to face the darkness. And perhaps he was cheered by keeping his eye on a chance of promotion to the fleet at Ravenna by and by, if he had good friends in Rome and survived the awful climate. Or think of a decent young citizen in a toga—perhaps too much dice, you know—coming out here in the train of some prefect, or tax-gatherer, or trader, even, to mend his fortunes. Land in a swamp, march through the woods, and in some inland post feel the savagery, the utter savagery, had closed round him—all that mysterious life of the wilderness that stirs in the forest, in the jungles, in the hearts of wild men. There's no initiation either into such mysteries. He has to live in the midst of the incomprehensible, which is also detestable. And it has a fascination, too, that goes to work upon him. The fascination of the abomination—you know. Imagine the growing regrets, the longing to escape, the power-less disgust, the surrender, the hate."

He paused.

"Mind," he began again, lifting one arm from the elbow, the palm of the hand outwards, so that, with his legs folded before him, he had the pose of a Buddha preaching in European clothes and without a lotus-flower—"Mind, none of us would feel exactly like this. What saves us is efficiency—the devotion to efficiency. But these chaps were not much account, really. They were no colonists; their administration was merely a squeeze, and nothing more, I suspect. They were conquerors, and for that you want only brute force—nothing to boast of, when you have it, since your strength is just an accident arising from the weakness of others. They grabbed what they could get for the sake of what was to be got. It was just robbery with violence, aggravated murder on a great scale, and men going at it blind—as is very proper for those

who tackle a darkness. The conquest of the earth, which mostly means the taking it away from those who have a different complexion or slightly flatter noses than ourselves, is not a pretty thing when you look into it too much. What redeems it is the idea only. An idea at the back of it; not a sentimental pretense but an idea; and an unselfish belief in the idea—something you can set up, and bow down before, and offer a sacrifice to. . . ."

He broke off. Flames glided in the river, small green flames, red flames, white flames, pursuing, overtaking, joining, crossing each other—then separating slowly or hastily. The traffic of the great city went on in the deepening night upon the sleepless river. We looked on, waiting patiently—there was nothing else to do till the end of the flood; but it was only after a long silence, when he said, in a hesitating voice, "I suppose you fellows remember I did once turn fresh-water sailor for a bit," that we knew we were fated, before the ebb began to run, to hear about one of Marlow's inconclusive experiences.

"I don't want to bother you much with what happened to me personally," he began, showing in this remark the weakness of many tellers of tales who seem so often unaware of what their audience would best like to hear; "yet to understand the effect of it on me you ought to know how I got out there, what I saw, how I went up that river to the place where I first met the poor chap. It was the farthest point of navigation and the culminating point of my experience. It seemed somehow to throw a kind of light on everything about me—and into my thoughts. It was somber enough too—and pitiful—not extraordinary in any way—not very clear either. No, not very clear. And yet it seemed to throw a kind of light.

"I had then, as you remember, just returned to London after a lot of Indian Ocean, Pacific, China Seas—a regular dose of the East—six years or so, and I was loafing about, hindering you fellows in your work and invading your homes, just as though I had got a heavenly mission to civilize you. It was very fine for a time, but after a bit I did get tired of resting. Then I began to look for a ship—I should think the hardest work on earth. But the ships wouldn't even look at me. And I got tired of that game too.

"Now when I was a little chap I had a passion for maps. I would look for hours at South America, or Africa, or Australia, and lose myself in all the glories of exploration. At that time there were many blank spaces on the earth, and when I saw one that looked particularly inviting on a map (but they all look that) I would put my finger on it and say, When I grow up I will go there. The North Pole was one of these places, I remember. Well, I haven't been there yet, and shall not try now. The glamor's off. Other places were scattered about the Equator, and in every sort of latitude all over the two hemispheres. I have been in some of them, and . . . well, we won't talk about that. But there was one yet—the biggest, the most blank, so to speak—that I had a hankering after.

"True, by this time it was not a blank space any more. It had got filled since my boyhood with rivers and lakes and names. It had ceased to be a blank space of delightful mystery—a white patch for a boy to dream gloriously over. It had become a place of darkness. But there was in it one river especially, a mighty big river, that you could see on the map, resembling an immense snake uncoiled, with its head in the sea, its body at rest curving afar over a vast country, and its tail lost in the depths of the land. And as I looked at the map of it in a shop window, it fascinated me as a snake would a bird—a silly little bird. Then I remembered there was a big concern, a Company for trade on that river. Dash it all!

I thought to myself, they can't trade without using some kind of craft on that lot of fresh water—steamboats! Why shouldn't I try to get charge of one? I went on along Fleet Street but could not shake off the idea. The snake had charmed me.

"You understand it was a Continental concern, that Trading Society; but I have a lot of relations living on the Continent, because it's cheap and not so nasty as it looks, they say.

"I am sorry to own I began to worry them. This was already a fresh departure for me. I was not used to get things that way, you know. I always went my own road and on my own legs where I had a mind to go. I wouldn't have believed it of myself; but, then—you see—I felt somehow I must get there by hook or by crook. So I worried them. The men said, 'My dear fellow,' and did nothing. Then—would you believe it?—I tried the women. I Charlie Marlow, set the women to work—to get a job. Heavens! Well, you see, the notion drove me. I had an aunt, a dear enthusiastic soul. She wrote: 'It will be delightful. I am ready to do anything, anything for you. It is a glorious idea. I know the wife of a very high personage in the Administration, and also a man who has lots of influence with,' etc. etc. She was determined to make no end of fuss to get me appointed skipper of a river steamboat, if such was my fancy.

"I got my appointment—of course; and I got it very quick. It appears the Company had received news that one of their captains had been killed in a scuffle with the natives. This was my chance, and it made me the more anxious to go. It was only months and months afterwards, when I made the attempt to recover what was left of the body, that I heard the original quarrel arose from a misunderstanding about some hens. Yes, two black hens. Fresleven—that was the fellow's name, a Dane—thought himself wronged somehow in the bargain, so he went ashore and started to hammer the chief of the village with a stick. Oh, it didn't surprise me in the least to hear this, and at the same time to be told that Fresleven was the gentlest, quietest creature that ever walked on two legs. No doubt he was; but he had been a couple of years already out there engaged in the noble cause, you know, and he probably felt the need at last of asserting his self-respect in some way. Therefore he whacked the old nigger mercilessly, while a big crowd of his people watched him, thunderstruck, till some man—I was told the chief's son—in desperation at hearing the old chap yell, made a tentative jab with a spear at the white man—and of course it went quite easy between the shoulder-blades. Then the whole population cleared into the forest, expecting all kinds of calamities to happen, while, on the other hand, the steamer Fresleven commanded left also in a bad panic, in charge of the engineer, I believe. Afterwards nobody seemed to trouble much about Fresleven's remains, till I got out and stepped into his shoes. I couldn't let it rest, though; but when an opportunity offered at last to meet my predecessor, the grass growing through his ribs was tall enough to hide his bones. They were all there. The supernatural being had not been touched after he fell. And the village was deserted, the huts gaped black, rotting, all askew within the fallen enclosures. A calamity had come to it, sure enough. The people had vanished. Mad terror had scattered them, men, women, and children, through the bush, and they had never returned. What became of the hens I don't know either. I should think the cause of progress got them, anyhow. However, through this glorious affair I got my appointment, before I had fairly begun to hope for it.

"I flew around like mad to get ready, and before forty-eight hours I was crossing the Channel to show myself to my employers, and sign the contract. In a very few hours I arrived in a city that always makes me think of a whited sepulcher. Prejudice no doubt. I had no difficulty in finding the Company's offices. It was the biggest thing in town, and every body I met was full of it. They were going to run an oversea empire, and make no end of coin by trade.

"A narrow and deserted street in deep shadow, high houses, innumerable windows with venetian blinds, a dead silence, grass sprouting between the stones, imposing carriage archways right and left, immense double doors standing ponderously ajar. I slipped through one of these cracks, went up a swept and ungarnished staircase, as arid as a desert, and opened the first door I came to. Two women, one fat and the other slim, sat on straw-bottomed chairs, knitting black wool. The slim one got up and walked straight at me—still knitting with downcast eyes—and only just as I began to think of getting out of her way, as you would for a somnambulist, stood still, and looked up. Her dress was as plain as an umbrella-cover, and she turned round without a word and preceded me into a waiting-room. I gave my name, and looked about. Deal table in the middle, plain chairs all round the walls, on one end a large shining map, marked with all the colors of a rainbow. There was a vast amount of red—good to see at any time, because one knows that some real work is done in there, a deuce of a lot of blue, a little green, smears of orange, and, on the East Coast, a purple patch, to show where the jolly pioneers of progress drink the jolly lager-beer. However, I wasn't going into any of these. I was going into the yellow. Dead in the center. And the river was there—fascinating—deadly —like a snake. Ough! A door opened, a white-haired secretarial head, but wearing a compassionate expression, appeared, and a skinny forefinger beckoned me into the sanctuary. Its light was dim, and a heavy writing-desk squatted in the middle. From behind that structure came out an impression of pale plumpness in a frock-coat. The great man himself. He was five feet six, I should judge, and had his grip on the handleend of ever so many millions. He shook hands, I fancy, murmured vaguely, was satisfied with my French. *Bon voyage.*

"In about forty-five seconds I found myself again in the waiting-room with the compassionate secretary, who, full of desolation and sympathy, made me sign some document. I believe I undertook amongst other things not to disclose any trade secrets. Well, I am not going to.

"I began to feel slightly uneasy. You know I am not used to such ceremonies, and there was something ominous in the atmosphere. It was just as though I had been let into some conspiracy—I don't know—something not quite right; and I was glad to get out. In the outer room the two women knitted black wool feverishly. People were arriving, and the younger one was walking back and forth introducing them. The old one sat on her chair. Her flat cloth slippers were propped up on a foot-warmer, and a cat reposed on her lap. She wore a starched white affair on her head, had a wart on one cheek, and silver-rimmed spectacles hung on the tip of her nose. She glanced at me above the glasses. The swift and indifferent placidity of that look troubled me. Two youths with foolish and cherry countenances were being piloted over, and she threw at them the same quick glance of unconcerned wisdom. She seemed to know all about them and about me too. An eerie feeling came over me. She seemed uncanny and fateful. Often far away there I thought of these two, guarding the door of Darkness, knitting black wool as for a warm pall, one introducing, introducing continuously to the unknown, the other scrutinizing the cheery and foolish faces with unconcerned old eyes. *Ave!* Old knitter of black wool. *Morituri te salutant.* Not many of those she looked at ever saw her again—not half, by a long way.

"There was yet a visit to the doctor. 'A simple formality,' assured me the secretary, with an air of taking an immense part in all my sorrows. Accordingly a young chap wearing his hat over the left eyebrow, some clerk I suppose—there must have been clerks in the business, though the house was as still as a house in a city of the dead—came from somewhere upstairs, and led me forth. He was shabby and careless, with ink-stains on the sleeves of his jacket, and his cravat was large and billowy, under a chin shaped like the toe of an old boot. It was a little too early for the doctor, so I proposed a drink, and thereupon he developed a vein of joviality. As we sat over our vermouths he glorified the Company's business, and by and by I expressed casually my surprise at him not going out there. He became very cool and collected all at once. 'I am not such a fool as I look, quoth Plato to his disciples,' he said sententiously, emptied his glass with great resolution, and we rose.

"The old doctor felt my pulse, evidently thinking of something else the while. 'Good, good for there,' he mumbled, and then with a certain eagerness asked me whether I would let him measure my head. Rather surprised, I said Yes, when he produced a thing like callipers and got the dimensions back and front and every way, taking notes carefully. He was an unshaven little man in a threadbare coat like a gaberdine, with his feet in slippers, and I thought him a harmless fool. 'I always ask leave, in the interests of science, to measure the crania of those going out there,' he said. 'And when they come back too?' I asked. 'Oh, I never see them,' he remarked; 'and, moreover, the changes take place inside, you know.' He smiled, as if at some quiet joke. 'So you are going out there. Famous. Interesting too.' He gave me a searching glance, and made another note. 'Ever any madness in your family?' he asked, in a matter-of-fact tone. I felt very annoyed. 'Is that question in the interests of science too?' 'It would be,' he said, without taking notice of my irritation, 'interesting for science to watch the mental changes of individuals, on the spot, but . . .' 'Are you an alienist?' I interrupted. 'Every doctor should be— a little,' answered that original imperturbably. 'I have a little theory which you Messieurs who go out there must help me to prove. This is my share in the advantages my country shall reap from the possession of such a magnificent dependency. The mere wealth I leave to others. Pardon my questions, but you are the first Englishman coming under my observation. . .' I hastened to assure him I was not in the least typical. 'If I were,' said I, 'I wouldn't be talking like this with you.' 'What you say is rather profound, and probably erroneous,' he said, with a laugh. 'Avoid irritation more than exposure to the sun. Adieu. How do you English say, eh? Good-bye. Ah! Good-bye. Adieu. In the tropics one must before everything keep calm.' . . . He lifted a warning forefinger. . . . 'Du calme, du calme. Adieu.'

"One thing more remained to do— say good-bye to my excellent aunt. I found her triumphant. I had a cup of tea—the last decent cup of tea for many days—and in a room that most soothingly looked just as you would expect a lady's drawing-room to look, we had a long quiet chat by the fireside. In the course of these confidences it became quite plain to me I had been represented to the wife of the high dignitary, and goodness knows to how many more people besides, as an exceptional and gifted creature—a piece of good fortune for the Company—a man you don't get hold of every day. Good Heavens! and I was going to take charge of a two-penny-halfpenny river-steamboat with a penny whistle attached! It appeared, however, I was also one of the Workers, with a capital—you know. Something like an emissary of light,

something like a lower sort of apostle. There had been a lot of such rot let loose in print and talk just about that time, and the excellent woman, living right in the rush of all that humbug, got carried off her feet. She talked about 'weaning those ignorant millions from their horrid ways,' till, upon my word, she made me quite uncomfortable. I ventured to hint that the Company was run for profit.

" 'You forget, dear Charlie, that the laborer is worthy of his hire,' she said brightly. It's queer how out of touch with truth women are. They live in a world of their own, and there had never been anything like it, and never can be. It is too beautiful altogether, and if they were to set it up it would go to pieces before the first sunset. Some confounded fact we men have been living contentedly with ever since the day of creation would start up and knock the whole thing over.

"After this I got embraced, told to wear flannel, be sure to write often, and so on—and I left. In the street—I don't know why—a queer feeling came to me that I was an impostor. Odd thing that I, who used to clear out for any part of the world at twenty-four hours' notice, with less thought than most men give to the crossing of a street, had a moment—I won't say of hesitation, but of startled pause, before this commonplace affair. The best way I can explain it to you is by saying that, for a second or two, I felt as though, instead of going to the center of a continent, I were about to set off for the center of the earth.

"I left in a French steamer, and she called in every blamed port they have out there, for, as far as I could see, the sole purpose of landing soldiers and custom-house officers. I watched the coast. Watching a coast as it slips by the ship is like thinking about an enigma. There it is before you—smiling, frowning, inviting, grand, mean, insipid, or savage, and always mute with an air of whispering, Come and find out. This one was almost featureless, as if still in the making, with an aspect of monotonous grimness. The edge of a colossal jungle, so dark green as to be almost black, fringed with white surf, ran straight, like a ruled line, far, far away along a blue sea whose glitter was blurred by a creeping mist. The sun was fierce, the land seemed to glisten and drip with steam. Here and there greyish-whitish specks showed up clustered inside the white surf, with a flag flying above them perhaps—settlements some centuries old, and still no bigger than pin-heads on the untouched expanse of their background. We pounded along, stopped, landed soldiers; went on, landed custom-house clerks to levy toll in what looked like a God-forsaken wilderness, with a tin shed and a flag-pole lost in it; landed more soldiers—to take care of the custom-house clerks presumably. Some, I heard, got drowned in the surf; but whether they did or not, nobody seemed particularly to care. They were just flung out there, and on we went. Every day the coast looked the same, as though we had not moved; but we passed various places—trading places—with names like Gran' Bassam, Little Popo; names that seemed to belong to some sordid farce acted in front of a sinister back-cloth. The idleness of a passenger, my isolation amongst all these men with whom I had no point of contact, the oily and languid sea, the uniform somberness of the coast, seemed to keep me away from the truth of things, within the toil of a mournful and senseless delusion. The voice of the surf heard now and then was a positive pleasure, like the speech of a brother. It was something natural, that had its reason, that had a meaning. Now and then a boat from the shore gave one a momentary contact with reality. It was paddled by black fellows. You could see from afar the white of their eyeballs glistening. They shouted, sang; their bodies streamed with perspiration; they

had faces like grotesque masks—these chaps; but they had bone, muscle, a wild vitality, an intense energy of movement, that was as natural and true as the surf along their coast. They wanted no excuse for being there. They were a great comfort to look at. For a time I would feel I belonged still to a world of straightforward facts; but the feeling would not last long. Something would turn up to scare it away. Once, I remember, we came upon a man-of-war anchored off the coast. There wasn't even a shed there, and she was shelling the bush. It appears the French had one of their wars going on thereabouts. Her ensign dropped limp like a rag; the muzzles of the long six-inch guns stuck out all over the low hull; the greasy, slimy swell swung her up lazily and let her down, swaying her thin masts. In the empty immensity of earth, sky, and water, there she was, incomprehensible, firing into a continent. Pop, would go one of the six-inch guns; a small flame would dart and vanish, a little white smoke would disappear, a tiny projectile would give a feeble screech—and nothing happened. Nothing could happen. There was a touch of insanity in the proceeding, a sense of lugubrious drollery in the sight; and it was not dissipated by somebody on board assuring me earnestly there was a camp of natives—he called them enemies!—hidden out of sight somewhere.

"We gave her her letters (I heard the men in that lonely ship were dying of fever at the rate of three a day) and went on. We called at some more places with farcical names, where the merry dance of death and trade goes on in a still and earthy atmosphere as of an overheated catacomb; all along the formless coast bordered by dangerous surf, as if Nature herself had tried to ward off intruders; in and out of rivers, streams of death in life, whose banks were rotting into mud, whose waters, thickened into slime, invaded the contorted mangroves, that seemed to writhe at us in the extremity of an impotent despair. Nowhere did we stop long enough to get a particularized impression, but the general sense of vague and oppressive wonder grew upon me. It was like a weary pilgrimage amongst hints for nightmares.

"It was upward of thirty days before I saw the mouth of the big river. We anchored off the seat of the government. But my work would not begin till some two hundred miles farther on. So as soon as I could I made a start for a place thirty miles higher up.

"I had my passage on a little sea-going steamer. Her captain was a Swede, and knowing me for a seaman, invited me on the bridge. He was a young man, lean, fair, and morose, with lanky hair and a shuffling gait. Ae we left the miserable little wharf, he tossed his head contemptuously at the shore. 'Been living there?' he asked. I said, 'Yes.' 'Fine lot these government chaps—are they not?' he went on, speaking English with great precision and considerable bitterness. 'It is funny what some people will do for a few francs a month. I wonder what becomes of that kind when it goes up country?' I said to him I expected to see that soon. 'So-o-o!' he exclaimed. He shuffled athwart, keeping one eye ahead vigilantly. 'Don't be too sure,' he continued. 'The other day I took up a man who hanged himself on the road. He was a Swede, too.' 'Hanged himself! Why, in God's name?' I cried. He kept on looking out watchfully. 'Who knows? The sun too much for him, or the country perhaps.'

"At last we opened a reach. A rocky cliff appeared, mounds of turned-up earth by the shore, houses on a hill, others with iron roofs, amongst a waste of excavations, or hanging to the declivity. A continuous noise of the rapids above hovered over this scene of inhabited devastation. A lot of people, mostly black and naked, moved about like ants. A jetty projected into the river. A blinding sunlight drowned all this at times in a sudden recrudescence of glare. 'There's your Company's station,' said the Swede, pointing to three wooden barrack-like structures on the rocky slope. 'I will send your things up. Four boxes did you say? So. Farewell.'

"I came upon a boiler wallowing in the grass, then found a path leading up the hill. It turned aside for the boulders, and also for an undersized railway truck lying there on its back with its wheels in the air. One was off. The thing looked as dead as the carcass of some animal. I came upon more pieces of decaying machinery, a stack of rusty rails. To the left a clump of trees made a shady spot, where dark things seemed to stir feebly. I blinked, the path was steep. A horn tooted to the right, and I saw the black people run. A heavy and dull detonation shook the ground, a puff of smoke came out of the cliff, and that was all. No change appeared on the face of the rock. They were building a railway. The cliff was not in the way or anything; but this objectless blasting was all the work going on.

"A slight clinking behind me made me turn my head. Six black men advanced in a file, toiling up the path. They walked erect and slow, balancing small baskets full of earth on their heads, and the clink kept time with their footsteps. Black rags were wound round their loins, and the short ends behind waggled to and fro like tails. I could see every rib, the joints of their limbs were like knots in a rope; each had an iron collar on his neck, and all were connected together with a chain whose bights swung between them, rhythmically clinking. Another report from the cliff made me think suddenly of that ship of war I had seen firing into a continent. It was the same kind of ominous voice; but these men could by no stretch of imagination be called enemies. They were called criminals, and the outraged law, like the bursting shells, had come to them, an insoluble mystery from the sea. All their meager breasts panted together, the violently dilated nostrils quivered, the eyes stared stonily uphill. They passed me within six inches, without a glance, with that complete, deathlike indifference of unhappy savages. Behind this raw matter one of the reclaimed, the product of the new forces at work, strolled despondently, carrying a rifle by its middle. He had a uniform jacket with one button off, and seeing a white man on the path, hoisted his weapon to his shoulder with alacrity. This was simple prudence, white men being so much alike at a distance that he could not tell who I might be. He was speedily reassured, and with a large, white, rascally grin, and a glance at his charge, seemed to take me into partnership in his exalted trust. After all, I also was a part of the great cause of these high and just proceedings.

"Instead of going up, I turned and descended to the left. My idea was to let that chain-gang get out of sight before I climbed the hill. You know I am not particularly tender; I've had to strike and to fend off. I've had to resist and to attack sometimes—that's only one way of resisting—without counting the exact cost, according to the demands of such sort of life as I had blundered into. I've seen the devil of violence, and the devil of greed, and the devil of hot desire; but, by all the stars! these were strong, lusty, red-eyed devils, that swayed and drove men—men, I tell you. But as I stood on this hillside, I foresaw that in the blinding sunshine of that land I would become acquainted with a flabby, pretending, weak-eyed devil of a rapacious and pitiless folly. How insidious he could be, too, I was only to find out several months later and a thousand miles farther. For a moment I stood appalled, as though by a warning. Finally I descended the hill, obliquely, towards the trees I had seen.

"I avoided a vast artificial hole somebody had been digging on the slope, the purpose of which I found it impossible to divine. It wasn't a quarry or a sandpit, anyhow. It was just a hole. It might have been connected with the philanthropic desire of giving the criminals something to do. I don't know. Then I nearly fell into a very narrow ravine, almost no more than a scar in the hillside. I discovered that a lot of imported drainage-pipes for the settlement had been tumbled in there. There wasn't one that was not broken. It was a wanton smash-up. At last I got under the trees. My purpose was to stroll into the shade for a moment; but no sooner within than it seemed to me I had stepped into the gloomy circle of some Inferno. The rapids were near, and an uninterrupted, uniform, headlong, rushing noise filled the mournful stillness of the grove, where not a breath stirred, not a leaf moved, with a mysterious sound—as though the tearing pace of the launched earth had suddenly become audible.

"Black shapes crouched, lay, sat between the trees, leaning against the trunks, clinging to the earth, half coming out, half effaced within the dim light, in all the attitudes of pain, abandonment, and despair. Another mine on the cliff went off, followed by a slight shudder of the soil under my feet. The work was going on. The work! and this was the place where some of the helpers had withdrawn to die.

"They were dying slowly—it was very clear. They were not enemies, they were not criminals, they were nothing earthly now—nothing but black shadows of disease and starvation, lying confusedly in the greenish gloom. Brought from all the recesses of the coast in all the legality of time contracts, lost in uncongenial surroundings, fed on unfamiliar food, they sickened, became inefficient, and were then allowed to crawl away and rest. These moribund shapes were free as air—and nearly as thin. I began to distinguish the gleam of the eyes under the trees. Then, glancing down, I saw a face near my hand. The black bones reclined at full length with one shoulder against the tree, and slowly the eyelids rose and the sunken eyes looked up at me, enormous and vacant, a kind of blind, white flicker in the depths of the orbs, which died out slowly. The man seemed young—almost a boy—but you know with them it's hard to tell. I found nothing else to do but to offer him one of my good Swede's ship's biscuits I had in my pocket. The fingers closed slowly on it and held—there was no other movement and no other glance. He had tied a bit of white worsted round his neck—Why? Where did he get it? Was it a badge—an ornament—a charm—a propitiatory act? Was there any idea at all connected with it? It looked startling round his black neck, this bit of white thread from beyond the seas.

"Near the same tree two more bundles of acute angles sat with their legs drawn up. One, with his chin propped on his knees, stared at nothing, in an intolerable and appalling manner: his brother phantom rested its forehead, as if overcome with a great weariness; and all about others were scattered in every pose of contorted collapse, as in some picture of a massacre or a pestilence. While I stood horror-struck, one of these creatures rose to his hands and knees, and went off on all-fours towards the river to drink. He lapped out of his hand, then sat up in the sunlight, crossing his shins in front of him, and after a time let his woolly head fall on his breastbone.

"I didn't want any more loitering in the shade, and I made haste towards the station. When near the buildings I met a white man, in such an unexpected elegance of get-up that in the first moment I took him for a sort of vision. I saw a high starched collar, white cuffs, a light alpaca jacket, snowy trousers, a clean necktie, and varnished boots. No hat. Hair parted, brushed, oiled, under a green-lined parasol held in a big white hand. He was amazing, and had a pen-holder behind his ear.

"I shook hands with this miracle, and I learned he was the Company's chief accountant, and that all the book-keeping was done at this station. He had come out for a moment, he said, 'to get a breath of fresh air.' The expression sounded wonderfully odd, with its suggestion of sedentary desk-life. I wouldn't have mentioned the fellow to you at all, only it was from his lips that I first heard the name of the man who is so indissolubly connected with the memories of that time. Moreover, I respected the fellow. Yes; I respected his collars, his vast cuffs, his brushed hair. His appearance was certainly that of a hairdresser's dummy; but in the great demoralization of the land he kept up his appearance. That's backbone. His starched collars and got-up shirt-fronts were achievements of character. He had been out nearly three years; and, later, I could not help asking him how he managed to sport such linen. He had just the faintest blush, and said modestly, 'I've been teaching one of the native women about the station. It was difficult. She had a distaste for the work.' Thus this man had verily accomplished something. And he was devoted to his books, which were in apple-pie order.

"Everything else in the station was in a muddle,—heads, things, buildings. Strings of dusty niggers with splay feet arrived and departed; a stream of manufactured goods, rubbishy cottons, beads, and brass-wire set into the depths of darkness, and in return came a precious trickle of ivory.

"I had to wait in the station for ten days—an eternity. I lived in a hut in the yard, but to be out of the chaos I would sometimes get into the accountant's office. It was built of horizontal planks, and so badly put together that, as he bent over his high desk, he was barred from neck to heels with narrow strips of sunlight. There was no need to open the big shutter to see. It was hot there too; big flies buzzed fiendishly, and did not sting, but stabbed. I sat generally on the floor, while, of faultless appearance (and even slightly scented), perching on a high stool, he wrote, he wrote. Sometimes he stood up for exercise. When a truckle-bed with a sick man (some invalided agent from up-country) was put in there, he exhibited a gentle annoyance. 'The groans of this sick person,' he said, 'distract my attention. And without that it is extremely difficult to guard against clerical errors in this climate.'

"One day he remarked, without lifting his head, 'In the interior you will no doubt meet Mr. Kurtz.' On my asking who Mr. Kurtz was, he said he was a first-class agent; and seeing my disappointment at this information, he added slowly, laying down his pen, 'He is a very remarkable person.' Further questions elicited from him that Mr. Kurtz was at present in charge of a trading-post, a very important one, in the true ivory-country, at 'the very bottom of there. Sends in as much ivory as all the others put together . . .' He began to write again. The sick man was too ill to groan. The flies buzzed in a great peace.

"Suddenly there was a growing murmur of voices and a great tramping of feet. A caravan had come in. A violent babble of uncouth sounds burst out on the other side of the planks. All the carriers were speaking together, and in the midst of the uproar the lamentable voice of the chief agent was heard 'giving it up' tearfully for the twentieth time that day. . . . He rose slowly. 'What a frightful row,' he said. He crossed the room gently to look at the sick man, and returning, said to me, 'He does not hear.' 'What! Dead?' I asked, startled. 'No, not yet,' he answered, with great composure. Then, alluding with a toss of the head to the tumult in the station-yard, 'When one has got to make correct entries, one comes to hate those savages—hate them to the death.' He remained thoughtful for a moment. 'When you see Mr. Kurtz,' he went on, 'tell him

from me that everything here'—he glanced at the desk—'is very satisfactory. I don't like to write to him—with those messengers of ours you never know who may get hold of your letter—at that Central Station.' He stared at me for a moment with his mild, bulging eyes. 'Oh, he will go far, very far,' he began again. 'He will be a somebody in the Administration before long. They, above —the Council in Europe, you know— mean him to be.'

"He turned to his work. The noise outside had ceased, and presently in going out I stopped at the door. In the steady buzz of flies the homeward-bound agent was lying flushed and insensible; the other, bent over his books, was making correct entries of perfectly correct transactions; and fifty feet below the doorstep I could see the still tree-tops of the grove of death.

"Next day I left that station at last, with a caravan of sixty men, for a two-hundred-mile tramp.

"No use telling you much about that. Paths, paths, everywhere; a stamped-in network of paths spreading over the empty land, through long grass, through burnt grass, through thickets, down and up chilly ravines, up and down stony hills ablaze with heat; and a solitude, a solitude, nobody, not a hut. The population had cleared out a long time ago. Well, if a lot of mysterious niggers armed with all kinds of fearful weapons suddenly took to travelling on the road between Deal and Gravesend, catching the yokels right and left to carry heavy loads for them, I fancy every farm and cottage thereabouts would get empty very soon. Only here the dwellings were gone too. Still, I passed through several abandoned villages. There's something pathetically childish in the ruins of grass walls. Day after day, with the stamp and shuffle of sixty pair of bare feet behind me, each pair under a 60-lb. load. Camp, cook, sleep; strike camp, march. Now and then a carrier dead in harness, at rest in the long grass near the path, with an empty water-gourd and his long staff lying by his side. A great silence around and above. Perhaps on some quiet night the tremor of far-off drums, sinking, swelling, a tremor vast, faint; a sound weird, appealing, suggestive, and wild—and perhaps with as profound a meaning as the sound of bells in a Christian country. Once a white man in an unbuttoned uniform, camping on the path with an armed escort of lank Zanzibaris, very hospitable and festive—not to say drunk. Was looking after the upkeep of the road, he declared. Can't say I saw any road or any upkeep, unless the body of a middle-aged negro, with a bullet-hole in the forehead, upon which I absolutely stumbled three miles farther on, may be considered as a permanent improvement. I had a white companion too, not a bad chap, but rather too fleshy and with the exasperating habit of fainting on the hot hillsides, miles away from the least bit of shade and water. Annoying, you know, to hold your own coat like a parasol over a man's head while he is coming to. I couldn't help asking him once what he meant by coming there at all. 'To make money, of course. What do you think?' he said scornfully. Then he got fever, and had to be carried in a hammock slung under a pole. As he weighed sixteen stone I had no end of rows with the carriers. They jibbed, ran away, sneaked off with their loads in the night—quite a mutiny. So, one evening, I made a speech in English with gestures, not one of which was lost to the sixty pairs of eyes before me, and the next morning I started the hammock off in front all right. An hour afterwards I came upon the whole concern wrecked in a bush—man, hammock, groans, blankets, horrors. The heavy pole had skinned his poor nose. He was very anxious for me to kill somebody, but there wasn't the shadow

of a carrier near. I remembered the old doctor—'It would be interesting for science to watch the mental changes of individuals, on the spot.' I felt I was becoming scientifically interesting. However, all that is to no purpose. On the fifteenth day I came in sight of the big river again, and hobbled into the Central Station. It was on a backwater surrounded by scrub and forest, with a pretty border of smelly mud on one side, and on the three others enclosed by a crazy fence of rushes. A neglected gap was all the gate it had, and the first glance at the place was enough to let you see the flabby devil was running that show. White men with long staves in their hands appeared languidly from amongst the buildings, strolling up to take a look at me, and then retired out of sight somewhere. One of them, a stout, excitable chap with black moustaches, informed me with great volubility and many digressions, as soon as I told him who I was, that my steamer was at the bottom of the river. I was thunderstruck. What, how, why? Oh, it was 'all right.' The 'manager himself' was there. All quite correct. 'Everybody had behaved splendidly! splendidly!'— 'You must,' he said in agitation, 'go and see the general manager at once. He is waiting.'

"I did not see the real significance of that wreck at once. I fancy I see it now, but I am not sure—not at all. Certainly the affair was too stupid—when I think of it—to be altogether natural. Still . . . But at the moment it presented itself simply as a confounded nuisance. The steamer was sunk. They had started two days before in a sudden hurry up the river with the manager on board, in charge of some volunteer skipper, and before they had been out three hours they tore the bottom out of her on stones, and she sank near the south bank. I asked myself what I was to do there, now my boat was lost. As a matter of fact, I had plenty to do in fishing my command out of the river. I had to set about it the very next day. That, and the repairs when I brought the pieces to the station, took some months.

"My first interview with the manager was curious. He did not ask me to sit down after my twenty-mile walk that morning. He was commonplace in complexion, in feature, in manners, and in voice. He was of middle size and of ordinary build. His eyes, of the usual blue, were perhaps remarkably cold, and he certainly could make his glance fall on one as trenchant and heavy as an axe. But even at these times the rest of his person seemed to disclaim the intention. Otherwise there was only an indefinable, faint expression of his lips, something stealthy—a smile—not a smile—I remember it, but I can't explain. It was unconscious, this smile was, though just after he had said something it got intensified for an instant. It came at the end of his speeches like a seal applied on the words to make the meaning of the commonest phrase appear absolutely inscrutable. He was a common trader, from his youth up employed in these parts—nothing more. He was obeyed, yet he inspired neither love nor fear, nor even respect. He inspired uneasiness. That was it! Uneasiness. Not a definite mistrust—just uneasiness—nothing more. You have no idea how effective such a . . . a . . . faculty can be. He had no genius for organizing, for initiative, or for order even. That was evident in such things as the deplorable state of the station. He had no learning, and no intelligence. His position had come to him— why? Perhaps because he was never ill . . . He had served three terms of three years out there . . . Because triumphant health in the general rout of constitutions is a kind of power in itself. When he went home on leave he rioted on a large scale—pompously. Jack ashore —with a difference—in externals only. This one could gather from his casual talk. He originated nothing, he could keep the routine going—that's all. But he was great. He was great by this little thing that it was impossible to tell what could control such a man. He never gave that secret away. Perhaps there was nothing within him. Such a suspicion made one pause—for out there there were no external checks. Once when various tropical diseases had laid low almost every 'agent' in the station, he was heard to say, 'Men who come out here should have no entrails.' He sealed the utterance with that smile of his, as though it had been a door opening into a darkness he had in his keeping. You fancied you had seen things—but the seal was on. When annoyed at mealtimes by the constant quarrels of the white men about precedence, he ordered an immense round table to be made, for which a special house had to be built. This was the station's messroom. Where he sat was the first place —the rest was nowhere. One felt this to be his unalterable conviction. He was neither civil nor uncivil. He was quiet. He allowed his 'boy'—an overfed young negro from the coast—to treat the white men, under his very eyes, with provoking insolence.

"He began to speak as soon as he saw me. I had been very long on the road. He could not wait. Had to start without me. The up-river stations had to be relieved. There had been so many delays already that he did not know who was dead and who was alive, and how they got on—and so on, and so on. He paid no attention to my explanations, and, playing with a stick of sealing-wax, repeated several times that the situation was 'very grave, very grave.' There were rumors that a very important station was in jeopardy, and its chief, Mr. Kurtz, was ill. Hoped it was not true. Mr. Kurtz was . . . I felt weary and irritable. Hang Kurtz, I thought. I interrupted him by saying I had heard of Mr. Kurtz on the coast. 'Ah! So they talk of him down there,' he murmured to himself. Then he began again, assuring me Mr. Kurtz was the best agent he had, an exceptional man, of the greatest importance to the Company; therefore I could understand his anxiety. He was, he said, 'very, very uneasy.' Certainly he fidgeted on his chair a good deal, exclaimed, 'Ah, Mr. Kurtz!' broke the stick of sealing-wax and seemed dumbfounded by the accident. Next thing he wanted to know 'how long it would take to' . . . I interrupted him again. Being hungry, you know, and kept on my feet too, I was getting savage. 'How can I tell?' I said. 'I haven't even seen the wreck yet—some months, no doubt.' All this talk seemed to me so futile. 'Some months,' he said. 'Well, let us say three months before we can make a start. Yes. That ought to do the affair.' I flung out of his hut (he lived all alone in a clay hut with a sort of verandah) muttering to myself my opinion of him. He was a chattering idiot. Afterwards I took it back when it was borne in upon me startlingly with what extreme nicety he had estimated the time requisite for the 'affair.'

"I went to work the next day, turning, so to speak, my back on that station. In that way only it seemed to me I could keep my hold on the redeeming facts of life. Still, one must look about sometimes; and then I saw this station, these men strolling aimlessly about in the sunshine of the yard. I asked myself sometimes what it all meant. They wandered here and there with their absurd long staves in their hands, like a lot of faithless pilgrims bewitched inside a rotten fence. The word 'ivory' rang in the air, was whispered, was sighed. You would think they were praying to it. A taint of imbecile rapacity blew through it all, like a whiff from some corpse. By Jove! I've never seen anything so unreal in my life. And outside, the silent wilderness surrounding this cleared speck on the earth struck me as something great and invincible, like evil or truth, waiting patiently for the passing away of this fantastic invasion.

"Oh, those months! Well, never mind. Various things happened. One evening a grass shed full of calico, cotton prints, beads, and I don't know what else, burst into a blaze so suddenly that you would have thought the earth had opened to let an avenging fire consume all that trash. I was smoking my pipe quietly by my dismantled steamer, and saw them all cutting capers in the light, with their arms lifted high, when the stout man with moustaches came tearing down to the river, a tin pail in his hand, assured me that everybody was 'behaving splendidly, splendidly,' dipped about a quart of water and tore back again. I noticed there was a hole in the bottom of his pail.

"I strolled up. There was no hurry. You see the thing had gone off like a box of matches. It had been hopeless from the very first. The flame had leaped high, driven everybody back, lighted up everything—and collapsed. The shed was already a heap of embers glowing fiercely. A nigger was being beaten near by. They said he had caused the fire in some way; be that as it may, he was screeching most horribly. I saw him, later, for several days, sitting in a bit of shade looking very sick and trying to recover himself: afterwards he arose and went out—and the wilderness without a sound took him into its bosom again. As I approached the glow from the dark I found myself at the back of two men, talking. I heard the name of Kurtz pronounced, then the words, 'take advantage of this unfortunate accident.' One of the men was the manager. I wished him a good evening. 'Did you ever see anything like it—eh? it is incredible,' he said, and walked off. The other man remained. He was a first-class agent, young, gentlemanly, a bit reserved, with a forked little beard and a hooked nose. He was stand-offish with the other agents, and they on their side said he was the manager's spy upon them. As to me, I had hardly ever spoken to him before. We got into talk, and by and by we strolled away from the hissing ruins. Then he asked me to his room, which was in the main building of the station. He struck a match, and I perceived that this young aristocrat had not only a silver-mounted dressing-case but also a whole candle all to himself. Just at that time the manager was the only man supposed to have any right to candles. Native mats covered the clay walls; a collection of spears, assegais, shields, knives, was hung up in trophies. The business entrusted to this fellow was the making of bricks—so I had been informed; but there wasn't a fragment of a brick anywhere in the station, and he had been there more than a year—waiting. It seems he could not make bricks without something, I don't know what—straw maybe. Anyway, it could not be found there, and as it was not likely to be sent from Europe, it did not appear clear to me what he was waiting for. An act of special creation perhaps. However, they were all waiting—all the sixteen or twenty pilgrims of them—for something; and upon my word it did not seem an uncongenial occupation, from the way they took it, though the only thing that ever came to them was disease—as far as I could see. They beguiled the time by backbiting and intriguing against each other in a foolish kind of way. There was an air of plotting about that station, but nothing came of it, of course. It was as unreal as everything else—as the philanthropic pretense of the whole concern, as their talk, as their government, as their show of work. The only real feeling was a desire to get appointed to a trading-post where ivory was to be had, so that they could earn percentages. They intrigued and slandered and hated each other only on that account—but as to effectually lifting a little finger—oh no. By Heavens! there is something after

all in the world allowing one man to steal a horse while another must not look at a halter. Steal a horse straight out. Very well. He has done it. Perhaps he can ride. But there is a way of looking at a halter that would provoke the most charitable of saints into a kick.

"I had no idea why he wanted to be sociable, but as we chatted in there it suddenly occurred to me the fellow was trying to get at something—in fact, pumping me. He alluded constantly to Europe, to the people I was supposed to know there—putting leading questions as to my acquaintances in the sepulchral city, and so on. His little eyes glittered like mica discs—with curiosity—though he tried to keep up a bit of superciliousness. At first I was astonished, but very soon I became awfully curious to see what he would find out from me. I couldn't possibly imagine what I had in me to make it worth his while. It was very pretty to see how he baffled himself, for in truth my body was full only of chills, and my head had nothing in it but that wretched steamboat business. It was evident he took me for a perfectly shameless prevaricator. At last he got angry, and, to conceal a movement of furious annoyance, he yawned. I rose. Then I noticed a small sketch in oils, on a panel, representing a woman, draped and blindfolded, carrying a lighted torch. The background was somber—almost black. The movement of the woman was stately, and the effect of the torchlight on the face was sinister.

"It arrested me, and he stood by civilly, holding an empty half-pint champagne bottle (medical comforts) with the candle stuck in it. To my question he said Mr. Kurtz had painted this—in this very station more than a year ago—while waiting for means to go to his trading-post. 'Tell me, pray,' said I, 'who is this Mr. Kurtz?'

" 'The chief of the Inner Station,' he answered in a short tone, looking away. 'Much obliged,' I said, laughing. 'And you are the brickmaker of the Central Station. Every one knows that.' He was silent for a while. 'He is a prodigy,' he said at last. 'He is an emissary of pity, and science, and progress, and devil knows what else. We want,' he began to declaim suddenly, 'for the guidance of the cause entrusted to us by Europe, so to speak, higher intelligence, wide sympathies, a singleness of purpose.' 'Who says that?' I asked. 'Lots of them,' he replied. 'Some even write that; and so *he* comes here, a special being, as you ought to know.' 'Why ought I to know?' I interrupted, really surprised. He paid no attention. 'Yes. To-day he is chief of the best station, next year he will be assistant-manager, two years more and . . . but I daresay you know what he will be in two years' time. You are of the new gang—the gang of virtue. The same people who sent him specially also recommended you. Oh, don't say no. I've my own eyes to trust.' Light dawned upon me. My dear aunt's influential acquaintances were producing an unexpected effect upon that young man. I nearly burst into a laugh. 'Do you read the Company's confidential correspondence?' I asked. He hadn't a word to say. It was great fun. 'When Mr. Kurtz,' I continued severely,' is General Manager, you won't have the opportunity.'

"He blew the candle out suddenly, and we went outside. The moon had risen. Black figures strolled about listlessly, pouring water on the glow, whence proceeded a sound of hissing; steam ascended in the moonlight; the beaten nigger groaned somewhere. 'What a row the brute makes!' said the indefatigable man with the moustaches, appearing near us. 'Serve him right. Transgression — punishment — bang! Pitiless, pitiless. That's the only way. This will prevent all conflagrations for the future. I was just telling the manager . . .' He noticed my companion, and became crestfallen all at once. 'Not in bed yet,' he said, with a kind of ser-vile heartiness; 'it's so natural. Ha! Danger—agitation.' He vanished. I went on to the river-side, and the other followed me. I heard a scathing murmur at my ear, 'Heaps of muffs—go to.' The Pilgrims could be seen in knots gesticulating, discussing. Several had still their staves in their hands. I verily believe they took these sticks to bed with them. Beyond the fence the forest stood up spectrally in the moonlight, and through the dim stir, through the faint sounds of that lamentable courtyard, the silence of the land went home to one's very heart—its mystery, its greatness, the amazing reality of its concealed life. The hurt nigger moaned feebly somewhere near by, and then fetched a deep sigh that made me mend my pace away from there. I felt a hand introducing itself under my arm. 'My dear sir,' said the fellow, 'I don't want to be misunderstood, and especially by you, who will see Mr. Kurtz long before I can have that pleasure. I wouldn't like him to get a false idea of my disposition. . . .'

"I let him run on, this papier-mâché Mephistopheles, and it seemed to me that if I tried I could poke my forefinger through him, and would find nothing inside but a little loose dirt, maybe. He, don't you see, had been planning to be assistant-manager by and by under the present man, and I could see that the coming of that Kurtz had upset them both not a little. He talked precipitately, and I did not try to stop him. I had my shoulders against the wreck of my steamer, hauled up on the slope like a carcass of some big river animal. The smell of mud, of primeval mud, by Jove! was in my nostrils, the high stillness of primeval forest was before my eyes; there were shiny patches on the black creek. The moon had spread over everything a thin layer of silver—over the rank grass, over the mud, upon the wall of matted vegetation standing higher than the wall of a temple, over the great river I could see through a somber gap glittering, glittering, as it flowed broadly by without a murmur. All this was great, expectant, mute, while the man jabbered about himself. I wondered whether the stillness on the face of the immensity looking at us two were meant as an appeal or as a menace. What were we who had strayed in here? Could we handle that dumb thing, or would it handle us? I felt how big, how confoundedly big, was that thing that couldn't talk and perhaps was deaf as well. What was in there? I could see a little ivory coming out from there, and I had heard Mr. Kurtz was in there. I had heard enough about it too—God knows! Yet somehow it didn't bring any image with it—no more than if I had been told an angel or a fiend was in there. I believed it in the same way one of you might believe there are inhabitants in the planet Mars. I knew once a Scotch sailmaker who was certain, dead sure, there were people in Mars. If you asked him for some idea how they looked and behaved, he would get shy and mutter something about 'walking on all-fours.' If you as much as smiled, he would—though a man of sixty—offer to fight you. I would not have gone so far as to fight for Kurtz, but I went for him near enough to a lie. You know I hate, detest, and can't bear a lie, not because I am straighter than the rest of us, but simply because it appals me. There is a taint of death, a flavor of mortality in lies—which is exactly what I hate and detest in the world—what I want to forget. It makes me miserable and sick, like biting something rotten would do. Temperament, I suppose. Well, I went near enough to it by letting the young fool there believe anything he liked to imagine as to my influence in Europe. I became in an instant as much of a pretense as the rest of the bewitched pilgrims. This simply because I had a notion it somehow would be of help to that Kurtz whom at the time I did not see—you understand. He was just a word for me.

I did not see the man in the name any more than you do. Do you see him? Do you see the story? Do you see anything? It seems to me I am trying to tell you a dream—making a vain attempt, because no relation of a dream can convey the dream-sensation, that commingling of absurdity, surprise, and bewilderment in a tremor of struggling revolt, that notion of being captured by the incredible which is of the very essence of dreams. . . ."

He was silent for a while.

". . . No, it is impossible; it is impossible to convey the life-sensation of any given epoch of one's existence—that which makes its truth, its meaning—its subtle and penetrating essence. It is impossible. We live, as we dream—alone. . . ."

He paused again as if reflecting, then added:

"Of course in this you fellows see more than I could then. You see me, whom you know. . . ."

It had become so pitch dark that we listeners could hardly see one another. For a long time already he, sitting apart, had been no more to us than a voice. There was not a word from anybody. The others might have been asleep, but I was awake. I listened, I listened on the watch for the sentence, for the word, that would give me the clue to the faint uneasiness inspired by this narrative that seemed to shape itself without human lips in the heavy night-air of the river.

". . . Yes—I let him run on," Marlow began again, "and think what he pleased about the powers that were behind me. I did! And there was nothing behind me! There was nothing but that wretched, old, mangled steamboat I was leaning against, while he talked fluently about 'the necessity for every man to get on.' 'And when one comes out here, you conceive, it is not to gaze at the moon.' Mr. Kurtz was a 'universal genius,' but even a genius would find it easier to work with 'adequate tools—

intelligent men.' He did not make bricks—why, there was a physical impossibility in the way—as I was well aware; and if he did secretarial work for the manager, it was because 'no sensible man rejects wantonly the confidence of his superiors.' Did I see it? I saw it. What more did I want? What I really wanted was rivets, by Heaven! Rivets. To get on with the work—to stop the hole. Rivets I wanted. There were cases of them down at the coast—cases—piled up—burst—split! You kicked a loose rivet at every second step in that station yard on the hillside. Rivets had rolled into the grove of death. You could fill your pockets with rivets for the trouble of stooping down—and there wasn't one rivet to be found where it was wanted. We had plates that would do, but nothing to fasten them with. And every week the messenger, a lone negro, letter-bag on shoulder and staff in hand, left our station for the coast. And several times a week a coast caravan came in with trade goods—ghastly glazed calico that made you shudder only to look at it, glass beads value about a penny a quart, confounded spotted cotton handkerchiefs. And no rivets. Three carriers could have brought all that was wanted to set that steamboat afloat.

"He was becoming confidential now, but I fancy my unresponsive attitude must have exasperated him at last, for he judged it necessary to inform me he feared neither God nor devil, let alone any mere man. I said I could see that very well, but what I wanted was a certain quantity of rivets—and rivets were what really Mr. Kurtz wanted, if he had only known it. Now letters went to the coast every week. . . . 'My dear sir,' he cried, 'I write from dictation.' I demanded rivets. There was a way—for an intelligent man. He changed his manner; became very cold, and suddenly began to talk about a hippopotamus; wondered whether sleeping on board the steamer (I stuck to my salvage night and day) I wasn't disturbed. There was an old hippo that had the bad habit of getting out on the bank and roaming at night over the station grounds. The pilgrims used to turn out in a body and empty every rifle they could lay hands on at him. Some even had sat up o'nights for him. All this energy was wasted, though. 'That animal has a charmed life,' he said; 'but you can say this only of brutes in this country. No man—you apprehend me?—no man here bears a charmed life.' He stood there for a moment in the moonlight with his delicate hooked nose set a little askew, and his mica eyes glittering without a wink, then, with a curt Good-night, he strode off. I could see he was disturbed and considerably puzzled, which made me feel more hopeful than I had been for days. It was a great comfort to turn from that chap to my influential friend, the battered, twisted, ruined, tin-pot steamboat. I clambered on board. She rang under my feet like an empty Huntley & Palmer biscuit-tin kicked along a gutter; she was nothing so solid in make, and rather less pretty in shape, but I had expended enough hard work on her to make me love her. No influential friend would have served me better. She had given me a chance to come out a bit—to find out what I could do. No, I don't like work. I had rather laze about and think of all the fine things that can be done. I don't like work—no man does—but I like what is in the work—the chance to find yourself. Your own reality—for yourself, not for others—what no other man can ever know. They can only see the mere show, and never can tell what it really means.

"I was not surprised to see somebody sitting aft, on the deck, with his legs dangling over the mud. You see I rather chummed with the few mechanics there were in that station, whom the other pilgrims naturally despised—on account of their imperfect manners, I suppose. This was the foreman—a boiler-maker by trade—a good worker. He was a lank, bony, yellow-faced man, with big intense eyes. His aspect was worried, and his head was as bald as the palm of my hand; but his hair in falling seemed to have stuck to his chin, and had prospered in the new locality, for his beard hung down to his waist. He was a widower with six young children (he had left them in charge of a sister of his to come out there), and the passion of his life was pigeon-flying. He was an enthusiast and a connoisseur. He would rave about pigeons. After work hours he used sometimes to come over from his hut for a talk about his children and his pigeons; at work, when he had to crawl in the mud under the bottom of the steamboat, he would tie up that beard of his in a kind of white serviette he brought for the purpose. It had loops to go over his ears. In the evening he could be seen squatted on the bank rinsing that wrapper in the creek with great care, then spreading it solemnly on a bush to dry.

"I slapped him on the back and shouted 'We shall have rivets!' He scrambled to his feet exclaiming 'No! Rivets!' as though he couldn't believe his ears. Then in a low voice, 'You . . . eh?' I don't know why we behaved like lunatics. I put my finger to the side of my nose and nodded mysteriously. 'Good for you!' he cried, snapped his fingers above his head, lifting one foot. I tried a jig. We capered on the iron deck. A frightful clatter came out of that hulk, and the virgin forest on the other bank of the creek sent it back in a thundering roll upon the sleeping station. It must have made some of the pilgrims sit up in their hovels. A dark figure obscured the lighted doorway of the manager's hut, vanished, then, a second or so after, the doorway itself vanished too. We stopped, and the silence driven away by the stamping of our feet flowed back again from the recesses

of the land. The great wall of vegetation, an exuberant and entangled mass of trunks, branches, leaves, boughs, festoons, motionless in the moonlight, was like a rioting invasion of soundless life, a rolling wave of plants, piled up, crested, ready to topple over the creek, to sweep every little man of us out of his little existence. And it moved not. A deadened burst of mighty splashes and snorts reached us from afar, as though an ichthyosaurus had been taking a bath of glitter in the great river. 'After all,' said the boiler-maker in a reasonable tone, 'why shouldn't we get the rivets? Why not, indeed! I did not know of any reason why we shouldn't. 'They'll come in three weeks,' I said confidently.

"But they didn't. Instead of rivets there came an invasion, an infliction, a visitation. It came in sections during the next three weeks, each section headed by a donkey carrying a white man in new clothes and tan shoes, bowing from that elevation right and left to the impressed pilgrims. A quarrelsome band of footsore sulky niggers trod on the heels of the donkey; a lot of tents, camp-stools, tin boxes, white cases, brown bales would be shot down in the courtyard, and the air of mystery would deepen a little over the muddle of the station. Five such instalments came, with their absurd air of disorderly flight with the loot of innumerable outfit shops and provision stores, that, one would think, they were lugging, after a raid, into the wilderness for equitable division. It was an inextricable mess of things decent in themselves but that human folly made look like the spoils of thieving.

"This devoted band called itself the Eldorado Exploring Expedition, and I believe they were sworn to secrecy. Their talk, however, was the talk of sordid buccaneers: it was reckless without hardihood, greedy without audacity, and cruel without courage; there was not an atom of foresight or of serious intention in the whole batch of them, and they did not seem aware these things are wanted for the work of the world. To tear treasure out of the bowels of the land was their desire, with no more moral purpose at the back of it than there is in burglars breaking into a safe. Who paid the expenses of the noble enterprise I don't know; but the uncle of our manager was leader of that lot.

"In exterior he resembled a butcher in a poor neighborhood, and his eyes had a look of sleepy cunning. He carried his fat paunch with ostentation on his short legs, and during the time his gang infested the station spoke to no one but his nephew. You could see these two roaming about all day long with their heads close together in an everlasting confab.

"I had given up worrying myself about the rivets. One's capacity for that kind of folly is more limited than you would suppose. I said Hang!—and let things slide. I had plenty of time for meditation, and now and then I would give some thought to Kurtz. I wasn't very interested in him. No. Still, I was curious to see whether this man, who had come out equipped with moral ideas of some sort, would climb to the top after all, and how he would set about his work when there."

II

"One evening as I was lying flat on the deck of my steamboat, I heard voices approaching—and there were the nephew and the uncle strolling along the bank. I laid my head on my arm again, and had nearly lost myself in a doze, when somebody said in my ear, as it were: 'I am as harmless as a little child, but I don't like to be dictated to. Am I the manager—or am I not? I was ordered to send him there. It's incredible.' . . . I became aware that the two were standing on the shore alongside the forepart of the steamboat, just be-

low my head. I did not move; it did not occur to me to move: I was sleepy. 'It *is* unpleasant,' grunted the uncle. 'He has asked the Administration to be sent there,' said the other, 'with the idea of showing what he could do; and I was instructed accordingly. Look at the influence that man must have. Is it not frightful?' They both agreed it was frightful, then made several bizarre remarks: 'Make rain and fine weather—one man—the Council—by the nose'—bits of absurd sentences that got the better of my drowsiness, so that I had pretty near the whole of my wits about me when the uncle said, "The climate may do away with this difficulty for you. Is he alone there?' 'Yes,' answered the manager; 'he sent his assistant down the river with a note to me in these terms: "Clear this poor devil out of the country, and don't bother sending more of that sort. I had rather be alone than have the kind of men you can dispose of with me." It was more than a year ago. Can you imagine such impudence?' 'Anything since then?' asked the other hoarsely. 'Ivory,' jerked the nephew; 'lots of it—prime sort—lots—most annoying, from him.' 'And with that?' questioned the heavy rumble. 'Invoice,' was the reply fired out, so to speak. Then silence. They had been talking about Kurtz.

"I was broad awake by this time, but, lying perfectly at ease, remained still, having no inducement to change my position. 'How did that ivory come all this way?' growled the elder man, who seemed very vexed. The other explained that it had come with a fleet of canoes in charge of an English half-caste clerk Kurtz had with him; that Kurtz had apparently intended to return himself, the station being by that time bare of goods and stores, but after coming three hundred miles, had suddenly decided to go back, which he started to do alone in a small dugout with four paddlers, leaving the half-caste to continue down the river with the ivory. The two

fellows there seemed astounded at anybody attempting such a thing. They were
at a loss for an adequate motive. As for
me, I seemed to see Kurtz for the first
time. It was a distinct glimpse: the
dugout, four paddling savages, and the
lone white man turning back suddenly
on the headquarters, on relief, on
thoughts of home—perhaps; setting his
face towards the depths of the wilderness, towards his empty and desolate
station. I did not know the motive.
Perhaps he was just simply a fine fellow
who stuck to his work for its own sake.
His name, you understand, had not been
pronounced once. He was 'that man.'
The half-caste, who, as far as I could
see, had conducted a difficult trip with
great prudence and pluck, was invariably alluded to as 'that scoundrel.' The
'scoundrel' had reported that the 'man'
had been very ill—had recovered im-
perfectly. . . . The two below me moved
away then a few paces, and strolled back
and forth at some little distance. I heard:
'Military post—doctor—two hundred
miles—quite alone now—unavoidable
delays—nine months—no news—strange
rumors.' They approached again, just as
the manager was saying, 'No one, as far
as I know, unless a species of wandering
trader—a pestilential fellow, snapping
ivory from the natives.' Who was it
they were talking about now? I gathered
in snatches that this was some man supposed to be in Kurtz's district, and of
whom the manager did not approve. 'We
will not be free from unfair competition till one of these fellows is hanged
for an example,' he said. 'Certainly,'
grunted the other; 'get him hanged!
Why not? Anything—anything can be
done in this country. That's what I say;
nobody here, you understand, here, can
endanger your position. And why? You
stand the climate—you outlast them all.
The danger is in Europe; but there before I left I took care to——' They
moved off and whispered, then their
voices rose again. 'The extraordinary
series of delays is not my fault. I did my

possible.' The fat man sighed, 'Very sad.'
'And the pestiferous absurdity of his
talk,' continued the other; 'he bothered
me enough when he was here. "Each
station should be like a beacon on the
road towards better things, a center for
trade of course, but also for humanizing,
improving, instructing." Conceive you—
that ass! And he wants to be manager!
No, it's——' Here he got choked by
excessive indignation, and I lifted my
head the least bit. I was surprised to
see how near they were—right under
me. I could have spat upon their hats.
They were looking on the ground, absorbed in thought. The manager was
switching his leg with a slender twig:
his sagacious relative lifted his head.
'You have been well since you came
out this time?' he asked. The other
gave a start. 'Who? I? Oh! Like a
charm—like a charm. But the rest—oh,
my goodness! All sick. They die so
quick, too, that I haven't the time to
send them out of the country—it's incredible!' 'H'm. Just so,' grunted the
uncle. 'Ah! my boy, trust to this—I say,
trust to this.' I saw him extend his
short flipper of an arm for a gesture
that took in the forest, the creek, the
mud, the river—seemed to beckon with
a dishonoring flourish before the sunlit face of the land a treacherous appeal
to the lurking death, to the hidden
evil, to the profound darkness of its
heart. It was so startling that I leaped
to my feet and looked back at the edge
of the forest, as though I had expected
an answer of some sort to that black
display of confidence. You know the
foolish notions that come to one sometimes. The high stillness confronted
these two figures with its ominous
patience, waiting for the passing away
of a fantastic invasion.

"They swore aloud together—out of
sheer fright, I believe—then, pretending
not to know anything of my existence,
turned back to the station. The sun
was low; and leaning forward side by
side, they seemed to be tugging painfully

uphill their two ridiculous shadows of unequal length, that trailed behind them slowly over the tall grass without bending a single blade.

"In a few days the Eldorado Expedition went into the patient wilderness, that closed upon it as the sea closes over a diver. Long afterwards the news came that all the donkeys were dead. I know nothing as to the fate of the less valuable animals. They, no doubt, like the rest of us, found what they deserved. I did not inquire. I was then rather excited at the prospect of meeting Kurtz very soon. When I say very soon I mean it comparatively. It was just two months from the day we left the creek when we came to the bank below Kurtz's station.

"Going up that river was like travelling back to the earliest beginnings of the world, when vegetation rioted on the earth and the big trees were kings. An empty stream, a great silence, an impenetrable forest. The air was warm, thick, heavy, sluggish. There was no joy in the brilliance of sunshine. The long stretches of the waterway ran on, deserted, into the gloom of overshadowed distances. On silvery sandbanks hippos and alligators sunned themselves side by side. The broadening waters flowed through a mob of wooded islands; you lost your way on that river as you would in a desert, and butted all day long against shoals, trying to find the channel, till you thought yourself bewitched and cut off for ever from everything you had known once—somewhere—far away—in another existence perhaps. There were moments when one's past came back to one, as it will sometimes when you have not a moment to spare to yourself; but it came in the shape of an unrestful and noisy dream, remembered with wonder amongst the overwhelming realities of this strange world of plants, and water, and silence. And this stillness of life did not in the least resemble a peace. It was the stillness of an implacable force brooding over an inscrutable intention. It looked at you with a vengeful aspect. I got used to it afterwards; I did not see it any more; I had no time. I had to keep guessing at the channel; I had to discern, mostly by inspiration, the signs of hidden banks; I watched for sunken stones; I was learning to clap my teeth smartly before my heart flew out, when I shaved by a fluke some infernal sly old snag that would have ripped the life out of the tin-pot steamboat and drowned all the pilgrims; I had to keep a look-out for the signs of dead wood we could cut up in the night for next day's steaming. When you have to attend to things of that sort, to the mere incidents of the surface, the reality—the reality, I tell you—fades. The inner truth is hidden—luckily, luckily. But I felt it all the same; I felt often its mysterious stillness watching me at my monkey tricks, just as it watches you fellows performing on your respective tight-ropes for—what is it? half a crown a tumble—"

"Try to be civil, Marlow," growled a voice, and I knew there was at least one listener awake besides myself.

"I beg your pardon. I forgot the heartache which makes up the rest of the price. And indeed what does the price matter, if the trick be well done? You do your tricks very well. And I didn't do badly either, since I managed not to sink that steamboat on my first trip. It's a wonder to me yet. Imagine a blindfolded man set to drive a van over a bad road. I sweated and shivered over that business considerably, I can tell you. After all, for a seaman, to scrape the bottom of the thing that's supposed to float all the time under his care is the unpardonable sin. No one may know of it, but you never forget the thump—eh? A blow on the very heart. You remember it, you dream of it, you wake up at night and think of it—years after—and go hot and cold all over. I don't pretend to say that steamboat floated all the time. More than once she had to wade for a bit, with twenty cannibals splashing around and pushing. We had enlisted some of these chaps on the way for a crew. Fine fellows—cannibals—in their place. They were men one could work with, and I am grateful to them. And, after all, they did not eat each other before my face: they had brought along a provision of hippo-meat which went rotten, and made the mystery of the wilderness stink in my nostrils. Phoo! I can sniff it now. I had the manager on board and three or four pilgrims with their staves—all complete. Sometimes we came upon a station close by the bank, clinging to the skirts of the unknown, and the white men rushing out of a tumble-down hovel, with great gestures of joy and surprise and welcome, seemed very strange—had the appearance of being held there captive by a spell. The word 'ivory' would ring in the air for a while—and on we went again into the silence, along empty reaches, round the still bends, between the high walls of our winding way, reverberating in hollow claps the ponderous beat of the stern-wheel. Trees, trees, millions of trees, massive, immense, running up high; and at their foot, hugging the bank against the stream, crept the little begrimed steamboat, like a sluggish beetle crawling on the floor of a lofty portico. It made you feel very small, very lost, and yet it was not altogether depressing, that feeling. After all, if you were small, the grimy beetle crawled on—which was just what you wanted it to do. Where the pilgrims imagined it crawled to I don't know. To some place where they expected to get something, I bet! For me it crawled towards Kurtz —exclusively; but when the steam-pipes started leaking we crawled very slow. The reaches opened before us and closed behind, as if the forest had stepped leisurely across the water to bar the way for our return. We penetrated deeper and deeper into the heart of darkness. It was very quiet there. At night some-

times the roll of drums behind the curtain of trees would run up the river and remain sustained faintly, as if hovering in the air high over our heads, till the first break of day. Whether it meant war, peace, or prayer we could not tell. The dawns were heralded by the descent of a chill stillness; the woodcutters slept, their fires burned low; the snapping of a twig would make you start. We were wanderers on a prehistoric earth, on an earth that wore the aspect of an unknown planet. We could have fancied ourselves the first of men taking possession of an accursed inheritance, to be subdued at the cost of profound anguish and of excessive toil. But suddenly, as we struggled round a bend, there would be a glimpse of rush walls, of peaked grass-roofs, a burst of yells, a whirl of black limbs, a mass of hands clapping, of feet stamping, of bodies swaying, of eyes rolling, under the droop of heavy and motionless foliage. The steamer toiled along slowly on the edge of a black and incomprehensible frenzy. The prehistoric man was cursing us, praying to us, welcoming us—who could tell? We were cut off from the comprehension of our surroundings; we glided past like phantoms, wondering and secretly appalled, as sane men would be before an enthusiastic outbreak in a madhouse. We could not understand because we were too far and could not remember, because we were travelling in the night of first ages, of those ages that are gone, leaving hardly a sign— and no memories.

"The earth seemed unearthly. We are accustomed to look upon the shackled form of a conquered monster, but there—there you could look at a thing monstrous and free. It was unearthly, and the men were—No, they were not inhuman. Well, you know, that was the worst of it—this suspicion of their not being inhuman. It would come slowly to one. They howled and leaped, and spun, and made horrid faces; but what thrilled you was just the thought of their humanity—like yours—the thought of your remote kinship with this wild and passionate uproar. Ugly. Yes, it was ugly enough; but if you were man enough you would admit to yourself that there was in you just the faintest trace of a response to the terrible frankness of that noise, a dim suspicion of there being a meaning in it which you—you so remote from the night of first ages—could comprehend. And why not? The mind of man is capable of anything—because everything is in it, all the past as well as all the future. What was there after all? Joy, fear, sorrow, devotion, valor, rage—who can tell?—but truth—truth stripped of its cloak of time. Let the fool gape and shudder—the man knows, and can look on without a wink. But he must at least be as much of a man as these on the shore. He must meet that truth with his own true stuff—with his own inborn strength. Principles? Principles won't do. Acquisitions, clothes, pretty rags—rags that would fly off at the first good shake. No; you want a deliberate belief. An appeal to me in this fiendish row—is there? Very well; I hear; I admit, but I have a voice too, and for good or evil mine is the speech that cannot be silenced. Of course, a fool, what with sheer fright and fine sentiments, is always safe. Who's that grunting? You wonder I didn't go ashore for a howl and a dance? Well, no—I didn't. Fine sentiments, you say? Fine sentiments be hanged! I had no time. I had to mess about with white-lead and strips of woolen blanket helping to put bandages on those leaky steam-pipes—I tell you. I had to watch the steering, and circumvent those snags, and get the tin-pot along by hook or by crook. There was surface-truth enough in these things to save a wiser man. And between whiles I had to look after the savage who was fireman. He was an improved specimen; he could fire up a vertical boiler. He was there below me, and, upon my word, to look at him was as edifying as seeing a dog

in a parody of breeches and a feather hat, walking on his hind legs. A few months of training had done for that really fine chap. He squinted at the steam-gauge and at the water-gauge with an evident effort of intrepidity—and he had filed teeth too, the poor devil, and the wool of his pate shaved into queer patterns, and three ornamental scars on each of his cheeks. He ought to have been clapping his hands and stamping his feet on the bank, instead of which he was hard at work, a thrall to strange witchcraft, full of improving knowledge. He was useful because he had been instructed; and what he knew was this—that should the water in that transparent thing disappear, the evil spirit inside the boiler would get angry through the greatness of his thirst, and take a terrible vengeance. So he sweated and fired up and watched the glass fearfully (with an impromptu charm, made of rags, tied to his arm, and a piece of polished bone, as big as a watch, stuck flatways through his lower lip), while the wooded banks slipped past us slowly, the short noise was left behind, the interminable miles of silence—and we crept on, towards Kurtz. But the snags were thick, the water was treacherous and shallow, the boiler seemed indeed to have a sulky devil in it, and thus neither that fireman nor I had any time to peer into our creepy thoughts.

"Some fifty miles below the Inner Station we came upon a hut of reeds, an inclined and melancholy pole, with the unrecognizable tatters of what had been a flag of some sort flying from it, and a neatly stacked wood-pile. This was unexpected. We came to the bank, and on the stack of firewood found a flat piece of board with some faded pencil-writing on it. When deciphered it said: 'Wood for you. Hurry up. Approach cautiously.' There was a signature, but it was illegible—not Kurtz—a much longer word. Hurry up. Where? Up the river? 'Approach cautiously.' We had not done so. But the warning could not have been meant for the place where it could be only found after approach. Something was wrong above. But what —and how much? That was the question. We commented adversely upon the imbecility of that telegraphic style. The bush around said nothing, and would not let us look very far, either. A torn curtain of red twill hung in the doorway of the hut, and flapped sadly in our faces. The dwelling was dismantled; but we could see a white man had lived there not very long ago. There remained a rude table—a plank on two posts; a heap of rubbish reposed in a dark corner, and by the door I picked up a book. It had lost its covers, and the pages had been thumbed into a state of extremely dirty softness; but the back had been lovingly stitched afresh with white cotton thread, which looked clean yet. It was an extraordinary find. Its title was, *An Inquiry into some Points of Seamanship,* by a man Towser, Towson —some such name—Master in His Majesty's Navy. The matter looked dreary reading enough, with illustrative diagrams and repulsive tables of figures, and the copy was sixty years old. I handled this amazing antiquity with the greatest possible tenderness, lest it should dissolve in my hands. Within, Towson or Towser was inquiring earnestly into the breaking strain of ships' chains and tackle, and other such matters. Not a very enthralling book; but at the first glance you could see there a singleness of intention, an honest concern for the right way of going to work, which made these humble pages, thought out so many years ago, luminous with another than a professional light. The simple old sailor, with his talk of chains and purchases, made me forget the jungle and the pilgrims in a delicious sensation of having come upon something unmistakably real. Such a book being there was wonderful enough; but still more astounding were the notes pencilled in the margin, and plainly referring to the text. I couldn't believe my eyes! They were in cipher! Yes, it looked like cipher. Fancy a man lugging with him a book of that description into this nowhere and studying it—and making notes—in cipher at that! It was an extravagant mystery.

"I had been dimly aware for some time of a worrying noise, and when I lifted my eyes I saw the wood-pile was gone, and the manager, aided by all the pilgrims, was shouting at me from the river-side. I slipped the book into my pocket. I assure you to leave off reading was like tearing myself away from the shelter of an old and solid friendship.

"I started the lame engine ahead. 'It must be this miserable trader—this intruder,' exclaimed the manager, looking back malevolently at the place we had left. 'He must be English,' I said. 'It will not save him from getting into trouble if he is not careful,' muttered the manager darkly. I observed with assumed innocence that no man was safe from trouble in this world.

"The current was more rapid now, the steamer seemed at her last gasp, the stern-wheel flopped languidly, and I caught myself listening on tiptoe for the next beat of the float, for in sober truth I expected the wretched thing to give up every moment. It was like watching the last flickers of a life. But still we crawled. Sometimes I would pick out a tree a little way ahead to measure our progress towards Kurtz by, but I lost it invariably before we got abreast. To keep the eyes so long on one thing was too much for human patience. The manager displayed a beautiful resignation. I fretted and fumed and took to arguing with myself whether or no I would talk openly with Kurtz; but before I could come to any conclusion it occurred to me that my speech or my silence, indeed any action of mine, would be a mere futility. What did it matter what any one knew or ignored? What did it matter who was manager? One gets sometimes such a flash of insight. The essentials of this affair lay deep under the surface, beyond my reach, and beyond my power of meddling.

"Towards the evening of the second day we judged ourselves about eight miles from Kurtz's station. I wanted to push on; but the manager looked grave, and told me the navigation up there was so dangerous that it would be advisable, the sun being very low already, to wait where we were till next morning. Moreover, he pointed out that if the warning to approach cautiously were to be followed, we must approach in daylight—not at dusk, or in the dark. This was sensible enough. Eight miles meant nearly three hours' steaming for us, and I could also see suspicious ripples at the upper end of the reach. Nevertheless, I was annoyed beyond expression at the delay, and most unreasonably too, since one night more could not matter much after so many months. As we had plenty of wood, and caution was the word, I brought up in the middle of the stream. The reach was narrow, straight, with high sides like a railway cutting. The dusk came gliding into it long before the sun had set. The current ran smooth and swift, but a dumb immobility sat on the banks. The living trees, lashed together by the creepers and every living bush of the undergrowth, might have been changed into stone, even to the slenderest twig, to the lightest leaf. It was not sleep—it seemed unnatural, like a state of trance. Not the faintest sound of any kind could be heard. You looked on amazed, and began to suspect yourself of being deaf—then the night came suddenly, and struck you blind as well. About three in the morning some large fish leaped, and the loud splash made me jump as though a gun had been fired. When the sun rose there was a white fog, very warm and clammy, and more blinding than the night. It did not shift or drive; it was just there, standing all round you like something solid. At eight or nine, perhaps, it lifted as

a shutter lifts. We had a glimpse of the towering multitude of trees, of the immense matted jungle, with the blazing little ball of the sun hanging over it—all perfectly still—and then the white shutter came down again. smoothly, as if sliding in greased grooves. I ordered the chain, which we had begun to heave in, to be paid out again. Before it stopped running with a muffled rattle, a cry, a very loud cry, as of infinite desolation, soared slowly in the opaque air. It ceased. A complaining clamor, modulated in savage discords, filled our ears. The sheer unexpectedness of it made my hair stir under my cap. I don't know how it struck the others: to me it seemed as though the mist itself had screamed, so suddenly, and apparently from all sides at once, did this tumultuous and mournful uproar arise. It culminated in a hurried outbreak of almost intolerably excessive shrieking, which stopped short, leaving us stiffened in a variety of silly attitudes, and obstinately listening to the nearly as appalling and excessive silence. 'Good God! What is the meaning——?' stammered at my elbow one of the pilgrims—a little fat man, with sandy hair and red whiskers, who wore side-spring boots, and pink pajamas tucked into his socks. Two others remained open-mouthed a whole minute, then dashed into the little cabin, to rush out incontinently and stand darting scared glances, with Winchesters at 'ready' in their hands. What we could see was just the steamer we were on, her outlines blurred as though she had been on the point of dissolving, and a misty strip of water, perhaps two feet broad, around her—and that was all. The rest of the world was nowhere, as far as our eyes and ears were concerned. Just nowhere. Gone, disappeared; swept off without leaving a whisper or a shadow behind.

"I went forward, and ordered the chain to be hauled in short, so as to be ready to trip the anchor and move the steamboat at once if necessary. 'Will they attack?' whispered an awed voice. 'We will all be butchered in this fog,' murmured another. The faces twitched with the strain, the hands trembled slightly, the eyes forgot to wink. It was very curious to see the contrast of expressions of the white men and of the black fellows of our crew, who were as much strangers to that part of the river as we, though their homes were only eight hundred miles away. The whites, of course greatly discomposed, had besides a curious look of being painfully shocked by such an outrageous row. The others had an alert, naturally interested expression; but their faces were essentially quiet, even those of the one or two who grinned as they hauled at the chain. Several exchanged short, grunting phrases, which seemed to settle the matter to their satisfaction. Their headman, a young, broad-chested black, severely draped in dark-blue fringed cloths, with fierce nostrils and his hair all done up artfully in oily ringlets, stood near me. 'Aha!' I said, just for good fellowship's sake. 'Catch 'im,' he snapped, with a bloodshot widening of his eyes and a flash of sharp teeth—'catch 'im. Give 'im to us.' 'To you, eh?' I asked; 'what would you do with them?' 'Eat 'im!' he said curtly, and, leaning his elbow on the rail, looked out into the fog in a dignified and profoundly pensive attitude. I would no doubt have been properly horrified, had it not occurred to me that he and his chaps must be very hungry: that they must have been growing increasingly hungry for at least this month past. They had been engaged for six months (I don't think a single one of them had any clear idea of time, as we at the end of countless ages have. They still belonged to the beginnings of time—had no inherited experience to teach them, as it were), and of course, as long as there was a piece of paper written over in accordance with some farcical law or other made down the river, it didn't

enter anybody's head to trouble how they would live. Certainly they had brought with them some rotten hippo-meat, which couldn't have lasted very long, anyway, even if the pilgrims hadn't, in the midst of a shocking hulla-baloo, thrown a considerable quantity of it overboard. It looked like a high-handed proceeding; but it was really a case of legitimate self-defence. You can't breathe dead hippo waking, sleeping, and eating, and at the same time keep your precarious grip on existence. Besides that, they had given them every week three pieces of brass wire, each about nine inches long; and the theory was they were to buy their provisions with that currency in river-side villages. You can see how *that* worked. There were either no villages, or the people were hostile, or the director, who like the rest of us fed out of tins, with an occasional old he-goat thrown in, didn't want to stop the steamer for some more or less recondite reason. So, unless they swallowed the wire itself, or made loops of it to snare the fishes with, I don't see what good their extravagant salary could be to them. I must say it was paid with a regularity worthy of a large and honorable trading company. For the rest, the only thing to eat—though it didn't look eatable in the least—I saw in their possession was a few lumps of some stuff like half-cooked dough, of a dirty lavender color, they kept wrapped in leaves, and now and then swallowed a piece of, but so small that it seemed done more for the look of the thing than for any serious purpose of sustenance. Why in the name of all the gnawing devils of hunger they didn't go for us—they were thirty to five—and have a good tuck-in for once, amazes me now when I think of it. They were big powerful men, with not much capacity to weigh the consequences, with courage, with strength, even yet, though their skins were no longer glossy and their muscles no longer hard. And I saw that something restraining, one of those human secrets that baffle probability, had come into play there. I looked at them with a swift quickening of interest—not because it occurred to me I might be eaten by them before very long, though I own to you that just then I perceived —in a new light, as it were—how unwholesome the pilgrims looked, and I hoped, yes, I positively hoped, that my aspect was not so—what shall I say?— so—unappetizing: a touch of fantastic vanity which fitted well with the dream-sensation that pervaded all my days at that time. Perhaps I had a little fever too. One can't live with one's finger everlastingly on one's pulse. I had often 'a little fever,' or a little touch of other things—the playful pawstrokes of the wilderness, the preliminary trifling before the more serious onslaught which came in due course. Yes; I looked at them as you would on any human being, with a curiosity of their impulses, motives, capacities, weaknesses, when brought to the test of an inexorable physical necessity. Restraint! What possible restraint? Was it superstition, disgust, patience, fear— or some kind of primitive honor? No fear can stand up to hunger, no patience can wear it out, disgust simply does not exist where hunger is; and as to superstition, beliefs, and what you may call principles, they are less than chaff in a breeze. Don't you know the devilry of lingering starvation, its exasperating torment, its black thoughts, its somber and brooding ferocity? Well, I do. It takes a man all his inborn strength to fight hunger properly. It's really easier to face bereavement, dishonor, and the perdition of one's soul —than this kind of prolonged hunger. Sad, but true. And these chaps too had no earthly reason for any kind of scruple. Restraint! I would just as soon have expected restraint from a hyena prowling amongst the corpses of a battlefield. But there was the fact facing me—the fact dazzling, to be seen, like the foam on the depths of the sea, like a ripple on an unfathomable enigma, a mystery greater—when I thought of it —than the curious, inexplicable note of desperate grief in this savage clamor that had swept by us on the river-bank, behind the blind whiteness of the fog.

Two pilgrims were quarrelling in hurried whispers as to which bank. 'Left.' 'No, no; how can you? Right, right, of course.' 'It is very serious,' said the manager's voice behind me; 'I would be desolated if anything should happen to Mr. Kurtz before we came up.' I looked at him, and had not the slightest doubt he was sincere. He was just the kind of man who would wish to preserve appearances. That was his restraint. But when he muttered something about going on at once, I did not even take the trouble to answer him. I knew, and he knew, that it was impossible. Were we to let go our hold of the bottom, we would be absolutely in the air—in space. We wouldn't be able to tell where we were going to— whether up or down stream, or across— till we fetched against one bank or the other—and then we wouldn't know at first which it was. Of course I made no move. I had no mind for a smash-up. You couldn't imagine a more deadly place for a shipwreck. Whether drowned at once or not, we were sure to perish speedily in one way or another. 'I authorize you to take all the risks,' he said, after a short silence. 'I refuse to take any,' I said shortly; which was just the answer he expected, though its tone might have surprised him. 'Well, I must defer to your judgment. You are captain,' he said, with marked civility. I turned my shoulder to him in sign of my appreciation, and looked into the fog. How long would it last? It was the most hopeless lookout. The approach to this Kurtz grubbing for ivory in the wretched bush was beset by as many dangers as though he had been an enchanted princess sleeping in a fabulous castle. 'Will they attack, do you think?' asked the manager, in a confidential tone.

"I did not think they would attack, for several obvious reasons. The thick fog was one. If they left the bank in their canoes they would get lost in it, as we would be if we attempted to move. Still, I had also judged the jungle of both banks quite impenetrable—and yet eyes were in it, eyes that had seen us. The river-side bushes were certainly very thick; but the undergrowth behind was evidently penetrable. However, during the short lift I had seen no canoes anywhere in the reach—certainly not abreast of the steamer. But what made the idea of attack inconceivable to me was the nature of the noise—of the cries we had heard. They had not the fierce character boding of immediate hostile intention. Unexpected, wild, and violent as they had been, they had given me an irresistible impression of sorrow. The glimpse of the steamboat had for some reason filled those savages with unrestrained grief. The danger, if any, I expounded, was from our proximity to a great human passion let loose. Even extreme grief may ultimately vent itself in violence—but more generally takes the form of apathy. . . .

"You should have seen the pilgrims stare! They had no heart to grin, or even to revile me; but I believe they thought me gone mad—with fright, maybe. I delivered a regular lecture. My dear boys, it was no good bothering. Keep a look-out? Well, you may guess I watched the fog for the signs of lifting as a cat watches a mouse; but for anything else our eyes were of no more use to us than if we had been buried miles deep in a heap of cotton-wool. It felt like it too—choking, warm, stifling. Besides, all I said, though it sounded extravagant, was absolutely true to fact. What we afterwards alluded to as an attack was really an attempt at repulse. The action was very far from being aggressive—it was not even defensive, in

the usual sense: it was undertaken under the stress of desperation, and in its essence was purely protective.

"It developed itself, I should say, two hours after the fog lifted, and its commencement was at a spot, roughly speaking, about a mile and a half below Kurtz's station. We had just floundered and flopped round a bend, when I saw an islet, a mere grassy hummock of bright green, in the middle of the stream. It was the only thing of the kind; but as we opened the reach more, I perceived it was the head of a long sandbank, or rather of a chain of shallow patches stretching down the middle of the river. They were discolored, just awash, and the whole lot was seen just under the water, exactly as a man's backbone is seen running down the middle of his back under the skin. Now, as far as I did see, I could go to the right or to the left of this. I didn't know either channel, of course. The banks looked pretty well alike, the depth appeared the same; but as I had been informed the station was on the west side, I naturally headed for the western passage.

"No sooner had we fairly entered it than I became aware it was much narrower than I had supposed. To the left of us there was the long uninterrupted shoal, and to the right a high steep bank heavily overgrown with bushes. Above the bush the trees stood in serried ranks. The twigs overhung the current thickly, and from distance to distance a large limb of some tree projected rigidly over the stream. It was then well on in the afternoon, the face of the forest was gloomy, and a broad strip of shadow had already fallen on the water. In this shadow we steamed up—very slowly, as you may imagine. I sheered her well inshore—the water being deepest near the bank, as the sounding-pole informed me.

"One of my hungry and forbearing friends was sounding in the bows just below me. This streamboat was exactly like a decked scow. On the deck there were two little teak-wood houses, with doors and windows. The boiler was in the fore-end, and the machinery right astern. Over the whole there was a light roof, supported on stanchions. The funnel projected through that roof, and in front of the funnel a small cabin built of light planks served for a pilot-house. It contained a couch, two camp-stools, a loaded Martini-Henry leaning in one corner, a tiny table, and the steering-wheel. It had a wide door in front and a broad shutter at each side. All these were always thrown open, of course. I spent my days perched up there on the extreme fore-end of that roof, before the door. At night I slept, or tired to, on the couch. An athletic black belonging to some coast tribe, and educated by my poor predecessor, was the helmsman. He sported a pair of brass earrings, wore a blue cloth wrapper from the waist to the ankles, and thought all the world of himself. He was the most unstable kind of fool I had ever seen. He steered with no end of a swagger while you were by; but if he lost sight of you, he became instantly the prey of an abject funk, and would let that cripple of a steamboat get the upper hand of him in a minute.

"I was looking down at the sounding-pole, and feeling much annoyed to see at each try a little more of it stick out of that river, when I saw my poleman give up the business suddenly, and stretch himself flat on the deck, without even taking the trouble to haul his pole in. He kept hold on it though, and it trailed in the water. At the same time the fireman, whom I could also see below me, sat down abruptly before his furnace and ducked his head. I was amazed. Then I had to look at the river mighty quick, because there was a snag in the fairway. Sticks, little sticks, were flying about—thick: they were whizzing before my nose, dropping below me, striking behind me against my pilot-house. All this time the river, the

shore, the woods were very quiet—perfectly quiet. I could only hear the heavy splashing thump of the stern-wheel and the patter of these things. We cleared the snag clumsily. Arrows, by Jove! We were being shot at! I stepped in quickly to close the shutter on the land-side. That fool-helmsman, his hands on the spokes, was lifting his knees high, stamping his feet, champing his mouth, like a reined-in horse. Confound him! And we were staggering within ten feet of the bank. I had to lean right out to swing the heavy-shutter, and I saw a face amongst the leaves on the level with my own, looking at me very fierce and steady; and then suddenly, as though a veil had been removed from my eyes, I made out, deep in the tangled gloom, naked breasts, arms, legs, glaring eyes—the bush was swarming with human limbs in movement, glistening, of bronzed color. The twigs shook, swayed, and rustled, the arrows flew out of them, and then the shutter came to. 'Steer her straight,' I said to the helmsman. He held his head rigid, face forward; but his eyes rolled, he kept on lifting and setting down his feet gently, his mouth foamed a little. 'Keep quiet!' I said in a fury. I might just as well have ordered a tree not to sway in the wind. I darted out. Below me there was a great scuffle of feet on the iron deck; confused exclamations; a voice screamed, 'Can you turn back?' I caught sight of a V-shaped ripple on the water ahead. What? Another snag! A fusillade burst out under my feet. The pilgrims had opened with their Winchesters, and were simply squirting lead into that bush. A deuce of a lot of smoke came up and drove slowly forward. I swore at it. Now I couldn't see the ripple or the snag either. I stood in the doorway, peering, and the arrows came in swarms. They might have been poisoned, but they looked as though they wouldn't kill a cat. The bush began to howl. Our wood-cutters raised a war-like whoop; the report of a rifle just at my back deafened me. I glanced over my shoulder, and the pilot-house was yet full of noise and smoke when I made a dash at the wheel. The fool-nigger had dropped everything to throw the shutter open and let off that Martini-Henry. He stood before the wide opening, glaring, and I yelled at him to come back, while I straightened the sudden twist out of that steamboat. There was no room to turn even if I had wanted to, the snag was somewhere very near ahead in that confounded smoke, there was no time to lose, so I just crowded her into the bank—right into the bank, where I knew the water was deep.

"We tore slowly along the overhanging bushes in a whirl of broken twigs and flying leaves. The fusillade below stopped short, as I had foreseen it would when the squirts got empty. I threw my head back to a glinting whiz that traversed the pilot-house, in at one shutter-hole and out at the other. Looking past that mad helmsman, who was shaking the empty rifle and yelling at the shore, I saw vague forms of men running bent double, leaping, gliding, distinct, incomplete, evanescent. Something big appeared in the air before the shutter, the rifle went overboard, and the man stepped back swiftly, looked at me over his shoulder in an extraordinary, profound, familiar manner, and fell upon my feet. The side of his head hit the wheel twice, and the end of what appeared a long cane clattered round and knocked over a little camp-stool. It looked as though after wrenching that thing from somebody ashore he had lost his balance in the effort. The thin smoke had blown away, we were clear of the snag, and looking ahead I could see that in another hundred yards or so I would be free to sheer off, away from the bank; but my feet felt so very warm and wet that I had to look down. The man had rolled on his back and stared straight up at me; both his hands clutched that cane.

It was the shaft of a spear that, either thrown or lunged through the opening, had caught him in the side just below the ribs; the blade had gone in out of sight, after making a frightful gash; my shoes were full; a pool of blood lay very still, gleaming dark-red under the wheel; his eyes shone with an amazing luster. The fusillade burst out again. He looked at me anxiously, gripping the spear like something precious, with an air of being afraid I would try to take it away from him. I had to make an effort to free my eyes from his gaze and attend to the steering. With one hand I felt above my head for the line of the steam whistle, and jerked out screech after screech hurriedly. The tumult of angry and warlike yells was checked instantly, and then from the depths of the woods went out such a tremulous and prolonged wail of mournful fear and utter despair as may be imagined to follow the flight of the last hope from the earth. There was a great commotion in the bush; the shower of arrows stopped, a few dropping shots rang out sharply—then silence, in which the languid beat of the stern-wheel came plainly to my ears. I put the helm hard a-starboard at the moment when the pilgrim in pink pajamas, very hot and agitated, appeared in the doorway. 'The manager sends me——' he began in an official tone, and stopped short. 'Good God!' he said, glaring at the wounded man.

"We two whites stood over him, and his lustrous and inquiring glance enveloped us both. I declare it looked as though he would presently put to us some question in an understandable language; but he died without uttering a sound, without moving a limb, without twitching a muscle. Only in the very last moment, as though in response to some sign we could not see, to some whisper we could not hear, he frowned heavily, and that frown gave to his black death-mask an inconceivably somber, brooding, and menacing expression.

The luster of inquiring glance faded swiftly into vacant glassiness. 'Can you steer?' I asked the agent eagerly. He looked very dubious; but I made a grab at his arm, and he understood at once I meant him to steer whether or no. To tell you the truth, I was morbidly anxious to change my shoes and socks. 'He is dead,' murmured the fellow, immensely impressed. 'No doubt about it,' said I, tugging like mad at the shoelaces. 'And by the way, I suppose Mr. Kurtz is dead as well by this time.'

"For the moment that was the dominant thought. There was a sense of extreme disappointment, as though I had found out I had been striving after something altogether without a substance. I couldn't have been more disgusted if I had travelled all this way for the sole purpose of talking with Mr. Kurtz. Talking with . . . I flung one shoe overboard, and became aware that that was exactly what I had been looking forward to—a talk with Kurtz. I made the strange discovery that I had never imagined him as doing, you know, but as discoursing. I didn't say to myself, 'Now I will never see him,' or 'Now I will never shake him by the hand,' but, 'Now I will never hear him.' The man presented himself as a voice. Not of course that I did not connect him with some sort of action. Hadn't I been told in all the tones of jealousy and admiration that he had collected, bartered, swindled, or stolen more ivory than all the other agents together? That was not the point. The point was in his being a gifted creature, and that of all his gifts the one that stood out pre-eminently, that carried with it a sense of real presence, was his ability to talk, his words—the gift of expression, the bewildering, the illuminating, the most exalted and the most contemptible, the pulsating stream of light, or the deceitful flow from the heart of an impenetrable darkness.

"The other shoe went flying unto the devil-god of that river. I thought, By Jove! it's all over. We are too late; he has vanished—the gift has vanished, by means of some spear, arrow, or club. I will never hear that chap speak after all—and my sorrow had a startling extravagance of emotion, even such as I had noticed in the howling sorrow of these savages in the bush. I couldn't have felt more of lonely desolation somehow, had I been robbed of a belief or had missed my destiny in life. . . . Why do you sigh in this beastly way, somebody? Absurd? Well, absurd. Good Lord! mustn't a man ever—— Here, give me some tobacco." . . .

There was a pause of profound stillness, then a match flared, and Marlow's lean face appeared, worn, hollow, with downward folds and dropped eyelids, with an aspect of concentrated attention; and as he took vigorous draws at his pipe, it seemed to retreat and advance out of the night in the regular flicker of the tiny flame. The match went out.

"Absurd!" he cried. "This is the worst of trying to tell . . . Here you all are, each moored with two good addresses, like a hulk with two anchors, a butcher round one corner, a policeman round another, excellent appetites, and temperature normal—you hear—normal from year's end to year's end. And you say, Absurd! Absurd be—exploded! Absurd! My dear boys, what can you expect from a man who out of sheer nervousness had just flung overboard a pair of new shoes? Now I think of it, it is amazing I did not shed tears. I am, upon the whole, proud of my fortitude. I was cut to the quick at the idea of having lost the inestimable privilege of listening to the gifted Kurtz. Of course I was wrong. The privilege was waiting for me. Oh yes, I heard more than enough. And I was right, too. A voice. He was very little more than a voice. And I heard—him—it—this voice—other voices—all of them were so little more than voices —and the memory of that time itself lingers around me, impalpable, like a dying vibration of one immense jabber, silly, atrocious, sordid, savage, or simply mean, without any kind of sense. Voices, voices—even the girl herself—now——"

He was silent for a long time.

"I laid the ghost of his gifts at last with a lie," he began suddenly. "Girl! What? Did I mention a girl? Oh, she is out of it—completely. They—the women I mean—are out of it—should be out of it. We must help them to stay in that beautiful world of their own, lest ours gets worse. Oh, she had to be out of it. You should have heard the disinterred body of Mr. Kurtz saying, 'My Intended.' You would have perceived directly then how completely she was out of it. And the lofty frontal bone of Mr. Kurtz! They say the hair goes on growing sometimes, but this—ah—specimen was impressively bald. The wilderness had patted him on the head, and, behold, it was like a ball—an ivory ball; it had caressed him, and—lo!—he had withered; it had taken him, loved him, embraced him, got into his veins, consumed his flesh, and sealed his soul to its own by the inconceivable ceremonies of some devilish initiation. He was its spoiled and pampered favorite. Ivory? I should think so. Heaps of it, stacks of it. The old mud shanty was bursting with it. You would think there was not a single tusk left either above or below the ground in the whole country. 'Mostly fossil,' the manager had remarked disparagingly. It was no more fossil than I am; but they call it fossil when it is dug up. It appears these niggers do bury the tusks sometimes—but evidently they couldn't bury this parcel deep enough to save the gifted Mr. Kurtz from his fate. We filled the steamboat with it, and had to pile a lot on the deck. Thus he could see and enjoy as long as he could see, because the appreciation of this favor had remained with him to the last. You should have heard him say, 'My ivory.' Oh yes, I heard him. 'My Intended, my ivory, my station, my river, my——' everything belonged to him. It made me hold my breath in expectation of hearing the wilderness burst into a prodigious peal of laughter that would shake the fixed stars in their places. Everything belonged to him—but that was a trifle. The thing was to know what he belonged to, how many powers of darkness claimed him for their own. That was the reflection that made you creepy all over. It was impossible—it was not good for one either—trying to imagine. He had taken a high seat amongst the devils of the land—I mean literally. You can't understand. How could you?—with solid pavement under your feet, surrounded by kind neighbors ready to cheer you or to fall on you, stepping delicately between the butcher and the policeman, in the holy terror of scandal and gallows and lunatic asylums—how can you imagine what particular region of the first ages a man's untrammelled feet may take him into by the way of solitude—utter solitude without a policeman—by the way of silence—utter silence, where no warning voice of a kind neighbor can be heard whispering of public opinion? These little things make all the great difference. When they are gone you must fall back upon your own innate strength, upon your own capacity for faithfulness. Of course you may be too much of a fool to go wrong—too dull even to know you are being assaulted by the powers of darkness. I take it, no fool ever made a bargain for his soul with the devil: the fool is too much of a fool, or the devil too much of a devil—I don't know which. Or you may be such a thunderingly exalted creature as to be altogether deaf and blind to anything but heavenly sights and sounds. Then the earth for you is only a standing place—and whether to be like this is your loss or your gain I won't pretend to say. But most of us are neither one nor the other. The earth for us is a place to live in, where we must put up with sights, with sounds, with smells, too, by Jove!—breathe dead hippo, so to speak, and not be contaminated. And there, don't you see? your strength comes in, the faith in your ability for the digging of un-ostentatious holes to bury the stuff in—your power of devotion, not to yourself, but to an obscure, back-breaking business. And that's difficult enough. Mind, I am not trying to excuse or even explain—I am trying to account to myself for—for—Mr. Kurtz—for the shade of Mr. Kurtz. This initiated wraith from the back of Nowhere honored me with its amazing confidence before it vanished altogether. This was because it could speak English to me. The original Kurtz had been educated partly in England, and—as he was good enough to say himself—his sympathies were in the right place. His mother was half-English, his father was half-French. All Europe contributed to the making of Kurtz; and by and by I learned that, most appropriately, the International Society for the Suppression of Savage Customs had entrusted him with the making of a report, for its future guidance. And he had written it too. I've seen it. I've read it. It was eloquent, vibrating with eloquence, but too high-strung, I think. Seventeen pages of close writing he had found time for! But this must have been before his—let us say—nerves went wrong, and caused him to preside at certain midnight dances ending with unspeakable rites, which—as far as I reluctantly gathered from what I heard at various times—were offered up to him—do you understand?—to Mr. Kurtz himself. But it was a beautiful piece of writing. The opening paragraph, however, in the light of later information, strikes me now as ominous. He began with the argument that we whites, from the point of development we had arrived at, 'must necessarily appear to them [savages] in the nature of supernatural beings—we approach them with the might as of a deity,' and so on, and so on. 'By the simple exercise of our will we can exert a power for good practically unbounded,' etc. etc. From

that point he soared and took me with him. The peroration was magnificent, though difficult to remember, you know. It gave me the notion of an exotic Immensity ruled by an august Benevolence. It made me tingle with enthusiasm. This was the unbounded power of eloquence —of words—of burning noble words. There were no practical hints to interrupt the magic current of phrases, unless a kind of note at the foot of the last page, scrawled evidently much later, in an unsteady hand, may be regarded as the exposition of a method. It was very simple, and at the end of that moving appeal to every altruistic sentiment it blazed at you, luminous and terrifying, like a flash of lightning in a serene sky: 'Exterminate all the brutes!' The curious part was that he had apparently forgotten all about that valuable postscriptum, because, later on, when he in a sense came to himself, he repeatedly entreated me to take good care of 'my pamphlet' (he called it), as it was sure to have in the future a good influence upon his career. I had full information about all these things, and, besides, as it turned out, I was to have the care of his memory. I've done enough for it to give me the indisputable right to lay it, if I choose, for an ever-lasting rest in the dust-bin of progress, amongst all the sweepings and, figuratively speaking, all the dead cats of civilization. But then, you see, I can't choose. He won't be forgotten. Whatever he was, he was not common. He had the power to charm or frighten rudimentary souls into an aggravated witch-dance in his honor; he could also fill the small souls of the pilgrims with bitter misgivings: he had one devoted friend at least, and he had conquered one soul in the world that was neither rudimentary nor tainted with self-seeking. No; I can't forget him, though I am not prepared to affirm the fellow was exactly worth the life we lost in getting to him. I missed my late helmsman awfully—I missed him even while his body was still lying in the pilot-house. Perhaps you will think it passing strange, this regret for a savage who was no more account than a grain of sand in a black Sahara. Well, don't you see, he had done something, he had steered; for months I had him at my back—a help—an instrument. It was a kind of partnership. He steered for me—I had to look after him, I worried about his deficiencies, and thus a subtle bond had been created, of which I only became aware when it was suddenly broken. And the intimate profundity of that look he gave me when he received his hurt remains to this day in my memory—like a claim of distant kinship affirmed in a supreme moment.

"Poor fool! If he had only left that shutter alone. He had no restraint, no restraint—just like Kurtz—a tree swayed by the wind. As soon as I had put on a dry pair of slippers, I dragged him out, after first jerking the spear out of his side, which operation I confess I performed with my eyes shut tight. His heels leaped together over the little door-step; his shoulders were pressed to my breast; I hugged him from behind desperately. Oh! he was heavy, heavy; heavier than any man on earth, I should imagine. Then without more ado I tipped him overboard. The current snatched him as though he had been a wisp of grass, and I saw the body roll over twice before I lost sight of it for ever. All the pilgrims and the manager were then congregated on the awning-deck about the pilot-house, chattering at each other like a flock of excited magpies, and there was a scandalized murmur at my heartless promptitude. What they wanted to keep that body hanging about for I can't guess. Embalm it, maybe. But I had also heard another, and a very ominous, murmur on the deck below. My friends the wood-cutters were likewise scandalized, and with a better show of reason—though I admit that the reason itself was quite inadmissible. Oh, quite! I had

made up my mind that if my late helmsman was to be eaten, the fishes alone should have him. He had been a very second-rate helmsman while alive, but now he was dead he might have become a first-class temptation, and possibly cause some startling trouble. Besides, I was anxious to take the wheel, the man in pink pajamas showing himself a hopeless duffer at the business.

"This I did directly the simple funeral was over. We were going half-speed, keeping right in the middle of the stream, and I listened to the talk about me. They had given up Kurtz, they had given up the station; Kurtz was dead, and the station had been burnt—and so on, and so on. The red-haired pilgrim was beside himself with the thought that at least this poor Kurtz had been properly revenged. 'Say! We must have made a glorious slaughter of them in the bush. Eh? What do you think? Say?' He positively danced, the bloodthirsty little gingery beggar. And he had nearly fainted when he saw the wounded man! I could not help saying, 'You made a glorious lot of smoke, anyhow.' I had seen, from the way the tops of the bushes rustled and flew, that almost all the shots had gone too high. You can't hit anything unless you take aim and fire from the shoulder; but these chaps fired from the hip with their eyes shut. The retreat, I maintained—and I was right—was caused by the screeching of the steam-whistle. Upon this they forgot Kurtz, and began to howl at me with indignant protests.

"The manager stood by the wheel murmuring confidentially about the necessity of getting well away down the river before dark at all events, when I saw in the distance a clearing on the river-side and the outlines of some sort of building. 'What's this?' I asked. He clapped his hands in wonder. 'The station!' he cried. I edged in at once, still going half-speed.

"Through my glasses I saw the slope of a hill interspersed with rare trees and perfectly free from undergrowth. A long decaying building on the summit was half buried in the high grass; the large holes in the peaked roof gaped black from afar; the jungle and the woods made a background. There was no enclosure or fence of any kind; but there had been one apparently, for near the house half a dozen slim posts remained in a row, roughly trimmed, and with their upper ends ornamented with round carved balls. The rails, or whatever there had been between, had disappeared. Of course the forest surrounded all that. The river-bank was clear, and on the water side I saw a white man under a hat like a cart-wheel beckoning persistently with his whole arm. Examining the edge of the forest above and below, I was almost certain I could see movements—human forms gliding here and there. I steamed past prudently, then stopped the engines and let her drift down. The man on the shore began to shout, urging us to land. 'We have been attacked,' screamed the manager. 'I know—I know. It's all right,' yelled back the other, as cheerful as you please. 'Come along. It's all right. I am glad.'

"His aspect reminded me of something I had seen—something funny I had seen somewhere. As I manœuvred to get alongside, I was asking myself, 'What does this fellow look like?' Suddenly I got it. He looked like a harlequin. His clothes had been made of some stuff that was brown holland probably, but it was covered with patches all over, with bright patches, blue, red, and yellow—patches on the back, patches on the front, patches on elbows, on knees; colored binding round his jacket, scarlet edging at the bottom of his trousers; and the sunshine made him look extremely gay and wonderfully neat withal, because you could see how beautifully all this patching had been done. A beardless, boyish face, very fair, no features to speak of, nose peeling, little blue eyes, smiles and frowns chasing each other over that open countenance like sunshine and shadow on a wind-swept plain. 'Look out, captain!' he cried; 'there's a snag lodged in here last night.' What! Another snag? I confess I swore shamefully. I had nearly holed my cripple, to finish off that charming trip. The harlequin on the bank turned his little pug-nose up to me. 'You English?' he asked, all smiles. 'Are you?' I shouted from the wheel. The smiles vanished, and he shook his head as if sorry for my disappointment. Then he brightened up. 'Never mind!' he cried encouragingly. 'Are we in time?' I asked. 'He is up there,' he replied, with a toss of the head up the hill, and becoming gloomy all of a sudden. His face was like the autumn sky, overcast one moment and bright the next.

"When the manager, escorted by the pilgrims, all of them armed to the teeth, had gone to the house, this chap came on board. 'I say, I don't like this. These natives are in the bush,' I said. He assured me earnestly it was all right. 'They are simple people,' he added; 'well, I am glad you came. It took me all my time to keep them off.' 'But you said it was all right,' I cried. 'Oh, they meant no harm,' he said; and as I stared he corrected himself, 'Not exactly.' Then vivaciously, 'My faith, your pilot-house wants a clean-up!' In the next breath he advised me to keep enough steam on the boiler to blow the whistle in case of any trouble. 'One good screech will do more for you than all your rifles. They are simple people,' he repeated. He rattled away at such a rate he quite overwhelmed me. He seemed to be trying to make up for lots of silence, and actually hinted, laughing, that such was the case. 'Don't you talk with Mr. Kurtz?' I said. 'You don't talk with that man—you listen to him,' he exclaimed with severe exaltation. 'But now——' He waved his arm, and in the twinkling of an eye was in the uttermost depths of despondency. In a moment he came up again with a jump, possessed himself of both my hands, shook them continuously, while he gabbled: 'Brother sailor . . . honor . . . pleasure . . . delight . . . introduce myself . . . Russian . . . son of an arch-priest . . . Government of Tambov . . . What? Tobacco! English tobacco; the excellent English tobacco! Now, that's brotherly. Smoke? Where's a sailor that does not smoke?'

"The pipe soothed him, and gradually I made out he had run away from school, had gone to sea in a Russian ship; ran away again; served some time in English ships; was now reconciled with the arch-priest. He made a point of that. 'But when one is young one must see things, gather experience, ideas; enlarge the mind.' 'Here!' I interrupted. 'You can never tell! Here I met Mr. Kurtz,' he said, youthfully solemn and reproachful. I held my tongue after that. It appears he had persuaded a Dutch trading-house on the coast to fit him out with stores and goods, and had started for the interior with a light heart, and no more idea of what would happen to him than a baby. He had been wandering about that river for nearly two years alone, cut off from everybody and everything. 'I am not so young as I look. I am twenty-five,' he said. 'At first old Van Shuyten would tell me to go to the devil,' he narrated with keen enjoyment; 'but I stuck to him, and talked and talked, till at last he got afraid I would talk the hind-leg off his favorite dog, so he gave me some cheap things and a few guns, and told me he hoped he would never see my face again. Good old Dutchman, Van Shuyten. I sent him one small lot of ivory a year ago, so that he can't call me a little thief when I get back. I hope he got it. And for the rest, I don't care. I had some wood stacked for you. That was my old house. Did you see?'

"I gave him Towson's book. He made as though he would kiss me, but restrained himself. 'The only book I had left, and I thought I had lost it,' he said, looking at it ecstatically. 'So many accidents happen to a man going about alone, you know. Canoes get upset sometimes—and sometimes you've got to clear out so quick when the people get angry.' He thumbed the pages. 'You made notes in Russian?' I asked. He nodded. 'I thought they were written in cipher,' I said. He laughed, then became serious. 'I had lots of trouble to keep these people off,' he said. 'Did they want to kill you?' I asked. 'Oh no!' he cried, and checked himself. 'Why did they attack us?' I pursued. He hesitated, then said shamefacedly, 'They don't want him to go.' 'Don't they?' I said curiously. He nodded a nod full of mystery and wisdom. 'I tell you,' he cried, 'this man has enlarged my mind.' He opened his arms wide, staring at me with his little blue eyes that were perfectly round."

III

"I looked at him, lost in astonishment. There he was before me, in motley, as though he had absconded from a troupe of mimes, enthusiastic, fabulous. His very existence was improbable, inexplicable, and altogether bewildering. He was an insoluble problem. It was inconceivable how he had existed, how he had succeeded in getting so far, how he had managed to remain—why he did not instantly disappear. 'I went a little farther,' he said, 'then still a little farther—till I had gone so far that I don't know how I'll ever get back. Never mind. Plenty time. I can manage. You take Kurtz away quick—quick—I tell you.' The glamor of youth enveloped his parti-colored rags, his destitution, his loneliness, the essential desolation of his futile wanderings. For months—for years—his life hadn't been worth a day's purchase; and there he was gallantly, thoughtlessly alive, to all appearance indestructible solely by the virtue of his few years and of his un-reflecting audacity. I was seduced into something like admiration—like envy. Glamor urged him on, glamor kept him unscathed. He surely wanted nothing from the wilderness but space to breath in and to push on through. His need was to exist, and to move onwards at the greatest possible risk, and with a maximum of privation. If the absolutely pure, uncalculating, unpractical spirit of adventure had ever ruled a human being, it ruled this be-patched youth. I almost envied him the possession of this mod-est and clear flame. It seemed to have consumed all thought of self so com-pletely, that, even while he was talking to you, you forgot that it was he—the man before your eyes—who had gone through these things. I did not envy him his devotion to Kurtz, though. He had not meditated over it. It came to him, and he accepted it with a sort of eager fatalism. I must say that to me it appeared about the most dangerous thing in every way he had come upon so far.

"They had come together unavoidably, like two ships becalmed near each other, and lay rubbing sides at last. I suppose Kurtz wanted an audience, because on a certain occasion, when encamped in the forest, they had talked all night, or more probably Kurtz had talked. 'We talked of everything,' he said, quite transported at the recollection. 'I forgot there was such a thing as sleep. The night did not seem to last an hour. Every-thing! Everything! . . . Of love too.' 'Ah, he talked to you of love!' I said, much amused. 'It isn't what you think,' he cried, almost passionately. 'It was in general. He made me see things— things.'

"He threw his arms up. We were on deck at the time, and the head-man of my wood-cutters, lounging near by, turned upon him his heavy and glitter-ing eyes. I looked around, and I don't know why, but I assure you that never, never before, did this land, this river, this jungle, the very arch of this blazing sky, appear to me so hopeless and so dark, so impenetrable to human thought, so pitiless to human weakness. 'And, ever since, you have been with him, of course?' I said.

"On the contrary. It appears their intercourse had been very much broken by various causes. He had, as he in-formed me proudly, managed to nurse Kurtz through two illnesses (he alluded to it as you would to some risky feat), but as a rule Kurtz wandered alone, far in the depths of the forest. 'Very often coming to this station, I had to wait days and days before he would turn up,' he said. 'Ah, it was worth waiting for!— sometimes.' 'What was he doing? ex-ploring or what?' I asked. 'Oh yes, of course'; he had discovered lots of vil-lages, a lake too—he did not know exactly in what direction; it was danger-ous to inquire too much—but mostly his expeditions had been for ivory. 'But he had no goods to trade with by that time,' I objected. 'There's a good lot of cartridges left even yet,' he answered, looking away. 'To speak plainly, he raided the country,' I said. He nodded. 'Not alone, surely!' He muttered some-thing about the villages round that lake. 'Kurtz got the tribe to follow him, did he?' I suggested. He fidgeted a little. 'They adored him,' he said. The tone of these words was so extraordinary that I looked at him searchingly. It was curious to see his mingled eagerness and re-luctance to speak of Kurtz. The man filled his life, occupied his thoughts, swayed his emotions. 'What can you expect?' he burst out; 'he came to them with thunder and lightning, you know— and they had never seen anything like it—and very terrible. He could be very terrible. You can't judge Mr. Kurtz as you would an ordinary man. No, no, no! Now—just to give you an idea—I don't mind telling you, he wanted to shoot me too one day—but I don't judge him.' 'Shoot you!' I cried. 'What for?' 'Well, I had a small lot of ivory the chief of that village near my house gave me. You see I used to shoot game for them. Well, he wanted it, and wouldn't hear reason. He declared he would shoot me unless I gave him the ivory and then cleared out of the country, because he could do so, and had a fancy for it, and there was nothing on earth to prevent him killing whom he jolly well pleased. And it was true too. I gave him the ivory. What did I care! But I didn't clear out. No, no. I couldn't leave him. I had to be careful, of course, till we got friendly again for a time. He had his second illness then. Afterwards I had to keep out of the way; but I didn't mind. He was living for the most part in those villages on the lake. When he came down to the river, sometimes he would take to me, and sometimes it was better for me to be careful. This man suffered too much. He hated all this, and somehow he couldn't get away. When I had a chance I begged him to try and leave while there was time; I offered to go back with him. And he would say yes, and then he would remain; go off on another ivory hunt; disappear for weeks; forget himself amongst these people—forget himself— you know.' 'Why! he's mad,' I said. He protested indignantly. Mr. Kurtz couldn't be mad. If I had heard him talk, only two days ago, I wouldn't dare hint at such a thing. . . . I had taken up my binoculars while we talked, and was looking at the shore, sweeping the limit of the forest at each side and at the back of the house. The consciousness of there being people in that bush, so silent, so quiet—as silent and quiet as the ruined house on the hill—made me uneasy. There was no sign on the face of nature of this amazing tale that was not so much told as suggested to me in desolate exclamations, completed by shrugs, in interrupted phrases, in hints ending in deep sighs. The woods were unmoved, like a mask—heavy, like the closed door of a prison—they looked with their air of hidden knowledge, of patient ex-

pectation, of unapproachable silence. The Russian was explaining to me that it was only lately that Mr. Kurtz had come down to the river, bringing along with him all the fighting men of that lake tribe. He had been absent for several months—getting himself adored, I suppose—and had come down unexpectedly, with the intention to all appearance of making a raid either across the river or down stream. Evidently the appetite for more ivory had got the better of the—what shall I say?—less material aspirations. However, he had got much worse suddenly. 'I heard he was lying helpless, and so I came up— took my chance,' said the Russian. 'Oh, he is bad, very bad.' I directed my glass to the house. There were no signs of life, but there were the ruined roof, the long mud wall peeping above the grass, with three little square window-holes, no two of the same size; all this brought within reach of my hand, as it were. And then I made a brusque movement, and one of the remaining posts of that vanished fence leaped up in the field of my glass. You remember I told you I had been struck at the distance by certain attempts at ornamentation, rather remarkable in the ruinous aspect of the place. Now I had suddenly a nearer view, and its first result was to make me throw my head back as if before a blow. Then I went carefully from post to post with my glass, and I saw my mistake. These round knobs were not ornamental but symbolic; they were expressive and puzzling, striking and disturbing—food for thought and also for vultures if there had been any looking down from the sky; but at all events for such ants as were industrious enough to ascend the pole. They would have been even more impressive, those heads on the stakes, if their faces had not been turned to the house. Only one, the first I had made out, was facing my way. I was not so shocked as you may think. The start back I had given was really nothing but a movement of surprise. I had expected to see a knob of wood there, you know. I returned deliberately to the first I had seen—and there it was, black, dried, sunken, with closed eyelids—a head that seemed to sleep at the top of that pole, and, with the shrunken dry lips showing a narrow white line of the teeth, was smiling too, smiling continuously at some endless and jocose dream of that eternal slumber.

"I am not disclosing any trade secrets. In fact the manager said afterwards that Mr. Kurtz's methods had ruined the district. I have no opinion on that point, but I want you clearly to understand that there was nothing exactly profitable in these heads being there. They only showed that Mr. Kurtz lacked restraint in the gratification of his various lusts, that there was something wanting in him—some small matter which, when the pressing need arose, could not be found under his magnificent eloquence. Whether he knew of this deficiency himself I can't say. I think the knowledge came to him at last—only at the very last. But the wilderness had found him out early, and had taken on him a terrible vengeance for the fantastic invasion. I think it had whispered to him things about himself which he did not know, things of which he had no conception till he took counsel with this great solitude—and the whisper had proved irresistibly fascinating. It echoed loudly within him because he was hollow at the core. . . . I put down the glass, and the head that had appeared near enough to be spoken to seemed at once to have leaped away from me into inaccessible distance.

"The admirer of Mr. Kurtz was a bit crest-fallen. In a hurried, indistinct voice he began to assure me he had not dared to take these—say, symbols—down. He was not afraid of the natives; they would not stir till Mr. Kurtz gave the word. His ascendancy was extraordinary. The camps of these people surrounded the place, and the chiefs came every day to see him. They would crawl . . . 'I don't want to know anything of the ceremonies used when approaching Mr. Kurtz,' I shouted. Curious, this feeling that came over me that such details would be more intolerable than those heads drying on the stakes under Mr. Kurtz's windows. After all, that was only a savage sight, while I seemed at one bound to have been transported into some lightless region of subtle horrors, where pure, uncomplicated savagery was a positive relief, being something that had a right to exist—obviously—in the sunshine. The young man looked at me with surprise. I suppose it did not occur to him that Mr. Kurtz was no idol of mine. He forgot I hadn't heard any of these splendid monologues on, what was it? on love, justice, conduct of life—or what not. If it had come to crawling before Mr. Kurtz, he crawled as much as the veriest savage of them all. I had no idea of the conditions, he said: these heads were the heads of rebels. I shocked him excessively by laughing. Rebels! What would be the next definition I was to hear? There had been enemies, criminals, workers—and these were rebels. Those rebellious heads looked very subdued to me on their sticks. 'You don't know how such a life tries a man like Kurtz,' cried Kurtz's last disciple. 'Well, and you?' I said. 'I! I! I am a simple man. I have no great thoughts. I want nothing from anybody. How can you compare me to . . . ?' His feelings were too much for speech, and suddenly he broke down. 'I don't understand,' he groaned. 'I've been doing my best to keep him alive, and that's enough. I had no hand in all this. I have no abilities. There hasn't been a drop of medicine or a mouthful of invalid food for months here. He was shamefully abandoned. A man like this, with such ideas. Shamefully! Shamefully! I—I—haven't slept for the last ten nights. . . .'

"His voice lost itself in the calm of the evening. The long shadows of the forest had slipped down-hill while we talked, had gone far beyond the ruined hovel, beyond the symbolic row of stakes. All this was in the gloom, while we down there were yet in the sunshine, and the stretch of the river abreast of the clearing glittered in a still and dazzling splendor, with a murky and overshadowed bend above and below. Not a living soul was seen on the shore. The bushes did not rustle.

"Suddenly round the corner of the house a group of men appeared, as though they had come up from the ground. They waded waist-deep in the grass, in a compact body, bearing an improvised stretcher in their midst. Instantly, in the emptiness of the landscape, a cry arose whose shrillness pierced the still air like a sharp arrow flying straight to the very heart of the land; and, as if by enchantment, streams of human beings—of naked human beings—with spears in their hands, with bows, with shields, with wild glances and savage movements, were poured into the clearing by the dark-faced and pensive forest. The bushes shook, the grass swayed for a time, and then everything stood still in attentive immobility.

" 'Now, if he does not say the right thing to them we are all done for,' said the Russian at my elbow. The knot of men with the stretcher had stopped too, half-way to the steamer, as if petrified. I saw the man on the stretcher sit up, lank and with an uplifted arm, above the shoulders of the bearers. 'Let us hope that the man who can talk so well of love in general will find some particular reason to spare us this time,' I said. I resented bitterly the absurd danger of our situation, as if to be at the mercy of that atrocious phantom had been a dishonoring necessity. I could not hear a sound, but through my glasses I saw the thin arm extended commandingly, the lower jaw moving, the eyes of that apparition shining darkly far in its bony head that nodded with grotesque jerks. Kurtz—Kurtz—that means 'short' in German—don't it? Well, the name was

as true as everything else in his life— and death. He looked at least seven feet long. His covering had fallen off, and his body emerged from it pitiful and appalling as from a winding-sheet. I could see the cage of his ribs all astir, the bones of his arm waving. It was as though an animated image of death carved out of old ivory had been shaking its hand with menaces at a motionless crowd of men made of dark and glittering bronze. I saw him open his mouth wide—it gave him a weirdly voracious aspect, as though he had wanted to swallow all the air, all the earth, all the men before him. A deep voiced reached me faintly. He must have been shouting. He fell back suddenly. The stretcher shook as the bearers staggered forward again, and almost at the same time I noticed that the crowd of savages was vanishing without any perceptible movement of retreat, as if the forest that had ejected these beings so suddenly had drawn them in again as the breath is drawn in a long aspiration.

"Some of the pilgrims behind the stretcher carried his arms—two shotguns, a heavy rifle, and a light revolvercarbine—the thunderbolts of that pitiful Jupiter. The manager bent over him murmuring as he walked beside his head. They laid him down in one of the little cabins—just a room for a bed-place and a camp-stool or two, you know. We had brought his belated correspondence, and a lot of torn envelopes and open letters littered his bed. His hand roamed feebly amongst these papers. I was struck by the fire of his eyes and the composed langour of his expression. It was not so much the exhaustion of disease. He did not seem in pain. This shadow looked satiated and calm, as though for the moment it had had its fill of all the emotions.

"He rustled one of the letters, and looking straight in my face said, 'I am glad.' Somebody had been writing to him about me. These special recommendations were turning up again. The volume of tone he emitted without effort, almost without the trouble of moving his lips, amazed me. A voice! a voice! It was grave, profound, vibrating, while the man did not seem capable of a whisper. However, he had enough strength in him—factitious no doubt—to very nearly make an end of us, as you shall hear directly.

"The manager appeared silently in the doorway; I stepped out at once and he drew the curtain after me. The Russian, eyed curiously by the pilgrims, was staring at the shore. I followed the direction of his glance.

"Dark human shapes could be made out in the distance, flitting indistinctly against the gloomy border of the forest, and near the river two bronze figures, leaning on tall spears, stood in the sunlight under fantastic head-dresses of spotted skins, warlike and still in statuesque repose. And from right to left along the lighted shore moved a wild and gorgeous apparition of a woman.

"She walked with measured steps, draped in striped and fringed cloths, treading the earth proudly, with a slight jingle and flash of barbarous ornaments. She carried her head high; her hair was done in the shape of a helmet; she had brass leggings to the knee, brass wire gauntlets to the elbow, a crimson spot on her tawny cheek, innumerable necklaces of glass beads on her neck; bizzare things, charms, gifts of witch-men, that hung about her, glittered and trembled at every step. She must have had the value of several elephant tusks upon her. She was savage and superb, wild-eyed and magnificent; there was something ominous and stately in her deliberate progress. And in the hush that had fallen suddenly upon the whole sorrowful land, the immense wilderness, the colossal body of the fecund and mysterious life seemed to look at her, pensive, as though it had been looking at the image of its own tenebrous and passionate soul.

"She came abreast of the steamer, stood still, and faced us. Her long shadow fell to the water's edge. Her face had a tragic and fierce aspect of wild sorrow and of dumb pain mingled with the fear of some struggling, half-shaped resolve. She stood looking at us without a stir, and like the wilderness itself, with an air of brooding over an inscrutable purpose. A whole minute passed, and then she made a step forward. There was a low jingle, a glint of yellow metal, a sway of fringed draperies, and she stopped as if her heart had failed her. The young fellow by my side growled. The pilgrims murmured at my back. She looked at us all as if her life had depended upon the unswerving steadiness of her glance. Suddenly she opened her bared arms and threw them up rigid above her head, as though in an uncontrollable desire to touch the sky, and at the same time the swift shadows darted out on the earth, swept around on the river, gathering the steamer in a shadowy embrace. A formidable silence hung over the scene.

"She turned away slowly, walked on, following the bank, and passed into the bushes to the left. Once only her eyes gleamed back at us in the dusk of the thickets before she disappeared.

" 'If she had offered to come aboard I really think I would have tried to shoot her,' said the man of patches nervously. 'I had been risking my life every day for the last fortnight to keep her out of the house. She got in one day and kicked up a row about those miserable rags I picked up in the store-room to mend my clothes with. I wasn't decent. At least it must have been that, for she talked like a fury to Kurtz for an hour, pointing at me now and then. I don't understand the dialect of this tribe. Luckily for me, I fancy Kurtz felt too ill that day to care, or there would have been mischief. I don't understand. . . . No—it's too much for me. Ah, well, it's all over now.'

"At this moment I heard Kurtz's deep voice behind the curtain: 'Save me!—

save the ivory, you mean. Don't tell me. Save *me!* Why, I've had to save you. You are interrupting my plans now. Sick! Sick! Not so sick as you would like to believe. Never mind. I'll carry my ideas out yet—I will return. I'll show you what can be done. You with your little peddling notions—you are interfering with me. I will return. I . . .'

"The manager came out. He did me the honor to take me under the arm and lead me aside. 'He is very low, very low,' he said. He considered it necessary to sigh, but neglected to be consistently sorrowful. 'We have done all we could for him—haven't we? But there is no disguising the fact, Mr. Kurtz has done more harm than good to the Company. He did not see the time was not ripe for vigorous action. Cautiously, cautiously—that's my principle. We must be cautious yet. The district is closed to us for a time. Deplorable! Upon the whole, the trade will suffer. I don't deny there is a remarkable quantity of ivory—mostly fossil. We must save it, at all events—but look how precarious the position is—and why? Because the method is unsound.' 'Do you,' said I, looking at the shore, 'call it "unsound method"?' 'Without doubt,' he exclaimed hotly. 'Don't you?' . . . 'No method at all,' I murmured after a while. 'Exactly,' he exulted. 'I anticipated this. Shows a complete want of judgment. It is my duty to point it out in the proper quarter.' 'Oh,' said I, 'that fellow—what's his name?—the brickmaker, will make a readable report for you.' He appeared confounded for a moment. It seemed to me I had never breathed an atmosphere so vile, and I turned mentally to Kurtz for relief—positively for relief. 'Nevertheless, I think Mr. Kurtz is a remarkable man.' I said with emphasis. He started, dropped on me a cold heavy glance, said very quietly, 'He *was*,' and turned his back on me. My hour of favor was over; I found myself lumped along with Kurtz as a partisan of methods for which

the time was not ripe: I was unsound! Ah! but it was something to have at least a choice of nightmares.

"I had turned to the wilderness really, not to Mr. Kurtz, who I was ready to admit, was as good as buried. And for a moment it seemed to me as if I also were buried in a vast grave full of unspeakable secrets. I felt an intolerable weight oppressing my breast, the smell of the damp earth, the unseen presence of victorious corruption, the darkness of an impenetrable night. . . . The Russian tapped me on the shoulder. I heard him mumbling and stammering something about 'brother seaman—couldn't conceal—knowledge of matters that would affect Mr. Kurtz's reputation.' I waited. For him evidently Mr. Kurtz was not in his grave; I suspect that for him Mr. Kurtz was one of the immortals. 'Well!' said I at last, 'speak out. As it happens, I am Mr. Kurtz's friend—in a way.'

"He stated with a good deal of formality that had we not been 'of the same profession,' he would have kept the matter to himself without regard to consequences. He suspected 'there was an active ill-will towards him on the part of these white men that——' 'You are right,' I said, remembering a certain conversation I had overheard. 'The manager thinks you ought to be hanged.' He showed a concern at this intelligence which amused me at first. 'I had better get out of the way quietly,' he said earnestly. 'I can do no more for Kurtz now, and they would soon find some excuse. What's to stop them? There's a military post three hundred miles from here.' 'Well, upon my word,' said I, 'perhaps you had better go if you have any friends amongst the savages near by.' 'Plenty,' he said. 'They are simple people—and I want nothing, you know.' He stood biting his lip, then: 'I don't want any harm to happen to these whites here, but of course I was thinking of Mr. Kurtz's reputation—

but you are a brother seaman and——'
'All right,' said I, after a time. 'Mr. Kurtz's reputation is safe with me.' I did not know how truly I spoke.

"He informed me, lowering his voice, that it was Kurtz who had ordered the attack to be made on the steamer. 'He hated sometimes the idea of being taken away—and then again . . . But I don't understand these matters. I am a simple man. He thought it would scare you away—that you would give it up, thinking him dead. I could not stop him. Oh, I had an awful time of it this last month.' 'Very well,' I said. 'He is all right now.' 'Ye-e-es,' he muttered, not very convinced apparently. 'Thanks,' said I; 'I shall keep my eyes open.' 'But quiet —eh?' he urged anxiously. 'It would be awful for his reputation if anybody here——' I promised a complete discretion with great gravity. 'I have a canoe and three black fellows waiting not very far. I am off. Could you give me a few Martini-Henry cartridges?' I could, and did, with proper secrecy. He helped himself, with a wink at me, to a handful of my tobacco. 'Between sailors—you know—good English tobacco.' At the door of the pilot-house he turned round—'I say, haven't you a pair of shoes you could spare?' He raised one leg. 'Look.' The soles were tied with knotted strings sandal-wise under his bare feet. I rooted out an old pair, at which he looked with admiration before tucking it under his left arm. One of his pockets (bright red) was bulging with cartridges, from the other (dark blue) peeped 'Towson's Inquiry,' etc. etc. He seemed to think himself excellently well equipped for a renewed encounter with the wilderness. 'Ah! I'll never, never meet such a man again. You ought to have heard him recite poetry—his own too it was, he told me. Poetry!' He rolled his eyes at the recollection of these delights. 'Oh, he enlarged my mind!' 'Good-bye,' said I. He shook hands and vanished in the night. Sometimes I ask myself whether I had ever really seen him— whether it was possible to meet such a phenomenon! . . .

"When I woke up shortly after midnight his warning came to my mind with its hint of danger that seemed, in the starred darkness, real enough to make me get up for the purpose of having a look round. On the hill a big fire burned, illuminating fitfully a crooked corner of the station-house. One of the agents with a picket of a few of our blacks, armed for the purpose, was keeping guard over the ivory; but deep within the forest, red gleams that wavered, that seemed to sink and rise from the ground amongst confused columnar shapes of intense blackness, showed the exact position of the camp where Mr. Kurtz's adorers were keeping their uneasy vigil. The monotonous beating of a big drum filled the air with muffled shocks and a lingering vibration. A steady droning sound of many men chanting each to himself some weird incantation came out from the black, flat wall of the woods as the humming of bees comes out of a hive, and had a strange narcotic effect upon my half-awake senses. I believe I dozed off leaning over the rail, till an abrupt burst of yells, an overwhelming outbreak of a pent-up and mysterious frenzy, woke me up in a bewildered wonder. It was cut short all at once, and the low droning went on with an effect of audible and soothing silence. I glanced casually into the little cabin. A light was burning within, but Mr. Kurtz was not there.

"I think I would have raised an outcry if I had believed my eyes. But I didn't believe them at first—the thing seemed so impossible. The fact is, I was completely unnerved by a sheer blank fright, pure abstract terror, unconnected with any distinct shape of physical danger. What made this emotion so overpowering was—how shall I define it?—the moral shock I received, as if something altogether monstrous, intolerable to thought and odious to the soul, had been thrust upon me unexpectedly. This lasted of course the merest fraction of a second, and then the usual sense of commonplace, deadly danger, the possibility of a sudden onslaught and massacre, or something of the kind, which I saw impending, was positively welcome and composing. It pacified me, in fact, so much that I did not raise an alarm.

"There was an agent buttoned up inside an ulster and sleeping on a chair on deck within three feet of me. The yells had not awakened him; he snored very slightly; I left him to his slumbers and leaped ashore. I did not betray Mr. Kurtz—it was ordered I should never betray him—it was written I should be loyal to the nightmare of my choice. I was anxious to deal with this shadow by myself alone—and to this day I don't know why I was so jealous of sharing with any one the peculiar blackness of that experience.

"As soon as I got on the bank I saw a trail—a broad trail through the grass. I remember the exultation with which I said to myself, 'He can't walk—he is crawling on all-fours—I've got him.' The grass was wet with dew. I strode rapidly with clenched fists. I fancy I had some vague notion of falling upon him and giving him a drubbing. I don't know. I had some imbecile thoughts. The knitting old woman with the cat obtruded herself upon my memory as a most improper person to be sitting at the other end of such an affair. I saw a row of pilgrims squirting lead in the air out of Winchesters held to the hip. I thought I would never get back to the steamer, and imagined myself living alone and unarmed in the woods to an advanced age. Such silly things—you know. And I remember I confounded the beat of the drum with the beating of my heart, and was pleased at its calm regularity.

"I kept to the track though—then stopped to listen. The night was very clear; a dark blue space, sparkling with dew and starlight, in which black things stood very still. I thought I could see a kind of motion ahead of me. I was strangely cocksure of everything that night. I actually left the track and ran in a wide semicircle (I verily believe chuckling to myself) so as to get in front of the stir, of that motion I had seen—if indeed I had seen anything. I was circumventing Kurtz as though it had been a boyish game.

"I came upon him, and, if he had not heard me coming, I would have fallen over him too, but he got up in time. He rose, unsteady, long, pale, indistinct, like a vapor exhaled by the earth, and swayed slightly, misty and silent before me; while at my back the fires loomed between the trees, and the murmur of many voices issued from the forest. I had cut him off cleverly; but when actually confronting him I seemed to come to my senses, I saw the danger in its right proportion. It was by no means over yet. Suppose he began to shout? Though he could hardly stand, there was still plenty of vigor in his voice. 'Go away—hide yourself,' he said, in that profound tone. It was very awful. I glanced back. We were within thirty yards from the nearest fire. A black figure stood up, strode on long black legs, waving long black arms, across the glow. It had horns—antelope horns, I think—on its head. Some sorcerer, some witch-man, no doubt: it looked fiendlike enough. 'Do you know what you are doing?' I whispered. 'Perfectly,' he answered, raising his voice for that single word: it sounded to me far off and yet loud, like a hail through a speaking-trumpet. If he makes a row we are lost, I thought to myself. This clearly was not a case for fisticuffs, even apart from the very natural aversion I had to beat that Shadow—this wandering and tormented thing. 'You will be lost,' I said—'utterly lost.' One gets sometimes such a flash of inspiration, you know. I did say the right thing, though indeed he could not have been more irretrievably lost than he was at this very moment, when the foundations of our intimacy were being laid—to endure—to endure—even to the end—even beyond.

" 'I had immense plans,' he muttered irresolutely. 'Yes,' said I; 'but if you try to shout I'll smash your head with——' There was not a stick or a stone near. 'I will throttle you for good,' I corrected myself. 'I was on the threshold of great things,' he pleaded, in a voice of longing, with a wistfulness of tone that made my blood run cold. 'And now for this stupid scoundrel——' 'Your success in Europe is assured in any case,' I affirmed steadily. I did not want to have the throttling of him, you understand—and indeed it would have been very little use for any practical purpose. I tried to break the spell—the heavy, mute spell of the wilderness—that seemed to draw him to its pitiless breast by the awakening of forgotten and brutal instincts, by the memory of gratified and monstrous passions. This alone, I was convinced, had driven him out to the edge of the forest, to the bush, towards the gleam of fires, the throb of drums, the drone of weird incantations; this alone had beguiled his unlawful soul beyond the bounds of permitted aspirations. And, don't you see, the terror of the position was not in being knocked on the head—though I had a very lively sense of that danger too—but in this, that I had to deal with a being to whom I could not appeal in the name of anything high or low. I had, even like the niggers, to invoke him—himself—his own exalted and incredible degradation. There was nothing either above or below him, and I knew it. He had kicked himself loose of the earth. Confound the man! he had kicked the very earth to pieces. He was alone, and I before him did not know whether I stood on the ground or

floated in the air. I've been telling you what we said—repeating the phrases we pronounced—but what's the good? They were common everyday words— the familiar, vague sounds exchanged on every waking day of life. But what of that? They had behind them, to my mind, the terrific suggestiveness of words heard in dreams, of phrases spoken in nightmares. Soul! If anybody had ever struggled with a soul, I am the man. And I wasn't arguing with a lunatic either. Believe me or not, his intelligence was perfectly clear—concentrated, it is true, upon himself with horrible intensity, yet clear; and therein was my only chance—barring, of course, the killing him there and then, which wasn't so good, on account of unavoidable noise. But his soul was mad. Being alone in the wilderness, it had looked within itself, and by Heavens! I tell you, it had gone mad. I had—for my sins, I suppose, to go through the ordeal of looking into it myself. No eloquence could have been so withering to one's belief in mankind as his final burst of sincerity. He struggled with himself too. I saw it—I heard it. I saw the inconceivable mystery of a soul that knew no restraint, no faith, and no fear, yet struggling blindly with itself. I kept my head pretty well; but when I had him at last stretched on the couch, I wiped my forehead, while my legs shook under me as though I had carried half a ton on my back down that hill. And yet I had only supported him, his bony arm clasped round my neck—and he was not much heavier than a child.

"When next day we left at noon, the crowd, of whose presence behind the curtain of trees I had been acutely conscious all the time, flowed out of the woods again, filled the clearing, covered the slope with a mass of naked, breathing, quivering, bronze bodies. I steamed up a bit, then swung down-stream, and two thousand eyes followed the evolutions of the splashing, thumping, fierce river-demon beating the water with its terrible tail and breathing black smoke into the air. In front of the first rank, along the river, three men, plastered with bright red earth from head to foot, strutted to and fro restlessly. When we came abreast again, they faced the river, stamped their feet, nodded their horned heads, swayed their scarlet bodies; they shook towards the fierce river-demon a bunch of black feathers, a mangy skin with a pendent tail—something that looked like a dried gourd; they shouted periodically together strings of amazing words that resembled no sounds of human language; and the deep murmurs of the crowd, interrupted suddenly, were like the responses of some satanic litany.

"We had carried Kurtz into the pilot-house: there was more air there. Lying on the couch, he stared through the open shutter. There was an eddy in the mass of human bodies, and the woman with helmeted head and tawny cheeks rushed out to the very brink of the stream. She put out her hands, shouted something, and all that wild mob took up the shout in a roaring chorus of articulated, rapid, breathless utterance.

" 'Do you understand this?' I asked.

"He kept on looking out past me with fiery, longing eyes, with a mingled expression of wistfulness and hate. He made no answer, but I saw a smile, a smile of indefinable meaning, appear on his colorless lips that a moment after twitched convulsively. 'Do I not?' he said slowly, gasping, as if the words had been torn out of him by a supernatural power.

"I pulled the string of the whistle, and I did this because I saw the pilgrims on deck getting out their rifles with an air of anticipating a jolly lark. At the sudden screech there was a movement of abject terror through that wedged mass of bodies. 'Don't! don't you frighten them away,' cried some one on deck disconsolately. I pulled the string time after time. They broke and ran, they leaped, they crouched, they swerved, they dodged the flying terror of the sound. The three red chaps had fallen flat, face down on the shore, as though they had been shot dead. Only the barbarous and superb woman did not so much as flinch, and stretched tragically her bare arms after us over the somber and glittering river.

"And then that imbecile crowd down on the deck started their little fun, and I could see nothing more for smoke.

"The brown current ran swiftly out of the heart of darkness, bearing us down towards the sea with twice the speed of our upward progress; and Kurtz's life was running swiftly too, ebbing, ebbing out of his heart into the sea of inexorable time. The manager was very placid, he had no vital anxieties now, he took us both in with a comprehensive and satisfied glance: the 'affair' had come off as well as could be wished. I saw the time approaching when I would be left alone of the party of 'unsound method.' The pilgrims looked upon me with disfavor. I was, so to speak, numbered with the dead. It is strange how I accepted this unforeseen partnership, this choice of nightmares forced upon me in the tenebrous land invaded by these mean and greedy phantoms.

"Kurtz discoursed. A voice! a voice! It rang deep to the very last. It survived his strength to hide in the magnificent folds of eloquence the barren darkness of his heart. Oh, he struggled! he struggled! The wastes of his weary brain were haunted by shadowy images now— images of wealth and fame revolving obsequiously round his unextinguishable gift of noble and lofty expression. My Intended, my station, my career, my ideas—these were the subjects for the occasional utterances of elevated sentiments. The shade of the original Kurtz frequented the bedside of the hollow sham, whose fate it was to be buried presently in the mold of primeval earth.

But both the diabolic love and the unearthly hate of the mysteries it had penetrated fought for the possession of that soul satiated with primitive emotions, avid of lying fame, of sham distinction, of all the appearances of success and power.

"Sometimes he was contemptibly childish. He desired to have kings meet him at railway stations on his return from some ghastly Nowhere, where he intended to accomplish great things. 'You show them you have in you something that is really profitable, and then there will be no limits to the recognition of your ability,' he would say. 'Of course you must take care of the motives—right motives—always.' The long reaches that were like one and the same reach, monotonous bends that were exactly alike, slipped past the steamer with their multitude of secular trees looking patiently after this grimy fragment of another world, the forerunner of change of conquest, of trade, of massacres, of blessings. I looked ahead—piloting. 'Close the shutter,' said Kurtz suddenly one day; 'I can't bear to look at this.' I did so. There was a silence. 'Oh, but I will wring your heart yet!' he cried at the invisible wilderness.

"We broke down—as I had expected—and had to lie up for repairs at the head of an island. This delay was the first thing that shook Kurtz's confidence. One morning he gave me a packet of papers and a photograph—the lot tied together with a shoe-string. 'Keep this for me,' he said. 'This noxious fool' (meaning the manager) 'is capable of prying into my boxes when I am not looking.' In the afternoon I saw him. He was lying on his back with closed eyes, and I withdrew quietly, but I heard him mutter, 'Live rightly, die, die . . .' I listened. There was nothing more. Was he rehearsing some speech in his sleep, or was it a fragment of a phrase from some newspaper article? He had been writing for the papers and meant to do so again, 'for the furthering of my ideas. It's a duty.'

"His was an impenetrable darkness. I looked at him as you peer down at a man who is lying at the bottom of a precipice where the sun never shines. But I had not much time to give him, because I was helping the engine-driver to take to pieces the leaky cylinders, to straighten a bent connecting-rod, and in other such matters. I lived in an infernal mess of rust, filings, nuts, bolts, spanners, hammers, rachet-drills—things I abominate, because I don't get on with them. I tended the little forge we fortunately had aboard; I toiled wearily in a wretched scrap-heap—unless I had the shakes too bad to stand.

"One evening coming in with a candle I was startled to hear him say a little tremulously, I am lying here in the dark waiting for death.' The light was within a foot of his eyes. I forced myself to murmur, 'Oh, nonsense!' and stood over him as if transfixed.

"Anything approaching the change that came over his features I have never seen before, and hope never to see again. Oh, I wasn't touched. I was fascinated. It was as though a veil had been rent. I saw on that ivory face the expression of somber pride, of ruthless power, of craven terror—of an intense and hopeless despair. Did he live his life again in every detail of desire, temptation, and surrender during that supreme moment of complete knowledge? He cried in a whisper at some image, at some vision—he cried out twice, a cry that was no more than a breath:

" 'The horror! The horror!'

"I blew the candle out and left the cabin. The pilgrims were dining in the mess-room, and I took my place opposite the manager, who lifted his eyes to give me a questioning glance, which I successfully ignored. He leaned back, serene, with that peculiar smile of his sealing the unexpressed depths of his meanness. A continuous shower of small flies streamed upon the lamp, upon the cloth, upon our hands and faces. Suddenly the manager's boy put his insolent black head in the doorway, and said in a tone of scathing contempt:

" 'Mistah Kurtz—he dead.'

"All the pilgrims rushed out to see. I remained, and went on with my dinner. I believe I was considered brutally callous. However, I did not eat much. There was a lamp in there—light, don't you know—and outside it was so beastly, beastly dark. I went no more near the remarkable man who had pronounced a judgment upon the adventures of his soul on this earth. The voice was gone. What else had been there? But I am of course aware that next day the pilgrims buried something in a muddy hole.

"And then they very nearly buried me.

"However, as you see, I did not go to join Kurtz there and then. I did not. I remained to dream the nightmare out to the end, and to show my loyalty to Kurtz once more. Destiny. My destiny! Droll thing life is—that mysterious arrangement of merciless logic for a futile purpose. The most you can hope from it is some knowledge of yourself—that comes too late—a crop of unextinguishable regrets. I have wrestled with death. It is the most unexciting contest you can imagine. It takes place in an impalpable greyness, with nothing underfoot, with nothing around, without spectators, without clamor, without glory, without the great desire of victory, without the great fear of defeat, in a sickly atmosphere of tepid scepticism, without much belief in your own right, and still less in that of your adversary. If such is the form of ultimate wisdom, then life is a greater riddle than some of us think it to be. I was within a hair's-breadth of the last opportunity for pronouncement, and I found with humiliation that probably I would have nothing to say. This is the reason why I affirm that Kurtz was a remarkable man. He had something to say. He said it. Since I had peeped

over the edge myself, I understand better the meaning of his stare, that could not see the flame of the candle, but was wide enough to embrace the whole universe, piercing enough to penetrate all the hearts that beat in the darkness. He had summed up—he had judged. 'The horror!' He was a remarkable man. After all, this was the expression of some sort of belief; it had candor, it had conviction, it had a vibrating note of revolt in its whisper, it had the appalling face of a glimpsed truth—the strange commingling of desire and hate. And it is not my own extremity I remember best—a vision of greyness without form filled with physical pain, and a careless contempt for the evanescence of all things—even of this pain itself. No! It is his extremity that I seem to have lived through. True, he had made that last stride; he had stepped over the edge, while I had been permitted to draw back my hesitating foot. And perhaps in this is the whole difference; perhaps all the wisdom, and all truth, and all sincerity, are just compressed into that inappreciable moment of time in which we step over the threshold of the invisible. Perhaps! I like to think my summing-up would not have been a word of careless contempt. Better his cry—much better. It was an affirmation, a moral victory paid for by innumerable defeats, by abominable terrors, by abominable satisfactions. But it was a victory! That is why I have remained loyal to Kurtz to the last, and even beyond, when a long time after I heard once more, not his own voice, but the echo of his magnificent eloquence thrown to me from a soul as translucently pure as a cliff of crystal.

"No, they did not bury me, though there is a period of time which I remember mistily, with a shuddering wonder, like a passage through some inconceivable world that had no hope in it and no desire. I found myself back in the sepulchral city resenting the sight of people hurrying through the streets to filch a little money from each other, to devour their infamous cookery, to gulp their unwholesome beer, to dream their insignificant and silly dreams. They trespassed upon my thoughts. They were intruders whose knowledge of life was to me an irritating pretense, because I felt so sure they could not possibly know the things I knew. Their bearing, which was simply the bearing of commonplace individuals going about their business in the assurance of perfect safety, was offensive to me like the outrageous flauntings of folly in the face of a danger it is unable to comprehend. I had no particular desire to enlighten them, but I had some difficulty in restraining myself from laughing in their faces, so full of stupid importance. I daresay I was not very well at that time. I tottered about the streets—there were various affairs to settle—grinning bitterly at perfectly respectable persons. I admit my behavior was inexcusable, but then my temperature was seldom normal in these days. My dear aunt's endeavors to 'nurse up my strength' seemed altogether beside the mark. It was not my strength that wanted nursing, it was my imagination that wanted soothing. I kept the bundle of papers given me by Kurtz, not knowing exactly what to do with it. His mother had died lately, watched over, as I was told, by his Intended. A clean-shaved man, with an official manner and wearing gold-rimmed spectacles, called on me one day and made inquiries, at first circuitous, afterwards suavely pressing, about what he was pleased to denominate certain 'documents.' I was not surprised, because I had had two rows with the manager on the subject out there. I had refused to give up the smallest scrap out of that package, and I took the same attitude with the spectacled man. He became darkly menacing at last, and with much heat argued that the Company had the right to every bit of information about its 'territories.' And, said he, 'Mr. Kurtz's knowledge of un-explored regions must have been necessarily extensive and peculiar—owing to his great abilities and to the deplorable circumstances in which he had been placed: therefore——' I assured him Mr. Kurtz's knowledge, however extensive, did not bear upon the problems of commerce or administration. He invoked then the name of science. 'It would be an incalculable loss if,' etc. etc. I offered him the report on the 'Suppression of Savage Customs,' with the postscriptum torn off. He took it up eagerly, but ended by sniffing at it with an air of contempt. 'This is not what we had a right to expect,' he remarked. 'Expect nothing else,' I said. 'There are only private letters.' He withdrew upon some threat of legal proceedings, and I saw him no more; but another fellow, calling himself Kurtz's cousin, appeared two days later, and was anxious to hear all the details about his dear relative's last moments. Incidentally he gave me to understand that Kurtz had been essentially a great musician. 'There was the making of an immense success,' said the man, who was an organist, I believe, with lank grey hair flowing over a greasy coat-collar. I had no reason to doubt his statement; and to this day I am unable to say what was Kurtz's profession, whether he ever had any—which was the greatest of his talents. I had taken him for a painter who wrote for the papers, or else for a journalist who could paint—but even the cousin (who took snuff during the interview) could not tell me what he had been—exactly. He was a universal genius—on that point I agreed with the old chap, who thereupon blew his nose noisily into a large cotton handkerchief and withdrew in senile agitation, bearing off some family letters and memoranda without importance. Ultimately a journalist anxious to know something of the fate of his 'dear colleague' turned up. This visitor informed me Kurtz's proper sphere ought to have been politics 'on the popular side.' He had furry straight eyebrows, bristly hair cropped short, an eyeglass on a broad ribbon, and, becoming expansive, confessed his opinion that Kurtz really couldn't write a bit— 'but Heavens! how that man could talk! He electrified large meetings. He had faith—don't you see?—he had the faith. He could get himself to believe anything—anything. He would have been a splendid leader of an extreme party.' 'What party?' I asked. 'Any party,' answered the other. 'He was an—an—extremist.' Did I not think so? I assented. Did I know, he asked, with a sudden flash of curiosity, 'what it was that had induced him to go out there?' 'Yes,' said I, and forthwith handed him the famous Report for publication, if he thought fit. He glanced through it hurriedly, mumbling all the time, judged 'it would do,' and took himself off with this plunder.

"Thus I was left at last with a slim packet of letters and the girl's portrait. She struck me as beautiful—I mean she had a beautiful expression. I know that the sunlight can be made to lie too, yet one felt that no manipulation of light and pose could have conveyed the delicate shade of truthfulness upon those features. She seemed ready to listen without mental reservation, without suspicion, without a thought for herself. I concluded I would go and give her back her portrait and those letters myself. Curiosity? Yes; and also some other feeling perhaps. All that had been Kurtz's had passed out of my hands: his soul, his body, his station, his plans, his ivory, his career. There remained only his memory and his Intended—and I wanted to give that up too to the past, in a way—to surrender personally all that remained of him with me to that oblivion which is the last word of our common fate. I don't defend myself. I had no clear perception of what it was I really wanted. Perhaps it was an impulse of unconscious loyalty, or the fulfilment of one of those ironic necessities

that lurk in the facts of human existence. I don't know. I can't tell. But I went.

"I thought his memory was like the other memories of the dead that accumulate in every man's life—a vague impress on the brain of shadows that had fallen on it in their swift and final passage; but before the high and ponderous door, between the tall houses of a street as still and decorous as a well-kept alley in a cemetery, I had a vision of him on the stretcher, opening his mouth voraciously, as if to devour all the earth with all its mankind. He lived then before me; he lived as much as he had ever lived—a shadow insatiable of splendid appearances, of frightful realities; a shadow darker than the shadow of the night, and draped nobly in the folds of a gorgeous eloquence. The vision seemed to enter the house with me—the stretcher, the phantom-bearers, the wild crowd of obedient worshippers, the gloom of the forests, the glitter of the reach between the murky bends, the beat of the drum, regular and muffled like the beating of a heart—the heart of a conquering darkness. It was a moment of triumph for the wilderness, an invading and vengeful rush which, it seemed to me, I would have to keep back alone for the salvation of another soul. And the memory of what I had heard him say afar there, with the horned shapes stirring at my back, in the glow of fires, within the patient woods, those broken phrases came back to me, were heard again in their ominous and terrifying simplicity. I remembered his abject pleading, his abject threats, the colossal scale of his vile desires, the meanness, the torment, the tempestuous anguish of his soul. And later on I seemed to see his collected languid manner, when he said one day, 'This lot of ivory now is really mine. The Company did not pay for it. I collected it myself at a very great personal risk. I am afraid they will try to claim it as theirs though. H'm. It is a difficult case. What do you think I ought to do—resist? Eh? I want no more than justice.' . . . He wanted no more than justice—no more than justice. I rang the bell before a mahogany door on the first floor, and while I waited he seemed to stare at me out of the glassy panel—stare with the wide and immense stare embracing, condemning, loathing all the universe. I seemed to hear the whisper cry, 'The horror! The horror!'

"The dusk was falling. I had to wait in a lofty drawing-room with three long windows from floor to ceiling that were like three luminous and be-draped columns. The bent gilt legs and backs of the furniture shone in indistinct curves. The tall marble fireplace had a cold and monumental whiteness. A grand piano stood massively in a corner; with dark gleams on the flat surfaces like a sombre and polished sarcophagus. A high door opened—closed. I rose.

"She came forward, all in black, with a pale head, floating towards me in the dusk. She was in mourning. It was more than a year since his death, more than a year since the news came; she seemed as though she would remember and mourn for ever. She took both my hands in hers and murmured, 'I had heard you were coming.' I noticed she was not very young—I mean not girlish. She had a mature capacity for fidelity, for belief, for suffering. The room seemed to have grown darker, as if all the sad light of the cloudy evening had taken refuge on her forehead. This fair hair, this pale visage, this pure brow, seemed surrounded by an ashy halo from which the dark eyes looked out at me. Their glance was guileless, profound, confident, and trustful. She carried her sorrowful head as though she were proud of that sorrow, as thought she would say, I—I alone know how to mourn for him as he deserves. But while we were still shaking hands, such a look of awful desolation came upon her face that I perceived she was one of those creatures

that are not the playthings of Time. For her he had died only yesterday. And, by Jove! the impression was so powerful that for me too he seemed to have died only yesterday—nay, this very minute. I saw her and him in the same instant of time—his death and her sorrow—I saw her sorrow in the very moment of his death. Do you understand? I saw them together—I heard them together. She had said, with a deep catch of the breath, 'I have survived'; while my strained ears seemed to hear distinctly, mingled with her tone of despairing regret, the summing-up whisper of his eternal condemnation. I asked myself what I was doing there, with a sensation of panic in my heart as though I had blundered into a place of cruel and absurd mysteries not fit for a human being to behold. She motioned me to a chair. We sat down. I laid the packet gently on the little table, and she put her hand over it. . . . 'You knew him well,' she murmured, after a moment of mourning silence.

" 'Intimacy grows quickly out there,' I said. 'I knew him as well as it is possible for one man to know another.'

" 'And you admired him,' she said. 'It was impossible to know him and not to admire him. Was it?'

" 'He was a remarkable man,' I said unsteadily. Then before the appealing fixity of her gaze, that seemed to watch for more words on my lips, I went on,' It was impossible not to——'

" 'Love him,' she finished eagerly, silencing me into an appalled dumbness. 'How true! how true! But when you think that no one knew him so well as I! I had all his noble confidence. I knew him best.'

" 'You knew him best,' I repeated. And perhaps she did. But with every word spoken the room was growing darker, and only her forehead, smooth and white, remained illumined by the unextinguishable light of belief and love.

" 'You were his friend,' she went on.

'His friend,' she repeated, a little louder. 'You must have been, if he had given you this, and sent you to me. I feel I can speak to you—and oh! I must speak. I want you—you who have heard his last words—to know I have been worthy of him. . . . It is not pride. . . . Yes! I am proud to know I understood him better than any one on earth—he told me so himself. And since his mother died I have had no one—no one—to—to——'

"I listened. The darkness deepened. I was not even sure whether he had given me the right bundle. I rather suspect he wanted me to take care of another batch of his papers which, after his death, I saw the manager examining under the lamp. And the girl talked, easing her pain in the certitude of my sympathy; she talked as thirsty men drink. I had heard that her engagement with Kurtz had been disapproved by her people. He wasn't rich enough or something. And indeed I don't know whether he had not been a pauper all his life. He had given me some reason to infer that it was his impatience of comparative poverty that drove him out there.

" '. . . Who was not his friend who had heard him speak once?' she was saying. 'He drew men towards him by what was best in them. She looked at me with intensity. 'It is the gift of the great,' she went on, and the sound of her low voice seemed to have the accompaniment of all the other sounds, full of mystery, desolation, and sorrow, I had ever heard—the ripple of the river, the soughing of the trees swayed by the wind, the murmurs of the crowds, the faint ring of incomprehensible words cried from afar, the whisper of a voice speaking from beyond the threshold of an eternal darkness. 'But you have heard him! You know!' she cried.

" 'Yes, I know,' I said with something like despair in my heart, but bowing my head before the faith that was in her, before that great and saving illusion that shone with an unearthly glow in the darkness, in the triumphant darkness from which I could not have defended her—from which I could not even defend myself.

" 'What a loss to me—to us!'—she corrected herself with beautiful generosity; then added in a murmur, 'To the world.' By the last gleams of twilight I could see the glitter of her eyes, full of tears—of tears that would not fall.

" 'I have been very happy—very fortunate—very proud,' she went on. 'Too fortunate. Too happy for a little while. And now I am unhappy for—for life.'

"She stood up; her fair hair seemed to catch all the remaining light in a glimmer of gold. I rose too.

" 'And of all this,' she went on mournfully, 'of all his promise, and of all his greatness, of his generous mind, of his noble heart, nothing remains—nothing but a memory. You and I——'

" 'We shall always remember him,' I said hastily.

" 'No!' she cried. 'It is impossible that all this should be lost—that such a life should be sacrificed to leave nothing—but sorrow. You know what vast plans he had. I knew of them too—I could not perhaps understand—but others knew of them. Something must remain. His words, at least, have not died.'

" 'His words will remain,' I said.

" 'And his example,' she whispered to herself. 'Men looked up to him—his goodness shone in every act. His example——'

" 'True,' I said; 'his example too. Yes, his example. I forgot that.'

" 'But I do not. I cannot—I cannot believe—not yet. I cannot believe that I shall never see him again, that nobody will see him again, never, never, never.'

"She put out her arms as if after a retreating figure, stretching them back and with clasped pale hands across the fading and narrow sheen of the window. Never see him! I saw him clearly enough then. I shall see this eloquent phantom as long as I live, and I shall see her too, a tragic and familiar Shade, resembling in this gesture another one, tragic also, and bedecked with powerless charms, stretching bare brown arms over the glitter of the infernal stream, the stream of darkness. She said suddenly very low, 'He died as he lived.'

"'His end,' said I, with dull anger stirring in me, 'was in every way worthy of his life.'

"'And I was not with him,' she murmured. My anger subsided before a feeling of infinite pity.

"'Everything that could be done——' I mumbled.

"'Ah, but I believed in him more than any one on earth—more than his own mother, more than—himself. He needed me! Me! I would have treasured every sigh, every word, every sign, every glance.'

"I felt like a chill grip on my chest. 'Don't,' I said, in a muffled voice.

"'Forgive me. I—I—have mourned so long in silence—in silence. . . . You were with him—to the last? I think of his loneliness. Nobody near to understand him as I would have understood. Perhaps no one to hear . . .'

"'To the very end,' I said shakily. 'I heard his very last words. . . .' I stopped in a fright.

"'Repeat them,' she murmured in a heart-broken tone. 'I want—I want—something — something — to — to live with.'

"I was on the point of crying at her, 'Don't you hear them?' The dusk was repeating them in a persistent whisper all around us, in a whisper that seemed to swell menacingly like the first whisper of a rising wind. 'The horror! The horror!'

"'His last word—to live with,' she insisted. 'Don't you understand I loved him—I loved him—I loved him!'

"I pulled myself together and spoke slowly.

"'The last word he pronounced was —your name.'

"I heard a light sigh and then my heart stood still, stopped dead short by an exulting and terrible cry, by the cry of inconceivable triumph and of unspeakable pain. 'I knew it—I was sure!' . . . She knew. She was sure. I heard her weeping; she had hidden her face in her hands. It seemed to me that the house would collapse before I could escape, that the heavens would fall upon my head. But nothing happened. The heavens do not fall for such a trifle. Would they have fallen, I wonder, if I had rendered Kurtz that justice which was his due? Hadn't he said he wanted only justice? But I couldn't. I could not tell her. It would have been too dark— too dark altogether. . . ."

Marlow ceased, and sat apart, indistinct and silent, in the pose of a meditating Buddha. Nobody moved for a time. "We have lost the first of the ebb," said the Director suddenly. I raised my head. The offing was barred by a black bank of clouds, and the tranquil waterway leading to the uttermost ends of the earth flowed somber under an overcast sky—seemed to lead into the heart of an immense darkness.

Virginia Woolf (1882–1941)

A ROOM OF ONE'S OWN

CHAPTER ONE

But, you may say, we asked you to speak about women and fiction—what has that got to do with a room of one's own? I will try to explain. When you asked me to speak about women and fiction I sat down on the banks of a river and began to wonder what the words meant. They might mean simply a few remarks about Fanny Burney; a few more about Jane Austen; a tribute to the Brontës and a sketch of Haworth Parsonage under snow; some witticisms if possible about Miss Mitford; a respectful allusion to George Eliot; a reference to Mrs. Gaskell and one would have done. But at second sight the words seemed not so simple. The title women and fiction might mean, and you may have meant it to mean, women and what they are like; or it might mean women and the fiction that they write; or it might mean women and the fiction that is written about them; or it might mean that somehow all three are inextricably mixed together and you want me to consider them in that light. But when I began to consider the subject in this last way, which seemed the most interesting, I soon saw that it had one fatal drawback. I should never be able to come to a conclusion. I should never be able to fulfil what is, I understand, the first duty of a lecturer —to hand you after an hour's discourse a nugget of pure truth to wrap up between the pages of your notebooks and keep on the mantelpiece for ever. All I could do was to offer you an opinion upon one minor point—a woman must have money and a room of her own if she is to write fiction; and that, as you will see, leaves the great problem of the true nature of woman and the true nature of fiction unsolved. I have shirked the duty of coming to a conclusion upon these two questions—women and fiction remain, so far as I am concerned, unsolved problems. But in order to make some amends I am going to do what I can to show you how I arrived at this opinion about the room and the money. I am going to develop in your presence as fully and freely as I can the train of thought which led me to think this. Perhaps if I lay bare the ideas, the prejudices, that lie behind this statement you will find that they have some bearing upon women and some upon fiction. At any rate, when a subject is highly controversial—and any question about sex is that—one cannot hope to tell the truth. One can only show how one came to hold whatever opinion one does hold. One can only give one's audience the chance of drawing their own conclusions as they observe the limitations, the prejudices, the idiosyncrasies of the speaker. Fiction here is likely to contain more truth than fact. Therefore I propose, making use of all the liberties and licenses of a novelist, to tell you the story of the two days that preceded my coming here—how, bowed down by the weight of the subject which you have laid upon my shoulders, I pondered it, and made it work in and out of my daily life. I need not say that what I am about to describe has no existence; Oxbridge is an invention; so is Fernham; "I" is only a convenient term for somebody who has no real being. Lies will flow from my lips, but there may perhaps be some truth mixed up with them; it is for you to seek out this truth and to decide whether any part of it is worth keeping. If not, you will of course throw the whole of it into the wastepaper basket and forget all about it.

Here then was I (call me Mary Beton, Mary Seton, Mary Carmichael or by any name you please—it is not a matter of any importance) sitting on the banks of a river a week or two ago in fine October weather, lost in thought. That collar I have spoken of, women and fiction, the need of coming to some conclusion on a subject that raises all sorts of prejudices and passions, bowed my head to the ground. To the right and left bushes of some sort, golden and crimson, glowed with the color, even it seemed burnt with the heat, of fire. On the further bank the willows wept in perpetual lamentation, their hair about their shoulders. The river reflected whatever it chose of sky and bridge and burning tree, and when the undergraduate had oared his boat through the reflections they closed again, completely, as if he had never been. There one might have sat the clock round lost in thought. Thought—to call it by a prouder name than it deserved—had let its line down into the stream. It swayed, minute after minute, hither and thither among the reflections and the weeds, letting the water lift it and sink it, until—you know the little tug—the sudden conglomeration of an idea at the end of one's line: and then the cautious hauling of it in, and the careful laying of it out? Alas, laid on the grass how small, how insignificant this thought of mine looked; the sort of fish that a good fisherman puts back into the water so that it may grow fatter and be one day worth cooking and eating. I will not trouble you with that thought now, though if you look carefully you may find it for yourselves in the course of what I am going to say.

But however small it was, it had, nevertheless, the mysterious property of its kind—put back into the mind, it became at once very exciting, and important; and as it darted and sank, and flashed hither and thither, set up such a wash and tumult of ideas that it was impossible to sit still. It was thus that I found myself walking with extreme rapidity across a grass plot. Instantly a man's figure rose to intercept me. Nor did I at first understand that the gesticulations of a curious-looking object, in a cut-away coat and evening shirt, were aimed at me. His face expressed horror and indignation. Instinct rather than reason came to my help; he was a Beadle; I was a woman. This was the turf; there was the path. Only the Fellows and Scholars are allowed here; the gravel is the place for me. Such thoughts were the work of a moment. As I regained the path the arms of the Beadle sank, his face assumed its usual repose, and though turf is better walking than gravel, no very great harm was done. The only charge I could bring against the Fellows and Scholars of whatever the college might happen to be was that in protection of their turf, which has been rolled for 300 years in succession, they had sent my little fish into hiding.

What idea it had been that had sent me so audaciously trespassing I could not now remember. The spirit of peace descended like a cloud from heaven, for if the spirit of peace dwells anywhere, it is in the courts and quadrangles of Oxbridge on a fine October morning. Strolling through those colleges past those ancient halls the roughness of the present seemed smoothed away; the body seemed contained in a miraculous glass cabinet through which no sound could penetrate, and the mind, freed from any contact with facts (unless one trespassed on the turf again), was at liberty to settle down upon whatever meditation was in harmony with the moment. As chance would have it, some stray memory of some old essay about revisiting Oxbridge in the long vacation brought Charles Lamb to mind—Saint Charles, said Thackeray, putting a letter of Lamb's to his forehead. Indeed, among all the dead (I give you my thoughts as they came to me), Lamb is one of the most congenial; one to whom one would have liked to say, Tell me then how you wrote your essays? For his essays are superior even to Max Beerbohm's, I thought, with all their perfection, because of that wild flash of imagination, that lightning crack of genius in the middle of them which leaves them flawed and imperfect, but starred with poetry. Lamb then came to Oxbridge perhaps a hundred years ago. Certainly he wrote an essay—the name escapes me—about the manuscript of one of Milton's poems which he saw here. It was *Lycidas* perhaps, and Lamb wrote how it shocked him to think it possible that any word in *Lycidas* could have been different from what it is. To think of Milton changing the words in that poem seemed to him a sort of sacrilege. This led me to remember what I could of *Lycidas* and to amuse myself with guessing which word it could have been that Milton had altered, and why. It then occurred to me that the very manuscript itself which Lamb had looked at was only a few hundred yards away, so that one could follow Lamb's footsteps across the quadrangle to that famous library where the treasure is kept. Moreover, I recollected, as I put this plan into execution, it is in this famous library that the manuscript of Thackeray's *Esmond* is also preserved. The critics often say that *Esmond* is Thackeray's most perfect novel. But the affection of the style, with its imitation of the eighteenth century, hampers one, so far as I remember; unless indeed the eighteenth-century style

was natural to Thackeray—a fact that one might prove by looking at the manuscript and seeing whether the alterations were for the benefit of the style or of the sense. But then one would have to decide what is style and what is meaning, a question which—but here I was actually at the door which leads into the library itself. I must have opened it, for instantly there issued, like a guardian angel barring the way with a flutter of black gown instead of white wings, a deprecating, silvery, kindly gentleman, who regretted in a low voice as he waved me back that ladies are only admitted to the library if accompanied by a Fellow of the College or furnished with a letter of introduction.

That a famous library has been cursed by a woman is a matter of complete indifference to a famous library. Venerable and calm, with all its treasures safe locked within its breast, it sleeps complacently and will, so far as I am concerned, so sleep for ever. Never will I wake those echoes, never will I ask for that hospitality again, I vowed as I descended the steps in anger. Still an hour remained before luncheon, and what was one to do? Stroll on the meadows? sit by the river? Certainly it was a lovely autumn morning; the leaves were fluttering red to the ground; there was no great hardship in doing either. But the sound of music reached my ear. Some service or celebration was going forward. The organ complained magnificently as I passed the chapel door. Even the sorrow of Christianity sounded in that serene air more like the recollection of sorrow than sorrow itself; even the groanings of the ancient organ seemed lapped in peace. I had no wish to enter had I the right, and this time the verger might have stopped me, demanding perhaps my baptismal certificate, or a letter of introduction from the Dean. But the outside of these magnificent buildings is often as beautiful as the inside. Moreover, it was amusing enough to watch the congregation assembling, coming in and going out again, busying themselves at the door of the chapel like bees at the mouth of a hive. Many were in cap and gown; some had tufts of fur on their shoulders; others were wheeled in bath-chairs; others, though not past middle age, seemed creased and crushed into shapes so singular that one was reminded of those giant crabs and crayfish who heave with difficulty across the sand of an aquarium. As I leant against the wall the University indeed seemed a sanctuary in which are preserved rare types which would soon be obsolete if left to fight for existence on the pavement of the Strand. Old stories of old deans and old dons came back to mind, but before I had summoned up courage to whistle —it used to be said that at the sound of a whistle old Professor —— instantly broke into a gallop—the venerable congregation had gone inside. The outside of the chapel remained. As you know, its high domes and pinnacles can be seen, like a sailing-ship always voyaging never arriving, lit up at night and visible for miles, far away across the hills. Once, presumably, this quadrangle with its smooth lawns, its massive buildings, and the chapel itself was marsh too, where the grasses waved and the swine rootled. Teams of horses and oxen, I thought, must have hauled the stone in wagons from far countries, and then with infinite labor the grey blocks in whose shade I was now standing were poised in order one on top of another, and then the painters brought their glass for the windows, and the masons were busy for centuries up on that roof with putty and cement, spade and trowel. Every Saturday somebody must have poured gold and silver out of a leathern purse into their ancient fists, for they had their beer and skittles presumably of an evening. An unending stream of gold and silver, I thought, must have flowed into this court perpetually to keep the stones coming and the masons working; to level, to ditch, to dig and to drain. But it was then the age of faith, and money was poured liberally to set these stones on a deep foundation, and when the stones were raised, still more money was poured in from the coffers of kings and queens and great nobles to ensure that hymns should be sung here and scholars taught. Lands were granted; tithes were paid. And when the age of faith was over and the age of reason had come, still the same flow of gold and silver went on; fellowships were founded; lectureships endowed; only the gold and silver flowed now, not from the coffers of the king, but from the chests of merchants and manufacturers, from the purses of men who had made, say, a fortune from industry, and returned, in their wills, a bounteous share of it to endow more chairs, more lectureships, more fellowships in the university where they had learnt their craft. Hence the libraries and laboratories; the observatories; the splendid equipment of costly and delicate instruments which now stands on glass shelves, where centuries ago the grasses waved and the swine rootled. Certainly, as I strolled round the court, the foundation of gold and silver seemed deep enough; the pavement laid solidly over the wild grasses. Men with trays on their heads went busily from staircase to staircase. Gaudy blossoms flowered in windowboxes. The strains of the gramophone blared out from the rooms within. It was impossible not to reflect—the reflection whatever it may have been was cut short. The clock struck. It was time to find one's way to luncheon.

It is a curious fact that novelists have a way of making us believe that luncheon parties are invariably memorable for something very witty that was said, or for something very wise that was done. But they seldom spare a word for what was eaten. It is part of the novelist's convention not to mention soup and salmon and ducklings, as if soup and salmon and ducklings were of no importance whatsoever, as if nobody ever smoked a cigar or drank a glass of wine. Here, however, I shall take the liberty to defy that convention and tell you that the lunch on this occasion began with soles, sunk in a deep dish, over which the college cook had spread a counterpane of the whitest cream, save that it was branded here and there with brown spots like the spots on the flanks of a doe. After that came the partridges, but if this suggests a couple of bald, brown birds on a plate you are mistaken. The partridges, many and various, came with all their retinue of sauces and salads, the sharp and the sweet, each in its order; their potatoes, thin as coins but not so hard; their sprouts, foliated as rosebuds but more succulent. And no sooner had the roast and its retinue been done with than the silent serving-man, the Beadle himself perhaps in a milder manifestation, set before us, wreathed in napkins, a confection which rose all sugar from the waves. To call it pudding and so relate it to rice and tapioca would be an insult. Meanwhile the wineglasses had flushed yellow and flushed crimson; had been emptied; had been filled. And thus by degrees was lit, halfway down the spine, which is the seat of the soul, not that hard little electric light which we call brilliance, as it pops in and out upon our lips, but the more profound, subtle and subterranean glow, which is the rich yellow flame of rational intercourse. No need to hurry. No need to sparkle. No need to be anybody but oneself. We are all going to heaven and Vandyck is of the company—in other words, how good life seemed, how sweet its rewards, how trivial this grudge or that grievance, how admirable friendship and the society of one's kind, as, lighting a good cigarette, one sunk among the cushions in the window-seat.

If by good luck there had been an ash-tray handy, if one had not knocked the ash out of the window in default, if things had been a little different from what they were, one would not have seen, presumably, a cat without a tail. The sight of that abrupt and truncated animal padding softly across the quadrangle changed by some fluke of the subconscious intelligence the emotional light for me. It was as if some one had let fall a shade. Perhaps the excellent hock was relinquishing its hold. Certainly, as I watched the Manx cat pause in the middle of the lawn as if it too questioned the universe, something seemed lacking, something seemed different. But what was lacking, what was different, I asked myself, listening to the talk. And to answer that question I had to think myself out of the room, back into the past, before the war indeed, and to set before my eyes the model of another luncheon party held in rooms not very far distant from these; but different. Everything was different. Meanwhile the talk went on among the guests, who were many and young, some of this sex, some of that; it went on swimmingly, it went on agreeably, freely, amusingly. And as it went on I set it against the background of that other talk, and as I matched the two together I had no doubt that one was the descendant, the legitimate heir of the other. Nothing was changed; nothing was different save only—here I listened with all my ears not entirely to what was being said, but to the murmur or current behind it. Yes, that was it—the change was there. Before the war at a luncheon party like this people would have said precisely the same things but they would have sounded different, because in those days they were accompanied by a sort of humming noise, not articulate, but musical, exciting, which changed the value of the words themselves. Could one set that humming noise to words? Perhaps with the help of the poets one could. A book lay beside me and, opening it, I turned casually enough to Tennyson. And here I found Tennyson was singing:

There has fallen a splendid tear
  From the passion-flower at the gate.
She is coming, my dove, my dear;
  She is coming, my life, my fate;
The red rose cries, "She is near, she is
    near";
  And the white rose weeps, "She is
    late";
The larkspur listens, "I hear, I hear";
  And the lily whispers, "I wait."

Was that what men hummed at luncheon parties before the war? And the women?

My heart is like a singing bird
  Whose nest is in a water'd shoot;
My heart is like an apple tree
  Whose boughs are bent with thickset fruit;
My heart is like a rainbow shell
  That paddles in a halcyon sea;
My heart is gladder than all these
  Because my love is come to me.

Was that what women hummed at luncheon parties before the war?

There was something so ludicrous in thinking of people humming such things even under their breath at luncheon parties before the war that I burst out laughing, and had to explain my laughter by pointing at the Manx cat, who did look a little absurd, poor beast, without a tail, in the middle of the lawn. Was he really born so, or had he lost his tail in an accident? The tailless cat, though some are said to exist in the Isle of Man, is rarer than one thinks. It is a queer animal, quaint rather than beautiful. It is strange what a difference a tail makes —you know the sort of things one says as a lunch party breaks up and people are finding their coats and hats. This one, thanks to the hospitality of the host, had lasted far into the afternoon. The beautiful October day was fading and the leaves were falling from the trees in the avenue as I walked through it. Gate after gate seemed to close with gentle finality behind me. Innumerable beadles were fitting innumerable keys into well-oiled locks; the treasure-house was being made secure for another night. After the avenue one comes out upon a road—I forget its name—which leads you, if you take the right turning, along to Fernham. But there was plenty of time. Dinner was not till half-past seven. One could almost do without dinner after such a luncheon. It is strange how a scrap of poetry works in the mind and makes the legs move in time to it along the road. Those words—

There has fallen a splendid tear
  From the passion-flower at the gate.
She is coming, my dove, my dear—

sang in my blood as I stepped quickly along towards Headingley. And then, switching off into the other measure, I sang, where the waters are churned up by the weir:

My heart is like a singing bird
  Whose nest is in a water'd shoot;
My heart is like an apple tree . . .

What poets, I cried aloud, as one does in the dusk, what poets they were!

In a sort of jealousy, I suppose, for our own age, silly and absurd though these comparisons are, I went on to wonder if honestly one could name two living poets now as great as Tennyson and Christina Rossetti were then. Obviously it is impossible, I thought, looking into those foaming waters, to compare them. The very reason why the poetry excites one to such abandonment, such rapture, is that it celebrates some feeling that one used to have (at luncheon parties before the war perhaps), so that one responds easily, familiarly, without troubling to check the feeling, or to compare it with any that one has now. But the living poets express a feeling that is actually being made and torn out of us at the moment. One does not recognize it in the first place; often for some reason one fears it; one watches it with keenness and compares it jealously and suspiciously with the old feeling that one knew. Hence the difficulty of modern poetry; and it is because of this difficulty that one cannot remember more than two consecutive lines of any good modern poet. For this reason—that my memory failed me—the argument flagged for want of material. But why, I continued, moving on towards Headingley, have we stopped humming under our breath at luncheon parties? Why has Alfred ceased to sing

She is coming, my dove, my dear?

Why has Christina ceased to respond

My heart is gladder than all these
Because my love is come to me?

Shall we lay the blame on the war? When the guns fired in August 1914, did the faces of men and women show so plain in each other's eyes that romance was killed? Certainly it was a shock (to women in particular with their illusions about education, and so on) to see the faces of our rulers in the light of the shell-fire. So ugly they looked—German, English, French—so stupid. But lay the blame where one will, on whom one will, the illusion which inspired Tennyson and Christina Rossetti to sing so passionately about the coming of their loves is far rarer now than then. One has only to read, to look, to listen, to remember. But why say "blame"? Why, if it was an illusion, not praise the catastrophe, whatever it was, that destroyed illusion and put truth in its place? For truth . . . those dots mark the spot where, in search of truth, I missed the turning up to Fernham. Yes indeed, which was truth and which was illusion, I asked myself. What was the truth about these houses, for example, dim and festive now with their red windows in the dusk, but raw and red and squalid, with their sweets and their boot-laces, at nine o'clock in the morning? And the willows and the river and the gardens that run down to the river, vague now with the mist stealing over them, but gold and red in the sunlight—which was the truth, which was the illusion about them? I spare you

the twists and turns of my cogitations, for no conclusion was found on the road to Headingley, and I ask you to suppose that I soon found out my mistake about the turning and retraced my steps to Fernham.

As I have said already that it was an October day, I dare not forfeit your respect and imperil the fair name of fiction by changing the season and describing lilacs hanging over garden walls, crocuses, tulips and other flowers of spring. Fiction must stick to facts, and the truer the facts the better the fiction —so we are told. Therefore it was still autumn and the leaves were still yellow and falling, if anything, a little faster than before, because it was now evening (seven twenty-three to be precise) and a breeze (from the south-west to be exact) had risen. But for all that there was something odd at work:

My heart is like a singing bird
Whose nest is in a water'd shoot;
My heart is like an apple tree
Whose boughs are bent with thick-
set fruit—

perhaps the words of Christina Rossetti were partly responsible for the folly of the fancy—it was nothing of course but a fancy—that the lilac was shaking its flowers over the garden walls, and the brimstone butterflies were scudding hither and thither, and the dust of the pollen was in the air. A wind blew, from what quarter I know not, but it lifted the half-grown leaves so that there was a flash of silver grey in the air. It was the time between the lights when colors undergo their intensification and purples and golds burn in windowpanes like the beat of an excitable heart; when for some reason the beauty of the world revealed and yet soon to perish (here I pushed into the garden, for, unwisely, the door was left open and no beadles seemed about), the beauty of the world which is so soon to perish, has two edges, one of laughter, one of anguish, cutting the heart asunder.

The gardens of Fernham lay before me in the spring twilight, wild and open, and in the long grass, sprinkled and carelessly flung, were daffodils and bluebells, not orderly perhaps at the best of times, and now wind-blown and waving as they tugged at their roots. The windows of the building, curved like ships' windows among generous waves of red brick, changed from lemon to silver under the flight of the quick spring clouds. Somebody was in a hammock, somebody, but in this light they were phantoms only, half guessed, half seen, raced across the grass—would no one stop her?—and then on the terrace, as if popping out to breathe the air, to glance at the garden, came a bent figure, formidable yet humble, with her great forehead and her shabby dress —could it be the famous scholar, could it be J—— H—— herself? All was dim, yet intense too, as if the scarf which the dusk had flung over the garden were torn asunder by star or sword—the flash of some terrible reality leaping, as its way is, out of the heart of the spring. For youth—

Here was my soup. Dinner was being served in the great dining-hall. Far from being spring it was in fact an evening in October. Everybody was assembled in the big dining-room. Dinner was ready. Here was the soup. It was a plain gravy soup. There was nothing to stir the fancy in that. One could have seen through the transparent liquid any pattern that there might have been on the plate itself. But there was no pattern. The plate was plain. Next came beef with its attendant greens and potatoes—a homely trinity, suggesting the rumps of cattle in a muddy market, and sprouts curled and yellowed at the edge, and bargaining and cheapening, and women with string bags on Monday morning. There was no reason to complain of human nature's daily food, seeing that the supply was sufficient and coal-miners doubtless were sitting down to less. Prunes and custard followed. And if any one complains that prunes, even when mitigated by custard, are an uncharitable vegetable (fruit they are not), stringy as a miser's heart and exuding a fluid such as might run in misers' veins who have denied themselves wine and warmth for eighty years and yet not given to the poor, he should reflect that there are people whose charity embraces even the prune. Biscuits and cheese came next, and here the water-jug was liberally passed round, for it is the nature of biscuits to be dry, and these were biscuits to the core. That was all. The meal was over. Everybody scraped their chairs back; the swing-doors swung violently to and fro; soon the hall was emptied of every sign of food and made ready no doubt for breakfast next morning. Down corridors and up staircases the youth of England went banging and singing. And was it for a guest, a stranger (for I had no more right here in Fernham than in Trinity or Somerville or Girton or Newnham or Christchurch), to say, "The dinner was not good," or to say (we were now, Mary Seton and I, in her sitting-room), "Could we not have dined up here alone?" for if I had said anything of the kind I should have been prying and searching into the secret economies of a house which to the stranger wears so fine a front of gaiety and courage. No, one could say nothing of the sort. Indeed, conversation for a moment flagged. The human frame being what it is, heart, body and brain all mixed together, and not contained in separate compartments as they will be no doubt in another million years, a good dinner is of great importance to good talk. One cannot think well, love well, sleep well, if one has not dined well. The lamp in the spine does not light on beef and prunes. We are all *probably* going to heaven, and Vandyck is, we *hope,* to meet us round the next corner—that is the dubious and qualifying state of mind that beef and prunes at the end of the day's work breed between them. Happily my friend, who taught science, had a cupboard where there was a squat bottle and little glasses—(but there should have been sole and partridge to begin with)—so that we were able to draw up to the fire and repair some of the damages of the day's living. In a minute or so we were slipping freely in and out among all those objects of curiosity and interest which form in the mind in the absence of a particular person, and are naturally to be discussed on coming together again—how somebody has married, another has not; one thinks this, another that; one has improved out of all knowledge, the other most amazingly gone to the bad—with all those speculations upon human nature and the character of the amazing world we live in which spring naturally from such beginnings. While these things were being said, however, I became shamefacedly aware of a current setting in of its own accord and carrying everything forward to an end of its own. One might be talking of Spain or Portugal, of book or racehorse, but the real interest of whatever was said was none of those things, but a scene of masons on a high roof some five centuries ago. Kings and nobles brought treasure in huge sacks and poured it under the earth. This scene was for ever coming alive in my mind and placing itself by another of lean cows and a muddy market and withered greens and the stringy hearts of old men—these two pictures, disjointed and disconnected and nonsensical as they were, were for ever coming together and combating each other and had me entirely at their mercy. The best course, unless the whole talk was to be distorted, was to expose what was in my mind to the air, when with good luck it would fade and crumble like the head of the dead king when they opened the coffin at Windsor. Briefly, then, I told Miss Seton about the masons who had been all those years on the roof of the chapel, and about the kings and queens and nobles bearing sacks of gold and silver on their shoulders, which they shovelled into the earth; and then how the great financial magnates of our own time came and laid cheques and bonds, I suppose, where the others had laid ingots and rough lumps of gold. All that lies beneath the colleges down there, I said; but this college, where we are now sitting, what lies beneath its gallant red brick and the wild unkempt grasses of the garden? What force is behind the plain china off which we dined, and (here it popped out of my mouth before I could stop it) the beef, the custard and the prunes?

Well, said Mary Seton, about the year 1860—Oh, but you know the story, she said, bored, I suppose, by the recital. And she told me—rooms were hired. Committees met. Envelopes were addressed. Circulars were drawn up. Meetings were held; letters were read out; so-and-so has promised so much; on the contrary, Mr. —— won't give a penny. The *Saturday Review* has been very rude. How can we raise a fund to pay for offices? Shall we hold a bazaar? Can't we find a pretty girl to sit in the front row? Let us look up what John Stuart Mill said on the subject. Can any one persuade the editor of the —— to print a letter? Can we get Lady —— to sign it? Lady —— is out of town. That was the way it was done, presumably, sixty years ago, and it was a prodigious effort, and a great deal of time was spent on it. And it was only after a long struggle and with the utmost difficulty that they got thirty thousand pounds together.[1] So obviously

---

[1] "We are told that we ought to ask for £30,000 at least. . . . It is not a large sum, considering that there is to be but one college of this sort for Great Britain, Ireland and the Colonies, and considering how easy it is to raise immense sums for boys' schools. But considering how few people really wish women to be educated, it is a good deal."—LADY STEPHEN, *Life of Miss Emily Davies*.

we cannot have wine and partridges and servants carrying tin dishes on their heads, she said. We cannot have sofas and separate rooms. "The amenities," she said, quoting from some book or other, "will have to wait."[2]

At the thought of all those women working year after year and finding it hard to get two thousand pounds together, and as much as they could do to get thirty thousand pounds, we burst out in scorn at the reprehensible poverty of our sex. What had our mothers been doing then that they had no wealth to leave us? Powdering their noses? Looking in at shop windows? Flaunting in the sun at Monte Carlo? There were some photographs on the mantel-piece. Mary's mother—if that was her picture —may have been a wastrel in her spare time (she had thirteen children by a minister of the church), but if so her gay and dissipated life had left too few traces of its pleasures on her face. She was a homely body; an old lady in a plaid shawl which was fastened by a large cameo; and she sat in a basket-chair, encouraging a spaniel to look at the camera, with the amused, yet strained expression of one who is sure that the dog will move directly the bulb is pressed. Now if she had gone into business; had become a manufacturer of artificial silk or a magnate on the Stock Exchange; if she had left two or three hundred thousand pounds to Fernham, we could have been sitting at our ease tonight and the subject of our talk might have been archaeology, botany, anthropology, physics, the nature of the atom, mathematics, astronomy, relativity, geography. If only Mrs. Seton and her mother and her mother before her had learnt the great art of making money and had left their money, like their fathers and their grandfathers before them, to found fellowships and lectureships and prizes and scholarships ap-propriated to the use of their own sex, we might have dined very tolerably up here alone off a bird and a bottle of wine; we might have looked forward without undue confidence to a pleasant and honorable lifetime spent in the shelter of one of the liberally endowed professions. We might have been exploring or writing; mooning about the venerable places of the earth; sitting contemplative on the steps of the Parthenon, or going at ten to an office and coming home comfortably at half-past four to write a little poetry. Only, if Mrs. Seton and her like had gone into business at the age of fifteen, there would have been—that was the snag in the argument—no Mary. What, I asked, did Mary think of that? There between the curtains was the October night, calm and lovely, with a star or two caught in the yellowing trees. Was she ready to resign her share of it and her memories (for they had been a happy family, though a large one) of games and quarrels up in Scotland, which she is never tired of praising for the fineness of its air and the quality of its cakes, in order that Fernham might have been endowed with fifty thousand pounds or so by a stroke of the pen? For, to endow a college would necessitate the suppression of families altogether. Making a fortune and bearing thirteen children—no human being could stand it. Consider the facts, we said. First there are nine months before the baby is born. Then the baby is born. Then there are three or four months spent in feeding the baby. After the baby is fed there are certainly five years spent in playing with the baby. You cannot, it seems, let children run about the streets. People who have seen them running wild in Russia say that the sight is not a pleasant one. People say, too, that human nature takes its shape in the years between one and

---

[2] Every penny which could be scraped together was set aside for building, and the amenities had to be postponed.—R. STRACHEY, *The Cause.*

five. If Mrs. Seton, I said, had been making money, what sort of memories would you have had of games and quarrels? What would you have known of Scotland, and its fine air and cakes and all the rest of it? But it is useless to ask these questions, because you would never have come into existence at all. Moreover, it is equally useless to ask what might have happened if Mrs. Seton and her mother and her mother before her had amassed great wealth and laid it under the foundations of college and library, because, in the first place, to earn money was impossible for them, and in the second, had it been possible, the law denied them the right to possess what money they earned. It is only for the last forty-eight years that Mrs. Seton has had a penny of her own. For all the centuries before that it would have been her husband's property—a thought which, perhaps, may have had its share in keeping Mrs. Seton and her mothers off the Stock Exchange. Every penny I earn, they may have said, will be taken from me and disposed of according to my husband's wisdom—perhaps to found a scholarship or to endow a fellowship in Balliol or Kings, so that to earn money, even if I could earn money, is not a matter that interests me very greatly. I had better leave it to my husband.

At any rate, whether or not the blame rested on the old lady who was looking at the spaniel, there could be no doubt that for some reason or other our mothers had mismanaged their affairs very gravely. Not a penny could be spared for "amenities"; for partridges and wine, beadles and turf, books and cigars, libraries and leisure. To raise bare walls out of the bare earth was the utmost they could do.

So we talked standing at the window and looking, as so many thousands look every night, down on the domes and towers of the famous city beneath us.

It was very beautiful, very mysterious in the autumn moonlight. The old stone looked very white and venerable. One thought of all the books that were assembled down there; of the pictures of old prelates and worthies hanging in the panelled rooms; of the painted windows that would be throwing strange globes and crescents on the pavement; of the tablets and memorials and inscriptions; of the fountains and the grass; of the quiet rooms looking across the quiet quadrangles. And (pardon me the thought) I thought, too, of the admirable smoke and drink and the deep armchairs and the pleasant carpets: of the urbanity, the geniality, the dignity which are the offspring of luxury and privacy and space. Certainly our mothers had not provided us with anything comparable to all this—our mothers who found it difficult to scrape together thirty thousand pounds, our mothers who bore thirteen children to ministers of religion at St. Andrews.

So I went back to my inn, and as I walked through the dark streets I pondered this and that, as one does at the end of the day's work. I pondered why it was that Mrs. Seton had no money to leave us; and what effect poverty has on the mind; and what effect wealth has on the mind; and I thought of the queer old gentlemen I had seen that morning with tufts of fur upon their shoulders; and I remembered how if one whistled one of them ran; and I thought of the organ booming in the chapel and of the shut doors of the library; and I thought how unpleasant it is to be locked out; and I thought how it is worse perhaps to be locked in; and, thinking of the safety and prosperity of the one sex and of the poverty and insecurity of the other and of the effect of tradition and of the lack of tradition upon the mind of a writer, I thought at last that it was time to roll up the crumpled skin of the day, with its arguments and its impressions and its anger and its laughter, and cast it into the hedge. A thousand stars were flashing across the blue wastes of the sky. One seemed alone with an inscrutable society. All human beings were laid asleep—prone, horizontal, dumb. Nobody seemed stirring in the streets of Oxbridge. Even the door of the hotel sprang open at the touch of an invisible hand—not a boots was sitting up to light me to bed, it was so late.

Jean Rhys (1894–)

WIDE SARGASSO SEA

PART ONE

They say when trouble comes close ranks, and so the white people did. But we were not in their ranks. The Jamaican ladies had never approved of my mother, "because she pretty like pretty self" Christophine said.

She was my father's second wife, far too young for him they thought, and, worse still, a Martinique girl. When I asked her why so few people came to see us, she told me that the road from Spanish Town to Coulibri Estate where we lived was very bad and that road repairing was now a thing of the past. (My father, visitors, horses, feeling safe in bed—all belonged to the past.)

Another day I heard her talking to Mr. Luttrell, our neighbor and her only friend. "Of course they have their own misfortunes. Still waiting for this compensation the English promised when the Emancipation Act was passed. Some will wait for a long time."

How could she know that Mr. Luttrell would be the first who grew tired of waiting? One calm evening he shot his dog, swam out to sea and was gone for always. No agent came from England to look after his property—Nelson's Rest it was called—and strangers from Spanish Town rode up to gossip and discuss the tragedy.

"Live at Nelson's Rest? Not for love or money. An unlucky place."

Mr. Luttrell's house was left empty, shutters banging in the wind. Soon the black people said it was haunted, they wouldn't go near it. And no one came near us.

I got used to a solitary life, but my mother still planned and hoped—perhaps she had to hope every time she passed a looking glass.

She still rode about every morning not caring that the black people stood about in groups to jeer at her, especially after her riding clothes grew shabby (they notice clothes, they know about money).

Then one day, very early, I saw her horse lying down under the frangipani tree. I went up to him but he was not sick, he was dead and his eyes were black with flies. I ran away and did not speak of it for I thought if I told no one it might not be true. But later that day, Godfrey found him, he had been poisoned. "Now we are marooned," my mother said, "now what will become of us?"

Godfrey said, "I can't watch the horse night and day. I too old now. When the old time go, let it go. No use to grab at it. The Lord make no distinction between black and white, black and white the same for Him. Rest yourself in peace for the righteous are not forsaken." But she couldn't. She was young. How could she not try for all the things that had gone so suddenly, so without warning. "You're blind when you want to be blind," she said ferociously, "and you're deaf when you want to be deaf. The old hypocrite," she kept saying. "He knew what they were going to do." "The devil prince of this world," Godfrey said, "but this world don't last so long for mortal man."

She persuaded a Spanish Town doctor to visit my younger brother Pierre who staggered when he walked and couldn't speak distinctly. I don't know what the doctor told her or what she said to him but he never came again and after that she changed. Suddenly, not gradually. She grew thin and silent, and at last she refused to leave the house at all.

Our garden was large and beautiful as that garden in the Bible—the tree of life grew there. But it had gone wild. The paths were overgrown and a smell of dead flowers mixed with the fresh living smell. Underneath the tree ferns, tall as forest tree ferns, the light was green. Orchids flourished out of reach or for some reason not to be touched. One was snaky looking, another like an octopus with long thin brown tentacles bare of leaves hanging from a twisted root. Twice a year the octopus orchid flowered—then not an inch of tentacle showed. It was a bell-shaped mass of white, mauve, deep purples, wonderful to see. The scent was very sweet and strong. I never went near it.

All Coulibri Estate had gone wild like the garden, gone to bush. No more slavery—why should *anybody* work? This never saddened me. I did not remember the place when it was prosperous.

My mother usually walked up and down the *glacis,* a paved roofed-in terrace which ran the length of the house and sloped upwards to a clump of bamboos. Standing by the bamboos she had a clear view to the sea, but anyone passing could stare at her. They stared, sometimes they laughed. Long after the sound was far away and faint she kept her eyes shut and her hands clenched. A frown came between her black eyebrows, deep—it might have been cut with a knife. I hated this frown and once I touched her forehead trying to smooth it. But she pushed me away, not roughly but calmly, coldly, without a word, as if she had decided once and for all that I was useless to her. She wanted to sit with Pierre or walk where she pleased without being pestered, she wanted peace and quiet. I was old enough to look after myself. "Oh, let me alone," she would say, "let me alone," and after I knew that she talked aloud to herself I was a little afraid of her.

So I spent most of my time in the kitchen which was in an outbuilding some way off. Christophine slept in the little room next to it.

When evening came she sang to me if she was in the mood. I couldn't always understand her patois songs—she also came from Martinique—but she taught me the one that meant "The little ones grow old, the children leave us, will they come back?" and the one about the cedar tree flowers which only last for a day.

The music was gay but the words were sad and her voice often quavered and broke on the high note. "Adieu." Not adieu as we said it, but *à dieu,* which made more sense after all. The loving man was lonely, the girl was deserted, the children never came back. Adieu.

Her songs were not like Jamaican songs, and she was not like the other women.

She was much blacker—blue-black with a thin face and straight features.

She wore a black dress, heavy gold earrings and a yellow handkerchief—carefully tied with the two high points in front. No other negro woman wore black, or tied her handkerchief Martinique fashion. She had a quiet voice and a quiet laugh (when she did laugh), and though she could speak good English if she wanted to, and French as well as patois, she took care to talk as they talked. But they would have nothing to do with her and she never saw her son who worked in Spanish Town. She had only one friend—a woman called Maillotte, and Maillotte was not a Jamaican.

The girls from the bayside who sometimes helped with the washing and cleaning were terrified of her. That, I soon discovered, was why they came at all—for she never paid them. Yet they brought presents of fruit and vegetables and after dark I often heard low voices from the kitchen.

So I asked about Christophine. Was she very old? Had she always been with us?

"She was your father's wedding present to me—one of his presents. He thought I would be pleased with a Martinique girl. I don't know how old she was when they brought her to Jamaica, quite young. I don't know how old she is now. Does it matter? Why do you pester and bother me about all these things that happened long ago? Christophine stayed with me because she wanted to stay. She had her own very good reasons you may be sure. I dare say we would have died if she'd turned against us and that would have been a better fate. To die and be forgotten and at peace. Not to know that one is abandoned, lied about, helpless. All the ones who died—who says a good word for them now?"

"Godfrey stayed too," I said. "And Sass."

"They stayed," she said angrily, "because they wanted somewhere to sleep and something to eat. That boy Sass! When his mother pranced off and left him here—a great deal *she* cared—why he was a little skeleton. Now he's growing into a big strong boy and away he goes. We shan't see him again. Godfrey is a rascal. These new ones aren't too kind to old people and he knows it. That's why he stays. Doesn't do a thing but eat enough for a couple of horses. Pretends he's deaf. He isn't deaf—he doesn't want to hear. What a devil he is!"

"Why don't you tell him to find somewhere else to live?" I said and she laughed.

"He wouldn't go. He'd probably try to force us out. I've learned to let sleeping curs lie," she said.

"Would Christophine go if you told her to?" I thought. But I didn't say it. I was afraid to say it.

It was too hot that afternoon. I could see the beads of perspiration on her upper lip and the dark circles under her eyes. I started to fan her, but she turned her head away. She might rest if I left her alone, she said.

Once I would have gone back quietly to watch her asleep on the blue sofa—once I made excuses to be near her when she brushed her hair, a soft black cloak to cover me, hide me, keep me safe.

But not any longer. Not any more.

These were all the people in my life—my mother and Pierre, Christophine, Godfrey, and Sass who had left us.

I never looked at any strange negro. They hated us. They called us white cockroaches. Let sleeping dogs lie. One day a little girl followed me singing, "Go away white cockroach, go away, go away." I walked fast, but she walked faster. "White cockroach, go away, go away. Nobody want you. Go away."

When I was safely home I sat close to the old wall at the end of the garden. It was covered with green moss soft as velvet and I never wanted to move again. Everything would be worse if I moved. Christophine found me there when it was nearly dark, and I was so stiff she had to help me to get up. She said nothing, but next morning Tia was in the kitchen with her mother Maillotte, Christophine's friend. Soon Tia was my friend and I met her nearly every morning at the turn of the road to the river.

Sometimes we left the bathing pool at midday, sometimes we stayed till late afternoon. Then Tia would light a fire (fires always lit for her, sharp stones did not hurt her bare feet, I never saw her cry). We boiled green bananas in an old iron pot and ate them with our fingers out of a calabash and after we had eaten she slept at once. I could not sleep, but I wasn't quite awake as I lay in the shade looking at the pool—deep and dark green under the trees, brown-green if it had rained, but a bright sparkling green in the sun. The water was so clear that you could see the pebbles at the bottom of the shallow part. Blue and white and striped red. Very pretty. Late or early we parted at the turn of the road. My mother never asked me where I had been or what I had done.

Christophine had given me some new pennies which I kept in the pocket of my dress. They dropped out one morning so I put them on a stone. They shone like gold in the sun and Tia stared. She had small eyes, very black, set deep in her head.

Then she bet me three of the pennies that I couldn't turn a somersault under water "like you say you can."

"Of course I can."

"I never see you do it," she said. "Only talk."

"Bet you all the money I can," I said.

But after one somersault I still turned and came up choking. Tia laughed and told me that it certainly look like I drown dead that time. Then she picked up the money.

"I did do it," I said when I could speak, but she shook her head. I hadn't done it good and besides pennies didn't buy much. Why did I look at her like that?

"Keep them then, you cheating nigger," I said, for I was tired, and the water I had swallowed made me feel sick. "I can get more if I want to."

That's not what she hear, she said. She hear all we poor like beggar. We ate salt fish—no money for fresh fish. That old house so leaky, you run with calabash to catch water when it rain. Plenty white people in Jamaica. Real white people, they got gold money. They didn't look at us, nobody see them come near us. Old time white people nothing but white nigger now, and black nigger better than white nigger.

I wrapped myself in my torn towel and sat on a stone with my back to her, shivering cold. But the sun couldn't warm me. I wanted to go home. I looked round and Tia had gone. I searched for a long time before I could believe that she had taken my dress—not my underclothes, she never wore any—but my dress, starched, ironed, clean that morning. She had left me hers and I put it on at last and walked home in the blazing sun feeling sick, hating her. I planned to get round the back of the house to the kitchen, but passing the stables I stopped to stare at three strange horses and my mother saw me and called. She was on the *glacis* with two young ladies and a gentleman. Visitors! I dragged up the steps unwillingly—I had longed for visitors once, but that was years ago.

They were very beautiful I thought and they wore such beautiful clothes that I looked away down at the flagstones and when they laughed—the gentleman laughed the loudest—I ran into the house, into my bedroom. There I stood with my back against the door and I could feel my heart all through me. I heard them talking and I heard them leave. I came out of my room and my mother was sitting on the blue sofa. She looked at me for some time before she said that I had behaved very oddly. My dress was even dirtier than usual.

"It's Tia's dress."

"But why are you wearing Tia's dress? Tia? Which one of them is Tia?"

Christophine, who had been in the pantry listening, came at once and was told to find a clean dress for me. "Throw away that thing. Burn it."

Then they quarrelled.

Christophine said I had no clean dress. "She got two dresses, wash and wear. You want clean dress to drop from heaven? Some people crazy in truth."

"She must have another dress," said my mother. "Somewhere." But Christophine told her loudly that it shameful. She run wild, she grow up worthless. And nobody care.

My mother walked over to the window. ("Marooned," said her straight narrow back, her carefully coiled hair. "Marooned.")

"She has an old muslin dress. Find that."

While Christophine scrubbed my face and tied my plaits with a fresh piece of string, she told me that those were the new people at Nelson's Rest. They called themselves Luttrell, but English or not English they were not like old Mr. Luttrell. "Old Mr. Luttrell spit in their face if he see how they look at you. Trouble walk into the house this day. Trouble walk in."

The old muslin dress was found and it tore as I forced it on. She didn't notice.

No more slavery! She had to laugh! "These new ones have Letter of the Law. Same thing. They got magistrate. They got fine. They got jail house and chain gang. They got tread machine to mash up people's feet. New ones worse than old ones—more cunning, that's all."

All that evening my mother didn't speak to me or look at me and I thought, "She is ashamed of me, what Tia said is true."

I went to bed early and slept at once. I dreamed that I was walking in the forest. Not alone. Someone who hated me was with me, out of sight. I could hear heavy footsteps coming closer and though I struggled and screamed I could not move. I woke crying. The covering sheet was on the floor and my mother was looking down at me.

"Did you have a nightmare?"

"Yes, a bad dream."

She sighed and covered me up. "You were making such a noise. I must go to Pierre, you've frightened him."

I lay thinking, "I am safe. There is the corner of the bedroom door and the friendly furniture. There is the tree of life in the garden and the wall green with moss. The barrier of the cliffs and the high mountains. And the barrier of the sea. I am safe. I am safe from strangers."

The light of the candle in Pierre's room was still there when I slept again. I woke next morning knowing that nothing would be the same. It would change and go on changing.

I don't know how she got money to buy the white muslin and the pink. Yards of muslin. She may have sold her last ring, for there was one left. I saw it in her jewel box—that, and a locket with a shamrock inside. They were mending and sewing first thing in the morning and still sewing when I went to bed. In a week she had a new dress and so had I.

The Luttrells lent her a horse, and she would ride off very early and not come back till late next day—tired out because she had been to a dance or a moonlight picnic. She was gay and laughing—younger than I had ever seen her and the house was sad when she had gone.

So I too left it and stayed away till dark. I was never long at the bathing pool, I never met Tia.

I took another road, past the old sugar works and the water wheel that had not turned for years. I went to parts of Coulibri that I had not seen, where there was no road, no path, no track. And if the razor grass cut my legs and arms I would think "It's better than people." Black ants or red ones, tall nests swarming with white ants, rain that soaked me to the skin—once I saw a snake. All better than people.

Better. Better, better than people.

Watching the red and yellow flowers in the sun thinking of nothing, it was as if a door opened and I was somewhere else, something else. Not myself any longer.

I knew the time of day when though it is hot and blue and there are no clouds, the sky can have a very black look.

I was bridesmaid when my mother married Mr. Mason in Spanish Town. Christophine curled my hair. I carried a bouquet and everything I wore was new—even my beautiful slippers. But their eyes slid away from my hating face. I had heard what all these smooth smiling people said about her when she was not listening and they did not guess I was. Hiding from them in the garden when they visited Coulibri, I listened.

"A fantastic marriage and he will regret it. Why should a very wealthy man who could take his pick of all the girls in the West Indies, and many in England too probably?" "Why *probably?*" the other voice said. "*Certainly.*" "Then why should he marry a widow without a penny to her name and Coulibri a wreck of a place? Emancipation troubles killed old Cosway? Nonsense—the estate was going downhill for years before that. He drank himself to death. Many's the time when—well! And all those women! She never did anything to stop him— she encouraged him. Presents and smiles for the bastards every Christmas. Old customs? Some old customs are better dead and buried. Her new husband will have to spend a pretty penny before the house is fit to live in—leaks like a sieve. And what about the stables and

the coach house dark as pitch, and the servants' quarters and the six-foot snake —saw with my own eyes curled up on the privy seat last time I was here. Alarmed? I screamed. Then that horrible old man she harbors came along, doubled up with laughter. As for those two children—the boy an idiot kept out of sight and mind and the girl going the same way in my opinion—a *lowering* expression."

"Oh I agree," the other one said, "but Annette is such a pretty woman. And what a dancer. Reminds me of that song 'light as cotton blossom on the something breeze,' or is it air? I forget."

Yes, what a dancer—that night when they came home from their honeymoon in Trinidad and they danced on the *glacis* to no music. There was no need for music when she danced. They stopped and she leaned backwards over his arm, down till her black hair touched the flagstones—still down, down. Then up again in a flash, laughing. She made it look so easy—as if anyone could do it, and he kissed her—a long kiss. I was there that time too but they had forgotten me and soon I wasn't thinking of them. I was remembering that woman saying "Dance! He didn't come to the West Indies to dance—he came to make money as they all do. Some of the big estates are going cheap, and one unfortunate's loss is always a clever man's gain. No, the whole thing is a mystery. It's evidently useful to keep a Martinique obeah woman on the premises." She meant Christophine. She said it mockingly, not meaning it, but soon other people were saying it—and meaning it.

While the repairs were being done and they were in Trinidad, Pierre and I stayed with Aunt Cora in Spanish Town.

Mr. Mason did not approve of Aunt Cora, an ex-slave-owner who had escaped misery, a flier in the face of Providence.

"Why did she do nothing to help you?"

I told him that her husband was English and didn't like us and he said, "Nonsense."

"It isn't nonsense, they lived in England and he was angry if she wrote to us. He hated the West Indies. When he died not long ago she came home, before that what could she do? *She* wasn't rich."

"That's her story. I don't believe it. A frivolous woman. In your mother's place I'd resent her behavior."

"None of you understand about us," I thought.

Coulibri looked the same when I saw it again, although it was clean and tidy, no grass between the flagstones, no leaks. But it didn't feel the same. Sass had come back and I was glad. They can *smell* money, somebody said. Mr. Mason engaged new servants—I didn't like any of them excepting Mannie the groom. It was their talk about Christophine that changed Coulibri, not the repairs or the new furniture or the strange faces. Their talk about Christophine and obeah changed it.

I knew her room so well—the pictures of the Holy Family and the prayer for a happy death. She had a bright patchwork counterpane, a broken-down press for her clothes, and my mother had given her an old rockingchair.

Yet one day when I was waiting there I was suddenly very much afraid. The door was open to the sunlight, someone was whistling near the stables, but I was afraid. I was certain that hidden in the room (behind the old black press?) there was a dead man's dried hand, white chicken feathers, a cock with its throat cut, dying slowly, slowly. Drop by drop the blood was falling into a red basin and I imagined I could hear it. No one had ever spoken to me about obeah—but I knew what I would find if I dared to look. Then Christophine came in smiling and pleased to see me. Nothing alarming ever happened and I forgot, or told myself I had forgotten.

Mr. Mason would laugh if he knew how frightened I had been. He would laugh even louder than he did when my mother told him that she wished to leave Coulibri.

This began when they had been married for over a year. They always said the same things and I seldom listened to the argument now. I knew that we were hated—but to go away . . . for once I agreed with my stepfather. That was not possible.

"You must have some reason," he would say, and she would answer "I need a change" or "We could visit Richard." (Richard, Mr. Mason's son by his first marriage, was at school in Barbados. He was going to England soon and we had seen very little of him.)

"An agent could look after this place. For the time being. The people here hate us. They certainly hate me." Straight out she said that one day and it was then he laughed so heartily.

"Annette, be reasonable. You were the widow of a slave-owner, the daughter of a slave-owner, and you had been living here alone, with two children, for nearly five years when we met. Things were at their worst then. But you were never molested, never harmed."

"How do you know that I was not harmed?" she said. "We were so poor then," she told him, "we were something to laugh at. But we are not poor now," she said. "You are not a poor man. Do you suppose they don't know all about your estate in Trinidad? And the Antigua property? They talk about us without stopping. They invent stories about you, and lies about me. They try to find out what we eat every day."

"They are curious. It's natural enough. You have lived alone far too long, Annette. You imagine enmity which doesn't exist. Always one extreme or the other. Didn't you fly at me like a little wild cat when I said nigger. Not nigger, nor even negro. Black people I must say."

"You don't like, or even recognize, the good in them," she said, "and you won't believe in the other side."

"They're too damn lazy to be dangerous," said Mr. Mason. "I know that."

"They are more alive than you are, lazy or not, and they can be dangerous and cruel for reasons you wouldn't understand."

"No, I don't understand," Mr. Mason always said. "I don't understand at all."

But she'd speak about going away again. Persistently. Angrily.

Mr. Mason pulled up near the empty huts on our way home that evening. "All gone to one of those dances," he said. "Young and old. How deserted the place looks."

"We'll hear the drums if there is a dance." I hoped he'd ride on quickly but he stayed by the huts to watch the sun go down, the sky and the sea were on fire when we left Bertrand Bay at last. From a long way off I saw the shadow of our house high up on its stone foundations. There was a smell of ferns and river water and I felt safe again, as if I was one of the righteous. (Godfrey said that we were not righteous. One day when he was drunk he told me that we were all damned and no use praying.)

"They've chosen a very hot night for their dance," Mr. Mason said, and Aunt Cora came on to the *glacis*. "What dance? Where?"

"There is some festivity in the neighborhood. The huts were abandoned. A wedding perhaps?"

"Not a wedding," I said. "There is never a wedding." He frowned at me but Aunt Cora smiled.

When they had gone indoors I leaned my arms on the cool *glacis* railings and thought that I would never like him very much. I still called him "Mr. Mason" in my head. "Goodnight white pappy," I said one evening and he was not vexed, he laughed. In some ways it was better before he came though he'd rescued us from poverty and misery. "Only just in

time too." The black people did not hate us quite so much when we were poor. We were white but we had not escaped and soon we would be dead for we had no money left. What was there to hate?

Now it had started up again and worse than before, my mother knows but she can't make him believe it. I wish I could tell him that out here is not at all like English people think it is. I wish . . .

I could hear them talking and Aunt Cora's laugh. I was glad she was staying with us. And I could hear the bamboos shiver and creak though there was no wind. It had been hot and still and dry for days. The colors had gone from the sky, the light was blue and could not last long. The *glacis* was not a good place when night was coming, Christophine said. As I went indoors my mother was talking in an excited voice.

"Very well. As you refuse to consider it, *I* will go and take Pierre with me. You won't object to that, I hope?"

"You are perfectly right, Annette," said Aunt Cora and that did surprise me. She seldom spoke when they argued.

Mr. Mason also seemed surprised and not at all pleased.

"You talk so wildly," he said. "And you are so mistaken. Of course you can get away for a change if you wish it. I promise you."

"You have promised that before," she said. "You don't keep your promises."

He sighed. "I feel very well here. However, we'll arrange something. Quite soon."

"I will not stay at Coulibri any longer," my mother said. "It is not safe. It is not safe for Pierre."

Aunt Cora nodded.

As it was late I ate with them instead of by myself as usual. Myra, one of the new servants, was standing by the sideboard, waiting to change the plates. We ate English food now, beef and mutton, pies and puddings.

I was glad to be like an English girl

but I missed the taste of Christophine's cooking.

My stepfather talked about a plan to import laborers—coolies he called them —from the East Indies. When Myra had gone out Aunt Cora said, "I shouldn't discuss that if I were you. Myra is listening."

"But the people here won't work. They don't want to work. Look at this place—it's enough to break your heart."

"Hearts have been broken," she said. "Be sure of that. I suppose you all know what you are doing."

"Do you mean to say—"

"I said nothing, except that it would be wiser not to tell that woman your plans—necessary and merciful no doubt. I don't trust her."

"Live here most of your life and know nothing about the people. It's astonishing. They are children—they wouldn't hurt a fly."

"Unhappily children do hurt flies," said Aunt Cora.

Myra came in again looking mournful as she always did though she smiled when she talked about hell. Everyone went to hell, she told me, you had to belong to her sect to be saved and even then—just as well not to be too sure. She had thin arms and big hands and feet and the handkerchief she wore round her head was always white. Never striped or a gay color.

So I looked away from her at my favorite picture, "The Miller's Daughter," a lovely English girl with brown curls and blue eyes and a dress slipping off her shoulders. Then I looked across the white tablecloth and the vase of yellow roses at Mr. Mason, so sure of himself, so without a doubt English. And at my mother, so without a doubt not English, but no white nigger either. Not my mother. Never had been. Never could be. Yes, she would have died, I thought, if she had not met him. And for the first time I was grateful and liked him. There are more ways than one of being happy, better perhaps to be peaceful and contented and protected, as I feel now, peaceful for years and long years, and afterwards I may be saved whatever Myra says. (When I asked Christophine what happened when you died, she said, "You want to know too much.") I remember to kiss my stepfather good-night. Once Aunt Cora had told me, "He's very hurt because you never kiss him."

"He does not look hurt," I argued. "Great mistake to go by looks," she said, "one way or the other."

I went into Pierre's room which was next to mine, the last one in the house. The bamboos were outside his window. You could almost touch them. He still had a crib and he slept more and more, nearly all the time. He was so thin that I could lift him easily. Mr. Mason had promised to take him to England later on, there he would be cured, made like other people. "And how will you like that" I thought, as I kissed him. "How will you like being made exactly like other people?" He looked happy asleep. But that will be later on. Later on. Sleep now. It was then I heard the bamboos creak again and a sound like whispering. I forced myself to look out of the window. There was a full moon but I saw nobody, nothing but shadows.

I left a light on the chair by my bed and waited for Christophine, for I liked to see her last thing. But she did not come, and as the candle burned down, the safe peaceful feeling left me. I wished I had a big Cuban dog to lie by my bed and protect me, I wished I had not heard a noise by the bamboo clump, or that I were very young again, for then I believed in my stick. It was not a stick, but a long narrow piece of wood, with two nails sticking out at the end, a shingle, perhaps. I picked it up soon after they killed our horse and I thought I can fight with this, if the worst comes to the worst I can fight to the end though the best ones fall and and that is another song. Christophine knocked the nails out, but she let me keep the shingle and I grew very fond of it, I believe that no one could harm me when it was near me, to lose it would be a great misfortune. All this was long ago, when I was still babyish and sure that everything was alive, not only the river or the rain, but chairs, looking-glasses, cups, saucers, everything.

I woke up and it was still night and my mother was there. She said, "Get up and dress yourself, and come down-stairs quickly." She was dressed, but she had not put up her hair and one of her plaits was loose. "Quickly," she said again, then she went into Pierre's room, next door. I heard her speak to Myra and I heard Myra answer her. I lay there, half asleep, looking at the lighted candle on the chest of drawers, till I heard a noise as though a chair had fallen over in the little room, then I got up and dressed.

The house was on different levels. There were three steps down from my bedroom and Pierre's to the dining-room and then three steps from the dining-room to the rest of the house, which we called "downstairs." The fold-ing doors of the dining-room were not shut and I could see that the big draw-ing-room was full of people. Mr. Mason, my mother, Christophine and Mannie and Sass. Aunt Cora was sitting on the blue sofa in the corner now, wearing a black silk dress, her ringlets were care-fully arranged. She looked very haughty, I thought. But Godfrey was not there, or Myra, or the cook, or any of the others.

"There is no reason to be alarmed," my stepfather was saying as I came in. "A handful of drunken negroes." He opened the door leading to the *glacis* and walked out. "What is all this," he shouted. "What do you want?" A hor-rible noise swelled up, like animals howling, but worse. We heard stones falling on to the *glacis*. He was pale when he came in again, but he tried to smile as he shut and bolted the door.

"More of them than I thought, and in a nasty mood too. They will repent in the morning. I foresee gifts of tama-rinds in syrup and ginger sweets to-morrow."

"Tomorrow will be too late," said Aunt Cora, "too late for ginger sweets or anything else." My mother was not listening to either of them. She said, "Pierre is asleep and Myra is with him. I thought it better to leave him in his own room, away from this horrible noise. I don't know. Perhaps." She was twisting her hands together, her wed-ding ring fell off and rolled into a corner near the steps. My stepfather and Mannie both stooped for it, then Man-nie straightened up and said, "Oh, my God, they get at the back, they set fire to the back of the house." He pointed to my bedroom door which I had shut after me, and smoke was rolling out from underneath.

I did not see my mother move she was so quick. She opened the door of my room and then again I did not see her, nothing but smoke. Mannie ran after her, so did Mr. Mason but more slowly. Aunt Cora put her arms round me. She said, "Don't be afraid, you are quite safe. We are all quite safe." Just for a moment I shut my eyes and rested my head against her shoulder. She smelled of vanilla, I remember. Then there was another smell, of burned hair, and I looked and my mother was in the room carrying Pierre. It was her loose hair that had burned and was smelling like that.

I thought, Pierre is dead. He looked dead. He was white and he did not make a sound, but his head hung back over her arm as if he had no life at all and his eyes were rolled up so that you only saw the whites. My stepfather said, "Annette, you are hurt—your hands . . ." But she did not even look at him. "His crib was on fire," she said to Aunt Cora. "The little room is on fire and Myra was not there. She has gone. She was not there."

"That does not surprise me at all," said Aunt Cora. She laid Pierre on the sofa, bent over him, then lifted up her skirt, stepped out of her white petticoat and began to tear it into strips.

"She left him, she ran away and left him alone to die," said my mother, still whispering. So it was all the more dreadful when she began to scream abuse at Mr. Mason, calling him a fool, a cruel stupid fool. "I told you," she said, "I told you what would happen again and again." Her voice broke, but still she screamed, "You would not listen, you sneered at me, you grinning hypocrite, you ought not to live either, you know so much, don't you? Why don't you go out and ask them to let you go? Say how innocent you are. Say you have always trusted them."

I was so shocked that everything was confused. And it happened quickly. I saw Mannie and Sass staggering along with two large earthenware jars of water which were kept in the pantry. They threw the water into the bedroom and it made a black pool on the floor, but the smoke rolled over the pool. Then Christophine, who had run into my mother's bedroom for the pitcher there, came back and spoke to my aunt. "It seems they have fired the other side of the house," said Aunt Cora. "They must have climbed that tree outside. This place is going to burn like tinder and there is nothing we can do to stop it. The sooner we get out the better."

Mannie said to the boy, "You frightened?" Sass shook his head. "Then come on," said Mannie. "Out of my way," he said and pushed Mr. Mason aside. Narrow wooden stairs led down from the pantry to the out-buildings, the kitchen, the servants' rooms, the stables. That was where they were going. "Take the child," Aunt Cora told Christophine, "and come."

It was very hot on the *glacis* too, they roared as we came out, then there was another roar behind us. I had not seen any flames, only smoke and sparks,

but now I saw tall flames shooting up to the sky, for the bamboos had caught. There were some tree ferns near, green and damp, one of those was smoldering too.

"Come quickly," said Aunt Cora, and she went first, holding my hand. Christophine followed, carrying Pierre, and they were quite silent as we went down the *glacis* steps. But when I looked round for my mother I saw that Mr. Mason, his face crimson with heat, seemed to be dragging her along and she was holding back, struggling. I heard him say, "It's impossible, too late now."

"Wants her jewel case?" Aunt Cora said.

"Jewel case? Nothing so sensible," bawled Mr. Mason. "She wanted to go back for her damned parrot. I won't allow it." She did not answer, only fought him silently, twisting like a cat and showing her teeth.

Our parrot was called Coco, a green parrot. He didn't talk very well, he could say *Qui est là? Qui est là?* and answer himself *Ché Coco, Ché Coco.* After Mr. Mason clipped his wings he grew very bad tempered, and though he would sit quietly on my mother's shoulder, he darted at everyone who came near her and pecked their feet.

"Annette," said Aunt Cora. "They are laughing at you, do not allow them to laugh at you." She stopped fighting then and he half supported, half pulled her after us, cursing loudly.

Still they were quiet and there were so many of them I could hardly see any grass or trees. There must have been many of the bay people but I recognized no one. They all looked the same, it was the same face repeated over and over, eyes gleaming, mouth half open to shout. We were past the mounting stone when they saw Mannie driving the carriage round the corner. Sass followed, riding one horse and leading another. There was a ladies' saddle on the one he was leading.

Somebody yelled, "But look the black

Englishman! Look the white niggers!," and then they were all yelling. "Look the white niggers! Look the damn white niggers!" A stone just missed Mannie's head, he cursed back at them and they cleared away from the rearing, frightened horses. "Come on, for God's sake," said Mr. Mason. "Get to the carriage, get to the horses." But we could not move for they pressed too close round us. Some of them were laughing and waving sticks, some of the ones at the back were carrying flambeaux and it was light as day. Aunt Cora held my hand very tightly and her lips moved but I could not hear because of the noise. And I was afraid, because I knew that the ones who laughed would be the worst. I shut my eyes and waited. Mr. Mason stopped swearing and began to pray in a loud pious voice. The prayer ended, "May Almighty God defend us." And God who is indeed mysterious, who had made no sign when they burned Pierre as he slept—not a clap of thunder, not a flash of lightning—mysterious God heard Mr. Mason at once and answered him. The yells stopped.

I opened my eyes, everybody was looking up and pointing at Coco on the *glacis* railings with his feathers alight. He made an effort to fly down but his clipped wings failed him and he fell screeching. He was all on fire.

I began to cry. "Don't look," said Aunt Cora. "Don't look." She stooped and put her arms round me and I hid my face, but I could feel that they were not so near. I heard someone say something about bad luck and remembered that it was very unlucky to kill a parrot, or even to see a parrot die. They began to go then, quickly, silently, and those that were left drew aside and watched us as we trailed across the grass. They were not laughing any more.

"Get to the carriage, get to the carriage," said Mr. Mason. "Hurry!" He went first, holding my mother's arm, then Christophine carrying Pierre, and Aunt Cora was last, still with my hand in hers. None of us looked back.

Mannie had stopped the horses at the bend of the cobblestone road and as we got closer we heard him shout, "What all you are, eh? Brute beasts?" He was speaking to a group of men and a few women who were standing round the carriage. A colored man with a machete in his hand was holding the bridle. I did not see Sass or the other two horses. "Get in," said Mr. Mason. "Take no notice of him, get in." The man with the machete said no. We would go to police and tell a lot of damn lies. A woman said to let us go. All this an accident and they had plenty witness. "Myra she witness for us."

"Shut your mouth," the man said. "You mash centipede, mash it, leave one little piece and it grow again . . . What you think police believe, eh? You, or the white nigger?"

Mr. Mason stared at him. He seemed not frightened, but too astounded to speak. Mannie took up the carriage whip but one of the blacker men wrenched it out of his hand, snapped it over his knee and threw it away. "Run away, black Englishman, like the boy run. Hide in the bushes. It's better for you." It was Aunt Cora who stepped forward and said, "The little boy is very badly hurt. He will die if we cannot get help for him."

The man said, "So black and white, they burn the same, eh?"

"They do," she said. "Here and hereafter, as you will find out. Very shortly."

He let the bridle go and thrust his face close to hers. He'd throw her on the fire, he said, if she put bad luck on him. Old white jumby, he called her. But she did not move an inch, she looked straight into his eyes and threatened him with eternal fire in a calm voice. "And never a drop of sangoree to cool your burning tongue," she said. He cursed her again but he backed away. "Now get in," said Mr. Mason. "You, Christophine, get in with the child." Christophine got in. "Now you," he said to my mother. But she had turned and was looking back at the house and when he put his hand on her arm, she screamed.

One woman said she only come to see what happen. Another woman began to cry. The man with the cutlass said, "You cry for her—when she ever cry for you? Tell me that."

But now I turned too. The house was burning, the yellow-red sky was like sunset and I knew that I would never see Coulibri again. Nothing would be left, the golden ferns and the silver ferns, the orchids, the ginger lilies and the roses, the rocking-chairs and the blue sofa, the jasmine and the honeysuckle, and the picture of the Miller's Daughter. When they had finished, there would be nothing left but blackened walls and the mounting stone. That was always left. That could not be stolen or burned.

Then, not so far off, I saw Tia and her mother and I ran to her, for she was all that was left of my life as it had been. We had eaten the same food, slept side by side, bathed in the same river. As I ran, I thought, I will live with Tia and I will be like her. Not to leave Coulibri. Not to go. Not. When I was close I saw the jagged stone in her hand but I did not see her throw it. I did not feel it either, only something wet, running down my face. I looked at her and I saw her face crumple up as she began to cry. We stared at each other, blood on my face, tears on hers. It was as if I saw myself. Like in a looking-glass.

"I saw my plait, tied with red ribbon, when I got up," I said. "In the chest of drawers. I thought it was a snake."

"Your hair had to be cut. You've been very ill, my darling," said Aunt Cora. "But you are safe with me now. We are all safe as I told you we would be. You must stay in bed though. Why are you wandering about the room? Your hair will grow again," she said. "Longer and thicker."

"But darker," I said.

"Why not darker?"

She picked me up and I was glad to feel the soft mattress and glad to be covered with a cool sheet.

"It's time for your arrowroot," she said and went out. When that was finished she took the cup away and stood looking down at me.

"I got up because I wanted to know where I was."

"And you do know, don't you?" she said in an anxious voice.

"Of course. But how did I get to your house?"

"The Luttrells were very good. As soon as Mannie got to Nelson's Rest they sent a hammock and four men. You were shaken about a good deal though. But they did their best. Young Mr. Luttrell rode alongside you all the way. Wasn't that kind?"

"Yes," I said. She looked thin and old and her hair wasn't arranged prettily so I shut my eyes, not wanting to see her.

"Pierre is dead, isn't he?"

"He died on the way down, the poor little boy," she said.

"He died before that," I thought but was too tired to speak.

"Your mother is in the country. Resting. Getting well again. You will see her quite soon."

"I didn't know," I said. "Why did she go away?"

"You've been very ill for nearly six weeks. You didn't know anything."

What was the use of telling her that I'd been awake before and heard my mother screaming *"Qui est là? Que est là?,"* then "Don't touch me. I'll kill you if you touch me. Coward. Hypocrite. I'll kill you." I'd put my hands over my ears, her screams were so loud and terrible. I slept and when I woke up everything was quiet.

Still Aunt Cora stayed by my bed looking at me.

"My head is bandaged up. It's so hot," I said. "Will I have a mark on my forehead?"

"No, no." She smiled for the first time. "That is healing very nicely. It won't spoil you on your wedding day," she said.

She bent down and kissed me. "Is there anything you want? A cool drink to sip?"

"No, not a drink. Sing to me. I like that."

She began in a shaky voice.

Every night at half past eight
  Comes tap tap tapping—

"Not that one. I don't like that one. Sing *Before I was set free*."

She sat near me and sang very softly, "Before I was set free." I heard as far as "The sorrow that my heart feels for—" I didn't hear the end but I heard that before I slept, "The sorrow that my heart feels for."

I was going to see my mother. I had insisted that Christophine must be with me, no one else, and as I was not yet quite well they had given way. I remember the dull feeling as we drove along for I did not expect to see her. She was part of Coulibri, that had gone, so she had gone, I was certain of it. But when we reached the tidy pretty little house where she lived now (they said) I jumped out of the carriage and ran as fast as I could across the lawn. One door was open on to the veranda. I went in without knocking and stared at the people in the room. A colored man, a colored woman, and a white woman sitting with her head bent so low that I couldn't see her face. But I recognized her hair, one plait much shorter than the other. And her dress. I put my arms round her and kissed her. She held me so tightly that I couldn't breathe and I thought, "It's not her." Then, "It must be her." She looked at the door, then at me, then at the door again. I could not say, "He is dead," so I shook my head. "But I am here, I am here," I said, and she said, "No," quietly. Then "No no no" very loudly and flung me from her. I fell against the partition and hurt myself. The man and the woman were holding her arms and Christophine was there. The woman said, "Why you bring the child to make trouble, trouble, trouble? Trouble enough without that."

All the way back to Aunt Cora's house we didn't speak.

The first day I had to go to the convent, I clung to Aunt Cora as you would cling to life if you loved it. At last she got impatient, so I forced myself away from her and through the passage, down the steps into the street and, as I knew they would be, they were waiting for me under the sandbox tree. There were two of them, a boy and a girl. The boy was about fourteen and tall and big for his age, he had a white skin, a dull ugly white covered with freckles, his mouth was a negro's mouth and he had small eyes, like bits of green glass. He had the eyes of a dead fish. Worst, most horrible of all, his hair was crinkled, a negro's hair, but bright red, and his eyebrows and eyelashes were red. The girl was very black and wore no head handkerchief. Her hair had been plaited and I could smell the sickening oil she had daubed on it, from where I stood on the steps of Aunt Cora's dark, clean, friendly house, staring at them. They looked so harmless and quiet, no one would have noticed the glint in the boy's eyes.

Then the girl grinned and began to crack the knuckles of her fingers. At each crack I jumped and my hands began to sweat. I was holding some school books in my right hand and I shifted them to under my arm, but it was too late, there was a mark on the palm of my hand and a stain on the cover of the book. The girl began to laugh, very quietly, and it was then that hate came to me and courage with the hate so that I was able to walk past without looking at them.

I knew they were following, I knew too that as long as I was in sight of Aunt Cora's house they would do nothing but stroll along some distance after me. But I knew when they would draw close. It would be when I was going up the hill. There were walls and gardens on each side of the hill and no one would be there at this hour of the morning.

Half-way up they closed in on me and started talking. The girl said, "Look the crazy girl, you crazy like your mother. Your aunt frightened to have you in the house. She sent you for the nuns to lock up. Your mother walk about with no shoes and stockings on her feet, she *sans culottes*. She try to kill her husband and she try to kill you too that day you go to see her. She have eyes like zombie and you have eyes like zombie too. Why you won't look at me." The boy only said, "One day I catch you alone, you wait, one day I catch you alone." When I got to the top of the hill they were jostling me, I could smell the girl's hair.

A long empty street stretched away to the convent, the convent wall and a wooden gate. I would have to ring before I could get in. The girl said, "You don't want to look at me, eh, I make you look at me." She pushed me and the books I was carrying fell to the ground.

I stooped to pick them up and saw that a tall boy who was walking along the other side of the street had stopped and looked towards us. Then he crossed over, running. He had long legs, his feet hardly touched the ground. As soon as they saw him, they turned and walked away. He looked after them, puzzled. I would have died sooner than run when they were there, but as soon as they had gone, I ran. I left one of my books on the ground and the tall boy came after me.

"You dropped this," he said, and smiled. I knew who he was, his name was Sandi, Alexander Cosway's son. Once I would have said "my cousin Sandi" but Mr. Mason's lectures had made me shy about my colored relatives. I muttered, "Thank you."

"I'll talk to that boy," he said. "He won't bother you again."

In the distance I could see my enemy's red hair as he pelted along, but he hadn't a chance. Sandi caught him up before he reached the corner. The girl had disappeared. I didn't wait to see what happened but I pulled and pulled at the bell.

At last the door opened. The nun was a colored woman and she seemed displeased. "You must not ring the bell like that," she said. "I come as quick as I can." Then I heard the door shut behind me.

I collapsed and began to cry. She asked me if I was sick, but I could not answer. She took my hand, still clicking her tongue and muttering in an ill-tempered way, and led me across the yard, past the shadow of the big tree, not into the front door but into a big, cool, stone-flagged room. There were pots and pans hanging on the wall and a stone fireplace. There was another nun at the back of the room and when the bell rang again, the first one went to answer it. The second nun, also a colored woman, brought a basin and water but as fast as she sponged my face, so fast did I cry. When she saw my hand she asked if I had fallen and hurt myself. I shook my head and she sponged the stain away gently. "What is the matter, what are you crying about? What has happened to you?" And still I could not answer. She brought me a glass of milk, I tried to drink it, but I choked. "Oh la la," she said, shrugging her shoulders and went out.

When she came in again, a third nun was with her who said in a calm voice, "You have cried quite enough now, you must stop. Have you got a handkerchief?"

I remembered that I had dropped it. The new nun wiped my eyes with a large handkerchief, gave it to me and asked my name.

"Antoinette," I said.

"Of course," she said. "I know. You are Antoinette Cosway, that is to say Antoinette Mason. Has someone frightened you?"

"Yes."

"Now look at me," she said. "You will not be frightened of me."

I looked at her. She had large brown eyes, very soft, and was dressed in white, not with a starched apron like the others had. The band round her face was of linen and above the white linen a black veil of some thin material, which fell in folds down her back. Her cheeks were red, she had a laughing face and two deep dimples. Her hands were small but they looked clumsy and swollen, not like the rest of her. It was only afterwards that I found out that they were crippled with rheumatism. She took me into a parlor furnished stiffly with straight-backed chairs and a polished table in the middle. After she had talked to me I told her a little of why I was crying and that I did not like walking to school alone.

"That must be seen to," she said. "I will write to your aunt. Now Mother St. Justine will be waiting for you. I have sent for a girl who has been with us for nearly a year. Her name is Louise—Louise de Plana. If you feel strange, she will explain everything."

Louise and I walked along a paved path to the classroom. There was grass on each side of the path and trees and shadows of trees and sometimes a bright bush of flowers. She was very pretty and when she smiled at me I could scarcely believe I had ever been miserable. She said, "We always call Mother St. Justine, Mother Juice of a Lime. She is not very intelligent, poor woman. You will see."

Quickly, while I can, I must remember the hot classroom. The hot classroom, the pitchpine desks, the heat of the bench striking up through my body, along my arms and hands. But outside I could see cool, blue shadow on a white wall. My needle is sticky, and creaks as it goes in and out of the canvas. "My needle is swearing," I whisper to Louise, who sits next to me. We are cross-stitching silk roses on a pale background. We can color the roses as we choose and

mine are green, blue and purple. Underneath, I will write my name in fire red, Antoinette Mason, née Cosway, Mount Calvary Convent, Spanish Town, Jamaica, 1839.

As we work, Mother St. Justine reads us stories from the lives of the Saints, St. Rose, St. Barbara, St. Agnes. But we have our own Saint, the skeleton of a girl of fourteen under the altar of the convent chapel. The Relics. But how did the nuns get them out here, I ask myself? In a cabin trunk? Specially packed for the hold? How? But here she is, and St. Innocenzia is her name. We do not know her story, she is not in the book. The saints we hear about were all very beautiful and wealthy. All were loved by rich and handsome young men.

". . . more lovely and more richly dressed than he had ever seen her in life," drones Mother St. Justine. "She smiled and said, 'Here Theophilus is a rose from the garden of my Spouse, in whom you did not believe.' The rose he found by his side when he awoke has never faded. It still exists." (Oh, but where? Where?) "And Theophilus was converted to Christianity," says Mother St. Justine, reading very rapidly now, "and became one of the Holy Martyrs." She shuts the book with a clap and talks about pushing down the cuticles of our nails when we wash our hands. Cleanliness, good manners and kindness to God's poor. A flow of words ("It is her time of life," said Hélène de Plana, "she cannot help it, poor old Justine.") "When you insult or injure the unfortunate or the unhappy, you insult Christ Himself and He will not forget, for they are His chosen ones." This remark is made in a casual and perfunctory voice and she slides on to order and chastity, that flawless crystal that, once broken, can never be mended. Also deportment. Like everyone else, she has fallen under the spell of the de Plana sisters and holds them up as an example to the class. I admire them. They sit so poised and imperturbable while she points out the excellence of Miss Hélène's coiffure, achieved without a looking-glass.

"Please, Hélène, tell me how you do your hair, because when I grow up I want mine to look like yours."

"It's very easy. You comb it upwards, like this and then push it a little forward, like that, and then you pin it here and here. Never too many pins."

"Yes, but Hélène, mine does not look like yours, whatever I do."

Her eyelashes flickered, she turned away, too polite to say the obvious thing. We have no looking-glass in the dormitory, once I saw the new young nun from Ireland looking at herself in a cask of water, smiling to see if her dimples were still there. When she noticed me, she blushed and I thought, now she will always dislike me.

Sometimes it was Miss Hélène's hair and sometimes Miss Germaine's impeccable deportment, and sometimes it was the care Miss Louise took of her beautiful teeth. And if we were never envious, they never seemed vain. Hélène and Germaine, a little disdainful, aloof perhaps, but Louise, not even that. She took no part in it—as if she knew that she was born for other things. Hélène's brown eyes could snap, Germaine's grey eyes were beautiful, soft and cow-like, she spoke slowly and, unlike most Creole girls, was very even-tempered. It is easy to imagine what happened to those two, bar accidents. Ah but Louise! Her small waist, her thin brown hands, her black curls which smelled of vetiver, her high sweet voice, singing so carelessly in Chapel about death. Like a bird would sing. Anything might have happened to you, Louise, anything at all, and I wouldn't be surprised.

Then there was another saint, said Mother St. Justine, she lived later on but still in Italy, or was it in Spain. Italy is white pillars and green water. Spain is hot sun on stones, France is a lady with black hair wearing a white dress because Louise was born in France

fifteen years ago, and my mother, whom I must forget and pray for as though she were dead, though she is living, liked to dress in white.

No one spoke of her now that Christophine had left us to live with her son. I seldom saw my stepfather. He seemed to dislike Jamaica, Spanish Town in particular, and was often away for months.

One hot afternoon in July my aunt told me that she was going to England for a year. Her health was not good and she needed a change. As she talked she was working at a patchwork counterpane. The diamond-shaped pieces of silk melted one into the other, red, blue, purple, green, yellow, all one shimmering color. Hours and hours she had spent on it and it was nearly finished. Would I be lonely? she asked and I said "No," looking at the colors. Hours and hours and hours I thought.

This convent was my refuge, a place of sunshine and of death where very early in the morning the clap of a wooden signal woke the nine of us who slept in the long dormitory. We woke to see Sister Marie Augustine sitting, serene and neat, bolt upright in a wooden chair. The long brown room was full of gold sunlight and shadows of trees moving quietly. I learnt to say very quickly as the others did, "offer up all the prayers, works and sufferings of this day." But what about happiness, I thought at first, is there no happiness? There must be. Oh happiness of course, happiness, well.

But I soon forgot about happiness, running down the stairs to the big stone bath where we splashed about wearing long grey cotton chemises which reached to our ankles. The smell of soap as you cautiously soaped yourself under the chemise, a trick to be learned, dressing with modesty, another trick. Great splashes of sunlight as we ran up the wooden steps of the refectory. Hot coffee and rolls and melting butter. But after the meal, now and at the hour of our death, and at midday and at six in the evening, now and at the hour of our death. Let perpetual light shine on them. This is for my mother, I would think, wherever her soul is wandering, for it has left her body. Then I remembered how she hated a strong light and loved the cool and the shade. It is a different light they told me. Still, I would not say it. Soon we were back in the shifting shadows outside, more beautiful than any perpetual light could be, and soon I learnt to gabble without thinking as the others did. About changing now and the hour of our death for that is all we have.

Everything was brightness, or dark. The walls, the blazing colors of the flowers in the garden, the nuns' habits were bright, but their veils, the Crucifix hanging from their waists, the shadow of the trees, were black. That was how it was, light and dark, sun and shadow, Heaven and Hell, for one of the nuns knew all about Hell and who does not? But another one knew about Heaven and the attributes of the blessed, of which the least is transcendent beauty. The very least. I could hardly wait for all this ecstasy and once I prayed for a long time to be dead. Then remembered that this was a sin. It's presumption or despair, I forget which, but a mortal sin. So I prayed for a long time about that too, but the thought came, so many things are sins, why? Another sin, to think that. However, happily, Sister Marie Augustine says thoughts are not sins, if they are driven away at once. You say Lord save me, I perish. I find it very comforting to know exactly what must be done. All the same, I did not pray so often after that and soon, hardly at all. I felt bolder, happier, more free. But not so safe.

During this time, nearly eighteen months, my stepfather often came to see me. He interviewed Mother Superior first, then I would go into the parlor dressed ready for a dinner or a visit to friends. He gave me presents when we parted, sweets, a locket, a bracelet, once a very pretty dress which, of course, I could not wear.

The last time he came was different. I knew that as soon as I got into the room. He kissed me, held me at arm's length looking at me carefully and critically, then smiled and said that I was taller than he thought. I reminded him that I was over seventeen, a grown woman. "I've not forgotten your present," he said.

Because I felt shy and ill at ease I answered coldly, "I can't wear all these things you buy for me."

"You can wear what you like when you live with me," he said.

"Where? In Trinidad?"

"Of course not. Here, for the time being. With me and your Aunt Cora who is coming home at last. She says another English winter will kill her. And Richard. You can't be hidden away all your life."

"Why not?" I thought.

I suppose he noticed my dismay because he began to joke, pay me compliments, and ask me such absurd questions that soon I was laughing too. How would I like to live in England? Then, before I could answer, had I learnt dancing, or were the nuns too strict?

"They are not strict at all," I said. "The Bishop who visits them every year says they are lax. Very lax. It's the climate he says."

"I hope they told him to mind his own business."

"She did. Mother Superior did. Some of the others were frightened. They are not strict but no one has taught me to dance."

"That won't be the difficulty. I want you to be happy, Antoinette, secure, I've tried to arrange, but we'll have time to talk about that later."

As we were going out of the convent gate he said in a careless voice, "I have asked some English friends to spend next winter here. You won't be dull."

"Do you think they'll come?" I said doubtfully.

"One of them will. I'm certain of that."

It may have been the way he smiled, but again a feeling of dismay, sadness, loss, almost choked me. This time I did not let him see it.

It was like that morning when I found the dead horse. Say nothing and it may not be true.

But they all knew at the convent. The girls were very curious but I would not answer their questions and for the first time I resented the nuns' cheerful faces.

They are safe. How can they know what it can be like *outside?*

This was the second time I had my dream.

Again I have left the house at Coulibri. It is still night and I am walking towards the forest. I am wearing a long dress and thin slippers, so I walk with difficulty, following the man who is with me and holding up the skirt of my dress. It is white and beautiful and I don't wish to get it soiled. I follow him, sick with fear but I make no effort to save myself; if anyone were to try to save me, I would refuse. This must happen. Now we have reached the forest. We are under the tall dark trees and there is no wind. "Here?" He turns and looks at me, his face black with hatred, and when I see this I begin to cry. He smiles slyly."Not here, not yet," he says, and I follow him, weeping. Now I do not try to hold up my dress, it trails in the dirt, my beautiful dress. We are no longer in the forest but in an enclosed garden surrounded by a stone wall and the trees are different trees. I do not know them. There are steps leading upwards. It is too dark to see the wall or the steps, but I know they are there and I think, "It will be when I go up these steps. At the top." I stumble over my dress and cannot get up. I touch a tree and my arms hold on to it. "Here, here." But I think I will not go any further. The tree sways and jerks as if it is trying to throw me off. Still I cling and the seconds pass and each one is a thousand years. "Here, in here," a strange voice said, and the tree stopped swaying and jerking.

Now Sister Marie Augustine is leading me out of the dormitory, asking if I am ill, telling me that I must not disturb the others and though I am still shivering I wonder if she will take me behind the mysterious curtains to the place where she sleeps. But no. She seats me in a chair, vanishes, and after a while comes back with a cup of hot chocolate.

I said, "I dreamed I was in Hell."

"That dream is evil. Put it from your mind—never think of it again," and she rubbed my cold hands to warm them.

She looks as usual, composed and neat, and I want to ask her if she gets up before dawn or hasn't been to bed at all.

"Drink your chocolate."

While I am drinking it I remember that after my mother's funeral, very early in the morning, almost as early as this, we went home to drink chocolate and eat cakes. She died last year, no one told me how, and I didn't ask. Mr. Mason was there and Christophine, no one else. Christophine cried bitterly but I could not. I prayed, but the words fell to the ground meaning nothing.

Now the thought of her is mixed up with my dream.

I saw her in her mended habit riding a borrowed horse, trying to wave at the head of the cobblestoned road at Coulibri, and tears came to my eyes again. "Such terrible things happen," I said. "Why? Why?"

"You must not concern yourself with that mystery," said Sister Maria Augustine. "We do not know why the devil must have his little day. Not yet."

She never smiled as much as the others, now she was not smiling at all. She looked sad.

She said, as if she was talking to herself, "Now go quietly back to bed.

Think of calm, peaceful things and try to sleep. Soon I will give the signal. Soon it will be tomorrow morning."

PART TWO

So it was all over, the advance and retreat, the doubts and hesitations. Everything finished, for better or for worse. There we were, sheltering from the heavy rain under a large mango tree, myself, my wife Antoinette and a little half-caste servant who was called Amélie. Under a neighboring tree I could see our luggage covered with sacking, the two porters and a boy holding fresh horses, hired to carry us up 2,000 feet to the waiting honeymoon house.

The girl Amélie said this morning, "I hope you will be very happy, sir, in your sweet honeymoon house." She was laughing at me I could see. A lovely little creature but sly, spiteful, malignant perhaps, like much else in this place.

"It's only a shower," Antoinette said anxiously. "It will soon stop."

I looked at the sad leaning cocoanut palms, the fishing boats drawn up on the shingly beach, the uneven row of whitewashed huts, and asked the name of the village.

"Massacre."

"And who was massacred here? Slaves?"

"Oh no." She sounded shocked. "Not slaves. Something must have happened a long time ago. Nobody remembers now."

The rain fell more heavily, huge drops sounded like hail on the leaves of the tree, and the sea crept stealthily forwards and backwards.

So this is Massacre. Not the end of the world, only the last stage of our interminable journey from Jamaica, the start of our sweet honeymoon. And it will all look very different in the sun.

It had been arranged that we would leave Spanish Town immediately after the ceremony and spend some weeks in one of the Windward Islands, at a small estate which had belonged to Antoinette's mother. I agreed. As I had agreed to everything else.

The windows of the huts were shut, the doors opened into silence and dimness. Then three little boys came to stare at us. The smallest wore nothing but a religious medal round his neck and the brim of a large fisherman's hat. When I smiled at him, he began to cry. A woman called from one of the huts and he ran away, still howling.

The other two followed slowly, looking back several times.

As if this was a signal a second woman appeared at her door, then a third.

"It's Caro," Antoinette said. "I'm sure it's Caro. Caroline," she called, waving, and the woman waved back. A gaudy old creature in a brightly flowered dress, a striped head handkerchief and gold earrings.

"You'll get soaked, Antoinette," I said.

"No, the rain is stopping." She held up the skirt of her riding habit and ran across the street. I watched her critically. She wore a tricorne hat which became her. At least it shadowed her eyes which are too large and can be disconcerting. She never blinks at all it seems to me. Long, sad, dark alien eyes. Creole of pure English descent she may be, but they are not English or European either. And when did I begin to notice all this about my wife Antoinette? After we left Spanish Town I suppose. Or did I notice it before and refuse to admit what I saw? Not that I had much time to notice anything. I was married a month after I arrived in Jamaica and for nearly three weeks of that time I was in bed with fever.

The two women stood in the doorway of the hut gesticulating, talking not English but the debased French patois they use in this island. The rain began to drip down the back of my neck adding to my feeling of discomfort and melancholy.

I thought about the letter which should have been written to England a week ago. Dear Father . . .

"Caroline asks if you will shelter in her house."

This was Antoinette. She spoke hesitatingly as if she expected me to refuse, so it was easy to do so.

"But you are getting wet," she said.

"I don't mind that." I smiled at Caroline and shook my head.

"She will be very disappointed," said my wife, crossed the street again and went into the dark hut.

Amélie, who had been sitting with her back to us, turned round. Her expression was so full of delighted malice, so intelligent, above all so intimate that I felt ashamed and looked away.

"Well," I thought. "I have had fever. I am not myself yet."

The rain was not so heavy and I went to talk to the porters. The first man was not a native of the island. "This a very wild place—not civilized. Why you come here?" He was called the Young Bull he told me, and he was twenty-seven years of age. A magnificent body and a foolish conceited face. The other man's name was Emile, yes, he was born in the village, he lived there. "Ask him how old he is," suggested the Young Bull. Emile said in a questioning voice, "Fourteen? Yes I have fourteen years master."

"Impossible," I said. I could see the grey hairs in his sparse beard.

"Fifty-six years perhaps." He seemed anxious to please.

The Young Bull laughed loudly. "He don't know how old he is, he don't think about it. I tell you sir these people are not civilized."

Emile muttered, "My mother she know, but she dead." Then he produced a blue rag which he twisted into a pad and put on his head.

Most of the women were outside their doors looking at us but without smiling. Somber people in a sombre place. Some of the men were going to their boats. When Emile shouted, two of them came towards him. He sang in a deep voice. They answered, then lifted the heavy wicker basket and swung it on to his head-pad singing. He tested the balance with one hand and strode off, barefooted on the sharp stones, by far the gayest member of the wedding party. As the Young Bull was loaded up he glanced at me sideways boastfully and he too sang to himself in English.

The boy brought the horses to a large stone and I saw Antoinette coming from the hut. The sun blazed out and steam rose from the green behind us. Amélie took her shoes off, tied them together and hung them round her neck. She balanced her small basket on her head and swung away as easily as the porters. We mounted, turned a corner and the village was out of sight. A cock crowed loudly and I remembered the night before which we had spent in the town. Antoinette had a room to herself, she was exhausted. I lay awake listening to cocks crowing all night, then got up very early and saw the women with trays covered with white cloths on their heads going to the kitchen. The woman with small hot loaves for sale, the woman with cakes, the woman with sweets. In the street another called *Bon sirop, Bon sirop,* and I felt peaceful.

The road climbed upward. On one side the wall of green, on the other a steep drop to the ravine below. We pulled up and looked at the hills, the mountains and the blue-green sea. There was a soft warm wind blowing but I understood why the porter had called it a wild place. Not only wild but menacing. Those hills would close in on you.

"What an extreme green," was all I could say, and thinking of Emile calling to the fishermen and the sound of his voice, I asked about him.

"They take short cuts. They will be at Granbois long before we are."

Everything is too much, I felt as I

rode wearily after her. Too much blue, too much purple, too much green. The flowers too red, the mountains too high, the hills too near. And the woman is a stranger. Her pleading expression annoys me. I have not bought her, she has bought me, or so she thinks. I looked down at the coarse mane of the horse . . . Dear Father. The thirty thousand pounds have been paid to me without question or condition. No provision made for her (that must be seen to). I have a modest competence now. I will never be a disgrace to you or to my dear brother the son you love. No begging letters, no mean requests. None of the furtive shabby manoeuvres of a younger son. I have sold my soul or you have sold it, and after all is it such a bad bargain? The girl is thought to be beautiful, she is beautiful. And yet . . .

Meanwhile the horses jogged along a very bad road. It was getting cooler. A bird whistled, a long sad note. "What bird is that?" She was too far ahead and did not hear me. The bird whistled again. A mountain bird. Shrill and sweet. A very lonely sound.

She stopped and called, "Put your coat on now." I did so and realized that I was no longer pleasantly cool but cold in my sweat-soaked shirt.

We rode on again, silent in the slanting afternoon sun, the wall of trees on one side, a drop on the other. Now the sea was a serene blue, deep and dark.

We came to a little river. "This is the boundary of Granbois." She smiled at me. It was the first time I had seen her smile simply and naturally. Or perhaps it was the first time I had felt simple and natural with her. A bamboo spout jutted from the cliff, the water coming from it was silver blue. She dismounted quickly, picked a large shamrock-shaped leaf to make a cup, and drank. Then she picked another leaf, folded it and brought it to me. "Taste. This is mountain water." Looking up smiling, she might have been any pretty English girl and to please her

I drank. It was cold, pure and sweet, a beautiful color against the thick green leaf.

She said, "After this we go down then up again. Then we are there."

Next time she spoke she said. "The earth is red here, do you notice?"

"It's red in parts of England too."

"Oh England, England," she called back mockingly, and the sound went on and on like a warning I did not choose to hear.

Soon the road was cobblestoned and we stopped at a flight of stone steps. There was a large screw pine to the left and to the right what looked like an imitation of an English summer house—four wooden posts and a thatched roof. She dismounted and ran up the steps. At the top a badly cut, coarse-grained lawn and at the end of the lawn a shabby white house. "Now you are at Granbois." I looked at the mountains purple against a very blue sky.

Perched up on wooden stilts the house seemed to shrink from the forest behind it and crane eagerly out to the distant sea. It was more awkward than ugly, a little sad as if it knew it could not last. A group of negroes were standing at the foot of the veranda steps. Antoinette ran across the lawn and as I followed her I collided with a boy coming in the opposite direction. He rolled his eyes, looking alarmed and went on towards the horses without a word of apology. A man's voice said, "Double up now double up. Look sharp." There were four of them. A woman, a girl and a tall, dignified man were together. Antoinette was standing with her arms round another woman. "That was Bertrand who nearly knocked you down. That is Rose and Hilda. This is Baptiste."

The servants grinned shyly as she named them.

"And here is Christophine who was my da, my nurse long ago."

Baptiste said that it was a happy day

and that we'd brought fine weather with us. He spoke good English, but in the middle of his address of welcome Hilda began to giggle. She was a young girl of about twelve or fourteen, wearing a sleeveless white dress which, just reached her knees. The dress was spotless but her uncovered hair, though it was oiled and braided into many small plaits, gave her a savage appearance. Baptiste frowned at her and she giggled more loudly, then put her hand over her mouth and went up the wooden steps into the house. I could hear her bare feet running along the veranda.

"Doudou, ché cocotte," the elderly woman said to Antoinette. I looked at her sharply but she seemed insignificant. She was blacker than most and her clothes, even the handkerchief round her head, were subdued in color. She looked at me steadily, not with approval, I thought. We stared at each other for quite a minute. I looked away first and she smiled to herself, gave Antoinette a little push forward and disappeared into the shadows at the back of the house. The other servants had gone.

Standing on the veranda I breathed the sweetness of the air. Cloves I could smell and cinnamon, roses and orange blossom. And an intoxicating freshness as if all this had never been breathed before. When Antoinette said "Come, I will show you the house" I went with her unwillingly for the rest of the place seemed neglected and deserted. She led me into a large unpainted room. There was a small shabby sofa, a mahogany table in the middle, some straight-backed chairs and an old oak chest with brass feet like lion's claws.

Holding my hand she went up to the sideboard where two glasses of rum punch were waiting for us. She handed me one and said, "To happiness."

"To happiness," I answered.

The room beyond was larger and emptier. There were two doors, one leading to the veranda, the other very slightly open into a small room. A big bed, a round table by its side, two chairs, a surprising dressing-table with a marble top and a large looking-glass. Two wreaths of frangipani lay on the bed.

"Am I expected to wear one of these? And when?'"

I crowned myself with one of the wreaths and made a face in the glass. "I hardly think it suits my handsome face, do you?"

"You look like a king, an emperor."

"God forbid," I said and took the wreath off. It fell on the floor and as I went towards the window I stepped on it. The room was full of the scent of crushed flowers. I saw her reflection in the glass fanning herself with a small palm-leaf fan colored blue and red at the edges. I felt sweat on my forehead and sat down, she knelt near me and wiped my face with her handkerchief.

"Don't you like it here? This is my place and everything is on our side. Once," she said, "I used to sleep with a piece of wood by my side so that I could defend myself if I were attacked. That's how afraid I was."

"Afraid of what?"

She shook her head. "Of nothing, of everything."

Someone knocked and she said, "It's only Christophine."

"The old woman who was your nurse? Are you afraid of her?"

"No, how could I be?"

"If she were taller," I said, "one of these strapping women dressed up to the nines, I might be afraid of her."

She laughed. "That door leads into your dressing-room."

I shut it gently after me.

It seemed crowded after the emptiness of the rest of the house. There was a carpet, the only one I had seen, a press made of some beautiful wood I did not recognize. Under the open window a small writing-desk with paper, pens, and ink. "A refuge" I was thinking when someone said, "This was Mr. Mason's room, sir, but he did not come

here often. He did not like the place."
Baptiste, standing in the doorway to the
veranda, had a blanket over his arm.

"It's all very comfortable," I said. He
laid the blanket on the bed.

"It can be cold here at night," he said.
Then went away. But the feeling of
security had left me. I looked round
suspiciously. The door into her room
could be bolted, a stout wooden bar
pushed across the other. This was the
last room in the house. Wooden steps
from the veranda led on to another
rough lawn, a Seville orange tree grew
by the steps. I want back into the
dressing-room and looked out of the
window. I saw a clay road, muddy in
places, bordered by a row of tall trees.
Beyond the road various half-hidden out-
buildings. One was the kitchen. No
chimney but smoke was pouring out
of the window. I sat on the soft narrow bed and listened. Not a sound
except the river. I might have been alone
in the house. There was a crude bookshelf made of three shingles strung together over the desk and I looked at the
books, Byron's poems, novels by Sir
Walter Scott, *Confessions of an Opium
Eater,* some shabby brown volumes, and
on the last shelf, *Life and Letters of . . .*
The rest was eaten away.

*Dear Father, we have arrived from Ja-
maica after an uncomfortable few days.
This little estate in the Windward
Islands is part of the family property
and Antoinette is much attached to it.
She wished to get here as soon as possible. All is well and has gone according
to your plans and wishes. I dealt of
course with Richard Mason. His father
died soon after I left for the West Indies
as you probably know. He is a good
fellow, hospitable and friendly; he
seemed to become attached to me and
trusted me completely. This place is very
beautiful but my illness has left me too
exhausted to appreciate it fully. I will
write again in a few days' time.*

I reread this letter and added a post-
script:

*I feel that I have left you too long
without news for the bare announcement
of my approaching marriage was hardly
news. I was down with fever for two
weeks after I got to Spanish Town.
Nothing serious but I felt wretched
enough. I stayed with the Frasers, friends
of the Masons. Mr. Fraser is an Englishman, a retired magistrate, and he insisted on telling me at length about
some of his cases. It was difficult to
think or write coherently. In this cool
and remote place it is called Granbois
(the High Woods I suppose) I feel better
already and my next letter will be longer
and more explicit.*

A cool and remote place . . . And I
wondered how they got their letters
posted. I folded mine and put it into a
drawer of the desk.

As for my confused impressions they
will never be written. There are blanks
in my mind that cannot be filled up.

It was all very brightly colored, very
strange, but it meant nothing to me.
Nor did she, the girl I was to marry.
When at last I met her I bowed, smiled,
kissed her hand, danced with her. I
played the part I was expected to play.
She never had anything to do with me
at all. Every movement I made was an
effort of will and sometimes I wondered
that no one noticed this. I would listen
to my own voice and marvel at it, calm,
correct but toneless, surely. But I must
have given a faultless performance. If
I saw an expression of doubt or curiosity it was on a black face not a white
one.

I remember little of the actual ceremony. Marble memorial tablets on the
walls commemorating the virtues of the
last generation of planters. All benevolent. All slave-owners. All resting in
peace. When we came out of the church

I took her hand. It was cold as ice in the hot sun.

Then I was at a long table in a crowded room. Palm leaf fans, a mob of servants, the women's head hand-kerchiefs striped red and yellow, the men's dark faces. The strong taste of punch, the cleaner taste of champagne, my bride in white but I hardly remember what she looked like. Then in another room women dressed in black. Cousin Julia, Cousin Ada, Aunt Lina. Thin or fat they all looked alike. Gold earrings in pierced ears. Silver bracelets jangling on their wrists. I said to one of them, "We are leaving Jamaica tonight," and she answered after a pause, "Of course, Antoinette does not like Spanish Town. Nor did her mother." Peering at me. (Do their eyes get smaller as they grow older? Smaller, beadier, more inquisitive?) After that I thought I saw the same expression on all their faces. Curiosity? Pity? Ridicule? But why should they pity me. I who have done so well for myself?

The morning before the wedding Richard Mason burst into my room at the Frasers as I was finishing my first cup of coffee. "She won't go through with it!"

"Won't go through with what?"

"She won't marry you."

"But why?"

"She doesn't say why."

"She must have some reason."

"She won't give a reason. I've been arguing with the little fool for an hour."

We stared at each other.

"Everything arranged, the presents, the invitations. What shall I tell your father?" He seemed on the verge of tears.

I said, "If she won't, she won't. She can't be dragged to the altar. Let me get dressed. I must hear what she has to say."

He went out meekly and while I dressed I thought that this would indeed make a fool of me. I did not relish going back to England in the role of rejected suitor jilted by this Creole girl. I must certainly know why.

She was sitting in a rocking chair with her head bent. Her hair was in two long plaits over her shoulders. From a little distance I spoke gently. "What is the matter, Antoinette? What have I done?"

She said nothing.

"You don't wish to marry me?"

"No." She spoke in a very low voice.

"But why?"

"I'm afraid of what may happen."

"But don't you remember last night I told you that when you are my wife there would not be any more reason to be afraid?"

"Yes," she said. "Then Richard came in and you laughed. I didn't like the way you laughed."

"But I was laughing at myself, Antoinette."

She looked at me and I took her in my arms and kissed her.

"You don't know anything about me," she said.

"I'll trust you if you'll trust me. Is that a bargain? You will make me very unhappy if you send me away without telling me what I have done to displease you. I will go with a sad heart."

"Your sad heart," she said, and touched my face. I kissed her fervently, promising her peace, happiness, safety, but when I said, "Can I tell poor Richard that it was a mistake? He is sad too," she did not answer me. Only nodded.

Thinking of all this, of Richard's angry face, her voice saying, "Can you give me peace?," I must have slept.

I woke to the sound of voices in the next room, laughter and water being poured out. I listened, still drowsy. Antoinette said, "Don't put any more scent on my hair. He doesn't like it." The other: "The man don't like scent? I never hear that before." It was almost dark.

The dining-room was brilliantly lit. Candles on the table, a row on the sideboard, three-branch candlesticks on the old sea-chest. The two doors on to the veranda stood open but there was no wind. The flames burned straight. She was sitting on the sofa and I wondered why I had never realized how beautiful she was. Her hair was combed away from her face and fell smoothly far below her waist. I could see the red and gold lights in it. She seemed pleased when I complimented her on her dress and told me she had it made in St. Pierre, Martinique. 'They call this fashion *à la Joséphine.*'

"You talk of St. Pierre as though it were Paris," I said.

"But it is the Paris of the West Indies."

There were trailing pink flowers on the table and the name echoed pleasantly in my head. Coralita Coralita. The food, though too highly seasoned, was lighter and more appetizing than anything I had tasted in Jamaica. We drank champagne. A great many moths and beetles found their way into the room, flew into the candles and fell dead on the tablecloth. Amélie swept them up with a crumb brush. Uselessly. More moths and beetles came.

"Is it true," she said, "that England is like a dream? Because one of my friends who married an Englishman wrote and told me so. She said this place London is like a cold dark dream sometimes. I want to wake up."

"Well," I answered annoyed, "that is precisely how your beautiful island seems to me, quite unreal and like a dream."

"But how can rivers and mountains and the sea be unreal?"

"And how can millions of people, their houses and their streets be unreal?"

"More easily," she said, "much more easily. Yes a big city must be like a dream."

"No, this is unreal and like a dream," I thought.

The long veranda was furnished with canvas chairs, two hammocks, and a wooden table on which stood a tripod telescope. Amélie brought out candles with glass shades but the night swallowed up the feeble light. There was a very strong scent of flowers—the flowers by the river that open at night she told me—and the noise, subdued in the inner room, was deafening. "Crac-cracs," she explained, "they make a sound like their name, and crickets and frogs."

I leaned on the railing and saw hundreds of fireflies—"Ah yes, fireflies in Jamaica, here they call a firefly La Belle."

A large moth, so large that I thought it was a bird, blundered into one of the candles, put it out and fell to the floor. "He's a big fellow," I said.

"Is it badly burned?"

"More stunned than hurt."

I took the beautiful creature up in my handkerchief and put it on the railing. For a moment it was still and by the dim candlelight I could see the soft brilliant colors, the intricate pattern on the wings. I shook the handkerchief gently and it flew away.

"I hope that gay gentleman will be safe," I said.

"He will come back if we don't put the candles out. It's light enough by the stars."

Indeed the starlight was so bright that shadows of the veranda posts and the trees outside lay on the floor.

"Now come for a walk," she said, "and I will tell you a story."

We walked along the veranda to the steps which led to the lawn.

"We used to come here to get away from the hot weather in June, July and August. I came three times with my Aunt Cora who is ill. That was after . . ." She stopped and put her hand up to her head.

"If this is a sad story, don't tell it to me tonight."

"It is not sad," she said. "Only some things happen and are there for always even though you forget why or when. It was in that little bedroom."

I looked where she was pointing but could only see the outline of a narrow bed and one or two chairs.

"This night I can remember it was very hot. The window was shut but I asked Christophine to open it because the breeze comes from the hills at night. The land breeze. Not from the sea. It was so hot that my night chemise was sticking to me but I went to sleep all the same. And then suddenly I was awake. I saw two enormous rats, as big as cats, on the sill staring at me."

"I'm not astonished that you were frightened."

"But I was not frightened. That was the strange thing. I stared at them and they did not move. I could see myself in the looking-glass the other side of the room, in my white chemise with a frill round the neck, staring at those rats and the rats quite still, staring at me."

"Well, what happened?"

"I turned over, pulled up the sheet and went to sleep instantly."

"And is that the story?"

"No, I woke up again suddenly like the first time and the rats were not there but I felt very frightened. I got out of bed quickly and ran on to the veranda. I lay down in this hammock. This one." She pointed to a flat hammock, a rope at each of the four corners.

"There was full moon that night—and I watched it for a long time. There were no clouds chasing it, so it seemed to be standing still and it shone on me. Next morning Christophine was angry. She said that it was very bad to sleep in the moonlight when the moon is full."

"And did you tell her about the rats?"

"No, I never told anyone till now. But I have never forgotten them."

I wanted to say something reassuring but the scent of the river flowers was overpoweringly strong. I felt giddy.

"Do you think that too," she said,

"that I have slept too long in the moonlight?"

Her mouth was set in a fixed smile but her eyes were so withdrawn and lonely that I put my arms round her, rocked her like a child and sang to her. An old song I thought I had forgotten:

Hail to the queen of the silent night,
Shine bright, shine bright Robin as you die.

She listened, then sang with me:

Shine bright, shine bright Robin as you die.

There was no one in the house and only two candles in the room which had been so brilliantly lit. Her room was dim, with a shaded candle by the bed and another on the dressing-table. There was a bottle of wine on the round table. It was very late when I poured out two glasses and told her to drink to our happiness, to our love and the day without end which would be tomorrow. I was young then. A short youth mine was.

I woke next morning in the green-yellow light, feeling uneasy as though someone were watching me. She must have been awake for some time. Her hair was plaited and she wore a fresh white chemise. I turned to take her in my arms, I meant to undo the careful plaits, but as I did so there was a soft discreet knock.

She said, "I have sent Christophine away twice. We wake very early here. The morning is the best time."

"Come in," she called and Christophine came in with our coffee on a tray. She was dressed up and looking very imposing. The skirt of her flowered dress trailed after her making a rustling noise as she walked and her yellow silk turban was elaborately tied. Long heavy gold earrings pulled down the lobes of her ears. She wished us good morning smiling and put the tray of coffee, cassava cakes and guava jelly on the round table. I got out of bed and went into the dressing-room. Someone had laid my dressing-gown on the narrow bed. I looked out of the window. The cloudless sky was a paler blue than I'd imagined but as I looked I thought I saw the color changing to a deeper blue. At noon I knew it would be gold, then brassy in the heat. Now it was fresh and cool and the air itself was blue. At last I turned away from the light and space and went back into the bedroom, which was still in the half dark. Antoinette was leaning back against the pillows with her eyes closed. She opened them and smiled when I came in. It was the black woman hovering over her who said, "Taste my bull's blood, master." The coffee she handed me was delicious and she had long-fingered hands, thin and beautiful I suppose.

"Not horse piss like the English madams drink," she said. "I know them. Drink drink their yellow horse piss, talk, talk their lying talk." Her dress trailed and rustled as she walked to the door. There she turned. "I send the girl to clear up the mess you make with the frangipani, it bring cockroach in the house. Take care not to slip on the flowers, young master." She slid through the door.

"Her coffee is delicious but her language is horrible and she might hold her dress up. It must get very dirty, yards of it trailing on the floor."

"When they don't hold their dress up it's for respect," said Antoinette. "Or for feast days or going to Mass."

"And is this a feast day?"

"She wanted it to be a feast day."

"Whatever the reason it is not a clean habit."

"It is. You don't understand at all. They don't care about getting a dress dirty because it shows it isn't the only dress they have. Don't you like Christophine?"

"She is a very worthy person no doubt. I can't say I like her language."

"It doesn't mean anything," said Antoinette.

"And she looks so lazy. She dawdles about."

"Again you are mistaken. She seems slow, but every move she makes is right so it's quick in the end."

I drank another cup of bull's blood. (Bull's blood, I thought. The Young Bull.)

"How did you get that dressing-table up here?"

"I don't know. It's always been here ever since I can remember. A lot of the furniture was stolen, but not that."

There were two pink roses on the tray, each in a small brown jug. One was full blown and as I touched it the petals dropped.

"Rose elle a vécu," I said and laughed. "Is that poem true? Have all beautiful things sad destinies?"

"No, of course not."

Her little fan was on the table, she took it up laughing, lay back and shut her eyes. "I think I won't get up this morning."

"Not get up. Not get up at all?"

"I'll get up when I wish to. I'm very lazy you know. Like Christophine. I often stay in bed all day." She flourished her fan. "The bathing pool is quite near. Go before it gets hot, Baptiste will show you. There are two pools, one we call the champagne pool because it has a waterfall, not a big one you understand, but it's good to feel it on your shoulders. Underneath is the nutmeg pool, that's brown and shaded by a big nutmeg tree. It's just big enough to swim in. But be careful. Remember to put your clothes on a rock and before you dress again shake them very well. Look for the red ant, that is the worst. It is very small but bright red so you will be able to see it easily if you look. Be careful," she said and waved her little fan.

One morning soon after we arrived, the row of tall trees outside my window were covered with small pale flowers too fragile to resist the wind. They fell in a day, and looked like snow on the rough grass—snow with a faint sweet scent. Then they were blown away.

The fine weather lasted longer. It lasted all that week and the next and the next and the next. No sign of a break. My fever weakness left me, so did all misgiving.

I went very early to the bathing pool and stayed there for hours, unwilling to leave the river, the trees shading it, the flowers that opened at night. They were tightly shut, drooping, sheltering from the sun under their thick leaves.

It was a beautiful place—wild, untouched, above all untouched, with an alien, disturbing, secret loveliness. And it kept its secret. I'd find myself thinking, "What I see is nothing—I want what it *hides*—that is not nothing."

In the late afternoon when the water was warmer she bathed with me. She'd spend some time throwing pebbles at a flat stone in the middle of the pool. "I've seen him. He hasn't died or gone to any other river. He's still there. The land crabs are harmless. People *say* they are harmless. I wouldn't like to—"

"Nor would I. Horrible looking creatures."

She was undecided, uncertain about facts—any fact. When I asked her if the snakes we sometimes saw were poisonous, she said, "Not those. The *fer de lance* of course, but there are none here," and added, "but how can they be sure? Do you think they know?" Then, "Our snakes are not poisonous. Of course not."

However, she was certain about the monster crab and one afternoon when I was watching her, hardly able to believe she was the pale silent creature I had married, watching her in her blue chemise, blue with white spots hitched up far above her knees, she stopped laughing, called a warning and threw a large pebble. She threw like a boy, with a sure graceful movement, and I looked down at very long pincer claws, jagged-edged and sharp, vanishing.

"He won't come after you if you keep away from that stone. He lives there. Oh it's another sort of crab. I don't know the name in English. Very big, very old."

As we were walking home I asked her who had taught her to aim so well. "Oh, Sandi taught me, a boy you never met."

Every evening we saw the sun go down from the thatched shelter she called the *ajoupa*, I the summer house. We watched the sky and the distant sea on fire—all colors were in that fire and the huge clouds fringed and shot with flame. But I soon tired of the display. I was waiting for the scent of the flowers by the river—they opened when darkness came and it came quickly. Not night or darkness as I knew it but night with blazing stars, an alien moon—night full of strange noises. Still night, not day.

"The man who owns Consolation Estate is a hermit," she was saying. "He never sees anyone—hardly ever speaks, they say."

"A hermit neighbor suits me. Very well indeed."

"There are four hermits in this island," she said. "Four real ones. Others pretend but they leave when the rainy season comes. Or else they are drunk all the time. That's when sad things happen."

"So this place is as lonely as it feels?" I asked her.

"Yes it is lonely. Are you happy here?"

"Who wouldn't be?"

"I love it more than anywhere in the world. As if it were a person. More than a person."

"But you don't know the world," I teased her.

"No, only here, and Jamaica of course. Coulibri, Spanish Town. I don't know the other islands at all. Is the world more beautiful, then?"

And how to answer that? "It's different," I said.

She told me that for a long time they had not known what was happening at Granbois. "When Mr. Mason came" (she always called her stepfather Mr. Mason) "the forest was swallowing it up." The overseer drank, the house was dilapidated, all the furniture had been stolen, then Baptiste was discovered. A butler. In St. Kitts. But born in this island and willing to come back. "He's a very good overseer," she'd say, and I'd agree, keeping my opinion of Baptiste, Christophine and all the others to myself. "Baptiste says . . . Christophine wants . . ."

She trusted them and I did not. But I could hardly say so. Not yet.

We did not see a great deal of them. The kitchen and the swarming kitchen life were some way off. As for the money which she handed out so carelessly, not counting it, not knowing how much she gave, or the unfamiliar faces that appeared then disappeared, though never without a large meal eaten and a shot of rum I discovered—sisters, cousins, aunts and uncles—if she asked no questions how could I?

The house was swept and dusted very early, usually before I woke. Hilda brought coffee and there were always two roses on the tray. Sometimes she'd smile a sweet childish smile, sometimes she would giggle very loudly and rudely, bang the tray down and run away.

"Stupid little girl," I'd say.

"No, no. She is shy. The girls here are very shy."

After breakfast at noon there'd be silence till the evening meal which was served much later than in England. Christophine's whims and fancies, I was sure. Then we were left alone. Sometimes a sidelong look or a sly knowing glance disturbed me, but it was never for long. "Not now," I would think. "Not yet."

It was often raining when I woke during the night, a light capricious shower, dancing playful rain, or hushed, muted, growing louder, more persistent, more powerful, an inexorable sound. But always music, a music I had never heard before.

Then I would look at her for long minutes by candlelight, wonder why she seemed sad asleep, and curse the fever or the caution that had made me so blind, so feeble, so hesitating. I'd remember her effort to escape. (*No, I am sorry, I do not wish to marry you.*) Had she given way to that man Richard's arguments, threats probably, I wouldn't trust him far, or to my half-serious blandishments and promises? In any case she had given way, but coldly, unwillingly, trying to protect herself with silence and a blank face. Poor weapons, and they had not served her well or lasted long. If I have forgotten caution, she has forgotten silence and coldness.

Shall I wake her up and listen to the things she says, whispers, in darkness. Not by day.

"I never wished to live before I knew you. I always thought it would be better if I died. Such a long time to wait before it's over."

"And did you ever tell anyone this?"

"There was no one to tell, no one to listen. Oh you can't imagine Coulibri."

"But after Coulibri?"

"After Coulibri it was too late. I did not change."

All day she'd be like any other girl, smile at herself in her looking-glass (*do you like this scent?*), try to teach me her songs, for they haunted me.

Adieu foulard, adieu madras, or *Ma belle ka di maman li.* My beautiful girl said to her mother (*No it is not like that. Now listen. It is this way.*). She'd be silent, or angry for no reason, and chatter to Christophine in patois.

"Why do you hug and kiss Christophine?" I'd say.

"Why not?"

"*I* wouldn't hug and kiss them," I'd say, "I couldn't."

At this she'd laugh for a long time and never tell me why she laughed.

But at night how different, even her voice was changed. Always this talk of death. (Is she trying to tell me that is the secret of this place? That there is no other way? She knows. She knows.)

"Why did you make me want to live? Why did you do that to me?"

"Because I wished it. Isn't that enough?"

"Yes, it is enough. But if one day you didn't wish it. What should I do then? Suppose you took this happiness away when I wasn't looking . . ."

"And lose my own? Who'd be so foolish?"

"I am not used to happiness," she said. "It makes me afraid."

"Never be afraid. Or if you are tell no one."

"I understand. But trying does not help me."

"What would?" She did not answer that, then one night whispered, "If I could die. Now, when I am happy. Would you do that? You wouldn't have to kill me. Say die and I will die. You don't believe me? Then try, try, say die and watch me die."

"Die then! Die!" I watched her die many times. In my way, not in hers. In sunlight, in shadow, by moonlight, by candlelight. In the long afternoons when the house was empty. Only the sun was there to keep us company. We shut him out. And why not? Very soon she was as eager for what's called loving as I was—more lost and drowned afterwards.

She said, "Here I can do as I like," not I, and then I said it too. It seemed right in that lonely place. "Here I can do as I like."

We seldom met anyone when we left the house. If we did they'd greet us and go on their way.

I grew to like those mountain people, silent, reserved, never servile, never

curious (or so I thought), not knowing that their quick sideways looks saw everything they wished to see.

It was at night that I felt danger and would try to forget it and push it away.

"You are safe," I'd say. She'd liked that—to be told "you are safe." Or I'd touch her face gently and touch tears. Tears—nothing! Words—less than nothing. As for the happiness I gave her, that was worse than nothing. I did not love her. I was thirsty for her, but that is not love. I felt very little tenderness for her, she was a stranger to me, a stranger who did not think or feel as I did.

One afternoon the sight of a dress which she'd left lying on her bedroom floor made me breathless and savage with desire. When I was exhausted I turned away from her and slept, still without a word or a caress. I woke and she was kissing me—soft light kisses. "It is late," she said and smiled. "You must let me cover you up—the land breeze can be cold."

"And you, aren't you cold?"

"Oh I will be ready quickly. I'll wear the dress you like tonight."

"Yes, do wear it."

The floor was strewn with garments, hers and mine. She stepped over them carelessly as she walked to her clothes press. "I was thinking, I'll have another made exactly like it," she promised happily. "Will you be pleased?"

"Very pleased."

If she was a child she was not a stupid child but an obstinate one. She often questioned me about England and listened attentively to my answers, but I was certain that nothing I said made much difference. Her mind was already made up. Some romantic novel, a stray remark never forgotten, a sketch, a picture, a song, a waltz, some note of music, and her ideas were fixed. About England and about Europe. I could not change them and probably nothing would. Reality might disconcert her, bewilder her, hurt her, but it would not be reality. It would be only a mistake, a misfortune, a wrong path taken, her fixed ideas would never change.

Nothing that I told her influenced her at all.

Die then. Sleep. It is all that I can give you. . . . I wonder if she ever guessed how near she came to dying. In her way, not in mine. It was not a safe game to play—in that place. Desire, Hatred, Life, Death came very close in the darkness. Better not know how close. Better not think, never for a moment. Not close. The same . . . "You are safe," I'd say to her and to myself. "Shut your eyes. Rest."

Then I'd listen to the rain, a sleepy tune that seemed as if it would go on for ever . . . Rain, for ever raining. Drown me in sleep. And soon.

Next morning there would be very little sign of these showers. If some of the flowers were battered, the others smelt sweeter, the air was bluer and sparkling fresh. Only the clay path outside my window was muddy. Little shallow pools of water glinted in the hot sun, red earth does not dry quickly.

"It came for you this morning early, master," Amélie said. "Hilda take it." She gave me a bulky envelope addressed in careful copperplate. *"By hand. Urgent"* was written in the corner.

"One of our hermit neighbors," I thought. "And an enclosure for Antoinette." Then I saw Baptiste standing near the veranda steps, put the letter in my pocket and forgot it.

I was later than usual that morning but when I was dressed I sat for a long time listening to the waterfall, eyes half closed, drowsy and content. When I put my hand in my pocket for my watch, I touched the envelope and opened it.

Dear Sir. I take up my pen after long thought and meditation but in the end the truth is better than a lie. I have this to say. You have been shamefully deceived by the Mason family. They tell you perhaps that your wife's name is Cosway, the English gentleman Mr. Mason being her stepfather only, but they don't tell you what sort of people were these Cosways. Wicked and detestable slave-owners since generations —yes everybody hate them in Jamaica and also in this beautiful island where I hope your stay will be long and pleasant and in spite of all, for some not worth sorrow. Wickedness is not the worst. There is madness in that family. Old Cosway die raving like his father before him.

You ask what proof I have and why I mix myself up in your affairs. I will answer you. I am your wife's brother by another lady, half-way house as we say. Her father and mine was a shameless man and of all his illegitimates I am the most unfortunate and poverty stricken.

My momma die when I was quite small and my godmother take care of me. The old mister hand out some money for that though he don't like me. No, that old devil don't like me at all, and when I grow older I see it and I think, Let him wait my day will come. Ask the older people sir about his disgusting goings on, some will remember.

When Madam his wife dies the reprobate marry again quick, to a young girl from Martinique—it's too much for him. Dead drunk from morning till night and he die raving and cursing.

Then comes the glorious Emancipation Act and trouble for some of the high and mighties. Nobody would work for the young woman and her two children and that place Coulibri goes quickly to bush as all does out here when nobody toil and labor on the land. She have no money and she have no friends, for French and English like cat and dog in these islands since long time. Shoot, Kill, Everything.

The woman call Christophine also from Martinique stay with her and an old man Godfrey, too silly to know what happen. Some like that. This young

Mrs. Cosway is worthless and spoilt, she can't lift a hand for herself and soon the madness that is in her, and in all these white Creoles, come out. She shut herself away, laughing and talking to nobody as many can bear witness. As for the litle girl, Antoinetta, as soon as she can walk she hide herself if she see anybody.

We all wait to hear the woman jump over a precipice "fini batt'e" as we say here which mean "finish to fight."

But no. She marry again to the rich Englishman Mr. Mason, and there is much I could say about that but you won't believe so I shut my mouth. They say he love her so much that if he have the world on a plate he give it to her —but no use.

The madness gets worse and she has to be shut away for she try to kill her husband—madness not being all either.

That sir is your wife's mother—that was her father. I leave Jamaica. I don't know what happen to the woman. Some say she is dead, other deny it. But old Mason take a great fancy for the girl Antoinetta and give her half his money when he die.

As for me I wander high and low, not much luck but a little money put by and I get to know of a house for sale in this island near Massacre. It's going very cheap so I buy it. News travel even to this wild place and next thing I hear from Jamaica is that old Mason is dead and that family plan to marry the girl to a young Englishman who know nothing of her. Then it seems to me that it is my Christian duty to warn the gentleman that she is no girl to marry with the bad blood she have from both sides. But they are white, I am colored. They are rich, I am poor. As I think about these things they do it quick while you still weak with fever at the magistrate's before you can ask questions. If this is true or not you must know for yourself.

Then you come to this island for your honeymoon and it's certain that the Lord put the thing on my shoul-

ders and that it is I must speak the truth to you. Still I hesitate.

I hear you young and handsome with a kind word for all, black, white, also colored. But I hear too that the girl is beautiful like her mother was beautiful, and you bewitch with her. She is in your blood and your bones. By night and by day. But you, an honorable man, know well that for marriage more is needed than all this. Which does not last. Old Mason bewitch so with her mother and look what happen to him. Sir I pray I am in time to warn you what to do.

Sir ask yourself how I can make up this story and for what reason. When I leave Jamaica I can read write and cypher a little. The good man in Barbados teach me more, he give me books, he tell me read the Bible every day and I pick up knowledge without effort. He is surprise how quick I am. Still I remain an ignorant man and I do not make up this story. I cannot. It is true.

I sit at my window and the words fly past me like birds—with God's help I catch some.

A week this letter take me. I cannot sleep at night thinking what to say. So quickly now I draw to a close and cease my task.

Still you don't believe me? Then ask that devil of a man Richard Mason three questions and make him answer you. Is your wife's mother shut away, a raging lunatic and worse besides? Dead or alive I do not know.

Was your wife's brother an idiot from birth, though God mercifully take him early on?

Is your wife herself going the same way as her mother and all knowing it?

Richard Mason is a sly man and he will tell you a lot of nancy stories, which is what we call lies here, about what happen at Coulibri and this and that. Don't listen. Make him answer— yes or no.

If he keep his mouth shut ask others for many think it shameful how that family treat you and your relatives.

I beg you sir come to see me for there is more that you should know. But my hand ache, my head ache and my heart is like a stone for the grief I bring you. Money is good but no money can pay for a crazy wife in your bed. Crazy and worse besides.

I lay down my pen with one last request. Come and see me quickly. Your obt servant. Daniel Cosway.

Ask the girl Amélie where I live. She knows, and she knows me. She belongs to this island.

I folded the letter carefully and put it into my pocket. I felt no surprise. It was as if I'd expected it, been waiting for it. For a time, long or short I don't know, I sat listening to the river. At last I stood up, the sun was hot now. I walked stiffly nor could I force myself to think. Then I passed an orchid with long sprays of golden-brown flowers. One of them touched my cheek and I remembered picking some for her one day. "They are like you," I told her. Now I stopped, broke a spray off and trampled it into the mud. This brought me to my senses. I leaned against a tree, sweating and trembling. "Far too hot today," I said aloud, "far too hot." When I came in sight of the house I began to walk silently. No one was about. The kitchen door was shut and the place looked deserted. I went up the steps and along the veranda and when I heard voices stopped behind the door which led into Antoinette's room. I could see it reflected in the looking-glass. She was in bed and the girl Amélie was weeping.

"Finish quickly," said Antoinette, "and go and tell Christophine I want to see her."

Amélie rested her hands on the broom handle. "Christophine is going," she said.

"Going?" repeated Antoinette.

"Yes, going," said Amélie. "Christophine don't like this sweet honeymoon house." Turning round she saw me and laughed loudly. "Your husban' he outside the door and he look like he see zombi. Must be he tired of the sweet honeymoon too."

Antoinette jumped out of bed and slapped her face.

"I hit you back white cockroach, I hit you back," said Amélie. And she did.

Antoinette gripped her hair. Amélie, whose teeth were bared, seemed to be trying to bite.

"Antoinette, for God's sake," I said from the doorway.

She swung round, very pale. Amélie buried her face in her hands and pretended to sob, but I could see her watching me through her fingers.

"Go away, child," I said.

"You call her child," said Antoinette. "She is older than the devil himself, and the devil is not more cruel."

"Send Christophine up," I said to Amélie.

"Yes master, yes master," she answered softly, dropping her eyes. But as soon as she was out of the room she began to sing:

The white cockroach she marry
The white cockroach she marry
The white cockroach she buy young
man
The white cockroach she marry.

Antoinette took a few steps forward. She walked unsteadily. I went to help her but she pushed me away, sat on the bed and with clenched teeth pulled at the sheet, then made a clicking sound of annoyance. She took a pair of scissors from the round table, cut through the hem and tore the sheet in half, then each half into strips.

The noise she made prevented me from hearing Christophine come in, but Antoinette heard her.

"You're not leaving?" she said.

"Yes," said Christophine.

"And what will become of me?" said Antoinette.

"Get up, girl, and dress yourself.

Woman must have spunks to live in this wicked world."

She had changed into a drab cotton dress and taken off her heavy gold earrings.

"I see enough trouble," she said. "I have right to my rest. I have my house that your mother give me so long ago and I have my garden and my son to work for me. A lazy boy but I made him work. Too besides the young master don't like me, and perhaps I don't like him so much. If I stay here I bring trouble and bone of contention in your house."

"If you are not happy here then go," said Antoinette.

Amélie came into the room with two jugs of hot water. She looked at me sideways and smiled.

Christophine said in a soft voice, "Amélie. Smile like that once more, just once more, and I mash your face like I mash plantain. You hear me? Answer me, girl."

"Yes, Christophine," Amélie said. She looked frightened.

"And too besides I give you bellyache like you never see bellyache. Perhaps you lie a long time with the bellyache I give you. Perhaps you don't get up again with the bellyache I give you. So keep quiet and decent. You hear me?"

"Yes, Christophine," Amélie said and crept out of the room.

"She worthless and good for nothing," said Christophine with contempt. "She creep and crawl like centipede."

She kissed Antoinette on the cheek. Then she looked at me, shook her head, and muttered in patois before she went out.

"Did you hear what the girl was singing?" Antoinette said.

"I don't always understand what they say or sing." Or anything else.

"It was a song about a white cockroach. That's me. That's what they call all of us who were here before their own people in Africa sold them to the slave traders. And I've heard English women call us white niggers. So between you I often wonder who I am and where is my country and where do I belong and why was I ever born at all. Will you go now please. I must dress like Christophine said."

After I had waited half an hour I knocked at her door. There was no answer so I asked Baptiste to bring me something to eat. He was sitting under the Seville orange tree at the end of the veranda. He served the food with such a mournful expression that I thought these people are very vulnerable. How old was I when I learned to hide what I felt? A very small boy. Six, five, even earlier. It was necessary, I was told, and that view I have always accepted. If these mountains challenge me, or Baptiste's face, or Antoinette's eyes, they are mistaken, melodramatic, unreal (England must be quite unreal and like a dream she said).

The rum punch I had drunk was very strong and after the meal was over I had a great wish to sleep. And why not? This is the time when everyone sleeps. I imagined the dogs the cats the cocks and hens all sleeping, even the water in the river running more slowly.

I woke up, thought at once of Antoinette and opened the door into her room, but she was sleeping too. Her back was towards me and she was quite still. I looked out of the window. The silence was disturbing, absolute. I would have welcomed the sound of a dog barking, a man sawing wood. Nothing. Silence. Heat. It was five minutes to three.

I went out following the path I could see from my window. It must have rained heavily during the night for the red clay was very muddy. I passed a sparse plantation of coffee trees, then straggly guava bushes. As I walked I remembered my father's face and his thin lips, my brother's round conceited eyes. They knew. And Richard the fool, he knew too. And the girl with her blank smiling face. They all knew.

I began to walk very quickly, then stopped because the light was different. A green light. I had reached the forest and you cannot mistake the forest. It is hostile. The path was overgrown but it was possible to follow it. I went on without looking at the tall trees on either side. Once I stepped over a fallen log swarming with white ants. How can one discover truth I thought and that thought led me nowhere. No one would tell me the truth. Not my father nor Richard Mason, certainly not the girl I had married. I stood still, so sure I was being watched that I looked over my shoulder. Nothing but the trees and the green light under the trees. A track was just visible and I went on, glancing from side to side and sometimes quickly behind me. This was why I stubbed my foot on a stone and nearly fell. The stone I had tripped on was not a boulder but part of a paved road. There had been a paved road through this forest. The track led to a large clear space. Here were the ruins of a stone house and round the ruins rose trees that had grown to an incredible height. At the back of the ruins a wild orange tree covered with fruit, the leaves a dark green. A beautiful place. And calm —so calm that it seemed foolish to think or plan. What had I to think about and how could I plan? Under the orange tree I noticed little bunches of flowers tied with grass.

I don't know how long it was before I began to feel chilly. The light had changed and the shadows were long. I had better get back before dark, I thought. Then I saw a little girl carrying a large basket on her head. I met her eyes and to my astonishment she screamed loudly, threw up her arms and ran. The basket fell off, I called after her, but she screamed again and ran faster. She sobbed as she ran, a small

frightened sound. Then she disappeared. I must be within a few minutes of the path I thought, but after I had walked for what seemed a long time I found that the undergrowth and creepers caught at my legs and the trees closed over my head. I decided to go back to the clearing and start again, with the same result. It was getting dark. It was useless to tell myself that I was not far from the house. I was lost and afraid among these enemy trees, so certain of danger that when I heard footsteps and a shout I did not answer. The footsteps and the voice came nearer. Then I shouted back. I did not recognize Baptiste at first. He was wearing blue cotton trousers pulled up above his knees and a broad ornamented belt round his slim waist. His machete was in his hand and the light caught the razor-sharp blue-white edge. He did not smile when he saw me.

"We look for you a long time," he said.

"I got lost."

He grunted in answer and led the way, walking in front of me very quickly and cutting off any branch or creeper that stopped us with an easy swing of his machete.

I said, "There was a road here once, where did it lead to?"

"No road," he said.

"But I saw it. A *pavé* road like the French made in the islands."

"No road."

"Who lived in that house?"

"They say a priest. Père Lilièvre. He lived here a long time ago."

"A child passed," I said. "She seemed very frightened when she saw me. Is there something wrong about the place?" He shrugged his shoulders.

"Is there a ghost, a zombi there?" I persisted.

"Don't know nothing about all that foolishness."

"There was a road here sometime."

"No road," he repeated obstinately.

It was nearly dark when we were

back on the red clay path. He walked more slowly, turned and smiled at me. It was as if he'd put his service mask on the savage reproachful face I had seen.

"You don't like the woods at night?"

He did not answer, but pointed to a light and said, "It's a long time I've been looking for you. Miss Antoinette frightened you come to harm."

When we reached the house I felt very weary.

"You look like you catch fever," he said.

"I've had that already."

"No limit to times you catch fever."

There was no one on the veranda and no sound from the house. We both stood in the road looking up, then he said, "I send the girl to you, master."

Hilda brought me a large bowl of soup and some fruit. I tried the door into Antoinette's room. It was bolted and there was no light. Hilda giggled. A nervous giggle.

I told her that I did not want anything to eat, to bring me the decanter of rum and a glass. I drank, then took up the book I had been reading, *The Glittering Coronet of Isles* it was called, and I turned to the chapter 'Obeah':

"A zombi is a dead person who seems to be alive or a living person who is dead. A zombi can also be the spirit of a place, usually malignant but sometimes to be propitiated with sacrifices or offerings of flowers and fruit." I thought at once of the bunches of flowers at the priest's ruined house. 'They cry out in the wind that is their voice, they rage in the sea that is their anger.'

"So I was told, but I have noticed that negroes as a rule refuse to discuss the black magic in which so many believe. Voodoo as it is called in Haiti— Obeah in some of the islands, another name in South America. They confuse matters by telling lies if pressed. The white people, sometimes credulous, pretend to dismiss the whole thing as nonsense. Cases of sudden or mysterious death are attributed to a poison known to the negroes which cannot be traced. It is further complicated by . . ."

I did not look up though I saw him at the window but rode on without thinking till I came to the rocks. People here call them Mounes Mors (The Dead Ones). Preston shied at them, they say horses always do. Then he stumbled badly, so I dismounted and walked along with the bridle over my arm. It was getting hot and I was tired when I reached the path to Christophine's two-roomed house, the roof shingled, not thatched. She was sitting on a box under her mango tree, smoking a white clay pipe and she called out, "It's you, Antoinette? Why you come up here so early?"

"I just wanted to see you," I said.

She helped me loosen Preston's girth and led him to a stream near by. He drank as if he were very thirsty, then shook himself and snorted. Water flew out of his nostrils. We left him cropping grass and went back to the mango tree. She sat on her box and pushed another towards me, but I knelt close to her touching a thin silver bangle that she always wore.

"You smell the same," I said.

"You come all this long way to tell me that?" she said. Her clothes smelled of clean cotton, starched and ironed. I had seen her so often standing knee deep in the river at Coulibri, her long skirt hitched up, washing her dresses and her white shifts, then beating them against the stones. Sometimes there would be other women all bringing their washing down on the stones again and again, a gay busy noise. At last they would spread the wet clothes in the sun, wipe their foreheads, start laughing and talking. She smelled too, of their smell, so warm and comforting to me (but he does not like it). The sky was dark blue through the dark green mango leaves, and I thought, "This is my place and this is where I belong and this is where I wish to stay." Then I thought, "What a beautiful tree, but it is too high up here for mangoes and it may never bear fruit," and I thought of lying alone in my bed with the soft silk cotton mattress and fine sheets, listening. At last I said, "Christophine, he does not love me, I think he hates me. He always sleeps in his dressing-room now and the servants know. If I get angry he is scornful and silent, sometimes he does not speak to me for hours and I cannot endure it any more, I cannot. What shall I do? He was not like that at first," I said.

Pink and red hibiscus grew in front of her door, she lit her pipe and did not answer.

"Answer me," I said. She puffed out a cloud of smoke.

"You ask me a hard thing, I tell you a hard thing, pack up and go."

"Go, go where? To some strange place where I shall never see him? No, I will not, then everyone, not only the servants, will laugh at me."

"It's not you they laugh at if you go, they laugh at him."

"I will not do that."

"Why you ask me, if when I answer you say no? Why you come up here if when I tell you the truth, you say no?"

"But there must be something else I can do."

She looked gloomy. "When man don't love you, more you try, more he hate you, man like that. If you love them they treat you bad, if you don't love them they after you night and day bothering your soul case out. I hear about you and your husband," she said.

"But I cannot go. He is my husband after all."

She spat over her shoulder. "All women, all colors, nothing but fools. Three children I have. One living in this world, each one a different father, but no husband, I thank my God. I keep my money. I don't give it to no worthless man."

"When must I go, where must I go?"

"But look me trouble, a rich white girl like you and more foolish than the rest. A man don't treat you good, pick up your skirt and walk out. Do it and he come after you."

"He will not come after me. And you must understand I am not rich now, I have no money of my own at all, everything I had belongs to him."

"What you tell me there?" she said sharply.

"That is English law."

"Law! The Mason boy fix it, that boy worse than Satan and he burn in Hell one of these fine nights. Listen to me now and I advise you what to do. Tell your husband you feeling sick, you want to visit your cousin Martinique. Ask him pretty for some of your own money, the man not bad-hearted, he give it. When you get away, stay away. Ask more. He give again and well satisfy. In the end he come to find out what you do, how you get on without him, and if he see you fat and happy he want you back. Men like that. Better not stay in that old house. Go from that house, I tell you."

"You think I must leave him?"

"You ask me so I answer."

"Yes," I said. "After all I could, but why should I go to Martinique? I wish to see England, I might be able to borrow money for that. Not from him but I know how I might get it. I must travel far, if I go."

I have been too unhappy, I thought, it cannot last, being so unhappy, it would kill you. I will be a different person when I live in England and different things will happen to me. . . . England, rosy pink in the geography book map, but on the page opposite the words are closely crowded, heavy looking. Exports, coal, iron, wool. Then imports and Character of Inhabitants. Names, Essex, Chelmsford on the Chelmer. The Yorkshire and Lincolnshire wolds. Wolds? Does that mean hills? How high? Half the height of ours, or not even that? Cool green leaves in the short cool summer. Summer. There are fields of corn like sugarcane fields, but gold color and not so tall. After summer the trees are bare, then winter and snow. White feathers falling? Torn pieces of paper falling? They say frost makes flower patterns on the window panes. I must know more than I know already. For I know that house where I will be cold and not belonging, the bed I shall lie in has red curtains and I have slept there many times before, long ago. How long ago? In that bed I will dream the end of my dream. But my dream had nothing to do with England and I must not think like this, I must remember about chandeliers and dancing, about swans and roses and snow. And snow.

"England," said Christophine, who was watching me. "You think there is such a place?"

"How can you ask that? You know there is."

"I never see the damn place, how I know?"

"You do not believe that there is a country called England?"

She blinked and answered quickly, "I don't say I don't *believe*, I say I don't *know*, I know what I see with my eyes and I never see it. Besides I ask myself is this place like they tell us? Some say one thing, some different, I hear it cold to freeze your bones and they thief your money, clever like the devil. You have money in your pocket, you look again and bam! No money. Why you want to go to this cold thief place? If there is this place at all, I never see it, that is one thing sure."

I stared at her, thinking, "but how can she know the best thing for me to do, this ignorant, obstinate old negro woman, who is not certain if there is such a place as England?" She knocked out her pipe and stared back at me, her eyes had no expression at all.

"Christophine," I said, "I may do as you advise. But not yet." (Now, I thought, I must say what I came to say.) "You knew what I wanted as soon as you saw me, and you certainly know now. Well, don't you?" I heard my voice getting high and thin.

"Hush up," she said. "If the man don't love you, I can't make him love you."

"Yes you can, I know you can. That is what I wish and that is why I came here. You can make people love or hate. Or . . . or die," I said.

She threw back her head and laughed loudly. (But she never laughs loudly and why is she laughing at all?)

"So you believe in that tim-tim story about obeah, you hear when you so high? All that foolishness and folly. Too besides, that is not for *béké*. Bad, bad trouble come when *béké* meddle with that."

"You must," I said. "You must."

"Hush up. Jo-jo my son coming to see me, if he catch you crying, he tell everybody."

"I will be quiet, I will not cry. But Christophine, if he, my husband, could come to me one night. Once more. I would make him love me."

"No *doudou*. No."

"Yes, Christophine."

"You talk foolishness. Even if I can make him come to your bed, I cannot make him love you. Afterward he hate you."

"No. And what do I care if he does? He hates me now. I hear him every night walking up and down the veranda. Up and down. When he passes my door he says, 'Goodnight, Bertha.' He never calls me Antoinette now. He has found out it was my mother's name. 'I hope you will sleep well, Bertha'— it cannot be worse," I said. "That one night he came I might sleep afterwards. I sleep so badly now. And I dream."

"No, I don't meddle with that for you."

Then I beat my fist on a stone, forcing myself to speak calmly.

"Going away to Martinique or England or anywhere else, that is the lie. He would never give me any money to go away and he would be furious if I asked him. There would be a scandal if I left him and he hates scandal. Even if I got away (and how?) he would force me back. So would Richard. So would everybody else. Running away from him, from this island, is the lie. What reason could I give for going and who would believe me?"

When she bent her head she looked old and I thought, "Oh Christophine, do not grow old. You are the only friend I have, do not go away from me into being old."

"Your husband certainly love money," she said. "That is no lie. Money have pretty face for everybody, but for that man money pretty like pretty self, he can't see nothing else."

"Help me then."

"Listen *doudou ché*. Plenty people fasten bad words on you and on your mother. I know it. I know who is talking and what they say. The man not a bad man, even if he love money, but he hear so many stories he don't know what to believe. That is why he keep away. I put no trust in none of those people round you. Not here, not in Jamaica."

"Not Aunt Cora?"

"Your aunty old woman now, she turn her face to the wall."

"*How do you know?*" I said. For that is what happened.

When I passed her room, I heard her quarreling with Richard and I knew it was about my marriage. "It's disgraceful," she said. "It's shameful. You are handing over everything the child owns to a perfect stranger. Your father would never have allowed it. She should be protected, legally. A settlement can be arranged and it should be arranged. That was his intention."

"You are talking about an honorable gentleman, not a rascal," Richard said.

"I am not in a position to make conditions, as you know very well. She is damn lucky to get him, all things considered. Why should I insist on a lawyer's settlement when I trust him? I would trust him with my life," he went on in an affected voice.

"You are trusting him with her life, not yours," she said.

He told her for God's sake shut up you old fool and banged the door when he left. So angry that he did not notice me standing in the passage. She was sitting up in bed when I went into her room. "Halfwit that the boy is, or pretends to be. I do not like what I have seen of this honorable gentleman. Stiff. Hard as a board and stupid as a foot, in my opinion, except where his own interests are concerned."

She was very pale and shaking all over, so I gave her the smelling salts on the dressing-table. They were in a red glass bottle with a gilt top. She put the bottle to her nose but her hand dropped as though she were too tired to hold it steady. Then she turned away from the window, the sky, the looking-glass, the pretty things on the dressing-table. The red and gilt bottle fell to the floor. She turned her face to the wall. "The Lord has forsaken us," she said, and shut her eyes. She did not speak again, and after a while I thought she was asleep. She was too ill to come to my wedding and I went to say good-bye, I was excited and happy thinking now it is my honeymoon. I kissed her and she gave me a little silk bag. "My rings. Two are valuable. Don't show it to him. Hide it away. Promise me."

I promised, but when I opened it, one of the rings was plain gold. I thought I might sell another yesterday but who will buy what I have to sell here? . . .

Christophine was saying, "Your aunty too old and sick, and that Mason boy worthless. Have spunks and do battle for yourself. Speak to your husband calm and cool, tell him about your

mother and all what happened at Coulibri and why she get sick and what
they do to her. Don't bawl at the man
and don't make crazy faces. Don't cry
either. Crying no good with him. Speak
nice and make him understand."

"I have tried," I said, "but he does
not believe me. It is too late for that
now" (it is always too late for truth, I
thought). "I will try again if you will
do what I ask. Oh Christophine, I am
so afraid," I said, "I do not know why,
but so afraid. All the time. Help me."

She said something I did not hear.
Then she took a sharp stick and drew
lines and circles on the earth under the
tree, then rubbed them out with her
foot.

"If you talk to him first I do what you
ask me."

"Now?"

"Yes," she said. "Now look at me.
Look in my eyes."

I was giddy when I stood up, and
she went into the house muttering and
came out with a cup of coffee.

"Good shot of white rum in that,"
she said. "Your face like dead woman
and your eyes red like *soucriant*. Keep
yourself quiet—look, Jo-jo coming, he
talk to everybody about what he hear.
Nothing but leaky calabash that boy."

When I had drunk the coffee I began
to laugh. "I have been so unhappy for
nothing, nothing," I said.

Her son was carrying a large basket
on his head. I watched his strong brown
legs swinging along the path so easily.
He seemed surprised and inquisitive
when he saw me, but he asked politely
in patois, was I well, was the master
in good health?

"Yes, Jo-jo, thank you, we are both
well."

Christophine helped him with the
basket, then she brought out the bottle
of white rum and poured out half a
tumblerful. He swallowed it quickly.
Then she filled the glass with water
and he drank that like they do.

She said in English, "The mistress is

going, her horse at the back there. Saddle him up."

I followed her into the house. There
was a wooden table in the outer room,
a bench and two broken-down chairs.
Her bedroom was large and dark. She
still had her bright patchwork counterpane, the palm leaf from Palm Sunday
and the prayer for a happy death. But
after I noticed a heap of chicken feathers
in one corner, I did not look round any
more.

"So already you frightened eh?" And
when I saw her expression I took my
purse from my pocket and threw it on
the bed.

"You don't have to give me money.
I do this foolishness because you beg
me—not for money."

"Is it foolishness?" I said, whispering
and she laughed again, but softly.

"If *béké* say it foolishness, then it
foolishness. *Béké* clever like the devil.
More clever than God. Ain't so? Now
listen and I will tell you what to do.

When we came out into the sunlight,
Jo-jo was holding Preston near a big
stone. I stood on it and mounted.

"Good-bye Christophine; good-bye
Jo-jo."

"Good-bye, mistress."

"You will come and see me very
soon, Christophine?"

"Yes, I will come."

I looked back at the end of the path.
She was talking to Jo-jo and he seemed
curious and amused. Nearby a cock
crew and I thought, "That is for betrayal, but who is the traitor?" She did
not want to do this. I forced her with
my ugly money. And what does anyone know about traitors, or why Judas
did what he did?

I can remember every second of that
morning, if I shut my eyes I can see
the deep blue color of the sky and the
mango leaves, the pink and red hibiscus,
the yellow handkerchief she wore round
her head, tied in the Martinique fashion
with the sharp points in front, but now
I see everything still, fixed for ever like

the colors in a stained-glass window. Only the clouds move. It was wrapped in a leaf, what she had given me, and I felt it cool and smooth against my skin.

"The mistress pay a visit," Baptiste told me when he brought my coffee that morning. "She will come back tonight or tomorrow. She make up her mind in a hurry and she has gone."

In the afternoon Amélie brought me a second letter.

Why you don't answer. You don't believe me? Then ask someone else— everybody in Spanish Town know. Why you think they bring you to this place? You want me to come to your house and bawl out your business before everybody? You come to me or I come—

At this point I stopped reading. The child Hilda came into the room and I asked her, "Is Amélie here?"

"Yes, master."

"Tell her I wish to speak to her."

"Yes, master."

She put her hand over her mouth as if to stifle laughter, but her eyes, which were the blackest I had ever seen, so black that it was impossible to distinguish the pupils from the iris, were alarmed and bewildered.

I sat on the veranda with my back to the sea and it was as if I had done it all my life. I could not imagine different weather or a different sky. I knew the shape of the mountains as well as I knew the shape of the two brown jugs filled with white sweet-scented flowers on the wooden table. I knew that the girl would be wearing a white dress. Brown and white she would be, her curls, her white girl's hair she called it, half covered with a red handkerchief, her feet bare. There would be the sky and the mountains, the flowers and the girl and the feeling that all this was a

nightmare, the faint consoling hope that I might wake up.

She leaned lightly against the veranda post, indifferently graceful, just respectful enough, and waited.

"Was this letter given to you?" I asked.

"No, master. Hilda take it."

"And is this man who writes a friend of yours?"

"Not my friend," she said.

"But he knows you—or says he does."

"Oh yes, I know Daniel."

"Very well then. Will you tell him that his letters annoy me, and that he'd better not write again for his own sake. If he brings a letter give it back to him. Understand?"

"Yes, master. I understand."

Still leaning against the post she smiled at me, and I felt that at any moment her smile would become loud laughter. It was to stop this that I went on, "Why does he write to me?"

She answered innocently, "He don't tell you that? He write you two letters and he don't say why he is writing? If you don't know then I don't know."

"But you know him?" I said. "Is his name Cosway?"

"Some people say yes, some people say no. That's what he calls himself."

She added thoughtfully that Daniel was a very superior man, always reading the Bible and that he lived like white people. I tried to find out what she meant by this, and she explained that he had a house like white people, with one room only for sitting in. That he had two pictures on the wall of his father and his mother.

"White people?"

"Oh no, colored."

"But he told me in his first letter that his father was a white man."

She shrugged her shoulders. "All that too long ago for me." It was easy to see her contempt for long ago. "I tell him what you say, master." Then she added, "Why you don't go and see him? It is much better. Daniel is a bad man and he will come here and make trouble for you. It's better he don't come. They say one time he was a preacher in Barbados, he talk like a preacher, and he have a brother in Jamaica in Spanish Town, Mr. Alexander. Very wealthy man. He own three rum shops and two dry goods stores." She flicked a look at me as sharp as a knife. "I hear one time that Miss Antoinette and his son Mr. Sandi get married, but that all foolishness. Miss Antoinette a white girl with a lot of money, she won't marry with a colored man even though he don't look like a colored man. You ask Miss Antoinette, she tell you."

Like Hilda she put her hand over her mouth as though she could not stop herself from laughing and walked away.

Then turned and said in a very low voice, "I am sorry for you."

"What did you say?"

"I don't say nothing, master."

A large table covered with a red fringed cloth made the small room seem hotter; the only window was shut.

"I put your chair near the door," Daniel said, "a breeze come in from underneath." But there was no breeze, not a breath of air, this place was lower down the mountain almost at sea-level.

"When I hear you coming I take a good shot of rum, and then I take a glass of water to cool me down, but it don't cool me down, it run out of my eyes in tears and lamentations. Why don't you give me an answer when I write to you the first time?" He went on talking, his eyes fixed on a framed text hanging on the dirty white wall, "Vengeance is Mine."

"You take too long, Lord," he told it. "I hurry you up a bit." Then he wiped his thin yellow face and blew his nose on a corner of the tablecloth.

"They call me Daniel," he said, still not looking at me, "but my name is Esau. All I get is curses and get-outs from that damn devil my father. My father old Cosway, with his white mar-

ble tablet in the English church at Spanish Town for all to see. It have a crest on it and a motto in Latin and words in big black letters. I never know such lies. I hope that stone tie round his neck and drag him down to Hell in the end. 'Pious,' they write up. 'Beloved by all.' Not a word about the people he buy and sell like cattle. 'Merciful to the weak,' they write up. Mercy! The man have a heart like stone. Sometimes when he get sick of a woman which is quickly, he free her like he free my mother, even he give her a hut and a bit of land for herself (a garden some call that), but it is no mercy, it's for wicked pride he do it. I never put my eyes on a man haughty and proud like that—he walk like he own the earth. 'I don't give a damn,' he says. Let him wait. . . . I can still see that tablet before my eyes because I go to look at it often. I know by heart all the lies they tell—no one to stand up and say, Why you write lies in the church? . . . I tell you this so you can know what sort of people you mix up with. The heart know its own bitterness but to keep it lock up all the time, that is hard. I remember it like yesterday the morning he put a curse on me. Sixteen years old I was and anxious. I start very early. I walk all the way to Coulibri—five six hours it take. He don't refuse to see me; he receive me very cool and calm and first thing he tell me is I'm always pestering him for money. This because sometimes I ask help to buy a pair of shoes and such. Not to go barefoot like a nigger. Which I am not. He look at me like I was dirt and I get angry too. 'I have my rights after all,' I tell him and you know what he do? He laugh in my face. When he finished laughing he call me what's-your-name. 'I can't remember all their names —it's too much to expect of me,' he says, talking to himself. Very old he look in the bright sunshine that morning. 'It's you yourself call me Daniel,' I tell him. 'I'm no slave like my mother was.'

" 'Your mother was a sly-boots if ever

there was one,' he says, 'and I'm not a fool. However the woman's dead and that's enough. But if there's one drop of my blood in your spindly carcass I'll eat my hat.' By this time my own blood at boiling point, I tell you, so I bawl back at him, 'Eat it then. Eat it. You haven't much time. Not much time either to kiss and love your new wife. She too young for you.' 'Great God!' he said and his face go red and then a kind of grey color. He try to get up but he falls back in his chair. He have a big silver inkstand on his desk, he throw it at my head and he curse me, but I duck and the inkstand hit the door. I have to laugh but I go off quick. He send me some money—not a word, only the money. It's the last time I see him."

Daniel breathed deeply and wiped his face again and offered me some rum. When I thanked him and shook my head he poured himself half a glassful and swallowed it.

"All that long time ago," he said.

"Why did you wish to see me, Daniel?"

The last drink seemed to have sobered him. He looked at me directly and spoke more naturally.

"I insist because I have this to say. When you ask if what I tell you is true, you will ask though you don't like me, I see that; but you know well my letter was no lie. Take care who you talk to. Many people like to say things behind your back, to your face they get frightened, or they don't want to mix up. The magistrate now, he know a lot, but his wife very friendly with the Mason family and she stop him if she can. Then there is my half brother Alexander, colored like me but not unlucky like me, he will want to tell you all sorts of lies. He was the old man's favorite and he prosper right from the start. Yes, Alexander is a rich man now but he keep quiet about it. Because he prosper he is two-faced, he won't speak against white people. There is that woman up

at your house, Christophine. She is the worst. She have to leave Jamaica because she go to jail: you know that?"

"Why was she sent to jail? What did she do?"

His eyes slid away from mine. "I tell you I leave Spanish Town, I don't know all that happen. It's something very bad. She is obeah woman and they catch her. I don't believe in all that devil business but many believe. Christophine is a bad woman and she will lie to you worse than your wife. Your own wife she talks sweet talk and she lies."

The black and gilt clock on a shelf struck four.

I must go. I must get away from his yellow sweating face and his hateful little room. I sat still, numb, staring at him.

"You like my clock?" said Daniel. "I work hard to buy it. But it's to please myself. I don't have to please no woman. Buy me this and buy me that—demons incarnate in my opinion. Alexander now, he can't keep away from them, and in the end he marry a very fair-colored girl, very respectable family. His son Sandi is like a white man, but more handsome than any white man, and received by many white people they say. Your wife know Sandi since long time. Ask her and she tell you. But not everything I think." He laughed. "Oh no, not everything. I see them when they think nobody see them. I see her when she . . . You going eh?" He darted to the doorway.

"No you don't go before I tell you the last thing. You want me to shut my mouth about what I know. She start with Sandi. They fool you well about that girl. She look you straight in the eye and talk sweet talk—and it's lies she tell you. Lies. Her mother was so. They say she worse than her mother, and she hardly more than a child. Must be you deaf you don't hear people laughing when you marry her. Don't waste your anger on me, sir. It's not I fool you, it's I wish to open your eyes. . . .

A tall fine English gentleman like you, you don't want to touch a little yellow rat like me eh? Besides I understand well. You believe me, but you want to do everything quiet like the English can. All right. But if I keep my mouth shut it seems to me you owe me something. What is five hundred pounds to you? To me it's my life."

Now disgust was rising in me like sickness. Disgust and rage.

"All right," he yelled, and moved away from the door. "Go then . . . get out. Now it's me to say it. Get out. Get out. And if I don't have the money I want you will see what I can do.

"Give my love to your wife—my sister," he called after me venomously. "You are not the first to kiss her pretty face. Pretty face, soft skin, pretty color —not yellow like me. But my sister just the same . . ."

At the end of the path out of sight and sound of the house I stopped. The world was given up to heat and to flies, the light was dazzling after his little dark room. A black and white goat tethered near by was staring at me and for what seemed minutes I stared back into its slanting yellow-green eyes. Then I walked to the tree where I'd left my horse and rode away as quickly as I could.

The telescope was pushed to one side of the table making room for a decanter half full of rum and two glasses on a tarnished silver tray. I listened to the ceaseless night noises outside, and watched the procession of small moths and beetles fly into the candle flames, then poured out a drink of rum and swallowed. At once the night noises drew away, became distant, bearable, even pleasant.

"Will you listen to me for God's sake," Antoinette said. She had said this before and I had not answered, now I told her, "Of course. I'd be the brute you doubtless think me if I did not do that."

"Why do you hate me?" she said.

"I do not hate you, I am most distressed about you, I am distraught," I said. But this was untrue, I was not distraught, I was calm, it was the first time I had felt calm or self-possessed for many a long day.

She was wearing the white dress I had admired, but it had slipped untidily over one shoulder and seemed too large for her. I watched her holding her left wrist with her right hand, an annoying habit.

"Then why do you never come near me?" she said. "Or kiss me, or talk to me. Why do you think I can bear it, what reason have you for treating me like that? Have you any reason?"

"Yes," I said, "I have a reason," and added very softly, "My God."

"You are always calling on God," she said. "Do you believe in God?"

"Of course, of course I believe in the power and wisdom of my creator."

She raised her eyebrows and the corners of her mouth turned down in a questioning mocking way. For a moment she looked very much like Amélie. Perhaps they are related, I thought. It's possible, it's even probable in this damned place.

"And you," I said. "Do you believe in God?"

"It doesn't matter," she answered calmly, "what I believe or you believe, because we can do nothing about it, we are like these." She flicked a dead moth off the table. "But I asked you a question, you remember. Will you answer that?"

I drank again and my brain was cold and clear.

"Very well, but question for question. Is your mother alive?"

"No, she is dead, she died."

"When?"

"Not long ago."

"Then why did you tell me that she died when you were a child?"

"Because they told me to say so and because it is true. She did die when I was a child. There are always two deaths, the real one and the one people know about."

"Two at least," I said, "for the fortunate." We were silent for a moment, then I went on, "I had a letter from a man who calls himself Daniel Cosway."

"He has no right to that name," she said quickly. "His real name, if he has one, is Daniel Boyd. He hates all white people, but he hates me the most. He tells lies about us and he is sure that you will believe him and not listen to the other side."

"Is there another side?" I said.

"There is always the other side, always."

"After his second letter, which was threatening, I thought it best to go and see him."

"You saw him," she said. "I know what he told you. That my mother was mad and an infamous woman and that my little brother who died was born a cretin, an idiot, and that I am a mad girl too. That is what he told you, isn't it?"

"Yes, that was his story, and is any of it true?" I said, cold and calm.

One of the candles flared up and I saw the hollows under her eyes, her drooping mouth, her thin, strained face.

"We won't talk about it now," I said. "Rest tonight."

"But we must talk about it." Her voice was high and shrill.

"Only if you promise to be reasonable."

But this is not the place or the time, I thought, not in this long dark veranda with the candles burning low and the watching, listening night outside. "Not tonight," I said again. "Some other time."

"I might never be able to tell you in any other place or at any other time. No other time, now. You frightened?" she said, imitating a negro's voice, singing and insolent.

Then I saw her shiver and remembered that she had been wearing a yellow silk shawl. I got up (my brain so clear and cold, my body so weighted and heavy). The shawl was on a chair in the next room, there were candles on the sideboard and I brought them on to the veranda, lit two, and put the shawl around her shoulders. "But why not tell me tomorrow, in the daylight?"

"You have no right," she said fiercely. "You have no right to ask questions about my mother and then refuse to listen to my answer."

"Of course I will listen, of course we can talk now, if that's what you wish." But the feeling of something unknown and hostile was very strong. "I feel very much a stranger here," I said. "I feel that this place is my enemy and on your side."

"You are quite mistaken," she said. "It is not for you and not for me. It has nothing to do with either of us. That is why you are afraid of it, because it is something else. I found that out long ago when I was a child. I loved it because I had nothing else to love, but it is as indifferent as this God you call on so often."

"We can talk here or anywhere else," I said, "just as you wish."

The decanter of rum was nearly empty so I went back into the dining-room, and brought out another bottle of rum. She had eaten nothing and refused wine, now she poured herself a drink, touched it with her lips then put it down again.

"You want to know about my mother, I will tell you about her, the truth, not lies." Then she was silent for so long that I said gently, "I know that after your father died, she was very lonely and unhappy."

"And very poor," she said. "Don't forget that. For five years. Isn't it quick to say. And isn't it long to live. And lonely. She was so lonely that she grew away from other people. That happens. It happened to me too but it was easier for me because I hardly remembered anything else. For her it was strange and frightening. And then she was so lovely. I used to think that every time she looked in the glass she must have hoped and pretended. I pretended too. Different things of course. You can pretend for a long time, but one day it all falls away and you are alone. We were alone in the most beautiful place in the world, it is not possible that there can be anywhere else so beautiful as Coulibri. The sea was not far off but we never heard it, we always heard the river. No sea. It was an old-time house and once there was an avenue of royal palms but a lot of them had fallen and others had been cut down and the ones that were left looked lost. Lost trees. Then they poisoned her horse and she could not ride about any more. She worked in the garden even when the sun was very hot and they'd say 'You go in now, mistress.' "

"And who were they?"

"Christophine was with us, and Godfrey the old gardener stayed, and a boy, I forget his name. Oh yes," she laughed. "His name was Disastrous because his godmother thought it such a pretty word. The parson said, 'I cannot christen this child Disastrous, he must have another name,' so his name was Disastrous Thomas, we called him Sass. It was Christophine who brought our food from the village and persuaded some girls to help her sweep and wash clothes. We would have died, my mother always said, if she had not stayed with us. Many died in those days, both white and black, especially the older people, but no one speaks of those days now. They are forgotten, except the lies. Lies are never forgotten, they go on and they grow."

"And you," I said. "What about you?"

"I was never sad in the morning," she said, "and every day was a fresh day for me. I remember the taste of milk and bread and the sound of the grandfather clock ticking slowly and the first time I had my hair tied with string because there was no ribbon left and no money to buy any. All the flowers in the world were in our garden and sometimes when I was thirsty I licked raindrops from the Jasmine leaves after a shower. If I could make you see it, because they destroyed it and it is only here now." She struck her forehead. "One of the best things was a curved flight of shallow steps that went down from the *glacis* to the mounting stone, the handrail was ornamented iron."

"Wrought iron," I said.

"Yes, wrought iron, and at the end of the last step it was curved like a question mark and when I put my hand on it, the iron was warm and I was comforted."

"But you said you were always happy."

"No, I said I was always happy in the morning, not always in the afternoon and never after sunset, for after sunset the house was haunted, some places are. Then there was the day when she saw I was growing up like a white nigger and she was ashamed of me, it was after that day that everything changed. Yes, it was my fault, it was my fault that she started to plan and work in a frenzy, in a fever to change our lives. Then people came to see us again and though I still hated them and was afraid of their cool, teasing eyes, I learned to hide it."

"No," I said.

"Why no?"

"You have never learned to hide it," I said.

"I learned to try," said Antoinette. Not very well, I thought.

"And there was that night when they destroyed it." She lay back in the chair, very pale. I poured some rum out and offered it to her, but she pushed the glass away so roughly that it spilled over her dress. "There is nothing left now. They trampled on it. It was a sacred place. It was sacred to the sun!" I began to wonder how much of all this was true, how much imagined, distorted. Certainly many of the old estate houses were burned. You saw ruins all over the place.

As if she'd guessed my thoughts she went on calmly, "But I was telling you about my mother. Afterwards I had fever. I was at Aunt Cora's house in Spanish Town. I heard screams and then someone laughing very loud. Next morning Aunt Cora told me that my mother was ill and had gone to the country. This did not seem strange to me for she was part of Coulibri, and if Coulibri had been destroyed and gone out of my life, it seemed natural that she should go too. I was ill for a long time. My head was bandaged because someone had thrown a stone at me. Aunt Cora told me that it was healing up and that it wouldn't spoil me on my wedding day. But I think it did spoil me for my wedding day and all the other days and nights."

I said, "Antoinette, your nights are not spoiled, or your days, put the sad things away. Don't think about them and nothing will be spoiled, I promise you."

But my heart was heavy as lead.

"Pierre died," she went on as if she had not heard me, "and my mother hated Mr. Mason. She would not let him go near her or touch her. She said she would kill him, she tried to, I think. So he bought her a house and hired a colored man and woman to look after her. For a while he was sad but he often left Jamaica and spent a lot of time in Trinidad. He almost forgot her."

"And you forgot her too," I could not help saying.

"I am not a forgetting person," said Antoinette. "But she—she didn't want me. She pushed me away and cried when I went to see her. They told me I made her worse. People talked about her, they would not leave her alone, they would be talking about her and stop if they saw me. One day I made up my mind to go to her, by myself. Before I reached her house I heard her crying. I thought I will kill anyone who is hurting my mother. I dismounted and ran quickly on to the veranda where I could look into the room. I remember the dress she was wearing—an evening dress cut very low, and she was barefooted. There was a fat black man with a glass of rum in his hand. He said, "Drink it and you will forget." She drank it without stopping. He poured her some more and she took the glass and laughed and threw it over her shoulder. It smashed to pieces. 'Clean it up,' the man said, 'or she'll walk in it.'

" 'If she walk in it a damn good thing,' the woman said. 'Perhaps she keep quiet then.' However she brought a pan and brush and swept up the broken glass. All this I saw. My mother did not look at them. She walked up and down and said, 'But this is a very pleasant surprise, Mr. Luttrell. Godfrey, take Mr. Luttrell's horse.' Then she seemed to grow tired and sat down on the rocking chair. I saw the man lift her up out of the chair and kiss her. I saw his mouth fasten on hers and she went all soft and limp in his arms and he laughed. The woman laughed too, but she was angry. When I saw that I ran away. Christophine was waiting for me when I came back crying. 'What you want to go up there for?' she said, and I said, 'You shut up devil, damned black devil from Hell.' Christophine said, 'Aie Aie Aie! Look me trouble, look me cross!' "

After a long time I heard her say as if she were talking to herself, "I have said all I want to say. I have tried to make you understand. But nothing has changed." She laughed.

"Don't laugh like that, Bertha."

"My name is not Bertha; why do you call me Bertha?"

"Because it is a name I'm particularly fond of. I think of you as Bertha."

"It doesn't matter," she said.

I said, "When you went off this morning where did you go?"

"I went to see Christophine," she said. "I will tell you anything you wish to know, but in a few words because words are no use, I know that now."

"Why did you go to see her?"

"I went to ask her to do something for me."

"And did she do it?"

"Yes." Another long pause.

"You wanted to ask her advice, was that it?"

She did not answer.

"What did she say?"

"She said that I ought to go away—to leave you."

"Oh did she?" I said, surprised.

"Yes, that was her advice."

"I want to do the best for both of us," I said. "So much of what you tell me is strange, different from what I was led to expect. Don't you feel that perhaps Christophine is right? That if you went away from this place or I went away—exactly as you wish of course—for a time, it might be the wisest thing we could do?" Then I said sharply, "Bertha, are you asleep, are you ill, why don't you answer me?" I got up, went over to her chair and took her cold hands in mine. "We've been sitting here long enough, it is very late."

"You go," she said. "I wish to stay here in the dark . . . where I belong," she added.

"Oh nonsense," I said. I put my arms round her to help her up, I kissed her, but she drew away.

"Your mouth is colder than my hands," she said. I tried to laugh. In the bedroom, I closed the shutters. "Sleep now, we will talk things over tomorrow."

"Yes," she said, "of course, but will you come in and say good night to me?"

"Certainly I will, my dear Bertha."

"Not Bertha tonight," she said.

"Of course, on this of all nights, you must be Bertha."

"As you wish," she said.

As I stepped into her room I noticed the white powder strewn on the floor. That was the first thing I asked her—about the powder. I asked what it was. She said it was to keep cockroaches away.

"Haven't you noticed that there are no cockroaches in this house and no centipedes? If you knew how horrible these things can be." She had lit all the candles and the room was full of shadows. There were six on the dressing-table and three on the table near her bed. The light changed her. I had never seen her look so gay or so beautiful. She poured wine into two glasses and handed me one but I swear it was before I drank that I longed to bury my face in her hair as I used to do. I said, "We are letting ghosts trouble us. Why shouldn't we be happy?" She said, "Christophine knows about ghosts too, but that is not what she calls them." She need not have done what she did to me. I will always swear that, she need not have done it. When she handed me the glass she was smiling. I remember saying in a voice that was not like my own that it was too light. I remember putting out the candles on the table near the bed and that is all I remember. All I will remember of the night.

I woke in the dark after dreaming that I was buried alive, and when I was awake the feeling of suffocation persisted. Something was lying across my mouth; hair with a sweet heavy smell. I threw it off but still I could not breathe. I shut my eyes and lay without moving for a few seconds. When I opened them I saw the candles burnt down on that abominable dressing-table, then I knew where I was. The door on to the veranda was open and the breeze was so cold that I knew it must be very early in the morning, before dawn. I was cold too, deathly cold and sick and in pain. I got out of bed without looking at her, staggering into my dressing-room and saw myself in the glass. I turned away at once. I could not vomit. I only retched painfully.

I thought, I have been poisoned. But it was a dull thought, like a child spelling out the letters of a word which he cannot read, and which if he could would have no meaning or context. I was too giddy to stand and fell backwards on to the bed, looking at the blanket which was of a peculiar shade of yellow. After looking at it for some time I was able to go over to the window and vomit. It seemed like hours before this stopped. I would lean up against the wall and wipe my face, then the retching and sickness would start again. When it was over I lay on the bed too weak to move.

I have never made a greater effort in my life than I made then. I longed to lie there and sleep but forced myself up. I was weak and giddy but no longer sick or in pain. I put on my dressing-gown and splashed water on my face, then I opened the door into her room.

The cold light was on her and I looked at the sad droop of her lips, the frown between her thick eyebrows, deep as if it had been cut with a knife. As I looked she moved and flung her arm out. I thought coldly, yes, very beautiful, the thin wrist, the sweet swell of the forearm, the rounded elbow, the curve of her shoulder into her upper arm. All present, all correct. As I watched, hating, her face grew smooth and very young again, she even seemed to smile. A trick of the light perhaps. What else?

She may wake at any moment, I told myself. I must be quick. Her torn shift was on the floor, I drew the sheet over her gently as if I covered a dead girl. One of the glasses was empty, she had drained hers. There was some wine left in the other which was on the dressing-table. I dipped my finger into it and tasted it. It was bitter. I didn't look at her again, but holding the glass went on to the veranda. Hilda was there with a broom in her hand. I put my finger to my lips and she looked at me with huge eyes, then imitated me, putting her own finger to her lips.

As soon as I had dressed and got out of the house I began to run.

I do not remember that day clearly, where I ran or how I fell or wept or

lay exhausted. But I found myself at last near the ruined house and the wild orange tree. Here with my head in my arms I must have slept and when I woke it was getting late and the wind was chilly. I got up and found my way back to the path which led to the house. I knew how to avoid every creeper, and I never stumbled once. I went to my dressing-room and if I passed anyone I did not see them and if they spoke I did not hear them.

There was a tray on the table with a jug of water, a glass and some brown fish cakes. I drank almost all of the water, for I was very thirsty, but I did not touch the food. I sat on the bed waiting, for I knew Amélie would come, and I knew what she would say: "I am sorry for you."

She came soundlessly on bare feet. "I get you something to eat," she said. She brought cold chicken, bread, fruit and a bottle of wine, and I drank a glass without speaking, then another. She cut some of the food up and sat beside me and fed me as if I were a child. Her arm behind my head was warm but the outside when I touched it was cool, almost cold. I looked into her lovely meaningless face, sat up and pushed the plate away. Then she said, "I am sorry for you."

"You've told me so before, Amélie. Is that the only song you know?"

There was a spark of gaiety in her eyes, but when I laughed she put her hand over my mouth apprehensively. I pulled her down beside me and we were both laughing. That is what I remember most about that encounter. She was so gay, so natural and something of this gaiety she must have given to me, for I had not one moment of remorse. Nor was I anxious to know what was happening behind the thin partition which divided us from my wife's bedroom.

In the morning, of course, I felt differently.

Another complication. Impossible. And her skin was darker, her lips thicker than I had thought.

She was sleeping very soundly and quietly but there was awareness in her eyes when she opened them, and after a moment suppressed laughter. I felt satisfied and peaceful, but not gay as she did, no, by God, not gay. I had no wish to touch her and she knew it, for she got up at once and began to dress.

"A very graceful dress," I said and she showed me the many ways it could be worn, trailing on the floor, lifted to show a lace petticoat, or hitched up far above the knee.

I told her that I was leaving the island soon but that before I left I wanted to give her a present. It was a large present but she took it with no thanks and no expression on her face. When I asked her what she meant to do she said, "It's long time I know what I want to do and I know I don't get it here."

"You are beautiful enough to get anything you want," I said.

"Yes," she agreed simply. "But not here."

She wanted, it seemed, to join her sister who was a dressmaker in Demerara, but she would not stay in Demerara, she said. She wanted to go to Rio. There were rich men in Rio.

"And when will you start all this?" I said, amused.

"I start now." She would catch one of the fishing boats at Massacre and get into town.

I laughed and teased her. She was running away from the old woman Christophine, I said.

She was unsmiling when she answered, "I have malice to no one but I don't stay here."

I asked her how she would get to Massacre. "I don't want no horse or mule," she said. "My legs strong enough to carry me."

As she was going I could not resist saying, half longing, half triumphant, "Well, Amélie, are you still sorry for me?"

"Yes," she said, "I am sorry for you. But I find it in my heart to be sorry for her too."

She shut the door gently. I lay and listened for the sound I knew I should hear, the horse's hoofs as my wife left the house.

I turned over and slept till Baptiste woke me with coffee. His face was gloomy.

"The cook is leaving," he announced.

"Why?"

He shrugged his shoulders and spread his hands open.

I got up, looked out of the window and saw her stride out of the kitchen, a strapping woman. She couldn't speak English, or said she couldn't. I forgot this when I said, "I must talk to her. What is the huge bundle on her head?"

"Her mattress," said Baptiste. "She will come back for the rest. No good to talk to her. She won't stay in this house."

I laughed.

"Are you leaving too?"

"No," said Baptiste. "I am overseer here."

I noticed that he did not call me "sir" or "master."

"And the litle girl, Hilda?"

"Hilda will do as I tell her. Hilda will stay."

"Capital," I said. "Then why are you looking so anxious? Your mistress will be back soon."

He shrugged again and muttered, but whether he was talking about my morals or the extra work he would have to do I couldn't tell, for he muttered in patois.

I told him to sling one of the veranda hammocks under the cedar trees and there I spent the rest of that day. Baptiste provided meals, but he seldom smiled and never spoke except to answer a question. My wife did not return. Yet I was not lonely or unhappy. Sun, sleep and the cool water of the river were enough. I wrote a cautious letter to Mr. Fraser on the third day.

I told him that I was considering a book about obeah and had remembered his story of the case he had come across. Had he any idea of the whereabouts of the woman now? Was she still in Jamaica?

This letter was sent down by the twice weekly messenger and he must have answered at once for I had his reply in a few days:

I have often thought of your wife and yourself. And was on the point of writing to you. Indeed I have not forgotten the case. The woman in question was called Josephine or Christophine Dubois, some such name and she had been one of the Cosway servants. After she came out of jail she disappeared, but it was common knowledge that old Mr. Mason befriended her. I heard that she owned or was given a small house and a piece of land near Granbois. She is intelligent in her way and can express herself well, but I did not like the look of her at all, and consider her a most dangerous person. My wife insisted that she had gone back to Martinique, her native island, and was very upset that I had mentioned the matter even in such a round-about fashion. I happen to know now that she has not returned to Martinique, so I have written very discreetly to Hill, the white inspector of police in your town. If she lives near you and gets up to any of her nonsense let him know at once. He'll send a couple of policemen up to your place and she won't get off lightly this time. I'll make sure of that. . . .

So much for you, Josephine or Christophine, I thought. So much for you, Pheena.

It was that half-hour after the sunset, the blue half-hour I called it to myself. The wind drops, the light is very beautiful, the mountains sharp, every leaf on every tree is clear and distinct. I was sitting in the hammock, watching, when Antoinette rode up. She passed me without looking at me, dismounted and went into the house. I heard her bedroom door slam and her handbell ring violently.

Baptiste came running along the veranda. I got out of the hammock and went to the sitting-room. He had opened the chest and taken out a bottle of rum. Some of this he poured into a decanter which he put on a tray with a glass.

"Who is that for?" I said. He didn't answer.

"No road?" I said and laughed.

"I don't want to know nothing about all this," he said.

"Baptiste!" Antoinette called in a high voice.

"Yes, mistress." He looked straight at me and carried the tray out.

As for the old woman, I saw her shadow before I saw her. She too passed me without turning her head. Nor did she go into Antoinette's room or look towards it. She walked along the veranda, down the steps the other side, and went into the kitchen. In that short time the dark had come and Hilda came in to light the candles. When I spoke to her she gave me an alarmed look and ran away. I opened the chest and looked at the rows of bottles inside. Here was the rum that kills you in a hundred years, the brandy, the red and white wine smuggled, I suppose, from St. Pierre, Martinique—the Paris of the West Indies. It was rum I chose to drink. Yes, it was mild in the mouth, I waited a second for the explosion of heat and light in my chest, the strength and warmth running through my body. Then I tried the door into Antoinette's room. It yielded very slightly. She must have pushed some piece of furniture against it, that round table probably. I pushed again and it opened enough for me to see her. She was lying on the bed on her back. Her eyes were closed and she breathed heavily. She had pulled the sheet up to her chin. On a chair beside the bed there was the empty decanter, a glass with some rum left in it and a small brass handbell.

I shut the door and sat down with my elbows on the table for I thought I knew what would happen and what I must do. I found the room oppressively hot, so I blew out most of the candles and waited in the half darkness. Then I went on to the veranda to watch the door of the kitchen where a light was showing.

Soon the little girl came out followed by Baptiste. At the same time the hand-bell in the bedroom rang. They both went into the sitting-room and I followed. Hilda lit all the candles with a frightened roll of the eyes in my direction. The handbell went on ringing.

"Mix me a good strong one, Baptiste. Just what I feel like."

He took a step away from me and said, "Miss Antoinette—"

"Baptiste, where are you?" Antoinette called. "Why don't you come?"

"I come as quick as I can," Baptiste said. But as he reached for the bottle I took it away from him.

Hilda ran out of the room. Baptiste and I stared at each other. I thought that his large protuberant eyes and his expression of utter bewilderment were comical.

Antoinette shrieked from the bedroom, "Baptiste! Christophine! Pheena, Pheena!"

"*Que komesse!*" Baptiste said. "I get Christophine."

He ran out almost as fast as the little girl had done.

The door of Antoinette's room opened. When I saw her I was too shocked to speak. Her hair hung uncombed and dull into her eyes which were inflamed and staring, her face was very flushed and looked swollen. Her feet were bare. However when she spoke her voice was low, amost inaudible.

"I rang the bell because I was thirsty. Didn't anybody hear?"

Before I could stop her she darted to the table and seized the bottle of rum.

"Don't drink any more," I said.

"And what right have you to tell me what I'm to do? Christophine!" she called again, but her voice broke.

"Christophine is an evil old woman and you know it as well as I do," I said. "She won't stay here very much longer."

"She won't stay here very much longer," she mimicked me, "and nor will you, nor will you. I thought you liked the black people so much," she said, still in that mincing voice, "but that's just a lie like everything else. You like the light brown girls better, don't you? You abused the planters and made up stories about them, but you do the same thing. You send the girl away quicker, and with no money or less money, and that's all the difference."

"Slavery was not a matter of liking or disliking," I said, trying to speak calmly. "It was a question of justice."

"Justice," she said. "I've heard that word. It's a cold word. I tried it out," she said, still speaking in a low voice. "I wrote it down. I wrote it down several times and always it looked like a damn cold lie to me. There is no justice." She drank some more rum and went on, "My mother whom you all talk about, what justice did she have? My mother sitting in the rocking-chair speaking about dead horses and dead grooms and a black devil kissing her sad mouth. Like you kissed mine," she said.

The room was now unbearably hot. "I'll open the window and let a little air in," I said.

"It will let the night in too," she said, "and the moon and the scent of those flowers you dislike so much."

When I turned from the window she was drinking again.

"Bertha," I said.

"Bertha is not my name. You are trying to make me into someone else, calling me by another name. I know, that's obeah too."

Tears streamed from her eyes.

"If my father, my real father, was alive you wouldn't come back here in a hurry after he'd finished with you. If he was alive. Do you know what you've done to me? It's not the girl, not the girl. But I loved this place and you have made it into a place I hate. I used to think that if everything else went out of my life I would still have this, and now you have spoilt it. It's just somewhere else where I have been unhappy, and all the other things are nothing to what has happened here. I hate it now like I hate you and before I die I will show you how much I hate you."

Then to my astonishment she stopped crying and said, "Is she so much prettier than I am? Don't you love me at all?"

"No, I do not," I said (at the same time remembering Amélie saying, "Do you like my hair? Isn't it prettier than hers?"). "Not at this moment," I said.

She laughed at that. A crazy laugh.

"You see. That's how you are. A stone. But it serves me right because didn't Aunt Cora say to me don't marry him. Not if he were stuffed with diamonds. And a lot of other things she told me. Are you talking about England, I said, and what about Grandpappy passing his glass over the water decanter and the tears running down his face for all the friends dead and gone, whom he would never see again. That was nothing to do with England that I ever heard, she said. On the contrary:

A Benky foot and a Benky leg
For Charlie over the water.
Charlie, Charlie,"

she sang in a hoarse voice. And lifted the bottle to drink again.

I said, and my voice was not very calm, "No."

I managed to hold her wrist with one hand and the rum with the other, but when I felt her teeth in my arm I dropped the bottle. The smell filled the room. But I was angry now and she saw it. She smashed another bottle against the wall and stood with the broken glass in her hand and murder in her eyes.

"Just you touch me once. You'll soon see if I'm a dam' coward like you are."

Then she cursed me comprehensively, my eyes, my mouth, every member of my body, and it was like a dream in the large unfurnished room with the candles flickering and this red-eyed wild-haired stranger who was my wife shouting obscenities at me. It was at this nightmare moment that I heard Christophine's calm voice.

"You hush up and keep yourself quiet. And don't cry. Crying's no good with him. I told you before. Crying's no good."

Antoinette collapsed on the sofa and went on sobbing. Christophine looked at me and her small eyes were very sad. "Why you do that eh? Why you don't take that worthless good-for-nothing girl somewhere else? But she love money like you love money—must be why you come together. Like goes to like."

I couldn't bear any more and again I went out of the room and sat on the veranda.

My arm was bleeding and painful and I wrapped my handkerchief round it, but it seemed to me that everything round me was hostile. The telescope drew away and said don't touch me. The trees were threatening and the shadows of the trees moving slowly over the floor menaced me. That green menace. I had felt it ever since I saw this place. There was nothing I knew, nothing to comfort me.

I listened. Christophine was talking softly. My wife was crying. Then a door shut. They had gone into the bedroom. Someone was singing "Ma belle ka di," or was it the song about one day and a thousand years. But whatever they were singing or saying was dangerous. I must protect myself. I went softly along the dark veranda. I could see Antoinette stretched on the bed quite still. Like a doll. Even when she threatened me with the bottle she had a marionette quality. "Ti moun," I heard and "Doudou ché," and the end of a head handkerchief made a finger on the wall. "Do do l'enfant do." Listening, I began to feel sleepy and cold.

I stumbled back into the big candle-lit room which still smelt strongly of rum. In spite of this I opened the chest and got out another bottle. That was what I was thinking when Christophine came in. I was thinking of a last strong drink in my room, fastening both doors, and sleeping.

"I hope you satisfy, I hope you well satisfy," she said, "and no good to start your lies with me. I know what you do with that girl as well as you know. Better. Don't think I frightened of you either."

"So she ran off to tell you I'd ill-treated her, did she? I ought to have guessed that."

"She don't tell me a thing," said Christophine. "Not one single thing. Always the same. Nobody is to have any pride but you. She have more pride than you and she say nothing. I see her standing at my door with that look on her face and I know something bad happen to her. I know I must act quick and I act."

"You seem to have acted, certainly. And what did you do before you brought her back in her present condition?"

"What did I do! Look! don't you provoke me more than I provoke already. Better not I tell you. You want to know what I do? I say *doudou*, if you have trouble you are right to come to me. And I kiss her. It's when I kiss her she cry—not before. It's long time she hold it back, I think. So I let her cry. That is the first thing. Let them cry—it eases the heart. When she can't cry no more I give her a cup of milk—it's lucky I have some. She won't eat, she won't talk. So I say, 'Lie down on the bed *doudou* and try to sleep, for me I can sleep on the floor, don't matter for me.' She isn't going to sleep natural that's certain, but I can make her sleep. That's what I do. As for what you do—you pay for it one day.

"When they get like that," she said, "first they must cry, then they must sleep. Don't talk to me about doctor, I know more than any doctor. I undress Antoinette so she can sleep cool and easy; it's then I see you very rough with her eh?"

At this point she laughed—a hearty merry laugh. "All that is a little thing —it's nothing. If you see what I see in this place with the machete bright and shining in the corner, you don't have such a long face for such a little thing. You make her love you more if that's what you want. It's not for that she have the look of death on her face. Oh no.

"One night," she went on, "I hold on a woman's nose because her husband nearly chop it off with his machete. I hold it on, I send a boy running for the doctor and the doctor come galloping at dead of night to sew up the woman. When he finish he tell me, 'Christophine you have a great presence of mind.' That's what he tell me. By this time the man crying like a baby. He says, 'Doctor I don't mean it. It just happened.' 'I know, Rupert,' the doctor says, 'but it mustn't happen again. Why don't you keep the damn machete in the other room?' he says. They have two small rooms only so I say, 'No, doctor—it much worse near the bed. They chop each other up in no time at all.' The doctor he laugh and laugh. Oh he was a good doctor. When he finished with that woman nose I won't say it look like before but I will say it don't notice much. Rupert that man's name was. Plenty Ruperts here you notice? One is Prince Rupert, and one who makes songs is Rupert the Rine. You see him? He sells his songs down by the bridge there in town. It's in the town I live when I first leave Jamaica. It's a pretty name eh—Rupert—but where they get it from? I think it's from old time they get it.

"That doctor an old-time doctor. These new ones I don't like them. First word in their mouth is police. Police—that's something I don't like."

"I'm sure you don't," I said. "But you

haven't told me yet what happened when my wife was with you. Or exactly what you did?"

"Your wife!" she said. "You make me laugh. I don't know all you did but I know some. Everybody know that you marry her for her money and you take it all. And then you want to break her up, because you jealous of her. She is more better than you, she have better blood in her and she don't care for money—it's nothing for her. Oh I see that first time I look at you. You young but already you hard. You fool the girl. You make her think you can't see the sun for looking at her."

It was like that, I thought. It was like that. But better to say nothing. Then surely they'll both go and it will be my turn to sleep—a long deep sleep, mine will be, and very far away.

"And then," she went on in her judge's voice, "you make love to her till she drunk with it, no rum could make her drunk like that, till she can't do without it. It's *she* can't see the sun any more. Only you she see. But all you want is to break her up."

(*Not the way you mean, I thought*)

"But she hold out eh? She hold out."

(*Yes, she held out. A pity*)

"So you pretend to believe all the lies that damn bastard tell you."

(*That damn bastard tell you*)

Now every word she said was echoed, echoed loudly in my head.

"So that you can leave her alone."

(*Leave her alone*)

"Not telling her why."

(*Why?*)

"No more love, eh?"

(*No more love*)

"And that," I said coldly, "is where you took charge, isn't it? You tried to poison me."

"Poison you? But look me trouble, the man crazy! She come to me and ask me for something to make you love her again and I tell her no I don't meddle in that for *béké.* I tell her it's foolishness."

(*Foolishness foolishness*)

"And even if it's no foolishness, it's too strong for *béké.*"

(*Too strong for* béké. *Too strong*)

"But she cry and she beg me."

(*She cry and she beg me*)

"So I give her something for love."

(*For love*)

"But you don't love. All you want is to break her up. And it help you break her up."

(*Break her up*)

"She tell me in the middle of all this you start calling her names. Marionette. Some word so."

"Yes, I remember, I did."

(*Marionette, Antoinette, Marionetta, Antoinetta*)

"That word mean doll, eh? Because she don't speak. You want force her to cry and to speak."

(*Force her to cry and to speak*)

"But she won't. So you think up something else. You bring that worthless girl to play with next door and you talk and laugh and love so that she hear everything. You meant her to hear."

Yes, that didn't just happen. I meant it.

(*I lay awake all night long after they were asleep, and as soon as it was light I got up and dressed and saddled Preston. And I came to you. Oh Christophine. O Pheena, Pheena, help me.*)

"You haven't yet told me exactly what you did with my—with Antoinette."

"Yes I tell you. I make her sleep."

"What? All the time?"

"No, no. I wake her up to sit in the sun, bathe in the cool river. Even if she dropping with sleep. I make good strong soup. I gave her milk if I have it, fruit I pick from my own trees. If she don't want to eat I say, 'Eat it up for my sake, *doudou.*' And she eat it up, then she sleep again."

"And why did you do all this?"

There was a long silence. Then she said, "It's better she sleep. She must sleep while I work for her—to make her well again. But I don't speak of all that to you."

"Unfortunately your cure was not successful. You didn't make her well. You made her worse."

"Yes I succeed," she said angrily. "I succeed. But I get frightened that she sleep too much, too long. She is not *béké* like you, but she is *béké*, and not like us either. There are mornings when she can't wake, or when she wake it's as if she still sleeping. I don't want to give her any more of—of what I give. So," she went on after another pause, "I let her have rum instead. I know that won't hurt her. Not much. As soon as she has the rum she starts raving that she must go back to you and I can't quiet her. She says she'll go alone if I don't come but she beg me to come. And I hear well when you tell her that you don't love her—quite calm and cool you tell her so, and undo all the good I do."

"The good you did! I'm very weary of your nonsense, Christophine. You seem to have made her dead drunk on bad rum and she's a wreck. I scarcely recognized her. Why you did it I can't say—hatred of me I suppose. And as you heard so much perhaps you were listening to all she admitted—boasted about, and to the vile names she called me. Your *doudou* certainly knows some filthy language."

"I tell you no. I tell you it's nothing. You make her so unhappy she don't know what she is saying. Her father old Mister Cosway swear like half past midnight—she pick it up from him. And once, when she was little she run away to be with the fishermen and the sailors on the bayside. Those men!" She raised her eyes to the ceiling. "Never would you think they was once innocent babies. She come back copying them. She don't understand what she says."

"I think she understood every word, and meant what she said too. But you are right, Christophine—it was all a very little thing. It was nothing. No machete here, so no machete damage. No damage at all by this time. I'm sure you took care of that however drunk you made her."

"You are a damn hard man for a young man."

"So you say, so you say."

"I tell her so. I warn her. I say this is not a man who will help you when he sees you break up. Only the best can do that. The best—and sometimes the worst."

"But you think I'm one of the worst, surely?"

"No," she said indifferently, "to me you are not the best, not the worst. You are—" she shrugged "—you will not help her. I tell her so."

Nearly all the candles were out. She didn't light fresh ones—nor did I. We sat in the dim light. I should stop this useless conversation, I thought, but could only listen, hypnotized, to her dark voice coming from the darkness.

"I know that girl. She will never ask you for love again, she will die first. But I Christophine I beg you. She love you so much. She thirsty for you. Wait, and perhaps you can love her again. A little, like she say. A little. Like you can love."

I shook my head and went on shaking it mechanically.

"It's lies all that yellow bastard tell you. He is no Cosway either. His mother was a no-good woman and she try to fool the old man but the old man isn't fooled. 'One more or less' he says, and laughs. He was wrong. More he do for those people, more they hate him. The hate in that man Daniel—he can't rest with it. If I know you coming here I stop you. But you marry quick, you leave Jamaica quick. No time."

"She told me that all he said was true. She wasn't lying then."

"Because you hurt her she want to hurt you back, that's why."

"And that her mother was mad. Another lie?"

Christophine did not answer me at once. When she did her voice was not so calm.

"They drive her to do it. When she lose her son she lose herself for a while and they shut her away. They tell her she is mad, they act like she is mad. Question, question. But no kind word, no friends, and her husban' he go off, he leave her. They won't let me see her. I try, but no. They won't let Antoinette see her. In the end—mad I don't know—she give up, she care for nothing. That man who is in charge of her he take her whenever he want and his woman talk. That man, and others. Then they have her. Ah there is no God."

"Only your spirits," I reminded her.

"Only my spirits," she said steadily. "In your Bible it say God is a spirit—it don't say no others. Not at all. It grieve me what happen to her mother, and I can't see it happen again. You call her a doll? She don't satisfy you? Try her once more, I think she satisfy you now. If you forsake her they will tear her in pieces—like they did her mother."

"I will not forsake her," I said wearily. "I will do all I can for her."

"You will love her like you did before?"

(*Give my sister your wife a kiss from me. Love her as I did—oh yes I did. How can I promise that?*) I said nothing.

"It's she won't be satisfy. She is Creole girl, and she have the sun in her. Tell the truth now. She don't come to your house in this place England they tell me about, she don't come to your beautiful house to beg you to marry with her. No, it's you come all the long way to her house—it's you beg her to marry. And she love you and she give you all she have. Now you say you don't love her and you break her up. What you do with her money, eh?" Her voice was still quiet but with a hiss in it when she said "money." I thought, of course, that is what all the rigmarole is about. I no longer felt dazed, tired,

half hypnotized, but alert and wary, ready to defend myself.

Why, she wanted to know, could I not return half of Antoinette's dowry and leave the island—"leave the West Indies if you don't want her no more."

I asked the exact sum she had in mind, but she was vague about that.

"You fix it up with lawyers and all those things."

"And what will happen to her then?"

She, Christophine, would take good care of Antoinette (and the money of course).

"You will both stay here?" I hoped that my voice was as smooth as hers.

No, they would go to Martinique. Then to other places.

"I like to see the world before I die."

Perhaps because I was so quiet and composed she added maliciously, "She marry with someone else. She forget about you and live happy."

A pang of rage and jealousy shot through me then. Oh no, she won't forget. I laughed.

"You laugh at me? Why you laugh at me?"

"Of course I laugh at you—you ridiculous old woman. I don't mean to discuss my affairs with you any longer. Or your mistress. I've listened to all you had to say and I don't believe you. Now, say good-bye to Antoinette, then go. You are to blame for all that has happened here, so don't come back."

She drew herself up tall and straight and put her hands on her hips. "Who you to tell me to go? This house belong to Miss Antoinette's mother, now it belong to her. Who you to tell me to go?"

"I assure you that it belongs to me now. You'll go, or I'll get the men to put you out."

"You think the men here touch me? They not damn fool like you to put their hand on me."

"Then I will have the police up, I warn you. There must be some law and order even in this God-forsaken island."

"No police here," she said. "No chain

gang, no tread machine, no dark jail either. This is free country and I am free woman."

"Christophine," I said, "you lived in Jamaica for years, and you know Mr. Fraser, the Spanish Town magistrate, well. I wrote to him about you. Would you like to hear what he answered?" She stared at me. I read the end of Fraser's letter aloud: "*I have written very discreetly to Hill, the white inspector of police in your town. If she lives near you and gets up to any of her nonsense let him know at once. He'll send a couple of policemen up to your place and she won't get off lightly this time . . .* You gave your mistress the poison that she put into my wine?"

"I tell you already—you talk foolishness."

"We'll see about that—I kept some of that wine."

"I tell her so," she said. "Always it don't work for *béké*. Always it bring trouble . . . So you send me away and you keep all her money. And what you do with her?"

"I don't see why I should tell you my plans. I mean to go back to Jamaica to consult the Spanish Town doctors and her brother. I'll follow their advice. That is all I mean to do. She is not well."

"Her brother!" She spat on the floor. "Richard Mason is no brother to her. You think you fool me? You want her money but you don't want her. It is in your mind to pretend she is mad. I know it. The doctors say what you tell them to say. That man Richard he say what you want him to say—glad and willing too, I know. She will be like her mother. You do that for money? But you wicked like Satan self!"

I said loudly and wildly, "And do you think that I wanted all this? I would give my life to undo it. I would give my eyes never to have seen this abominable place."

She laughed. "And that's the first damn word of truth you speak. You

choose what you give, eh? Then you choose. You meddle in something and perhaps you don't know what it is." She began to mutter to herself. Not in patois. I knew the sound of patois now.

She's as mad as the other, I thought, and turned to the window.

The servants were standing in a group under the clove tree. Baptiste, the boy who helped with the horses and the little girl Hilda.

Christophine was right. They didn't intend to get mixed up in this business.

When I looked at her there was a mask on her face and her eyes were undaunted. She was a fighter, I had to admit. Against my will I repeated, "Do you wish to say good-bye to Antoinette?"

"I give her something to sleep— nothing to hurt her. I don't wake her up to no misery. I leave that for you."

"You can write to her," I said stiffly.

"Read and write I don't know. Other things I know."

She walked away without looking back.

All wish to sleep had left me. I walked up and down the room and felt the blood tingle in my finger-tips. It ran up my arms and reached my heart, which began to beat very fast. I spoke aloud as I walked. I spoke the letter I meant to write.

"I know now that you planned this because you wanted to be rid of me. You had no love at all for me. Nor had my brother. Your plan succeeded because I was young, conceited, foolish, trusting. Above all because I was young. You were able to do this to me . . ."

But I am not young now, I thought, stopped pacing and drank. Indeed this rum is mild as mother's milk or father's blessing.

I could imagine his expression if I sent that letter and he read it.

"Dear Father," I wrote. *"We are leaving this island for Jamaica very shortly.*

*Unforeseen circumstances, at least un-
foreseen by me, have forced me to make
this decision. I am certain that you
know or can guess what has happened,
and I am certain you will believe that
the less you talk to anyone about my
affairs, especially my marriage, the better. This is in your interest as well as
mine. You will hear from me again.
Soon I hope."*

Then I wrote to the firm of lawyers I
had dealt with in Spanish Town. I told
them that I wished to rent a furnished
house not too near the town, commo-
dious enough to allow for two separate
suites of rooms. I also told them to engage a staff of servants whom I was prepared to pay very liberally—so long as
they keep their mouths shut, I thought
—provided that they are discreet, I
wrote. My wife and myself would be in
Jamaica in about a week and expected
to find everything ready.

All the time I was writing this letter
a cock crowed persistently outside. I
took the first book I could lay hands on
and threw it at him, but he stalked
a few yards away and started again.

Baptiste appeared, looking towards
Antoinette's silent room.

"Have you got much more of this
famous rum?"

"Plenty rum," he said.

"Is it really a hundred years old?"

He nodded indifferently. A hundred
years, a thousand all the same to *le bon
Dieu* and Baptiste too.

"What's that damn cock crowing
about?"

"Crowing for change of weather."

Because his eyes were fixed on the
bedroom I shouted at him, "Asleep,
dormi, dormi."

He shook his head and went away.

He scowled at me then, I thought.
I scowled too as I re-read the letter I had
written to the lawyers. However much
I paid Jamaican servants I would never
buy discretion. I'd be gossiped about,

sung about (but they make up songs
about everything, everybody. You should
hear the one about the Governor's
wife). Wherever I went I would be
talked about. I drank some more rum
and, drinking, I drew a house surrounded
by trees. A large house. I divided the
third floor into rooms and in one room
I drew a standing woman—a child's
scribble, a dot for a head, a larger one
for the body, a triangle for a skirt, slanting lines for arms and feet. But it was
an English house.

English trees. I wondered if I ever
should see England again.

Under the oleanders . . . I watched
the hidden mountains and the mists
drawn over their faces. It's cool today;
cool, calm and cloudy as an English summer. But a lovely place in any weather,
however far I travel I'll never see a
lovelier.

The hurricane months are not so
far away, I thought, and saw that tree
strike its roots deeper, making ready
to fight the wind. Useless. If and when
it comes they'll all go. Some of the
royal palms stand (she told me).
Stripped of their branches, like tall
brown pillars, still they stand—defiant.
Not for nothing are they called royal.
The bamboos take an easier way, they
bend to the earth and lie there, creaking,
groaning, crying for mercy. The contemptuous wind passes, not caring for
these abject things. (*Let them live.*)
Howling, shrieking, laughing the wild
blast passes.

But all that's some months away. It's
an English summer now, so cool, so
grey. Yet I think of my revenge and
hurricanes. Words rush through my
head (deeds too). Words. Pity is one
of them. It gives me no rest.

Pity like a new-born babe striding
the blast.

I read that long ago when I was young
—I hate poets now and poetry. As I
hate music which I loved once. Sing

your songs, Rupert the Rine, but I'll not listen, though they tell me you've a sweet voice. . . .

Pity. Is there none for me? Tied to a lunatic for life—a drunken lying lunatic—gone her mother's way.

"She loves you so much, so much. She thirsty for you. Love her a little like she say. It's all that you can love—a little."

Sneer to the last, Devil. Do you think that I don't know? She thirsts for *anyone*—not for me . . .

She'll loosen her black hair, and laugh and coax and flatter (a mad girl. She'll not care who she's loving). She'll moan and cry and give herself as no sane woman would—or could. *Or could.* Then lie so still, still as this cloudy day. A lunatic who always knows the time. But never does.

Till she's drunk so deep, played her games so often that the lowest shrug and jeer at her. And I'm to know it—I? No, I've a trick worth two of that.

"She love you so much, so much. Try her once more."

I tell you she loves no one, anyone. I could not touch her. Excepting as the hurricane will touch that tree—and break it. You say I did? No. That was love's fierce play. Now I'll do it.

She'll not laugh in the sun again. She'll not dress up and smile at herself in that damnable looking-glass. So pleased, so satisfied.

Vain, silly creature. Made for loving? Yes, but she'll have no lover, for I don't want her and she'll see no other.

The tree shivers. Shivers and gathers all its strength. And waits.

(There is a cool wind blowing now —a cold wind. Does it carry the babe born to stride the blast of hurricanes?)

She said she loved this place. This is the last she'll see of it. I'll watch for one tear, one human tear. Not that blank hating moonstruck face. I'll listen. . . . If she says good-bye, perhaps adieu. *Adieu*—like those old-time songs she sang. Always *adieu* (and all songs say it). If she too says it, or weeps, I'll

take her in my arms, my lunatic. She's mad but *mine, mine.* What will I care for gods or devils or for Fate itself. If she smiles or weeps or both. *For me.*

Antoinetta—I can be gentle too. Hide your face. Hide yourself but in my arms. You'll soon see how gentle. My lunatic. My mad girl.

Here's a cloudy day to help you. No brazen sun.

No sun . . . No sun. The weather's changed.

Baptiste was waiting and the horses saddled. That boy stood by the clove tree and near him the basket he was to carry. These baskets are light and waterproof. I'd decided to use one for a few necessary clothes—most of our belongings were to follow in a day or two. A carriage was to meet us at Massacre. I'd seen to everything, arranged everything.

She was there in the *ajoupa*; carefully dressed for the journey, I noticed, but her face blank, no expression at all. Tears? There's not a tear in her. Well, we will see. Did she remember anything, I wondered, feel anything? (That blue cloud, that shadow, is Martinique. It's clear now . . . Or the names of the mountains. No, not mountain. *Morne*, she'd say. "Mountain is an ugly word— for them." Or the stories about Jack Spaniards. Long ago. And when she said, "Look! The Emerald Drop! That brings good fortune." Yes, for a moment the sky was green—a bright green sunset. Strange. But not half so strange as saying it brought good fortune.)

After all I was prepared for her blank indifference. I knew that my dreams were dreams. But the sadness I felt looking at the shabby white house—I wasn't prepared for that. More than ever before it strained away from the black snake-like forest. Louder and more desperately it called: Save me from destruction, ruin and desolation. Save me from the long slow death by ants. But what are you doing here you folly? So near the forest. Don't you know that this is a dangerous place? And that the dark forest always wins? Always. If you don't, you soon will, and I can do nothing to help you.

Baptiste looked very different. Not a trace of the polite domestic. He wore a very wide-brimmed straw hat, like the fisherman's hats, but the crown flat, not high and pointed. His wide leather belt was polished, so was the handle of his sheathed cutlass, and his blue cotton shirt and trousers were spotless. The hat, I knew, was waterproof. He was ready for the rain and it was certainly on its way.

I said that I would like to say good-bye to the little girl who laughed— Hilda. "Hilda is not here," he answered in his careful English. "Hilda has left— yesterday."

He spoke politely enough, but I could feel his dislike and contempt. The same contempt as that devil's when she said, 'Taste my bull's blood." Meaning that will make you a man. Perhaps. Much I cared for what they thought of me! As for her, I'd forgotten her for the moment. So I shall never understand why, suddenly, bewilderingly, I was certain that everything I had imagined to be truth was false. False. Only the magic and the dream are true—all the rest's a lie. Let it go. Here is the secret. Here.

(*But it is lost, that secret, and those who know it cannot tell it.*)

Not lost. I had found it in a hidden place and I'd keep it, hold it fast. As I'd hold her.

I looked at her. She was staring out to the distant sea. She was silence itself.

Sing, Antoinetta. I can hear you now.

Here the wind says it has been, it has been
And the sea says it must be, it must be
And the sun says it can be, it will be
And the rain . . . ?

"You must listen to that. Our rain knows all the songs."
"And all the tears?"

"All, all, all."

Yes, I will listen to the rain. I will listen to the mountain bird. Oh, a heart-stopper is the solitaire's one note—high, sweet, lonely, magic. You hold your breath to listen . . . No . . . Gone. What was I to say to her?

Do not be sad. Or think Adieu. Never Adieu. We will watch the sun set again —many times, and perhaps we'll see the Emerald Drop, the green flash that brings good fortune. And you must laugh and chatter as you used to do— telling me about the battle off the Saints or the picnic at Marie Galante—that famous picnic that turned into a fight. Or the pirates and what they did between voyages. For every voyage might be their last. Sun and sangoree's a heady mixture. Then—the earthquake. Oh yes, people say that God was angry at the things they did, woke from his sleep, one breath and they were gone. He slept again. But they left their treasure, gold and more than gold. Some of it is found—but the finders never tell, because you see they'd only get one-third then: that's the law of treasure. They want it all, so never speak of it. Sometimes precious things, or jewels. There's no end to what they find and sell in secret to some cautious man who weighs and measures, hesitates, asks questions which are not answered, then hands over money in exchange. Everybody knows that gold pieces, treasures, appear in Spanish Town— (here too). In all the islands, from nowhere, from no one knows where. For it is better not to speak of treasure. Better not to tell them.

Yes, better not to tell them. I won't tell you that I scarcely listened to your stories. I was longing for night and darkness and the time when the moon-flowers open.

Blot out the moon,
Pull down the stars.
Love in the dark, for we're for the dark
So soon, so soon.

Like the swaggering pirates, let's make the most and best and worst of what we have. Give not one-third but everything. All—all—all. Keep nothing back. . . .

No, I would say—I knew what I would say. "I have made a terrible mistake. Forgive me."

I said it, looking at her, seeing the hatred in her eyes—and feeling my own hate spring up to meet it. Again the giddy change, the remembering, the sickening swing back to hate. They bought me, *me* with your paltry money. You helped them to do it. You deceived me, betrayed me, and you'll do worse if you get the chance . . . (*That girl she look you straight in the eye and talk sweet talk—and it's lies she tell you. Lies. Her mother was so. They say she worse than her mother.*)

. . . If I was bound for hell let it be hell. No more false heavens. No more damned magic. You hate me and I hate you. We'll see who hates best. But first, first I will destroy your hatred. Now. My hate is colder, stronger, and you'll have no hate to warm yourself. You will have nothing.

I did it too. I saw the hate go out of her eyes. I forced it out. And with the hate her beauty. She was only a ghost. A ghost in the grey daylight. Nothing left but hopelessness. *Say die and I will die. Say die and watch me die.*

She lifted her eyes. Blank lovely eyes. Mad eyes. A mad girl. I don't know what I would have said or done. In the balance—everything. But at this moment the nameless boy leaned his head against the clove tree and sobbed. Loud heartbreaking sobs. I could have strangled him with pleasure. But I managed to control myself, walk up to them and say coldly, "What is the matter with him? What is he crying about?" Baptiste did not answer. His sullen face grew a shade more sullen and that was all I got from Baptiste.

She had followed me and she answered. I scarcely recognized her voice.

No warmth, no sweetness. The doll had a doll's voice, a breathless but curiously indifferent voice.

"He asked me when we first came if we—if you—would take him with you when we left. He doesn't want any money. Just to be with you. Because—" She stopped and ran her tongue over her lips, "he loves you very much. So I said you would. Take him. Baptiste has told him that you will not. So he is crying."

"I certainly will not," I said angrily. (God! A half-savage boy as well as . . . as well as . . .)

"He knows English," she said, still indifferently. "He has tried very hard to learn English."

"He hasn't learned any English that I can understand," I said. And looking at her stiff white face my fury grew. "What right have you to make promises in my name? Or to speak for me at all?"

"No, I had no right, I am sorry. I don't understand you. I know nothing about you, and I cannot speak for you. . . ."

And that was all. I said good-bye to Baptiste. He bowed stiffly, unwillingly and muttered—wishes for a pleasant journey, I suppose. He hoped, I am sure, that he'd never set eyes on me again.

She had mounted and he went over to her. When she stretched her hand out he took it and still holding it spoke to her very earnestly. I did not hear what he said but I thought she would cry then. No, the doll's smile came back—nailed to her face. Even if she had wept like Magdalene it would have made no difference. I was exhausted. All the mad conflicting emotions had gone and left me wearied and empty. Sane.

I was tired of these people. I disliked their laughter and their tears, their flattery and envy, conceit and deceit. And I hated the place.

I hated the mountains and the hills, the rivers and the rain. I hated the sunsets of whatever color, I hated its beauty and its magic and the secret I would never know. I hated its indifference and the cruelty which was part of its loveliness. Above all I hated her. For she belonged to the magic and the loveliness. She had left me thirsty and all my life would be thirst and longing for what I had lost before I found it.

So we rode away and left it—the hidden place. Not for me and not for her. I'd look after that. She's far along the road now.

Very soon she'll join all the others who know the secret and will not tell it. Or cannot. Or try and fail because they do not know enough. They can be recognized. White faces, dazed eyes, aimless gestures, high-pitched laughter. The way they walk and talk and scream or try to kill (themselves or you) if you laugh back at them. Yes, they've got to be watched. For the time comes when they try to kill, then disappear. But others are waiting to take their places, it's a long, long line. She's one of them. I too can wait—for the day when she is only a memory to be avoided, locked away, and like all memories a legend. Or a lie.

I remember that as we turned the corner, I thought about Baptiste and wondered if he had another name—I'd never asked. And then that I'd sell the place for what it would fetch. I had meant to give it back to her. Now—what's the use?

That stupid boy followed us, the basket balanced on his head. He used the back of his hand to wipe away his tears. Who would have thought that any boy would cry like that. For nothing. Nothing.

PART THREE

"They knew that he was in Jamaica when his father and his brother died," Grace Poole said. "He inherited everything, but he was a wealthy man before that. Some people are fortunate, they said, and there were hints about the woman he brought back to England with him. Next day Mrs. Eff wanted to see me and she complained about gossip. I don't allow gossip. I told you that when you came. Servants will talk and you can't stop them, I said. And I am not certain that the situation will suit me, madam. First when I answered your advertisement you said that the person I had to look after was not a young girl. I asked if she was an old woman and you said no. Now that I see her I don't know what to think. She sits shivering and she is so thin. If she dies on my hands who will get the blame? Wait, Grace, she said. She was holding a letter. Before you decide will you listen to what the master of the house has to say about this matter. 'If Mrs. Poole is satisfactory why not give her double, treble the money,' she read, and folded the letter away but not before I had seen the words on the next page, 'but for God's sake let me hear no more of it.' There was a foreign stamp on the envelope. 'I don't serve the devil for no money,' I said. She said, 'If you imagine that when you serve this gentleman you are serving the devil you never made a greater mistake in your life. I knew him as a boy. I knew him as a young man. He was gentle, generous, brave. His stay in the West Indies has changed him out of all knowledge. He has grey in his hair and misery in his eyes. Don't ask me to pity anyone who had a hand in that. I've said enough and too much. I am not prepared to treble your money, Grace, but I am prepared to double it. But there must be no more gossip. If there is I will dismiss you at once. I do not think it will be impossible to fill your place. I'm sure you understand.' Yes, I understand, I said.

"Then all the servants were sent away and she engaged a cook, one maid and you, Leah. They were sent away but how could she stop them talking? If you ask me the whole county knows. The rumors I've heard—very far from *the truth. But I don't contradict, I know better than to say a word. After all the house is big and safe, a shelter from the world outside which, say what you like, can be a black and cruel world to a woman. Maybe that's why I stayed on."*

The thick walls, she thought. Past the lodge gate a long avenue of trees and inside the house the blazing fires and the crimson and white rooms. But above all the thick walls, keeping away all the things that you have fought till you can fight no more. Yes, maybe that's why we all stay—Mrs. Eff and Leah and me. All of us except that girl who lives in her own darkness. I'll say one thing for her, she hasn't lost her spirit. She's still fierce. I don't turn my back on her when her eyes have that look. I know it.

In this room I wake early and lie shivering for it is very cold. At last Grace Poole, the woman who looks after me, lights a fire with paper and sticks and lumps of coal. She kneels to blow it with bellows. The paper shrivels, the sticks crackle and spit, the coal smolders and glowers. In the end flames shoot up and they are beautiful. I get out of bed and go close to watch them and to wonder why I have been brought here. For what reason? There must be a reason. What is it that I must do? When I first came I thought it would be for a day, two days, a week perhaps. I thought that when I saw him and spoke to him I would be wise as serpents, harmless as doves. "I give you all I have freely," I would say, "and I will not trouble you again if you will let me go." But he never came.

The woman Grace sleeps in my room. At night I sometimes see her sitting at the table counting money. She holds a gold piece in her hand and smiles. Then she puts it all into a little canvas bag with a drawstring and hangs the bag round her neck so that it is hidden in her dress. At first she used to look at me before she did this but I always pre-

tended to be asleep, now she does not trouble about me. She drinks from a bottle on the table then she goes to bed, or puts her arms on the table, her head on her arms, and sleeps. But I lie watching the fire die out. When she is snoring I get up and I have tasted the drink without color in the bottle. The first time I did this I wanted to spit it out but managed to swallow it. When I got back into bed I could remember more and think again. I was not so cold.

There is one window high up—you cannot see out of it. My bed had doors but they have been taken away. There is not much else in the room. Her bed, a black press, the table in the middle and two black chairs carved with fruit and flowers. They have high backs and no arms. The dressing-room is very small, the room next to this one is hung with tapestry. Looking at the tapestry one day I recognized my mother dressed in an evening gown but with bare feet. She looked away from me, over my head just as she used to do. I wouldn't tell Grace this. Her name oughtn't to be Grace. Names matter, like when he wouldn't call me Antoinette, and I saw Antoinette drifting out of the window with her scents, her pretty clothes and her looking-glass.

There is no looking-glass here and I don't know what I am like now. I remember watching myself brush my hair and how my eyes looked back at me. The girl I saw was myself yet not quite myself. Long ago when I was a child and very lonely I tried to kiss her. But the glass was between us—hard, cold and misted over with my breath. Now they have taken everything away. What am I doing in this place and who am I?

The door of the tapestry room is kept locked. It leads, I know, into a passage. That is where Grace stands and talks to another woman whom I have never seen. Her name is Leah. I listen but I cannot understand what they say.

So there is still the sound of whispering that I have heard all my life, but these are different voices.

When night comes, and she has had several drinks and sleeps, it is easy to take the keys. I know now where she keeps them. Then I open the door and walk into their world. It is, as I always knew, made of cardboard. I have seen it before somewhere, this cardboard world where everything is colored brown or dark red or yellow that has no light in it. As I walk along the passages I wish I could see what is behind the cardboard. They tell me I am in England but I don't believe them. We lost our way to England. When? Where? I don't remember, but we lost it. Was it that evening in the cabin when he found me talking to the young man who brought me my food? I put my arms round his neck and asked him to help me. He said, "I didn't know what to do, sir." I smashed the glasses and plates against the porthole. I hoped it would break and the sea come in. A woman came and then an older man who cleared up the broken things on the floor. He did not look at me while he was doing it. The third man said drink this and you will sleep. I drank it and I said, "It isn't like it seems to be."—"I know. It never is," he said. And then I slept. When I woke it was a different sea. Colder. It was that night, I think, that we changed course and lost our way to England. This cardboard house where I walk at night is not England.

One morning when I woke I ached all over. Not the cold, another sort of ache. I saw that my wrists were red and swollen. Grace said, "I suppose you're going to tell me that you don't remember anything about last night."

"When was last night?" I said.

"Yesterday."

"I don't remember yesterday."

"Last night a gentleman came to see you," she said.

"Which of them was that?"

Because I knew that there were strange people in the house. When I took the keys and went into the passage I heard them laughing and talking in the distance, like birds, and there were lights on the floor beneath.

Turning a corner I saw a girl coming out of her bedroom. She wore a white dress and she was humming to herself. I flattened myself against the wall for I did not wish her to see me, but she stopped and looked around. She saw nothing but shadows, I took care of that, but she didn't walk to the head of the stairs. She ran. She met another girl and the second girl said, "Have you seen a ghost?"—"I didn't see anything but I thought I felt something."—"That is the ghost," the second one said and they went down the stairs together.

"Which of these people came to see me, Grace Poole?" I said.

He didn't come. Even if I was asleep I would have known. He hasn't come yet. She said, "It's my belief that you remember much more than you pretend to remember. Why did you behave like that when I had promised you would be quiet and sensible? I'll never try and do you a good turn again. Your brother came to see you."

"I have no brother."

"He said he was your brother."

A long long way my mind reached back.

"Was his name Richard?"

"He didn't tell me what his name was."

"I know him," I said, and jumped out of bed. "It's all here, it's all here, but I hid it from your beastly eyes as I hide everything. But where is it? Where did I hide it? The sole of my shoes? Underneath the mattress? On top of the press? In the pocket of my red dress? Where, where is this letter? It was short because I remembered that Richard did not like long letters. Dear Richard please take me away from this place where I am dying because it is so cold and dark."

Mrs. Poole said, "It's no use running

around and looking now. He's gone and he won't come back—nor would I in his place."

I said, "I can't remember what happened. I can't remember."

"When he came in," said Grace Poole, "he didn't recognize you."

"Will you light the fire," I said, "because I'm so cold."

"This gentleman arrived suddenly and insisted on seeing you and that was all the thanks he got. You rushed at him with a knife and when he got the knife away you bit his arm. You won't see him again. And where did you get that knife? I told them you stole it from me but I'm much too careful. I'm used to your sort. You got no knife from me. You must have bought it that day when I took you out. I told Mrs. Eff you ought to be taken out."

"When we went to England," I said.

"You fool," she said, "this is England."

"I don't believe it," I said, "and I never will believe it."

(That afternoon we went to England. There was grass and olive-green water and tall trees looking into the water. This, I thought, is England. If I could be here I'd get well again and the sound in my head would stop. Let me stay a little longer, I said, and she sat down under a tree and went to sleep. A little way off there was a cart and horse—a woman was driving it. It was she who sold me the knife. I gave her the locket round my neck for it.)

Grace Poole said, "So you don't remember that you attacked this gentleman with a knife? I said that you would be quiet. 'I must speak to her,' he said. Oh he was warned but he wouldn't listen. I was in the room but I didn't hear all he said except 'I cannot interfere legally between yourself and your husband.' It was when he said 'legally' that you flew at him and when he twisted the knife out of your hand you bit him. Do you mean to say that you don't remember any of this?"

I remember now that he did not recognize me. I saw him look at me and his eyes went first to one corner and then to another, not finding what they expected. He looked at me and spoke to me as though I were a stranger. What do you do when something happens to you like that? Why are you laughing at me? "Have you hidden my red dress too? If I'd been wearing that he'd have known me."

"Nobody's hidden your dress," she said. "It's hanging in the press."

She looked at me and said, "I don't believe you know how long you've been here, you poor creature."

"On the contrary," I said, "only I know how long I have been here. Nights and days and days and nights, hundreds of them slipping through my fingers. But that does not matter. Time has no meaning. But something you can touch and hold like my red dress, that has a meaning. Where is it?"

She jerked her head towards the press and the corners of her mouth turned down. As soon as I turned the key I saw it hanging, the color of fire and sunset. The color of flamboyant flowers. "If you are buried under a flamboyant tree," I said, "your soul is lifted up when it flowers. Everyone wants that."

She shook her head but she did not move or touch me.

The scent that came from the dress was very faint at first, then it grew stronger. The smell of vetivert and frangipanni, of cinnamon and dust and lime trees when they are flowering. The smell of the sun and the smell of the rain.

. . . I was wearing a dress of that color when Sandi came to see me for the last time.

"Will you come with me?" he said. "No," I said, "I cannot."

"So this is good-bye?"

Yes, this is good-bye.

"But I can't leave you like this," he said, "you are unhappy."

"You are wasting time," I said, "and we have so little."

Sandi often came to see me when that man was away and when I went out driving I would meet him. I could go out driving then. The servants knew, but none of them told.

Now there was no time left so we kissed each other in that stupid room. Spread fans decorated the walls. We had often kissed before but not like that. That was the life and death kiss and you only know a long time afterwards what it is, the life and death kiss. The white ship whistled three times, once gaily, once calling, once to say good-bye.

I took the red dress down and put it against myself. "Does it make me look intemperate and unchaste?" I said. That man told me so. He had found out that Sandi had been to the house and that I went to see him. I never knew who told. "Infamous daughter of an infamous mother," he said to me.

"Oh put it away," Grace Poole said, "come and eat your food. Here's your grey wrapper. Why they can't give you anything better is more than I can understand. They're rich enough."

But I held the dress in my hand wondering if they had done the last and worst thing. If they had *changed* it when I wasn't looking. If they had changed it and it wasn't my dress at all—but how could they get the scent?

"Well don't stand there shivering," she said, quite kindly for her.

I let the dress fall on the floor, and looked from the fire to the dress and from the dress to the fire.

I put the grey wrapper round my shoulders, but I told her I wasn't hungry and she didn't try to force me to eat as she sometimes does.

"It's just as well that you don't remember last night," she said. "The gentleman fainted and a fine outcry there was up here. Blood all over the place and I was blamed for letting you attack him. And the master is expected in a few days. I'll never try to help you

again. You are too far gone to be helped."

I said, "If I had been wearing my red dress Richard would have known me."

"Your red dress," she said, and laughed.

But I looked at the dress on the floor and it was as if the fire had spread across the room. It was beautiful and it reminded me of something I must do. I will remember I thought. I will remember quite soon now.

That was the third time I had my dream, and it ended. I know now that the flight of steps leads to this room where I lie watching the woman asleep with her head on her arms. In my dream I waited till she began to snore, then I got up, took the keys and let myself out with a candle in my hand. It was easier this time than ever before and I walked as though I were flying.

All the people who had been staying in the house had gone, for the bedroom doors were shut, but it seemed to me that someone was following me, someone was chasing me, laughing. Sometimes I looked to the right or to the left but I never looked behind me for I did not want to see that ghost of a woman who they say haunts this place. I went down the staircase. I went further than I had ever been before. There was someone talking in one of the rooms. I passed it without noise, slowly.

At last I was in the hall where a lamp was burning. I remember that when I came. A lamp and the dark staircase and the veil over my face. They think I don't remember but I do. There was a door to the right. I opened it and went in. It was a large room with a red carpet and red curtains. Everything else was white. I sat down on a couch to look at it and it seemed sad and cold and empty to me, like a church without an altar. I wished to see it clearly so I lit all the candles, and there were many. I lit them carefully from the one I was carrying but I couldn't reach up to the chandelier. I looked round for the altar for with so many candles and so much red, the room reminded me of a church. Then I heard a clock ticking and it was made of gold. Gold is the idol they worship.

Suddenly I felt very miserable in that room, though the couch I was sitting on was so soft that I sank into it. It seemed to me that I was going to sleep. But I imagined that I heard a footstep and I thought what will they say, what will they do if they find me here? I held my right wrist with my left hand and waited. But it was nothing. I was very tired after this. Very tired. I wanted to get out of the room but my own candle had burned down and I took one of the others. Suddenly I was in Aunt Cora's room. I saw the sunlight coming through the window, the tree outside and the shadows of the leaves on the floor, but I saw the wax candles too and I hated them. So I knocked them all down. Most of them went out but one caught the thin curtains that were behind the red ones. I laughed when I saw the lovely color spreading so fast, but I did not stay to watch it. I went into the hall again with the tall candle in my hand. It was then that I saw her—the ghost. The woman with streaming hair. She was surrounded by a gilt frame but I knew her. I dropped the candle I was carrying and it caught the end of a tablecloth and I saw flames shoot up. As I ran or perhaps floated or flew I called help me Christophine help me and looking behind me I saw that I had been helped. There was a wall of fire protecting me but it was too hot, it scorched me and I went away from it.

There were more candles on a table and I took one of them and ran up the first flight of stairs and the second. On the second floor I threw away the candle. But I did not stay to watch. I ran up the last flight of stairs and along the passage. I passed the room where they brought me yesterday or the day before yesterday, I don't remember. Perhaps it was long ago for I seemed to know the house well. I knew how to get away

from the heat and the shouting, for there was shouting now. When I was out on the battlements it was cool and I could hardly hear them. I sat there quietly. I don't know how long I sat. Then I turned round and saw the sky. It was red and all my life was in it. I saw the grandfather clock and Aunt Cora's patchwork, all colors, I saw the orchids and the stephanotis and the jasmine and the tree of life in flames. I saw the chandelier and the red carpet downstairs and the bamboos and the tree ferns, the gold ferns and the silver, and the soft green velvet of the moss on the garden wall. I saw my doll's house and the books and the picture of the Miller's Daughter. I heard the parrot call as he did when he saw a stranger, *Qui est là? Qui est là?* and the man who hated me was calling too, Bertha! Bertha! The wind caught my hair and it streamed out like wings. It might bear me up, I thought, if I jumped to those hard stones. But when I looked over the edge I saw the pool at Coulibri. Tia was there. She beckoned to me and when I hesitated, she laughed. I heard her say, You frightened? And I heard the man's voice, Bertha! Bertha! All this I saw and heard in a fraction of a second. And the sky so red. Someone screamed and I thought, *Why did I scream?* I called "Tia!" and jumped and woke.

Grace Poole was sitting at the table but she had heard the scream too, for she said, "What was that?" She got up, came over and looked at me. I lay still, breathing evenly with my eyes shut. "I must have been dreaming," she said. Then she went back, not to the table but to her bed. I waited a long time after I heard her snore, then I got up, took the keys and unlocked the door. I was outside holding my candle. Now at last I know why I was brought here and what I have to do. There must have been a draught for the flame flickered and I thought it was out. But I shielded it with my hand and it burned up again to light me along the dark passage.

Jorge Luis Borges (1899–)

THE LOTTERY IN BABYLON

Like all men in Babylon, I have been proconsul; like all, a slave. I have also known omnipotence, opprobrium, imprisonment. Look: the index finger on my right hand is missing. Look: through the rip in my cape you can see a vermilion tattoo on my stomach. It is the second symbol, Beth. This letter, on nights when the moon is full, gives me power over men whose mark is Gimmel, but it subordinates me to the men of Aleph, who on moonless nights owe obedience to those marked with Gimmel. In the half light of dawn, in a cellar, I have cut the jugular vein of sacred bulls before a black stone. During a lunar year I have been declared invisible. I shouted and they did not answer me; I stole bread and they did not behead me. I have known what the Greeks do not know, incertitude. In a bronze chamber, before the silent handkerchief of the strangler, hope has been faithful to me, as has panic in the river of pleasure. Heraclides Ponticus tells with amazement that Pythagoras remembered having been Pyrrhus and before that Euphorbus and before that some other mortal. In order to remember similar vicissitudes I do not need to have recourse to death or even to deception.

I owe this almost atrocious variety to an institution which other republics do not know or which operates in them in an imperfect and secret manner: the lottery. I have not looked into its history; I know that the wise men cannot agree. I know of its powerful purposes what a man who is not versed in astrology can know about the moon. I come from a dizzy land where the lottery is the basis of reality. Until today I have thought as little about it as I have about the conduct of indecipherable divinities or about my heart. Now, far from Babylon and its beloved customs, I think with a certain amount of amazement about the lottery and about the blasphemous conjectures which veiled men murmur in the twilight.

My father used to say that formerly— a matter of centuries, of years?—the lottery in Babylon was a game of plebeian character. He recounted (I don't know whether rightly) that barbers sold, in exchange for copper coins, squares of bone or of parchment adorned with symbols. In broad daylight a drawing took place. Those who won received silver coins without any other test of luck. The system was elementary, as you can see.

Naturally these "lotteries" failed. Their moral virtue was nil. They were not directed at all of man's faculties, but only at hope. In the face of public indifference, the merchants who founded these venal lotteries began to lose money. Someone tried a reform: The interpolation of a few unfavorable tickets in the list of favorable numbers. By means of this reform, the buyers of numbered squares ran the double risk of winning a sum and of paying a fine that could be considerable. This slight danger (for every thirty favorable numbers there was one unlucky one) awoke, as is natural, the interest of the public. The Babylonians threw themselves into the game. Those who did not acquire chances were considered pusillanimous, cowardly. In time, that justified disdain was doubled. Those who did not play were scorned, but also the losers who paid the fine were scorned. The Company (as it came to be known then) had to take care of the winners, who could not cash in their prizes if almost the total amount of the fines was unpaid. It started a lawsuit against the losers. The judge condemned them to pay the original fine and costs or spend several days in jail. All chose jail in order to defraud the Company. The bravado of a few is the source of the omnipotence of the Company and of its metaphysical and ecclesiastical power.

A little while afterward the lottery lists omitted the amounts of fines and limited themselves to publishing the days of imprisonment that each unfavorable number indicated. That laconic spirit, almost unnoticed at the time, was of capital importance. *It was the first appearance in the lottery of nonmonetary elements.* The success was tremendous. Urged by the clientele, the Company was obliged to increase the unfavorable numbers.

Everyone knows that the people of Babylon are fond of logic and even of symmetry. It was illogical for the lucky numbers to be computed in round coins and the unlucky ones in days and nights of imprisonment. Some moralists reasoned that the possession of money does not always determine happiness and that other forms of happiness are perhaps more direct.

Another concern swept the quarters of the poorer classes. The members of the college of priests multiplied their stakes and enjoyed all the vicissitudes of terror and hope; the poor (with reasonable or unavoidable envy) knew that they were excluded from that notoriously delicious rhythm. The just desire that all, rich and poor, should participate equally in the lottery, inspired an indignant agitation, the memory of which the years have not erased. Some obstinate people did not understand (or pretended not to understand) that it was

a question of a new order, of a necessary historical stage. A slave stole a crimson ticket, which in the drawing credited him with the burning of his tongue. The legal code fixed that same penalty for the one who stole a ticket. Some Babylonians argued that he deserved the burning irons in his status of a thief; others, generously, that the executioner should apply it to him because chance had determined it that way. There were disturbances, there were lamentable drawings of blood, but the masses of Babylon finally imposed their will against the opposition of the rich. The people achieved amply its generous purposes. In the first place it caused the Company to accept total power. (That unification was necessary, given the vastness and complexity of the new operations.) In the second place, it made the lottery secret, free and general. The mercenary sale of chances was abolished. Once initiated in the mysteries of Baal, every free man automatically participated in the sacred drawings, which took place in the labyrinths of the god every sixty nights and which determined his destiny until the next drawing. The consequences were incalculable. A fortunate play could bring about his promotion to the council of wise men or the imprisonment of an enemy (public or private) or finding, in the peaceful darkness of his room, the woman who begins to excite him and whom he never expected to see again. A bad play: mutilation, different kinds of infamy, death. At times one single fact—the vulgar murder of C, the mysterious apotheosis of B—was the happy solution of thirty or forty drawings. To combine the plays was difficult, but one must remember that the individuals of the Company were (and are) omnipotent and astute. In many cases the knowledge that certain happinesses were the simple product of chance would have diminished their virtue. To avoid that obstacle, the agents of the Company made use of the power of suggestion and magic. Their steps, their maneuverings, were secret. To find out about the intimate hopes and terrors of each individual, they had astrologists and spies. There were certain stone lions, there was a sacred latrine called Qaphqa, there were fissures in a dusty aqueduct which, according to general opinion, *led to the Company;* malignant or benevolent persons deposited information in these places. An alphabetical file collected these items of varying truthfulness.

Incredibly, there were complaints. The Company, with its usual discretion, did not answer directly. It preferred to scrawl in the rubbish of a mask factory a brief statement which now figures in the sacred scriptures. This doctrinal item observed that the lottery is an interpolation of chance in the order of the world and that to accept errors is not to contradict chance: it is to corroborate it. It likewise observed that those lions and that sacred receptacle, although not disavowed by the Company (which did not abandon the right to consult them), functioned without official guarantee.

This declaration pacified the public's restlessness. It also produced other effects, perhaps unforeseen by its writer. It deeply modified the spirit and the operations of the Company. I don't have much time left; they tell us that the ship is about to weigh anchor. But I shall try to explain it.

However unlikely it might seem, no one had tried out before then a general theory of chance. Babylonians are not very speculative. They revere the judgments of fate, they deliver to them their lives, their hopes, their panic, but it does not occur to them to investigate fate's labyrinthine laws nor the gyratory spheres which reveal it. Nevertheless, the *unofficial* declaration that I have mentioned inspired many discussions of judicial-mathematical character. From some one of them the following conjecture was born: If the lottery is an intensification of chance, a periodical infusion of chaos in the cosmos, would it not be right for chance to intervene in all stages of the drawing and not in one alone? Is it not ridiculous for chance to dictate someone's death and have the circumstances of that death—secrecy, publicity, the fixed time of an hour or a century—not subject to chance? These just scruples finally caused a considerable reform, whose complexities (aggravated by centuries' practice) only a few specialists understand, but which I shall try to summarize, at least in a symbolic way.

Let us imagine a first drawing, which decrees the death of a man. For its fulfillment one proceeds to another drawing, which proposes (let us say) nine possible executors. Of these executors, four can initiate a third drawing which will tell the name of the executioner, two can replace the adverse order with a fortunate one (finding a treasure, let us say), another will intensify the death penalty (that is, will make it infamous or enrich it with tortures), others can refuse to fulfill it. This is the symbolic scheme. In reality *the number of drawings is infinite*. No decision is final, all branch into others. Ignorant people suppose that infinite drawings require an infinite time; actually it is sufficient for time to be infinitely subdivisible, as the famous parable of the contest with the tortoise teaches. This infinity harmonizes admirably with the sinuous numbers of Chance and with the Celestial Archetype of the Lottery, which the Platonists adore. Some warped echo of our rites seems to have resounded on the Tiber: Ellus Lampridius, in the *Life of Antoninus Heliogabalus*, tells that this emperor wrote on shells the lots that were destined for his guests, so that one received ten pounds of gold and another ten flies, ten dormice, ten bears. It is permissible to recall that Heliogabalus was brought up in Asia Minor, among the priests of the eponymous god.

There are also impersonal drawings, with an indefinite purpose. One decrees that a sapphire of Taprobana be thrown into the waters of the Euphrates; another, that a bird be released from the roof of a tower; another, that each century there be withdrawn (or added) a grain of sand from the innumerable ones on the beach. The consequences are, at times, terrible.

Under the beneficent influence of the Company, our customs are saturated with chance. The buyer of a dozen amphoras of Damascene wine will not be surprised if one of them contains a talisman or a snake. The scribe who writes a contract almost never fails to introduce some erroneous information. I myself, in this hasty declaration, have falsified some splendor, some atrocity. Perhaps, also, some mysterious monotony . . . Our historians, who are the most penetrating on the globe, have invented a method to correct chance. It is well known that the operations of this method are (in general) reliable, although, naturally, they are not divulged without some portion of deceit. Furthermore, there is nothing so contaminated with fiction as the history of the Company. A paleographic document, exhumed in a temple, can be the result of yesterday's lottery or of an age-old lottery. No book is published without some discrepancy in each one of the copies. Scribes take a secret oath to omit, to interpolate, to change. The indirect lie is also cultivated.

The Company, with divine modesty, avoids all publicity. Its agents, as is natural, are secret. The orders which it issues continually (perhaps incessantly) do not differ from those lavished by impostors. Moreover, who can brag about being a mere impostor? The drunkard who improvises an absurd order, the dreamer who awakens suddenly and strangles the woman who sleeps at his side, do they not execute, perhaps, a secret decision of the Company? That silent functioning, comparable to God's, gives rise to all sorts of conjectures. One abominably insinuates that the Company has not existed for centuries and that the sacred disorder of our lives is purely hereditary, traditional. Another judges it eternal and teaches that it will last until the last night, when the last god annihilates the world. Another declares that the Company is omnipotent, but that it only has influence in tiny things: in a bird's call, in the shadings of rust and of dust, in the half dreams of dawn. Another, in the words of masked heresiarchs, *that it has never existed and will not exist.* Another, no less vile, reasons that it is indifferent to affirm or deny the reality of the shadowy corporation, because Babylon is nothing else than an infinite game of chance.

Translated by John M. Fein

Julio Cortázar (1914-)

THE NIGHT FACE UP

*And at certain periods they went out to hunt enemies; they called it the war of the blossom.**

Halfway down the long hotel vestibule, he thought that probably he was going to be late, and hurried on into the street to get out his motorcycle from the corner where the next-door superintendent let him keep it. On the jewelry store at the

---

* The war of the blossom was the name the Aztecs gave to a ritual war in which they took prisoners for sacrifice. It is metaphysics to say that the gods see men as flowers, to be so uprooted, trampled, cut down.—ED.

corner he read that it was ten to nine; he had time to spare. The sun filtered through the tall downtown buildings, and he—because for himself, for just going along thinking, he did not have a name—he swung onto the machine, savoring the idea of the ride. The motor whirred between his legs, and a cool wind whipped his pantslegs.

He let the ministries zip past (the pink, the white), and a series of stores on the main street, their windows flashing. Now he was beginning the most pleasant part of the run, the real ride: a long street bordered with trees, very little traffic, with spacious villas whose gardens rambled all the way down to the sidewalks, which were barely indicated by low hedges. A bit inattentive perhaps, but tooling along on the right side of the street, he allowed himself to be carried away by the freshness, by the weightless contraction of this hardly begun day. This involuntary relaxation, possibly, kept him from preventing the accident. When he saw that the woman standing on the corner had rushed into the crosswalk while he still had the green light, it was already somewhat too late for a simple solution. He braked hard with foot and hand, wrenching himself to the left; he heard the woman scream, and at the collision his vision went. It was like falling asleep all at once.

He came to abruptly. Four or five young men were getting him out from under the cycle. He felt the taste of salt and blood, one knee hurt, and when they hoisted him up he yelped, he couldn't bear the pressure on his right arm. Voices which did not seem to belong to the faces hanging above him encouraged him cheerfully with jokes and assurances. His single solace was to hear someone else confirm that the lights indeed had been in his favor. He asked about the woman, trying to keep down the nausea which was edging up into his throat. While they carried him face up to a nearby pharmacy, he learned that the cause of the accident had gotten only a few scrapes on the legs. "Nah, you barely got her at all, but when ya hit, the impact made the machine jump and flop on its side . . ." Opinions, recollections of other smash-ups, take it easy, work him in shoulders first, there, that's fine, and someone in a dust-coat giving him a swallow of something soothing in the shadowy interior of the small local pharmacy.

Within five minutes the police ambulance arrived, and they lifted him onto a cushioned stretcher. It was a relief for him to be able to lie out flat. Completely lucid, but realizing that he was suffering the effects of a terrible shock, he gave his information to the officer riding in the ambulance with him. The arm almost didn't hurt; blood dripped down from a cut over the eyebrow all over his face. He licked his lips once or twice to drink it. He felt pretty good, it had been an accident, tough luck; stay quiet a few weeks, nothing worse. The guard said that the motorcycle didn't seem badly racked up. "Why should it," he replied. "It all landed on top of me." They both laughed, and when they got to the hospital, the guard shook his hand and wished him luck. Now the nausea was coming back little by little; meanwhile they were pushing him on a wheeled stretcher toward a pavilion further back, rolling along under trees full of birds, he shut his eyes and wished he were asleep or chloroformed. But they kept him for a good while in a room with that hospital smell, filling out a form, getting his clothes off, and dressing him in a stiff, greyish smock. They moved his arm carefully, it didn't hurt him. The nurses were constantly making wisecracks, and if it hadn't been for the stomach contractions he would have felt fine, almost happy.

They got him over to X-ray, and twenty minutes later, with the still-damp negative lying on his chest like a black tombstone, they pushed him into surgery. Someone tall and thin in white came over and began to look at the X-rays. A woman's hands were arranging his head, he felt that they were moving him from one stretcher to another. The man in white came over to him again, smiling, something gleamed in his right hand. He patted his cheek and made a sign to someone stationed behind.

It was unusual as a dream because it was full of smells, and he never dreamt smells. First a marshy smell, there to the left of the trail the swamps began already, the quaking bogs from which no one ever returned. But the reek lifted, and instead there came a dark, fresh composite fragrance, like the night under which he moved, in flight from the Aztecs. And it was all so natural, he had to run from the Aztecs who had set out on their manhunt, and his sole chance was to find a place to hide in the deepest part of the forest, taking care not to lose the narrow trail which only they, the Motecas, knew.

What tormented him the most was the odor, as though, notwithstanding the absolute acceptance of the dream, there was something which resisted that which was not habitual, which until that point had not participated in the game. "It smells of war," he thought, his hand going instinctively to the stone knife which was tucked at an angle into his girdle of woven wool. An unexpected sound made him crouch suddenly stock-still and shaking. To be afraid was nothing strange, there was plenty of fear in his dreams. He waited, covered by the branches of a shrub and the starless night. Far off, probably on the other side of the big lake, they'd be lighting the bivouac fires; that part of the sky had a reddish glare. The sound was not repeated. It had been like a broken limb. Maybe an animal that, like himself, was escaping from the smell of war. He stood erect slowly, sniffing the air. Not a sound could be heard, but the fear was still following,

as was the smell, that cloying incense of the war of the blossom. He had to press forward, to stay out of the bogs and get to the heart of the forest. Groping uncertainly through the dark, stooping every other moment to touch the packed earth of the trail, he took a few steps. He would have liked to have broken into a run, but the gurgling fens lapped on either side of him. On the path and in darkness, he took his bearings. Then he caught a horrible blast of that foul smell he was most afraid of, and leaped forward desperately.

"You're going to fall off the bed," said the patient next to him. "Stop bouncing around, old buddy."

He opened his eyes and it was afternoon, the sun already low in the oversized windows of the long ward. While trying to smile at his neighbor, he detached himself almost physically from the final scene of the nightmare. His arm, in a plaster cast, hung suspended from an apparatus with weights and pulleys. He felt thirsty, as though he'd been running for miles, but they didn't want to give him much water, barely enough to moisten his lips and make a mouthful. The fever was winning slowly and he would have been able to sleep again, but he was enjoying the pleasure of keeping awake, eyes half-closed, listening to the other patients' conversation, answering a question from time to time. He saw a little white pushcart come up beside the bed, a blond nurse rubbed the front of his thigh with alcohol and stuck him with a fat needle connected to a tube which ran up to a bottle filled with a milky, opalescent liquid. A young intern arrived with some metal and leather apparatus which he adjusted to fit onto the good arm to check something or other. Night fell, and the fever went along dragging him down softly to a state in which things seemed embossed as through opera glasses, they were real and soft and, at the same time, vaguely distasteful; like sitting in a boring movie and thinking that, well, still, it'd be worse out in the street, and staying.

A cup of a marvelous golden broth came, smelling of leeks, celery and parsley. A small hunk of bread, more precious than a whole banquet, found itself crumbling little by little. His arm hardly hurt him at all, and only in the eyebrow where they'd taken stitches a quick, hot pain sizzled occasionally. When the big windows across the way turned to smudges of dark blue, he thought it would not be difficult for him to sleep. Still on his back so a little uncomfortable, running his tongue out over his hot, too-dry lips, he tasted the broth still, and with a sigh of bliss, he let himself drift off.

First there was a confusion, as of one drawing all his sensations, for that moment blunted or muddled, into himself. He realized that he was running in pitch darkness, although, above, the sky crisscrossed with treetops was less black than the rest. "The trail," he thought. "I've gotten off the trail." His feet sank into a bed of leaves and mud, and then he couldn't take a step that the branches of shrubs did not whiplash against his ribs and legs. Out of breath, knowing despite the darkness and silence that he was surrounded, he crouched down to listen. Maybe the trail was very near, with the first daylight he would be able to see it again. Nothing now could help him to find it. The hand that had unconsciously gripped the haft of the dagger climbed like a fen scorpion up to his neck where the protecting amulet hung. Barely moving his lips, he mumbled the supplication of the corn which brings prayer to Her Very Highness, to the distributor of all Motecan possessions. At the same time he felt his ankles sinking deeper into the mud, and the waiting in the darkness of the obscure grove of live oak grew intolerable to him. The war of the blossom had started at the beginning of the moon and had been going on for three days and three nights now. If he

managed to hide in the depths of the forest, getting off the trail further up past the marsh country, perhaps the warriors wouldn't follow his track. He thought of the many prisoners they'd already taken. But the number didn't count, only the consecrated period. The hunt would continue until the priests gave the sign to return. Everything had its number and its limit, and it was within the sacred period, and he on the other side from the hunters.

He heard the cries and leaped up, knife in hand. As if the sky were aflame on the horizon, he saw torches moving among the branches, very near him. The smell of war was unbearable, and when the first enemy jumped him, leaped at his throat, he felt an almost-pleasure in sinking the stone blade flat to the haft into his chest. The lights were already around him, the happy cries. He managed to cut the air once or twice, then a rope snared him from behind.

"It's the fever," the man in the next bed said. "The same thing happened to me when they operated on my duodenum. Take some water, you'll see, you'll sleep all right."

Laid next to the night from which he came back, the tepid shadow of the ward seemed delicious to him. A violet lamp kept watch high on the far wall like a guardian eye. You could hear coughing, deep breathing, once in a while a conversation in whispers. Everything was pleasant and secure, without the chase, no . . . But he didn't want to go on thinking about the nightmare. There were lots of things to amuse himself with. He began to look at the cast on his arm, and the pulleys that held it so comfortably in the air. They'd left a bottle of mineral water on the night table beside him. He put the neck of the bottle to his mouth and drank it like a precious liqueur. He could now make out the different shapes in the ward, the thirty beds, the closets with glass doors. He guessed that his fever was down, his face felt cool. The cut over the eyebrow barely hurt at all, like a recollection. He saw himself leaving the hotel again, wheeling out the cycle. Who'd have thought that it would end like this? He tried to fix the moment of the accident exactly, and it got him very angry to notice that there was a void there, an emptiness he could not manage to fill. Between the impact and the moment that they picked him up off the pavement, the passing out or what went on, there was nothing he could see. And at the same time he had the feeling that this void, this nothingness, had lasted an eternity. No, not even time, more as if, in this void, he had passed across something, or had run back immense distances. The shock, the brutal dashing against the pavement. Anyway, he had felt an immense relief in coming out of the black pit while the people were lifting him off the ground. With pain in the broken arm, blood from the split eyebrow, contusion on the knee; with all that, a relief in returning to daylight, to the day, and to feel sustained and attended. That was weird. Someday he'd ask the doctor at the office about that. Now sleep began to take over again, to pull him slowly down. The pillow was so soft, and the coolness of the mineral water in his fevered throat. The violet light of the lamp up there was beginning to get dimmer and dimmer.

As he was sleeping on his back, the position in which he came to did not surprise him, but on the other hand the damp smell, the smell of oozing rock, blocked his throat and forced him to understand. Open his eyes and look in all directions, hopeless. He was surrounded by an absolute darkness. Tried to get up and felt ropes pinning his wrists and ankles. He was staked to the ground on a floor of dank, icy stone slabs. The cold bit into his naked back, his legs. Dully, he tried to touch the amulet with his chin and found they had stripped him of it. Now he was lost, no prayer could save him from the final . . . From afar off, as though filtering through

the rock of the dungeon, he heard the great kettledrums of the feast. They had carried him to the temple, he was in the underground cells of Teocalli itself, awaiting his turn.

He heard a yell, a hoarse yell that rocked off the walls. Another yell, ending in a moan. It was he who was screaming in the darkness, he was screaming because he was alive, his whole body with that cry fended off what was coming, the inevitable end. He thought of his friends filling up the other dungeons, and of those already walking up the stairs of the sacrifice. He uttered another choked cry, he could barely open his mouth, his jaws were twisted back as if with a rope and a stick, and once in a while they would open slowly with an endless exertion, as if they were made of rubber. The creaking of the wooden latches jolted him like a whip. Rent, writhing, he fought to rid himself of the cords sinking into his flesh. His right arm, the strongest, strained until the pain became unbearable and he had to give up. He watched the double door open, and the smell of the torches reached him before the light did. Barely girdled by the ceremonial loincloths, the priests' acolytes moved in his direction, looking at him with contempt. Lights reflected off the sweaty torsos and off the black hair dressed with feathers. The cords went slack, and in their place the grappling of hot hands, hard as bronze; he felt himself lifted, still face up, and jerked along by the four acolytes who carried him down the passageway. The torchbearers went ahead, indistinctly lighting up the corridor with its dripping walls and a ceiling so low that the acolytes had to duck their heads. Now they were taking him out, taking him out, it was the end. Face up, under a mile of living rock which, for a succession of moments, was lit up by a glimmer of torchlight. When the stars came out up there instead of the roof and the great terraced steps rose before him, on fire with cries and dances, it would be the end. The passage was never going to end, but now it was beginning to end, he would see suddenly the open sky full of stars, but not yet, they trundled him along endlessly in the reddish shadow, hauling him roughly along and he did not want that, but how to stop it if they had torn off the amulet, his real heart, the life-center.

In a single jump he came out into the hospital night, to the high, gentle, bare ceiling, to the soft shadow wrapping him round. He thought he must have cried out, but his neighbors were peacefully snoring. The water in the bottle on the night table was somewhat bubbly, a translucent shape against the dark azure shadow of the windows. He panted, looking for some relief for his lungs, oblivion for those images still glued to his eyelids. Each time he shut his eyes he saw them take shape instantly, and he sat up, completely wrung out, but savoring at the same time the surety that now he was awake, that the night nurse would answer if he rang, that soon it would be daybreak, with the good, deep sleep he usually had at that hour, no images, no nothing . . . It was difficult to keep his eyes open, the drowsiness was more powerful than he. He made one last effort, he sketched a gesture toward the bottle of water with his good hand and did not manage to reach it, his fingers closed again on a black emptiness, and the passageway went on endlessly, rock after rock, with momentary ruddy flares, and face up he choked out a dull moan because the roof was about to end, it rose, was opening like a mouth of shadow, and the acolytes straightened up, and from on high a

waning moon fell on a face whose eyes wanted not to see it, were closing and opening desperately, trying to pass to the other side, to find again the bare, protecting ceiling of the ward. And every time they opened, it was night and the moon, while they climbed the great terraced steps, his head hanging down backward now, and up at the top were the bonfires, red columns of perfumed smoke, and suddenly he saw the red stone, shiny with the blood dripping off it, and the spinning arcs cut by the feet of the victim whom they pulled off to throw him rolling down the north steps. With a last hope he shut his lids tightly, moaning to wake up. For a second he thought he had gotten there, because once more he was immobile in the bed, except that his head was hanging down off it, swinging. But he smelled death, and when he opened his eyes he saw the blood-soaked figure of the executioner-priest coming toward him with the stone knife in his hand. He managed to close his eyelids again, although he knew now he was not going to wake up, that he was awake, that the marvelous dream had been the other, absurd as all dreams are—a dream in which he was going through the strange avenues of an astonishing city, with green and red lights that burned without fire or smoke, on an enormous metal insect that whirred away between his legs. In the infinite lie of the dream, they had also picked him up off the ground, someone had approached him also with a knife in his hand, approached him who was lying face up, face up with his eyes closed between the bonfires on the steps.

BLOW-UP

It'll never be known how this has to be told, in the first person or in the second, using the third person plural or continually inventing modes that will serve for nothing. If one might say: I will see the moon rose, or: we hurt me at the back of my eyes, and especially: you the blond woman was the clouds that race before my your his our yours their faces. What the hell.

Seated ready to tell it, if one might go to drink a bock over there, and the typewriter continue by itself (because I use the machine), that would be perfection. And that's not just a manner of speaking. Perfection, yes, because here is the aperture which must be counted also as a machine (of another sort, a Contax 1.1.2) and it is possible that one machine may know more about another machine than I, you, she—the blond—and the clouds. But I have the dumb luck to know that if I go this Remington will sit turned to stone on top of the table with the air of being twice as quiet that mobile things have when they are not moving. So, I have to write. One of us all has to write, if this is going to get told. Better that it be me who am dead, for I'm less compromised than the rest; I who see only the clouds and can think without being distracted, write without being distracted (there goes another, with a grey edge) and remember without being distracted, I who am dead (and I'm alive, I'm not trying to fool anybody, you'll see when we get to the moment, because I have to begin some way and I've begun with this period, the last one back, the one at the beginning, which in the end is the best of the periods when you want to tell something).

All of a sudden I wonder why I have to tell this, but if one begins to wonder why he does all he does do, if one wonders why he accepts an invitation to lunch (now a pigeon's flying by and it seems to me a sparrow), or why when someone has told us a good joke immediately there starts up something like a tickling in the stomach and we are not at peace until we've gone into the office across the hall and told the joke over again; then it feels good immediately, one is fine, happy, and can get back to work. For I imagine that no one has explained this, that really the best thing is to put aside all decorum and tell it, because, after all's done, nobody is ashamed of breathing or of putting on his shoes; they're things that you do, and when something weird happens, when you find a spider in your shoe or if you take a breath and feel like a broken window, then you have to tell what's happening, tell it to the guys at the office or to the doctor. Oh, doctor, every time I take a breath . . . Always tell it, always get rid of that tickle in the stomach that bothers you.

And now that we're finally going to tell it, let's put things a little bit in order, we'd be walking down the staircase in this house as far as Sunday, November 7, just a month back. One goes down five floors and stands then in the Sunday in the sun one would not have suspected of Paris in November, with a large appetite to walk around, to see things, to take photos (because we were photographers, I'm a photographer). I know that the most difficult thing is going to be finding a way to tell it, and I'm not afraid of repeating myself. It's going to be difficult because nobody really knows who it is telling it, if I am I or what actually occurred or what I'm seeing (clouds, and once in a while a pigeon) or if, simply, I'm telling a truth which is only my truth, and then is the truth only for my stomach, for this impulse to go running out and to finish up in some manner with, this, whatever it is.

We're going to tell it slowly, what happens in the middle of what I'm writing is coming already. If they replace me, if, so soon, I don't know what to say, if the clouds stop coming and something else starts (because it's impossible that this keep coming, clouds passing continually and occasionally a pigeon), if something out of all this . . . And after the "if" what am I going to put if I'm going to close the sentence structure correctly? But if I begin to ask questions, I'll never tell anything, maybe to tell would be like an

652 INTRODUCTION TO IMPRESSIONISM

answer, at least for someone who's reading it.

Roberto Michel, French-Chilean, translator and in his spare time an amateur photographer, left number 11, rue Monsieur-le-Prince Sunday November 7 of the current year (now there're two small ones passing, with silver linings). He had spent three weeks working on the French version of a treatise on challenges and appeals by José Norberto Allende, professor at the University of Santiago. It's rare that there's wind in Paris, and even less seldom a wind like this that swirled around corners and rose up to whip at old wooden venetian blinds behind which astonished ladies commented variously on how unreliable the weather had been these last few years. But the sun was out also, riding the wind and friend of the cats, so there was nothing that would keep me from taking a walk along the docks of the Seine and taking photos of the Conservatoire and Sainte-Chapelle. It was hardly ten o'clock, and I figured that by eleven the light would be good, the best you can get in the fall; to kill some time I detoured around by the Ile Saint-Louis and started to walk along the quai d'Anjou, I stared for a bit at the hôtel de Lauzun, I recited bits from Apollinaire which always get into my head whenever I pass in front of the hôtel de Lauzun (and at that I ought to be remembering the other poet, but Michel is an obstinate beggar), and when the wind stopped all at once and the sun came out at least twice as hard (I mean warmer, but really it's the same thing), I sat down on the parapet and felt terribly happy in the Sunday morning.

One of the many ways of contesting level-zero, and one of the best, is to take photographs, an activity in which one should start becoming an adept very early in life, teach it to children since it requires discipline, aesthetic education, a good eye and steady fingers. I'm not talking about waylaying the lie like any old reporter, snapping the stupid silhouette of the VIP leaving number 10 Downing Street, but in all ways when one is walking about with a camera, one has almost a duty to be attentive, to not lose that abrupt and happy rebound of sun's rays off an old stone, or the pigtails-flying run of a small girl going home with a loaf of bread or a bottle of milk. Michel knew that the photographer always worked as a permutation of his personal way of seeing the world as other than the camera insidiously imposed upon it (now a large cloud is going by, almost black), but he lacked no confidence in himself, knowing that he had only to go out without the Contax to recover the keynote of distraction, the sight without a frame around it, light without the diaphragm aperture or 1/250 sec. Right now (what a word, *now*, what a dumb lie) I was able to sit quietly on the railing overlooking the river watching the red and black motorboats passing below without it occurring to me to think photographically of the scenes, nothing more than letting myself go in the letting go of objects, running immobile in the stream of time. And then the wind was not blowing.

After, I wandered down the quai de Bourbon until getting to the end of the isle where the intimate square was (intimate because it was small, not that it was hidden, it offered its whole breast to the river and the sky), I enjoyed it, a lot. Nothing there but a couple and, of course, pigeons; maybe even some of those which are flying past now so that I'm seeing them. A leap up and I settled on the wall, and let myself turn about and be caught and fixed by the sun, giving it my face and ears and hands (I kept my gloves in my pocket). I had no desire to shoot pictures, and lit a cigarette to be doing something; I think it was that moment when the match was about to touch the tobacco that I saw the young boy for the first time.

What I'd thought was a couple seemed

much more now a boy with his mother, although at the same time I realized that it was not a kid and his mother, and that it was a couple in the sense that we always allegate to couples when we see them leaning up against the parapets or embracing on the benches in the squares. As I had nothing else to do, I had more than enough time to wonder why the boy was so nervous, like a young colt or a hare, sticking his hands into his pockets, taking them out immediately, one after the other, running his fingers through his hair, changing his stance, and especially why was he afraid, well, you could guess that from every gesture, a fear suffocated by his shyness, an impulse to step backwards which he telegraphed, his body standing as if it were on the edge of flight, holding itself back in a final pitiful decorum.

All this was so clear, ten feet away— and we were alone against the parapet at the tip of the island—that at the beginning the boy's fright didn't let me see the blond very well. Now, thinking back on it, I see her much better at that first second when I read her face (she'd turned around suddenly, swinging like a metal weathercock, and the eyes, the eyes were there), when I vaguely understood what might have been occurring to the boy and figured it would be worth the trouble to stay and watch (the wind was blowing their words away and they were speaking in a low murmur). I think that I know how to look, if it's something I know, and also that every looking oozes with mendacity, because it's that which expels us furthest outside ourselves, without the least guarantee, whereas to smell, or (but Michel rambles on to himself easily enough, there's no need to let him harangue on this way). In any case, if the likely inaccuracy can be seen beforehand, it becomes possible again to look; perhaps it suffices to choose between looking and the reality looked at, to strip things of all their unnecessary clothing. And surely all that is difficult besides.

As for the boy I remember the image before his actual body (that will clear itself up later), while now I am sure that I remember the woman's body much better than the image. She was thin and willowy, two unfair words to describe what she was, and was wearing an almost-black fur coat, almost long, almost handsome. All the morning's wind (now it was hardly a breeze and it wasn't cold) had blown through her blond hair which pared away her white, bleak face—two unfair words—and put the world at her feet and horribly alone in front of her dark eyes, her eyes fell on things like two eagles, two leaps into nothingness, two puffs of green slime. I'm not describing anything, it's more a matter of trying to understand it. And I said two puffs of green slime.

Let's be fair, the boy was well enough dressed and was sporting yellow gloves which I would have sworn belonged to his older brother, a student of law or sociology; it was pleasant to see the fingers of the gloves sticking out of his jacket pocket. For a long time I didn't see his face, barely a profile, not stupid —a terrified bird, a Fra Filippo angel, rice pudding with milk—and the back of an adolescent who wants to take up judo and has had a scuffle or two in defense of an idea or his sister. Turning fourteen, perhaps fifteen, one would guess that he was dressed and fed by his parents but without a nickel in his pocket, having to debate with his buddies before making up his mind to buy a coffee, a cognac, a pack of cigarettes. He'd walk through the streets thinking of the girls in his class, about how good it would be to go to the movies and see the latest film, or to buy novels or neckties or bottles of liquor with green and white labels on them. At home (it would be a respectable home, lunch at noon and romantic landscapes on the walls, with a dark entryway and a mahogany umbrella stand inside the door) there'd be the slow rain of time, for studying, for being mama's hope, for looking like dad, for writing to his aunt in Avignon. So that there was a lot of walking the streets, the whole of the river for him (but without a nickel) and the mysterious city of fifteen-year-olds with its signs in doorways, its terrifying cats, a paper of fried potatoes for thirty francs, the pornographic magazine folded four ways, a solitude like the emptiness of his pockets, the eagerness for so much that was incomprehensible but illuminated by a total love, by the availability analogous to the wind and the streets.

This biography was of the boy and of any boy whatsoever, but this particular one now, you could see he was insular, surrounded solely by the blond's presence as she continued talking with him. (I'm tired of insisting, but two long ragged ones just went by. That morning I don't think I looked at the sky once, because what was happening with the boy and the woman appeared so soon I could do nothing but look at them and wait, look at them and . . .) To cut it short, the boy was agitated and one could guess without too much trouble what had just occurred a few minutes before, at most half-an-hour. The boy had come onto the tip of the island, seen the woman and thought her marvelous. The woman was waiting for that because she was there waiting for that, or maybe the boy arrived before her and she saw him from one of the balconies or from a car and got out to meet him, starting the conversation with whatever, from the beginning she was sure that he was going to be afraid and want to run off, and that, naturally, he'd stay, stiff and sullen, pretending experience and the pleasure of the adventure. The rest was easy because it was happening ten feet away from me, and anyone could have gauged the stages of the game, the derisive, competitive fencing; its major attraction was not that it was happening but in foreseeing its denouement. The boy would try to end it by pretending a date, an obligation, what-

ever, and would go stumbling off disconcerted, wishing he were walking with some assurance, but naked under the mocking glance which would follow him until he was out of sight. Or rather, he would stay there, fascinated or simply incapable of taking the initiative, and the woman would begin to touch his face gently, muss his hair, still talking to him voicelessly, and soon would take him by the arm to lead him off, unless he, with an uneasiness beginning to tinge the edge of desire, even his stake in the adventure, would rouse himself to put his arm around her waist and to kiss her. Any of this could have happened, though it did not, and perversely Michel waited, sitting on the railing, making the settings almost without looking at the camera, ready to take a picturesque shot of a corner of the island with an uncommon couple talking and looking at one another.

Strange how the scene (almost nothing: two figures there mismatched in their youth) was taking on a disquieting aura. I thought it was I imposing it, and that my photo, if I shot it, would reconstitute things in their true stupidity. I would have liked to know what he was thinking, a man in a grey hat sitting at the wheel of a car parked on the dock which led up to the footbridge, and whether he was reading the paper or asleep. I had just discovered him because people inside a parked car have a tendency to disappear, they get lost in that wretched, private cage stripped of the beauty that motion and danger give it. And nevertheless, the car had been there the whole time, forming part (or deforming that part) of the isle. A car: like saying a lighted streetlamp, a park bench. Never like saying wind, sunlight, those elements always new to the skin and the eyes, and also the boy and the woman, unique, put there to change the island, to show it to me in another way. Finally, it may have been that the man with the newspaper also became aware of what was happening and would, like me, feel that malicious sensation of waiting for everything to happen. Now the woman had swung around smoothly, putting the young boy between herself and the wall, I saw them almost in profile, and he was taller, though not much taller, and yet she dominated him, it seemed like she was hovering over him (her laugh, all at once, a whip of feathers), crushing him just by being there, smiling, one hand taking a stroll through the air. Why wait any longer? Aperture at sixteen, a sighting which would not include the horrible black car, but yes, that tree, necessary to break up too much grey space . . .

I raised the camera, pretended to study a focus which did not include them, and waited and watched closely, sure that I would finally catch the revealing expression, one that would sum it all up, life that is rhythmed by movement but which a stiff image destroys, taking time in cross section, if we do not choose the essential imperceptible fraction of it. I did not have to wait long. The woman was getting on with the job of handcuffing the boy smoothly, stripping from him what was left of his freedom a hair at a time, in an incredibly slow and delicious torture. I imagined the possible endings (now a small fluffy cloud appears, almost alone in the sky), I saw their arrival at the house (a basement apartment probably, which she would have filled with large cushions and cats) and conjectured the boy's terror and his desperate decision to play it cool and to be led off pretending there was nothing new in it for him. Closing my eyes, if I did in fact close my eyes, I set the scene: the teasing kisses, the woman mildly repelling the hands which were trying to undress her, like in novels, on a bed that would have a lilac-colored comforter, on the other hand she taking off his clothes, plainly mother and son under a milky yellow light, and everything would end up as usual, perhaps, but maybe everything would go otherwise,

and the initiation of the adolescent would not happen, she would not let it happen, after a long prologue wherein the awkwardnesses, the exasperating caresses, the running of hands over bodies would be resolved in who knows what, in a separate and solitary pleasure, in a petulant denial mixed with the art of tiring and disconcerting so much poor innocence. It might go like that, it might very well go like that; that woman was not looking for the boy as a lover, and at the same time she was dominating him toward some end impossible to understand if you do not imagine it as a cruel game, the desire to desire without satisfaction, to excite herself for someone else, someone who in no way could be that kid.

Michel is guilty of making literature, of indulging in fabricated unrealities. Nothing pleases him more than to imagine exceptions to the rule, individuals outside the species, not-always-repugnant monsters. But that woman invited speculation, perhaps giving clues enough for the fantasy to hit the bullseye. Before she left, and now that she would fill my imaginings for several days, for I'm given to ruminating, I decided not to lose a moment more. I got it all into the view-finder (with the tree, the railing, the eleven-o'clock sun) and took the shot. In time to realize that they both had noticed and stood there looking at me, the boy surprised and as though questioning, but she was irritated, her face and body flat-footedly hostile, feeling robbed, ignominiously recorded on a small chemical image.

I might be able to tell it in much greater detail but it's not worth the trouble. The woman said that no one had the right to take a picture without permission, and demanded that I hand her over the film. All this in a dry, clear voice with a good Parisian accent, which rose in color and tone with every phrase. For my part, it hardly mattered whether she got the roll of film or not, but anyone who knows me will tell you, if you want anything from me, ask nicely. With the result that I restricted myself to formulating the opinion that not only was photography in public places not prohibited, but it was looked upon with decided favor, both private and official. And while that was getting said, I noticed on the sly how the boy was falling back, sort of actively backing up though without moving, and all at once (it seemed almost incredible) he turned and broke into a run, the poor kid, thinking that he was walking off and in fact in full flight, running past the side of the car, disappearing like a gossamer filament of angel-spit in the morning air.

But filaments of angel-spittle are also called devil-spit, and Michel had to endure rather particular curses, to hear himself called meddler and imbecile, taking great pains meanwhile to smile and to abate with simple movements of his head such a hard sell. As I was beginning to get tired, I heard the car door slam. The man in the grey hat was there, looking at us. It was only at that point that I realized he was playing a part in the comedy.

He began to walk toward us, carrying in his hand the paper he had been pretending to read. What I remember best is the grimace that twisted his mouth askew, it covered his face with wrinkles, changed somewhat both in location and shape because his lips trembled and the grimace went from one side of his mouth to the other as though it were on wheels, independent and involuntary. But the rest stayed fixed, a flour-powdered clown or bloodless man, dull dry skin, eyes deepset, the nostrils black and prominently visible, blacker than the eyebrows or hair or the black necktie. Walking cautiously as though the pavement hurt his feet; I saw patent-leather shoes with such thin soles that he must have felt every roughness in the pavement. I don't know why I got down off the railing, nor very well why I de-

cided to not give them the photo, to refuse that demand in which I guessed at their fear and cowardice. The clown and the woman consulted one another in silence: we made a perfect and unbearable triangle, something I felt compelled to break with a crack of a whip. I laughed in their faces and began to walk off, a little more slowly, I imagine, than the boy. At the level of the first houses, beside the iron footbridge, I turned around to look at them. They were not moving, but the man had dropped his newspaper; it seemed to me that the woman, her back to the parapet, ran her hands over the stone with the classical and absurd gesture of someone pursued looking for a way out.

What happened after that happened here, almost just now, in a room on the fifth floor. Several days went by before Michel developed the photos he'd taken on Sunday; his shots of the Conservatoire and of Sainte-Chapelle were all they should be. Then he found two or three proof-shots he'd forgotten, a poor attempt to catch a cat perched astonishingly on the roof of a rambling public urinal, and also the shot of the blond and the kid. The negative was so good that he made an enlargement; the enlargement was so good that he made one very much larger, almost the size of a poster. It did not occur to him (now one wonders and wonders) that only the shots of the Conservatoire were worth so much work. Of the whole series, the snapshot of the tip of the island was the only one which interested him; he tacked up the enlargement on one wall of the room, and the first day he spent some time looking at it and remembering, that gloomy operation of comparing the memory with the gone reality; a frozen memory, like any photo, where nothing is missing, not even, and especially, nothingness, the true solidifier of the scene. There was the woman, there was the boy, the tree rigid above their heads, the sky as sharp as the stone of the parapet, clouds and stones melded into a single substance and inseparable (now one with sharp edges is going by, like a thunderhead). The first two days I accepted what I had done, from the photo itself to the enlargement on the wall, and didn't even question that every once in a while I would interrupt my translation of José Norberto Allende's treatise to encounter once more the woman's face, the dark splotches on the railing. I'm such a jerk; it had never occurred to me that when we look at a photo from the front, the eyes reproduce exactly the position and the vision of the lens; it's these things that are taken for granted and it never occurs to anyone to think about them. From my chair, with the typewriter directly in front of me, I looked at the photo ten feet away, and then it occurred to me that I had hung it exactly at the point of view of the lens. It looked very good that way; no doubt, it was the best way to appreciate a photo, though the angle from the diagonal doubtless has its pleasures and might even divulge different aspects. Every few minutes, for example when I was unable to find the way to say in good French what José Norberto Allende was saying in very good Spanish, I raised my eyes and looked at the photo; sometimes the woman would catch my eye, sometimes the boy, sometimes the pavement where a dry leaf had fallen admirably situated to heighten a lateral section. Then I rested a bit from my labors, and I enclosed myself again happily in that morning in which the photo was drenched, I recalled ironically the angry picture of the woman demanding I give her the photograph, the boy's pathetic and ridiculous flight, the entrance on the scene of the man with the white face. Basically, I was satisfied with myself; my part had not been too brilliant, and since the French have been given the gift of the sharp response, I did not see very well why I'd chosen to leave without a complete demonstration of the rights, privileges and prerogatives of citizens. The important thing, the really important thing was having helped the kid to escape in time (this in case my theorizing was correct, which was not sufficiently proven, but the running away itself seemed to show it so). Out of plain meddling, I had given him the opportunity finally to take advantage of his fright to do something useful; now he would be regretting it, feeling his honor impaired, his manhood diminished. That was better than the attentions of a woman capable of looking as she had looked at him on that island. Michel is something of a puritan at times, he believes that one should not seduce someone from a position of strength. In the last analysis, taking that photo had been a good act.

Well, it wasn't because of the good act that I looked at it between paragraphs while I was working. At that moment I didn't know the reason, the reason I had tacked the enlargement onto the wall; maybe all fatal acts happen that way, and that is the condition of their fulfillment. I don't think the almost-furtive trembling of the leaves on the tree alarmed me, I was working on a sentence and rounded it out successfully. Habits are like immense herbariums, in the end an enlargement of 32 × 28 looks like a movie screen, where, on the tip of the island, a woman is speaking with a boy and a tree is shaking its dry leaves over their heads.

But her hands were just too much. I had just translated: "In that case, the second key resides in the intrinsic nature of difficulties which societies . . ." —when I saw the woman's hand beginning to stir slowly, finger by finger. There was nothing left of me, a phrase in French which I would never have to finish, a typewriter on the floor, a chair that squeaked and shook, fog. The kid had ducked his head like boxers do when they've done all they can and are waiting for the final blow to fall; he had turned up the collar of his overcoat and seemed more a prisoner than ever, the perfect victim helping promote the catastrophe. Now the woman was talking into his ear, and her hand opened again to lay itself against his cheekbone, to caress and caress it, burning it, taking her time. The kid was less startled than he was suspicious, once or twice he poked his head over the woman's shoulder and she continued talking, saying something that made him look back every few minutes toward that area where Michel knew the car was parked and the man in the grey hat, carefully eliminated from the photo but present in the boy's eyes (how doubt that now) in the words of the woman, in the woman's hands, in the vicarious presence of the woman. When I saw the man come up, stop near them and look at them, his hands in his pockets and a stance somewhere between disgusted and demanding, the master who is about to whistle in his dog after a frolic in the square, I understood, if that was to understand, what had to happen now, what had to have happened then, what would have to happen at that moment, among these people, just where I had poked my nose in to upset an established order, interfering innocently in that which had not happened, but which was now going to happen, now was going to be fulfilled. And what I had imagined earlier was much less horrible than the reality, that woman, who was not there by herself, she was not caressing or propositioning or encouraging for her own pleasure, to lead the angel away with his tousled hair and play the tease with his terror and his eager grace. The real boss was waiting there, smiling petulantly, already certain of the business; he was not the first to send a woman in the vanguard, to bring him the prisoners manacled with flowers. The rest of it would be so simple, the car, some house or another, drinks, stimulating engravings, tardy tears, the awakening in hell. And there was nothing I could do, this time I could do absolutely

nothing. My strength had been a photograph, that, there, where they were taking their revenge on me, demonstrating clearly what was going to happen. The photo had been taken, the time had run out, gone; we were so far from one another, the abusive act had certainly already taken place, the tears already shed, and the rest conjecture and sorrow. All at once the order was inverted, they were alive, moving, they were deciding and had decided, they were going to their future; and I on this side, prisoner of another time, in a room on the fifth floor, to not know who they were, that woman, that man, and that boy, to be only the lens of my camera, something fixed, rigid, incapable of intervention. It was horrible, their mocking me, deciding it before my impotent eye, mocking me, for the boy again was looking at the flour-faced clown and I had to accept the fact that he was going to say yes, that the proposition carried money with it or a gimmick, and I couldn't yell for him to run, or even open the road to him again with a new photo, a small and almost meek intervention which would ruin the framework of drool and perfume. Everything was going to resolve itself right there, at that moment; there was like an immense silence which had nothing to do with physical silence. It was stretching it out, setting itself up. I think I screamed, I screamed terribly, and that at that exact second I realized that I was beginning to move toward them, four inches, a step, another step, the tree swung its branches rhythmically in the foreground, a place where the railing was tarnished emerged from the frame, the woman's face turned toward me as though surprised, was enlarging, and then I turned a bit, I mean that the camera turned a little, and without losing sight of the woman, I began to close in on the man who was looking at me with the black holes he had in place of eyes, surprised and angered both, he looked, wanting to nail me onto the air, and at that instant I happened to see something like a large bird outside the focus that was flying in a single swoop in front of the picture, and I leaned up against the wall of my room and was happy because the boy had just managed to escape, I saw him running off, in focus again, sprinting with his hair flying in the wind, learning finally to fly across the island, to arrive at the footbridge, return to the city. For the second time he'd escaped them, for the second time I was helping him to escape, returning him to his precarious paradise. Out of breath, I stood in front of them; no need to step closer, the game was played out. Of the woman you could see just maybe a shoulder and a bit of the hair, brutally cut off by the frame of the picture; but the man was directly center, his mouth half open, you could see a shaking black tongue, and he lifted his hands slowly, bringing them into the foreground, an instant still in perfect focus, and then all of him a lump that blotted out the island, the

tree, and I shut my eyes, I didn't want to see any more, and I covered my face and broke into tears like an idiot.

Now there's a big white cloud, as on all these days, all this untellable time. What remains to be said is always a cloud, two clouds, or long hours of a sky perfectly clear, a very clean, clear rectangle tacked up with pins on the wall of my room. That was what I saw when I opened my eyes and dried them with my fingers: the clear sky, and then a cloud that drifted in from the left, passed gracefully and slowly across and disappeared on the right. And then another, and for a change sometimes, everything gets grey, all one enormous cloud, and suddenly the splotches of rain cracking down, for a long spell you can see it raining over the picture, like a spell of weeping reversed, and little by little, the frame becomes clear, perhaps the sun comes out, and again the clouds begin to come, two at a time, three at a time. And the pigeons once in a while, and a sparrow or two.

Alain Robbe-Grillet (1922–   )

THE SECRET ROOM

to Gustave Moreau

The first thing to be seen is a red stain, of a deep, dark, shiny red, with almost black shadows. It is in the form of an irregular rosette, sharply outlined, extending in several directions in wide outflows of unequal length, dividing and dwindling afterward into single sinuous streaks. The whole stands out against a smooth, pale surface, round in shape, at once dull and pearly, a hemisphere joined by gentle curves to an expanse

of the same pale color—white darkened by the shadowy quality of the place: a dungeon, a sunken room, or a cathedral —glowing with a diffused brilliance in the semidarkness.

Farther back, the space is filled with the cylindrical trunks of columns, repeated with progressive vagueness in their retreat toward the beginning of a vast stone stairway, turning slightly as it rises, growing narrower and narrower as it approaches the high vaults where it disappears.

The whole setting is empty, stairway and colonnades. Alone, in the foreground, the stretched-out body gleams feebly, marked with the red stain—a white body whose full, supple flesh can be sensed, fragile, no doubt, and vulnerable. Alongside the bloody hemisphere another identical round form, this one intact, is seen at almost the same angle of view; but the haloed point at its summit, of darker tint, is in this case quite recognizable, whereas the other is entirely destroyed, or at least covered by the wound.

In the background, near the top of the stairway, a black silhouette is seen fleeing, a man wrapped in a long, floating cape, ascending the last steps without turning around, his deed accomplished. A thin smoke rises in twisting scrolls from a sort of incense burner placed on a high stand of ironwork with a silvery glint. Nearby lies the milk-white body, with wide streaks of blood running from the left breast, along the flank and on the hip.

It is a fully rounded woman's body, but not heavy, completely nude, lying on its back, the bust raised up somewhat by thick cushions thrown down on the floor, which is covered with Oriental rugs. The waist is very narrow, the neck long and thin, curved to one side, the head thrown back into a darker area where, even so, the facial features may be discerned, the partly opened mouth, the wide-staring eyes, shining with a fixed brilliance, and the mass of long, black hair spread out in a complicated wavy disorder over a heavily folded cloth, of velvet perhaps, on which also rest the arm and shoulder.

It is a uniformly colored velvet of dark purple, or which seems so in this lighting. But purple, brown, blue also seem to dominate in the colors of the cushions—only a small portion of which is hidden beneath the velvet cloth, and which protrude noticeably, lower down,

beneath the bust and waist—as well as in the Oriental patterns of the rugs on the floor. Farther on, these same colors are picked up again in the stone of the paving and the columns, the vaulted archways, the stairs, and the less discernible surfaces that disappear into the farthest reaches of the room.

The dimensions of this room are difficult to determine exactly; the body of the young sacrificial victim seems at first glance to occupy a substantial portion of it, but the vast size of the stairway leading down to it would imply rather that this is not the whole room, whose considerable space must in reality extend all around, right and left, as it does toward the faraway browns and blues among the columns standing in line, in every direction, perhaps toward other sofas, thick carpets, piles of cushions and fabrics, other tortured bodies, other incense burners.

It is also difficult to say where the light comes from. No clue, on the columns or on the floor, suggests the direction of the rays. Nor is any window or torch visible. The milkwhite body itself seems to light the scene, with its full breasts, the curve of its thighs, the rounded belly, the full buttocks, the stretched-out legs, widely spread, and the black tuft of the exposed sex, provocative, proffered, useless now.

The man has already moved several steps back. He is now on the first steps of the stairs, ready to go up. The bottom steps are wide and deep, like the steps leading up to some great building, a temple or theater; they grow smaller as they ascend, and at the same time describe a wide, helical curve, so gradually that the stairway has not yet made a half-turn by the time it disappears near the top of the vaults, reduced then to a steep, narrow flight of steps without handrail, vaguely outlined, moreover, in the thickening darkness beyond.

But the man does not look in this direction, where his movement nonetheless carries him; his left foot on the second step and his right foot already touching the third, with his knee bent, he has turned around to look at the spectacle for one last time. The long, floating cape thrown hastily over his shoulders, clasped in one hand at his waist, has been whirled around by the rapid circular motion that has just caused his head and chest to turn in the opposite direction, and a corner of the cloth remains suspended in the air as if blown by a gust of wind; this corner, twisting around upon itself in the form of a loose S, reveals the red silk lining with its gold embroidery.

The man's features are impassive, but tense, as if in expectation—or perhaps fear—of some sudden event, or surveying with one last glance the total immobility of the scene. Though he is looking backward, his whole body is turned slightly forward, as if he were continuing up the stairs. His right arm —not the one holding the edge of the cape—is bent sharply toward the left, toward a point in space where the balustrade should be, if this stairway had one, an interrupted gesture, almost incomprehensible, unless it arose from an instinctive movement to grasp the absent support.

As to the direction of his glance, it is certainly aimed at the body of the victim lying on the cushions, its extended members stretched out in the form of a cross, its bust raised up, its head thrown back. But the face is perhaps hidden from the man's eyes by one of the columns, standing at the foot of the stairs. The young woman's right hand touches the floor just at the foot of this column. The fragile wrist is encircled by an iron bracelet. The arm is almost in darkness, only the hand receiving enough light to make the thin, outspread fingers clearly visible against the circular protrusion at the base of the stone column. A black metal chain running around the column passes through a ring affixed to the bracelet, binding the wrist tightly to the column.

At the top of the arm a rounded shoulder, raised up by the cushions, also stands out well lighted, as well as the neck, the throat, and the other shoulder, the armpit with its soft hair, the left arm likewise pulled back with its wrist bound in the same manner to the base of another column, in the extreme foreground; here the iron bracelet and the chain are fully displayed, represented with perfect clarity down to the slightest details.

The same is true, still in the foreground but at the other side, for a similar chain, but not quite as thick, wound directly around the ankle, running twice around the column and terminating in a heavy iron ring embedded in the floor. About a yard farther back, or perhaps slightly farther, the right foot is identically chained. But it is the left foot, and its chain, that are the most minutely depicted.

The foot is small, delicate, finely modeled. In several places the chain has broken the skin, causing noticeable if not extensive depressions in the flesh. The chain links are oval, thick, the size of an eye. The ring in the floor resembles those used to attach horses; it lies almost touching the stone pavement to which it is riveted by a massive iron peg. A few inches away is the edge of a rug; it is grossly wrinkled at this point, doubtless as a result of the convulsive, but necessarily very restricted, movements of the victim attempting to struggle.

The man is still standing about a yard away, half leaning over her. He looks at her face, seen upside down, her dark eyes made larger by their surrounding eyeshadow, her mouth wide open as if screaming. The man's posture allows his face to be seen only in a vague profile, but one senses in it a violent exaltation, despite the rigid attitude, the silence, the immobility. His back is slightly arched. His left hand, the only one visible, holds up at some distance from the body a piece of cloth, some dark-colored piece of clothing, which drags on the carpet, and which must be the long cape with its gold-embroidered lining.

This immense silhouette hides most of the bare flesh over which the red stain, spreading from the globe of the breast, runs in long rivulets that branch out, growing narrower, upon the pale background of the bust and the flank. One thread has reached the armpit and runs in an almost straight, thin line along the arm; others have run down toward the waist and traced out, along one side of the belly, the hip, the top of the thigh, a more random network already starting to congeal. Three or four tiny veins have reached the hollow between the legs, meeting in a sinuous line, touching the point of the V formed by the outspread legs, and disappearing into the black tuft.

Look, now the flesh is still intact: the black tuft and the white belly, the soft curve of the hips, the narrow waist, and, higher up, the pearly breasts rising and falling in time with the rapid breathing, whose rhythm grows more accelerated. The man, close to her, one knee on the floor, leans farther over. The head, with its long, curly hair, which alone is free to move somewhat, turns from side to side, struggling; finally the woman's mouth twists open, while the flesh is torn open, the blood spurts out over the tender skin, stretched tight, the carefully shadowed eyes grow abnormally larger, the mouth opens wider, the head twists violently, one last time, from right to left, then more gently, to fall back finally and become still, amid the mass of black hair spread out on the velvet.

At the very top of the stone stairway, the little door has opened, allowing a yellowish but sustained shaft of light to enter, against which stands out the dark silhouette of the man wrapped in his long cloak. He has but to climb a few more steps to reach the threshold.

Afterward, the whole setting is empty, the enormous room with its purple shadows and its stone columns proliferating in all directions, the monumental staircase with no handrail that twists upward, growing narrower and vaguer as it rises into the darkness, toward the top of the vaults where it disappears.

Near the body, whose wound has stiffened, whose brilliance is already growing dim, the thin smoke from the incense burner traces complicated scrolls in the still air: first a coil turned horizontally to the left, which then straightens out and rises slightly, then returns to the axis of its point of origin, which it crosses as it moves to the right, then turns back in the first direction, only to wind back again, thus forming an irregular sinusoidal curve, more and move flattened out, and rising, vertically, toward the top of the canvas.

THE COLLECTED WORKS OF
BILLY *The* KID

Michael Ondaatje (1943-   )

Editors' note:

If the following pages look rather strange to you, the effect is intentional, for the message of this narrative is to some degree visual as well as verbal.

We have used the Norton edition (a photocopy of the original House of Anansi edition) as our own photocopy; the pages of continuous prose, as well as pictures, borders, diagrams, and significant white spaces, are in facsimile. With the author's approval, several pairs of shorter poems and prose pieces that were originally printed separately on successive pages are arranged on a single page in our edition.

Author's note:

The death of Tunstall, the reminiscences by Paulita Maxwell and Sallie Chisum on Billy, are essentially made up of statements made to Walter Noble Burns in his book *The Saga of Billy the Kid* published in 1926. The comment about taking photographs around 1870-80 is by the great Western photographer L. A. Huffman and appears in his book *Huffman, Frontier Photographer*. (Some of the photographs in this book are his.) The last piece of dialogue between Garrett and Poe is taken from an account written by Deputy John W. Po in 1919 when he was the President of the National Bank of Roswell, New Mexico. The comic book legend is real.

With these basic sources I have edited, rephrased, and slightly reworked the originals. But the emotions belong to their authors.

I send you a picture of Billy made with the Perry shutter as quick as it can be worked — Pyro and soda developer. I am making daily experiments now and find I am able to take passing horses at a lively trot square across the line of fire — bits of snow in the air — spokes well defined — some blur on top of wheel but sharp in the main — men walking are no trick — I will send you proofs sometime. I shall show you what can be done from the saddle without ground glass or tripod — please notice when you get the specimens that they were made with the lens wide open and many of the best exposed when my horse was in motion.

These are the killed.

(By me) —
Morton, Baker, early friends of mine.
Joe Bernstein. 3 Indians.
A blacksmith when I was twelve, with a knife.
5 Indians in self defence (behind a very safe rock).
One man who bit me during a robbery.
Brady, Hindman, Beckwith, Joe Clark,
Deputy Jim Carlyle, Deputy Sheriff J. W. Bell.
And Bob Ollinger. A rabid cat
birds during practice,

These are the killed.

(By them) —
Charlie, Tom O'Folliard
Angela D's split arm,
                    and Pat Garrett
sliced off my head.
Blood a necklace on me all my life.

Christmas at Fort Sumner, 1880. There were five of us together then. Wilson, Dave Rudabaugh, Charlie Bowdre, Tom O'Folliard, and me. In November we celebrated my 21st birthday, mixing red dirt and alcohol — a public breathing throughout the night. The next day we were told that Pat Garrett had been made sheriff and had accepted it. We were bad for progress in New Mexico and cattle politicians like Chisum wanted the bad name out. They made Garrett sheriff and he sent me a letter saying move out or I will get you Billy. The government sent a Mr. Azariah F. Wild to help him out. Between November and December I killed Jim Carlyle over some mixup, he being a friend.

Tom O'Folliard decided to go east then, said he would meet up with us in Sumner for Christmas. Goodbye goodbye. A few days before Christmas we were told that Garrett was in Sumner waiting for us all. Christmas night. Garrett, Mason, Wild, with four or five others. Tom O'Folliard rides into town, leaning his rifle between the horse's ears. He would shoot from the waist now which, with a rifle, was pretty good, and he was always accurate.

Garrett had been waiting for us, playing poker with the others, guns on the floor beside them. Told that Tom was riding in alone, he went straight to the window and shot O'Folliard's horse dead. Tom collapsed with the horse still holding the gun and blew out Garrett's window. Garrett already halfway downstairs. Mr. Wild shot at Tom from the other side of the street, rather unnecessarily shooting the horse again. If Tom had used stirrups and didnt swing his legs so much he would probably have been locked under the animal. O'Folliard moved soon. When Garrett had got to ground level, only the horse was there in the open street, good and dead. He couldnt shout to ask Wild where O'Folliard was or he would've got busted. Wild started to yell to tell Garrett though and Tom killed him at once. Garrett fired at O'Folliard's flash and took his shoulder off. Tom O'Folliard screaming out onto the quiet Fort Sumner street, Christmas night, walking over to Garrett, no shoulder left, his jaws tilting up and down like mad bladders going. Too mad to even aim at Garrett. Son of a bitch son of a bitch, as Garrett took clear aim and blew him out.

Garrett picked him up, the head broken in two, took him back upstairs into the hotel room. Mason stretched out a blanket neat in the corner. Garrett placed Tom O'Folliard down, broke open Tom's rifle, took the remaining shells and placed them by him. They had to wait till morning now. They continued their poker game till six a.m. Then remembered they hadnt done anything about Wild. So the four of them went out, brought Wild into the room. At eight in the morning Garrett buried Tom O'Folliard. He had known him quite well. Then he went to the train station, put Azariah F. Wild on ice and sent him back to Washington.

In Boot Hill there are over 400 graves. It takes
the space of 7 acres. There is an elaborate gate
but the path keeps to no main route for it tangles
like branches of a tree among the gravestones.

300 of the dead in Boot Hill died violently
200 by guns, over 50 by knives
some were pushed under trains — a popular
and overlooked form of murder in the west.
Some from brain haemorrhages resulting from bar fights
at least 10 killed in barbed wire.

In Boot Hill there are only two graves that belong to women
and they are the only known suicides in that graveyard

The others, I know, did not see the wounds appearing in the sky, in the air. Sometimes a normal forehead in front of me leaked brain gasses. Once a nose clogged right before me, a lock of skin formed over the nostrils, and the shocked face had to start breathing through mouth, but then the mustache bound itself in the lower teeth and he began to gasp loud the hah! hah! going strong — churned onto the floor, collapsed out, seeming in the end to be breathing out of his eye — tiny needle jets of air reaching into the throat. I told no one. If Angela D. had been with me then, not even her; not Sallie, John, Charlie, or Pat. In the end the only thing that never changed, never became deformed, were animals.

MMMMMMMM mm thinking
moving across the world on horses
body split at the edge of their necks
neck sweat eating at my jeans
moving across the world on horses
so if I had a newsman's brain I'd say
well some morals are physical
must be clear and open
like diagram of watch or star
one must eliminate much
that is one turns when the bullet leaves you
walk off see none of the thrashing
the very eyes welling up like bad drains
believing then the moral of newspapers or gun
where bodies are mindless as paper flowers you dont feed
or give to drink
that is why I can watch the stomach of clocks
shift their wheels and pins into each other
and emerge living, for hours

When I caught Charlie Bowdre dying
tossed 3 feet by bang bullets giggling
at me face tossed in a gaggle
he pissing into his trouser legs in pain
face changing like fast sunshine o my god
o my god billy I'm pissing watch
your hands
                      while the eyes grew all over his body

Jesus I never knew that did you
the nerves shot out
the liver running around there
like a headless hen jerking
brown all over the yard
seen that too at my aunt's
never eaten hen since then

Blurred a waist high river
foam against the horse
riding naked clothes and boots
and pistol in the air

Crossed a crooked river
loving in my head
ambled dry on stubble
shot a crooked bird

Held it in my fingers
the eyes were small and far
it yelled out like a trumpet
destroyed it of its fear

After shooting Gregory
this is what happened

I'd shot him well and careful
made it explode under his heart
so it wouldnt last long and
was about to walk away
when this chicken paddles out to him
and as he was falling hops on his neck
digs the beak into his throat
straightens legs and heaves
a red and blue vein out

Meanwhile he fell
and the chicken walked away

still tugging at the vein
till it was 12 yards long
as if it held that body like a kite
Gregory's last words being

get away from me yer stupid chicken

Tilts back to fall
black hair swivelling off her
shattering the pillow
Billy she says
the tall gawky body spitting electric
off the sheets to my arm
leans her whole body out
so breasts are thinner
stomach is a hollow
where the bright bush jumps
this is the first time
bite into her side leave
a string of teeth marks
she hooks in two and covers me
my hand locked
her body nearly breaking off my fingers
pivoting like machines in final speed

later my hands cracked in love juice
fingers paralysed by it arthritic
these beautiful fingers I couldnt move
faster than a crippled witch now

The barn I stayed in for a week then was at the edge of a farm and had been deserted it seemed for several years, though built of stone and good wood. The cold dark grey of the place made my eyes become used to soft light and I burned out my fever there. It was twenty yards long, about ten yards wide. Above me was another similar sized room but the floors were unsafe for me to walk on. However I heard birds and the odd animal scrape their feet, the rotten wood magnifying the sound so they entered my dreams and nightmares.

But it was the colour and light of the place that made me stay there, not my fever. It became a calm week. It was the colour and the light. The colour a grey with remnants of brown — for instance those rust brown pipes and metal objects that before had held bridles or pails, that slid to machine uses; the thirty or so grey cans in one corner of the room, their ellipses, from where I sat, setting up patterns in the dark.

When I had arrived I opened two windows and a door and the sun poured blocks and angles in, lighting up the floor's skin of feathers and dust and old grain. The windows looked out onto fields and plants grew at the door, me killing them gradually with my urine. Wind came in wet and brought in birds who flew to the other end of the room to get their aim to fly out again. An old tap hung from the roof, the same colour as the walls, so once I knocked myself out on it.

For that week then I made a bed of the table there and lay out my fever, whatever it was. I began to block my mind of all thought. Just sensed the room and learnt what my body could do, what it could survive, what colours it liked best, what songs I sang best. There were animals who did not move out and accepted me as a larger breed. I ate the old grain with them, drank from a constant puddle about twenty yards away from the barn. I saw no human and heard no human voice, learned to squat the best way when shitting, used leaves for wiping, never ate flesh or touched another animal's flesh, never entered his boundary. We were all aware and allowed each other. The fly who sat on my arm, after his inquiry, just went away, ate his disease and kept it in him. When I walked I avoided the cobwebs who had places to grow to, who had stories to finish. The flies caught in those acrobat nets were the only murder I saw.

And in the barn next to us there was another granary, separated
by just a thick wood door. In it a hundred or so rats, thick rats,
eating and eating the foot deep pile of grain abandoned now and
fermenting so that at the end of my week, after a heavy rain
storm burst the power in those seeds and brought drunkenness
into the minds of those rats, they abandoned the sanity of eating
the food before them and turned on each other and grotesque
and awkwardly because of their size they went for each other's
eyes and ribs so the yellow stomachs slid out and they came
through that door and killed a chipmunk — about ten of them
onto that one striped thing and the ten eating each other before
they realised the chipmunk was long gone so that I, sitting on
the open window with its thick sill where they couldnt reach me,
filled my gun and fired again and again into their slow wheel
across the room at each boommm, and reloaded and fired again
and again till I went through the whole bag of bullet supplies —
the noise breaking out the seal of silence in my ears, the smoke
sucked out of the window as it emerged from my fist and the
long twenty yard space between me and them empty but for the
floating bullet lonely as an emissary across and between the
wooden posts that never returned, so the rats continued to wheel
and stop in the silences and eat each other, some even the bullet.
Till my hand was black and the gun was hot and no other
animal of any kind remained in that room but for the boy in the
blue shirt sitting there coughing at the dust, rubbing the sweat
of his upper lip with his left forearm.

PAULITA MAXWELL: THE PHOTOGRAPH

*In 1880 a travelling photographer came through Fort Sumner.
Billy posed standing in the street near old Beaver Smith's saloon.
The picture makes him rough and uncouth.*

*The expression of his face was really boyish and pleasant.
He may have worn such clothes as appear in the picture out on
the range, but in Sumner he was careful of his personal appearance and dressed neatly and in good taste. I never liked the
picture. I don't think it does Billy justice.*

Not a story about me through their eyes then. Find the
beginning, the slight silver key to unlock it, to dig it out.
Here then is a maze to begin, be in.

Two years ago Charlie Bowdre and I criss-crossed the Canadian
border. Ten miles north of it ten miles south. Our horses stepped
from country to country, across low rivers, through different
colours of tree green. The two of us, our criss-cross like a whip
in slow motion, the ridge of action rising and falling, getting
narrower in radius till it ended and we drifted down to Mexico
and old heat. That there is nothing of depth, of significant
accuracy, of wealth in the image, I know. It is there for a
beginning.

She leans against the door, holds
her left hand at the elbow
with her right, looks at the bed

on my sheets — oranges
peeled half peeled
bright as hidden coins against the pillow

she walks slow to the window
lifts the sackcloth
and jams it horizontal on a nail
so the bent oblong of sun
hoists itself across the room
framing the bed the white flesh
of my arm

she is crossing the sun
sits on her leg here
sweeping off the peels

traces the thin bones on me
turns toppling slow back to the pillow
Bonney Bonney

I am very still
I take in all the angles of the room

January at Tivan Arroyo, called Stinking Springs more often.
With me, Charlie, Wilson, Dave Rudabaugh. Snow. Charlie
took my hat and went out to get wood and feed the horses. The
shot burnt the clothes on his stomach off and lifted him right
back into the room. Snow on Charlie's left boot. He had taken
one step out. In one hand had been an axe, in the other a pail.
No guns.

Get up Charlie, get up, go and get one. No Billy. I'm tired,
please. Jesus watch your hands Billy. Get up Charlie. I prop him
to the door, put his gun in his hand. Take off, good luck Charlie.

He stood there weaving, not moving. Then began to walk in a
perfect, incredible straight line out of the door towards Pat and
the others at the ridge of the arroyo about twenty yards away.
He couldnt even lift his gun. Moving sideways at times but
always always in a straight line. Dead on Garrett. Shoot him
Charlie. They were watching him only, not moving. Over his
shoulder I aimed at Pat, fired, and hit his shoulder braid. Hadnt
touched him. Charlie hunched. Get up Charlie kill him kill him.
Charlie got up poking the gun barrel in snow. Went straight
towards Garrett. The others had ducked down, but not Garrett
who just stood there and I didnt shoot again. Charlie he knew
was already dead now, had to go somewhere, do something, to
get his mind off the pain. Charlie went straight, now closer to
them his hands covered the mess in his trousers. Shoot him
Charlie shoot him. The blood trail he left straight as a knife cut.
Getting there getting there. Charlie getting to the arroyo,
pitching into Garrett's arms, slobbering his stomach on Garrett's
gun belt. Hello Charlie, said Pat quietly.

Snow outside. Wilson, Dave Rudabaugh and me. No windows,
the door open so we could see. Four horses outside.

Jim Payne's grandfather told him that he met Frank James
of the James Brothers once.

It was in a Los Angeles movie theatre. After the amnesty he
was given, Frank had many jobs. When Jim's grandfather
met him, he was the doorman at the Fresco Theatre.

GET YOUR TICKET TORN UP BY FRANK JAMES the poster said,
and people came for that rather than the film. Frank would say,
'Thanks for coming, go on in'.

Jim's grandfather asked him if he would like to come over and
have a beer after the film, but Frank James said 'No, but thank
you' and tore up the next ticket. He was by then an alcoholic.

Miss Angela Dickinson of Tucson
tall legs like a dancer
set the 80's style
by shaving them hairless
keeps saying
I'm too tall for you Billy
but we walk around a bit
buy a bottle and she stands
showing me her thighs
look Billy look at this
she folded on the sheet
tapping away at her knees
leans back waving feet at me
catching me like a butterfly
in the shaved legs in her Tucson room

A river you could get lost in
and the sun a flashy hawk
on the edge of it

a mile away you see the white path
of an animal moving through water

you can turn a hundred yard circle
and the horse bends dribbles his face
you step off and lie in it propping your head

till dusk and cold and the horse shift you
and you look up and moon a frozen bird's eye

H is stomach was warm
remembered this when I put my hand into
a pot of luke warm tea to wash it out
dragging out the stomach to get the bullet
he wanted to see when taking tea
with Sallie Chisum in Paris Texas

With Sallie Chisum in Paris Texas
he wanted to see when taking tea
dragging out the stomach to get the bullet
a pot of luke warm tea to wash it out
remembered this when I put my hand into
his stomach was warm

Pat Garrett, ideal assassin. Public figure, the mind of a doctor, his hands hairy, scarred, burned by rope, on his wrist there was a purple stain there all his life. Ideal assassin for his mind was unwarped. Had the ability to kill someone on the street walk back and finish a joke. One who had decided what was right and forgot all morals. He was genial to everyone even his enemies. He genuinely enjoyed people, some who were odd, the dopes, the thieves. Most dangerous for them, he understood them, what motivated their laughter and anger, what they liked to think about, how he had to act for them to like him. An academic murderer — only his vivacious humour and diverse interests made him the best kind of company. He would listen to people like Rudabaugh and giggle at their escapades. His language was atrocious in public, yet when alone he never swore.

At the age of 15 he taught himself French and never told anyone about it and never spoke to anyone in French for the next 40 years. He didnt even read French books.

Between the ages of 15 and 18 little was heard of Garrett. In Juan Para he bought himself a hotel room for two years with money he had saved and organised a schedule to learn how to drink. In the first three months he forced himself to disintegrate his mind. He would vomit everywhere. In a year he could drink two bottles a day and not vomit. He began to dream for the first time in his life. He would wake up in the mornings, his sheets soaked in urine 40% alcohol. He became frightened of flowers because they grew so slowly that he couldnt tell what they planned to do. His mind learned to be superior because of the excessive mistakes of those around him. Flowers watched him.

After two years he could drink anything, mix anything together and stay awake and react just as effectively as when sober. But he was now addicted, locked in his own game. His money was running out. He had planned the drunk to last only two years, now it continued into new months over which he had no control. He stole and sold himself to survive. One day he was robbing the house of Juanita Martinez, was discovered by her, and collapsed in her living room. In about six months she had un-iced his addiction. They married and two weeks later she died of a consumption she had hidden from him.

What happened in Garrett's mind no one knows. He did not drink, was never seen. A month after Juanita Garrett's death he arrived in Sumner.

PAULITA MAXWELL:

> I remember the first day Pat Garrett ever set foot in Fort Sumner. I was a small girl with dresses at my shoe-tops and when he came to our house and asked for a job, I stood behind my brother Pete and stared at him in open eyed wonder; he had the longest legs I'd ever seen and he looked so comical and had such a droll way of talking that after he was gone, Pete and I had a good laugh about him.

His mind was clear, his body able to drink, his feelings, unlike those who usually work their own way out of hell, not cynical about another's incapacity to get out of problems and difficulties. He did ten years of ranching, cow punching, being a buffalo hunter. He married Apolinaria Guitterrez and had five sons. He had come to Sumner then, mind full of French he never used, everything equipped to be that rare thing — a sane assassin sane assassin sane assassin sane assassin sane assassin sane

*(Miss Sallie Chisum, later Mrs. Roberts, was living in Roswell
in 1924, a sweet faced, kindly old lady of a thousand memories
of frontier days.)*

ON HER HOUSE

*The house was full of people all the time
the ranch was a little world in itself
I couldn't have been lonesome if I had tried*

*Every man worth knowing in the Southwest,
and many not worth knowing, were guests
one time or another.
What they were made no difference in their welcome.
Sometimes a man would ride up in a hurry
eat a meal in a hurry and depart in a hurry*

*Billy the Kid would come in often
and sometimes stayed for a week or two.
I remember how frightened I was the first time he came.*

Forty miles ahead of us, in almost a straight line, is the house. Angela D and I on horses moving towards it, me bringing her there. Even now, this far away, I can imagine them moving among the rooms. It is nine in the morning. They are leaning back in their chairs after their slow late Saturday breakfast. John with the heels of his brown boots on the edge of the table in the space he cleared of his plate and cup and cutlery, the cup in his hands in his lap. The table with four plates — two large two small. The remnants of bacon fat and eggs on the larger ones, the black crumbs of toast butter and marmalade (Californian) on the others. One cup in a saucer, one saucer that belonged to the cup that is in John Chisum's hands now. Across the table on the other side is Sallie, in probably her long brown and yellow dress, the ribbon down her front to the waist with pale blue buttons, a frill on either side of her neck along her shoulders. By now she would have moved the spare chair so she too could put her feet up, barefoot as always, her toes crinkling at the wind that comes from the verandah door. Her right arm would be leaning against the table and now and then she'll scrape the bottom of her cup against the saucer and drink some of the coffee, put it down and return the fingers of her right hand to bury them in the warm of her hair. They do not talk much, Sallie and John Chisum, but from here I can imagine the dialogue of noise — the scraping cup, the tilting chair, the cough, the suction as an arm lifts off a table breaking the lock that was formed by air and the wet of the surface.

On other days they would go their own ways. Chisum would be up earlier than dawn and gone before Sallie even woke and rolled over in bed, her face blind as a bird in the dark. It was only later, when the sun eventually reached the bed and slid over her eyes, that she slowly leaned up to find her body, clothesless, had got cold and pulling the sheet from the strong tuck fold at the foot of the bed brings it to her, wraps it around her while she sits in bed, the fists of her feet against her thighs trying to discover which was colder — the flesh at her feet or the flesh at her thighs, hugging the sheet to her tight until it would be a skin. Pretending to lock her arms over it as if a tight dress, warming her breasts with her hands through the material.

Once last year seeing her wrapped I said, Sallie, know what a mad man's skin is? And I showed her, filling the automatic indoor bath with warm water and lifting her and dropping her slow into the bath with the sheet around her and then heaving her out and saying that's what it is, that white thing round you. Try now to dig yourself out of it. Placed her in the bed and watched her try to escape it then.

On weekdays anyway, she'd sit like that on the bed, the sheet tight around her top and brought down to her belly, her legs having to keep themselves warm. Listening for noises around the house, the silence really, knowing John had gone, just leaving a list of things he wanted her to do. She would get up and after a breakfast that she would eat wandering around the house slowly, she would begin the work. Keeping the books, dusting his reading books, filling the lamps in the afternoon — they being emptied in the early morning by John to avoid fire danger when the sun took over the house and scorched it at noon, or dropping sideways in the early afternoon sent rays horizontal through the doors and windows. No I forgot, she had stopped that now. She left the paraffin in the lamps; instead had had John build shutters for every door and window, every hole in the wall. So that at eleven in the morning all she did was close and lock them all until the house was silent and dark blue with sunless quiet. For four hours. Eleven till three. A time when, if inside, as I was often, your footsteps sounded like clangs over the floors, echoes shuddering across the rooms. And Sallie like a ghost across the room moving in white dresses, her hair knotted as always at the neck and continuing down until it splayed and withered like eternal smoke half way between the shoulder blades and the base of cobble spine.

Yes. In white long dresses in the dark house, the large bones somehow taking on the quietness of the house. Yes I remember. After burning my legs in the fire and I came to their house, it must have been my second visit and Sallie had begun using the shutters at eleven. And they brought the bed out of the extra bedroom and propped me up at one end of the vast living room of their bungalow. And I sat there for three days not moving an inch, like some dead tree witnessing the tides or the sun and the moon taking over from each other as the house in front of me changed colour — the night, the early morning yellow, the gradual move to dark blue at 11 o clock, the new white 4 o clock sun let in, later the gradual growing dark again.

For three days, my head delirious so much I thought I was going blind twice a day, recognizing no one, certainly not the Chisums, for I had been brought out cold and dropped on their porch by someone who had gone on without waiting even for water for himself. And Sallie I suppose taking the tent sheet off my legs each morning once the shutters closed. No. Again. Sallie approaching from the far end of the room like some ghost. I didn't know who it was, a tray of things in her right hand, a lamp in the other carrying them. Me screaming stop stop STOP THERE you're going to *fall* on me! My picture now sliding so she with her tray and her lamp jerked up to the ceiling and floated down calm again and jerked to the ceiling and floated down calm again and continued forward crushing me against the wall only I didnt feel anything yet. And Sallie I suppose taking the sheet off my legs and putting on the fan so they became cold and I started to feel them again. Then starting to rub and pour calamine like ice only it felt like the tongue of a very large animal my god I remember each swab felt like the skin and flesh had been moved off completely leaving only raw bone riddled with loose nerves being blown about and banging against each other from just her slow breath.

In the long 20 yard living-dining room I remember the closing of shutters, with each one the sudden blacking out of clarity in a section of the room, leaving fewer arcs of sun each time digging into the floor. Sallie starting from one end and dis-appearing down to the far end leaving black behind her as she walked into the remaining light, making it all a cold darkness. Then in other rooms not seen by me. Then appearing vast in the thick blue in her long white dress, her hands in the pockets strolling in the quiet, because of her tallness the hips moving first, me at the far end all in black.

Her shoes off, so silent, she moves a hand straying over the
covers off John's books, till she comes and sits near me and puts
her feet up shoeless and I reach to touch them and the base of
them is hard like some semi-shelled animal but only at the base,
the rest of her foot being soft, oiled almost so smooth, the thin
blue veins wrapping themselves around the inside ankle bone
and moving like paths into the toes, the brown tanned feet of
Sallie Chisum resting on my chest, my hands rubbing them,
pushing my hands against them like a carpenter shaving wood
to find new clear pulp smelling wood beneath. My own legs
black with scars. And down the room, the parrot begins to talk
to itself in the dark, thinking it is night.

She had lived in that house fourteen years, and every year she demanded of John that she be given a pet of some strange exotic breed. Not that she did not have enough animals. She had collected several wild and broken animals that, in a way, had become exotic by their breaking. Their roof would have collapsed from the number of birds who might have lived there if the desert hadnt killed three quarters of those that tried to cross it. Still every animal that came within a certain radius of that house was given a welcome, the tame, the half born, the wild, the wounded.

I remember the first night there. John took me to see the animals. About 20 yards away from the house, he had built vast cages, all in a row. They had a tough net roof over them for the day time when they were let out but tended to stay within the shade of their cages anyway. That night John took me along and we stepped off the porch, left the last pool of light, down the steps into the dark. We walked together smoking his long narrow cigars, with each suck the nose and his mustache lighting up. We came to the low brooding whirr of noise, night sleep of animals. They were stunning things in the dark. Just shapes that shifted. You could peer into a cage and see nothing till a rattle of claws hit the grid an inch from your face and their churning feathers seemed to hiss, and a yellow pearl of an eye cracked with veins glowed through the criss crossed fence.

One of the cages had a huge owl. It was vast. All I could see
were its eyes — at least 8″ apart. The next morning however,
it turned out to be two owls, both blind in one eye. In those dark
cages the birds, there must have been 20 of them, made a steady
hum all through the night — a noise you heard only if you were
within five yards of them. Walking back to the house it was
again sheer silence from where we had come, only now we knew
they were moving and sensing the air and our departure. We
knew they continued like that all night while we slept.

Half way back to the house, the building we moved towards
seemed to be stuffed with something yellow and wet. The night,
the dark air, made it all mad. That fifteen yards away there were
bright birds in cages and here John Chisum and me walked,
strange bodies. Around us total blackness, nothing out there
but a desert for seventy miles or more, and to the left, a few
yards away, a house stuffed with yellow wet light where within
the frame of a window we saw a woman move carrying fire in
a glass funnel and container towards the window, towards the
edge of the dark where we stood.

(To come) to where eyes will
move in head like a rat
mad since locked in a biscuit tin all day
stampeding mad as a mad rats legs
bang it went was hot
under my eye
was hot small bang did it
almost a pop
I didnt hear till I was red
had a rat fyt in my head
sad billys body glancing out
body going as sweating white horses go
reeling off me wet
scuffing down my arms
wet horse white
screaming wet sweat round the house
sad billys out
floating barracuda in the brain

With the Bowdres

She is boiling us black coffee
leaning her side against the warm stove
taps her nails against the mug
Charlie talking on about things
and with a bit the edge of my eye
I sense the thin white body of my friend's wife

Strange that how I feel people
not close to me
as if their dress were against my shoulder
and as they bend down
the strange smell of their breath
moving across my face
or my eyes
magnifying the bones across a room
shifting in a wrist

Getting more difficult
things all over crawling
in the way
gotta think through
the wave of ants on him
millions a moving vest up his neck
over his head down his back
leaving a bright skull white smirking
to drop to ankles
ribs blossoming out like springs
the meat from his eyes

Last night was dreamed into a bartender
with an axe I drove into glasses of gin lifted up to be tasted

I have seen pictures of great stars,
drawings which show them straining to the centre
that would explode their white
if temperature and the speed they moved at
shifted one degree.

Or in the East have seen
the dark grey yards where trains are fitted
and the clean speed of machines
that make machines, their
red golden pouring which when cooled
mists out to rust or grey.

The beautiful machines pivoting on themselves
sealing and fusing to others
and men throwing levers like coins at them.
And there is there the same stress as with stars,
the one altered move that will make them maniac.

Mistuh. . .Patrick. . .Garrett ! ! !

Mescalaro territory is a flat region, no rivers, no trees, no grass.
In August the winds begin and at that time everybody who can
moves away. If you stayed, you couldnt see the sun for weeks
because, if opened, your eyes would be speckled and frosted
with sand. Dust and sand stick to anything wet as your eyeball,
or a small dribble from your nostril, a flesh wound, even sweat
on your shirt. A beard or mustache weighs three times as much
after you are caught in the storms. Your ears are so blocked that
you cannot hear for a good while afterwards, which is just as
well for all there is is the long constant screech and scream of
wind carrying anything it can lift.

I had been caught in the Mescalero that August for two days.
Blindfolding the horse I veered it east when the storm let down,
came to stony land and tumbleweed. Tumbleweed wont survive
in the Mescalero for it is blasted to pieces in minutes. But here,
tumbleweed moved like tires out of nowhere; you could be
knocked off your horse by them. In another half day I got to the
Chisum ranch. Had been there once a few years earlier and
had liked them very much. It was, anyway, the only place you
could have superb meals which became even better by your
realisation that there was nothing near them for almost a 100
miles. I arrived at their house mind blasted, and spent those
strange three hours while the Chisums rushed around me,
giving me drinks, gesturing towards the bath they had poured —
all in total silence for I heard nothing, only the wind I
remembered from 24 hours back — before my ears had been
gradually sprayed and locked. I put my head under water and
weaved about, the hot water stinging even more my red face.
Drunk on water, I staggered from the tub and passed out
on the bed.

Sallie came in when I was waking and threw me a towel. Can
you hear now? I nodded. Her voice like piercing explosions.
Yes, but softly, I said. She nodded. We got visitors, she said.
Do you know him? William Bonney? He's brought his girl-
friend that he plans to marry. My mind awake then. I'd of course

heard of him. But leaning back to think of it, I fell asleep. Sallie must have covered me up properly with a sheet because I woke up a long while later and was warm. I could hear the boy Bonney arguing with John.

I joined them just as they were finishing dinner. Bonney seemed relaxed and dressed very well, his left heel resting on his right knee. He ate corn, drank coffee, used a fork and knife alternately — always with his right hand. The three days we were together and at other times in our lives when we saw each other, he never used his left hand for anything except of course to shoot. He wouldn't even pick up a mug of coffee. I saw the hand, it was virgin white. Later when we talked about it, I explained about how a hand or muscle unused for much work would atrophy, grow small. He said he did fingers exercises subconsciously, on the average 12 hours a day. And it was true. From then on I noticed his left hand churning within itself, each finger circling alternately like a train wheel. Curling into balls, pouring like waves across a tablecloth. It was the most hypnotising beautiful thing I ever saw.

He jumped up, and introduced himself informally to me, not waiting for Chisum to, and pointed out Angie. She was a good 6″ taller than him, a very big woman, not fat, but big bones. She moved like some fluid competent animal.

Bonney was that weekend, and always was, charming. He must, I thought, have seduced Angie by his imagination which was usually pointless and never in control. I had expected him to be the taciturn pale wretch — the image of the sallow punk that was usually attached to him by others. The rather cruel smile, when seen close, turned out to be intricate and witty. You could never tell how he meant a phrase, whether he was serious or joking. From his eyes you could tell nothing at all. In general he had a quick, quiet humour. His only affectation was his outfit of black clothes speckled with silver buttons and silver belt lock. Also his long black hair was pulled back and tied in a knot of leather.

It was impossible to study the relationship he had with the large tall Angie. After dinner they sat in their chairs. He would usually be hooked in ridiculous positions, feet locked in the chair's arms, or lying on the floor with his feet up. He could never remain in one position more than five minutes. Angie alternately never moved violently like Billy. Only now and then she shifted that thick body, tucked her legs under those vast thighs that spread like bags of wheat, perfectly proportioned.

After an evening of considerable drinking we all retreated to our rooms. And the next morning, Billy and Angie who had been planning to leave, decided to stay. I was glad as I didnt understand either of them and wanted to see how they understood each other. At breakfast a strange thing happened that explained some things.

Sallie had had a cat named Ferns who was very old and had somehow got pains in its shoulders during the last two days. I looked at it after breakfast and saw it had been bitten by a snake. It was in fact poisoned and could not live. It already had gone half blind. John decided then to kill it and lifted the half paralysed body to take it outside. However, once out, the cat made a frantic leap, knowing what was going to happen, fell, and pulled itself by two feet under the floor boards of the house. The whole of the Chisum house was built in such a way that the house stood on a base which was 9″ off the ground. The cat was heard shifting underneath those floors and then there was silence. We all looked under the boards from the side of the house, seeing into the dark, but we couldnt see Ferns and couldnt crawl under to get him. After a good hour, from the odd thrashing, we knew the cat was still alive and in pain. It would I theorized probably live for a day and then die. We sat around on the verandah for a while and then Billy said, do you want me to kill it. Sallie without asking how said yes.

He stood up and took off his boots and socks, went to his room, returned, he had washed his hands. He asked us to go into the living room and sit still. Then he changed his mind and asked us to go out of the house and onto the verandah and keep still and quiet, not to talk. He began to walk over the kitchen floor, the living room area, almost bent in two, his face about a foot from the pine floorboards. He had the gun out now. And for about half an hour he walked around like this, sniffing away it seemed to me. Twice he stopped in the same place but continued on. He went all over the house. Finally he came back to a spot near the sofa in the living room. We could see him through the window, all of us. Billy bent quietly onto his knees and sniffed carefully at the two square feet of floor. He listened for a while, then sniffed again. Then he fired twice into the floorboards. Jumped up and walked out to us. He's dead now Sallie, dont worry.

Our faces must have been interesting to see then. John and Sallie were thankful, almost proud of him. I had a look I suppose of incredible admiration for him too. But when I looked at Angie, leaning against the rail of the verandah, her face was terrified. Simply terrified.

Down the street was a dog. Some mut spaniel, black and white. One dog, Garrett and two friends, stud looking, came down the street to the house, to me.

Again.

Down the street was a dog. Some mut spaniel, black and white. One dog, Garrett and two friends came down the street to the house, to me.

Garrett takes off his hat and leaves it outside the door. The others laugh. Garrett smiles, pokes his gun towards the door. The others melt and surround.
All this I would have seen if I was on the roof looking.

You know hunters
are the gentlest
anywhere in the world

they halt caterpillars
from path dangers
lift a drowning moth from a bowl
remarkable in peace

in the same way assassins
come to chaos neutral

Snow outside. Wilson, Dave Rudabaugh and me. No windows,
the door open so we could see. Four horses outside. Garrett
aimed and shot to sever the horse reigns. He did that for 3 of
them so they got away and 3 of us couldnt escape. He tried for
5 minutes to get the reigns on the last horse but kept missing.
So he shot the horse. We came out. No guns.

One morning woke up
Charlie was cooking
and we ate not talking
but sniffing wind
wind so fine
it was like drinking ether

we sat hands round knees
heads leaned back taking lover wind
in us sniffing and sniffing
getting high on the way
it crashed into our nostrils

This is Tom O'Folliard's story, the time I met him, eating red dirt to keep the pain away, off his body, out there like a melting shape in the sun. Sitting, his legs dangling like tails off the wall. Out of his skull.

What made me notice him was his neck. Whenever he breathed the neck and cheek filled out vast as if holding a bag of trapped air. I introduced myself. Later he gave me red dirt. Said want to hear a story and he told me. I was thinking of a photograph someone had taken of me, the only one I had then. I was standing on a wall, at my feet there was this bucket and in the bucket was a pump and I was pumping water out over the wall. Only now, with the red dirt, water started dripping out of the photo. This is his story.

At fifteen he took a job with an outfit shooting wild horses. They were given a quarter a head for each one dead. These horses grazed wild, ate up good grass. The desert then had no towns every 50 miles. He sucked the clear milk out of a chopped cactus, drank piss at times. Once, blind thirsty, O'Folliard who was then 17 killed the horse he sat on and covered himself in the only liquid he could find. Blood caked on his hair, arms, shoulders, everywhere. Two days later he stumbled into a camp.

Then half a year ago he had his big accident. He was alone on the Carrizoza, north of here; the gun blew up on him. He didnt remember anything after he saw horses moving in single file and he put the gun to his shoulder. Pulling the trigger the gun blew to pieces. He was out about two days. When he woke up, he did because he was vomiting. His face was out to here. From that moment, his horse gone, he lived for four days in the desert without food or water. Because he had passed out and eaten nothing he survived, at least a doctor told him that. Finding water finally, he drank and it poured out of his ear. He felt sleepy all the time. Every two hours he stopped walking and fell asleep placing his boots into an arrow in the direction he was going. Then he would get up, put boots on and move on. He said he would have cut off his left hand with a knife to have something to eat, but he realised he had lost too much blood already.

He killed lizards when he got onto rock desert. Then a couple
of days later the shrubs started appearing with him following
them, still sleeping every two hours. First village he came to
was Mexican. José Chavez y Chavez, blacksmith. The last thing
O'Folliard noticed was Chavez sandbagging him in the stomach.
O'Folliard going out cold. When he woke José had him in a
bed, his arms trapped down.

Chavez had knocked out Tom as he had gone to throw himself
in water which would have got rid of his thirst but killed him
too. Chavez gave it to him drop by drop. A week later he let
Tom have his first complete glass of water. Tom would have
killed Chavez for water during that week. When he finally got
to a doctor he found all the muscles on the left side of his face
had collapsed. When he breathed, he couldnt control where
the air went and it took new channels according to its fancy and
formed thin balloons down the side of his cheek and neck.
These fresh passages of air ricocheted pain across his face every
time he breathed. The left side of his face looked as though it had
melted by getting close to fire. So he chewed red dirt constantly,
his pockets were full of it. But his mind was still sharp, the pain
took all the drug. The rest of him was flawless, perfect. He was
better than me with rifles. His feet danced with energy. On a
horse he did tricks all the time, somersaulting, lying back. He
was riddled with energy. He walked, both arms crooked over a
rifle at the elbows. Legs always swinging extra.

MISS SALLIE CHISUM : ON BILLY

I was sitting in the living room
when word was brought he had arrived.
I felt in a panic. I pictured him
in all the evil ugliness
of a bloodthirsty ogre.
I half expected he would slit my throat
if he didnt like my looks.

I heard John saying with a wave of his hand,
Sallie, this is my friend, Billy the Kid.
A good looking, clear-eyed boy stood there
with his hat in his hand, smiling at me.

I stretched out my hand automatically to him,
and he grasped it in a hand as small as my own

Crouching in the 5 minute dark
can smell him smell that mule sweat
that stink need a shotgun
for a searchlight to his corner

Garrett? I aint love-worn
torn aint blue I'm waiting
smelling you across the room
to kill you Garrett going
to take you from the knee up
leave me   my dark   AMATEUR!

A motive? some reasoning we can give to explain all this violence. Was there a source for all this? yup —

"Hill leaped from his horse and, sticking a rifle to the back of Tunstall's head blew out his brains. Half drunk with whisky and mad with the taste of blood, the savages turned the murder of the defenceless man into an orgy. Pantillon Gallegos, a Bonito Cañon Mexican, hammered in his head with a jagged rock. They killed Tunstall's horse, stretched Tunstall's body beside the dead animal, face to the sky, arms folded across his breast, feet together. Under the man's head they placed his hat and under the horse's head his coat carefully folded by way of pillows. So murdered man and dead horse suggested they had crawled into bed and gone to sleep together. This was their devil's mockery, their joke — ghastly, meaningless. Then they rode back to Lincoln, roaring drunken songs along the way.

"Lucky for Billy the Kid and Brewer that they had gone hunting wild turkeys, else they would have shared Tunstall's fate. From a distant hillside they witnessed the murder."

To be near flowers in the rain
all that pollen stink buds
bloated split
leaves their juices
bursting the white drop of spend
out into the air at you
the smell of things dying flamboyant
smell stuffing up your nose
and up like wet cotton in the brain
can hardly breathe nothing
nothing thick sugar death

In Mexico the flowers
like brain the blood drained out
packed with all the liquor perfume
sweat like lilac urine smell
getting to me from across a room

if you cut the stalk
your face near it
you feel the puff of air escape
the flower gets small smells sane
deteriorates in a hand

When Charlie Bowdre married Manuela, we carried them
on our shoulders, us on horses. Took them to the Shea
Hotel, 8 rooms. Jack Shea at the desk said
Charlie — everythings on the house, we'll give you the
Bridal.
No no, says Charlie, dont bother, I'll hang onto her ears
until I get used to it.
                    HAWHAWHAW

White walls neon on the eye
1880   November 23   my birthday

    catching flies with my left hand
    bringing the fist to my ear
    hearing the scream grey buzz
    as their legs cramp their
    heads with no air
    so eyes split and release

    open fingers
    the air and sun hit them like pollen
    sun flood drying them red
    catching flies
    angry weather in my head, too

I remember this midnight at John Chisum's. Sallie was telling me about Henry. They had had it imported from England by ship, then train, then Sallie had met the train and brought it the last seventy miles in a coach. Strangest looking thing she said. It could hardly walk up a stair at first because it was so heavy and long. Its tail, which was dark brown with an amber ridge all down the middle of its length, stood up like a plant, so when he moved up and down hills the first thing you saw was this tail. In the house, John's clock banged away in the kitchen, the noise and whir reeling out onto us on the porch. John and Sallie, the mut Henry, and me. I had come in that morning.

They call it a bassett says Sallie, and they used to breed them in France for all those fat noblemen whose hounds were too fast for them when they went hunting. So they got the worst and slowest of every batch and bred them with the worst and slowest of every other batch and kept doing this until they got the slowest kind of hound they could think of. Looks pretty messy to me, I said. John scratched his groin awkwardly but politely — I mean not many would have noticed if they hadnt been on the lookout, expecting it as it were. John began a story.

When I was in New Orleans during the war I met this character who had dogs. I met him because I was a singer then, and he liked to sing, so we used to sing together quite a lot. He seemed a pretty sane guy to me. I mean, he didnt twitch or nothing like that. Well, a month or two after I left New Orleans, I got a note from another friend who sang with us once in a while, and he said Livingstone, who was the first singer, had been eaten by his dogs. It was a postcard and it didnt say anymore. When I was in New Orleans again, 2 or 3 years later I found out.

Livingstone had been mad apparently. Had been for a couple of years, and, while he couldnt fight in the war — he had a limp from a carriage accident — he hung around the soldiers like me. There was a rumour though that the reason he was not accepted was because no one that knew him would trust him with a gun. He had almost killed his mother with a twelve bore, fortunately only shooting an ugly vase to pieces and also her foot. (Her surgeon's bills were over $40 for he took nearly three hours getting all the buckshot out of her thighs because she wouldnt let anyone go any further than her knees, not even a professional doctor.) After that, Livingstone stayed away from guns, was embarrassed by it all I suppose, and besides the episode was a joke all over town.

Some time later he bought a spaniel, one of the American kind. A month later he bought another. He said he was going to start breeding dogs, and his mother, pleased at even a quirk of an ambition, encouraged him. But she didnt realize what he had been really doing until after his death and even then the vet had to explain it to her once more. Livingstone, and this was at the same time as he sang with me in the evenings, had decided to breed a race of mad dogs. He did this by inbreeding. His mother gave him money to start the business and he bought this wooden walled farm, put a vast fence around an area of 50 square feet, and keeping only the two original dogs he had bought, literally copulated them into madness. At least not them but their pups, who were bred and re-bred with their brothers and sisters and mothers and uncles and nephews. Every combination until their bones grew arched and tangled, ears longer than their feet, their tempers became either slothful or venomous and their jaws were black rather than red. You realize no one knew about this. It went on for two or three years before the accident. When people asked him how the dogs were coming along, he said fine; it was all a secret system and he didnt want anyone looking in. He said he liked to get a piece of work finished before he showed it to people. Then it was a surprise and they would get the total effect. It was like breeding roses.

You are supposed to be able to tell how inbred a dog is by the width of their pupils and Livingstone knew this, for again he picked the two most far gone dogs and bred them one step further into madness. In three years he had over 40 dogs. The earlier ones he just let loose, they were too sane. The rest, when the vet found them, were grotesque things — who hardly moved except to eat or fornicate. They lay, the dogs, when they found his body, listless as sandbags propped against the 14 foot fence Livingstone had built. Their eyes bulged like marbles; some were blind, their eyes had split. Livingstone had found that the less he fed them the more they fornicated, if only to keep their mind off the hunger. These originally beautiful dogs were gawky and terrifying to that New Orleans vet when he found them. He couldnt even recognize that they had been spaniels or were intended to be. They didnt snarl, just hissed through the teeth — gaps left in them for they were falling out. Livingstone had often given them just alcohol to drink.

His mother continued to give him money for his business, which still of course hadnt turned a penny. He had never sold a dog and lived alone. He came into town on Thursdays for food and on Thursday evenings when I was stationed in New Orleans he sang with me. We usually drank a lot after the bouts of singing. And again, even when drunk he never showed any sign of madness or quirkiness. As if he left all his madness, all his perverse logic, behind that fence on his farm and was washed pure by the time he came to town every Thursday. Many he had known when younger said how much more stable he had become, and that now they probably would accept him in the army. He told me he had a small farm he ran, never mentioning dogs. Then usually about three in the morning or around then he went back home to the house next to those 40 mad dogs, clinically and scientifically breeding the worst with the worst, those heaps of bone and hair and sexual organs and bulging eyes and minds which were chaotic half out of hunger out of liquor out of their minds being pressed out of shape by new freakish bones that grew into their skulls. These spaniels, if you could call them that now, were mostly brown.

When they found Livingstone there was almost nothing left of him. Even his watch had been eaten by one of the dogs who coughed it up in the presence of the vet. There were the bones of course, and his left wrist — the hand that held the whip when he was in the pen — was left untouched in the middle of the area. But there was not much else. The dust all over the yard was reddish and his clothes, not much left of those, scattered round.

The dogs too were blood hungry. Though this scene was discovered, they reckoned, two days after the event occurred, some of the dogs had been similarly eaten. The vet went into the house, got Livingstone's shot gun, the same one that had spread bullets into his mother's leg, couldnt find any bullets, went into town, bought bullets, didnt say a word in town except got the sheriff with him and rode back. And they shot all the dogs left, refusing to go into the pen, but poking the gun through the planks in the fence and blowing off the thirty heads that remained alive whenever they came into range or into the arc that the gun could turn to reach them. Then they went in, dug a pit with a couple of Livingstone's shovels, and buried everything. 40 dogs and their disintegrated owner.

The clock inside whirred for a half second and then clunked 1 o clock. Sallie got up and walked down the steps of the porch. Henry could deal with the steps now, went down with her and they walked into the edge of the dark empty desert. John rocked on in his chair. I was watching Sallie. She bent down, put her hands under Henry's ears and scratched his neck where she knew he liked it. She bent down further to his ear, the left one, the one away from us, and said, very quietly, I dont think John heard it it was so quiet, Aint that a nasty story Henry, aint it? Aint it nasty.

Up with the curtain
down with your pants
William Bonney
is going to dance

Hlo folks —'d liketa sing my song about the lady Miss A D
you all know her — her mind the only one in town high on
the pox

Miss Angela D has a mouth like a bee
she eats and off all your honey
her teeth leave a sting on your very best thing
and its best when she gets the best money

Miss Angela Dickinson
blurred in the dark
her teeth are a tunnel
her eyes need a boat

Her mouth is an outlaw
she swallow your breath
a thigh it can drown you
or break off your neck

Her throat is a kitchen
red food and old heat
her ears are a harp
you tongue till it hurt

Her toes take your ribs
her fingers your mind
her turns a gorilla
to swallow you blind

(thankin yew

Angela — hand shot open
water blood on my shoulder
crying quiet
O Bonney you bastard Bonney
kill him Bonney kill him

this from Angela
she saying this when their bullet for me
split her wrist so flesh burst out

Watching me do it.
Took knife and opened the skin
more, tugged it back
on the other side of her arm
to pick the bullets out
3 of them
like those rolled pellet tongues of pigeons

look at it, I'm looking into your arm
nothing confused in there
look how clear
Yes Billy, clear

So we are sitting slowly going drunk here on the porch. Usually it was three of us. Now five, our bodies on the chairs out here blocking out sections of the dark night. And the burn from the kerosene lamp throwing ochre across our clothes and faces. John in the silent rocking chair bending forward and back, one leg tucked under him, with each tilt his shirt smothering the light and spiralling shadows along the floor. The rest of us are quieter. Garrett sits on the sofa with Sallie the quietest of us all. He doesnt talk much I've noticed and mostly listens. Sallie her legs out resting on the chair at the ankles, the long skirt falling like a curtain off her legs and touching the floor. The cat shifts in her lap. And just to my left, her leg dangling off the rail she sits on, Angela D, the long leg about a foot to my left swaying, the heel tapping the wooden rail.

The thing here is to explain the difference of this evening. That in fact the Chisum verandah is crowded. It could of course hold a hundred more, but that John and Sallie and I have been used to other distances, that we have talked slowly through nights expecting the long silences and we have taken our time thinking the replies. That one was used to the space of black that hung like cotton just off the porch lights' spill. At 1 or 2 then Sallie would get up and bring me the cat and leave to make coffee and get ready for bed. And come back with the three cups and changed into her nightgown, always yellow or white with fabulous bows at her shoulders and the front of her neck. And then hunch up the gown over her folded legs so we joked at her looking like a pelican or some fat bird with vast stomach and short legs. But she didnt move from that, said her legs against herself kept herself warm for the wind had begun now, a slight flapping against the house. And it is now one and Sallie gets up and the cat stays on the sofa in the warm pool of material where she was. And Angela stretches and says bed I guess and I say no we are having coffee now and she leans back and later Sallie brings mugs in on a tray this time. And we all laugh a little cos Garrett has fallen asleep. Nobody noticed it in the semi dark. He hasnt moved an inch. Just the eyes closed. But the coffee tonight doesnt do much for the drink. That is, we are all pretty loaded here and in fact we go back to the whisky. And my throat now feels nothing as the drinks go down. I wonder how Angie

can balance on the rail; as I do, she slips down near me and tho
I cant see Sallie's eyes I think she must be watching us.

We sit here drinking on, after the coffee. Garrett here but asleep,
Sallie, John, and the two of us. My eyes are burning from the
pain of change and the whisky and I cant see very well, John's
rocker is going slow but his checkered shirt leaves just a red arc
daze like some blurred picture. I remember, when they took the
picture of me there was a white block down the fountain road
where somebody had come out of a building and got off the
porch onto his horse and ridden away while I was waiting
standing still for the acid in the camera to dry firm.

So, bed, says John and we say yes and sit for a bit longer, then
Sallie wakes Garrett and we all get up and go to our rooms.
And Angie I find is high as hell and stumbling hanging onto my
shoulder. In the room we have been given the same bed I was
given when alone. Angie says she'll have to sleep on top of me
or me on top of her. And I say I'm too drunk for a balancing act
Angie.O fooo she says and buttons open my shirt and her hands
are like warm gloves on my back, soft till she uses her nails to
scratch me towards her and I come and start giggling, wait the
bathroom hold it. Yes, she says laughing. Quiet Sallie's in the
next room, got ears like anything.

On the can I have to sit cos I know I cant pee straight. Before I
finish she comes in and straddles me and drops her long hair
into my open shirt as we slip our tongues into each others
mouths. Her skirt over both of us and the can. Billy come on.
mmm I say yes, get up first. No. Shit Angie. No. And slowly
and carefully she lifts her legs higher and hangs them on tight
to my shoulders like clothespins. Come on Angie I'm drunk 'm
not a trapeze artist. Yes you are. No. And slowly I lift her up
pressing her to me. The smell of her sex strong now daubing
my chest and shirt where she rubs it. Youre too heavy for this I
think, and we move careful to the floor, she leaning back like
timber, lifts her legs to take clothes off and I grab the skirt and
pull it over her head. Let me out Billy. Out Billy.Quiet she's next
door. No! I know you Billy you! Youre fucking her. No Angie,
no, I say, honest Angie you got too much, and enter her like a
whale with a hat on, my drowning woman my lady who drowns,
and take my hat off.

Waking in the white rooms of Texas after a bad night must be like heaven I think now. About 9 o clock and the room looks huge like the sun came in and pushed out the walls, now the sun — as if reflected off the bushes outside — hitting and swirling on the white walls and the white sheets on the bed as I can see when I put my head up.

I'm sure everyone in the house threw up last night. All except Garrett anyway. The whisky and coffee and whisky again did in our communal stomach and the bathroom last night was like a confession box. At one point Angela was in the can and Sallie and I stood in the hall, leaning against the wall, eyes half closed, she in a nightgown of white with silver flowers on it and a bow of grey trailing down to her stomach. The hall also grey as nobody wants the light on for our eyes are shifting like old half

dried blood under their lids and Sallie's even put her hair over
her face for more shade. And in my blur she looks lovely there,
her body against the cold stone wall, leaning there, her arms
folded, the wrists snuggled into her elbows and her gown down
to her white feet scratching at each other. Me in a towel, having
now to sit cos I keep slipping down the wall.

Hurry up Angela, Sallie hits the door. More noises in there like
an engine starting up. I cant wait, I said, I'll go outside. No reply.
And I move through the dark house hitting stools with my feet
and hanging onto chairs on my way, cant see a goddam. Realize
walls are there just before I hit them and the dog comes out of a
corner and along with me licking my bare feet.

Outside with only a towel on and the wind is lifting the sand
and lashing me around. I select a spot and start throwing up,
the wind carrying it like a yellow ribbon a good foot to my right.
The acid burning my gums and tongue on the way out. Stop.
Put my fingers into the mushrooms of my throat and up it comes
again and flies out like a pack of miniature canaries. A flock.
A covey of them, like I'm some magician or something. This is
doing nothing for my image is it. Here I am ¾s naked in a towel
vomiting 10 yards from the house, to my left a fucking big
desert where nothing is except wind picking up sand and dust
and the smell off dead animals a hundred miles away and aiming
it at me and my body.

And this bloody dog goes over and sniffs it and then meth-
odically begins to eat, preparing no doubt his appetite for
tomorrow morning, while now, it puts the machinery in me that
organizes my throwing up to sleep, as if I hadnt drunk a thing
in a year. I kick the dog away but it comes back to the meal. I
cant yell cos my mouth is dry. I try and then the muscles heave
deep down and up it comes like a daisy chain whipping out as it
gets free into the slip stream of the wind and collapses on the
ground right in front of the dog who is having the time of his
life. The end. I leave the dog and move back into the now warm
of the house, sand on my feet and collapse into my bed. And
Angela's there and Sallie wasnt in the hall so I guess she's in
there or back in bed. And just as I drop off I hear John getting
up and staggering in the dark.

So it was a bad night. But this morning the room is white and silvery shadows roll across the ceiling. All is clean except our mouths and I move to the basin and rinse out last night's throat and pee down the drain and struggle back to bed, and Angela D is golden and cool beside me the sheet over her stomach like a skirt and her arm out straight over the edge of the bed like a peninsula rich with veins and cooler than the rest of her for it has been in the path of the window's wind all night.

She is so brown and lovely, the sun rim blending into lighter colours at her neck and wrists. The edge of the pillow in her mouth, her hip a mountain further down the bed. Beautiful ladies in white rooms in the morning. How do I wake her? All the awkwardness of last night with the Chisums gone, like my head is empty, scoured open by acid. My head and body open to every new wind direction, every nerve new move and smell. I look up. On the nail above the bed the black holster and gun is coiled like a snake, glinting also in the early morning white.

The street of the slow moving animals
while the sun drops in perfect verticals
no wider than boots
The dogs sleep their dreams off
they are everywhere
so that horses on the crowded weekend
will step back and snap a leg

/ while I've been going on
the blood from my wrist
has travelled to my heart
and my fingers touch
this soft blue paper notebook
control a pencil that shifts up and sideways
mapping my thinking going its own way
like light wet glasses drifting on polished wood.

The acute nerves spark
on the periphery of our bodies
while the block trunk of us
blunders as if we were
those sun drugged horses

I am here with the range for everything
corpuscle muscle hair
hands that need the rub of metal
those senses that
that want to crash things with an axe
that listen to deep buried veins in our palms
those who move in dreams over your women night
near you, every paw, the invisible hooves
the mind's invisible blackout   the intricate never
the body's waiting rut.

           The eyes bright scales
(watch)   bullet claws coming
           at me like women fingers
           part my hair slow
           go in slow in slow,
           leaving skin in a puff
           behind and the slow
           as if fire pours out
           red grey brain the hair slow
           startled by it all pour
           Miss Angela D her eyes like a boat
           on fire her throat is a kitchen
           warm on my face heaving
           my head mouth out
           she swallows your breath
           like warm tar pour
           the man in the bright tin armour star
           blurred in the dark
           saying stop jeesus jesus jesus JESUS

           This nightmare by this 7 foot high doorway
           waiting for friends to come
           mine or theirs
           I am 4 feet inside the room
           in the brown cold dark
           the doorway's slide of sun
           three inches from my shoes
           I am on the edge of the cold dark
           watching the white landscape in its frame
           a world that's so precise
           every nail and cobweb
           has magnified itself to my presence

Waiting
nothing breaks my vision
but flies in their black path
like inverted stars,
or the shock sweep of a bird
that's grown too hot
and moves into the cool for an hour

If I hold up my finger
I blot out the horizon
if I hold up my thumb
I'd ignore a man who comes
on a three mile trip to here
The dog near me breathes out
his lungs make a pattern of sound
when he shakes
his ears go off like whips
he is outside the door
mind clean, the heat
floating his brain in fantasy

I am here on the edge of sun
that would ignite me
looking out into pitch white
sky and grass overdeveloped to meaninglessness
waiting for enemies' friends or mine

There is nothing in my hands
though every move I would make
getting up slowly walking
on the periphery of black
to where weapons are
is planned by my eye

A boy blocks out the light
in blue shirt and jeans
his long hair over his ears
face young like some pharoah

I am unable to move
with nothing in my hands

We moved in a batch now. Not just Dave Rudabaugh, Wilson and me, but also Garrett, deputies Emory and East, seven others I'd never seen and Charlie lying dead on the horse's back, his arms and legs dangling over the side, tied, so he wouldnt fall off. A sheet covered him to stop him drying too much in the sun. That was a bad week after that. Charlie having taken my hat had got it busted to pieces, so no hat for me as we moved back and forward, side to side over the county, avoiding people and law. Lynchers were out now and, bless him, Garrett didnt want that. So we moved along the Carrizozo plains to the slopes of Oscuros, stayed one night by Chupadero mesa, back to the Carrizozo, passed the Evan tribe, followed now the telegraph to Punta de la Glorietta but over 40 lynchers there. So we moved, no hat for me, uncomfortable times for all of us.

Horses and trains horses and trains. Dave, Wilson and me, our legs handcuffed with long 24″ chains under the horse, our hands bound to the bridle. Five days like that. We had to pee as we sat, into our trousers and down the horse's side. We slept lying forward on the horse's neck. All they did to stop us going mad from saddle pain was alternate saddles, or let us ride bareback one day and a saddle the next. All going grey in the eyes. My horse hating me, the chain under his belly, as much as I hated him.

On the fifth day the sun turned into a pair of hands and began to pull out the hairs in my head. Twist pluck twist pluck. In two hours I was bald, my head like a lemon. It used a fingernail and scratched a knife line from front to back on the skin. A hairline of blood bubbled up and dried. Eleven in the morning then. The sun took a towel and wiped the dried dribble off, like red powder on the towel now. Then with very thin careful fingers it began to unfold my head drawing back each layer of skin and letting it flap over my ears.

The brain juice began to swell up. You could see the bones and grey now. The sun sat back and watched while the juice evaporated. By now the bone was dull white, all dry. When he touched the bone with his fingers it was like brushing raw nerves. He took a thin cold hand and sank it into my head down past the roof of my mouth and washed his fingers in my tongue. Down the long cool hand went scratching the freckles and warts in my throat breaking through veins like pieces of long glass tubing, touched my heart with his wrist, down he went the liquid yellow from my busted brain finally vanishing as it passed through soft warm stomach like a luscious blood wet oasis, weaving in and out of the red yellow blue green nerves moving uncertainly through wrong fissures ending pausing at cul de sacs of bone then retreating slow leaving the pain of suction then down the proper path through pyramids of bone that were there when I was born, through grooves the fingers spanning the merging paths of medians of blue matter, the long cool hand going down brushing cobwebs of nerves the horizontal pain pits, lobules gyres notches arcs tracts fissures roots' white insulation of dead seven year cells clinging things rubbing them off on the tracts of spine down the cool precise fingers went into the cistern of bladder down the last hundred miles in a jerk breaking through my sacs of sperm got my cock in the cool fingers pulled it back up and carried it pulling pulling flabby as smoke up the path his arm had rested in and widened. He brought it up fast half tearing the roots off up the coloured bridges of fibres again, charting the slimy arm back through the pyramids up locked in his fingers up the now bleeding throat up squeezed it through the skull bones, so there I was, my cock standing out of my head. Then he brought his other hand into play I could feel the cool shadow now as he bent over me both his hands tapering into beautiful cool fingers, one hand white as new smelling paper the other 40 colours ochres blues silver from my lung gold and tangerine from the burst ear canals all that clung to him as he went in and came out.

The hands were cold as porcelain, one was silver old bone stripped oak white eastern cigarettes white sky the eye core of sun. Two hands, one dead, one born from me, one like crystal, one like shell of snake found in spring. Burning me like dry ice.

They picked up the fold of foreskin one hand on each side and began the slow pull back back back back *down* like a cap with ear winter muffs like a pair of trousers down boots and then he let go. The wind picked up, I was drowned, locked inside my skin sensitive as an hour old animal, could feel everything, I could hear everything on my skin, as I sat, like a great opaque ostrich egg on the barebacked horse. In my skin hearing

Garrett's voice near me on the skin whats wrong billy whats
wrong, couldnt see him but I turned to where I knew he was. I
yelled so he could hear me through the skin. Ive been fucked.
Ive been fuckd Ive been fucked by Christ almighty god Ive been
good and fucked by Christ. And I rolled off the horse's back like
a soft shell-less egg wrapped in thin white silk and I splashed
onto the dust blind and white but the chain held my legs to the
horse and I was dragged picking up dust on my wet skin as I
travelled in between his four trotting legs at last thank the
fucking christ, in the shade of his stomach.

Garrett moved us straight to the nearest railroad depot. We had
to wait one night for the train that would take us to Messilla
where they would hold the trial. The Polk Hotel there was a
bright white place with a wide courtyard and well. The deputies
went down in the bucket and washed themselves. They removed
Charlie off his horse. Garrett took over and washed the dried
blood off the animal. Garrett ordered a box for Charlie Bowdre.
Then he made me drink liquids and paste. They had to carry the
three of us from the horses to the beds — we couldn't walk after
the week on horses. I was to share a room with Garrett and
Emory.

Your last good bed Billy, he said, pick your position. I did, face
and stomach down. He chained me to the bed. He taped my
fingers so thick I couldnt get them through a trigger guard even
if they gave me a gun. Then he went out and looked after
Wilson who had broken both ankles when the horse stumbled
collapsing on his chained legs.

It is afternoon still, the room white with light. My last white
room, the sun coming through the shutters making the white
walls whiter. I lie on my left cheek looking to that light. I cannot even see the door or if Emory has stayed behind. The bed
vast. Went to sleep, my body melting into it. I remember once
after Charlie and I stopped talking we could hear flies buzzing
in their black across a room, and I remember once, one night in
the open I turned to say goodnight to Charlie who was about ten
yards away and there was the moon balanced perfect on his nose.

It is the order of the court that you
be taken to Lincoln and confined to
jail until May 13th and that on that
day between the hours of sunrise and
noon you be hanged on the gallows
until you are dead dead dead
And may God have mercy on your
soul

said Judge Warren H. Bristol

THE TEXAS STAR MARCH 1881

THE KID TELLS ALL

'EXCLUSIVE JAIL INTERVIEW'

INTERVIEWER: Billy...

BONNEY: Mr. Bonney please.

I: Mr. Bonney, I am from the *Texas Star*. You are now how old?

B: 21.

I: When is your birthday?

B: November 23rd. On that lap I'll be 22.

I: You were reported as saying, as adding, to that phrase — 'If I make it' when asked that question before.

B: Well, sometimes I feel more confident than at others.

I: And you feel alright now...

B: Yes, I'm ok now.

I: Mr. Bonney, when you rejected Governor Wallace's offer of an amnesty, were you aware of the possibility that your life would continue the way it has?

B: Well, I don't know; Charlie, Charlie Bowdre that is, said then that I was a fool not to grab what I could out of old Wallace. But what the hell. It didn't mean too much then anyway. All Wallace was offering me was protection from the law, and at that time the law had no quarrels with me, so it seemed rather silly.

I: But you were wanted for cattle rustling weren't you?

B: Yes, but, well let me put it this way. I could only be arrested if they had proof, definite proof, not just stories. They had to practically catch me with stolen cattle in my bed. And when you rustle, you can see law coming a good two miles away. All I had to do was ride off in the opposite direction and that would have been that.

I: But couldn't they catch you with them when you sold them?

B: Well I don't do, I didn't do the selling — I sold them off before they reached the market.

I: How were, or with whom were you able to do that?

B: I'd rather not mention names if you don't mind.

(Here Mr. Bonney withdrew a black cigarette, lit it, and grinned charmingly, then retreated behind his enigmatic half smile, a smile which was on the verge of one. These smiles of 'Billy the Kid' are well known and have become legendary among his friends in this area. Sheriff Garrett has an explanation for this:

"Billy has a denture system which is prominent, buck teeth you at the paper would call it. So that even when he has no intention of smiling his teeth force his mouth into a half grin. Because of this, people are always amazed at his high spirits in a time of stress." Mrs. Celsa Guitterrez adds to this:

"When Billy was 18, a man named John Rapsey ('. . . . head' as he was affectionately called afterwards) broke his (Billy's) nose with a bottle. Billy was knocked unconscious and Rapsey escaped. Bowdre who was with him, to ease the pain when he came to, fed him some tequila, made him drunk. Billy didn't get his nose fixed for three days as Bowdre accompanying him on the tequila also got drunk and forgot all about the broken nose. As a result, when Billy finally got to Sumner to get it fixed his breathing channels, or whatever, were clogged. After that he rarely breathed through his nose again, and breathed by sucking the air in through his mouth, or through his teeth as it seemed. If you were near him when he was breathing heavily — when excited or running, you could hear this hissing noise which was quite loud.")

B: Anyway, Wallace offered me protection from the law, and the only law I knew in Fort Sumner was the Murphy faction which would certainly not uphold Wallace if they found me in a dark street without guns. (Laugh)

I: Did you get on well with Wallace?

B: He was ok.

I: What do you mean by that?

B: Just that he was straight about it all. I mean he was disappointed of course that I couldn't agree, but I think he saw my point. I don't think he thought much of Murphy's men, or trusted them either.

I: But right now you've threatened to kill him if you escape this hanging?

B: WHEN I escape, yes.

I: Why?

B: Well, I've been through all this before. I've already made a statement. But anyway, again. In my trial three weeks ago, the charge that was brought against me was for shooting Sheriff Clark, etc. Now Wallace offered me parole, or amnesty or whatever *after* this shooting. As you know there were no real witnesses of any murder on my part after that incident. But the fact is that the Clark shooting took place during the Lincoln County war — when EVERYBODY was shooting. I mean no one brought charges against those who shot McSween or Tunstall. Now Wallace when he spoke to me admitted that, while he couldn't condone what was done during those three days, he understood that both sides were guilty, and like a state of war there was no criminal punishment that could be genuinely brought against me without bringing it against everyone connected with that war. Two wrongs make a right, right? Now they find that because they cannot charge me with anything else that'll stick they charge me for something that happened during a war. A fact that your Governor Wallace realises and I'm sure privately admits and still won't do anything about.

I: Why do you suppose he doesn't do anything to pardon you now?

B: (Giggling) Well I suppose he's been wished into thinking that I've been pretty nasty since. But the point is that there is no legal proof to all this later stuff. The evidence used was unconstitutional.

I: Do you have a lawyer, I mean working on an appeal now?

B: Slip me a gun and I will have — don't print that.

I: Mr. Bonney, or may I call you Billy. . .

B: No.

I: Mr. Bonney, do you believe in God?

B: No.

I: Why not, and for how long haven't you?

B: Well I did for a long time, I mean in a superstitious way, same way I believe in luck for instance. I couldn't take the risk you see. Like never wearing anything yellow. So before big fights, or even the most minor as well as the really easy ones, I used to cross myself and say, "God please don't let me die today." I did this fast though so no one would see me, see what I was doing. I did this pretty well every day from the age of 12 till I was 18. When I was 18, I had a shooting match with Tom O'Folliard, the prize was a horse. Now it was with rifles and Tom is excellent with them and I wanted that horse very much. I prayed every day. Then I lost the bet with Tom.

I: Do you worry about what will happen after death now you don't believe in God?

B: Well I try to avoid it. Though I suppose not. I guess they'll just put you in a box and you will stay there forever. There'll be nothing else. The only thing I wish is that I could hear what people say afterwards. I'd really like that. You know, I'd like to be invisible watching what happens to people when I am not around. I suppose you thing that's simple minded.

I: Are you happy, or at least were you happy? Did you have any reason for going on living, or were you just experimenting?

B: I don't know whether I'm happy or not. But in the end that is all that's important — that you keep testing yourself, as you say — experimenting on how good you are, and you can't do that when you want to lose.

I: Is that all you looked forward to?

B: Yes I suppose so. And my friends. I enjoy people and being with friends.

I: Is it true that you were going to get married and move east when you were arrested?

B: As I say I don't want to cause trouble, and though I'm not saying about the first part of the question, I *had* intended to leave the area cos people kept coming up to me and saying I was going to get it for what I had done to their friends. Bob Ollinger who's worked his way into being my jailer. He had a close friend who was killed in the Lincoln County war.

I: Who do you consider your friends now, now that Bowdre and O'Folliard are dead?

B: Well I have some. Dave Rudabaugh wherever he is. I guess he's locked up too somewhere. They won't tell me. A couple of guys here and there. A couple of ladies.

I: Garrett?

B: Well Pat's right now a . . . . head. We used to be friends as you probably know. He's got senile. He's getting a lot of money for cleaning the area up — of us supposedly. No I don't think much of him now.

I: He's said that he gave you all plenty of opportunity to get out of New Mexico before he began hunting you.

B: Yeahhhh but one) you don't go around using mutual friends to trap an old friend and two) I love the country around here and Fort Sumner. . .all my friends are here. I'd go now, cos some I thought were friends were really pretty hypocritical.

I: What about pastimes? Did you have many when you were free? Did you like books, music, dancing?

B: Dancing I like, I'm a pretty good dancer. Fond of music too. There's a Canadian group, a sort of orchestra, that is the best. Great. Heard them often when I was up there trying to get hold of a man who went by the name of Captain P————.* Never found him. But that group will be remembered a long time.

I: How about you, do you think you will last in people's memories?

B: I'll be with the world till she dies.

I: But what do you think you'll be remembered as? I mean don't you think that already several feel you are morally vulgar? I mean all these editorials about you. . . .

B: Well. . .editorials. A friend of Garrett's, Mr. Cassavates or something, said something bout editorials. He said editorials don't do anything they just make people feel guilty.

I: That's rather good.

B: Yes. It is.

Am the dartboard
for your midnight blood
the bones' moment
of perfect movement
that waits to be thrown
magnetic into combat

a pencil
harnessing my face
goes stumbling into dots

No the escape was no surprise to me. I expected it. I really did,
we all did I suppose. And it is now in retrospect difficult to
describe. You've probably read the picture books anyway, seen
the films, of how he did it. What he did was to seduce young
Bell into a cardgame, shot him, then shot Ollinger returning
from lunch. Nobody cared about Ollinger, but Bell was liked.
You know how Ollinger used to kill people? He'd go up to them
about to shake hands, then grab their right hand with his left,
lift out his pistol and fire into the chest. He had hated Billy
ever since the Lincoln County War. So Bell and Ollinger died
and Billy escaped. Also on the way out of town he hit a man
named Ellery Fleck in the face, with his rifle, for no reason at all.
He was probably elated.

One funny thing happened apparently (I was out of town).
Billy's hands were still chained, and jumping onto a horse to
escape he lost his balance and fell off — right in front of the
crowd who refused to do anything but watch. In that crowd
nobody cracked a smile. Three or four kids helped him catch the
horse and held it while he got on carefully. Then with the rifle
cradled in his arms he made the horse walk slowly over
Ollinger's body and went.

MISS SALLIE CHISUM :

GOOD FRIENDS :

As far as dress was concerned
he always looked as if
he had just stepped out of a bandbox.

In broadbrimmed white hat
dark coat and vest
grey trousers worn over his boots
a grey flannel shirt
and black four-in-hand tie
and sometimes — would you believe it ? —
a flower in his lapel.

A COURTEOUS LITTLE GENTLEMAN:

I suppose it sounds absurd to speak
of such a character as a gentleman,
but from beginning to end
of our long relationship,
in all his personal relations with me,
he was the pink of politeness
and as courteous a little gentleman
as I ever met.

There was a brook full of fish
that ran under the house
across a corner of the kitchen
and I often sat on the back porch
in a rocking chair, with Billy
to bait my hook for me,
and caught a string of perch for dinner.

(Garrett had stuffed birds. Not just the stringy Mexican vultures
but huge exotic things. We would sometimes be with him when
they arrived. He would have them sent to him frozen in boxes.
The box was wooden, a crate really, and with great care after
bringing it back from the station, he would remove the nails.
He first took out the 8″ of small crushed ice and said look. And
it would be a white seagull. It was beautifully spread in the ice,
not a feather out of place, its claws extended and brittle from
the freezing. Garrett melted it and split it with a narrow knife,
parting the feathers first, and with a rubber glove in his right
hand removed the body. He then washed the rotted blood from
the wings, the outside, and then took it out onto the verandah
to dry.)

MISS SALLIE CHISUM : PAT GARRETT

A tremendously tall man.

Despite his crooked mouth
and crooked smile which
made his whole face seem crooked

he was a remarkably handsome man.

BILLY THE KID & PAT GARRETT ; SOME FINAL THOUGHTS :

I knew both these men intimately.
There was good mixed in with the bad
in Billy the Kid
and bad mixed in with the good
in Pat Garrett.

No matter what they did in the world
or what the world thought of them
they were my friends.
Both were worth knowing.

Sound up. Loud and vibrating in the room. My ears picking up all the burning hum of flies letting go across the room. The mattress under Pete Maxwell shifting its straw, each blade loud in its clear flick against another. Even the now and then crack at the glass as the day's heat evaporates from the window against the dark of the desert.

And then that breathing, not Maxwell's but *the other's*. The breathing precise but forced into quiet but regular streams. Think of the dark air going up through the nose, down to the stomach rolling around on itself, and then up and out like a fountain spilling through his teeth hissssssssssss sssssssssssssss

MMMmmmmmmm. In the final minutes. It is Texas midnight. A large large square, well and buckets centre. The houses and sheds in rows making up the square. The long narrow porch running all around. Up to the well rides Pat Garrett and deputies Poe and Mackinnon. Scuffling slow, smoking as they dismount gentle and leave the horses and walk to the large hut which is Maxwell's room. They pass the dog.

This is a diagram then of Maxwell's, Pete Maxwell's, room. Bed here against the wall, here's the window where he put his hand through. And here, along here, is the porch. While this, about 20 yards away, is the Guitterrez home. Garrett, Poe, and Mackinnon stop near Maxwell's door. On some vague tip Garrett has come to ask Maxwell where he thinks Billy is hiding out — where in the territory is he — he's been escaped 3 months and nobody's seen him. Garrett leaves the deputies sitting smoking on the porch, flicks away his own cigar and goes into the dark room where Maxwell is asleep *Meanwhile*

Billy is just yards away drinking with Celsa Guitterrez. He came in about an hour ago, he wears only his trousers and guns, hot night. They decide she will cook him something and he offers to go cut some meat. Carrying a knife in his left hand, and barefoot, he is up and begins walking towards the ice house. Passing the Maxwell room he sees the two men outside. Quien es? They do not answer. Again the question. No answer. Billy backs off the porch into Maxwell's room and heads towards his friend's sleeping.

In the dark room Garrett has wakened and is questioning the dazed Maxwell. In fact as Billy enters he is crouching by Maxwell's bed. Quienes son esos hombres afuera, Pete? Garrett recognises the voice. He does the one thing that will save him. Quietly, with his long legs, he climbs over Maxwell's body and gets into bed between Maxwell and the wall. With his rifle in his hands he watches the darkness, trying to make out the shape that is moving towards him. Billy moves over barefoot and asks Pete again. Quienes son esos hombres afuera?

Maxwell doesn't say a word. He can feel Garrett's oiled rifle barrel leaning against his cheek. Billy shakes Maxwell's shoulder and then he hears the other person's breathing. As the only other woman on the ranch, apart from Celsa Guitterrez is Paulita Maxwell — Pete's sister — he doesn't know what to think. Paulita? Pete Maxwell gives a nervous giggle full of fear which Billy mistakes for embarrassment. Paulita! Jesus Christ. He leans forward again and moves his hands down the bed and then feels a man's boots. O my god Pete quien es?

He is beginning to move back a couple of yards in amazement. Garrett is about to burst out laughing so he fires, leaving a powder scar on Maxwell's face that stayed with him all his life.

Outside
   the outline of houses
   Garrett running from a door
   — all seen sliding round
   the screen of a horse's eye

NOW dead centre in the square is Garrett with Poe — hands in back pockets — argues, nodding his head and then ALL TURNING as the naked arm, the arm from the body, breaks through the window. The window — what remains between the splits — reflecting all the moving too.

Guitterrez goes to hold the arm but it is manic, breaks her second finger. His veins that controlled triggers — now tearing all they touch.

The end of it, lying at the wall
the bullet itch frozen in my head

my right arm is through the window pane
and the cut veins awake me
so I can watch inside and through the window

Garrett's voice going Billy Billy
and the other two dancing circles
saying we got him we got him the little shrunk bugger

the pain at my armpit I'm glad for
keeping me alive at the bone
and suns coming up everywhere out of the walls and floors
Garrett's jaw and stomach   thousands

of lovely perfect sun balls
breaking at each other click
click click click like Saturday morning pistol cleaning
when the bullets hop across the bed sheet and bounce and click

click and you toss them across the floor like . . . up in the air
and see how many you can catch in one hand the left

oranges reeling across the room AND I KNOW I KNOW
it is my brain coming out like red grass
this breaking where red things wade

Paulita Maxwell

*An old story that identifies me as Billy the Kid's
sweetheart has been going the rounds for many years.
Perhaps it honours me; perhaps not; it depends on how
you feel about it. But I was not Billy the Kid's sweetheart
I liked him very much — oh, yes — but I did not love
him. He was a nice boy, at least to me, courteous, gallant,
always respectful. I used to meet him at dances; he was
of course often at our home. But he and I had not
thought of marriage.*

*There was a story that Billy and I had laid our plans to
elope to old Mexico and had fixed the date for the night
just after that on which he was killed. There was another
tale that we proposed to elope riding double on one
horse. Neither story was true and the one about eloping
on one horse was a joke. Pete Maxwell, my brother, had
more horses than he knew what to do with, and if Billy
and I had wanted to set off for the Rio Grande by the
light of the moon, you may depend upon it we would at
least have had separate mounts. I did not need to put my
arms around any man's waist to keep from falling off a
horse. Not I. I was, if you please, brought up in the
saddle, and plumed myself on my horsemanship.*

Imagine if you dug him up and brought him out. You'd see very
little. There'd be the buck teeth. Perhaps Garrett's bullet no
longer in thick wet flesh would roll in the skull like a marble.
From the head there'd be a trail of vertebrae like a row of pearl
buttons off a rich coat down to the pelvis. The arms would be
cramped on the edge of what was the box. And a pair of handcuffs holding ridiculously the fine ankle bones. (Even though
dead they buried him in leg irons). There would be the silver
from the toe of each boot.

His legend a jungle sleep

Billy the Kid and the Princess

The Castle of the Spanish girl called 'La Princesa' towered above the broad fertile valley . . . in the looming hills there were gold and silver mines . . . . Truly, the man chosen to rule beside the loveliest woman in Mexico would be a king. The girl had chosen William H. Bonney to reign with her . . . but a massive brute named Toro Cuneo craved that honor. . .

There'd been a cattle war in Jackson County . . . He'd settled a beef with three gunquick brothers near Tucson. . . and he was weary of gunthunder and sudden death! Billy the Kid turned his cayuse south . . . splashed across the drought dried Rio Grande . . . and let the sun bake the tension out of his mind and body.

"See them sawtooth peaks, Caballo? There's a little town yonder with a real cold cerveza and a fat lady who can cook Mexican food better'n anybody in the world! This lady also got a daughter . . . una muchacho . . . who's got shinin' black hair and a gleam in her brown eyes I want to see again."

And on a distant hill . . .
"He comes, be ready Soto."

"Gunshots . . . a 45 pistol! Runaway! It's a girl! She's goin' to take a spill! Faster Chico!"
"AAAAAHH!"
"Hang on . . . I got yuh! . . . You're okay now Señorita."
"Gracias, Señor. You are so strong and brave . . . and very gallant!"

"Thanks, I heard shots . . . Did they scare your cayuse into runnin' away?"

"I think I can stand now, Señor . . . if you will put me down."

"Huh? Oh sorry, Señorita. I'm Billy Bonney, Señorita. I'm from up around Tucson."

"I am Marguerita Juliana de Guelva y Solanza, la Princesa de Guelva."

"La Princesa? A *real* princess?"

"I am direct descendent of King Phillip of Spain. By virtue of Royal land grants, I own this land west for 200 leagues, south for 180 leagues. It is as large as some European kingdoms . . . larger than two of your American states . . . I am still a little weak. Ride with me to the castle, Señor Bonney."

"*There* Señor Bonney . . . my ancestral home. The castle and the valley farther than you can see . . . I have 20,000 cattle, almost as many horses and herds of goats, pigs, chickens. Everything my people need to live."

"WHOOOEEE! The Governor's mansion up at Phoenix would fit in one end o' that wickiup."

"Come on, Yanqui! It is late . . . you must have dinner with me."

"ATTENTION! HER EXCELLENCY RETURNS!"
Thinks: "She's got a regular army!"

The man called Billy the Kid is not impressed by the magnificent richness of his surroundings. The golden cutlery means nothing . . . The priceless china and crystal matter not, and the food cooked by a French chef? — PFAAGGH!
Thinks: "I'd sooner be in Mama Rosa's kitchen eatin' tortillas an' chile with Rosita battin' them dark eyes at me!"

"This table needs a man like you, Señor Bonney. Others have occupied that chair but none so well as you."

"Gracias, Princesa . . . but I'd never feel right in it . . . if you know what I mean."

"I propose a toast, my gringo friend . . . to our meeting . . . to your gallant rescue of me!"

"I reckon I can't let a lady drink alone, Princesa."

CRASH! ! !

"He could have sunk it in my neck just as easy . . . Start talkin' hombre 'fore I say *my* piece about that knife throwing act!"

"I am a man of action, not words, gringo! I weel crack your ribs . . . break your wrists . . . then send you back where you belong!"

"Come on, animal, I want to finish dinner!"

SOCK! !

Thinks: "If I can nail him quick I'll take the fight out of him . . . PERFECT!"

That was his Sunday punch . . . and Toro laughed at it! Now, Billy the Kid knows he's in for a struggle!

"He's got a granite jaw which means . . . I'll have to weaken him with powerful hooks to the stomach! OOooWwww!" THUD!

"Now it's my turn!"

"If he lays a hand on me .. ."

SWISSS!

SOCK!

"I keel you gringo!"

Thinks: "My head . . . he busted my jaw!"

TOCK!

Thinks: "He's a stomper . . ."

"I keel your pet gringo Excellencia!"

"Yuh'll take me tuh death maybe, hombre!"

"You no escape Toro now!"

"I didn't figure on escapin' Toro!"

CRACK!

"Over you go, Toro!" "Olé! Olé!"

CRASH!

"Sorry I busted the place up some, Princesa."

"You are mucho hombre, Yanqui, very much man! A man like you could help me rule this wild kingdom! Will you remain as my guest for a time?"
"I come down here to rest up some. I reckon I can do that here as well as in Mama Rosa's cantina."
(Kiss)
"That was to thank you for protecting me from Toro Cueno. I must not go on being formal with you . . ."

In the next few days, Billy the Kid was with La Princesa often. Long rides through wild country . . .
"Wait princess . . . don't get ahead of me!"
"EEEEEeeii! !"
"Duck, princess!"
BANG! BANG!
"Once more Chivoto, you have saved my life, this time from that cougar. You have won my love!"
"Hold on, ma'am . . ."
Before Billy the Kid can defend himself, La Princesa Marguerita has taken him in her arms and . . . .

"It was the Kid who came in there on to me," Garrett told Poe,
"and I think I got him."

"Pat," replied Poe, "I believe you have killed the wrong man."

"I'm sure it was the Kid," responded Garrett, "for I knew his
voice and could not have been mistaken."

Poor young William's dead
with a fish stare, with a giggle
with blood planets in his head.

The blood came down like river ride
long as Texas down his side.
We cleaned him up when blood was drier
his eyes looked up like turf on fire.

We got the eight foot garden hose
turned it on, leaned him down flat.
What fell away we threw away
his head was smaller than a rat.

I got the bullets, cleaned him up
sold them to the Texas Star.
They weighed them, put them in a pile
took pictures with a camera.

Poor young William's dead
with blood planets in his head
with a fish stare, with a giggle
like he said.

It is now early morning, was a bad night. The hotel room seems large. The morning sun has concentrated all the cigarette smoke so one can see it hanging in pillars or sliding along the roof like amoeba. In the bathroom, I wash the loose nicotene out of my mouth. I smell the smoke still in my shirt.

Critical Guide

Features of Literary Language

In our introduction to this text, we said that modern artists were interested in exploring what is primary in human experience. You may well be asking yourself, "If these modern artists are so concerned with representing the primary, why is so much of their art so obscure?" Our introductions to the three sections of this book should have suggested an answer. Modern artists want to make us critically aware of the way language shapes and reflects our definitions of reality, and this critical awareness depends upon uses of language which tend to disturb normal, almost unconscious processes of reading and understanding. In contrast with traditional literature, modern literature makes us question our dependency on old conventions and reading habits.

In the pages that follow, we describe some of the important features of literary language and show you their effect on the process of reading and understanding. Knowing these will not make reading easier—in fact, they may make reading a more complex and time-consuming project—but they should start you working in a direction that can yield valid insights into the meaning of a work of art.

DRAMATIC SITUATION

We said in our Introduction to Modernism that we wanted to describe our social context, ourselves as speakers and our intended audience, before defining our attitudes toward literature. This kind of identification of speaker and audience is necessary in literature as well as in general introductions, but literature's complexity requires a more precise definition of both ordinary or expository and artistic contexts.

Let's begin by looking at ordinary language. Any sort of verbal message, from presidential conference to casual conversation, is a social act. Speech act theorists say there are three levels in the verbal message: words, intent, and effect. For example, a swimming coach who says "Go jump in the lake" is doing three distinct things:

1. Making a sentence (words).
2. Giving a command, which might also be given with a whistle signal (intent).
3. Causing someone to enter the water (effect).

The audience is probably willing to comply with this command since it is an acceptable sentence in understandable language coming from a reasonable authority.

Now compare an ordinary command like "Go jump in the lake" with a similar grammatical construction in W. B. Yeats's "Sailing to Byzantium":

> Consume my heart away; sick with
>   desire
> And fastened to a dying animal
> It knows not what it is; and gather me
> Into the artifice of eternity.

Literary speech is obviously not judged successful by the same standard as ordinary discourse, for if we did not distinguish literary speech acts from actual ones we would assume we are being requested to devour a diseased portion of Yeat's anatomy. Unlike "Go jump in the lake," there is no reasonable action that we as readers could take in response to Yeats's request. The real Yeats makes the words, of course, but he is not performing them, and they do not apply to us directly.

He is not commanding us to do anything with his speech acts within the poem. In literature, as opposed to life, the speech act is dislocated from its immediate practical objective, as Richard Ohmann best explains: "What he [the artist] does is something like putting words in another's mouth. Yet the other does not really exist. More precisely, the writer puts out imitation speech acts *as if* they were being performed by someone. Since that someone has no prior existence, in effect he is largely creating the assignment of speech acts." The author creates a speaker who talks to a similarly created audience, and this is the social context in which the literary speech act is performed. The imaginary world the writer creates and the reader recognizes is called the *dramatic situation* of a poem or a article, or work of fiction.

Literary dramatic situation includes four parts: the author, the speaker or persona (see Glossary), the speaker's audience, and the particular reader who happens to be studying the literary work. The following chart identifies the dramatic situation of several poems included in this anthology:

POEM	AUTHOR	SPEAKER	AUDIENCE	READER
1. Sylvia Plath's "Daddy": "Daddy, I have had to kill you."				
	Plath	anonymous daughter	dead father	us
2. T. S. Eliot's "The Love Song of J. Alfred Prufrock": "Let us go then, you and I"				
	Eliot	Prufrock	himself	us
3. Ted Hughes's "In Laughter": "but it's only human."				
	Hughes	Crow	unidentified audience	us
4. W. B. Yeats's "The Circus Animals' Desertion": "I sought a theme and sought for it in vain."				
	Yeats	bard	his readers	us

A brief consideration of this chart will reveal that the position of the author and reader remains the same in each case; therefore, the interest of dramatic situation resides in the interaction of speaker and audience. For example, the authority of the father is the rather obvious focus of the poem "Daddy." Prufrock's monologue implies self-investigation. Hughes's use of a crow as a speaker dramatizes the necessity of distinguishing between author and persona; even though the audience is anonymous, the reader cannot assume the role of the audience. Yeats plays upon the bardic voice by referring continually to his own poetic works. If we have not read as many Yeats poems as the bard's audience has, "Circus Animals" will be less meaningful for us.

As these examples indicate, dramatic situation can play a complex function in determining the meaning of a poem. In prose, the speaker is termed a *narrator*. Applying the same chart, we note that a work such as *Heart of Darkness* employs two dramatic situations. In the opening pages of the novel, the categories are as follows:

AUTHOR	NARRATOR	AUDIENCE	READER
Conrad	a member of the "Nellie" party, an "I"	undefined listener or reader	us

The narrator soon limits his comments to retelling Marlow's story, using Marlow's words, and a second dramatic situation takes over:

AUTHOR	NARRATOR	AUDIENCE	READER
Conrad	Marlow	"I," a lawyer, an accountant, the Director of Companies	us

The interaction between the narrators then becomes a subject of interest. How does the narrator evaluate Marlow, and is he correct?

Now look at Andy Doppelt's and Bob Mandel's essays as they refer to the treatment of the dramatic situation in Sillitoe's *The Loneliness of the Long-Distance Runner.* They discuss the way the device of the found manuscript makes us evaluate Smith's character. You might consider this question as well: What if the author were not designated as Sillitoe but instead as "Crazylegs" Smith? How would that redefine the role of audience and reader?

FIGURATIVE LANGUAGE

When you identify an imaginary situation for language, you are reacting to the artful quality of that language. Artificial framing devices such as the title of a book or the appearance of the poem on a page announce the distinction between literary expression and practical information, and we all recognize fundamental distinctions between literary and ordinary language. No one really thinks or speaks in poetic rhyme, meter, or sentence structure, for example. Ordinary language is not constructed so that patterns of imagery or meaning repeat themselves. The presence of such features tells us that language is not simply conveying information but is carefully selected and arranged by a particular artist to convey particular emotions, attitudes, ideas, and values.

The term *figurative language* has traditionally been used to describe certain major features that distinguish literary language. The basic unit of figurative language is the *metaphor,* or the verbal comparison of two apparently unlike objects, persons, or ideas. We should recognize from the beginning that all language is metaphorical since its sounds or letters stand for concepts. If we use the words "green grass" to describe an object in our physical environment, these words

are signs for things (otherwise we would have to point to grass or carry some of it around in order to make ourselves understood). The configuration of ten letters "green grass" is not an object in itself but a sign for an object. After admitting that language is fundamentally metaphorical, we make certain additional assumptions about literal and metaphorical uses of these verbal signs. "Green grass" makes a literal statement about your lawn, but when we use a term like "green thumb" to indicate a good gardener, we are using language metaphorically. We are comparing a part of human anatomy with a concept about gardening; the word "green" brings associations about the fertility of objects like green grass, and fertility is the property common to the otherwise unlike thumb and successful gardener. I. A. Richards has provided conventional terms for designating relationships in metaphor. He would call "good gardener" the tenor or the idea to be conveyed and "green thumb" the vehicle, the phrase which communicates the idea. The vehicle of this metaphor is so commonly used that we understand its meaning automatically and rarely consider the clash of ideas involved in the comparison.

In literary language, the author does not depend on this kind of familiar or "dead" metaphor to produce meaning but seeks to disrupt our habitual response to language and make us realize unfamiliar, perhaps new meanings for words. You have probably never heard melting ice described as a lizard before. When Robert Frost makes this comparison in "A Hillside Thaw," you will have to stop and examine the vehicle to determine what trait these two very different concepts share. What does it mean when the clause, "the sun lets go/Ten million silver lizards," takes the place of "the sun melts the snow"?

Metaphor is only one of many ways of expressing verbal comparisons, however. When Lawrence refers to a snake as "a king in exile, uncrowned in the underworld," suggesting that it shares human attributes, he is using *personification.* When a poet makes a comparison explicit with "like" or "as," we call this kind of comparison a *simile.* In "The Love Song of J. Alfred Prufrock," Eliot calls attention to his speaker's processes of association by a simile: ". . . the evening is spread out against the sky/*Like* a patient etherized upon a table." When Sylvia Plath makes a sow into the emblem of all womanhood by saying that only a hero out of a romance is mighty enough to mate with her, she is using extravagant comparison or *hyperbole.* In "A High-Toned Old Christian Woman," Stevens relies on *metonymy* for his effect. In the lines, "Take a moral law and make a nave of it,/ And from the nave build haunted heaven," he substitutes parts and consequences of things for the things themselves ("nave" for "church," for example) to show how a religion develops out of the human conscience.

We have listed just a few rhetorical terms, not to suggest that reading literature requires your mastering a large literary vocabulary, but to suggest the many ways in which poets can make verbal comparisons. You should find them useful but not completely adequate equipment for understanding most artistic language. You can not simply substitute familiar language for an unusual vehicle and make an adequate statement of the meaning of a poem. Take these lines from Dylan Thomas as an example: "The force that through the green fuse drives the flower/ Drives my green age." Thomas' use of "green" to describe "fuse" and "age" is something we cannot possibly understand out of its poetic context, for it is Thomas' own special use of language. Anyone who uses these terms after him will be borrowing his words, and people familiar with his poetry will recognize the allusion. The meanings of words in this kind. of personalized language are not as immediately apparent as those in ordinary speech or prose; you may have to read the poem several times in order to arrive at the particular meaning of "green." You will have to examine the ways in which it is repeated, the words with which it is associated, and those to which it is opposed.

None of our selections in this text

will yield simple truths—most literary art cannot be reduced to an easy paraphrase. Clear examples of classic metaphoric substitutions are especially rare in modern poetry. The following discussions are designed to help you understand and describe the meaning of poetic language without reducing the complexity of the work of art.

CONNOTATION AND DENOTATION

Language with a practical purpose is limited by the situation that it is to effect. Ordinarily we try to construct unambiguous statements that eliminate alternative meanings and restrict the audience's understanding to the one meaning we intend. In writing *about* literature, for example, the goal of convincing the reader that you know what you are talking about makes it important to express ideas in language that cannot be misinterpreted. In good expository prose you eliminate the necessity to "interpret" at all; you leave no question concerning what a word or sentence means. But literary language is different, for in a work of literature the artist does not eliminate alternative meanings. When Marlow says of Kurtz, "He had kicked himself loose from the earth," what does this sentence from *Heart of Darkness* tell us? Is Marlow announcing Kurtz's death and possible suicide, describing the loftiness of Kurtz's mind, or suggesting that the man was simply mad? Because literary language is not restricted by the practicalities of an actual social situation but in fact generates its own imaginary context or dramatic situation, literary language tends to expand rather than limit the meaning of words and strings of words. Conrad's sentence could suggest all three possibilities and even more. Literary language is usually capable of sustaining more than one meaning, and this multiplicity is generally considered a valuable quality in literature, as you will see in the section on ambiguity.

Multiple meanings for words and phrases are often a consequence of the difference between the connotation (implied, associative meaning) and the denotation (literal meaning) of language.

Kurtz has not succeeded in a struggle to jump from the ground as the language denotes. The meaning of the sentence derives from the connotations of "kicked," "loose," and "earth," suggestions of strenuous detachment from material existence. Particularly in poetry, a phrase or sentence may be unintelligible if we consider denotation alone, but if we substitute the connotations (possible characteristics associated with a word) for its literal meaning, the line will begin to make sense. Dylan Thomas's language is particularly nonsensical when read in terms of its denotations. Look at the first lines of "The Force That Through the Green Fuse Drives the Flower," for example. It is easy to imagine a green fuse even though it is certainly a peculiarity, but how can an abstraction such as "age" be green?

Let's first try to establish a literal meaning by substituting common definitions, synonyms found in the dictionary, for the important words:

| THE | agent FORCE | THAT | THROUGH | THE | ultramarine GREEN | combustible cord FUSE |

| propels DRIVES | THE | blossom FLOWER | propels DRIVES | MY | ultramarine GREEN | years AGE |

Absolute nonsense. Now do the same thing, but instead of the specific meaning of the word, substitute qualities associated with the word:

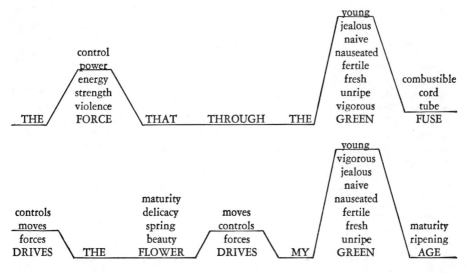

Connotations link the adjectives and nouns. In the context of "young" and "flower," "fuse" must mean stalk. Similarly, when "green" is associated with "age," it must signify youth. As we see that most of the important words have associations with natural growth, the lines begin to make sense:

THE GREEN FUSE DRIVES THE FLOWER, DRIVES MY GREEN AGE . . .

The power that makes the flower grow from the stalk controls my youth.
THE FORCE THAT THROUGH

Of course, this procedure will not yield meaning that is complete in any sense, because the lines that follow this one will also use language rich in connotations. After careful reading, some of their connotations will change or add to the meaning we have already established. The repetition of the subject "force" with the verb "blasts" in line two activates connotations of violence rather than simply of power; it calls up an alternate connotation of "fuse," its combustible nature.

By selecting consistent connotations of particular words we will be able to make sense of the entire poem. When you follow this procedure in order to arrive at a description of the poem's meaning, you can then demonstrate that your description is not mere opinion but a concrete statement of meaning generated by the specific words of the poem itself.

This method of deriving meaning through consistent selection of word connotation applies equally to poetry and prose. For example, these two sentences appear near the conclusion of Lawrence's "The Woman Who Rode Away":

> But what she felt was that fanged inverted pinnacle of ice, hanging from the lip of the dark precipice above. And behind the great rope of ice she saw the leopard-like figures of priests climbing the hollow cliff face, to the cave that like a dark socket bored a cavity, an orifice, half-way up the crag.

Since the woman described is about to be ritually sacrificed in order to become a messenger to the gods, how are her executioners depicted? Notice the sexual connotation of words used to describe the cave—"lip," "socket," "cavity," and "orifice"—and decide how they support the idea that she is being born into another, purely spiritual life. In this case, the sinister description of the priests and their environment modifies the idea of renewed life and beneficial sacrifice central in the Indian myth that organizes the story.

SEMANTIC CATEGORIES

Semantics is the study of meaning. Our discussion of connotation showed that literary discourse exploits multiple meanings. If single words may have several associations, it follows that their meanings will continue to expand when words are joined to form sentence chains, paragraphs or stanzas, whole poems, and works of prose fiction. The many alternative meanings theoretically possible in literary language seem to suggest a kind

of semantic chaos, but in fact literature is as highly organized as any other system of meaning such as science, law, or religion.

Every attempt to determine or convey meaning entails some organization of experience in terms of likeness and difference. The study of zoology, for example, organizes the animal kingdom by placing all animals with a backbone in one category and those without one in another. Subcategories are formed on the basis of breathing apparatus, method of reproducing and feeding the young, and so on until the entire animal kingdom is described in a tree structure which may be studied systematically. The anthropologist Levi-Strauss has concluded that organizing phenomena into sets of binary oppositions is the fundamental human method of making sense of anything. Therefore when an artist produces a fictive world in words, it will exhibit the same principles of opposition as other systems of meaning. Since literary language is suggestive and multiple, however, the oppositions will often be implied rather than overtly stated. When we write about a work of art we must make the implied oppositions in the organization of the work explicit.

How do we describe the "ideas" of Yeats's "Crazy Jane Talks with the Bishop"? We are on more solid ground if we describe the organization that is actually there in the poem rather than speculating about what "Yeats is trying to say." In the first stanza of the poem most of the nouns belong to opposing categories:

Stanza I

Bishop	breasts
heavenly mansion	veins
	foul sty

A reasonable first step in determining what the poem is about is to name these categories: The bishop and the heavenly mansion have spiritual connotations whereas the list on the right suggests physical life, particularly animal sexuality. We can now hypothesize that the poem may be about the relationship between the two categories, spirituality and sexuality. Let us finish classifying:

                    Stanza I
Bishop   breasts
heavenly mansion   veins
                        foul sty

                    Stanza II
fair   foul
                        friends
                        graves
                        bed
                        bodily lowliness
                        heart's pride

                    Stanza III
love   Love's mansion
                        place of excrement
                        everything sole
                        and whole

As we complete the process of distinguishing words according to their spiritual and sexual connotations, a problem becomes apparent. Almost everything seems to belong on the physical side of the opposition. "Fair" and "foul" are usually opposed, but only words belonging to the category foul appear in this poem: "bed," "grave," "bodily lowliness," and "heart's pride" amplify "foul," whereas "fair" remains an empty category—nothing fair is described. In the final stanza "love" appears twice and could be placed in both categories, but Love with a capital L, which asserts its relative importance over lower-case "love," must be placed with "excrement" in the "foul" category. In the same stanza, "mansion" is no longer associated with "heaven" but also belongs in the "place of excrement."

Now we can make sense of the two problematic statements, "fair needs foul" and "nothing can be sole or whole/That has not been rent." Since everything in the poem (all that is "sole and whole") is ultimately categorized as physical, the spiritual category is simply a denial of the flesh, a mere reaction rather than a genuine thing in itself. The conventional opposition between flesh and spirit is thus a false one in Yeats's poem since the spiritual has no reality. We can now see how language generates the dramatic situation of the poem: Crazy Jane opposes the authority of the bishop's normal middle-class morality. Hers is the voice of wisdom because she has done more living than the bishop (she has been "rent").

Determining the semantic opposition that produces the meaning of the poem is commonly called a "thematic analysis." Often when people talk about themes in literature, however, they choose superficial terms, and the thematic exercise then becomes a sloppy and arbitrary process. The key lies in choosing the oppositions which can be supported with the most evidence. Although we choose our own rather than the artist's labels for semantic categories, this does not mean that our exercise is based on mere opinion or that one such exercise is as good as any other. If your oppositions account for the structure of the entire poem, you know you have an important theme.

VALUE MARKINGS

In our discussion of "Crazy Jane Talks with the Bishop," we noted the opposition between the two speakers. In fact, the bishop not only seeks to establish his difference from Crazy Jane, but he also wants to convert her to what he considers to be a more desirable system of religious values. Jane is to leave her "foul sty" for a "heavenly mansion," leave the negative for the positive dwelling. The language of ordinary discourse works in much the same way, implying value markings through word selection.

Among the features or connotations that adhere to certain words are those which signify plus or minus evaluation: that is, green when connoting fertility is conventionally marked positive, while in another context green may signify nausea which is a minus or undesirable state. In a paint box, of course, the color green will not be marked. The terms "crazy" and "bishop" are respectively marked negative and positive in our culture, and we can view the action of this poem as a reevaluation of this conventional value system so that the values signified by "bishop" are redefined as undesirable.

Think of a scale of the more and less complimentary synonyms for "female human being" and the way they project a particular attitude:

1. Lady
2. Woman
3. Chick
4. Dolly
5. Piece

"Woman" presently has a positive connotation because of its directness, and in the past "lady" was considered a compliment because of its reference to the British nobility. Notice the kinds of reductions inherent in the derogatory terms: chick or animal; dolly or inanimate, merely playful object; piece or inanimate part rather than whole. A choice among these five terms will indicate how a speaker feels about women. In the same way, we can determine a sense of value from choice of language in literary works. The bishop's effete character is defined by his speech.

We have said that the structure of Yeats's poem empties the Bishop's arguments so that all objects in the poem belong in Crazy Jane's categories. We feel that Jane has won the argument because of the way semantic categories are manipulated. If we therefore feel that Yeats sides with Jane, it is because we assume that the structure of the poem represents the working out of the author's opinions. We posit a hypothetical Yeats or *implied author* who shifts the positive love from the Bishop's to Jane's domain. In other words, we feel that the values conveyed through connotations and categories of language reveal Yeats's point of view, and in order to know what he "intended" we merely have to give a complete and accurate account of what he wrote. What he means is what he says.

In most cases, values are not so clearly marked as Crazy Jane's "fair and foul," however, and we must deduce the marking of words in their particular context. Look at the distribution of value markings in the following passage from *The Time Machine:*

... the Upper-world man had drifted towards his feeble prettiness, and the Under-world to mere mechanical industry ... The Under-world being in contact with machinery, which, however perfect, still needs some little thought outside habit, had probably retained perforce rather more initiative, if less of every other human character, than the Upper.

Wells posits two societies; each is a mixture of the positive and negative. If we wish to deduce the ideal of the implied author, we obviously must combine the beneficial traits of both.

POSITIVE	NEGATIVE
initiative	feeble prettiness
human character	mechanical industry
thought	habit

A desirable society must be industrious and productive without sacrificing the humanistic virtues. If we look at the language of both the time traveler and the narrator, we will see why this kind of deduction is essential.

Narrator: And I have by me, for my comfort, *two strange white flowers—* *shrivelled now,* and brown and flat and brittle—to witness that even when mind and strength had gone, *gratitude and a mutual tenderness* still lived on in the *heart* of man.

Time Traveller: Here I was more in my element, for rising on either side of me were the *huge bulks of big machines* all greatly corroded and many broken down, but some still fairly complete. You know I have a certain weakness for *mechanism* ...

The narrator obviously prefers passive sentimentality in contrast with the time traveller's active mechanism, but neither accurately represents the values of the implied author. The narrator possesses the humane characteristics but not the industry of the ideal we deduced from the description of the upper world; the time traveller possesses just the opposite.

"A Boy and His Dog," like *The Time Machine,* posits an upper and lower world. From the values connoted by the language of this work, can you deduce the values of an implied author?

AMBIGUITY

We have said that language with a practical purpose is limited by the specific situation it is supposed to effect. If a swimming coach says "Go jump in the lake," you will probably do just that. If an irritated friend gives you the same command, you will know it means something like "Get lost" or "I'm annoyed with you at the moment." The phrase "Go jump in the lake" has two possible meanings, one literal and the other a common cliché or metaphor, and we know which meaning applies because of practical context. In literature, particularly in poetry, this practical context is often missing, and the literary context will allow the two possibilities to apply simultaneously. When at least two meanings are suggested by one word, phrase, or larger semantic unit, we say that the unit is ambiguous. In ordinary speech, we seek an economy of accurate, recognizable expression by eliminating the confusion of dual meanings. In literature, the artist who wants to stimulate the critical activity of the reader will create language with multiple possibilities for meaning.

Ambiguity is most obvious in verbal puns. Look in *Heart of Darkness* for the narrator's description of the significance of the Thames as it embodies "The dreams of men, the seed of commonwealths, the germs of empires." The word "germs" can suggest either fertility or disease, two contradictory possibilities in meaning. The two possibilities come from different semantic categories, one suggesting life and the other death, which obviously have opposite value markings. If we attempt to solve this ambiguity by looking at the context of "germ," we find that there is no literary resolution to the contradiction. The suggestion of fertility is supported by "seed of commonwealth,"

but this positive value is countered by the larger context of the passage. The men who sail the Thames bear "the sword," and the river flows by a "monstrous town" that is "marked ominously on the sky." This particular instance of ambiguity is significant in terms of the overall structure of *Heart of Darkness,* since one of its major themes involves civilization's ambiguous position as sustainer of life in Europe and initiator of death in Africa. Significant acts such as Marlow's lie and Kurtz's death must be evaluated in terms of this structural contradiction.

Since civilization is simultaneously judged positive and negative, *Heart of Darkness* could be said to contain two conflicting normative judgments. Kurtz may be heroic in his freedom from false restraints, or he may be flawed in comparison with the practical, civilized survivor, Marlow. Because both judgments are supported by extensive and convincing evidence, any effort to prove one rather than admit both seems rather artificial. Normative judgment is relative to the individual.

This kind of relativity is absent in both realistic and expressionistic works. The norm will be given in realism; we know the ignorance of the newspaper account in "Scoop." Normative judgment is generally indecipherable or simply absent in expressionistic works. The artistic state in "Byzantium" simply *is,* and we cannot deduce values from the poem.

PLOT

If you understand dramatic situation, the connotative and denotative properties of words, thematic structure, and the ways literature effects value judgments, you can go a long way toward determining the meaning of poetic or literary language, as distinguished from the meaning of informal or practical speech. Few people mistake artistic for ordinary language when it comes to poetry, for while ordinary language is simply *used* by any speaker or writer, poetry announces the fact that it is a structure *created* by a particular author. To see what we mean, perform this simple experiment. First read the newspaper account, "Severed Hand

Banned at Art Exhibit," at the beginning of the Introduction to Realism, and then compare it to the same statement converted into something approximating poetic form:

Severed Hand Banned at Art Exhibit

The Sidney Opera House has refused to let a
Severed hand
Be shown at a national art show
At the House,

But an art dealer says he has bought
The hand
And will display if for two weeks.

We assume that the newspaper account is conveying factual information about the real world, but poetic form suggests that the words were selected and arranged to express some idea or emotion of the author.

Prose narrative can involve the reader in a problem that poetry avoids. In fiction, the artist often conceals the artificiality of form and appears to be offering factual information. Prose is closer to ordinary language, and in narrative form, characters often perform rather ordinary actions. For these reasons, students are often led to describe and judge fictive events as if they were real events. The following discussions of plot, character, and narration should introduce you to the art of narrative and help you avoid the mistake of treating literary events as if they were actual events.

Much of the interest in reading fiction comes from discovering what happens next and how things turn out. The plot of a narrative creates this sense that something is happening, and skillful storytellers control the amount and timing of the information they convey in order to manipulate the reader's response. The mystery writer, for example, will withhold parts of the story so that you seek an answer further in the text. The author may even create a mystery and never resolve it, as Cortázar does in "The Night Face Up." If we the audience decide that Cortázar's young man is really dreaming in the hospital or that he is killed in an Aztec ritual, we are assuming the artist's role and making up the ending. Other stories, like Farrell's "A Front-Page Story," deliberately eliminate all mystery and along with it any possibility of alternative endings. Ruth Summer is dead when the story begins, and we witness the contribution of all acts toward this inevitable end.

Since the extent and timing of the information we receive is obviously central to the meaning of the narrative, it is important first of all to define plot and separate it from more general concepts of history or story. To begin with, look at the sequence of central events in Faulkner's short *Bildungsroman,* "Barn Burning."

Faulkner's story follows a straight chronology of events. The plot follows a causal sequence: The initial barn burning leads to a trial, whose outcome necessitates the family's flight from town, which in turn opens the opportunity of meeting the Sartoris family. The same pattern of revenge which initiated the plot threatens to repeat itself at the Sartoris estate. We see the conclusion of the story in terms of the development of the boy towards a tragic kind of maturity. He learns that he must betray his father in order to halt this primitive cycle of vengeance. Sillitoe's *The Loneliness of the Long-Distance Runner* indicates a similar progression in the mind of the central character, but geographic progression is no longer tied directly to mental development. Although Smith thinks best while running, his imprisonment forces him to do his running in circles, and his mind ranges from the present race course to locales of his past. A diagram indicating the major sequence of events in the plot, as opposed to the story line which takes Smith from a childhood picnic to his current jail term, will suggest the way a story's chronology may be manipulated in order to indicate the developing independence of the narrator's mind.

Chronological story line	*Plot*
1. Picnic	8. Begins recollecting and writing
2. Father's death	5. Running
3. Robbery	6. Conversation with governor
4. Imprisonment	7. Decides to lose race
5. Running	1. Picnic
6. Conversation with governor	3. Robbery
7. Decides to lose race	4. Imprisonment
8. Begins recalling and writing	9. Race begins
9. Race begins	2. Father's death
10. Loses	10. Loses
11. Release	11. Release
12. Successful robberies	12. Successful robberies
13. Speculates about publishing book	13. Speculates about publishing book
14. Finishes book	14. Finishes book
15. Unsuccessful robbery, or	
16. Friend betrays him	
17. Publication of book	

You can see that the time shifts of the plot disrupt a chronological arrangement of fictive data. These shifts link past and present events in an achronological order representing Smith's mental processes. This order suggests that Smith's fate, in contrast with that of Faulkner's protagonist, is not determined by external laws of cause and effect. The meaning of the story for both Smith and his reader lies in the arrangement of external events to express Smith's needs and values, which are denied by the rules governing his environment. But the reader may question the kind of psychological causality operating here. Has Smith learned from the past so that he can redefine success in his own working-class terms in the present, or is he simply repeating the naive pattern of his old mistakes?

A special plot pattern in which a movement in time and space denotes character development is called a "quest." In this kind of plot, some initial deficiency must be rectified. The plot consists of a series of obstacles, such as a battle with a villain or a difficult task, which are overcome by the character. During this process the hero or heroine loses weakness and acquires some virtue. The basic unit of the plot is confrontation   contests   acquisition. "The Woman Who Rode Away" is a good example of a story plotted according to the quest pattern: The woman, initially prevented from developing psychologically and spiritually, sheds her middle-class identity through her difficult initiation into the Indian religion.

Literal journey: Middle-class ———> Primitive Indian tribe
industrial society

Symbolic journey: Materialistic ———> Fertile environment
wasteland   (character has spiritual
(character has   attributes)
physical attributes)

Most twentieth-century artists who use the quest pattern depict heroic action ironically rather than straightforwardly. The woman indeed acquires spiritual attributes; she becomes a goddess, but to do this she sacrifices all personal identity and even her life. In becoming a more than human heroine, she is destroyed. Fitzgerald's use of the pattern in "Winter Dreams" is equally qualified. He shows that the heroic pattern is a deceptive dream when the hero seeks middle-class goals.

CHARACTER

Our discussion of the quest suggests that we are more interested in what events say about a character's potentialities and limitations than simply in what happens next. We cannot really describe plot without considering character, and this convention can create as many problems for the reader as any other aspect of fiction, even though character is its most familiar and understandable aspect. An author may make the verbal account of a character's adventures seem to happen to a real person, but it is important to recognize that character is made up of language. A sound character analysis will always be based on this assumption.

Étienne Souriau's theory of dramatic functions provides a useful basis for describing character. According to this concept, any event in literature is composed of six functions:

1. The "will" or agent of the action.
2. The desired "object" to be acquired in the action.
3. The beneficiary or "destination" of the action.
4. The "opposition" to the action.
5. The "arbiter" who decides if the action is successful.
6. The "helper" who assists the agent.

In his essay at the end of the critical guide, Bob Mandel uses dramatic roles to prove his point about Sillitoe's central character, Smith. This method is particularly useful in analyzing episodic fiction where it appears uncertain where the action leads and what it means. Success in applying these functions depends upon your being able to find literal evidence of their distribution. For example, in determining "the will" or agent of the action, you must find in the text an explicit expression of the character's desire for something, such as saying "I want." You should of course abandon the method if a meaningful pattern does not emerge.

The episodic nature of Anderson's *Winesburg, Ohio* makes Souriau's roles particularly useful as a critical method. The short stories each describe a different "grotesque" character, and we can determine what Anderson is saying about human nature through these characters by distributing the dramatic roles in "Hands." Wing Biddlebaum is designated the "will" by various verbs of desire: "He *hungered* for the presence of the boy," George Willard, the "object" of desire. Society had judged this will as deviant before when Wing, formerly called Adolf Meyers, tried to enlighten other schoolboys in his role as teacher. Expelled from his old community and trying to repress the hands which indicate his desire in his new community, Wing similarly judges his former role as affectionate schoolteacher to be a threat to social acceptance. He represses his former behavior: "he felt the hands were to *blame*." Thus we can say that Wing is a character encompassing two opposing roles, and Anderson has even given him two names to make this problem apparent. Distribution of dramatic functions reveals the composition of the grotesque character:

1. Will: Wing Biddlebaum
2. Object: George Willard
3. Destination: Wing Biddlebaum
4. Opposition: Adolf Meyer's hands
5. Arbiter: Wing Biddlebaum
6. Helper: none

Wing desires friendship and an end to isolation, but in his society a show of intense emotion obstructs relationships. It only makes sense that when the roles of will, opposition, and arbiter are performed by the same character, there will be no end to isolation. When judgment opposes desire, there can be no chance for successful completion of the action, and no outside character has a chance to help. If you want to talk about the theme of isolation and community, these roles will help you to define in precise terms the problems the story poses.

For most readers the meaning of events in a story depends upon what kind of "person" is performing the action or affected by it. Another way of describing character is by determining the types which compose it. A description of a character is never a complete catalogue of physical or psychological features. A few details generally suffice. As members of a society we share a vocabulary of character traits on which we depend in order to identify other people as well as ourselves. When you describe someone as "broad-shouldered," "shifty-eyed," or "pushy," your audience receives a concept of character from just a single detail. Certain details evoke in all of us a bundle of associated physical features, behavior patterns, and psychological traits, and an artist who wants to create a character draws upon this vocabulary of types or "flat" characters. In a character that we consider realistic or "round," several often conflicting types are encompassed in one figure, where many aspects of a personality interact and conflict as they do in Wing Biddlebaum. This technique creates the illusion of depth.

Fitzgerald's Judy Jones is another such character. She is composed of two recognizable types. Her admirer Dexter thinks she is a sentimental heroine as found in nineteenth-century romances, but she behaves like a careless, insincere, and cruel aristocrat. She looks like a sympathetic heroine, but her behavior stems from an unsympathetic character type. Dexter desires both the social features and the sentimental ones that Judy represents, but the story explores the impossibility of combining domestic love and aristocratic freedom in one character. In the course of the story, Dexter loses his own sentimental attributes as he gains wealth, and Judy's development works the other way around. She becomes "more of a human being" through a degrading marriage to one of Dexter's colleagues. Fitzgerald's story shows that attractive social and economic features are absolutely in conflict with the internal qualities of sympathy and responsibility. We can describe the thematic organization of this story in terms of its treatment of characters.

First opposition: Sentiment ⟷ Aristocratic freedom

Dexter   Judy

Second opposition: Sympathy ⟷ Wealth

An artist like Fitzgerald develops round characters to show that social or fictional stereotypes are false and oversimplified representations of human nature.

In some literature flat characters prevail. The expressionist, assuming that one cannot know or accurately represent another personality, uses characters simply to express personal ideas and attitudes. These characters correspond exactly to a concept, and the author trims away all superfluous or "realistic" features so that this idea is clear. A Morlock in Wells's *The Time Machine* or a Topeka citizen in "A Boy and his Dog" are not intended to represent human beings at all but to express, in the first instance, the author's view of pure survival instincts, and in the second, pure impractical sentimentality. These characters are actually more like the symbolic creatures of Yeats's poetry than the social types in Fitzgerald, Faulkner, or Sillitoe. Even though they have retained some recognizable social features, they behave allegorically, like the demons and angels of myth and dream.

In impressionist fiction the classic round character also undergoes a strange transformation. A character like Kurtz will offer a field of variant possibilities: He is the hero who does not falter in a quest for knowledge, but he is also the hollow man who cannot maintain the values of civilization in the face of the temptations of the wilderness. Antoinette, the narrator in *Wide Sargasso Sea*, is far more complex a personality than the character type described by Jane Eyre. These novels seem to suggest that personality and character are two very different things. In the impressionist novel, the social type used to describe a given character will tell us more about the narrator who uses character conventions than about the "personality" being described. The following discussion of narration (how a story gets told) explains further techniques modern authors have developed to represent personality and consciousness in fiction.

NARRATION

Since Aristotle, the customary distinction drawn between the lyric and the drama is that the lyric *tells* (this is called *diegesis*) and the drama and all other visual arts *show (mimesis)*. In dramatic forms authors show rather than tell us what they mean by having all language come from characters. No speech directly expresses the author's view. In contrast, poetic form and techniques make the reader always aware that the poem is written by an author, not created by a character. We assume that the language in the poem tells us how the writer thinks or feels. Aristotle maintained, and most critics still agree, that narrative is a combination of *mimesis* and *diegesis*. Prose fiction therefore presents the reader with some unique difficulties: Since fiction is usually a combination of showing and telling, the speaker or source of language can be difficult to determine.

Why should we be concerned with these distinctions? Actually, we make daily judgments about the quality of the information we receive: Does it tell us something about the world, or does it show something about the character of the teller? We always take the source of information into account. Had a George Washington instead of Richard Nixon told us, "I am not a crook," more people probably would have believed him. In fiction, language works the same way; we must familiarize ourselves with the various kinds of narration in order to distinguish who is responsible for the words we read and thus to understand the way we should read them.

There are basically two ways a story can be written or told to us:

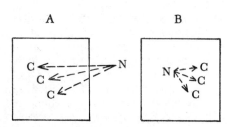

A   B

Figure A is an illustration of the relationship between characters and narrator in omniscient third-person narrative. Here, the narrative source is an implied or imaginary author. Such narrators are called "omniscient" because their knowledge is not limited by the fictive world they are describing, and they knows things no single character could. In Farrell's "The Scoop," for example, the narrator provides whole personal histories and alludes to a large social context: "At that time *The Questioner* was conducting, as a circulation stunt, one of its wars on crime." Such narrators never call attention to themselves as personalities but seem merely to recount the events of history. Anderson's narrator in *Winesburg, Ohio* is similarly omniscient, but artfully intrudes in the first person to guide the reader to truths submerged beneath the appearances of the characters: "Let us look briefly into the story of the hands. Perhaps our talking of them will arouse the poet who will tell the hidden wonder story of the influence for which the hands were but the fluttering pennants of promise." We trust Anderson's narrator, who has the wisdom and insight of the traditional storyteller, and we trust the scientific objectivity of Farrell's narrator. We never question the accuracy of the statements they make.

Figure B illustrates the relationship between characters and narrator in first-person narration. Here the narrator explicitly says "I" or "me" and is generally restricted to the fictional world being described. Unlike the omniscient narrator, this kind of narrator exists within the fictive world as a character. For example, Alan Sillitoe's *The Loneliness of the Long-Distance Runner* is narrated by Smith. Supposedly he is the source of all the information we receive and is the central character as well, but the student essays by Bob Mandel and Andy Doppelt dispute the reliability of Smith's information. Does Smith express the values which the implied author advocates, or is Smith self-deceived, a character whose words we should view critically? When a character speaks, he or she is usually expressing a subjective opinion, and this is of course why most newspaper accounts, textbooks, and critical essays are written in the third person—to imply omniscience and avoid our questioning the authority of the source.

Each of these two types of narration has several variations, and the two can be combined. In "The Snows of Kilimanjaro" the narrator is omniscient; at least he describes characters and dialogue no single character on the scene could know. But the knowledge we received from the narrator is sometimes deliberately limited to Harry's awareness. When this happens, the effect is very similar to the dramatic effect of first-person narration. For example, this sentence, "The cot the man lay on was in the shade of a mimosa tree," is not something Harry is likely to think or say, for he himself is described in the third person ("the man") as if presented by an outside source. However, in the sentence, "But if he lived he would never write about her, he knew that now," Harry is the source of information, and we can easily translate the sentence into the first person: "If I live I will never write about her, I know that now." The narrator appears to transcribe Harry's thoughts rather than provide the information himself. Other parts of the story, printed in italics, appear to be the direct expression of Harry's unspoken thoughts and reveries. In a sentence like *"Shoot me, Harry, for Christ sake shoot me,"* not only the information but the language itself seems to come directly from Harry's memory. This combination of omniscient and limited narration enables the author to dramatize not only the speech of his character but also his thoughts, even those subjective experiences he does not know consciously.

When authors like Hemingway and Faulkner describe their characters' thoughts in a way that only the character himself would, they approach description of the *stream of consciousness* or nonverbal activities of the character's mind. One way this illusion is achieved is by shifting to the language of a character and leaving out the tag clause, "he thought." In *A Portrait of the Artist as a Young Man,* we know that a child cannot be responsible for the literary language we read, but the narrator's language frequently remains within the limits of the child's diction and seems to follow the associative processes of his mind. When the narrator

says, "He was baby tuckoo. The moocow came down the road where Betty Byrne lived: she sold lemon platt," we know that the statement could be tagged, "Stephen thought." But without this reminder of the narrator's presence we lose a sense that the story is being told at all and feel that the inner world of the character is dramatically shown to us.

In order to show the effect of reality on the mind of a character, the impressionist often uses the device of the twice-told tale. The narrator of *Heart of Darkness* retells Marlow's recollection of his journey to Africa and encounter with Kurtz. The physical journey which takes place in the fictive past is reconstructed as a process of recollection in the fictive present as Marlow tells his story. We get not only the physical experience but its effect on Marlow's mind. This makes it difficult, if not impossible, for the reader to determine what really happened—was Kurtz really a fascinating man of genius, or does attraction for him reveal a weakness in Marlow's character? In *Wide Sargasso Sea,* Rhys uses two different narrators with conflicting subjective views. Rochester's resentment at being saddled with a mad, adulterous wife is understandable according to his English standards, but in Rhys's novel the madwoman demands equal sympathy. We see her marriage to an Englishman strain a mind that would have been peaceful in the convent. We do not have to agree with one view and condemn the other in her novel, because both narrators have been twisted by a marriage system based on economic rather than psychological needs.

If in impressionist fiction we have problems discerning the objective from the subjective experience and deciding whether to accept subjective responses and judgements as reliable, later fictions in this tradition deliberately complicate this situation. Do we have one or several narrators in Cortázar's "Blow-Up"? If one, who is he, an author or a character? And if several, how can we tell who is speaking when? Whoever is doing the talking, he promises the reader in the first sentence that the puzzle concerning the narrative source cannot be solved: "It'll never be known how this has to be told, in the first or the third person plural or continually inventing modes that will serve for nothing." The reader is drawn into an endless process of constructing plots which might reveal the identity of the narrative personality, but the author has refused to name a single source. If we posit a mind as the teller of the story, it is a personality that *we* rather than the author construct.

Now look at Ondaatje's *The Collected Works of Billy the Kid.* When you trace the sources of the various documents that make up his history, you will find that it is impossible to deduce either the personality of the long-dead historical character or that of his narrator. The story has many origins, all of them artificial.

Essay Writing

The reading processes we have discussed will help you arrive at an idea of what a given work of art means, but often this is only the beginning. You will find that thorough understanding of a poem or narrative comes only after you have tried to write about it. When mathematicians solve difficult problems, they do not work them out in their heads but use pencil and paper, trial and error, until all the pieces have been put together. They make their discoveries while trying to prove their hypotheses, and your task will be very similar. You want to prove your own hypothesis about a literary work by gathering and organizing evidence. In this way, writing an English paper becomes a practice in understanding the ways language creates the effect of truth and an exercise in producing that effect yourself. You can then adapt this method of argumentation to those required in other disciplines. In other words, if you can write a good English paper, you ought to be able to write a good essay on just about anything.

The first thing you want to remember when beginning to write a college English paper is that you are inevitably involved in a "dramatic situation." You are writing to an educated audience who will construct an implied author from your use of the language. And if you write like a fool, the audience will take this as pretty good evidence that you are one. You are communicating a sense of yourself as a reader and writer, as a literate person, and we assume that you want this image to be positive, to have authority. Your

essay must be logical and convincing, and it must be written in prose that is correct in grammar, spelling, and diction. How could you expect to convince a reader that you have something to say about complex literary subject matter if your own writing suggests ignorance of the basic rules of written English? The main thing to keep in mind is your desire to communicate your ideas as clearly and accurately as possible. But sometimes students have difficulty in writing ideas that they could explain with perfect clarity in conversation. Their grammar is fine, they have solid ideas, but they find something in the written word that blocks their natural ability for argumentation. If you know you honestly have something to say and are not just making up words to fill the required number of pages, then certain practical techniques can assist you in getting what you feel to be a valid idea onto paper. Start gathering notes—pieces of evidence, ideas for an argument, possible conclusions—until you see a way to arrange many of these notes into an outline that supports one central idea or thesis. Once you have gone through this preparation for writing—reading the poem or narrative closely, logically arranging and revising your assertions, eliminating extraneous material and selecting the most convincing evidence—your essay will not only be valid and convincing, but it will be much easier to write. You will know what you want to say and in what order you want to say it. If you are still uneasy about whether or not your final language will actually communicate the ideas you have so carefully prepared, take this practical suggestion offered by many of our students. Read your draft aloud to an attentive friend before typing the final copy. By watching for visible signs of confusion, you will be able to determine when you are losing your listener and where your statements need clarification or examples. Have this friend explain what message he has actually received from your words, and see how this compares with what you intended to say. Once you have handed in a typed manuscript, it is too late to retract, reorganize, and clarify; the argument must stand on its own. Your friend's criticism can help you prepare for this end.

There are many handbooks full of specific rules concerning essay writing, but we feel that it is impossible to simply tell someone how to write. However, we can show how general writing principles apply in specific examples. We will begin by identifying the parts of a good argument about literature with reference to one of our students' essays. The linguist A. A. Hill has stated a useful rule for writing an argument about literature: "The best statement of design in a poem [and in narrative or drama] is that which is most complete, most consistent, and in a rather special sense, most simple." Hill's criteria more or less conform to most definitions of hypothesis and proof. In a good argument, the writer is able to account for all the data without contradicting himself and without bending the data to fit a theory that is complex because it is somehow inaccurate. There are many good arguments possible within these limits, but when you read a poem or narrative thoroughly and begin to formulate a thesis, you should discover one approach that you believe best fulfills Hill's criteria. This one idea in all probability is the one you can convert into your best expository prose and organize according to the following general principles.

I. THESIS

The good essay presupposes a worthwhile idea or thesis upon which to build an argument. The essays you will be asked to write undoubtedly will be limited in scope in comparison with the complexity of the works you are reading. It is impossible to say everything that can be said, so your thesis should be carefully focused, an aspect of essay writing that requires ingenuity, creativity, and a considerable amount of work. Everyone begins with a subjective response to a work of art, but by the time writing begins, concern should have shifted from "how does the story make *me* feel?" to a more objective consideration of how the composition of the work of art produces this effect on an audience. This is not an arbitrary or haphazard process but is best when conducted in the logical and empirical manner evident in Marybeth Spencer's essay, "Conflicting Values Systems in 'Barn Burning.'" After a close reading of the text and some experimentation with outlines, Spencer decided that all the data of the story could be explained by positing an opposition between the father's primitive ideals and those of civilization.

II. PROOF

In the body of the argument, you show the logical steps which justify your thesis assumption. This entails the use of evidence, much like the proceedings of a jury trial. In her second paragraph, for example, Spencer refers to specific passages that support her assertion that the father is emotional, illogical, violent, yet has a sense of family integrity that appeals to the boy. Her authority as an accurate reader is established by this use of textual evidence, in an argument that then shows the opposing civilized values of Major deSpain and apparent resolution of the conflict with the boy's acquisition of the language of civilization. As you read this paper, you should be able to see that it was written from this preconsidered outline:

I.   Thesis: Character's developing verbal abilities represent developing conflict between emotional and social values.
II. Proof:
  A. Tribal values represented by father
     1. Primitive nature of justice
     2. Priority of instincts

3. Preference for action
4. Continuation of violence
B. Civilized values represented by Major deSpain
   1. Democratic nature of justice
   2. Priority of reason
   3. Preference for language
   4. Maintenance of order
C. Developing conflict
   1. Loyalty of blood
   2. Effects of socialization
   3. Continuation of conflict
III. Conclusion: Rules of civilization, called into question by story.

III. CONCLUSIONS

The most common misconception about the conclusion is that it is merely a repetition of the thesis; you should view a conclusion as an opportunity to show that all your work has a purpose. Pretend for a moment that you are grading Spencer's paper. After her fourth paragraph you might say, "So what? What does it matter if one boy learns to speak in one short story?" In her conclusion, Spencer explains the meaning of the boy's successful struggle to speak out for reason. She shows that in this story the achievement of verbal power is not without sacrifice, for Faulkner ultimately undermines the value which growing-up stories traditionally place on the acquisition of reason and verbal ability. Spencer's completeness, consistency, straightforwardness, as well as her correct use of English, convinced us that her essay accurately describes the meaning conveyed by the design of the story, and as a bonus, her analysis made the story interesting. We have printed Spencer's essay for you in correct MLA (Modern Language Association) form to show exactly what an essay should look like when typed up according to manuscript specifications.

In addition to Spencer's, we have included other model essays demonstrating ways in which a good argument about literature may be constructed. We realize that not everyone will agree with the style or argument of every paper, but we think most teachers will feel that each essay is written in mature prose, each shows evidence of careful reading and consideration of the text, and each has something reasonable yet sophisticated to say. Because these arguments are well written, it is easy to recognize the critical methods or strategies used by their authors. Marybeth Spencer, as we have shown, uses a basically thematic approach. By close examination of the language of the story, she shows that all the important elements in it can be explained in terms of the values placed on two opposing categories. The success of her argument does not mean that many different but equally good essays cannot be written about this story. For example, Bob Mandel's paper was inspired by his disagreement with Andy Doppelt's analysis of Smith in "The Loneliness of the Long-distance Runner," and we consider their papers to be approximately equal in quality. Mandel's judgment of Smith is based on the nature of the parts of the narrative and their interrelationship. He uses Souriau's dramatic roles to describe the meaning of these elements as he compares Smith's role to that of other characters within an event and then defines a kind of progress or development in the roles Smith assumes. True, Smith does not progress by mastering social conventions as a character usually does in a *bildungsroman,* but Smith's defiance of athletic conventions, not to mention the law, is a sign of truer development, given the working-class background of Sillitoe's hero. Doppelt's view of Smith differs from Mandel's because Doppelt has not based his judgment solely on the arrangement of elements within the story. He views Smith as a version of the Marxist hero and finds him deficient in terms of this external model. We can see that the arguments of the other student essays can be similarly distinguished according to their internal analyses of their external criteria for judgment.

As different as the papers by Lam, Youngers, Hanson, and Haack seem, their methods are quite similar. They began by examining the relationship of the parts within a specific work of art. Using conventions described in the Critical Guide or one of the introductions to a section of this book, they decided what parts are functional or most important in producing the meaning or effect of the work in question. Catherine Lam and Annette Haack, for example, focus on the plots of stories by Lawrence, Fitzgerald, and Cortázar. In their essays, both argue that the use of a causally improbable plot (usually a convention of fantasy) to produce the effect of realism is central to the meaning of these works. They prove that when realistic plot conventions are modified as they are in these stories, the fiction is not unrealistic but forces the reader to change his conventional notion of what reality is. Similarly, you can see that Sid Youngers' application of a poetic technique, the "objective correlative," to drama credibly explains the uniquely abstract or nonrepresentational quality of Beckett's *Act Without Words.* Jane Hanson's analysis of one precise feature, fire imagery, distinguishes the contemporary *Wide Sargasso Sea* from the more traditional novel, *Jane Eyre.* Notice that she does not merely prove that fire is associated with warmly positive things in Rhys's novel, but she uses this evidence to prove something important about the novel's meaning: namely, that *Wide Sargasso Sea* overturns a traditionally repressive view of the female character. As you read these essays, notice how each begins with a proposition concerning the way a formal convention or use of language affects communication. Each traces the use of this convention through the work of art, showing that it explains the function of most of the important elements composing that work and arriving at a verifiable statement of its meaning.

Andy Doppelt and Anne Quinn, in contrast, see the work of art as a version of another, external theory such as a political or psychological system. Doppelt argues that Sillitoe's hero falls short of the Marxist ideal, an ideal not defined within the work of art itself. Quinn investigates the relationship between the treatment of women in two of Sexton's poems and the female role as it is defined in Freud's *Outline of Psycho-Analysis.* She selects that evidence from the poem which demonstrates the Freudian pattern of the Electra complex. Thus she is not interested so much in what the particular composition of linguistic material in the poems *means* as in its *significance.* What place does the poem have among theories describing female psychology? Quinn sees the poems as a protest against oppressive social roles that Freud and children's fairy tales establish for women. Even though Barry Lessin's concern for the function of various elements such as narrator and plot resembles the kind of formal analysis demonstrated by the first group of essays we discussed; he uses impressionist fiction as a philosophical or political theory as well as a form of narrative art and establishes the place of *Heart of Darkness* in this larger context. Lessin's paper does not comprehensively analyze the relationship of parts to whole in Conrad's novel but selects those elements of the narrative that define Conrad's concept of history and compares it to more standard concepts. The similarity between the two ways of analyzing literature Lessin's paper reveals brings us to an important point concerning the use of external standards for judgment. Doppelt and Quinn convinced us that their applications of Marxist and Freudian theories are not arbitrary. Their close readings of the literary works in question show that there is a relationship between the literature and the extraliterary models they have chosen. Whenever you make comparisons between a poem or narrative and another system of meaning, such as politics, psychology, philosophy, or religion, you run the risk of revealing more about yourself, your personal beliefs and ideologies than you do about the work of art. In critical writing, where the object is to arrive at some new understanding of an art work that can be communicated to others, the best statement of its significance as well as that of its formal meaning will originate in a close investigation of the language of the text itself.

Student Essays

Marybeth Spencer
English 208
May 26, 1976

1
CONFLICTING VALUE SYSTEMS
IN "BARN BURNING"
Marybeth Spencer

Through the use of a limited third-person narration in the short story "Barn Burning," William Faulkner presents a value struggle between a man's moral obligation to tribal ethic (the family) and his natural inclination toward the "good life" of civilization. This conflict is manifest in the maturation process of the protagonist, a young boy, and is expressed in various levels of his consciousness. On one level he is bound emotionally to the ideals of his father, feeling that the bond of blood and therefore the moral commitment to family is stronger than all other ties. However, on another level he is bound to his natural desire for the order, logic, and reason that can be found in civilization. Faulkner presents the emotional bond as chaotic, destructive, and changeable as exemplified in the boy's father and his irrational actions. This is opposed to the boy's desire for a life containing permanence, control, and rationalism as associated with the verbal reason and logic of law. Through the boy's developing value system Faulkner implies that a person's greatest commitment is to the verbalization of his conscious experiences.

The tribal ethic is exemplified in the relationship of the boy with his father. The father is presented as a character who values actions over words and is constantly involved in the traditional eye-for-an-eye struggle. His irrational behavior is tied to the illogical reasoning he employs, such as his perception of fire as "the one weapon for the preservation of integrity, else breath were not worth the breathing, and hence to be regarded with respect and used with discretion."[1] Because the father deals in emotions and actions, he cannot verbalize experience. This is exemplified in his manner of speech. Faulkner characterizes his voice as cold and harsh, and the father utilizes it rarely, using it only to say "something unprintable and vile, addressed to no one" (p. 5). Because the father cannot verbalize his emotions, he resorts to actions such as the violence he enacts on the boy: "His father struck him with the flat of his hand on the side of the head, hard but without heat" (p. 9). The boy perceives the irrational acts of his father, and this undermines the ideals his father stands for and preaches: "You got to stick to your own blood or you ain't going to have any blood stick to you" (p. 9). In this way the bond of blood is equated with violent, irrational actions. This undercuts the boy's feeling of moral obligation to

his father and leads him to describe their relationship as "despair and grief, the old fierce pull of blood" (p. 3).

In opposition to these ideals are those values of civilization manifested in law. These are symbolized in the boy's perceptions of Major deSpain's house. He views it as a "courthouse," a place where reason prevails over actions and therefore where his father would be powerless: "They are safe from him. People whose lives are a part of this peace and dignity are beyond his touch" (p. 11). The spell he attributes to the house has the power to allow the boy to forget "his father and the terror and despair both" (p. 11). In this way Faulkner presents the ideals of reason, logic, and justice as possessing a much greater value than any other possible ideals.

This establishes the competing and conflicting value system within the boy's developing consciousness. He is torn between the primitive ethic of action and blood and the verbal reason and logic of civilization. The resolution of this con-

---

[1] William Faulkner, "Barn Burning," in *Selected Short Stories of William Faulkner* (New York: The Modern Library, 1961), p. 8. All subsequent references are to this edition and appear in the text.

flict is demonstrated in the maturation of the boy and his growing ability to verbalize his conscious experiences. Initially upon the realization that his father is an arsonist, the boy converts his emotions into actions, as presented in the fight scene where he defends his father's honor, "scrabbling up to see the other boy in full flight and himself already leaping into pursuit" (p. 6). He struggles against verbalizing this reality even in his own mind: " 'Forever,' he thought. 'Maybe he's done satisfied now, now that he has' . . . stopping himself, not to say it aloud even to himself" (p. 7). Ultimately the boy converts his thoughts from actions into words: "The boy did not move. Then he could speak. 'What . . .' he cried. 'What are you . . .'" (p. 23). This verbalization of his conscious experiences is the climax of the boy's maturation. He has finally made a commitment to the rationalism of civilization, as opposed to the irrational emotions of the tribal ethic.

Through the opposing values systems presented by Faulkner in the maturation of the central character we are led to conclude that the most important growth of an individual occurs through the verbalization of his conscious experiences. It is only through language that these experiences become reality. Therefore, as Faulkner presents it, only words can render a person capable of logic and reason. This premise is undermined, however, by the ambiguous feelings the boy retains after verbalization of his conscious reality: "the grief and despair now no longer terror and fear but just grief and despair" (p. 26). In this way Faulkner forces the reader to deduce that not all the values of conscious experience lie in verbal expression. Therefore the boy's commitment to the linguistic reason and logic of civilization is not the ultimate answer to his conflict. In this way Faulkner undermines the reality of the conscious experiences presented in his narrative form itself.

2

IS THE LONG DISTANCE
RUNNER A REVOLUTIONARY
HERO?
Andy Doppelt

Alan Sillitoe's *The Loneliness of the Long Distance Runner* is a story about an alienated, lower-class Englishman named Smith and his life in a Borstal. The plot centers around a cross-country race in which Smith is running for the honor of the Borstal's governor. But this story is not just about a race and a jail; rather it is a series of thoughts and recollections that occur in Smith's mind. We see the entire story through Smith's eyes, yet we must remember that he is alienated, angered, and biased. The key to understanding the work is to note the divergences between what Smith tells us and what the author shows us about Smith's acts and thoughts. These divergences allow the author indirectly to interject his values and judgments of the character as well as give us deep insights into the character's thoughts and deeds. By piecing together all of Smith's thoughts, ideas, and subsequent acts, one cannot only gain an understanding of the story but can also conclude that Smith's naivete and distorted mind deceive and harm him.

Understanding Smith's conception of himself is a necessary foundation for gaining insight into the character and the plot. Smith, remember, comes from a society in which the capitalist, ruling class oppresses and exploits the lower, working class. Smith, belonging to the latter group, thus views his characteristics as part of this "us versus them" conflict. Not only does he claim that he is extremely smart and clever; he also maintains that he is more cunning and honest than the governor. Smith professes that true honesty is to be honest to yourself, saying, "You should think about nobody and go on your own way, not on a course marked out for you by other people." This allegiance to himself and others like him leads him to say that he is, at times, a warm and loyal person:

> I'm not hard-hearted (in fact I've helped a few blokes in my time with the odd quid, fag, or shelter from the rain when they've been on the run) but I'm boggered if I'm going to risk being put in the cells just for trying to give the governor a bit of advice he don't deserve.

Overall, Smith's view of himself is that of a good, clever person, better than those above him.

More important than these attributes, however, Smith primarily considers himself as a revolutionary hero. He is against the rich and for the poor (a kind of a Robin Hood ideal). He sacrifices material and physical benefits for his ideals (as exemplified by his being in the Borstal and deliberately losing the race yet never regretting these actions). The race especially illustrates several of his revolutionary ideals. Since winning the race will benefit only the governor, Smith has to be true to himself and deliberately lose the race. Smith has an overall negative view of the race in that he is forced to compete against other working-class Borstal Boys, who are just like him, for the benefit of the governor (this is strongly against Marxist proletarian ethics). These firm, rebellious commitments will, according to the Marxists, eventually lead to an uprising of the oppressed working class and a greatly improved society.

However, Sillitoe shows contradictions in Smith's character between what he says and what he actually does, thus undermining Smith's conception of himself as a true revolutionary hero. Although his goal, to take from the rich and give to the poor, is very noble, Smith actually does the reverse! He robs a poor neighborhood baker, not an upper-class capitalist. When he gets the money, he wants to spend it on a hotel room, thus giving the money to a wealthy person (the owner of the hotel) instead of his fellow working-class people. Another fault in his reasoning is shown by the fact that he does not want his story published. In order to bring about any social change, others must know of his thoughts and experiences. Since he is confined to a Borstal, his only means of communication with the outside world is through the written word. If his story is not made public, however, nobody will know of his efforts and everything he does will go to waste. Finally, observe the kind of society he wishes to establish when he said "in the end the governor is going to be doomed while blokes like me will take the pickings of his roasted bones and dance like maniacs around the Borstal's ruins." This vengeful, violent, chaotic society is not at all what revolutionary Marxists wish to establish. Smith's actions, therefore, show that while he thinks he is a revolutionary hero, his thoughts are actually opposite to those of the true revolutionary Marxists.

Smith most clearly demonstrates the hypocrisy and contradiction of his revolutionary ideals when he chooses to idolize his father as a true revolutionary model. The details of his father's bloody death appear, for the first time in several years, while Smith is running the race. Smith recalls how much courage and "guts" his father had when he was extremely ill yet defied the doctors who wished to hospitalize him. His father's defiance of authority and sacrifice of physical comfort thus become not only a model but also an inspiration for Smith when he says, "By God I'll stick this out like my dad stuck out his pain and kicked them doctors down the stairs: if he had guts for that then I've got guts for this." But observe where this courage led his father—to a painful, bloody death. Granted, he had a great deal of courage, but this defiance resulted in much more than just a loss of physical comfort and other personal benefits. This man died; obviously, he was oblivious of any possible consequences of his actions. Yet Smith selects this man as his model for a revolutionary hero when, in fact, this "model" lacked the common sense and prudence that a true revolutionary hero should possess.

These divergences between what Sillitoe shows us and what Smith tells us lead us to conclude that Sillitoe is a bit critical of Smith. He is not, however, against Smith in the sense that he is on the governor's side. Rather, Sillitoe is critical of Smith because of Smith's failure to follow the true ideals of a revolutionary hero. A true revolutionary hero will, among other things, sacrifice material and personal benefits for an ideal, work against the rich and for the poor, compensate cleverness for various weaknesses, and seek to establish a more civilized society where the capitalists will no longer oppress and exploit the working-class people. Smith claims that he believes in these ideals, yet his actions show that he does not practice them fully. Notice that Sillitoe never directly steps in and tells us when he approves or disapproves of Smith's thoughts and actions. Simply by developing divergences between the character's thoughts and acts, the author helps us to reason out several conclusions about the character and the values presented in the story.

3
*A DIFFERENT VIEW
OF SMITH
Bob Mandel*

Some readers view the character Smith in Alan Sillitoe's story, *The Loneliness of the Long-Distance Runner,* as an antihero. Smith does not possess any preeminent virtues, such as strength or morality, of a literary hero. Smith, however, is appealing to this kind of reader because he is seen as the underdog—poor, uneducated, and powerless—who stands up to a foe larger than himself in order to assert his worthiness as a human being. Other readers see contradictions in Smith's character and contradictions between Smith as the narrator and Sillitoe the author, and conclude that Smith is unreliable and not a hero. For example, Smith appears to have a split personality: a public face and a private one. To the Governor, Smith appears to want to win the race; privately he does not. In the same way Smith seems naive about the qualities he possesses. Will Smith "have more fun and fire" in his life than the Governor, or is the author just showing how foolish Smith is? Smith claims he is cunning, but the author shows a character who gets caught when the stolen money he stuffed up a drainpipe falls out in front of a policeman. Moreover, Smith states that he is in a war, yet he robs the baker who is on his side.

Though this kind of reader finds some valid contradictions in Smith's character, he does not look for possible textual explanations, except to say that the author does not agree with the narrator. Many of these contradictions in Smith's character can be explained with reference to the roles—Will, Opposition, Object, Destination, Arbiter, Helper—that Souriau developed in *Situations Dramatique*. They will help explain what Smith learns about himself and his relationship to his environment, how he adapts, and what he still must learn.

The major scene of the story is the Borstal race in which Smith is competing against other runners from different Borstals. Souriau's roles could define the act in the following way:

Scene	Will	Opposition	Object	Destination	Arbiter	Helper
Normal race	Runner	Other runners	To win	Runner	Nature	Coach
Smith's view	Smith	Governor	To be treated like a human being	Smith	Smith	None

In a normal race the opposition is the other runners, but Smith sees the governor as his opposition because, as Smith says, "the governor talks to me when he comes on his rounds, almost as he'd talk to his prize race horse." Smith's object or desire is not to win the race but to be treated as a human being. Smith says, "I'll lose that race, because I'm not a race horse at all, and I'll let him know it." In addition, Smith states, "I'm a human being and I've got thoughts and secrets and bloody life inside me that the Governor doesn't know is there." Because Smith decides to lose the race, the race in a sense is fixed, and Smith becomes the judge of whether he'll obtain his object. Therefore, Smith learns in the Borstal "that it's war between me and them," a war over which Smith would like to have some control. A constructive reader must decide if Smith's perception of the events is believable and if losing the race is a heroic act. To recall previous criticisms, Smith, by purposely losing the race in front of the Governor, refutes the charge that he has a split personality. He merely delays revelation of this private desire for dramatic effect.

The situation of the race and Smith's life outside the Borstal are similar, except for the fact that money, which he needs for food, clothing, and shelter, becomes an additional desire in the latter. After Smith leaves the Borstal, he has three career options to obtain his objects—racing, working, and stealing. It is true that he could join the army, but Smith comes down with pleurisy which keeps him out. Before the Borstal race Smith thinks about racing as a career: "I realized it might be possible to do such a thing, run for money, trot for wages on piece work at a bob a puff rising bit by bit to a guinea a gasp and retiring through old age at thirty-two because of lace-curtain lungs, a football heart, and legs like varicose beanstalks." Besides seeing the physical harm in racing, Smith perceives that racing will not allow him to escape the war he finds himself in. Smith imagines that even though he is the best runner in the world, "bullets that can go faster than any man running, coming from a copper's rifle planted in a tree, winged me and split my gizzard in spite of my perfect running." Moreover, it is the running and not racing that allows Smith to engage in a creative activity. Smith can put on a spurt at the end of a race "because I feel that up till then I haven't been running and that I've used up no energy at all." Though energy is expended in running, Smith psychologically does not feel any deterioration to his body, unlike in racing. Moreover, through running Smith is able to create art in the form of his story. Just one sentence takes "a few hundred miles of long-distance ‧ running." In this context, running allows Smith to utilize both his mind and body to its fullest potential, but it will not provide the money he needs to live in society. On the other hand, racing will provide the money he needs but not the necessary creative activity that he finds in running.

Another possible career for Smith is to become a worker. When Smith's father dies from cancer of the throat, the factory sends his family five hundred dollars; but Smith sees that it was his father "who'd done the suffering and dying for such a lot of lolly." Even before his father died, Smith sweated his "thin guts out on a milling machine with the rest of them." The only payment in the work process for Smith was physical deterioration and underutilization of his mental capacity. It is true that Smith would receive money for his work, but it would not be enough to compensate for the physical damage or to satisfy his desire for money, which increases through watching television. With the money Smith's family had received, they bought a television whose "adverts on the telly had shown us how much more there was in the world to buy than we'd ever dreamed of when we'd looked into shop windows but hadn't seen all there was to see because we didn't have the money to buy it with anyway. And the telly made all these things seem twenty times better than we'd ever thought they were." Since racing and working do not provide him with either enough money or a creative activity, Smith chooses stealing to obtain his objects.

Again, if stealing as a general concept is considered a scene in the story, Souriau's roles could define the act in the following way:

Scene	Will	Opposition	Object	Destination	Arbiter	Helper
Stealing	Smith (Out-law)	In-laws	Money	Smith	Smith's ability Cops	None

Stealing will provide Smith with money (if he is not caught) and a creative activity. In the following Smith sees stealing as a craft: "I worked out my systems and hiding-places while pushing scrubbing-brushes around them Borstal floors, planned my outward life of innocence and honest work, yet at the same time grew perfect in the razor-edges of my craft for what I knew I had to do once free." Stealing is similar to running for Smith in that he uses his mind to create a plan and then carries it out; both mind and body are utilized. Unlike the situation while running, he is opposed by the "In-laws" of which "there are thousands . . . over the poxeaten country, in shops, offices, railway stations, cars, houses, pubs—In-law blokes like you and them, all on the watch for Out-law blokes like me and us." Although Smith might get caught, he had decided that being an "Out-law" is the best way to live because he can both have the money and engage in a creative activity.

Although Smith has found a way to exist in his environment, it is apparent to both the reader and Smith that Smith lives in isolation. In both the Borstal race and Smith's future work, stealing, Smith has no helper. Smith knows this and is willing to live with it when he says, "I'm a long-distance runner, crossing country all on my own no matter how bad it feels." At the end of the story, however, Smith's knowledge and the reader's knowledge diverge, and the reader learns how totally alone Smith is. What happens is that Smith says he is going to give this story to a pal with the condition that if Smith gets caught by the cops, his pal will try to get the story published. If Smith never gets caught, his pal will keep the story to himself. Smith believes that his pal will never give him away because "he's lived in our terrace for as long as I can remember, and he's my pal. That I do know." Assuming that the publication would be considered the last scene of the story, there are two possible ways that the book gets published. The first is that Smith gets caught and his friend gets the story published. This is possible because although Smith claims that he is cunning, he knows that he would always "be tripped up sooner or later no matter how many" traps he escaped. On the other hand, if Smith is not caught by the police, then his friend has betrayed him (since we know the book is published), and Souriau's roles look like this:

Scene	Will	Opposition	Object	Destination	Arbiter	Helper
Publication (Smith not caught)	Smith	Pal	Story not to be published	Smith	Pal	Pal

What is apparent is that Smith's pal is his Opposition, Arbiter, and Helper, that friend-to-friend relationships in this environment break down, and that Smith is more alone than he imagines. Thus, Smith is obviously not Sillitoe's "socialist hero" who disdains money and is caught up in the workers' cause. Rather, Smith is a character who is poor, who finds himself in an environment where luxuries exist for the wealthy, and who tries his best to adapt. In a sense, this story is only a section of Smith's quest for self-identity. Though Smith has found a creative and profitable activity in stealing and though he recognizes that because of the war between the "In-laws" and the "Out-laws" he must live alone, he does not understand how totally alone he is and how ultimately impotent his actions must be because of his isolation.

4
*REALITY IN LITERATURE:
"THE WOMAN WHO RODE
AWAY" AND "WINTER
DREAMS"*
Catherine May Ngor Lam

Readers generally find fiction more acceptable if it conforms to their idea of ordinary life as governed by laws of cause and effect. They accept causal probability as signifying reality, whereas any plot that is causally improbable is taken as an illusion, a dream, something that is unreal. However, this criterion is illogical since fiction by definition is something unreal. It is only an embodiment of ideas. In fact, it is in the idea behind the plot that reality lies. We can illustrate this by contrasting the plot of "The Woman Who Rode Away" with "Winter Dreams."

In "The Woman Who Rode Away," the plot is highly mythical. A character, *she,* wanders into a long-forgotten savage Indian valley out of "a foolish romanticism more unreal than a girl's." The valley turns out to be a magic green place for the woman, as opposed to the wasteland she formerly experienced. This change of landscape can be regarded as a projection of her mind. She is released from her sexual repression as she gradually adopts the Indian myths. This is because the Indian myth is in fact a deification of fertility: "When the man gets a woman, the sun goes into the cave of the moon, and that is how everything in the world starts." Sexual union is pure, reaching beyond time and space, since it is a part of nature. This notion is reflected in the landscape, where "The whole valley glittered intolerably with pure snow," in contrast with the "pinkish, stark dry and abstract" Mexican city. The woman "did not feel shamed in her nakedness. Because nobody felt ashamed." The sexual union, in turn, is only part of the union between man and nature—his source of life and nourishment. The human sacrifice at the end of the novel embodies this idea. Unlike the lifeless caves of the silverwork which symbolize man disfiguring and raping nature, the "funnel-shaped cavity" with the "fanged inverted pinnacle" of ice, symbolizes the perfect union of man, woman, and nature: "Womanhood was to be cast once more into the great stream of impersonal sex and impersonal passion." All these myths about the environment become reality to the woman. Once more she feels the life and consciousness which had "mysteriously stopped with her marriage." She becomes very sensuous and feels as if "she were diffusing out deliciously into the harmony of things," but she has little sensation of the sacrifice. The sacrifice to her is merely a process of transition, changing her state of existence in the universe of which already she is a part. Thus, if reality is the realm of experience which gives life its meaning, reality for the woman in the book must lie in the mythical, causally improbable Indian valley.

Fitzgerald's "Winter Dreams," on the other hand, takes place in ordinary American society. Details such as Mr. T. A. Hedrick's initials create the illusion of historical realism. The plot concerning an unsuccessful love story is causally probable and represents a recognizable social reality. However, Judy Jones, functioning like the Indians in "The Woman Who Rode Away," serves to reveal Dexter's mind. She proves to be an illusion, defining Dexter's American dream.

Dexter feels deprived since his mother is a Bohemian peasant. He is convinced that he will forever be "the rough strong stuff from which they [men with rich origins] eternally sprang." He wants to be a mythic American hero, the socially successful urbanite: "he wanted the glittering things themselves." Dexter sees in Judy his ideal, since "She was not a girl who could be 'won.'" She cannot be earned; she is simply bestowed like grace from God or white magic. "Whatever Judy wanted, she went after with the full pressure of her charm," and she "was entertained only by the gratification of her desires." She possesses the aggressiveness and willful pleasure-seeking which define an American urban hero, qualities Dexter wants to possess. Dexter seeks psychological fulfillment in Judy; their love is "surfeit that would demand more surfeit." Consequently, the physical separation from Judy does not really hurt Dexter since she is only a projection of himself. It is her loss of willfulness and beauty, the falling apart of his illusion, that strikes him at last. With the fading away of her magic charm, his notion of reality is opened to reexamination. She has always been an illusion, and "the dream was gone." Ironically, Judy, the object of a causally probable plot, proves to be nothing more than part of a dream. The reader is deceived into accepting her as a probable lover for Dexter since she is described in socially realistic terms. We are then like Dexter himself, who does not understand what he is after until the very end of the story. His mind is preoccupied by his heroic dream to the extent that he idealizes Judy when he first meets her. He sees what he wants to see and builds up for himself a distorted reality. This reality will only be questioned when it comes into sharp conflict with the objective world.

Thus, causal probability does not necessarily make the story more real. Both more and less probable plots are only embodiments of ideas. They are fictions which never can be real. Reality lies in the idea created through the interaction of the character with his environment and how he perceives that world. Causal improbability may define a unique state of mind, and thus a deviant's view of the world is no less real in fiction than an objective, socially accepted view. These stories suggest that life for every individual is a constant struggle to construct his own reality.

5
THE FAIRY TALE
TRANSFORMED: A WOMAN'S
NIGHTMARE
Anne D. Quinn

In childhood, there are certain stories and images of womanhood that are "taught," enforcing roles and determining a social reality. To be a good person or a complete individual is not enough; little girls are supposed to behave in one way and little boys another. As Freud said in An Outline of Psychoanalysis, "For distinguishing between male and female in mental life we make use of what is obviously an inadequate empirical and conventional equation: We call everything that is strong and active male, and everything that is weak and passive female." In the seemingly innocent and primitive mode of literature, the fairy tale, these roles and expectations are both rigidly and clearly defined. A child's view of reality is limited; so quite naturally the fairy tale seems real. It becomes a part of his world and thus is transformed into social fact. The dangerous and damaging aspect of both Freudian analysis and Grimm's Fairy Tales is seen when the implicit attitudes of these myths shape the social reality. As children get older, they find life not as simple and magical as fairy tales portray it to be. Material goods are not gained through good luck and a wish; not everyone who is "devout and good" is rewarded with a handsome prince, and a husband and wife do not always "live happily ever after." These myths cause damage to the living human psyche, for they do not allow for the growth and understanding of the child. By believing in eternal youthfulness and happiness, the child cannot attain a realistic perception of life.

In two examples, "Cinderella" and

"Briar Rose" from the *Grimm's Fairy Tales,* Anne Sexton demonstrates the nightmarish consequences of fairy tales becoming a social and psychological reality. She changes their meaning and the values they communicate concerning the role of women in order to transform that role. By incorporating Freudian language into the fairy tale, Sexton implies that one is as mythical as the other, although one seems to be scientific fact and the other merely fiction. She uses colloquialism and contemporary words for a comic effect to satirize the conventions of these mythologies. The transformed portrayal of the fairy tale represents a transformed portrayal of women.

Through the use of Freudian language, Sexton illustrates the psychological realism of fairy tales. This is exemplified in "Briar Rose" in terms of the Electra complex, for when the prince found the "sleeping beauty": "He kissed Briar Rose/ and she woke up crying:/ Daddy! Daddy!/ Presto! She's out of prison!" The Electra complex determines that a woman will "choose her husband for his paternal characteristics and be ready to recognize his authority." To clarify this predominant pattern, other symbols are used. Sexton speaks of a young girl, "She's on a voyage./ She is swimming further and further back. . . ." In Freudian terms, swimming (in dream analysis) refers to a desire to return to the mother's womb. The word "prick," which appears twice in "Briar Rose," and the metaphor, "so that I do not know that brutal place/ where I lie down with cattle prods,/ the hole in my cheek open," both have blatant sexual connotations. By applying these concepts to the fairy tale, Sexton reveals the limited concept of women implied in Freudian language.

To demonstrate the social realism embedded in fairy tales, Sexton employs contemporary details. She replaces traditional and formal language with contemporary language and colloquialism. The "once upon a time . . ." is transformed to:

You always read about it: the plumber with twelve children who wins the Irish Sweepstakes. From toilets to riches. That story.

The evil fairy in "Briar Rose" is portrayed as a modern horror: "The thirteenth fairy, her fingers as long and thin as straws,/ her eyes burnt by cigarettes,/ her uterus an empty teacup." Magic, too, is dealt with on a naturalistic level:

The eldest went into a room to try the slipper on but her big toe got in the way so she simply sliced it off and put on the slipper. The prince rode away with her until the dove told him to look at the blood pouring forth. That is the way with amputations. They don't just heal up like a wish.

Because of her contemporary tone and matter-of-fact approach, the awful consequences of making a fairy tale into social and economic reality become evident. *Grimm's Fairy Tales* similarly present women as incomplete, empty creatures with no other motives or desires than marriage and babies: "Next came the ball, as you all know./ It was a marriage market./ The prince was looking for a wife."

Sexton applies these same fantasy techniques of characterization in *Transformations,* but only to criticize the fairy tale characters by revealing their flatly artificial lives. She accomplishes this by following the fairy tale and preserving much of the Grimms' language. In *Grimm's Fairy Tales:* "When the wedding was going to take place, the two false sisters came and wanted to curry favor with her and take part in her good fortune. . . . Afterwards when they were coming out of the church, the elder was on the left, the younger on the right, and the doves picked out the the other eye of each of them." The same story in Sexton's *Transformations* follows:

At the wedding ceremony the two sisters came to curry favor and the white dove pecked their eyes out. Two hollow spots were left like soup spoons.

Sexton thus uses comic treatment to satirize the characters so that they are distinguishd from real people: "Cinderella was their maid./ She slept on the sooty hearth each night/ and walked around looking like Al Jolson . . ." By satirizing these women and their roles, she shows they are mere masks. She treats their situations flippantly also, for like the characters, they are mere charades:

She [the thirteenth fairy] made this prophecy: The princess shall prick herself on a spinning wheel in her fifteenth year and then fall dead.
Kaputt!

In contrast to *Grimm's Fairy Tales,* Sexton's version implies that her female characters do have a personality and a psyche. They are potentially more than just pretty maidens with plastic, hollow bodies, always sitting and smiling. They take on human characteristics:

Briar Rose was an insomniac . . . She could not nap òr lie in sleep without the court chemist mixing her some knock-out drops and never in the prince's presence.

However, Sexton also illustrates that when human characters lead fairy tale lives, they deserve fairy tale endings:

Cinderella and the prince lived, they say, happily ever after, like two dolls in a museum case never bothered by diapers or dust, never arguing over the timing of an egg, never telling the same story twice, never getting a middle-aged spread, their darling smiles pasted on for eternity. Regular Bobbsey Twins. That story.

This ending, however, is less than positive in Sexton's version of the story.

Because her poems deal with a psychological reality, Sexton reveals a very nightmarish consequence of living in such a mythical world. "Briar Rose" directly alludes to the Electra complex. Freud, like the Grimm Brothers, has a false definition of the happy ending because he fails to account for the reality of the female psyche. The poet/persona in "Briar Rose" speaks this repressed truth:

But if you kissed her on the mouth her eyes would spring open and she'd call out: Daddy! Daddy! Presto! She's out of prison. . . . Each night I am nailed into place and I forget who I am. Daddy? That's another kind of prison. It's not the prince at all, but my father drunkenly bent over my bed, circling the abyss like a shark, my father thick upon me like some sleeping jelly fish.

Through the transformation of fairy tales, Sexton is able to demonstrate that the traditional presentation of women is primitive and naive. She has placed the fairy tale into a social and psychological context in order to exhibit the damaging limitations in its definition of woman. Because myths often shape one's view toward reality, Sexton has established the need for a transformation of all myths in order for the social and psychological reality to change.

6
THE FORM AS THE MESSAGE IN "ACT WITHOUT WORDS"
Sid Youngers

In his play *Act Without Words,* Beckett presents a microcosmic view of life and he does so through objective correlative. The man's relationship to the objects he is confronted with points to a frame of mind which cannot be adequately described by words (the inadequacy of words is seen in the fact that the play lacks dialogue entirely). Moreover, the entire play is merely a vehicle through which the reader gains the extremely pessimistic insight that when cut off from his traditional religious explanations of being, man is lost.

While the appearance and disappearance of the tree, scissors and boxes could be attributed to chance, there is certainly some unidentified force guiding the man's activity in the play. He is "flung backwards onto the stage." This force is represented by the whistle which rules out any independent action taken by the man. The force is not, however, merely a symbol for God. In fact, it is the unconventional treatment of this omnipotent force normally associated with the Christian "God" that allows this work its meaning.

The God of Christian ethic is a provider, overseer, and beneficiary of mankind. The force or power in this play is a frustrater. The man is repeatedly called off stage, only to be "flung back on," and he is never allowed to clip his nails. The nature of this force is such, too, that the traditionally favorable qualities of ambition, purposefulness, and dignity are stifled in this man. When the man seeks an improvement in his condition, such as gaining shade or water, he is forbidden it: "He turns, sees rope, reflects, goes to it, climbs up it and is about to reach carafe when rope is let out and deposits him back on ground." The man is continually humbled through the pratfalls he takes: "The big cube is pulled from under him and he falls." Even when his only purpose is suicide, and he "runs his finger along blade of scissors, goes and lays them on small cube, turns aside, opens his collar and frees his neck," he is not allowed to do so: "The small cube is pulled up and disappears in the flies, carrying away the scissors."

Upon being confronted by this unidentifiable and anticonventional power in the play, the man is not frustrated. No word describes his situation properly. For this reason, Beckett deals not with words, but solely with the action responsible for creating an emotion beyond words. The action is not symbolic of any other. It is unique and serves as the medium by which he transfers the desired feeling to the audience. The conclusion of the play is extremely pessimistic. The man is without dignity, ambition, or purpose. "He does not move." This, though, is not the source of pessimism. He is lost only in that without the traditional religious explanation of existence, his life appears meaningless to the audience. In this way, the form of the play is the content, for the audience becomes aware of its own limitations in identifying the true value of existence when it sees none for the man in the play.

7
THE UNRELIABILITY OF
HISTORY REVEALED THROUGH
EVALUATION OF HEART OF
DARKNESS
Barry Lessin

An impressionistic literary work relies on active participation by its reader-audience. Forced to explain various ambiguities, the reader must "reconstruct" certain aspects of the narration and make up his own version of the fictional "reality," of what occurs in the story. Often, no effective judgment can be made concerning the validity of these constructed "realities," and a single judgment must therefore be discounted when looking at the meaning of the literary work as a whole. Thus it is the active evaluation process that is the primary purpose of the work because the reader's constructive experience is not always the same. Evaluation of Joseph Conrad's novel, *Heart of Darkness,* shows the destruction of the so-called reliability of the traditional story-teller as a dictator of the truth. The passivity of the audience receiving the "official truth" is disturbed, and the reader is forced to question the reliability of the storyteller's version of history.

Heart of Darkness is seemingly structured to provide the reader with an organized direction for his understanding of the events that take place in the novel. It is written as a "layered story" in which the narrator describes a situation where an old seaman, Marlow, tells a group of his friends a story about a personal experience that took place in the fictive past. In his description of Marlow, the narrator shows an obvious respect and reverence for the old seaman: "He had the pose of a Buddah preaching in European clothes and without a lotus flower." To the narrator Marlow "resembled an idol." By using an old storyteller, wise from the rich experiences of a long life, to reflect back on a past event with supposed new understanding, Conrad presents the reader with an established character upon whom he can depend for understanding and value judgments of the fictional narrative.

Furthermore, the novel has an historical reference, an objective set of events which enable the reader to judge the accuracy of Marlow's narration. Thus the reader should be able to distinguish any subjective distortions imposed on the events reported by Marlow. During the nineteenth century, France and Belguim engaged in economic exploitation of the Congo territory in Africa. In the fictional recount of this historical event, Marlow is a young man hired by a trading company to serve as the captain of a trading steamboat in the Congo. Through the account of Marlow's experiences in Africa, the reader sees the events of this historical period from the perspective of a fictional "eyewitness," a traditional source of reliability. Marlow describes how he embarked on the river, "deeper and deeper into the heart of darkness" to get to "a very important [trade] station in jeopardy" to bring back Mr. Kurtz, "the chief of the inner station . . . a prodigy . . . an emissary of pity, and science, and progress." The story related by the "old" Marlow attempts to find the "true" historical reality, for the storyteller shows that information is concealed from the public by the government version of the "official truth": "the International Society for the Suppression of Savage Customs had entrusted him [Kurtz] with the making of a report, for its future guidance. . . . It was eloquent, vibrating with eloquence . . . But this must have been before his— let us say—nerves went wrong and caused him to preside at certain midnight dances with unspeakable rites, which . . . were offered up to him."

The chronology of history is reflected in the chronology of Marlow's journey away from civilization to Kurtz's stronghold in the African jungle. Young Marlow embarks on a physical journey to find Kurtz and must overcome many obstacles along the way, including mechanical failures with the steamship, natural phenomena such as fog and snags in the river, and an attack by a tribe of African natives: "We cleared the snags clumsily. Arrows, by Jove! We were being shot at!" The old storyteller Marlow, on the other hand, embarks on a mental quest to understand the meaning of his past adventures in the Congo. The old seaman is plagued and confused by his attempts to perceive the evil of the tyranny used to "civilize" the Congo: "It was the farthest point of navigation and the culminating point of my experience. It seemed somehow to throw a kind of light onto everything about me—and into my thoughts. It was somber enough too—and pitiful—not extraordinary in any way—not very clear either."

Through this continuous chronological narration of his experiences, Marlow moves from certainty to uncertainty and is faced with the paradox that Kurtz, the "ardent civilizer," is a savage tyrant,

"grubbing for ivory in the wretched bush." Marlow initially becomes confused about the effect of the colonization on the Congo as he observes the black slaves at the company station, half way up the river: "they were not criminals—nothing but black shadows of disease and starvation, lying confused in the greenish gloom." Later in his journey Marlow is confused over the "restraint" of the "black fellows of our crew," cannibals who "must be very hungry": "Why in the gnawing devils of hunger didn't they go for us?" The reader sees Marlow's development from confusion to understanding of the paradoxical nature of the human mind, and thus to perception of the cause of Kurtz's actions: "Kurtz lacked restraint in the gratification of his various lusts." This is what caused the "original," "gifted" Mr. Kurtz to "preside at certain midnight dances ending with unspeakable rites" and to place "heads on the stakes . . . black, dried, sunken with closed eyelids."

In *Heart of Darkness,* then, literary conventions such as the use of the seemingly omnipotent, wise storyteller, historical reference, and the continuity of physical and mental quests enable the reader to determine the various levels of events which constitute the "true reality" of the situation that occurred with the colonial exploitation of the Congo, as compared to the "official" version recorded in history. At the end of the story, however, the reader does not naively accept the storyteller Marlow's assessment of events. The old seaman had proclaimed, "You know I hate, detest, and can't bear a lie, not because I am straighter than the rest of us, but simply because it appals me." As a young agent, however, he pretends to have influence in Europe, thinking, "it was great fun." Eventually he lies to protect the late Kurtz's "image" with his fiancée: "The last word he pronounced was—your name." This divergence between what the older Marlow says about himself and what the younger Marlow does causes the reader to doubt the reliability of the storyteller's narration, for how can one tell when a known liar is telling the truth? The reader also notices Marlow's fascination with Kurtz. Marlow claims that, "Mr. Kurtz was no idol of mine," but he actually admires him: "He had summed it up—he had judged 'the horror'! He was a remarkable man . . . I have remained loyal to Kurtz to the last, and even beyond, when a long time after I heard no more, not his own voice, but the echo of his magnificent eloquence."

Here, Marlow's reliability as a storyteller is again thrown into serious doubt. The reader is uncertain whether Marlow praises Kurtz or curses him. The ambiguities surrounding Marlow's narration of the events that occurred in Africa caused the reader to construct a new version of the "reality" of the story. History is thrown into doubt, for which explanation can be regarded as the "official truth"? Thus in the novel, *The Heart of Darkness,* Joseph Conrad shows that history can be seen as a myth perceived and recorded differently by different observers of the same events. There can be no singular, universal truth, only different versions of history constructed and influenced by the limitations of the human mind.

8
THE VALUE OF FIRE IN WIDE SARGASSO SEA
Jane Hanson

Wide Sargasso Sea is Jean Rhys's version of the story behind the mysterious "lunatic" in Charlotte Brontë's nineteenth-century novel, *Jane Eyre.* Rhys's story, published in 1966, is that of Rochester's wife Antoinette. *Wide Sargasso Sea* depicts a young woman who was taken from her homeland of Jamaica to her husband's home in England. Her life is seen in three parts: her early years, her years of marriage, and her life in the attic of Thornfield Hall. Antoinette emerges in a different light from that seen in Brontë's novel; her character is more fully developed, and the reader gains more sympathy for her situation. Rhys, in rewriting the story of Rochester's marriage, changes some of the values Brontë expresses. The use of fire shows this reversal of values. In Brontë's story fire is traditionally depicted as negative; it is destructive. In *Wide Sargasso Sea* fire takes on opposite meanings. Throughout the novel fire

emerges as a symbol of safety, purity, and Antoinette's love of her past.

Jean Rhys takes the character of Rochester's wife and, by showing her background, makes her a round character instead of Brontë's flat one. Antoinette's early life was not exceptionally secluded. She was the first to admit this fact. She said, "My father, visitors, horses, feeling safe in bed—all belonged to the past." After the death of her father when she was very young, Antoinette's life became one of isolation. Her mother would call their situation "marooned." When visitors did come Antoinette said, "I had longed for visitors once, but that was years ago." She wanted isolation because it protected her: "Once I made excuses to be near her when she (her mother) brushed her hair, a soft black cloak to cover me, hide me, keep me safe. But not any longer. Not any more." Very rarely as a child or even when she was older did she feel safe. At many times she expressed her feelings of fear. When her mother married Mr. Mason she began to like him for what he had done to reduce her fears: "There are more ways than one of being happy, better perhaps to be peaceful, and contented, and protected, as I feel now." If given the choice, she would have exchanged normal social existence for a secluded stay in a convent: " 'You can't be hidden away all your life,' Mr. Mason said to her. 'Why not?' Antoinette thought to herself." To her the convent was safety. As she looked at the nuns she contemplated, "They are safe. How can they know what it can be like 'outside'?"

In the narrative of Antoinette's early life, fire is associated with safety. When Antoinette was rejected by the strange Negroes, Tia became her friend and brought the safety of fire with her friendship: "Sometimes we left the bathing pool at midday, sometimes we stayed till late afternoon. Then Tia would light a fire." Fire thus symbolizes the hearth, as well as the purity, of the vestal virgin. While waiting for the comforting presence of her servant, Antoinette emphasizes the positive value that the flame of a candle signifies:

I left a light on the chair by my bed and waited for Christophine, for I liked to see her last thing. But she did not come and as the candle burned down, the safe feeling left me. I wish I had a big Cuban dog to lie by my bed and protect me.

This protective aspect of fire is not violated, even under circumstances where fire would conventionally be conceived as negative; as the plantation was burning Aunt Cora continually comforted Antoinette by putting her arms around her and saying, "Don't be afraid, you are quite safe." Because of these few instances of fire in Antoinette's early life, fire continues to represent these positive values of safety and protection in successive monologues.

As Antoinette grew older her love for her Jamaican homeland also grew, and her feelings as stated during her younger years flourished. As a young child her surroundings had protected her:

I am safe . . . There is the tree of life in the garden and the wall green with moss. The barrier of the sea. I am safe. I am safe from strangers.
When I was safely home I sat close to the old wall at the end of the garden. It was soft as velvet and I never wanted to move again.

Her island became more than just the protection of isolation it once had given her; it became her life. When she showed Rochester her home she told him, "I love it more than anywhere in the world. As if it were a person. More than a person."

Because fire came to represent the safety and isolation of Antoinette's past and of her island, fire in *Wide Sargasso Sea* is associated with natural beauty and love. Even the fireflies were called "La Belle." Antoinette continually commented on the beauty of fire, as she did when she said, "in the end flames shoot up and they are beautiful." In Thornfield Hall when Antoinette asked Grace Poole to light a fire because she was cold, she was asking for more than heat to warm her physical coldness; she was asking for emotional comfort. The heat of the fire corresponded to the warmth of the Jamaican sun and also to the spiritual warmth connected with the island. The warm island was contrasted with England—"a cold dark dream." The red and yellow of the fire brought images of the "blazing colors of the flowers" and Jamaica's red earth. The fact that fire in her memory represents not only life but Antoinette's personal identity is implied by her having written her name on a sampler in "fire red."

In Jean Rhys's novel Antoinette is given an identity which she does not have in *Jane Eyre*. Even her name is different; she is named Antoinette, but her husband chooses to call her Bertha. In *Jane Eyre*, she is referred to as Bertha or the lunatic wife. Rhys presents Antoinette as a fully developed character, shaped by events and surroundings, rather than as a woman who has inherited madness. In *Jane Eyre* Bertha's life is ended with a fire at Thornfield Hall. This same fire is the ending of *Wide Sargasso Sea*, but the fire has different values in the two novels. Brontë uses fire in its destructive sense. The fire was set by the lunatic Bertha, seemingly to spite Rochester and the governess whom he loved. The fire was described by a spectator:

A dreadful calamity! such an immense quantity of valuable property destroyed: hardly any of the furniture could be saved. The fire broke out at dead of night, and before the engines arrived from Millcote, the building was one mass of flame. It was a terrible spectacle: I witnessed it myself.

During the fire Bertha climbed to the roof but then jumped to her death as Rochester approached her. Rochester became blind and crippled as a result of the fire.

Rhys shows that by choosing fire in the end, Antoinette's goal was not to destroy Rochester's life or her own, but it was to bring back her past. Fire reminded her of her past, just as her red dress brought from Jamaica revived fond memories: "If I had been wearing my red dress Richard would have known me." Even the fragrance of the stored dress reminded her of home:

The scent that came from the dress was very faint at first, then it grew stronger. The smell of vertivert and frangipanni, of cinnamon and dust and lime, trees when they are flowering. The smell of the sun and smell of the rain.

The dress, fire, and sunset as symbols all become intertwined when she described the dress as "the color of fire and sunset." The sunset had been connected with fire earlier when Rochester described the sunset by saying, "We watched the sky and the distant sea on fire—all colors were in that fire and huge clouds shot with flame." The burning sunset also gave Antoinette the satisfactions of fire. At the end of *Wide Sargasso Sea* spreading the fire was Antoinette's last and desperate move to recapture the life that Rochester had stolen from her. At first she said, "There was a wall of fire protecting me." As it spread it encompassed more; it encompassed her whole life:

> Then I turned around and saw the sky. It was red and all my life was in it. I saw the grandfather clock and Aunt Cora's patchwork. I saw the orchids and stephanotis and the jasmine and the tree of life in flames. I saw the chandelier and the tree ferns, the gold ferns.

In both *Jane Eyre* and *Wide Sargasso Sea* fire is a key symbol associated with Rochester's wife. However, it is clear that the symbol of fire creates different images in the two novels. In *Jane Eyre* Brontë uses fire to represent negative values such as passion, irrationality, destruction, and even hell. When Mr. Brocklehurst had asked young Jane what hell was, she had answered, "A pit full of fire." The fire in *Jane Eyre* destroys the placid, mannered, male-dominated surface of social life. In *Wide Sargasso Sea* Rhys reverses these values attributed to fire; fire becomes safety, love, individuality, and liberation from English male domination.

9
THE READER'S ROLE IN CORTÁZAR'S "THE NIGHT FACE UP"
Annette Haack

In "The Night Face Up," Cortázar confronts the reader with a situation that would be impossible in real life, that of a person's existing in two distinct worlds simultaneously. The reader senses a conflict between the separate situations and attempts to resolve it by judging one as the fictive reality and one as the fictive imaginary. Cortázar leads the reader into doing this, and yet he exercises his power as author and creator of fiction by making such an attempt futile.

Cortázar superimposes two events that both mirror and contrast with each other; like a collage, this magnifies aspects of both events. Through the narrator, he suggests the dramatic situation of a man in a hospital who is having nightmares about being chased by enemy Aztecs. The story begins with an experience that the reader can identify with as being "real"; therefore, the reader initially has little cause for doubt concerning what kind of event is represented in the story. In every case, the narrator ends the hospital scene with the protagonist falling asleep and begins the Indian scene with reference to dreams or confusion. By paralleling the plots of the scenes, the author maintains a suggestive explanation. In both plots, the protagonist has similar experiences, such as being restrained by cords on his arms, being approached by a man carrying a knife-like utensil in his hand, and being carried a long way while lying face up on his back. Both share elements of pain and fear as well as images like flashing light and blood. Comments by the character in the next bed strengthen the idea of a dream: "You're going to fall off the bed. Stop bouncing around, old buddy." It is reasonable that a person of contemporary society could dream about an uncivilized society of the past; however, it is unlikely that a savage person could imagine such an accurate depiction of an industrial society of the future. Therefore, the reader continues to read the Indian scenes as a dream. However, aspects of the story remain which refute rather than support the reader's conventional reaction that the hospital is indeed the story's reality. Some of these are expressed by the narrator himself. For example, we are told that "it was unusual as a dream because it was full of smells, and he never dreamt smells," and "what tormented him most was the odor, as though, notwithstanding the absolute acceptance of the dream, there was something that resisted that which was not habitual, which until that point had not participated in the game." Although it is true that dreams seldom contain smells, a hospital environment could afford unusual stimuli for a dream. Still, the presence of odors is repeatedly stressed and thus begins to create doubts within the reader's mind concerning the fixed relationship of dream and reality.

By contrast, the hospital scenes emphasize the sense of sight more than the sense of smell. They contain a full rainbow of colors, whereas the Indian scenes consist of only black and red images. The primary sensation in the hospital is heat, while coldness is dominant in the jungle. Light versus darkness is also developed. These extreme contrasts focus on differences between the two scenes that make it more difficult for the reader to accept the simple explanation of a dream.

The narrator generates more suspicions within the reader in another way, one which also foreshadows the end of the story. He tells us that "between the impact and the moment that they picked him up off the pavement, the passing out or what went on, there was nothing he could see . . . as if, in this void, he had passed across something, or run back immense distances." Foreshadowing is again used in a hiatus: "Now he was lost, no prayer could save him from the final. . . ." Here the reader must complete the sentence.

Other features of the story are not consistent with the reader's premature conclusion. The conventions of a dream are defied in the way it is presented. First, the Indian scenes are not written as a "stream of consciousness" but in chronologically coherent and very concrete prose. Secondly, the native scenes occur in separate episodes, while dreams typically do not follow each other in sequence. Thirdly,

the author gives both Indian and contemporary scenes equal importance by dividing the story evenly between them; he even splits the strongest points of the story, the initial scene and the final scene, between the two plots. Because the structure of the story does not express a dream method, a weaker impression of dream is created in the reader.

Through his narrative form, Cortázar uses several phrases that add to the ambiguity of the dramatic situation. In the jungle, the protagonist hears an unexpected sound "like a broken limb." Similes that refer to the Aztec scene occur throughout the hospital experience: "He felt thirsty, as though he'd been running for miles." The concept of "Her Very Highness," who looks over the Motecans, is repeated in the room: "A violet lamp kept watch high on the far wall like a guardian eye." With the help of such words, the reader is led to think about both plots simultaneously, regardless of which scene is being described; in the final paragraph, the reader is confronted directly with this coexistence. This ending is not a true surprise, though, precisely because of previous transgression of the line between conventions for representing the "real" and the "imaginary."

Cortázar does not resolve the story in the sense of telling exactly what has happened. In this way, the story is an "open" one, allowing the reader to construct his own version. However, because no conclusion by the reader can be proven, the story remains a mystery. Through the defamiliarization of a motorcycle accident, Cortázar forces the reader to play a constructive role throughout the whole story, not only in the last paragraph; he is supporting the impressionist idea that there is value not only in the plot of a work, but more importantly, there is value in the experience of reading itself.

Index
of
Useful Literary Terms

● *Absurdism:* 248, see *Grotesque.*

● *Aesthetic Distance:* the degree of separation between art and reality as determined by the work's literary conventions. Art refers to reality but it 'is necessarily different from it. The furor created by the severed hand displayed at the Australian exhibition (see the Introduction to Realism) indicates that we do not want art to be too real, that the mere placing of a human hand into a museum setting is not a sufficient artistic convention. We prefer as a work of art a hand created from pigment and displayed on canvas encased in a frame. In literature, conventions such as impersonation (see *Persona*), meter, or allusion operate in much the same way as a frame on a picture. They are traditional devices which separate art from reality and, indeed, make art possible. Many works termed "realistic" exhibit a relatively low degree of aesthetic distance because they deal primarily with an objective, material world as their source and appear to treat it without artistic conventions. The narrative voice in "Charlie Simpson's Apocalypse" is specified to be that of Joe Eszterhas, writer of this particular article for the *Rolling Stone.* Not only are the speaker and narrator equated, identifying the article as journalism rather than fiction, but the fragmentary, highly colloquial, and often sexually explicit language Eszterhas employs breaks literary linguistic convention and reduces aesthetic distance. Often a label of "obscenity" results from this kind of lowered aesthetic distance.

In comparison, an expressionist work such as T. S. Eliot's *The Waste Land* establishes a high degree of aesthetic distance through its poetic form and frequent, highly complex use of literary, historical, and anthropological allusions. Eliot never lets us forget that his work is literary, and readers dismayed by high aesthetic distance may attack the poetry of Pound and Eliot for "intellectualism." The degree of aesthetic distance attributed to a work is not constant but can change with time and audience. Lawrence's fiction seemed shockingly frank to its first readership but may seem quaintly conventional to a reader today.

● *Alienation:* a philosophical, sociological, and psychological concept originating with Hegel and Marx. Karl Marx in his *Economic and Philosophic Manuscripts* of 1844 defines alienation as the act of transforming the products of human activity—commodities, institutions, and ideas, including art—into objects which are independent of people and govern their lives. Capitalism causes this distortion of natural social and psychological existence: "The less you *are,* the more you *have;* the less you express your own, the greater is your *alienated* life—the greater is the store of your estranged being. Everything which the political economist takes from you in life and in humanity, he replaces for you in *money* and in *wealth;* and all the things which you cannot do, your money can do. It can eat and drink, go to the dance hall and the theatre; it can travel, it can appropriate art, learning, and the treasures of the past, political power. . . ." Our separation from the products of human labor, implying the separation of consciousness from action, of the individual from the essential self, is often termed self-alienation.

Twentieth-century artists commonly acknowledge estrangement from self and community as the modern human condition, but artistic expressions of this condition are as divergent as the possibilities for escape from alienation they project. Writers in the tradition of social realism, like D. H. Lawrence, Alan Sillitoe, or Sherwood Anderson, agree with Marxist assumptions that alienation is pathological and can be remedied only by social change. Their fiction dramatizes the morbidity of the isolated consciousness and envisions its reintegration by such means as the return to a precapitalist tribal society in "The Woman Who Rode Away" or the future proletarian revolution heralded in *The Loneliness of the Long-Distance Runner.* Impressionist and expressionist writers are accused by the Marxists of accepting or approving of alienation, as we see in Georg Lukács' argument that "the ideology of most modernist writers asserts the unalterability of outward reality," so that "human activity is, *a priori,* rendered impotent and robbed of meaning." Poets like Eliot and Yeats, however, believed that the source as well as the solution to the problem of alienation is in the human consciousness; consequently they removed themselves from the sphere of political action in order to create universal symbols that could function like a religion as the basis for a communal consciousness or spirit. Other artists, like Joyce, Hughes, or Ellison, seem to enjoy the eccentric or sociopathic since extreme alienation produces those distortions of external convention essential to art.

● *Allegory:*   757, see Utopia.

● *Allusion:*   a reference within a literary work to any historical, mythical, or artistic person, place, or thing in order to amplify or expand a subject. When the narrator alludes to Henry David Thoreau in Joe Eszterhas' article, he provides a literary and philosophical base for Charlie's love of the land he is not allowed to own. This explicit reference associates Thoreau's passive civil disobedience and reverence for the simple and natural with Charlie's character, but when Charlie's frustration takes the form of multiple murder, we recognize that the Thoreau allusion is ironic. Jesse Bentley in "Godliness" from *Winesburg, Ohio* explicitly invokes a Biblical comparison by identifying himself with Jesse, the father of David, but his sacrificial rites indirectly allude to the story of Abraham and Isaac. The reader aware of the similarity in the plots of

the two stories will fear for David Hartley's life when Jesse forces him into sacrificing a lamb. Similarly, readers will completely miss Anderson's ironic comment on Jesse's religious attitudes at the end of the story if they do not see that Jesse has assumed the role of Goliath, the enemy of David, rather than that of the Biblical father. The direct allusions thus tell us how Jesse assesses his own character, while the indirect allusions to the Bible represent the view of the implied author and show Jesse to be dangerously deluded.

Allusion can be used to decrease aesthetic distance and make the fictive world familiar. Ellison does not want his reader to miss the fact that he is not merely indulging in fantasy but criticizing contemporary culture in his post-World War III societies. He uses allusions to endow the strange futuristic landscape with features and qualities of the present. Vic's roverpak is ironically called "Our Gang," an allusion to the innocently mischievous youths of the film series of the thirties and forties, and this gang is contrasted with the world of the "downunders," who are the kind of people who make "Myrna Loy and George Brent kind of flicks," "clean stuff with even married people sleeping in twin beds." Ellison's bizarre societies become more comprehensible when described in terms of popular movies.

Allusion can also increase aesthetic distance and restrict comprehension to a select readership. Eliot's use of arcane allusions from history, religion, anthropology, and literature make *The Waste Land* fully comprehensible only after an arduous education and many readings. The author himself supplies notes for his readers to encourage the effort of reading. By placing allusions as obstacles in the path of the common reader, Eliot forces upon us a difficult task resembling that of the questing hero: We have to assimilate and bring to life nearly all our cultural heritage in order to read *The Waste Land,* and this feat would accomplish Eliot's purpose of cultural revitalization—if we do not throw up our hands in despair first.

● *Ambiguity:*   504, 748, 753.

● *Angry young men:*   in the middle

1950's, a loosely-defined group of English writers that caught the public's attention. They were generally of working-class origin, they all took a militant stand against a middle-class, genteel "Bloomsbury" tradition and a middle-class control of the literary market place. They were labeled "angry young men" by one hostile critic, and another referred to their "maggoty" style. To the urbane and erudite Somerset Maugham they were "scum." Colin Wilson, the self-educated son of a factory worker, published *The Outsider* in 1956, and the term "outsider" has come to be associated with their alienated posture: "the Outsider cannot live in the comfortable, insulated world of the bourgeois, accepting what he sees and touches as reality. 'He sees too deep and too much,' and what he sees is essentially chaos." John Osborne's play, *Look Back in Anger,* Kingsley Amis's novel, *Lucky Jim,* and Alan Sillitoe's *The Loneliness of the Long-Distance Runner* are representative works of a group which has been seen as an English equivalent to the American Beat writers.

● *Archetype:* an image that recalls basic psychological events common to all people and all cultures. A character or pattern of images or events is labeled archetypal if it causes the reader to recognize in it a psychic phenomenon so fundamental that it has never been absent from literature, religion, myth, and dream. Carl Jung originated the theory of archetypes, referring to the human "collective unconscious" as the source for these "primordial images." This kind of image antedates all the forms or devices that have been or can be used to express it, and the reader recognizes an archetype only if the particular character, symbol, or plot being considered leads to recollection of an underlying pattern or profound experience that consistently seeks expression in art.

Sir James Frazer's *The Golden Bough* established an anthropological base for a fundamental archetype, the vegetative cycle of death and rebirth. The primitive mind saw the cycle of the seasons as the life of a god who ruled nature but who was subject to the power of death, although this death was not lasting, and the god was capable of undergoing resurrection. Jessie L. Weston's *From Ritual to Romance* presented this cycle as the foundation of the Christian pattern of spiritual rebirth and of the hero's quest for the Holy Grail in romance narratives. T. S. Eliot's *The Waste Land* is the major contemporary version of the archetypal vegetative cycle, but the contemporary poet sees consciousness as separate from nature and thus not subject to its revitalizing processes, as the opening lines suggest:

> April is the cruellest month, breeding
> Lilacs out of the dead land, mixing
> Memory and desire, stirring
> Dull roots with spring rain.

The sophisticated urban consciousness is unable to see in this world any affirmation of the rebirth assumed by primitives or poets living in an age of faith. Lawrence's "The Woman Who Rode Away" uses an Indian myth to explore one woman's desire to fulfill this same archetypal pattern.

A hero or heroine who descends into the underworld seeking rebirth often encounters dark irrational forces objectified in a Devil archetype. Kurtz in *Heart of Darkness,* for example, embodies the destructive energy of the uncontrolled psyche, and it is necessary for Marlow to "step back from the edge" of Kurtz's experience in order to reenter the upper world of rational control.

● *Art for art's sake:* 243.

● *Avant garde:* 10.

● *Beat movement:* A group of writers in the 1950s, who with an energy their "angry young" English counterparts lacked, assaulted the world of accepted academic, middle-class, white-collar good taste. The movement was so broadly based that its ambience was seen by some to characterize an era. The "Beat Generation" emerged in the East with Allen Ginsberg, Jack Kerouac, Gregory Corso, and William Burroughs, and in the West with poets such as Lawrence Ferlinghetti and Robert Duncan. A contemporary account of the phenomenon, such as Seymour Krim's 1960 introduction to his collection, *The Beats,* reveals the style and principles of this movement:

> Beat writing . . . didn't come out of nowhere, even though it hit us that way; it came, grew, then overthrew the gags of taste and repression out of an awful soul-need that couldn't be petted and then put back in its cage by

psychiatry. Life had radically changed in America and the world to the point where many of the old cowardices seemed absurd to the unbribed cub scouts who had just entered the front-lines of adulthood; but literary expression still went through its standard i-dotting and comma-kneeling practices (*The New Yorker* being the prime tortured example of the Cramped Way of Writing Life) while the hallucinatory fires of actual 1950ish reality were levelling to the ground many of the old-fashioned consolations in writing, in living, in the world itself. Something had to give. It did. Some young guys with nothing to lose—since all seemed lost to them already!—and with the dangerous virtue of daring to believe in what they experienced even though it might land them in jail or the loony-bin, started sending out messages with the faith that what they were wailing was REALER. . . . It [their writing] was intimate as a love note, a private erotic fantasy, a tenor-talking jazz side— it was actual communication from living soul to swinging living soul, and nuts to all outdated formal restraints and laughable writing conventions, all so pitiable irrelevant and coy and *in the way.*

The hip slang is dated, and the enthusiasm now seems a bit windy and presumptuous, but no one can deny the impact on our culture of the Beat sensibility as expressed by such writers as Mailer, Ginsberg, Kerouac, and Ferlinghetti. The Beats' attempt to be "realer" also led to their concern with exploring a personal world and expressing visionary and "beatific" states of mind. The only predecessors they would claim were radical visionaries like William Blake and Walt Whitman. The Hippie culture was their direct descendent.

● *Bildungsroman:* 8, 244, 754, 762.
● *Bloomsbury group:* As Virginia Woolf's husband, Leonard, explains in his autobiography, most of the group lived for a time in the Bloomsbury district of London "within a few minutes walk of one another." The group was united by friendship rather than "a common doctrine and object, or purpose artistic or social." The economist John Maynard Keynes, philosophers G. E. Moore and Bertrand Russell, essayist Lytton Strachey, novelists

Virginia Woolf, V. Sackville West, and E. M. Forster, critics Clive Bell and Roger Fry, and publisher Leonard Woolf are the principals of this famous circle of intellectuals. They met regularly but informally and exchanged enlightened, liberal, often eccentric views about art, philosophy, and politics from about 1906 until the 1930's. The word "Bloomsbury," as Leonard Woolf notes, "was and is currently used as a term—usually of abuse." There is indeed a whole literary tradition beginning with modernists such as Wyndam Lewis or Ezra Pound and the miner's son D. H. Lawrence that is distinguished by attitudes hostile to those of the upper-class Bloomsbury intellectuals. These antagonistic artists might give the pejorative label "Bloomsbury" to any tacit approval of the British class system or any sign of the late nineteenth century obsession with genteel style and wit. In spite of the genuinely liberal nature of the cause in a work like Virginia Woolf's *A Room of One's Own,* writers as early as Lawrence and as recent as Sillitoe often use "Bloomsbury" as a synonym for "reactionary."

● *Elegy:*   in classical literature, a poem with formal, serious subject matter written in a particular elegiac meter. Today, an elegy must simply be solemn in tone and concerned with the death of an individual or, perhaps, an age. Dylan Thomas, for example, defies tradition by refusing to mourn the death of a particular child in London but conforms in his lament for the death awaiting us all. Lawrence's autobiographical elegy, "Bavarian Gentians," arrives at a consolation based on the pagan assumption that anything natural is part of an ever-renewing life process and not mortal as Thomas asserts.

Milton's *Lycidas* is used as the model

for the pastoral elegy, identified by the following features: (1) The disconsolate shepherd speaker invokes the muses. (2) Nature itself mourns the death of another shepherd, often a poet himself. (3) The mourners form a procession. (4) The shepherd speaker laments the failings of the age in which the poet died unappreciated. (5) The speaker finds consolation for his grief, usually with reference to some form of immortality. Elements of the pastoral elegy are obvious in Auden's "In Memory of W. B. Yeats." The "dead of winter" suggests nature's mourning and the poet receives a kind of consolation when "in the deserts of the heart" the "healing fountain" starts, but Auden adapts the elegiac pattern to a contemporary wasteland setting. Yeats's poetry survives because the destructive social and political forces of contemporary society deem it worthless: "it survives/ In the valley of its making where executives/ Would never want to tamper." Auden's elegy is correspondingly cynical and colloquial, a far cry from Milton's very formal lament:

> Earth, receive an honored guest:
> William Yeats is laid to rest.
> Let the Irish vessel lie
> Emptied of its poetry.

● *Epic:* a long, formal narrative poem of national or historical significance. Northrop Frye in *Anatomy of Criticism* describes the epic scope as the full cycle of the life and death of an individual as well as a nation. In Homer's folk epic *The Odyssey,* we see Odysseus span the Mediterranean with adventures involving monsters, figures from the underworld, and the gods, with the fate of his nation ultimately at issue. The action of the epic begins *in medias res* or in the middle of things, and the epic persona maintains a distanced and objective perspective on the subject matter. Major oral or folk epics include the *Iliad, Beowulf,* and *Song of Roland,* and important written or literary epics include Dante's *Divine Comedy* and Milton's *Paradise Lost.* Eliot's *The Waste Land* might be termed a contemporary epic, for the title suggests the cycle from a deathly wasteland to a living green world. But an old mythology does not provide the means for this contemporary

poet to represent a continuous cultural process. In the traditional sense, it is a failed epic, but the poem is an appropriate epic for a fragmented culture.

The opening stanza of the section "A Game of Chess" fulfills all the requirements of a subsidiary epic convention, the epic simile, in which the vehicle (see "Figurative language" in the Critical Guide) of the simile, "The chair she sat in, like a burnished throne,/ Glowed on the marble," is extended and elaborated far beyond the necessity of defining the tenor. When the woman upon the chair first speaks and says, "My nerves are bad tonight," the irony of comparing a regal classical throne with the functional chair of a modern urban home is obvious.

Hart Crane's *The Bridge* can be read as an attempt to create a national mythology of geographical landmarks, historical events, and legendary figures of America. This attempt to unify symbolically the progress of such a diverse culture as our own is certainly in the epic spirit. A work like William Carlos Williams' *Paterson* which represents all of American culture in one town in New Jersey or James Joyce's *Ulysses* which embodies all of Anglo-Irish culture in one day's stroll through Dublin are examples of modern variations on the epic tradition.

● *Exposition:* the beginning of a work of drama or prose fiction, where the artist exposes the laws determining the progress of the fiction, particularly in terms of point of view (see "Narration" in the Critical Guide), character, landscape, and image patterns. When Joyce's *A Portrait of the Artist as a Young Man* begins "Once upon a time and a very good time it was there was a moocow coming down along the road," it is obvious that the narrative voice has been adapted to the diction and the fairy tale clichés of childhood speech. We expect the rest of the work to investigate the acquisition of language by one particular speaker because of this unique introduction to character through point of view. In the first sentences of Lawrence's "Odour of Chrysanthemums," in contrast, a conventional narrator focuses upon the negative images of an industrialized landscape: "The small locomotive engine, Number 4, came *clanking, stumbling* down from Selston with seven full wagons. It appeared round the corner with loud *threats* of speed. . . . The trucks *thumped heavily* past, one by one, with *slow inevitable* movement, as she stood *insignificantly trapped* between the *jolting* black wagons and the hedge. . . ." From these few sentences, the beginning of the exposition, we form different expectations concerning the two works. Lawrence's speaker will probably investigate the meaning of a wasteland created from realistic material objects; whereas the Joyce passage reflects the innocence of a child who will inevitably grow and change. Changes in the speaker's use of language itself will be an issue in Joyce, but since Lawrence's language follows traditional literary conventions in diction, syntax ,and value-marked imagery, his focus will probably be the effect of that landscape on his characters.

● *Figurative language:*   747.

● *Framed tale:* a story within a story. This embedding of one narrative within another functions like the frame around a picture by making the reader aware that the embedded tale is just that, a fiction. The first-person narrator of *Heart of Darkness* locates the time, place, and dramatic audience for Marlow's tale of the Congo, and in doing so he increases both the believability as well as the artifice of Marlow's story by endowing Marlow with the authority of a world traveler and the artfulness of an experienced tale teller. The frame narrator's initial observations serve as an exposition for Marlow's narration by describing it as "inconclusive." When Marlow falls silent, the narrator observes that the "offing was barred by a black bank of clouds, and the tranquil waterway leading to the uttermost ends of the earth flowed somber under an overcast sky—seemed to lead into the heart of an immense darkness." This final description of the landscape seems to summarize the tale and its significance to the frame narrator. The final passage of Sillitoe's *The Loneliness of the Long-Distance Runner* creates a kind of open frame. Since Smith states that his narrative will be published only if he is sent back to prison because a friend has been entrusted with the manuscript, we readers

construct a frame situation to account for our being able to read Smith's story. Smith is either in prison, or he has naively misjudged his companion.

● *The grotesque:* art that combines elements from incompatible categories. The result is an often obscene physical or psychological abnormality that generates an ambivalent response. We cannot decide if the work is comic and intended to amuse, or if it is horrible and demands our disgust or terror. Franz Kafka's *The Metamorphosis* is perhaps the most famous example of this phenomenon in modern literature. The story begins:

> As Gregor Samsa awoke one morning from uneasy dreams he found himself transformed in his bed into a gigantic insect. He was lying on his hard, as it were armor-plated, back and when he lifted his head a little he could see his dome-like brown belly divided into stiff arched segments on top of which the bed quilt could hardly keep in position and was about to slide off completely. His numerous legs, which were pitifully thin compared to the rest of his bulk, waved helplessly before his eyes.[1]

Throughout the course of the story, we are never told how or why Gregor was turned into a cockroach. We are simply left with a world strongly resembling our own in most respects but one where strange and unnatural aberrations sometimes occur. The grotesque is closely related to several of the literary modes and techniques represented in this collection. Grotesque effects are used in critical realism when the artist wants to estrange the reader by disturbing conventional modes of perception. Wilfred Owen combines idealistic and grossly physical images to produce such an effect in "Greater Love" when he says, "Your slender attitude/ Trembles not exquisite like limbs knife-skewed."

The grotesque character is often a caricature, or a character in which a single feature or two is exaggerated to proportions that are both ridiculously and horribly incompatible with human nature as normally conceived. A good example is Flannery O'Connor's Lucynell, a thirty-

[1] Translation by Willa and Edwin Muir.

year-old retarded woman who has the appearance of a beautiful adolescent and the behavior of a dumb animal: ". . . the old woman said, "Don't Lucynell look pretty? Looks like a baby doll.' Lucynell was dressed up in a white dress that her mother had uprooted from a trunk and there was a Panama hat on her head with a bunch of red wooden cherries on the brim. Every now and then her placid expression was changed by a sly isolate little thought like a shoot of green in the desert." Jesse Bently in Anderson's "Godliness" is a grotesque psychological portrait. In his attempt to make ritual sacrifice of the lamb, Jesse's religious fanaticism becomes exaggerated to ridiculous and horrible proportions.

Extreme satire and parody tend to become grotesque. "Apple Tragedy," Hughes's irreverent version of the events in *Genesis,* ridicules traditionally prim attitudes toward sexuality, but it also conveys a strange revulsion from human mating procedure. As a result, we don't know whether to respond with amusement or disgust to the poem's violently abusive treatment of the Biblical material.

A sense of the Absurd is produced when the grotesque is not limited to a character but seems to take on cosmic proportions. In Pinter's *A Slight Ache,* events are controlled by a disgusting matchseller who arrives mysteriously every morning at seven to stand by the gate of a respectable couple's home. For no apparent reason at all, the quite ordinary wife takes him on as her mate, and her dispossessed husband goes off into the world with a tray of soggy matches. The world of the play, like that of Kafka's story, is both familiar in the details that compose it and utterly alien in the rules by which it operates. The artist presents familiar elements in a peculiar and disturbing light and refuses to rationalize them.

● *Haiku:* like the English sonnet, the Japanese lyric called the haiku adheres to a prescribed form and is part of a complex literary tradition. The haiku was of interest to Western modernists on two counts. First, it appealed to the late-Victorian interest in Oriental art. Turn-of-the-century artists such as Aubrey Beardsley imitated the conventions of Japanese ink drawings in an attempt to communicate a sense of the exotic or forbidden. This borrowing from Eastern traditions can be seen as part of a general rejection of Western culture. Secondly and more importantly, early twentieth-century poets sought an artistic form to clearly and directly convey an image ("that which presents an intellectual and emotional complex in an instant of time"). The haiku's form—three lines of five, seven, and five syllables respectively—was admired for its lack of intellectual verbiage. Pound's "In a Station of the Metro" and the discrete parts of Stevens' "Thirteen Ways of Looking at a Blackbird" stylistically resemble the Japanese form. The Chinese character, or ideogram, was also interesting to Pound, who mistakenly generalized that the entire written language was a concrete pictorial expression. In *The Pound Era,* Hugh Kenner argues that I. A. Richards' famous definition of metaphor as the uniting of "two *things,* tenor and vehicle," is based on a similar misapprehension of the Chinese language, and the assumption that the ideogram produced a uniquely vivid impression by combining discrete images led to Soviet filmmaker Sergei Eisenstein's theory of montage.

● *Hero:* the character who functions as "will" or protagonist. In ancient Greek literature, "hero" specifically meant the offspring of a god mated with a human woman. This half-human, half-divine composition indicates a broad principle that holds true for every literary hero: he must possess human properties so that ordinary readers may identify with his anxieties and struggles, but he must also have some exemplary quality that distinguishes him from the common lot. Initially, the hero has rather ordinary features, but while seeking a remedy to some social or personal problem or deficiency, he forms a heroic character. By defeating a powerful opposition or overcoming the obstacles of a difficult task, the hero either acquires the attributes required for a heroic feat, or learns to use his own strengths in the correct way (which amounts to the same thing).

Traditionally, heroes project the dominant values of their society. When bravery is highly prized, the physical hero is recognized. When cleverness is valued, a mental hero triumphs. We find an ethical hero produced by a culture that exalts morality. And when feelings are granted priority, we have a sentimental hero. However, when the values of the dominant culture are as subject to criticism as they are in twentieth century art, the heroic pattern becomes radically modified. These are some of the variations produced by twentieth-century artists:

1. *The ironic hero* successfully fulfills the heroic pattern only to discover that the goal he has reached is highly questionable. We see this in Conrad's Kurtz, who initially believed he had "a power for good practically unbounded" but dies recognizing "the horror" of his accomplishments. Similarly in Fitzgerald's "Winter Dreams," pursuit of the traditional goals of wealth and power leads to a recognition of their falseness and corruption, not to any lofty or gratifying achievement.

2. In a society where all values are in doubt, the *antihero* projects a denial of value and a refusal of all action as his virtues. It is questionable whether Beckett's character in "Act without Words" can even be termed a "protagonist." Unlike the traditional dramatic hero, he does not want to act at all. He is thrown back onto the stage after trying to escape. He does not desire heroic virtues but dramatizes the simplest cravings for water or death. These are manipulated by some mysterious "director" until the subject falls into complete apathy. He learns to desire nothing at all.

3. *The artist hero* is recognized as hero to the degree that he distinguishes himself from the traditional values of his society. Ability to overcome convention is his measure of sensitivity and perception and is the necessary foundation for artistic creativity. Stephen's only achievement in Joyce's *A Portrait of the Artist as a Young Man* is that he is unable to conform to the ordinary models of achievement and virtue and becomes his own unique standard.

4. All these forms of the hero project alienation to one degree or another, but the *alienated hero* acquires heroic status simply by combatting the establishment. Eszterhas' Charlie Simpson is unlike Christ, a model ethical hero, in every conceivable way except in his challenge to the overwhelming power of the social establishment. Ellison's "A Boy and His Dog" shows just how ethically equivocal this kind of rebel can become.

5. *The Marxist hero* is a form of alienated hero in whom moral and mental virtue becomes equated with violent conflict with the middle-class establishment. Sillitoe's Smith is not refusing all values but is fighting for superior social goals, those furthering the freedom of the working class from middle-class oppression. Smith initially is persuaded to adopt middle-class goals and become a physical hero, a runner, but the fruits of his labor, the trophy, will benefit neither himself nor his fellows. Winning would only aid his oppressor. Smith then becomes a mental hero as he rejects these goals and enters into conflict with the ruling class by means of his wits and words.

6. Rather than coalescing into a distinct heroic type, the character of the *fragmented hero* disintegrates as he adopts a role valued by his society. Rather than developing a more complete, whole personality as he becomes socialized, Faulkner's protagonist in "Barn Burning" is split in two. The social models valued by society conflict with his primitive heritage. This process of fragmentation is of course very similar to what happens to Kurtz in *Heart of Darkness,* and it can be seen in extreme form in Ondaatje's *The Collected Works of Billy the Kid,* where the hero is only a collection of fantasies, types, behavior patterns, and literary modes which yield no coherent personality. Billy is a hero because he embodies all the conflicts of his society.

● *Hyperbole:* 748.

● *Imagery:* Verbal representations of things known through the five senses. Wallace Stevens' "Sunday Morning" evokes an awareness of sound or the absence of it with the phrases "Chant" and "holy hush"; an awareness of light and color with "sunny" and "green"; and a sense of taste and smell with "pungent oranges." The absence of tactile images, words evoking the sense of touch, communicates a sense of insubstantiality about the leisure-class life depicted in this poem. In contrast, the nightmare world of Wright's "Man Who Lived Underground" achieves palpability through this kind of language, emphasized in the following passage: ". . . he waded with taut muscles, his feet *sloshing* over the *slimy* bottom, his shoes *sinking* into *spongy* slop, the slate-colored water *cracking* in creamy foam against his knees." Sections of Hart Crane's *The Bridge* rely heavily upon kinesthetic imagery in order to capture the rapid flux of American culture and to convey a sense that the poet's eye is sweeping across time and space:

> . . . —and whistling down the tracks a headlight rushing with the sound—can you imagine—while an express makes time like SCIENCE—COMMERCE AND THE HOLYGHOST RADIO ROARS IN EVERY HOME WE HAVE THE NORTHPOLE WALL-STREET AND VIRGINBIRTH WITHOUT STONES OR WIRES OR EVEN RUNning brooks connecting ears and no more sermons windows flashing roar breathtaking—as you like it . . . eh?

The sense of energy and motion apparent in this passage suggests that imagery is important in conveying both physical and psychological states. The artist can convey a confusion of sense and indicate either madness or heightened perception, as Wright does in 'The Man Who Lived Underground." In his cave, the man *hears* as well as sees the sparkle of diamonds. Or the artist may use the absence of sensory imagery to depict despair and disillusionment, as Fitzgerald does at the end of "Winter Dreams." For an example of the way in which an image can become a pattern which helps to develop and reveal the meaning of an entire novel, see Jane Hanson's student essay on "The Value of Fire in *Wide Sargasso Sea*."
● *Imagism*: 245.
● *Implied author*: 752.
● *Irony*: saying one thing but meaning another. When Marlow describes the Company's chief accountant, a man who manages to wear starched collars in the midst of the jungle while viciously exploiting the Africans, as a "miracle," he does not mean that the man is marvelous or semidivine. In the context of Marlow's developing awareness of European corruption, we know that this particular remark must be taken as a bleak irony. The accountant would more appropriately be described as a demon. Wayne C. Booth in

A Rhetoric of Irony posits five general ways of recognizing this kind of ironic statement in literature. (1) The author may warn readers not to take words literally. Joe Eszterhas' combination of the Biblical term "apocalypse" with the ordinary, rather casual name "Charlie Simpson" suggests that neither the normality of the name nor the cataclysmic implications of the event should be taken straightforwardly. The strange combination of terms in the title warns the reader to consider the context of what follows. (2) The author may create irony by contradicting known fact. When the baton twirler in "Twirling at Ole Miss" assumes that there is no limit to the number of times a baton can spin before hitting the ground, her ignorance of physical law is taken ironically. (3) Contradictory facts within the work of art may create ironies. Jesse Bentley, for example, sees himself as some kind of Biblical Jesse to his grandson's David in "Godliness," but it is ironic that Jesse becomes a threatening Goliath rather than a compassionate father and must be stoned by the boy. (4) Clashes of style within the work may indicate irony. Southern describes the very limited skill of baton twirling as an "almost forgotten *l'art pour l'art*" which remains "an area of human endeavor absolutely sufficient unto itself" in the midst of "a tedious labyrinth of technical specialization." There is an obvious clash between the subject and the jargon and literary allusion with which it is described. If the clash involves mocking another literary work rather than two styles within the same work, the result is parody. The title of Redgrove's "Thirteen Ways of Looking at a Blackboard" announces that it will be a comic imitation of Stevens' previous poem. (5) A statement in a work may contradict the beliefs or values you feel you can impute to the implied author, allowing you to judge an assertion or a character's statement as ironic. Given the various ways in which human failings have been explored in *The Time Machine*, the narrator's assertion that "gratitude and a mutual tenderness" will live on "in the heart of man" can only be ironic. All five methods of identifying irony depend upon the reader's close attention to language and its context and critical awareness of the potential differences between stated and implied values.

● *Künstlerroman:* 244.

● *Landscape:* description of a place or locale. Because landscape in literature is always described by a persona, a specified character, or an implied author (see "Value Markings" in the Critical Guide), any discussion of its function must take into account the nature of the perceiving intelligence. The method of landscape description will necessarily shift according to the reality the artist wants to represent. A realistic work such as Sillitoe's *The Loneliness of the Long-Distance Runner* will concentrate upon the physical environment which fosters the character's beliefs and behavior. Lawrence's "The Woman Who Rode Away," an example of psychological realism, objectifies the malaise of a middle-class woman; there are flowers in the wasteland of the silver mine, but they "were never very flowery to her." By having her see "great green-covered, unbroken mountains" in "the midst of lifeless isolation," Lawrence shows the degree to which psychological states determine the external environment perceived.

Expressionist landscape similarly refers to the mental state of its perceiver rather than the physical object, but in expressionism landscape does not afford a standard against which to measure the character's deviation. All we get are the distortions. The landscape describes only the egocentric imaginings of Joyce's artist-protagonist as he walks a gloomy corridor with eyes "weak and tired with tears so that he could not see" and sees that the "portraits of the saints and great men" are "looking down on him silently as he passed." Artists like Wells and Ellison abandon the conventions of realistic landscape and use landscape symbolically as in dream or fantasy.

An impressionist such as Conrad in *Heart of Darkness* will mediate between the individual perceiver's response and the material object that elicited it by focusing on the process of perception itself. In the following passage, notice the time lag between the speaker's perception, the barrage of physical data, and his understanding of the way in which his environment is being transformed: "Then I had to look at the river mighty quick, because there was a snag in the fairway. Sticks, little sticks, were flying about—thick: they were whizzing before my nose, dropping below me, striking behind me against my pilot-house. All this time the river, the shore, the woods, were very quiet—perfectly quiet. I could only hear the heavy splashing thump of the stern-wheel and the patter of these things. We cleared the snag clumsily. Arrows, by Jove! We were being shot at!"

● *Linguistic realism:* 7, 16.

● *Lost generation:* The phrase specifically refers to a community of expatriot artists living in post-Warld War I Paris. "You are all a lost generation" serves as an epigraph to Ernest Hemingway's *The Sun Also Rises,* and in his *A Moveable Feast* he recollects the conversation in which Gertrude Stein coined the expression:

It was when we had come back from Canada and were living in the rue Notre-Dame-des-Champs and Miss Stein and I were still good friends that Miss Stein made the remark about the lost generation. She had some ignition trouble with the old Model T Ford she then drove and the young man who worked in the garage and had served in the last year of the war had not been adept, or perhaps had not broken the priority of other vehicles, in repairing Miss Stein's Ford. Anyway, he had not been *sérieux* and had been corrected severely by the *patron* of the garage after Miss Stein's protest. The *patron* had said to him, "You are all a *génération perdue.*"

"That's what you are. That's what you all are," Miss Stein said. "All of you young people who served in the war. You are a lost generation."

"Really?" I said.

"You are," she insisted. "You have no respect for anything. You drink yourselves to death. . . ."

The era is remarkable for an abundance of diverse and high quality literary talent. Writers like Hemingway, Fitzgerald, and Joyce exerted an almost tyrannical influence on later writers who grew up reading their books; Ezra Pound, E. E. Cummings, and Hart Crane are also representative of the era. Many of these artists tended to ignore the public or perplex it with deliberately private and inaccessible art; others treated established ideals irreverently to dramatize their sense of disillusionment. Harry's boozey reflections on the war and on story writing in "The Snows of Kilimanjaro" reflect the attitudes of disillusion, failure, and alienation shared by many of these novelists and their characters. Dexter's last words in "Winter Dreams" could easily have been said by many of these artists in their works or in personal conversation:

> "Long ago," he said, "long ago, there was something in me, but now that thing is gone. Now that thing is gone, that thing is gone. I cannot cry. I cannot care. That thing will come back no more."

● *Lyric:* Originally, the term *"lyric"* designated those poems sung by an individual Greek poet accompanied by a lyre. Today the term commonly describes short, subjective (perhaps ecstatic), non-dramatic, non-narrative poems. The rather inclusive term defines a speaker's general attitude rather than a specific poetic form, although this attitude can indeed be manifest in prescribed patterns such as the sonnet or elegy, which might be considered subcategories of the lyric. The title of Eliot's "The Love Song of J. Alfred Prufrock" deliberately evokes the lyric tradition but with ironic effect since his speaker, Prufrock, is unable to speak, much less "sing," about love. A persona such as Yeats's in "Sailing to Byzantium" is the more typical in his brief description of his personal fascination with artifice. In Auden's elegy, "In Memory of Sigmund Freud," the speaker's mourning for a lost genius expands the brief, emotional origins of the lyric into a complex analysis of intellectual history and the purpose of art.
● *Marxist realism:*   9, 15, See also *Hero* and *Alienation.*
● *Metaphor:*   246, 747.
● *Metonymy:*   748.
● *Myth:* Anthropologist Claude Levi-Strauss, father of the new research in mythology, dismisses the old methods: "Myths are still widely interpreted in conflicting ways: collective dreams, the outcome of a kind of esthetic play, the foundation of ritual. . . . Mythological figures are considered as personified abstractions, divinized heroes or decayed gods. Whatever the hypothesis, the choice amounts to reducing mythology either to an idle play or to a coarse kind of speculation." Levi-Strauss sees myth as a kind of picture language, much as Freud regards the figures of a dream, where the primitive mind symbolically resolves problems that cannot be resolved in real life: "The purpose of myth is to provide a logical model capable of overcoming a contradiction." An element in a myth is drawn from a classification system, based on physical perception and basic qualities, by which the savage mind organizes the universe. These symbols behave like those of a dream where the objective is to overcome a contradiction within the system by formulating a mediating term. What usually happens is that the opposition is reformulated until it produces some symbol that incorporates both of the opposing ideas. According to the new anthropology, this is the way the stories we call myths are produced. We can say, for example, that Christ mediates between the idea of man's divine origin and his earthly one because Christ is both flesh and immortal. The Virgin and Holy Ghost are restatements of the ideas of earthly and divine parentage that enable the formulation of the messiah figure.

Levi-Strauss's theories are important to people interested in narrative because they offer an explanation of why each culture produces narrative as well as how the meaning of the narratives produced by a culture is determined. His notion of myth as the search for a term that mediates a binary opposition is for many theorists the foundation of investigations of narrative structure. You can see the close relationship between the structure of myth as Levi-Strauss defines it and the pattern of the traditional quest where a heroic character is formed through overcoming an opposing villain, and you can also see that Levi-Strauss has redefined theme for literary criticism. Lawrence's use of the quest pattern in "The Woman Who Rode Away" reveals the way in which a narrative seeks to resolve a cultural contradiction. The woman is initially an economic token defining a system of human relationships based on money. But this produces an opposition, for her "consciousness had stopped growing." The narrative seeks to overcome this opposition by shifting to an Indian community organized on religious or spiritual principles. Here the woman is a spiritual token or "Goddess," but this does not resolve the conflict. In becoming a symbol of spirit, she must completely sacrifice her physical identity, which generates further opposition in the reader, if not in the narrative itself. Lawrence's narrative does not produce a term resolving the opposition between economic and spiritual concepts of man existing in our culture. The woman is exclusively one or the other, but never the desired "whole woman."

● *Mythic displacement:* In the view of critic Northrop Frye, art is generated from certain basic conflics in the human condition. Perhaps the most essential conflict involves the fact that human beings desire to live but know they must die. In artistic embodiments of this anxiety, an imaginary battle becomes the nature metaphor for the conflict. The battle might be depicted through a set of fictional characters and situations in a spectrum of literary forms ranging from "mythic" through "romance" to "realistic" possibilities. For example, a sun god of light and goodness might battle bravely but unsuccessfully with a black monster of darkness, night, and annihilation. From this level, we might "displace" the story into "romance" by making the protagonists more human, more complete, giving details of description and character beyond those absolutely necessary for the mythic core of opposition. Here a white knight whose purity lends him supernatural powers but who is otherwise described as a credible man fights a black dragon of unnatural power. Wells's angelic Eloi and demonic Morlocks are an example of conflicting forces in twentieth century romance. We might displace the story even further toward "realism" by having a perfectly normal young black worker battle a white landowner's son for his rightful wife, as we see in Toomer's "Blood-burning Moon." In this story you'll notice that the black man represents the positive values and the white, the destructive power.

But note the curious paradox in realism by displacement: the "real" part of the story or the fundamental human anxiety is a core of mythic opposition. As the story adds descriptive detail and causal probability, it moves further away from its motivating opposition. The more "realistic" the story becomes, the less "real" its embodiment of the mythic core.

● *Narration:* 758.
● *Narrator:* 503, 746, 753, 758.
● *Naturalism:* 15, 501.
● *New journalism:* (sometimes termed "participatory" or "advocacy journalism") a label for various innovative journalistic modes that became fashionable in the early and mid-sixties. Terry Southern, Joan Didion, and Joe Eszterhas are new journalist included in this collection; Hunter S. Thompson's *Hell's Angels,* Ed Sanders' biography of the Charles Manson "family," Gay Talese's *Honor Thy Father,* Norman Mailer's accounts of the political conventions, George Plimpton's *Paper Lion,* Tom Wolfe's *The Kandy-Kolored Tangerine Flake Streamline Baby,* and Seymour Krim's *Shake It for the World, Smartass* are other well-known examples that suggest the nature of the genre. The dying *New York Herald Tribune*'s Sunday Magazine served as one of the birthplaces of the movement, and although Joan Didion's "Some Dreamers of the Golden Dream" was published in the equally respectable *Saturday Evening Post,* for obvious reasons much of this writing has appeared in ideologically left-of-center intellectual periodicals like *The New York Review of Books;* papers with a bohemian aura like *The Village Voice,* the *Los Angeles Free Press,* and Paul Krassner's *The Realist;* popular slick magazines like *Esquire;* and the modish radical *Rolling Stone* (see 17).
● *Normative judgment:* 753.
● *Objective correlative:* 245, 763.
● *Paradox:* an apparently self-contradictory statement that ultimately admits to reasonable meaning rather than absurdity. Wallace Stevens' "Thirteen Ways of Looking at a Blackbird" is structured upon a series of paradoxes. When the persona states that "A man and a woman/ Are one./ A man and a woman and a blackbird/ Are one," he is perhaps discussing their placement in the same perceptual frame or the blackbird's status as universally applicable symbol, but he is not making a mistake in arithmetic. When the narrator of "The Woman Who Rode Away" notes that the woman saw "great green-covered, unbroken mountain-hills,

and in the midst of the lifeless isolation, the sharp pinkish mounds of the dried mud from the silver-works," the contradiction between the adjective "green" and her sense of "lifeless isolation" reveals her alienated mental state rather than her visual error. The significance of the story as a whole might be stated in paradoxical terms involving the need to experience literal death in order to find spiritual life. The term "living death" that expresses the woman's alienation from her wasteland environment is itself a specific form of paradox, the *oxymoron,* in which contraries or antitheses are combined.

● *Parody:*   See *Irony* and *The grotesque.*

● *Pastoral convention:*   as defined by William Empson in *Some Versions of the Pastoral,* when an author from the upper, educated class writing for a similarly sophisticated audience endorses the values of a simpler, less sophisticated society of shepherds, rustics, savages, children, workers, or even the insane. The pastoral convention involves the creation of two opposed worlds. The sophisticated urban world of the author and his audience is contrasted with a more natural imagined world which has some virtue lacking in the "real" society.

In "Hands," a twentieth century example; Sherwood Anderson opposes Wing Biddlebaum's actual existence to one Wing imagines in which "men lived again in a kind of pastoral golden age":

> Across a green open country came clean-limbed young men, some afoot, some mounted upon horses. In crowds the young men came to gather about the feet of an old man who sat beneath a tree in a tiny garden and who talked to them.

In the simpler imagined world, men are free to express their ideas and emotions, whereas in the urban society of Winesburg this kind of intimacy is suppressed as deviant. We can see that the imagined world does not refer so much to the historical reality of pagan life as it does to some anxiety present in Wing's present-day social life. Anderson's pastoral posits a society superior in its natural simplicity to the oppressive society of his readership.

More often in twentieth century literature, the pastoral is used ironically. Fitzgerald's hero, Dexter Green, yearns for a promised society free of sexual and class restrictions. The green world proves to be no more than a personal wish-fulfillment dream, however, and the hero is spiritually and morally broken in the effort to achieve this ideal state: "In a sort of panic he pushed the palms of his hands into his eyes and tried to bring up a picture of the waters lapping on Sherry Island and the moonlit veranda, and gingham on the golf-links and the dry sun and the gold color of her neck's soft down."

● *Persona:*   the speaker of a poem or work of fiction. As the section on dramatic situation in the critical guide demonstrates, this speaker cannot be identified with the author. Even the most seemingly sincere or spontaneous thoughts are artfully designed to isolate and dramaticaly represent a specific state of mind. For this reason, it is more accurate to identify the "I" of a poem as the speaker of a lyric or "persona," a term derived from the Latin word for the mask used by an actor when he impersonated a character. This labeling of the persona (or narrator in prose) distinguishes the poetic or narrative consciousness from the thoughts and opinions of the artist in all his human complexity. The persona of Wilfred Owen's "Greater Love" is not Owen himself but the constructed voice of some soldier or simply someone confronted with the horrors of war. In a work such as *The Loneliness of the Long-Distance Runner,* Sillitoe creates a character named Smith as his narrator. When Smith as the storyteller tells us that he is "clever" but his actions in the story show us that he makes some errors in judgment, Smith is revealed as a limited and therefore possibly "unreliable" narrator (see "Narration" in the Critical Guide).

● *Personification:*   748.

● *Plot:*   15, 503, 753.

● *Poètes maudits:*   10.

● *Point of view:*   752, 758.

● *Pornography:*   5, 247.

● *Psychological realism:*   15, 16.

● *Quest:*   755.

● *Romance:*   See *Mythic displacement.*

● *Romantic movement:*   5, 246.

● *Round and flat characters:*   757.

● *Science fiction:*   247. See also *Utopia and dystopia.*

● *Semantic categories:*   750.

● *Simile:*   748.

● *Sonnet:* a lyric poem of fourteen lines of iambic pentameter verse. It requires elaborate end-rhyming patterns which can be loosely divided into two basic groups: the *abba abba ccd ccd* pattern of a Petrarchan or Italian sonnet, and the *abab cdcd efef gg* pattern of the Shakespearean or English sonnet. Although twentieth-century sonnets rarely conform to these precise rhyme schemes, Yeats's "Leda and the Swan" might be termed a Petrarchan sonnet and Frost's "Acquainted with the Night" Shakespearean. Both forms of the sonnet are based upon an epigrammatic structure which divides the Petrarchan sonnet into an eight-line exposition or posing of the problem (octave) and a six-line commentary or reply (sestet). The Shakespearean divides into a twelve-line exposition and a witty, two-line reply (couplet). The epigrammatic effect of Yeats's Petrarchan sonnet balances the octave's description of the circumstance of Zeus's visitation with a sestet which reveals the historical and philosophical implications of the immediate event. The repetition of the first line of the poem as its last emphasizes the couplet as the logical closure of a Shakespearean sonnet like "Acquainted with the Night." In terms of content, "Leda and the Swan" could be seen as an ironic reaction to the courtly love sonnet's traditional love theme, and Frost's poem is a secular version of the meditative tradition of the holy sonnets by poets such as Donne and Hopkins. The sonnet's traditional subject matter, logical structure, regular meter, complex rhyme scheme, and prescribed length make it one of the most "artificial" of art forms (see *Aesthetic distance*). When writing a sonnet, the poet expects that the reader will instantly recognize this form and all the rules defining it.

● *Utopia and dystopia:* Utopian fictions possess the optimism of myths about an earthly paradise or "golden age," but the utopian author, conscious of a gap between the real world and the possibility of a perfect one, must invent literary devices to lend credibility to this fantastic ideal. With popularization of theories of evolution in the nineteenth century, the idea of an earthly paradise began to seem realistically attainable, and utopian fiction came into its own. These theories provided a scientific basis for assuming the possibility of human perfection; the mere passage of time should provide transformation of man's actual condition into a desired one. The evolutionary metaphor is thus a ready-made device for drawing the fantastic within the reach of causal probability. Works like Bernard Shaw's *Back to Methuselah* and Wells's *A Modern Utopia* affirmed optimistic middle-class assumptions that time would produce a superman and that human ignorance and evil would disappear as man achieved superior biological development.

The dystopia or anti-utopia is, as the name implies, a form of utopia and derives its meaning from inversion of the concept and conventions of utopian fiction. Dystopian fiction is produced when the artist turns with horror on a future we have been trained to desire, as Irving Howe argues in *A World More Attractive*. This fiction is intended to show that the evolutionary process is inevitable, but the result of biological, social, and scientific progress is more likely to be a barbaric, totalitarian, or mechanized state than the desired utopian model. Dystopian writers feel that a convincing representation of the future must preserve the structure of the actual present but exaggerate and modify certain features in the manner of a nightmare. They are interested primarily in conveying a theory and not in realistically representing the social subject matter itself. In *The Time Machine* and "A Boy and His Dog," character and plot are close to those of simple allegory. These authors use only two basic character types, and plot is similarly restricted to express a personal bias (see plot and character in the critical guide). The two exaggerated character types, representing opposition of physical power and culture, project an acute social division and refute the utopian superman by having the dominant type turn out to be a merciless cannibal.